A COMPLETE COURSE IN FRESHMAN ENGLISH

A COMPLETE COURSE IN FRESHMAN ENGLISH

Harry Shaw

FORMERLY DIRECTOR, WORKSHOPS IN COMPOSITION
NEW YORK UNIVERSITY,
AND LECTURER IN ENGLISH, COLUMBIA UNIVERSITY

SEVENTH EDITION

HARPER & ROW, PUBLISHERS
New York, Evanston, San Francisco, and London

A COMPLETE COURSE IN FRESHMAN ENGLISH, Seventh Edition

STANDARD BOOK NUMBER: 06-045974-3

LIBRARY OF CONGRESS CATALOG CARD NUMBER: 72-9394

Grateful acknowledgment is hereby made to the following publishers and individuals for permission to reprint the material specified:

Agnes Rogers Allen. *Lines to a Daughter—Any Daughter* by Agnes Rogers Allen. From *Harper's Magazine,* February 1947. Reprinted by permission.

Paul McClelland Angle. *Lincoln at Gettysburg* by Paul McClelland Angle. From *The Lincoln Reader.* Copyright 1947 by Paul M. Angle. Reprinted by permission of Rutgers University Press.

W. H. Auden. *Ballad* by W. H. Auden. From *On This Island.* Reprinted by permission of Random House, Inc. Copyright 1937 by Random House, Inc. *Musée des Beaux Arts* by W. H. Auden. From *Another Time.* Reprinted by permission of Random House, Inc. Copyright 1940 by W. H. Auden.

Joan Baez. *Song for a Small Voyager* by Joan Baez. From *McCall's Magazine,* January 1971. Reprinted by permission of Folklore Productions, Inc.

Russell Baker. *The Cosmonauts' Whiskers* by Russell Baker. From *All Things Considered.* Copyright 1965 by the New York Times Company. Published by J. B. Lippincott Company.

James Baldwin. *The Fire Next Time* by James Baldwin. From *The Fire Next Time.* Copyright © 1962, 1963 by James Baldwin. Reprinted by permission of the publisher, The Dial Press.

Morris Bishop. *The Reading Machine* by Morris Bishop. Copyright 1947 by *The New Yorker Magazine.* Reprinted through the courtesy of the author.

Paul Brodeur. *The Spoiler* by Paul Brodeur. From *The New Yorker,* January 8, 1966. Reprinted by permission; © 1966 The New Yorker Magazine, Inc.

Gwendolyn Brooks. *The Preacher: Ruminates Behind the Sermon.* From *The World of Gwendolyn Brooks* by Gwendolyn Brooks. Copyright © 1945 by Gwendolyn Brooks Blakely. By permission of Harper & Row, Publishers, Inc.

Ivor Brown. *The Case for Greater Clarity in Writing* by Ivor Brown. From *The New York Times Book Review,* July 30, 1950. Reprinted by permission.

Joyce Cary. *The Myth of the Mass Mind* by Joyce Cary. Copyright © 1952 by Harper and Brothers. Reprinted by permission of Curtis Brown, Ltd.

Stuart Chase. *Not Quite Utopia* by Stuart Chase. From *The Most Probable World* by Stuart Chase. Copyright © 1968 by Stuart Chase. Reprinted by permission of Harper & Row, Publishers, Inc.

John Ciardi. *Hatred* by John Ciardi. From *The Saturday Review,* August 1, 1970. Copyright 1970 by Saturday Review, Inc.

Kenneth B. Clark. *Dark Ghetto* by Kenneth B. Clark. Abridged from *Dark Ghetto,* Harper & Row, copyright © 1965 by Kenneth B. Clark.

Norman Cousins. *The Computer and the Poet* by Norman Cousins. From *The Saturday Review,* July 23, 1966. Copyright 1966 by Saturday Review, Inc.

Countee Cullen. *Yet Do I Marvel* by Countee Cullen. From *Color* by Countee Cullen. Reprinted by permission of Harper & Row, Publishers.

E. E. Cummings. *old age sticks* by E. E. Cummings. From *95 Poems,* © 1958 by E. E. Cummings. Reprinted by permission of Harcourt Brace Jovanovich, Inc.

Current Biography, Editors of. *Ralph Nader: Dedicated Man* by the Editors of *Current Biography.* Reprinted by permission from *Current Biography Yearbook,* 1968. Copyright © 1968, 1969 by the H. W. Wilson Company.

Eliot Daley. *What Produced Those Pot-Smoking, Rebellious, Demonstrating Kids?* by Eliot Daley. Reprinted with permission from *TV Guide* ® *Magazine.* Copyright © 1970 by Triangle Publications, Inc., Radnor, Pennsylvania.

Wayne H. Davis. *Overpopulated America* by Wayne H. Davis. From *The New Republic,* January 10, 1970. © by Wayne H. Davis. Reprinted by permission of the author.

Garrett De Bell. *A Future That Makes Ecological Sense* by Garrett De Bell. From *The Environmental Handbook,* edited by Garrett De Bell. Copyright © 1970 by Garrett De Bell. Reprinted by permission of Ballantine Books, Inc.

Richard Eberhart. *1934* by Richard Eberhart. From *Selected Poems* by Richard Eberhart. Reprinted by permission of Oxford University Press.

T. S. Eliot. *Journey of the Magi* by T. S. Eliot. From *Collected Poems, 1909–1962,* by T. S. Eliot. Copyright 1936 by Harcourt, Brace & World, Inc.; copyright 1963, 1964 by T. S. Eliot. Reprinted by permission of the publishers.

Ralph Ellison. *The Old Man's Words Were Like a Curse* by Ralph Ellison. Copyright 1947 by Ralph Ellison. Reprinted from *Invisible Man* by Ralph Ellison, by permission of Random House, Inc.

William Faulkner. *Man Will Prevail* by William Faulkner. Reprinted from *The Faulkner Reader,* copyright 1954 by William Faulkner, through the courtesy of Random House, Inc. *A Rose for Emily* by William Faulkner. Copyright 1930 by *Forum Magazine.* Reprinted by permission of Random House, Inc.

Thomas Hornsby Ferril. *Freudian Football* by Thomas Hornsby Ferril. From *The Rocky Mountain Herald,* Denver, Colorado. Reprinted by permission of the author.

John Fischer. *Survival U* by John Fischer. Copyright © 1969 by Minneapolis Star Tribune Co., Inc. Reprinted from the September 1969 issue of *Harper's Magazine* by permission of the author.

Robert Frost. *Mending Wall* and *The Road Not Taken* by Robert Frost. From *Complete Poems of Robert Frost.* Copyright 1930, 1949 by Henry Holt & Company, Inc. Reprinted by permission of the publishers. *My Objection to Being Stepped On.* Copyright © by Robert Frost. Reprinted by permission of Henry Holt & Company, Inc.

William Golding. *Thinking as a Hobby* by William Golding. Copyright © 1961 by The Curtis Publishing Company. Reprinted by permission of Curtis Brown, Ltd.

Edwin Granberry. *A Trip to Czardis* by Edwin Granberry. From *Forum,* April 1932. Reprinted by permission of the publishers.

Robert F. Haugh. *Conrad's "Youth"* by Robert F. Haugh. From *Joseph Conrad: Discovery in Design* by Robert F. Haugh. Copyright 1957 by the University of Oklahoma Press.

Ernest Hemingway. *In Another Country* by Ernest Hemingway. Copyright 1927, 1955 by Charles Scribner's Sons. Reprinted from *Men Without Women* by Ernest Hemingway, by permission of Charles Scribner's Sons.

Lisa Hobbs. *Love and Liberation* by Lisa Hobbs. From *Love and Liberation* by Lisa Hobbs. Copyright © 1970 by Lisa Hobbs. Used with permission of McGraw-Hill Book Company.

Gerard Manley Hopkins. *Hurrahing in Harvest* and *God's Grandeur* by Gerard Manley Hopkins. From *Poems of Gerard Manley Hopkins.* Oxford University Press. Reprinted by permission of the publisher.

A. E. Housman. *Oh, When I Was in Love with You, When I Was One-and-Twenty, With Rue My Heart Is Laden, "Terence, This Is Stupid Stuff"* by A. E. Housman. From *A Shropshire Lad* by A. E. Housman. Reprinted by permission of Henry Holt & Company, Inc.

Langston Hughes. *Dream Variations* by Langston Hughes. Copyright 1926 by Alfred A. Knopf, Inc. and renewed 1954 by Langston Hughes. Reprinted from *Selected Poems* by Langston Hughes, by permission of the publisher. *Refugee in America.* Copyright 1943 by The Curtis Publishing Company. Reprinted from *Selected Poems,* by Langston Hughes, by permission of Alfred A. Knopf, Inc.

Aldous Huxley. *Comfort* by Aldous Huxley. From *Proper Studies,* Harper & Row. Copyright 1927, 1955 by Aldous Huxley. Reprinted by permission of Harper & Row and Chatto & Windus.

Randall Jarrell. *A Camp in the Prussian Forest* by Randall Jarrell. Reprinted with the permission of Farrar, Straus & Giroux, Inc. from *The Complete Poems* by Randall Jarrell, copyright © 1955 by Randall Jarrell, copyright © 1969 by Mrs. Randall Jarrell.

LeRoi Jones. *Preface to a Twenty-Volume Suicide Note* by LeRoi Jones. Copyright © 1961 by LeRoi Jones. Reprinted by permission of Corinth Books.

William T. Keeton. *Cultural and Biological Evolution* by William T. Keeton. Reprinted from *Biological Science* by William T. Keeton. Copyright © 1967 by W. W. Norton & Company, Inc. By permission of W. W. Norton & Company, Inc.

Helen Keller. *The Story of My Life* by Helen Keller. From *The Story of My Life* by Helen Keller. Copyright 1903, 1931 by Helen Keller. Reprinted by permission of Doubleday & Company, Inc.

Martin Luther King, Jr. *I Have a Dream* by Martin Luther King, Jr. Copyright © 1963 by Martin Luther King, Jr. Reprinted by permission of Joan Daves.

Louis Kronenberger. *Fashions in Vulgarity* by Louis Kronenberger. From *The Cart and the Horse,* 1961, Alfred A. Knopf, Inc. Reprinted by permission of the author.

Clare Boothe Luce. *A Vision of the Year 2000* by Clare Boothe Luce. From *McCall's Magazine,* January 1966. Reprinted by permission of the author and the publisher.

Archibald MacLeish. *Riders on Earth Together, Brothers in the Eternal Cold* by Archibald MacLeish. Copyright © 1968 by the New York Times Company. Reprinted by permission.

Russell Maloney. *Inflexible Logic* by Russell Maloney. Copyright © 1940 by The New Yorker Magazine, Inc. Reprinted by permission.

Marya Mannes. *How Do You Know It's Good?* by Marya Mannes. From the book *But Will It Sell?* by Marya Mannes. Copyright © 1964 by Marya Mannes. Reprinted by permission of J. B. Lippincott Company.

Edgar Lee Masters. *Lucinda Matlock* and *Petit, the Poet* by Edgar Lee Masters. From *Spoon River Anthology,* The Macmillan Company, 1915. Reprinted by special permission of Mrs. Edgar Lee Masters.

W. S. Merwin. *The Bones* by W. S. Merwin. From *The Drunk in the Furnace* by W. S. Merwin. Copyright © by W. S. Merwin. Reprinted by permission of Harold Ober Associates and David Higham Associates, Ltd.

Edna St. Vincent Millay. *Love Is Not All: It Is Not Meat Nor Drink* by Edna St. Vincent Millay. From *Collected Poems,* Harper & Row. Copyright 1931, 1958 by Edna St. Vincent Millay and Norma Millay Ellis.

John Moffitt. *Seeing New* by John Moffitt. © 1961 by John Moffitt. From his volume *The Living Seed,* by permission of Harcourt Brace Jovanovich, Inc.

Paul Amos Moody. *An Open Letter to Students* by Paul Amos Moody. From *Introduction to Evolution,* 3rd edition, by Paul Amos Moody. Copyright 1953 by Harper & Row, Publishers, Inc. Copyright © 1962, 1970 by Paul Amos Moody. Reprinted by permission of Harper & Row, Publishers, Inc.

Marianne Moore. *Silence* by Marianne Moore. From *Collected Poems.* Copyright 1951 by Marianne Moore. Reprinted by permission of the publishers, The Macmillan Company. *Poetry* by Marianne Moore. From *Collected Poems.* Copyright 1935 by Marianne Moore, renewed 1963 by Marianne Moore and T. S. Eliot. Reprinted with permission of The Macmillan Company.

H. H. Munro. *The Open Window* by "Saki" (H. H. Munro). From *The Short Stories of Saki* by H. H. Munro. Copyright 1950 by The Viking Press, Inc. Reprinted by permission of The Viking Press, Inc.

Dorothy Parker. *Résumé* by Dorothy Parker. From *The Portable Dorothy Parker.* Copyright 1926, 1954 by Dorothy Parker. Reprinted by permission of The Viking Press, Inc.

Max Rafferty. *The Five Main Purposes of Education* by Max Rafferty. From *Max Rafferty on Education,* copyright 1968 by The Devin-Adair Company. Reprinted by permission of the publisher.

Estelle Ramey. *A Remarkable and Marvelous Sex* by Estelle Ramey. Appeared in *McCall's* magazine, January 1971, under the title "What Did Happen at the Bay of Pigs?" Reprinted by permission.

James Reston. *A Fable* by James Reston. From *The New York Times,* February 12, 1961. Copyright © 1961 by the New York Times Company. Reprinted by permission.

Adrienne Rich. *The Roofwalker* by Adrienne Rich. Reprinted from *Snapshots of a Daughter-in-Law* by Adrienne Rich. By permission of W. W. Norton & Company, Inc. Copyright © 1956, 1957, 1958, 1959, 1960, 1961, 1962, 1963, 1967 by Adrienne Rich Conrad.

Theodore Roethke. *Her Longing* by Theodore Roethke. From *The Far Field.* Copyright © by Beatrice Roethke as administratrix of the estate of Theodore Roethke. Reprinted by permission of Doubleday & Company, Inc. *I Waited* by Theodore Roethke. Copyright © 1956 by Kenyon College. From *The Far Field* by Theodore Roethke. Reprinted by permission of Doubleday & Company, Inc.

Richard H. Rovere. *Wallace* by Richard H. Rovere. From *The New Yorker,* February 4, 1950. Reprinted by permission; copyright © 1950 The New Yorker Magazine, Inc.

Carl Sandburg. *Cool Tombs* by Carl Sandburg. From *Cornhuskers.* Copyright 1918 by Henry Holt & Company, Inc. Copyright 1946 by Carl Sandburg. By permission of the publishers. *Chicago* by Carl Sandburg. From *Chicago Poems.* Copyright 1916 by Henry Holt & Company, Inc. Copyright 1944 by Carl Sandburg. Reprinted by permission of the publishers.

David Sarnoff. *The New Computerized Age: No Life Untouched* by David Sarnoff. From *The Saturday Review,* July 23, 1966. Copyright 1966 by Saturday Review, Inc.

Anne Sexton. *The Addict* by Anne Sexton. *From Live or Die,* copyright © 1966 by Anne Sexton. Reprinted by permission of the publisher, Houghton Mifflin Company.

Karl Shapiro. *Buick* by Karl Shapiro. From *Person, Place and Thing* by Karl Shapiro. Copyright 1941 by Karl Shapiro. Reprinted by permission of Random House, Inc.

Stephen Spender. *Daybreak* and *Oh Young Men Oh Young Comrades* by Stephen Spender. From *Ruins and Visions.* Reprinted by permission of Random House, Inc. Copyright 1942 by Stephen Spender.

Gloria Steinem. *What It Would Be Like If Women Win* by Gloria Steinem. From *Time Magazine,* August 31, 1970. Reprinted by permission of *Time,* the Weekly Newsmagazine; © Time, Inc., 1970.

Wallace Stevens. *The Emperor of Ice-Cream* by Wallace Stevens. Reprinted from *Harmonium* by Wallace Stevens, by permission of Alfred A. Knopf, Inc. Copyright 1923, 1931 by Alfred A. Knopf, Inc.

Caskie Stinnett. *On the Beach* by Caskie Stinnett. Reprinted with the permission of Bernard Geis Associates from *Back to Abnormal* by Caskie Stinnett. Copyright 1963 by Caskie Stinnett.

Deems Taylor. *The Monster* by Deems Taylor. From *Of Men and Music.* Copyright 1937 by Deems Taylor. Reprinted by permission of Simon and Schuster, publishers.

Harold Taylor. *What Is Wrong with the University?* by Harold Taylor. From *How To Change Colleges* by Harold Taylor. Copyright © 1971 by Harold Taylor. Reprinted by permission of Holt, Rinehart and Winston, Inc.

Dylan Thomas. *Especially When the October Wind* and *Death Shall Have No Dominion* by Dylan Thomas. From *Collected Poems of Dylan Thomas.* Copyright 1953 by Dylan Thomas and published by New Directions. Reprinted by permission of the publishers.

James Thurber. *The Moth and the Star* by James Thurber. Copyright © 1940 by James Thurber, copyright © 1968 by Helen Thurber. From *Fables for Our Time,* published by Harper & Row. Originally printed in *The New Yorker.*

E. B. White. *A Letter to Henry David Thoreau* by E. B. White. From *One Man's Meat,* Harper & Row, 1942. Reprinted by permission.

Thornton Wilder. *The Long Christmas Dinner* by Thornton Wilder. From *The Long Christmas Dinner and Other Plays in One Act* by Thornton Wilder. Copyright 1931 by Yale University Press and Coward-McCann, Inc.; renewed 1959 by Thornton Wilder. Reprinted by permission of Harper & Row, Publishers, Inc.

William Butler Yeats. *When You Are Old* and *The Lake Isle of Innisfree* by William Butler

Yeats. From *Collected Poems,* copyright 1956 by The Macmillan Company. Reprinted by permission of the publishers.

Robert F. Young. *Chicken Itza* by Robert F. Young. Originally appeared in *Playboy Magazine,* January 1972. Copyright © by *Playboy*. Reprinted by permission of the author and his agent, Theron Raines.

FOREWORD

The first edition of *A Complete Course in Freshman English* appeared more than three decades ago. During this time, emphasis in first-year college English has shifted, now here, now there: semantics, communication, introduction to literature, speed and skill in reading, linguistics, *explication de texte,* grammar by rote and by workbook drill, esthetics, and rhetoric, together with an influx of paperbacks of widely varying content and technique. Each of these approaches has made a contribution to the course; several of them still do.

During these same three decades, the first-year course in English has been attacked and defended. Some able educators have urged that the freshman composition course be abolished—advice that some colleges have followed. Other institutions and departments of English have shortened the course to one semester. Still others have discarded efforts to teach the writing of narration, description, exposition, and argument and have made the course a prolonged reading project with writing assignments directed to comments on selections read.

However the course is taught and no matter what its directives and goals, thousands of teachers and presumably hundreds of thousands of former first-year students might vigorously maintain that it is not only the most important course in the English department but in the entire college curriculum. These same loyal supporters might also admit that a course in freshman English, *any* course in freshman English, is imperfect—just as is any other human institution or any other discipline.

Although nearly every page of this seventh edition of *A Complete Course* has been markedly altered from its counterpart in the first edition, I continue to believe that the fundamental objective of the course is, or should be, training in clear thinking, intelligent and creative reading, and—that optimum without which nothing else really matters—clear, effective, and appropriate writing and rewriting. Emphasis on speech has been increased in this edition and that on "correctness" has been decreased. But the volume remains a carefully interrelated rhetoric, handbook, and collection of readings in which writing, revising, and reading are linked as stages of a dynamic and ongoing process.

The economy, common sense, and convenience of this articulation are still apparent after six major revisions. The present seventh edition offers a thorough reworking of the elements of that plan—emendation, addition, deletion, expansion—but no basic changes in scope or purpose.

This edition rides no hobby horse. Instead, it offers work in English of such variety that the individual instructor can evolve any of several courses in accordance with his own predilections, tastes, interests, and teaching methods as they are related to departmental objectives and the needs of a particular section or class.

It would be an unusual class that could assimilate every approach presented and could utilize every device afforded in this purposefully *complete*, many-sided volume. Freshman English is not a cut-and-dried course, nor should it ever be. The thousands who teach it have varied methods and aims; students have diverse needs; the shared experiences of teachers and the findings of contemporary researchers demand that flexibility, not rigidity, be a hallmark of the strong and unwavering discipline underlying any English course worthy of its name. Ample work in freshman English is offered here, plenty and to spare, but the individual teacher is urged to use this volume in accordance with his own judgment and professional experience.

Part One (the rhetoric) is more succinct than most rhetorics. And yet its comparative brevity permits a vigorous survey of those principles—and only those—that seem genuinely important. In each of the ten chapters of this part, students are urged, implicitly or explicitly, to apply what they are learning to their own writing habits and processes.

Part Two (the handbook) is intended for actual use in the classroom; it is also a reference section for students doing assignments. It will be noted that the final fifteen sections of the handbook (56–70) are designed to be helpful to all students in all college classes.

Part Three is intended primarily as a reference work and as a supplement to Part Two. Like Part One, Parts Two and Three are comparatively brief. Emphasis upon relatively few essentials of effective writing (and speaking) should help students more than will discussion of minor errors and less dominant aims of effective communication. Such concentration may also assist the instructor in selecting from a mass of material available elsewhere only those items of true significance and immediate need. Every item in Parts Two and Three can be used for study, for reference, and for correcting papers.

Another guiding principle of these parts should be mentioned: they adopt a "middle-of-the-road" approach that may seem too reactionary to some and too liberal to others. Staying in the middle of the road can be fatal on a highway, but perhaps not on the highway to better composition. This approach is based on many years of teaching experience and hundreds of talks with teachers throughout the country over more than three decades. Obviously, added attention is given in this book to the findings and recommendations of linguists and lexicographers, but the present edition does not claim to be in the avant-garde of linguistic theory, nor does it try to stretch its purpose beyond those already mentioned in this Foreword.

The writing of college-trained people is expected to be somewhat different, on occasion, from informal speech. This is a normal, justified expectation. No matter what some lexicographers and linguists heatedly maintain, an attitude of "anything goes" can be, and repeatedly is, costly to students in business and social affairs. The late Will Rogers was genuinely humorous when he remarked: "A lot of people who don't say *ain't,* ain't eatin'." And yet, in certain clearly defined circumstances, using *ain't,* misspelling a word, employing an unidiomatic expression, or saying *went* when *gone* is indicated can cost a job, advancement, a social opportunity, or even a potential friend. English composition has many values, one of which is practicality.

In short, the credo of Parts One, Two, and Three is that expressed by Theodore M. Bernstein, staff editor for *The New York Times,* in *Watch Your Language:*

> To be sure, the English language is a changing and growing thing. All its users have, of course, a perceptible effect upon it. But in changing and growing it needs no contrived help from chitchat columnists or advertising writers or comic strip artists or television speakers. It will evolve nicely by itself. If anything, it requires protection from influences that try to push it too fast. There is need, not for those who would halt its progress altogether, but for those who can keep a gentle foot on the brake and a guiding hand on the steering wheel. . . .

Part Four contains a diversified, representative, and even exciting collection of readings. Obviously, more material is included than most classes can possibly absorb, but overabundance will provide opportunity to assign only those selections especially useful to a particular class. The aim has been to make selections that represent good writing, that appeal to students, and that stimulate class discussion and foster imitation of writing techniques. At times, selections were made as much on the basis of interest and provocativeness as of purely literary qualities. Also, in addition to much material that is recent, I have chosen several selections that through the years have proved their value in the classroom. Still another of my purposes was to represent major types of writing and thus provide an adequate introduction to literature itself.

In successive editions, selections that have become "dated" or have not proved sufficiently stimulating have been removed and new ones have been added. In this edition appear new essays, critical articles, biographical sketches, short stories, plays, and poems.

In short, this edition of *A Complete Course in Freshman English* has been thoroughly revised and updated. But it retains its original plan, scope, and purpose. May it help to encourage and give light, insight, and confidence to all who use it—students and teachers engaged in a common goal.

H.S.

CONTENTS

Part Four. A COLLECTION OF READINGS FOR WRITERS

PART ONE

A BRIEF MANUAL OF RHETORICAL PRINCIPLES

CHAPTER 1

GETTING UNDER WAY

Through practice, and only through practice, can you or anyone else effectively learn any necessary or worthwhile activity: talking, walking, playing games, dancing, thinking—and writing. Even such automatic activities as breathing, eating, and sleeping can be changed and improved through practice and training—as many singers, public speakers, athletes, teachers of yoga, and marriage counselors can testify.

Freshman English provides practice in those writing experiences that are an essential part of every educated person's basic equipment. The primary aim of this course is to give you practice in the clear and effective expression of *your own* ideas, emotions, and reactions. You will have some reading to do in order to stock your mind with ideas that may be thought about and assimilated to give you experiences as real and important as any job or position or physical activity. In addition, the course will teach you much about both listening and speaking. But its primary purpose is to help you write well.

Actually, you may have had little experience in formal writing, although you have been speaking since infancy. What you say and how you say it may sometimes be neither clear nor effective, yet such shortcomings rarely result from lack of practice in speaking. But few students entering college have made more than isolated and fragmentary writing efforts in the past, no matter how much they may have composed in their minds. The slim total may consist of an occasional composition (theme) or book report or "research" paper, a few letters, a job application or two, answers on school examinations, and the like.

Laboratory work is the method a physical scientist employs to turn theory into fact. Field work is an important means by which a social scientist translates theories and formulas into techniques and tools. Chemists and biologists and sociologists and engineers and home economists use retorts, microscopes, case studies, testing machines, and demonstration homes to relate theory to reality. For those who wish to use English clearly and effectively, the prescribed laboratory work is the writing of papers.

When writing is done well it becomes an art; even when done poorly or only adequately, it reflects personal characteristics and is subject to individual differences. But mere knowledge of words and their ways is worthless unless it can be applied. The word, the sentence, and the paragraph are only means to an end—the bricks, planks, or stones that make up a house. No one can be said to write well until he can achieve a completed whole, an entire composition.

Many a beginning student of biology or chemistry or physics has been appalled at how rapidly his instructor set him to performing laboratory work. Such a student, feeling inadequate in both knowledge and technique, might wonder how he will learn or remember hundreds and hundreds of immediately needed facts.

Similarly, some beginning composition students feel unprepared to write papers because they have many facts about grammar, diction, spelling, and structure to learn or relearn, many details to keep in mind. And yet the only way to learn to write is to write; and the sooner the process is started, the quicker the design and purpose of writing become clear. When you begin to write, you are already on the way to becoming a practical and effective handler of language.

Speaking and writing are important forms of behavior, and the different ways we perform these acts tell much about us: our standards of taste, our education, our judgment, and our goals. When George Bernard Shaw wrote *Pygmalion,* he insisted that it was Eliza's Cockney speech which "kept her in her place." The theme of the play is that proper training in speaking could change Eliza's entire existence. Proper training in writing, such as you will receive in this course, is not likely to alter *your* entire existence, but it will make you more interesting to yourself and to others.

Writing has at least two dimensions. The first is *literacy:* the ability to spell, to punctuate, to follow acceptable conventions of word choice and usage, to employ words in their everyday meanings. Writing that lacks literacy tends to be slovenly, irritating, and incomprehensible. Although *literate* English is in a sense negative—the ability *not* to make mistakes—it is no minor achievement. Do not almost all of us wish to "write acceptably" just as we desire to "make a good appearance" and not be thought dull, boring, and lacking a sense of humor?

Another dimension of writing is *competence.* Competence involves the ability to conceive, arrange in order, and clearly explain ideas; to handle and control language as a means of expressing thought and feeling; to define a quality; to support an idea; to express differences of mood and emotion and meaning. Every student in freshman English should be literate. Those who already write literately when they enter the course can seek varying and greater degrees of competence.

In short, this course should help you:

1. To present ideas in clearly constructed sentences
2. To develop and expand these ideas into organized units of paragraphs and compositions
3. To gain confidence that these ideas will be understood, respected, and fairly evaluated
4. To free your writing of grammatical and mechanical errors

Sometimes during the course you may begin to lose heart. You need not be discouraged, for writing is difficult—difficult for everyone regardless of his training and experience. Voltaire, a French essayist and philosopher, wrote:

> The necessity of saying something, the embarrassment produced by the consciousness of having nothing to say, and the desire to exhibit ability, are three things sufficient to render even a great man ridiculous.

Disappointments may come as often as triumphs during freshman English. Try to accept both as a part of the effort, excitement, and, yes, fun, involved in mastering a worthwhile skill.

Also, try not to think of writing as a complicated series of do's and don'ts, a long list of thou shalt not's. Instead, approach writing as what it is: a useful medium that will help you to communicate clearly and interestingly to and with others. What activity could be more important to you or to anyone?

CHAPTER 2

UNCOVERING IDEAS: WHERE TO LOOK

Three basic problems are involved in all writing: getting ideas, getting material, and writing. These steps are closely related, so closely that they may be expressed as two steps: (1) discovering what we think (or think we think) about people, places, events, and ideas; and (2) communicating our thoughts to readers. The first step is *thinking;* the second is *writing.* The two are inseparably linked.

Before writing comes thinking. Thinking itself should begin with *self-evaluation,* a basic approach to all self-expression, whether in writing or speaking. We need to do what a good storekeeper does periodically: take stock.

It is difficult to get at the truth about oneself. Unearthing the facts requires digging, hard thinking, and careful reflecting. And when you have arrived at some truth about yourself, or what you believe is the truth, when you have evaluated what some experience or person has done to shape your thought and life, it may take courage to put on paper what you have found. All of us keep a curtain between ourselves and others, we hide behind masks, we keep to ourselves some secret part of self—even when we think we are being open. Such caution (or self-preservation) is normal; in some areas of thought and experience it may be both wise and necessary.

But how refreshing to writer and reader to discover an honest revelation rather than a set of standard pretenses! Many analyses of character and attitudes are predictable because they result from a search for what is considered expected and recognizable rather than for what is individual and distinctive. One freshman English teacher has remarked that if you remove the pronouns in most personal compositions, it is impossible to tell whether the writer is a man or a woman. Even if some of your innermost thoughts and feelings must be kept sacred, you should be able to reveal others without incriminating yourself.

A good place to start with self-analysis is to think about what the members of your family mean and have meant to you, what friends you have and what kind of people they are, what you have obtained from your schooling thus far, and what your ideas (or lack of them) are about religion, drugs, politics, love, marriage, sports, hobbies. The ideas you have now may change in a few months or even a few days, but that does not matter. What is important is that you take the first step in becoming a writer, the first step in learning to communicate your thoughts and feelings effectively: Find out things about yourself that, perhaps, you have never realized before.

Consider these ten questions:

1. What are my *social* beliefs? (Do I really like people? What kinds of people? What qualities do my friends have? Do I like men better than women or women better than men? Do I like children—as a general rule, occasionally, never? *Why* do I hold these attitudes?)
2. What are my *religious* beliefs? (Do I believe in God? If so, am I a transcendentalist, a Baptist, a Roman Catholic, or do I simply believe in some sort of Supreme Mind? If not, am I agnostic or atheistic? *Why* do I hold these beliefs?)
3. What are my *political* beliefs? (Am I interested in national and international politics? Am I a reactionary, a conservative, a liberal, a radical, or an extremist in politics? What do I mean by these terms? *Why* do I hold these attitudes?)
4. What are my *moral* beliefs? (Do I subscribe to, and practice, the "Golden Rule"? Do I believe that "Honesty is the best policy" or that "The end justifies the means?" What do I really think of the Ten Commandments as a guide for human conduct? Do I know all ten? Do I believe in the single or double standard? Do I believe in the sanctity of marriage? in romantic love? in free love? *Why* do I hold these attitudes?)
5. What do I want to be, and to be doing, five (ten) years from now? *Why?*
6. What do I expect to be, and to be doing, five (ten) years from now? *Why?*
7. What, for me, is the single major problem facing the world today? Why have I selected this from the many possible choices?
8. What would constitute for me the greatest happiness I can imagine? the greatest disaster? *Why?*
9. Am I an observant person, alert to what is going on about me? Am I capable of self-analysis and criticism? Am I open-minded—tolerant of other people and their ideas? Am I capable of reflection and meditation? Am I aware of my limitations?
10. How did I get to be the way I am? What were (or are) the principal events, persons, and places that have molded my life thus far?

What you find out about yourself in pondering such questions as these may disappoint, disgust, or excite you. But it is impossible to give them serious thought without having dozens of ideas occur to you. These ideas may be unformed and shaky, but many of them will be topics about which you could write with some interest and possibly some pleasure.

You will always find that what you have to write about comes from your own experience, observation, imagination, and reflection. Naturally, we get many of our ideas from others through discussions or conversations, interviews or lectures, or reading. But we must absorb all this material and make it our own. Otherwise, what we write will not be ours but someone else's. True originality is not so much a matter of substance as of individualized treatment. The most interesting and effective subjects for compositions are those about which we either have some knowledge or genuinely want to learn something. Writing is made out of the ideas and impressions we have obtained from various sources and made a part of ourselves.

You cannot avoid writing about yourself or revealing yourself in many ways. When you write a paper that, for example, explains or defines something, you can write objectively, but even then you will be giving your personal explanation, telling what that something means to you. Anatole France, the French novelist and satirist, once wrote that, to be frank, even the critic ought to say: "Gentlemen, I am going to speak of myself apropos of Shakespeare, apropos of Racine, or of Goethe."

Recently, a college freshman stormed away from a serious argument with his parents about life styles and attitudes. The student and his parents held opposing points of view about nearly every subject that had come up: morals, habits, manners, politics—even food and drink. As the student fumed in his room, he recalled that his next writing assignment was an autobiographical paper dealing with someone who had had an important influence on his life. He thought of writing about his parents, but then began to reflect that age and circumstances caused "generation gaps" other than between those under and over thirty. After pondering this interesting idea, he turned in to his instructor a composition of which this is the first part:

> When I began to take stock of all the friends whom I have had, I quickly came to the conclusion that Jerry was the most important and had exerted the greatest influence upon my life. His family moved to my block when I was only 10. Jerry was 15 at the time, but the fact that he was so much older than I seemed to make no difference to him. I was highly flattered that he seemed to like me, and I haunted his house day after day. We took long walks together, on which he would tell me stories from Cooper's *Leather-Stocking Tales*. They were Jerry's improvisations, of course, and it was years later that I realized Jerry was paraphrasing. Doubtless, Cooper would have been annoyed had he known what twists Jerry gave to his stories, but then again, he might not have been, for Jerry had a quick imagination and an excellent sense of what parts of the stories would especially appeal to a 10-year-old whose mind was full of Indians, pioneer forts, and even pirates and buried gold.
>
> Jerry never seemed to mind giving me so much of his time and, although he had many other friends, he always made me feel that I was his special crony. He taught me all I still know about birds and flowers; he came over to read to me every day when I broke my leg and had to stay in the house for weeks. His ideas about people and moving pictures and even food and clothes were my ideas. I gradually came to feel that Jerry meant more to me than either my father or mother did. During that whole first year of our acquaintance he never said or did an unkind thing to me, and I began to look up to him as I would have to a god.

The idyllic friendship recounted here did not continue, and the story of its breakup is the meat of the paper. The writer traced that one year's beautiful friendship and then described a change that began to come over Jerry. When Jerry became sixteen, his interests and tastes shifted; he grew concerned with girls and dancing and things that to an eleven-year-old were unimportant. Annoyed at attempts to keep the friendship going, he finally had to hurt the younger boy's feelings before the latter could understand that they had to come to a real parting of the ways.

The composition is a nostalgic account of a long-dead relationship such as you and I and millions of other people have experienced. And it is because we have all had such an experience that we are interested in this one. Possibly you have not had many unusual experiences. But you are an individual, and things seem different to you. Freshman English can enable you to see how your mind works, how your thoughts are different from those of everyone else. It is in precisely this area that you will find ideas for writing.

In addition to thinking about the ten questions listed earlier, give some attention to these idea-provoking items:

Memories. Can you recall how someone, or some place, or some idea seemed to you at some earlier time in your life? What can you remember about the day you entered first grade? The first (or most memorable) Christmas you can recollect? The most cruel (or kindest) thing anyone ever did to you? Your first date? The day Martin Luther King, Jr., was shot?

People and places. Who is the most entertaining (or dullest or most arrogant) person you have ever known? What one person did you most admire when you were ten years old? Whom do you most admire today? What is the most beautiful (or appealing or restful) place you have ever seen? What is, or once seemed, the most shocking sight in your home town?

Incidents and events. What was the most appalling accident you have ever witnessed? What event in your life provided the greatest excitement? sense of achievement? biggest disappointment? worst embarrassment? Of all the incidents in your life, which one do you remember with the greatest pleasure? the most shame? If you could relive one day (or one hour) in your life, what would that day (or hour) be?

Imagination and daydreaming. If you could be any person in the world for a day (or month) whom would you choose to be? With what one person who has ever lived would you most like to have an imaginary conversation? If you had free choice and unlimited resources, in what city or century would you most like to spend a week or a year? What is your idea of a perfect day?

None of these topics and questions is guaranteed to produce workable ideas, but your mind probably will be triggered by a few of them. What remains to be done is testing this idea to see if it is usable *and* getting hold of material for its development.

CHAPTER 3

MAKING A SELECTION

Every writer has had the experience of coming across what seemed an excellent idea and developing it with great care, only to discover that others were not interested and that his paper did not "come across." Perhaps it is true that everything has interest for someone, but it is also true that some ideas (topics) are more interesting than others and can be presented more effectively.

How do you select ideas that have a better chance for success than others and that you can handle with some ease and sureness?

Select an interesting idea (topic).

This somewhat vague suggestion can be made specific. First, does the topic interest you yourself? It is difficult to write effectively unless you are actually interested in the material. Vagueness, aimlessness, dullness, and sketchiness are the hallmarks of uninterested writing; force and vigor come naturally when you are engrossed in your subject.

You may not be interested in labor unions, for example, but if you have a friend who has lost his job because of joining or not joining a union, you are likely to write about unions with genuine interest. Perhaps you seldom have even thought about South America, but if you become friends with a Brazilian, you may discover that that continent and his country have a new interest, meaning, and appeal for you.

Of course, you will be required to write papers on ideas in which you are not really interested; but when you are *choosing* a topic, select one that genuinely appeals to you. Then ask yourself, will the topic interest your readers, that is, your classmates and instructor? A writer needs to spend considerable time analyzing his readers' likes and dislikes, planning ways to interest them in his ideas or to present ideas in which they are already interested.

It is short-sighted to argue that what seems clear and interesting to you as a writer will always appeal to your readers, for in writing to please only ourselves we frequently are too easily pleased. Most professional writers and editors have undergone an apprenticeship that has made them reasonably certain their tastes reflect those of their readers—and yet they always do keep their readers in mind. If you lose sight of your reader, you may fail to communicate.

As a writer, you will never be judged by your private vision, only by that part of it which shows on paper. It is a mistake for a writer to sit around admiring his mental processes, his extraordinary insights, his captivating ideas. A reader is not sitting around in any such admiring state. His demand is "show me," and he is quite justified in his insistence.

Men and women are first of all interested in themselves. This belief is not cynical so much as it is part of the law of self-preservation. Your reader, any reader, is constantly looking for, and interested in, ideas to which he can relate and by which he can measure himself. Nearly everything that we see and hear we identify with ourselves if we possibly can. What, for example, does anyone first look for in a photograph of a meeting he has attended? What does one think about on seeing an advertisement for a dress or suit other than "How will that look on me?" or "Can I afford it?" or "Will I like it?"

What are some other compelling ideas and interests, matters to which your readers are nearly always attuned and to which their responses will usually be quick and strong? The late Joseph Pulitzer, famed newspaper publisher and editor, once stated that the most effective topics for front-page treatment are murders, sex, wills, and how the rich spend their money. The newspaper with the largest circulation in the United States, *The New York Daily News*, adheres fairly closely to this somewhat sensational formula. In freshman English, however, you and your instructor will probably settle on more prosaic topics. The following list may suggest ideas and provide tests for measuring the appeal to others of what you have already chosen to write about:

1. Timely topics—either new ideas or recent facts, or the development of some old idea by emphasizing its relation to recent developments.
2. People—unique, prominent, or familiar.
3. Important matters—those that involve the life and property of others and that have a relation to the reader's own welfare.
4. Conflict—contests between people, those between man and nature, and internal conflicts (within the person).
5. Amusements and hobbies.

An examination of current popular magazines will provide further evidence of what apparently interests people in general. Many topics constantly treated in periodicals will not be good topics for you, but they do provide insights into people's tastes and concerns: health (how to get and keep it), catastrophes (everything from accidents to obituary columns), self-improvement, religion and religious or ethical experiences, relationships between the sexes, money (who has it, how he got it, what he does with it). With such clues to readers' interests, it should not be difficult to select ideas appealing to others or to remember that certain topics will require added effort to make them come alive.

Select a topic (idea) about which you know something.
Ideas and material derived from personal experience, observation, and thought can be not only parts of compositions but papers complete in themselves. If you write about something you actually know, something you have thought or seen or heard, you have a head start on presenting your material effectively.

Just as one cannot expect to handle a tool or machine expertly without some previous experience, so one cannot expect to write effectively without some experience or first-hand acquaintance with the topic of the composition. John R. Tunis' books and articles on sports are based on many years of direct observation and study; the late Kenneth Roberts' stories of Arundel—*The Lively Lady, Arundel, Captain Caution*—came out of Roberts' personal familiarity with the Kennebunk, Maine, area, his considerable study and research, and careful observation of people. Herman Melville shipped as a sailor in 1839. Two years later he sailed around Cape Horn in the whaler *Acushnet,* and the following year was "captured" by cannibals in the South Seas. These experiences—and his keen observation of men and the sea—he used in *Typee,* in *Redburn,* and in his great novel *Moby Dick.*

Every good writer resorts to his own experience for ideas—to those things he knows or has thought or seen or heard. Remember, however, that your own special experiences (hobbies, jobs, personal relationships, dates, parties, volunteer work, travels, and the like) are quickly exhausted as writing materials unless you can develop from them some new aspects of thought, new insights, and novel conclusions and judgments. Almost any of your particular experiences will quickly become wearisome even to you unless you can develop some awareness that has meaning above and beyond the incident itself.

Not long ago a class in freshman English was asked to write a paper describing someone whom each writer knew well. Every student in the class except one understandably wrote about a parent or close friend. One girl, a capable student, got the idea of writing about a classmate of whom she knew little but who interested her. She began to observe this student, to talk with her after class, to speculate about her background, interests, and possible future. As a result of observation, curiosity, and reflection, she came to know her subject better and finally produced this unusually good character sketch:

> She is thin and short and dark, of a peculiar kind of ugliness which comes and goes, suddenly terribly apparent as she laughs and talks vivaciously, oddly dis-

appearing as she sits quietly, a queer lonely look on her face. What goes on inside a person such as she? Is she unhappy? *Can* she be happy? Does she ever pause to wonder whether she will be loved, whether someone will sit beside her and call her large beaked nose, her frizzed, lumpy hair, her black, un-pretty eyes beautiful?

She is perhaps too obviously charming. Her face lights up as she talks; her conversation is pert and clever. Somehow one gets the feeling as one looks at her that from behind those darting black eyes a strange, lonely person is watching with deadly earnestness. If there is a person behind the lively, alert face it will be, or is already, warped and misshapen by the conditions of its existence. Sometimes she must think of theaters at night with their attractively dressed, perfumed women, men made mysterious by the dim lights and the silence. She must think of pale roads winding by dark country places. Of Fifth Avenue at night. Of dirty, poorly lit restaurants. Of walks along chilly, deserted streets. Perhaps she will feel some ache of longing in her small, immature body. And perhaps she will write a passionate love story of frustrated desire.

It is easy to visualize her in later life. She will be thoroughly familiar with every new movement in art, literature, music. She will have seen the best shows when everyone else is still waiting for two tickets for that coming Saturday night. She will have read the best books before everyone else has had time to run into his bookstore to see if there is a copy in stock. At the parties to which her married friends will invite her, she will talk vivaciously to her friends' husbands, or to the young men who have been sent to sit with her. She will grow desperate with eagerness to keep this or that man by her side, as she sees his eyes grow blank in uncomprehending politeness. And in her despair she will know that he is not worthy of her, that she is far finer, more intelligent, more interesting than ten of such as he.

But when regard for appearances begins to disappear, she will embark on a long series of lunches with her girl friends, matinées with them, evening movies with her mother, or her sisters. She will perhaps continue writing. Her energies, directed solely at this one field, will fan her native talent into a certain blaze, and she will undoubtedly become a popular, if not an artistic success. Prosperity will agree with her. She will grow plump. Her angular face will lose its drawn, rouged hollows, and her figure will reveal some charm in its small, but pigeon-like contours. She will become more sure of herself—less anguished in her efforts to amuse. Perhaps when she is 35 or 40 she will marry, and continue to write, the habit having become ingrown. Her husband will sincerely admire her; her talent will be a constant source of pleasure to him. Such a little thing, and you should see how hard she works! She will be happy perhaps, but the feeling will come upon her again and again that she has missed something in her youth which she can never now replace. The bitterness which was hidden so well when she went to college will sink deeper and deeper behind the growing pudginess; gradually it may disappear. It was hard anyway to see any grand surge of emotion behind such spare angularity and tininess. But sometime she will write a nostalgic novel of young love and feel the better for it.

But all her bird-like motions, her bright little remarks, will be put to good use. All the things she dreamed of saying as a girl, all the little actions which she hoped men would see and admire, her smallness, now an asset, all these she will direct at her stout, slumberous husband, who will be pricked into laughter by the needle-like sharpness of her character.

Select a topic (idea) that you can handle adequately.

It is difficult, even impossible, to write an effective 500-word paper on a subject that requires 5,000 words. If you choose a big idea and fail to limit it, you are likely to become discouraged and to write sketchily and illogically. You may select a topic that is interesting to both you and your reader and that you know something about; yet it may not be a good paper simply because you cannot handle it adequately within the limits prescribed by your professor. "College Demonstrations," "Professional Football," and "The History of My Hometown" are examples of such topics. They cannot be treated in a short paper; and even if the paper is to be lengthy, they will require more extended research than you can or will undertake.

The word *theme* is not applied to freshman English papers so often as it once was, but instructors still insist that prepared papers should stick to one subject and treat it adequately. The very word *theme* implies a single, well-defined phase of a subject. Be careful not to select an idea so large and inclusive that it cannot possibly be treated in a short theme. "Aviation," for example, is a hopelessly broad topic; limited to "Aviation in America," it is still too large, perhaps even for a book; "The Career of Wilbur Wright" might be developed in a very long paper; "That Last Flight of ———" would be more suitable for ordinary treatment. Limit a topic to an aspect you can develop with reasonable thoroughness and unity in the space at your command. A small composition on a large subject is necessarily fragmentary, disconnected, and ineffective. This problem of limiting a topic, partly a matter of idea and partly one of selecting material, is discussed in following chapters.

CHAPTER 4

SHAPING THE TOPIC

After you have hit upon a workable idea (whether through luck, hard thinking, or having had a topic assigned), the first step is to decide what it involves and what you plan to do with it. The second step is to secure material for developing that idea and fulfilling your purpose with it.

There should be an objective for your paper other than the completion of a required assignment, for there can be no such thing as good *purposeless* writing. How you determine your purpose will control and direct your selection of material. Every composition is a project for communicating to some clearly defined person, or group of persons, a series of thoughts, facts, or emotions. Thus, writing is either a search for ways to accomplish a central aim or, as it all too often is, a setting down of words according to mechanical requirements. Simply completing a routine assignment will neither bring credit to you nor provide any pleasure for your readers.

Ask these four questions about any idea (topic) you select:

1. What special characteristics distinguish my topic?
2. What am I trying to do with it?
3. For what specific reader(s) am I developing it?
4. How can I best convey my purpose and meaning to my reader(s)?

Your answers to these questions may be vague at first, but stick with them. Thinking about them is a form of *pre*writing, a valuable part of the process of self-expression. Also keep in mind three other considerations:

1. What is the required length of the paper?
2. How much do I really know about the topic?
3. Where can I get more information about it?

Your task will become simpler if you will *limit* the topic to some phase that can be handled properly in the number of words assigned. As has been pointed out, some topics are too general or too big to be handled in brief space.

Don't sit down to think about what you will write; think the topic through in the prewriting stages and then sit down to write what you have thought. If this sounds like a vague suggestion, consider these five specific steps:

1. Determine the central purpose of your paper.

In a single sentence (which may or may not be included in the actual paper), state your central purpose, your controlling idea. That is, what is the *theme* of the theme? A *thesis sentence* will enable you to grasp, identify, and state your central purpose. On the general subject of "Part-time Employment," for example, you might try a plan like this:

Limited subject: "How I Got a Summer Job."
Possible title: "I Earn and Learn."
Reader: A next-door neighbor one year younger than you.
Length: 500 words.
Thesis sentence: Those who plan ahead and apply early can get a summer job.

This subject is too broad to be treated fully in a brief composition, but your purpose is clearly stated: You can, through an account of your own experiences, show your neighbor how to get the summer job he or she wants. Your basic decision has now been made; your purpose will control the choice of material to be used in your paper and the effect that that material will have on your reader.

2. List details that might be used.

In determining your purpose, make an inventory of what you know and what you will need to find out. Your list might consist of ten or more items that could be used, arranged in no particular order:

1. Qualifications for getting a job
2. Timing the campaign
3. Discovering job opportunities (want ads, government bulletins, high school or college employment office)
4. People who can help
5. Making applications
6. Preparing for an interview
7. Carrying out the interview
8. Difficulties in being interviewed
9. Following up job prospects
10. Use of supporting letters

Such a listing provides an overview of your topic. After thinking about such a list, you may decide to limit your previously stated central purpose even further and settle on the topic "How to Find Out about Summer Jobs." You would then concentrate on item 3 and eliminate the others. Or you might concentrate on items 6 to 8 and confine your paper to "Being Interviewed Is Frightening" or "Tough Interviewers I Have Known." A valuable result of listing developing material is limiting a subject to manageable proportions.

3. Choose a consistent method of development.

For the paper suggested here (a summer job), an informal narrative approach is probably best. But such a method of development will not work for all topics. Some ideas require definition of terms and a serious, critical approach. Some require argument, reasons for and against this or that cause or action.

Some subjects can be developed humorously; some require descriptive details; some require comparison and contrast. Whatever method you select—and remember that that is determined by topic *and* reader—be consistent in its use. Also, when you have finished writing, check to see that you have consistently maintained the method selected.

Be steadfast in your primary aim: to inform, or amuse, or persuade, or ridicule, or whatever. One purpose is enough for any one composition.

Decide on the basic form of writing you will use. If you wish to argue, omit narrative detail that adds nothing to your central purpose. If you wish to tell a story, use little argument and exposition—and none that has no direct relationship to your aim.

Try to make your theme unified in tone and mood. Tragedy and comedy, dignity and farce, pathos and ridicule are difficult to mingle in a short paper. A solemn page on Robert F. Kennedy's assassination probably should not contain any references at all to his lively undergraduate days. A farcical paper on night-club humor will lack unity if you add serious thoughts about the plight of minority groups.

4. Choose material with a specific reader in mind.

Always keep your prospective reader in mind. Usually, your readers will be your instructor and classmates, but you may be asked to write for someone else. Whoever your reader, how much does he already know about your topic? What can you write that will be freshly informative? interesting? appealing? If you are writing on a subject about which your reader knows little or nothing, what background information should you supply? What terms need defining? What technical material had best be omitted to avoid confusing your reader? What kinds of illustrations, examples, and descriptive details will help make the subject as clear to your reader as it is to you?

You can save yourself time and trouble by *always* deciding in advance just whom you are writing for. It's wasteful to unearth material that is not needed for your central purpose. It's even more wasteful to gather material already well known to your readers. Regardless of who your readers are, however, you will need specific details to shore up the purpose, the thesis, you have in mind. You will need concrete material and factual evidence to support a position or idea. No writer can be effective without ample substance, more than he needs or can use.

5. Be honest about the material you gather.

When you come across an idea new to you, state your indebtedness in your own or in quoted words. Taking the ideas and words of another and passing them on as your own is *plagiarism.* It is *thievery.* Sometimes you can acknowledge a source with a mere phrase: "As Salinger suggests, . . ." Sometimes you will need to make fuller acknowledgment in a footnote. But borrow, don't steal, and do indicate who the lender is.

It is equally important that in gathering material from others you think about it and try to state in your own words what you have learned. It is unnecessary to acknowledge every item of information you glean: you do not need to cite some authority if you write that water is wet or the earth is round. But you should always put information of whatever kind through your own thought processes and usually should express it in your own words.

CHAPTER 5

FINDING THE MATERIAL

You now have a topic. You have limited it to suitable proportions. You have decided what you propose to do with it. You have settled upon a method of developing it. Having taken these prewriting steps, you now face the challenging problem of gathering ample material for expanding your idea into a full-length paper.

You are still not ready for actual writing, but you are well on your way. You know—to some degree—what you are going to write about, what your purpose is, and how you hope to accomplish what you have set out to do. Even more significantly, you have eliminated ideas that could only slow you up.

Where can you get the material needed? There are only two sources: yourself and others.

Many people feel that their own ideas and experiences are not significant or interesting. Others have a false modesty and so refuse to consider subjects in terms of their own experience. Actually, personal experience provides a freshness and interest that is hard to equal. The writer's own *observation, curiosity, imagination,* and *reflection* provide material that can capture the reader's attention as very little "second-hand knowledge" is able to do.

Indeed, it is impossible for one to write wholly objectively; the writer necessarily puts something of himself into everything he writes. The more of himself he puts into his writing—that is, his own ideas, reactions, and observations—the more likely he is to write with full, interesting, concrete detail.

It is likely that your powers of observation, your curiosity, your imagination, and your willingness to reflect have not been developed fully. Freshman English gives you a chance to develop these assets and to use them increasingly powerfully in your writing.

Observation—accurate, clear, and usable observation—means looking at something long and carefully enough really to see what you are looking at. Most of us settle for fleeting observations, for just a surface view. We fail to pay close attention. The only person who should legitimately have difficulty in observing is one who is blind and deaf and without the ability to taste, touch, or smell. Yet many of us go through life half-dead, not really seeing and hearing what is going on around us. Without this ability to observe, we can never describe fully or effectively; with it, we have only the problem of selecting from a mass of details those that will most accurately indicate what we wish to convey. Guy de Maupassant, in telling of his apprenticeship as a writer and the assistance Flaubert gave him, wrote:

> Talent is enduring patience. It is a matter of looking at that which one wishes to express long enough and with sufficient attention to discover in it an aspect no one has seen. Everything has its unexplored elements, because we are accustomed to see things with the eyes of others. The least thing contains something of the unknown. Find it! To describe a blazing fire or a tree on the plain, let us live with that fire and that tree until they no longer resemble for us any other fire or tree. This is the way one becomes original.
>
> Furthermore, having laid down the truth that in the entire world there are no two grains of sand, two flies, two hands, or two noses exactly alike, he [Flaubert] compelled me to describe an object so particularized as to distinguish it from all others of its species and class. He used to say, "When you pass a grocer seated on his doorstep, or a concierge smoking his pipe, or a cab stand, show me that grocer and that concierge in all their physical appearance and in all their moral nature so that I shall not mistake that grocer and that concierge for any other, and make me see by a single word wherein a cab horse differs from the fifty others that go before and come after him."

As children, each of us had a desire to learn and to know, but as we grew older our *curiosity*, our inquisitiveness, lessened. Most of us tend to accept (or reject) people and situations and ideas without really digging into them, without asking questions and seeking specific details. We fall back on general impressions. The student who wrote the sketch in Chapter 3 used her powers of observation and her curiosity so fully that she produced an interesting, idea-filled "A" theme from material most of us would not even have noticed enough to think about.

In a workaday, practical existence, few of us use *imagination*—our ability to form mental images of what is not actually present in real life. No sets of exercises exist for genuinely training the imagination, yet this capacity is one of the richest sources of writing material. Everyone daydreams, but imagination can be more immediately useful and practical than daydreaming because it can be applied to real-life persons, situations, and circumstances. Try following through on such speculations as "What would happen if . . ." and "I wonder why. . . ."

Reflection is another name for careful thinking. Don Marquis, an American writer and humorist, once remarked: "If you make people think they're thinking, they'll love you. If you really make them think, they'll hate you." Careful thinking *is* hard work, but it has no peer as a source of writing material. If you give solid, prolonged thought to events in your life, to situations about you every day, to people whom you know and see regularly, an astonishing amount of material will appear.

Although a writer necessarily obtains much material from his own observation, curiosity, imagination, and reflection, he cannot neglect the material he can get from others, unless he is a recognized authority on the particular topic.

An easy and often pleasant way of getting material from other people is *discussion*—an interchange of ideas, a give-and-take resulting in expanded thought and new ideas. Classroom discussions are an excellent source of material. For comments on exchanging ideas with others, see Part Two, Sections 65 and 66.

Interviewing is another means of quickly and easily getting material for writing. The formal interview has gradually gone out of fashion, even in newspapers and magazines where it was once so prevalent. But a form of interview—a sort of clipped version—forms the basis of many television and radio talk shows. Interviewing a person and accurately recording his statements may be difficult, but it does train the ear, the eye, and the memory. Truman Capote attributed much of the success of his *In Cold Blood* to the thoroughness and efficiency of the interviewing techniques that underlie most of this thriller.

Meeting and talking with people is valuable, too, in developing a universally helpful knowledge of human nature. You do not need to know and have access to famous people in order to conduct interviews. Conversation with a fellow student, a college employee, the proprietor of a nearby store, a bus driver, or the cashier at a movie theater may produce extremely good material.

Another important way of getting content is *reading*. Certainly reading will intensify and expand your own ideas. It may also suggest entirely new lines of thought that, when reflected upon, can be used as your own. One good source of material (a combination of conversation and reading) is discussing with your classmates and instructor the ideas in reading assignments and their significance (see Part Two, Section 64).

Still other important sources of content are audiovisual media: radio and television programs, films, phonograph records, tape recordings, and works of art such as paintings and sculptures. These are also expressions of the experiences and thoughts of other people and are prime sources of material. For special information, especially when writing a longer research paper, you might want to write a letter of inquiry to a company or a recognized authority.

Using these various sources—especially discussion and reading—you can write why you agree or disagree or what your own opinions and beliefs are. But in drawing upon the experiences and reflections of others, remember to make them your own by assimilating ideas and expressing them in your own words.

CHAPTER 6

BUILDING A PARAGRAPH

A paragraph is a sequence of related sentences, a logical unit developing one thought or a part of one thought. It is a group, or bundle, of sentences tied together for the convenience of readers: a visual unit.

The structural unit of the paragraph is the sentence; the structural unit of a paper is the paragraph. Since a composition has, or should have, a central aim, one particular point to make or idea to reveal, it follows that each paragraph within a paper is likely to develop only one phase of this thought rather than an idea complete in itself. For this reason, training in writing paragraphs is often begun with assignments requiring the development of a single idea, with building one paragraph which can stand alone but may be one of a group.

Good paragraphing is a real aid to clarity. Properly separated groups of sentences let the writer plot his course and see the progress he is making. They serve the reader by making the structure and development of ideas apparent. Paragraphing involves some of the principles of punctuation in the sense that it separates certain ideas from others because of their structural relationships; it furnishes the reader signposts to guide him along the writer's paths of thought.

The sentence is the unit of writing, but the paragraph is the unit of thought. In fact, the heart of learning to write effectively is found in paragraph development. The secret of the effective writer—if he may be said to have a secret—is his ability to form a thought, however fragmentary or vague, and then to develop it so that it is clear, helpful, and interesting to his readers.

Hasn't everyone had the experience of making a statement or writing a sentence and then halting, aware that it needs expansion, certain that the one idea standing alone seems bare and incomplete, but not knowing what to say or write to "flesh it out"? This problem is the core of the writing process. It's what freshman English is all about. It's what any course in writing and most courses in speaking are all about.

Suppose, for example, the thought occurs to you, as well it might, that "the calendar is a foolish invention." But if you express this idea to yourself or say it aloud to someone, it obviously needs further comment. Can you explain what you mean? Add a thought or two to it? Build it into a paragraph? After some thought, you may be able to write this much:

> The calendar is a foolish invention. It tells us that the new year begins in winter. But everyone knows that school and business start afresh in the autumn, and nature has its rebirth in spring.

This is still an only partly clothed idea, but it has a little something to wear.

Again, suppose that you have just finished reading some material dealing with the philosophy that underlay the birth of the United States. Musing on the types of freedom envisioned by the Founding Fathers, you may think that your own freedom today seems limited. This is a tenable idea. What can you say or write to make clear what you have in mind? Here is what a capable writer, John Ciardi, has said on this subject:

> Americans are still born free, but their freedom neither lasts as long nor goes as far as it used to. Once the infant is smacked on the bottom and lets out his first taxable howl, he is immediately tagged, footprinted, blood-tested, classified, certificated, and generally taken in census. By the time that squawler has drawn the breath of adulthood he must have some clerk's permission to go to school or stay away, ride a bike, drive a car, collect his salary, carry a gun, fish, get married, go into the army or stay out, leave or re-enter the country, fly a plane, operate a power boat or a ham radio, buy a piece of land, build a house or knock one down, add a room to the house he has bought, burn his trash, park his car, keep a dog, run his business, go bankrupt, practice a profession, pick the wildflowers, bury the garbage, beg in the streets, sell whiskey in his store, peddle magazines from house to house, walk across a turnpike from one of his fields to another now that the state has divided him—the list is endless. Even in death his corpse must be certificated and licensed before the earth may swallow him legally. Freedom is no longer free but licensed.

Perhaps after reading some essay about science or nature you may reflect that you never have been able to understand why Nature is usually considered kind when you have often found her cruel. This is a legitimate concept; can you explain what you mean? Perhaps so, perhaps not. This is a paragraph from what Eric Hoffer said in an article about his war with nature:

> All through adult life I have had a feeling of revulsion when told how nature aids and guides us, how like a stern mother she nudges and pushes man to fulfil her wise designs. As a migratory worker from the age of eighteen I knew nature as

ill-disposed and inhospitable. If I stretched on the ground to rest, nature pushed its hard knuckles into my sides, and sent bugs, burrs, and foxtails to make me get up and be gone. As a placer miner I had to run the gantlet of buckbrush, manzanita, and poison oak when I left the road to find my way to a creek. Direct contact with nature almost always meant scratches, bites, torn clothes, and grime that ate its way into every pore of the body. To make life bearable I had to interpose a protective layer between myself and nature. On the paved road, even when miles from anywhere, I felt at home. I had a sense of kinship with the winding, endless road that cares not where it goes or what its load.

After reading some selection dealing with progress, you may reflect that you feel uneasy about the rapid changes evident everywhere. Can you express your fears in a sentence and develop them in a paragraph? Here is what a noted writer, E. B. White, managed to do with this concept:

> We were encouraged at reading the prediction that this country would be out of gas in about ten years. There is probably nothing in the report. Still, it bucks a man up. We can now dismiss the revolting picture of the postwar world which has been painted for us—a world agitated by an unlimited supply of petrol and by the spirit of total motion. The automobile, the helicopter, the family plane, the stratoliner, and the folding house which flaps together and jumps around from place to place have been woven into a dream in Technicolor by the excitable prophets of industry. They push this dream down our throats at every turn of the page. Unless a man believes that the highest form of life is that which darts about, he can face the future only with an effort of will. As for us, we are an exponent of the sit-still, or stay-where-you-are, theory of life and have always had more respect for the horned toad than for the black ant. The bicycle is our idea of a decent acceleration of the normal body movements and the Model T Ford is the highest point to which we deem it advisable to develop the gas engine. We therefore hail with cries of unprincipled joy the news of the drying up of the wells. Ah, lovely wilderness, if only it were true!

It should be clear, then, that writing a good paragraph depends upon your own thinking. You must train your mind to deal fully and logically with an idea, or series of ideas, to develop concepts and relate them to each other. Learning to write well depends in large part on learning to think well.

Suppose, for example, that you have decided to write something about your friend George. Having made your decision, you then must ask, "What can I say about him?" After considerable reflection, you might come up with five statements about George, each of them indicating one aspect of your subject. You phrase these thoughts:

1. He is tall, strong, athletic.
2. He has always been interested in how things work and is now studying mechanical engineering at college.
3. He is generous and fun-loving but lacks will power.
4. The outstanding influence on his life has been his mother, who has always pampered him.
5. He is completely sincere in his belief that success can be measured only in terms of money, and consequently he cares little for so-called culture.

The five sentences about George will mean little to the reader until they are expanded into paragraphs. Their shaping and expansion require thought, more thought than is ordinarily used in conversation. These five ideas indicate different and interesting characteristics and should serve as the nucleus of an effective description. Your writing problem is to arrange and develop these statements and combine them into a whole. Your "developed" statements will be the paragraphs of your paper. Your composition will be as effective, and only as effective, as the individual paragraphs. It is as simple, and as difficult, as that.

A well-constructed paragraph, like good diction or a good sentence, should be *clear* and *effective*—characteristics dependent upon careful thinking. Let us take a closer look at the elements that give paragraphs clarity and effectiveness.

CHAPTER 7

SHAPING THE PARAGRAPH

Effective paragraphs have four major characteristics: (1) a central idea and purpose, (2) adequate development, (3) absence of any unrelated material, and (4) proper proportion and length.

A paragraph should have a central idea and purpose expressed (or implied) in a topic (or thesis) sentence.

A thesis or topic sentence states the point of the paragraph. It contains the heart of the idea that is developed in the other sentences of the paragraph. (If such a sentence does not actually appear in a paragraph, one can be made by a reader who can sum up for himself the central thought and purpose.)

Such a sentence may appear at various places within the paragraph, although usually it is the first sentence because it can prepare the reader for what is to come. In the following paragraphs, note the position of each topic sentence, and especially note how each serves to unify and clarify the content of the entire paragraph.

> *The two most expressive things about him were his mouth and the pockets of his jacket.* By looking at his mouth, one could tell whether he was plotting evil or had recently accomplished it. If he was bent upon malevolence, his lips were all puckered up, like those of a billiard player about to make a difficult shot. After the

deed was done, the pucker was replaced by a delicate, unearthly smile. How a teacher who knew anything about boys could miss the fact that both expressions were masks of Satan I'm sure I don't know. Wallace's pockets were less interesting than his mouth, perhaps, but more spectacular in a way. The side pockets of his jacket bulged out over his pudgy haunches like burro hampers. They were filled with tools—screwdrivers, pliers, files, wrenches, wire cutters, nail sets, and I don't know what else. In addition to all this, one pocket always contained a rolled-up copy of *Popular Mechanics,* while from the top of the other protruded *Scientific American* or some such other magazine. His breast pocket contained, besides a large collection of fountain pens and mechanical pencils, a picket fence of drill bits, gimlets, kitchen knives, and other pointed instruments. When he walked, he clinked and jangled and pealed.

From *Wallace,* by Richard Rovere

The author discusses "the two most expressive things" about Wallace in one paragraph; the paragraph is unified by the topic sentence and its statement of content and implied purpose.

The room in which I found myself was very large and lofty. The windows were long, narrow, and pointed, and at so vast a distance from the black oaken floor as to be altogether inaccessible from within. Feeble gleams of encrimsoned light made their way though the trellised panes, and served to render sufficiently distinct the more prominent objects around; the eye, however, struggled in vain to reach the remoter angles of the chamber, or the recesses of the vaulted and fretted ceiling. Dark draperies hung upon the walls. The general furniture was profuse, comfortless, antique, and tattered. Many books and musical instruments lay scattered about, but failed to give any vitality to the scene. I felt that I breathed an atmosphere of sorrow. *An air of stern, deep, and irredeemable gloom hung over and pervaded all.*

From *The Fall of the House of Usher,*
by Edgar Allan Poe

Placing the topic sentence at the end makes the effect of the paragraph more dramatic: inductive arrangement presents evidence piece by piece and is summarized in the final sentence.

In the face of this, one may ask: Why does the great and universal fame of classical authors continue? The answer is that *the fame of classical authors is entirely independent of the majority.* Do you suppose that if the fame of Shakespeare depended on the man in the street it would survive a fortnight? *The fame of classical authors is originally made, and it is maintained, by a passionate few.* Even when a first-class author has enjoyed immense success during his lifetime, the majority have never appreciated him so sincerely as they have appreciated second-rate men. He has always been reenforced by the ardor of the passionate few. And in the case of an author who has emerged into glory after his death, the happy sequel has been due solely to the obstinate perseverance of the few. They could not leave him alone; they would not. They kept on savoring him, and talking about him, and buying him, and they generally behaved with such eager zeal, and they were so authoritative and sure of themselves, that at last the majority grew accustomed to the sound of his name and placidly agreed to the proposition that he was a genius; the majority really did not care very much either way.

From *Why a Classic Is a Classic,*
by Arnold Bennett

Suppose, however, that we had called that same animal a "mongrel." The matter is more complicated. We have used a word which objectively means the same as "dog of mixed breed," but which also arouses in our hearers an emotional attitude of disapproval toward that particular dog. *A word, therefore, cannot only indicate an object, but can also suggest an emotional attitude toward it.* Such suggestion of an emotional attitude does go beyond exact and scientific discussion because our approvals and disapprovals are individual—they belong to ourselves and not to the objects we approve or disapprove of. An animal which to the mind of its master is a faithful and noble dog of mixed ancestry may be a "mongrel" to his neighbor whose chickens are chased by it.

From *Emotional Meanings,* by Robert Thouless

As an easy check on the presence or absence of a topic sentence and its effective phrasing, reread carefully each paragraph that you write. Put in the margin (and later remove) the key words that indicate the subject of the paragraph. Or boldly print the topic at the beginning of each paragraph.

One test of a good paragraph is that it must be so unified that its central thought *can* be expressed in a topic sentence, even if the sentence itself does not appear. Only thus can you be certain that you have kept to the subject; only thus can the reader follow clearly the development of your idea. But keep in mind that a topic sentence contains merely the main point, or points, of a paragraph, not every idea mentioned.

A good paragraph consists of an idea developed by pertinent detail. Neither repetition of the central idea nor vague generalizations will build a good paragraph. Each of the paragraphs quoted above supports its central idea with details. All too frequently, compositions consist of a few topic sentences, perhaps adequate in themselves but thin in genuine material.

Adequate substance consists of definite ideas, impressions, and observations. Generalizations are frequently trite, vague, and ineffective. Note the lack of substance in this student paragraph:

> Cheating never pays. After all, "honesty is the best policy"; also when one gets something for nothing he does not appreciate it. I think that every student should be on his own, even if his "own" is not good enough for him to pass his courses. One should be honest, no matter what the cost. The student who thinks cheating is a sin only when it is detected is fooling nobody but himself. Sooner or later, his sins will find him out, and he will have nobody but himself to blame.

The student rewrote this paragraph with greater effectiveness when he used a specific illustration:

> Cheating never pays. A friend of mine, whom we shall call John, thought that it did. He once said to me: "Why should I study when it is so easy to get the desired results without work? The only sin in cheating is being caught." And so John was dishonest all through his four years at school. But when he took the college board examinations, he could not cheat because the proctors were efficient. He failed and was bitterly disappointed, because he wanted very badly to enter ——— College. Now he believes, as I do, that cheating never pays.

In your study of history or science, it may have occurred to you that in the past some daring thinker or some new discovery or invention has been ridiculed. Such shortsightedness and contempt now seem savage and unbelievable, just as men of the twenty-first century may regard some of our oversights and intolerances as incredible. Not long ago, a freshman seized upon the idea that some great thinkers and innovators have been laughed at or scorned by their contemporaries. He did some reading and jotted down some of his findings about these subjects: de Forest, the locomotive, the automobile, Daguerre, the vacuum tube, Murdoch, coal gas, and Socrates. These notes, combined with some hard thinking and rewriting, enabled him to produce this paragraph filled with solid, informative, arresting substance:

> History follows a disturbing pattern of denouncing great discoveries, only to honor them after the discoverers themselves are destroyed or ridiculed by their detractors. For centuries, men have honored the teachings of Socrates as preserved in the *Dialogues* of Plato, but the man himself was condemned to death for corrupting youth with his novel ideas. Lee de Forest was prosecuted for using the mails to defraud because he wrote that his vacuum tube "would transmit the human voice across the Atlantic." And this was as recent as 1913! Daguerre, the creator of photography, was committed to an insane asylum for insisting that he could transfer a likeness to a tin plate. The automobile was opposed because agriculture was felt to be doomed by a vehicle that ate neither oats nor hay. Stephenson's locomotive was denounced on the grounds that its speed would shatter men's minds and bodies. The eminent Sir Walter Scott called William Murdoch a madman for proposing to light the streets of London with coal gas, and the great Emperor Napoleon laughed off the idea as a "crazy notion." Some churchmen argued against the plan as being blasphemous, since God had divided the light from darkness. And some physicians insisted coal-gas lights would induce people to stay out late and catch cold. Who are the heretics and madmen of the 1960s who will be honored and acclaimed a decade or century from now?

Various methods of developing topic sentences involve using different kinds of material in different ways. All methods of paragraph development have essentially the same purpose, however, and the different technical names to label material are of little importance and less help. The primary aim in writing paragraphs is to make the reader see exactly and fully the ideas contained in the expressed or implied topic sentences. The only test of the substance of a paragraph is that of communication. *Define* if the terms are not clear; *explain in detail* if the idea is difficult or abstruse; *give instances and examples* that will relate to the reader's experience and understanding; *compare* or *contrast* the idea with something the reader already knows.

Experienced writers do not say to themselves: "Now I shall give an illustration and example to develop the thought of this paragraph." Many writers would find it almost impossible to define and explain the kinds of substance they use. Nevertheless, a good writer does put flesh on the bare bones of a topic sentence. He asks himself, "What could I do to get across my idea more clearly?" Then his mind sorts through all the available examples and evidence to weed out the most convincing and effective.

A paragraph should contain only material directly related to the main thought.

Our minds do not always work logically. We may think of an idea, possibly an important one, that should appear in the paper we are writing but that does not bear upon the subject at hand. If it is included where it does not belong, a reader who is prepared for discussion of topic A will be confused by a remark concerning topic B. Two examples:

> Lake-of-the-Woods is an excellent place for the sportsman to spend the summer. If you like to fish, there are all kinds of fresh-water fish to be found, the most common of which is the pike. A few miles away, up in the mountains, the streams are filled with brook trout. *For people who like to winter-fish, there is ice-fishing nearly every day.* People who are fishing there for the first time can obtain guides, leaving the town early in the morning before the weather gets hot and returning in the cool of the evening.
>
> Our government is primarily one of lawyers and bureaucrats who seem to feel that any attempt to root out gobbledygook is an attack upon their own livelihood. The present tax law, a creation of lawyers, is gleefully enforced by bureaucrats. *The Social Security Act was passed in 1935 and has had several major amendments since then.* Since nobody, including lawyers, knows exactly what our tax code means, lawyers can enjoy never-ending litigation.

Any idea that is not related to the main thought of the paragraph should be omitted or placed in another paragraph where it does belong. The only test for unity is this: does the statement refer to the thought contained in the expressed or implied topic sentence? Let each paragraph develop and convey its own idea—and no other.

The proportions and lengths of paragraphs in a composition should be determined by a writer's purpose and by the significance of paragraph ideas.

However much an idea appeals to the writer, dwelling at length upon it may distort its significance for the reader. Here are five suggestions for proportioning paragraphs:

1. View the subject as a whole before writing.
2. Allot a tentative number of words for the development of each paragraph, but be ready to change this allotment when necessary.
3. Determine the central purpose of each paragraph in communicating ideas to your reader.
4. Lengthen a paragraph if its central idea seems to need amplification, illustration, definition, or any other sort of material that will make clear to your reader what is in your mind.
5. Shorten a paragraph if it does not possess enough significance, even though the words in it appeal to you.

Paragraph length, like paragraph proportion, should be regulated by a writer's purpose and the significance of its ideas. No specific rule is valid, except this one: do not thoughtlessly or artificially avoid either long or short paragraphs, but keep away from series of either. A successive group of short paragraphs will soon become monotonous and will create an impression of sketchy, inadequate development. Long paragraphs all too often contain unrelated material and thus violate the principle of paragraph unity.

CHAPTER 8

PULLING TOGETHER IDEAS: WRITING A COMPLETE PAPER

No one can be said to write well until he can compose a completed whole, an entire composition. An automobile is more than the sum of its parts; a composition is more than the sum of its words, sentences, and paragraphs. Dependent though it is on units of construction, a paper needs more than these. It needs a sense of wholeness and integrity; the separate parts must *unite;* they must work well together.

If you have carefully studied the preceding chapters, you are prepared to write a competent paper. The pitfalls to avoid and the goals for which to strive are pinpointed in those chapters and in the sections of Part Two.

As an overall checklist to apply to any composition you may write, ask these questions and try to answer them honestly and completely:

1. Does my paper have a definite *central purpose* (that is, have I carefully analyzed the topic)?
2. Does my paper have *ample material?*
3. Is this material (substance) *arranged* in a clear, orderly, and logical way?
4. Is this paper *unified?*
5. Is my composition *clear* in all its parts?
6. Is the material presented so interestingly that it will *appeal* to its readers?
7. Is my paper *correct* in grammatical and mechanical details?

The key words in these questions are italicized. Your own common sense will tell you what these key words involve. As a kind of case study in writing a paper, however, let's go through an exercise together.

Assume that you have decided to write (or have been assigned) a composition about some college activity that interests you. Assume further that you realize this broad general subject must be narrowed to some specific topic that can be handled adequately in the space of 400 to 500 words. Before you can even consider the first question suggested above, you must perform some prewriting tasks.

Perhaps one particular college activity will spring immediately to mind. If it doesn't, however, you might begin by jotting down a list of something like the following:

Wide and general subject:	College activities
General subject:	College-sponsored community work
	Sports
	Classes and studies
	Student organizations

Thus far, you have broken up a broad subject into four areas that are representative of a dozen or more that could be listed. But the subject is still too general.

Assume then that you narrow "Student organizations" to a less general topic. Your list might read:

College government
College dramatics
Intramural sports
Special interest clubs (Women's Liberation, Black Awareness, Weaving, Pottery, Modern Dance, Camera, and so on)
Departmental clubs (Biology, French, Russian, Debating, and so on)
Musical organizations

Many other groups could be named, but you have limited a wide subject to topics that might be handled in lengthy compositions. The subject, however, can be restricted even more. For instance, "Musical Organizations" can be reduced to a list like this:

The college choir
Rock groups
Jazz groups
Concert groups
The student chorus
All-campus musical shows
The college glee club*

Now let's assume that you decide to write about "The College Glee Club." At last you are ready to tackle the first question to be asked: What is to be the *central purpose* of my paper?

* Singing groups go by different names in different colleges. Where "glee club" appears in the following paragraphs, substitute if necessary the name applicable in your school.

You can write an autobiographical paper about how or why you joined the glee club, or at least tried out for it. You can explain how to become a member. You can argue that the glee club contributes to the reputation and public image of the college throughout the state or section of the country in which it is located.

You decide, however, that you wish to write a paper that will show how much pleasure, relaxation, and musical education can be derived from glee club activity.

You can now proceed with these steps:

Limited subject: The College Glee Club
Possible title: Let's Sing
Reader: Other students in this college who might be recruited for the glee club
Length: 400–500 words
Thesis sentence: This college's glee club provides an opportunity to have fun, find relaxation, and improve one's musical education.
Specific purpose: To convince fellow students that glee club membership will be helpful and pleasurable to them and profitable to the college.

The assignment is well under way; many writers would say that it is more than half completed. Having selected and analyzed a suitable topic, you now have several items to consider, according to the questions listed earlier in this chapter.

Material. From your own experience, observation, imagination, curiosity, and thinking and from the remarks of others you can select facts, testimony, quotations, impressions, arguments, examples, incidents, and case histories to explain the pleasure, excitement, and enrichment that come from participating in glee club activities. You should gather more material than you can use and then select those items that will contribute most effectively to the central purpose of your paper.

Arrangement. Almost any kind of order and arrangement may be used, provided it makes sense and is clear to your readers. For further suggestions and information, see Part Two, Section 68.

Unity. Remember the central purpose of your theme. Stick to it. Do not tell about the difficulties encountered in learning some particular selection, the miserable experience you had on some bus during a glee club trip, the lack of interest of some members of the club, and so forth. Nothing should appear in your paper that does not contribute to its prime purpose.

Clarity. You are writing with specific readers in mind. (1) Probably you should avoid terms like *fugue, counterpoint,* and *obbligato;* if you must use them, define them simply and clearly. (2) Make sure that your ideas are based on fact and that beliefs and opinions are clearly identified as such. (3) Avoid generalizations, false assumptions, and the like. For further comment on "muddy" thinking, see Part Two, Section 56.

Appeal. Readers expect more than mere clarity. The human mind, someone once remarked, has an extraordinary capacity for resisting information. Exposition, which has as its primary purpose imparting information, thus possesses limitations that other forms of writing do not have. The story teller has a chain of incidents and an emotional appeal to rely on; the descriptive writer can appeal to the senses; the debater has strong convictions to discuss and often can make a frank display of his own personality. Since the expository writer has none of these aids, he must be resourceful in finding ways to interest his reader. He must use narrative and descriptive material to make his information pleasing; wherever possible, he must strive to get a new approach to the subject; he must make occasional use of humor and satire. Material that is dull, dry, and commonplace is not readily communicable to others.

Seldom do we remember a writer's or speaker's generalities or moralizings, but we recall vividly the stories he tells, the illustrative jokes, the revealing incidents, the re-creations of dialogue, the pertinent anecdotes he injects into his writing or speech. We may recall little of the Bible, but we are likely to keep forever in mind, once read, stories about Joseph, about David and Goliath, about Daniel in the den of lions, about Ruth or the prodigal son.

If you can make your paper *interesting*, you can be certain that it will appeal to your readers regardless of their previous interest—or lack of it—in glee clubs in general and yours in particular.

Correctness. Everyone—yes, everyone—makes mistakes in writing. Most writers are aware of this fact and perform mopping-up operations on their "finished" compositions. For suggestions about these essential steps, see Part Two, Section 69.

Errors should be corrected before you submit a paper to your instructor. Carefully read it—perhaps more than once—as a check against these questions:

1. Does my paper contain any unjustified sentence fragments? (Part Two, Section 41)
2. Does my paper contain any fused sentences? (Part Two, Section 43)
3. Have I avoided all comma splices? (Part Two, Section 42)
4. Is the punctuation in my theme logical and necessary? (Part Two, Sections 21–34)
5. Have I checked to make sure that my theme contains no glaring errors in grammar—agreement, reference of pronouns, correct verb forms, correct case of pronouns, and so on? (Part Two, Sections 12–20)
6. Is the sentence construction accurate and clear—no misplaced or dangling modifiers, split constructions, faulty parallelism, faulty coordination or subordination, illogical constructions, inconsistencies in tense, and so on? Have I avoided choppiness? (Part Two, Sections 44–55)
7. Is the diction as correct, clear, and effective as I can make it? (Part Two, Sections 36–39)
8. Have I checked the spelling of all words? (Part Two, Section 35)
9. Have I proofread the theme carefully, checking painstakingly to eliminate all careless errors? (Part Two, Section 69)

If you are a person who, in reading your paper aloud, is likely to give it a satisfactory interpretation regardless of how it is written, try having a friend read your composition to you. You can judge from the reader's interpretation whether the communication is registering correctly and effectively.

Allow as much time as possible to elapse between writing a paper and revising it. If there is sufficient time between the two steps (the actual composition and the suggested rereadings), you can approach your work more objectively. Errors not seen before will be prominent in rereading. Every writer has noted that he can detect errors in another's work more easily than he can in his own. If you will allow your paper to "jell," you can see it almost as objectively as you can the compositions of someone else.

An inexperienced person tends to think that a writer just writes and that something is wrong with him if his words do not pour out on paper in complete, final, and correct form. And yet most writers, and certainly most skilled professional writers, have testified that writing is painful, time-consuming labor. If an experienced professional writer can get on paper only a few hundred words during a full working day, he feels encouraged and even elated. Consider this comment from a Nobel Prize winner, John Steinbeck:

> Many years of preparation preceded the writing of *Grapes of Wrath*. I wrote it in one hundred days, but the preparation, false starts, and wasted motion took two and a half years. The actual writing is the last process.

Effective writing requires time, effort, and careful thinking. But reasonable amounts of these ingredients will produce astonishing results. Few satisfactions in life will exceed that of really getting across to others what you think and feel about something that is important to you. Probably you don't intend to become a professional writer, but you do expect to take your rightful place in a world that needs communication between people as much as it needs anything else.

CHAPTER 9

DEFINING STYLE

If you were asked why you are taking freshman English, chances are that you would give one of two answers: "Because it is required" or "To improve my writing style." Let the wisdom or folly of requiring freshman English be debated elsewhere. Just what do we mean when we refer to "style in writing"? And indeed, how *can* one improve the writing style he already has?

WHAT STYLE MEANS

The term *style* has been defined in many ways but never to everyone's satisfaction, since every speaker and writer has his own notion of its precise meaning. Do you agree with Lord Chesterfield that "style is the dress of thought"? With Whitehead's comment that "style is the ultimate morality of mind"? With Cardinal Newman's "style is a thinking out into language"? With Jonathan Swift's suggestion that "proper words in proper places make the true definition of a style"? Or with the most quoted definition of all, Buffon's "the style is the man himself" (*Le style est l'homme même*)? Do any of these definitions provide you with a useful, helpful idea?

Probably the word *style* means to you something more or less than any of these statements, or something entirely different. When you say that so-and-so has no style, or has poor style, rarely are you referring to his or her manner of writing and speaking. Probably you are commenting on a manner of acting or appearing or behaving (dressing, greeting someone, dancing), an individual's complex or combination of attitudes and actions. If this is what is meant, then style for you refers to the *way* one does or expresses something. It singles out for notice or comment the particular and individual manner in which someone does or says something, whatever that something may be.

Can we say that style consists, at least in part, of what a person adds to or subtracts from a particular activity: walking, eating, conversing, writing? Of the ways in which what one person does or says differ from the ways in which someone else does or says that same something? If style in general means "manner or mode," can we say that literary style is a way of putting thoughts into words, a characteristic manner of expression or construction in writing and speaking?

Style is the influence of personality upon subject matter. *Your style is what you as an individual contribute to the expression of what you have in mind to say and write.*

Perhaps even this simple definition does not express what you mean by *style*. You may conceive of style as the removal from your work of so-called errors and weaknesses rather than the addition of grace, strength, and other elements that you think should be reserved for professional writers. Style to you may mean correct spelling, suitable punctuation, the absence of errors in tense or agreement or the principal parts of verbs.

That is, to some persons good style implies writing that is free of language impurities, that is aseptic, harmless because it has no such "microorganisms" as comma faults and localisms. Many teachers and many more students would agree that attaining such a style—sterile, flat, and colorless though it usually is—is a praiseworthy aim, one representing a distinct step forward, even though the student is striving for something limited and largely negative.

Style should mean more than the negative aspects of writing and speaking, the mere avoidance of mistakes in usage and mechanics. "Improving" one's style involves correctness and appropriateness, but it embraces more than this. What characteristics of style can a first-year college student reasonably hope to attain? And how can he go about acquiring these characteristics?

First, may we agree that the primary aim of writing, its dominant purpose, is communicating ideas from the mind of the writer to that of the reader? If we agree, then it follows that anything and everything which blocks or slows down communication should be removed; anything and everything which eases or increases communication should be used. Therefore, we try to eliminate the errors—the faulty diction, illogical sentence structure, nonstandard usage—that distort or bury our meaning or that so attract our reader's attention that his mind is turned from what we are trying to convey. In addition, we employ whatever devices of style we can in order to smooth and speed our message to our readers' minds.

Scores of devices can help us communicate. The most important elements contributing to effective and pleasing style can be classified under four headings:

simplicity, conversational quality, individuality, and concreteness. Other characteristics could be listed, but even these four goals involve refinements of style that can take a lifetime to perfect.

SIMPLICITY

Simplicity does not mean "writing down" to the reader and underestimating either his intelligence or his knowledge. It does mean expressing one's ideas in terms that are clear, logical, and specifically geared to the level (age, education, and so on) of the persons for whom one is writing.

If a subject is so technical that technical terms cannot be avoided, use them—but define them without employing a tone or method insulting to the reader's intelligence. The level of your reading audience will determine how many such terms should be defined and in what detail.

If you have a choice between a long and a short word, use whichever is clearer and more exact—usually, but not always, the short word. Short words are more often clear and sharp, like signs chiseled in the face of a rock; in much writing, and especially in speaking, they are crisp and filled with zest, saying what they "mean" and leaving as little doubt as possible in the mind of reader or hearer. But whether we use long or short words, diction should be as simple and clear as we can make it so that our ideas will move smoothly.

In college you hear and read many words previously unknown to you. Impressed, you may attempt what hundreds of thousands of others have done: to employ such expressions in speaking and writing not so much for their actual value as to show others how smart you are, how "educated" you are becoming. Enlarging one's vocabulary and using new words purposefully are both worthwhile activities—but they lose meaning when they are pursued for reasons of vanity, self-esteem, or "culture climbing."

No truer statement about simplicity in style exists than this: "A book has one leg on immortality's trophy when the words are for children but the meanings are for men." Simplicity without substance is childish; but great thoughts, like great inventions of whatever kind, achieve much of their effectiveness and power through simplicity. Can you think of any great work of literature, of any great scientific discovery, that is unnecessarily and arbitrarily complex and involved? A good literary selection or an important scientific discovery may be beyond our understanding, but each probably is as simple as it can be and still be what it is.

Other devices for achieving simplicity in style are discussed in Part Two of this book. Try to apply them in your own papers. In selections in Part Four you can observe and study simplicity of diction, sentence structure, organization, and logic—all contributing directly and powerfully to the process of communication.

CONVERSATIONAL QUALITY

More than most of us realize, the *conversational* quality of what we read adds an appeal that helps us to grasp the ideas being presented. Conversation is not necessarily informal and relaxed, but good conversation is never so elevated in tone that one feels condescended to. Have you noticed that some essays by eighteenth- and nineteenth-century writers, even ones considered great and timeless, seem formal and pontifical? That essays of more recent vintage are often more relaxed, less didactic and "preachy"?

This difference in attitude toward both subject and reader is partly a matter of diction and sentence structure, but even more a result of later authors' descending from their pedestals. Such a statement does not imply that only recent essays have a conversational quality and thus are enjoyable to read. Nor does it mean that a good writer, of whatever era, will figuratively remove his jacket and necktie. It does imply that most effective writers have tried not to sound stuffy and ponderous, that without losing their dignity they have labored to infuse a human, friendly quality into their writing. Conversational quality means ease of expression, not sloppy thought; consideration for the reader as one "thinking with" the author and not as a person both ignorant and stupid.

John R. Tunis, one of the more popular and esteemed professional writers of recent years, has said that he tries to write an essay or magazine article as though he were conversing with a dinner companion. By this, he explained, he meant that he tries to use words and expressions that are not dull and stuffy, that he anticipates and answers in his writing the questions his companion would actually raise in conversation, that he provides illustrations and examples designed to keep the attention of his listener and make him or her actually *see* what he is attempting to communicate. An even greater writer of an earlier time, Laurence Sterne, wrote in *Tristram Shandy:* "Writing, when properly managed [and, being Sterne, he put in parentheses] (as you may be sure I think mine is) is but another name for conversation."

Huxley's "The Method of Scientific Investigation" (Part Four) is notable for its conversational quality. But conversational quality does not appear only in writing derived from lectures. Notice the relaxed and even quietly intimate quality of Frost's "Mending Wall" (Part Four). Such pieces do not "descend to the level" of any reader. Like many other selections in Part Four, they use the conversational device of "thinking with the reader" and thus achieve a degree of communication otherwise impossible.

INDIVIDUALITY

Related to the device of conversational tone is *individuality*, which is often a virtue and, occasionally, a vice in writing. Individuality implies "subjectivity"; when a writer is subjective he is inward-centered and applies his own standards and judgments. A highly subjective writer tends to ignore the needs and appeals of his readers and thinks exclusively of himself, his thoughts, his needs, his aspirations. Such a tendency—the direct opposite of the stylistic quality inherent in conversation—is a definite flaw.

On the other hand, the individuality growing from subjectivity can help in developing a writing style that is effectively communicative. When we read nonfiction such as essays and articles, we want and need to get the author's opinions, not merely a statement of facts, principles, and statistics. We may be dozing through a dull lecture, a flat recital of facts, but we tend to come awake when the lecturer begins to recount a personal experience, to give an eyewitness account, to express his opinions—in short, when he becomes a human being and stops being an automaton or robot.

No reader, and especially no instructor in freshman English, wishes to be confronted with material that possesses no spark of the writer's individuality, his personality, his subjective processes of thought and reasoning. Nothing is more dull and hence less communicative than a composition that "goes through the motions" of setting down borrowed or plagiarized facts for the required number of words with no obvious stamp of the author's mind and personality. Even a research paper, one based on sources other than the writer's thought and experience, will communicate effectively only if and when it reveals the author's conclusions and judgments.

Prose is seldom wholly objective (unless, of course, it is merely copied from reference sources). However, an excessively subjective composition can be as ineffective as a wholly objective one. If a writer parades his opinions to the exclusion of all other considerations, if his work is studded with "I," if he is not in some respects reader-centered, he commits the error of subjectivity. If his writing is dull, lifeless, static, almost or totally devoid of emotion or personality, he commits the error of objectivity. Both errors are serious, and striking the delicate balance between them is no easy task.

But it can be done. Not one of the selections in Part Four lacks at least some degree of individuality. Unless they possessed strong and clear elements of personality and individuality, not one of the informal essays appearing there, nor any of the short stories, poems, or plays, would have any claim to fame whatever.

Do such comments about individuality suggest that one must be *original* in his writing style? The answer, both "yes" and "no," depends upon what is meant by "original." No one—teacher, student, college administrator, or even political agitator—can reasonably be expected to produce wholly new, entirely fresh ideas and novel ways of conveying them. No one can do this often; perhaps no one now alive can do this *ever*. If he could, he would be as misunderstood as Galileo or Socrates and might lose his job or his life. But originality can and does also mean "independent thought," "individual insight," "constructive imagination." Each of these elements is attainable by nearly everyone. Goethe has wisely summed up this matter of individuality and originality:

> The most original authors of modern times are such not because they create anything new but only because they are able to say things in a manner as if they had never been said before.

You are yourself and no one but yourself. If what you write, or say, reveals in some degree the imprint of your own personality, your particular individuality, then it will have never been said before in quite the same way. It will possess a genuinely important stylistic quality without which it would be dull and spiritless.

CONCRETENESS

Each of us has repeatedly read material that seemingly "made sense" but that left us with only a vague, fuzzy impression of what the author apparently intended us to absorb. Try as we might, we could not come to grips with the author's meaning. We felt we were dealing with cotton wool or some such soft and flabby substance that we could not grasp, handle, and move about in our own thought processes. Discouraged or annoyed, we may have decided that the selection had no meaning and no message for us and thus gone on to something else.

One major cause of such a reaction is lack of *concreteness* in writing. The author we were trying unsuccessfully to read may have been using abstract words to express general ideas; he may have forgotten, if indeed he ever knew, that readers' minds respond most readily to the specific, the tangible, the concrete. For example, when we are hungry we don't think of "nutrition" or "nourishment" or even of "food." We think of steak or baked potatoes or chocolate cake.

Actually, we learned everything we know as itemized bits of experience. When we were small, a parent or some other older person pointed out to us a dog, said "See the dog," and ever afterward, a d-o-g had some particular and special meaning for us. Your concept of a "dog" and that of anyone else will differ, but each item of experience in our private store of meanings has a definite, concrete application. In contrast, we feel baffled by abstract words and expressions that have no direct connection with our own backgrounds.

Abstract words are useful in discussing certain ideas and are especially common in such subjects as philosophy and the social sciences, but usually they are less exact, less meaningful, and consequently less effective than concrete words. Because they refer to specific and actual objects or concepts, concrete words have meanings more or less solidly established in the minds of both writer and reader. "Something worn on the human body between shoulders and chin" is rather vague but not entirely abstract. The concept can be made less vague by referring to a *collar* and more concrete by mention of a *ruff, shawl collar, long point, spread collar,* and *button-down.* The word *neckwear* can refer to a "rather long narrow length of soft material such as silk or wool, worn about the neck and usually under a collar." If a speaker or writer uses *necktie,* he is somewhat more specific; if he uses *four-in-hand, bow tie, white tie,* or *necktie party,* he is being even more concrete.

Abstract words possess varying degrees of definiteness. Such words as *countryside, fear,* and *security* are not particularly specific, but they have more understandable connections with the experiences of most people than terms like *culture, duty, truth,* and *honor.* The word *carrier,* defined as a means of conveying and transporting, is somewhat abstract but can be made less so by using such terms as *truck, car, motorcycle,* and *handcar,* or *mule, tank, bus, half-track,* and *kayak.*

Good writers sometimes use an abstract term because nothing else will fit and then immediately make it more communicative by providing a concrete example of what is meant or by translating its meaning into terms less abstract and vague. Suppose, for example, that you contend that government should intervene as little as possible in our economy and thus you employ the term *laissez-faire*. Is this expression abstract or concrete? An effective writer, Stuart Chase, unwilling to take a chance on his readers' understanding of the term, used it but immediately equated it with a city that had "no traffic system," one where every driver was on his own. Chase then explained *enforced competition* as a system in which "traffic cops protect little cars"; *governmental regulation* as similar to "traffic cops advising drivers how to drive"; *government ownership* as a procedure in which "a traffic officer throws the driver out and gets behind the wheel himself." You may agree or disagree with the writer's definitions and analogies, but at least you know what he means and have been entertained while finding out.

Much of what we remember from our reading of literature—especially of essays, articles, and biography—consists of incidents and anecdotes originally designed by the author to reinforce some abstract concept. For example, once you have read it, you cannot forget "The Monster" (Part Four), because the author uses one incident, anecdote, and illustration after another to drive home his concept of this particular "monster," Richard Wagner. Writing can rarely be more concrete than this—and hence more readable, understandable, and entertaining. The appeal of short stories, plays, novels, and of much poetry lies in the fact that understandable, flesh-and-blood persons are involved in understandable problems and face understandable conflicts. What happens to people, why it happens, and what the results are seem real and exciting to us because happenings are narrated and described in concrete, specific terms that we can grasp as readily as we can observe or face problems and situations in our immediate lives.

Nine-tenths of all good writing consists of being concrete and specific. The other tenth doesn't really matter.

CHAPTER 10

DEVELOPING AN EFFECTIVE INDIVIDUAL STYLE

Assuming that you now know something about style and its desirable elements, what next? You might begin by asking: what is my style now and how do I go about improving it?

What your present style is should concern both you and your instructor. An important aim of freshman English is to make you aware of your stylistic strengths and weaknesses, to help you increase the former and decrease the latter. All the writing you and your classmates do, under the guidance of your teacher, should aid you both to remove flaws and to increase clarity and effectiveness. The best method of improving your style—best because it is most direct, most specific, and most logical—is to write and keep writing under the practiced eye and hand of your instructor.

As you continue your week-after-week improvement, try to keep constantly in mind the stylistic qualities singled out for attention in the previous chapter: simplicity, conversational quality, individuality, and concreteness.

Two other methods of improving style deserve comment. Neither is as direct as writing under supervision, but both are important. One method is *imitation;* the other is *analysis.*

IMITATION

Every writer must acquire his own style. Indeed, you already have a style, even if it pleases neither you nor your teacher. Your style possesses qualities (good and bad) peculiarly your own. It has developed with you as you have grown and matured. Your style reflects your personality, your character, your whole mode of thought. It may reflect these attributes improperly, unfairly, or obscurely, but reflect them it does. And yet your personality, character, and attitudes of thought have changed through the years and will continue to do so. Your style can be altered and improved to reflect these changes.

A mature style, such as you probably desire, is difficult to attain by conscious means. But one deliberate method of improving style is to select some writer, or writers, whose work you admire and then attempt to model your own writing upon it. If you adopt the style of another slavishly, you become a mere imitator, an inevitable second-rater. But it may be possible through imitation to learn what characteristic qualities of style are most natural and effective for you and thus improve your own work. Some writer represented in Part Four may appeal strongly to you; if so, try to imitate his or her style, but not so closely that you become only a parodist. Your study should be interpretive rather than imitative; your own approach should never be overshadowed by that of the writer being studied.

Many excellent writers claim to have become so by imitating the work of others. Robert Louis Stevenson, one of the all-time master stylists in English literature, once wrote:

> When I read a book or passage with some distinction, I must sit down at once and ape that quality. Thus I got practice in harmony, in rhythm, and in construction, playing the sedulous ape to Lamb, to Wordsworth, to Defoe, to Hawthorne, to Baudelaire.

In his *Autobiography,* Benjamin Franklin referred to his attempts to paraphrase some of the *Spectator* papers (essays by the eighteenth-century English writers Joseph Addison and Richard Steele) and then wrote:

> But I found I wanted a stock of words, or a readiness in recollecting and using them, which I thought I should have acquired before that time if I had gone on making verses; since the continual occasion for words of the same import, but of different length, to suit the measure, or of different sound for the rhyme, would have laid me under a constant necessity of searching for variety; and also have tended to fix that variety in my mind, and make me master of it. Therefore I took some of the tales and turned them into verse; and, after a time, when I had pretty well forgotten the prose, turned them back again.

In selecting an author whom you would like to imitate, search for one whose stylistic qualities seem natural and unforced for you. Effective style is natural: your style is the imprint of *your* personality upon *your* subject matter. If you are a restrained, laconic person who speaks tersely and sees things objectively, perhaps Hemingway could serve as a model. If your turn of mind is ironic, if you see the absurdity and pretense in much of modern-day living, if you prefer understatement, then E. B. White might be a possible model for imitation.

In trying to improve your style by imitating some admired author, be careful to grasp more than a superficial impression of that author's style. That is, before you go far with imitation as a technique, stop to analyze just what it is you are striving for.

ANALYSIS

Second only to actual writing as an effective method of improving one's style is careful analysis of good literary work. Such elements as figures of speech, transitional devices, length of sentences, length of words, and concrete or abstract nouns are easily detected. Other qualities are more pervasive than these but can still be discovered and analyzed: humor, irony, conciseness, rhythm, monotony, imagery, and quotable remarks such as epigrams and wisecracks. Analyzing a competent writer's style for the occurrence or absence of such elements and qualities may help you to discover weaknesses in your own writing.

The analysis of a given selection should begin with careful, attentive reading. This should be followed by a second reading that is more analytical than the first. This time you should actually note, list, and count such matters as kinds of words and sentences, uses of figurative language, and the like. In this second reading you undoubtedly will notice qualities of style you skipped over before. You can see how the author achieves his effects because you now know the stylistic elements he employed. In this kind of reading you should be rewarded with specific ideas for improving your own style. Section 64 of Part Two, especially that part called "Reading as a Writer," will help you at this stage.

Let's be specific. Assume that you admire the work of Ernest Hemingway and think that you would like to try imitating his style. Before setting out on this task, turn to Hemingway's "In Another Country" (Part Four) and analyze the varied elements that make it what it is.

After a careful study of this short story, most readers would agree that it possesses at least three of the four characteristics discussed in the preceding chapter: simplicity, conversational quality, and concreteness. Some readers may feel that it lacks individuality because the author nowhere injects his personality into the story. And yet, in his choice of subject matter and in the obvious, although unstated, implications of the narrative, Hemingway does reveal something of his attitudes and is not entirely removed from the action. (Actually, the story is largely autobiographical.)

Even more specifically, what does analysis reveal about particular elements of style in this story?

Sentence structure. With few exceptions, the sentences are simple or compound. A reader has to search hard for a complex or compound-complex sentence. In the first paragraph, for example, each of the six sentences is compound. Most of the sentences are short, or fairly short, and not one is really lengthy. Nearly every sentence follows the standard order of subject-verb-object. None are in transposed word order, periodic, or inverted form.

Vocabulary. The words Hemingway uses are easily understandable. Not every word is short and simple, but few polysyllabic expressions appear. Words of three or four syllables occur, but notice, for instance, that of the 17 words in the opening sentence, 16 have only one syllable. In the second sentence, 12 of the 14 words are monosyllabic. Of the 106 words in the entire first paragraph, only 13 have two syllables and only 1, *electric,* has three. Diction throughout the story is not always so consistently brief, but it stays simple.

Nouns and verbs are uniformly concrete and specific. No abstract words appear, except for two in Italian (*fratellanza* and *abnegazione*)—and these the author characteristically debunks by translating "with the adjectives removed." (One might have expected in a story with this setting and substance references to such terms as patriotism, duty, sacrifice, and honor.) Few adjectives appear, and adverbs are scarce. (When the major responds to the doctor, he says "No"—nothing is added to indicate how "No" was said.) Few figures of speech are used, and those that do appear are either submerged or unusually concrete: "powdered in the fur," "like hunting-hawks," "hand like a baby's."

Rhythm. As is pointed out elsewhere, the first paragraph has a rhythm that is almost measured. The same statement can be made of other descriptive passages in the story, for example, paragraphs 2, 3, 6, and 7. This effect of rhythm is achieved by the use of simple and compound sentences that tend to balance the sound of the prose and by a sense of movement: the story reads almost like a record being played.

Organization. The organization is as straightforward as prose can be. The story begins at a certain point in time, unfolds its action in chronological order, and ends when it has made its point: "The Major . . . only looked out of the window."

Tone. The style is objective, but the story itself reveals that the author has made value judgments about war, courage, and suffering. These judgments, however, are implicit rather than explicit. This story is an example of flat, objective, almost terse reporting, done with precision, conciseness, restraint, and accuracy.

Such analysis can dig deeper and be carried further, but perhaps enough has been said to prove that style can be probed and dissected. It *is* possible to see *how* an author achieves his effects through the technical handling of specific subject matter with a controlling central purpose.

Now try your hand at a selection by an author whose style is quite different from that of Hemingway. Joseph Conrad, like Hemingway, revered courage and often wrote of men facing physical and mental dangers. Careful analysis of the sentence structure of "Youth" (Part Four), of its vocabulary, imagery, and tone will uncover marked differences from those of "In Another Country."

For example, the first paragraph of "Youth" consists of one sentence of 45 words—longer than any sentence in "In Another Country." Of these 45 words, 11 contain more than one syllable and 1 has five syllables, longer than any word in "In Another Country." The vocabulary and sentence structure of this opening paragraph set a tone of leisurely development throughout the story—of explanation, description, and even argument—that is nowhere developed in Hemingway's shorter, compact tale.

Analysis does not suggest that one of these stories is better than the other, but it does show how the two differ in technique. Both are notable for their rhythmic flow and chronological development, but these elements are handled differently in the two stories. Careful analysis, more detailed than is indicated here, is invaluable in studying these and other literary selections.

For still another attempt at analysis, consider Huxley's "The Method of Scientific Investigation" (Part Four). It, too, can be dissected for its sentence structure, diction, imagery, rhythm, and tone. After analyzing these elements, however, you may still wonder how it manages to explain a complex idea so clearly and interestingly. The answer lies largely in its organization:

1. The thesis is stated in the first sentence and is repeated in different words in the second. The remainder of paragraph 1 is a clarification of this thesis by a comparison between the mental processes of scientists and storekeepers.
2. In the second paragraph, Huxley identifies the principal operations of the scientific method. He then restates the thesis of the essay in the light of this identification.
3. Paragraph 3 presents an example which will serve as an introduction for the discussion that is to follow.
4. In the fourth paragraph, the author analyzes the example given in paragraph 3 and relates it to the methods identified in paragraph 2. The resulting "law" parallels the "laws" of science. This paragraph concludes by extending the example to show an analogy (likeness) to the process of verifying any scientific investigation.
5. The fifth paragraph restates the similarity of methods used in the example and in scientific inquiry and concludes with yet another statement of the thesis, this time in the light of the entire essay.

Any worthwhile selection can be analyzed for its style, its technique, and the elements that make it more than merely "correct" and readable. In other words, study of an essay, story, or poem can reveal why and how it becomes *memorable*.

Style and meaning are always closely related. There are obvious relationships between the individuality of a writer and his style just as there are obvious traits of style that are characteristic of science fiction, advertising copy, and legal briefs. Qualities of language and elements of style directly affect the emphasis, tone, precision, suggestiveness, and intensity of the message being conveyed, the story being told, the idea being developed. Accurate understanding of a selection depends to some degree upon an aware and sensitive response to the style in which it is presented.

Analysis of effective style may not immediately improve your writing, but it will enormously improve your reading ability. This in itself is genuine progress.

PART TWO

A HANDBOOK OF WRITING AND REWRITING

GRAMMAR

That everyone should be able to read and write is now a basic assumption of our economic, political, and social system. Try to get a decent job, cast an intelligent vote, run for public office, or move up to a higher social level and you will discover how essential it is to read and write in a modern industrial democracy such as ours.

You *must* be literate. You will be judged by the literate character of your speaking and your writing. And literate writing, among many other things, is *grammatical.* This section attempts to present an approach to English grammar that will provide a clear sense of how English sentences are written.

Grammar is ordinarily understood as a series of statements of the way a language works; English grammar is "the English way of saying things." That is, grammar concerns the forms of words; their use in phrases, clauses, and sentences; their tenses, cases, and other changes in form. The word *grammar,* which comes from the Greek word *gramma* ("letter," "written symbol"), now means the structure of an entire given language.

Sentences are composed of words. Grammar classifies words as *parts of speech.* They are grouped according to the purpose they serve, or how they convey meaning *as words.*

Naming words:	Nouns and pronouns
Asserting words:	Verbs
Modifying words:	Adjectives and adverbs
Joining words:	Conjunctions and prepositions
Exclamatory words:	Interjections

But words work together to convey meaning. Grammar is also concerned with explaining how the parts of speech can be grouped together in sentences. Structures involving groups of words, that is, *phrases* and *clauses,* are essential to mature sentence construction, so that we must see how parts of speech are placed with one another to produce these structures.

Finally, words take on basic functions in the sentence, which is the central unit of meaning in all writing. How the parts of speech function in the sentence as a whole is what grammar is all about.

When you begin to write sentences, you become impressed with a significant difference between speaking and writing. Writing is a more formal mode of communicating than speaking. In ordinary conversation you rely on vocal impressions, surrounding circumstances, what the hearer knows of you and the subject of the discussion, and the opportunity to explain in response to questions if your meaning is not clear. What many educated people might consider acceptable in informal speech they would frown upon if it appeared in writing. An attitude of "anything goes" in speech does not apply in most writing situations.

As a college student, you are expected to use language well; an important part of education is learning to make words work for you. If you are a native speaker of English, you know, and have known from an early age, much about the grammatical patterns of your language. You use certain structures without conscious thought or knowledge of what they involve. But in freshman English, you have an unrivaled opportunity to refresh your knowledge of grammar, to learn new subtleties of the language, and to relearn what has slipped from your mind.

1. NOUNS

A *noun* (derived from the Latin word *nomen,* meaning "name") designates or names a person, place, or thing; a quality, idea, or action; an event or point in time.

1a. CHARACTERISTICS OF NOUNS

Nouns are usually preceded by such words as *the, a, an, my, your, his, her, some, each, every, their, this, that.*

Certain nouns have characteristic endings (*-al, -tion, -ness, -ment, -ure, -dom, -ism, -ance,* for example) that distinguish them from corresponding verbs or adjectives: *arrive, arrival; determine, determination; depart, departure; real, realism; rely, reliance; wise, wisdom.*

Nouns and identically spelled verbs may sometimes be differentiated by accent. The first member in each of these pairs of words is a noun, the second a verb; *per′mit, permit′; rec′ord, record′; sur′vey, survey′; ob′ject, object′.*

Nouns are found in set positions, such as before a verb (a *mouse* roars), after a verb (wash the *shirt*), or after a preposition (working for *money*).

Nouns may be singular or plural in number. The plural of most English nouns is obtained by adding *-s* or *-es* to the singular form: *girls, books, trees, fields, peaches.* Some nouns have only one form for both the singular and the plural: *deer, sheep, moose.* Some nouns have irregular plurals: *oxen, children, mice.* Some actually have no plurals: *fun, furniture.*

Nouns have four genders: (1) masculine (*man, boy*), (2) feminine (*girl, woman*), and (3) neuter (*chalk, earth*). When a noun may be either masculine or feminine, it has a (4) common gender (*teacher, friend*).

Nouns have three cases: nominative (subject), objective, and genitive (possessive). In English, nouns have a common form for both the nominative and the objective case. An apostrophe is used to designate a noun in the genitive case: *Jack's, boat's, neighbor's.*

1b. CLASSIFICATION OF NOUNS

A *common* noun is a name given to all members of a class: *dozen, infant, farm, street, city, boy, structure.* Common nouns can be recognized as such because they do *not* begin with a capital letter (except at the beginning of a sentence or as part of a name).

A *proper* noun names a particular member of a class; it *does* begin with a capital: *Rover, Michael, Twin Cedars, Roosevelt Freeway, Atlanta, Bob Dylan, Eiffel Tower.*

An *abstract* noun is the name of a quality or general idea that cannot be known directly by the senses: *faith, happiness, courage, fear, love.*

Concrete nouns name material (tangible) things that can be perceived by one or more of the senses: *fire, aroma, notebook, hamburger, stone, record, cake.*

A *collective* noun names a group of individuals. Although it refers to more than one, it is singular in form: *pair, committee, squad, team, crowd, crew, assembly.*

2. PRONOUNS

A *pronoun* (from the Latin *pro* and *nomen,* meaning "for a name") is not easy to define because this part of speech includes groups of quite different words.

2a. FUNCTIONS OF PRONOUNS

A pronoun is a word that can be replaced by a noun in a particular sentence or other group of words. Pronouns can function like nouns as subjects and objects; many pronouns also have plural forms and a genitive (possessive) case formed with *s.* A pronoun, then, acts in the place of a noun.

2b. KINDS OF PRONOUNS

Pronouns are classified as personal, relative, demonstrative, interrogative, reflexive, intensive, indefinite, and reciprocal.

Personal pronouns refer to an individual or individuals. Personal pronouns have thirty case forms, some of which include all genders and some with special forms for masculine, feminine, and neuter. Personal pronouns also can be labeled first person, second person, third person. First person pronouns indicate the speaker or writer, either singular or plural (*I, we*). Second person pronouns indicate the person or persons spoken to and have identical forms for singular and plural (*you, you*). Gender (or sex) is the same for all first and second person pronouns. Third person pronouns indicate the person or persons spoken of or written about. Third person pronouns involve considerations of number and gender, as shown in this table:

	Singular		
	Nominative	*Genitive*	*Objective*
1st person	I	my, mine	me
2nd person	you	your, yours	you
3rd person			
masculine	he	his	him
feminine	she	her, hers	her
neuter	it	its	it
	Plural		
1st person	we	our, ours	us
2nd person	you	your, yours	you
3rd person			
(all genders)	they	their, theirs	them

Relative pronouns relate or connect the clauses they introduce to independent clauses (see Section 8). For instance, a relative pronoun connects an adjective clause to an antecedent (the noun or pronoun to which a pronoun refers or for which it is substituted).

The flyer *who* served in the Korean War is now an airline official.
Radar equipment *that* is to be used for ships must be installed carefully.
The Elm Street group, *which* collected the most old clothing, was awarded a prize.
The person *whose* book I found lives in my dorm.
The man *that* (or *whom*) I saw was named Alexander Watts.

The same forms—*who, whose, whom, which, that*—serve for gender or number; their having gender or being singular or plural depends upon their antecedents. The choice of a relative pronoun is also largely determined by its antecedent. *Who, whose,* and *whom* are used to refer to persons. *Which* is used to refer to inanimate objects, animals, and groups of persons. *That* may refer to either things or persons.

Who, which, and *that* are frequently used relative pronouns; *whoever, whomever, whichever,* and *whatever* are less often used. *Whosoever, whichsoever,* and *whatsoever* are seldom used today.

Demonstrative pronouns point out and identify nouns or other pronouns. The important demonstrative pronouns are *this* and *that* (singular), *these* and *those* (plural), and *such* (singular or plural).

> *This* is the way to clean a window.
> *That* is my new television set.
> *These* are your books; *those* on the table are mine.
> *Such* are the problems of college.

An *interrogative* pronoun (*who, whom, whose, which, what,* and occasionally *whoever, whichever, whatever*) introduces a question.

> *Who* shall demand that a pardon be granted?
> *Which* is the route we should take from Detroit?
> *What* do you have in mind?
> *Whose* is that red Jaguar?

A *reflexive pronoun* is used to refer to the subject of a sentence or clause. It is a compound of one of the personal pronouns plus *self* or *selves: myself, yourself, himself, herself, itself, ourselves, yourselves, themselves.* An *intensive* pronoun is used to draw particular attention to a noun. Intensives take the same forms as reflexives.

> His laboratory assistant burned *himself.*
> They appointed *themselves* as law enforcement officers.
> The nurse *herself* was at fault.
> We employees *ourselves* are wholly responsible.

Indefinite pronouns are less specific in reference and less exact in meaning than other pronouns. It is often difficult to pin down a precise antecedent for an indefinite pronoun. Among the more frequently used are *all, another, any, anyone, anything, everybody, everyone, everything, few, many, nobody, none, one, several, some, each.* The pronoun *one* and its compound forms, and compound forms built on the element *-body,* form the possessive in the same way as nouns (*anybody's, everyone's*).

> Of all those involved in the accident, *none* was seriously injured.
> *Someone* should be in charge of refreshments at the dance.

A *reciprocal* pronoun completes an interchange of action involved in the predicate. This interchange can be seen in the following sentences, which include the only reciprocal pronouns in English:

> The blonde and the brunette complemented *each other.*
> The members of the group shouted at *one another.*

3. VERBS AND VERBALS

A *verb* is a word which, through the addition of endings or internal changes, specifies actions or events that take place in time. A verb may also be defined as any member of a class of words (parts of speech) that typically expresses action, state, or a relation between two objects or ideas. A verb also functions as the main element of a predicate (see Section 10). When inflected, a verb exhibits changes indicating tense, tone, voice, mood, and agreement with its subject or object.

A *verbal* is a verb that cannot serve as a predicate. The three kinds of verbals are participles, gerunds, and infinitives.

3a. KINDS OF VERBS

Verbs may be classified as transitive, intransitive, or linking.

A *transitive* verb is regularly followed by a noun or pronoun (the object) that completes the action specified by the verb.

> John *played* the *drums*.
> Tony *has* a part-time *job* after classes.
> The mechanic *removed* the *carburetor* from the engine.

A transitive verb shows the relationship existing between the noun or pronoun (the subject) that performs the action specified by the verb and the noun or pronoun that follows it (the object). In a sentence like "John played the drums," *played* expresses the nature of the relationship between *John* and *drums*.

An *intransitive* verb does not need to be followed by a noun or pronoun to make complete sense in the sentence in which it appears.

> The halfback *ran* through the line.
> Mike *walked* down the road.

Many verbs can be used in either a transitive or intransitive sense.

> We *read* the magazine with great care. [Transitive]
> We *read* until late at night. [Intransitive]
> I *won* the first game. [Transitive]
> I *won* easily. [Intransitive]

A *linking* verb shows the relationship between the subject and the noun that follows it. The noun that follows a linking verb is sometimes called the *predicate* noun. Frequently, a linking verb expresses the relationship existing between the subject and an adjective following it (the *predicate* adjective). Linking verbs are further discussed in Section 16.

3b. CHARACTERISTICS OF VERBS

English verbs have a base form called the *infinitive* form. It is sometimes preceded by the word *to;* for example, *to talk, to walk, to cook, to change*. There are three principal forms in addition to the base form (see Section 15). These forms have certain inflectional endings.

The *present* tense of English verbs is the same as the base form: *to run, run; to talk, talk; to hide, hide*. The *past* tense of English verbs varies, depending upon whether the verb is *regular* or *irregular*. In regular verbs, the past tense is formed by adding the ending *-ed* (or *-d* or *-t*) to the base form: *walk, walked; originate, originated; lend, lent*. The past tense of irregular verbs differs from word to word and must be learned individually. Most past tense forms of irregular verbs are familiar to native speakers of English: *throw, threw; tear, tore; say, said; go, went.*

The *past participle* of regular verbs is identical to the past tense: *organize, organized, organized; arrange, arranged, arranged; solve, solved, solved; mean, meant, meant.* The past participle of irregular verbs differs from word to word and must be learned individually. It is always the form that is used with the verb *have:* have *gone, written, torn, run, sung, drawn, done.* English verbs also have a *present participial* form that is formed by adding *-ing* to the base: *have, having; go, going; rain, raining; talk, talking.*

Verbs in English have one other characteristic inflectional ending. When a verb in the present tense follows the words *he, she,* or *it,* or a noun that may be substituted for them, the letter *-s* (or *-es* with some verbs) is added to the base form: *speak, speaks; run, runs; go, goes; laugh, laughs.*

In the present tense, an English verb changes its inflectional ending when the subject changes from singular to plural.

> A bird *sings.* Birds *sing.* Jack *goes.* Bill and Jack *go.*
> Josie *plays* the piano. The girls *play* the piano.

Certain *prefixes* and *suffixes* are used with verbs. The prefixes *en-* and *be-* are often used with verbs: *en*force, *en*able, *en*title, *be*come, *be*friend, *be*head. The suffixes *-(i)fy, -ate,* and *-ize* commonly signal verbs: test*ify,* ver*ify,* clar*ify,* segreg*ate,* oper*ate,* civil*ize,* colon*ize,* symbol*ize.*

Verb markers, or *auxiliaries,* frequently signal verbs. The most common auxiliaries in English are *be* (and all its forms), *have, do, can, could, shall, should, will, would, may, might, must,* and *ought* (see Section 16).

3c. VOICE

Transitive verbs are classified as to *voice.* A verb is in the *active* voice when the noun or pronoun that names the performer of the action specified by the verb is the actual subject of the verb.

> We *built* a hut in the woods.
> The engineers *have developed* new types of electrical circuits.
> The Beatles *helped* to lessen Britain's balance of payments problem.

A verb is in the *passive* voice when its grammatical subject is not the actual performer of the activity specified by the verb. When verbs appear in the passive voice, the noun that names the actual performer of the action either appears in a prepositional phrase at the end of the sentence or is not given at all. The noun that names the actual performer of the action of passive verbs can be determined by changing the verb to the active voice.

> The firm was run by one man. [Passive]
> One man ran the firm. [Active]
> The money was found in the subway. [Passive]
> Kathleen found the money in the subway. [Active]

NOTE: The passive voice always consists of some form of the verb *be* followed by a past participle.

3d. MOOD

The *mood* of a verb makes clear the manner in which the writer or speaker thinks of the action (see Part Three).

3e. TENSE

Tense indicates the time of the action or state of existence expressed by the verb. Tense can be thought of as either simple or progressive. The *simple* tenses designate actions that are occurring now, have occurred in the past, or will occur in the future. The *progressive* tenses designate continuing action in present or past time (see Section 17).

3f. VERBALS

A *participle* is a word that functions either as a verb or as an adjective. The present participle always ends in *-ing* (*laughing, throwing*). The past participle is the third principal part of a verb (*laughed, thrown*). The perfect participle consists of *having* or *having been* plus the past participle (*having laughed, having been thrown*). Some past participles end in *-ed;* others in *-n;* still others change the vowel (*sung*); and some change their form completely (*sought*). When the participle takes an object or is modified by an adverb, the group of words forms a *participial phrase* (see Section 7).

A *gerund* is a verbal noun. Gerunds have the same form as present or perfect participles but are used as nouns instead of adjectives.

> *Studying* is hard work.
> *Saying* that studying is hard work is easy.

A gerund may take an object and be modified by an adverb or adjective.

> *Cleaning* the *river bank* was the goal of the sophomores.
> *Stamping out drug abuse* is *difficult*.
> *Eating well* is *desirable*.

An *infinitive* is the form of the verb usually preceded by *to*. An infinitive may be used as a noun, an adjective, or an adverb.

> His greatest fear is *to die*. [Noun]
> John had three dollars *to spend*. [Adjective]
> Harvey was disappointed *to have failed*. [Adverb]

Sometimes the word *to* is omitted from the infinitive.

> Let him *go* with you.
> Will they make him *resign*?
> Help me *decorate* the Christmas tree.

The infinitive may take an object and be modified by an adverb or an adverbial phrase or clause.

> *To find the missing lens* we searched for twenty minutes.
> Susie and Joe struggled *to swim faster*.
> The debris began *to accumulate along the highway*.
> Arthur plans *to wait until we write him*.

4. ADJECTIVES AND ADVERBS

Certain words and groups of words are used within a sentence to specify, qualify, or otherwise determine the meaning of another word. This relationship is known grammatically as *modification.*

A modifier does not change or alter the meaning of the word it modifies; it simply makes the meaning of the word more exact and specific within the sentence or in a group of sentences. The parts of speech whose basic functions are to modify are *adjectives* and *adverbs.*

4a. ADJECTIVES

An *adjective* modifies a noun or pronoun by describing, limiting, or in some other closely related way making meaning more nearly exact. An adjective may indicate quality or quantity, may identify or set limits. Adjectives are therefore of three general types: descriptive (a *red* hat, a *hard* lesson, a *damaged* thumb); limiting (the *fourth* period, her *former* home, *many* times); proper (an *American* play, a *Colorado* melon).

Some *adjectives*—indeed, most—have endings that mark them as adjectives. The more important of these include

-y: rocky, funny, dreamy, fussy, muddy
-ful: harmful, faithful, hurtful, sinful
-less: stainless, timeless, lawless, guiltless
-en: golden, wooden, given, hidden, rotten
-able (*-ible*): favorable, desirable, credible
-ive: obtrusive, submissive, impulsive
-ous: amorous, ridiculous, generous, marvelous
-ish: womanish, selfish, Danish, fortyish
-al: cordial, optional, experimental, judicial
-ic: metric, philosophic, authentic, artistic
-ary: primary, visionary, contrary, secondary
-some: meddlesome, tiresome, handsome, troublesome.

An adjective may modify a noun directly ("this *yellow* light thrown upon the color of his ambitions") or indirectly ("the survivors, *weary* and *emaciated,* moved feebly toward the ship"). In sentences such as "The water felt *cold*" and "The corn is *ripe,*" each adjective is related to the subject, the word it modifies, by a linking verb. (A linking verb has little meaning of its own; it functions primarily as a connection between subject and predicate noun or predicate adjective.) In the sentences above, *cold* and *ripe* are called *predicate adjectives* or *complements* (see Section 16).

4b. ADVERBS

An *adverb* modifies a verb, adjective, or other adverb by describing or limiting to make meaning more exact. Adverbs usually tell *how, when, where, why, how often,* or *how much.* In "A low cry came *faintly* to our ears," the adverb modifies the verb *came.* In "Close the door *very* softly," the adverb modifies the adverb *softly.*

Adverbs have the following characteristics: (1) They are commonly, but not always, distinguished from corresponding adjectives by the suffix *-ly: bad, badly; sure, surely; cold, coldly.* (2) Certain adverbs are distinguished from corresponding nouns by the suffixes *-wise* and *-ways: endways, sideways, lengthwise.* (3) Certain adverbs are distinguished from corresponding prepositions in not being connected to a following noun: He ran *up* (adverb); he ran *up* the street (preposition). (4) Like adjectives, but unlike nouns and verbs, adverbs may be preceded by words of the *very* group (intensifiers): The *most exotically* dressed girl passed by; he went *right* by (see Section 19).

5. CONJUNCTIONS

A *conjunction* is a linking word used to connect words or groups of words in a sentence.

Conjunctions are of two main kinds: *coordinating,* which join words or groups of words of equal rank, such as *and, but, for, or, nor, either, neither, yet;* and *subordinating,* which join dependent clauses to main clauses, such as *if, since, because, as, while, so that, although, unless.* Certain coordinating conjunctions used in pairs are called *correlative* conjunctions: *both . . . and, either . . . or, neither . . . nor, as . . . as, so . . . as, whether . . . or, not only . . . but also.*

Conjunctions and conjunctive adverbs

Another kind of conjunction is the *conjunctive adverb,* a type of adverb that can also be used as a conjunction joining two independent clauses. Some examples are *accordingly, also, anyhow, besides, consequently, furthermore, hence, however, indeed, likewise, moreover, nevertheless, still, then, therefore, thus.*

The most commonly used conjunctions and conjunctive adverbs together with the ideas they express are these:

1. Continuation of thought: *and, both . . . and, not only . . . but also, also, besides, furthermore, in addition, indeed, likewise, moreover, similarly, whereby, whereupon.*
2. Contrast: *although, but, however, instead, nevertheless, not only . . . but also, notwithstanding, still, whereas, yet.*
3. Affirmative alternation: *anyhow, either . . . or, else, moreover, or, still, whereas, whether.*
4. Negative alternation: *except that, however, instead, neither, neither . . . nor, nevertheless, nor, only, whereas.*
5. Reason, result, purpose, cause: *accordingly, as, as a result, because, consequently, for, hence, inasmuch as, in order that, since, so, so that, that, thereby, therefore, thus, whereas, why.*
6. Example: *for example, indeed, in fact, namely.*
7. Comparison: *indeed, in fact, moreover, so . . . as, than.*
8. Time: *after, as long as, as soon as, before, henceforth, meanwhile, once, since, then, until, when, whenever, while.*
9. Place: *whence, where, wherever, whither.*
10. Condition: *although, as if, as though, if, lest, once, provided, providing, though, unless.*

11. Concession: *although, insofar as, notwithstanding the fact that, though, unless, while.*

6. PREPOSITIONS

A preposition is a linking word used to show the relationship of a noun or pronoun to some other word in the sentence. Prepositions show position or direction (*at, with, to, from*) or indicate cause or possession (*because of, of*). The literal meaning of the word is indicated by its form: *pre* (before) and *position.*

A preposition is nearly always followed by a noun or pronoun (or the equivalent), with which it forms a unit. An exception is the use of prepositions in certain inverted structures with *who* (*whom*), *which,* and *what: Whom* are you going with? (With whom are you going?); *What's* it made of? (Of what is it made?).

The following list contains the prepositions commonly used in English: *about, above, across, after, against, along, alongside, amid, among, around, at, before, behind, below, beneath, beside, besides, between, beyond, but, by, concerning, despite, down, during, ere, except, excepting, for, from, in, inside, into, like, near, notwithstanding, of, off, on, onto, outside, over, per, regarding, save, since, through, throughout, till, to, toward, under, underneath, until, unto, up, upon, with, within, without.*

Here are some examples:

> Please keep this idea *between* you and me.
> I couldn't find the book anywhere *in* the classroom.

A few less often used prepositions are *compound:*

> What is the name of the street *across from* the bandstand?
> He was late *owing to* unavoidable circumstances.
> *Apart from* cardiac weakness, Jim is in excellent health.

7. PHRASES

A phrase, which usually serves as a part of speech, is a group of related words that does not contain a subject and predicate. Phrases may be classified as to use and form.

7a. USE

A *noun* phrase is used in a sentence as subject or object: *Making a lot of money* is his goal in life. [The italicized phrase is the subject of *is.*] He likes *making a lot of money.* [Here the phrase is the object of *likes.*]

An *adjective* (*adjectival*) phrase is used in a sentence as a single adjective would be: The boys *in this dormitory* are noisy and thoughtless. [The phrase modifies the noun *boys.*]

An *adverb* (*adverbial*) phrase is used in a sentence to modify a verb, adjective, or adverb: We spent our vacation *on a farm.* [The phrase modifies the verb *spent;* it answers the question "where?"]

7b. FORM

A *prepositional* phrase is one beginning with a preposition; it may be used as an adjective or adverb and (rarely) as a noun: The book *on the desk* is mine. [Adjective; what book?] He strode *into the room.* [Adverb; strode where?] *Without smiling* was his way of showing irritation. [Noun; subject of *was.*]

A *participial* phrase takes its name from an initial or important word: *Racing like mad,* we barely caught the bus. *Having run the last mile,* we caught the bus.

A *gerundial* phrase takes its name from the gerund it contains: *Playing at Forest Hills* was his highest aim in sports. The crowd enjoyed *her expert twirling of a baton.*

An *infinitive* phrase takes its name from the infinitive it contains: *To make friends* is a worthwhile undertaking.

An *absolute* phrase is one that is not directly attached to any other word in a sentence: John left quickly, *his objection now being a matter of record.*

8. CLAUSES

A clause is a group of words having a subject and predicate. Some clauses are independent (main, principal); others are dependent (subordinate).

8a. INDEPENDENT CLAUSES

An independent clause is one that makes a complete grammatical statement and can stand alone. It may appear within a sentence or as a sentence itself:

> *A doctor's firmest diagnosis often is only an educated guess.*
>
> Although only a cynic would say so, *a doctor's firmest diagnosis often is only an educated guess.*

8b. DEPENDENT CLAUSES

A dependent clause is one that is incapable of standing alone, one that depends for its meaning upon the remainder of the sentence in which it appears. Dependent (subordinate) clauses function as nouns, adjectives, and adverbs.

NOUN CLAUSE

> *What you said* is not true. [Subject of *is;* equivalent to "your remark."]
>
> I do not believe *that you are my friend.* [Object of *believe.*]
>
> Your suggestion *that you are really lazy* surprises me. [In apposition with *suggestion.* This clause can also be considered *adjectival,* since it identifies and explains the word *suggestion.*]

ADJECTIVE CLAUSE

> Girls *who have hair they consider their fortune* may have eyes that really draw interest. [The italicized clause modifies *girls.*]
>
> The players think he is a coach *who should be taken with a grain of salt.* [Clause modifies *coach.*]

ADVERBIAL CLAUSE

How can I look up a word *when I don't know how to spell it?* [Clause modifies the verb *look up.*]

You can read more rapidly *than I can.* [Clause modifies the adverb *rapidly.*]

Steak is usually more expensive *than fish is.* [Clause modifies the adjective *expensive.*]

Accompanied by subordinating conjunctions (see Section 5), adverbial clauses can express the following relationships:

1. Time: *when, before, while, since. When one rows a boat,* he must keep firmly seated. [Adverbial clause modifies *must keep.*]
2. Place: *where, wherever.* After finding the Honda *where I had left it,* I hurried back into the shop. [Adverbial clause modifies gerund *finding.*]
3. Manner: *as, as if.* He kicked the can *as if it were a football.* [Adverbial clause modifies verb *kicked.*]
4. Condition: *if, so, unless, provided that. Unless you telephone now,* service will be cut off. [Adverbial clause modifies verb *will be cut off.*]
5. Cause: *because, as, since.* The train, three hours late *because the engine had broken down,* was full of angry passengers. [Adverbial clause modifies adjective *late.*]
6. Purpose: *in order that, so that.* The students worked all day *so that the gym would be decorated for the party.* [Adverbial clause modifies verb *worked.*]
7. Result: *that, so that, so . . . that.* We were *so* hungry *that we ate stale bread.* [Adverbial clause modifies adjective *hungry.*]
8. Degree or comparison: *than, as much as, as . . . as, just as.* Priscilla walked farther *than you did.* [Adverbial clause modifies adverb *farther.*]
9. Concession: *though, although. Although he did not score,* he made the most exciting play of the game. [Adverbial clause modifies verb *made.*]

9. SENTENCES

Traditionally, a sentence has been defined as "a group of words containing a subject and predicate and expressing a complete thought." However, some "sentences" accepted as such by almost everybody do not contain both an expressed subject and predicate. Furthermore, what exactly is a "complete thought"? The "completeness" of a thought frequently depends upon what statements precede or follow it.

All that accurately and fairly can be said is that a sentence is a stretch of prose (or poetry, for that matter) which a capable writer punctuates by beginning with a capital letter and ending with a terminal mark (see Section 21) and which an educated reader will recognize and accept as a "sentence" (see Section 41).

9a. SENTENCE MEANING AND PURPOSE

Sentences may be classified according to meaning and purpose. A *declarative* sentence states a fact or makes an assertion: *The car has eight cylinders.* An *interrogative* sentence asks a question: *Does the car have eight cylinders?* An *imperative* sentence expresses an entreaty or command: *Please lend me the money now.*

Move over! An *exclamatory* sentence expresses strong feeling: *Oh, if he were only my friend! Thank goodness, you are safe!*

9b. SENTENCE WORD ORDER

Sentences may be classified according to the arrangement of their content. A sentence in which the words are so set down that the meaning is not completed until the end or near the end is called *periodic.* A sentence so constructed that the thought may be completed before the end is termed *loose.*

Our conversation and informal writing contain many more loose sentences than periodic. Yet a periodic sentence does provide suspense and variety; it holds the attention of reader or listener and contributes to stylistic effectiveness. Although a natural form of expression, the periodic sentence tends to become monotonous and forced and should not be overused.

> Act quickly or you will be too late to buy the food you wish. [Loose]
>
> He liked to play chess and bridge, but more than either he enjoyed swimming when the surf was not rough. [Loose]
>
> If you do not wish to pay this debt, please say so. [Periodic]
>
> According to a former college president, to be at home in all lands and ages; to count Nature a familiar acquaintance and Art a familiar friend; to gain a standard for the appreciation of other men's work and the criticism of one's own; to make friends among men and women of one's own age who are to be the leaders in all walks of life; to lose one's self in generous enthusiasm and to cooperate with others for common ends; and to form character under professors who are dedicated—these are the returns of a college for the best four years of one's life. [Periodic]

A *balanced sentence* is so constructed that similar or opposing thoughts have similar structure. Such a sentence is sometimes used to make a statement especially emphatic and for comparisons and contrasts.

> You can take a man out of the country; you can't take the "country" out of a man.
>
> You may call him the man who invented evil, but I would say he is the man whom evil invented.

9c. SENTENCE STRUCTURE

Sentences may be classified according to grammatical structure as simple, compound, complex, or compound-complex.

A *simple* sentence contains only one subject (simple or compound) and one predicate (simple or compound) and expresses one thought: *The road is dusty. The boy and the girl ate and drank.*

A *compound* sentence contains two or more independent clauses. The clauses of a compound sentence are grammatically capable of standing alone, but they are closely related parts of one main idea: *She read* and *I listened to the radio. The nights are long* but *the days seem short.*

A *complex* sentence contains one independent clause and one or more dependent (subordinate) clauses: *Carol said that she had walked for several blocks. He is an athlete whose muscles are unusually pliant.*

A *compound-complex* sentence contains two or more independent clauses and one or more dependent clauses: *Since the day was unpleasant, Judy looked at TV* and *Ned wrote several letters.*

9d. SENTENCE PATTERNS

The series of words that comprise a sentence can convey meaning in English only because certain of those words are structurally related to one another in such a way that they state or imply something about the subject. The patterns indicate the order in which these structural relationships are placed in English. Sentence patterns specify the types of words that must be present in a statement before it may be called a sentence. In English, there are seven basic predication (stating, implying) patterns:

Pattern 1:

Subject	*Predicate*
People	talk.
Dogs	run.

Pattern 2:

Subject	*Predicate*	*Direct Object*
Chris	tutors	Jennifer.
You	need	me.

Pattern 3:

Subject	*Predicate*	*Indirect Object*	*Direct Object*
John	gives	Babs	presents.
Susan	wrote	him	letters.
The instructor	assigned	Steve	poetry.

Pattern 4:

Subject	*Linking Verb*	*Predicate Noun*
Ed	is	a pilot.
She	was	the office manager.
John	will be	a teacher.

Pattern 5:

Subject	*Linking Verb*	*Predicate Adjective*
Dogs	are	loving.
Roses	smell	delightful.
It	seems	all right.

Pattern 6:

Subject	*Predicate*	*Direct Object*	*Object Complement*
Louise	named	her fish	Percy.
John	called	his friend	a fool.
Joan	considered	Will	her friend.

Pattern 7:

Subject	*Predicate*	*Direct Object*	*Adjective Complement*
Mr. Anderson	painted	the house	green.
Josie	thought	her boyfriend	handsome.
Bob	considered	the situation	difficult.
Henry	made	the garden	beautiful.

Several types of modifiers may be used to expand the basic elements of any of these seven patterns.

They may be definite and indefinite articles and other noun markers. Articles attach themselves to and signal nouns (see Section 1). The sentence without articles or noun markers is unusual.

> *The* boys built *a* shack. [Pattern 2]
> *My* brother lost *his* comb. [Pattern 2]

Single-word adjectives and adverbs frequently modify the elements of the basic patterns.

> The *energetic* boys *quickly* built a lean-to. [Pattern 2]
> She is an *accomplished* pianist. [Pattern 4]
> They elected a *capable* man judge. [Pattern 6]
> He works *well*. [Pattern 1]

Phrases of various kinds (see Section 7) frequently modify the basic words in patterns.

> *In the morning*, they left *for Naples*. [Pattern 1]
> *Hoping to win the cup*, Tom entered the race. [Pattern 2]
> New Orleans, *a truly beautiful city*, is a popular place *for tourists*. [Pattern 4]
> *To get there on time*, Rocky told the driver *to speed it up*. [Pattern 2]
> He gave his father a present *by staying out of trouble*. [Pattern 3]

Clauses of various kinds (see Section 8) frequently modify basic words in patterns.

> *Because he had failed twice already*, Seth lost his desire to try again. [Pattern 2]
> Athens, *which enjoys a temperate climate*, is the capital of Greece. [Pattern 4]
> She always fought *for what she believed in*. [Pattern 1]

When infinitive and gerund phrases or noun clauses serve as either subjects or objects, they may be considered as integral parts of basic patterns. Note the following examples:

> *To forgive* is divine. [Pattern 5]
> The team tried *to win*. [Pattern 2]
> *Developing new territories* was the sales manager's primary responsibility. [Pattern 4]
> They tried *growing hybrid roses*. [Pattern 2]
> *That he won* was clear. [Pattern 5]
> He knew *what to do*. [Pattern 2]

Any essential part of a sentence pattern may be compounded through the use of a correlative conjunction (see Section 5). Compound subjects, predicates, and complements are considered as single units so far as the patterns are concerned.

9e. VARIATIONS IN SENTENCE PATTERNS

There are a few other common types of sentences, a knowledge of which will complete your understanding of the English sentence.

THE PASSIVE VARIATION

Sentences employing a verb in the passive voice are common in English; they are usually developed from Pattern 2 sentences. The passive variation is formed by moving the direct object into the subject position and by making the subject into the object of a preposition in a prepositional phrase. The verb also changes to the passive voice, which is always made up of a form of the verb *to be* followed by the past participle:

Subject	*Predicate*	*(Prepositional Phrase)*
The line	was hit	(by Jim).
The treasure	was hidden	(by Captain Kidd).
The men	were scolded	(by the corporal).

The prepositional phrases appear in parentheses because they are optional. In some passive sentences, the prepositional phrase is omitted.

Pattern 6 and pattern 7 sentences can also be changed into the passive voice. Note the changes that occur in the following examples:

Pattern 6: Louise named her fish Percy.
The fish was named Percy (by Louise).
Pattern 7: Mr. Anderson painted his house green.
The house was painted green (by Mr. Anderson).

When a pattern 2 sentence is changed into the passive, it may be considered a pattern 1 sentence. When patterns 6 and 7 are changed, the revisions may be considered as patterns 4 and 5, respectively.

THE QUESTION VARIATION

Sentences that ask questions are as common in English as in any other language. The question variation follows certain set patterns in English.

If in an affirmative statement a verb has one or more auxiliaries, the first auxiliary is switched so that it comes before the subject. Here are some examples:

Affirmative: The game was won.
The arrest will be made.
The house could have been repainted.
The guest has eaten.
Questions: Was the game won?
Will the arrest be made?
Could the house have been repainted?
Has the guest eaten?

If the affirmative statement contains no auxiliary, some form of the verb *do* is placed in front of the subject. Here are some examples:

Affirmative: The boy runs fast.
Bill helps his friends.
Joe flew an airplane.
Sam likes physics.

Questions: Does the boy run fast?
Does Bill help his friends?
Did Joe fly an airplane?
Does Sam like physics?

These same rules apply when questions begin with common question words like *where, when, why,* and *how.*

THE IMPERATIVE VARIATION

The imperative mood in English also constitutes another basic variation that may appear in any of the seven basic patterns. The imperative is commonly viewed as having the subject "you" understood or implied. Here is an example of the imperative variation in each of the seven basic patterns:

Begin! [Pattern 1]
Begin the game! [Pattern 2]
Give him a chance. [Pattern 3]
Be a doctor. [Pattern 4]
Remain silent. [Pattern 5]
Name the dog Willie. [Pattern 6]
Color his face red. [Pattern 7]

10. GLOSSARY OF GRAMMATICAL TERMS

The following list briefly defines those elements of grammar that are most often and most importantly involved in the writing of English sentences. Several of the items are treated in greater detail at appropriate places within the text itself.

Absolute expression. An absolute expression (also called nominative absolute) is one that has a thought relationship but no direct grammatical relationship with the remainder of the sentence in which it occurs. An absolute expression is usually composed of a noun or pronoun and a participle: *The game being lost,* we left the stadium. *The purpose of our field trip having been explained,* we set out with enthusiasm.

Accusative. A case name meaning the same as the *objective* case (see Section 14). The term *accusative case* is rare in English, but it is common in the study of such foreign languages as Latin and German.

Active voice. The form of an action-expressing verb which tells that the subject does or performs the action (see Section 18).

Agreement. Correspondence, or sameness, in number, gender, and person. When a subject agrees with its verb, they are alike in having the same *person* (first, second, or third) and *number* (singular or plural). Pronouns agree not only in person and number, but also in *gender* (see Sections 12 and 13).

Martha is my cousin.
Martha and *Sue are* my cousins.
A *woman* hopes to retain *her* youthful appearance.
Many *women* retain *their* youthful appearance.
Gary is one of those *boys who are* always well-mannered.

Antecedent. The substantive (noun or pronoun) to which a pronoun refers is its antecedent (see Section 13).

The *girl* has lost *her* chance. [*Girl* is the antecedent of *her*.]
Remember that *pronouns* agree with *their* antecedents in gender, number, and person. [*Pronouns* is the antecedent of *their*.]

Appositive. A substantive added to another substantive to identify or explain it. It is said to be "in apposition."

One important product, *rubber*, is in short supply in that country. [*Rubber* is in apposition with *product*.]
More hardy than wheat are these grains—*rye, oats,* and *barley*. [*Rye, oats,* and *barley* are in apposition with *grains*.]

An appositive agrees with its substantive in number and case. It is set off by commas if its relationship is loose (nonrestrictive) and is used without punctuation if the relationship is close (restrictive) (see Section 25o).

Article. The articles (*a, an, the*) may be classed as adjectives because they possess limiting or specifying functions. *A* and *an* are indefinite articles; *the* is the definite article: *a* phonograph, *an* error, *the* surgeon.

Auxiliary. A verb used to "help" another verb in the formation of tenses, voice, mood, and certain precise ideas. *Be* (*am, is, are, was, were, been*), *have* (*has, had*), *do* (*does*), *can, could, may, might, shall, should, will, would, must, ought, let, used* are examples (see Section 16).

He *has* left town for the weekend.
We *should have been* working with the stevedores on the dock.
Will you please turn off the light?

Case. A term referring to the forms that nouns or pronouns have (nominative, possessive, objective) to indicate their relation to other words in the sentence (see Section 14).

Clause. A group of words containing a subject and predicate and forming part of a sentence (see Section 8).

When the cheering stopped, *Effie was sad.* [Independent]
This is the present *that I bought.* [Dependent adjective clause]
Wherever we go, we shall have trouble. [Dependent adverb clause]
Maury insisted *that he tried his best.* [Dependent noun clause]

Collective noun. The name of a group composed of individuals but considered as a unit: *class, audience, jury.*

Common noun. A noun naming a member or members of a general or common group: *automobile, coat, quintet.*

Comparison. The change in form of an adjective or adverb to indicate greater or smaller degrees of quantity, quality, or manner (see Section 19e).

Complement. A word or expression used to complete the idea indicated or implied by a verb. A *predicate* complement (sometimes called *subjective* complement) may be a noun, a pronoun, or an adjective that follows a linking verb and describes or identifies the subject of that verb. An *object* (*objective*) complement may be a noun or adjective that follows the direct object of a verb and completes the meaning.

> Mr. Black is a *lawyer*.
> Jane is *mournful*.
> The club members are *youthful*.
> They called the dog *Willie*.
> We dyed the dress *green*.

Complex sentence. A sentence containing one independent clause and one or more dependent clauses (see Section 9c).

Compound sentence. A sentence containing two or more clauses that could stand alone (see Section 9c).

Compound-complex sentence. A sentence containing two or more independent clauses and one or more dependent clauses (see Section 9c): You may send candy, or you may send flowers, but you must certainly send something to Mother because she expects a gift.

Conjugation. The changes in the form or uses of a verb to show tense, mood, voice, number, and person. See these terms in this glossary and in sections 3, 17, 18.

Conjunction. A part of speech that serves as a linking or joining word to connect words or groups of words (see Section 5).

Conjunctive adverb. An adverb that can also be used as a conjunction coordinating two independent clauses: *also, furthermore, nevertheless, besides, however, therefore, thus, so, consequently, hence, likewise, still, then, moreover.* For example: The library is open on Saturday; *therefore* you can take the books back then.

Context. The parts of a piece of writing or of speech that precede or follow a given word or passage with which they are directly connected. If we say that such and such a passage in a novel is obscene but that in its *context* it is significant and not shocking, we mean that what comes before or follows provides meaning which is important, even essential, to understanding and judgment.

Copula. A word or set of words that acts as a connecting link (see Section 16).

Declension. The inflectional changes in the form or use of a noun or pronoun to indicate case, number, and person. "To decline" means to give these grammatical changes.

Case	*Singular*	*Plural*
Nominative	man, I, who	men, we, who
Possessive	man's; my, mine; whose	men's; our, ours; whose
Objective	man, me, whom	men, us, whom

Determiner. A determiner may be an article (*a, an, the*), a possessive (*my, your, its, their, hers, his*), a demonstrative (*this, that, those*). In general, a determiner is any member of a subclass of adjectival words that limits the noun it modifies and that usually is placed before descriptive adjectives.

Direct address. In this construction, also called the *vocative,* the noun or pronoun shows to whom speech is addressed: "*Jimmy,* where are you?" "What did you say, *Mother*?" "After you mow the grass, *Fred,* please take out the garbage."

Direct quotation. A quotation that reproduces the exact words written or spoken by someone: "Please use your dictionary more often," the office manager said. "These letters will all need to be retyped."

Ellipsis (elliptical clause). The omission of a word or words that are not needed because they are understood from other words or from context. In the following examples, the words shown in brackets are often omitted in speaking and writing.

> Some drove to Miami, others [drove] to Palm Beach.
> While [we were] swimming, we agreed to go to a movie later.

Expletive. A word or phrase added either to fill out a sentence or to provide emphasis. The latter function is performed by exclamatory or profane expressions. The more frequently employed function of the expletive is complementary, however; in this sense, *surely, indeed, why,* and *yes* may be considered expletives. *It* and *there* are commonly used as expletives:

> *It* was Alice sitting there.
> *It* is a truism that men love freedom.
> *There* are 2,400 people present.

Some grammarians further classify *it.* For example, the late Professor Paul Roberts discussed "impersonal *it,*" "situation *it,*" and "expletive *it,*" illustrating each as follows:

Impersonal: It is raining.
It is Wednesday.
It snowed last night.
Situation: It was Ben who started the trouble.
It's Lois and the children.
Was it the cat?
Expletive: It is hard to believe that Dave is sixteen.
It is true that we were once great friends.

Finite verb. A verb form or verb phrase that serves as a predicate; it has number and person. The nonfinite verb form cannot serve as a predicate. Nonfinite forms are participles, gerunds, and infinitives (see Section 3f).

Gender. The gender of nouns and pronouns is determined by sex. A noun or pronoun denoting the male sex is called *masculine: man, boy, lord, executor, he.* A noun or pronoun indicating the female sex is called *feminine: woman, girl, lady, executrix, she.* Nouns that denote no sex are referred to as *neuter: house, book, tree, desk, lamp, courage.* Some nouns and pronouns may be either masculine or feminine and are said to have *common* gender: *child, teacher, friend, doctor, visitor, it, they.*

Genitive. A case name meaning the same as *possessive* (see Section 14).

Gerund. A verbal noun ending in *-ing* (*speaking, singing*). Because the gerund has the same form as the present participle, note the difference in their functions: the participle is a verbal *adjective;* the gerund is a verbal *noun.* A gerund can take an object and be modified by an adverb; as a noun, it can be the subject or object of a verb or the object of a preposition (see Section 3f).

Playing basketball is good exercise.
All the skiers enjoy *eating.*

Idiom. The usual forms of expression of a language; the characteristic way in which it is put together. In speaking of French idiom, for example, we refer to such a distinct usage as putting the adjective after its noun or the fact that an adjective in French has forms for singular and plural and for masculine and feminine gender. *Idiom* also refers to expressions that are accepted but that differ from usual constructions, such as *a hot cup of tea, how do you do,* and *jump the gun* (see Section 38e).

Impersonal construction. A method of phrasing in which neither a personal pronoun nor a person as noun is stated as the actor. The passive voice is used, or words like *it* or *there* (see *Expletive*).

I have four reasons for my decision. [Personal]
There are four reasons for this decision. [Impersonal]

We must consider two suggestions. [Personal]
It is necessary to consider two suggestions. [Impersonal]

Indirect object. A noun or pronoun that precedes the direct object of a verb and before which the word *to* or *for* is understood. When an indirect object follows the direct object, a preposition (*to, for*) is actually used: Yesterday I bought *him* a soda. Yesterday I bought a soda for *him.*

Indirect question. Restatement by one person of a direct question asked by another: When will you pay me? [Direct] Joe asked when I would pay him. [Indirect]

Indirect quotation. Restatement by one person in his own words of the words written or spoken by someone else: Eileen said, "I'll be there on Sunday." [Direct] Eileen said that she will be here on Sunday. [Indirect]

Infinitive. A word that functions as both verb and noun and that also may be employed as an adjectival or adverbial modifier. The infinitive is usually introduced by the sign *to: to* speak,, *to* sing (see Section 3f). Like a *gerund,* an infinitive can take an object and be modified by an adverb; in its function as a noun, it can be the subject or object of a verb and the object of a preposition.

Will you please *return* by the next plane. [Please *to return;* infinitive as verb and part of predicate]
The person *to see* is the manager. [Infinitive as adjective]
She is waiting *to tell* us of her recent trip. [Infinitive as adverb]

Inflection. (1) A change in the form of a word to show a change in use or meaning. *Comparison* is the inflection of adjectives and adverbs; *declension* is the inflection of nouns and pronouns; *conjugation* is the inflection of verbs. (2) A change in the pitch or tone of voice (see Section 59).

Intensifier. A word or element used to strengthen, increase, or enforce meaning. *Certainly* and *extremely* are examples of intensifiers.

Interjection. The interjection (1) has no grammatical connection with the remainder of the sentence, and (2) expresses emotion—surprise, dismay, disapproval, anger, fear. Grammarians distinguish two kinds of interjections. First are those forms used only as interjections, never occurring otherwise in speech: *oh, ouch, tsk-tsk, psst, whew, alas.* Some of these contain sounds not used otherwise in English and consequently difficult to represent in writing; *tsk-tsk,* for example, is an inadequate representation of the clucking sound made to indicate disapproval. Second are the forms that occur sometimes as interjections and sometimes as other parts of speech: *goodness, well, my.* The two groups are hard to separate, since many words now used only as interjections originate from other parts of speech: *Alas,* for example, has its root in a word meaning "wretched."

Intonation. See *Pitch.*

Intransitive verb. See *Transitive verb.*

Irregular verb. Sometimes called *strong* verbs, irregular verbs do not follow a regular pattern in forming their principal parts. Instead, these are usually formed by a change in the vowel: *see, saw, seen; choose, chose, chosen.* Your dictionary is your guide (see Section 15).

Juncture. This word has several meanings, all of which involve the act or state of "joining" or "connecting." In linguistics, juncture indicates that words as we speak them are not usually separated to the extent that they are in writing. Our words tend to flow together without the pauses that in writing are shown by spaces. For example, if we speak the sentence quoted in Section 44a, "The person who can do this well deserves praise," we would need briefly to interrupt our flow of sound after either *this* or *well* in order to be fully understood. Such interruptions vary in length and are frequently combined with variations in *pitch.*

Linking verb. This verb is also called a *joining* verb, a *copula,* a *copulative* verb, or a *coupling* verb. It does not express action but only a state of being. It serves to link the subject with another noun (predicate noun), pronoun (predicate pronoun), or adjective (predicate adjective). These words following the linking verb are called predicate complements or subjective complements. Common linking verbs are the forms of *to be, look, seem, smell, sound, appear, feel, become, grow, prove, turn, remain, stand* (see Section 16).

Modify. To limit or describe or qualify a meaning in some other specific and closely related way, adjectives are used with nouns and pronouns and adverbs are used with verbs, adjectives, and other adverbs. Limiting: *five* acres, the *only* meal. Descriptive: *blue* skies, *large* houses, speak *rapidly* (see Section 4).

Mood. A characteristic of verbs, revealing how action or expression is thought of: as a fact (*indicative* mood), as a possibility or something desired (*subjunctive* mood), or as a command or request (*imperative* mood). Other kinds of expression are possible through use of certain auxiliary verbs.

> He *is* my friend. [Indicative]
> I wish I *were* with you. [Subjunctive]
> *Drop* that cigarette. [Imperative]

Morpheme. Any word or part of a word not further divisible into smaller meaningful elements: *boy, -ish* in *boyish; ad-, mit* in *admit.*

Morphology. The patterns of word formation in language, including derivation and inflection. Morphology and syntax together form a basic division of grammar.

Nonfinite verb. A verb form that cannot serve as predicate, since it shows neither person nor grammatical number. Nonfinite verb forms—the verbals—are gerunds, participles, and infinitives (see Section 3f).

Nouns. See specific kinds of nouns (Section 1b).

Number. The change in the form of a noun, pronoun, or verb to show whether one or more than one is indicated. The formation of the plural of nouns is discussed in Section 1; the few pronouns that have plural forms are listed in Section 2.

Plurals of verbs are relatively simple. Main verbs have the same form for singular and plural except in the third person singular, present tense, which ends in *-s* (*talks, thinks*) or occasionally *-es* (*goes*). Of the verb *to be,* in the present tense, *am* (first person) and *is* (third person) are singular, *are* is second person singular and first, second, and third person plural; in the past tense, *was* is first and third person singular, *were* is second person singular and first, second, and third person plural. Of the verb *to have, has* is the third person singular, present tense form. Of the verb *to do, does* is the third person singular, present tense form. Use a dictionary when in doubt concerning the singular or plural form of a noun, pronoun, or verb.

Object. The noun, pronoun, noun phrase, or noun clause following a transitive verb or a preposition.

> Your book is on the *floor.* [Object of preposition]
> She struck *him* with a newspaper. [Object of verb]
> I see *what you think.* [Object of verb]

A *simple* object is a substantive alone; a *complete* object is a simple object together with its modifiers; a *compound* object consists of two or more substantives.

> The Popes built the *house.* [Simple]
> The Popes built *the large yellow house on the slope.* [Complete]
> The Popes built *the house and the barn.* [Compound]

Object complement. A word, usually a noun or adjective, used after the direct object of certain verbs and intended to complete the meaning of a sentence: We have chosen Margie *leader.* Let me make this story *simple.*

Participle. A verb form having the function either of a verb used as part of the predicate or of an adjective. The three forms are *present, past,* and *perfect* participle (see Section 3f).

> The player *swinging* the bat is Henry.
> I have *finished* my essay.
> *Having finished* my essay, I turned it in.

Parts of speech. Words are classified according to their use in larger units of thought, that is, sentences. This functional division results in the so-called parts of speech; every word in the English language belongs to one or more of these parts of speech. There are eight such parts: *noun, pronoun, verb, adjective, adverb, conjunction, preposition, interjection.*

Many words are always used in a certain way, as a particular part of speech. But since our language is constantly changing, the functions of words reflect that change. *Chair,* for example, is usually thought of as a noun (a seat, a position), yet the poet A. E. Housman tells of carrying a victorious athlete "shoulder-high" in a parade through his hometown:

> The time you won your town the race
> We *chaired* you through the market-place.

Words *name, assert, modify,* and *join.* To determine what part of speech a given word is, observe how the word is used in a sentence of which it is a part.

Passive voice. The form of an action-expressing verb which tells that the subject does not act but is acted upon. Literally and actually, the subject is *passive* (see Section 18).

Person. The change in the form of a pronoun or verb—sometimes merely a change in use, as with verbs—to indicate whether the "person" used is the person speaking (*first* person), the person spoken to (*second* person), or the person or thing spoken about (*third* person): *I* read, *you* read, *he* reads, *we* read, *you* read, *they* read, *it* plays.

Phoneme. A *phone* is an individual speech sound; a *phoneme* is one of the set of the smallest units that distinguish one word from another in sound. Two phonemes in English are the *b* of *boat* and the *c* of *coat*. Linguists differ in their analysis of the sounds of our language but are generally agreed that some fifty phonemes exist in English.

Phonetics. The science of speech sounds and their production.

Phrase. A group of related words not containing a subject and a predicate and serving as a single part of speech (see Section 7).

Pitch. The combination of pitch, stress, and juncture forms what is known as *intonation,* an important item in any analysis of spoken language. Intonation means "the significant speech pattern or patterns resulting from pitch sequences and pauses (juncture)." Pitch is closely connected with stress; the latter, which refers to loudness, may be primary, secondary, tertiary, or weak (neutral). One linguist (Paul Roberts) used the sentence "The White House is a white house" to indicate the different emphases given *White House* and *white house*. Pitch is usually numbered from 1 to 4 (low to high or high to low, depending upon what linguist is speaking or writing). Pitch signals help in distinguishing spoken questions from statements, just as question marks and periods do in writing.

Plural. See *Number.*

Possessive. The case form of nouns and pronouns indicating ownership or some form of idiomatic usage: the *man's* hat, a *week's* vacation, *my* job (see Section 14).

Predicate. The verb or verb phrase in a sentence that makes a statement—an assertion, an action, a condition, a state of being—about the subject. A *simple* predicate is a verb or verb phrase alone, without an object or modifiers; a *complete* predicate consists of a verb with its object and all its modifiers; a *compound* predicate consists of two or more verbs or verb phrases.

> The next player drove the ball 200 yards down the fairway. [*Drove* is the simple predicate; *drove the ball 200 yards down the fairway* is the complete predicate.]
>
> I *wrote* the theme last night and *submitted* it this morning. [Compound predicate]

Predicate adjective. An adjective used in the predicate after a linking verb; this adjective modifies or qualifies the subject: Today seems *colder* than yesterday. The players appear *ready* for the match.

Predicate complement. Also called *subjective* complement. A predicate noun or pronoun, or a predicate adjective.

Reference. In linguistics, a word used with pronouns and their antecedents to indicate the relationship between them. The pronoun *refers* to the antecedent; the antecedent is indicated or *referred to* by the pronoun (see Section 52).

Regular verb. Also called *weak* verbs, these are the most common verbs in English. They usually form their past tense and past participle by adding *-d, -ed,* or *-t* to the present infinitive form: *move, moved, moved; walk, walked, walked; mean, meant, meant* (see Section 15).

Rhetoric. The art or science of literary uses of language, the body of principles and theory concerning the presentation of facts and ideas in clear, effective, and pleasing language. Rhetoric is only loosely connected with grammar and correctness and with specific details of the mechanics of writing.

Along with logic and grammar, rhetoric made up the basic trivium of medieval study, but it had been important long before this. The founder of rhetoric, Corax of Syracuse, laid down fundamental principles for public speech and debate in the fifth century B.C. In a rhetoric written more than three hundred years before the Christian era, Aristotle described it as the art of giving effectiveness and persuasiveness to truth rather than to the speaker. (The word *rhetoric* comes from a Greek word, *rhetor,* meaning "orator.") Aristotle believed that rhetoric depended upon, and derived from, proof and logic and that its values could be taught as systematized principles. He distinguished between the appeal of rhetoric to man's intellect and the presentation of ideas emotionally and imaginatively, which he discussed in his treatment of poetics.

Many philosophers and orators through the centuries, however, have tried to make rhetoric a mere tool of argumentation and persuasiveness. Plato condemned rhetoric because he felt that many who practiced it used questionable techniques; he also quoted Socrates as declaring rhetoric to be "superficial." This tendency to downgrade rhetoric still persists; when we say something is "mere rhetoric," we mean it is something empty, showy, without genuine substance. Although it is undeniable that some modern politicians and writers use tricks of presentation to conceal lack of thought and outright dishonesty, it is equally true that *how* we say or write something is important; that legitimate and time-tested rhetorical devices can increase the value and appeal of our writing and speaking; that although rhetoric without intellect is ineffective, so, too, are fact unadorned and opinion presented bare.

Rhetorical question. A query designed to produce an effect and not to draw an answer. It is used to introduce a topic or emphasize a point; no answer is expected.

Root. The base of a word, a morpheme to which may be added prefixes and suffixes. An approximate synonym for *base* and *root* in this sense is *stem;* all mean the part of a word to which suffixes and prefixes are added or in which phonetic changes are made. Thus we say that *love* is the root (stem or base) of the word *loveliness, form* of the word *deform,* and so on (see Section 58d).

Simple sentence. A sentence containing one subject (simple or compound) and one predicate (simple or compound) (see Section 9c).

Singular. See *Number.*

Stress. See *Pitch.*

Strong verb. See *Irregular verb.*

Subject. The person or thing (noun, pronoun, noun phrase, noun clause) about which a statement or assertion is made in a sentence or clause. A *simple* subject is the noun or pronoun alone; a *complete* subject is a simple subject together with its modifiers; a *compound* subject consists of two or more nouns, pronouns, noun phrases, noun clauses.

Substantive. An inclusive term for noun, pronoun, verbal noun (gerund, infinitive), or a phrase or a clause used like a noun. The following are examples of substantives:

My *hat* is three years old. [Noun]
They will leave tomorrow; in fact, *everyone* is leaving tomorrow. [Pronouns]
Your *playing* is admired. [Gerund]
To better myself is my *purpose.* [Infinitive, noun]
From Chicago to Los Angeles is a long distance. [Noun phrase]
What you think is *no problem of mine.* [Noun clause, noun phrase]
Do *you* know *that he is a thief?* [Pronoun, noun clause]

Syllable. In phonetics, a segment of speech uttered with one impulse of air pressure from the lungs; in writing, a character or set of characters (letters of the alphabet) representing one sound. That is, a syllable is the smallest amount or unit of speech or writing.

Syntax. The arrangement of words in a sentence to show their relationship. It is a rather vague and general term, but one for which our language has no adequate substitute. Syntax is a branch of grammar.

Tense. The time of the action or the state of being expressed by the verb: present, past, future, present perfect, past perfect, future perfect. The first three of these six are sometimes named the *simple* or *primary* tenses; the last three are sometimes named the *compound* or *secondary* or *perfect* tenses (see Section 17).

Tone. A word used to distinguish a characteristic of tenses of verbs, indicating within any one tense or time limit emphasis or progress or simple time (see Section 17).

Transitive verb. Verbs are classified as either transitive or intransitive. A *transitive* verb is regularly accompanied by a direct object that completes the meaning of the verb: They *refused* his resignation. An *intransitive* verb requires no direct object: He *will obey.* Whether a verb is transitive or intransitive depends upon meaning, upon the idea the writer wishes to show: *will obey* in "He *will obey* our orders" is transitive.

Verb. See specific kinds of verbs; see also Sections 3, 15, 16, and 17.

Verb phrase. A verb together with an auxiliary or auxiliaries, or with its object or its modifiers: *is going, was finished, shall have taken, will have been taken, studied the assignments, flows slowly, whispers nonsense to himself.* Distinguish between a *verb phrase* and a *verbal* (participle, infinitive, gerund).

Verbal. The verb forms—participles, gerunds, infinitives. These serve at times as adjectives, adverbs, nouns, parts of the predicate—but *never* as a predicate alone (see Section 3f).

Skiing is delightful. [Gerund used as a noun]
To succeed is exciting. [Infinitive used as a noun]
The *shaking* house may collapse. [Participle used as an adjective]
Sandy was glad *to have come.* [Infinitive used as an adverb]

Voice. See *Active voice, Passive voice.*

Weak verb. See *Regular verb.*

Word order. An English sentence consists not of a string of words in free relationship to one other, but of groups of words arranged in patterns. Words in an English sentence have meaning because of their position. That is, they have one meaning in one position, another meaning in another position, and no meaning in still another position (see Sections 44, 45, 46).

EXERCISES

I

Parts of speech, grammatical functions. Use a capital letter to indicate that the word, phrase, or clause italicized in each sentence below has the grammatical function of: A—a noun (*naming* word), B—a finite verb (*asserting* word), C—an adjective (*modifying* word, D—an adverb (*modifying* word), E—a preposition or a conjunction.

1. I *am* ready to help you at any time.
2. He was charged with driving too *fast* for road conditions.
3. I had still another *reason* for calling you.
4. It is of primary importance in swimming *to learn* to breathe properly.
5. You read faster *than* I do.
6. I don't want the people *sitting* over there to hear this.
7. You can *at least* try.
8. Who is *in charge* around here?
9. The best seat will go to *whoever comes first.*
10. *Insofar as* information is available, we will keep you posted.

II

Follow the directions given above.

1. Someone *has to have been monkeying* with this set, the way it works now.
2. *Doing* what other people expect you to do is his idea of morality.
3. *To whatever extent* I can help you, you can count on me.
4. The aphorism that truth lies *at the bottom of the cup* is often misleading.
5. *Whomever you want to invite* will be all right with me.
6. Courage *at two o'clock in the morning,* according to Napoleon, is the kind that counts.
7. To get up and *try* again, no matter how often you fail, is the mark of a hero.
8. I will repeat my last remark for the benefit of those *who came in late.*
9. These supplies, *however you came by them,* are going to prove useful.
10. We usually admire the people who like us; we do not always admire those *we like.*

III

Recognition of verbals. Each of the following sentences contains two verbals. Pick out each verbal and classify it by an identifying letter: G—gerund, P—participle, I—infinitive.

1. Dressed in his football uniform, Martin seemed to be unusually muscular.
2. Thinking that her mother was not at home, the little girl went to the cupboard to get a handful of her favorite cookies.
3. Am I to understand that cleaning out an attic is a simple procedure?
4. Running full before the wind in a stiff breeze, the sailor was determined not to jibe.
5. Training a puppy to go out at regular intervals takes patience and vigilance.
6. Jay earned money to put himself through college by composing rock tunes.
7. His throat parched, John tried to unstick his tongue from the roof of his mouth.
8. Having calculated the risk, the gambler decided to put all his chips on one throw of the dice.
9. To appear as tall as the soprano, the tenor had to wear elevator shoes.
10. Refreshed after a night's sleep, the astronauts found the going easier.

IV

Recognition and classification of phrases. Underline the phrases in the following sentences. Indicate the form of each phrase: Prep—prepositional, Par—participial, Ger—gerund, Inf—infinitive. Then indicate the function of each phrase: N—noun, Adj—adjective, Adv—adverb. Each sentence contains two such phrases.

1. At last a gentle rain fell upon the dry fields.
2. Students usually have to study at night.
3. Martin played most of the game with a broken finger.
4. The son of the circus strong man wanted to feed the elephants.
5. Putting both hands into the box, Jane pulled out all the candy she could grasp.
6. Rowing a boat is a good way to develop shoulder muscles.
7. Billy stepped importantly from the plane into a waiting car.
8. To breed a champion hog is the dream of many 4-H Club members.
9. Having packed his bags, Errol phoned for a bellboy.
10. The thing I like most about clothes is buying them.

V

Recognition and classification of dependent clauses. Underline the dependent clauses in the following sentences. Classify each such clause: N—noun clause, Adj—adjective clause, Adv—adverb clause. Each sentence contains two dependent clauses.

1. When Jim telephoned, I was in the basement with the men who were cleaning up the mess.
2. What we wanted most was to find the cherry tree we had seen the day before.
3. Although the seal dived into the pool after her, Gladys, who was a strong swimmer, still had hope of getting the fish.
4. If you have finished your tirade, Dick, I suggest that we join the party.
5. I can't see why anyone would want it, since it isn't really oblong.
6. After the party was over, Stanley looked around for the girl who had come with him.
7. When he threw me out of the house, I realized that he just didn't want to buy a television set.
8. It was clear that Ken was a little uncouth, but we needed a man who could manage the turnstiles.
9. It doesn't matter why he got in; we have to decide how we're going to get him out.
10. Until we know otherwise, we must assume that Sellers is not on our side.

VI

Kinds of sentences. Indicate the kind of sentence formed by each of the following groups of words, using these symbols: S–single, Cp–compound, Cx–complex; CC–compound-complex.

1. After we had been driving for miles on the rolling, twisting road, a wave of nausea suddenly swept over me.
2. My brother hurries through dinner, changes into old clothes, and works in the lab for two hours.
3. Since Jack could scarcely distinguish a yellow-bellied sapsucker from a double-breasted blue serge, he was asked to resign from the Birdwatchers' Club.
4. Smiling nonchalantly, the little man tossed the bundle over his left shoulder.
5. No one could understand how the chickens escaped, but Polly knew.
6. Some students do not know how to use the card catalog, and they waste time looking for books in the library.
7. The symbol of Martin's club is a corn cob pipe.
8. When the group reached the ski hut, some people built a fire, and others prepared dinner.
9. The forecast was for fair and warmer weather, but the day dawned dark and cool.
10. We don't know, but we suspect that the dean's wife has rebellious thoughts.

VII

Sentence patterns. Determine the sentence patterns in the following expanded sentences. Write the code for each pattern, following this example:

> Mary thoughtfully bought her best friend a tiny doll. Answer: Subject, predicate, indirect object, direct object. [Pattern 3]

1. Because they had to leave before sunrise, the explorers assembled their equipment the night before.
2. Gray, seeing that it was too early to get up, fell asleep for another few minutes.
3. The President awarded the hero the nation's highest decoration.
4. Although Tom had attempted to change her mind, Joy still thought him an extraordinary fool.
5. Mrs. Morris considered the former convict honest.
6. When Andy came home, the house was a mess.
7. Several men had applied for the job without success.
8. The cold water tasted wonderful.
9. Virtue is its own reward.
10. Having looked all over town and having been convinced that a good used car could not be found for fifty dollars, the boys, disillusioned but not completely hopeless, went home.

USAGE

Will Rogers (1879–1935), an American humorist and homespun philosopher, once remarked: "A lot of people who don't say *ain't*, ain't eatin'." In today's society, however, nearly everyone recognizes the importance of using what is commonly called "good" or "accepted" English. The use of "good English" will not guarantee success in any area of your life; but whatever goals you set, ignorance of standard practices in speech and writing will make those goals more difficult to attain. It is important to choose and use those expressions and grammatical forms that will let your hearers and readers know precisely what you are trying to communicate. Usage that interferes with communication, usage that weakens or destroys a favorable image of you as speaker or writer should be avoided.

11. LEVELS OF USAGE

The most common violations of acceptable usage occur in these sentence situations:

1. Subject and verb agreement
2. Pronoun and antecedent agreement
3. The case of pronouns

4. Principal parts of verbs
5. Linking and auxiliary verbs
6. Tense of verbs
7. Active and passive voice
8. Use of adjectives and adverbs
9. Use of conjunctions

These nine grammatical structures are discussed in the sections that follow (12–20). Concentrate on them. Other situations that might cause violations of standard usage can be safely ignored, at least for now.

11a. APPROPRIATE LEVELS OF USAGE

The appropriateness (suitability, fitness) of language is determined by the subject being discussed, by who is speaking or writing to whom, and by the situation involved. In one set of circumstances, it might be appropriate to say, for instance, "beat it," or "get lost," or "scram." In another situation, it would be appropriate to say "please leave," or "goodbye," or even "au revoir." The appropriateness of a given level of usage depends upon the *what, who,* and *where* of a particular setting or circumstance.

What expressions and grammatical forms should be employed on what occasions? Although attitudes toward usage have become less rigid in recent years, almost everyone has faced many situations in which a knowledge of acceptable, reputable English is either desirable or essential. You may not wish or need to use "correct" English at all times, but you should at least know what preferred usage directs both when you are conversing with other people and when you are writing business letters, class papers, minutes of club meetings, and all compositions designed to be read by others.

In neither speaking nor writing should you appear stuffy and overly precise. There is, or should be, however, a marked difference between the *what* and *how* of communicating in relaxed conversation and in writing for formal and semi-formal occasions. Material in Sections 12–20 is not designed to put your speech and writing into a straitjacket. It is designed to inform you about what's what in contemporary standard English usage.

11b. VARIOUS LEVELS OF USAGE

Each of us employs a different level of usage depending upon whether we are speaking or writing, upon who are our audience and readers, and upon the kind of occasion. As Professor John S. Kenyon has pointed out, what are commonly grouped together in one class as different levels of language are combinations of two categories: cultural levels and functional varieties.

CULTURAL LEVELS

Among cultural levels may be included narrowly local dialect, ungrammatical speech, illiterate speech, slovenly vocabulary and construction, exceptional pronunciation, and excessive and unskillful use of slang. On a higher level is the language used generally by educated people over wide areas; it is both clear and grammatically correct. These two cultural levels are called *substandard* and *standard* language, respectively.

FUNCTIONAL VARIETIES

The term *level* does not properly apply to functional varieties: colloquial, familiar, formal, legal, scientific. As Professor Kenyon suggests, these varieties are equally suitable for their respective functions and do not depend on the cultural status of the users.

In a general and practical sense, the most helpful distinction is between informal and formal ways of speaking and writing. Five levels may be mentioned, but it is not easy to say precisely where one ends and another begins.

1. Carefully selected written English. Thoughtfully prepared and painstakingly edited books and magazines exhibit this level of usage. In addition, the writing of many educated men and women in all parts of the country falls into this category, which is largely (but not exclusively) the usage described and recommended in the sections that follow.

2. General written English. Most newspapers, radio and television scripts, business letters and reports, and several widely circulated magazines employ this second level of usage. It does not have all the polish of carefully selected written English, but it is generally acceptable and represents the level all students should try to attain in written work.

3. Choice spoken English. This is the language heard in serious or formal addresses and talks and in the conversation of educated people who normally apply the requirements of carefully selected written English to the spoken variety. It is neither so "correct" nor so inflexible as the two earlier varieties mentioned, because oral English is nearly always freer than is written English.

4. General spoken English. Most fairly well educated people employ this level in ordinary conversation. It is somewhat more easygoing than level 3, employs more newer and shorter forms (slang, contractions), and is sometimes referred to as "colloquial."

5. Substandard English. This is a term used to characterize illiterate or vulgar expressions. Such expressions, associated with the uneducated, appear also in the speech of many educated persons who choose to express themselves this way.

The distinctions just made can be labeled at their centers but run together at their extremes. Further, most expressions are identical on all levels. One who says or writes "I spoke slowly" is using an expression that has no distinct level of usage. The five categories can, however, be illustrated:

Carefully selected written English:	I shall not go.
General written English:	I will not go.

Choice spoken:	I'll not go.
General spoken:	I'm not going to go.
Substandard:	I ain't gonna go.

In addition to being modified by the general distinction between formal and informal usage, language is encased in rules about grammatical structure and word choice that are themselves modified by considerations of time, place, and situation. In general, word usage and grammatical structure should be in *current, national,* and *reputable* use. No standards of usage are absolute and unvarying. The usage recommended in the sections that follow, however, is that which is employed by most careful, thoughtful speakers and writers.

12. SUBJECT AND VERB AGREEMENT

Agreement means "the state of being in accord," "conformity." As applied to grammar, the term means "correspondence in person, number, gender, or case." Thus, when a subject agrees with its predicate, both subject and predicate verb have the same *person* (first, second, third) and *number* (singular or plural).

Few problems of agreement between subject and predicate arise, because English verbs (except *to be*) have only one form for singular and plural and for all persons except the third person singular present. But what few errors do occur are important. Usually, errors in agreement appear for two reasons: (1) The writer or speaker is confused about the *number* of the subject because of the presence of other words; or (2) he uses a verb to agree not with the grammatical form of a subject but with its meaning. You need to know what the *true* subject is and whether it is singular or plural. Look for the person or thing about which the verb makes a statement. When you find it, you have the subject. A subject is always either a noun, a word or group of words used as a noun, or a pronoun.

"Our *basketball team* [subject] *plays* [verb] twenty games each year." In the preceding sentence, the subject and the verb are easy to find, but in some sentences the subject comes after the verb or is separated from the verb by other words. Before you try to make the verb agree with the subject, be sure that you have the *real* subject.

12a. A PREDICATE (VERB) NORMALLY AGREES WITH ITS SUBJECT IN PERSON AND NUMBER

The *owners* greedily *ask* too high a price. [*Owners* and *ask* are in the third person and are plural in number.]

I agree to pay your asking price. [*I* and *agree* are in the first person and are singular in number.]

He agrees to pay the asking price. [*He* and *agrees* are in the third person and are singular in number.]

Section 12a states the general rule. The following sections deal with variations and situations likely to cause trouble.

12b. A VERB SHOULD *NOT* AGREE WITH A NOUN THAT INTERVENES BETWEEN IT AND THE SUBJECT

The *cause* for all the noise and confusion *were* not obvious. [Substitute *was* for *were; cause,* the subject, is singular.]

I, together with Eleanor and Sally, *are* going. [Substitute *am* for *are; I* is the true subject.]

The *child,* as well as the other members of the family, *were* frightened. [Substitute *was* for *were; child* is the true subject of the sentence.]

12c. SINGULAR PRONOUNS REQUIRE SINGULAR VERBS

The following pronouns are singular: *another, anybody, anyone, anything, each, either, everybody, everyone, everything, many a one, neither, nobody, no one, one, somebody, someone.*

Each *has* his duty to perform.
No one *was* present at the time.
One of you *is* mistaken.

None (literally *no one* and also meaning "not any") may be followed by either a singular or a plural verb. Today, it is as frequently followed by a plural verb as by one in the singular, especially when the phrase that modifies *none* contains a plural noun (*none of the men*). The standard rule, however, is that *none* requires a singular verb.

Agreement based on meaning and agreement based on grammatical form sometimes conflict. In the sentence, "*Each* of the boys in this group *is* sixteen years old," *each* and *is* are in grammatical agreement. But in "*Each* of the boys in this group *are* sixteen years old," *are* is plural because the meaning of "each of the boys" is construed to be "all of the boys." A somewhat similar principle may be illustrated thus: "*Everyone* in the apartment house tuned *his* TV [or *their* TVs] to that channel." Careful speakers and writers follow grammatical agreement in such sentences, but agreement based on meaning is becoming acceptable in informal speech and writing.

12d. NOUNS PLURAL IN FORM BUT SINGULAR IN MEANING REQUIRE A SINGULAR VERB

Authorities differ about the number of many such nouns. A good rule, according to usage, is "when in doubt, use a singular verb." The following are nearly always used with singular verbs: *physics, economics, mathematics, news, politics, whereabouts, mechanics, ethics, mumps, stamina, headquarters.*

Physics, they were told, *is* the study of heat, light, sound, mechanics, and electricity.

The sad *news was* broadcast at noon.

12e. SUBJECTS PLURAL IN FORM THAT INDICATE A QUANTITY OR NUMBER REQUIRE A SINGULAR VERB WHEN THE SUBJECT IS REGARDED AS A UNIT

Four-fifths of the area *is* under water.
Two from five *leaves* three.

12f. TWO OR MORE SUBJECTS JOINED BY *AND* REQUIRE A PLURAL VERB

"Both Ed and Bob *are* running for office" is an example. When two subjects form a single thought or have a closely related meaning, however, a singular verb is frequently used: His kindness and generosity *is* well known.

12g. SINGULAR SUBJECTS JOINED BY *OR* OR *NOR, EITHER . . . OR,* AND *NEITHER . . . NOR* USUALLY REQUIRE A SINGULAR VERB

Either Mimi or Dick *is* at fault.
Neither the boy nor his father *was* found guilty.

12h. IF THE SUBJECTS DIFFER IN NUMBER OR PERSON, THE VERB AGREES WITH THE NEARER SUBJECT

Neither Phil nor the other boys *know*.
They or I *am* liable for damages.
Either Sue or some of her classmates *are* willing to go.

12i. RELATIVE PRONOUNS REFERRING TO PLURAL ANTECEDENTS GENERALLY REQUIRE PLURAL VERBS

Each of *those* who *are* there should listen carefully.
He is one of the most able *students* who *have* ever attended this school.

If *only* or some similar qualifying word precedes *one*, the verb in the subordinate clause is singular:

He is the *only one* of those in this class who *listens* carefully.

12j. A VERB DOES NOT AGREE WITH A PREDICATE NOUN

The best part of a children's party *is* the ice cream and cake.
Ice cream and cake *are* the best part of a children's party.

12k. AFTER THE EXPLETIVE *THERE*, THE VERB IS SINGULAR OR PLURAL ACCORDING TO THE NUMBER OF THE SUBJECT THAT FOLLOWS. A SINGULAR VERB SHOULD APPEAR AFTER THE EXPLETIVE *IT*

There *are* [not *is*] strong sentiments in his favor.
There *were* [not *was*] baseball, tennis, and swimming.
In the field there *stands* [not *stand*] a towering tree.
It *is* [not *are*] the girls who must wash the dishes.

12l. A COLLECTIVE NOUN TAKES A SINGULAR VERB WHEN THE GROUP IS REGARDED AS A UNIT, A PLURAL VERB WHEN THE INDIVIDUALS OF THE GROUP ARE REGARDED SEPARATELY

Common collective nouns are *army, assembly, clergy, committee, company, couple, crew, crowd, family, flock, group, herd, jury, mob, multitude, orchestra, pair, personnel, squad, team, union.* Most of these nouns also have plural forms: *army, armies; assembly, assemblies; company, companies; crowd, crowds; team, teams;* and so on.

Without the *-s,* they are considered singular and take a singular verb and singular pronouns when the collection of individuals is thought of as a unit, as a whole; they are considered plural and take a plural verb and plural pronouns when the members of the group are thought of as individuals, acting separately.

> The jury [a unit] *is* going to reach a verdict soon.
> The jury [members] *have* ordered their suppers and are going to eat them in the jury room.
> The committee *has* appointed a new chairman.
> The committee *have* been unwilling to charge for personal expenses.
> The couple at the head table *is* named Burden.
> The couple *were* assigned to simple tasks during the service.
> The crew *has asked* him to help with coaching.
> The crew *are coming* on board in a few hours.
> The family *was named* Gregson.
> The family *were seated* at the dinner table.

12m. SOME NOUNS OF FOREIGN ORIGIN HAVE DISTINCTIVE FORMS FOR SINGULAR AND PLURAL

Singular	*Plural*
basis	bases
datum	data
phenomenon	phenomena
criterion	criteria
synopsis	synopses
alumnus	alumni
thesis	theses

> *Synopses* of two stories *were* submitted.
> The *alumni were* in favor of building the stadium.

NOTE: *Data* is correctly used as a plural, but many educated speakers and writers now use it as a singular.

13. PRONOUNS AND ANTECEDENTS

An *antecedent* (derived from Latin words meaning "going before") is the substantive (noun or pronoun) to which a pronoun refers or for which it is substituted. The agreement of pronouns and antecedents causes at least as much difficulty as that of subjects and verbs.

13a. A PRONOUN AGREES WITH ITS ANTECEDENT IN GENDER, NUMBER, AND PERSON

The meaning of the pronoun will not be clear unless it has the same gender, number, and person as the noun for which it stands.

Orlon is an important synthetic material. *It* is said to be better than nylon. [*It* refers to *orlon,* the antecedent. Both *orlon* and *it* are neuter gender, singular number, third person.]

The woman put on *her* coat. [Singular antecedent, feminine, third person.]
The women put on *their* coats. [Plural antecedent, feminine, third person.]
The man removed *his* hat. [Masculine, singular, third person.]
The boys raised *their* voices. [Masculine, plural, third person.]

Pronouns do not necessarily agree with their antecedents in case. In the sentences above, *woman, women, man,* and *boys,* are nominative; *her, their,* and *his* are possessive (see Section 14).

13b. SINGULAR PRONOUNS REFER TO SINGULAR ANTECEDENTS

The words *each, either, neither, somebody, anyone, anybody, everybody,* and *nobody* are singular, and a pronoun referring to any one of these words should be singular (*he, his, him, she, her, it*).

Has anyone here forgotten *his* promise?
Everybody is expected to do *his* share.

In the second sentence, *everybody* may refer to men and women. In informal English one could say, "Everybody is expected to contribute *their* share," even though, strictly speaking, *his* is preferred. One may write, "Everybody is expected to contribute his or her share," although this construction sounds artificial and even awkward. Note that even when this "singular pronoun–singular antecedent" rule is relaxed, as it often is, the verb remains singular.

Everybody *wears* shoes on their feet.
Each of the contestants *was* accompanied by their manager.

13c. A COLLECTIVE NOUN USED AS AN ANTECEDENT TAKES A SINGULAR PRONOUN IF THE GROUP IS THOUGHT OF AS A UNIT AND A PLURAL PRONOUN IF IT IS THOUGHT OF IN TERMS OF ITS INDIVIDUAL MEMBERS

The group of girls was shouting *its* praises. [The group acted as a unit.]
The group of girls raised *their* umbrellas. [The group acted as individuals.]
The class was divided in *its* [not *their*] opinion of the speaker.
Members of the class *were* divided in *their* [not *its*] opinions of the speaker.

If a collective noun is used with a singular verb, all pronouns referring to it are singular; if the verb used is plural, all pronouns referring to the antecedent should be plural.

Doubtful: The family *was* discussing *their* problems.
Right: The family *was* discussing *its* problems.
Right: The family *were* discussing *their* problems.

13d. *WHO* REFERS TO PERSONS, *WHICH* REFERS TO THINGS, AND *THAT* REFERS TO PERSONS OR THINGS

The person *who* told me the facts is your mother.
That magazine, *which* is the one you lent me, contains some very dull stories.

The flier *that* took her plane on a record-breaking trip has been given an award.

13e. A NOUN OR AN INDEFINITE PRONOUN USED AS AN ANTECEDENT TAKES A PRONOUN IN THE THIRD PERSON

Nouns and indefinite pronouns are in the third person except when used in direct address or in apposition with a pronoun of the first or second person. A phrase such as *of us* or *of you* between the pronoun and its antecedent does not affect the person of the pronoun.

Informal: If a man wants to succeed, *you* must work hard.
Right: If a man wants to succeed, *he* must work hard.
Informal: Neither of you has finished *your* lunch.
Right: Neither of you has finished *his* lunch.

13f. A PRONOUN AGREES WITH THE NEARER OF TWO ANTECEDENTS

Occasionally, two antecedents, different in gender or number, occur in one sentence. With two antecedents and only one pronoun, the pronoun referring to the nearer antecedent should be used.

He hated everybody and everything *that* caused his defeat.
He hated everything and everybody *who* caused his defeat.
Either Jack or his sisters will lose *their* chance to go.
Either Jack's sisters or he will lose *his* chance to go.
In this cool room, neither the gardenia nor the roses will lose *their* freshness.

13g. *WHAT* SHOULD NOT BE USED TO REFER TO AN EXPRESSED ANTECEDENT

Substandard: The stationery *what* you sent me as a Christmas present arrived yesterday.
Right: The stationery *that* you sent me arrived last week.
Right: I heard *what* you said.

14. CASE OF PRONOUNS

Case is one of the forms that a noun or pronoun takes to indicate its relationship to other words in the sentence. There are three important cases in English: nominative (subjective): genitive (possessive); and accusative (objective).

A noun or pronoun is in the *nominative* case (subject of a sentence) when it indicates the person or thing acting; in the *genitive* (possessive) case when it denotes the person or thing owning or possessing; in the *accusative* (objective) case when it indicates the person or thing acted upon.

There is no change in the form of a noun to denote the nominative and objective cases. Word order in the sentence provides the only clue:

The child rode his tricycle. [*Child* is in the nominative case, *tricycle* in the objective.]

The tricycle was ridden by the child. [*Tricycle* is in the *nominative* case, *child* in the objective.]

The possessive case does involve a change in the form of a noun: *child's*. But the case of nouns usually causes little trouble.

Grammatical problems arise because many pronouns, unlike nouns, have distinct forms for the nominative and objective cases. Such problems appear most frequently with *personal* pronouns (*I, you, he, me, him*) and with *relative* and *interrogative* pronouns (*who, whom, whose*).

Nominative case

14a. THE SUBJECT OF A SENTENCE OR A CLAUSE IS IN THE NOMINATIVE CASE

If the subject is a noun, just write the noun; if the subject is a pronoun, you still should have little trouble:

> He and *I* [not *me*] volunteered to go.
> *Who* [not *whom*] is speaking, please?

14b. A PREDICATE COMPLEMENT IS IN THE NOMINATIVE CASE

A predicate complement is a noun (no difficulty with case), a pronoun (nominative case, essentially), or a predicate adjective (no case involved) used after a linking verb (see Section 16). After a linking verb, use only the nominative case of a pronoun:

> That was *she* [not *her*] calling on the telephone.
> It was *they* [not *them*] who invited us to dinner.

In informal speech one often hears (and perhaps says), "It's me" or "This is me," or "That's him." Such expressions are growing more acceptable, but careful speakers and writers continue to use the nominative case in such constructions. If saying "It's I" sounds stilted to you, why not say "It's" or "This is" and follow with your name?

Objective case

14c. THE OBJECT OF A VERB OR PREPOSITION IS IN THE OBJECTIVE CASE

All nouns and the pronouns *it* and *you* cause no difficulty in this construction, because they are the same in the nominative and objective cases. But carefully choose between *who* and *whom, I* and *me, she* and *her, he* and *him, they* and *them, we* and *us*.

> *Whom* did the police blame for the accident?
> The superintendent accused *me*.
> That is a blow to *her*.
> A group of *us* is going to the lecture.
> Did you invite both *him* and *her* to our party?
> To *whom* did you mention our party?

14d. THE INDIRECT OBJECT OF A VERB IS IN THE OBJECTIVE CASE

An indirect object is a noun or pronoun before which *to* or *for* is expressed or understood.

Give *me* a fuller explanation, please.
If you do *him* a favor, he will not be grateful.
Tell *whom* my bad luck? Didi? I certainly shall not.

14e. THE SUBJECT, OBJECT, OR OBJECTIVE COMPLEMENT OF AN INFINITIVE IS IN THE OBJECTIVE CASE

Whom did you take him to be? [That is, you did take *him* to be *whom?*]
His father made *him* say that. [*Him* is the subject of *to say.*]
I was eager to kiss *her*. [*Her* is the object of *to kiss.*]
Did Jack think him to be *me?* [*Me* is the objective complement of *to be.*]

Nominative or objective case

So far, so good; now we come to the real trouble spots. If you do not fully understand the function of pronouns, particularly *who, whoever, whom,* and *whomever,* now is the time to learn once and for all.

14f. *WHO* AND *WHOEVER* ARE USED AS SUBJECTS OF VERBS OR AS PREDICATE PRONOUNS; *WHOM* AND *WHOMEVER* ARE USED AS OBJECTS OF VERBS AND OF PREPOSITIONS

The following sentences illustrate correct use of *who* and *whoever:*

The question of *who* is eligible is unimportant. [*Who* is the subject of *is;* the entire clause *who is eligible* is the object of the preposition *of.*]

This article offers good advice to *whoever* will accept it. [*Whoever* is the subject of *will accept;* the clause *whoever will accept it* is the object of *to.*]

A stranger here, he does not know *who* is *who*. [The first *who* is the subject of *is;* the second *who* is a predicate pronoun.]

These sentences illustrate proper use of *whom* and *whomever:*

That is the boy *whom* I saw at the beach last summer. [*Whom* is the direct object of *saw:* I saw *whom.*]

Jack always tells his problems to *whomever* he meets. [*Whomever* is the direct object of *meets:* He meets *whomever.*]

Give the present to *whomever* you wish. [*Whomever* is the object of the preposition *to.*]

The case of a pronoun must not be affected by words that come between the pronoun and its antecedent. The case of a word always depends upon its *use* in a sentence.

Jill asked Gray *who* he thought would be elected. [Check by omitting *he thought.*]

Who do you think is responsible for that decision? [Check by omitting *do you think.*]

I winked at the girl *whom* no one thought we had invited. [Check by omitting *no one thought.*]

Current usage studies indicate that the distinction between *who* and *whom* is breaking down, partly because keeping them straight is difficult and partly because many people start a sentence or clause with *who*, not knowing how they are going to end. One dictionary says of *whom:* "The objective case of *who;* in colloquial usage, now often replaced by *who*." (*Webster's New World Dictionary*)

14g. AN APPOSITIVE SHOULD BE IN THE SAME CASE AS THE NOUN OR PRONOUN IT IDENTIFIES OR EXPLAINS

We, *you* and *I*, are silly to take this chance.
The coach gave both of us, *Fred* and *me*, a stern lecture.
A few of us, those *whom* you asked, are delighted to accept.

14h. AN ELLIPTICAL CLAUSE OF COMPARISON, PRECEDED BY *THAN* OR AS, REQUIRES THE CASE CALLED FOR BY THE EXPANDED CONSTRUCTION

An elliptical clause is one with a word or more missing; the omitted word or words are understood from other parts of the sentence.

You are as strong as *I* (am). [Nominative]
This story interested you more than (it interested) me. [Objective]
I do not love her as much as *he* (loves her). [Nominative]

Genitive (possessive) case

14i. A NOUN OR PRONOUN LINKED IMMEDIATELY WITH A GERUND SHOULD BE IN THE POSSESSIVE CASE

She dislikes *your* being more organized than she is.
The coach praised John for *his* taking extra practice sessions.

When the use of a possessive with a gerund causes awkwardness, rephrase the sentence:

Awkward: No rules exist against *anyone's* in this class speaking his mind.
Improved: No rules exist against any class *member's* speaking his mind.

14j. THE POSSESSIVE CASE OF AN INANIMATE OBJECT IS USUALLY TO BE AVOIDED

Awkward: The *tree's* leaves were turning brown.
This machine will quickly wax and polish the *dance hall's* floor.
Improved: The leaves *of the tree* were turning brown.
This machine will quickly wax and polish the floor *of the dance hall* (or *the dance hall floor*.)

14k. THE POSSESSIVE CASE IS USED IN ACCORDANCE WITH ESTABLISHED IDIOM

Despite the suggestion given in Section 14j, such expressions as the following are idiomatic and thus completely acceptable: *a day's work, a moment's notice, a dime's worth, a stone's throw, a summer's work, at his wits' end, three years' experience, tomorrow's weather report, the law's delay, two semesters' study.*

15. PRINCIPAL PARTS OF VERBS

In every language, verbs have principal parts, sometimes three (as in German), sometimes five (as in Spanish, Italian, and French). An English verb has three principal parts: present tense (present infinitive), past tense, past participle (*go, went, gone*). A good way to recall these parts is to substitute those of any verb for the following:

I play today.	I swim today.
I played yesterday.	I swam yesterday.
I have played every day this week.	I have swum every day this week.

15a. THE PAST TENSE AND PAST PARTICIPLE OFTEN HAVE DIFFERENT FORMS

The past tense and past participle of most English verbs are formed by adding *-d, -ed,* or *-t* to the present infinitive: *ask, asked, asked; deal, dealt, dealt.* Such verbs are called *regular,* or *weak,* verbs. Verbs that form the past tense and past participle by a vowel change as well as by the occasional addition of an ending are called *irregular,* or *strong,* verbs: *do, did, done; ride, rode, ridden.* The following are incorrect:

The dog *has bit* the child seriously. [Should be *has bitten*]
Joe *drunk* a pint of cold milk. [Should be *drank*]
Snow *has fell* for 22 hours. [Should be *has fallen*]

When in doubt about the correct forms of the past tense or past participle, consult a dictionary. If no additional forms follow the main entry, the verb is regular.

15b. THE ENDING OF A REGULAR VERB SHOULD NOT BE OMITTED

We are *supposed* [not *suppose*] to arrive on time.
Yesterday I *asked* [not *ask*] for another examination.

15c. THE PRINCIPAL PARTS OF FREQUENTLY USED REGULAR AND IRREGULAR VERBS REQUIRE STUDY

Following is a list of fifty troublesome verbs. Each can be put into the three expressions suggested in the beginning of this section, sometimes with amusing results.

Present Tense	*Past Tense*	*Past Participle*
bear	bore	borne (born, *given birth to*)
begin	began	begun
bid	bid	bid (*as in an auction*)
bid	bade	bidden (*as in a command*)
bite	bit	bitten (bit)
blow	blew	blown

Present Tense	*Past Tense*	*Past Participle*
break	broke	broken
burst	burst	burst
catch	caught	caught
choose	chose	chosen
come	came	come
dig	dug	dug
dive	dived	dived
do	did	done
drag	dragged	dragged
draw	drew	drawn
drink	drank	drunk
drown	drowned	drowned
eat	ate	eaten
fall	fell	fallen
fly	flew	flown
forget	forgot	forgotten (forgot)
freeze	froze	frozen
get	got	got (gotten)
go	went	gone
hang	hung	hung (*object*)
hang	hanged	hanged (*person*)
know	knew	known
lay	laid	laid
lead	led	led
lend	lent	lent
lie	lay	lain (*recline*)
lie	lied	lied (*falsehood*)
lose	lost	lost
pay	paid	paid
raise	raised	raised
ride	rode	ridden
rise	rose	risen
run	ran	run
set	set	set
sing	sang	sung
sit	sat	sat
speak	spoke	spoken
swim	swam	swum
take	took	taken
tear	tore	torn
wake	waked (woke)	waked (woke)
wear	wore	worn
wring	wrung	wrung
write	wrote	written

16. LINKING AND AUXILIARY VERBS

Most verbs assert (indicate) action, but some express a static condition or state of being. Nearly all such "inactive" verbs are *linking* verbs (also called *copulative* or *joining* verbs). A linking verb can "couple" two nouns or pronouns or a noun and an adjective: This *is* my brother. The dog *looks* sick.

The most common linking verb is *to be*. Other linking verbs are *appear, become, feel, grow, look, prove, remain, seem, smell, sound, stand, taste, turn.* Still other verbs occur in only a limited number of linking contexts: *slam* shut, *ring* true. The same verb can assert action and serve as a link:

> The sky *looks* overcast today. [Linking]
> Jane *looks* closely at every page she reads. [Action]
> We *felt* downcast over our defeat. [Linking]
> Marian *felt* her way through the dark room. [Action]

Another variety of verb that can cause trouble is the *auxiliary* verb, one that "helps out" another verb in forming tenses, voice, mood, and certain precise ideas. Usually an auxiliary verb has little meaning of its own but it does change the meaning of the main verb it accompanies.

> The man of the soil *has been* pushed more and more out of the American economy.
> A careful analysis of the oxygen content *should have been* made at the time.

Commonly used auxiliary verbs

The meanings of all commonly used auxiliary verbs are contained in a dictionary. Such verbs and their uses may be summarized as follows:

1. *To be*. Used in all tenses in forming the progressive tone and the passive voice.
2. *Can*. Used to express ability or power or the idea of "being able to": I *can* meet him at noon. My daddy *can* fix anything.
3. *Could*. Used as a kind of "past" tense of *can* to express the same ideas in a weaker manner: Beverly *could* not haul in the heavy anchor. My daddy *could* fix anything if he wanted to fix it.
4. *Dare*. Used, usually with *say*, to express probability: I *dare* say that's true. I *dare* say the choice will be easy to make.
5. *To do*. Used to express emphasis [emphatic tone] in the present and past tenses: Please *do* come to see us soon. She *did* send me a birthday card this year. Also used to avoid repetition of a verb or full verb expression: John slept as soundly as I *did*. We shall start out when you *do*.
6. *To have*. Used in the present perfect, past perfect, and future perfect tenses; also in the perfect infinitive and the perfect participle: He *has* gone, *had* gone, will *have* gone; to *have* gone, *having* gone.
7. *Let*. Used to express the ideas of "allowing" or "permitting," "suggesting," or "ordering": *Let* me go now. *Let's* have a picnic. *Let* me think about that. *Let* her finish her supper.
8. *May*. Used to express permission: *May* I have your coat? You *may* keep the book. Also used to express probability or a wish: It *may* hurt for a while. *May* your trip be a pleasant one!
9. *Might*. Used as a kind of "past" tense of *may* to express the same ideas of possibility or probability in a weaker manner: You *might* try tutoring handicapped children.
10. *Must*. Used to express obligation or compulsion: Every person *must* help in the dispensary. You *must* list your assets. Also used to express reasonable certainty: Jim was here promptly, so he *must* have set his alarm clock. I hear thunder; there *must* be a storm coming.
11. *Need*. Used to express necessity or obligation: I *need* not give her my name. They *need* only to speak up and speak out. *Note:* As auxiliary verb, the third person singular form is also *need:* He *need* not take my suggestion.

12. *Ought.* Used to express duty or obligation; one of the few auxiliary verbs followed by the sign of the infinitive (*to*) with the main verb: you *ought* to learn mechanics. Everyone *ought* to know that story. *Note: Have* and *had* are never used before *ought* or *must*. Wrong: I *had ought* to start working. Right: I *ought to have started* working long ago.
13. *Shall.* Used as the precise auxiliary for the first person, future and future perfect tenses: We *shall* start the trip tomorrow. Also used in the second and third persons to express command or determination: You *shall* be prompt in the future.
14. *Should.* Used as a kind of "past" tense of *shall,* in the first person, but weaker in emphasis: I *should* not scold the children. I *should* hope for the best. Also used frequently in a conditional meaning: If I *should* make other plans, I shall let you know. If Jack *should* want food, we can provide some. Used as well in all three persons to express duty or propriety or necessity: You *should* organize your work. She *should* be proud of him. And used in all three persons to express expectation: We *should* be flying over Spokane now. The letter *should* reach her on Monday.
15. *Used.* In the past tense only, *used* expresses custom or habitual action: I *used* to cry a lot when I was little. It *used* to rain every day in Portland.
16. *Will.* Used as the precise auxiliary for the second and third persons, future and future perfect tenses. You *will* go, *will* have gone; he *will* go, *will* have gone; they *will* go, *will* have gone. Also used in all three persons to express willingness or consent: I *will* take the examination.
17. *Would.* Used as a kind of "past" tense of *will,* in the second and third persons, but less strong in meaning: You *would* scarcely care about them. *Note:* If the verb in the independent clause is in the past tense, use *would* to express futurity in the dependent clause; if the verb in the independent clause is in the present tense, use *will* in the dependent clause: Willie *told* me that he *would* write. Willie *tells* me that he *will* write.
    Used frequently in a conditional meaning, or after a conditional clause: If you *would* agree, they *would* be reassured. If the traffic were heavy, he *would* take another route. If I could, I *would.* Used to express determination: He *would* try, no matter how difficult the assignment appeared to be. Also used in all three persons to express repeated or habitual action: In the winter we *would* skate every day. And used infrequently to express wish or desire: *Would* that we all had done otherwise!

17. TENSE AND TONE

Tense indicates the time of the action or time of the static condition (state of being) expressed by a verb. The three divisions of time—past, present, future—are shown in English by six tenses. The three primary, or simple, tenses are the *present* tense, the *past* tense, and the *future* tense. The three secondary, or compound, tenses are the *present perfect,* the *past perfect,* and the *future perfect.*

Within some tenses, verbs also have certain tones that express precisely what the writer wishes to say: *simple* tone (*I study*); *progressive* tone (*I am studying*); and *emphatic* tone (*I do study*).

17a. THE CORRECT TENSE IS NEEDED TO EXPRESS PRECISE TIME

Unlike a highly inflected language, such as German, English has few tense forms; English verbs reveal change in tense only by inflection or by the use of auxiliary words (see Section 16). Difficulty with tense usage arises from not knowing the functions of the six tenses or from not thinking carefully about the exact time element involved. The following table shows the tenses needed to convey precise ideas.

ACTIVE VOICE

Present:	I see (am seeing)
Past:	I saw (was seeing)
Future:	I shall see (shall be seeing)
Present perfect:	I have seen (have been seeing)
Past perfect:	I had seen (had been seeing)
Future perfect:	I shall have seen (shall have been seeing)

PASSIVE VOICE

Present:	I am seen (am being seen)
Past:	I was seen (was being seen)
Future:	I shall be seen
Present perfect:	I have been seen
Past perfect:	I had been seen
Future perfect:	I shall have been seen

VERBALS (NONFINITE VERB FORMS)

Present infinitive:	to see (to be seeing)
Perfect infinitive:	to have seen (to have been seeing)
Present participle:	seeing [none]
Past participle:	seen [none]
Perfect participle:	having seen (having been seeing)
Present gerund:	seeing [none]
Perfect gerund:	having seen (having been seeing)

Present tense indicates that the action or condition is going on or exists now.

He *walks* to his office every day.
The truth *is* known.

Past tense indicates that an action or condition took place or existed at some definite time in the past.

She *mailed* the package yesterday.
The summer of 1972 *was* hot.

Future tense indicates that an action will take place, or that a certain condition will exist, in the future:

We *shall leave* at noon tomorrow.
Our glee club *will be singing* there next month.

The future may be stated by the present tense accompanied by an adverb (or adverbial phrase) of time. Such constructions as the following are common:

I am going to San Diego soon.
This Thursday the boat leaves for Honolulu.

Present perfect tense indicates that an action or condition was begun in the past and has just been completed or is still going on. The time is past but it is connected with the present. The present perfect tense *presupposes* some relationship with the present.

> You *have been* a nuisance all your life.
> The weather *has been* too cold for hiking in the woods.
> I *have* long *been* an Alfred Hitchcock addict.

Past perfect tense indicates that an action or condition was completed at a time now past. It indicates action "two steps back"—that is, the past perfect tense presupposes some relationship with an action or condition expressed in the past tense.

> The roads were impassable because ice sheets *had formed* during the night.
> He lived in Berkeley. He *had been* there for several months.

Future perfect tense indicates that an action or condition will be completed at a future time.

> I *shall have died* by that time.
> The weather *will have changed* before you leave.

The three secondary, or compound, tenses always indicate *completed* action, whether it be in the present (present perfect tense), in the past (past perfect tense), or in the future (future perfect tense).

17b. THE CORRECT TONE IS NEEDED TO EXPRESS PRECISE MEANING

The *simple* tone is a concise statement of a "snapshot" action of a verb, or immediate or unspecified time: I *talk* (present tense), I *talked* (past tense), I *shall talk* (future tense), I *have talked* (present perfect tense), I *had talked* (past perfect tense), I *shall have talked* (future perfect tense).

The *progressive* tone forms in each of the six tenses are built by using proper tense forms of the verb *to be* followed by the present participle of the main verb: I *am talking, was talking, shall be talking, have been talking, had been talking, shall have been talking.*

The *emphatic* tone forms are expressed by the verb *to do* and the present infinitive of the main verb. The emphatic tone is used in only present and past tenses: I *do talk*, I *did talk*.

17c. TENSES SHOULD APPEAR IN PROPER SEQUENCE

When only one verb is used in a sentence, it should express the precise time involved. When two or more verbs appear in a sentence, they should be consistent in tense (see Section 51a). Most important, remember that the tense of a verb in a subordinate clause depends on the tense of the verb in the main clause.

The present tense is used in a dependent clause to express a general truth: Some people did not believe that the earth *is* a planet. The present tense is used alone to express a universal or "timeless" truth: Thought *makes* the whole dignity of man.

Do not allow the tense of a verb to be in the past when it should be present:

Last summer, I visited a small village in France; the houses *were* old and picturesque. (It is conceivable that the village has been destroyed, but is that what is meant? Use instead: The houses there *are* old and picturesque.) Passages in some short stories and novels are written in the present tense although the action occurred in time which is past. This use of what is called the *historical present* sometimes makes narrative more vivid, but it quickly becomes monotonous.

Use a present infinitive except when the infinitive represents action completed before the time of the governing verb.

> I intended *to see* [not *to have seen*] you about it.
> Everyone is pleased *to have had* you as a visitor.

A present participle indicates action at the time expressed by the verb; a past participle indicates action before that of the verb.

> *Traveling* all over the world, he *sees* many remarkable people.
> *Having been* a good student, he *was* able to get many letters of recommendation.

When narration in the past tense is interrupted for reference to a preceding event, use the past perfect tense.

> In April they *pruned* the trees that *had been damaged* by sleet.
> He *told* me that he *had been* ill for a month.

As a summary, these two formulas for the sequence of tenses may be helpful to you:

PAST ←——————— PRESENT ———————→ FUTURE
PAST PERFECT ←——————— PAST ———————→ FUTURE

18. VOICE

As explained in Section 3c, verbs are classified as to voice. A verb is in the *active* voice when the subject is the performer of the action or is in the condition or state named. In the *passive* voice, the subject does nothing, is inactive or passive, and has something done to it.

> The engineers *threw* a bridge across the river. A bridge *was thrown* across the river by the engineers.
> The lookout *sighted* the ship on the horizon. The ship on the horizon *was sighted* by the lookout.
> Tom *laid* the book on the table. The book *was laid* on the table by Tom.
> We *rested* on the beach.

In the first three examples above, the point of view and the emphasis are quite different. The verbs that are *active* stress the doers of the action—*engineers, lookout,* and *Tom;* the verbs that are *passive* stress the recipients of the action—*bridge, ship,* and *book.*

Choice of active or passive voice depends upon context, upon relative importance of the doer and the recipient of the action. Since intransitive verbs rarely fulfill the conditions that make verbs active or passive, only transitive verbs can have a passive voice. In the last example above, the intransitive verb *rested* is in the active voice because the subject, *we,* is in the state or condition named.

18a. INTRANSITIVE VERBS DO NOT APPEAR IN PASSIVE VOICE CONSTRUCTIONS

Substandard: Your books have been lain on the table.
The puppy was sat on a chair.
Correct: Your books have been laid on the table.
The puppy was made to sit on a chair.

18b. THE PASSIVE VOICE IS USED IN IMPERSONAL CONSTRUCTIONS

Writing is impersonal when it avoids use of personal pronouns; it is completely impersonal when it avoids even the use of the indefinite pronouns like *one, someone, everybody,* or nouns like a *person,* a *student.* In certain kinds of writing, as in recording laboratory experiments, giving conclusions, making recommendations, and the like, impersonal expression may be desirable and is achieved by using the passive voice. The agent or doer is usually not expressed, only implied.

The experiment *was performed* in order to . . .
The following facts *were obtained* . . .
The results *were tabulated,* and from them the following conclusions *were reached* . . .

18c. OVERUSE OF THE PASSIVE VOICE IS INEFFECTIVE

Doers and agents are usually more appealing than those who sit still and do nothing. The active voice normally provides greater force, strength, and life than does the passive. Use the active voice whenever you wish to imply action, mental or physical; use the passive voice in impersonal writing (These results *were noticed*) and as little elsewhere as possible. Your reader will prefer "Fred *kissed* Joy passionately" to "Joy *was kissed* passionately by Fred." Fred and Joy probably do not care what voice you use and may be sorry you mentioned them, but it is likely that Joy was as "active" as Fred.

18d. VOICE CONSTRUCTIONS SHOULD BE CONSISTENT

Clear, effective use of voice is mainly a matter of being consistent. Do not, therefore, shift needlessly from active to passive voice or from passive to active. Not only is such shifting annoying and troublesome to the reader, but it causes a needless and ineffective shifting from one subject to another in clauses and sentences.

Faulty: You should follow a budget, and much money will be saved.
When a person approaches the mountains, a blue haze can be seen in the distance.
Join the Navy and the world will be seen—through a porthole!
Improved: You should follow a budget, and you will save much money.
If you follow a budget, you will save much money.

When a person approaches the mountains, he can see a blue haze in the distance.
Join the Navy and see the world—through a porthole!

19. ADJECTIVES AND ADVERBS

Ordinarily, it is not difficult to determine when an adjective or adverb should be used. *Adjectives* "go with" nouns and pronouns; *adverbs* "go with" verbs, adjectives, and other adverbs (see Section 4). Difficulty in the use of adjectives and adverbs occurs in three situations: (1) After a linking verb (see Section 16), an adjective is used if reference is to the subject, an adverb if reference is to the verb. (2) Idiomatic usage (see Section 38e) often violates the distinction between adjectives and adverbs. (3) Several adjectives and adverbs have similar or identical forms.

19a. AN ADJECTIVE DOES NOT MODIFY A VERB

The form of a word does not always reveal whether it is an adjective or adverb. Most words ending in *-ly* are adverbs, but *holy, sickly, fatherly,* and *manly* are adjectives. Also, some adjectives and adverbs have the same form: *quick, fast, little, early, kindly* (see Section 19d). Finally, a few adverbs have two forms quite different in meaning: *late, lately; sharp, sharply.*

He drives his car too *rapid*. [*Rapidly,* an adverb, should modify the verb *drives; rapid* is an adjective.]
She dresses *neat* when she is going to a party. [Use *neatly.*]
Shakespeare's Portia acted *womanly*. [Use *in a womanly way.*]
The teacher spoke *abrupt* to me. [Use *abruptly.*]

19b. AN ADJECTIVE DOES NOT MODIFY ANOTHER ADJECTIVE

Judy is a *real* keen chess player. [Use *really,* an adverb.]
That is a *sturdy* tailored overcoat. [Use *sturdily.*]
Dick drove his car *plenty* fast. [Use *very,* or *quite,* or *exceedingly.*]

19c. AFTER SUCH VERBS AS *APPEAR, BE, BECOME, FEEL, LOOK, SEEM, SMELL, TASTE,* THE MODIFIER SHOULD BE AN ADJECTIVE IF IT REFERS TO THE SUBJECT, AN ADVERB IF IT DESCRIBES OR DEFINES THE VERB

This coffee tastes *good*. [Adjective]
The hall looked *beautiful*. [Adjective]
Jim appeared *sick* when he left the room. [Adjective]
She looked at him *lovingly*. [Adverb]
Karen feels *intensely* that she was slighted. [Adverb]
Joe tasted *carefully* before he swallowed. [Adverb]

19d. CERTAIN WORDS MAY BE EITHER ADJECTIVES OR ADVERBS

Sue was a *little* girl. [Adjective]
Please come a *little* nearer. [Adverb]

Bob was a *kindly* man. [Adjective]
Bob spoke *kindly* to everyone. [Adverb]
Get here quickly; be an *early* bird. [Adjective]
I hope you will come *early*. [Adverb]

19e. ACCURACY IS REQUIRED IN THE USE OF COMPARATIVES AND SUPERLATIVES

Grammatically, comparison is the change in form of an adjective or adverb to indicate greater or smaller degrees of quantity, quality, or manner. The change is commonly indicated by the endings *-er* and *-est* or by the use of adverbial modifiers: *more, most, less, least*. The three degrees of comparison are *positive, comparative,* and *superlative*.

Positive	*Comparative*	*Superlative*
silly [adj.]	sillier	silliest
soon [adv.]	sooner	soonest

In comparisons that indicate *less* of quality, the words *less* and *least* are used with all adjectives and adverbs that can be compared.

ill	less ill	least ill
afraid	less afraid	least afraid

Most adjectives and adverbs of one syllable form the comparative degree by adding *-er* and the superlative degree by adding *-est*.

tall	taller	tallest
tough	tougher	toughest

Adjectives of two syllables usually add *-er* for the comparative and *-est* for the superlative, but some such adjectives have two forms for both comparative and superlative.

manly	manlier or more manly	manliest or most manly
rotten	more rotten or rottener	most rotten or rottenest

Adverbs that end in *-ly* and adjectives of more than two syllables usually form the comparative and superlative by prefixing *more* and *most*.

rapidly	more rapidly	most rapidly
efficient [adj.]	more efficient	most efficient

Some adjectives and adverbs form their changes irregularly.

good [adj.]	better	best
well [adv.]	better	best
bad [adj.]	worse	worst
badly [adv.]	worse	worst

The comparative is used for comparing two persons or objects or actions; the superlative is used for comparing more than two.

I bought two new outfits. Which do you think is *more attractive?*
Which of your brothers is the *better* sportsman?

Caribbean water is *greener* than Atlantic water.
Susan's was the *most artistic* of all the flower arrangements.

In informal English, the superlative is often used when only two things are compared.

A few adjectives like *parallel, unique, square, round,* and *equal* are logically incapable of comparison because their meaning is absolute. Two lines, actions, or ideas are parallel or they are not. They cannot logically be *more* parallel. However, these words have somewhat lost their superlative force and in informal English are often compared. Even good writers use adverbs like *entirely* or *quite* before them.

20. CONJUNCTIONS

Conjunctions, especially those that join clauses, must be carefully selected, for they always show logical relationships of ideas. A careless writer will frequently use *and* where the relationship of clauses needs a more accurate expression, probably by use of subordination. In the following sentences, compare meaning and emphasis:

The search for the chemical formula has been rewarding, *and* further investigation will make the rewards even greater.

Although the search for the chemical formula has been rewarding, further investigation will make the rewards even greater.

For further discussion of the exact meaning of various conjunctions, see Section 5.

20a. CORRELATIVE CONJUNCTIONS SHOULD CORRELATE ONLY TWO IDEAS

Doubtful: Both her loveliness, charm, good humor, *and* talent attracted us. [Delete *both* or two of the first three subjects.]
Neither noise, a crowded room, *nor* the disdain of his roommate could keep Mark from concentrating on calculus. [Delete one of the first two subjects or rephrase the sentence.]

20b. CONJUNCTIVE ADVERBS SHOULD NOT JOIN WORDS, PHRASES, OR DEPENDENT CLAUSES

Doubtful: The worst things are poverty, disease, ignorance, *also* prejudice. [Should be . . . ignorance, *and* prejudice.]
John had lost two big contracts; *still* was making money. [Should be . . . *but* he was still making money.]

20c. THE USE OF *LIKE* AS A SUBORDINATING CONJUNCTION IS DUBIOUS

In recent years the use of *like* in clauses of comparison has greatly increased (It looks *like* he might succeed). In standard English, however, *like* is used as a preposition with no verb following: He looks *like* an athlete. For clauses of comparison, use *as* or *as if* in strictly formal English.

> My wet shoes felt *as if* [not *like*] they weighed a ton.
> I am named for my father *as* [not *like*] my father was named for his.
> You must do *as* [not *like*] I tell you.

EXERCISES

I

Agreement and case. In this exercise apply the standards of edited English rather than those of informal speech. Consider word contractions acceptable if they are in standard form. In the space at the left, write a capital letter to indicate that the sentence shows an error connected with: A—agreement of the subject and predicate; B—agreement of pronoun and antecedent; C—case indicating subject or object; D—case (genitive) indicating possession or attribution; E—none of these: The sentence is acceptable as it stands.

1. He is the only one of the people on this block who do not take the morning paper.
2. Aunt Tilda was really eloquent on the subject of Bert coming in late for dinner.
3. Either the operators or the foreman are to blame for the accident.
4. The spring series of lectures on Elizabethan dramatists was well attended.
5. We suspected the perpetrator of this joke to be either his sister or he.
6. You should keep the drainpipe's slant to about one-quarter inch to the foot.
7. Eight slices of pie divided by four make two apiece.
8. Everybody working on Sunday or a holiday will have their pay doubled.
9. I asked Sally if that was her brother or she who came in.
10. He said that whomever he stayed with would have to get used to him getting up early.
11. Father told Hy and me that we would be well rewarded for the weeks work.
12. The worst of my worries and difficulties was that nobody would believe me.
13. I finally collared the dog, after a week's watching, who had been digging up the garden.
14. It became clear to Mack and I that none of the fish in that pond was going to take a hook.
15. Either chemistry or physics is required in the third year.
16. Give these old skates to whomever you think can use them.
17. What I have written down here are the things you are to bring back from town.
18. Neither Parsons nor I am eligible for the scholarship.
19. Either you or Dolly swims better than her.
20. He is one of those people who have to be told everything twice.

II

Verbs, adjectives, adverbs, conjunctions. In this exercise, following current standard usage, *shall* and *will* or *should* and *would* are regarded as interchangeable forms in the first person; you will not be asked to distinguish them. In the second and third persons, *shall* still implies determination and *should*, obligation. In the space at the left, use a capital letter to indicate that the sentence contains an error involving: A—the form of a verb (confusion of principal parts, wrong mood, or use of a substandard form); B—tense or sequence of tenses; C—use of adjective for adverb or vice versa, or the wrong form of either; D—misuse of conjunctions (preposition or coordinating conjunction used for subordination, and so on); E—none of these: The sentence is acceptable as it stands.

1. He looked as if he were about to explode, but with an apparent superhuman effort he controlled himself.
2. If I knew then what I know now, we would never have drifted apart.
3. I have never learned to play a piece of music, like you can, at first sight.
4. He has lived for several years in the Arctic before he settled down here, and has many fascinating stories to tell about his life there.
5. If I had had her experiences, I would write a book—maybe several books.
6. Before the party started, I made the irritating discovery that someone had got into the refrigerator and drank most of the cokes.
7. He's a very retiring neighbor and never comes over without I ask him to call on us.
8. We would have liked to have Jed on our team, but he's too prejudice to join us.
9. If we keep very quiet and talk soft enough, we may get close enough to take a picture.
10. Only in recent years was it discovered that the more distant galaxies seemed to be receding from us at enormous speeds.
11. If I would have known you were coming to town, I'd have got tickets for a play.
12. I had never swum in the ocean before, and I was surprised at how bitterly it tasted.
13. I can remember having the same experience; however, you'll get use to it.
14. I'm sorry the Petersons have already left; I should have liked to have seen them.
15. It's surprising how swiftly the time has passed, and I can hardly realize that at the end of the month I'll be here a whole year.
16. In the part of the country where I was born, every boy wanted to have a rifle, a pony, moreover a couple of good dogs.
17. If the fishing here turns out to be as good as I have heard of its being last year, I shall not have wasted my time in coming so far.
18. She was the wittiest and intelligentest speaker whom up to that time I had ever listened to.
19. After a long discussion that grew fairly warm at times, it was voted that the club president was directed to invite two speakers, on opposite sides of the question.
20. I wouldn't have tried to ride your bicycle, had I known the chain was broke.

III

Exact connectives. In each sentence below, a blank indicates the omission of a connective word or phrase. In the space at the left, write a capital letter to indicate the expression that fits the context and most precisely shows the relation between the two parts of the sentence. Do not overlook correct punctuation.

1. Several teams on the Coast appear to be almost exactly balanced this year; ________ I wouldn't be surprised if the season ended in a three-way tie for the title. [A—of course/B—moreover,/C—in fact,/D—for example,/E—anyway]
2. A translation of a Latin passage into English is usually much longer than the original, ________English uses separate words to express relations that in Latin are shown by inflections. [A—primarily because/B—chiefly for the reason that/C—although/D—consequently,/E—in any case,]
3. The difference is that the writer of ordinary fiction is permitted to introduce genuine surprises now and then, just as life does, ________the writer of detective stories is required to play strictly fair with the reader and present only solutions that have been clued beforehand. [A—but/B—however,/C—in contrast,/D—whereas/E—on the contrary,]
4. It is a good rule of style to choose short, homely words instead of showy ones; ________one should avoid an obviously affected, Hemingwayesque simplicity. [A—in

any case,/ B—at the same time,/ C—whenever possible,/ D—in contrast,/ E—notwithstanding,]

5. Nobody knows how the public will react to the proposal of a guaranteed annual income; ________ I'm not sure how I feel about it myself. [A—however that may be,/ B—in any event,/ C—consequently,/ D—for that matter,/ E—at the same time,]

IV

Review. Each sentence below, continued through five lettered segments, contains an error in grammar. (You are to apply the standard of *edited* English rather than that of informal speech, but contractions are acceptable if they are in standard form.) In the space at the left, use a capital letter to indicate the segment with the error.

1. (A) Had I known that you were taking (B) the same route to school as we, (C) I'd have suggested you riding (D) in the same car with (E) John and me.
2. (A) He lay looking like something (B) the cat had dragged in, (C) having swum too far and (D) drank enough salt water (E) to make anybody feel bad.
3. (A) The latest of his exploits is (B) to have caught four touchdown passes (C) in one game, though he has been (D) looking so good lately that I (E) was not much surprise to hear of it.
4. (A) He was an effective storyteller (B) who we knew had traveled a great deal, (C) and his account of adventures (D) among savage tribesmen were (E) thrilling to both Joey and me.
5. (A) He failed in algebra because he is (B) one of those people who begin to study (C) too late, but if he had started earlier (D) and worked harder, (E) he may have passed the course with ease.
6. (A) Once in possession of the house, I (B) planned to make great changes, and (C) would have completed them (D) if I didn't run out of money (E) before I had well begun.
7. (A) We were held spellbound by the glass blower, (B) marveling at how he could work so fast and careful (C) in turning out little colored animals; (D) there is not many an artist who combines (E) so much speed and expertness.
8. (A) They're now freshmen in college, and (B) their chief worry is whether four years (C) from now they're going to be as many jobs (D) available to graduates as there are at present, (E) but I think there're going to be plenty of jobs.
9. (A) The intellectual level of foreign movies, (B) according to many critics, (C) are usually superior to (D) that of those produced in America, (E) especially in the category of satire.
10. (A) The members of the early class (B) and we in ours learned too late that (C) if we had listened to the assignments (D) and wrote up all the reports listed in them (E) we might not have landed in the mess we're in now.

V

Review. Each sentence below, continued through four lettered segments, may contain an error in grammar. (Apply the standard of *edited* English.) In the space at the left, use a capital letter to indicate the segment containing an error, if any. If there are no errors in the sentence, write key E.

1. (A) The contract will be awarded to whoever (B) submits the lowest estimate, and (C) I hope it will effect a greater saving (D) than last years economies.
2. (A) There is not many a person (B) who I have found believes (C) that a simple yes or no (D) are the best answers.
3. (A) It hardly seemed serious enough (B) to Tom and me to justify (C) us writing Dad to suggest that he (D) attend the hearing.

4. (A) As soon as the lake appeared quiet (B) enough, we swam out to the boat (C) and began to dive for the motor, (D) which had sunk in ten feet of water.
5. (A) The least of my fears was that (B) I might lose my way, for although I (C) had never taken this path in the dark before, (D) I was use to every turn and dip in it.
6. (A) He has taught in this college (B) for years before attracting (C) national notice, but has since (D) become our principal ornament.
7. (A) He is one of those people (B) who find it easy to (C) look wise and sound plausible (D) on all sorts of topics.
8. (A) The dean told Ted and me that he would (B) have had the apartment ready if we gave him a little (C) earlier notice, since everybody knows that it (D) takes time to get such a place looking clean.
9. (A) This short course of lectures (B) on the new math have led us to conclude (C) that such instruction proves ineffective unless (D) the students' interest is enforced by regular tests.
10. A state of ill-concealed hostility (B) exist so far between these two new nations, (C) and unless we can reconcile their demands, (D) serious harm threatens both them and us.

PUNCTUATION AND MECHANICS

Punctuation originally developed because, without it, written language was unable to indicate or reproduce certain definite and clear qualities of speech. We can always tell, for example, from a person's voice whether he is making a statement or asking a question. But in writing we would not know which sentence made a statement and which asked a question unless we saw a period at the end of one and a question mark terminating the other. We also know that a pause, or a rising inflection, means something in speech.

These and other meanings and qualities in speech are reproduced in writing by certain marks of punctuation. In addition, since English is not a highly inflected language, the meaning of a sentence and the relationships of its parts are revealed primarily by word order. But word order is flexible, and punctuation is required to suggest the grouping of words and phrases in a sentence that conveys meaning.

Punctuation is not arbitrary and mechanical; it is an integral part of writing. You cannot sprinkle your writing with punctuation marks and expect it to be fully understood.

Usage varies with individual writers, but certain basic principles remain steadfast. These principles may be called "descriptive rules," since they have been formulated from hundreds and thousands of examples of punctuation as applied by reputable authors and, much more important, by professional editors and type compositors. When we have enough examples of one use of a certain mark of punctuation, we state this as a general principle or rule: "Use the . . ." or "*Always* use the . . ."; when most of our examples agree, we say: "The mark is *usually* used . . ."; when examples are insufficient to make a generalization, we say: "The mark is *occasionally* used . . ."

What is usually considered correct spelling is also fixed in usage. Just as punctuation usage is based upon the practice of editors and compositors who normally follow one or more of a group of standardized books of rules, spelling practices, too, are made rigid by the same professional groups. For this reason, and also because spelling is partly a problem in mechanics, it is treated among the sections that follow.

The most important marks of punctuation are these:

.	Period	,	Comma
?	Question mark	;	Semicolon
!	Exclamation point	:	Colon
—	Dash	" "	Double quotation marks
-	Hyphen	' '	Single quotation marks
'	Apostrophe	( )	Parentheses

The use, misuse, and overuse of each of these marks are discussed in the sections that follow. In addition, other items involving punctuation and the mechanics of writing are also discussed: italics, capital letters, brackets, abbreviations, numbers, and miscellaneous marks.

21. END STOPS

An *end stop* is a mark of punctuation used at the end of a sentence. Sometimes also referred to as *terminal marks,* end stops are usually a period, question mark, or exclamation point. More than 95 percent of all sentences end with a period, regardless of where they appear or who writes them. But the other two end stops have special, limited uses.

Victor Hugo, the nineteenth-century French writer, is said to have written the shortest letter on record. Wishing to know how his latest novel was selling, he sent a sheet of paper to his publisher on which appeared a single question mark. His publisher, pleased to report good news, replied with a single exclamation point.

If you wish to know your standing with an absent sweetheart, you might imitate Hugo's letter, but you run the risk of receiving in reply another question mark or, worse luck, a period.

21a. A PERIOD APPEARS AT THE END OF A DECLARATIVE SENTENCE

His trip began with an inspection of the missile base.
Dick prefers winter to summer vacations.

21b. A PERIOD IS USED AFTER MOST ABBREVIATIONS

Mr. and Mrs. Richard Soule
Mary E. Bisacca, M.D. (b. 1905, d. 1960)
Oct. 15, Ariz., bbl., Ave., St.

21c. PERIODS SHOULD BE USED PROPERLY IN AN OUTLINE

A period should appear after each number or letter symbol in an outline. Use no period at the end of a line in a topic outline, but do place one at the end of each sentence in a sentence or paragraph outline. (See Section 68.)

21d. THREE SPACED PERIODS INDICATE AN INTENTIONAL OMISSION

Such periods, called *ellipses* or *ellipsis periods* or the *ellipsis mark,* indicate an omission of one or more words within a sentence or quotation. If the omission ends with a period, use four spaced periods.

> "Some books are to be tasted, others . . . swallowed, and some few . . . chewed and digested."
>
> The day wore on from sunrise to late afternoon. . . .

21e. A PERIOD IS USED BEFORE A DECIMAL, TO SEPARATE DOLLARS AND CENTS, AND TO PRECEDE CENTS WRITTEN ALONE

5.26 percent $4.38 $0.65

21f. THE EXCLAMATION POINT MAY END A FORCEFUL INTERJECTION OR INDICATE SURPRISE OR VIGOROUS EMOTION

So you have really decided to go!
What an incredibly rude remark!
May I ask you—please!—to help me now.

21g. A QUESTION MARK SHOULD APPEAR AT THE END OF EVERY DIRECT QUESTION

Does Janice really love Henry?
Pat asked, "May I go with you today?"
You said—did I understand you?—that you were ill.

21h. QUESTION MARKS MAY INDICATE A SERIES OF QUERIES IN THE SAME SENTENCE OR PASSAGE

> Are you going? Is your sister? John? Mimi?
>
> Do you remember when car windshields opened to let in the breeze? When men wore garters? When grandmothers were elderly?

21i. END STOPS HAVE SPECIFIC PURPOSES

Use a period, not an exclamation point, after a mildly imperative sentence: *Take your time and work carefully.* Use a period, not a question mark, after an indirect question: *Please tell me what he said and how he said it.* Use a period, not a question mark, after a polite request or only superficially interrogative sentence: "*May I have your hat*" is one of many expressions more often prompted by courtesy than by curiosity.

21j. END STOPS SHOULD NOT BE OVERUSED

Do not use a period at the end of a theme title. Do not use end stops (especially the period) to punctuate sentence fragments (see Section 41). Avoid using a question mark enclosed in parentheses to indicate doubt, uncertainty, or a humorous meaning (see Section 29).

Use the exclamation point sparingly. The emotion, surprise, or command expressed should be strong to warrant the exclamation point. Also, an exclamation point after a long sentence looks silly; most of us don't have sufficient breath to exclaim more than a few words at a time.

22. THE SEMICOLON

The semicolon is a stronger mark of punctuation than the comma; it signifies a greater break or longer pause between sentence elements. It is not, however, so forceful as terminal marks of punctuation.

The semicolon has definitely established uses that are not difficult to master. Remember: the semicolon is used only between elements of equal rank; it is entirely a mark of coordination, of separation, of division. It is never used to introduce, enclose, or end a statement.

22a. THE SEMICOLON SEPARATES INDEPENDENT CLAUSES NOT JOINED BY A SIMPLE CONJUNCTION

> In most contracts, the large print giveth; the small print taketh away.
>
> "Children begin by loving their parents; as they grow older they judge them; sometimes they forgive them."
>
> —Wilde

22b. THE SEMICOLON SEPARATES INDEPENDENT CLAUSES JOINED BY A CONJUNCTIVE ADVERB

Conjunctive adverbs, special kinds of adverbs that can also be used as conjunctions, include *also, anyhow, as a result, besides, consequently, for example, furthermore, hence, however, in addition, indeed, in fact, instead, likewise, meanwhile, moreover, namely, nevertheless, otherwise, similarly, still, then, therefore, thus.*

> He tried for two months to learn to use a Comptometer; *then* he quit trying and admitted his failure.
>
> This job is not simple; *however,* it is exciting and rewarding.
>
> Jim's sister is a busy girl; *in fact,* she works harder than he does.

22c. THE SEMICOLON APPEARS BETWEEN INDEPENDENT CLAUSES THAT ARE LENGTHY OR CONTAIN INTERNAL PUNCTUATION

As long as war is regarded as wicked, it will have its fascination; when it is looked upon as vulgar, it will cease to be popular.

—Wilde

Whatsoever thy hand findeth to do, do it with thy might; for there is no work, nor device, nor knowledge, nor wisdom, in the grave, whither thou goest.

—Ecclesiastes

It is easy in the world to live after the world's opinion; it is easy in solitude to live after our own; but the great man is he who, in the midst of the crowd, keeps with perfect sweetness the independence of solitude.

—Emerson

22d. THE SEMICOLON SEPARATES PHRASES AND CLAUSES OF CONSIDERABLE LENGTH AND ALSO SERIES OF WORDS IN WHICH COMPLETE CLEARNESS IS DESIRED

Those chosen to receive awards were Shirley Blackman, who had not missed a day from work; Louise Wether, who had made the most suggestions for improving efficiency; Jack Smythe, who had the best record among all the salesmen.

22e. THE SEMICOLON SHOULD NOT BE OVERUSED

The semicolon is a particular mark with quite definite uses. Like all other marks, it should be neither incorrectly used nor overused. Especially avoid using semicolons in the following ways:

1. To set off phrases or dependent clauses unless for specific purposes indicated above. Ordinarily, the semicolon has the same function as a period: it indicates a complete break, the end of one thought and the beginning of another. One fairly safe guide may be stated: *no period, no semicolon.* Setting off dependent clauses or phrases with semicolons will confuse your readers.

Inasmuch as Joe has a fiery temper; we have to be careful what we say to him. [Dependent clause]

Being careful to observe all traffic regulations; I am considered a good driver. [Participial phrase]

The excitement of our mock political campaign having died down; we once again turned our attention to our jobs. [Absolute phrase]

To correct semicolon errors like these, use a comma or no punctuation; a comma is preferable.

2. As a mark of introduction.

My purpose is simple; to succeed in life.
Dear Sir; Dear Mr. Woods; Gentlemen; [In business letters]

Substitute colons or commas for the semicolons.

3. As a summarizing mark.

Answering the phone, typing, filing; these were my duties that summer.

Use a dash or a colon, not a semicolon.

23. THE COLON

The colon is a mark of expectation or addition. Its primary function is to signal the reader that the next group of words will fulfill what the last group promised. What comes after the colon is usually explanatory or illustrative material that has been prepared for by a word, or words, preceding the colon.

The major uses of the colon are these: (1) To introduce lists, tabulations, enumerations; (2) to introduce a word, a phrase, or even a to-be-emphasized clause; (3) to precede an example or clarification of an idea suggested before the colon; (4) to introduce a restatement of a preceding phrase or clause; (5) to spell out details of a generalization; (6) to introduce a formal quotation.

23a. THE COLON INTRODUCES A WORD, PHRASE, OR CLAUSE AND APPEARS AFTER AN INTRODUCTORY STATEMENT WHICH SHOWS THAT SOMETHING IS TO FOLLOW

My goal in this job is simple: success.
Only one course remains: to get out of here at once.
This is my problem: what do I do now?
Do this before you leave: check your passport, buy traveler's checks, have your smallpox vaccination.

23b. THE COLON SEPARATES INTRODUCTORY WORDS FROM A LONG OR FORMAL QUOTATION THAT FOLLOWS

Jefferson concluded his First Inaugural Address as follows: "And may that Infinite Power which rules the destinies of the universe lead our councils to what is best and give them a favorable issue for your peace and prosperity."

23c. THE COLON ACTS AS A SEPARATING MARK IN SPECIAL SITUATIONS

1. In business letters, the salutation is separated from the body of the letter by a colon. (*Dear Sir: Dear Mr. James: Gentlemen:*). It is customary to place a comma after the salutation of a friendly or personal letter (*Dear Jim,*), but the colon is not so formal a mark as to repulse friendship. Use either a colon or a comma after the salutation in such letters.

2. Titles and subtitles of books may be separated by a colon (*The English Novel: A Panorama; Education for College: Improving the High School Curriculum*).

3. Hour and minute figures in writing time may be separated by a colon (10:15 A.M.; 4:46 P.M.).

4. Acts and scenes of plays may be separated by a colon (Shakespeare's *Twelfth Night*, II:v).

5. Chapters and verses of the Bible may be separated by a colon (*Exodus*, 12:31).

6. Volume and page references may be separated by a colon (*The History of the English Novel*, IV:77).

7. A publisher's location and name may be separated by a colon (New York: W. W. Norton & Company).

8. In stating proportions, both a single colon and double colon may be used (2:4::4:8).

23d. THE COLON SHOULD NOT BE OVERUSED

The colon is a useful mark adding clarity to writing, but it should be employed to accomplish only the purposes suggested in Section 23a–c. Used in other constructions, the colon becomes both obstructive and intrusive.

1. Do not place a colon between a preposition and its object.

> I am fond *of: New Orleans, Seattle,* and *Denver.* [There is no need for the colon or any other mark of punctuation after *of*.]

2. Do not place a colon between a verb and its object or object complement.

> He liked to *watch: TV plays, movies,* and *football games.* [Use no mark of punctuation after *watch.*]
>
> She likes a number of activities, *such as: swimming, dancing,* and *cooking.* [Use no mark of any kind after *such as.*]

24. THE DASH

The dash (—) is used to indicate a sudden interruption in thought, a sharp break, or a shift in thought. It has been called "the interruption, the mark of abruptness, the sob, the stammer, and the mark of ignorance."

Some other mark of punctuation can always be substituted for a dash. It does have functions roughly equivalent to those of a comma and does resemble a period, exclamation point, and question mark in certain situations. However, a dash provides a certain air of surprise or emotional tone and, if used sparingly, adds movement, or a sense of movement, to writing. But it is rightly called a "mark of ignorance," since it is used indiscriminately and too often.

The dash is the only common mark of punctuation not on the standard typewriter keyboard. To type a dash, use two hyphens; no space precedes or follows the hyphens.

24a. A DASH INDICATES A BREAK OR SHIFT IN THOUGHT

> When I was in college—but I have already talked about that.
>
> Do we—can we—dare we ask for more money?
>
> I started to say, "But—" "But me no *but's!*" roared the supervisor.

24b. A DASH INTRODUCES A WORD OR GROUP OF WORDS TO BE EMPHASIZED

> What he needed most he never got—love.
>
> This is our most serious question—can we find a buyer for our product?

In such constructions as these, either a colon or comma could be used; the dash adds vigor, emphasis, and a tonal quality of emotion.

24c. DASHES SET OFF STRONGLY DISTINGUISHED PARENTHETICAL MATERIAL

I think—no, I am positive—that you should go.

My mother can bandage that—she's a trained nurse, you know—so that it won't hurt at all.

If you do succeed—and try hard!—telephone me right away.

Through clandestine channels—a small man wearing red suspenders—I discovered that the idea originated with one of the secretaries.

A pair of commas or parentheses could replace the dashes in each of these sentences, but they would not so sharply set off and distinguish the parenthetical material.

24d. DASHES OF VARIOUS LENGTHS INDICATE OMISSION OF LETTERS AND WORDS AND CONNECT COMBINATIONS OF LETTERS AND FIGURES

Senator S—— was from my hometown.
We were in one d—— of a spot when that happened.
June–October (June to or through October)
She lived in that city 1970–1972.
Ed used to fly the New York–Dallas run.

Do not use a dash in such expressions as those above when the word *from* or *between* appears.

From May to (or through) August [Not *From May–August*]
Between 1956 and 1963 [Not *Between 1956–1963*]

25. THE COMMA

The comma, serving many different purposes, is the most widely used of all punctuation marks. Because of its varied uses, it is the most troublesome of the marks. And yet this mark of punctuation, more than any of the others, can and does help to make clear the meaning of writing. Its overuse and misuse also obscure meaning more than the mishandling of any other mark. If you can master even the basic uses of the comma—and you can—no other mark of punctuation will hold any terrors for you.

Always used within the sentence, the comma serves four purposes: to introduce, to separate, to enclose, to show omission.

Before undertaking study of these four purposes of the comma, consider six basic principles of comma use. Learning these six fundamental applications of the comma will not solve all problems with this mark, but doing so will solve the majority of them.

1. Use a comma to separate long independent clauses in a compound sentence.

Jack has not replied to my letter, nor do I think that he ever will.

She tried to interest him in the stock, but he insisted that he would invest his money in real estate.

2. Use a comma to set off a long introductory phrase or clause from an independent clause that follows.

A retiring and unusually timid man, he refused even to consider the nomination.

When they had finished eating dinner and washing the dishes, they left for the theater.

3. Use a pair of commas to set off words and groups of words inserted within a sentence.

The manager did not say that, as you would know if you had listened carefully, nor did he even hint at it.

On that occasion, it seems, he was driving carelessly.

4. Use commas to divide elements in a series.

He blushed, stammered, and finally looked away.

Joe collected a change of clothing, shoes, and golf gear before he set off for the day.

5. Use commas with transposed initials, with titles, in dates, and the like.

Both Smythe, H. M., and Smythe, J. W., were nominated for the position.
Dexter Lenci, M.D., and Francis Coffin, D.D., attended the services.
The boys sailed for Europe on June 22, 1970.

6. Use a comma, or commas, to prevent misreading.

The morning after a policeman came to the door.
In 1965 361 men from this town entered military service.

These two sentences can be unscrambled, but even momentary misreading will be prevented if commas follow *after* and *1965*.

Each of these six principles is more fully explained and illustrated in sections that follow, together with additional comment, exceptions, and still other examples of comma usage.

Commas to introduce

25a. A COMMA INTRODUCES A WORD, PHRASE, OR, ON OCCASION, A CLAUSE

He needed only one thing, encouragement.

Only one course is left, to get a job.

She had an important decision to make, whether she should take the job or go on for an advanced degree.

25b. A COMMA INTRODUCES A STATEMENT OR QUESTION THAT IS PRECEDED BY A MENTAL QUESTION OR MUSING ALOUD

She thought to herself, I cannot afford to fail.
I wondered, should I tell the coach about my leg?

25c. A COMMA INTRODUCES A SHORT QUOTATION

Jack replied, "I'll never play chess with him again." If the "Jack replied" or "he said" or an equivalent expression follows the quotation, it is separated by a comma unless a question mark or exclamation point is needed.

> "I'll never play chess with him again," Jack replied.
> "Do you think I'll ever play chess with him again?" Jack replied.

If the "Jack replied" or its equivalent is inserted between two parts of a quotation, it is enclosed by commas unless a stronger mark of punctuation is called for.

> "I'll never play chess with him again," Jack replied, "unless he apologizes first."
> "I'll never play chess with him again," Jack replied; "he insulted me."

When the quotation being introduced is long or formal, use a colon rather than a comma (see Section 23b).

Commas to separate

25d. A COMMA SEPARATES INDEPENDENT CLAUSES JOINED BY SUCH CONJUNCTIONS AS *AND, BUT, YET, NEITHER, NOR, OR*

> She did not like her work, and her distaste for it was evident to everyone.
> It is one of the busiest streets in town, but motorists should avoid it because it is filled with potholes.

This use of the comma is one of the most frequently illustrated in all writing. However, its very frequency allows considerable flexibility in application. For example, if the clauses are short, the comma may be omitted before the conjunction. But how short is short? If each clause consists of four or five words or less, obviously each is short. If the clauses consist of only subject and predicate, the comma is usually omitted.

> The grass grew and the flowers bloomed.
> Janet did not come nor did Harry.

Even long clauses connected by a conjunction are sometimes written without a comma if their thought relationship is close or if the subject of both clauses is the same.

> Stephen dressed as carefully as he could for he wished to make a good impression on the personnel manager.

25e. A COMMA SEPARATES AN INTRODUCTORY MODIFYING PHRASE OR ADVERBIAL CLAUSE FROM THE INDEPENDENT CLAUSE THAT FOLLOWS

> By working hard and pleasing his employers, Steve got several promotions.
> When you have finished with this load, start on that one.

The introductory phrase should be a modifying one and should contain a verb form in order to be followed by a comma. "Earning a big salary" contains a verb form, *earning,* but it does not modify in such a sentence as "Earning a big salary was his goal" and therefore does not require a following comma. Similarly, "because of poor health" does not contain a verb form, and although it modifies in such a sentence as "Because of poor health the man could not work," it is not followed by a comma.

Also note that the comma follows only *introductory adverbial* clauses. Use no comma in a sentence such as "That you were late for work this morning is not my fault"; the noun clause, "that you were late for work this morning," is the subject of the verb *is* and should not be separated from what follows (see Section 25t).

25f. COMMAS SEPARATE WORDS, PHRASES, AND CLAUSES IN A SERIES

I chose a tray, selected my food, and paid the cashier.

In the huge jail were what seemed miles of narrow, sunless, low-ceilinged corridors.

Because of his morbid curiosity he read all he could find about Jesse James, John Dillinger, Jumbo, two-headed calves, and the Cardiff Giant.

In this book Mark Twain revealed the gloom, pessimism, skepticism, and fury that darkened his last years.

Some writers omit the comma before the conjunction and punctuate such series as those illustrated as "A, B *and* C," "A, B *or* C." Greater clarity—the main purpose of punctuation—is usually achieved by the comma before the conjunction. For this reason its use is recommended. A variation on this series is three or more items with the last two not joined by a conjunction. Commas are used after each member except the last: *This general store sells groceries, clothing, fishing supplies, camp equipment.*

25g. A COMMA SEPARATES TWO OR MORE ADJECTIVES WHEN THEY EQUALLY MODIFY THE SAME NOUN

She wore an old, dirty dress and a new, pretty, expensive coat.

When the adjectives do not modify equally—that is, when they are not coordinate —use no commas:

A large green bug settled on the torn autumn leaf.

It is not always easy to determine whether modifying adjectives are really coordinate. One test is mentally to insert the coordinate conjunction *and* between adjectives; only if it naturally fits should you use a comma. In the illustrative sentence immediately above, you can fit *and* between *large* and *green* and between *torn* and *autumn,* but the fit does not seem natural. *Large,* for example, seems to modify *green bug.* Also, truly coordinate adjectives can be reversed: *torn autumn leaf* makes sense whereas *autumn torn leaf* does not.

25h. COMMAS SEPARATE CONTRASTED ELEMENTS IN A SENTENCE

Such elements may be letters, numbers, words, phrases, or clauses.

The word begins with an *s*, not a *c*.
The answer should be 26, not 25.
Your error is due to carelessness, not ignorance.
Put your hat on the shelf, not on the floor.
The harder he tried, the less he succeeded.

25i. A COMMA SEPARATES WORDS OR OTHER SENTENCE ELEMENTS THAT MIGHT BE MISREAD

Sentences in which commas are needed to prevent misreading are usually faulty in construction and should be rephrased. At times, however, a comma is essential to clarify meaning; without commas, the following sentences would be at least momentarily misunderstood:

The stock advanced five points, to 21. [The comma makes clear that the range of advance was 16 upward, not between five and 21.]
Instead of scores, hundreds telephoned the station.
He arrived on February 10, 1786.
The day after, the supervisor was absent himself.
In 1971, 331 people took this same test.
They prefer an education to drills and forced marches, and college dormitories to army barracks.
Soon after, she got up and left the house.

25j. A COMMA, OR COMMAS, MAY SEPARATE THOUSANDS, MILLIONS, AND SO ON, IN WRITING FIGURES

In this contest 4,962 entries were received.
The deficit that year amounted to $8,786,982,000.

Commas are used with all numbers of four or more digits except telephone numbers, years, house numbers, and page numbers.

Her number is 256–1847.
He was born in 1962.
She lives at 11002 Prospect Avenue.

The comma is also usually omitted from certain numbers in specialized use: motor number 136592; zip code number 10654; serial number 825364; 8.0946 inches; 8/1200 of an inch.

Commas to enclose

25k. COMMAS MAY ENCLOSE PARENTHETICAL WORDS, PHRASES, OR CLAUSES

A parenthetical expression (word, phrase, clause) may be omitted from a sentence without materially affecting meaning. Usually, but not always, a parenthetical expression may shift its position in a sentence without changing meaning.

However, the order was not filled that day.
The order, *however,* was not filled that day.
Oh, *yes,* I shall be glad to go.
You are, *on the other hand,* well suited for this work.
I believe, *whether or not you care for my opinion,* that our company was mistaken in its policy.

Parenthetical elements vary in intensity; you may indicate their relative strength by punctuation. Many expressions, for example, are so weak that they require no punctuation.

In fact I agree with you.
The foreman *also* believed that you tried.

25l. COMMAS ENCLOSE INSERTED SENTENCE ELEMENTS

Inserted sentence elements are similar to parenthetical words, phrases, and clauses but normally are more essential to the meaning of the sentence than are the latter. They do not restrict the meaning of the sentence but they do add some degree of emphasis. Such emphatic expressions are set off by commas to indicate that they are considered forceful. Again, an inserted sentence element may interrupt or delay the meaning of a sentence, withholding (or suspending) important material until near the end of a sentence. Finally, an inserted sentence element may be transposed and thus require punctuation unnecessary in normal word order.

He is an honest man, a man of complete integrity, and has my full confidence. [Emphatic]
He is an honest man, not only because he keeps the letter of the law, but because he exceeds even the teachings of the Golden Rule. [Suspending]
A sports car, small and sleek and fast, was what he liked to drive. [Transposed]

25m. COMMAS ENCLOSE NONRESTRICTIVE PHRASES AND CLAUSES

As a broad distinction, nonrestrictive phrases and clauses do not limit or actually restrict the word or words they modify, whereas restrictive phrases and clauses do.

Denver, *which is the capital of Colorado,* has an altitude of one mile.
The city *that is the capital of Colorado* has an altitude of one mile.

In the first of these sentences, the italicized clause may be omitted without materially affecting central meaning; the purpose of the clause is to supply additional information. But the clause in the second sentence is essential; it identifies, it tells *what* city "has an altitude of one mile." True, the italicized clause in the second sentence could be omitted and a grammatically complete sentence would remain, but it would lack full meaning. Therefore we say that the clause in the first sentence is *nonrestrictive* and we enclose it in commas to set it off from the remainder of the sentence. The second is *restrictive* and should not be enclosed by commas or by any other mark of punctuation.

If you will carefully note comma usage in the following sentences, the principle of restrictive and nonrestrictive phrases and clauses should become clear:

Our son Stephen, *who was seventeen last year,* hopes to become a physician.
Our son *who was seventeen last year* hopes to become a physician.
The books *that I own* are all paperbacks.
The books, *those that I own,* are all paperbacks.
The suit *lying there on my bed* has had long wear.
The suit, *a blue one lying there on my bed,* has had long wear.
The woman *sitting in the front row* is a secretary.
The woman wearing a green dress and hat, *sitting in the front row,* is a secretary.

25n. COMMAS ENCLOSE ABSOLUTE PHRASES

A phrase is called *absolute* when it stands apart and conveys only its own meaning. It belongs in a sentence but has no specific grammatical relationship to other words it accompanies.

The performance over, we rose to leave.
He entered the office, *hat in hand,* to seek the job.
They were lonely that year, *their only son being away on military duty.*

25o. COMMAS ENCLOSE WORDS IN APPOSITION

Words in apposition follow another word or group of words and serve to identify or explain them. A word in apposition is a noun or pronoun, or a phrase acting as one of these two parts of speech, that provides explanation and is usually nonrestrictive in function. When the words in apposition actually limit or restrict meaning, then no enclosing commas are used.

James Greene, *our foreman,* was a kindly man. [Nonrestrictive]
Our foreman, *James Greene,* was a kindly man. [Nonrestrictive]
Foreman James Greene was a kindly man. [Restrictive]
Barry Smith, *Republican,* is a senator from Ohio.
My assignment, *to wash all the dishes,* seemed endless.
Here comes Mary Perry, *our gardening expert.*

25p. COMMAS ENCLOSE VOCATIVES

A *vocative* is a noun, pronoun, or noun phrase used in direct address; that is, a vocative indicates to whom something is said. A vocative may appear at various positions within a sentence.

Mr. Noble, may I ask you a question?
May I, *Mr. Noble,* ask you a question?
May I ask you a question, *Mr. Noble?*
Let me tell you, *all of you workers,* that you have done a splendid job.

25q. COMMAS ENCLOSE INITIALS OR TITLES FOLLOWING A PERSON'S NAME

Joseph Clardy, Ph.D., and Robert Furth, D.D., are on the school board.
The letter was addressed to Marion High, Esq.
Miriam Jones, chairman, was a handsome woman.
Are you referring to Roosevelt, T., or Roosevelt, F. D.?
James Exeter, Jr., was chosen as the first speaker.

25r. COMMAS ENCLOSE FULL DATE AND PLACE CITATIONS

He left on July 20, 1970, for a trip around the world.
He lives in Columbia, Missouri, having been transferred there from Akron, Ohio.
Her new home is at 1607 Ravinia Road, Peru, Illinois.

No commas are needed before or after zip code numbers. The second comma must be used when the state follows town or city and when the year follows both month and day. When only month and year are used, employ no commas at all.

Punctuation in the date line of a letter is optional. Formerly it was common practice to write *June 6, 1970;* now the form *6 June 1970* is increasingly popular. Both are acceptable. For the sake of clarity, always separate two numerals; where a word intervenes, the comma may be omitted, as shown, if you prefer.

Commas to indicate omission

25s. COMMAS MAY HELP TO AVOID WORDINESS AND FAULTY REPETITION

Most sentences which require a comma to make clear that something has been left out are poorly constructed and should be rephrased. In some instances, however, using a comma to show omission helps to avoid wordiness.

In this office are 10 workers; in that, 16. [The comma clearly and correctly replaces the words *one are*.]
Smith is a collector of taxes; Jones, of stamps; Duane, of women.
He takes his work seriously, himself lightly.
A decade ago they were rich and powerful; only five years later, poor and weak.

Unnecessary commas

You should be able to justify the appearance of every comma you use. It is as great a sin against clarity to overuse or misuse commas as it is to omit them where they are needed as an organic part of writing.

25t. UNNECESSARY COMMAS

Do not use a comma before the first or after the last member of a series.

Chromatic colors include, red, green, purple, and brown.
The tea was a cold, sweet, refreshing, drink.

Omit the first comma in the first sentence; the last in the second.

Do not use a comma to separate a subject from its predicate. No comma is needed in any of these sentences:

We requested that the road be paved.
I quickly learned what sort of man he was.
They soon found the weather to be too cold.

Do not use a comma before the indirect part of a quotation. No comma is needed in a sentence such as this: *The candidate stated that he was against higher taxes.*

Do not use a comma between two independent clauses where a stronger mark of punctuation (semicolon, period) is required (see Section 42). This misuse, sometimes called the "comma fault" or "comma splice," always causes confusion. Use a semicolon or period for the misused comma in such a statement as this: *The foreman told me to be there early, I told him I couldn't.*

Do not use a comma, or pair of commas, with words in apposition that are actually restrictive. The italicized words in the following examples really limit, identify, or define; to enclose them with commas is a mistake:

> My sister *Margaret* is a lovely woman.
> Shakespeare's play *Macbeth* is one of his greatest.
> Eleanor *of Aquitaine* was the mother of Richard *the Lion-Hearted.*

Do not use a comma indiscriminately to replace a word omitted. On occasion, a comma can correctly and clearly be substituted for a word or even a group of words, but rarely can it take the place of pronouns such as *that, who, whom, which.* In "Robin said, he would come to see me soon," the comma is incorrectly used for *that;* in "The person, I saw was a friend of mine," *whom* should replace the comma. "He thought, that child was sick" should be written "He thought that that child was sick." Actually, both comma and pronoun can be omitted in such constructions.

Do not use a comma in any situation unless it adds to clarity and understanding. This is a catchall suggestion. Admittedly vague, it should call attention to the fact that comma usage is slowly growing more and more "open." Every comma in the following sentences can be justified, but each could equally well be omitted since clarity is not affected in the slightest degree.

> Naturally, the first thing you should do, after reporting for work, is to see the supervisor.
>
> After the play, Martha and I went home, by taxicab, because we wanted, at all costs, to avoid subway crowds.

Commas are the most frequently used and the most important for clarity of all marks of punctuation. Use them when necessary to make your meaning clear, but avoid using them when they interrupt or slow down thought or make a page of writing look as though someone had used a comma shaker.

26. THE APOSTROPHE

The apostrophe, a mark of punctuation and a spelling symbol, has two uses: (1) To form the possessive (genitive) case of nouns and of certain pronouns; (2) to indicate omission of a letter or letters from words and of a figure or figures from numerals.

26a. AN APOSTROPHE AND S FORM THE POSSESSIVE CASE OF A NOUN (SINGULAR OR PLURAL) NOT ENDING IN S

children, children's	horse, horse's
doctor, doctor's	town, town's

Children's shoes are often expensive.

26b. ONLY AN APOSTROPHE FORMS THE POSSESSIVE CASE OF A PLURAL NOUN ENDING IN S

boys, boys' students, students'
ladies, ladies' weeks, weeks'
The *boys'* coats are in the closet.

26c. AN APOSTROPHE ALONE OR AN APOSTROPHE AND S FORM THE POSSESSIVE OF SINGULAR NOUNS ENDING IN S

Robert Burns, Robert Burns' (*or* Burns's)
Charles, Charles' (*or* Charles's)
She liked *Francis'* looks and *Burns'* (*or* Burns's) poems.

Usage varies, but the "standard rule" is that proper names of one syllable ending in an *s* sound add an apostrophe and *-s: Marx's* books, *Keats's* poetry, Robert *Burns's* songs. In words of more than one syllable ending in *s* add the apostrophe only: *Demosthenes'* orations, *Sophocles'* plays.

26d. IN COMPOUND NOUNS THE APOSTROPHE AND S ARE ADDED TO THE LAST ELEMENT OF THE EXPRESSION, THE ONE NEAREST THE OBJECT POSSESSED

my son-in-law's boat King Henry IV's funeral
somebody else's ticket the city manager's duty

26e. AN APOSTROPHE MAY SHOW THAT LETTERS OR FIGURES HAVE BEEN OMITTED

aren't (are not) they're (they are)
don't (do not) shouldn't (should not)

This use of the apostrophe is reflected in the most misspelled short and simple word in the English language. *It's* means "it is" and can never be correctly used for *its* in the possessive sense: When a dog wags *its* tail, that is a sign *it's* happy. Never write the letters *i-t-s* without thinking whether or not you mean "it is."

26f. AN APOSTROPHE AND S INDICATE THE PLURALS OF NUMERALS, LETTERS, AND WORDS CONSIDERED AS WORDS

Small children cannot always make legible *5's*.
Uncrossed *t's* look like *l's*.
He uses too many *and's* and *but's* in speaking.

Note: Some authorities recommend that such numerals, letters, and words be pluralized with an *s* alone except when such a practice would result in confusion, as in this sentence: In the first paragraph you have written five *As* and four *Is*. When no confusion is likely, write *in the 1970's* or *in the 1970s, by one's and two's* or *by ones and twos,* and so forth.

26g. AN APOSTROPHE IS NOT USED IN FORMING THE PLURAL OF NOUNS AND THE POSSESSIVE CASE OF PERSONAL AND RELATIVE PRONOUNS

The Browns [not Brown's] came to see us.

Correct: ours, yours, his, hers, its, theirs, whose
Incorrect: our's, ours', your's, yours', his', her's, hers', their's, theirs', who's [unless you mean *who is*]

27. QUOTATION MARKS

Quotation marks, both double (" ") and single (' '), are marks of enclosure for words, phrases, clauses, sentences, and even paragraphs and groups of paragraphs. By definition, *quotation* means repeating (or copying) what someone has said or written. Quotation marks are a device used principally to indicate the beginning and end of material so quoted.

27a. QUOTATION MARKS ENCLOSE EVERY DIRECT QUOTATION AND EACH PART OF AN INTERRUPTED QUOTATION

"What will my starting salary be?" I asked the manager.

"Well," he replied, "I'm not sure." Then, pausing, he inquired, "What do you think is fair?"

27b. IN DIALOGUE, A SEPARATE PARAGRAPH IS NEEDED FOR EACH CHANGE OF SPEAKER

Mr. Gray was sitting at his desk when his assistant, Ned, walked into the room.

"Mr. Gray," announced Ned, "the Johnson contract has just come through."

"Why, that's great, Ned," said Mr. Gray, feeling as though he wanted to shout from the window for the only really good news he had heard in a week.

Then Ned crushed him by adding, "But they want some additional concessions from us."

27c. IF A DIRECT QUOTATION EXTENDS FOR MORE THAN ONE PARAGRAPH, QUOTATION MARKS SHOULD APPEAR AT THE BEGINNING OF EACH PARAGRAPH BUT AT THE END OF ONLY THE LAST

"To measure and mark time has always been a concern of people. Early systems for noting the passage of time were based on the sun, stars, and moon.

"Egyptian priests established a year of 365 days as early as 4200 B.C. and based their calculations on the passage of the seasons, the sun's shadow, and the behavior of stars.

"Under Julius Caesar, astronomers prepared the Julian calendar in which 12 months were given arbitrary lengths and every fourth year was made a leap year."

27d. QUOTATION MARKS ENCLOSE WORDS WITH A WIDELY DIFFERENT LEVEL OF USAGE

No matter what its level of usage, if a word is appropriate use it with no quotation marks as a form of apology. In rare instances, however, you may wish to switch to an expression requiring enclosure.

> The person who has "had it" so far as all religion is concerned looks with impatience on the role that religion has played in man's progress toward self-mastery.

27e. QUOTATION MARKS MAY ENCLOSE CHAPTER HEADINGS AND THE TITLES OF ARTICLES, SHORT STORIES, AND SHORT POEMS

When both chapter heading and book are mentioned, or title of article (story, poem) and magazine, book and magazine names should be indicated by italics (underlining) (see Section 30).

> He found the quotation from Longfellow's "The Children's Hour" in Bartlett's *Familiar Quotations.*
>
> Grant Wood's famed painting, "American Gothic," was recently reproduced in *American Heritage.*
>
> His most famous short story is called "The Devil and Daniel Webster." It first appeared in the *Saturday Evening Post* and was later published in a book entitled *Thirteen O'Clock.*

27f. SINGLE QUOTATION MARKS ENCLOSE A QUOTATION WITHIN A QUOTATION

On rare occasions when you may have to punctuate a quotation within a quotation within a quotation, the correct order is double marks, single marks, double marks. If you need more sets than this, rephrase your sentence so as not to lose your reader entirely.

> The coach said, "When you say, 'I'll be there on time,' I expect you to mean what you say."
>
> The coach went on, "Then this player asked, 'What did the coach mean when he said, "Jim, be there on time"?' "

27g. QUOTATION MARKS SHOULD BE PLACED CORRECTLY WITH REFERENCE TO OTHER MARKS

The comma and the period always come *inside* quotation marks. This rule never varies and applies even when only the last word before the comma or period is enclosed. A question mark, exclamation point, or dash comes *outside* quotation marks unless it is part of the quotation. A single question mark comes inside quotation marks when both the nonquoted and quoted elements are questions. The semicolon and colon come *outside* quotation marks.

Are you thoroughly confused? Perhaps these illustrations will help:

> "Please lend me the money now," she said. "I won't need it tomorrow."
> The pumpkin was rated "excellent," but I felt it was only "good."
> Did Jim ask, "Have I enough money?"
> What is meant by "an eye for an eye"?
> The performance was an utter "flop"!

"My performance was a 'flop'!" she exclaimed.

Study the following paragraphs in Stevenson's "Markheim": the first, third, and fifth.

Read Thoreau's "Brute Neighbors"; as a nature lover, you will appreciate it.

28. THE HYPHEN

The hyphen is a mark of separation used between parts of a word. Its most frequent use, however, is to join two or more separate words to form a compound. As a largely mechanical device, serving as a mark of punctuation and as an aid in spelling, the hyphen is essential to correct, clear writing.

28a. YOUR DICTIONARY WILL INDICATE WHETHER A WORD COMBINATION IS WRITTEN AS A COMPOUND WITH A HYPHEN, AS ONE WORD, OR AS TWO SEPARATE WORDS

The general principle of word-joining derives from actual usage. When two (or more) words first become associated with a single meaning, they are written separately. As they become more of a unit in thought and writing, they are usually hyphenated. Finally, they tend to be spelled as one word. The evolution may be seen in the following examples, the third word in each series now being the accepted form: *base ball, base-ball, baseball; rail road, rail-road, railroad.* This general principle, however, does not always hold; many common expressions are still written as two separate words: *mother tongue, girl scout, in fact, high school.*

28b. A HYPHEN IS USED TO SEPARATE (ACTUALLY, JOIN) THE PARTS OF MANY COMPOUND WORDS

There is neither a shortcut nor an all-inclusive rule for spelling compound words. It may help to know that the present-day tendency is to avoid using hyphens whenever possible. It may also help to know that seven groups, or classes, of words ordinarily require hyphens (but check the dictionary for individual items).

1. Two or more words modifying a substantive (noun) and used as a single adjective: *fast-moving, bluish-gray, first-rate, un-American, wild-eyed, soft-spoken, wind-blown.*
2. Compound nouns: *by-product, sister-in-law, looker-on, ex-president.*
3. Compound words with *half, quarter,* or *self* as the first element: *half-asleep, quarter-final, self-sacrifice.*
4. Compound words made from a single capital letter and a noun or participle: *A-flat, F-sharp, T-shirt, X-ray, U-turn, H-bomb.*
5. Improvised compounds: *know-it-all, never-say-die, never-to-be-forgotten.*
6. Compound numerals from *twenty-one* through *ninety-nine.*
7. Compounds formed from the numerator and denominator of fractions: *three-fourths, two-thirds.*

28c. A HYPHEN IS USED TO INDICATE THE DIVISION OF A WORD BROKEN AT THE END OF A LINE

When using a division hyphen at the end of a line, keep the following rules in mind:

1. Always divide according to pronunciation: knowl-edge, *not* know-ledge; ste-nog-ra-pher, *not* sten-og-ra-pher; sten-o-graph-ic, *not* ste-nog-ra-phic.
2. Place the hyphen at the end of the first line, never at the beginning of the second.
3. Never divide a monosyllable. Write such words as *breath, ground, laughed, strength,* and *through* in their entirety on the first line; if this is not possible, carry the whole word over to the next line. Also, such parts of words as *-geous* (advantageous) and *-tious* (contentious) cannot be divided.
4. Do not divide a one-letter syllable from the remainder of the word. A word such as *about* does have two syllables, *a-bout,* but it should not be broken up. Do not divide other two-syllable words such as *able, among, enough, item, many, unit, very.*
5. Do not divide on a syllable with a silent vowel. The ending *-ed* is not fully pronounced in many words and should not be separated from the word of which it is a part. Avoid breaking up such words as *asked, attacked, climbed, massed, yelled.*
6. Do not divide a word with only four letters. Such a word can usually be crowded into the first line, if necessary. If space does not permit, carry over to the second line in their entirety such words as *also, into, open, real, veto.*
7. Divide two consonants standing between vowels when pronunciation warrants. This principle is illustrated by words such as *alter-native, exis-ten-tialism, struc-ture, strin-gent.*
8. Present participles may be divided before their *-ing* ending: *ask-ing, carry-ing, giv-ing, sing-ing, talk-ing, walk-ing.*
9. Most prefixes and suffixes may be divided from main words.
10. Do not divide sums of money.
11. Do not divide initials in abbreviations for names or as parts of proper names.
12. Do not divide units of time.

29. PARENTHESES AND BRACKETS

Parentheses ( ) are curved punctuation marks principally used to enclose explanatory matter in a sentence. They signal to a reader what a speaker means when he says "by the way" or "incidentally." Such material is important enough to be included but is not intended to be a part of the main statement and often has no direct grammatical relationship to the sentence in which it appears.

Brackets [ ] are editorial marks used primarily to enclose comments, corrections, or additions to quoted material. The mark is often used in professional and academic writing but has limited use elsewhere.

Brackets should never be confused with marks of parenthesis, which have entirely different uses. Parentheses enclose your own parenthetical material; brackets set off material inserted by you in writing you are quoting.

29a. PARENTHESES MAY ENCLOSE MATERIAL ONLY REMOTELY CONNECTED WITH ITS CONTEXT

This illustration (see p. 35) is quite clear.

Your attitude (I am certain it is important) should be carefully explained.

This issue of the magazine (September 1971) is particularly interesting.

This politician (about whom I shall have more to say later) is not worth your support.

The general properties of sets of continuous real numbers (which exclude imaginary numbers such as those based on the square root of −1) are called mathematical analysis.

You may set off incidental (parenthetical) material by commas, dashes, or marks of parenthesis. Your choice will depend upon the closeness of the relationship between the material inserted and the remainder of the sentence. No specific rule can be stated, but commas are ordinarily used to enclose parenthetical material closely related in thought and structure to the sentence in which it occurs. Dashes enclose parenthetical material that more abruptly breaks into the sentence. Parentheses are used to enclose material more remote in thought and structure or material that runs to some length or may itself contain internal punctuation.

29b. PARENTHESES MAY ENCLOSE NUMERALS OR LETTERS INDICATING DIVISIONS

Two parentheses are the standard usage; do not use only the second.

The committee decided to (1) adopt the suggested budget, (2) set a date for the next meeting, (3) adjourn.

He left hurriedly for several reasons: (*a*) poor health, (*b*) lack of money, (*c*) dull companions, (*d*) a job in the city.

29c. PARENTHESES MAY ENCLOSE SUMS OF MONEY WHEN ACCURACY IS ESSENTIAL

Sums of money repeated for accuracy and enclosed in parentheses occur most often in business writing and in legal papers. Ordinarily, you need not resort to this device; either words or numerals will suffice.

His total bill was four hundred dollars ($400).
The wholesale price is eighty cents (80¢) per dozen.

29d. BRACKETS ARE USED TO ENCLOSE A COMMENT INSERTED IN A QUOTED PASSAGE

The speaker then said, "I am annoyed [obviously he was furious, not merely annoyed] by the neglect of our officials."

The foreman then remarked, "You may have the rest of the day off. [Cheers.] But you must report for work on time tomorrow."

29e. BRACKETS MAY ENCLOSE CORRECTIONS IN QUOTED MATTER

If the person whom you are quoting has made an error, or what you consider an error, you can add a correction and enclose it in brackets. If you wish not to make a correction but merely to call attention to an error, you may use the Latin word *sic,* which means "thus," and enclose it in brackets.

"In 1776 on the tenth [fourth] day of July, the Declaration of Independence was signed."

"I was born in 1938," the candidate wrote," in Walthum [Waltham], Massachusatts [Massachusetts], and have lived there all my life."

"I am of English decent [*sic*] and am proud of my heritage."

29f. BRACKETS MAY ENCLOSE ADDITIONS TO A QUOTED PASSAGE

The advertisement read: "These shirts [oxford cloth, button-down collars] were designed by Oleg Rastrobi."

"The jury awarded £200 [$560] to the plaintiff."

"Later in the play," the lecturer continued, "he [Hotspur] is killed."

"They [the Germans] were not any more at fault than their collaborators [the Russians]," the speaker concluded.

30. ITALICS

In longhand and typewritten copy, certain words and groups of words should be underlined to correspond to the conventions of using italic type. These conventions, however, have never been standardized, and the use of italic type varies widely from publication to publication.

To a printer, italic type means letters with a slope to the right that look different from the so-called roman type ordinarily used. To a reader, italic type indicates that some word or group of words has been singled out for emphasis or other distinction.

30a. THE FOLLOWING GROUPS AND CLASSES OF WORDS SHOULD BE UNDERLINED

1. Titles of books and magazines: *Foundations of Western Thought, All the King's Men, Saturday Review, The Atlantic Monthly.*
2. Titles of plays, operas, long poems, and motion pictures: *Strange Interlude* (play), *The Girl of the Golden West* (opera), *Paradise Lost* (long poem), *Born Free* (motion picture).
3. Names of ships, trains, and aircraft: the *Caronia* (steamship), the *City of Denver* (train), the *Bermuda Clipper* (aircraft).
4. Names of newspapers: *The New York Times, The San Francisco Chronicle.*
5. Names of legal cases: *John Doe* v. *Mary Doe* (note that "v." is not underlined).
6. Scientific names: *Ursus arctos* (European brown bear), *Canis familiaris* (a plain *dog* to you and me).

30b. FOREIGN WORDS AND PHRASES SHOULD BE UNDERLINED

Zeitgeist [German for "spirit of the time"]
Honi soit qui mal y pense [French for "Evil to him who evil thinks"]
This statue has a *je ne sais quoi* quality about it.
Foreign students have to arrive at a *modus vivendi.*

Thousands of words and phrases have been so thoroughly absorbed into the English language that they need no longer be italicized. Such words as these can safely be written without italics (underlining), but check the dictionary for individual items: alias, bona fide, carte blanche, delicatessen, en route, et cetera, ex officio, gratis, hors d'oeuvres, matinee, mores, prima facie, sauerkraut, status quo, vice versa.

30c. UNDERLINE ITEMS FOR SPECIFIC REFERENCE OR EMPHASIS

The word is spelled *dollar;* it should have been *collar*.

Is this a *6* or a *9*?

The advertiser who wrote *Come Dye With Me* should have been a cleaner, not a funeral director.

Whatever you think, *whatever you even suspect,* keep to yourself for the present.

The late Will Rogers was genuinely humorous when he said: "Don't gamble. Take all your savings, buy some good stock, and hold it until it goes up. Then sell it. *If it doesn't go up, don't buy it.*"

31. CAPITALS

Usage for capitalization is not fixed and unchanging; exceptions occur for almost every "standard" rule. For example, a recent printing of the *U.S. Government Printing Office Style Manual* devotes thirty-seven pages to the use of capitals and thoughtfully adds blank pages on which one may make notes of exceptions and variations.

Despite the confusion, however, there are certain basic principles and there is also a clearly discernible trend: in general, books, magazines, and especially newspapers are using fewer and fewer capitals than they once did.

31a. THE FIRST WORD OF EVERY SENTENCE, INCLUDING EVERY QUOTED SENTENCE, IS CAPITALIZED

The engine needs repair.

He asked, "Does the engine need repair?"

When only part of a direct quotation is included within a sentence, or when the quotation is a grammatical part of the sentence, it is usually not begun with a capital letter.

The reporter told me that the official said he felt "fine" but thought that he should "take it easy" for a few weeks.

He agreed that "politics makes strange bedfellows."

31b. PROPER NOUNS ARE CAPITALIZED

1. Names of people and titles used for specific persons: George Washington, Theodore Roosevelt, the President, Senator Smith, Treasurer H. W. Jones, General Eisenhower, Mr. Chairman, Father, Mother. Note that with the exceptions of direct address and the President of the United States, titles used alone are not usually capitalized: the senator, the treasurer, the general.
2. Names of countries, states, regions, localities, other geographic areas, and the like (but not compass direction): United States, Illinois, the Far East, the Dust Bowl, the Midwest, the Solid South, the Rocky Mountains, the Sahara Desert, the Connecticut River, Lake Michigan, to the east.
3. Names of streets: Michigan Boulevard, Fifth Avenue, Old Mill Road.
4. Names of the Deity and personal pronouns referring to Him: God, Heavenly Father, Son of God, Jesus Christ, Savior, His, Him, Thy, Thine.

5. Names for the Bible and other sacred writings: Bible, the Scriptures, Book of Genesis, Revelations, Koran. (Note that these are not italicized.)
6. Names of religions and religious groups: Protestantism, Roman Catholicism, Presbyterian, Jesuit, Unitarian.
7. Names of the days and the months (but *not* the seasons): Monday, Tuesday; January, February; summer, winter.
8. Names of schools, universities, colleges: Woodberry Forest School, California Institute of Technology, Davidson College, Boston University.
9. Names of historical events, eras, and holidays: Revolutionary War, Christian Era, Middle Ages, Renaissance, Fourth of July, Labor Day.
10. Names of races, organizations, and members of each: Indian, Malay, League of Women Voters, American Academy of Science, National League, San Francisco Giants, Big Ten Conference, an Elk, a Socialist (*but* the league, the conference, socialism).
11. Vivid personifications: Fate, Destiny, the power of Nature, the paths of Glory, the chronicles of Time.
12. Trade names (check the dictionary for individual cases): Ry-Krisp, Wheaties, Tide, Sunkist, Frigidaire, Coca Cola.

31c. THE FIRST WORD OF EVERY LINE OF POETRY IS USUALLY CAPITALIZED

And we are here as on a darkling plain,
Swept with confused alarms of struggle and flight
Where ignorant armies clash by night.

Matthew Arnold

31d. EACH IMPORTANT WORD IN THE TITLE OF A BOOK, PLAY, MAGAZINE, AND MUSICAL COMPOSITION SHOULD BE CAPITALIZED

Do not capitalize prepositions, conjunctions, and articles except at the beginning or end of the title or unless they consist of five or more letters: *Romeo and Juliet, The Moonlight Sonata, Good Housekeeping, The Web of Earth, The Iceman Cometh, The Return of the Native, Caught Between Storms, Mr. Pim Passes By.*

32. ABBREVIATIONS

Abbreviations, shortened forms of words and phrases, help save time and space. Ordinarily, you will have more time and space than you know what to do with; in formal papers such as reports and themes you should use abbreviations carefully and sparingly. Especially avoid using so many abbreviations that your writing appears telegraphic in style and offensive to your reader's eye. Write out words in full, unless condensation seems necessary or the spelled-out words are unconventional, like *Mister* for *Mr.*

32a. ONLY ACCEPTABLE ABBREVIATIONS SHOULD BE USED IN FORMAL WRITING

As a general rule, spell out all words and phrases that would be puzzling if abbreviated and abbreviate correctly all terms that are often encountered and readily understood in shortened form by everyone.

In the following list, some abbreviations are acceptable in any style of writing, some only in informal writing, and some should not be used at all because they may cause confusion. For example, the abbreviations *Mr.* and *Mrs.* are acceptable at all times; the abbreviations *c.* and *ct.* (for cent or cents) are suitable only in informal writing; the abbreviation *civ.* should never be used since it can stand for civics, civilization, and civil (as in civil engineer).

Addresses: Ave., Blvd., Rd., St., Ct., Pl., Ter.
Calendar divisions: Mon., Mar.
Geographic names: U.S.A., Calif., St. Louis, N.Y.C., S.F.
Measurements: mi., P.M., bbl., oz., in.
Money: ¢, c., ct., $, dol.
Names and titles: Mr., Mrs., Dr., Col., Litt.D.
School subjects: chem., comp. lit., math., bot., Fr., Western Civ.

32b. A PERIOD IS USED AFTER MOST ABBREVIATIONS
Most standard abbreviations require a period, but note these exceptions:

Ordinal numbers: 2nd, 4th, and so on
Shortened forms: ad, phone, lab, exam
Specialized forms: TV, NBC, UNESCO, FBI, UNICEF
Contractions: don't, haven't, isn't, aren't
Nicknames: Joe, Al, Ned, Ben

32c. CONTRACTIONS SHOULD BE AVOIDED IN FORMAL WRITING
Sometimes considered colloquial, contractions are questionable in unusually precise formal writing. Do not, however, avoid such contractions as *won't, shouldn't,* and *can't* to the extent of making your writing seem artificial and pretentious.

33. NUMBERS

The practice of spelling out numbers or of using figures is more a matter of convention and custom than of correctness. However, representing numbers *is* a matter of mechanics, and a troublesome one at that.

Since there are no exact rules, it is better to adopt a general system and to use it consistently. In arriving at a formula that will cover most of your uses of numerals, remember these generally accepted principles: (1) Never begin a sentence with a figure. (2) In general, use words for numbers between one and ninety-nine; use figures above. (3) When a number can be expressed in not more than two words, spell it out. (4) When a number can be expressed in no less than three words, use figures. (5) Arabic numerals are generally preferable to Roman numerals.

33a. WORDS ARE USED TO REPRESENT NUMBERS IN SPECIAL USES
Spell out isolated numbers less than 100.

At least three men should be nominated for secretary.
We can choose one of six magazines to read.

Spell out indefinite expressions or round numbers (figures are also acceptable, however).

This theater will seat two or three thousand persons *or* This theater will seat 2,000 or 3,000 persons.
The mid-fifties will probably be known as the atomic fifties *or* The mid-50s will probably be known as the atomic 50s.
Right now I could use a hundred dollars *or* Right now I could use $100.

Spell out one number or related numbers at the beginning of a sentence.

Three of our officers are from Syracuse.
Twenty to thirty employees will be away on an inspection trip to Detroit.

Spell out numbers preceding a compound modifier containing a figure and fractions standing alone.

To line this wall, we need twelve ¼-inch pieces of plywood.
Our tent is supported by two 8-foot poles.
Be sure that the plywood is one-half inch thick.
I live about one-fourth of a mile from the highway.

33b. FIGURES ARE USED TO REPRESENT NUMBERS IN SPECIAL USES

Use figures for isolated numbers of 100 or more.

At least 250 people attended the meeting at the school.
The amount is 120 times what it was in 1968.

Use figures for dates, including the day or the day and the year.

Please report for duty by July 1.
I worked there from May 1 to October 15, 1971.

Use figures for house, room, telephone, and zip code numbers; for highway and comparable numbers.

She lives at 472 Old Mill Road; her telephone number is 534-6061.
She was in Room 2145 at the Ansonia Hotel, Columbia, North Dakota 58360.
We were driving on Route 46.
The best programs will be found on Channel 20.

Use figures for measurements, for time, for percentages, for money, for chapter and page numbers.

Standard typewriter paper is 8½ by 11 inches in size.
The package weighed 6 pounds 4 ounces.
He needed a 5-foot pole, ¼-inch wire, and 2-inch board.
9:00 P.M., 2:35 A.M., half-past 5
11 o'clock [not 11 o'clock A.M. or 11 A.M. in the morning]
5 hours 8 minutes 12 seconds; 6 years 3 months 21 days
8 percent, one-half of 1 percent, 5¼ percent return
You waste 5 to 10 percent of your lunch hour.
$5.60, $0.60, 60 cents, $4 per dozen, 28¢ apiece
Chapter 7, p. 121, pp. 15–30, p. 1123

33c. FIGURE-AND-LETTER COMBINATIONS SHOULD BE USED APPROPRIATELY

Occasionally, you will need to write figures and letters in combination, especially in expressing ordinal numbers (first, 1st; second, 2nd). Such combinations are correctly used in tables, sometimes in numbering items in a list, sometimes in dates (but not when the year immediately follows), and usually in expressing a numbered street from 10th on.

> Your April 15th request [*or* your request of April 15] has been noted.
> Your request of April 15, 1970, has been noted.
> 28 Prospect Road, corner of 10th Street and Fifth Avenue, 105 Fifth Avenue, North 210th Street

34. MISCELLANEOUS MARKS

Certain marks serve purposes in writing that are more concerned with spelling or pronunciation or mechanics than with punctuation as such.

34a. ACCENT MARKS SHOULD BE USED WHERE SPELLING REQUIRES THEM

In careful writing, each of these words and expressions would carry a special mark:

> Acute accent (é): blasé, début, éclair, fiancé, fiancée, passé
> Grave accent (à): à la carte, frère, suède
> Circumflex (ê): bête noire, raison d'être, table d'hôte
> Cedilla (ç): façade, Français, garçon, soupçon
> Dieresis (ö): Chloë, naïve
> Tilde (ñ): cañon, mañana, señor
> Umlaut (ö): Die Walküre, Tannhäuser

34b. AN ASTERISK (*) IS USED FOR FOOTNOTES AND TO INDICATE OMISSION

The asterisk is a conspicuous mark occasionally used to indicate omission (three spaced asterisks between paragraphs) or to call attention to something requiring comment in a footnote or elsewhere. In footnotes it is part of the symbol sequence (*, †, ‡, **, §) used with tabular or mathematical material, or when there are two kinds of footnotes, explanatory (symbol) and reference (number). The asterisk should not be used for ordinary reference footnotes.

34c. A CARET (‸) MAY BE USED TO INSERT AN OMISSION

Place the caret below the line at the point of omission and write the inserted expression directly above or in the margin.

34d. AN AMPERSAND (&) SHOULD NOT APPEAR IN MOST FORMAL WRITING

A mechanical mark meaning "and," an ampersand is designed to save space. Except in business writing, reports, reference works, and company names, its use should be avoided.

34e. CERTAIN MECHANICAL AND TYPOGRAPHICAL MARKS HAVE SPECIALIZED USES

1. The *brace* ({) is used to enclose words, lines, or figures to be considered together.
2. The *breve* (ŭ) is a mark over a letter to show that it is short or to indicate a specific pronunciation.
3. A *macron* (ō) is a horizontal line over a vowel to indicate that it has a long sound.
4. A *virgule* (/) is a short slanting stroke used in fractions (3/4); in expressions such as "and/or"; to separate lines of poetry when they are written solid rather than as separate lines; and in dates (7/4/76). The virgule is sometimes called a *bar,* a *slant,* a *slash,* and a *diagonal.*

35. SPELLING

Correct spelling is essential for intelligent communication in writing. Misspelling is not the most serious error a writer can commit, but some teachers, some friends and acquaintances, and nearly all employers can and do consider it a major fault.

If you really have a desire to learn to spell perfectly you can, provided:

1. You can pronounce such words as *adopt* and *adapt* so that they will not sound exactly alike.
2. You can look at such words as *respectfully* and *respectively* and in a single glance, without moving your eyes, detect the difference between them.
3. You can sign your name without looking at the paper on which you are writing and without even consciously thinking about what you are doing.
4. You can learn a simple rhyme, such as "Thirty days hath September. . . ."
5. You can remember that a compl*i*ment is "what *I* like to get."
6. You can equip yourself with a reliable desk dictionary.
7. You can learn what a syllable is and proofread your writing syllable by syllable.

If you can honestly meet all these conditions, you can learn to spell *without ever making a mistake;* if you can meet only some, you can still double or quadruple your spelling efficiency.

The first and most important step in correct spelling is to form the desire to learn, really to want to become a competent speller; the second is to devote the necessary time to learning; the third is to use all available means to learn. (If you are chronically and consistently a poor speller, your instructor may recommend a special book that deals solely with spelling problems and provides spelling exercises.)

In addition to desire, time, and means, it should be easy to improve if you habitually do these seven things:

1. Pronounce words correctly.
2. Mentally *see* words as well as hear them.
3. Use a dictionary to fix words in your memory.
4. Use memory devices (mnemonics) to help remember troublesome words.
5. Learn a few spelling rules.

6. Write words carefully in order to avoid errors caused not by ignorance but by carelessness.
7. *List* and *study* the words you most frequently misspell.

35a. PROPER PRONUNCIATION IS AN AID IN CORRECT SPELLING

Actually, mispronouncing words causes more trouble than does a difference between the spelling and the sound of a correctly pronounced word. It is probably improper pronunciation that would make you write *calvary* when you mean *cavalry*. *Affect* and *effect* look somewhat alike, but they do have different pronunciations as well as different meanings. A *dairy* is one thing; a *diary* is another. There is some reason why, from the sound of the word, you might spell *crowd* as "croud" or *benign* as "benine," but there may be no reason except poor pronunciation for spelling *shudder* as "shutter," *propose* as "porpose," or *marrying* as "marring."

Spelling consciousness, an awareness of words, depends in part on correct pronunciation. Properly pronouncing the following words will help some persons to spell them correctly; mispronouncing them will cause nearly everyone spelling trouble: carton, cartoon; celery, salary; color, collar; concur, conquer; elicit, illicit; finally, finely; minister, minster; pastor, pasture; plaintiff, plaintive; sink, zinc; specie, species; tenet, tenant.

Here are seven specific suggestions to keep in mind:

1. Do not add vowels or consonants in pronouncing such words as *athletics, disastrous, height,* and *similar,* and you will not misspell them as "ath*a*letics" or "ath*e*letics," "disast*e*rous," "heigh*th*," and "simil*i*ar."
2. Do not omit consonants in pronouncing such words as *environment, February, government,* and *library.*
3. Do not omit syllables in pronouncing *accidentally, criticism, laboratory, miniature, sophomore,* and you will not misspell them as "accidently," "critcism," "labratory" or "labortory," "minature," and "sophmore."
4. Carefully examine words that contain silent letters: *subtle, muscle, pneumonia, psychology, handsome, would, solemn, listen,* and many, many others.
5. Watch the prefixes of words: *perform* and *perhaps* (not *preform* and *prehaps*), *prefix* (not *perfix*), *proposal* (not *porposal*).
6. Beware of words containing lightly stressed syllables: *dollar, grammar, mathematics, professor.* Exaggerate the trouble spots: *dollAr, grammAr, mathEmatics, professOr.*
7. Form the habit of pronouncing and spelling troublesome words syllable by syllable, writing them, and then pronouncing them aloud in order to relate the sound to the spelling.

35b. WORDS SHOULD BE SEEN AS WELL AS HEARD

The ability to visualize words, to see them in the mind's eye, is the hallmark of the good speller. When a word is mentioned, a proficient speller can "see" the word in full detail, every letter standing out, as though it were written down before him. Here is a method of learning to see words mentally:

1. With your eyes on the word being studied, pronounce it carefully. If you don't know the proper pronunciation, consult a dictionary.
2. Study each individual letter in the word; if the word has more than one syllable, separate the syllables and focus on each one in turn.
3. *Close your eyes* and pronounce and spell the word either letter by letter or syllable by syllable, depending on its length.
4. Look at the word again to make certain that you have recalled it correctly.
5. Practice this alternate fixing of the image and its recall until you are certain that you can instantly "see" the word under any circumstances and at any time.

Such a procedure is especially valuable when dealing with tricky words that add or drop letters for no apparent reason, that contain silent letters, or that transpose or change letters without logical cause: *explain* but *explanation, curious* but *curiosity, proceed* but *procedure, maintain* but *maintenance, pronounce* but *pronunciation, fire* but *fiery.*

The most frequent error in visualizing words is mistaking one word for another to which it bears some resemblance: *accept* and *except; adapt* and *adopt; affect* and *effect; all together* and *altogether; beach* and *beech; breath* and *breathe; council* and *counsel; formally* and *formerly; its* and *it's; loose* and *lose; pillar* and *pillow; statue, stature,* and *statute; want, wont,* and *won't.*

Literally thousands of "look-alikes" and "sound-alikes" such as these demand that you become visual-minded if you wish to improve your spelling.

35c. A DICTIONARY IS AN IMPORTANT AID IN CORRECT SPELLING

When you are doubtful about the spelling of any word, you should check it immediately in your dictionary. You should not, however, have to spend half your writing time flipping pages of the dictionary rather than communicating. Intelligent use of a dictionary can help to prevent trouble. That is, certain approaches to the vast amount of knowledge recorded in a dictionary can fix helpful principles and patterns in your mind so that you do not have to consult it for, at most, more than 5 percent of the words you use. Certain facts about word derivations, prefixes, suffixes, plurals, apostrophes, hyphens, and capitalization can be learned easily—facts that apply to large numbers and classes of words and that help to improve your spelling in wholesale fashion (see Section 57).

35d. MEMORY DEVICES HELP IN REMEMBERING TROUBLESOME WORDS

One kind of memory device has the rather imposing name of *mnemonics.* The word is pronounced "ne-MON-iks" and comes from a Greek word meaning "to remember." A *mnemonic* is a special aid to memory, a memory "trick" based on what psychologists refer to as "association of ideas," remembering something by associating it with something else. You have been using mnemonics most of your life.

A mnemonic will be most helpful when you base it upon some happening or some person in your life. That is, you must invent, or use, only mnemonics that have a *personal* association of ideas.

Here are a few examples of mnemonics. They may not help you because they have no personal association, but they will provide ideas for the manufacture of your own:

all right: Two words. Associate with *all correct* or *all wrong.*
argument: I lost an *e* in that *argument.*
business: Business is no *sin.*
compliment: A compl*i*ment is what *I* like to get.
corps: Don't kill a live body of men with an *e* (corpse).
dessert: Strawberry sundae (double *s*).
piece: Have a *piece* of *pie.*
potatoes: Potatoes have eyes and *toes.*
together: To + get + her.
vaccine: Va*cc*ine is measured in *c*ubic *c*entimeters (*cc*'s).

35e. SOME SPELLING RULES ARE HELPFUL

If you happen to study carefully a number of words that have similar characteristics, you can make some generalizations about their spelling. In fact, observers have been doing just this for more than a century, with the result that nearly fifty spelling rules have been formulated.

Generalizations about the groupings of letters that form classes of words do help some people to spell more correctly. The five basic rules given below are of particular value in spelling correctly certain classes of words.

WORDS CONTAINING *ei* OR *ie*

About 1,000 fairly common words contain *ei* or *ie.* It helps to know that *ie* occurs in about twice as many words as *ei,* but the problem is not thereby fully solved. The basic rule may be stated in this well-known verse:

Write *i* before *e*
Except after *c*
Or when sounded like *a,*
As in *neighbor* and *weigh.*

This rule, or principle, applies only when the pronunciation of *ie* or *ei* is a long *e* (as in *he*) or the sound of the *a* in *pale.*

Here is another way to summarize the rule and its reverse: When the sound is long *e* (as in *piece*) put *i* before *e* except after *c.* When the sound is not long *e* (as it is not in *weigh*) put *e* before *i.*

Still another way to state the principle is this: When the *e* sound is long, *e* comes first after *c,* but *i* comes first after all other consonants: ceiling, conceit, conceive, deceit, perceive, receipt, receive; achieve, aggrieve, cashier, chandelier, handkerchief, hygiene, reprieve, retrieve.

This much of the rule is fairly simple. The last two lines of the verse refer to words in which *ei* sounds like *a.* Fortunately, only a few everyday words, such as the following, fall in this group: chow mein, eight, feint, freight, heinous, neighbor, reign, rein, veil, vein, weight.

A few words are exceptions to this basic *ei-ie* rule or are not fully covered by the verse. The best advice is to learn the following words by some method other than trying to apply the rule, which doesn't work: either, Fahrenheit, fiery, financier, height, leisure, neither, protein, seize, sleight, stein, weird.

FINAL *e*

Hundreds of everyday words end in *e*, and thousands more consist of such words plus suffixes: *care, careful; hope, hopeful.* In our pronunciation nearly all *e*'s at the ends of words are silent: *advice, give, live.* Actually the usual function of a final silent *e* is to make the syllable long: *rate* but *rat, mete* but *met, bite* but *bit, note* but *not.*

Final silent *e* is usually dropped before a suffix beginning with a vowel but is usually retained before a suffix beginning with a consonant.

advise, advising
amuse, amusing, amusement
argue, arguing
arrive, arrival
bare, barely, bareness
believe, believable
care, careful, careless
come, coming
desire, desirable
dine, dining
excite, exciting
extreme, extremely
ice, icy
like, likable
love, lovable
move, movable
owe, owing
purchase, purchasing
safe, safety
sincere, sincerely
use, usable, useless
value, valuable
whole, wholesome
zone, zoning

This basic rule is clear enough, but it does not cover all words ending in silent *e*. Here are additions and exceptions to the general principle.

Silent *e* is retained when *ing* is added to certain words, largely to prevent them from being confused with other words.

> *dye, dyeing,* to contrast with *die, dying*
> *singe, singeing,* to contrast with *sing, singing*
> *tinge, tingeing,* to contrast with *ting, tinging*

Silent *e* is retained in still other words before a suffix beginning with a vowel. Sometimes this is done for the sake of pronunciation, sometimes for no logical reason at all: acre, acreage; cage, cagey; courage, courageous; here, herein; mile, mileage; service, serviceable; shoe, shoeing.

FINAL *y*

Words ending in *y* preceded by a consonant usually change *y* to *i* before any suffix except one beginning with *i:* angry, angrily; beauty, beautiful; carry, carries, carrying; dignify, dignified, dignifying; happy, happier, happiness; lucky, luckier, luckily; marry, married, marriage; pity, pitiful, pitying.

Words ending in *y* preceded by a vowel do not change *y* to *i* before suffixes or other endings: annoy, annoyed, annoyance; betray, betrayal, betraying; buy, buyer, buying.

Here are some everyday words that follow neither part or the "final *y*" principle: baby, babyhood; busy, busyness; day, daily; lay, laid; shy, shyly, shyness.

DOUBLING FINAL CONSONANT

Most words of one syllable and words of more than one that are accented on the last syllable, when ending in a single consonant (except *x*) preceded by a single vowel, double the consonant before adding an ending beginning with a vowel. This is a complicated rule but a helpful one, as may be seen: *run, running; plan, planning; forget, forgettable.* Several important exceptions, however, should be noted: *transfer, transferable; gas, gases.* Note, also, that the rule applies only to words accented on the last syllable: *refer, referred,* but *reference; prefer, preferred,* but *preference.*

"ONE-PLUS-ONE" RULE

When a prefix ends in the same letter with which the main part of the word begins, be sure that both letters are included. When the main part of a word ends in the same consonant with which a suffix begins, be sure that both consonants are included. When two words are combined, the first ending with the same letter with which the second begins, be sure that both letters are included. Here are some examples: accidentally, bathhouse, bookkeeping, cruelly, dissatisfied, irresponsible, misspelling, overrated, really, roommate, suddenness, unnecessary.

The only important exception to this rule is *eighteen,* which, of course, is not spelled "eighttteen." Also, keep in mind that three of the same consonant are never written solidly together: *cross-stitch,* not "crossstitch"; *still life* or *still-life,* not "stilllife."

35f. CARELESSNESS IS A PRIMARY CAUSE OF MISSPELLING

When writing, you concentrate on what you are trying to say and not on such matters as grammar, punctuation, and spelling. This concentration is both proper and understandable. But in your absorption you are quite likely to make errors of various sorts, including some in spelling, that result from haste or carelessness, not ignorance.

Since many English words really are difficult to spell, we should be careful with those we actually know; yet it is the simple, easy words nearly everyone *can* spell that cause over half the errors made. Listed below are twelve words or phrases repeatedly found misspelled. They are so easy that you are likely to look at them scornfully and say "I would never misspell any one of them." The fact is that you probably do misspell some of these words on occasion, or other words just as simple.

a lot, *not* alot	research, *not* reaserch
all right, *not* alright	religion, *not* regilion
doesn't, *not* does'nt	surprise, *not* supprise
forty, *not* fourty	thoroughly, *not* throughly
high school, *not* highschool	whether, *not* wheather
ninety, *not* ninty	wouldn't, *not* would'nt

35g. LIST AND STUDY THE WORDS YOU MOST FREQUENTLY MISSPELL

Learning to spell is an individual, highly personal matter. One attack on correct spelling will work for one person but not for another. Perhaps it would be more precise to say that although certain words cause trouble for a majority of people, any list of commonly misspelled words will contain some that give you no difficulty and omit others that do. The best list of words for you to study is the one you prepare yourself to meet your own needs and shortcomings.

According to one estimate, only a basic 1,000 words appear in 90 percent of all writing. Several of these words appear in the following list of frequently misspelled words. You might start your list of "personal demons" with words in this group that are troublesome for you.

absence	choose	forty	magazine
absurd	coming	fourth	marriage
accepted	copies	friend	mathematics
across	courtesy	frivolous	meant
afraid	cried	fulfilled	messenger
all right	decide	furniture	minute
already	definite	generally	misspelled
altogether	descend	governor	mortgage
always	describe	grammar	mountain
amateur	desirable	guard	muscle
among	despair	hammer	mystery
anxiety	destroy	handkerchief	necessary
anxious	develop	heroes	neighbor
apartment	difficulties	humorous	neither
apparatus	dining room	hurried	niece
argument	disabled	imaginary	nineteen
arithmetic	disagree	immediately	ninety
arrival	divide	independent	ninth
assemblies	doesn't	influence	oblige
audience	during	intellectual	occasionally
awkward	easily	invitation	occurred
beginning	eighth	itself	offered
believe	embarrass	jewelry	omission
biscuit	enemies	judgment	opportunity
brief	excellent	knowledge	paid
business	exercise	laboratory	parallel
buying	existence	ladies	partner
cafeteria	experience	laid	peculiar
captain	familiar	library	perhaps
certain	fierce	lightning	pilgrim
cheerful	fiery	loneliness	pleasant
chief	foreign	lying	possession

potato	riding	strength	twelfth
prison	running	stretch	until
privilege	safety	strictly	using
probably	seize	studying	usually
pronunciation	sense	summarize	village
realize	sentence	superstitious	villain
really	separate	surely	Wednesday
receive	shepherd	surprise	woman
repetition	shining	thorough	women
replied	shoulder	toward	writer
representative	similar	tragedy	writing
respectfully	sincerely	tries	written
rhyme	speech	truly	yacht

EXERCISES

I

Periods and related marks. Each entry in the pairs below may contain a mistake in the use of periods, question marks, or exclamation points. In space at the left, use a capital letter to indicate that of the two sentences: A—the first only is acceptable; B—the second only is acceptable; C—both are acceptable; D—neither is acceptable.

1. Will you please refer to the Simmons file for the requested information. As I prepared to drive away, Father asked me if I hadn't forgotten something?
2. Mrs Ethel Richardson agreed to serve as secretary at the meeting. The skid marks measured 18 yd. 2 ft. 4 in.
3. NASA announced a delay of the moon shot because of overcast skies. As soon as Porter arrived, he asked us if we had bought our diving equipment.
4. "Many provisions . . . for governmental intervention in the economy, once regarded as startling and dangerous, have now come to be commonplace and routine . . ." The FRB announced a rise in the bank discount rate to 5.5 percent.
5. The title of his theme, "The Can-Opener Culture.", seemed to me too comprehensive for a short essay. On your way out, would you please post this letter for me!
6. How many times have I asked you not to slam that door! Just as Bert had said, there was a good record player in the cabin, but his record collection contained nothing but—ugh!—country music.
7. Instead of addressing the letter to Mr. Henry Tripp, 1256 So. Euclid Ave., you would show your correspondent more respect by spelling out the address fully. A frequent and well-intended social query—haven't you lost some weight lately?—can never actually be pleasing, since it implies that the hearer was too fat before or is too thin now.
8. How can we make you comfortable? Something to eat? A magazine? Television? Or would you like just to be let alone? She was always asking her guests if they didn't believe in extrasensory perception?
9. Did the Weather Bureau say it will rain today? Isn't that a pity?
10. Will you kindly let me know as soon as Emerson returns to his office. You expect me to meet her plane at 2:30 AM? Impossible!

II

Semicolon, colon, dash. Each item below begins with a correct sentence; you are to rewrite it as directed. In space at the left, use a capital letter to indicate that the shift from the original to the rewritten sentence requires you to: A–insert, or change a mark to, a semicolon or semicolons; B–insert, or change a mark to, a colon or colons; C–insert, or change a mark to, a dash or dashes; D–take out one of the marks above, or change it to a comma; E–keep the same punctuation as in the original.

1. The facts of her childhood were hardly ideal: she was born into poverty, abandoned at the age of six, and reared in an orphanage. [Take out *she was.*]
2. At high school he starred in all the sports offered: football, basketball, and track. [Take out *all the sports offered.*]
3. Now listen to this carefully: send word to me at once if the drill brings up any gravel or even coarse sand from the well. [Put *now listen to this carefully* after *me.*]
4. The wind had veered to the east and raised a scattering of whitecaps on the bay; a canoe crossing looked too dangerous to try. [Change *had* to *having.*]
5. Not all people, it has been found, can roll the tip of the tongue into the shape of a tube; this ability, being hereditary, cannot be acquired by practice–nor does it appear to be good for anything, for that matter. [Insert *and* after *tube.*]
6. A cat when lapping up milk cups its tongue backward, not, as many suppose, forward, in a rapid series of dipping and raking motions; this fact is one of the curious revelations of high-speed photography. [Take out *this fact is.*]
7. You can hardly be a success in politics without being your own convinced disciple, but the reverse proposition is unfortunately not true. [Change *but* to *however.*]
8. The accident occurred at 12 minutes after three in the afternoon. [Put the time in numerical and abbreviated form.]
9. The army expects of its rank and file one thing above all, and that is obedience. [Take out *and that is.*]
10. Because of a rainy spell construction was halted for a week, so we were free from Monday through Friday. [Change *so* to *consequently.*]

III

Commas to introduce or to separate. Each item below begins with a correct sentence; you are to rewrite it as directed. Make only changes required by the directions. In space at the left, use a capital letter to indicate that the rewritten sentence, compared with the original, has: A–lost a mark of punctuation; B–gained a mark of punctuation; C–changed one mark of punctuation to another (for example, a comma to a semicolon); D–more than one change in punctuation; E–the same amount and kind of punctuation as before. *Example:* As soon as I get home from work, I will wash the car. [Start the rewritten sentence with the words *I will.*] *Explanation:* The rewritten sentence reads: I will wash the car as soon as I get home from work. [A comma has been *lost,* so the answer is A.]

1. I have arranged your interview with Adderley, and I will take you to see him on Monday. [Take out the second *I.*]
2. I have arranged your interview with Adderley, and he will see you on Monday. [Take out *and.*]
3. Adderley is the only man you have yet to interview. [Start the sentence: *There is only one man whom you.*]
4. Arrowheads were often made of obsidian (volcanic glass) in the absence of metal. [Start the sentence: *In the absence.*]
5. Yesterday the Sioux City stockyards reported taking in 400 cattle and 300 sheep. [Multiply each figure by 10.]
6. He still owes more than $600. [Multiply the figure by 100.]
7. Willow bark contains various amounts of salicylic acid and was long used as an analgesic before the discovery of aspirin. [Insert *it* after *and.*]

8. "Should I really trust him with the secret?" I wondered aloud. [Start the sentence with *I wondered* and take out *aloud.*]
9. Let me know as soon as the undercoat is dry, and I will finish painting the car. [Start the sentence: *As soon as.*]
10. "For all I know," he said, "I may drive the old car for another year." [Change *For all I know* to *I haven't decided yet.*]

IV

Commas to enclose or set off. Each item below begins with a correct sentence; you are to rewrite it as directed. Make no changes except those required by the directions. In space at the left, write a capital letter to indicate that the rewritten sentence, compared with the original, has: A–lost one comma, B–lost two commas, C–gained one comma, D–gained two commas, E–the same amount of punctuation as before.

1. My uncle Harvey is a policeman. [Insert *maternal* after *My.*]
2. Mr. Vertigo Spinn
   Churn Agitators, Inc.
   1313 Rolls Avenue
   Centrifuge, Ohio
   [To this address add the zip code number *43605.*]
3. The announced lineup for Tuesday's game had James Carter at second base and Alvin Carter in left field. [Insert the phrase (*no relation*) after *Alvin Carter.*]
4. The new name in the lineup for Tuesday's game was J. Carter. [Put Carter's initial *after* the surname.]
5. Mr. Larkin called while you were out, and in a very bad temper, too. [Insert *you may as well know* after *and.*]
6. The course in English composition is not addressed to a specific and generally agreed-on subject matter. [Insert *like physics or chemistry* after *not.*]
7. I had to stay home that afternoon and supervise the Two Demons, as we call the twins, Mother having decided to get her hair done. [Start the sentence: *Mother having decided.*]
8. The giant panda is not a bear or, for that matter, closely related to any familiar animal. [Insert *as many suppose* after *not.*]
9. There is an association with members on both sides of the Atlantic whose sole purpose is to rescue the reputation of King Richard III from the calumnies of Tudor-minded historians. [Insert *an earnest and active one* after *association.*]
10. In this statement Mr. Tompkins has raised a question that deserves our earnest consideration. [Change *has* to *you have.*]

V

Restriction and nonrestriction. Each item below begins with a correct sentence; you are to rewrite it as directed. Make no changes except those required by the directions. In space at the left, write a capital letter to indicate that the rewritten sentence, compared with the original, has: A–lost a comma, B–lost two commas, C–gained a comma, D–gained two commas, E–the same number of commas as before (possibly none).

1. A boat which leaks may be dangerous. [Change *A* to *John's.*]
2. The members of the senior class, who were wearing caps and gowns, were enjoying the mingled feelings of pride and absurdity usual on such occasions. [By the management of punctuation alone, make it clear that some members of the senior class were *not* wearing caps and gowns.]

3. About a century ago, a lawless class of young bloods (called "scorchers") who burnt up the streets on high-wheeled bicycles were the subject of angry editorials. [Insert *at speeds as high as 15 miles per hour* after *bicycles.*]
4. I did not call on the Haskins just because Miriam was staying with them. [Make it clear that the speaker did *not* call on the Haskins.]
5. The men of the first group who had already crossed the creek signaled for the others to follow them. [Make it clear that *all* the men of the first group had crossed the creek.]
6. More than half the people who take up the doctor's time, it is said, have nothing specifically discoverable wrong with them. [Change *people* to *patients.*]
7. The protein-deficiency diseases which afflict the populations of many backward countries are often caused by lack of a single amino acid, lysine. [Change *The protein-deficiency diseases* to *Diseases associated with underconsumption of proteins.*]
8. Protein-deficiency diseases are often caused by lack of an amino acid, lysine, which is abundant in meat but scanty in some cereals. [Put *lysine* at the end of the sentence.]
9. Since Howard arrived, nobody at our summer hotel has lacked amusement, for he is infinitely diverting. [Put *since Howard arrived* after *amusement.*]
10. Since prices have increased along with them, recent increases in wages may not mean additional purchasing power. [Shift the words preceding the comma to the end of the sentence.]

VI

Quotation marks and related marks. Each sentence below may contain a mistake in the use of quotation marks, italics, or some other mark. In space at the left, write a capital letter to indicate that in the sentence: A–quotation marks are missing, superfluous, or misplaced with respect to accompanying punctuation; B–italic indicators are missing or superfluous; C–some other mark or letter is missing or superfluous; D–a wrong mark is used (for example, italics instead of quotation marks); E–none of these: the sentence is acceptable as it stands.

1. There's a favorable review of "The Nylon Jungle," an Italian movie now featured at the Araby Theatre, in today's Chicago *Spectator*.
2. "In those days," she said, "you had to send the children to school in Switzerland in order to qualify as a member of the *haute monde*."
3. With an expression of intense hauteur, she said, "Do you really imagine that eating pie a la mode is the custom of all Americans"?
4. "Who was it," he asked, "that said, 'People will give up making war only when it comes to be regarded as vulgar.' ?"
5. She replied, "I think it was Oscar Wilde;" then after a pause, "however, I'd better look it up to make sure."
6. Interviewed aboard the Queen Mary at his departure, the Prince said, "Americans are very clever people; they can understand my English but I can't understand theirs."
7. Paraphrasing William James, he said, "If you want to kick a bad habit, you should enlist pride in support of will power by announcing the decision publicly."
8. "Different as they look," said Professor Fitts, "the words sporran and purse are etymologically related."
9. The popular aphorism "nice guys finish last" is attributed to Leo Durocher.
10. "Are you absolutely sure," demanded the prosecutor, "that you heard the woman cry, 'It was Gerald–I *saw* him!' ?"

VII

Marks of enclosure. Each sentence below may contain a mistake in the use of parentheses, brackets, or punctuation associated with them (a comma used with a parenthesis). In the space at the left, write a capital letter to indicate that the sentence: A—lacks a necessary mark or marks; B—has a superfluous mark or marks; C—uses a wrong mark or marks (some other mark[s] should have been used); D—misplaces a mark or marks with respect to accompanying punctuation or text; E—is acceptable as it stands.

1. It's an interesting coincidence that these same years of political jitteriness [the middle 50's] abounded also in sightings of saucers from outer space and other unidentified flying objects.
2. Professor White's exploits as a secret courier during World War II were recounted in an earlier issue of the same magazine [see January 26, 1958].
3. "It was with genuine regret," wrote the General, "that I then lay (*sic*) down the burdens of command."
4. Mrs. Hawkins is the recognized dictator of our little town's society (this is the same person, believe it or not, whom you knew in high school as Mary Trotter.)
5. Pentwater, Michigan, once a lumber shipping center and one of the busiest ports on the lake, is now a quiet resort community.
6. The short stories of Saki (Hector Hugh Munro), are among the wittiest ever written.
7. Writes Professor Bloch: "There can be little doubt that the Whig aristocracy of the eighteenth century led the best *all-around* [my emphasis] life ever enjoyed by any class anywhere."
8. "When Monroe uttered his famous Doctrine in 1822 (actually 1823), he can have had but little idea of the interpretations that subsequent administrations would put on it."
9. I know exactly where we left the car; it was just opposite a little shop with the sign, I'm not likely to forget it, "Antiques and Junque."
10. Although Timmy accepted my veto of his plan to trap old Mr. McDowell in an elephant pit, (I said it might break his neck), I could see that he privately regarded my objection as frivolous and cowardly.

VIII

Mechanics. Each sentence below may contain a mistake in the use of hyphens, apostrophes, capitals, abbreviations, numbers, or special marks such as the acute accent, circumflex, or cedilla. A "wrong mark" in the key listed below includes also the wrong form, such as a capital instead of a small letter, a spelled-out number instead of an Arabic figure, and so on. In the space at the left, write a capital letter to indicate that the sentence: A—lacks a necessary mark or marks; B—has a superfluous mark or marks; C—uses a wrong mark or form (some other should have been used); D—misplaces a mark or marks; E—is acceptable as it stands.

1 May'nt we come in now?
2. We visited the Trent's last night.
3. Among teen-agers, a passion for nonconformity can coexist comfortably with passive submission to the mores of the clique or gang.
4. I told my Mother I would be home early.
5. There were 4 absentees on Monday.
6. The lowest temperature recorded for this day was on January 12th, 1940.
7. Professor Clark is preeminent in his field.

8. The President appoints the members of the cabinet.
9. It was an easily-forgotten novel.
10. Senora Madura was accompanied by her husband, the Ambassador.
11. He secured a loan at the rate of five and one-half percent.
12. Examples of highly visual writing are easily found in Keats's poetry.
13. You should be more self-reliant and not take second hand advice.
14. The store specializes in boys' and womens' wear.
15. Thucydides' history of the Peloponnesian war is fascinating reading.
16. I finally figured out that he was my ex-brother-in-law's first cousin.
17. The Secretary stated in a hearing of the Senate Foreign Relations Committee that he had no ready-made solutions of our problems in the East.
18. According to Simmons' report, twenty-two cartons are missing.
19. Most under-developed countries lie south of the Tropic of Cancer.
20. Afterwards Father asked me where I had picked up such half-baked ideas.

IX

Spelling. Supply the missing letter in each of the following words.

1. ab_____ence
2. absor_____tion
3. excell_____nt
4. apol_____gy
5. calend_____r
6. cem_____tery
7. compar_____tive
8. Ba_____tist
9. exigen_____y
10. han_____kerchief
11. iden_____ity
12. min_____ature
13. opt_____mistic
14. caf_____teria
15. sacr_____legious
16. sep_____rate
17. sim_____lar
18. temper_____ment
19. dorm_____tory
20. disinfect_____nt

X

Spelling. Indicate with an 0 each word in the following list that is spelled correctly. Correct the misspelled words.

1. alright
2. analogous
3. appelation
4. business
5. commited
6. conscientious
7. developement
8. ecstasy
9. innoculate
10. occasionally
11. pantomime
12. paralel
13. pidgeon
14. questionaire
15. renege
16. rythmical
17. scurrulous
18. symetrical
19. temperature
20. tendency

XI

Spelling. Supply for each of the following words forms like this: *pray, prays, prayed, praying*. Some of the verbs are irregular.

1. concur
2. notice
3. tax
4. cry
5. begin
6. happen
7. argue
8. have
9. marry
10. swim

XII

Spelling rules. In each group of three words below, one may be misspelled. Find the misspelled word; then decide which rule, if any, applies to it. In the space at the left, write a capital letter to indicate that the correct spelling of the word falls under the rule treating: A—*ei* or *ie,* according to a preceding letter and pronunciation of the vowels; B—final *e* or final *y* when a suffix is added; C—doubling the final consonant (or not) when a suffix is added; D—exceptional spelling required to preserve the pronunciation of the word; E—none of these: The correct spelling of the word is contrary to rule.

1. conceive
drooping
changable
2. neighbor
benefited
sieze
3. briefing
writing
layed
4. beleiving
looted
lovable
5. annoyance
alloted
extremely
6. likelyhood
weighing
fighting
7. grievous
forgetable
happiness
8. kercheif
reference
meanness
9. canceled
noticable
luckily
10. leaving
ladylike
developed

THE WORD

When you engage in a conversation, or write a letter, report, theme, or other composition, you have something to say and some interest and purpose in expressing that something, whatever it is. Therefore, you call on your word supply, your vocabulary or stock of words, and select those expressions that will communicate to others what you have in mind.

This process of selecting is called *diction:* the choice of a word or group of words for the expression of ideas. Thus defined, diction applies to both speaking and writing, although "diction" has further meanings when applied to speech, since it involves voice control, voice expression, and even pronunciation and enunciation. (The term *diction* comes from the Latin *dictio,* meaning "saying," "word." The root *dict* is familiar to us in words like *dictate, Dictaphone, dictator,* and *dictionary.*)

Thinking and diction are inseparable because we cannot think without using words. In one sense, then, our thinking can be no better than our word supply. Oliver Wendell Holmes, the great jurist, once said, "A word is the skin of a living thought."

Because there are many words to choose from, because many ideas require expression in different shades of meaning and emphasis, and because errors should be avoided, diction is troublesome for all writers and speakers. Just as a builder carefully selects materials for the construction of a house, so must a writer make a real effort to choose carefully the words he uses. Effective communication, the primary aim of all writing and speaking, is impossible without effective choice and use of words.

Diction, like sentences, should be *correct, clear,* and *effective,* but no standards can be absolute. Our language is constantly changing. Also, diction, like fashions in dress and food, is influenced by changes in taste. Again, what is acceptable in daily speech and conversation may not be suitable in written form. The use of this or that word cannot be justified by saying that it is often heard or seen in print. Advertisements, newspapers, magazines, and even some "good" books may exhibit faulty diction.

As you study the following sections on the word, keep your dictionary constantly at hand. You may disagree with some of the statements made in Sections 36–40, but it is sensible to be guided—at least at first—by the work of those authors and speakers of the past and present whose skill in communicating commands respect.

Common problems in choosing and using words may be summarized as follows: (1) Words should be in *current* use (Section 36). (2) Words should be in *national* use (Section 37). (3) Words should be in *reputable* use (Section 38). (4) Words should be *exact and emphatic* (Section 39). For quick reference, a glossary of words often confused or misused is given in Section 40.

36. CURRENT USE

One of several requirements of good usage is that words must be understandable to readers and listeners of the present time. Words do go out of style and out of use; you must have struggled with the meanings of words used by Shakespeare and other writers of earlier times. Except for doubtful purposes of humor, avoid using antiquated expressions.

36a. OBSOLETE WORDS

An *obsolete* word is one that has completely passed out of use; an *obsolescent* word is one in the process of becoming obsolete. One dictionary may label a word as "obsolete," another may call the same word "archaic." Does your dictionary include *infortune* for *misfortune, garb* for *personal bearing, prevent* for *precede, anon* for *coming, twifallow* for *plow again?*

36b. ARCHAIC WORDS

An *archaic* word is an old-fashioned word, one that has passed from ordinary language, although it may still appear in legal and Biblical expressions. Effective, up-to-date writing will never contain expressions such as these: *enow* for *enough, gramercy* for *thank you, methinks* for *it seems to me, lief* for *willing, oft* or *ofttimes* for *often, wot* for *know, glister* for *glisten, whilom* for *formerly, bedight* for *array, pease* for *pea.*

36c. POETIC WORDS

Words that have been (and are still occasionally) used in poetry but not in prose are known as *poetic diction.* Since early in the nineteenth century, much poetic diction has been imaginative combinations of words rather than isolated words themselves.

"Poetic" words, sometimes so designated in dictionaries, are usually archaic words found in poetry composed in or intended to create the aura of a remote past. Examples are contractions such as *'tis, 'twas;* the use of *-st, -est, -th, -eth* endings on present-tense verbs: *dost, would'st, doth, leadeth;* and words like *'neath, oft, ofttimes, ope,* and *glebe.*

36d. NEOLOGISMS

A *neologism* is a newly coined word or phrase or an established word or phrase employed in a new meaning. Not all neologisms are contrived and artificial, but the majority are. Several well-known columnists and broadcasters repeatedly concoct neologisms. So do many sports commentators and advertising copywriters. Their productions are frequently colorful, attention-getting, and picturesque, but few of them prove permanently valuable.

New words are coined in various ways. Some are adaptations of common words: *millionheiress.* Some, the so-called portmanteau words, are combinations of common words: *brunch* (*br*eakfast and l*unch*), *smog* (*sm*oke and f*og*), *slanguage* (*slang* and lan*guage*). Some are formed from the initial letters of common words: *loran* (*lo*ng *ra*nge *n*avigation), *radar* (*ra*dio *d*etecting *a*nd *r*anging). Some are virtually new formations, like *gobbledygook,* modeled on the meaningless sounds made by a turkey. Some are comparatively unknown, despite their creation by eminent speakers and writers: *clouderpuffs* (a sky full of round soft clouds), by Conrad Aiken; *popaganda* (Father's Day), by Edward Anthony; *globilliterate* (one ignorant of world affairs), by Norman Corbin.

Discoveries, new inventions, and occupations inspire new coinages: *A-bomb, rhombatron, realtor, beautician.* Registered trade names or trademarks are in the same classification: *Dacron, Technicolor, Kodak.* Events, like economic depressions and wars, create words: *jeep, foxhole, blitz.*

New words that appear in dictionaries may have no label or be labeled "slang" or "colloquial." (Some neologisms, like *motel,* change to permanent status and become common words.) Until a "new" word is widely accepted in present (current) use, it is best to avoid using it. Like some slang, most neologisms are "here today, gone tomorrow." How recently have you heard or read such neologisms as *cinemaddict* (lover of films), *aristobrat* (son or daughter of rich parents), *publicator* (press agent), and *tube steak* (the hot dog)? These lines from Alexander Pope are sound advice:

> In words, as fashions, the same rule will hold,
> Alike fantastic if too new or old:
> Be not the first by whom the new are tried,
> Nor yet the last to lay the old aside.

37. NATIONAL USE

It is important to use words that are generally understandable throughout the entire country. Words and expressions understandable to us may, to others, be localisms, technical terms, or Anglicisms. Also, idiomatic expressions acceptable in one part of the country may not be understood elsewhere. If you habitually use such expressions as the following in your speech and writing, drop them from your vocabulary, unless they are needed for some definite stylistic effect: the localisms *calculate, reckon,* and *guess* (for think or suppose); such semi-technical words as *half-volley, eagle, double steal, full gainer, birdie, switch tacks* (unless these terms are used in direct reference to various sports); such Anglicisms as *bonnet* (hood of a car), *biscuits* (cookies), *bowler* (derby), and *lift* (elevator).

Actually, if English is to remain a world language, it is important that words have not only national, but international, acceptance. Some observers have mentioned that we have, among many varieties, what might be called "Oxford English," "Australian English," and "New York English." When Confucius was asked what his first deed would be if he were to be made Emperor of China, he replied, "I would reestablish the precise meaning of words." Such an aim was impossible then and is impossible now. The difficulty of worldwide acceptance of word meanings is illustrated by this remark: "I was mad about my flat." In England it means "I liked my apartment"; in the United States it would usually mean "I was angry because I had a punctured tire."

An Americanism such as *lickety-split* is more vivid and picturesque than "fast" or "rapid," but its meaning might be unclear in Wales, South Africa, or New Zealand. Even in our own country, the problem is not always simple. Would everyone understand this sign posted in a North Carolina country store: "Kwittin credit till I get my outins in"? To those who can translate, however, the sentence is more quaint and expressive than "I shall extend no further credit to anyone who has not made full payment for goods already received."

37a. INAPPROPRIATE LOCALISMS

A *localism* is a word or phrase used and understood in a particular section or region. It may also be called a *regionalism* or a *provincialism.*

The western, southwestern, southern, and northeastern areas of the United States are rich in localisms that add flavor to speech but that may not be understood in other areas. Such expressions are difficult for a native of one of these areas to detect; as a writer or speaker he accepts them as reputable and assumes them to be generally understood, since he himself has known and used them from childhood. Although such words and combinations of words may not always be explained in print, dictionaries do label or define many words according to the geographical area where they are common. Examples:

Western: *grubstake* (supplies or funds furnished a prospector), *coulee* (narrow, steep-walled valley), *rustler* (cattle thief), *dogie, dogy* (motherless calf), *sagebrush* (a flower of the aster family).

Southwest:	*mesa* (flat-topped rocky hill with steeply sloping sides), *mustang* (small, hardy, half-wild horse), *longhorn* (formerly a variety of cattle), *mesquite* (spiny tree or shrub), *maverick* (an unbranded animal).
South:	*butternuts* (a kind of brown overalls), *granny* (a nurse), *lightwood* (pitchy pine wood), *corn pone* (corn bread), *hoecake* (a cake of Indian meal), *chunk* (throw), *tote* (carry), *poke* (sack).
Northeastern:	*down-easter* (a native of New England, especially of Maine), *selectman* (a town official), *choose* (wish).

Should localisms ever be used? The only satisfactory test is appropriateness. If you live in an area or address people in an area where localisms are easily understood, they are appropriate in speaking and informal writing. But in formal writing for such a geographical area, and in formal and informal speaking and writing intended to be understandable in other areas, avoid localisms in the interests of clarity.

37b. INAPPROPRIATE NATIONALISMS

A further extension of localism is *nationalism,* a term here describing expressions common in or limited to English used by one of the English-speaking nations. *Americanism* and *Briticism* refer to words or word meanings common, respectively, in the United States and in the British Isles; logically, other labels might be *Canadianisms, Australianisms, New Zealandisms,* and *South Africanisms.*

A two-volume reference work, *A Dictionary of Americanisms on Historical Principles,* records American usage—words of American origin and words with a distinctively American meaning, *American* here referring only to the United States. All reliable dictionaries, however, label many expressions *U.S., Chiefly U.S., British, Chiefly Brit.* or *Scotch.* Examples:

Americanisms:	*catchup* (tomato sauce); *levee* (an embankment); *calaboose* (prison, jail); *stump* (travel to electioneer); *bellhop; caboose; gangster; haberdasher; gusher.*
Briticisms:	*accumulator* (storage battery); *tube* (subway); *croft* (small enclosed field); *petrol* (gasoline), *stay-in strike* (sit-down strike).
Scotch dialect:	*bairn* (child); *canty* (cheerful); *auld* (old); *bree* (broth); *awee* (a little while).

Advice to avoid inappropriate nationalisms does not apply to American words and phrases but to those of other English-speaking countries when such words and phrases would not be readily understood in your writing.

37c. INAPPROPRIATE SHOPTALK

The specialized or technical vocabulary and idioms of those in the same work or the same way of life is known as *shoptalk,* the language people use in discussing their particular line of activity. To *talk shop* is the verb form of this expression.

Avoid introducing into writing words and expressions peculiar to, or understood only by, members of a particular profession, trade, science, or art. Legal jargon, medical jargon, and sports jargon, for example, have special meanings for people in those particular fields or occupations. So do more than forty other classifications of words that have special subject labels: astronomy, entomology, psychology, engineering, and so on. Examples of technical words are *sidereal* (astronomy), *broadside* (nautical), *lepidopterous* (zoology). Some have crept into popular use: *telescope* (astronomy), *virtuoso* (music and art), *stereo* (sound reproduction), *analog computer* (electronics).

A specialist writing for specialists uses many technical words. If he is writing for others in the same general field, he will use fewer technical terms, or less difficult ones, and will define the more specialized terms. If he is writing for the nonspecialist and the general reader, he will use no technical terms at all or will define the ones he does use.

If you are a science major writing a class paper, do not introduce and leave unexplained such terms as *diastrophism* (geology), *stratus* (meteorology), *cuprous* (chemistry), *coniferous* (botany).

37d. OVERUSE OF FOREIGN WORDS AND PHRASES

For Americans, a foreign word or phrase is one from a non-English language. Tens of thousands of foreign words have come into our language from Greek, Latin, and French, and thousands more have come from other languages. Depending upon your dictionary, you will find from 40 to 150 foreign-language abbreviations used for word origins and meanings.

Two things happen to these foreign words and phrases: (1) If they have been widely used or used over a long period, or both, they are Anglicized and become a part of our everyday language, recorded in dictionaries like any common word. (2) If the conditions of (1) have not been met, the word or phrase remains foreign: as such, it is indicated in dictionaries as foreign, partly as a guide for a writer to use italics if he uses the word or phrase (see Section 30). Anglicized examples: a priori, à la mode, blitz, chef, habitué, smorgasbord. Non-Anglicized examples: *Anno Domini, fait accompli, cause célèbre, ex libris, mañana, Weltschmerz.*

Use common sense in employing foreign words and phrases. If the word or phrase has been Anglicized or if no good English equivalent exists, use it. But why *merci beaucoup for* "thank you" or *Auf Wiedersehen* for "good-by"? Even *a* or *an* serves better than *per:* "$5 *an* hour." Do not use such foreign expressions merely to impress the reader.

38. REPUTABLE USE

A writer's vocabulary is the *number* of words he can command; a writer's diction is the *kind* of words he uses. As is pointed out at other places in this book, the first, most important, and fairest test of a word is usage. But usage must be "reputable"; that is, in diction one should follow standards set by that large body of accomplished speakers and writers who we have reason to believe know the language best. These standards rule out a number of words that most of us have in our vocabularies. In compensating for their loss, however, we may fall into other errors. That is, in substituting reputable expressions for disreputable ones, we may forget that the *primary* purpose of all writing is communication and that usage must be appropriate as well as reputable. This section is designed to help you avoid certain errors that may creep in as you begin to sort and expand your vocabulary.

38a. ILLITERACIES

Illiteracies are words and phrases not normally accepted in either informal or standard usage. Also called *barbarisms* and *vulgarisms, illiteracies* are characteristic of uneducated speech; they are to be avoided in writing unless put into the mouths of people being characterized. Illiteracies are not necessarily coarse and are frequently effective, but they should not be used without specific purpose.

Dictionary-makers apply different restrictive labels to "illiterate" or "vulgar" English; what may be marked *illiterate* in one dictionary may be termed *colloquial* or *dialect* in another. And because most dictionaries primarily record "standard" usage, many illiteracies are not listed at all.

The following words and phrases are illiteracies: acrossed, ain't, anywheres, as how, being as, being as how, borned, brung, to burgle, concertize, couldn't of, disremember, drownded, drug [past tense of *drag*], et [past tense of *eat*], excessible, fellers, hadn't ought, hisself, I been *or* I done, irregardless, mistakened, nohow, nowheres, ourn, snuck [past tense of *sneak*], them's [for *those are*], them there, this here.

38b. COLLOQUIALISMS

A *colloquialism* is a conversational word or phrase permissible in, and often indispensable to, an easy, informal style of speaking and writing. A colloquialism is not substandard, not illiterate; it is an expression more often used in speech than in writing and more appropriate in informal than formal speech and writing. The origin of the word is Latin *colloquium,* for "conversation." Our word *colloquy* means "speaking together"; the word *loquacious* means "given to talking, fond of talking."

Dictionary words and phrases are marked as colloquial (*Colloq.*) when the editors judge them to be more common in speech than in writing or more suitable in informal than formal discourse. A large number of words and phrases are so labeled. The term applies to many expressions because informal English has a wide range and because editors differ in interpretations of their findings. Certain contractions, such as *don't, shouldn't,* and *won't,* are considered "acceptable" colloquialisms; others, however, such as *'tis, 'twas, 'twere,* should be avoided in even informal writing. No objective rule or test will tell you when to use a colloquialism and when not to. In general, use a colloquialism when your writing would otherwise seem stiff and artificial.

The following are examples of colloquialisms (as in dictionaries and linguistic studies, no attempt is made to indicate their comparative rank): angel (financial backer), brass (impudence), freeze (stand motionless), don't, jinx, enthuse, phone, ad, gumption, cute, hasn't got any, brass tacks (facts), show up, try and, take a try at, alongside of, flabbergast, fizzle, flop, root for, make out, fill the bill.

You might use any or all of these colloquialisms if you are reporting the conversation of a person who would characteristically speak them. You might use one or more of them in informal writing where the tone is light or humorous or breezy. But if you use any colloquialisms at all, use only a few and be certain that they are in keeping with the purpose and tone of your writing.

38c. SLANG

Slang is a label for a particular kind of colloquialism (see Section 38b).

Characteristics of slang include flippant or eccentric humor; forced, fantastic, or grotesque meanings; novelty; attempts to be colorful, fresh, and vivid. Such expressions may capture the popular fancy or some segment of it (college slang, musical slang, baseball slang), but in the main they are substandard. Even so, slang may for a while be used over a broad area, and a large number of words and phrases bear the "slang" label in dictionaries. If such expressions survive, they may in time receive the respectable label "colloquial." Some of the following examples appear in dictionaries with the "slang" label; some may appear there eventually; and some will not appear at all, because their vogue is too short-lived.

Neologisms (newly coined words): *scrumptious, wacky, shyster, mooch, beatnik, razz, oops, hornswoggle, goofy, payola, scram, nix, teenybopper, pizzaz.* [Not all newly coined words, however, are slang. See Section 36d].

Words formed from others by abbreviation or by adding endings to change the part of speech: *VIP* (Very Important Person), *psych out, groovy, snafu* (situation normal; all fouled up), *phony, chintzy, nervy, mod.*

Words in otherwise acceptable use given extended meanings: *chicken, grind, corny, guts, lousy, swell, buck, bean, jerk, square, guy, grub, sack, blow, grease, tough, cat, fuzz, pad.*

Words formed by compounding or coalescing two or more words: *whodunit, stash* (store and cache), *egghead, sweedle* (swindle and wheedle), *high-hat, attaboy* (that's the boy), *screwball.*

Phrases made up of one or more newly coined words (neologisms) and one or more acceptable ones: *goof off, pork barrel, blow one's top, bum steer, shoot the bull, live it up, get in orbit, deadbeat, have a ball, off one's rocker, conk out, jam session, cut out, shoot the works, cool it.*

Slang, although popular, has little place in formal writing or even in effective informal writing. First, many slang words and expressions last for a brief time and then pass out of use, becoming unintelligible to many readers and listeners. Second, using slang expressions keeps you from searching for the exact words you need to convey your meaning. To refer to a person as a "creep" hardly expresses exactly or fully any critical judgment or intelligent description. Third, slang does not serve the primary aim of writing: conveying a clear and exact message from writer to reader. Finally, slang is not suitable in most formal or careful informal writing because it is not in keeping with the context. Words should be appropriate to the audience, the occasion, and the subject.

There are, however, some arguments in favor of slang in certain situations.

It does express feeling. It also makes effective short cuts in expression and often prevents artificiality in writing. Furthermore, it should be used in recording dialogue to convey the flavor of speech actually used.

38d. MIXED FIGURES

A figure of speech is a method of using words out of their literal, or ordinary, sense in order to suggest a picture or image. "He is a saint" and "sleeping like a baby" are illustrations of, respectively, the two most common figures of speech: *metaphor* and *simile.* A *metaphor* is a term applied to something to which it is not literally applicable. Associated with *metaphor* in meaning, a *simile* expresses direct comparison of two unlike things by using the words *like, as,* or *as if:* She is *like* a china doll.

Several figures of speech appear in both writing and speaking in addition to metaphor and simile. The following paragraphs describe the most common ones.

Synecdoche is a figure of association: it is the use of a part or an individual for the whole class or group, or the reverse. Part for whole: We have fifty *head* of cattle on our farm. Whole for part: Central defeated Gardner in the home-coming game (that is, the two schools did not play, but their football teams did).

Metonymy is a figure of association, somewhat like synecdoche. It is the use of the name of one thing for that of another suggested by it: We all agree that the tailor *sews a fine seam* (that is, does good tailoring).

Personification is giving nonhuman objects the characteristics of a human being: The waves *murmured,* and the moon *wept* silver tears.

Hyperbole is "exaggeration, or a statement exaggerated imaginatively, for effect; not to be taken literally." Some similes and metaphors express hyperbole: The young student, innocent *as a newborn babe,* eagerly accepted the challenge.

Because figurative language is colorful and imaginative, it adds vigor and effectiveness to writing. But do not think of figurative language as a mere ornament of style; do not use it too frequently; do not shift abruptly from figurative to literal language; and bear in mind that a direct, simple statement is usually preferable to a series of figures and always preferable when the figures are artificial, trite, or overly elaborate. Many similes are trite phrases or clichés: *happy as a lark, cool as a cucumber, busy as a bee, mad as a wet hen, quick as a wink, smooth as silk, right as rain, quiet as a mouse, hot as blazes* (see Section 39i).

Mixed figures are those in which the images suggested by words and phrases are obviously unrelated. Similes or metaphors are especially likely to become mixed through inconsistency, over-elaborateness, and incongruity. Here are examples of mixed and inappropriate figures:

> After football season many a football player who was a tidal wave on the football field has to put his nose to the grindstone and study.
>
> Although Judy can dance like a nymph, our ballet coach threw her out of the group like an old shoe.
>
> By milking from Ned all the money we could, we killed the goose that lays the golden eggs.

Do not confuse, perplex, or attempt to amuse readers (or hearers) by combining images that cannot possibly be related. See Sections 39k, 51e.

38e. IDIOMATIC USAGE

English *idiom* or *idiomatic* English concerns words used in combination with others. Of Greek origin, the word *idiom* meant "a private citizen, something belonging to a private citizen, personal," and, by extension, something individual and peculiar. Idiomatic expressions, then, conform to no laws or principles describing their formation. An idiomatic expression may violate grammar or logic or both and still be acceptable because the phrase is familiar, deep-rooted, widely used, and easily understandable—for the native born. "How do you do?" is, for example, an accepted idiom, although an exact answer would be absurd.

A few generalized statements may be made about the many idiomatic expressions in our language. One is that several words combined may lose their literal meaning and express something only remotely suggested by any one word: *birds of a feather, blacklist, lay up, toe the line, make out, bed of roses, dark horse, heavy hand, open house, read between the lines, no ax to grind, hard row to hoe.*

A second statement about idioms is that parts of the human body have suggested many of them: *burn one's fingers, all thumbs, fly in the face of, stand on one's own feet, keep body and soul together, keep one's eyes open, step on someone's toes, rub elbows with, get one's back up, keep one's chin up.*

A third generalization is that hundreds of idiomatic phrases contain adverbs or prepositions with other parts of speech. Here are some examples: *walk off, walk over, walk-up; run down, run in, run off, run out; get nowhere, get through, get off.*

agree	*to* a proposal
	on a plan
	with a person
contend	*for* a principle
	with a person
	against an obstacle
differ	*with* a person
	from something else
	about or *over* a question
impatient	*for* something desired
	with someone else
	of restraint
	at someone's conduct
rewarded	*for* something done
	with a gift
	by a person

Usage should conform to the idiomatic word combinations that are generally acceptable. A good dictionary contains explanations of idiomatic usage following key words that need such explanation, even though interpretations of particular expressions may differ from dictionary to dictionary. Examples of idiomatic and unidiomatic expressions containing troublesome prepositions or other forms are the following:

Idiomatic	*Unidiomatic*
accord with	accord to
according to	according with
acquaint with	acquaint to
adverse to	adverse against
aim to prove	aim at proving
among themselves	among one another
angry with (a person)	angry at (a person)
as regards	as regards to
authority on	authority about
blame me for it	blame it on me
cannot help talking	cannot help but talk
comply with	comply to
conform to, with	conform in
correspond to (a thing)	correspond with (a thing)
desirous of	desirous to
graduated from (high school)	graduated (high school)
identical with	identical to
in accordance with	in accordance to
in search of	in search for
prefer (one) to (another)	prefer (one) over (another)
prior to	prior than
responsible for, to	responsible on
superior to	superior than
treat of (a subject)	treat on (a subject)
unequal to	unequal for

39. INEXACT AND INEFFECTIVE DICTION

Some (perhaps many) of the words you speak and write may be in current, national, and reputable use and yet be neither exact nor effective.

The exact use of words depends upon *clear thinking*. If we have only a vague idea, we are likely to choose for its expression the first words that come to mind. But if we know *exactly* what we have in mind, we will search for the word or words that will most accurately express what we mean to say.

For example, consider one of the overworked words in our language, *pretty*. We speak of a pretty girl, a pretty flower, a pretty day, and so on. The word *pretty* carries a somewhat general meaning and cannot be called incorrect. But does it express exactly what we mean to convey? Perhaps it would be more accurate to say that a certain girl is *attractive,* or *beautiful,* or *personable,* or *charming,* or *exquisite,* or *fair,* or *sensuous,* or *dainty,* or *engaging*. These words are not all synonyms for *pretty,* but perhaps one of them would more exactly express an impression than the now trite and ineffective *pretty*.

In the preface to *Pierre et Jean*, Guy de Maupassant wrote:

> Whatever one wishes to say, there is one noun only by which to express it, one verb only to give it life, one adjective only which will describe it. One must

search until one has found them, this noun, this verb, this adjective, and never rest content with approximations, never resort to trickery, however happy, or to illiteracies, so as to dodge the difficulty.

Words stand for ideas and not *directly* for objects or actions. The basic elements of words are (1) the word itself, which is a sign or symbol; (2) the idea in the mind which the word suggests or for which it stands; (3) the real objects the idea concerns. Sometimes confusion or misunderstanding results because these distinctions are not recognized; the word as a sign or symbol is mistaken for the idea or for the real thing, or the idea is mistaken for the real object. We must be careful in writing—and in listening and in reading—to make sure that both the transmitter and the receiver of the communication understand exactly the sense in which a word is used and the meaning that it has. For example, one of the objects of alchemy (medieval chemical science) was to find the "philosopher's stone" by which alchemists thought they could transmute base metals into gold. The words *philosopher's stone,* then, stood for an idea; no such real stone was ever found to exist. The trite expression to indicate disapproval of an action, "That's not my idea of fun," illustrates the separation of the second and third elements; the person speaking would, perhaps, call the action "a bore" or "hard work" or something similar.

To determine the exact word for the context, you must become aware of shades of meaning, of distinctions that clarify the idea for which you wish to use the word as symbol. When you want to describe a surface that, from every point of view, lies on a line corresponding to or parallel with the horizon, will you use *flat, plane, level, even, flush,* or *smooth?* Always choose the word that shows most exactly the meaning you intend.

Sometimes the first word that comes to mind is the most nearly exact which can be used; more often it is not. Also, remember that a word means to the reader what the reader thinks it means, not necessarily what the writer thinks.

Again, a word may be exact and yet be lacking in force, animation, and strength. It is reasonably "exact" to refer to a dog as being *of mixed breed* but more lively and emphatic to refer to it as a *mongrel.* Effective writing is vigorous and positive and uses colorless words only as necessary. Emphatic diction requires expressive nouns, verbs, adjectives, and adverbs.

The following sections are designed to help you make your writing and speech more exact *and* effective. As you study them, remember that not only may exact diction be unemphatic but vigorous and forceful diction may be inexact.

39a. IMPROPRIETIES

Improprieties are recognized (standard) English words misused in function or meaning. One classification of improprieties includes words acceptable as one part of speech but unacceptable as another: nouns improperly substituted for verbs, verbs for nouns, adjectives for nouns, adjectives for adverbs, adverbs for adjectives, prepositions for conjunctions. Another includes misuses of principal parts of verbs. Such improprieties have been called "coined grammar."

A word identified as more than one part of speech may be so used without question, but a word should not be moved from one part of speech and placed in another until standard usage has sanctioned this new function. Examples of grammatical improprieties:

Nouns used as verbs:	*grassing* a lawn, *suppering,* to *party, ambitioned, passengered,* to *suspicion,* to *suicide*
Verbs used as nouns:	*eats,* a *repeat,* a *sell, advise,* an *invite*
Adjectives used as adverbs:	dances *good, awful* short, real pretty
Verb forms:	*come* for *came, don't* for *doesn't, says* for *said, done* for *did, hadn't ought, set* for *sit, of* for *have, seen* for *saw.*

Another classification of improprieties includes words similar to other words and used inaccurately in their place. Such words include homonyms and homographs. *Homonyms* are two words that have the same or almost the same pronunciation, but are different in meaning, in origin, and frequently in spelling; for example, *real* and *reel; made* and *maid; hour, our,* and *are; accept, except.*

Homographs are two or more words that have the same spelling but are different in meaning, origin, and perhaps pronunciation. Examples: *slaver* (a dealer in slaves) and *slaver* (drool or drivel); *arms* (parts of the body) and *arms* (weapons); *bat* (club, cudgel) and *bat* (flying rodent). Homographs cannot cause misspelling, but they can cause confusion or ambiguity.

Near-homonyms may also cause confusion: *farther* for *further, father* for *farther, genial* for *general, stationary* for *stationery, morass* for *morose, loose* for *lose, imminent* for *eminent, aisle* for *isle, allude* for *elude, climactic* for *climatic.*

39b. SPECIFIC AND GENERAL WORDS

A specific word names a narrow concept; a general word names a broad concept. *House* is a general word, whereas *castle, chalet, lodge, mansion, hut, shack,* and *villa* are specific. A *red* dress may be *carnelian, cerise, crimson, magenta, scarlet,* or *vermilion.* A conventional verb such as *walk* is general; more specific (and occasionally more effective) are such words as *flounce, mince, prance, saunter, shamble, stagger, stride, stroll, strut, totter,* and *traipse.*

Specific words are more exact and usually more effective than general words, but writing can become overloaded with highly charged concepts. The second of the following sentences is more exact and emphatic than the first, but it is too specific to be genuinely effective:

> There was an old boat moving through the heavy sea.
>
> Like a lady wrestler among thieves, the tanker *Isobel Ann* lunged into each massive green wave and, with a grunt of ancient rage, flung the Arctic-spawned monster over her scaling brown shoulder.

39c. CONCRETE AND ABSTRACT WORDS

A concrete word expresses something tangible, usually perceivable by one or more of the senses: *encrusted, forsythia, gargle, guillotine, lemony, waddle.* An abstract word suggests no really tangible image or impression: *duty, honor, leave, move, persuasion, slow, truth.*

Concrete words are specific, and specific words are frequently concrete; abstract words are general, and general words are often abstract. Ordinarily, and within reason, choose the specific, concrete word over the general, abstract one (see Section 39b).

This sentence is correct in form and clear in meaning:

> If you have committed a crime, escape to the woods with ammunition and clothing. People there will give you food and you need worry about nothing.

Notice the greater exactness and effectiveness of these sentences from Merimée's short story, "Mateo Falcone":

> If you have killed a man, go into the *maquis* of Porto-Vecchio with a good gun and powder and shot. You will live there quite safely, but don't forget to bring along a brown cloak and hood for your blanket and mattress. The shepherds will give you milk, cheese, and chestnuts, and you need not trouble your head about the law or the dead man's relatives, except when you are compelled to go down into the town to renew your ammunition.

39d. EXAGGERATION

Exaggeration is the act of magnifying, overstating, and going beyond the limits of truth. In writing, exaggeration is used to intensify or strengthen meaning: *starved* or *famished* for "hungry," *a million thanks, abject adoration.*

In most instances, exaggeration actually misrepresents and is neither exact nor effective: I thought I'd die laughing. Exaggeration occasionally may be used effectively, but it is more often misleading. Be on guard when using such words as *amazing, awful, fantastic, gigantic, gorgeous, horrible, marvelous, overwhelming, phenomenal, staggering, terrible, thrilling, tremendous,* and *wonderful.* These words, and scores more like them, appear often in what is unkindly called "schoolgirl style"—a manner of writing characterized by gushiness, exaggeration, and overuse of intensifiers.

39e. AFFECTATION

Affectation is artificial behavior designed to impress others, a mannerism for effect that involves some kind of show or pretense. In language, it is evident in the use of words and expressions not customary or appropriate for the speaker or writer employing them. Getting rid of words and expressions that are not reputable and simultaneously trying to increase the vigor and appeal of one's speech and writing are worthwhile endeavors. Deliberately trying to be different or learned or impressive often results in misinterpretation, confusion, and annoyance. Pretense is a greater sin against expressive English than even "bad grammar."

For example, a recent magazine article contained this paragraph:

> The opportunity for options in life distinguishes the rich from the poor. Perhaps through better motivation, the upper levels of the poor could be tempted onto the option track. It is important to motivate such people close to the breakthrough level in income because they are closest to getting a foot on the option ladder.

What this writer probably meant was "The more money you have, the more choices you have." He used reputable expressions, but he fell into the greater error of affectation.

39f. EUPHEMISMS

A *euphemism* is a softened, bland, inoffensive expression used instead of one that may suggest something unpleasant. In avoiding the use of such nonreputable expressions as *croak, kick the bucket,* and *take the last count,* you may be tempted to write *pass away* or *depart this life.* Unless religious dictates prevent, use the short, direct word *die.* Other examples of euphemisms to be avoided: *prevaricate* for *lie, watery plain* for *sea* or *ocean, expectorate* for *spit, mortician* for *undertaker, lowing herd* for *cattle, villatic fowl* for *chicken, separate from school* for *expel, abdomen* for *belly, love child* for *illegitimate.*

Here is a short list of expressions recently noted in magazine and newspaper articles and advertisements, together with possible translations into useful English:

preowned car (secondhand car)
senior citizens (old people)
problem skin (acne)
motion discomfort (nausea)
extrapolation (educated guess)
sanitary engineer (garbageman)
creative conflict (civil rights demonstration)
custodial engineer (janitor)
experienced tires (retreads or recaps)
collection correspondent (bill collector)
comfort station (public toilet)
mortical surgeon (undertaker)
cardiovascular accident (stroke)
archivist (library worker)
food preparation center (kitchen)

39g. EMOTIONAL MEANINGS

Nearly all words mean more than they seem to mean; they possess associated meanings, a sort of periphery of suggestive, or connotative, values. The bare, literal meaning of a word is its *denotation.* The *connotation* of a word is the suggestions and associations that have surrounded it. For example, a dictionary definition of the word *gold* is "A precious yellow metal, highly malleable and ductile, and free from liability to rust." This is its denotation. But with *gold* have long been associated color, riches, power, happiness, evil, unhappiness.

All good writers avail themselves of the latent magic in words, but connotative values are intricate and must be watched. If you do not employ connotation, your writing will be flatter and more insipid than it should be. But misinterpretation or misunderstanding can result from failure to consider the values of words.

Writers of advertising are skillful in using emotionally charged words. The slogan "Pure as the tear that falls upon a sister's grave" pretended, as one writer has pointed out, to describe the quality of an advertised wine. Read literally, the remark is far from complimentary, but the writer was trying to evoke a sentimental, buying response to the words *pure, tear,* and *sister.*

39h. JARGON AND GOBBLEDYGOOK

Jargon is a general term sometimes applied to mixed linguistic forms for communication between speakers who do not know each other's language—for example, *pidgin English* and *lingua franca.* It refers as well to speaking and writing that contain a number of expressions unfamiliar to the general reader (the jargon of sports, the jargon of atomic physicists) and to writing filled with long words (polysyllabication) and circumlocutions (indirect or roundabout expressions).

"Short words are words of might." This observation—wise but no truer than most generalizations—does not imply that long words should never be used; it does suggest that long words are more likely than short ones to be artificial, affected, and pretentious. The user of jargon will write "The answer is in the negative" rather than "No." For him, "worked hard" is "pursued his tasks with great diligence"; "bad weather" is "unfavorable climatic conditions"; "food" becomes "comestibles"; "fire" becomes "devouring element"; "a meal" becomes "succulent viands" or "a savory repast." The jargoneer also employs what has been called "the trick of elegant variation": he may call a spade a spade the first time but then refer to "an agricultural implement." In a paper on Lord Byron, he will use such variations as "that great but uneven poet," "the gloomy master of Newstead," and "the meteoric darling of society."

It is impossible always to use concrete words (see Section 39c), but be certain you mean precisely what you say in writing such usually vague words as *asset, case, character, condition, degree, factor, instance, nature, personality, persuasion, quality, state,* and *thing.* It is likely you will never really have to use such expressions as these: *according as to whether, along the line of, in connection with,* and *in regard to.*

Gobbledygook (or *gobbledegook*) is a special kind of jargon: generally unintelligible, wordy, inflated, and obscure verbiage. Jargon is always undesirable but is often understandable; gobbledygook is likely to be meaningless or quite difficult to decipher. The word was coined by a former United States congressman, grown weary of involved government reports, who apparently had in mind the throaty sound made by a male turkey.

The term is increasingly applied to governmental and bureaucratic pronouncements that have been referred to as "masterpieces of complexity." For example, the phrase "the chance of war" in gobbledygook might be "in the regrettable eventuality of failure of the deterrence policy." But gobbledygook is not confined to bureaucratic circles. Here is a direct quotation from a financial adviser concerning shares of stock: "Overall, the underlying pattern, notwithstanding periods of consolidation, remains suggestive of at least further selective improvement over the foreseeable future." What he meant: "Selected stocks will increase in price."

A plumber, an often-told story goes, wrote to inform an agency of the United States government that he had found hydrochloric acid good for cleaning out pipes. Some bureaucrat responded with this gobbledygook: "The efficiency of hydrochloric acid is indisputable, but the corrosive residue is incompatible with metallic permanence." The plumber responded that he was glad the agency agreed. After several more such letters, an official finally wrote what he should have originally: "Don't use hydrochloric acid. It eats the inside out of pipes."

Here, in gobbledygook, are two well-known proverbs:

Feathered bipeds of similar plumage will live gregariously.

Too great a number of culinary assistants may impair the flavor of the consommé.

Can you translate them into the direct English of the originals?

39i. TRITENESS

Triteness applies to words and expressions that are worn out from overuse. A trite expression is sometimes called *hackneyed language* or a *cliché*. The origins of the words *triteness, hackneyed,* and *cliché* are illuminating: the first comes from the Latin word *tritus,* the past participle of *terere,* which means "to rub, to wear out"; *hackneyed* is derived from the idea of a horse or carriage let out for hire, devoted to common use, and thus worn out in service; *cliché* comes from the French word *clicher,* meaning "to stereotype."

Thus trite language resembles slang in that both are rubber stamps, "stereotyped plates" of thought and expression. Clichés may be tags from common speech, or overworked quotations, or outworn phrases from newspapers. They save the writer the task of stating exactly what he means, but their use results in writing that is both stale and ineffective. Such words and phrases may seem humorous; they are, indeed, often used for humor or irony. Used seriously, they suggest that the speaker or writer is naïve.

Familiarity with trite words and expressions is likely to cause them to occur to us more readily than others that are more effective. Look suspiciously upon each word or phrase that leaps to mind until you can be certain the expression is exact and unhackneyed. Hundreds and hundreds of examples could be cited, but here are some colorful expressions now ineffective from overuse:

brave as a lion	like a blundering idiot
brown as a berry	like a duck out of water
cold as ice	like a newborn babe
fight like a tiger	pure as new-fallen snow
free as the air	strong as an ox
gentle as a lamb	trees like sentinels
green as grass	wild as a March hare

Here are more trite words and phrases:

a must, all boils down to, all in all, along this (that) line, and things like that, any manner or means, aroused our curiosity, as a matter of fact.

battle of life, beating around the bush, believe me, bigger and better things, bitter end, bright and early, brings to mind, butterflies in my stomach, by leaps and bounds

center of attraction, chills (shivers) up and down my spine, come into the picture, come to life, comfortable living, conspicuous by its absence

dear old (high school, college, Alma Mater), depths of despair, doomed to disappointment, dull thud

each and every, every walk of life

fair land of ours, few and far between, fill the shoes of, first and foremost, fond memories, force of circumstances get our (their) wires crossed, give it a try, give out (up), goes without saying, grand and glorious, great (guy, job, thrill, and so on), green with envy

hang one on, hapless victim, honest to goodness

in dire straits, in glowing terms, in the best of health, in the long run, in this day and age, interesting (surprising) to note, intestinal fortitude, irony of fate

last but not least, last straw, leaves little to be desired, live it up

mad dash for, main underlying reason, make the world a better place, many and varied, meets the eye, modern world of today (our), more than pleased, Mother Nature

Nature in all her splendor, necessary evil, never a dull moment, nick of time, nipped in the bud, no fooling, no respecter of persons, no thinking man, none the worse for wear

out of this world

packed in like sardines, pounding like a hammer, proud possessor, psychological moment

race, creed, or color (race, belief, or national origin), raining cats and dogs, real challenge, really a thrill, rise majestically

sad to relate, sadder but wiser, safe to say, setting the scene, sigh of relief, sight to behold, sit up and take notice, suffice it to say

take a back seat for no one, take pen in hand, the time of my life, the worse for wear, thing of the past, this old world of ours, through thick and thin, tired but happy, top it off

wait with bated breath, wee small hours of the morning, wends his way, wide open spaces, with a bang, with fear and trembling, wonderful (time, day, meal, and so on), wonders of Nature, words fail to express, wunderbar

39j. WORDINESS

To be effective, diction must be economical. Writing should not be sketchy, nor should necessary words be omitted, but wordiness weakens the force and appeal of expression.

In Shakespeare's *Hamlet,* old Polonius announces:

> Therefore, since brevity is the soul of wit,
> And tediousness the limbs and outward flourishes,
> I will be brief.

In this context, *wit* means "understanding" or "wisdom." That is, being brief and to the point is the only way effectively to express genuine thought. See Section 55.

Conciseness alone does not guarantee good writing, but it is difficult, even impossible, to write forcefully when using three or four words where one would be sufficient. Lincoln's Gettysburg Address contains only 267 words. The Ten Commandments are expressed in 75 words. The Golden Rule contains 11 words. The moral of "few words for many" is in the following: To the simple question of whether rules should be observed, an administrator wrote, "The implementation of sanctions will inevitably eventuate in subsequent repercussions." What he might have said, simply, was "Yes."

Our conversation is normally more wordy than formal writing should be because in speaking we do not have, or take, time to be economical and direct. Here are a few expressions that we probably use often in speaking but that should be made concise in writing:

Reduce these	*To these*
a certain length of time	a certain time
are of the opinion	believe
I would appreciate it if	please
in the event that	if
it is interesting to note that	[begin with the word after *that*]
on condition that	if
at the present time	now
under date of June 5	June 5
for the amount of	for
in lieu of	instead
before long	soon

39k. FIGURES OF SPEECH

Figures of speech are referred to as the ornaments of prose. And yet they are ornaments often used. We use figurative language when, for example, we speak of a *heavy* heart, a *heavy* silence, *heavy* grief, *heavy* style, *heavy* rain, a *heavy* sky, a *heavy* sound, a *heavy* grade, *heavy* food, *heavy* features, or *heavy* humor. The literal meaning of the word *heavy* is "weighty, of high specific gravity," a meaning only remotely connected with some of the above-mentioned uses of the word. Much of our language is consciously or unconsciously figurative; sometimes it is even awkward and illogical (see Section 38d).

A writer's obligation is to convey sensible comments clearly. But good writers search for words that stimulate the reader's imagination. These words, having connotative values, suggest associated meanings: *baby sister,* not *girl; enigma,* not *problem; home,* not *house; breechloader,* not *gun; mother,* not *woman.*

40. GLOSSARY OF DICTION

The following glossary, alphabetically arranged for easy reference, contains words and expressions often misused or confused. The list, not all-inclusive, is a capsule discussion of some common violations of good usage. If the material given below does not apply to your problem, if you want more detailed information, or if you do not find listed the word or phrase you are seeking, consult your dictionary.

A few of these expressions are always to be avoided, but many are unacceptable only in formal English. Remember especially that no stigma attaches to the label "colloquial"; it indicates that a given expression is more appropriate in conversation and in informal discourse than it is in formal writing.

Usage is so constantly changing that expressions now restricted in some way may later be considered standard. Furthermore, because no dictionary or textbook (including this one) is a final authority, some usages are disputed. Probably no two linguists would agree on all the comments that follow. But this illustrative list should be serviceable as a starter; to it you may add from time to time other words and expressions.

A, an. The choice between *a* and *an* depends on the initial sound of the word that follows. *An* should be used before a vowel sound, *a* before a word beginning with a consonant sound: *an* adult, *a* picture; *an* honor, *a* historian.

Ability, capacity. *Ability* means the power to do something, physical or mental (*ability* to speak in public). *Capacity* is the ability to hold, contain, or absorb (a room filled to *capacity*).

Absolutely. This word means "completely," "perfectly," "wholly." In addition to being greatly overused as an intensifier, it is both faulty and wordy in an expression such as "absolutely complete." Never use *absolutely* or any other such modifier with words like *complete, perfect, unique* (see *Unique*).

Accept, except. *Accept* means "to receive" or "to agree with"; *except* means "to omit" or "to exempt." (I will not *accept* your offer. The men were punished but Ned was *excepted.*) As a preposition, *except* means "other than." (Everyone *except* me was on time.)

Ad. A colloquial abbreviation, much used, for *advertisement*. In strictly formal writing, avoid such abbreviations as *ad, auto* for *automobile, phone* for *telephone, exam* for *examination.*

Ad lib. This verb, meaning "to improvise," "to extemporize," is both overused and colloquial. It is derived from the Latin phrase *ad libitum,* meaning "at pleasure," and is appropriately used in music to mean "freely." Avoid using *ad lib* to mean adding words and gestures not in the script or not intended to be said or otherwise expressed.

Advise. This word, meaning "to counsel," "to give advice to," is overused in business letters and other forms of communication for "tell," "inform." (I am pleased to *inform* [not *advise*] you that the check has been received.)

Affect, effect. As a verb, *affect* means "to influence," or "to assume." (This book has *affected* my thinking.) *Effect* as a verb means "to cause" and as a noun means "result." (Your good work will *effect* an improvement in your mark for the term. This play will have a good *effect* on youth.)

Ain't. This contraction is considered illiterate, dialectal, or colloquial and is cautioned against in standard English, both written and spoken. The word, which stands for *am not,* is often informally used even by educated people, but it has not been accepted in the sense that *isn't* (for *is not*), *aren't* (for *are not*), and *weren't* (for *were not*) have been.

Alibi. Used colloquially to mean "an excuse or any kind of defense," the word precisely and correctly should be used to mean "a plea or fact of having been elsewhere when an offense was committed." *Alibi* is often used in the loose sense mentioned above and is now a trite and jaded expression.

All right, alright. The former expression is correct but has been overworked to mean "satisfactory" or "very well." *Alright* is analogous to *altogether* and *already* (both standard words) but is not yet an acceptable word in standard usage.

Almost. See *Most, almost.*

Already, all ready. The former means "earlier," "previously." (When she arrived, her friend had *already* left.) *All ready* means "all are ready." (They will leave when they are *all ready.*)

Altogether, all together. *Altogether* means "wholly," "completely." (He was not *altogether* pleased with his purchase.) *All together* means "all in company" or "everybody in one place." (The family was *all together* for the holidays.)

Alumnus, alumna. An *alumnus* is a male graduate; an *alumna* is a woman graduate. The respective plurals are *alumni* and *alumnae.* To refer to graduates of a school as *alum* or *alums* is colloquial or slangy.

Among, between. The former shows the relationship of more than two objects; *between* refers to only two or to more than two when each object is considered in its relationship to others. (We distributed the candy *among* the six children. We divided the candy *between* Jill and Gray. Understanding *between* nations is essential.)

Amount, number. The former is used of things involving a unified mass—bulk, weight, or sums. (What is the *amount* of the bill?) *Number* is used of things that can be counted in individual units. (I have a *number* of hats and coats.)

And etc. A redundant expression. *Etc.* is an abbreviation for the Latin phrase *et cetera,* meaning "and so forth." Omit the *and* in *and etc.*

And how. A slang expression indicating strong feeling or approval. Avoid its use in standard English; it is both informal and trite.

And/or. Primarily a business and legal expression, *and/or* is objected to by purists and other especially fastidious users of English. It is somewhat vague and also has business connotations objectionable to some people. Although it is a useful time-saver, in formal English you should avoid using it.

And which, that, who; but which, that, who. Correct sentence structure provides that these phrases should appear in clauses only if preceded by clauses that also contain *which, that,* or *who.* ("This is the first book *that* I bought *and that* I treasure," not "This is the first book I bought *and that* I treasure.") See Section 48d.

Anyway, anyways. *Anyway* means "in any case," "anyhow." (She was planning to go *anyway.*) *Anyways* has the same meaning as *anyway,* but it is considered either dialectal or colloquial when used to mean "in any case."

Apt, liable, likely. *Apt* suggests fitness or tendency. (She is *apt* in arithmetic.) *Liable* implies exposure to something burdensome or disadvantageous. (You are *liable* for damages.) *Likely* means "expected," "probable." (We are *likely* to have snow next month.) *Likely* is the most commonly used of the three terms. Distinction in meaning has broken somewhat, but *apt* and *liable* used in the sense of "probable" are sometimes considered colloquial or dialectal.

As. One of the most overworked words in the English language. It is a perfectly good word, but *since, because,* and *when* are more exact and effective conjunctions. (*Since* [not *As*] it was snowing, we decided to stay indoors.) *As* is often misused in place of *that* or *whether.* (I doubt *that* [not *as*] I can go.) In negative comparisons some writers prefer *so . . . as* to *as . . . as.* (He is not *so* heavy *as* his brother.) In general, use *as* sparingly; nearly always a more exact and effective word can be found.

As good as, if not better than. A correctly phrased but awkward and mixed comparison. A statement will be more effective when *If not better* is put at the end. (*Awkward:* My work is *as good as, if not better than,* your work. *Improved:* My work is *as good as yours, if not better.*)

Awful, awfully, abominably. These and such other expressions as *terrible, ghastly,* and *horrible* are loose, overworked intensifiers. If you really need an intensifier, use *very* (which see).

Bad, badly, ill. *Bad* is an adjective meaning "not good," "not as it should be." *Badly* is an adverb meaning "harmfully," "wickedly," "unpleasantly," "inefficiently." *Ill* is both an adjective and an adverb and means "sick," "tending to cause harm or evil," or "in a malevolent manner," "wrongly." (She was very *ill.*) *Bad* and *badly* are often incorrectly used with the verb *feel.* (I feel *bad* today"—not *badly,* unless you mean that your sense of touch is impaired.)

Badly. A colloquial expression for "very much." Avoid its use in this sense in formal writing and speaking.

Balance, remainder. The latter term means "what is left over." *Balance* has many meanings, but its use as "remainder" is considered colloquial. (He ate the *remainder* [not *balance*] of the meal.)

Be sure and. This expression is considered both colloquial and unidiomatic. (When you get there, *be sure to* [not *sure and*] write to me.)

Being as. A colloquial or illiterate substitute for *since, because, inasmuch as,* and so on. (*Since* [not *Being as*] I have some money, I'll lend you some.)

Beside, besides. *Beside* is normally a preposition meaning "by the side of." *Besides* is an adverb meaning "moreover," and, infrequently, is a preposition meaning "except." (The old man sat *beside* the stove. I can't go because I have no money, and *besides* I don't feel well.)

Between. See *Among, between.*

Blame me for it, blame it on me. Both of these expressions are in everyday use, but only the former is considered idiomatically correct and proper. *Blame it on me* is either dialectal or colloquial.

Broke. This word has standard uses, but it is a colloquialism or slang when used to mean "out of money." To *go broke* (become penniless) and *go for broke* (dare or risk everything) are slangy expressions.

Bunch. A colloquialism for "a group of people," "crowd," or "set." (Our *set*—or *group* or *crowd* or *gang*—was closely knit at that time.)

But which. See *And which.*

Calculate, reckon, guess. These words are localisms for "think," "suppose," and "expect." Each of the words has standard and acceptable meanings, but in the senses indicated here they should always be avoided except in informal conversation.

Can, may, might. *Can* suggests "ability," physical and mental. (He *can* make good progress if he tries hard enough.) *May* implies permission or sanction. (The office manager says that you *may* leave.) The distinction between *can* and *may* (ability vs. permission) is illustrated in this sentence: Lee thinks that you *can*, and you *may* try if you wish. *May* also expresses possibility and wish (desire): It *may* snow today (possibility); *may* you have a pleasant time (wish, desire). *Might* is used after a governing verb in the past tense, *may* after a governing verb in the present tense: He *says* that you *may* try; he *said* that you *might* try.

Cancel out. Omit the *out.* This wordy expression is often used, perhaps by analogy with *cross out* or *strike out.*

Cannot help, cannot help but. The first of these expressions is preferable in such statements as "I *cannot help* talking about my trip." The *but* should be omitted since its addition can result in a double negative: Use *cannot help* and *can but.*

Can't hardly. Omit the *not.* (I *can* hardly hear you.) *Can't hardly* is a double negative.

Capital, capitol. The first of these words may be employed in all meanings except that of "a building." A *capitol* is an edifice, a building. (He raised new *capital* for the company. The sight-seeing bus passed the state *capitol.* Sacramento is the *capital* of California.)

Case. This word (other than indicating the forms of pronouns and nouns) has many vague meanings. *Case, phase, factor, instance, nature, thing* are prime examples of jargon. *To case,* in the sense of "examine carefully," is slang. Don't use *case the joint* in standard English.

Common, mutual. The former means "belonging to many or to all." *Mutual* means "reciprocal." (Airplanes are *common* carriers. Our respect and love were *mutual.*) Avoid the redundancy of this kind of statement: He and I entered into a *mutual* agreement.

Compare, contrast. *Compare* is used to point out likenesses, similarities (used with the preposition *to*), and to examine two or more objects to find likenesses or differences (used with the preposition *with*). *Contrast* always points out differences. (The poet *compared* his lady *to* a wood thrush. The teacher *compared* my paper *with* Henry's and found no signs of copying. In *contrast* to your work, mine is poor.)

Complected. This abomination may be considered an illiteracy or a dialectal expression. The standard word is *complexioned.* (Janet was dark-*complexioned.*)

Complement, compliment. *Complement* implies something that completes. (This jewelry will *complement* your dress.) A *compliment* is flattery. (Beulah enjoyed the *compliment* paid to her.)

Contact, contacted. Each of these words has perfectly proper uses, but as business terms they have been overworked. Possible substitutes are *communicate with, call, call upon, telephone.*

Continual, continuous. In some uses these words are interchangeable. A subtle distinction is that *continual* implies "a close recurrence in time," "in rapid succession," and that *continuous* implies "without interruption." (The *continual* ringing of the doorbell bothers me. The ticking of the watch was *continuous.*)

Continue on. This is a wordy phrase. *Continue* means "to endure," "to last." Hence *on* is unnecessary to convey full meaning.

Contrast. See *Compare, contrast.*

Convince, persuade. The former means "to overcome the doubts of." *Persuade* implies "influencing a person to an action or belief." (I am *convinced* that you are right and you have *persuaded* me to help you.) *Convince to* is not idiomatic. (*Wrong:* I *convinced* him *to* see the play. *Right:* I *persuaded* him *to* see the play. I *convinced* him *that* he should see the play.)

Cool. In the sense of "lacking warmth," "moderately cold," and several other meanings, *cool* is a useful and correct word. But it is informal or slangy when used to mean "actual" (a *cool* million dollars), "great," and "excellent." It is also highly informal in such debatable expressions as "cool cat" and "cool customer."

Council, counsel. *Council* means "an assembly," "a group." (This is a *council* of citizens.) *Counsel* is both a noun and a verb and means "advice" or "to advise." (The physician gave me expensive *counsel.* The manager will *counsel* fast action by the board of directors.)

Cute. This is an overworked and somewhat vague word that generally expresses approval. Probably *charming, clever, attractive, winsome, piquant, pleasing, vivacious,* or one of a dozen other adjectives would come nearer the meaning you have in mind.

Data. This word was originally the plural of the Latin *datum* and means "facts and figures from which conclusions may be drawn." Purists consider the word to be plural and use it with a plural verb, but its use with a singular verb is becoming more widespread. (*These* data *are* not reliable. *This* data *is* not reliable.)

Des′ert, desert′, dessert′. These three words involve problems in spelling, pronunciation, and meaning. The first, with accent on the first syllable, means "barren ground." (The *desert* is 100 miles wide.) *Desert* (with accent on the second syllable) means "to abandon." (Don't ever *desert* your true friends.) *Dessert* (note the double *s*) is "the last course of a lunch or dinner." (Apple pie is his favorite *dessert.*)

Different from, than, to. *Different than* and *different to* are considered colloquial by some authorities, improper and incorrect by others. Even so, these idioms have long literary usage to support them, and certainly they are widely used. No one ever objects on any grounds to *different from.* Use *different from* and be safe, never sorry.

Disinterested, uninterested. The former means "unbiased," "not influenced by personal reasons." *Uninterested* means "having no interest in," "not paying attention." (The minister's opinion was *disinterested.* I was completely *uninterested* in the play.) As a colloquialism, a somewhat inexact one, *disinterested* is often used in the sense of "uninterested," "indifferent."

Disregardless. See *Irregardless, disregardless.*

Disremember. An illiteracy. Never use this word in standard English.

Done, don't. The principal parts of this verb are *do, did, done. Done* is frequently used incorrectly as the past tense of *do.* (We *did* [not *done*] our work early today.) *Don't* is often used incorrectly for *doesn't.* (It *doesn't* [not *don't*] make much difference to me.)

Due to. Some authorities label this phrase "colloquial" when it is used to mean "because of." Nevertheless, it is widely used in this sense by capable speakers and writers. Purists prefer such expressions as *owing to, caused by, on account of,* and *because of.* If you wish your English to be above any possible criticism, avoid using *due to* as a preposition. (Tension there was *caused by* [not *due to*] racial unrest that had been building for decades.) Most important, remember that *due to the fact that* is a wordy way of saying the short and simple word *since* (see *Fact that*).

Each . . . are. *Each,* even if not followed by *one,* implies "one." Any plural words used in modifying phrases do not change the number. (Each *is* [not *are*] expected to contribute *his* time. *Each one* of you *is* a fraud.)

Either . . . or, neither . . . nor. The former means "one of two." *Neither* means "not one of two." *Or* is used with *either, nor* with *neither.* The use of *either . . . or* and *neither . . . nor* in coordinating more than two words, phrases, or clauses is sanctioned by some dictionaries but not by others. (*Either* of you *is* satisfactory for the role. *Neither* the boys *nor* the girls wished to dance.)

Emigrate, immigrate. The former means "to leave"; the latter means "to enter." (Our janitor *emigrated* from Poland in 1938. Many people have tried to *immigrate* to this country in the last decade.) The corresponding nouns, *emigration* and *immigration,* are similarly distinguished in meaning.

Enthuse. This word is a formation derived from "enthusiasm." Most dictionaries label *enthuse* as colloquial, although it is shorter and more direct than preferred locutions such as *be enthusiastic about* or *become enthusiastic over.* Even so, the word is greatly overused and somewhat "gushy"; do not use it in formal English.

Envelop, envelope. The verb *en-vel'op* (accent on the second syllable) means "to cover," "to wrap." (Fire will soon *envelop* the entire block.) *En'-vel-ope* (accent on first syllable) is a noun meaning "a covering." (Put a stamp on this *envelope.*)

Except. See *Accept, except.*

Fact that, the fact remains that. Roundabout, wordy substitutes for *that* and *the fact is,* respectively (see *Due to*).

Farther, further. These words are interchangeable in meaning, but unusually precise writers and speakers prefer *farther* to indicate space, a measurable distance. *Further* indicates "greater in degree, quantity, or time" and also means "moreover" and "in addition to." (We walked two miles *farther.* Let's talk about this *further.*)

Feature. As both verb and noun, *feature* is an overworked colloquialism in the sense of "emphasize" or "emphasis." *Feature* is slang in the expression "Can you feature that?" meaning, presumably, "Can you imagine that?"

Fed up. An expressive but slangy term meaning "to become disgusted, bored." Don't use it in formal or scholarly writing.

Feel. This useful word appears in several expressions that are colloquial or dialectal. In standard English avoid using *feel of* (for *feel*), *feel like* (for *wish to, desire*), *feel up to* (for *feel capable of*).

Fewer, less. Both of these words imply a comparison with something larger in number or amount. Although *less* is widely used in place of *fewer,* particularly in informal writing and in speech, the distinction between them seems useful. *Fewer* applies to number. (*Fewer* horses are seen on the streets these days.) *Less* is used in several ways: *less* material in the dress, *less* coverage, *less* than a dollar. (The *less* money we have the *fewer* purchases we can make.)

Figuratively. This word means "metaphorically," "representing one thing in terms of another," "not literally." (*Figuratively* speaking, you acted like a mouse.) (See *Literally.*)

Fine. This word is much overused in the general sense of approval. It is colloquial when used as an adverb: Mona sang *well* [not *fine* or *just fine*].

Firstly, secondly. These words are acceptable, but most skilled users of the language prefer *first* and *second* because they are just as accurate and are shorter. *First of all* is a wordy expression.

First-rate, second-rate. These words suggesting rank or degree of excellence are vastly overused. *First-rate* is colloquial in the sense of "very good" or "excellent" or "very well."

Fix. This is a word of many meanings. In standard English it means "to make fast." As a verb, it is informal (colloquial) when used to mean "to arrange matters," "to get revenge on," "to repair." As a noun, it is used colloquially for "difficulty," "predicament" and is a slang term for an injection of a narcotic.

Flunk. A colloquialism for "to fail" and "failure," this word should not appear in standard English as either verb or noun.

Folks. This word is colloquial when used to refer to "relatives" and "family." Both dialectal and colloquial is the expression *just folks,* meaning "simple and unassuming people." *Folksy* is a colloquial word for "sociable."

Foreword, forward. A *foreword* is a "preface" or "introduction." *Forward* suggests "movement onward." (This book needs no *foreword.* The crowd surged *forward.*)

Formally, formerly. The first term means "in a formal manner," "precisely," "ceremonially." The latter means "in the past." (The defendant bowed *formally* to the judge. Betty was *formerly* an employee of that company.)

Former, latter. *Former* and *latter* refer to only two units. To refer to a group of more than two items, use *first* and *last* to indicate order.

Fort, forte. *Fort* means an "enclosed place," a "fortified building." *Forte* means "special accomplishment or ability." (The Indians burned the settlers' *fort.* His *forte* is playing the violin.)

Free from, free of. The former is idiomatically correct. *Free of* is considered either colloquial or dialectal.

Free gratis. *Gratis* means "without payment," "free." Use either *free* or *gratis,* not both.

Funny. A common and useful word but one that is vastly overworked. Its use to mean "strange," "queer," "odd," "remarkable" is considered colloquial. Its primary meaning is "humorous" or "comical."

Further. See *Farther, further.*

Genius, genus. The former refers to great ability. (Bach was a man of *genius.*) *Genus* refers to class or kind. (What is the *genus* of this plant?)

Good, well. The former is an adjective with many meanings: a *good* time, *good* advice, *good* Republican, *good* humor. *Well* functions as both adjective and adverb. As an adjective it means "in good health," and as an adverb it means "ably" or "efficiently." (I feel *well* once again. The sales force worked *well* in this campaign.)

Got, gotten. The principal parts of *get* are *get, got, got* (or *gotten*). Both *got* and *gotten* are acceptable words; your choice will depend upon your speech habits or on the rhythm of the sentence you are writing or speaking. *Got* is colloquial when used to mean "must," "ought," "own," "possess," and many other terms. (I *ought* [not *got*] to go.) (See *Have got to.*)

Gourmand, gourmet. These words have to do with eating, but they are different in meaning. A *gourmand* is a large eater. (Diamond Jim Brady was a *gourmand,* often eating for three hours at a time.) A *gourmet* is a fastidious eater, an epicure. (As a French chef, he considers himself a *gourmet.*)

Graduate. This word has several meanings, all of which are in some way related to marking in steps, measuring. Idiom decrees that one *graduate from* (not *graduate*) a school.

Grand. This word means "imposing," "magnificent," "noble." It is overused as a vague counter word meaning "delightful" or "admirable." *Grand* is colloquial in such expressions as *look grand, a grand time, feel grand.*

Gratis. See *Free gratis.*

Guess. See *Calculate, reckon, guess.*

Guy. This word has several meanings, but we most often use it colloquially to refer to a man, boy, or individual generally. Some experts regard this use of the word as slang; it should be avoided in standard English.

Hang, hung. The principal parts of *hang* are *hang, hung, hung.* However, when the word refers to the death penalty, the parts are *hang, hanged, hanged.* (The draperies are *hung.* The murderer was *hanged.*)

Have got to. A colloquial and redundant expression for "must," and so on. (I *must* [not *have got to*] do my laundry today.) (See *Got, gotten.*) *Have* is a useful verb and appears in many expressions we use constantly. In standard English we should avoid using such expressions as *have a check bounce, have cold feet, have a lot on the ball, have it in for someone.* In these expressions the *have* is only partly responsible for the colloquialism.

Healthful, healthy. These words are often used interchangeably, but *healthful* precisely means "conducive to health"; *healthy* means "possessing health." In other words, places and foods are *healthful,* people and animals are *healthy.* (I wonder whether he is a *healthy* person because he lives in a *healthful* climate.)

Highbrow. See *Lowbrow, highbrow.*

Home, homey. Do not loosely use *home* for *house.* Do not omit the preposition in such an expression as *I am at home.* Most important, remember that *homey* is a colloquial word for *homelike.*

Human, humane. The word *human* refers to a person. Some especially careful or precise writers and speakers do not use the word alone to refer to man as man; they say or write *human being.* However, the practice of using the word alone as a noun has a long and respectable background. *Humane* means "tender," "merciful," "considerate." (His treatment of the prisoners was *humane.*)

Hunch. This word has acceptable meanings as both verb and noun. In the sense of "a premonition or feeling that something is going to happen," it is informal and should be avoided in standard English.

I.e., e.g., viz., N.B., P.S. These and many other abbreviations commonly appear in writing. Although abbreviations are not recommended for formal writing, many of them are useful shortcuts. For "that is," we use the abbreviation *i.e. E.g.* is an abbreviation meaning "for example." *Viz.* is an abbreviation meaning "namely." *N.B.* stands for Latin *nota bene,* meaning "note well." *P.S.* is the abbreviation for "postscript"; *P.SS.* stands for "postscripts."

If, whether. In standard English, *if* is used to express conditions; *whether,* usually with *or,* is used in expressions of doubt and in indirect questions expressing conditions. (*If* it doesn't snow, we shall go [simple *condition*]. We have been wondering *whether* we would reach our sales quota [doubt]. I asked *whether* the doctor had arrived [indirect question].)

Immigrate. See *Emigrate, immigrate.*

Imply, infer. To *imply* is to suggest a meaning hinted at but not explicitly stated. (Do you *imply* that I am not telling the truth?) To *infer* is to draw a conclusion from statements, circumstances, or evidence. (After that remark, I *infer* that you no longer agree.)

Impractical. See *Unpractical.*

In, into. The former is used to indicate motion within relatively narrow or well-defined limits. (She walked up and down *in* her room for an hour.) *In* is also used when a place is not mentioned. (The airplane came *in* for a landing.) *Into* usually follows a verb indicating motion to a place. (When Marion strode *into* the room, everyone fell silent.)

In back of. This phrase is colloquial for "behind." However, *in the back of* and *in front of* are considered standard terms, although both are wordy. *Behind* and *before* are shorter and nearly always will suffice. (*Behind* [not *in back of*] the office was the storeroom. *Before* [or *in front of*] the house was a tree.)

In line, on line. The first of these idiomatic terms is more widely used than the second throughout the United States. (Jim stood *in line* with the other boys.)

However, *on line* may be used if doing so causes no confusion to your reader or listener. The word *line* appears in expressions that are considered colloquial or dialectal: *come into line* (meaning "to correspond" or "agree"), *get a line on* (meaning "to find out about").

In regards to. Omit the *s* in *regards.* Better yet, substitute *concerning* or *about* for the entire phrase; one word is usually more effective than three (see *Regard, regards*).

In search for, in search of. Both of these expressions are commonly used, but the latter is the preferred idiom.

Individual. See *Party, person, individual.*

Inferior than, to. The former is not standard idiom; the latter is. (This oil is *inferior to* [not *than*] that.)

Ingenious, ingenuous. *Ingenious* means "talented," "resourceful," or "tricky." (This is an *ingenious* computation device.) *Ingenuous* means "innocent," "frank," or "naïve." (Sally is an *ingenuous* little girl.)

Inside of, off of, outside of. The *of* in each of these expressions is superfluous. (*Inside* [not *inside of*] the barn the horses are eating hay. The boy fell *off* [not *off of*] his *tricycle.*) When *inside* and *outside* are not prepositional, the *of* should be included: the *outside of* the house, the *inside of* the tent.

Irregardless, disregardless. Each of these words is an illiteracy. That is, neither is a standard word and neither should be used under any circumstances, formal or informal. The prefixes *ir-* and *dis-* are both incorrect and superfluous in these constructions. Use *regardless.*

Is, was, were. Parts of the verb *to be*. It may help you to remember that *is* is singular in number, third person, present tense. (He [or *She* or *It*] *is* in the room.) *Was* is singular, first or third person, past tense. (I [or *He* or *She* or *It*] *was* in the room.) *Were* can be either singular or plural, second person in the singular and all three persons in the plural, and is in the past tense. (*You* [both singular and plural] *were* in the room. *We* [or *You* or *They*] *were* in the room.) The two most frequent errors in using *to be* are employing *was* for *were,* and vice versa, and using *is* in the first or second person instead of in the third, where it belongs.

Is when, is where. These terms are frequently misused, especially in giving definitions. Grammatically, the fault may be described as using an adverbial clause in place of the noun phrase or clause that is called for. "A subway *is where* you ride under the ground" can be improved to "A subway *is* an electric railroad beneath the surface of the streets." "Walking *is when* you move about on foot" can be improved to "Walking *is the act of* [or *consists of*] *moving* about on foot."

It stands to reason. A cliché.

It's me. Please turn immediately to Section 14b.

Job. This word is frequently and inexactly used in the sense of "achievement." The chief objection to it is its overuse to cover many general and vague meanings. Furthermore, *job* is colloquial when used to mean "affair" and slang when applied to a robbery. In short, *job* is a useful word, but it should be employed carefully and sparingly. Consult your dictionary.

Kid. This word means "a young goat," in which sense it is rarely used. But *kid* in two other senses is one of the most ubiquitous words in the language. We use it to refer to a "child or young person" and we use *to kid* when we mean "to tease, banter, jest with." In both uses the word is dubious in standard English.

Kind of a, sort of a. In these phrases the *a* is superfluous. Logically, the main word (which can be *kind, sort,* or *type*) should indicate a class, not one thing. (*What kind of* [not *what kind of a*] party is this?) Although *kind of* and *sort of* are preferred in this construction, these same phrases are often used colloquially to mean "almost," "rather," "somewhat." (She was *rather* [not *kind of*] weary. Martha was almost [not *sort of*] resigned to going.)

Knock. In the primary sense of "strike" and in several other meanings, *knock* is a legitimate word on any level of usage. We should avoid its use in such phrases and terms as *to knock* (colloquial for "to criticize"), *to knock about* (colloquial for "to wander"), and *to knock down* (colloquial in the sense of "to embezzle" or "to steal"). *Knock off,* meaning "to stop," as in "to knock off work," is ever more frequently heard, but it is still considered colloquial by most authorities.

Lab. Colloquial for *laboratory* (see *Ad*).

Later, latter. The spelling of these words is often confused. They also have different meanings. *Later* refers to time. (He arrived at the office *later* than I did.) For *latter,* see *Former, latter.*

Lead, led. These words show the confusion that our language suffers because of using different symbols to represent one sound. *Lead* (pronounced lēd) is the present tense of the verb and causes little or no difficulty. *Led* (pronounced like the name of the metal) is the past tense and is often misspelled with *ea.* (*Lead* the blind man across the street. He *led* the blind man across the street yesterday.)

Learn, teach. Standard English requires a distinction in meaning between these words. (I'll *learn* the language if you will *teach* me.) *To learn* someone something is an illiteracy.

Least, lest. The former means "smallest," "slightest." The latter means "for fear that." (He did not give me the *least* argument. Give me your picture *lest* I forget how you look.)

Leave, let. Both words are common in several idiomatic expressions implying permission, but *let* is standard whereas *leave* is not. (*Let* [not *leave*] me go with you.)

Legible, readable. These terms are synonymous in the meaning of "capable of being deciphered or read with ease." *Readable* has the additional meaning of "interesting or easy to read." (Your handwriting is *legible*. This book is *readable*.)

Lend. See *Loan, lend.*

Less. See *Fewer, less.*

Lest. See *Least, lest.*

Let. This word, with a primary meaning of "allow," "permit," has many legitimate uses. Such phrases involving *let* as the following, however, are colloquial and should not be used in standard English; *let on* (in the sense of "pretend"), *let out* (as in "school *let out*"), *let up* (meaning "cease"). *To let one's hair down* is both colloquial and trite (see also *Leave, let*).

Liable. See *Apt, liable, likely.*

Like. See Section 20c.

Line. This standard word has several nonstandard uses. It is considered slang in such expressions as *get into line* (meaning both "agree" and "behave properly"); *get a line on; he gave* [*or fed*] *her a line.*

Literally. This word not only is overused but also is confused with *figuratively*. It is an antonym of the latter and really means "not imaginatively," "actually" (see *Figuratively*).

Loan, lend. Many careful writers and speakers use *loan* only as a noun (to make a *loan*) and *lend* as a verb (to *lend* money). Because of constant and widespread usage, *loan* is now considered a legitimate verb to be avoided only in strictly formal English.

Loose, lose, loss. *Loose* means "not fastened tightly." (This is a *loose* connection.) *Lose* means "to suffer the loss of." (Don't *lose* your hard-earned money.) *Loss* means "a deprivation," "a defeat," "a reverse." (The coach blamed me for the *loss* of the ball.)

Lots of, a lot of, a whole lot. These terms are colloquial for "many," "much," "a great deal." The chief objection to their use is that each is a vague, general expression.

Lousy. This word actually means "infested with lice." It is constantly used as a slang expression, however, to mean "dirty," "disgusting," "contemptible," "poor," "inferior," and "well supplied with" (as in "*lousy* with money"). Use it in only the most informal of informal conversations. You can startle or impress your friends by using *pediculous*.

Lowbrow, highbrow. These terms are being used so increasingly in both writing and speaking that presumably they will, in time, be accepted as standard usage. Their status now is that of either slang or colloquialisms, depending upon the authority consulted. For a while, at least, do not use them in formal writing and speaking. *Lowbrow* refers to a person lacking, or considered to lack, cultivated and intellectual tastes. Naturally, *highbrow* is applied to those who do have such attainments. Both terms are frequently used in a derisive or derogatory manner.

Luxuriant, luxurious. The former term refers to abundant growth; *luxurious* pertains to luxury. (The undergrowth was *luxuriant.* The furnishings were *luxurious.*)

Mad. This short and useful word has many acceptable meanings such as "insane," "frantic," and "frenzied." Most authorities consider *mad* to be colloquial when it is used to mean "angry" or "furious." (I was *angry with*—or *furious with*—[not *mad at*] him.)

May. See *Can, may, might.*

Maybe, may be. The former means "perhaps." (*Maybe* you will finish your task early today.) *May be* (two words) is used to express possibility. (It *may be* going to snow today.)

Memorandum. This word, which is of Latin origin and means "short note" or "record of events," has two plurals, both acceptable in standard English: *memoranda, memorandums.* Abbreviations are *memo* (singular) and *memos* (plural).

Might of. An illiteracy. (If you had asked, I *might have* [not *might of*] accompanied you.) (See *Would of.*)

Moral, morale. As an adjective, the former has a meaning of "good," "proper." (Frances' *moral* code was high.) *Morale* refers to a condition, state of being, or attitude. (The *morale* in this college is excellent.)

Most, almost. *Most* is the superlative of *many* and *much* and means "greatest in amount, quality, or degree." *Almost* means "very nearly," "all but." *Most* is colloquial when used for *almost.* (He has *almost* [not *most*] finished his assignment.)

Muchly. An illiteracy. Despite the fact that you may often hear the word, it really doesn't exist—at least not in standard English. Use *much* instead.

Must. As a noun, this word is no longer considered slang by most authorities, but it is tiresomely overused to mean something essential or necessary, as in "This movie is a *must.*"

Neither . . . nor. See *Either . . . or.*

Nice. This is a word with many meanings, including "agreeable," "pleasant," "attractive," and "delightful." Its overuse indicates the need for more specific substitutes.

No place, nowhere. The former is a perfectly sound phrase (There's *no place* like home), but in standard English it cannot be a synonym for *nowhere.* (She could find her purse *nowhere* [not *no place*].) Be certain to spell *nowhere* correctly; *nowheres* is as dialectal as *no place.*

O, oh. The former is usually part of a vocative (direct address), is normally capitalized, and is rarely followed by any mark of punctuation. *Oh* is an interjection, may be followed by a comma or exclamation point, and is capitalized according to the usual rules. (*O* Mickey! You don't really mean that. Yet, *oh,* what hatred we had for him! *Oh,* what a chance!)

Off of. See *Inside of.*

O.K. This everyday term is colloquial or business English for "all right," "correct," "approved." It is occasionally spelled *OK, okay, okeh.* The terms *oke* and *okey-doke* are slang. For the debatable origin of *O.K.*, see any standard dictionary.

Oral, aural, verbal. *Oral* means "spoken." (The order was *oral,* not written.) *Aural* means "received through the ear," or "pertaining to the sense of hearing." (After the concussion, Jane's *aural* sense was below normal.) *Verbal* means "of, in, or by means of words." In such a sentence as "Our contract was *verbal,*" it loosely means "unwritten." *Oral* and *verbal* are often confused in everyday use.

Out loud. *Aloud* is considered more nearly standard English. *Out loud* is colloquial and not entirely idiomatic.

Outside of. See *Inside of.*

Overuse of so. *So* is correctly used as a conjunctive adverb with a semicolon preceding, and it is frequently used between independent clauses with only a comma before it. The chief objection to *so* in such constructions is simply overuse. In constructions like those below, *so* can often be replaced by *therefore, thus, accordingly,* and the like, or predication may be reduced. See Section 48e.

Ineffective: The bridge was out on Route 8, *so* we had to make a long detour on Highway 20.
Improved: Since the bridge was out on Route 8, we had to make a long detour on Highway 20.

In correcting the overuse of *so,* guard against a worse error, that of using another conjunctive adverb with a comma before it and thus writing an unjustifiable comma splice: The bridge was out on Route 8, therefore we had to make a long detour on Highway 20. [Use a semicolon or a period.]

Sometimes *so* is misused when the writer means *so that* or *in order that.*

Ineffective: Do people want the legislators to spend more money *so* they themselves can pay higher taxes?
Improved: Do people want the legislators to spend more money *in order that* they themselves can pay higher taxes?

Paid, payed. *Paid* is the past tense and past participle of the verb *pay.* (He *paid* all his bills promptly.) *Payed* is used only in the sense of to *pay* out a cable or line. (He *payed* out the anchor line slowly.)

Party, person, individual. Except in telephone and legal language, *party* implies a group and should not be used to refer to one person except in a colloquial sense. *Individual* refers to a single, particular person. As nouns, *individual* and *person* are synonymous. As an adjective, *individual* means "single," "separate," and is therefore unnecessary and repetitious when used to modify *person* or when "each" has been used. Both *individual person* and *each individual member* are wordy.

Pass out. In the sense of "to faint" or "to become unconscious," *pass out* is a useful term but, as slang, should not appear in standard English.

Passed, past. The former is the past tense of the verb *to pass;* in its use as a verb, the latter is the past participle. (The car *passed* us at 70 miles per hour. Your troubles are now *past.*) *Pass* is not only a verb; it is also a noun. In one or the other of these two categories, it appears in many expressions that are either colloquial or slangy, among them *a pretty pass, make a pass at, pass out* (which see), *pass up, pass the buck.*

Percent. This word (from Latin *per centum,* meaning "by the hundred") is now spelled as one word. *Percent* is colloquial when used as a substitute for *percentage* (the noun). *Percentage* is colloquial when used in the meaning of "profit" or "advantage," as in "What's the *percentage* in hard work?"

Personal, personnel. The former means "private," "individual." (The employer granted me a *personal* interview.) *Personal* is a much overused word. Perhaps because we wish to belong, to show a close relationship with someone, we say or write such sentences as "He is a *personal* friend of mine." The *personal* should be omitted. *Personnel* means "a body of persons," usually a group employed in any work, establishment, enterprise, or service. (The *personnel* of this firm was [or possibly *were*] carefully chosen.)

Phony. As both adjective and noun, this word is slang. As a quick and easy substitute for "not genuine," "fake," *phony* is so often used that, presumably, it will in time be acceptable in standard English. Until then, no.

Plan on going, plan to go. Both of these expressions are in everyday use, but the former is considered colloquial and idiomatically not so sound as *plan to go.*

Principal, principle. The former means "a sum of money" or "a chief person." As an adjective, *principal* means "main" or "chief." *Principle* is always a noun meaning "a governing rule or truth," "a doctrine." (The *principal* of that school was a man of *principle.*)

Prior than, prior to. Both terms are in common use but only the latter has the sanction of accepted idiom.

Proposition. A mathematical term colloquially much overused for *affair, offer, project, undertaking, proposal,* and similar words.

Quiet, quit, quite. *Quiet* means "still" or "calm." (It was a *quiet* meeting.) *Quit* means "to stop," "to desist." (Did you *quit* working?) *Quite* means "positively," "entirely." (I am *quite* certain there is a burglar in the house.)

Quite a. This phrase is colloquial when used to mean "more than." In standard English avoid using such phrases as *quite a few, quite a bit,* and *quite a party.*

Rabbit, rarebit. A *rabbit* is a rodent of the hare family. In standard English there is no such word as *rarebit*. It frequently appears in the phrase *Welsh rarebit* (a dish of melted cheese on toast) but only because of faulty etymology; the correct phrase is *Welsh rabbit*. *Rare* and *bit,* however, can be correctly used as two words. (That was a *rare bit* of comedy.)

Raise, raze, rise. *Raise* means "to elevate," "to lift." (Please *raise* your eyes and look at me.) *Raze* means "to tear down." (The wreckers will *raze* this building.) *Rise* means "to get up." (When the chairman enters, everyone should *rise*.) Strictly, the word *raise* is never a noun; a few purists therefore consider it colloquial to refer to a *raise* in wages. When referring to bringing up children, *rear, raise,* and *bring up* may all be used. *Rear* is preferred in this connection, although *bring up* is also standard; *raise* is colloquial. To *raise Cain, raise the roof, raise a rumpus,* and *raise the devil* are all slang. *To get a rise out of* someone or something is also slang.

Rang, wrung. *Rang* is the past tense of the verb *ring,* meaning "to give forth a sound." (He *rang* the bell for ten minutes.) *Wrung* is the past tense of the verb *wring,* "to press or squeeze." (She *wrung* out the clothes before hanging them on the line.)

Real. In the sense of "really" or "very," *real* is an impropriety. (Are you *really*—or *very*—[not *real*] certain of your figures?) Adverbial use of *real* is, however, increasing steadily.

Reason is because. In standard English, the construction beginning "the reason is . . ." is followed by a noun or a noun clause usually introduced by *that*. Yet we often hear such a sentence as "I couldn't go; the *reason was because* I had to work." In spite of its form, the construction introduced by *reason was* is a noun clause rather than an adverbial one. But such a use should appear only in colloquial speech. Standard writing requires "I couldn't go; the *reason was that* I had to work."

Reason why. A redundant expression. Omit *why* and, in most constructions, also omit *reason*. "The *reason why* I like this job is the salary I get" can be improved by writing "I like this job because of the salary."

Receipt, recipe. Both words mean "a formula" or "directions for making or preparing something." Fastidious users of the language prefer *recipe,* but in this meaning the terms are interchangeable. *Receipt* also means "a written acknowledgment of something received." It is considered badly overworked business jargon in such an expression as "we are in *receipt* of."

Reckon. See *Calculate, reckon, guess.*

Refer, refer back. *Refer* means "to direct attention" or "to make reference"; therefore, *back* is superfluous. (Please *refer* [not *refer back*] again to my statement.) The same kind of faulty diction is evident in *repeat again* and *return back.*

Regard, regards. The former is used with *as* to mean "consider" or "think." (I *regard* her *as* my best friend.) *In regard to* and *with regard to* are idiomatically sound, but both phrases are wordy and jargonistic. In these same phrases, *regards* is nonstandard. Restrict your use of *regards* to the plural form of the noun *regard* and the singular form of the verb.

Repeat again. See *Refer, refer back.*

Respectfully, respectively. The former means "in a respectful manner." (My detailed statement is *respectfully* submitted.) *Respectively* means "severally" or "in specified order." (*Farewell, au revoir,* and *auf Wiedersehen* are ways of saying good-by in, respectively, English, French, and German.)

Return back. See *Refer, refer back.*

Rise. See *Raise, raze, rise.*

Said, same, such. As an adjective, *said* is used in legal writing but is considered to be jargon in standard English. Unless you're a lawyer (or a lawyer's secretary), avoid such expressions as *said party, said person,* and *said proposal. Same* as a pronoun is also characteristic of legal and business use. Lawyers may insist upon its retention, but businessmen in general and you in particular should avoid such expressions as "check enclosed in payment for *same.*" *Such* may be an adjective, an adverb, and a pronoun—all with standard uses. It is considered colloquial, however, when used in place of a demonstrative. (I could not tolerate *that* [not *such*].) *Such* is also colloquial when used as an intensifier. (She is *a very* [not *such a*] charming person.)

Saw, seen. The principal parts of *to see* are *see, saw, seen. Seen* is improperly used as the past tense; *saw* is incorrect as the past participle. (I *saw* [not *seen*] you yesterday. I *have seen* [not *have saw*] you every day this week.)

Sensual, sensuous. The former refers to gratification of bodily pleasures or appetites. *Sensuous* suggests the appeal of that which is pleasing to the senses. (In his abandon he indulged in every *sensual* excess he could imagine. He loved the *sensuous* music.)

Set. See *Sit, set.*

Setup. In the sense of "an easy victory," this term is slang. More importantly, *setup* is now being used widely to refer to anything related to organization, conditions, or circumstances. (What's the new *setup?*) The term is vague, at best. Try to find something less used and more exact.

Shall, will. Distinctions in the use of *shall* and *will* have largely broken down, but a few careful speakers and writers still observe them. Use *shall* in the first person and *will* in the second and third persons to express simple futurity. (I *shall* go.

You [or He] *will* go.) For emphasis, to express determination, command, intention, or promise, use *will* in the first person and *shall* in the second and third persons. (I *will* speak, no matter what the result may be. You *shall* speak—meaning "you *must* speak.") See Section 16.

Should of. See *Would of.*

Should, would. In general, use *should* and *would* according to the rules for *shall* and *will* (which see). The following may be helpful:

1. *Should* is used to express obligation (I *should* read more than I do); expectation, a corollary of obligation (they *should* be here by this time); condition (if he *should* speak, listen carefully); and simple future, first person only (I *should* like to go).

2. *Would* is used to express habitual action (he *would* walk in the woods every day); condition, *after* a conditional clause (if the weather were good, he would walk in the park); determination (he *would* do it, no matter how much we protested); wish or desire (*would* I had gone with you); and simple future, second and third persons only (he said that he *would* go). If the governing verb is in the past tense, use *would* to express futurity, as above. If the governing verb is in the present tense, use *will:* he *indicates* that he *will* help us. See Section 16.

Sit, set. *Sit,* predominantly an intransitive verb, not requiring an object, has the meaning of "to place oneself." *Set,* predominantly a transitive verb, requiring an object, means "to put" or "to place." (*Set* the book on the table and come *sit* here.) *Set* used for *sit* in the meaning shown is dialectal or an impropriety. However, both words have several special meanings. For example, *set* has an intransitive use: The sun *sets* early tonight.

Snafu. Military slang for "*s*ituation *n*ormal, *a*ll *f*ouled *u*p."

So. See *Overuse of so.*

So as. See *As.*

Sort of a. See *Kind of a.*

Stationary, stationery. The former means "having a fixed or unmoving position." (This rock is *stationary.*) *Stationery* means "paper for writing." (This is new *stationery.*)

Statue, stature, statute. A *statue* is a sculptured likeness. (This is a *statue* of Robert E. Lee.) *Stature* is often use figuratively (a man of moral *stature*). A *statute* is a law. (This *statute* forbids kissing in public.)

Sure. This word is used as adjective or adverb, but it is colloquial in the sense of "surely," "certainly," "indeed." (He was *certainly* [not *sure*] angry with the policeman.) *Sure* is also colloquial in such expressions as *sure enough* (meaning both "certainly" and "real") and *sure-fire* (meaning "certain to be successful"). (See *Be sure and.*)

Sure thing, a. A slang expression.

Swell. This word is not acceptable in standard English as a modifier. It is colloquial when used to mean "stylish," "fashionable," and it is slang when used as a general term of approval meaning "excellent." (That was *an excellent* [not *a swell*] meal.) In the meaning of "conceited," *swelled head* is considered colloquial or slangy.

Take. *Take* is a good, simple, useful word, but it appears in many expressions that are substandard. For example, *take and* is a colloquial and wordy expression. In the sentence, "He *took and* beat the horse unmercifully," *took and* should be omitted. *Take* is colloquial or dialectal in *he took sick, she takes well* (she photographs well), *the day's take* (money or profit received), *take someone for* (cheat), *take it* (withstand difficulty, hardship), *take it lying down* (submit without protest), *take it on the chin* (undergo punishment or pain), *take it out of* (tire, exhaust), *take it out on* (make another suffer), *take on* (show emotion such as sorrow or anger), *take in* (tricky), *take-off* (an amusing or mocking imitation), *taking* (contagious, said of a disease).

Take it easy. A trite expression that is used *ad nauseam.* So, also, is *take my word for it.*

Tasteful, tasty. The former means "having or showing good taste, sense, or judgment." *Tasty* means "flavorful," "savory," "having the quality of tasting good." (The reception was a *tasteful* affair and the food served at it was *tasty.*) *Tasteful* for *tasty* is in rare or archaic use; *tasty* for *tasteful* is colloquial.

Their, there, they're. These simple and common words cause much difficulty, but they are easy to keep straight. *Their* is a possessive pronoun. (This is *their* house.) *There* means "in or at that place." (Were you *there* when she arrived?) *They're* is a contraction of *they are.* (We are disappointed because *they're* not coming.)

Then, than. These words are often confused in writing and sometimes in pronunciation. *Than* is a conjunction used in clauses of comparison. (He worked better today *than* he did yesterday.) *Then* is an adverb of time. (We *then* went to a restaurant.)

Thusly. An illiteracy. Use *thus.*

Till, until, 'til. Each of these words means "up to the time of." *Till* and *'til* (a shortened form of *until*) have the same pronunciation and are more often used within a sentence than at the beginning. *Until* more often appears at the beginnings of sentences and is sometimes considered somewhat more formal than its two synonyms. All three terms are correct in standard English.

To, too, two. Correct use of these words is a matter of careful spelling. *To* is a preposition (*to* the store) and the sign of an infinitive (*to* work). *Too* is an adverb meaning "also" or "overabundance of." (We *too* are working, but Jack is *too* lazy *to* get up.) *Two* is the number after one. (The *two* men were *too* tired *to* go.)

Try and, try to. The correct idiom is *try to.* However, *try and* is in everyday use and has been for a century. Standard English would have you write "*Try to* [not *try and*] finish your work early."

Uninterested. See *Disinterested.*

Unique. This word means "having no like or equal" and expresses absoluteness as do words such as *round, square, perpendicular.* Logically, therefore, the word *unique* cannot be compared; something cannot be "more unique," "less unique," "more round," "less round." If a qualifying word such as *nearly* is used, the illogicality is removed. "This is the *most unique* painting in the museum" is not standard, but "This is the *most nearly unique* painting . . ." is.

Unmoral, amoral, immoral. *Unmoral* means "having no morality," "nonmoral," "unable to distinguish right from wrong." Thus we may say that an infant or a mentally disordered person is *unmoral. Amoral* means "not concerned with moral standards," "not to be judged by criteria or standards of morality." Morons and animals, for example, may be called *amoral. Immoral* means "wicked," "contrary to accepted principles of right and wrong." The acts of thieves, murderers, and embezzlers may be called immoral.

Unpractical, impractical, impracticable. The first two of these terms are interchangeable, although *impractical* is considered by some writers as being more formal. Each means "not practical," "lacking practical usefulness or wisdom." *Impracticable* means "not capable of being carried out, used, or managed." (The piccolo player was a good man but thoroughly *impractical.* The manager considered my plan *impracticable.*)

Until. See *Till.*

Up. This useful little word appears in many verb-adverb combinations (*grow up, give up, take up, use up*). In other phrases it adds nothing to the meaning of the verb; *up* is colloquial in such expressions as *choose up, divide up, finish up, wait up*. *On the up and up* is slang. *Up against* (meaning "face to face with") and *up against it* (meaning "in difficulty") are colloquial. *Up on* (meaning "informed about") and *up to* (meaning "scheming" or "plotting") are colloquial. *Up-and-coming* and *up one's alley* are other phrases to avoid in standard English. *Open up* is wordy in the sense of "give access to" and is colloquial when used to mean "speak freely."

Used to, used to could. In the phrase *used to,* the *d* is often elided in speaking so that it sounds like *use to.* In writing, the *d* must be included. *Used to could* is an illiteracy; write *used to be able.*

Very. *Very,* like *so, surely, too, extremely, indeed,* has been so overused that it has lost some of its value as an intensifier. Use these words sparingly and thoughtfully; consider whether your meaning isn't just as emphatic without them: (You are [very] positive about the matter.) *Very* is used colloquially to qualify participles; formal use has adverbs like *much* or *greatly.* Do not substitute *plenty* or *mighty* for any use of *very.*

Colloquial: I was *very annoyed* with myself.
Formal: I was *much annoyed* with myself.
Colloquial: I am *very torn* between the desire to speak my mind and the desire to keep out of trouble.
Formal: I am *greatly torn* between . . .

Wait on. In the sense of "serve," this is an acceptable phrase. (I have to *wait on* the customers now.) In the sense of "await" or "wait for," the phrase is dialectal or colloquial. (Please hurry; I don't want to *wait for* [not *wait on*] you.)

Want for, want in, want out. The *for* in *want for* is dialectal. (He *wants* [not *wants for*] to see the circus.) Neither *want in* nor *want out* is acceptable in formal English. (The dog *wants to get out* [not *wants out*].)

Way, ways. The former is colloquial when used to mean "away." (The mine is *away* [not *way*] across the state.) The following phrases involving *way* are also colloquial: *in a bad way, come my way* (achieve success), *act the way he does. Ways* is a dialectal substitute for *way* in such an expression as "a long ways to the river."

Well. See *Good, well.*

Where. This is a useful word, but it should not be substituted for *that* in standard English. (We noted *that* [not *where*] the umpire made a mistake.)

Where at. As two words this phrase is redundant for *where.* In standard English avoid such a statement as "Janet did not know *where* she was *at.*"

Whether. See *If, whether.*

Who, whom. The former is the nominative case; the latter, the objective. When in doubt, try as a memory device the substitution of *he* for *who* and *him* for *whom,* since the proper use of *he* and *him* is more easily recognized: I wonder *who* [or *whom*?] I should invite. I should invite *him.* Therefore: I wonder *whom* I should invite. See Section 14f.

Who's, whose. The former is a shortened form of *who is.* (*Who's* ahead in the office pool?) *Whose* is the possessive case of *who.* (*Whose* toes did I step on?)

Will, would. See *Shall, will; Should, would.*

Wise. This word is an acceptable adjective but is nonstandard in such expressions as *a wise guy, get wise to, get wise, put wise to, wise up, wisecrack.*

-wise. This suffix has many standard uses and appears in such fully acceptable words as *clockwise* and *sidewise.* Unfortunately, it has been greatly overused in recent years and appears in scores of awkward and strained neologisms: *ideawise, travelwise, saleswise, timewise.*

Worst kind, worst sort, worst way. Slang terms for *very much, greatly, intensely,* and the like.

Would. See *Should, would.*

Would of, could of, might of, should of. These terms are all illiteracies probably resulting from attempts to represent what is pronounced. In rapid and informal speech, that is, *would have* (*would've*) has the sound of *would of.* In each phrase, *have* should replace *of.*

You all. In the sense of "all of you," this phrase has a recognized and standard plural meaning. When used to refer to one person, it may be considered either dialectal or an illiteracy.

You know. This is a tiresomely overused expression, a conversational filler that really adds nothing to most statements with whch it is used.

EXERCISES

I

Areas of usage. In this exercise, assume that the standard of word choice is that of careful but not overformal or affectedly "fine" American speech or writing. By this standard, each of the sentences below contains one or more questionable expressions. In the space at the left, write a capital letter to indicate that in order to make the sentence acceptable, you would have to substitute (in one or more places): A—the correct form of a word or phrase (for an impropriety or illiteracy); B—a current American expression (for a regional, British, or old-fashioned one); C—a more formal expression (for slang, argot, or jocular usage); D—a fresher or simpler expression (for hackneyed language or occupational jargon); E—a more straightforward or frank expression (for a euphemism, a would-be elegance, or affectedly fine writing). If the sentence fits more than one category, choose the first one it fits.

1. In this crowning victory, the veteran left-hander gave everything he had.
2. I resent your calling me a dropout, being that actually I was thrown out.
3. In the little town where I grew up, a courthouse idler could achieve lasting distinction by unusual distance and accuracy of expectoration.
4. We made two stops to take on petrol during the race.
5. The gathering at Harold's was supposed to be a cram session, but I'm afraid we spent most of the time just goofing off.
6. Having finally reached the top of the divide, we all got out and left the car cool off.
7. Everybody wanted to ride with Claude, because he really drives a boss car.
8. Mr. Powers is out of the office today, but I reckon you can see him tomorrow.
9. I have observed that fanatics or radicals in any political cause tend to prevaricate when it suits their purposes.
10. In response to your inquiry regarding our ability to supply earth-moving equipment immediately, I wish to state that the answer is in the affirmative.

II

Improprieties and mistaken identities. Each sentence in the pairs below may contain careless or faulty diction. In the space at the left, write a capital letter to indicate that of the two sentences: A—the first only is acceptable; B—the second only is acceptable; C—both are acceptable; D—neither is acceptable.

1. I found the book rather *dissatisfying.* I don't like the *hustling and bristling* to and from work in rush-hour crowds.
2. I have nothing to gain by the deal, and my curiosity is entirely *disinterested.* There are usually many causes of an *economical* depression.
3. Football had a *derogative* influence on his study habits. Whether you go or stay is *immaterial* to me.
4. Thanksgiving makes me conscious of *materialistic* things that I usually take for granted. He easily passed the *entry* requirements of the college.
5. The movies supply *vicarious* pleasures. I was interested in the close *contrast* exhibited by many details of their two lives.
6. I was embarrassed by that *phase* of the incident. While in England he *frequented* the British Museum.
7. The two events are entirely *disassociated.* Although you can't see it move, a glacier is in *continual* motion; it never stops.
8. A really accurate *translation* of a poem is impossible. The conductor started the second movement with a *flourish* of his baton.
9. Information *achieved* from libraries is sooner forgotten than that from life. It was truly a *pathetic* case.
10. He *obtained* his goal of getting a job in the circus. He was too *reticent* to take part in sports.

III

Idiomatic usage. Each sentence in the numbered pairs below may contain an example of nonstandard idiomatic usage. In the space at the left, write a capital letter to indicate that: A—the first sentence only is acceptable; B—the second sentence only is acceptable; C—both sentences are acceptable; D—neither sentence is acceptable.

1. I could not agree to his proposal that we nominate Sellers for vice-president. He thought Sellers was the best candidate, but I could not agree with him.
2. I am often impatient with being delayed in expressway jams. My father is often impatient with me.
3. Prior to the final test, we were given several review exercises to study. Of approximately three subjects, he passed only English.
4. When John forgets a date with me, I get angry at him. He is annoyed with me when I am late.
5. I prefer cooked breakfast food over the dry cereals. I don't like this hat, and wish I hadn't bought it during a spur of the moment.
6. Obedience to the traffic laws saves a driver from tickets and fines. Less and less original dramatic programs are broadcast on television.
7. Mother often tells me I am prone toward sloppiness in doing my chores. She always adds that I seem oblivious to her criticism.
8. Statistics show that fewer licenses for horse-drawn vehicles are issued each year. A well-trained horse is always obedient of commands given it.
9. Many people who are expert at swimming are not able to dive well. He was angry that she was unmindful of his wishes.
10. Everybody was surprised to find him capable to play the piano so well. She was astonished that he thought her careless about his feelings.

IV

Figures of speech. Each sentence below contains figurative language (metaphor or simile) that may and may not be effective. In the space at the left, write a capital letter to indicate your judgment of the figurative language. (If the sentence fits more than one category, choose the first one it fits.) A—bad because mixed (combines two or more incompatible images); B—bad because *incongruous or absurd* (produces an effect not intended by the writer); C—bad because trite (weakened by overuse); D—reasonably fresh and effective (or at least not obviously faulty).

1. Collins took the pass over his shoulder and, running like a deer, covered the 50 yards to the goal line unmolested.
2. Many people are prevented by poverty from pursuing the higher fields of education.
3. While we talked, the kittens continued their intricate game, skittering back and forth over the floor like blown leaves.
4. Her smile disclosed a perfect row of teeth that shone like diamonds.
5. The social bridge between them was now so far apart that neither felt like keeping up the correspondence.
6. The poor schoolmaster was destined to be unlucky in love, and after a year his headlong pursuit of Miss Darby ended in flat disappointment.
7. Mrs. Peebles ruled her husband with an iron hand, and during her lectures the unfortunate man couldn't get a word in edgewise.
8. It was one of those stinging cold Arizona nights, with a sky full of the enormous desert stars shuddering and, I imagined, blowing on their hands.
9. From my experience as a player and coach, I would say that poor footwork is the greatest stumbling block in learning to play tennis.
10. The romantic intentions of the summer night were embarrassingly obvious—not a ripple on the dreaming lake, and a little mood music coming from the leaves overhead.

V

The exact word. In each of the following sentences you are to supply the missing word from the list given below it. In the space, write a capital letter to indicate the word that most *exactly* fits the meaning and idiom of the context.

1. I have decided to ignore his criticism entirely, and nothing he can say will ______ me to make a reply. [A–aggravate/ B–irritate/ C–provoke/ D–exasperate/ E–nettle]
2. His failure to show up at the eight o'clock class was a rather frequent ______. [A–event/ B–incident/ C–accident/ D–episode/ E–occurrence]
3. Carrying the surveying equipment proved to be an awkward and exhausting task; before we had gone far I began to wish that I had chosen a less ______ load. [A–heavy/ B–weighty/ C–ponderous/ D–massive/ E–cumbersome]
4. It takes more courage to be patient and persevering under long-continuing ______ than to face a momentary danger boldly. [A–calamity/ B–misfortune/ C–disaster/ D–mischance/ E–catastrophe]
5. Something was preventing the water from entering our part of the irrigation system, and it took us several hours to locate and remove the ______. [A–obstacle/ B–impediment/ C–obstruction/ D–hindrance/ E–barrier]
6. It was some comfort to him that nobody else would ever know, but for a long time his conscience continued to ______ him with having betrayed his better nature by a selfish act. [A–blame/ B–censure/ C–condemn/ D–reprove/ E–reproach]
7. Having been left alone and with nothing in particular to do, he decided to spend the afternoon in an aimless ______ through the surrounding fields and woods. [A–excursion/ B–ramble/ C–tour/ D–trip/ E–jaunt]
8. It is impossible to call a person or family ______ without implying that there is something at least faintly absurd or pretentious about them. [A–polite/ B–urbane/ C–cosmopolitan/ D–genteel/ E–well-bred]
9. These shameless elderly gossips were never known to spare an ounce of charity for anybody outside their own circle, but they spent endless time on one another's aches, pains, and operations in loud expressions of ______. [A–commiseration/ B–sympathy/ C–compassion/ D–condolence/ E–pity]
10. This silly piece of criticism has neither seriousness of argument nor decency of manner, and the writer's comments are to be dismissed as merely ______. [A–trifling/ B–playful/ C–petty/ D–frivolous/ E–insignificant]

THE SENTENCE

All writing of whatever kind—paragraphs, themes, reports, research papers, personal and business letters, and answers to most examination questions—is dependent upon a basic unit of expression, the sentence. Effective sentences, in turn, depend upon (1) a knowledge of sentence structure, what might be called "sentence sense," and (2) experience and practice in reading effective sentences and in phrasing your own.

Talking about the qualities of sentences is an artificial activity. Actually, good sentences are as much a matter of personality and judgment as of rules and requirements. Good sentences will come when you know what you want to say, have some interest in what you know or think, and want to share that knowledge and understanding with your reader.

Naturalness and ease should be primary goals in sentence writing, but it will help to review three major characteristics of good sentences. A sentence should be *correct, clear,* and *effective*. These somewhat vague and general qualities can be pinpointed.

Correctness

First, what in the structure, the form, of a sentence can prevent its being considered correct by customary standards? The three faults usually considered most glaring are *incompleteness* (Section 41), the *comma splice* (Section 42), and the *fused sentence* (Section 43). Learning what these three offenses are and how to correct or avoid them will ensure minimum correctness in sentence structure.

Clearness

Second, what in the form and phrasing of sentences can come between you and your reader, thwarting communication and leaving your reader baffled or annoyed or both? *Clearness* in sentence structure is discussed under the following headings: *misplaced modifiers* (Section 44), *dangling modifiers* (Section 45), *split constructions* (Section 46), *faulty parallelism* (Section 47), *faulty coordination* (Section 48), *faulty subordination* (Section 49), *illogical constructions* (Section 50), *consistency* (Section 51), and *reference of pronouns* (Section 52).

Effectiveness

And, yet, correctness and clearness are only minimum characteristics of a good sentence. If you wish to achieve a varied, flexible, pleasing style that will always be appropriate to your purpose and your readers, consider other qualities that make writing more than just inoffensive and understandable. That is, you must learn also to write *effectively*. Three major violations of effectiveness are discussed in Section 53 (*choppiness*), Section 54 (*lack of unity*), Section 55 (*wordiness*). Avoiding these three kinds of sentence ineffectiveness is, again, a minimum achievement.

These requirements may be reduced to seven statements that cover all the really basic qualities of effective sentences:

1. A sentence should be *complete* (Section 41).
2. A sentence should be *properly punctuated* (Sections 42, 43).
3. A sentence should have its *words in proper order*. (Sections 44, 45, 46).
4. A sentence should be *logical in structure* (Sections 47, 48, 49, 50).
5. A sentence should be *consistent in structure* (Sections 51, 52, 53).
6. A sentence should be *unified* (Section 54).
7. A sentence should be *concise* (Section 55).

Other characteristics of genuinely effective sentences are adequate *transition* between sentences, *parallelism, variety* in length and form, and the *position* and *arrangement* of words in a sentence. Examine each of these last-named topics in every sentence that you compose. Doing so will pay dividends as you acquire ease and naturalness in composing sentences that convey ideas and information with smoothness and grace.

41. INCOMPLETENESS (SENTENCE FRAGMENT)

The word *sentence* can mean "a stated opinion." By this definition, all words, or groups of words, that "make sense" to your reader or listener can be called sentences. But remember these two requirements for a *complete* sentence: (1) It must have both a subject and a predicate (verb) that actually appear or are clearly implied (understood); (2) it must not begin with a connecting word such as *although, as, because, before,* and *while* unless an independent clause follows immediately in the same construction (see Section 9).

This is a complete sentence: *Dick has bought a new jacket.* Omit *Dick* (subject) or *has bought* (verb) and not enough remains to make a full sentence. Also, substituting for *has bought* a compound participle such as *having bought* produces an incomplete statement: *Dick having bought a new jacket.* If a word such as *although* precedes *Dick,* the sentence is incomplete for another reason. The clause, *although Dick has bought a new jacket,* expresses an idea, but it depends on some other statement and is not capable of standing alone. If you don't like Dick, you might write: *Although Dick has bought a new jacket, his appearance has not been improved.*

41a. A PHRASE IS NOT A SENTENCE

A phrase is only part of a full sentence. It should be attached to, or should be expressed within, the sentence of which it is a part. Or the phrase should be made complete in itself by adding what is needed, usually a subject or verb or both.

Incorrect: My last year in high school I studied for hours every night. *Getting ready for college entrance tests.*

Correct: My last year in high school I studied for hours every night, *getting ready for college entrance tests.*

Incorrect: *Winter being mild last year.* I had to start mowing the lawn weeks earlier than usual.

Correct: *Winter being mild last year,* I had to start mowing the lawn weeks earlier than usual.

Winter was mild last year, and I had to start mowing the lawn weeks earlier than usual.

41b. A DEPENDENT CLAUSE IS NOT A SENTENCE

Adverbial and adjective clauses can never stand alone; they always *depend* upon something else for completeness. Correcting a dependent clause fragment often involves no change in wording; sometimes, changing a capital to a small letter and a period to a comma or to no mark at all will correct the error. Sometimes, you may prefer to make a dependent adverbial clause into an independent clause by omitting a subordinating conjunction and to make an independent clause of an adjective clause by changing the relative pronoun to a personal one (see Section 8).

Incorrect: I had no money for the trip. *When suddenly Jack paid me what he had borrowed.* [Adverbial]

Because the course is difficult. We do not advise you to enroll in it. [Adverbial]

Dick has talked with Coach Barnett. *Who thinks Dick's prospects for making the team are good.* [Adjective]

Sue lived in Akron for five years. *From which her family moved to Atlanta.* [Adjective]

Correct: I had no money for the trip. Suddenly Jack paid me what he had borrowed.

Because the course is difficult, we do not advise you to enroll in it.
The course is difficult. We do not advise you to enroll in it.
Dick has talked with Coach Barnett. He thinks Dick's prospects for making the team are good.
Sue lived in Akron for five years, from which her family moved to Atlanta.

41c. A STATEMENT SHOULD NOT BEGIN WITH ONE CONSTRUCTION AND THEN SHIFT TO ANOTHER

You may begin a statement and then, forgetting where you and your thoughts are, keep adding words but stop before giving meaning to the words with which you started. In such an unfinished construction, examine carefully what you have written to discover what is missing.

Incomplete: Some of the students from abroad, not being used to central heating, and also wearing heavy clothes.
Improved: Some of the students from abroad, not being used to central heating, and also wearing heavy clothes, were often uncomfortably warm.

41d. SOME SENTENCE FRAGMENTS ARE JUSTIFIABLE

Many kinds of statements convey a full thought without an actual or implied subject or verb. Such expressions as *Ouch, Hello, Good-by, Never again, But to continue* can and do make clear, often effective, statements. Fragments appear in plays, short stories, and novels because they are mirrors of normal conversation.

Context is important in asking and answering questions and in providing details after a general statement. The following dialogue contains several fragments that are justifiable:

"Where did you get those shoes?"
"At Finchley's."
"On sale?"
"But of course."
"How much?"
"My secret, for now."

You may complain that your instructor marks all fragments (also known as "period faults") as incorrect, even though you may claim to use them for stylistic effect. Most teachers will approve your use of fragments after you have demonstrated your knowledge of sentence completeness.

42. COMMA SPLICE

Writing correctly is difficult now and always has been. You are required to write complete sentences with no unjustifiable fragments. But you are also expected to write full sentences *one at a time*. When your mind is racing or wandering, this is no simple chore.

Like the sentence fragment (period fault), the *comma splice* is an error in sentence construction and a flaw in punctuation. But the splice is no ordinary misuse of the comma; it consists of using a comma to join what really are two sentences. That is, a comma splices (joins) statements that should be separated by a period or joined by a semicolon, a colon, or a conjunction *and* a comma (see Sections 21–25).

42a. UNJUSTIFIABLE COMMA SPLICES

The comma splice, or "comma fault," appears in several forms:

1. Two statements that are related by content but that have little or no actual grammatical relationship.
2. Two related statements, the second of which begins with a personal pronoun whose antecedent is in the first.
3. Two related statements, the second of which begins with a demonstrative pronoun or adjective (*this, that, these,* and so on).
4. Two statements, the second of which contains, or begins with, a conjunctive adverb (*however, then,* and so on).

In order of the faults given above, consider these comma splices:

> A meeting of the Sigma Society is scheduled for tonight, many important items are on the agenda.
> The physician examined the patient carefully, he did not say a word.
> Drive carefully when you near the bridge, this is very narrow.
> I was late for the lecture, however, Mr. James did not scold me.

The comma splice error can be corrected in several ways:

1. Use a period after the first statement and a capital letter at the beginning of the second.
2. Use a semicolon between the statements.
3. Subordinate one of the statements and retain the comma.
4. Insert a conjunction between statements, or as a substitute for the conjunctive adverb, and retain the comma.

Each of the four comma splices above can be corrected by more than one of these methods. However, you should avoid a series of short, jerky sentences; you should never attempt to show a cause-and-effect relationship where it does not exist and without proper subordination.

42b. A COMMA SPLICE IS JUSTIFIABLE WHEN IT IS EFFECTIVE AND APPROPRIATE

An occasional comma splice can be both suitable and stylistically valid. Many writers and professional editors carefully avoid all comma splices of whatever kind; your instructor may urge you to do likewise. Even so, a case can be made for using a comma in such constructions as these:

> I worked, I struggled, I failed.
> That is Alice, this is Betty.
> We are not going to the library, we are going to class.

43. FUSED SENTENCES

A sentence should express only one thought or a group of closely related thoughts. A violation of this principle is writing two complete sentences with no mark of punctuation whatever between them. This grammatical error confuses a reader because the writer has not indicated where one complete thought ends and another begins. Some instructors consider the fused sentence a more serious flaw than the comma splice: the writer of a spliced sentence has at least realized the need for punctuation of some sort, even though what he uses is inadequate and incorrect.

43a. TWO SENTENCES REQUIRE ADEQUATE PUNCTUATION BETWEEN THEM

A sentence is, or should be, a complete, meaningful statement and must usually be followed by a terminal mark, a full stop: period, question mark, exclamation point.

Incorrect: Late that same month the dam broke thousands of people were left homeless in the resulting flood.
After two days they left London for Copenhagen this city is the capital of Denmark.

It is possible to understand these two fused sentences, but lack of separation between their parts causes at least momentary confusion. Each may be written as two separate statements with a period between them. Or, if you wish to connect their ideas more closely, you may use punctuation that is not terminal.

Correct: Late that same month the dam broke. Thousands of people were left homeless in the resulting flood.
After two days they left London for Copenhagen; this city is the capital of Denmark.
After two days they left London for Copenhagen, the capital of Denmark.

43b. A FUSED SENTENCE IS NOT CORRECTED BY PLACING A COMMA BETWEEN ITS PARTS

A comma splice is almost as serious an offense as a fused sentence. A comma is insufficient in a sentence such as this: *He was in California last year he lived in San Diego*. After the word *year* you may *not* use a comma. Your instructor may insist that you use a period or may permit a semicolon, colon, or dash.

44. MISPLACED MODIFIERS

Words in an English sentence have meaning largely because of their position. That is, they have one meaning in one position, another meaning in another position, and little or no meaning in still another position. Some linguists maintain that the true basis of English grammar is word order. "My *first* roommate's name was Bill" has a meaning different from "My roommate's *first* name was Bill." Again, changing the position of only one word results in ideas that are quite unalike: I was invited to a dance *tonight*. I was *tonight* invited to a dance.

Try to keep related words together so that your readers may see the connection you have in mind; try to place every modifier so that logically and naturally it is associated with the word or phrase it modifies.

44a. THE "SQUINTING MODIFIER"

A modifier "squints" when it "looks both ways" and may refer to either of two parts of a sentence. Consider this sentence: The person who can do this *well* deserves praise.

Well may modify either *can do* or *deserves.* You should revise. One way to clear up the confusion is to add *certainly* after *well.* Now the adverb *well* modifies *can do,* and the adverb *certainly* applies to *deserves.* Such a construction involves *juncture,* a term you should consult in Section 10 (Glossary of Grammatical Terms).

Take another example: The repairman who does his work quietly *from the point of view of the housewife* is worthy of praise. The "squinting" italicized phrases should appear at the beginning or end of the sentence, which will still be wordy and awkward but at least understandable.

44b. THE POSITION OF SUCH WORDS AS *EVEN, HARDLY, NOT, ONLY, SCARCELY*

Words such as these are usually associated with the word or phrase immediately following or preceding. In this sentence, *he hardly has enough strength for the work, hardly* may be thought to modify *has;* it should logically modify the adjective *enough.* To remove any possible doubt, write: He has *hardly* enough strength for the work.

Here is a sentence containing eleven words: *Only the foreman told me to finish the job before noon.* In it the word *only* can appear in every position from one through eleven: The *only* foreman told me . . . , the foreman *only* told me . . . , the foreman told *only* me . . . , and so on. The position of *only* will provide eleven somewhat different meanings for the sentence. (Note that placing it in the sixth position causes a split infinitive, perhaps not a very sound idea. See Section 46a.)

44c. THE POSITION OF PHRASES AND CLAUSES

By failing to place phrases as near as they should have to words modified, writers of the following hardly expressed what presumably they intended to:

> Last month the Capitol was closed for alterations to all visitors. [*To all visitors* should appear after *closed;* the resulting sentence will be no gem, but at least confusion will disappear.]
>
> The President discussed everyday affairs and people whom you and I know *as simply as a little child.* [Place the italicized phrase after *discussed* or at the beginning of the sentence.]

45. DANGLING MODIFIERS

Any misplaced word, phrase, or clause dangles in the sense that it hangs loosely within a sentence. The word another word or group of words is intended to modify should never be taken for granted; it should be expressed and it should be placed so that your readers can easily make the intended association.

The term *dangling* applies especially to verbal phrases and elliptical clauses, the correct position of which depends upon logical, careful thinking (see Sections 7, 8).

45a. DANGLING VERBAL PHRASES

Sentences containing dangling verbal phrases may be corrected in three ways: (1) by expanding the verbal phrase to a dependent clause; (2) by supplying the substantive (noun or pronoun) that the dangling phrase *should* modify; (3) by placing the construction so near the supplied substantive that no confusion is possible.

Incorrect: *Walking down the aisle,* the curtain rose. [Participial phrase]
To play tennis well, a good racquet is needed. [Infinitive phrase]
By exercising every day, your health will improve. [Gerund phrase]

Correct: While we were walking down the aisle, the curtain rose.
Walking down the aisle, John saw the curtain rise.
We, walking down the aisle, saw the curtain rise. [This revision is no great improvement because it widely separates subject and verb. See Section 46c.]

The two other incorrect sentences given may also be improved by one of the three methods suggested. Most of us don't mind making an error, but we do dislike being thought incoherent or ludicrous, both of which these sentences definitely are.

When a verbal phrase is used to denote a general action rather than a specific one, it is *not* considered a dangling modifier: *Considering everything,* his suggestion was reasonable.

45b. DANGLING ELLIPTICAL CLAUSES

Ellipsis means "an omission." An elliptical clause is one without a subject, or verb, or both; it dangles unless the implied (understood) subject is the same as that of the main clause.

Incorrect: *When 19 years old,* my grandfather died.
While working last night, the lights went out.
Before thoroughly warmed up, you should not race a motor.

To correct such confused sentences, insert in the dangling clause the needed subject and verb, or change the subject (or subject and verb) in the main clause.

When I was 19 years old, my grandfather died.
When 19 years old, I grieved because my grandfather had died.
While I was working last night, the lights went out.
Before it is thoroughly warmed up, you should not race a motor.
You should thoroughly warm up a motor before you race it.

46. SPLIT CONSTRUCTIONS

Separating, or splitting, closely related parts of a sentence is not always incorrect. But splitting verbs in a verb phrase, the two parts of an infinitive, and a preposition and its object often results in awkwardness and lack of clarity. Whenever possible, keep logically related elements together.

46a. THE SPLIT INFINITIVE

When a word, phrase, or clause comes between the sign of the infinitive, *to,* and a verb, the construction is called a *split infinitive.* Reputable speakers and writers occasionally split an infinitive; consequently, this error is no longer considered as grave as it once was. Also, on rare occasions, you must split an infinitive to make clear and exact what you have in mind. For example, in this sentence, "Martha wants *to really see* Tod in person," moving *really* to any other place in the sentence would change the meaning or weaken the effectiveness of the sentence.

Normally, however, no sound reason exists for putting an adverb or phrase or other group of words between *to* and a verb. "He requested us to *as soon as possible* leave the building" would be clearer and more natural if the italicized words were moved to the end of the sentence.

46b. SEPARATING THE PARTS OF A VERB PHRASE

An auxiliary verb and main verb form a frequent pattern in English (see Section 16). Splitting such a verb phrase is rarely effective and usually results in an awkward construction. In sentences such as the following, the italicized words should be brought together:

There was the boy we *had* before we left *seen* in the park. [There was the boy we *had seen* in the park before we left.]

This building *has,* although it is hard to believe, *been* here for more than a century. [This building *has been, or* Although it is hard to believe, this building *has been.*]

46c. THE UNNECESSARY SEPARATION OF SUBJECT AND VERB, PREPOSITION AND OBJECT

Separation of such elements is occasionally justifiable. But in awkward and generally ineffective sentences like the following, the italicized elements should be brought together:

Jack, as soon as he heard the question, *raised his hand.* [Subject and verb]

Mabel crept *into,* although she was terrified, *the frail canoe.* [Preposition and object]

Mary *asked,* even before I could finish, *what I really meant.* [Subject and object]

46d. COORDINATE ELEMENTS SHOULD BE PLACED TOGETHER

When two clauses or phrases of approximately equal strength and importance are used in a sentence, avoid putting one at the beginning of the sentence and the other at the end. The italicized phrases and clauses in these sentences should be brought together and be joined by *and:*

Although he was an ardent golfer, he could never break 90, *although he practiced daily.*

With fair weather, we should have a pleasant journey, *with good luck.*

47. FAULTY PARALLELISM

In writing, the word *parallelism* suggests "similarity," "close resemblance." When two or more ideas in a sentence are related in form and purpose, they can and should be phrased in the same grammatical form.

> Jill is *sweet* but *noisy*. [Words]
> Gray loves to read both *at home* and *at school*. [Phrases]
> Joy was shocked when she discovered *that one tire was flat* and *that the jack was missing*. [Clauses]

47a. SENTENCE ELEMENTS COORDINATE IN RANK SHOULD BE PARALLEL IN STRUCTURE

An infinitive phrase should be coordinate with an infinitive phrase, a dependent clause with a dependent clause, and so on.

> Harry liked *to swim* and *to fish*. [Not Harry liked *to swim* and *fishing*. But the second *to* can be omitted, if desired.]
>
> Ned hoped *that he might earn a good reputation* and *that he might make a lot of money*. [Not Ned hoped that he *might earn* a good reputation and *to make* a lot of money.]

47b. PARTIAL PARALLELISM

Make certain that *each* element in a series is similar in form and structure to *all* others in the same series.

> Steve has worked as a camp counselor, tennis coach, and has served as a bank teller. [Revise this sentence to read: Steve has worked as a camp counselor, tennis coach, and bank teller.]
>
> That TV play was dramatic, exciting, and had an involved plot. [Revise this sentence to read: That TV play was dramatic, exciting, and involved in plot.]

47c. MISLEADING PARALLELISM

The same structural form should not be used for sentence elements of unequal value. Be especially careful in handling a series of elements that may appear to modify the same element when they are not actually parallel.

Ineffective: They left quickly, and they had a good automobile.
For your sake, for $25 I will assist you.
We bought that set from a local dealer and with a good walnut finish.

Improved: They left quickly in a good automobile.
For your sake, I will assist you to the extent of $25.
We bought that set from a local dealer; it has a good walnut finish.

47d. SENTENCE ELEMENTS FOLLOWING CORRELATIVE CONJUNCTIONS SHOULD BE PARALLEL IN FORM

The four common pairs of correlatives are *both-and, either-or, neither-nor,* and *not only-but also*. Each member of each of these pairs should be followed immediately by the same grammatical form: two words, two similar phrases, two similar clauses.

Faulty: I *neither* have the time *nor* the money to make the trip.
Either you can read the story at the library *or* in your own room.
Not only when I am tired *but also sick,* I like to watch TV.
Improved: I have *neither* the time *nor* the money to make the trip.
You can read the story *either* at the library *or* in your own room.
Not only when I am tired *but also* when I am sick, I like to watch TV.

48. FAULTY COORDINATION

The adjective *coordinate* means "of equal importance or rank." If you think carefully, you can express your ideas in constructions which will show their varying importance; you can subordinate minor ideas so that important ones may be emphasized.

Excessive coordination is monotonous, often childish, frequently ineffective. Inaccurate and illogical coordination will give your readers incorrect impressions of the relationship of your ideas and their relative degrees of significance.

48a. STRINGY, "RUN-ON" SENTENCES

Do not overwork the compound sentence. An immature writer, such as a college student is striving not to be, might say, "We bought a color TV set, and it was a beauty, and it had a 21-inch screen." Such a sentence is strung out, it runs on and on. As a mature writer, you should learn to reduce predication, that is, to convert an independent to a dependent clause, change a phrase to a word, and so on: We bought a beautiful color TV set with a 21-inch screen. (See Section 55.)

48b. "SEESAW" SENTENCES

"Seesaw" sentences take their name from the familiar playground device. Such sentences move alternately up and down and quickly become monotonous. A passage such as this cries out for reduced predication (see Section 48a):

> We thought of going to a dance, but we didn't have enough money. Next we decided to take a walk, but a heavy rain prevented that. We bought some soft drinks, and we went to John's house to watch TV. Soon John started snoring, and I became bored and restless.

48c. INACCURATE COORDINATION

The *exact* coordinating conjunction is required to relate two sentence elements. For example, do not use *and* if *but* is the exact connective.

> Joe wanted to go to the game, *but* [not *and*] he had to study.
> We had an interruption, *or* [not *but*] we would have finished sooner.

48d. FALSE COORDINATION: A RELATIVE CLAUSE IS NOT JOINED TO ITS PRINCIPAL CLAUSE BY *AND, BUT,* OR *OR.*

And, but, or, and other coordinating conjunctions may properly connect only elements of equal rank. The most frequent and most distressing violation of this principle is the so-called *and which* construction. Never use *and which* or *that, but which* or *that, and who, but who,* unless you have written a preceding *which, that,* or *who* clause.

This is a beautiful tennis court, *and that* we enjoy using. [The simplest method of correcting this sentence is to omit *and* and also the comma, since the clause is restrictive. Or you can supply a preceding *that* clause: This is a beautiful tennis court that is open to all and that we enjoy using. Even better, cut out some of the deadwood: We enjoy playing tennis on this beautiful court.]

48e. THE OVERUSE OF *SO* AS A CONJUNCTION

So is a good and useful word but it comes to mind *so* easily and *so* often (have you noticed?) that is is often overused. To avoid a plethora of *so*'s, occasionally substitute such a connective as *accordingly, so that, therefore, thus.* One or more of these connectives could substitute for *so* in such a series of monotonous statements as this:

He didn't have a date, *so* he didn't plan to go to the dance.
He began to feel lonely in his room, *so* he went to the library.
He soon grew bored, fell asleep, and *so* got little work done.

49. FAULTY SUBORDINATION

The term *subordination* means "the act of placing in a lower class or rank." When a writer selects one idea for primary emphasis in a sentence, he automatically decides to subordinate others in the same sentence. If he doesn't, his sentences will appear in primer style like those of children just learning to talk (see Section 48a).

Even though you can detect what is probably a main idea and what is subordinate, you will still have trouble unless you can distinguish between main and dependent clauses, between clauses and phrases, between phrases and single words (see Section 55).

Careful, thoughtful, mature writing normally contains much subordination. But errors in the use of subordination are easy to make. The following are some major pitfalls to avoid:

49a. A COORDINATE IDEA IN A SUBORDINATE FORM

Undesirable: He was short and fat, *while* his sister was tall and slender.
Born in Ohio in 1935, he became a resident of Utah in 1970.
Improved: He was short and fat, *but* his sister was tall and slender.
He was short and fat; his sister was tall and slender.
He was short and fat, *whereas* his sister was tall and slender.
He was born in Ohio in 1935, *but* became a resident of Utah in 1970.
He was born in Ohio in 1935 *and* became a resident of Utah in 1970.

49b. THE MAIN IDEA OF A SENTENCE IN A SUBORDINATE FORM; A SUBORDINATE IDEA IN A MAIN CLAUSE

Upside-down subordination (an accurate, expressive term) exists when an idea of less importance is placed in a main clause and a more important idea in a subordinate clause. Sometimes it is difficult to determine which is which. Usually, the most dramatic incident and the effect, rather than the causes, are major ideas.

Preliminaries, such as time and place, are usually minor (or at least less important) considerations.

Ineffective: We were getting tired of walking when suddenly we saw an oncoming car.
I was halfway across the river when I saw a water moccasin.
Improved: When we were getting tired of walking, we saw an oncoming car.
When (just as) I was halfway across the river, I saw a water moccasin.

49c. EXCESSIVE SUBORDINATION

Sentence elements should be suitably linked, but they should not be built like an accordion or, to vary the simile, like stairs—one step attached to the one just above.

Ineffective: These are orchids that were grown in Hawaii, where there is an excellent climate, and which were flown here today.
Improved: These orchids, grown in Hawaii where there is an excellent climate, were flown here today.
These orchids, grown in Hawaii's excellent climate, were flown here today.

50. ILLOGICAL CONSTRUCTIONS

Construction in sentence writing refers to the grouping of words with other words or word formations. An *illogical construction* involves a grouping of words that (1) is contrary to reason, (2) violates some principle of regularity, (3) fails to make good sense, (4) omits an important word or words, (5) adds an element which has no grammatical function, (6) substitutes a dependent clause functioning as one part of speech for another.

No wonder there are so many types of illogical constructions: our minds are often inadequate, but they are all we have for thinking.

You can expect your readers to give careful attention, but you cannot expect them to untangle mixed and involved constructions or to correct your mistakes in logic. (Your instructor will do precisely this, but try to avoid the penalty he will inflict for having to do so.)

The six kinds of illogical and mixed constructions just mentioned can be broken into ten groups for careful examination.

50a. OMISSION OF A NECESSARY VERB

In both speaking and writing, we often omit words without necessarily being illogical or unclear. "He always has worked hard and always will [work hard]" is understandable without the bracketed words. But it is doubtful that the following sentence could be considered complete: The floor is swept and the dishes washed. In this sentence, *is* is understood to accompany *washed*. But *dishes is washed* is wrong. We should write: The floor is swept and the dishes *are* washed.

I never have and probably never will write good letters. [The word *written* should be added after have.]

50b. OMISSION OF CERTAIN WORDS ESSENTIAL FOR THE CLEAR EXPRESSION OF MEANING

If a necessary article, pronoun, conjunction, or preposition is omitted, your meaning will not be clear or, worse, may be misinterpreted.

The President and Chief Executive received us. [This sentence may mean that one person is both President and Chief Executive. If you mean to indicate two people, add *the* after *and.*]

I have interest and regard for your work. [Add *in* after *interest.*]

She asked that question be repeated. [Add another *that* before *question.*]

50c. OMISSION OF WORDS NECESSARY IN A COMPARISON

Doubtful: He is so wealthy.
Your report was the greatest success.
His feet are bigger than any boy in town.

Clearer: He is quite wealthy.
He is so wealthy that he never needs to think about money.
Your report was a great success.
Your report was the greatest success of any received thus far.
His feet are bigger than those of any other boy in town.

50d. CONFUSING BLENDS

Certain blends may creep into anyone's writing. *Regardless* and *irrespective* are good words but are often faultily blended into *irregardless. In spite of* and *despite* may be illogically blended into *despite of: Despite of* what you say, I am not convinced. Blending *where* (meaning *at* or *in which*) with *at which* results in expressions such as "*Where* does she live *at*?" and "The town *where* I live *in*."

50e. MIXED OR DOUBLE COMPARISON

A confused construction may occur when a writer tries to include two comparisons in the same statement. Good usage permits a double comparison in the same sentence but only when the second appears after the first has been completed.

Illogical: The Battle of Stalingrad was *one of the greatest if not the greatest* single conflict of all time.

Preferable: The Battle of Stalingrad was *one of the greatest* single conflicts of all time, *if not the greatest.*

50f. IT SHOULD BE CLEAR WHETHER AN OBJECT OR TERM BEING COMPARED IS OR IS NOT PART OF A CLASS OR GROUP

Avoid including within the class or group the object or term being compared, if it is part of the group. Use the word *other*.

Illogical: Helen is prettier than any girl in the school.
Clear: Helen is prettier than any other girl in the school.

When the superlative degree is involved, do not use *other;* this degree indicates that the object compared is included within the group.

Illogical: Helen is the prettiest of all the other girls in the school.
Clear: Helen is the prettiest of all the girls in the school.

50g. DOUBLE NEGATIVES

Everyday speech is filled with expressions such as "haven't scarcely" and "can't help but." These are forms of what is called the *double negative,* two negative terms in the same statement. The double negative was used repeatedly by Chaucer, Shakespeare, and many other great writers of the past. It still appears regularly in correct French. Double negatives in English today, however, are considered out of style and unacceptable.

You are not likely to write, or often hear, such expressions as "I didn't see nobody" and "I didn't get none." You should avoid such commonly used and less obviously illiterate expressions as "I did *not* have *but* two," "one *can't* help *but*," "*not scarcely* enough," and "*not hardly* any."

50h. USING AN ADVERBIAL CLAUSE AS A NOUN CLAUSE

Dependent clauses function as parts of speech; to substitute an adverbial clause for a noun clause is as illogical as to use an adverb in place of a noun.

Dubious: *Because she had no new dress* was the reason Joy stayed at home.
Eleanor noted *where the paper says* that it will snow tonight.
Correct: Joy stayed at home *because she had no new dress.*
That she had no new dress was the reason Joy stayed at home.
Eleanor noted *that the paper says* it will snow tonight.

50i. USING AN ADVERBIAL CLAUSE IN PLACE OF A NOUN OR NOUN PHRASE

This suggestion is closely related to that given in Section 50h and is made for the same reason. *When, where,* and *because* clauses are chief offenders in this form of illogicality.

Dubious: Stealing is *when* (is *where*) one takes the property of another without permission and with stealth.
My high fever was *because* I was in a weak condition.
Clear: Stealing is taking the property of another without permission and with stealth.
Stealing is the act of taking the property . . .
My weak condition caused my high fever.
That I was in a weak condition was the cause . . .

50j. A NOUN CLAUSE, NOT A SENTENCE, SHOULD BE THE SUBJECT OR COMPLEMENT OF *IS* AND *WAS*

A quotation may be the subject or complement of *is* and *was:* "When I have fears that I may cease to be" is a line from Keats' famous poem. Ordinarily, however, you should convert a sentence into a noun clause (or, rarely, a noun phrase) in this construction.

Illogical: I had lost my nerve was the reason I did not try.
Fred's only hope is he will get his allowance today.

Improved: The reason that I did not try was that I had lost my nerve.
Fred's only hope is that he will get his allowance today.
Fred has only one hope: getting his allowance today.

51. CONSISTENCY

Consistency in a sentence means that its parts are in agreement, are similar, and that they must remain so unless there is good reason for shifting them. You should be consistent (avoid shifts) in tense, subject and voice, number, person or class of pronouns, and figures of speech.

51a. UNNECESSARY SHIFTS IN TENSE

Tense (see Section 17) indicates the time of a verb: past, present, future, present perfect, and so on. Do not shift unnecessarily from past time to present or from present to past or back and forth between the two.

Jill was striding along when suddenly a motorcycle turned the corner. It *careens* wildly down the street, twisting as if its rider *is* unconscious. Jill leaped to the sidewalk. [Change *careens* to *careened, is* to *were.*]

51b. SHIFTING THE SUBJECT OR VOICE IN A SENTENCE

Voice (see Section 18) is a term indicating whether the subject is acting (active) or is acted upon (passive). Consistency in voice within a sentence usually removes a major cause of shifts in subject. Ordinarily you should have one subject in a sentence and should use one voice (the active voice is usually more effective). After you select them, stay with them throughout the sentence.

Faulty: The furnace burns little coal, and Joe says it is fully reliable.
As you look across the street, lighted windows can be seen.
Improved: Joe says that the furnace burns little coal and is fully reliable.
As you look across the street, you can see lighted windows.

51c. UNNECESSARY SHIFTS IN NUMBER

A common error in the use of number is a thoughtless shift from plural to singular or from singular to plural, or failure to make pronouns and antecedents agree in number.

A small child can be a joy, but *they require* constant attention. [Change *they* to *it* or *he* or *she, require* to *requires.*]

If men really try their best, *he is* bound to succeed. [Change *he* to *they* and *is* to *are.*]

51d. SHIFTING THE PERSON OR CLASS OF PRONOUNS

A shift in pronoun reference violates the general rule that pronouns and antecedents must agree in person. The most common occurrence of this fault is shifting from the third person to the second.

If *one* tries hard enough, *you* will usually succeed. [*One* is an indefinite pronoun in the third person; *you* is a personal pronoun in the second person. The sentence should read: "If *you* try hard enough, *you* . . ." or "If *one* tries hard enough, *he* . . ."]

51e. SHIFTS IN FIGURES OF SPEECH

You should not change suddenly from literal speech to figurative language or vice versa. When you do use a figure of speech, you should not suddenly shift the figure (see Section 38d). By not sustaining one figure of speech, we obtain such an inconsistent and confused statement as this:

> She got into a rut and felt all at sea when she lost her job. [Whoever *she* is has trouble, but we can be of little help because we are laughing too hard at the weird description of her predicament. Perhaps this will be an improvement: She felt depressed and uncertain when she lost her job.]

52. REFERENCE OF PRONOUNS

The word *reference* is used with pronouns and their antecedents to indicate the relationship between them. A pronoun *refers* to an antecedent; the latter is *referred* to by a pronoun. The relationship of a pronoun to its antecedent must be clear and unmistakable.

52a. DOUBLE REFERENCE FOR A PRONOUN

Double reference occurs when there are two possible antecedents for a pronoun. Such ambiguous reference can be corrected by (1) repeating the antecedent, (2) using a synonym for the antecedent, (3) changing sentence construction.

Not clear: She took the eggs from the cartons and placed them on the counter.
Better: She took the eggs from the cartons and placed the cartons [or the *eggs*, if that is what you mean] on the counter.
She took the eggs from the cartons and placed the latter on the counter.
She removed the eggs and placed the cartons on the counter.

52b. IMPLIED REFERENCE FOR A PRONOUN

Implied reference occurs when an antecedent is not actually expressed and must be inferred from the context (what precedes or follows). The most common form of implied reference is using *this, that, what,* and *which* to refer to an entire preceding statement rather than to some specific word (usually a noun) in that statement. Such a fault may be corrected by (1) summing up the idea of a preceding statement in a noun that then becomes the antecedent, (2) making the statements coordinate, (3) rephrasing the sentence.

Not clear: Her sister is a nurse. *This* is the profession she intends to enter.
Better: Her sister is a nurse. *Nursing* is the profession she intends to enter.
Her sister is a nurse; she intends to be one too.
Because her sister is a nurse, she intends to study nursing also.

52c. VAGUE REFERENCE FOR A PRONOUN

Every pronoun (especially *that, these, which, those, it*) should refer clearly to its antecedent or should be made clear by some other statement in the sentence.

Not clear: Janet's remark gave Joe *that* sinking feeling.
In this editorial *it* states that taxes are increasing.
Better: Janet's remark gave Joe a sinking feeling.
Janet's remark depressed Joe.
Janet's remark gave Joe that sinking feeling which comes from despair.
This editorial states that taxes are increasing.
That taxes are increasing is the theme of this editorial.

52d. INDEFINITE USE OF *YOU, IT, THEY*

In informal speech it is permissible to use such an expression as "*you* can always try harder," even though no particular person or group is addressed. Everyday speech is filled with statements such as "*it* says on the radio it will snow tonight" and "in this town *they* have plenty of fun."

In writing, however, it is preferable to use *one* or *person* rather than *you* if you wish to refer to no particular individual or group. Also, *it* should usually have an appropriate antecedent, unles you are using the impersonal *it* (*it* is raining). *They* should always have a definite antecedent.

Undesirable: When *you* become a Girl Scout, *you* learn many interesting facts.
In this TV program *it* showed the horrors of drug addiction.
They say that men prefer blondes.
Better: When *one* [or a *girl*] becomes a Girl Scout, *she* learns many interesting facts.
This TV program showed the horrors of drug addiction.
Some people say that men prefer blondes.

52e. THE PRONOUN *IT* AND IMPERSONAL *IT*

Using impersonal *it* (see *Expletive* in Section 10) and the pronoun *it* in the same sentence may cause confusion.

Vague: We can send the refrigerator today, or we can keep it in the factory for a few days if *it* is necessary.
Better: We can send the refrigerator today, or we can keep *it* for a few days.

In informal English, *it* sometimes refers to an idea instead of a single antecedent.

Informal: He was nervous, but he tried not to show *it*.
Formal: He was nervous, but he tried not to show *uneasiness*.

53. CHOPPINESS

An occasional short sentence is effective. A series of short sentences not only is monotonous but often gives unwanted emphasis to some comparatively unimportant ideas that should be subordinated.

53a. A SERIES OF SHORT, JERKY SENTENCES

Evaluate the ideas in short, jerky sentences and then coordinate or subordinate them in a longer unified sentence.

Faulty: It was dark. She was afraid to enter the room. She called her brother. He did not answer her. She was more terrified than ever.

We have an eighty-acre farm located in southern Virginia. Besides the eighty acres, we lease a neighbor's farm of fifty acres. Our farm is in the rolling country. We have to terrace our land. On our farm we have a small wood. This wood has a creek running through it. There are two hills on both sides of our farm. We therefore call our farm "Green Valley Farm." Our farm is shaped like the state of Texas. The creek we call the Little Rio Grande.

Better: Because it was dark, she was afraid to enter the room. When she called her brother, he did not answer her, and consequently she was more terrified than ever.

In southern Virginia we have an eighty-acre farm, to which we have added fifty more acres leased from a neighbor. The rolling land, which we have to terrace, is flanked by two hills; hence the name "Green Valley Farm." Running through a small wood on our property is a creek which, because the farm is shaped like the state of Texas, we call the Little Rio Grande.

53b. A SERIES OF SENTENCES CONTAINING SHORT, JERKY INDEPENDENT CLAUSES

"Correcting" a series of short, jerky sentences by combining them into compound sentences is no improvement. Short jerky clauses can be as ineffective as short, jerky sentences (see Section 48b).

Faulty: I work in a supermarket, and my job is stocking shelves. I have many friends there, but perhaps my best friend is Warren. He has a good disposition, which I don't.

There were two ways to reach the cone: one was by cable car, the other was by car and foot. Mother and I chose the latter. The road was under construction; once we had to wait for a load of stone to be unloaded before we could pass.

Improved: I work in a supermarket where I stock shelves. Of all my friends there, Warren, who has the good disposition I lack, is perhaps the best.

Of the two ways to reach the cone, one by cable car and the other by car and foot, Mother and I chose the latter. The road was under construction, and once we had to wait for a load of stone to be unloaded before we could pass.

54. UNITY

Unity means "oneness, singleness of purpose." A sentence should contain a single thought or a group of closely related thoughts.

Unity has little to do with length; a long sentence may be unified and a short one ununified. This long sentence forms a unit of thought: Although Lee liked her fellow employees, especially Mary Ellen and Harvey, she was tired of working and decided to resign and marry Henry. But this short sentence lacks unity: Mary Ellen was a good worker, and she had a friend named Henry.

54a. RAMBLING SENTENCES WITH MANY DETAILS

Faulty: He was reared in Southport, a village in Connecticut, which has only about 1,000 inhabitants, but which has a famous yacht club, three churches, an excellent public library, several tree-lined residential streets, and a good motel, being located just off U.S. Highway 95.

As I grew older, my desire to play basketball grew also, and when I entered high school I was too small to play my first two years of school, being only five feet tall, so I had to sit on the bench, but later in high school I began to grow, and before I graduated my senior year I was playing center on the first team, for I had grown 13 inches in two years.

Improved: He was reared in Southport, Connecticut, a village of about 1,000 inhabitants which is located just off U.S. Highway 95. Southport has several tree-lined residential streets, an excellent public library, a motel, three churches, and a famous yacht club.

Although my interest in basketball had grown with the years, I discovered upon entering high school that my physical growth had not kept pace with my desire to play. For two years my five-foot frame glumly occupied the bench. That before I graduated I was playing center on the first team I contend is due to a genuine, if familiar, miracle: in the years between I had grown 13 inches.

54b. UNRELATED IDEAS IN THE SAME SENTENCE

You can achieve unity in a sentence containing unrelated ideas by showing some evidence of relationship or by subordinating one idea. If the ideas are not closely related and relationship cannot logically be indicated, place them in separate sentences: If no relationship whatever is evident, omit one of the ideas.

Faulty: His father was a jolly man, and he was a good doctor.
Improved: His father, a jolly man who cheered up his patients, was a good doctor.
His father was a jolly man. He was also a good doctor.

55. CONCISENESS

Concise means "brief," "condensed," "to the point." In sentence structure, *conciseness* implies that much is said in few words. See Section 39j.

Good writing results from a wealth of ideas and economy in words, not from scarcity of thought and a flood of words. Even fairly well-constructed sentences can be improved by removing nonessential words, by using direct word patterns, by economizing on modifiers. A sentence such as "My typing had the effect of making the boss regret the decision that had led him to hire me" can be shortened to "My typing made the boss regret hiring me"—a reduction from nineteen words to eight.

55a. REDUCING PREDICATION

Reducing predication means decreasing the number of words used to make a statement. Consider these suggestions:

1. Combine two short sentences into one.

From: He was a mechanic in a repair shop. He specialized in carburetor adjustment.
To: He was a garage mechanic, specializing in carburetor adjustment.

2. Reduce a compound or complex sentence to a simple sentence.

From: Sarah Bernhardt was for many years an excellent actress, and everyone admired her talent.
Everyone admired the talent of Sarah Bernhardt, who was for many years an excellent actress.
To: Everyone admired the talent of Sarah Bernhardt, for years an excellent actress.

3. Reduce a clause to a phrase.

From: a haze that resembled the color of smoke
To: a haze the color of smoke

4. Reduce a phrase to a single word.

From: a haze the color of smoke
To: a smoke-colored haze

5. Reduce two or more words to one.

From: a foreman in the Department of Shipping
To: a shipping foreman

55b. UNNECESSARY DETAILS

Using unnecessary details is known as *prolixity*. A prolix sentence obscures or weakens the main idea.

Wordy: Last winter the intramural squash tournament was won by Central High's Barry Stebbins with a racquet he had purchased two months before from a friend of his who had bought a new one made of catgut and who sold Barry his old one for $8.50.
Improved: Last winter the intramural squash tournament was won by Central High's Barry Stebbins with a racquet he had bought from a friend for $8.50.
Still better: Last winter Central High's Barry Stebbins won the intramural squash tournament with a second-hand racquet.

55c. USELESS REPETITION OF AN IDEA

The needless repetition of an idea without providing additional force or clearness is called *tautology*. This flaw is obvious in the following sentence: This entirely new and novel innovation in our program will delight our TV viewing audience; it has just been introduced for the first time and will cause pleasure to many people who will be watching.

Faulty: Peggy was anxious for Jack to succeed and eager that he do so.
In all necessary essentials the work is completed and finished.
Improved: Peggy was eager for Jack to succeed.
In all essentials the work is completed.

EXERCISES

I

Sentence recognition. In each of the numbered passages below, *printed here without internal punctuation,* you are to count the sentences. Some of the passages are incomplete (sentence fragments). In the space at the left of each item, put a capital letter to indicate that the passage contains: A—one sentence, B—two sentences, C—three sentences, D—four or more sentences, E—no sentence (a sentence fragment).

1. Ever since primitive man decided that it was easier to raise his own meat than to go out and hunt wild game there have been herdsmen and farmers who have had to build fences which moreover had to be maintained.
2. Fence building and fence repairing whether they concern stone walls living thorn hedges rail fences barbed wire or electric barriers to be installed and kept in good condition.
3. About the time young Abraham Lincoln was splitting oak and walnut logs into rails for "worm" fences middle western farmers began to hear of a small thorny tree native to the Arkansas River region that could be grown in dense hedges to enclose horses cattle sheep and hogs because the Osage (Wazhazhe or "war people") Indians inhabited that region it was called the Osage Orange.
4. The Osage orange is a medium-sized tree occasionally it reaches 50 feet in height and two feet in diameter it has glossy simple leaves they are about twice as long as broad.
5. The twigs armed with many straight stout sharp thorns about three-quarters of an inch long and orange-brown in color.
6. The large wrinkled orange-like green fruit four or five inches in diameter as well as the leaves and twigs contain a milky juice that is quite bitter commonly known as "hedge apples" these heavy and hard fruits are used by boys as missiles for mimic warfare and other purposes they are not edible.
7. The only tree of its kind in the world although it is distantly related to mulberries and figs and silkworms feed as readily on its leaves as on those of the mulberry.
8. Some of these trees have yellowish male flowers which bear pollen that is carried by bees to other trees with greenish female flower heads the ones which produce the "oranges."
9. Growing well on many kinds of soil throughout most of the United States sprouts from roots or shoots grown from seed or cuttings in nurseries are planted in one or two rows several inches apart where a hedge fence is wanted once or twice a year these are trimmed to form a dense hedge about four feet high and two feet wide the "whips" or sprouts being sometimes planted at an angle to create an interwoven lattice-like living fence.
10. If farmers neglect the trimming the hedges grow rapidly to become havens for birds and other wildlife the trees so produced however are valuable as posts for wire fences because Osage orange is more durable in the soil than any other wood many such fences having lasted more than 50 years without a single rotten post since they occupy and shade too much valuable cropland most such overgrown hedges have been removed in recent years.

II

Fragments, comma splices, fused sentences. In each pair of sentences, one is faulty. Faulty sentences are of three kinds: (1) sentence fragments, (2) comma splices, (3) fused sentences. Find the faulty sentences in the numbered items and on a separate sheet rewrite each in an acceptable form. Then indicate the nature of your revisions by inserting in the space on the left a capital letter to show that the item contains: A—a sentence fragment that could be best corrected by changing the form of one word (changing a participle to a finite verb, for example); B—a sentence fragment that could be best corrected by joining it to the preceding or following sentence (with appropriate changes in punctuation and capitalization); C—a sentence fragment that could be best corrected by rewriting (to make its structure complete); D—a comma splice (to be corrected by changing the punctuation or by inserting a connective word); E—a fused sentence (to be corrected by inserting appropriate punctuation or by inserting a connective word).

1. I was wrong in thinking the ice was thick enough to skate on, it was not. Fortunately the water was not very deep, and I scrambled ashore without much trouble.
2. Insurance statistics prove that women drive more safely than men. However, it will take more than statistics to convince me, in fact I just don't believe it.
3. It turns out you were right I forgot to return the book to the library. But I seldom make such mistakes, and I can't imagine how it happened.
4. The natives had a kind of lie-detector test, in which the suspected culprit was required to chew dry rice. The theory being that a bad conscience prevents or slows the flow of saliva.
5. An electric dryer is cheaper to buy than a gas dryer, however, it is more expensive to operate. So the salesman told me, at any rate.
6. Contrary to common belief, a bent stick always breaks first on the inside of the curve, not the outside. Because the tensile strength of wood is much greater than its compressive strength.
7. The use of silver rather than paper dollars was until recently common in the western states, especially for games of chance. "Iron dollars," as the old-timers called them.
8. People tend to hum or whistle tunes that were popular when they were about 20 years old. And are seldom conscious of doing so.
9. Ben and Sam often quarreled violently then they would make up and act as if nothing had happened. After I got to know them I decided that they were just putting on a show, the customers having no suspicion of their intention.
10. A very interesting speech, whatever you may think of the opinions expressed. But most of the audience, I believe, came away unconvinced.

III

Word order and dangling elements. Each of the numbered sentences below is faulty, either in the order of words or in the way in which modifiers are attached to the remainder of the sentence. Find the faulty sentences and on a separate sheet rewrite each in acceptable form. Then, for each item, in the space at the left write a capital letter to show that the sentence contains: A—a word or phrase so placed as to give the sentence two or more meanings; B—separated parallel elements giving the sentence an awkward effect; C—a split construction: the separation of words that come together in normal speech patterns; D—a dangling modifier, although the thing modified is named in the sentence; E—an elliptical dangling modifier: the thing modified is not named in the sentence.

1. I, after only a couple of days in Paris, was delighted to find my French coming back with a rush, although some of the slang baffled me, of course.
2. Fish are easy to catch in these waters when using the right bait.
3. After the first week, Professor White almost knows every student in his class.
4. Traveling by air all the way, the trip around the world was completed by Mallard in only eight days.

5. Although not trusting by nature, I gave Vic the loan because he seemed to be in dire want, although I didn't know him very well.
6. The woods were at last left behind, and, looking westward, an unbroken expanse of prairie sloped down to the river.
7. If I'm not imposing on your time, I'd like to take a look at the old Hackett house this afternoon, if you're willing to go with me.
8. I took hold of the sharp-finned fish that was struggling on the line with my bare hands.
9. We were stuck in the expressway jam for half an hour, and, while fuming helplessly in the line of cars, the airplane took off without us.
10. To play your best game, you have only to firmly keep in mind that your opponent is just as nervous as you are.

IV

Parallelism and word order. Most of the numbered sentences below contain faults of parallelism. Some sentences are acceptably constructed. For each sentence, in the space at the left write a capital letter to indicate that in order to make the sentence acceptable you would have to: A—insert a necessary word or words; B—take out a superfluous word or words; C—change the form of one or more verbs or verbals; D—change the order of the words; E—do nothing: the sentence is acceptable as it stands. If so instructed, rewrite each faulty sentence on a separate sheet.

1. The problem these days is found not so much in choosing a college as gaining admittance to the college chosen.
2. Fired up by the hope that Father would be vastly impressed (and perhaps disposed to reward me accordingly), I swept the basement, cleaned out the garage, and then I carried all the trash to the alley.
3. In the debate on Latin American policy, he said that either we must gamble on supporting the non-Communist Left or reconcile ourselves to alliances with military dictatorships.
4. Working on my stamp collection is in my opinion much more interesting than to watch television.
5. The most reliable sources of humor, as every jokesmith knows, are surprise at incongruity, the release of forbidden impulses (such as cruelty), and irreverence toward custom or authority.
6. Expressways not only cost far more than improved public transportation but often create more problems than they solve.
7. The referee tossed the coin, acted out the usual choices of the opposing field captains, and the all-important game was under way.
8. It is well to invest in a variety of enterprises rather than putting all your eggs in one basket.
9. Either one has to be 65 or blind in order to claim an extra personal exemption.
10. In navigation, finding your latitude is vastly easier than to determine your longitude, which depends on knowing exactly what time it is somewhere else.

V

Coordination and subordination. Each numbered sentence below may present a problem in coordination or subordination of parts. Find the faults and on a separate sheet rewrite each item in an acceptable form. Then, for each sentence, in the space at the left write a capital letter to indicate that in order to make the sentence acceptable you would have to: A—subordinate one or more of the parts, to correct an effect of monotony; B—change a conjunction, to join the parts more logically or correctly; C—put the main thought or idea in an independent instead of a dependent clause; D—rearrange the dependent or subordinate elements, to correct an effect of trailing off weakly; E—do nothing: the sentence is acceptable as it stands.

1. The judge announced that my entry had won, after he had explained the points used in judging and had commended the runners-up in a manner satisfying to everybody.
2. I was a freshman, and I didn't know my way around, so my roommate drew a map of the campus for me, but I got lost on my way to my first class.
3. Quick reactions are important in driving, but actually the surest mark of a good driver is that he rarely has to do anything quickly.
4. They cause interference in television reception, which is the reason that high-speed motors in household appliances and tools were not employed after about 1950.
5. The idea of the Peace Corps at first met much criticism, but which virtually disappeared when the program was well under way.
6. The old-fashioned cooking stoves burned wood, so the temperature was difficult to control, but our grandmothers cooked wonderful meals on them, and they didn't complain.
7. We had been asked to bring the charcoal and lighting fluid, and in the hurry of packing the other picnic things I forgot them.
8. As much as I dislike his managerial tone of speaking, I have to admit that Harvey's ideas are usually sound and that we might have made a mess of the project without him.
9. People with an ax to grind often say that you can't legislate morality, though it must be obvious that a vast amount of traditionally accepted legislation has precisely that purpose.
10. The downed fliers were finally sighted and rescued, after they had spent ten miserable days on the raft and had survived only through the ingenuity of Lieutenant Morrison, who devised a method of catching fish.

VI

Illogical constructions. Each numbered sentence below may contain one of the following faults: (1) an illogical construction (a faulty sentence plan or two sentence plans blended together); (2) an undesirable shift in person, number, tense, or voice; (3) a pronoun to which the reference is vague or missing. Some sentences are acceptable as they stand. For each sentence, in the space at the left write a capital letter to indicate that in order to correct the sentence you would: A—insert a necessary word or take out a superfluous word; B—change the wording to effect consistency (correct an undesirable shift in point of view); C—rework the sentence to make the reference of a pronoun clear or correct; D—change the basic plan of the sentence so that its parts are logically united; E—do nothing: the sentence is acceptable as it stands. If so instructed, rewrite each faulty sentence on a separate sheet.

1. Just as Martin thought he had paid off his month's debts, they sent him another bill.
2. My chief criticisms of your story are that it has too little narrative interest and too many lush descriptions.
3. The subject which you are best in, you are likely to spend the most time on it.
4. When I serve my time in the Army, I hope they send me to Hawaii.
5. This is probably the only large city which you can pass between extremes of wealth and poverty by walking only a block or two.
6. We were much put out to discover that the boys had got into the refrigerator and drank almost all the cokes before the party started.

7. In this editorial it says that the first principle of foreign policy is to refrain from doing what is clearly wrong.
8. One of the chief causes of rigidity in international relations is that every government becomes the prisoner of its own propaganda.
9. The tourist can now cross the Straits in a few minutes by bridge, whereas they often used to wait hours for a ferry.
10. The winter I won both the skating and skiing trophies was my greatest athletic achievement.

VII

Conciseness. Most of the sentences below contain deadwood of one kind or another that should be cut out or trimmed. Some sentences are already about as concise as they can be made. On a separate sheet, rewrite each wordy sentence in acceptable form. Then in the space at the left write a capital letter to indicate that you have made the sentence more concise by: A–taking out something that repeats an idea already expressed; B–taking out a qualifying tag that adds no real information or interest; C–reducing a predication to a phrase or word; D–doing nothing: the sentence is already concise.

1. The information that has been put together in this report should be immediately given to the sales department.
2. In the modern world of today, we are subject to many pressures unknown to our ancestors.
3. To me, this magazine contains an excess of advertising over other printed matter.
4. The most widespread and long-continuing use of competitive civil-service examinations occurred in the old Chinese Empire.
5. In the early sixties, intercollegiate athletics became not much more than an appendage, so to speak, of commercial television.
6. It was obvious to everyone that Violet resembled her maternal grandmother on her mother's side.
7. One of the reasons it took Odysseus many years to get home was that ships were then so rigged that they could sail only with a favoring wind.
8. Frankly, if I were in the situation that you are in, I would give the boss a piece of my mind and let him do whatever he liked about it.
9. Dixon turned out to be an abominable cook, and by the end of the week we had more or less decided to take turns at the job and give him something else to do.
10. The Schmidt camera, which combines the reflective and refractive principles and which was invented only a few years ago, is the first basic innovation in telescope design since the eighteenth century.

SPECIAL PROBLEMS AND PURPOSES

As you write papers and study Sections 1–55 it may occur to you that the problem of writing English is like that of repairing a worn tire: you repair one leak only to have air escape through other holes.

Despite attempts to cover all conceivable approaches to writing and to pigeonhole them in conveniently studied sections, some problems overlap and others remain unattended. For example, a flaw in diction may involve pronunciation or mechanics or grammar or sentence structure, or all four simultaneously. In addition, what is studied about diction in one section might not apply with full meaning if your purpose in writing were different or if your task were the preparation of a quite distinct form of paper or report. Even if you were able to master every problem involving grammar, usage, punctuation, mechanics, diction, and sentence structure, your task would not be completed.

What you are striving for is an application of individual principles of writing, "rules" about what to do and what not to do, so as to achieve completed wholes: effective paragraphs and entire papers of varied sorts. Such an accomplishment depends upon more than routine attention to specific *do's* and *don't's*. Several related but distinct aims, patterns, ideas, and forms applying to writing can be neither forced into pigeonholes nor neglected because they fit no particular mold. Such purposes and problems are briefly discussed in Sections 56–70.

Each of these has a distinct contribution to make to the study of composition and to other college courses. Each is important, not only for now, but for the future.

56. THINKING

"We do not think enough about thinking, and much of our confusion is the result of current illusions in regard to it." Thus begins a famous essay, "On Various Kinds of Thinking," by James Harvey Robinson.

Perhaps we do not think enough about thinking because thinking is hard work, because we seem to get along fairly well without doing much of it—possibly because we think we are thinking when actually we are doing nothing of the sort.

Errors in thinking and reasoning can destroy fact-finding and process-describing papers; they can ruin argumentative papers and speeches that try to establish a case, to prove a point. We are often only too ready to ignore, twist, or exaggerate evidence. Some errors in reasoning violate that rare and valuable commodity, plain common sense. Other errors involve logic.

You may consider yourself a rational person and believe that every statement you make and every sentence you write is reasonable. If so, think again. Neither you nor I nor anyone else can make every statement fully reasonable because reasoning is based upon facts or what are considered facts. And facts, or assumed facts, change with time. For example, the facts of medicine or physics or population growth or air pollution only a few years ago are hardly the *facts* today. Reasoning is also based upon conclusions drawn from facts; yet the conclusions one reasonable man draws from a given set of facts may differ widely from those of another man.

Clearly, then, you cannot make your every statement reasonable. But at least you can avoid making statements that are obviously questionable; and if you do make such a statement, you should be prepared to defend it. You should make your meaning clear by offering evidence. You can usually avoid statements based on faulty premises, those based on false analogy, those involving mere generalizations. How logical, for example, are these statements?

> All automobiles should have governors limiting their speed to 50 miles an hour. [What about police cars? ambulances? fire trucks?]
>
> Since football is the most dangerous of all sports, my parents refused to allow me to play it. [Overlook the possible parental muddleheadedness: What about water polo? bullfighting? skin diving?]
>
> Steve knows all there is to know about stocks and bonds. [All? Absolutely nothing he doesn't know?]
>
> Gambling is a bad habit; everyone should avoid it because habits are bad. [Can you prove gambling is a bad habit? Are habits bad? all habits? What about the habit of paying your debts? telling the truth?]

You may also believe that you possess a logical mind. Indeed, if you accept a definition of logic as "logical reasoning," you may be partially right. If you agree with this quotation from *Alice's Adventures in Wonderland,* you certainly are right:

"Contrariwise," continued Tweedledee, "if it was so, it might be; and if it were so, it would be; but if it isn't, it ain't. That's logic."

Induction and deduction

It is more likely, however, that you—like all other people—use and abuse two common methods of thinking every day. These methods are *induction* and *deduction*.

The former seeks to establish a general truth, an all-embracing principle or conclusion. The inductive process begins by using observation of specific facts, which it classifies. From a sufficient number of these facts, or particulars, the inductive process leads into a general principle, a comprehensive conclusion. Movement of thought is from the *particular* to the *general*.

Deduction, conversely, tries to show how a particular statement is true because it is part of, and leads down from, a general principle or truth. Movement of thought is from the *general* to the *particular*.

In *inductive* reasoning a set of particulars is studied experimentally and, from observations made, a general principle is drawn or formed. For example: Every horse I have seen has four legs; therefore, I can expect all horses to have four legs. In *deductive* reasoning an accepted general statement, which may be true or false, is applied to a particular situation or case. For example: All horses are animals; this is a horse; therefore, this is an animal.

Processes of thought such as these may seem different from your own thinking processes. Nevertheless, all men do reason this way. For example, early in history, men became convinced that no one lives forever, that sooner or later all men die. Through inductive thinking, mankind arrived at a general conclusion: All men are mortal.

A generalization as well established as this, one that needs neither reexamination nor further testing, may be used as a starting point, that is, a *premise* in deductive thinking. In light of the general truth that all men are mortal, we examine the future of a man named Ned Weston. This deductive process may be expressed in the form of a *syllogism*.

Major premise: All men are mortal.
Minor premise: Ned Weston is a man.
Conclusion: Ned Weston is mortal.

Although we do not arrange our thoughts in syllogisms such as the one just illustrated, we reason in much the same way. For example, we assume that events encountered in the future will be like those met with in the past. What, indeed, is the real meaning of the saying, "A burnt child dreads the fire"?

In induction, the possibility of exceptions always exists, but those general conclusions reached by inductive processes are usually acceptable. When you write "most honor graduates of high school do well in college," you cannot be certain because you cannot have examined all records of past and present students and cannot be positive about the future. But the statement is probable. So is the inductive conclusion that no two people have identical fingerprints or footprints, although this statement, too, is only theoretically capable of being positively proved.

Through inductive reasoning, the laws (that is, the principles, the generalized and descriptive statements) of any science, such as chemistry and physics, have been arrived at. Through deductive reasoning they are applied in particular situations: the launching of a space rocket, the manufacture of a computer, the development of a vaccine. In pure and applied science, such reasoning is virtually foolproof. But loopholes do occur where human beings and human behavior are concerned.

56a. LOGICAL LOOPHOLES

Here is brief comment on nine of the more common offenses against straight and logical thinking.

1. HASTY GENERALIZATION

The most prevalent error in inductive reasoning is observing only a few instances and then jumping to an invalid conclusion. For instance, you know a few athletes whom you consider stupid; does it follow that all, or even most, athletes are mentally deficient? What is the specific evidence for labeling certain groups "hippie freaks," "irresponsible women drivers," "dumb blondes," "male chauvinist pigs"? What is the evidence for "every schoolboy knows . . ." or "all good Americans realize . . ." or "statistics show . . ."?

2. NON SEQUITUR

A major error in deductive thinking is the "it does not follow" assumption. *Non sequitur* is an inference or conclusion that does not proceed from the premises or materials upon which it is apparently based. This fallacy can be caused by a false major premise and by a minor premise that is only apparently related to the major premise. For example, some good professional writers admit to being poor spellers. Are you justified in concluding that you, too, also a poor speller, are destined to be a good professional writer? These syllogisms illustrate the *non sequitur* flaw in thinking:

> All members of X club are conceited.
> Frances is not a member of X club.
> Therefore, Frances is not conceited.
>
> Some members of X club are conceited.
> Frances is a member of X club.
> Therefore, Frances is conceited.

3. POST HOC, ERGO PROPTER HOC

A name applied to a variation of hasty generalization, *post hoc, ergo propter hoc* means in English "after this, therefore on account of this." The error it involves is to hold that a happening which precedes another must naturally or necessarily be its cause or that when one event follows another the latter event is the result of the first. "I have a cold today because I got my feet wet yesterday." "No wonder I had bad luck today; I walked under a ladder yesterday." The Roman Empire fell after the birth and spread of Christianity. Would anyone argue that Christianity alone directly caused the fall of Rome? Those who do—and many have—make the *post hoc, ergo propter hoc* mistake in reasoning.

4. BIASED OR SUPPRESSED EVIDENCE

Facts that furnish ground for belief and that help to prove an assumption or proposition constitute evidence. An obvious flaw in reasoning is selecting evidence from questionable sources or omitting evidence that runs contrary to the point you wish to make. The testimony of dedicated yoga disciples is in itself not sufficient to prove that practicing yoga promotes a peaceful mind or a healthful, happy life. What do those who do not practice yoga think? What do doctors and philosophers think? other authorities? recent converts? those who once practiced yoga and have given it up?

Figures and statistics can lie if evidence is biased or suppressed. Many of the so-called truths we hear and read have been prepared by paid propagandists and directly interested individuals or groups. Biased and suppressed evidence has caused everyone to recognize that "figures don't lie, but liars figure."

5. DISTINGUISHING FACT FROM OPINION

A fact is based on actuality of some sort, a *verifiable* event or statement, whereas opinion is an inference that may be mingled with a supposed fact. That Ernest Hemingway was "an American writer" is a statement which can be proved. That Hemingway was "the greatest American novelist of the twentieth century" is only an opinion of those who hold it. That Thomas Jefferson was President from 1801 until the inauguration of James Madison in 1809 is a fact; that Jefferson was "our greatest President" is a matter of opinion. A favorite device of many writers and speakers is to mingle opinions with facts and thus obscure the difference between them.

6. BEGGING THE QUESTION

This flaw in thinking consists of taking a conclusion for granted before it is proved or assuming in the propositions (premises) that which is to be proved in the conclusion. A question as "Should a vicious man like Charles Grundy be allowed to hold office?" is "loaded" because it assumes what needs to be proved. Common forms of begging the question are *slanting, name calling,* and *shifting the meaning of a word.*

Using unfairly suggestive words to create an emotional attitude (as in the application of *vicious* to Charles Grundy, above) is a form of slanting. It is also a form of *argumentum ad hominem,* a Latin phrase meaning "argument against the person." That is, it is an argument against the person who may hold an opinion rather than against the opinion itself: Only an idiot would believe that.

Guard against using or fully believing such suggestive words and phrases as *bigoted, saintly, progressive, reactionary, undemocratic ideas,* or *dangerous proposal.* Use them if you have supporting evidence; accept them if the proof offered seems valid. Otherwise, avoid slanting in writing and be on your guard when reading and listening.

Name calling is closely allied to slanting. It appeals to prejudice and emotion rather than to the intellect. It employs "good" words to approve and accept, "bad" words to condemn and reject. In writing and reading, be cautious in using such terms as *two-faced, yes man, angel in disguise, rabble rouser, benefactor, do-gooder,* and so on.

Shifting the meaning of a word consists of using the same word several times with a shift in meaning designed to confuse the reader or listener. A *conservative* disposed to preserve existing conditions and to agree with gradual rather than abrupt changes is one thing; a *conservative* unswervingly opposed to all progress, a reactionary, is another. Student *unions* are one thing; labor *unions* are another. Should every citizen vote the Republican ticket because ours is a great *republic* or vote the *Democratic* ticket because this is a great *democracy?*

7. EVADING THE ISSUE

This error in logic is most common in heated arguments. It consists of ignoring the point under discussion and making a statement that has no bearing on the argument. If you tell a friend that he drives too fast and he responds that you are a poor driver yourself, he has evaded the issue. He may be right, but he has neither met your objection nor won the argument. Such argument is especially common in political campaigns. It is easy to sidestep an issue and launch a counterattack.

8. FAULTY ANALOGY

Because two objects or ideas are alike in one or more respects, they are not necessarily similar in some further way. *Analogy* (partial similarity) can be both accurate and effective; otherwise we could not employ either similes or metaphors. But when we use figurative-language analogy, we do not expect such a figure of speech to *prove* anything.

In the kind of writing most of us do most of the time, an analogy is chiefly useful as an illustration. In many analogies, differences outweigh similarities. "Why do we need social security? Do we help trees when they lose their leaves in autumn winds? Do we provide assistance to dogs and horses in their old age? Don't some tribes kill people when they are too old to be useful?" Such analogy as this is obviously absurd, but even more literal analogies than this can be ridiculous. You may, for example, reason that since the honor system has worked well in several small colleges, it will work equally well in large universities. Are the similarities between the schools either superficial or less important than the differences? The whipping post was a deterrent to crime in seventeenth-century New England. Is it false analogy to suggest that similar punishment should be inflicted on twentieth-century criminals and dope addicts?

9. TESTIMONIALS

Citing statements from historical personages or well-known contemporaries is not necessarily straight thinking. In an attempt to bolster an argument, we are quick to employ such terms as *authorities have concluded, science proves, doctors say, laboratory tests reveal.* George Washington, Thomas Jefferson, and Abraham Lincoln—justly renowned as they are—might not have held economic, social, and political views necessarily valid in the twentieth century. Douglas MacArthur was a great military strategist, but something he said about combustion engines may be less convincing than the words of a good local mechanic. Is an authority in one field an oracle of wisdom about any subject on which he speaks or writes? As a witness for or against an important educational policy, how effective would an eminent surgeon be? a football hero? a TV personality? If you were writing an attack on vaccination, would you reasonably expect the opposition of George Bernard Shaw to outweigh the pronouncements of the entire medical profession?

But even where there is little question of the validity of authority, be careful to see that neither bias nor the time element weakens your presentation. Some businessmen and labor leaders are experts on economic problems, but their particular interests might prevent their having the impartiality, the objectivity, of a disinterested observer. As for timing, remember that in many fields of human activity and knowledge, authorities soon become obsolete. Charles Darwin no longer has the last word on evolution; Sigmund Freud is not universally considered the final authority in psychoanalysis.

56b. CHECKLIST FOR WRITTEN WORK

Before submitting a paper, apply the following comments so as to forestall their being made by your instructor:

1. The statement needs qualification; it is too sweeping or dogmatic. (This comment refers to assertions that are not altogether false or irresponsible but simply cover too much ground too positively and need to be guarded with a limiting phrase or clause specifying the degree of certainty warranted, taking account of possible exceptions, or confining the generalization to what you are reasonably sure of.)
2. The facts cited are not such as are likely to be accepted on your bare assertion. You should supply informally in the current of your development some authority, occupational experience, or other reason why you should be believed.
3. Your argument is good so far as it goes, but it is unconvincing because you have failed to dispose of some obvious and overriding argument that can be made on the other side. Your case is strengthened when you evaluate your own argument and show that you have disposed of possible alternatives.
4. The evidence supplied is pertinent but falls far short of proof. One good reason does not build a case.
5. There is such a thing as being too specific if you do not make clear what generalization is supported by the instances given. A well-developed train of thought works back and forth between the general and the specific, showing the connections and applications intended at each point.
6. Your treatment here is obviously marked by particular bias and prior emotional

commitment. This does not necessarily make your conclusions false, but it does make them all suspect.

7. Your approach here is essentially moralistic and directive rather than analytical. No law exists against preaching, but distinguish preaching from investigation, analysis, and reasoning.
8. Here you are exploring religious or philosophical questions that have been discussed for thousands of years without being resolved. You of course have a right to try your hand at them, but don't expect an easy success, and remember that no certain conclusions are possible when the assumptions with which you start out are untestable.[1]

EXERCISES

How would you reply to the following statements? What logical loophole is involved in each?

1. In reply to Mr. Marsh's claim that his administration is prepared to help the poor, I wish to point out that he has never been hungry in his entire life, that he has inherited a vast fortune, and that his children attend exclusive private schools.
2. Ladies and gentlemen of the jury, the prosecution is prepared to prove to you that this heartless murderer who sits before you is guilty as charged.
3. From the courses I have taken this semester, I feel I am correct in stating that college professors are hopeless idealists.
4. Oliver Wendell Holmes, Jr., the Supreme Court Justice, was a greater American than his father, the poet, essayist, and doctor.
5. Dean Smither's wife is beautiful; she is, however, a sober looking woman. Therefore, I am convinced that she is unhappily married.
6. Courses in marriage and the family cannot prepare men and women for marriage. To try to educate them for marriage is like trying to teach them to swim without letting them go into the water. It just can't be done!
7. Dissecting animals is an evil, wicked practice. How would you like it if someone snipped off your arm, leg, or finger?
8. *First student:* Do you feel that there is a relationship between intelligence and high grades? *Second student:* There is no sense discussing this subject. Those who earn high grades are dull, uninteresting bookworms.
9. Depraved and inhuman as they are, boxing matches must be banned by the American people.
10. Lazy students often flunk out of college. My roommate is one of the laziest students I have ever met. Therefore, he is flunking because of his laziness.

57. USING A DICTIONARY

To speak and write competently, everyone needs as a guide a reliable dictionary. No one knows all the words in the English language. Whether often or occasionally, every user of language needs help with the meaning, spelling, pronunciation, and use of a particular word.

A dictionary is a book containing a selection of words, normally arranged alphabetically, concerning which information about meanings and a wealth of

[1] For these suggestions the person largely responsible is Professor Macklin Thomas of the Department of Higher Education, Chicago.

other material is given. In one sense, a reliable dictionary is a guide to standard English, "the practice of the socially accepted, those who carry on the important affairs of English-speaking people."[1] But a dictionary is an authority largely in the sense that it *records* and *interprets* English words and phrases. Carefully prepared dictionaries do not prescribe or dictate usage but rather indicate what is considered general language practice.

57a. CHOOSING A RELIABLE DICTIONARY

Suitable dictionaries are what economists refer to as "durable goods." It is well worth paying a few dollars to buy a good, hardbound dictionary that you can keep and use for many years. A pocket dictionary is almost worthless, except as a quick guide to spelling and pronunciation. Equip yourself with a sufficiently large dictionary (approximately 100,000 entries), published by a reliable firm. These, for example, are good dictionaries:

The American College Dictionary (New York: Random House)
The American Heritage Dictionary of the English Language (New York: The American Heritage Publishing Company; text edition, Houghton Mifflin Company)
Funk & Wagnalls Standard College Dictionary (New York: Funk & Wagnalls: text edition, Harcourt, Brace & Jovanovich)
The Random House Dictionary of the English Language, College Edition (New York: Random House)
Webster's Seventh New Collegiate Dictionary (Springfield, Mass.: G. & C. Merriam Company)
Webster's New World Dictionary of the American Language (Cleveland: World Publishing Company)

57b. INTERPRETING AND USING A DICTIONARY

If you have never done so before, examine your dictionary carefully. Read its table of contents; examine the information given on the inside of the front and back covers; at least skim the prefatory pages as well as any supplementary materials at the back. Then read thoughtfully any editorial sections it contains: "general introduction," "guide to the use of this dictionary," "guide to pronunciation," or "explanatory notes." You may be astonished to discover resources of which you were previously unaware.

For any word listed in an adequate dictionary, each of the first five of the following items is given. For many words, some of the next five kinds of information are provided:

1. Spelling	6. Level(s) of meaning
2. Syllabication	7. Derivation (origin)
3. Pronunciation	8. Synonyms
4. Part(s) of speech	9. Antonyms
5. Meaning(s)	10. Other information

You should actually *study* each word you look up. Take your time. It requires only a moment to learn the spelling, pronunciation, or one meaning of a word.

[1] Charles C. Fries, *The American College Dictionary* (New York: Random House), p. xxv.

But hasty examination will prevent your mastering the word and making it a part of your active vocabulary. Time spent in learning words thoroughly will save time, errors, and annoyance later.

1. SPELLING

The basic or "entry" word is ordinarily given in black (boldface) type. Associated with the main entry may be other words in black type indicating run-on entries (endings such as *-er* and *-like* may be added—*begin, beginner; clerk, clerk-like*) and alternative entries of variant forms (*Bosporus, Bosphorus; diagram, -gramed, -graming* or *-grammed, -gramming*). Note especially that:

1. The plurals of nouns are given if a noun forms its plural other than by adding *-s* or *-es*.
2. The comparative and superlative degrees of adjectives and adverbs are given if a spelling change is made in the addition of *-er, -est*.
3. The past tense, past participle, and present participle of verbs are given if these forms differ from the present-tense form or if the spelling changes in the addition of an ending.
4. Many compound words spelled with a hyphen or as one word or as two words are so indicated.

When a word has two or more spellings, the preferred spelling form is usually given first. Sometimes the variant spelling is also placed separately as a vocabulary entry.

The spelling of proper names (people, places, and so on) is given either in the regular place in the alphabetical listing or in a special section or sections at the back, depending upon the dictionary.

2. SYLLABICATION

Learn to distinguish between the light mark or dot (·) used to separate syllables (ri·dic·u·lous) and the hyphen (-) used to show that the word is a compound (*hard-fisted*). All reliable dictionaries use the dot system of indicating syllabication; some substitute for the dot in the vocabulary entry an accent mark after the stressed syllable.

Knowledge of syllabication is important in two ways: it helps in the pronunciation of words, which in turn helps in correct spelling, and it shows where to divide words if division is necessary at ends of lines (see Section 28).

3. PRONUNCIATION

Pronunciation is based upon accent or emphasized syllables and upon the sound given to letters or letter combinations. Both accent marks and syllabication dots are included in the entry word by some dictionaries; other dictionaries carry only the syllabication dots in the entry word and include the accent marks in the pronunciation word.

Learn to distinguish the accent marks: primary or heavy stress is shown by a heavy mark (**ʹ**) and secondary or less heavy stress by a light (ʹ) or double (ʺ)

mark: com**′**pass′, com**′**pass″, dif**′**fer′, dif**′**fer″; spell**′**ing′, spell**′**ing″; pro′nounce**′**, pro″nounce**′**.

Pronunciation of sounds is more complicated than accent. The fact that twenty-six alphabetical letters are used in 250 common spellings of sounds is evidence that everyone needs help. Linguists have developed systems whereby forty to sixty symbols, depending upon the dictionary, are adequate to solve most pronunciation problems.

Most dictionaries list a "pronunciation" word in parentheses just after the entry word. It is a respelling of the word, giving the sounds of vowels and consonants by syllables and according to the pronunciation key that the dictionary has adopted. Familiarize yourself with this key in your dictionary. For foreign words or those newly adopted from a foreign language, your dictionary may include a separate key for foreign sounds.

Learn to interpret diacritical marks (ë), which are placed over the second of two consecutive vowels when each vowel is pronounced separately. As a variant method hyphens may be used instead. Examples: *naïve, reënforce* or *re-enforce, preëminence* or *pre-eminence.* As such words become common, diacritical marks or the hyphen may be left out in spelling the word, as in *preeminence.*

Generally, when two or more pronunciations of a word are included, the one more commonly used is given first. A variant pronunciation may occasionally be labeled *British* or *Chiefly British* to show that this pronunciation is the common one in Great Britain.

4. PARTS OF SPEECH

Since all English words are parts of speech, the part of speech of every entry is generally given. If the word is used as more than one part of speech, such information is provided, with the particular meaning or meanings under each explained. Also shown are the singular or plural forms of many nouns, the comparative and superlative degrees of many adjectives and adverbs, and the correct use of verbs as transitive, or intransitive, or both. Here are some of the more common abbreviations for this information:

act.	active	*interj.*	interjection	*prep.*	preposition
adj.	adjective	*masc.*	masculine	*pres.*	present
adv.	adverb	*n.*	noun	*prin. pts.*	principal parts
art.	article	*neut.*	neuter	*pron.*	pronoun
auxil.	auxiliary	*nom.*	nominative	*refl.*	reflexive
compar.	comparative	*obj.*	objective	*rel.*	relative
conj.	conjunction	*part.*	participle	*sing.*	singular
def.	definite	*pass.*	passive	*subj.*	subjunctive
fem.	feminine	*perf.*	perfect	*superl.*	superlative
fut.	future	*pers.*	person or personal	*v.*	verb
indef.	indefinite	*pl.*	plural	*v.i.*	verb intransitive
indic.	indicative	*poss.*	possessive	*v. imp.*	verb impersonal
inf.	infinitive	*pp.*	past participle	*v.t.*	verb transitive
intens.	intensive	*pred.*	predicate		

If you are uncertain of the meaning of some of these grammatical terms, see the sections on grammar, especially Section 10.

5. MEANINGS

Words may have one or more of the following meanings: a traditional meaning, a historical meaning, a figurative meaning, a special meaning, or a new meaning. Note the various definitions giving both usual and specialized meanings. Learn the method used in the order of definitions—for example, by part of speech, by historical development of meaning, by frequency of occurrence, or by general to specialized meaning. Master, too, the significance of definitions preceded by Arabic numbers or by letters of the alphabet. Note the method of entry for capitalized and small-letter words, for homographs (words spelled alike but having different meanings) and homonyms (words spelled differently but pronounced alike), and for all words having a superficial resemblance. Although all these may have similar spellings or pronunciations, their meanings are quite different. Place the meaning of the word into the context of your encounter with it in reading and listening.

Hyphenated words and two or more words forming phrases that have idiomatic, specialized, or figurative meaning are explained in the regular alphabetical listing, either entered separately or put under the main word. In most dictionaries, abbreviations and foreign words or phrases also are included in their alphabetical position.

6. LEVEL(S) OF MEANING

Entry in a dictionary is not a guarantee that a word is in good use or that its special meanings are suitable in current English. Your dictionary enables you to weigh the appropriateness of a word by the absence or presence of a restrictive label. Some words have no labels, and others have labels for certain meanings or for use as a certain part of speech. Any word not given a restrictive label is acceptable in formal and informal English. Any word labeled "colloquial" is usually suitable in *all* informal speech and writing. All other labels are guides to special uses of the word. Four classifications of restrictive labels are common:

1. *Geographical* labels indicate a country or region of a country where the word is in general use: *Chiefly U.S., British, Scotch, New England, Southwest, Western U.S., dialect,* and so on.
2. *Time* labels indicate that the word is no longer used, is disappearing from use, or is still used but has a quaint form or meaning: *obsolete, obsolescent, archaic.* Words having no time label are in current use.
3. *Subject* labels show that a specialized word or word meaning belongs to a limited area of knowledge such as science, technology, craft, sport, and the like. As many as 100 of these labels are used, including *astronomy, biology, electrical engineering, architecture, dentistry, painting,* and *football.*
4. *Cultural* labels indicate whether the word or a special meaning is substandard or suitable as informal English: *illiterate, slang, dialect* (which may be geographical also), *colloquial, poetic, literary.* Absence of any such label signifies that the word is acceptable in formal and informal writing and speaking.

There is no Supreme Court in language to which a final appeal can be made; lexicographers can only use their best judgment in collecting and interpreting data on language. Dictionaries may therefore differ in the labels they give to certain words or certain meanings.

Some dictionaries carry brief comments on levels of meaning and the usage problems involved. Here, for example, is such an entry extracted from the listing for the word *due:*[2]

> ***Usage:*** The phrase *due to* is always acceptable when *due* functions as a predicate adjective following a linking verb: *His hesitancy was due to fear.* But objection is often made when *due to* introduces an adverbial phrase that assigns the reason for, or cause of, the action denoted by a nonlinking verb: *He hesitated due to fear.* The adverbial construction typified by the second example is termed unacceptable in writing by 84 per cent of the Usage Panel, though it is widely employed informally. Generally accepted alternatives to *due to,* in such examples, are *because of, on account of, through,* and *owing to.*

7. DERIVATION (ORIGIN)

The origin of a word—in linguistics, its *etymology*—may be twofold: (1) less commonly, a narrative account of how a word was formed or was given its meaning (see in your dictionary, for example, *derrick, burke, macadam, radar*), or (2) whenever known, the ancestral or foreign languages through or from which the word evolved to its English form. Old English, Latin, Greek, German, and French have contributed heavily to modern English, but several other languages have also had a part—Italian and Spanish, for example.

Such derivations, generally entered between brackets near the beginning or at the end of the vocabulary entry, help to fix the meaning and spelling of words in your mind. Learn the more common abbreviations with which your dictionary indicates them: *OE* (*Old English*), *L.* (*Latin*), *Gk.* (*Greek*), *Sp.* (*Spanish*), and so on. Learn also the space-saving short cuts: *b.* (*blended of*), *f.* (*formed from*), *t.* (*taken from*), < (*derived from*), and so on.

8. SYNONYMS

Words that in one or more of their definitions have the same or similar meanings as other words are called *synonyms.* Make a study of synonyms; often these approximate equivalents have significant differences in meaning that enable you to choose exact and emphatic words (see Section 39). So important is this study that whole books have been compiled for the benefit of writers and speakers, such as *Webster's Dictionary of Synonyms, Crabb's English Synonyms,* and *Roget's International Thesaurus of English Words.*

Dictionaries include the listings and often brief discussions of hundreds of

[2] From *The American Heritage Dictionary of the English Language,* p. 403. © 1969, 1970, 1971 by American Heritage Publishing Co., Inc. Reprinted by permission.

synonyms; they indicate differences in meaning of apparently similar words and signify by a number which usage is part of synonymous meaning.

9. ANTONYMS

Antonyms are pairs of words that have opposite or negative meanings: *man-woman, man-boy, man-beast, man-God, holy-unholy.* These opposite meanings are not all-inclusive: a word may be an antonym of another only in a certain restricted meaning. One antonym of *man* concerns sex; another, age; another, biology; another, religion.

10. OTHER INFORMATION

Other information that may be carried as part of an entry or as separate entries in the main part of your dictionary includes abbreviations; biographical names; capitalized words and words spelled with both capitals and small letters; cross references to words listed elsewhere; examples of word use in phrases and sentences; foreign words and phrases (usually labeled as such or given a special symbol); geographical names; homographs and homonyms; meaning of idiomatic phrases; prefixes, suffixes, and other combining word elements; and, for some words, graphic or pictorial illustrations.

EXERCISES

I

Look through your dictionary to find out what kinds of information it contains and where that information is located. Then answer the following questions:

1. Give the full title, the edition, and the copyright date of your dictionary.
2. Is there a section explaining how to use the dictionary? On what pages?
3. Is there a guide (key) to pronunciation? Where?
4. What is orthography? Does your dictionary have a section on orthography? Where?
5. Is there an explanation of the abbreviations used in the dictionary? Where?
6. In the definitions of words of more than one meaning, in what order are the meanings arranged?
7. Does your dictionary give biographical facts on famous people? Where?
8. Does your dictionary explain foreign words and phrases? Where?
9. Is there a discussion of punctuation? Where?
10. What is an etymology? In the word entries in your dictionary, where are the etymologies placed?

II

Prepare an oral or written report, as directed, in which you explain each detail of the following entry.[3] Be certain to account for all numbers, marks of punctuation, and abbreviations.

[3] By permission. From *Webster's Seventh New Collegiate Dictionary,* copyright 1965 by G. & C. Merriam Company, Publishers of the Merriam-Webster Dictionaries.

[1] **spell**\'spel\ *n* [ME, talk, tale. fr. OE: akin to OHG *spel* talk, tale. Gk *apeilē* boast] **1 a** : a spoken word or form of words believed to have magic power : INCANTATION **b** : a state of enchantment **2** : a strong compelling influence or attraction
[2] **spell** *vt* : to put under a spell : BEWITCH
[3] **spell** *vb* **spelled**\'speld, 'spelt\ **spell·ing** [ME *spellen,* fr. OF *espeiler,* of Gme origin; akin to OE *spell* talk] *vt* **1** : to read slowly and with difficulty **2 a** : to find out by study : DISCOVER **b** : COMPREHEND, UNDERSTAND **3 a** : to name the letters of in order; *also* : to write or print the letters of in order **b** : to make up (a word) : FORM **4** : MEAN, SIGNIFY ~ *vi* : to form words with letters
[4] **spell** *vb* **spelled**\'speld\ **spell·ing** [ME *spelen.* *fr.* OE *spelian:* akin to OE *spala* substitute] *vt* **1** : to take the place of for a time : RELIEVE **2** : to allow an interval of rest to : REST ~ *vi* **1** : to work in turns **2** : to rest from work or activity for a time
[5] **spell** *n* **1** a *archaic* : a shift of workers **b** : one's turn at work **2 a** : a period spent in a job or occupation **b** *chiefly Austral* : a period of rest from work, activity, or use **3 a** : an indeterminate period of time **b** : a stretch of a specified type of weather **4** : a time colored by some state of body or mind : FIT

58. BUILDING A VOCABULARY

Lack of mastery of words prevents the full expression of hundreds of impressions, thoughts, and feelings that come to us as results of our observation and thinking. But although most people wish to increase and strengthen their vocabularies, few are willing to make a real effort to do so. There are no easy methods of acquiring and mastering a good vocabulary. Occasionally looking up a word in the dictionary will help very little; sitting down in a burst of enthusiasm to memorize, at random, scores of words from it is also valueless. Perhaps the most direct way to broaden vocabulary is to learn to use the words we already have in our potential vocabularies.

Each of us has three vocabularies. First, there is our *active,* or *speaking,* vocabulary. This is our productive word stock, the words we use daily in speech. Second, there is our *writing* vocabulary. This also is active in that we use it habitually in our writing, even though it contains some words that we seldom use in speech. In addition to these two active, or productive, vocabularies, each of us has a *potential,* or *recognition,* vocabulary.

Using this potential vocabulary (the largest of the three), we can understand speakers and can read and understand books, magazines, and newspapers. But in our reading and listening we encounter many words which we recognize and of which we have some understanding, possibly from the context, but which we would be unable to use in our own speaking and writing. Until we use such words, however—put them into circulation, that is—they are not really ours.

To get words from our potential into our active vocabularies requires systematic effort, but it is the logical way to begin vocabulary improvement. Words in a recognition vocabulary already have made some impression on our consciousness; they are already partly ours. Their values, although still vague to us, can be made exact and accurate. Furthermore, quite likely they are words that we shall want in our vocabularies. Probably we have come across them time and again. They are not unusual or esoteric; they are words that have *use* value.

We have both to learn, and to learn how to use, such words before they can become parts of our active vocabularies. Try reading the current issue of one of your favorite magazines and underlining all the words in it that you do not use very often. Then try to give a working definition of each word and to use the word in a sentence. Even the most intelligent readers usually discover when they put themselves through this test that they have simply assumed that they know words which in fact they do not know. Probably a few of the words that you underlined will be esoteric and generally useless, but most of them will be useful ones that you can add to your working vocabulary relatively easily. Set out to master these words; move them from your potential to your active vocabulary.

Actually, acquiring an active vocabulary of considerable range is not so formidable a task as it may seem. A reliable scholar has revealed that even Shakespeare, that master of diction, used fewer than 17,000 words in all his plays. And yet, as the late S. Stephenson Smith[1] pointed out, the "average" American knows about 10,000 words—the words most common in newspapers, general magazines, and daily speaking.

Mr. Smith reported that certain magazines—*Saturday Review*, the *Atlantic Monthly, Harper's Magazine*—assume that their readers command the vocabulary of the "average" college graduate: 20,000–25,000 words. Naturally, these are not always the same words; an English major and a premedical student are quite likely to possess somewhat different vocabularies upon graduation from college.

However, a number of careful studies have revealed that certain basic words are used most frequently in writing and speaking. One such study, Thorndike and Lorge's *The Teacher's Word Book of 30,000 Words,* contains from 10,000 to 15,000 words that are known to nearly every adult. It is reasonable to assume, therefore, that you have a vocabulary of about this size. With this number as a starter, you can begin to build.

College courses will provide many opportunities for you to double the size of your vocabulary. Words new to you appear on every page of the daily newspaper. Conversations and lectures will be full of them. Television and radio programs fill the air with them. Try to master them not only because doing so will enrich your reading, writing, and speaking, but because a good vocabulary will be important to you throughout life. A scientific investigator, Johnson O'Connor, has written:

> An extensive knowledge of the exact meanings of English words accompanies outstanding success in this country more often than any other single characteristic which the Human Engineering Laboratory has been able to isolate and measure.

58a. USING A DICTIONARY

Wide reading and intelligent listening should lead straight to a good dictionary (see Section 57).

[1] S. Stephenson Smith, *The Command of Words,* 2nd ed. (New York: Thomas Y. Crowell, 1949).

If in reading you dislike to "break the chain of thought" by looking up words in a dictionary (although the very necessity for using a dictionary has already broken that chain), jot down unfamiliar words and look them up as soon as possible. Keeping a notebook nearby is a good idea. Be sure, after you have thoroughly studied a new word, to use it in speaking and writing until it is yours. Adding words to one's stock can be fascinating, but there must be a systematic and constant exercise of your will to study and use what you have acquired.

58b. SYNONYMS AND ANTONYMS

Collecting lists of synonyms and distinguishing among their meanings is an effective, and often entertaining, way to enlarge your vocabulary. Most good dictionaries include listings and often brief discussions of hundreds of synonyms. When looking up a word, carefully study the treatment of those synonym entries that sometimes follow the definitions. If you do this, you may be able to choose a more exact and effective word for the occasion at hand and also add a useful word to your active vocabulary.

For example, after becoming aware of synonyms, will you necessarily have to write that the girl is *cute*, the game *thrilling*, the idea *interesting*, the dress *sexy* or *mod*, the play *exciting*? A study of synonyms for *old* might add to your vocabulary these, among other words: *immemorial, aged, ancient, aboriginal, decrepit, antique, hoary, elderly, patriarchal, venerable, passé, antiquated*, and *antediluvian*.

Similarly, studying antonyms will improve your understanding and also contribute to vocabulary growth. For example, seeking antonyms for *praise* may add to your vocabulary such words as *vilify, stigmatize, lampoon, abuse, censure, blame, deprecate, condemn, impugn, denigrate, disparage*, and *inveigh against*. Even such a simple word as *join* has numerous approximate opposites, among them *uncouple, separate, sunder, unyoke, cleave, disconnect*, and *dissever*.

58c. PREFIXES AND SUFFIXES

Another method of adding to your vocabulary is to make a study of prefixes and suffixes.

A *prefix* is an element placed before a word or root to make another word of different function or meaning. (The prefix *pre* means *before: pre-American, premeditate, premature.*)

Knowledge of the meanings of some of the hundreds of prefixes in English words is of enormous value in quickly getting at the sense of unfamiliar words. Following is a list of common prefixes, together with one or more approximate meanings and illustrative words:

a-	not	amoral, anonymous
ad-	to, against	adverse, adjective
ambi-	around, both	ambiguous, ambidextrous
ante-	before	antedate, anteroom
anti-	opposite	antisocial, antiwar
audio-	hearing	audiovisual, audition

auto-	self, same	autograph, autobiography
bene-	well, good	beneficial, benefit
bio-	life	biography, biology
circum-	about, around	circumstance, circumflex
co-	complement of	comaker, co-signer
col-	together	collateral, collection
com-	in association	combine, compare
de-	away, down, from	demerit, degrade
dis-	apart, not, away	disbar, disability
ec- (*ex-*)	from, out of	eccentric, exhale
en- (*em-*)	in, on, into	enact, empower
epi-	upon, before	epigram, epilogue
ex-	out of, from	exclaim, excommunicate
extra-	beyond, without	extrajudicial, extrasensory
hemi-	half	hemisphere, hemiplegia
hyper-	beyond the ordinary	hypercritical, hypersensitive
il-	not	illogical, illegitimate
im-	opposed, negative	immoral, imbalance
inter-	among, between	interdepartmental, intercollegiate
intra-	within	intramural, intravenous
ir-	not, opposed	irreligious, irreducible
meta-	along with, among	metaphysics, metamorphism
mono-	one, alone	monochrome, monologue
neo-	new, recent	neophyte, neolithic
para-	beside	paragraph, parachute
per-	through, thoroughly	pervert, perfect
peri-	about, beyond	perimeter, perigee
poly-	many	polygon, polysyllable
post-	behind, after	postscript, postgraduate
pro-	for, forward	proclivity, proceed
pseudo-	false	pseudoclassic, pseudonym
re-	backward, again	revert, return
retro-	backward	retrogress, retroactive
semi-	half	semidetached, semicolon
super-	above, beyond	supernatural, supersensitive
syn-	together, with	synthesis, syndrome
tel- (*tele-*)	distant	telegraph, telecast
trans-	across, beyond	transcend, transmit
ultra-	beyond, in excess of	ultraviolet, ultrasonic
un-	not, reverse of	unfair, unbend

A *suffix* is an element that is placed after a word or word root to make a term of different use or meaning. For example, the suffix *-age* has a general meaning of "belonging to." *Postage* (*post* plus *age*) has to do with a series of stations along a route that receive and send mail. With this sense of *-age* in mind, words such as *coinage, fruitage, spoilage,* and *bondage* become clear. Common suffixes include these:

-ana	Americana, collegiana	*-hood*	childhood, priesthood
-ance	connivance, nonchalance	*-ice*	apprentice, novice
-dom	kingdom, freedom	*-ish*	British, girlish
-er	loiterer, embezzler	*-ism*	barbarism, plagiarism
-fold	maniford, twofold	*-ity*	civility, nobility
-ful	beautiful, harmful	*-let*	bracelet, ringlet
-graph	monograph, lithograph	*-like*	lifelike, childlike

-logy	trilogy, theology	*-some*	twosome, quarrelsome
-ness	kindness, preparedness	*-ward*	toward, afterward
-phone	telephone, megaphone	*-ways*	always, sideways
-polis	metropolis, megalopolis	*-wise*	clockwise, sidewise
-ship	friendship, statesmanship	*-y*	dreamy, infamy

58d. COMBINING FORMS

A *combining form* is a term for a word element that rarely appears independently but forms part of a longer word. *Graph*, for example, is a combining form that appears in such words as *photograph* and *lithography*. Knowing the meanings of such forms as the following will help in increasing your vocabulary:

anima	life, breath	animal, animation
aqua	water	aquarium, aqualung
aristos	the best	aristocrat, aristocracy
beatus	blessed	beatitude, beatification
bios	life	biosphere, biopsy
causa	cause	causal, causation
culpa	fault	culprit, culpable
decem	ten	December, decennial
domus	house	domestic, domicile
ego	I	egoism, egocentric
facilis	easy	facile, facilitate
gramma	letter	grammar, grammatical
hostis	enemy	hostile, hostility
lex	law	legal, legalize
liber	book	library, libretto
locus	place	local, locality
mater	mother	matriarch, maternal
navis	ship	navy, navigate
opus	work	operation, opera
pedi	foot	pedometer
petra	rock	petroleum, petrology
plus, pluris	more	plural, plurality
populus	people	population, populate
sanctus	holy	sanctuary, sanctify
sophia	wisdom	sophomore, sophisticated
tacitus	silence	tacit, taciturn
thermo	heat	thermometer, thermal
umbra	shade	umbrella, umbrage
vita	life	vital, vitamin

EXERCISES

I

Select in each series the word or word group that is closest in meaning to the word italicized in the phrase. Check your list of answers with a dictionary.

1. *propriety* of actions [property/ properness/ standard/ principle/ behavior]
2. I replied *glibly* [fast/ profound/ slowly/ loudly/ fluently]
3. your reasoning is *erroneous* [incorrect/ convincing/ right/ pleasing/ learned]
4. *edified* by the sermon [pleased/ disgusted/ saddened/ amused/ uplifted]

5. these fruits are *indigenous* [common/ expensive/ sweet/ native/ nonexistent]
6. *harassed* by upperclassmen [praised/ ignored/ loved/ guided/ tormented]
7. completely *exasperated* [thoughtful/ exalted/ pleased/ worn out/ angered]
8. a *sagacious* decision [shrewd/ foolish/ unanimous/ necessary/ overdue]
9. to eat *voraciously* [rapidly/ slowly/ politely/ indifferently/ greedily]
10. with much *vehemence* [pettiness/ violence/ venom/ expression/ ease]
11. religious *intolerance* [unwillingness/ uneasiness/ narrowmindedness/ faith/ sincerity]
12. *ostensibly* confused [much/ unexpectedly/ professedly/ possibly/ stupidly]
13. an *antiquated* building [rustic/ outdated/ magnificent/ modern/ haunted]
14. to *dominate* a conversation [improve/ interrupt/ participate in/ rule/ object to]
15. a *boon* to mankind [legacy/ blessing/ boost/ friend/ curse]
16. a *lucrative* occupation [dull/ interesting/ overcrowded/ lucky/ profitable]
17. we *subjugated* the natives [educated/ clothed/ conquered/ harassed/ victimized]
18. the action was *deplorable* [useless/ desirable/ regrettable/ necessary/ decisive]
19. the child wept *copiously* [little/ abundantly/ often/ secretly/ openly]
20. complete *annihilation* [destruction/ praise/ anger/ despair/ victory]
21. a *peculiarity* of manners [politeness/ quality/ genuineness/ change/ oddity]
22. acting *flippantly* [pertly/ half-scared/ half-apologetically/ flinchingly/ stupidly]
23. a *beatific smile* [silly/ flashing/ beaming/ blissful/ sincere]
24. to *succumb* to a disease [overcome/ yield to/ ignore/ be immune to/ be cured of]
25. a *colossal* undertaking [approved/ amazing/ huge/ impossible/ secret]

II

Define and use in sentences each of these words:

1. ominous
2. trepidation
3. idyllic
4. brainwashing
5. plausible
6. pervasive
7. envisaged
8. despotism
9. technological
10. nihilistic

III

1. The word *allow* has several synonyms, among them *let, permit, suffer,* and *tolerate.* Are there other synonyms for *let*?
2. The word *choice* has many synonyms. List at least five.
3. The following words have many meanings: *appeal, fix, point, keep, sweep.* Prepare for class an oral or written discussion of *one* of these words. Which meanings seem most common? Which seem most unusual? In what idiomatic phrases do these words appear?
4. Give one antonym for each of the following: *arrive, atrocious, arrogant, dark, latent, solitary, sophisticated, temporary, weak, wordy.*
5. Give the meaning of each of the following prefixes and list five common words containing each prefix: *bi-, cross-, non-, pre-, sub-.*
6. Give the meaning of each of the following suffixes and list five common words containing each suffix: *-al, -est, -less, -ist, -ment.*

59. PRONUNCIATION

For each of us, words actually live in oral rather than in printed or handwritten form. It is a rare person who does not speak a hundred or a thousand times more often than he writes, who does not listen more than he reads. Consequently, pronunciation, the act of making the sounds of speech, is the direct, immediate, and constant concern of everyone. People spend more time in speaking and listening than in any other pursuits of their lives (breathing and possibly sleeping excepted).

And yet, even if one wished to, it would be impossible for him to speak *the* English language or even "American English." Everyone's speech reflects the characteristics of a specific locality, individual background, and particular social group. Everyone learns and usually hangs on to certain speech patterns that are uniquely his own, patterns derived from the members of his family, the locality or localities in which he grew up, the schools he attended, his acquaintances, his occupation, and his hobbies and recreations.

That is, no such thing as total conformity in pronunciation is possible because every speaker of a language employs his own dialect. Every pronouncer of words, no matter what his native language is, has a speech pattern peculiar to him at a specific period of his life. One's individual speech pattern is known as his *idiolect,* his unique way of forming the sounds of speech. To the expert, the speech sounds of no two persons are, or ever can be, identical.

59a. NO SINGLE PRONUNCIATION STANDARD EXISTS

With many millions of idiolects in daily use, no way of sounding a given word can be said to be its only correct pronunciation. True, nearly everyone pronounces more than 90 percent of all words in general use in about the same way, so nearly the same that for all practical purposes the pronunciation could be called identical. And yet a trained ear would detect differences. Also, even if pronunciations of individual words seem identical, they would change and shift as they appeared in connected speech (talk, that is) because people speak at different rates and with differing emphasis on specific words.

The distinctive speech patterns of sections of the United States involve flavor and color more than substance, so that communication between speakers in different areas creates no real problem. But individual systems of pronunciation can and do exist throughout the country, no one of which can flatly be called "standard" or "universal" or "correct."

59b. WHAT IS CORRECT PRONUNCIATION?

The only accurate answer to this question is that the pronunciation of any word or phrase is correct if it is one used by a majority of educated speakers under similar sets of circumstances in a particular major speech area. This definition suggests that there is more than one "correct" pronunciation for the majority of words about which differences exist.

It is a basic principle of all experts on pronunciation, including the makers of dictionaries, that the one and only test for correctness is *usage*. Rules, tradition, spelling, or word derivation may help the speaker, but they carry no weight if they differ from the accepted usage.

59c. TACKLING THE PROBLEM OF PRONUNCIATION

If you have a good ear and spend considerable time listening to speakers in person and on radio and television, you can learn the pronunciation of many troublesome words. This method of learning-by-ear has several flaws, however, among which two may be mentioned: (1) Not every effective speaker, including broadcasters and telecasters, has faultless pronunciation. (2) In any particular conversation, speech, or broadcast, you may not hear the words you wish and need to learn to pronounce.

Although no reputable dictionary is, or claims to be, an infallible guide to pronunciation, no one should ignore its findings; every serious student should study it carefully. In actual fact the surest, most economical way to learn pronunciation is to consult your dictionary *when the need arises.* Do not worry about the pronunciation of any word until you read it, hear it, or anticipate the need for it in your own speech.

What such words will be must vary from person to person. No two people have the same vocabulary; no two people make the same demands on language because no two can have the same audience or identical things to say. As a conscientious student of pronunciation, you will make your own list of trouble spots. Looking up words as you need to and entering them alphabetically (or by some other method that appeals to you) in your own notebook is the most efficient way to improve your pronunciation.

Every modern American dictionary presents its own system of recording pronunciation. Your first move should be to familiarize yourself with that system. Read the essay on pronunciation that every reliable dictionary contains. Study the full pronunciation key. Examine the abbreviated pronunciation key at the bottom of each page or each alternate page. Only after you have taken these steps will you be able to use your dictionary intelligently as a guide in pronunciation.

Pronunciation, as you already know and as your dictionary will again inform you, depends upon the *sound* given to alphabetical letters or letter combinations and upon *accent* of emphasized syllables. The best-known set of symbols for transcribing the sounds of language is the International Phonetic Alphabet (IPA). This "alphabet," applicable to all languages, is highly accurate, but it is likely that the ordinary speaker and writer will find it somewhat cumbersome and involved.

Your most sensible approach will be to study the "pronunciation word" that appears in parentheses immediately after an entry word. It is a respelling of the word, giving the sounds of vowels and consonants, by syllables, according to the pronunciation key of the particular dictionary. As an indication of the kinds of information provided about pronunciation in your dictionary, see how it represents the varied sounds of, say, the letter *o*. You will find that the sounds of *o* are indicated by some or all of these symbols:

o—as in *odd, hot, lot, ox*
ō—as in *go, open, over, no*
ô—as in *oil, order, horn, ought*
o͝o—as in *took, book, look, poor*
o͞o—as in *pool, ooze, boot, too*

Each of the signs (symbols) appearing with words in a pronunciation key is a kind of diacritical mark. (The word *diacritical* comes from a Greek term meaning "capable of distinguishing," "distinctive.") Still other signs, or points, are occasionally added to letters to indicate a particular sound value. Among these are the *circumflex* (raison d'être); the *tilde* (cañon); *umlaut* (schön), and the *cedilla* (façade) (see Section 34). Some dictionaries supply these and other diacritical marks with individual entries; other dictionaries provide a separate key for foreign sounds. All diacritical marks are, of course, only approximations of sounds. Once you have studied the dictionary entry, try saying the word aloud. Then listen for its use in someone's speech and try it out in your own to fix the sounds firmly in your mind.

The matter of stress, or accent, is much less involved than the pronunciation of sounds. But it is important. Examine the method your dictionary employs for indicating where accents fall in given entries. Some dictionaries provide both accent marks and syllabication periods (dots) in the entry word. Others use only dots to indicate syllabication in the entry word and insert accent marks in the "pronunciation word." Learn the methods your dictionary has provided for indicating heavy (primary) stress and less heavy (secondary) stress.

When two or more pronunciations of an entry are provided, the pronunciation more generally used may or may not be given first. One reliable current dictionary shows first the pronunciation its compilers consider the one most widespread in "general American" usage. Another equally reliable dictionary lists first the pronunciation most prevalent in Eastern speech (along the North Atlantic seaboard). Any pronunciation shown is "standard," although some dictionaries do make a distinction by preceding a given pronunciation with the word *also.* Pronunciations also are sometimes labeled *British,* or *Chiefly British,* or with some other indication of regional usage.

Pronunciation, or what may be called the sound system of language, is important, although relatively less so for the average speaker than diction or what is broadly called grammar. And yet phonology, the sound system of language, really *is* "the grammar of speech." Every user of language will find gaps in his knowledge when he encounters certain words and will be doubtful about pronunciation. And the most reliable and systematic way to tackle pronunciation is consistent and informed use of a dictionary. Four other suggestions, however, may be helpful:

First, try to form the habit of listening carefully to the speech you hear. When you hear an unfamiliar word that interests you, when you hear a pronunciation different from your own, when you hear what you think is an error in pronunciation, you should promptly haul out a dictionary. It is possible to improve pronunciation greatly just by listening, especially when one is listening to educated and truly informed speakers.

Second, try experimenting with listening to yourself. Many of us never *really* hear what we say. If you make a conscious effort, you can hear the sounds of your own voice and can judge its quality. You can question your accent, vowel formation, articulation, and inflection. If careful listening to your voice inhibits you from speaking (everyone becomes self-conscious at times), try recording your voice on a tape recorder. What you learn may be significant.

Third, become aware of your pronunciation without becoming frightened or overly self-conscious at your method of speaking. Remember that your primary aim should be, as H. W. Fowler wrote, "to speak as your neighbors do, not better."

Fourth, and finally, try to avoid the careless, slovenly, and sometimes uninformed habits of pronunciation that do make nearly everyone seem less intelligent and less aware than he really is.

EXERCISES

I

From your dictionary copy the "pronunciation word" for each of the following:

1. economics
2. gnaw
3. chic
4. advertisement
5. coupon
6. grimace
7. data
8. chiropodist
9. acumen
10. au gratin

II

Each of the following has more than one pronunciation. What does each pronunciation indicate about the part of speech and the meaning?

1. appropriate
2. contrast
3. minute
4. object
5. subject
6. moderate
7. address
8. transfer
9. refuse
10. present

III

What is the pronunciation shown in your dictionary for each of the following proper names?

1. Eire
2. Kilimanjaro
3. Puerto Rico
4. Yangtze
5. Valkyrie
6. Socrates
7. Daguerre
8. Riviera
9. Liszt
10. Van Gogh

60. USING A LIBRARY

The word *library* comes from Latin *liber*, meaning "book." Actually, a library is a depository, a treasury of the written word and the recording of thought in manuscripts, pictures, phonograph records, tape recordings, microfilm, and all varieties of print.

The heart of any library is its collection of books and bound magazines. But a library is more than a static collection of volumes. Finding out the resources of your college library and getting to know them is inseparable from the widening of intellectual horizons. Learning to use a library intelligently will lead to a more exciting, less monotonous, far richer life. In a sense, libraries are a symbol of civilization; thanks to them, we can stand on the shoulders of giant thinkers of the past and present.

Libraries differ greatly in actual content and physical arrangement, yet the basic principles that determine their organization have been sufficiently standardized to enable you to use *any* library intelligently provided you understand the following: (1) the physical arrangement, (2) the card catalog and its uses, (3) the uses of periodical indexes, (4) reference books and their resources.

60a. PHYSICAL ARRANGEMENT

Before losing time through a trial-and-error method of discovering the resources of the library you use, devote a free hour (or several of them) to a tour of its physical arrangement. Your use of a library, *any* library, will be more efficient if you know the location of the items you are almost certain to use. Also, a tour of the library will uncover stores of information that you may wish to investigate later.

Examine the main reading room, reserved-book room, study alcoves, reference section, and periodical room. Your particular library may not be arranged to include such divisions, but it will have an equivalent organization, on either a smaller or larger scale. You should find out where the desk is located at which books are charged out for home or classroom use, where the card catalog is located, where current magazines and newspapers are filed or racked. Books of fiction (novels and stories) are arranged in most libraries in sections to themselves, shelved alphabetically by author; find out if your library employs this system. Stroll in the room or section where reference books are located and discover the kind and location of books there.

Your library may have available a guide, handbook, or pamphlet that explains the organization of the library and that sets forth regulations for its use. If so, examine it carefully. In addition, both your instructor and the librarian will be equipped and eager to answer any reasonable questions you may have about the physical arrangement of the library and the most efficient means of using its resources.

60b. THE CARD CATALOG

A large library contains a vast amount of material of varied kinds. Even a small library has a wealth of resources that will bewilder the outsider. The key to this treasure (or at least its collection of books and bound magazines) is the card catalog. This index to a library consists of 3-by-5 cards filed alphabetically in long trays or drawers and located in a series of filing cabinets. Book information may be found in a card catalog in three ways: (1) by author, (2) by title, (3) by subject.

In most libraries, every nonfiction book is represented by at least three cards, identical except that certain lines giving subject headings and joint author may be typed across the top. If you know the author or the title of a book, you will obtain needed information most easily from an author or title card. If you know the name of neither, consult the subject card for books dealing with the subject about which you are seeking information.

In addition to telling you what books are in the library, the card catalog provides the call number by means of which each book is located on the shelves. Many libraries are arranged so that all (or some) of their books are placed on open shelves easily accessible to readers. If this is the system used in your library, then the call number will help you quickly locate the volume you are seeking. In other libraries, the main collection of books is shelved in closed stacks; in order to get a book, you fill out a "call slip" furnished by the library and present it at the Circulation or Loan desk. A library worker will then locate the book by using its call number, and the book will be lent to you.

In every library, books are arranged according to a system, the notational expression of which is the first part of the call number. The two classification systems most commonly used in the United States are the Dewey Decimal classification and the Library of Congress classification. Some knowledge of each is helpful because you probably will use different libraries at different times.

In the Dewey Decimal system, fields of knowledge are arranged in ten groups, including one group for reference or general books. Each major class and each subclass is represented by a three-digit number. Further subdivisions are indicated by numbers actually following a decimal point. On a separate line beneath the Dewey number will be found the author and book number. Books are classified in the Dewey Decimal system as follows:

000–099	General works (encyclopedias, periodicals, and so on)
100–199	Philosophy (psychology, and so on)
200–299	Religion (mythology)
300–399	Social sciences (economics, government, and so on)
400–499	Language (linguistics, dictionaries, and so on)
500–599	Pure science (mathematics, chemistry, and so on)
600–699	Applied science (engineering, aviation, and so on)
700–799	Arts and recreation (painting, music, and so on)
800–899	Literature (poetry, plays, and so on)
900–999	History (Travel, 910–919; Biography, 920–929)

In the Dewey Decimal system, each book has its own call number. For instance, American literature has the subclassification 810–819. An edition of Longfellow's translation of the *Divine Comedy* has the call number 811 and beneath this the author and book number L86d. The 811 is the Dewey Decimal classification. The L86d is the author and book number; *L* is the first letter of the author's name, and *d* is the first letter of the title.

The Library of Congress classification uses letters of the alphabet followed by other letters or by Arabic numerals. The following are its main classes:

A.	General works	M.	Music
B.	Philosophy, religion	N.	Fine arts
C.	History, auxiliary sciences	P.	Language and literature
D.	History, topography (except American)	Q.	Science
E., F.	American history	R.	Medicine
G.	Geography, anthropology	S.	Agriculture, husbandry
H.	Social sciences	T.	Technology
J.	Political science	U.	Military science
K.	Law	V.	Naval science
L.	Education	Z.	Bibliography, library science

In this system, PS 303–324 is devoted to American poetry; PS 700 on, to individual authors; PS 2250–2298, to Henry W. Longfellow. Longfellow's *Evangeline* has the call number PS 2263.

Some libraries use a strictly alphabetical order for filing cards, but most of them follow the rules outlined below.

All libraries file by entry, that is, according to what appears first on the card, whether author, subject, or title. Articles that comprise the first word of a title are ignored; most libraries file letter-by-letter to the end of the word. This means that the title card *The American Way* would be filed in front of the subject card *AMERICANISMS*, just as all cards beginning with New York would be filed in front of cards with Newark as the entry word. Libraries that use a system of strictly alphabetical order would, of course, file *-isms* before *way* and *-ark* before *York*. It may be noted that encyclopedias, as well as library catalogs, differ in this fundamental rule. Abbreviations and numerals are filed just as they would be if the words they represent were spelled out.

Books that are *about* an author (considered subject entries and typed in red or in black capitals) are filed after books that are *by* that author.

Author cards having the same surname as the entry word are filed according to the given name; always note carefully the first name, or at least the initials, of an author and the *exact* title of the book you wish.

When an entry name is the same, all authors by that name precede all subjects, and all subjects come before all titles. Hence, Washington, George (books by), WASHINGTON, GEORGE (books about), *Washington Merry-go-round* (title) are filed in that order.

60c. PERIODICAL INDEXES

Current and recent issues of magazines are often displayed in libraries, sometimes in a periodical room. Older issues of magazines and of some newspapers are normally bound in book form. Some libraries own microfilm records of one or more leading newspapers. To find what you wish in them, consult *periodical indexes.* These are helpful guides to articles and other items that otherwise might lie buried.

When you consult a periodical index, turn first to the front; here you will find lists of the periodicals indexed and helpful, full instructions for use of the volume.

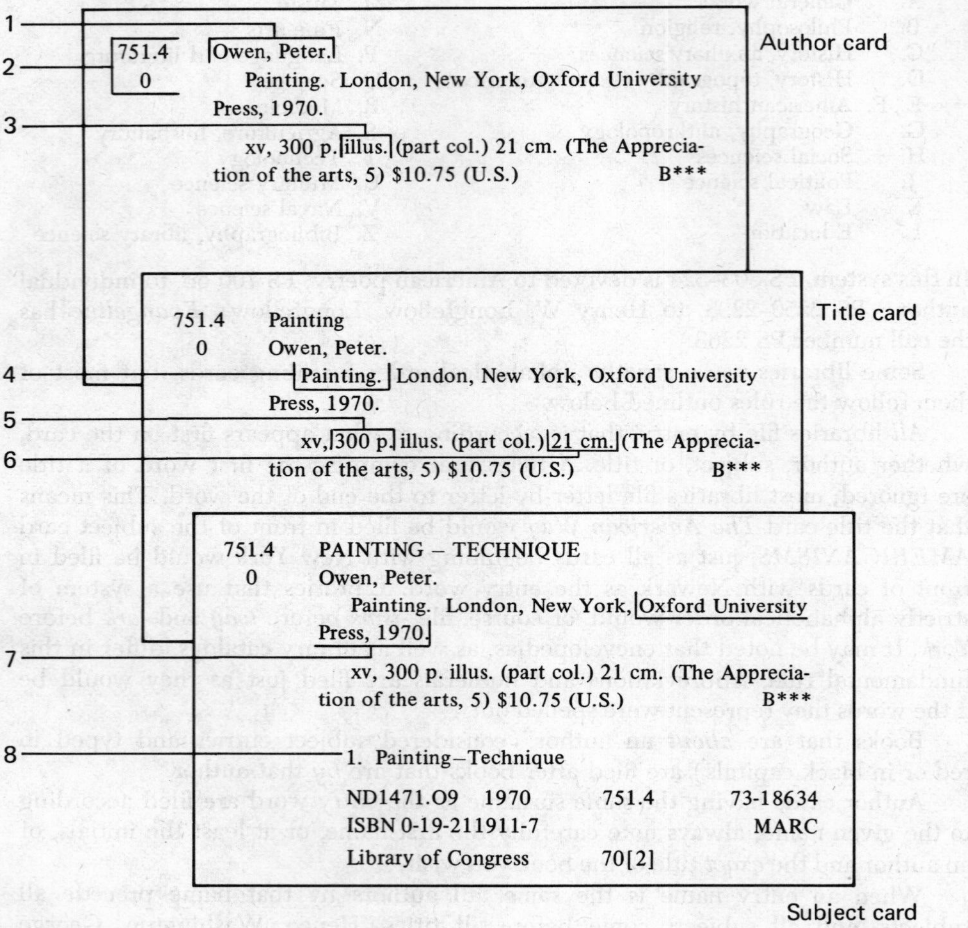

1. Author
2. Call number
3. Illustrations
4. Title
5. Number of pages
6. Size of page
7. Place of publication, name of publisher, date of publication
8. Other headings under which the book is listed

For example, here are two entries from *Readers' Guide to Periodical Literature* and their meanings:

Author entry: MANCHESTER, Harland
What you should know about flammable fabrics. Read Digest 90:37–8+ My '67

This entry means that Harland Manchester published an article entitled "What You Should Know About Flammable Fabrics" in the *Reader's Digest* for May

1967. The volume number is 90. The article begins on page 37 and continues on page 38 and later pages.

Subject entry: MARINE painting
Frederick Waugh. America's most popular marine painter. G. R. Havens IL Am Artist 31:30–7+ Ja '67

An illustrated article on the subject *MARINE* painting entitled "Frederick Waugh, America's Most Popular Marine Painter," by G. R. Havens, will be found in volume 31 of *American Artist,* pages 30–37 (continued on later pages of the same issue) of the January 1967 number.

Indexes are of two kinds. *General* indexes list the contents of magazines and a few newspapers of widespread circulation and interest. Unless you are working on some highly specialized and rather unusual subject, a general index, such as *The Readers' Guide to Periodical Literature, Facts on File, The New York Times Index,* or *The Social Sciences and Humanities Index,* probably will meet your needs. *Special* indexes, occasionally more helpful than general ones, restrict themselves to coverage of one particular area. *Agricultural Index, Applied Science and Technology Index, Art Index, Chemical Abstracts, Engineering Index,* and *Psychological Abstracts* are examples of special indexes.

Here is an annotated list of the ten periodical indexes likely to be of most use to you. (If your library does not subscribe to them, consult the librarian about your specific needs and interests. The librarian may be able to make other suggestions or provide adequate substitute material.)

1. *Annual Magazine Subject-Index,* 1907–1949. A subject index, until discontinued, to a selected list—dealing mainly with history, travel, and art—of American and British periodicals and professional or cultural society publications.
2. *Bibliographic Index, A Cumulative Bibliography of Bibliographies,* 1937——. A subject index to separately published bibliographies, and to bibliographies included each year in several hundred books and approximately 1,500 periodicals.
3. *Public Affairs Information Service Bulletin,* 1915——. A cumulative subject index to current books, pamphlets, periodicals, government documents, and other library material in the fields of economics and public affairs.
4. *Facts on File,* 1940——. A weekly world news digest with cumulative index, including world, national, and foreign affairs, Latin America, finance and economics, art and science, education and religion, sports, obituaries, and other miscellany.
5. *Index to Legal Periodicals,* 1908——. A cumulative subject and author index to articles in law journals.
6. *The Social Sciences and Humanities Index,* formerly the *International Index to Periodicals,* 1907——. A cumulative author and subject index to articles in domestic and foreign periodicals dealing with literature, history, social science, religion, drama, and pure science. It is really a supplement to *Readers' Guide,* below.
7. *The New York Times Index,* 1913——. A cumulative guide to events of national importance by reference to day, page, and column of *The New York Times.* Material is entered by subjects, persons, and organizations. The only index to an American newspaper, it is an indirect guide to events in other newspapers.
8. *Nineteenth Century Readers' Guide to Periodical Literature,* 1890–1899, with supplementary indexing, 1900–1922, 2 vols.

9. *Poole's Index to Periodical Literature*. 7 vols. An index of articles, by subject only, in American and British periodicals from 1802 to 1906.
10. *Readers' Guide to Periodical Literature*, 1900——. A cumulative index, most useful to the general reader, to over 100 popular and semipopular magazines. Entries are according to author, subject, and fiction title.

60d. REFERENCE BOOKS

Any book can be used for reference, but those that merit the name are condensed, authoritative, conveniently arranged, and up to date. (The preparation of a genuine reference book is expensive in time, money, and effort. It cannot be revised and reprinted often and therefore is not always strictly current.)

In many libraries, reference books are available on shelves open to students or on tables in a special reference section. Your instructor, or the school or reference librarian, can tell you which of the scores of reference books at hand are likely to be most helpful with a particular subject. In addition, if your library has a copy of any of the following titles, examine it carefully for useful, time-saving hints on using reference books:

American Library Association: *Ready Reference Collection*. Chicago: American Library Association, 1962.

Barton, Mary Neill: *Reference Books: A Brief Guide for Students and Other Users of the Library*, 6th ed. Baltimore: Enoch Pratt Free Library, 1966.

Hoffman, Hester R.: *Reader's Adviser and Bookman's Manual*, 10th ed. New York: R. R. Bowker, 1964.

Murphey, Robert W.: *How and Where To Look It Up*. New York: McGraw-Hill, 1958.

Winchell, Constance M.: *Guide to Reference Books*, 8th ed. Chicago: American Library Association, 1967. Supplements.

Reference works are so numerous and so varied in content and quality that it would be impossible to discuss all of them. But you should become acquainted with such important works as these:

General Encyclopedias

Collier's Encyclopedia. 20 vols. kept up to date with an annual volume, *Collier's Year Book Covering National and International Events*.

Columbia Encyclopedia, 2nd ed.

Columbia-Viking Desk Encyclopedia, 2nd ed.

Encyclopaedia Britannica. 24 vols. Kept up to date with an annual volume, *Britannica Book of the Year, a Record of the March of Events*.

Encyclopedia Americana. 30 vols. Kept up to date with an annual volume, *The Americana Annual, an Encyclopedia of Current Events*.

International Encyclopedia of the Social Sciences, 17 vols.

New International Encyclopedia. 25 vols. Kept up to date with an annual volume, *New International Year Book, a Compendium of the World's Progress*.

Seligman, Edwin R. A., and Alvin Johnson (eds.): *Encyclopaedia of the Social Sciences* (commonly known as ESS). 15 vols. Less comprehensive than the volumes listed above, it deals with many subjects directly and indirectly related to the social sciences.

General Dictionaries

Funk and Wagnalls New Standard Dictionary of the English Language.

Murray, Sir James A. H. *et al.* (eds.): *A New English Dictionary on Historical*

Principles, reissued as *The Oxford English Dictionary.* 13 vols. (Commonly referred to as the NED or OED.)
The Random House Dictionary of the English Language.
Webster's New International Dictionary of the English Language.

Yearbooks

(These are in addition to the annual yearbooks of the various encyclopedias.)
Annual Register: A Review of Public Events at Home and Abroad (British).
Europa Yearbook. 2 vols. Vol I, Europe; Vol. II, Africa, The Americas, Asia, Australasia.
Information Please Almanac. Miscellaneous information in compact form.
International Yearbook and Statesmen's Who's Who. Data on countries and political leaders.
Reader's Digest Almanac and Yearbook. Miscellaneous information.
Statesman's Year-book: Statistical and Historical Annual of the States of the World. Over 100 annual volumes have been published.
United Nations Yearbook.
World Almanac and Book of Facts. Miscellaneous information.

Your library probably has additional encyclopedias, handbooks, and dictionaries. Special reference works are available dealing with subjects such as biography, business and economics, education, drama and the theater, history, language, literature, music and the dance, painting and architecture, philosophy and psychology, religion, and science. Some of these special subject reference books will be extremely useful. Ferret them out. Once again, a good reference book is the place where you should start—but only *start*—any research project you have (see Sections 61, 62).

EXERCISES

1. Make a floor plan of the main reading room of your library, showing the location of shelves, tables, and any special sections devoted to particular kinds of books or periodicals.
2. Answer these questions about the book represented by this card:

598.294
B **Bruun, Bertel.**
Birds of Europe. Text by Bertel Bruun. Paintings by Arthur Singer. Consultant editor: Bruce Campbell. New York, Golden Press [1971, c1969]

320 p. col. illus. 30 cm. $16.95

1969 ed. published in London and New York by the Hamlyn Publishing Group under title: British & European birds in colour. Bibliography: p. 313-315.

1. Birds—Europe I. Singer, Arthur, illus. II. Title

QL690.A1B77 1971 598.294 74-147881
MARC

Library of Congress 72 [4]

A. What is the call number of this book?
B. Where was this book published? By whom? In what year?
C. What information is suppied about an earlier edition of this book?
D. How many pages does the book contain? What is the page size?
E. Is the book illustrated?
F. Does the book contain a bibliography?
G. Under what other cards in the card catalog might this book be found?

3. Copy the following, leaving enough space where the dashes occur to fill in needed material. Find the information in your library, after you have filled in the blanks or have had them filled in for you by your instructor. Write after each of the ten items the exact source of your information.
A. Give the birthplace, university attended, and date of death of ______.
B. ______ was discoverer (or inventor) of ______.
C. ______ was first published in the year ______, in the city of ______.
D. ______ University was founded in ______.
E. ______ was elected Vice-President of the United States in ______. He was a candidate of the ______ party.
F. The scenes of action in Shakespeare's play ______ are ______.
G. Two books about ______ are by, respectively, ______ and ______. For each, give the nationality of author and year and place of publication.
H. ______ is the manufacturing center in ______ of (the product) ______.
I. ______ of ______ University received his undergraduate training at ______ and did his graduate study at ______. He holds the degrees of ______ from ______.
J. At one time or another ______ has been a part of, or has belonged to, three different countries: ______, ______, and ______.

61. THE RESEARCH PAPER

The word *research* came into our language from an Old French word, *cercher,* meaning to seek or search, and the prefix *re-* (again). Research may be defined as "intensive search with the purpose of becoming certain."

The essentials of research are as natural as eating and sleeping. On your own, you have gone from one store to another to locate the suit or dress or hat that looked best on you and was the best bargain. You have tried out various restaurants, soft drinks, and movie theaters in what are actually research projects. In a sense, isn't even dating a problem in research?

After you have had some practice in writing, you may be assigned a *research paper* (also called a *term paper* or *library paper*). This will be somewhere between 1,500 and 6,000 words, depending on the subject and the limit set by your teacher. You will be asked to make a careful search for information about a particular subject and then to present and interpret what you have found out. The result should be more than a mere reading report or a hodgepodge of quotations and summaries. An effective paper is an orderly, systematic study undertaken for a specific purpose.

To turn out a good research paper takes time. It is a task you cannot do hastily or postpone until the last moment. It means choosing a suitable subject and knowing how and where to inform yourself about it. It means knowing how to take efficient notes on reading and having a clear conception of what belongs to your subject and what does not. Further, preparing a good paper requires the patience and will to write and rewrite.

As overwhelming as this task may appear, it can be both interesting and rewarding if you have a genuine interest in your subject and the curiosity to get at the facts behind it. Researching a subject and coming upon a missing fact you have been hunting for has the fascination of detective work. Students who approach a research assignment with reluctance sometimes become so engrossed in their subject that they find it difficult to make themselves stop gathering information.

The preparation of a research paper involves five major steps: (1) choosing and analyzing a subject, (2) investigating the subject carefully, (3) taking notes, (4) preparing an outline, and (5) writing and revising.[1]

61a. SELECTING AND ANALYZING A SUBJECT

Select a subject that is neither too large nor too small. Some subjects can be treated adequately in 1,000 words; trying to develop such subjects in 5,000 words results in padding and dull repetition. On the other hand, subjects such as "Aviation," "The Social Security Act," "Vietnam," and "Professional Basketball" are obviously too broad and inclusive. Countless students have discovered to their chagrin that trying to handle such a topic in 5,000 words is like using a teaspoon to catch rainwater. Trying to tackle too broad a subject is probably one of the most common errors in writing term papers.

Select a subject in which you are already interested or in which you think you can become interested. Also, even though it interests you, do not select a subject so technical or abstruse that your readers cannot be interested in it.

Select a subject about which sufficient material is available in your own college library (see Section 60).

Be fairly sure that your investigation will lead you to a set of conclusions. A research paper, like an ordinary theme, should have a central thesis, a controlling idea. Any assembling of materials anticipates the support of some proposition, of some general idea or statement. The facts you gather should lead to conclusions, the most significant part of any research paper.

61b. MAKING A THOROUGH INVESTIGATION OF THE SUBJECT

Pressed for time, you are not likely to collect more than a small part of the material available on any important subject. Amassing all that has been written on a fairly significant topic might require a year, a decade, a lifetime. But, within reason and time limitations, you should make a thorough search for information. A research paper is valueless if it merely dips into a subject. Using an encyclo-

[1] These steps constitute a complex operation. The pages that follow provide only a sketchy indication of the problems involved. Your instructor may supplement this section with classroom lectures and other specific teaching aids or may refer you to books dealing solely with research papers. If your instructor does assign one of a dozen such books, study it carefully. Preparing a research paper, and understanding fully what you are doing and the implications of your work, is one of the most valuable intellectual experiences college can offer.

pedia and investigating a topic are far different things. Here are questions you should ask:

Where can I find a good résumé of this subject? It is sound practice to get an overall view of a subject, a general background of information, in beginning an investigation. Most often you should start with an encyclopedia article. If your topic is not covered in a general or special subject encyclopedia, you may find the needed summary in a magazine article or chapter from a book.

But in starting with an encyclopedia article, do not assume that the *Britannica* is the final word, the source of all wisdom. It is a great and monumental general work, but the *Encyclopedia of the Social Sciences* or the *Dictionary of American History* might provide a better general view of your particular subject. No matter what the source, start with a nucleus of information to guide you in making the genuine investigation to follow.

What books are in the library on my topic? Begin your search in the card catalog for books given in the bibliography following the résumé article just mentioned. If you will note the subject headings appearing at the bottoms of the cards you consult, you can choose those titles that seem useful. If a suitable subject heading eludes you, try looking in the catalog for a title card under the key word of your topic.

You probably have had some experience with card catalogs in libraries. During college, you will have many opportunities to become familiar with this extraordinary key for unlocking the fabulous resources of a library. If you need help in familarizing yourself with a card catalog, a librarian or your instructor will assist you and may even suggest one of a number of useful pamphlets or books dealing with this remarkable device (see Section 60b).

What reference materials will help? Try to prevent as much fumbling and waste of time as possible. Reference materials, available in most libraries in large quantities, are excellent, time-saving aids. If you are confused, ask your librarian for help. A good reference librarian will suggest, for example, that if your topic has been discussed in Congress you should consult the *Congressional Quarterly;* that the *Harvard Guide to American History* is a timesaver in another area; that both *The Reference Shelf* and *Editorial Research Reports* treat topics of current public interest. *The Essay and General Literature Index* is a boon to harried researchers. Annual supplements to general encyclopedias such as the *Britannica* and the *Americana* provide invaluable reference materials (see Section 60d.)

How can I locate material recently written on my topic? When looking for recent material, you might begin by examining recent issues of the *Readers' Guide to Periodical Literature.* You can then compare what is listed there with entries in the *International Index to Periodicals* and *Bulletin of the Public Affairs Information Service* (P.A.I.S.). In addition, depending on your topic, you might consult entries in the *Art Index, Agricultural Index, Education Index, Applied Science and Technology Index,* and *Business Periodical Index* (see Section 60c).

Answering, and following up, the four questions just posed will provide a good start on your research. But the references listed above will not answer all your questions or provide all the guidelines needed; they represent only the beginning of your investigation. You have located some primary sources. Now you have to read and absorb what you have collected. As you read, you must take notes.

61c. TAKING CAREFUL NOTES FROM READING

Note-taking should be a process of careful thinking, not a hasty scribbling of jumbled ideas or scratchy jottings here and there in a notebook. You should read carefully and thoughtfully when doing research; both the materials and methods of your notes should reflect equal care and thoughtfulness.

MATERIALS

Index cards (3-by-5, preferably larger) can be easily shuffled into place according to subject outline; some students, however, prefer to take notes on half-size or full-size sheets of paper. Whichever material you choose, place no more than one note on a card or sheet or half-sheet of paper. *Never* use both sides of the card or paper; if the quotation or the information needed requires more space than the card or sheet allows, continue on card or sheet 2, which should be clearly marked with the same heading.

METHODS

Each book or other source used should be entered on a separate card or sheet, *in full bibliographical detail,* giving full name of the author, title, place of publication, publisher, and date. Include the number of pages in the book or article on this master card. With this complete information about each source used, the reference on the individual notes can be somewhat shortened, and all the information needed for your bibliography will be assured. You will, then, have two files of cards: one, a master file that will include *all* bibliographical detail on each book or article used (this file can be arranged in order later for your bibliography); the other, a file containing notes taken for the body of your paper.

Before you begin to take notes on a book, study its Preface and Contents. Skim through each chapter or article first, then read carefully and take notes as needed. Often the index of a book saves time if you are careful not to overlook any possible entry for the subject being searched.

Record accurately and fully the details of the information you will need, and do it the first time. Notes must be *legible,* so that they cannot be misinterpreted later, and *full,* so that you will not have to make repeated trips to the library to verify them. If you quote, *use quotation marks* to avoid wondering later whether your note represents your summary or whether it is in the author's words. Your notes should be *organized* under tentative headings; each should indicate its source by author, title, and page.

Condense your notes. Make frequent use of topic sentences and summaries. Think about what you are reading and then make the note as concise as possible.

Rearrange and regroup your notes as work proceeds. In effect, this regrouping and perhaps discarding (tentatively only, for it is a mistake to destroy what you

Webster, Margaret

<u>Shakespeare Without Tears</u>. New York: McGraw-Hill Book Company, Inc., 1942. 319 p.

The Elizabethan Stage

"When Shakespeare came to London around the year 1587... the Elizabethan stage... was in an extremely fluid condition."

Margaret Webster, <u>Shakespeare Without Tears</u>, New York, McGraw-Hill, 1942, p. 19

The Elizabethan Stage

James Burbage, about 1576 began plans for a building to be used primarily for plays.

Marchette Chute, <u>Shakespeare of London</u>, New York, E.P. Dutton, 1949, p. 29

may have second thoughts about later) amounts to making a preliminary outline.

Distinguish fact and opinion in your reading and in the notes made. Consider the point of view of each author, judge whether he proves his points, note the date of publication. Not all cards will note material directly quoted; but all should be so worded that there will be no confusion in your mind later as to what *you* said or thought and what the *author* said or what his meaning was.

61d. PREPARING AN OUTLINE FOR A RESEARCH PAPER

You will probably make a number of tentative outlines as your work proceeds, but only after you have investigated thoroughly and taken notes carefully and fully can you make a final outline of your paper. When you are ready to state conclusions and have some idea of the framework of the entire structure, you can rearrange your notes (if carefully taken) under suitable headings. From these you can readily prepare a topic or sentence outline. Never, repeat, *never* attempt to write a research paper without some form of outline as a guide (see Section 68).

The following is a list of items that should appear in the majority of outlines for research papers. It is not an outline itself but merely an indication of contents a suitable outline will cover, a checklist of items to keep in mind.

1. Purpose of investigation
2. Importance (significance) of the subject
3. Background (history) of the subject
4. The investigation itself—chronological developments, description of apparatus, and so on
5. Conclusions—generalized statements based on the findings of your study

61e. WRITING AND REWRITING

Your paper is the end result of all your reading and note taking. Even if the final outline is well designed and sufficiently detailed, and even if your notes are arranged to follow its divisions, you should, however, write a first draft as a working copy to get material down on paper to see how it looks and sounds. Leave one or two spaces between the lines for revisions. You can then make changes in sequence, strengthen your beginning, eliminate overlapping details, or make your discussion more effective in any other needed way.

A research paper is an objective presentation of the facts about a subject. Its point of view is *impersonal.* Ordinarily, do not refer to yourself as "I" or to the reader as "you." If you refer to either—and you should rarely do so—speak of "the writer" or "the present writer" and "the reader."

Write in as clear and straightforward a manner as you can. A research paper need not be stiff, overformal, or pedantic. It can be enlivened by touches of irony, humor, or a well-turned phrase. Most research papers are duller than they need be. A good research paper is a living, tangible accomplishment. You may be delightfully surprised at your success in mastering one phase of a subject and communicating it with clarity, vigor, and appeal.

SPECIMEN PAGE

Two conditions of special import help account for the violence of the attack upon witchcraft in colonial Massachusetts. One was the particular body of religious beliefs held by Puritans. The other traced from frontier conditions in early New England.

First, it is noteworthy that intellectual leaders as well as the "common herd" among Puritans considered the Bible the infallible word of God.[1] They accepted without any question whatever such a Mosaic pronouncement as "Thou shalt not suffer a witch to live."[2] Few Puritans in New England, and hardly more in the mother country, even considered challenging current theology. Newton's law of gravitation was not used as an argument against the possibility of witches riding the sky on broomsticks. Many Puritans believed that individuals could, and did, enter into compacts with the Devil. They believed in a personal devil, as described by Phillips:

> A gentleman clothed in black with horns on his head, cloven hoofs, and a forked tail, whom you might meet by ill luck almost any dark night.[3]

Puritans listened and believed when Cotton Mather spoke these awesome words:

> We should every one of us be a dog and a witch, too, if God should leave us to ourselves. It is the mere grace of God, the chains of which refrain us from bringing the chains of darkness upon our souls.[4]

[1] George Lyman Kittredge, Witchcraft in Old and New England (New York, 1929), pp. 329–330.

[2] Exodus, 22:18 (King James translation).

[3] James Duncan Phillips, Salem in the Seventeenth Century (Boston, 1933), p. 290.

[4] Cotton Mather, Memorable Provinces, Relating to Witchcraft and Possessions (Boston, 1689). Quoted from David Levin, What Happened in Salem? (New York, 1960), pp. 96–97.

Such a pronouncement was similar to hundreds of others which filled the Puritan air and inclined hearers to hatred, fear, and persecution.

The other important condition intensifying the attack upon witches involves the hardships of frontier living in early New England . . .

61f. DOCUMENTING THE RESEARCH PAPER

In addition to writing as clearly as possible, you must also document the borrowed materials you use. Documentation involves the use of both footnotes and a bibliography.

The purpose of a *footnote* is to mention the authority for some fact stated or to develop some point referred to in the body of a paper. A *bibliography* is an alphabetical list containing the names of all works (sometimes grouped according to classes or categories) quoted from or generally used in the preparation of the paper. Every formally prepared research paper should include a bibliography begun on a separate page and placed at the end of the theme. For detailed information on footnotes and bibliographies, see Part Three, the Guide to Terms and Usage.

62. REPORT WRITING

A *report* is an account or statement describing in adequate detail an event, situation, or circumstance, usually as the result of observation or inquiry. As a verb, *report* literally means to "carry back" and more generally means to "relate what has been learned by seeing and investigating."

If you witness a person entering a thicket where you have noticed a reptile and cry, "Look out for the snake," you have produced an efficient report. That is, you have clearly, briefly, and effectively conveyed important and useful information on a single topic about which you have become knowledgeable.

Report writing, however, is usually less simple and spontaneous than this warning about a snake. It may involve two or three pages of expository writing or, possibly, many pages bound in a folder containing pictures, diagrams, and charts. Regardless of length or form, report writing and letter writing (see Section 63) are likely to be the two forms that you will use and depend upon most in later life.

A report can appear in the form of a research paper (Section 61) or a letter (Section 63) or even a précis (Section 67), but most often it is a summary of activity based on an experiment or an investigation. For example, activities of any organized group may require reports. Whether you are an officer in a civic group, a chairman of a union committee, an accountant, or a research scientist, you will do a better job if you can submit a well-prepared, well-written report.

62a. PLANNING A REPORT

A good report contains enough accurate and pertinent information to accomplish the job designed—and not one bit more. In order to ensure adequate but not excess coverage, outline the report before you begin or frame one as you proceed (see Section 68). No satisfactory report was ever written without some sort of plan prepared in advance or developed as the writing progressed.

Such a scheme for an informal report might cover these questions:

1. Who asked you to study the problem? When? Why?
2. Precisely what is the subject to be reported on?
3. How was the investigation made? (Authorities consulted, people interviewed, places visited, tests made, reading done)
4. What are the specific results or recommendations?

In a formal or lengthy report, a summary of methods used to obtain information and of results or recommendations comes first. This summary is followed by the main body of the report, which discusses these summary points in detail. A list of topics on "Club Conditions in This College" might resemble this:

1. Summary
2. Members of the investigating committee
3. Methods of conducting the survey
4. Number and kinds of clubs investigated
5. Means of selecting club members
6. Activities of the clubs involved in this study
7. Club contributions to the college
8. Clubs and elections
9. Clubs and the community
10. Effects of clubs on the student body

62b. SUMMARIZING A REPORT

The plan of an effective report is usually dictated by the opening summary, an illustration of which follows:

> The purpose of this report is to determine (1) whether the program designed to give new employees an understanding of the products and social significance of the company has actually justified its cost in time and money; and (2) whether changes are needed to improve the program if it is retained.
>
> The investigation has been based on four sources of information: (1) interviews with employees who have completed the program; (2) interviews with supervisory personnel: (3) statistical comparisons of work efficiency between those who have and have not taken the program; (4) published reports on related programs at four other industrial centers.
>
> The report establishes the value of the program and recommends its continuation. Suggestions for improvement: (1) Top-level executives should contribute more actively to the program through individual interviews with employees and by lectures to groups. (2) Greater use of visual-aid material is needed to ex-

plain certain complex company operations. (3) The orientation course should be extended by two weeks.

Brief and informal reports do not require written summaries, but every report should be so organized and presented that it *can* be summarized in some such fashion as that shown.

62c. SELECTIVITY

No report reveals everything known about any subject; a good report writer indicates ability as much by what he omits as by what he includes. Nevertheless, no competent reporter regrets collecting more material than he can use; only if he collects more than he needs can he "write from strength" by having in reserve more than he requires.

62d. OBJECTIVITY

An investigator who knows in advance what answers he wishes to get and uses data to support his predetermined point of view is neither a competent nor a fair reporter. A report should be approached without personal prejudice; results and recommendations should be based on materials collected and assembled with an open mind. An effective report contains no exaggerations and few superlatives. The reliable report writer presents facts as clearly as possible and phrases recommendations without resort to argument and appeals to emotion.

62e. DIRECTNESS

Each paragraph in a report should begin with a topic sentence. A reader who, after absorbing the opening summary, wishes to examine in detail a particular part of the report should be able to locate that part at once by glancing at topic sentences only. The writer of a good report comes to each point at once and adds no unnecessary details.

62f. VISUAL REPRESENTATION

Some reports present opportunities for graphic representation. You do not need to develop professional skill in visual representation, but you should be aware that charts, maps, drawings, graphs, photographs, and diagrams may be helpful. If your report would be aided by the use of illustrative material, discuss the matter with your instructor or consult a reliable reference book on the graphic representation of data.

63. WRITING LETTERS

During their college years, many students write more letters than all other forms of writing combined: examinations, compositions, and reports. After they leave college, they are likely to write even more letters than they did in college—if they do any writing at all. So widely used a form of communication deserves careful attention: from the standpoint of utility only, training in no other kind of writing is more important.

As with all that you write, your letters unmistakably reflect and comment upon you. What you say and how you say that something, the paper you use, the appearance of your handwriting or typing, even the way you affix a postage stamp suggest your personality and your attitude, just as do your voice, diction, facial expression, and gestures.

Two main kinds of letters are *informal* (friendly) and *business* letters. Conventional patterns of *formal* correspondence (invitations to weddings and elaborate receptions and replies to such invitations, for example) might be considered a third form; however, such formal correspondence can usually be handled best through efficient stationers or engravers (who have standardized invitation forms) or through a counselor or standard reference work on etiquette.

63a. INFORMAL LETTERS

Writing a friendly letter is a highly personal act. But since "the best way to have a friend is to be one," you should not write letters that seem to say: "Here, take this. I owe you a letter, but what can I say in the limited time I have? It's messy and thin and almost incoherent—but I have a headache and also a test coming up." Your letters reflect you, and if you want them to do you justice, you should consider the following suggestions.

1. *Take your time*. No one can write a careful, interesting letter in 10 minutes. Instead of writing *five* notes in 30 minutes, try writing only *one* letter in the same length of time.
2. *Think about your reader*. A personal letter has to use a number of *I's* and *me's,* but try also to express interest in what your reader is doing or seeing or thinking.
3. *Give details*. Genuine information about one interesting conversation or one event might be more appealing to your reader than a series of hasty, unformed, kaleidoscopic, random comments about a dozen different matters.
4. *Make your letters appropriate*. Do not thoughtlessly write the same thing to every correspondent. Ninki might be interested in one subject, Robin in another, Marion and Herbert in still a third. Keep in mind the tastes and interests of your reader.
5. *Write legibly*. A letter that no one can understand is not a form of communication at all.

63b. BUSINESS LETTERS

The purpose of a business letter is to convey a message clearly. Your primary concern as a writer of business letters is with *presentation* and *content,* that is, with the order and expression of your material and with the subject matter itself. There are many kinds of business letters, among them order letters, inquiries, claims, sales letters, adjustment letters, credit letters, collection letters, letters of recommendation, and letters of application. All these are written to a form now standardized in the six parts described in the following material.

PRESENTATION

1. The *heading* contains the sender's *full* address and the date, usually placed in the upper right-hand of the sheet, an inch or more below the top edge, flush

with the right margin, and typed or written single space. On stationery with a letterhead, only the date is entered, either flush with the right-hand margin or centered under the letterhead.

2. The *inside address,* that is, the name, preceded by a proper title, and the address of the person or company written to should appear flush with the left-hand margin of the paper, usually two or four lines below the heading but sometimes farther, depending upon the length of the letter. If only the last name of the person written to is known, the letter is directed to the firm and an attention line, consisting of *Attention: Mr.* —— or *Attention of Mr.* ——, is inserted two lines below the address and two lines above the greeting. It has no bearing on the greeting, which is determined by the first line of the inside address.

3. The *greeting* or *salutation* is placed two lines below the inside address, flush with the left-hand margin, and is usually punctuated with a colon. It should be in harmony with the first line of the inside address and the general tone of the letter: for example, when writing to a man, correct forms would be *Dear Sir* or, preferably, *Dear Mr.* ——. To a woman, one would write *Dear Madam* or *Dear Miss, Mrs.,* or *Ms.* ——.

4. The *body,* the message of the letter, begins two lines below the greeting. It is commonly single-spaced (although short messages on a large sheet may be double-spaced) and double-spaced between paragraphs, which may be in block form or indented. Long messages are never continued on the back of a sheet but are carried over to a second sheet that should contain at least two lines in addition to the complimentary close and signature and that should carry in a top line some sort of identification, such as the addressee's initials, page number, and the date.

5. The *complimentary close,* usually placed at the middle or slightly to the right of the middle of the page, two or three lines below the last line of the body, harmonizes with the formality or semiformality of the greeting. Correct forms, capitalized in the first word only and usually followed by a comma, include *Your truly, Very truly yours, Yours sincerely, Cordially yours, Cordially,* and so on. (*Cordially yours* is often used among business friends and by older people writing to younger.) Independent of the last paragraph, the close should not be linked to it by participial phrases such as "*Thanking you in advance, I am,*" and so on.

6. The *signature,* unless a letter is mimeographed or is plainly a circular, is handwritten and is placed directly below the complimentary close. If the name is typed in, four spaces should be allowed for signature. Traditionally, an unmarried woman placed *Miss* in parentheses before her name, and a married woman either placed *Mrs.* in parentheses before her name or signed her full name followed by her married name. With the advent of the abbreviation *Ms.,* however, women have begun omitting any indication of their marital status and (like men) placing no title before their written or typed name. For both men and women, the business title often is placed after the typed name: *General Manager, Superintendent,* and so on.

STATIONERY AND TYPING

A good business letter, correct and attractive in form, reflects thoughtfulness for the reader. Unruled, white paper of good quality and standard size (8½ × 11 inch) or half-size (8½ × 5½ inch) contributes to this impression of courtesy, as does neat typing with fresh black ribbon, or legible longhand in black or blue-black ink. Materials of unusual size and color are a distraction to the reader. The layout of the letter should be balanced on the page, with margins at least an inch wide and with the right-hand margin as even as possible.

In writing a business letter, you may arrange the lines of the heading and of the inside address according to the *full block* or the *modified block system.* In both, the second and third lines of the heading and of the inside address, respectively, begin directly underneath the beginning of the first line. In the full block form, all the parts of the letter, including the heading, complimentary close, and signature, begin at the left-hand margin. In the modified block form, the heading, complimentary close, and signature are in their conventional place, on the right side of the letter.

Rarely seen in a present-day business letter is the formerly popular *indented* system, in which each line of the heading and of the inside address is indented a few spaces to the right of the line preceding it.

HEADING, ADDRESS, AND ENVELOPE

Heading and inside and outside addresses should be punctuated consistently according to the *open* or *closed* system. In the open system, no commas or final periods, except after abbreviations, are used after the separate lines, and some letter-writers prefer, also, to omit the colon after the salutation and the comma after the complimentary close. In the closed system, commas are placed after each line of the heading and inside address, except the last, at the end of which a period is used. Open punctuation is used more frequently today.

Finally, as a business correspondent you should observe convention in folding the letter and inserting it in its envelope: For the standard large envelope, fold the lower third of the letter over the message and fold the top third to within a half-inch of the creased edge. For the standard small envelope, fold the lower part of the page to within a half-inch of the upper edge; then fold from the right slightly more than one-third so that the left folded portion will come slightly short of the right creased edge. Attention to such details may seem tedious and unnecessary, but it does make opening and reading your letter as easy as possible, so that your reader may focus his entire attention on what you have to say.

CONTENT

Since a business letter conveys information by precise exposition, the general rules of effective writing apply to it as well as to other types of composition. Your very first paragraph should include a statement of your subject or purpose and any pertinent background information that will clarify your message.

After making your purpose evident, your letter should reveal your thoughts in logical, easily followed units, with short, separate paragraphs for separate ideas. The letter should close strongly and effectively with a complete sentence—a direct question, an invitation, a restatement of the subject, or an important comment.

A cogent business letter contains no hackneyed, worn-out "business" expressions such as these, sometimes referred to as "letter-killers": *am pleased to advise, beg to acknowledge, contents noted, enclosed please find, in receipt of, thank you in advance, under separate cover, wish to advise.* Instead, it is written in an informal, soundly idiomatic style, using much the same language that is used in a business conversation over the telephone.

In composing a business letter, whether your subject is a one-sentence request, a multiple-item order, a detailed inquiry, or a job application with a request for an interview, you should be brief, clear, and exact. Here is an example of a letter of application. Note how the writer comes to the point as quickly as possible and how he then proceeds without delay to describe himself and his qualifications. Here also are examples of an order letter and a claims letter. Note how all the necessary information—but no more than is necessary—is supplied clearly and concisely.

Stenton College
Columbus, Illinois 62328
February 10, 19--

Mr. Joseph R. Stolpe, President
Stolpe Homes, Incorporated
180 Walnut Boulevard
Olympia, Illinois 10198

Dear Mr. Stolpe:

Mr. Earl Winant, a member of the Olympia Realty Board, has informed me that your firm plans this summer to build a number of homes on the old Bloomfield estate, which you recently acquired, and that you will need an additional builder's assistant. I should like to apply for that position.

A resident of Olympia, I am now at Stenton College, where I plan to major in architecture. I am a graduate of the Hilltop School in Cardiff, Pennsylvania, where as a student for three years I completed one year of regular and two years of advanced mechanical drawing. The small student body at Hilltop was responsible for construction of the school itself, and so I participated in the building, wiring, and plumbing of a 10-room dormitory, a science building, and a farmhouse that was converted into classrooms. I also was the designer and builder of the photography lab.

During the past two summers, I have been employed by Hummel Brothers, in nearby Darwin, as carpenter's helper. My duties with the firm included roofing, insulating, digging foundations, flooring, painting, and electrical work. I also drove their 2½-ton pick-up truck.

My age is 19. I am in excellent health, am 5'10" tall, and weigh 160 pounds. I own my own tools, and you can depend on my working with them intelligently and skillfully.

We shall have our mid-semester recess during the week beginning March 15. I can come to your office then for an interview, and shall do so at any time agreeable to you. When would be most convenient?

Very truly yours,

Robert A. Dennison

References: Professor M. G. Farkes, Stenton College, Columbus, Illinois 62253
Mr. Rutherford Parsons, Hilltop School, Cardiff, Pennsylvania 18967 (Director of Construction Activities)
Mr. Conrad Hummel, Hummel Brothers, 120 Main Street, Darwin, Illinois 62195
Mr. Earl Winant, Olympia Realty Board, Olympia, Illinois 62198

ORDER LETTER

240 King Street
Maryville, Delaware 19721
April 9, 19——

White Garment Company
8639 West Street
New York, New York 10017

Gentlemen:

Please send me, by parcel post, four pairs of ladies' nylon hose, 15 Denier, size 9, medium length, suntan color. In payment I enclose a money order for six dollars ($6).

Yours very truly,

(Miss) Jane Smith

CLAIMS LETTER

R.F.D. 6
Lansom, Pennsylvania 18231
November 15, 19——

The Tryco Department Store
49 East Tenth Street
New York, New York 10015

Gentlemen:

On November 9 I purchased in your radio department a Vinson radio, table model R-350, with brown plastic case. The radio arrived promptly, but I am disappointed to find that it does not operate on DC current. It was my understanding that the Model R-350 is designed to operate on either AC or DC, but I find that the accompanying instructions indicate only AC. I am returning the radio at once in the hope that it can be exchanged for a set suitable for DC wiring.

If there has been a misunderstanding and the R-350 does not operate on DC current, I shall have to choose another model. If that is the case I hope that I may have a refund, since I shall not be in New York again for several months. I hope, however, that you will be able to supply an R-350 model that will fill my needs.

Very truly yours,

Edward J. Ryan, Jr.

64. READING

Reading and writing are two aspects of the same process—the communication of thoughts, moods, and emotions. When you write effectively you convey your ideas and feelings to others; when you read well you receive from others their ideas and feelings. Since reading and writing are inseparably linked, it is important that in trying to learn to write well you learn to read well.

An American university president recently remarked that at one period in the history of this country our leaders "found time to read and demonstrated in their own lives and works the utility as well as the delight of reading. The four master-builders—Hamilton, John Adams, Jefferson, and Madison—were probably the four most widely read men of their age." Were they great because they were well read, or well read because they were great?

It has not been proved that all great writers have been efficient readers, but generations of college students have demonstrated a striking parallelism between efficient reading and effective writing. Furthermore, although motion pictures, radio, television, and varied audiovisual materials may eventually alter the situation, at least we know that a good general education cannot now be imparted to anyone unable to read both accurately and reflectively. *In Heroes and Hero-Worship,* Thomas Carlyle stated, "If we think of it, all that a university can do for us is still but what the first school began doing—teach us to *read.*"

Learning to read efficiently is a long and arduous process. Perhaps it should be, for reading is almost miraculous when we consider that through it we have at our command and for our use much of the best that has been thought and written by the greatest minds of many centuries.

Efficient reading demands the ability to concentrate, to use our intellectual curiosity, to visualize as we read so that images come to life and take on extra dimensions. Perhaps most important of all, efficient reading involves organizing and retaining ideas and impressions gained from the printed page.

64a. READING TO COMPREHEND

Much of our reading is not accurate or reflective. When we read a light short story or novel, a mystery story or a comic book, we are usually seeking relaxation and quite naturally skip and skim. But when we attempt similarly to read meaty fiction and drama, closely reasoned essays and biography, and carefully and concisely wrought poems, we become confused or receive all too little of the meaning intended. Desultory and inattentive reading is proper when applied to unimportant writing; the danger is that frequently we attempt to read anything and everything at the same speed and with the same degree of concentration.

Any difficulty and burdensomeness of reading, however, is of small import next to the pleasure that it can and does afford many millions of readers. After all, reading is one of the few pure pleasures known to mankind. Reading is a voluptuous delight for the initiated, a pastime that, in the words of Sir Philip Sidney, "holdeth children from play and old men from the chimney corner."

Remember that some who feast on light fiction and comic books do not so much "skip and skim" as merely read without concentrated attention and reflection. Also, although you may not be among their number, many persons actually read for sheer pleasure works dealing with science, history, biography, philosophy, and the like. One's active sympathies and intellectual curiosity strongly affect *what* and *how* one reads.

In reading to understand, to comprehend, one should keep in mind that everyone ought to learn to read well enough to: (1) gain and understand accurate information and ideas; (2) recognize the organization and style of what he is reading; (3) interpret what he is reading in terms of his own experience; (4) analyze and evaluate what he is reading.

Whether we read for relaxation, information, or both, our aim should be to use our time intelligently. More than three centuries ago, Francis Bacon wrote wisely on the relationship of reading and writing:

> Read not to contradict and confute; nor to believe and take for granted; nor to find talk and discourse; but to weigh and consider. Some books are to be tasted, others to be swallowed, and some few to be chewed and digested; that is, some books are to be read only in parts; others to be read, but not curiously; and some few to be read wholly, and with diligence and attention. Some books also may be read by deputy, and extracts made of them by others; but that would be only in the less important arguments, and the meaner sort of books; else distilled books are like common distilled waters, flashy things. Reading maketh a full man; conference a ready man; and writing an exact man. And therefore, if a man write little, he had need have a great memory; if he confer little, he had need have a present wit; and if he read little, he had need have much cunning, to seem to know what he doth not.

64b. SPEED IN READING

Reading effectively is reading with both speed and comprehension. You will soon discover, if you have not already done so, that one of the main differences between college and high school work lies in the amount of reading required. It has been estimated that college students today have more than five times as much required reading as did those of 1900. You may feel that you are floundering in a sea of words: as a college freshman you will be asked to read some 4 million words in textbooks, collateral volumes, and source books. Reading is required in all but about 10 percent of your college studies. Assignments of several thousand words each in such courses as history, economics, sociology, and political science will force you to increase your reading speed, even if you already are a rapid reader.

By a conspiracy of silence in high schools and colleges, until recently little attention was given to rapid reading. But the necessity for skipping and scanning at last has been recognized; educators are aware that success in college depends in part upon one's reading speed.

Our rate of reading is connected with the number of fixations that our eyes make as they move across a page. Our aim should be to reduce the number of fixations, to read not word-by-word but by thought phrases. As we lengthen the span of our eye movements, our reading rate will increase and so will our comprehension. We will be reading not in isolated units but in context. A skillful reader seldom has to refer to the beginning of a sentence he has finished; he will have carried the thought through in one rapid series of lengthened glances. The best advice, of course, is to "read with your head, not with your eyes"; so doing will increase comprehension by reducing fixations of the eyes and increasing concentration. Practice finding main ideas in a passage and separating them from subordinate thoughts; learn to find key words and key sentences and to distinguish them from merely illustrative material. The assignments in many of your courses will provide you with ample opportunity for such practice.

64c. READING DIFFICULTIES

You may encounter hindrances to effective reading. For example, if, after concentrated reading for a short time, your eyes feel tired or begin to smart, or your head begins to ache, you should consult an ophthalmologist or oculist. Again, good posture while reading will help to prevent muscular weariness and incorrect breathing. Also, you need a good light for reading, one that both illuminates the page without glare and does not shine directly into your eyes.

You may have fallen into the bad habit of pronouncing words as you read silently. Few, if any, "lip movers" can read with either comprehension or speed. If you suspect yourself of this acquired fault, have someone observe you and then try to break this bad habit. Daydreaming, napping, and just plain letting your mind wander are enemies of reading with either speed or comprehension. Good reading is as much a matter of concentrated attention as it is anything else.

64d. READING AS A READER

When you read *as a reader* your purposes should be to acquire information, to form opinions, to draw conclusions. You stock your mind with ideas for use in thinking, discussion, and writing. You look for new problems, answers to questions, visual details that widen your experience and understanding. Careful reading of any selection should help you to partial understanding of the author's life and background, to a statement of central theme and purpose, to a concept of the organization of main divisions and supporting material. This kind of reading must be painstakingly careful. In *Translating Literature into Life,* Arnold Bennett wrote:

> What is the matter with our reading is casualness, languor, preoccupation. We don't give the book a chance. We don't put ourselves at the disposal of the book. It is impossible to read properly without using all one's engine-power. If we are not tired after reading, common sense is not in us. How should one grapple with a superior and not be out of breath?
>
> But even if we read with the whole force of our brain, and do nothing else, common sense is still not in us, while sublime conceit is. For we are assuming that, without further trouble, we can possess, coordinate, and assimilate all the ideas and sensations rapidly offered to us by a mind greater than our own. The assumption has only to be stated in order to appear in its monstrous absurdity. Hence it follows that something remains to be done. This something is the act of reflection. Reading without subsequent reflection is ridiculous; it is equally a proof of folly and of vanity.

Bennett here used the word *reflection* to mean *evaluation*. Reading to absorb ideas is important in itself but it is not enough; we should also read to answer these questions: (1) What is the author attempting to do? (2) How well does he succeed in his attempt? (3) What value has the attempt? Effective reading is critical reading, a many-sided evaluation of scope, material, and purpose.

64e. READING AS A WRITER

When you read *as a writer* you should focus your attention not only upon the specific approaches already noted but also upon the author's technique, his methods of manipulating material. It should become habitual for you to study a writer's choice and use of words, his sentence and paragraph structure, even such relatively prosaic matters as punctuation and mechanics. Look consciously for the methods by which he secures his effects: aids to interest such as humor, irony, anecdote; appeals to emotions; the logicalness of the presentation. Reading as a writer involves reading thoroughly, imaginatively, creatively. It implies a consideration of subject matter, style (the imprint of the author's personality on subject matter), and technique.

For additional comment on reading as a writer, see Chapters 9 and 10 in Part One.

65. LISTENING

You do a lot of reading and writing in college, and possibly much talking, but you listen more often than you do anything else. College essentially provides an opportunity to listen. Certainly, much of what we know—including the prime ability to speak our language—has come through our ears.

65a. ACTIVE LISTENING

When people talk to you, they are usually affected by how you listen. If you are attentive, you assist the speaker in saying exactly what he has on his mind. Inattentiveness acts as a damper on the person talking; he will sometimes stop, or he will find it more difficult to express his ideas.

Try this simple experiment. In an empty room, try talking aloud to yourself about some simple fact. Your words may not flow smoothly, and you will undoubtedly become confused. Ask someone into the room and explain the same fact to him. You will find doing so far less difficult than before. We all need listeners; without them we are mentally lost as we talk.

When you are on the listening end, you have a responsibility for producing effective communication. But remember that good listening is not easily faked. Facial expressions, posture, eye movements, and gestures betray the poor listener or support the good one.

65b. LISTENING AS A LEARNING TOOL

A friend may have a large store of knowledge to offer if you will only listen. The person who sits next to you on a bus or train or airplane may be an authority on a subject, and if you listen attentively, he will often pass along a wealth of information. Your college staff has experts in many fields; most of them will take time outside of classes to pass on what they know if they think you care. People usually are flattered and eager to share their knowledge.

Listening is sometimes a faster, more efficient means of gathering information than reading. If you need to know something about a subject quickly, you can often find an authority on it to ask. He is likely to speak in terms that you can understand. He may also select and consolidate information from his broad field of knowledge to give you an accurate, generalized view of the subject; for you to do the same through reading might take weeks or months of research. And, of course, if you don't understand his discourse, you can ask questions for immediate clarification; as a reader you cannot question the writer so easily. Also, many times a listener can obtain valuable information not easily found in written form.

Writing that may seem dull and difficult to understand as you read it can often be understood and appreciated if you listen to it. Shakespeare's plays prove this point. They were written to be heard and are at a disadvantage when presented simply as words on a page. However, if you can first hear one of the plays, and then read it, your experience is enhanced, and your chances of appreciating Shakespeare are much better. It's not difficult to find a friend who will join you in reading aloud. Also, if you have a record player, you might investigate the many available records of famous authors reading their own writings or accomplished actors reading classical literature.

Good listening is one of the best-known ways for improving language facility. Perhaps this fact stems from early childhood when we learned to talk by listening to and imitating our elders. The principle remains valid throughout our lives. Listen to persons who are accomplished speakers, either in public speaking situations or in conversation. At college you will hear many such speakers; and the more carefully you listen to them, the more you will be able to improve your own oral facility.

65c. LISTENING HABITS

You may have acquired some habits that thwart your attempts in learning to listen while listening to learn. These habits will be less difficult to overcome if you are aware of them.

1. *Supersensitive listening.* Some persons refuse to listen to anything that does not agree with their own private thoughts. Hearing statements that they do not like, they immediately begin to plan a rebuttal and stop listening to what the speaker has to say. Perhaps they should make it a policy to hear the speaker out. When he has finished, they can make final judgments.

2. *Avoiding difficult explanations.* If something is difficult to understand, many listeners tend to give up too easily. They blame the speaker for not making his points clearer. The remedy: go out of your way to hear material that is hard to grasp. Stick with the subject from beginning to end; force yourself to listen. Listening requires practice just as writing does.

3. *Premature dismissal of a subject as uninteresting.* If a speaker's material seems dry, some of us use that impression as rationalization for not listening. We feel that if the speaker's material is not stimulating, he must not have anything worth hearing. Yet, as someone once remarked, there are no uninteresting subjects, only uninterested people. When one forms the habit of listening attentively, many previously dull subjects seem to take on new life. Have you never become friends with, or even fallen in love with, someone whom you used to consider dull and uninteresting?

4. *Finding fault with a speaker's delivery or appearance.* Sometimes we become so deeply involved in a speaker's delivery or appearance that we cannot concentrate on what he or she is saying. If his manner or appearance creates an unfavorable impression, we lose interest. Conversely, a speaker's looks or manner may cause fantasies that distract us with equal loss of comprehension. The most important task in listening is to learn what the speaker says, not how he says it or how he looks when saying it.

65d. TAKING NOTES ON LECTURES

Many persons fail at taking notes because they try to write down too much of what is being said. Some students feel that they should transcribe as many of the lecturer's words as possible in order to make a good set of notes. Or they feel that they should *outline* the lectures they hear. In either case, the note-taker cannot be effective. He concentrates too much on the mechanical process of writing when he should be listening and thinking about what he hears. As a result, he receives some parts of a lecture, obtains garbled versions of other parts, and completely misses a large percentage of it. The efficient note-taker spends far more time listening than he does writing.

A means of properly apportioning time between listening and writing during a lecture is found in the *précis* system of note-taking (see Section 67). This system involves listening for the period of time it requires the speaker to make a point and then writing down that point in a one-sentence summary. A lecture is usually organized so that the speaker makes a series of points (they might be compared with the topic sentences of written paragraphs) which support a main idea. If you catch these points and summarize them in a complete sentence, you will make efficient notes from the lectures you hear.

This kind of note-taking requires considerable practice. Actually, the time to listen and the time to write become more obvious as you learn to recognize how a lecture is organized. As you become adept at précis-writing you will find your notes increasingly useful. Not only will they lead you to the central ideas contained in the lectures; they will also help you to remember through mental association the facts and figures that should be in your mind simply because you were listening and not writing constantly during the lectures.

Here are a couple of worthwhile tips: (1) Leave plenty of space around each sentence that you write in your notebook. (2) As soon as possible after a lecture, review the précis notes and expand them with whatever they bring to mind from the lecture. In this way you will produce a more complete set of notes depending less on memory, yet your note-taking will not have blocked your listening.

65e. LISTENING OUTSIDE THE CLASSROOM

Good listening is as important at home, in one's dormitory or student center, and on the street as it is in the classroom and laboratory. When you leave school, your ability to listen may become more important than ever. An adult spends at least half his communication time in listening. That poor listeners are expensive and expendable employees is a cruel fact of the business world.

Indeed, many of our most important affairs depend on listening. What does a jury do? It listens, sometimes to millions of words of testimony, and then makes up its mind about the case on trial. The way one votes in an election depends to a large extent on his ability to listen.

66. SPEAKING

The way you talk tells more about you than any other activity of your life. What you say—and how you say it—are more revealing of your intelligence, personality, and character than the ways you dress, eat, walk, read, or make your living. Knowing how to read and write are significant accomplishments for anyone, but neither is an *essential* part of anyone's existence. Communicating with others through some sort of speech signals *is* essential.

Everyone reading this book presumably can write, obviously can read, and certainly can communicate with others. Most people spend many school years learning to read and write, but few of us have ever paid much attention to learning how to talk. We have talked since infancy, and now we assume that it is as "simple" and as "natural" as breathing. It isn't.

More time, opportunities, money, and friendships are lost through careless, slovenly, inaccurate speech than through any other activity of people's lives. Because no one can speak perfectly (any more than he can read or write perfectly), this condition will persist. And yet everyone can learn to speak with greater confidence, fewer errors, and more genuine communication if he will only study his speech habits and give the problem of talking with others the attention it fully deserves.

This section is designed to make a start in helping you get rid of any bad speech habits you may have and to confirm and strengthen you in your good ones.

Improving talk is a life-long occupation, but here are "ten commandments" that will serve as constant, never-failing guides in learning to speak effectively.

1. *Pronounce words carefully.* More errors, inaccuracies, and misunderstandings are caused by carelessness and haste than by ignorance or inadequate vocabulary. Give speech the care and attention it deserves (see Section 59).
2. *Speak to be heard.* If something is worth saying, it deserves to be heard. Don't shout, but don't mumble. Say, don't slur.
3. *Look alive.* If you show interest in what you are saying and talk in lively tones, animation will invigorate your talk and stimulate your hearers.
4. *Take your time.* Your tongue is slower than your mind, but it is quicker than your listener's ear. Nearly everyone speaks rapidly, drops syllables, slurs words, and runs thoughts together in headlong haste. Slow down.
5. *Learn to listen.* Talk should be a two-way street. It is not only courteous to listen to others; learning to listen is the most effective means known to man for gathering facts, acquiring ideas—and improving speech (see Section 65). It is how you learned to talk in the first place. Open your ears.
6. *Vary your approach.* The sole requirement of effective speech is that it should communicate. The tone of your voice and your choice and use of words should vary from situation to situation, from person to person. At times, your speech should be racy and pungent; at other times, deliberate and formal (see Section 11). Talk should be appropriate. Shift gears.
7. *Be concise.* Most statements of any kind are wordy. All of us repeat an idea in identical or similar words—and then say it again (see Section 55). Talk should not be cryptic and mysteriously abrupt, but it should be economical. Make it snappy!
8. *Be specific.* Much of our speech is indefinite, not clearly expressed, uncertain in meaning. Even when we have a fairly good idea of what we wish to say, we don't seek out those exact and concrete words that would convey what we have in mind (see Section 39b). Try to use words that have precise meaning. Don't be vague.
9. *Be original.* It's impossible for anyone to conceive of a wholly new idea or to express an old one in fresh, original diction. And yet the greatest single error in "saying it right" is the use of trite, worn-out expressions that have lost their first vigor, picturesqueness, and appeal (see Section 39i). Avoid clichés. Don't be a rubber stamp.
10. *Have something to say.* With rare exceptions, people tend to talk more—and say less—than they should. After all, speech is only the faculty or power of speaking. The ability to talk is one thing; thoughts and emotions are another. Spinoza wrote that mankind would be happier if the power in men to be silent were the same as that to speak; that "men govern nothing with more difficulty than their tongues." It was a wise person who remarked at a meeting that it was better for him to remain silent and be suspected a fool than to speak and remove all possible doubt. Think first.

Keeping these "ten commandments" is within the capacity of anyone free from major speech defects. If you can keep any one of these "commandments" better than you did before, you have taken a long step toward improvement. If you can keep any five of them, you are an above-average speaker.

66a. ORAL AND WRITTEN COMPOSITION

Although speaking and writing have many common characteristics, a brief consideration of how they differ may help to improve both written and oral communication. A speech is not merely "an essay walking on its hind legs"; there are some essential differences between oral and written composition.

The speaker is usually concerned with the attention of a group; the writer, with that of one individual at a time. A group is slower in getting meanings than the individual member, and the speaker must make allowances for this. Furthermore, each audience constitutes a special problem, and the speaker must take into account its size, average age, educational level, and special interests. Writing at its best is nearly universal in its appeal, but speaking is usually best when it is clearly adapted to immediate listeners.

Oral style differs from written style. The speaker must be instantly intelligible. His hearers cannot go back and meditate on a sentence or try to figure out its meaning; if they do so, they are sure to lose what follows. The speaker's sentences, as a rule, are shorter and his language usually is simpler and more direct than the writer's. Reader and writer are separated, but speaker and listener are thrown into close association. An alert speaker can watch the facial expressions of his audience and thus get feedback, which is totally lacking in a writer-reader relationship. On the other hand, the reader is usually alone, relatively comfortable, and free from distractions, while the listener is physically distracted by other members of the audience. Even when he is quietly at home listening to a speech over TV or the radio, it is more difficult for the listener to give close attention to it than to the printed page, which he can always reread if his attention wanders. Many more people are eye-minded than are ear-minded.

The speaker's voice is an important consideration in oral communication, one that has no exact parallel in the written form. And the speaker's use of his body, which also is important in establishing communication with his audience, has no bearing whatever upon writing.

66b. CONVERSATION

Who is the best conversationalist you know? What are the characteristics of his or her language? If you reply honestly, you will probably select a person whose speech seems *forceful* or *vivid* to you, someone who talks *clearly,* someone whose conversation is *smooth* or even *logical* or *precise* or *animated.* Few will select a person whose talk is notably *correct;* rarely will any comment be made on the niceties of conventional grammar, on violations of established usage, on subject-verb agreement or the right case of pronouns. True, the person whom you choose may be a user of correct English—more often than not he will be—but your remarks will not be "he uses correct English" nearly so often as "he's interesting to listen to" or "he knows how to get his ideas across." "Bad grammar" affects most of us far less than do pompous language, longwindedness, affectation, and insincerity. Correctness is helpful, but it is a limited goal in diction. The best speakers—and best writers—are those who in addition to using words correctly also use them clearly, vividly, and forcefully.

Conversation should be a genuine meeting of the minds. It has little in common with mere talkativeness or chattering about dates, clothes, or the weather. Good conversation is a stimulating pastime, especially when it concerns genuine ideas or problems and represents a frank interchange of information and opinion. Don't aim for mere glibness as a conversational goal; superficiality may enable you to "get by" in a group discussion, it may save you the trouble of defending your opinions, but it wastes your time and that of your companions.

How can you become a good conversationalist?

Be sincere and straightforward but also tactful and courteous. A group of people will seldom agree about anything of real consequence; and if they did, a conversation about it would probably be dull. A spirited discussion may be, and often is, argumentative. However, you can state your opinions and defend them firmly without hurting the feelings of those who differ with you. Frankness that verges on rudeness is never in good taste, nor is the brusque person welcome in a discussion. Flat contradiction is rude, but it is possible to differ with your neighbor and still engage in a friendly discussion.

You will often engage in conversation with one person, even at a large party. You may be left with the guest of honor at a reception, a professor at a college mixer, a stranger at a dinner party. If you are, instead of trying to interest him in yourself and your problems, why not find out as much about him as you tactfully can? It is human to be flattered at another's interest in us, and few people fail to respond if that interest seems genuine.

Analyze every conversation you have an opportunity to hear or engage in. Notice that the best conversationalists are usually those who have the largest fund of interesting experiences or the greatest familiarity with the subjects of most interest to the people in your circle. Listen and observe.

Read as much as you can; a good daily paper, worthwhile magazines, books that are attracting attention. Keep informed about matters likely to be discussed among your acquaintances: current events, political affairs, personalities in the limelight, general economic and business conditions, new styles, changes on college campuses, sporting events, current music, art, and literature. Try to remember good stories you hear or read, funny or interesting incidents that happen to you or your friends, amusing or significant happenings you see or read about.

Above all, *practice* conversing; join in good conversation every chance you have.

66c. GROUP DISCUSSION

Hundreds of thousands of Americans received their first opportunity to speak in public through *group discussions*. The function of a group discussion, which may have varying degrees of formality and informality, is to pool the information of a group to find a satisfactory solution to the problem at hand.

Various types of public discussion are in general use today, but all call for the same type of preparation. A general topic and the specific problem for discussion are chosen. Possible solutions are usually presented by speakers assigned in advance. After more or less prolonged debate on these solutions, a plan of action or an agreement on policy is reached, if possible.

1. The *single-leader type*. This kind of program often follows an important speech and always heightens interest in it. Here an open-forum period is allowed

during which members of the audience may ask questions of the speaker or differ with him. The speaker himself may preside at the forum period, or a chairman may act as moderator and refer questions to the speaker. Or a meeting may be called to discuss a problem of local interest, and some elected or appointed member of the group may take charge of the meeting, acting as both chairman and discussion leader. His function is to state the problem or problems involved, to recognize speakers, to keep things going, to see that all important phases of the problem are considered, to ensure that no one monopolizes the time, to prevent unpleasant conflicts, and to guide the discussion to some sort of conclusion. Most assemblies and parliamentary bodies follow a system of this type, usually governed by specific rules.

2. The *town meeting* type. A group of experts—usually four—discusses opposing attitudes toward some important public question; each is given at least one opportunity to reply to the other's arguments, and the audience is then given an opportunity to enter the discussion and to question the speakers. A moderator presides over the meeting, introduces the speakers, and controls the audience discussion.

3. The *panel,* or *round-table,* type. A group of experts, literally sitting around a table, discusses various aspects of the topic selected. The discussion is informal and resembles a spirited conversation. The speakers have no time limit when they speak, and they may speak as many times as they choose—unless they threaten to monopolize the discussion. The function of the chairman is to keep the discussion moving forward, to keep the various members of the panel participating, to sift out points of agreement if possible, and to summarize the argument for the audience at the end. Such panel discussions occur frequently on television and radio.

4. The *debate.* Formal debate has many characteristics in common with more informal panel discussions. But it is closely controlled by rules. The proposition for debate is carefully worded to provide a direct clash and to prevent ambiguity; opposing members are organized into teams, each with a captain; each speaker is allowed to speak twice in a prescribed order; a rigid time limit is imposed for each speech; and a judge, or board of judges, usually awards a decision to the team that has "played the game" more skillfully. Although this form of intellectual sport has unquestioned values for its participants, it is available only to relatively few students and has little direct application to everyday life.

EXERCISES

1. Listen to what you consider a typical conversation between two friends or acquaintances. Summarize it for the class, using direct quotations if you can. Criticize the conversation from the point of view of Section 66b.
2. Find one example of a good conversation in a short story or novel. Tell why you think it is interesting and effective.

3. Listen to a television or radio speaker who interests you. Prepare a report, oral or written as your instructor directs, that analyzes this speaker's performance in the light of comments made in Section 66.
4. Find an interesting modern speech in a collection or in an issue of *Vital Speeches*. List the rhetorical devices the speaker used (see Chapter 9 for a discussion of such devices).
5. Prepare a three-minute speech to be delivered in class on a subject you have previously used for a composition. Hand in, in advance, an outline of the speech and a summary of the differences between the speech and the composition on which you based it.

67. PRÉCIS AND PARAPHRASE

Two forms of writing that have proved effective methods of study for many persons are the précis and the paraphrase. Neither technique is so often assigned as a writing task as it once was, but both devices are worth consideration.

The précis

A *précis* (the form is both singular and plural and is pronounced "pray-see") is a brief summary of the essential thought of a longer composition. It is a miniature of the original that reproduces in the same mood and tone the basic ideas of the original passage. The writer of a précis does not interpret or comment; his function is to provide a reduction of the author's exact meaning without omitting any important details.

In taking lecture notes, in doing library research, and in preparing homework assignments, you have been making and using précis for several years, perhaps without knowing or employing the term itself. (In Molière's play, *The Bourgeois Gentleman,* a character exclaims "Good Heavens! For more than forty years I have been speaking prose without knowing it.") By whatever name (précis, summary, digest), the technique of condensing material is an invaluable aid to every student.

In studying, you have probably discovered that some selections can be reduced satisfactorily, but others are so tightly knit that condensation is virtually impossible. You can make précis of novels, short stories, speeches, or essays, but not of material that is especially compactly and epigrammatically written. Material that has already been summarized, edited, or abridged is particularly difficult to handle because "continual distillation" cannot accurately indicate the essential thought of the original composition.

67a. READ THE SELECTION CAREFULLY

The major purpose of a précis is to present faithfully, as briefly and clearly as possible, the important ideas of the selection being "cut down." In order to grasp the central ideas, you must read carefully, analytically, and reflectively.

Look up the meanings of all words and phrases about which you are in doubt. Do not skim, but look for important or key expressions. Before starting to write, you must, to use Sir Francis Bacon's phrase, "chew and digest" the selection, not merely "taste" it or "swallow" it whole in a single gulp. You must see how the material has been organized, what devices the writer has used, what kinds of illustrations support the main thought. (These suggestions are, of course, those you would follow every time you concentrate on reading and thinking intelligently.)

67b. USE YOUR OWN WORDS

Quoting sentences—perhaps topic sentences—from each paragraph results in a sentence outline, not a précis. You must use your own words for the most part, although you may want to quote key words or phrases. Ordinarily, the phrasing of the original will not be suitable for your purposes. Once you have mastered the thought of the selection, your problem is one of original composition. You are guided and aided by the order and wording of the material, but the précis itself represents your own analysis and statement of the main thought.

67c. LIMIT THE NUMBER OF WORDS USED

Nothing of real importance can be omitted, but remember that a précis must be a condensation. The length of a condensation cannot arbitrarily be determined, but most prose can be reduced by two-thirds to three-fourths. Some verse is so compact that it can be condensed hardly at all; other verse can be shortened more than good prose.

67d. FOLLOW THE PLAN OF THE ORIGINAL

In order to be faithful to your selection, preserve its proportion and order. Changing the author's plan will distort its essence. Resist the temptation to rearrange facts and ideas. Try to preserve the original mood, content, order, and tone.

67e. USE EFFECTIVE ENGLISH

The condensation should not be a jumble of disconnected words and faulty sentences. It should be a model of exact and emphatic diction and clear, effective sentence construction, because it must be intelligible to a reader who has not seen the original. It is not likely to be so well written as the original, but it should read smoothly and possess compositional merit of its own.

The following is a précis made by a student. Criticize it in terms of the suggestions given above.

ORIGINAL

> But as for the bulk of mankind, they are clearly devoid of any degree of taste. It is a quality in which they advance very little beyond a state of infancy. The first thing a child is fond of in a book is a picture, the second is a story, and the third a jest. Here then is the true Pons Asinorum, which very few readers ever get over. (69 words)
>
> —Henry Fielding

PRÉCIS

> Most people lack taste; they remain childlike. Readers, like children, rarely ever get over the "bridge of asses" constituted by pictures, stories, and jokes. (24 words)

EXERCISE

Write a précis of the following selection, reducing it to approxmiately one-third of its present length.

> A third kind of thinking is stimulated when anyone questions our beliefs and opinions. We sometimes find ourselves changing our minds without any resistance or heavy emotion, but if we are told that we are wrong we resent the imputation and harden our hearts. We are incredibly heedless in the formation of our beliefs, but find ourselves filled with an illicit passion for them when anyone proposes to rob us of their companionship. It is obviously not the ideas themselves that are dear to us, but our self-esteem, which is threatened. We are by nature stubbornly pledged to defend our own from attack, whether it be our person, our family, our property, or our opinion. A United States Senator once remarked to a friend of mine that God Almighty could not make him change his mind on our Latin-American policy. We may surrender, but rarely confess ourselves vanquished. In the intellectual world at least, peace is without victory.
>
> Few of us take the pains to study the origin of our cherished convictions; indeed, we have a natural repugnance to so doing. We like to continue to believe what we have been accustomed to accept as true, and the resentment aroused when doubt is cast upon any of our assumptions leads us to seek every manner of excuse for clinging to them. *The result is that most of our so-called reasoning consists in finding arguments for going on believing as we already do.* (242 words)
>
> —James Harvey Robinson, "On Various Kinds of Thinking"

The paraphrase

The *paraphrase* is another type of "report on reading." The term is derived from Greek terms loosely meaning "writing (or speaking) on this model."

A paraphrase is unlike a précis in that the latter is a digest of the essential meaning of an original passage, whereas a paraphrase is a full-length statement of that meaning. It is a free rendering of the sense of a passage, fully and proportionately, but in different words.

The paraphrase is frequently used to make clear wording that is vague and obscure; it is a process of simplification and modernization. Each of you has read a particularly difficult poem or discussion in prose that you could not make sense of until you put it into your own words. After you did so, its meaning was clear, and you felt that you had actually translated the passage into your own thought processes.

Much of the discussion in English and social science classrooms begins with a paraphrasing of the ideas expressed in assignments from textbooks. In other words, every student has almost daily need for reshaping source material to suit his purposes and aims.

In making a paraphrase:

67f. READ AND REREAD THE ORIGINAL PASSAGE

It is impossible properly to paraphrase a passage until you have mastered its essential content, until you are familiar with its purposes, organization, and method of getting at the central idea. Just as in making a précis, read as well and think as consistently as you can. Some phrases and sentences you will probably have to reread several times, carefully and reflectively, before their meaning will "come alive" for you. If the passage contains obscure words and allusions about which you are in doubt, consult a dictionary or other reference book to determine their meanings.

67g. USE YOUR OWN WORDS

Try to find understandable equivalents for words and phrases that are obscure, but do not strain for synonyms. Repeat words whose meaning is unmistakably clear; restrict your changes to passages that actually require simplifying or modernizing. For instance, the phrase *chacun à son goût* may be changed to "each to his own taste." Do not fail to make necessary changes just because it is difficult to do so.

67h. OMIT NOTHING OF IMPORTANCE

A paraphrase is a restatement and, as such, should contain the essential thought of the original in its entirety. Omitting significant detail results in distortion.

67i. ADD NOTHING THAT IS NOT IN THE ORIGINAL

Interpretation and explanation should be confined to making clear what the original author had in mind and should not convey the paraphraser's additional ideas. Whether you like or dislike what the writer has said, whether you agree or disagree with him, whether you think his logic is sound or faulty—these considerations do not enter into the making of the paraphrase.

To make a paraphrase does not mean that you cease to think; it means that your thinking produces a full-length statement of another's meaning.

67j. FOLLOW THE ORIGINAL

Keep as closely as clarity will permit to the form and tone of the original. If necessary, recast the passage; but be careful not to distort or to parody. Obviously, a paraphraser can hardly hope to achieve the same mood and tonal quality as the author of, say, a great poem, but he should try to preserve as much of these existing qualities as possible.

67k. USE GOOD ENGLISH

Any paraphrase of a good poem or prose passage is worth far less than the original; but the better the paraphrase, the less the difference between it and the original. In addition to careful reading and constructive thinking, the making of a good paraphrase, just as of an effective précis, requires exact writing.

The following is a paraphrase made by a student. Criticize it in terms of the suggestions given above.

ON FIRST LOOKING INTO
CHAPMAN'S HOMER

Much have I travell'd in the realms of gold,
And many goodly states and kingdoms seen;
Round many western islands have I been

Which bards in fealty to Apollo hold.
Oft of one wide expanse had I been told
That deep-brow'd Homer ruled as his demesne:
Yet did I never breathe its pure serene
Till I heard Chapman speak out loud and bold:
Then felt I like some watcher of the skies
When a new planet swims into his ken;
Or like stout Cortez, when with eagle eyes
He stared at the Pacific—and all his men
Look'd at each other with a wild surmise—
Silent, upon a peak in Darien.

—John Keats

PARAPHRASE

I have read widely in the great classics of literature and have noted many examples of great poetry. I had often been told of the work of Homer and the poetry which he had created, but I never really understood or appreciated its great beauty and power until I read Chapman's translation. Then I felt as awed as some astronomer who unexpectedly discovers a new planet, or as surprised and speechless as Cortez (Balboa) and his followers were when they saw the Pacific Ocean for the first time, from Panama.

EXERCISE

Write a paraphrase on the following sonnet:

CXVI

Let me not to the marriage of true minds
Admit impediments. Love is not love
Which alters when it alteration finds,
Or bends with the remover to remove:
O, no! it is an ever-fixèd mark
That looks on tempests and is never shaken;
It is the star to every wand'ring bark,
Whose worth's unknown, although his height be taken.
Love's not Time's fool, though rosy lips and cheeks
Within his bending sickle's compass come;
Love alters not with his brief hours and weeks,
But bears it out even to the edge of doom:—
If this be error and upon me proved,
I never writ, nor no man ever loved.

—William Shakespeare

68. OUTLINING

No one can write an effective paper without some sort of plan for it. This plan can be formal or informal, sketchy or detailed, written or "just in one's head." It can be prepared in advance of writing or can be made from what has been written. But a plan of some sort, made and followed at some time, is essential in the preparation of any composition more than a paragraph in length.

One useful means of planning a paper is a formal outline. Some people object to outlining; they insist that preparing a formal outline steals valuable time from actual writing and that an outline acts as a brake on the free flow of their ideas. Both objections make some sense. But time spent on an outline will be more than repaid when one begins to write. Also, few of us always think logically. We *need* some definite control over random ideas that pop into our heads.

An outline does not have to be detailed or elaborate. If you are writing a paper in class or an essay answer on an examination, only five minutes may be devoted to preparing a rough "sketch" outline that will certainly be informal and yet may pay dividends. Nor need an outline be followed slavishly; it should be your servant, not your master. As you write you may see that certain changes in plan are necessary and effective. Work *from* an outline, not *for* it.

It is as illogical to say that you can't prepare an outline until after you read what you have written as it is to say you can't tell what you're going to say until after you have said it. Making a comment first and not thinking about it until later gets people into serious trouble every day.

68a. USE OF A THESIS SENTENCE

A thesis sentence suggests the material to be developed. It need not be all-inclusive, but it should indicate something of the scope of what is to come and also your purpose. A thesis sentence carefully prepared in advance will make easier your task in preparing an outline. In addition, it will serve as a constant check against the unity and coherence of the outline and paper that follow.

In outlining, three kinds are often used: *topic, sentence,* and *paragraph* outlines.

68b. TOPIC OUTLINE

A topic outline, consisting of words and phrases, is perhaps more helpful to the writer than either sentence or paragraph outlines. A topic outline may be quite simple, as in the following example:

MY FIRST DAY AT WORK

I. Sleeplessness the night before
II. Early morning preparation
III. The trip to work
IV. Getting started
V. How the day went

Such a scheme is really a "sketch" outline, but it may be made more elaborate. In fact, the expanded outline that follows could contain five or six main heads instead of the two shown.

MY FIRST DAY AT WORK

Thesis sentence: The first day at work is a nervous ordeal, but it can be endured because tension and worry pass away.

I. Prework jitters
  A. The night before
    1. Setting the alarm clock
    2. Sleeplessness
    3. Thoughts of failing

B. The next morning at home
   1. Hurried dressing
   2. A bolted breakfast

II. The workday
   A. Getting to work
      1. A run for the bus
      2. My nervousness and other riders' composure
   B. The first hour
      1. Meeting the foreman
      2. Inability to understand
      3. Helpfulness of another worker
      4. Gradual easing of tension
   C. How the day went
      1. Slow passage of time
      2. Lunch hour
      3. Afternoon exhaustion
      4. Quitting time
      5. Satisfied feeling
      6. Readiness for tomorrow

68c. SENTENCE OUTLINE

A sentence outline consists of complete sentences, not words and phrases. It is likely to be clearer to the writer than a topic outline and is more helpful to a reader who wishes to make useful suggestions.

For illustrative purposes, here is how Part I of the topic outline in Section 68b could appear in a sentence outline:

MY FIRST DAY AT WORK

I. I was nervous and jittery the night before I was to begin work.
   A. I set the alarm clock and turned in early.
   B. I could not get to sleep and tossed restlessly.
   C. My mind was tortured with fears of not being able to do the job.

II. The next morning I was tired and still nervous.
   A. I dressed hurriedly and clumsily.
   B. I did not feel like eating but bolted my breakfast.

68d. PARAGRAPH OUTLINE

A paragraph outline consists of groups of sentences (perhaps mainly topic sentences) indicating the contents of entire paragraphs. Such an outline may be used in planning your own composition, but it is perhaps even more helpful in setting down summary sentences to indicate the thought of successive paragraphs in a selection being studied.

In the paragraph outline, material is not classified into major headings and subheadings; rather, the topic of each paragraph is simply listed in the order in which it is to appear. For illustration, here is a specimen paragraph outline of Part II of the topic outline in Section 68b:

1. Dashing from the breakfast table, I made a run for the bus.
2. My inner fears and worries had me in a turmoil, but other riders on the bus seemed calm and even casual.
3. The foreman was gruff, and my worries increased.

4. My hands were sweaty and my knees felt weak so that I couldn't catch on to what I was supposed to do.
5. A man nearby saw my confusion and kindly showed me, slowly and clearly, what my job was.
6. As I began to catch on, my hands stopped sweating and I began to feel easier in mind and body.
7. The morning passed slowly, and I thought lunchtime would never come.
8. During the afternoon, my muscles grew more and more tired, and I had to hang on until quitting time.
9. As I walked to catch the bus home, I felt satisfied that I had met the test of the first day and could meet the challenge of the next without fear.

68e. CORRECT OUTLINE FORM

Any outline that clearly reveals the structure of a theme is effective, so that "correctness" in form is more often a matter of convention than of logic. Writers, however, have tended to follow certain conventions:

1. Outlining is division; subdivision means division into at least two parts. If a single minor topic (subhead) must be mentioned, express it as part of the major heading or add another subhead.
2. Use parallel phrasing. Do not use a word or phrase for one topic, a sentence for another. Topic, sentence, and paragraph outlines should be consistent in structure throughout.
3. Avoid meaningless headings such as *Introduction, Conclusion, Reasons,* and *Effects.* If you feel they must appear, add specific explanatory subheads.
4. The first main heading of the outline should not repeat the title of the paper. If the idea expressed in the title logically should appear in the outline, at least rephrase it.
5. Avoid putting into a subhead any matter that should appear in a larger division; even more important, do not list in a main heading material belonging in a subdivision.
6. Follow conventional uses of *indentation, symbols,* and *punctuation.*

Study the specimen outlines in this section. Note the use of Roman numerals beginning flush left in a topic outline. Observe that capital letters (A, B, C) indicate the first series of subdivisions, and study their indentation. If needed, the next series of subdivisions is indicated by Arabic numerals (1, 2, 3). If still further subdivision is needed, use small letters (a, b, c). Observe that a period follows each numeral or letter and, in sentence and paragraph outlines, each sentence.

EXERCISES

1. Expand this "sketch" outline for a paper on getting a summer job as a waiter into a full topic outline:

TIPS ON SUMMER TABLES

I. How to apply
II. Learning the job
III. Problems with people

IV. Monetary rewards
V. Leisure-time activities

2. Make a sentence outline from the "sketch" outline in Exercise I.
3. Make a paragraph outline of the first two main sections of the sentence outline prepared for Exercise 2.

69. REVISION AND PROOFREADING

In everything you write for English or any other class in college, errors of one sort or another are inevitable. Mistakes crop up in the reports, examinations, themes, tests, and letters you write—just as they may in anything written by anyone anytime and anywhere. Not even a skilled professional writer can plan, write, and proofread all at one time.

"There is no such thing as good writing; there is only good rewriting." Some students will object to this statement. They will mention an occasion when they really "got going" and turned out an effective first, last, and only draft. Or they will say, "I wrote this paper in an hour and got a B grade on it; here's one that took four hours and was marked D." Or they will recall that Shakespeare never "blotted a line" or that this or that writer was said never to have rewritten his material.

The writer of a good "hour" theme probably had composed it in his mind many times before setting it down on paper. He had thought it through; he had written mentally while walking, eating, dressing, even bathing. His "quickly written" paper was not quickly written at all, even though he thought it was rapidly put on paper.

69a. REVISION

If time permits (and usually it does if you allow for it), revise or rewrite at least some parts of every paper you prepare for any college course, any lengthy examination that you take, and any important letter that you write.

Three kinds of alteration are possible when you revise a paper. *You can substitute,* you can *delete,* and you can *add.* When your reasons for making such changes are considered, certain subdivisions appear.

One such subdivision consists of asking questions like those listed in Chapter 8 and then making necessary changes. Another subdivision of changes consists of questions like these: (1) Have I chosen a suitable subject and narrowed it so that in the number of words I have at my disposal I can provide a clear and reasonably complete account of what my reader expects or has a right to expect? (2) Have I followed an orderly plan in writing, working from either a mental or written outline? Have I divided the treatment into related parts and written at least one paragraph on each? (3) Is each of my paragraphs adequate in material, unified in substance, correctly proportioned?

Still another group of alterations consists of efforts to achieve greater accuracy of expression, or more clarity, so as to drive home more forcefully to a reader a particular point, idea, mood, or impression. In this sort of revision, you check and recheck your choice of words; you revise the word order and structure of a sentence or group of sentences; you alter a figure of speech to make an image sharper or clearer; you add a bit of dialogue or an incident or anecdote to reinforce an idea; you remove a section that seems stale and ineffective; you alter the position of sentences within paragraphs or the order of paragraphs in the entire paper.

Consider this example of revision. An English instructor asked students to write a paragraph with this topic sentence: "Lying is bad policy." One student wrote the following:

> Lying is bad policy. When you tell one lie, you usually have to tell a dozen more to cover up the first one. Even when you try your best to keep from getting caught, you usually wind up red-faced or red-handed. Sometimes the penalty for telling a lie can be severe. Telling the truth may hurt, but it's the only sure way to avoid trouble.

The instructor commented that the paragraph was free from grammatical errors but that it was dull and repetitious. The writer improved it greatly in this revision:

> Lying is bad policy. A friend of mine applied for a summer job last year and told a lie about his previous experience when he filed his application. A week after he had started work, his supervisor discovered my friend's claim was false and fired him instantly. My friend not only lost his job, but he couldn't bear to explain what had really happened. Furthermore, it was then too late to get another job and he was miserable all summer long. Now he knows, as I do, that lying is a bad and foolish policy.

69b. PROOFREADING

When we read, we usually see merely the outlines, or shells, of words. Only poor readers need to see individual letters as such; most of us comprehend words and even groups of words at a glance. But have you ever noticed how much easier it is for you to detect errors in someone else's writing than in your own? This may be because in reading someone else's writing you are *looking* for mistakes. Or it may be that you look more carefully at the writing of someone else than at your own because you are unfamiliar with it and have to focus more sharply in order to comprehend. You already "know" what you are saying.

Whatever the reason for closer scrutiny, in proofreading we narrow the range of our vision and thereby pick up mistakes hitherto unnoticed. In short, we detect careless errors not by reading but by *proofreading*.

Much of the effectiveness of proofreading depends upon the spread of your vision. The following triangle will show you how wide your vision (sight spread) is. Look at the top of the triangle and then down. How far down can you go and still identify each letter in each line at a *single* glance? Your central vision is as wide as the line above the one where you cannot identify each letter *without moving your eyes at all.*

a
a r
a r d
a r d c
a r d c f
a r d c f g
a r d c f g x
a r d c f g x y
a r d c f g x y z
a r d c f g x y z p
a r d c f g x y z p w

People differ in their range of vision as they do in nearly everything else. But many people have difficulty in identifying more than six letters at a single glance. Some have a span of vision embracing only three or four letters. Whatever your span, you should not try to exceed it when you are carefully checking for errors. If you do, you are reading—perhaps with excellent understanding—but you are not *proofreading*.

Only proofreading will enable you to eliminate errors caused not by ignorance or stupidity but by carelessness.

70. TAKING TESTS AND EXAMINATIONS

Tests have become a part of your life. There is no escaping them. As a student, you face a test of one sort or another nearly all the time, whether it be ten brief questions intended to check on a reading assignment or a two-hour essay examination designed to evaluate a semester's work.

Tests and examinations, however, are not confined to course work in college. Tests are used by employers to evaluate skills and aptitudes necessary for various types of jobs. Most of you, no matter what you do, will continue to take tests for a long time to come.

It is obvious that study is the best preparation for examinations and tests. Tests used for college admission and for employment evaluation, however, attempt mainly to determine general knowledge and ability. Detailed study of specific subject matter is impossible.

But you can prepare for tests by acquainting yourself with the kinds of questions that are likely to be asked, the general types of tests and exams that are available and are widely used. Without some basic knowledge of what tests are like, you cannot live comfortably with them or avoid the tensions that waste energy.

Before taking any test or exam try to find out from your instructor, or from students who have taken the course before, answers to questions such as these:

1. What will the test cover?
2. How long will it be?
3. Will the test require writing or will it be true-false, multiple choice, or some other type that can be scored by electronic test-scoring equipment?
4. Will there be a penalty for wrong answers?

5. What weight will be given to accuracy and fullness of answers as contrasted with the form, appearance, and style of any writing required?

70a. TESTS

When taking a test, one can do little to disguise the fact that he doesn't know the material involved. And yet he can do much to weaken his performance. In an excellent guide, *The Effective Student* (Harper & Row, 1966), Dr. H. Chandler Elliott provides these suggestions for failing a test even when one knows the answers:

1. Arrive in a daze due to an (ineffectual) attempt to "cover" the whole course during the night. Your noble efforts will placate the Powers Above, whatever the effect on the examiner.
2. Try to counteract the daze by extra coffee, or by pep pills. This will make you feel awfully clever, however scrambled your presentation.
3. Scan the questions in a flash. If you do misread, your answer will be brilliant enough to rate full credit anyway.
4. Plunge straight ahead without plan or schedule, relying on your unerring instinct. If you run short at the end, write "No more time!" and the examiner will pro-rate what you have done.
5. Don't take instructions seriously; for example, if a diagram is required, give three pages of writing instead. You do it so much better, and the poor, stupid examiner will not know the difference.
6. Write with such frantic speed as to be illegible (a faint pencil helps here). The examiner will assume you are correct on points that he cannot read.
7. On objective, short-answer examinations, make *A*'s that look like *H*'s, *C*'s like *G*'s, *7*'s like 9's, *V*'s like *II*'s, and so on. Obviously your answer must be right, so anyone can see that you mean *A*, *7*, or whatnot.
8. Spend the time saved by the foregoing techniques using long-winded flowery phrases, digressing, and padding. This impresses an examiner far more than a few extra facts.
9. Put an addition to some question at the back, especially after some blank, unnumbered pages. A reader will instinctively realize that you know more than just the first part.
10. Leave out part of a question. You are too rushed to attend to such details.
11. Do not sign your paper. The examiner will rather enjoy a little break from routine, trying to identify it.

Suggestions for taking tests sensibly and effectively include these:

1. Carefully read all questions and instructions before beginning to write. (This suggestion will not apply to all types of standardized, objective tests and examinations.)
2. Budget your time. Follow a thought-out schedule carefully. Leave a margin of safety.
3. Write as clearly and legibly as you can.
4. Look over the test upon completion. Correct errors; check to make sure that nothing is omitted; add afterthoughts of importance.

70b. ESSAY QUESTIONS

No type of test or examination question frightens students so much as an essay question. Nearly everyone would rather take objective tests than be faced with questions that demand lengthy answers in intelligible prose.

Essay questions, however, are necessary because they test for the type of information that objective questions tend to ignore. An essay question enables the tester to determine a student's ability to put facts into perspective, to generalize from the data he has assembled, and to draw subjective conclusions from the content of his study. The essay question is also used to measure how well a student is able to communicate in writing.

You should approach an essay question with the same care that you give any written assignment. Read the question carefully. You must determine exactly what it is the question seeks to discover and the general type of information the answer requires. It is also good practice to sketch out an outline before you begin to write. The preliminary steps in answering an essay question are as important as they are in planning a formal composition.

Perhaps the most difficult step in an essay answer is the framing of the first sentence of the first paragraph. It is frequently possible to restate the central part of the question as the opening sentence. Note the following question:

> In a famous definition of the tragic hero, Aristotle pointed out that he was a man who was not preeminently virtuous or just, but one who came to his tragic end not through some essential lack of goodness but through some error of judgment. How well do you feel that Julius Caesar measures up or fails to measure up to Aristotle's definition? Use incidents from the play to support your judgment.

Depending upon your judgment, the central part of the question might be expressed as the first sentence of your answer as follows: *Caesar fits (or does not fit) perfectly Aristotle's definition of the tragic hero.*

Some essay questions merely require you to provide factual data. Most, however, demand that you come to a conclusion or formulate a judgment based upon your study; you must see to it that your conclusions are concretely supported by pertinent facts and examples. Moreover, the relationship between your supporting facts and your conclusion must be evident. Note that the sample question above directs the student to support his answer by citing incidents and details from Shakespeare's *Julius Caesar.*

For example, you may write that Caesar's judgment was affected by his vanity and pride. In an essay answer, such a statement should be supported by specific mention of instances where Caesar is boastful, where he denies that he is ever afraid of anything. You know that fear is a basic human emotion and you might point out that, in his denial of fear, Caesar is actually denying his own humanity. Your conclusion is that his confidence in his superiority over all other men warped his judgment and was thus a major cause of his downfall.

Or you may feel that Caesar's errors of judgment resulted from rashness and imprudence in not paying attention to warnings that might have saved his life. You should cite one or more instances in which Caesar ignores the superstitions and traditions in which he firmly believed but which he rashly overlooked when tempted by the offer of a crown.

On the other hand, you may feel that Caesar does not really fit Aristotle's definition of the tragic hero at all. It may seem to you that in spite of his pride, vanity, rashness, and ruthless ambition, Caesar is actually a noble figure and that others, not he, are responsible for the tragedy that occurs. If this is your belief, then you should give examples of, for instance, the raw courage and spiritual power that made him a magnificent figure. You might point out that at the end of the play Brutus himself speaks of the triumph of Caesar's spirit. Caesar's body is destroyed, but his spirit lives on.

Whatever your approach, your answer should consist of a conclusion, or series of conclusions, based on examples and citations that precisely set forth what you are trying to communicate.

Little relationship exists between length of answer and its worth. Common sense indicates that there is merit in brevity. Many students have a tendency to expand their essay answers, believing that those who evaluate them will be favorably disposed by bulk. On the contrary, those who must read essay answers are impressed by pertinent material economically expressed.

EXERCISE

The following essay questions are representative of the type that you might encounter on semester or year-end examinations. Choose one and answer it as best you can, paying particular attention to the structure of your answer. Keep in mind that you would be graded for both content and the quality of the writing.

1. Plot has been defined as a series of causally related events working up to a conclusion. A distinction may then be drawn between story and plot. Events that are chronologically related to each other comprise what we call "story." "The king died and then the queen died" constitutes the essentials of story. "The king died and then the queen died because of grief" constitutes plot. By referring to a short story or novel you have read recently, isolate at least five events that constitute plot, indicating how each is causally related to the rest. Explain each relationship in some detail.
2. Many literary works express a theme that the author wishes the reader to understand. Identify the theme presented in a work you have read recently. Support your judgment by referring to specific incidents in the work.
3. Relate the following quotation to one of the works you have read recently.

   > Every man who knows how to read has it in his power to magnify himself, to multiply the ways in which he exists, to make his life full, significant, and interesting.
   >
   > —Aldous Huxley

PART THREE

A GUIDE TO TERMS AND USAGE

This Guide contains items in alphabetical order that fall into six sometimes overlapping groups:

1. Entries on grammatical constructions with recommendations for effective usage: *and which; is, was, were; is when, is where;* and so on.

2. Entries for groups of words with similar spelling characteristics; *-able, -ible; -efy;* silent letters; *k* inserted; *ise, -ize, -yze;* and so on.

3. Definitions and discussions of grammatical terms and expressions. If the term has been developed fully elsewhere (adjective, adverb), there is no entry here; consult the general index.

4. Brief articles of general interest to the writer, bearing on problems of composition: manuscript form, plagiarism, history of English, footnotes, bibliographies, linguistics, and so on.

5. Brief comments on rhetorical matters: accordion sentence, cadence, parallelism, schoolgirl style, wordiness, and so on.

6. Brief discussions of various literary genres and techniques designed to help the writer of papers and reader of literary selections: autobiography, imagery, novel, satire, symbolism, and so on.

Abbreviations. A shortened form of a word or phrase, such as *Mr.* for *Mister* and *S.C.* for *South Carolina.* Abbreviations, except such common ones as *Mr.* and *Dr.,* are normally unacceptable in standard writing and should never be overused (see Section 32).

-able. The ending should usually be *-able* if the base (root) is a complete word: *eat + able*. For example: *acceptable, available, dependable, detestable, peaceable*.

The ending should usually be *-able* if the base (root) is a complete word lacking a final *e: desire + able = desirable*. For example: *believable, deplorable, excitable, likable, sizable*.

The ending should usually be *-able* if the base (root) ends in *i* (the original word may have ended in *y*): *enviable*. If this rule were not followed, we would have a double *i* (*ii*). For example: *appreciable, classifiable, dutiable, reliable, sociable*.

The ending should usually be *-able* if the base (root) has other forms with the sound of long *a: demonstrate, demonstrable*. This principle will be helpful only if you actually sound out another form (or forms) of the root word to see whether it has (or they have) the long *a* sound: *abominate, abominable; estimate, estimable*. For example: *delectable, durable, impregnable, inflammable, inseparable*.

The ending should usually be *-able* if the base (root) ends in hard *c* or hard *g*. Hard *c* is sounded like the *c* in *cat;* hard g has the sound of g in *get*. The following words illustrate this principle: *amicable, applicable, implacable, indefatigable*.

These principles cover most of the fairly common words that have *-able* endings. But if you wish to be able to spell all words ending with *-able*, study the following by some other method—rules won't help much: *affable, equitable, formidable, indomitable, inevitable, inscrutable, insuperable, memorable, palpable, portable, probable, vulnerable*. (See also *-ible*.)

Abstract. A word or phrase is *abstract* when it is not concrete (definite and specific) in meaning, when it applies to a quality thought of as being apart from any material object: *honor, mercy, beauty* (see Section 39c).

As a noun, *abstract* means a brief statement of the essential contents of an article, speech, book (see *Summary*).

Abstract noun. The name of a thing not evident to one of the senses, such as a quality or condition: *duty, happiness, glory, freedom* (see *Concreteness*).

Accent. This word has several meanings, two of which apply particularly to English speech or writing. We may say that someone has an *accent*, by which we mean his distinguishing regional or national manner of pronouncing or the tone of his voice (a Southern *accent*). Accent also means the emphasis (by pitch or stress or both) given to a particular syllable or word when speaking it. Thus we say "Please *accent* that word more clearly" or "The *accent* in the word *refer* is on the second syllable."

Accent mark. A mark used to distinguish between various sounds of the same letter. Thus we add a stroke above the letter *a* to show that it has a long sound as in the word *fāme.* An accent mark is related to *Diacritical mark,* which see (see also Section 34).

Accordion sentence. A sentence that, like an accordion, is alternately pulled out and pressed together. It is caused by faulty subordination (see *Section* 49).

Ad-. This prefix (see Section 58c) alters its form according to the root word to which it is attached. Before a root beginning with *sc* or *sp,* the *d* is dropped: *ascent, aspire.* Before *c, f, g, l, n, p,* and *t,* the *d* is assimilated (becomes the same as the following letter): *accommodate, affix, aggression, allegation, announce, appoint, attend.*

A.D., B.C. *Anno domini,* Latin for "in the year of the Lord," is represented by the letters *A.D.* "Before Christ" is abbreviated to *B.C.*

Added vowels. Some words are misspelled because in pronouncing them an extra vowel is added. Here are some especially common errors to be wary of:

> *Athletic* (physically active and strong) should not be spelled "athaletic" or "atheletic."
> *Entrance* (act or point of coming in) should not be spelled "enterance."
> *Explanation* (interpretation) should not be spelled "explaination."
> *Grievous* (sad to hear, deplorable) should not be spelled "grievious."
> *Hundred* (the number) should not be spelled "hundered."
> *Laundry* (washing of clothes) should not be spelled "laundery" or "laundary."
> *Monstrous* (huge, enormous) should not be spelled "monsterous."
> *Partner* (associate) should not be spelled "partener."
> *Remembrance* (souvenir, keepsake) should not be spelled "rememberance."

Affixes. This term embraces both prefixes and suffixes. *Prefixes* are syllables added at the beginnings of words to alter or modify their meanings, or, occasionally, to form entirely new words. For example, we add the prefix *de-* to the word *form* and make *deform. Suffixes* are syllables added at the ends of words to alter their meanings, to form new words, or to show grammatical function (part of speech). Thus we add *-ly* to *like* and form *likely.*

The readiness with which prefixes and suffixes are tacked on to root words in the English language is an indication of the freedom in word formation that has characterized our language for many centuries. For example, consider the word *recession.* This is derived from a Latin word *cedere* (*cessus*), which has the general meaning of "go." To this base we add the prefix *re-,* which has a generalized meaning of "back" or "again," and the suffix *-ion,* an ending which shows that the word is a noun. Related to *recession* are many words with still other prefixes and suffixes but all with a similar root, or base: *recede, recess, recessive, concession, procession, secession.*

A knowledge of the ways in which prefixes and suffixes are added to words will increase your vocabulary and improve your spelling (see Section 58c).

Alliteration. Repetition of an initial sound in two or more words of a phrase, sentence, or line of poetry: *Ada ambled across the avenue.* In poetry, alliteration is often effective; in prose, it is usually considered an affectation.

-ally, -ly. Because these endings appear so often in commonly used words, they account for a large number of misspellings.

The suffix *-ly* is used to form an adverb from an adjective: *poor* + *ly* = *poorly*. If the adjective ends in *l*, *-ly* is tacked on to the complete root, thus producing an *-lly* ending. For example: *accidentally, finally, naturally, personally.*

The suffix *-ly* is added to basic words ending in silent *e*, the *e* being retained. For example: *absolutely, completely, entirely, scarcely.*

If an adjective ends in *-ic*, its adverbial form ends in *-ally*. The only exception to this simple rule is *publicly;* you must fix this word in your visual memory. Here are examples of adverbs formed from adjectives with *-ic* endings: *academically, basically, grammatically.*

The following adverbs do not completely follow the principles just enumerated; fix them in your visual memory: *duly, only, possibly, terribly, truly, wholly.*

A.M., a.m.; P.M., p.m. The first expression, spelled with either capitals or lowercase letters, means "before noon" (from the Latin *ante meridiem*). *P.M.* or *p.m.* means "noon to midnight" (from the Latin *post meridiem*). Both are clear indicators of time and are not followed by such expressions as "in the morning." Figures, not words, are conventionally used: We left at 7 *A.M.* (see Section 33).

Ambiguity. A word or other expression whose meaning is doubtful, uncertain, capable of being misunderstood or of being understood in more than one sense. Ambiguous expressions occur often in speech and writing: getting rid of them is one of the prime objects of all writers who wish to be effective. An antonym of ambiguity is *clearness* (clarity), which see.

Americanism. A word or phrase peculiar to the English language as developed in the United States. Americans use *er* in words such as *theater* and *center;* the English are more likely to write *theatre* and *centre*. Americans double fewer consonants (*wagon, traveler*) than the English (*waggon, traveller*). We also write *favor* and *humor*, not *favour* and *humour*.

Many minor differences exist between the language generally used in England and in the United States. For Americans to adopt British methods of pronunciation, British spelling, and British vocabulary is generally an affectation.

Analogy. This word suggests "partial resemblance" and implies similarity in some respect between things otherwise unlike. In linguistics, *analogy* is the process by which new or less familiar words, constructions, or pronunciations conform with older ones. Thus we form *energize* from *energy* by analogy with *apologize* from *apology*. Reasoning by analogy can cause serious blunders in logic (see Section 56a).

Analysis of a sentence. Theoretically, you should be able to analyze a sentence both by words and by groups of words—*if you know grammar*.

Consider the following sentence: *The little old lady across the street is carefully knitting a sweater for her grandson, who is a newsboy.* A grammatical analysis of this sentence is as follows:

The is a definite article modifying the noun *lady*. *Little* and *old* are adjectives modifying the noun *lady*. *Lady* is a noun used as subject of the sentence. *The little old lady* is the complete subject of *is knitting*.

Across is a preposition introducing the prepositional phrase; *the,* a definite article modifying the noun *street; street,* a noun used as object of the preposition *across*. The entire prepositional phrase, *across the street,* is used as an adjective modifying *lady*.

Is is an auxiliary verb that with the present participle *knitting* forms the present progressive tense, active voice, and is the predicate of the sentence. *Carefully* is an adverb modifying the verb phrase *is knitting*.

A is an indefinite article modifying *sweater,* which is a noun used as direct object of the verb phrase *is knitting*.

For is a preposition; *her,* a possessive pronoun, third person singular feminine, refers to *lady* and modifies *grandson; grandson,* a noun, is the object of the preposition *for*. The entire prepositional phrase, *for her grandson,* is used as an adverb modifying *is knitting,* if we think of the phrase as being closely associated with and tied to the verb phrase *is knitting*. If, however, we think of *for her grandson* as being closely associated with *sweater,* then both by logic and by common sense we can call it a phrase used as an adjective modifying *sweater*.

Who is a relative pronoun, nominative case, referring to *grandson* and used as the subject of *is; is* is a linking verb; *a* is an indefinite article modifying *newsboy;* and *newsboy* is a predicate noun after a linking verb. The group of words, *who is a newsboy,* is an adjective clause modifying *grandson*.

The entire sentence is *complex* in its grammatical structure (see *Diagraming*).

-ance, -ence. The suffixes *-ance* and *-ence* are added to root words (verbs) to form nouns: *attend, attendance; prefer, preference.* There is no single guiding principle in the choice of *-ance* or *-ence*. Correct pronunciation is of no help. The only safe procedure is to consult a dictionary and to try to form good visual images of *-ance* and *-ence* words.

One helpful principle, and one only, is this: If a verb ends in *r* preceded by a single vowel and is accented on the last syllable, it forms its noun with *-ence*. For example: *abhorrence, conference, deterrence.*

And which, that, who; but which, that, who. Correct sentence structure provides that these phrases should appear in clauses only if preceded by clauses that also contain *which, that,* or *who.* ("This is the first book *that* I bought *and that* I treasure," not "This is the first book I bought *and that* I treasure.") (See Section 48d.)

Anecdote. The *anecdote* is a narrative bit told or written to illustrate some specific point. Its chief characteristic is that it presents individuals in an action which illustrates some definite idea, illuminates some aspect of personality or character. Every effective anecdote has a single point; in each, the dialogue, setting, and characters are subordinate to the main point. The anecdote rarely stands alone, but it is a powerful method of making understandable a difficult idea.

Ante-, anti-. The first of these prefixes is of Latin origin and means "before," "prior." *Anti-* is from the Greek and means "opposite," "against." Note these different spellings: *antebellum* (before the war), *antemeridian* (before noon, A.M.), *anteroom* (room before another room), *antiaircraft, antibiotic, anticlimax.*

Antecedent. This word means literally "going before." The substantive (noun or pronoun) to which a pronoun refers is its antecedent (see Section 13).

Anticlimax. A drop, often sudden and unexpected, from a dignified or important idea or situation to a trivial one. In fiction and drama, *anticlimax* involves action that is in disappointing contrast to a previous moment of intense interest; in a story or play, it is anything that follows the climax (the decisive, culminating struggle and resolution of conflict).

Antithesis. This word means "opposition" or "contrast" of thoughts. "You are smart, but I am stupid" illustrates the meaning of the term. Shakespeare's "Fair is foul, and foul is fair" suggests what rhetorical power the device can have.

Apostrophe. A figure of speech in which a person not present or a nonhuman object is addressed (spoken to). Instances of *apostrophe* in poetry are invocations to the muses and in oratory to the shades of men such as Julius Caesar, Thomas Jefferson, and Abraham Lincoln. Wordsworth's "London, 1802" begins "Milton! Thou shouldst be living at this hour." (Milton died in 1674).

Appropriateness. In writing or speaking, this term means using words and constructions that are fit, suitable, proper. The appropriateness of language is determined by the subject being discussed, the situation or medium for discussion, the reader or listener, the writer or speaker.

-ar, -er, -or. These suffixes have various origins, functions, and meanings. Their most common shared meaning denotes an actor, a doer, "one who." Following are examples of words ending in *-ar, -er, -or* that are often misspelled.

altar	grammar	popular
calendar	liar	scholar
collar	particular	vinegar
dollar	peculiar	vulgar
advertiser	consumer	messenger
baker	employer	officer
beginner	examiner	partner
carrier	lecturer	teacher
actor	creditor	inferior
aggressor	debtor	investigator
anchor	dictator	janitor
contributor	harbor	radiator

Arabic numerals. See *Roman numerals.*

Argument. A reason or reasons offered for or against something. Argument refers to a discussion in which there is disagreement and suggests the use of logic and a statement of facts to refute or support a position or point. *Argument* is one of the forms of discourse, the others being *narration, exposition,* and *description* (all of which see).

-ary, -ery. This suffix problem is simple. Many hundreds of English words end in *-ary.* Only eight fairly common words end in *-ery.* Learn these *-ery* words by whatever device works best for you; spell all others with *-ary.* The eight are *cemetery, confectionery, distillery, dysentery, every, millinery, monastery, stationery.*

Now if you end all other words with *-ary,* you'll be right every time, unless you happen to use such a rare word as *philandery.* You will have no spelling problems with the endings of such words as *auxiliary, boundary, dictionary, elementary, honorary, imaginary, library, secretary,* and *voluntary.*

Assonance. A partial or approximate similarity of sound. *Assonance* occurs in words like *fate* and *make,* in which partial rhyme is achieved because the stressed vowel sounds are alike but the consonant sounds are different.

Autobiography. This type of writing is an account of oneself written by oneself. The author of an *autobiography* presents (or tries to present) a continuous narrative of what he considers the major (or most interesting) events of his life. Usually, an autobiographer reveals about himself only what he is willing to have known and remembered.

Autobiography resembles other literary forms: biography, diaries, letters, journals, and memoirs. A *biography* is the written history of a person's life composed by someone else; the other four related forms are recollections set down by the subject himself. An *autobiography* and a *memoir* are usually lengthy, organized narratives prepared for others to read, but the latter is more likely to focus on one phase of a person's life than on the whole of it. A typical memoir also emphasizes the subject's relationship to notable persons or events more than do most autobiographies, which are likely to be more self-centered and introspective. A *diary* is a day-to-day or week-to-week chronicle of events and is thus closely related to a *journal;* the diary is usually more intimate than a journal and more deliberately chronological than autobiography. *Letters* are epistles, notes, and memoranda exchanged among friends and acquaintances; they afford an insight the intimacy of which varies with the personality of the writer, the identity of his correspondent, and the possibility of publication.

Awkwardness. A general term of disapproval that implies clumsiness, ungainliness, lack of grace and smoothness.

Balanced sentence. A sentence so written that certain thoughts or ideas have similar phrasing for purposes of comparison, contrast, or emphasis. (A wise man changes direction; a fool never does.)

Barbarism. A word or expression not standard in a language as, for example, "youse" for *you* (see Section 38a).

B.C. See *A.D.*

Beginning, ending of sentence. Avoid beginning or ending a sentence with weak and relatively unimportant words or ideas. Sentences should usually be built with the most important idea at the beginning or end, the places where the attention of the reader is most keen. You should remember, however, that transitional words and phrases, although seemingly colorless, are really significant and frequently deserve beginning positions.

Prepositions, parenthetical expressions, and most conjunctions are usually not pivotal or important words. Thus you should place them within the sentence, although you should avoid artificiality and awkwardness in so doing. There is no sensible rule against beginning a sentence with *and* or *but.* Normally, however, the beginning position should be given to a more emphatic word.

Ineffective: He had no money to buy the meal *with.* [It is not incorrect to end a sentence with a preposition, but this sentence will be more effective if rearranged so that due emphasis is given the relatively important word *meal:* He had no money with which to buy the meal.]
Ineffective: *However,* he will pass, the professor says.
Better: The professor says, *however,* that he will pass.

Standard advice is never to begin a sentence with a numeral. This admonition seems largely a matter of typography or a printing convention. It is a good rule to follow, however, since beginning with a numeral sometimes causes momentary confusion.

To avoid monotony, do not begin a number of successive sentences with the same word or phrase. Avoid especially overuse of the outworn beginnings *there is, there are, it is, this, the, he,* and *we.*

Awkward: It is just the trip he had planned. It is just the day for the trip. It is the consummation of all his hopes.
Improved: It is just the trip he had planned and just the day for the trip, a consummation of all his hopes.

Bibliography. A list of books or articles, or both, relating to a particular subject. In a research paper, a bibliography is an alphabetical list, sometimes grouped into categories, containing the names of all works quoted from or generally used in its preparation. Every formally prepared research paper should contain a bibliography placed at the end and begun on a separate page.

Bibliographical items should be arranged correctly and consistently. Usage varies, but unless your instructor rules otherwise, follow these suggestions:

1. Arrange items alphabetically by last names of the authors. Each surname is followed by a comma, then by the author's given name(s) or initials.
2. If the author's name is not given and not known, list the item by the first word (except *a, an, the*) in the title. List titles by the same author alphabetically, using a blank line about three-fourths of an inch long in place of the author's name after its first appearance.
3. A period follows the author's complete name.
4. The title of a book is followed by a period.
5. Place of publication is followed by a colon and the name of the publisher and the date, the latter elements separated by a comma.

The following are examples of citations of books and of articles from periodicals.

BIBLIOGRAPHY

Books

Chute, Marchette. *Shakespeare of London.* New York: E. P. Dutton & Co., 1949.
Dictionary of American Biography. Ed. Dumas Malone. New York: Charles Scribner's Sons, 1928–37.
Magill, Frank N. (ed.) *Masterpieces of World Literature in Digest Form.* First Series, 348–350. New York: Harper & Row, 1952.
Partridge, Eric. *Shakespeare's Bawdy.* New York: E. P. Dutton & Co., 1948.

Articles

Cohen, Hennig. "Why Isn't Melville for the Masses?" *The Saturday Review,* 16 Aug. 1969, pp. 19–21.
Hamblin, Dora Jane. "History's Biggest Literary Whodunit," *Life,* 24 April 1964, p. 69.
Levy, Alan. "The Would-Be Writer Industry," *The Reporter,* 24 Oct. 1963, p. 48.
Wilson, James Southall. "Devil Was in It," *American Mercury,* October, 1931, pp. 215–220.

Biography. A written account of a person's life or an account of the lives of any small and closely knit group, such as a family. *Biography* is thus a subtype of history, "a continuous, systematic narrative of past events as relating to a particular people, country, period, or person"; a subdivision of biography itself is *autobiography,* which see. Thomas Carlyle once defined history as "the essence of innumerable biographies," and Emerson wrote "There is properly no history, only biography."

Blend. This term refers to a mixing, fusing, or mingling of elements or varieties, as a *blend of tea.* In language, it means a word or construction formed by fusing two or more words: *motel* from *motor hotel.* Some blends have been accepted in standard English; others have not.

Boner. A slang term for "a stupid mistake," "a silly blunder." The person who referred to the *plastic* in his socks committed a blunder ("pulled a boner") by not writing *elastic* (see *Malapropism*).

Book review. A description, evaluation, and analysis of a book. These are the questions an effective book review should answer:

1. What was the author trying to do?
2. How well did he succeed in his attempt?
3. What value has the attempt?

An answer to the first question should be a discussion of the scope and purpose of the book. What material is covered? What material is stressed? What was the author's apparent purpose in writing the book?

The second question requires comment not so much on material as on manner. What stylistic faults and excellencies does the book possess? Is it convincing, persuasive, dull? Would some readers find the book excellent, others think it inferior? What readers? Why?

The third question may be answered by a discussion of the theme and purpose of the book. Here you may criticize an author for having written a light romance instead of a novel of social significance, or vice versa. But remember: fairness demands that you first evaluate a book in terms of what it is designed to be. Later, if you wish, you may point out the worthiness or unworthiness of the attempt (see *Criticism*).

There are three different kinds, or methods, of book reviewing. The first is the method of the reporter; that is, the reviewer reports on the book as an item of news. He tells what the book contains, perhaps in the form of a précis or résumé; he tells something of the author and his method of handling material. This type of review is not critical. It reports, in some detail, the observable facts about the author and contents of the book and does little else.

Another method, the one most frequently expected by college instructors, is that of combining reportorial details with some critical comment. The writer of this kind of review not only reports but also explains, interprets, and evaluates the book in terms of its material, its style, its scope, and its purpose. Such a review is ordinarily composed of about 50 percent summary and 50 percent evaluation.

The third method has been called the "springboard review." This type of criticism deals only slightly with the actual book under consideration; the "reviewer" uses it merely as a convenient starting point from which he launches into a critical essay that ranges far afield. For example, a "springboard reviewer," in considering a book on war, may make a few comments about the book and then proceed to a discussion of other books on war, or the dominant psychology of war novels, or even to an analysis of the causes of international friction.

The good review is usually a blend of these three methods. It contains some reportorial detail and some critical comment. It also compares and contrasts the book and its author with other similar or dissimilar books and authors, in an attempt to "place" the book and its special contribution.

Brief. The special form of outline used in argument is called a *brief,* but it has precisely the purpose and function that a topic or sentence or paragraph outline has. The brief differs from an ordinary outline only by using conjunctions (*for,* most notably) to reveal precise relationships between developing ideas. The brief is a complete statement of every phase of the argument, including definite indication of the proof that is to be supplied. Thus it may be called a "plan of attack."

In its simplest form, a brief consists of a stated conclusion followed by a statement of evidence, fact, or reason:

A. John must have received his allowance this month, for
   1. He has paid off his debt to me, and
   2. He has bought a new pair of shoes.

A lengthy argument will require a lengthy series of interlocking statements, usually arranged under headings of *introduction, argument,* and *conclusion.* But the purpose of the brief is always the same: to present a close line of argument in a clearly revealed series of related ideas.

Business English. The forms, conventions, idioms, and customs peculiar to communication in trade and industry. Business English is, or should be, merely standard English applied to the specific needs of industry and trade. However, its mechanical forms are so fixed and standardized that reference to a book on the subject is required for thorough knowledge (see Section 63).

But which, but who. See *And which.*

Cacophony. A harsh, jarring sound. Generally considered discordant are words like *flak, clack, hiss, wrangle, gutter, gaseous, spinach,* and *squash.* The antonym of *cacophony* is *euphony* (which see).

Cadence. The rhythmic flow, or sequence, of sounds in writing and speaking. *Cadence* has been broadened in meaning to refer to the time, measure, sequence, or beat of any rhythmical activity (dancing, rowing, marching). Specifically, *cadence* suggests the particular rhythm of prose and free verse and is a convenient term to designate the measured repetition of emphasis and accent in writing or speaking that is not altogether metrical (as in poetry). Used as a natural, inherent alternation of stressed and unstressed syllables in prose writing and in speaking, *cadence* is a pleasing stylistic quality; overly stressed, it develops artificial and "sing-song" effects.

Caricature. This term suggests ludicrous distortion of a particular feature, or features, of the characteristics of a person or idea. The word is derived from Italian *caricare* ("to load") and may be called a "loaded" or "overloaded" representation. *Caricature* is more often associated with drawing, as in cartoons, than with literature, but in each medium exaggeration is used for comic effect.

-cede, -ceed, -sede. These endings cause a large number of misspellings, but the problem they present is simple because so few words are involved. Only twelve words in the language end in the sound "seed," and not all of these are in common use.

First, only one word in English ends in *-sede: supersede.* It has this ending because of its origin; it comes from the Latin verb *sedere,* meaning "to sit." As with many other borrowed words in English, it maintains some connection with its source. Second, only three of the twelve words ending with the "seed" pronunciation are spelled *-ceed: exceed, proceed,* and *succeed.* Finally, the eight remaining words end in *-cede,* and of these only half are in everyday use: *accede, antecede, cede, concede, intercede, precede, recede, secede.*

It won't help in spelling the *-ceed* and *-cede* words to know their origin, but it will help in avoiding a *-sede* ending: the eleven *-ceed* and *-cede* words derive not from *sedere* (as *supersede* does) but from the Latin *cedere,* meaning "to go." Thus *pre* + *cede* means "to go or come before," *inter* + *cede* means "to go or come between," and so on.

Circumlocution. A lengthy, indirect, roundabout way of expressing something. An effective and clear synonym for this term is *deadwood;* a pedantic synonym is *periphrasis.* Vigorous and emphatic sentences are lean and direct; they contain no wordy expressions. "The sort of lightweight metal they employ in the making of kitchen utensils" can be more directly expressed by the single word *aluminum* (see Section 55).

Clearness. A fundamental virtue of writing and speaking is *clearness,* but the term is not easy to explain. Making your sentences clear involves such matters as *unity, completeness, coordination, word order, transition,* and the like. And yet writing sentences that are free from muddiness, haziness, and cloudiness; that are easily and distinctly understood; that are entirely logical; that have no ambiguity or obscurity—such style results less from avoiding mistakes than from qualities of mind and heart that cannot readily be described or learned.

Climactic order. Ideas arranged in the order of their importance so as to secure climax. Climax is attained when ideas in a sentence are so arranged that each succeeding idea has greater force than its predecessor. Avoid arranging the elements of a sentence so that it "sags," or loses force at the end. See *Climax.*

Unemphatic: In this collision some died agonizing deaths; some received serious injuries; and a few were barely scratched.
Better: A few were barely scratched in this collision; but some received serious injuries; and some died agonizing deaths.
Unemphatic: We were frightened by the noise: the crashing of the thunder, the pouring of the rain, and the steady blowing of the wind.
Better: We were frightened by the noises: the steady blowing of the wind, the pouring of the rain, and the crashing of the thunder.

The effectiveness of a sentence depends not entirely on the position of any single word or idea but on the arrangement of the whole sentence. The *sense* of the sentence must always be considered; the statement must be correct and clear. Effectiveness cannot be gained by a thoughtless or artificial attempt to employ the suggestion mentioned here; it will help to increase effectiveness only if its use does not destroy correctness, clearness, and naturalness.

Climax. The most intense or highest point in the development of some action, either physical or mental. In literature, *climax* is the moment in a play, novel, short story, or narrative poem at which a crisis comes to its point of greatest intensity and is in some manner resolved. The term is an index of emotional response from reader or spectator and is also a designation of the turning point in action. See *Climactic order.*

Close and open punctuation. Writing in which as few marks of punctuation as possible are used is said to be punctuated in *open* style; writing that employs no incorrect marks but omits none which could legitimately be used is called *close* in its punctuation.

The terms *open* and *close* have a somewhat specialized meaning when applied to business letters. Punctuation of the heading and of both inside and outside addresses usually follows the *open* system. No commas or final periods, except after abbreviations, are used after the separate lines, and some letter writers prefer also to omit the colon after the salutation and the comma after the complimentary close. The *close* system, in which commas are used after each line of the heading and inside address, except the last, at the end of which a period is used, is rarely considered standard business usage (see Section 63b).

Composition. A composition is a carefully planned and executed literary, artistic, or musical product. The term may refer to any piece of writing that has a definite theme.

Conciseness. This term refers to the quality of brevity, terseness. Writing is *concise* when it expresses much thought in few words. Succinct writing is both brief and comprehensive (see Section 55).

Concreteness. Concrete words, in contrast to abstract terms, are those that name objects or persons which can be seen, touched, and so on—*train, filing clerk, store, apple.* Each of these words has at least a slightly different meaning for each of us, but they have a "core" of reality that is readily understood. And yet your idea and mine of such abstract words as *goodness, duty,* and *sophistication* may differ widely. For this reason, concrete words are more exact than abstract ones, and concreteness is a valued quality in writing (see Section 39c).

Conjugation. The changes in the form and uses of a verb to show tense, mood, voice, number, and person.

Connotation. This word applies to the overtones of words—values and meanings that are suggested rather than specifically expressed in a dictionary definition. For example, San Francisco is "a seaport city in northern California," but the name itself has such connotations as "Golden Gate," "Chinatown," "Barbary Coast," "Gateway to the Orient," and "Earthquake of 1906." Connotative words have implied, suggestive, associated meanings, in contrast to *denotative* words.

Consonant. In phonetics, a *consonant* has a sound in which the breath is somewhat restricted or even stopped. Consonant sounds may be constrasted with *vowel* sounds, which are made with less friction and fuller resonance. The vowels in our alphabet are *a, e, i, o, u,* and sometimes *y.* All the other letters are consonants (see *Vowel*).

Consonants dropped. See *Dropped consonants.*

Contraction. A shortened form of a word, such as *can't* for *cannot, I'll* for *I shall* or *I will.* Large numbers of contractions seem out of place in standard English except when used to convey the actual tone and flavor of dialogue. A few are used in this book to avoid stiffness and artificiality.

Counter word. This expression means a term that is used in a vague sense of approval or disapproval but without any exact meaning. Many counter words are slang and all are trite: *swell, lousy, nice, terrible, ghastly, cool.* Counter words are prevalent in advertising and colloquial speech but are rarely suitable for standard writing.

Criticism. Criticism is a part of everyone's daily life. We exercise critical faculties every time we choose a meal in the cafeteria, decide how to spend the afternoon, or buy an article of clothing. We read one book in preference to another; we choose the subway rather than the bus—all these are acts involving some sort of criticism.

In a broader and more exact sense, criticism is thoughtful, many-sided evaluation. The word *critic* comes from the Greek *kritikós,* meaning "a judge." Thus, criticism is a process that weighs, evaluates, judges. Contrary to some opinion, it does not deal only with faults. Sound criticism mentions good qualities as well as bad, virtues as well as faults. It should not set out to praise or condemn; rather, it weighs faults and merits and then passes a considered judgment.

In writing criticisms of books, plays, concerts and recitals, radio and television programs, and motion pictures, you should remember that your comments must be based on knowledge. It is unfair to review a book or a motion picture, for example, without first having read (or listened and looked) with care and thoughtfulness. You must give whatever it is that you are reviewing a fair and thorough trial. The best criticism is thoughtful, detached, impersonal—not unreasoning and biased.

But critical writing is also emotional and personal. As individuals, we all have prejudices of some sort as a result of our heredity and environment. We must be on guard against our prejudices, but of course it is impossible not to react according to our individual traits. The best criticism is an amalgam of objectivity and subjectivity; it should be impersonal and yet it must be subjective (see *Book review*).

De-, dis-, dys-. These prefixes will cause spelling problems when you don't distinguish clearly between root words beginning with *s* and the prefixes themselves. Note these spellings: *describe* (write down), *de + scribe; despoil* (strip, rob), *de + spoil; dissemble* (disguise), *dis + semble; dissimilar* (unlike), *dis + similar.*

Only about thirty common words begin with *diss-*, but ten times as many begin with *dis-*. Only three common words (and their derivatives) begin with *dys-: dysentery, dyspepsia, dystrophy* (as in *muscular dystrophy*).

Here is a simple rule: When the prefixes *dis-* and *mis-* are added to a root word beginning with *s*, neither *s* should be omitted: *dissatisfied, misstep.* When they are added to roots not beginning with an *s*, use only one *s: disappear, misfortune.*

Deadwood. This word actually means, of course, dead wood on trees; by extension, it has come to mean anything that is useless or burdensome (see Section 55). In writing, it is a convenient label for wordiness and is applied to words and phrases that add little or nothing to the sentence in which they appear: *this is a topic that* may be written *this topic; the fact that I came* may be written *my coming; in the year of 1970* may be written *in 1970.* See *Wordiness.*

Declension. The changes in the form or use of a noun or pronoun to indicate case, number, and person. To *decline* means to give these grammatical changes.

Definition. The typical dictionary definition has three parts: *term, genus, differentia.* From the standpoint of logic, a good definition is made only by placing the term to be defined in the class or kind to which it belongs (genus) and then giving a statement of the individual characteristics that distinguish the term from other members of the genus. Thus, "Braille [the term] is a system of printing or transcribing [the genus] in which the characters are represented by raised letters [the differentia]."

In practice, most definitions are made less formally and exactly than this. Sometimes we use synonyms, explaining one term with the aid of other words that mean the same, or almost the same, thing. Thus we say that a *mendicant* is a *beggar,* or that *to pilfer* means *to steal.*

On occasion, however, it is necessary to be more precise than this. A definition does not have to be formal in order to define; a satisfactory definition can overlook both genus and differentia. Such a definition can be made by collecting examples or instances of the term. If asked to define a *laser,* you could perhaps best define it for the lay reader by citing examples of how it works. Or if asked to define *honesty,* you might well cite instances of people who revealed honesty in their actions. You can also define satisfactorily by telling at some length what a thing is not, or by comparing and contrasting the term with something known and familiar (extended simile or metaphor).

Denotation. The exact, literal meaning of a word as contrasted with its *connotation,* or suggestive meaning. Thus, *home* has a denotative meaning of "house," "apartment," "fixed dwelling place." Its connotation might be "refuge," "place of peace," "retreat," "haven of rest" (see *Connotation*).

Derivation. See *Words, origins of.*

Description. To *describe* someone or something is to convey an impression or image that reveals the appearance, nature, and attributes of the person or thing under discussion. *Description* is one of the four forms of discourse (which see).

Diacritical mark. A diacritical mark, point, or sign is attached to a letter or character to distinguish it from another of the same form or to give it a particular phonetic value or indicate stress. For example, diacritical marks are used to show the sound of *a* as in *cär* and *a* as in *āble.*

Diagraming. A mechanical device to aid in identifying words as parts of speech, in identifying phrases and clauses, and in indicating in a sentence the uses or functions of these words, phrases, and clauses (see *Analysis of a sentence*). The parts of a sentence are put on lines in the positions indicated in the following skeleton diagram. The three most important parts of the sentence (subject, predicate, object) are usually put on a horizontal line; any modifiers are appropriately placed on lines underneath.

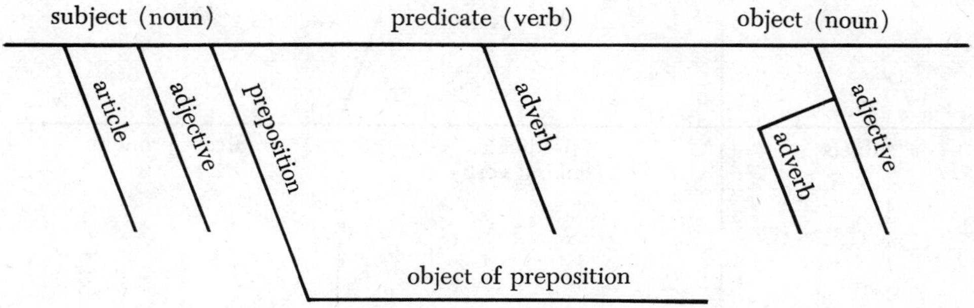

Filled in, such a diagramed sentence might read:

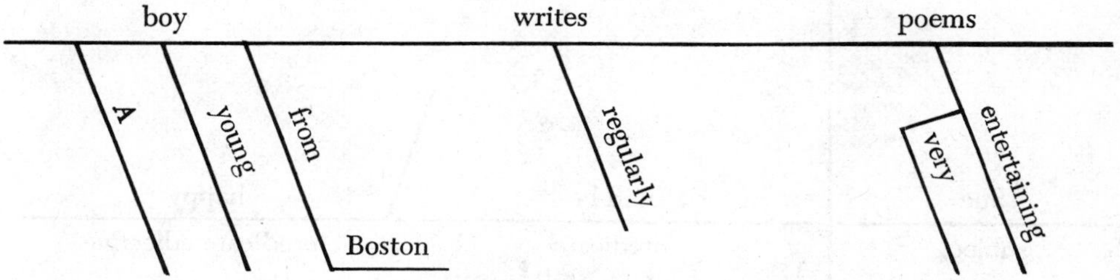

A young boy from Boston regularly writes very entertaining poems.

The simple subject, the simple predicate, the direct object, the object complement, the predicate noun or pronoun, and the predicate adjective are written on the main horizontal line. (If you have forgotten the meanings of these terms, look up each one at its appropriate place in this book.) Subject and predicate are separated by a perpendicular line intersecting the horizontal line. The direct object is separated from the verb by a short perpendicular line extending up from the horizontal line. The object complement, the predicate noun or pronoun, or the predicate adjective is set off by a short slanting line extending up to the left from the horizontal line. The following diagrams illustrate the principles just stated:

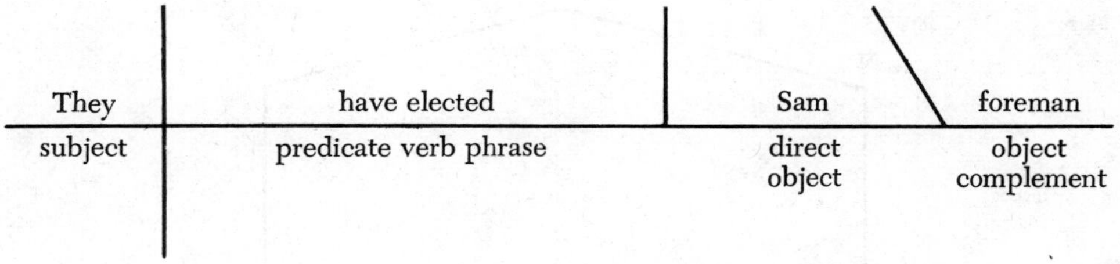

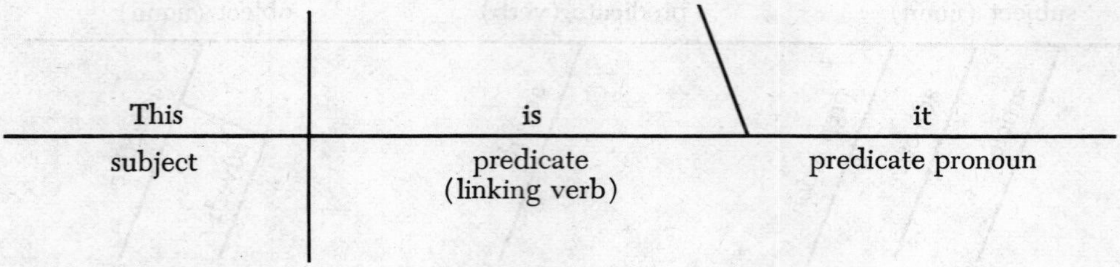

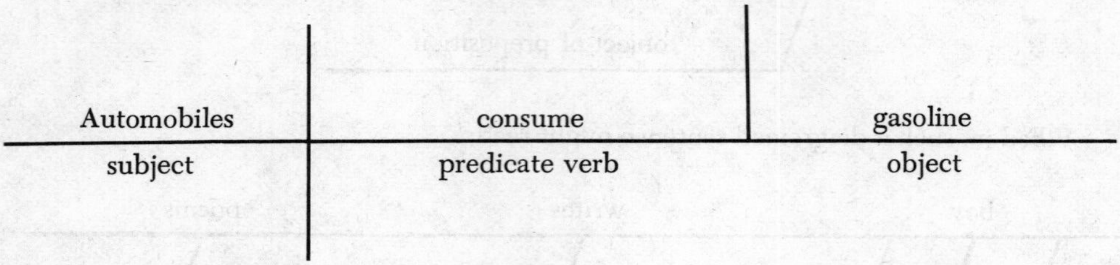

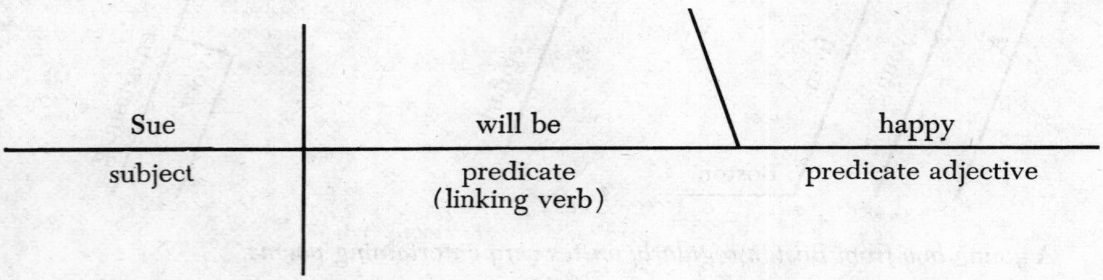

Another method of diagraming consists of placing each word in a sentence in a box. This plan results in a set of boxes, each enclosed in another box except the last, which encloses the entire sentence.

Still another method of diagraming is accomplished by the use of lines branching like the limbs of trees. The first branching is from the sentence (S) to the subject (noun or noun phrase, N or NP) and the predicate (verb or verb phrase, V or VP). Further branchings reveal as many levels and varieties of structural relationships as the sentence to be diagramed involves.

The simplest tree diagram is obviously of a two-word sentence such as "Children play." A tree diagram of this sentence is as follows:

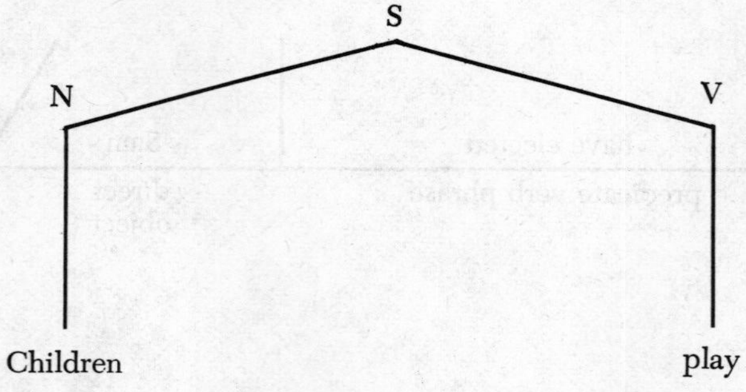

For a longer sentence, a tree diagram would look like this:

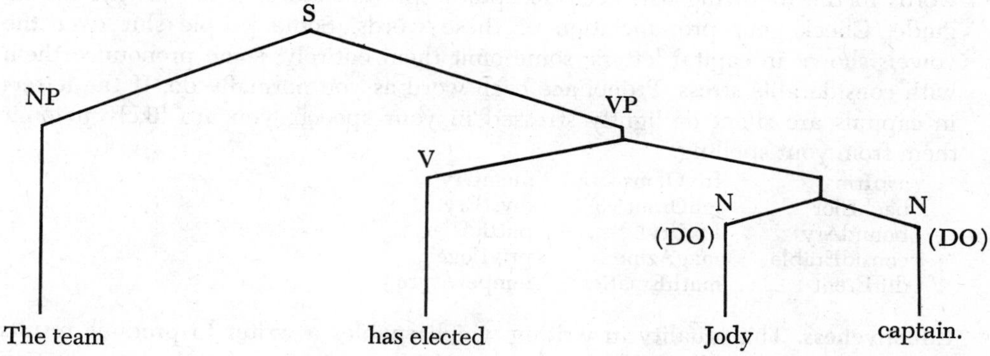

In this diagram, the sentence consists of a noun phrase (NP) and a verb phrase (VP). The latter contains both a direct object (DO) and an object complement (also DO), both referring to the same person. Thus the two are joined by a horizontal line.

Dialogue. Conversation, talking together. *Dialogue* (also spelled *dialog*) refers to passages of talk in a story, novel, or play. Fixed rules apply to the paragraphing and punctuation of dialogue (see Section 27).

Ditto marks. The word *ditto* means "the same" or "a duplicate." Ditto marks (″) are used in itemized lists and tables to show that a word, figure, or passage above is to be repeated. (In typewritten manuscript use quotation marks to represent ditto marks.) Ditto marks are less used than formerly and are advised against in ordinary writing.

Double negative. This construction consists of the use of two negative words in the same statement: He *couldn't* find his friend *nowhere*. Actually, a double negative can intensify and enforce a negative sense, but it is considered a colloquial or substandard form of expression in current English usage (see Section 50g).

Dropped consonants. If our visual memory of words is stronger than our auditory image, well and good. But when a letter is incorrectly omitted in pronouncing a word, we have to be on guard. The following representative list of words should be studied carefully. In each word the "offending" consonant is set as a capital letter; try to pronounce it fully, sounding it out as an aid to your auditory memory. (Admittedly, some of the consonants are really silent and are difficult to pronounce.)

accepT	emPty	lanDlord
aCquire	fasCinate	nesTle
anD	granDfather	ofTen
authenTic	hanDful	promPt
condemN	kePt	tenTative

Dropped vowels. Educated speakers often drop vowels in pronouncing some words in the following list; even acceptable pronunciation is not always a sure guide. Check your pronunciation of these words. Some people slur over the vowels shown in capital letters; some omit them entirely; some pronounce them with considerable stress. Pronounce each word as you normally do. If the letters in capitals are silent or lightly stressed in your speech, you are likely to omit them from your spelling.

aspIrin	frivOlous	memOry
bachElor	ignOrant	mystEry
boundAry	luxUry	particUlar
considErable	magAzine	privIlege
diffErent	mathEmatics	temperAture

Effectiveness. That quality in writing which enables a writer to produce results intended or expected. The primary aim of all writing is clear communication from writer to reader. Writing that most nearly meets this ideal is most effective.

It is possible to write sentences that are clear and correct and yet not effective. Effectiveness is a somewhat vague and elusive quality that is dependent upon many sentence characteristics. The qualities contributing most to effectiveness in sentences are conciseness, parallelism, consistency, variety in structure, and position and arrangement of words.

-efy, -ify. These two suffixes cause much spelling trouble, but the problem is simple when it is looked at clearly. Actually, only four words you are likely to use end in *-efy* (and you probably won't use them every day, either). All the remainder, without exception, end in *-ify*.

Learn by whatever method seems best these four words and spell all others with *-ify: liquefy* (to make or become liquid); *putrefy* (to make or become rotten); *rarefy* (to make or become rare); *stupefy* (to make or become insensible). Words built on these four tend to retain the *e* spelling: *liquefy, liquefies, liquefied, liquefying, liquefaction.*

Emphasis. Force of thought, feeling, action, or expression. In writing and speaking, emphasis depends less upon force than upon careful diction, position and arrangement of words, effective repetition, and the use of intensifiers. Emphasis is one of the most desired of all qualities in writing and speaking and one of the most difficult to define or attain. In sentence structure it implies accurately conveying your ideas to your reader or listener; it involves leading your reader to see your thoughts in the same relative importance in which you see them.

English, history of. The English we speak and write is descended from that spoken and written by immigrants from England, Scotland, and Ireland who founded the British colonies in this country in the seventeenth century. Their language, in turn, came from the dialects of ancient Germanic tribes.

For about a thousand years before the Christian era, our linguistic ancestors were semisavages wandering through northern Europe. These tribes, consisting of Angles, Saxons, and Jutes, spoke several dialects of what is known as Low German, or Plattdeutsch. They had some contact with the Roman Empire and promptly began a process that has continued unabated to the present day: they started borrowing words from Latin and placing them in their own vocabularies. We still use many everyday words borrowed by these tribes, such as *bishop, butter, cheese, plum, kettle, street, fork, cook.*

When their empire began to weaken, the Romans had to give up occupancy of what we now know as England, and the Germanic tribes, commonly called Anglo-Saxons, began to move in. We know little about the arrival of the Anglo-Saxons in England in the fifth century A.D., but we do know that after the year 600 they were partially converted to Christianity and that borrowing from Latin became even more pronounced. To what was then Anglo-Saxon, or Old English, were added many words that are in use today, such as *alms, anthem, martyr, palm, priest.*

England even then was considered an attractive and desirable place, and Norsemen from Denmark and the Scandinavian peninsula began a long series of hit-and-run raids. Forays of the Norsemen continued until the eleventh century, with the linguistic result that many Norse words were added to the language—for example, *crawl, egg, law, race, scowl, tree.* Even our pronouns *they, them,* and *their* are of Norse origin. So is our suffix *-by,* the Danish word for "farm" or "town," which appears in names such as *Derby.*

Another event of great importance to our language was the Norman Conquest. The Normans, originally from Scandinavia, settled in northern France in the tenth century and adopted the French language. In 1066 they crossed the English Channel and became the masters of England. French became the language of the nobility, the court, and polite society, although the common people continued to use English. Our language was profoundly affected by the introduction of French; literally thousands of words were added to the English vocabulary between 1100 and 1500. A few examples will serve to show this borrowing: *bacon, baptism, biscuit, blanket, bucket, chess, curtain, fault, flower, government, grammar, incense, lamp, lease, logic, parson, religion, scarlet, surprise, towel.*

Beginning about 1500, the discovery of new lands brought many thousands of other new words to the English language. Words from such remote regions as India, China, Africa, and North America enriched the language tremendously. Among familiar words borrowed, for example, from the North American Indians may be mentioned *Connecticut, Massachusetts, Monongahela, squaw, tomahawk, wampum.*

In short, during the past thousand years our language has far more than tripled its size. Words have come pouring into the language from French, Latin, Greek, Hebrew, Arabic, and a score of other tongues.

This brief comment on English is inadequate as linguistic history, but at least it may make clear a dominant reason why spelling and pronunciation are so far apart. When these many thousands of words first arrived in English, they often appeared with the spellings, or phonetic (sound) approximations of the spellings, that they originally had and that did not always conform to the customs of English. Sometimes the spellings of words were modified to conform to the English tongue; many times they were not. The English language is thus a linguistic grab bag with tremendous range and flexibility. See *Old English, Middle English,* and *Modern English.*

Etymology. The origin and development of a word; tracing a word back as far as possible by means of comparative *linguistics* (which see). (See also *Words, origins of.*)

Euphemism. The substitution of a mild, bland, inoffensive expression for a blunt or harsh one. *To depart this life* is a euphemism for *to die.*

Euphony. Agreeableness of sound; a speech sound pleasing to the ear. *Euphony* is largely a negative quality in English prose; it consists of avoiding unpleasant sounds such as sibilants, guttural expressions, and the like. Euphonious words selected by some writers: *vermilion, melody, nevermore, cuspidor, cellar door, moonlight.* The antonym of *euphony* is *cacophony* (which see).

Exaggeration. The act of magnifying, overstating, or going beyond the limits of truth. In writing, exaggeration is used not so much to deceive as to intensify or strengthen meaning: *starved* or *famished* for "hungry"; *a million thanks, abject adoration.*

Exposition. A kind of writing that defines, explains, and interprets. As contrasted with other basic forms of discourse, *exposition* is all writing that does not primarily describe an object, tell a story, or maintain a position. It includes much of what we read: magazine articles, news stories, textbooks, editorials.

Fallacy. From a Latin word meaning "to deceive," *fallacy* names a false or misleading notion, belief, or argument. In logic, a *fallacy* is any of various kinds of erroneous reasoning that make arguments unsound (see Section 56).

Fine writing. A term applied to writing that is incorrectly thought to be free of all impurities and blemishes because it has been made perfect. Actually, "fine" writing is artificial, affected, and overcareful. It results from the use of pompous and long words, from euphemisms, from the use of too many modifiers, from the overuse of foreign words and Briticisms.

Flashback. A scene inserted into a play, novel, or short story representing an earlier event. A *flashback* is a narrative device that "flashes back" to the presentation of an incident that occurred prior to the opening scene of a literary work. Such a flashback may be developed through a reverie, a recollection by a character, a dream sequence, or dialogue.

Footnote. The purpose of a footnote is to mention the authority for some fact stated or to develop some point referred to in the body of a paper.

Generally known facts or quotations do not require footnotes, but you must avoid *plagiarism* (which see). Unless the idea and the phrasing are your own, refer the reader to some source for your statement. To be entirely honest, acknowledge every source of indebtedness even when no direct quotation is used.

On occasion, you may wish to develop, interpret, or refute some idea but not want an extended comment to clutter up the body of your paper. Use a footnote.

How many footnotes should appear in a research paper? One investigation may call for twice as many as another. Some pages of your paper may require a half-dozen or more footnotes; others may need none or only one or two. Acknowledge credit where it is due and supply discussion footnotes where they are needed for understanding.

Methods of footnoting are numerous, but whatever system you employ should be consistent throughout your paper and immediately clear to any intelligent reader.

For books, standard usage favors this form: (1) author's Christian name or initials followed by surname, (2) title of book (in italics) and number of edition, (3) place of publication, (4) name of publisher, (5) date of publication, (6) volume and page reference. In the first illustration below all six items are shown. In the next four, item 4 is optionally omitted.

In listing information about periodical material, place the title of the article or story after the author's name and before the name of the periodical. The title is put in quotation marks; the name of the magazine is italicized (underlined). Study the correct forms for listing the following kinds of information:

Books

[1] Henry Louis Mencken, *The American Language,* 4th ed. (New York: Alfred A. Knopf, 1936), p. 168.

[1] John Tasker Howard and Arthur Mendel, *Our American Composers* (New York, 1941), p. 82.

[1] Douglas S. Freeman, *George Washington* (New York, 1948) II, 142.

[1] *Letters from W. H. Hudson,* ed. Edward Garnett (New York, 1923), p. 62.

[1] Homer, *The Odyssey,* trans. George Herbert Palmer (Boston, 1891), p. 46.

Articles (Essays, Stories)

[1] Walter D. Edmonds, "Arrival of the Lily Dean," *The Saturday Evening Post,* 7 May 1938, p. 5.

[1] "Personality Tests," *Life,* 7 Oct. 1946, p. 35.

[1] Katherine Mansfield, "Bliss," *A Study of the Short Story,* ed. Henry S. Canby and Alfred Dashiell (New York: Henry Holt, and Company, Inc., 1935), p. 303.

Your instructor may prefer a shorter form or one in which the information is arranged differently. For example, he may require you to omit the author's first name, the place of publication, or the name of the publisher. After the form has been decided upon, be consistent in its use.

In documenting your research paper, you may be urged by your instructor to use abbreviations wherever possible for increased efficiency. The main, or primary, forms shown above may well be used less often than short-cut versions. For example:

Ibid.: the same. If a footnote refers to the same source as the one referred to in the footnote immediately preceding, the abbreviation *ibid.* (from the Latin *ibidem,* meaning "in the same place") may be used. If the volume, page, title, and author are the same, use *ibid.* alone. If the volume and page differ, use, for example, "*Ibid.*, III, 206." *Ibid.* usually comes at the beginning of a footnote and is capitalized for that reason only.

Op. cit.: the work cited. After the first full reference to a given work, provided no other work by the same author is mentioned in the paper, succeeding references may be indicated by the author's surname followed by *op. cit.* (from the Latin *opere citato,* meaning "in the work cited") and the volume and page: Jones, *op. cit.*, IV, 19; Hasty, *op. cit.*, p. 94. However, *op. cit.* does no real work, and its use is being discarded in favor of a note containing only the author's last name and the page number involved: Burke, p. 230.

Passim: "everywhere," "throughout." It is to be used when no specific page reference can be given.

Loc. cit.: the place cited. If the reference is to the exact passage covered by an earlier reference not immediately preceding, use *loc. cit.* (from the Latin *loco citato,* meaning "in the place cited"). *Loc. cit.*, like *op. cit.*, seems wordy and is gradually being discarded in research writing. Actually, *ibid.* can do anything which *loc. cit.* can.

Some style manuals dealing with documentation recommend that *ibid.* and *passim* no longer be italicized (underlined). Two of the best and most influential manuals making this suggestion are *The MLA Style Sheet,* compiled by William R. Parker, formerly executive secretary of the Modern Language Association, first published in 1951, second edition published in 1970; and *A Research Manual for College Studies and Papers,* by Cecil B. Williams, 3rd edition, 1963. You should follow the specific instructions given by your own instructor in this and other matters of documentation. Here are some common abbreviations:

p. (*plural,* pp.): page (pages)
l. (*plural,* ll.): line (lines)
vol.: volume
ch. (*plural,* chs.): chapter (chapters)
ff.: following
v.: verse
ante: before
art.: article
sec. (*plural,* secs.): section (sections)
n. (*plural,* nn.): note (notes)

In the text, a footnote is indicated by an Arabic numeral placed above and to the right of the word to be commented upon. If the reference is to a quotation, place the numeral at the end of the passage. Before the actual footnote at the bottom of the page repeat the number used in the text.

Footnotes may be numbered consecutively throughout the manuscript or separately for each page. Follow the directions issued by your instructor.

Footnotes may be put at the bottoms of pages, between the lines in the manuscript proper, or all together at the end of the paper. Most instructors prefer the first of these methods. If the footnotes are placed at the bottom of the page, they should not be crowded. Always leave a clearly defined space between the text and the footnotes.

Foreshadowing. Showing, indicating, or suggesting beforehand. In a literary work, *foreshadowing* provides a hint of what is to occur later.

Forms of discourse. It is conventional to divide writing into four forms of discourse (communication of thought by words). The forms—description, exposition, narration, argument—are rarely found in a pure or unmixed state; even a novel, which is basically narrative, usually contains much description and some exposition and argument. Each of the four forms is briefly discussed at an appropriate place in this Guide.

"Frying pan error." A term used by some teachers to characterize an error resulting from an attempt to correct an original mistake. For example, if you attempt to correct a fused sentence by inserting a comma, you have not improved matters much, if at all. The term is derived from an expression used in *Don Quixote,* "Lest we leap out of the frying pan into the fire," and generally implies "getting into even more serious trouble by trying to correct a mistake already made."

Homographs. Two words that have the same spelling but different meanings, origins, and perhaps pronunciations; *air* (atmosphere) and *air* (melody), *lead* (to conduct) and *lead* (metal).

Homonyms. Two words that have close or identical pronunciation but different meanings, origins, and frequently spellings: *pale* and *pail, sew* and *so, steal* and *steel.*

Hyperbole. An extravagant expression not intended to be taken literally; an obvious and deliberate exaggeration: *as old as time* (see *Exaggeration*).

-ible. For comment on the problem of *-able* or *-ible,* see *-able.*

The ending should usually be *-ible* if the base (root) is not a complete word. Contrast this principle with the first rule under *-able:* If the base is a complete word, add *-able; mail + able = mailable.* If the base is not a complete word, add *-ible: ris + ible = risible, poss + ible = possible.* For example: *audible, compatible, feasible, infallible, negligible, terrible.*

The ending should usually be *-ible* if the base (root) ends in *ns: respons + ible = responsible.* For example: *comprehensible, defensible, ostensible, sensible.*

The ending should usually be *-ible* if the base (root) ends in *-miss.* Comparatively few words belong in this category. Here are three examples: *admissible, permissible, transmissible.* With roots not ending in *-miss,* but closely related, are such words with *-ible* endings as *accessible, compressible, irrepressible,* and *possible* (which also fits under group 1, above).

The ending should usually be *-ible* if *-ion* can be added to the base (root) without intervening letters: *collect, collection, collectible.* A number of words (roots) form nouns by the immediate addition of *-ion.* All such words form adjectives ending in *-ible.* For example: *accessible, convertible, corruptible, inexhaustible, reversible, suggestible.* You should note that this principle is tricky: if *-ion* cannot be added to the root without intervening letters the *-able* ending is more likely, as in *present, presentation, presentable.*

The ending should usually be *-ible* if the base (root) ends in soft *c* or soft *g.* This principle should be compared with the rule under *-able.* A soft *c* sounds like an *s* (*force*); a soft *g* sounds like a *j* (*tangent*). The following words contain a soft *c* or a soft *g* (also note that, with few exceptions, the roots are not complete words): *eligible, forcible, incorrigible, invincible, irascible.*

Just as there are a few exceptions to the rules for *-able* endings, so are there for words ending in *-ible.* Among those words that, by rule, should end in *-able* but do not are the following: *collapsible, contemptible, discernible, gullible, inflexible, irresistible.*

Imagery. The forming of mental images, figures, or likenesses of things; the use of language to represent descriptively actions, persons, objects, and ideas. Any effective writer, especially a poet, is a maker of pictures in words, but he can, and does, appeal to senses other than that of sight.

Incident. An *incident* is a short narrative told for its own sake. Not concerned with making a point, it deals with a single, simple situation. Its primary emphasis is upon the character of the narrator or some person involved in the action, or upon the action itself.

Informal essay. A composition without set form or obvious pattern that also goes by the names of *familiar* essay, *light* essay, and *personal* essay. Subject matter for an informal essay is infinite; it may reflect any of a thousand moods or feelings.

Although informal essays make no pretensions toward learning or instruction, the best of them are stylistically polished and imply more than they state.

Irony. A figure of speech in which the literal (denotative) meaning of a word or statement is the opposite of that intended. In literature, *irony* is a technique of indicating an intention or attitude opposed to what is actually stated. Aristotle defined *irony* as "a dissembling toward the inner core of truth"; Cicero supplied a simpler and more helpful explanation: "Irony is the saying of one thing and meaning another."

Irregular plurals. Here is a representative list of words with irregular or nonsensical plurals that follow none of the principles stated under *Plurals* (which see):

bison, bison	louse, lice	series, series
brother, brothers, brethren	madame, mesdames	sheep, sheep
child, children	man, men	species, species
deer, deer	moose, moose	swine, swine
foot, feet	mouse, mice	tooth, teeth
goose, geese	scissors, scissors	trousers, trousers

Is, was, were. Parts of the verb *to be*. It may help you to remember that *is* is singular in number, third person, present tense. (*He* [or *She* or *It*] *is* in the room.) *Was* is singular, first or third person, past tense. (*I* [or *He* or *She* or *It*] *was* in the room.) *Were* can be either singular or plural, second person in the singular and all three persons in the plural, and is in the past tense. (*You* [both singular and plural] *were* in the room. *We* [or *You* or *They*] *were* in the room.) The two most frequent errors in using *to be* are employing *was* for *were* and vice versa, and using *is* in the first or second person instead of in the third, where it belongs.

Is when, is where. These terms are frequently misused, especially in giving definitions. Grammatically, the fault may be described as using an adverbial clause in place of the noun phrase or clause that is called for. "A subway *is where* you ride under the ground" can be improved to "A subway *is* [or *involves*] an electric railroad beneath the surface of the streets." Walking *is when* you move about on foot" can be improved to "Walking *is the act of* [or *consists of*] *moving* about on foot."

-ise, -ize, -yze. Some 500 fairly common words in our language end in *-ise, -ize, -yze.* How can one master all these spellings, especially since correct pronunciation provides no help at all?

The best approach is to isolate the comparatively few words ending in *-yze* and *-ise* and to remember that *-ize* is by far the most common suffix and that the chances of its being correct are mathematically excellent.

Only four fairly common words in English end in *-yze,* and of them you will normally use only two: *analyze, catalyze, electrolyze, paralyze.*

No clear "rules" exist for choosing between *-ise* and *-ize* endings. But although well over 400 words end in *-ize,* there are only one-tenth as many with an *-ise* suffix.

1. Combinations with *-cise: excise, exercise, exorcise, incise.* These *-cise* words are so spelled because they derive from Latin *incisus,* meaning "cut."
2. Combinations with *guise: disguise.*
3. Words ending in *-mise: compromise, demise, premise, surmise.*
4. Words ending in *-prise: apprise, comprise, emprise, enterprise, reprise, surprise.*
5. Combinations with *-rise: arise, moonrise, sunrise, uprise.*
6. Words ending in *-vise: advise, devise, improvise, revise, supervise.* These *-vise* words (except for *devise*) are derived from the Latin *visus,* "see."

7. Words ending in *-wise: contrariwise, lengthwise, likewise, otherwise, sidewise.*
8. Miscellaneous combinations with *-ise: advertise, chastise, despise, franchise, merchandise.*

This makes a total of less than forty common words ending *-yze* and *-ise*. All others with this suffix pronunciation end in *-ize*. Here are a few of the hundreds of words with this ending in American spelling: *agonize, apologize, authorize, baptize, generalize, harmonize, legalize, pasteurize, patronize, realize, recognize.*

Its, it's, its'. This little three-letter combination causes more errors than any other grouping of letters in the English language. However, the distinctions among them are simple and easily learned. *Its* is the possessive form of *it*. (The dress has lost *its* shape.) *It's* is a contraction of *it is* and should never be used unless it means precisely this. (I think *it's* [*it is*] going to rain.) *Its'?* There is no such form or word in the language. (See Section 26e.)

Journalese. A style of writing supposed to characterize newspaper usage. Good newspaper writing is terse, accurate, complete, and frequently employs relatively short sentences. Faults of some *journalese* are triteness, forced humor, neologisms, wordiness, and occasional resort to polysyllabication. Some newspaper writing is wordy and lazy, but much is vigorous and effective, remarkably so since it is prepared under pressure of time.

K inserted. The letter *k* is usually added to words ending in *c* before a suffix beginning with *e, i,* or *y*. This is done in order to prevent mispronunciation; note the different pronunciations, for example, of *picnicking* and *icing*. Only a few common words are involved in this rule, but they are frequently misspelled: *colic, colicky; frolic, frolicked, frolicking; mimic, mimicked, mimicking; panic, panicky; picnic, picnicked, picnicker; politic, politicking; traffic, trafficked, trafficking.*

This rule must be applied carefully. Note, for example, the words *frolicsome* and *mimicry*. There is no reason to add *k*, since the *c* remains hard.

Linguistics. The science of language. English linguistics is a study of the structure and development of the English language and its relationship to other languages. Involved in linguistics are *etymology, morphology, phonetics, semantics,* and *syntax*.

Linguistics is derived from the Latin word *lingua,* meaning "tongue," "language." The very origin of the word implies that linguistics and its practitioners, *linguists,* are more concerned with speech and its sounds than with language in written form; a tenet of linguistics is that language is primarily a matter of speech.

The word *structural* applied to linguistic study and analysis implies that a system, or series, of patterns in spoken language can be isolated and described. In structural grammar, emphasis is first placed on form (system) and then on meaning. To a structuralist, words and their functions are classified by formal and structural means (changes in the form of a word, noting the ways it can be used in a sentence) with no particular regard for the meanings involved. That is, in structural grammar, *the cat's meow* and *the dat's meow* would receive similar attention because of the form and function of *cat* and *dat*, even though the latter is meaningless.

Structuralists recognize four *form* classes of words that correspond approximately to the parts of speech known as nouns, verbs, adjectives, and adverbs. All other words—mainly prepositions, pronouns, and interjections—are called *function* or *structure* words, since their purpose is to supply information about the relationships of parts of a sentence made up of the form classes of words. Function words, such as *a, the, enough,* and *after,* have little meaning by themselves but do provide clues to the structure of a sentence; they provide a framework into which form class words can be dropped. Such combinations of function and form words result in three kinds of structures: noun, verb, and modifier structures. All *substantives* are noun structures; verb structures consist of words of the verb form class together with such function words as linking verbs; modifier structures are words from adjective or adverb form classes.

Structural linguists classify sentences according to the structures they contain and the arrangement of these structures. Such classification results in several different kinds of *patterns* (subject-verb, subject-verb-predicate adjective, and so on).

Another kind of grammar, called *transformational,* attempts to outline the processes by which sentences are formed. Transformational grammar assumes that basic sentence patterns, called *kernel sentences,* can be transformed into more involved sentence patterns by combination or addition. This scientific approach to grammar provides rules for forming kernel sentences, for combining or otherwise altering kernel sentences into transformed sentences, and for making resultant transformations understandable and "pronounceable."

Regardless of its particular label or approach, each kind of "scientific" or "modern" linguistics emphasizes *word order* and the specific patterns of words and phrases. This emphasis on structure and pattern, on position and function, has resulted in terminology which is somewhat different from that of traditional grammar. For an example, study the entry for *Noun* in Section 1; the seven characteristics given there of this part of speech constitute an approach to one form of modern linguistics, a form that may be called "scientific" since it is based on observation rather than upon formal Latin tradition.

At the present time, lack of agreement among linguists prevents any concrete, fully coherent description of modern linguistics—its undeniable achievements and its potential contribution to a study of language. But since description of our language should be as accurate as possible, hopefully some agreed-upon form of scientific linguistics will eventually improve, strengthen, or even replace our "traditional grammar" with its inconsistencies and inaccuracies.

Malapropism. Ridiculous misuse of words, usually resulting from confusion of words similar in sound but different in meaning: *progeny* for *prodigy, dual* for *duel.* The word comes from the name of a character in Sheridan's play, *The Rivals*—Mrs. Malaprop (see *Boner*).

Manuscript. Literally, a letter, report, document, or book written by hand (from Latin words for "hand" and "writing"). *Manuscript* is now used to mean composition prepared by hand or on the typewriter, as contrasted with type. The word may be abbreviated *MS.* (plural *MSS.*).

Manuscript form. What you have to say and the way you say that something, whatever it is, are the important elements in writing. But neatness, legibility, and orderly method are also important. Try to give to your ideas the outward form that will ensure ready communication and a favorable response. If your instructor or department has given instructions for preparing manuscript, follow those directions carefully and exactly. Otherwise, use the following suggestions as a guide.

Paper. Use prescribed paper or standard-sized stationery, 8½ by 11 inches, preferably a good grade of white bond that will take a clean impression. Write on only one side of the sheet.

Title. Center the title on the first line or about two inches from the top of the page. Capitalize the first word and all other important words (see Section 31d). Do not use a period after the title but do use a question mark or exclamation point, if appropriate.

Beginning. Start the theme with an indented paragraph about one inch below the title. In the first sentence, avoid vague reference to the title.

Margins. Leave a frame of white space *all around each page.* On the left, the margin should be one inch or that shown by the printed vertical line on standard theme paper. On the right and at the bottom of each page, the margins should be at least one-half inch. Keep the margins fairly uniform.

Indentation. Set in (indent) the first line of every paragraph a uniform distance; one inch is suggested. On the second and following pages, indent the first line only if it begins a paragraph.

Indicate a paragraph division not shown by placing the sign ¶ before the word beginning the paragraph. Cancel a paragraph division by placing "No ¶" in the left margin. Preferably, use neither mark; recopy the page, correcting the indentation.

Insertions. Use a caret (‸) when inserting something omitted. Preferably, recopy the page (see Section 34c).

Cancellation. Draw a neat line through material you wish to omit. Do not use brackets or parentheses to cancel words.

Order. Number pages with an Arabic numeral in the upper right-hand corner of each page. The first page is usually not numbered; if it is, place the number at the bottom center.

Legibility. If the paper is handwritten: (1) Use a good pen with black or blue-black ink. (2) Do not crowd your writing by running words together; do not write consecutive lines too closely together; leave ample margins. (3) The consecutive letters in a word should be joined. (4) Take your time. Most of us can form letters correctly and clearly if we take pains. Dot every lower-case *i* and *j* (with dots, not circles); cross every *t;* do not hurriedly write small letters for capitals, and vice versa.

All of us are likely to make errors even in the final draft of a page. If the errors are numerous, correct them, of course. Preferably, recopy an entire page if it contains numerous erasures, blurs, and canceled or inserted words.

Typescript is more legible than handwriting and, with rare exceptions, neater. In addition, you can detect mistakes in typescript more easily than in handwriting. If you do not know how to type, learning might be an excellent investment of time and money. If you do type, be certain to double-space all lines; quotations of more than four lines, however, should be single-spaced and set apart from the text by extra lines of space above and below.

After you have completed a paper—and preferably some time after—reread it carefully, word by word. The changes you make as a result of doing so may raise your grade several points (see Section 69).

Mechanics. The technical aspect of something as, in writing, the mechanical aspects of paragraphing, capitalization, use of italics, figures for numbers, and the like.

Metaphor. A figure of speech in which a term or phrase is applied to something to which it is not literally applicable. This is done in order to suggest a resemblance: *She is a perfect lamb. Metaphor* and *simile* are allied in meaning; a *simile* also expresses resemblance but does so by using *as, as if, like: She is like a delicate flower.*

Unfortunately, most metaphors are either strained or trite. Many figures of speech are often "mixed"; standard advice is to sustain one figure and not suddenly shift to another.

Metonymy. The use of the name of one thing for that of another to which it has some relationship: *The White House* for *office of the Presidency, bottle* for *milk* or *strong drink.*

Middle English. The English language spoken and written during the period from approximately A.D. 1100 to 1500. It differs markedly in pronunciation, spelling, and grammar from *Modern English* (our language since about 1500).

About the time that Anglo-Saxons were settling in England, similar Northmen were migrating to Normandy, on the northern coast of France (see *Old English*). In a century and a half, they succeeded not only in absorbing some elements of French civilization but also in adopting the French language. After their victory in the Battle of Hastings (1066), these Normans sought not to dispossess the English, as earlier Scandinavians had done, but rather to become their masters. Feudalism was imposed, a French aristocracy largely replaced the English nobility, and a new judicial system was established. Because it was the tongue of the ruling class, French was the only acceptable language for affairs of the church, government, society, and education. The common people continued to speak English, but their dialect underwent dramatic changes as it gradually dropped inflections and became more and more simplified. By about 1500, the end of the period known as Middle English, many thousands of French and French-modified Latin words had been assimilated into native speech. An educated guess is that half the vocabulary used by Geoffrey Chaucer (ca. 1340–1400) consisted of Old French and Anglo-French words.

Though more familiar to our eyes than the version quoted from King Alfred's time (see *Old English*), the Lord's Prayer as John Wycliffe (ca. 1320–1384) set it down in the first translation into English of the entire Bible is still difficult to read:

> Oure fadir that art in heuenes, halwid be thi name; thi kyngdom cumme to; be thi wille don as in heuen and in erthe; zif to vs this day ouer breed oure other substaunce; and forzeue to vs oure dettis as we forzeue to oure dettours; and leede vs nat in to temptacioun, but delyuere vs fro yuel. Amen.

By way of contrast, here is the Lord's Prayer as it appeared in Matthew VI:9–13 of the King James or Authorized Version of the Bible, published in 1611:

9. After this manner therefore pray ye: Our Father which art in heaven, Hallowed be thy name.
10. Thy kingdom come. Thy will be done on earth, as it *is* in heaven.
11. Give us this day our daily bread.
12. And forgive us our debts, as we forgive our debtors.
13. And lead us not into temptation, but deliver us from evil: For thine is the kingdom, and the power, and the glory, for ever. Amen.

Modern English. English evolved to its present state through processes of growth and decay, of expansion and simplification. As with human beings, the growth did not come smoothly but in spurts, sometimes dramatic, interspersed with calm periods in which changes were barely perceptible. Such a "spurt" in the development of English followed the innovation of printing from movable type, introduced into England in 1476 by William Caxton. So rapid was the effect of this method of producing books that in less than two centuries there were over 20,000 titles in English, and when Shakespeare wrote his plays, between a third and a half of the population could read. Cheaper books, more available education for the middle classes, and trade with new lands caused a deep change in linguistic development: the language became more uniform and was thus enabled to spread.

In the Middle English period, the most drastic changes in English had been grammatical: complex inflections and systems of conjugations and declensions had been pared away, and the language had moved toward clearer, more direct expression heavily based upon word order and intonation. True, remnants of the old structure can be found even today: the plural endings shown by *foot, feet; tooth, teeth; ox, oxen; mouse, mice;* and the tense formation shown by *shake, shook, shaken.* But if some examples like these may be cited, many thousands more attest to an evolved regularity, simplification, and standardization.

Unlike Middle English, however, which had survived a relatively massive injection of French import words, modern English drastically changed in vocabulary. Increased trade, popular education, and above all the effects of the Renaissance gave the language an enormous appetite.

Our modern English vocabulary is roughly half Germanic (English and Scandinavian) and half Romance (Latin and French). The Scandinavians gave us such common words as *awkward, egg, bread, kid, crook, scare, ugly, ill, call, scrub,* and *want.* Words from the French are so numerous as to be virtually uncountable, but include *city, charity, interior, action, grace, dinner, merge, price, spouse,* and *residence. Acrobat, catarrh,* and *magic* are Greek; so are *arithmetic, astronomy, rhetoric, music, theater, drama,* and *scene*—words that acknowledge ancient Greece as the cradle of liberal arts. Latin, the language of scholars and churchmen, supplied our earliest loan words, and today the language abounds with them as well as a Latin terminology for such sciences as biology, botany, chemistry, engineering, and medicine.

But English has ranged even wider for loans; we are sometimes surprised to find that the words *cruller, golf,* and *wagon* are Dutch; that *seersucker* and *shawl* are Persian; that *piano, balcony,* and *granite* come from Italy; and that *cork, mosquito,* and *vanilla* were imported from Spain. The Australians have given us *boomerang,* the Mexicans *chocolate,* the Malaysians *bamboo* and *gingham,* and our own American Indians *chipmunk, moccasin, hominy,* and *moose.* The list is virtually endless.

English-speaking peoples have never attempted to keep their language pure. Some critics attribute this tendency to linguistic laziness, to a preference for adopting scraps of other languages rather than for designing new words from native material. Others say that modern English simply grew too fast for the resources of the language. Because of this, our English possesses extraordinary richness, clarity, and flexibility. It lends itself to continuous simplification and at the same time welcomes terms from any language that will enhance the expression of an idea. It is a truly cosmopolitan tongue.

Monologue. Talk or discourse by a single speaker is called a *monologue.* For example, an entire poem may consist of the thoughts (speech) of one person; in a play an actor may speak alone for a protracted period (see *Dialogue*).

Monosyllable. A word of one syllable, such as *yes, no, through* (see *Polysyllable*).

Mood. The mood (or mode) of a verb indicates the manner in which a statement is made. Thus, if we wish merely to express a fact or ask a question of fact, we use the *indicative* mood: The building *is* tall. [Statement] *Is* the building tall? [Question] If we wish to express a desire or a condition contrary to fact, we use the *subjunctive* mood: Oh, how I wish I *were* in Austria! [Desire] If I *were* rich, I should give you your wish. [Contrary to fact] If we wish to give a command, we use the *imperative* mood: *Shut* the gate, please.

The indicative and imperative moods are not troublesome, and the use of the subjunctive has largely disappeared. However, careful speakers and writers employ the subjunctive to express the precise manner in which they make their statements. *Were* and *be* are the only distinct subjunctive forms now in general use, although our speech still retains numerous subjunctive forms in sayings handed down from times when this mood was more widely used: Heaven *forbid,* if need *be, suffice* it to say, *come* what may.

As indicated above, use the subjunctive mood, not the indicative, to express a condition contrary to fact. Also use the subjunctive in expressions of *supposition* and to indicate that a condition is *highly improbable* even though not completely contrary to fact: He worked as if he *were* never going to have another opportunity. Suppose he *were* to ask you to go with him!

Use the subjunctive in clauses introduced by *as though* or *as if* to express doubt and uncertainty: He talks as if he *were* the only clever person in the house.

Use the subjunctive in *that* clauses expressing necessity or a parliamentary motion: It is essential that he *appear* at the meeting of the group. I move that the contractors *be authorized* to proceed with the work.

As indicated above, use the subjunctive mood to express a desire (wish, volition). In parallel constructions, do not shift the mood of verbs: If I *were* in your position and *was* not prevented, I should certainly speak up. [Change *was* to *were*.]

Differences between the indicative and subjunctive may be illustrated thus:

Indicative	*Subjunctive*
I take (am taken)	(if) I take (be taken)
you take (are taken)	(if) you take (be taken)
he, she, it takes (is taken)	(if) he, she, it take (be taken)
we take (are taken)	(if) we take (be taken)
I took (was taken)	(if) I took (were taken)
I am, we are	(if) I be, we be
you are, you are	(if) you be, you be
he is, they are	(if) he be, they be
I was, we were	(if) I were, we were

Narration. One of the forms of discourse (which see) that relates or recounts events: novels, short stories, plays.

Novel. A lengthy fictitious prose narrative portraying characters and presenting an organized series of events and settings. A work of fiction less than 30,000 to 40,000 words is usually considered a short story, novelette, or tale, but the *novel* has no real maximum length. Every *novel* is an account of life; every novel involves conflict, characters, action, settings, plot, and theme.

Old English. The English language of the period before A.D. 1100. Often called *Anglo-Saxon,* it is as foreign to the native speaker and writer of Modern English as German or Latin.

The Angles, Saxons, and Jutes who began their invasion of the lowlands of Britain in the fifth century were Germanic tribes from northwest Germany and Denmark: the Saxons came from the Holstein district of Germany, the Jutes from Jutland (a part of Denmark), and the Angles from Schleswig, also a German state at the base of the Danish peninsula. The Angles, called *Angli* in Latin and Germanic, gave the name *Engla-land* to the new country; by A.D. 1000 the name was acknowledged by all the Germanic peoples who had settled there. It was from the mixing and mingling of Germanic dialects, after the occupation was complete and intercourse with the continent was largely discontinued, that English sprang. After the year 600, when St. Augustine introduced Christianity and the islands now known as Great Britain had undergone at least partial Christian conversion, a superstructure of adopted Latin words began to give the language a new dimension.

Contrary to what one might expect from relatively primitive and nomadic tribes, Old English comprised a remarkably large vocabulary, estimated by scholars to have amounted to almost 50,000 words. This "word hoard," as some Anglo-Saxons picturesquely called it, was partly attributable to a talent for modifying and joining two base words to form a new one; thus, Anglo-Saxons were able to express new, occasionally even sophisticated, concepts through the use of familiar material. For example, a native word, *God*, was combined with *spell*, meaning "message," to make *Godspell*, "message of God," or, in modern English, *Gospel*. Other related words were *godcund*, "divine"; *godferht*, "pious"; *godspellian*, "preach the gospel"; *godsunu*, "godson." The words *gospel* and *godson* are found in modern English, whereas other secondary words have been supplanted.

If an Anglo-Saxon were heard speaking his native tongue today, he might be dimly understood; however, because of different spellings, heavy inflections, and the use of symbols no longer in existence, written Old English appears at least as foreign as do French and Latin. Even so, many words are recognizable: *hete* (hate), *weorc* (work), *sāwol* (soul), *fȳr* (fire), *heofan* (heaven). A noun, *gelīca*, whose modern counterpart is *like*, was inflected, that is, given numerous changes to denote its use as an adjective, a verb, an adverb, or a preposition. Today's English depends more heavily upon word order than inflection to convey meaning, but our word *like* nevertheless has the same functional versatility: I won't deal with his *like* (noun); as *like* as two peas (adjective); we *like* her (verb); more *like* forty than thirty (adverb); cry *like* a baby (preposition).

The Lord's Prayer, here given in the dialect spoken about the time of King Alfred (ninth century), is largely foreign-appearing:

Fæder ūre þū þe eart on heofonum, sī þin nama gehalgod.
Father our thou that art on heavens, be thy name hallowed.

Tobecume þīn rīce. Gewurþe þīn willa on eorþan swā swā on
Come thy kingdom. Be done thy will on earth just as on

heofonum. Urne gedæghwāmlīcan hlāf syle ūs tō dæg. And forgyf heavens. Our daily bread give us to-day. And forgive

ūs ūre gyltas, swā swā wē forgyfaþ ūram gyltendum. And ne
us our guilts, just as we forgive those guilty to us. And do not

gelæd þū ūs on costnunge, ac ālȳs ūs of yfele. Sōþlīce.
lead thou us into temptation, but unloose us from evil. Verily.

1. The character þ, called a "thorn," has the sound of modern *th.*
2. Despite differences in spelling (and thus in pronunciation) several of the words are easily recognizable: *Faeder, forgyf,* and so on.
3. Inflectional endings are frequent. *Heofonum,* for example, is a plural dative.
4. Old English contains few words borrowed from Latin or any other source. For example, *costnunge* was a native word which, of course, has been replaced by a later borrowing from Latin, *temptation.*

Old English survived an invasion of Scandinavians in the ninth century, but it was very nearly swallowed up by the great Norman Conquest in 1066. This was an onslaught by people militarily and politically superior to the defenders. The eventual result was a vast change in the character of English, a change so profound that the language of the Old English period, which may be said to have ended about 1100, resembled the language at the end of the Middle English period (about 1475) far less than Middle English resembles our own. (See *Middle English, Modern English, Origins of English*).

Onomatopoeia. The formation of a word by imitating sound associated with the object or action named: *tinkle, buzz, whir, chickadee.*

Open punctuation. See *Close and open punctuation.*

Origins of English. Because the English language is our rightful heritage we often take it for granted. And yet the origins and development of our language comprise an interesting story with which everyone who uses English should become at least slightly acquainted. Our language is a priceless legacy that, in a continuous process of growth and change, has come down to us from beyond antiquity.

Although our interest in the language we have inherited may be slight, and our concern about the origins of language itself even less than that, thousands of scholars have debated for centuries about the beginnings of speech. As of now, no one yet knows who "invented" language or when and how it came into existence. Arguments about the birth of speech have been so varied, so vigorous, and so fruitless that scholars today hold that language was never *invented* at all; they contend that it is apparently so native to man that it began to spring up in many ways and many forms when vertebrates attempted to become human and that, indeed, man has had language of one sort or another ever since he could really be called human. Humanity and language may be only two aspects of the same thing. If so, language may be considered one way of defining man.

Ancient Greeks studied their own language and wrote useful and sound grammars of it during the five centuries immediately preceding the Christian era. (These Greek grammarians gave us the eight parts of speech we still study.) But they had no better idea than we do today where language actually originated and, furthermore, knew little about languages other than their own.

The Old Testament indicates that God and Adam began talking as soon as Adam was created, but the Bible does not suggest what language they used. Later in the Bible, we are informed that the Lord "confounded" the languages of certain people so as to prevent their erecting a building into the sky (the Tower of Babel), but most linguists feel that this account has more theological than philological meaning.

And yet a few actual facts about language were positively known for many years before the Christian era. It was clear to students that Latin was a different language from Greek. It was later recognized that Latin had changed from Classical times to such an extent that the tongue had become Italian in its native peninsula, French as it was spoken in what was then known as Gaul, and Spanish and Portuguese as it was used on the Iberian peninsula. Learned scholars argued that if these languages shared Latin as a father, it was reasonable to assume that Latin, too, must have had a father at some time and in some place.

In fact, reasoned some scholars, might not all languages have descended from a single parent language as all men are said to descend from Adam and Eve? Precisely this assumption by philologists has led to the conviction that indeed there was at one time a vast system of tongues known as Indo-European, a complex language family in which grammatical structures and vocabularies of the various branches basically corresponded.

This Indo-European family of languages flourished on the plains of eastern Europe north of the Black Sea several thousand years before the Christian era. The group includes many culturally and politically important tongues, especially those of the Italic, Hellenic, Slavic, Indo-Iranian, and Germanic branches. (It is from the last-named that English has directly descended.) Scholars can only guess at the exact makeup of this ancient progenitor language, but when some of the cuneiform writings of Sanskrit, a member tongue, were uncovered, diligent students found valuable leads to the nature of Indo-European which point to the fact that English, if not a direct lineal descendant, is undeniably related to it through its connection with Germanic dialects.

It should be remembered that "Indo-European" probably never existed as a specific spoken and written language and that it is a fabrication of linguistic scholars. Furthermore, scholars are uncertain about the peoples who have been labeled "Indo-Europeans"; even their name has been coined for them. Apparently, these were a seminomadic people who lived in what we would call an almost barbaric state. And yet the highly inflected tongue they are reputed to have used has accounted for most of the languages of Europe and many of the most important languages in North and South America, Asia, and Australia.

It should also be remembered that the figure of speech "language family" is an approximate description of linguistic relationships and not an exact reference. A parent language, such as Indo-European, does not produce an offspring at a specific time and place in the manner that a mother bears a child.

When history dawned over western and northwestern Europe, the territory we now know as England, Scotland, and Ireland was inhabited by tribes of fishermen and hunters known as Celts. Invading Romans succeeded in conquering most of these tribes, but the Roman Empire began to decline after several centuries. When the last of the Romans left the islands during the fifth century, Germanic peoples began to move west to take over the forsaken areas.

Before they invaded Britain, these Germanic tribes, from one of whose dialects our English language was derived, had lived mainly along the shores of the Baltic Sea in northern Germany. They were a fierce and nomadic people, savage in their ways, who at least ten centuries before the birth of Christ had been roaming the fields and forests of northern Europe. Three of these tribes—the Angles, Saxons, and Jutes—spoke dialects that differed from each other but were related. Furthermore, in the course of their later wanderings over the European continent, the Germani, as they were called, encountered traders and soldiers from then-dominant Rome, from whom they borrowed and incorporated into their own speech such practical words as *wine, cheap, cook,* and *anchor*. These early Latin borrowings began a process of continuous word adoption that is still a characteristic of English today. See *Old English, Middle English, Modern English*.

Parallelism. Parallelism means "like construction for like ideas." You will convey your precise meaning to your readers, surely and effectively, if you construct your sentences so that the reader can immediately see what ideas are of equal importance. Parallel construction for like ideas is indispensable to clear, grammatically correct, effective sentences. Parallel movement, correctly handled, is one means of attaining an emphatic, vigorous style.

The simplest form of parallelism involves two or more words in a series. Using more complex forms, the writer can make two or more phrases parallel, or two or more dependent clauses, or two or more independent clauses, or two or more sentences.

Words: Henry is *slow* but *thorough*. The American colors are *red, white,* and *blue*.
Phrases: Every afternoon my grandfather is at the barbershop *telling yarns about his youth* or *hearing the yarns that his cronies tell*.
Dependent clauses: I was desperate *when I arrived late in town* and *when I found there were no desirable rooms available*.
Independent clauses: Julius Caesar's most famous statement was this: *"I came, I saw, I conquered."*
Sentences: Alfred, Lord Tennyson was the British poet who wrote lyrics in his early life and dramas in his closing years. Robert Browning was the British poet who wrote dramas in his early career and other forms of poetry in his later life.

As an effective test for true parallelism, draw lines under parallel elements. Then draw a corresponding number of lines in parallel form and write the underlined words on these parallel lines. Examples from the illustrations above:

Every afternoon my grandfather is at the barbershop
telling yarns about his youth
or
hearing the yarns that his cronies tell.
Julius Caesar's most famous statement was this:
I came,
I saw,
I conquered.

Parenthetical statement. A word, phrase, clause, or sentence that is inserted in or added to a statement grammatically complete without it. Such a statement is usually enclosed by parentheses, commas, or dashes.

Patterns. In the sense of style, model, or form, patterns appear in every example of speech and writing that anyone is capable of producing. In grammar, *sentence patterns* indicate the basic kinds of words appearing in sentences and their structural relationship (see Section 9d and *Linguistics*).

Periodic sentence. A sentence with its parts arranged so that its meaning is not clear or complete until the end or nearly the end.

Personification. A figure of speech in which abstractions, animals, ideas, and inanimate objects are endowed with human form, character traits, or sensibilities. In personification, an entirely imaginary creature or person may also be conceived of as representing an idea or object. A kind of metaphor, personification is a frequent resource in poetry and occasionally appears in other types of writing as well.

Persuasion. A form of argumentation that is designed to convince, to arouse, to attain a specific goal. Persuasion attempts to prevail on listeners or readers to do something, to react positively, and to bring such conviction that the recipient will think, believe, and be moved to respond actively. Persuasion usually combines an appeal to emotions with an appeal to the intellect.

Plagiarism. The act of taking and passing off as one's own the thoughts and writings of someone else. It may be interesting to note that the word comes from a Latin term meaning "kidnaper." It might also be well to remember that "copying from one source is plagiarism; copying from two or more is research" is an inaccurate and dishonest observation.

Plurals. You may find it fairly easy to spell the singular of a word but have trouble forming and correctly spelling its plural. This is quite understandable, since many English words form plurals in unusual ways. You can "look it up" in a dictionary when you are puzzled, but a few principles of plural-forming can be easily mastered (see also *Irregular plurals*).

1. The plural of most nouns is formed by adding *s* to the singular: *bed, beds; cracker, crackers; hat, hats.*
2. Nouns ending with a sibilant or *s* sound (*ch, sh, s, x, z*) form their plurals by adding *es: box, boxes; bush, bushes; church, churches; loss, losses; tax, taxes.*
3. Nouns ending in *y* preceded by a consonant usually change *y* to *i* before adding *es: activity, activities; fly, flies; library, libraries.*
4. Nouns ending in *y* preceded by a vowel usually add *s* without changing the final *y: alley, alleys; key, keys; toy, toys.*
5. Nouns ending in *o* preceded by a vowel add *s* to form their plurals: *cameo, cameos; radio, radios.*
6. Nouns ending in *o* preceded by a consonant often add *es* to form their plurals: *cargo, cargoes; echo, echoes; hero, heroes; mosquito, mosquitoes; potato, potatoes; tornado, tornadoes.*
7. Some nouns ending in *o* preceded by a consonant, including most musical terms, add *s* to form their plurals: *alto, altos; banjo, banjos; concerto, concertos; dynamo, dynamos; piano, pianos; silo, silos; soprano, sopranos; zero, zeros.*
8. Nouns ending in *f* form their plurals in such variable ways that you should always consult your dictionary when in doubt. Nouns ending in *ff* usually add *s*. Most nouns ending in *fe* change *fe* to *ve* and add *s*. For example: *belief, beliefs; half, halves* (*halfs*); *leaf, leaves; life, lives; loaf, loaves; roof, roofs; self, selves; tariff, tariffs.*

P.M. See *A.M.*

Point of view. (1) A specified position or method of consideration and appraisal; (2) an attitude, judgment, or opinion.

In literature, *point of view* has several special meanings: (1) *physical* point of view has to do with the position in time and space from which a writer approaches, views, and describes his material; (2) *mental* point of view involves an author's feeling and attitude toward his subject; (3) *personal* point of view concerns the relationship through which a writer narrates or discusses a subject, whether first, second, or third person.

In personal point of view, several arrangements are possible. If a writer assumes the point of view of a character, he becomes an "author participant" and usually writes in the first person. This is the point of view of Defoe's *Robinson Crusoe*, in which the author relates what happened to him and reveals his own feelings in his own words. If the writer adopts the point of view of a minor character, he becomes an "author observant" who sits on the sidelines and reports the story. In several of Conrad's stories, the narrator observes more than he participates. When an author selects an impersonal point of view and detaches himself completely, he becomes Godlike, an "author omniscient"; he sees all, hears all, knows all.

Polysyllable. A word having more than three *syllables*. A monosyllable is a word of only one syllable. Good writing requires words of varying length, but polysyllabic words should never be used merely to make an impression.

Portmanteau word. A word made by telescoping or blending two or more words: *dandle* from *dance* and *handle, aristobrat* from *aristocrat* and *brat* (see *Blend*).

Progressive verb form. A statement of continuing action or state of being within a tense, formed by the proper forms of the auxiliary *to be* followed by the present participle: We *are preparing* our reports today. Tommy *was playing* chess when I arrived.

Prolixity. The state or quality of being tedious, long, or wordy; speaking or writing at great length (see *Circumlocution, Conciseness, Deadwood,* and *Tautology*).

Proportion. The comparative relationship between things or magnitudes as to size, quantity, number, emphasis, and the like. In writing, proportion usually refers to the relationship between length and emphasis of paragraphs or to the amounts of space given development of different ideas in a letter or report.

Protagonist. The leading character of a drama, novel, or other literary work. *Protagonist* in Greek meant "first combatant"; such a person is not always the hero of a work, but he (or she) is always the principal and central character. The rival of a protagonist is an *antagonist.*

Redundancy. An excess; too many words to express an idea; superabundance; superfluity (see *Prolixity* and the entries listed there).

Rhyme. Words or verses that agree in their terminal (end) sounds. Rhyme occurs when the accented vowels of two words and all succeeding sounds in the words are identical: *rain, strain; pill, still.*

Rhythm. Uniform recurrence of a beat or accent. Good writers of prose occasionally create rhythmic patterns by the use of devices such as balanced sentences, euphony, variety in sentence length and structure, and transitional aids.

Roman numerals. Our numbers (1, 2, 3, 4) came to us from the Arabs and are called Arabic numerals. Roman numerals are used occasionally for numbering the preliminary pages of a book, marking year dates, and indicating acts of plays, volume numbers of books, and so on.

> George I, George II, and George III reigned in the eighteenth century; George V and George VI, in the twentieth.
>
> Prince Hal and Falstaff first appear in Act I, Scene 2, of Shakespeare's *Henry IV, Part I.*
>
> This imposing building bears the date when it was constructed—MDCCCLXXIV.

Notice how Roman numerals are formed: a repeated letter repeats its value; a letter placed after one of greater value adds to it; a letter placed before one of greater value subtracts from it; a dashline over a letter denotes "multiplied by 1,000."

ROMAN NUMERALS

I	1	XCV	95
II	2	XCIX	99
III	3	C	100
IV	4	CL	150
V	5	CC	200
VI	6	CCC	300
VII	7	CD	400
VIII	8	D	500
IX	9	DC	600
X	10	DCC	700
XV	15	DCCC	800
XIX	19	CM	900
XX	20	M	1,000
XXV	25	MD	1,500
XXX	30	MM	2,000
XL	40	MMM	3,000
L	50	MMMM	4,000
LXXXV	85	$\overline{V}$	5,000
LXXXIX	89	$\overline{M}$	1,000,000
XC	90		

Sagging sentence. A sagging sentence loses force as it proceeds and tapers off at the end. This flaw results primarily from improper word order (see *Climactic order*).

Sarcasm. A form of irony; bitter and often harsh derision. *Sarcasm* consists of sneering or cutting remarks; it is always personal, always jeering, and always intended to hurt.

Satire. The ridiculing of folly, stupidity, or vice; the use of irony, sarcasm, or ridicule for exposing or denouncing the frailties and faults of mankind. *Satire* is a literary manner, or technique, that blends humor and wit with a critical attitude toward human activities and institutions. It is a general term, one usually considered to involve both moral judgment and a desire for improvement.

Schoolgirl style. An unkind term for a manner of writing characterized by gushiness, exaggeration, and overuse of intensifiers. Counter words, triple underlinings, exclamation points, and dashes are used freely.

Schwa. See *Unstressed vowels*.

-sede. See *-cede*.

Semantics. Semantics is the study of word meanings and changes of meaning. Specifically, semantics (1) refers to that branch of linguistics (which see) that deals with word meanings and historical changes in meaning and (2) involves a study of the relations among signs (words, symbols), their meanings, and the mental or physical actions called forth by them. As the science of meanings, semantics is contrasted with *phonetics,* the science of speech sounds and their production.

Man, so far as we now know, is the only creature capable of inventing symbol systems—such as mathematics and the English language—with which to record and evaluate his past and present and to plan his future.

The conscious and systematic study of the role of human symbols in the lives of individuals and groups is known as general semantics. The word *semantics* comes from the Greek *semainein,* "to mean," "to signify." But general semantics is concerned with meanings more than merely in their dictionary sense. It involves several kinds of meaning, both verbal and nonverbal, and their importance in our private lives and our public affairs.

Like words, sentences too have meanings, and so do paragraphs, chapters, essays, songs, plays, poems, and books. But you cannot find the meaning of a paragraph or a poem by looking up in a dictionary the meaning of each of its words. Nor will you, as the late Wendell Johnson remarked, find the meaning of a particular sunset in the dictionary: you will find it only in yourself—in your own feelings and thoughts, in what you say and do. The meanings of words are no more in the words than is the meaning of a willow tree in a willow; the meanings of words are in the person who responds to them, or writes them, just as the meanings of "a green meadow are the children who chase butterflies across it, the artist who paints it, the cows who graze upon it, or the old soldier who remembers the battle that once was fought across its green slope" (Johnson).

To the general semanticist, the study of words is not simply the study of words, or paintings, or musical scores. Rather, the study of words includes a study of human beings and what words and paintings and musical scores mean to them. To discover what such things mean to people is to observe what people do to, with, and about them. Therefore, general semantics deals with *symbolic behavior,* its patterns, its principles, its effects on man and his world, and with the conditions of its changes from time to time in the lives of men and their societies.

Sentence patterns. See *Patterns, Linguistics.*

Shifts. This is a term applied to *shifted constructions* and refers to elements that have the same relationship to the statement being made but not the same grammatical structure. Adjectives should be paralleled by adjectives, nouns by nouns, and so on; shifting from one form to another may confuse a reader (see Section 51).

Shoptalk. The specialized or technical vocabulary and idioms of those in the same way of life (see Section 37c).

Silent letters. Some spelling authorities believe that the single greatest cause of misspelling connected with pronunciation is the silent letter. Sounds have been dropping out of our language for many centuries, but their disappearance has affected pronunciation much more than spelling. Actually, many letters no longer pronounced in certain words persist in our spelling. For example, the *l* in words such as *could, would,* and *should* has been silent for hundreds of years.

The problem is compounded when we realize that the majority of the letters of our alphabet appear as silent letters in one word or another.

a is silent in *dead*	*l* is silent in *salmon*
b is silent in *doubt*	*m* is silent in *mnemonics*
c is silent in *scene*	*n* is silent in *column*
d is silent in *handsome*	*o* is silent in *too*
e is silent in *come*	*p* is silent in *raspberry*
f is silent in *off*	*t* is silent in *often*
g is silent in *sign*	*u* is silent in *guess*
h is silent in *honest*	*w* is silent in *answer*
i is silent in *weird*	*ch* is silent in *yacht*
k is silent in *knife*	*gh* is silent in *bough*

Most silent letters should cause little difficulty in spelling. If you are visual-minded, you will automatically put a *k* in *knee* or a g in *gnat*. But some letters that are silent, or are so lightly sounded as to be almost unheard, do cause trouble. Here is a list of some common words that, in the pronunciation of most educated people, contain silent letters:

benign	ghastly	knit	psychology
bomb	gnat	knob	through
condemn	gnaw	knock	thumb
daughter	hymn	know	wrap
dough	indebted	knuckle	wreck
dumb	knack	plumber	wrench
eight	knee	pneumonia	wring
fourth	kneel	psalm	write

Sketch. The *sketch* is a study of character, setting, or mood. It contains little action or plot and places emphasis on descriptive details. Unlike the anecdote, it is not concerned with making a point or illustrating a thesis; unlike the incident, it puts emphasis upon characterization to the virtual exclusion of action.

Speech sounds. Scholars are agreed that the total number of speech sounds used by those who speak English is about fifty. To express these sounds we have only twenty-six letters in our alphabet, but they appear in about 250 spelling combinations. For example, there are eleven ways of spelling the sound of long *e*, the initial sound in *equal: eve, seed, read, receive, people, key, quay, police, piece, amoeba, Caesar.*

Actually, some relationship often exists between sound and spelling; a large number of words are spelled exactly as they sound, and many others have sounds and spellings almost alike. The words *bat, red,* and *top* are spelled as they sound to most people. Many longer words are also spelled as they sound, especially if you break them into syllables: *lone-li-ness, mem-o-ry, part-ner.*

Moreover, many words that differ most in sound and spelling are those you rarely use. Like almost everyone else, including good spellers, you look up such words in a dictionary before attempting to write them; they do not have to be learned. Few people can spell, on demand, such words as *flocculent* and *phthisic.* They consult a dictionary. So should you.

Stream of consciousness. A manner of writing in which a character's perceptions and thoughts are presented as occurring in random form. In this technique, ideas and sensations are revealed without regard for logical sequences, distinctions between various levels of reality (sleep, waking), or syntax. *Stream of consciousness,* a phrase coined by William James in his *Principles of Psychology* (1890), attempts to set forth the inner thoughts of a character in the seemingly haphazard fashion of everyday thinking.

Structural linguistics. See *Linguistics.*

Style. This term has been defined in many ways but never satisfactorily, since every writer and speaker has his own notion of its meaning. In general, *style* is a "manner or mode of expression in language, a way of putting thoughts into words." It also refers to a specific or characteristic manner of expression or construction. An author's or speaker's style is the impress (influence) of his personality upon his subject matter.

Think of *mood* and *impression* as the mental or physical atmosphere that a writer creates to surround his reader and wants the reader to receive. Think of *style,* which occasionally may include mood and impression, as mainly the manner in which a writer expresses himself. In that expression, variety of phrase, clause, and sentence pattern is not only consistent but desirable. Consistency in style is also a matter of word choice. What kind of style are you aiming at? Formal? Conversational? Simple? Archaic? Quaint? Whimsical? Flippant? Humorous? Breezy? Breathless? Concise? Whatever it is, be consistent in choosing and arranging words.

Subject. The person or thing (noun, pronoun, noun phrase, noun clause) about which a statement or assertion is made in a sentence or clause. A *simple* subject is the noun or pronoun alone. A *complete* subject is a simple subject together with its modifiers. A *compound* subject consists of two or more nouns, pronouns, noun phrases, noun clauses.

> The *ranch house* is for sale. [Simple subject]
> The *yellow ranch house on the hill* is for sale. [Complete subject]
> The *yellow ranch house and two acres of land* are for sale. [Compound subject]
> *What you think and what you want* are no concern of mine. [Compound subject]

Subordination. Like appropriate coordination, appropriate subordination contributes to clear and effective writing by showing the relationship of less important to more important ideas.

Careful, thoughtful writing contains much subordination. Actually, the work of nearly all skilled writers abounds in subordination. Such work clearly communicates to readers because they can see what the relationships involved really are. Two important steps: (1) Avoid faulty subordination (see Section 49); (2) reduce predication (see Section 55a).

Summary. "You went to the movies last night, didn't you? What was the picture about?" "What did you do in the city this afternoon?" "Write a brief statement concerning the essential ideas in Thackeray's essay on Addison." All such questions, asked in conversation and on examinations, require summarizing answers —an indispensable form of communication.

Brief, comprehensive presentations of facts may be called summaries. A summary is a terse restatement of main points, as, for example, a summary of a chapter. It is related in meaning to *digest, résumé,* and *synopsis,* although the last-named is usually applied to a compressed statement of the plot of a play, story, or novel, rather than to expository prose.

Symbolism. The practice of representing objects or ideas by symbols or of giving things a symbolic (associated) character and meaning. John Bunyan built all of his *The Pilgrim's Progress* on symbolism: it is the story of man's progress through life to heaven or hell as told through the adventures of Christian Faithful, Mr. Worldly Wiseman, and others who symbolize man in his various guises.

Tautology. Needless repetition of an idea in a different word, phrase, clause, or sentence (see *Deadwood*).

Technical terms. Terms that have special meanings for people in particular fields, occupations, or professions. Special subject labels are attached by dictionaries to such words in the fields of astronomy, engineering, psychology, and the like. Technical terms should be used sparingly in writing for the general public and, when so employed, may be underlined or enclosed in quotation marks—at least the first time they are used—and usually should be defined (see Section 37c).

Telegraphic style. The clipped, abbreviated style employed in telegrams to save on words: [Your] letter [has been] received. [I am] answering immediately. [Please accept my warm] regards.

Theme. This word means "topic," "subject." When, for example, we speak of the *theme* of a play or a musical composition, we mean its controlling idea, its central subject matter and content. Also, a short essay, such as a school composition, is known as a *theme.*

Thesis. A proposition stated or laid down and intended to be discussed, defended, and proved. *Thesis* is also a somewhat loose synonym for *theme* in the sense of "subject" or "content."

Titles. Just as a topic sentence is frequently helpful in keeping on the track within the paragraph, a well-chosen title may help one stick to his subject throughout a composition. But the title has another important function. A well-chosen title is an effective means of gaining the attention of the reader. Give your theme a good title, not a mere tag, and you have already taken an important step in making the whole composition more effective.

The term *subject* is broader and more inclusive than the word *title.* If the instructor asks for a composition on "My Reading Habits," he has assigned a *subject,* not a *title,* and you should sharpen this subject to a more specific and more interesting title. Conversely, if the actual title of a theme is assigned, you must discover precisely what subject it covers. Do not assume that the title of a specific composition should be the same as the assigned general subject.

A title should not be misleading; it should give at least a hint of the contents of the theme. Do not announce a title and then develop ideas that bear no relation whatever to it. As has been pointed out, a good title is an effective aid in interesting the reader. Some writers miss this opportunity by using titles that are too *long:* "How to While Away an Afternoon Among the Stacks of the Belton Library" is certainly less effective than "Browsing in the Belton Library." Other writers use titles that are too *vague* and *commonplace:* "Political Activity on College Campuses," "A Camping Trip," "The Federal Constitution," "Contemporary Values." To be effective, a title must usually be short and fresh and definite.

Tone. The word *tone* has many different meanings, one of which refers to the general or prevailing character, trend, or quality of social or moral behavior: the academic tone of this college. In writing, *tone* is used to refer to the character or appeal or point of view of a given selection and of its author. Specifically, tone in this sense has approximately the meaning of "attitude" and refers to the approach of the writer to his material and to the effect he intends his work to have on his audience.

When the tone of a piece of writing is serious, ironic, solemn, playful, formal, intimate, or informal, obviously the selection and its effect on readers are strongly influenced. The word is applied not only to an author but to the work itself and to the various stylistic elements and devices (such as sentence structure, diction, imagery, and the like) that in combination contribute to character and appeal.

In a different sense, the word *tone* distinguishes a characteristic of tenses of verbs, indicating within any one tense emphasis or progress or simple time: I still *do* work. I *was leaving* when you called. I *mailed* the package (see Section 17b).

Topic sentence. A *topic sentence,* or statement, gives the subject of a paragraph. It states, suggests, or in some other way indicates the heart, the core, of the idea to be developed.

Usually, the first sentence of a paragraph is the topic sentence. However, a topic sentence need not be a *sentence* at all: the subject of a paragraph may be suggested in a dependent clause, in a phrase, even in a single word. Also, a topic sentence need not be actually expressed; even so, every good, unified paragraph is so well knit that a reader, reflecting, can sum up the central thought of the paragraph in his own words.

Transformational grammar. See *Linguistics.*

Transition. Passage from one area, position, state, or stage to another. In writing and speaking, *transition* refers to methods by which writer and speaker bridge gaps between what has been covered and what is to come.

Unity. A term meaning "oneness." In writing and speaking, *unity* refers to sentences, paragraphs, reports, and the like that stick to their subjects (see Section 54).

Unnecessary capitals. Capitals are often overused or wrongly used (see Section 31).

If the reference is to any one of a class of persons or things rather than to a specific person or thing, do not capitalize the noun or the adjective: He is a general. He is General John Jones. I am going to a theater. I am going to the Bijou Theater.

Do not capitalize names of points of the compass unless they refer to a specific geographical section: He lives in the West. He walked south along the avenue.

Do not capitalize nouns such as *father* and *mother* if they are preceded by a possessive: My father is a tall man. Your sister thinks I am quiet, but Grandma says I talk entirely too much.

Unnecessary commas. Comma usage varies with different writers, but every comma used must be needed for sense construction. Modern punctuation usage omits more commas than formerly; therefore, be able to account for each comma you use (see *Close and open punctuation* and Section 25t).

Unstressed vowels. No words in English are more often misspelled than those that contain unstressed (or lightly stressed) vowels. An unstressed vowel, like the *a* in *dollar,* is uttered with little force; its sound is faint, indistinct, blurred.

A technical name and symbol, *schwa* (ə), are used to indicate this sound of unstressed vowels. It resembles a kind of "uh," a quiet sound much less vigorous than the stronger "uh" sound found in such words as *flood* and *rush.* This unstressed vowel sound may be represented in spelling by any one of the vowels.

a: gramm*a*r, sof*a*, *a*bove, *a*go, *a*long
e: corn*e*r, mod*e*l, *e*stablish, syst*e*m
i: nad*i*r, per*i*l, or*i*gin, san*i*ty
o: profess*o*r, spons*o*r, *o*ccur, gall*o*n
u: murm*u*r, sulf*u*r, lux*u*ry, foc*u*s, circ*u*s

The letter *y* is sometimes a vowel also. Its unstressed sound is illustrated in the word *martyr.*

Although the schwa sound "uh" is the most frequent unstressed vowel sound, it is not the only one. An unstressed *i* sound appears in such words as *solid* but is not always spelled as *i;* note, for example, such words as *private, women,* and *busy.* Here is a representative list of everyday words often misspelled because of the unstressed vowels they contain:

accident	humorous
actor	hunger
applicant	hypocrisy
arithmetic	loafer
benefit	maintenance
busy	martyr
calendar	mathematics
category	medicine
clamor	monastery
comparative	optimism
describe	private
despair	privilege
develop	propaganda
dilute	repetition
discipline	respectable
distress	ridiculous
dollar	separate
ecstasy	solid
excellent	swindler
existence	terror

Vowel. In phonetics, a speech sound articulated so that there is a clear channel for the voice through the middle of the mouth. In spelling and grammar, a letter representing such a sound: *a, e, i, o, u,* and sometimes *y* (see *Consonant*).

Vowels added. See *Added vowels.*

Vowels dropped. See *Dropped vowels.*

Vowels unstressed. See *Unstressed vowels.*

Vulgarism. A term derived from the Latin *vulgus,* meaning "the common people." A *vulgarism* is a word or expression occurring only in common colloquial usage or in coarse speech (see Section 38a).

Wordiness. A sentence may be complete and unified and still be ineffective because it is wordy. Clear, effective sentences demand accuracy of thought and conciseness of expression. This does not mean that you should use a *telegraphic style* (which see). Nor does it mean that all sentences must be brief; a sentence of 100 words may be concise and one of 10 may be wordy. But sentences are rarely effective when they contain superfluous words or ideas.

Eliminate unnecessary words, turn clauses into phrases, and use word-saving suffixes. For example, you would not refer to "a great, big, enormous man." Probably the last adjective alone would suffice. "Any typist who is qualified can become a member of the secretarial staff" may be shortened to "Any qualified typist can become a secretary." And a sentence such as "I was waiting for his telephone call until I became frantic" can be written "I was waiting frantically for his telephone call." If such condensation violates meaning, it should not be employed. But you hold readers only when your sentences are lean and vigorous (see Section 55).

Words, origins of. An account of the history of a word, its origin and derivation, is known as its *etymology* (which see). Knowing what a word "comes from" is an aid in building vocabulary and in spelling. For example, the word *preparation* is derived from the Latin prefix *prae-* ("before hand") plus *parare* ("to make ready"). Knowing this fact and accenting the first *a* in *parare* may help you to spell the word correctly: *preparation*, not "preperation."

Similarly, our word *dormitory* (a building containing sleeping rooms) is derived from the Latin word *dormitorium.* Noting the first *i* in this Latin word, and perhaps also knowing that the French word for sleep is *dormir,* may help you to spell *dormitory* with an *i* and not an *a.*

Here are simplified comments on the origins of five words to illustrate vocabulary building and spelling aids:

Calendar. This word is descended from the Latin word *calendarium,* meaning "account book." Note the second *a;* we frequently misspell the word as *calender* (a perfectly good word with an entirely different meaning).

Consensus. This word comes from the same Latin root as *consent* (*con* + *sentire,* "to feel"). Note the *s* in *sentire* and you will not spell the word "concensus," as is frequently done.

Equivalent. This word may be easier for you to spell if you remember that it means "equal in value" and is derived from the prefix *equi-* and the Latin verb *valere.* Accent the *val* sound in *valere* and connect it with *value.*

Extravagance. This word is composed of *extra-* ("beyond") and the Latin participle *vagans* (*vagari,* "to wander"). *Extravagance* means "wandering beyond limits." Accent the letters *v-a-g* in the root word to ensure correct spelling.

Finis. This synonym for "end" has the same origin as the words *definite* and *finite.* Accent the *i* sound and remember the two *i*'s in this word.

Zeal. A word meaning "interest," "devotion," and "enthusiasm," *zeal* is what you need in learning to write correctly, clearly, effectively, and appropriately. You can learn if you will really try. Freshman English makes no demands beyond the ability of the average student. Hundreds of thousands of students before you have benefited from the course. With *zeal,* why not you?

PART FOUR

A COLLECTION OF READINGS FOR WRITERS

THE ESSAY

NOTES ON READING

The essay may be called a brief, expository prose composition, usually devoted to reflection on life and man's ideas about human existence.

Referring to the essay as a "prose composition" may give the impression that it is dull and even academic. The essay may at times be prosaic (written in prose that is largely unimaginative), but at its best it is never dull. It may even become poetic. Many effective essayists draw upon such resources of poetry as rhythm and figurative language.

Nor should one stress the "expository" nature of the essay. Often an essay employs narration and description and loosely resembles a short story. Depending upon the writer's purpose and subject matter, an essay may use description and narration fully as much as exposition and argumentation.

The essay is usually notable for its brevity. But brevity is relative, and essays vary in length. Some are often little more than a few paragraphs, but many essays cover page upon page with solid prose.

The word *essay* comes from an Anglo-French word, *assayer*, meaning "to try or test." When, in 1580, the French writer Montaigne published his first collection of wise sayings, each dealing with a single topic, he called it *Essais*. Since that time, the word *essay* has been used to indicate any short prose discussion.

As the word itself suggests, *prose* progresses; that is, it carries an idea forward. (In Latin, the word *prosa,* from which *prose* is derived, means "straightforward"; the Latin verb *provertere* means to "turn forward.") An essay, therefore, tries to state and carry forward an idea or series of ideas.

By contrast, the term *verse* comes from Latin *versus,* a "turning." Poetry in a literal sense "stops" at the end of a line, turns back upon itself, and *reverses* its position to the beginning of the next line. In seeking the shaping thought of an essay, we look to its sentences; in reading a poem we concentrate on elements that provide richness of detail and memorable, concentrated expressions of thought and experience. Poetry and prose are different methods for giving shape and form to ideas.

The most marked characteristic of the essay is its tendency toward reflection; it may be called the literature of thought as distinct from the literature of action. This latter distinction is especially valid, as a comparison of the essay and short story illustrates. In brevity the essay resembles the short story, but resemblance may end there. For although the essay may, on occasion, employ narrative, it rarely presents ideas in story form—in terms, that is, of character and incident. It may be thought of as a thinking about ideas rather than an acting out of ideas.

A classification of essays indicates how difficult the essay is to define. An attempt to divide essays according to subject matter results in immediate confusion, for the subjects of the essay are legion.

Hardly more successful in classifying essays is trying to group them in broad fields of interest: politics, history, nature, philosophy, travel, science, and so on. To list essays as informative, didactic, and reflective is no less confusing, for here divisions overlap. Some essays may be called didactic. They may also be regarded as reflective or even as personal. Attempts to break down the essay into various types and subtypes are successful only as they demonstrate the flexibility and range of this literary genre.

Essays may, however, be divided into two broad classes, *informal* and *formal.* And this division is perhaps the most useful, since it draws attention to questions of manner and purpose, especially manner.

A formal essay is a composition written in a conventionally restrained, thoughtful, and analytical style. It obviously reflects the attitudes and opinions of its author but is written in a less personal and more objective manner than other types of prose compositions.

The informal essay, with its colloquial, chatty style, its friendly air, suggests confidential talk, even confession. It suggests relaxation and entertainment, too, and the laughter that comes of taking the world not too seriously. That this type of essay is sometimes called genial, familiar, or intimate is an indication of its nature. It is often spoken of, moreover, as the personal essay. For even more so than lyric poetry, the informal essay is frequently autobiographical, reflecting the peculiar notions, whims, and prejudices of the author and often recording his actual experiences. Usually written in the first person, the familiar essay is free in its use of the pronoun *I.*

Whether it is informal or formal, whether it aims to instruct, entertain, or persuade, the essay has long since won for itself an important place among literary genres. For three centuries, major writers have used it in one way or another to clarify or defend their views, to record their impressions of life, and to portray themselves.

Before the twentieth century, many essays were preachy in style, heavy in diction, and complex in structure. More recent essayists, however, try to express what they have in mind in terms that are simple, clear, logical, and specifically adapted to the persons for whom they are writing.

In structure, modern essays tend to start with an expressed or implied thesis sentence and proceed logically from the known to the unknown, from the near to the remote, from the present to the future or the past, or from abstract statement or generalization to specific example. In tone, the typical modern essay is more relaxed, less pontifical, and less didactic than were most of its predecessors. The twentieth-century essay is notable for its ease of expression, although not laxity of thought; it exhibits consideration for the reader as one "thinking with" the author. Not every modern essay fully reveals the personality of its author, but no modern essayist fails to present something of his particular and unmistakable individuality.

Problems and Points of View

A LETTER TO HENRY DAVID THOREAU

E. B. White

ELWYN BROOKS WHITE (1899–   ) was born in Mount Vernon, New York. After his graduation from Cornell in 1921, Mr. White traveled about and held several positions, including a reporter's job on the *Seattle Times* and work as a production assistant in an advertising agency. He is well known for his contributions to *The New Yorker* and for such books as *The Lady Is Cold* (1929), *Is Sex Necessary?* (1929 and 1950, with James Thurber), *Every Day Is Saturday* (1934), *The Fox of Peapack* (1938), *One Man's Meat* (1942 and 1944), *Stuart Little* (1945), *Charlotte's Web* (1952), *The Second Tree from the Corner* (1953), *The Points of My Compass* (1962), and *The Trumpet of the Swan* (1970).

1 Miss Nims, take a letter to Henry David Thoreau.[1] Dear Henry: I thought of you the other afternoon as I was approaching Concord doing fifty on Route 62. That is a high speed at which to hold a philosopher in one's mind, but in this century we are a nimble bunch.[2]

2 On one of the lawns in the outskirts of the village a woman was cutting the grass with a motorized lawn mower. What made me think of you was that the machine had rather got away from her, although she was game enough, and in the brief glimpse I had of the scene it appeared to me that the lawn was mowing the lady. She kept a tight grip on the handles, which throbbed violently with every explosion of the one-cylinder motor, and as she sheered around bushes and lurched along at a reluctant trot behind her impetuous[3] servant, she looked like a puppy who had grabbed something that was too much for him. Concord hasn't changed much, Henry; the farm implements and the animals still have the upper hand.

3 I may as well admit that I was journeying to Concord with the deliberate intention of visiting your woods; for although I have never knelt at the grave of a philosopher nor placed wreaths on moldy poets, and have often gone a mile out of my way to avoid some place of historical interest, I have always wanted to see Walden Pond. The account which you left of your sojourn[4] there is, you will be amused to learn, a document of increasing pertinence;[5] each year it seems to gain a little headway, as the world loses ground. We may all be transcendental[6] yet, whether we like it or not. As our common complexities increase, any tale of individual simplicity (and yours is the best written and the cockiest) acquires a new fascination; as our goods accumulate, but not our well-being, your report of an existence without material adornment takes on a certain awkward credibility.[7]

4 My purpose in going to Walden Pond, like yours, was not to live cheaply or to live dearly there, but to transact some private business with the fewest obstacles. Approaching Concord, doing forty, doing forty-five, doing fifty, the steering wheel held snug in my palms, the highway held grimly in my vision, the crown of the road now serving me (on the right-hand curves), now defeating me (on the lefthand curves), I began to rouse myself from the stupefaction[8] which a day's motor journey induces. It was a delicious evening, Henry, when the whole body is one sense, and imbibes delight through every pore, if I may coin a phrase.[9] Fields were richly brown where the harrow,[10] drawn by the stripped Ford, had lately sunk its teeth; pastures were green; and overhead the sky had that same everlasting great look which you will find on page 144 of the Oxford Pocket Edition.[11] I could feel the road entering me, through tire, wheel, spring, and cushion; shall I have intelligence with earth too? Am I not partly leaves and vegetable mold myself?—a man of infinite horsepower, yet partly leaves.

5 Stay with me on 62 and it will take you into Concord. As I say, it was a delicious evening. The snake had come forth to die in a bloody S on the highway, the wheel upon its head, its bowels flat now and exposed. The turtle had come up too to cross the road and die in the attempt, its hard shell smashed under the rubber blow, its intestinal yearning (for the other side of the road) forever squashed. There was a sign by the wayside which announced that the road had a "cotton surface." You wouldn't know what that is, but neither, for that matter, did I. There is a cryptic[12] ingredient in many of

our modern improvements—we are awed and pleased without knowing quite what we are enjoying. It is something to be traveling on a road with a cotton surface.

6 The civilization round Concord today is an odd distillation[13] of city, village, farm, and manor. The houses, yards, fields look not quite suburban, not quite rural. Under the bronze beech and the blue spruce of the departed baron grazes the milch goat of the heirs. Under the porte-cochère[14] stands the reconditioned station wagon; under the grape arbor sit the puppies for sale. (But why do men degenerate ever? What makes families run out?)[15]

7 It was June and everywhere June was publishing her immemorial[16] stanza: in the lilacs, in the syringa, in the freshly edged paths and the sweetness of moist beloved gardens, and the little wire wickets that preserve the tulips' front. Farmers were already moving the fruits of their toil into their yards, arranging the rhubarb, the asparagus, the strictly fresh eggs on the painted stands under the little shed roofs with the patent shingles. And though it was almost a hundred years since you had taken your ax and started cutting out your home on Walden Pond, I was interested to observe that the philosophical spirit was still alive in Massachusetts: in the center of a vacant lot some boys were assembling the framework of a rude shelter, their whole mind and skill concentrated in the rather inauspicious helter-skeleton[17] of studs and rafters. They too were escaping from town, to live naturally, in a rich blend of savagery and philosophy.

8 That evening, after supper at the inn, I strolled out into the twilight to dream my shapeless transcendental dreams and see that the car was locked up for the night (first open the right front door, then reach over, straining, and pull up the handles of the left rear and the left front till you hear the click, then the handle of the right rear, then shut the right front but open it again, remembering that the key is still in the ignition switch, remove the key, shut the right front again with a bang, push the tiny keyhole cover to one side, insert key, turn, and withdraw). It is what we all do, Henry. It is called locking the car. It is said to confuse thieves and keep them from making off with the laprobe. Four doors to lock behind one robe. The driver himself never uses a laprobe, the free movement of his legs being vital to the operation of the vehicle; so that when he locks the car it is a pure and unselfish act. I have in my life gained very little essential heat from laprobes, yet I have ever been at pains to lock them up.

9 The evening was full of sounds, some of which would have stirred your memory. The robins still love the elms of New England villages at sundown. There is enough of the thrush in them to make song inevitable[18] at the end of the day, and enough of the tramp to make them hang round the dwellings of men. A robin, like many another American, dearly loves a white house with green blinds. Concord is still full of them.

10 Your fellow-townsmen were stirring abroad—not many afoot, most of them in their cars; and the sound which they made in Concord at evening was a rustling and a whispering. The sound lacks steadfastness and is wholly unlike that of a train. A train, as you know who lived so near the

Fitchburg[19] line, whistles once or twice sadly and is gone, trailing a memory in smoke, soothing to ear and mind. Automobiles, skirting a village green, are like flies that have gained the inner ear—they buzz, cease, pause, start, shift, stop, halt, brake, and the whole effect is a nervous polytone[20] curiously disturbing.

11 As I wandered along, the *toc toc*[21] of ping-pong balls drifted from an attic window. In front of the Reuben Brown house a Buick was drawn up. At the wheel, motionless, his hat upon his head, a man sat, listening to Amos and Andy on the radio (it is a drama of many scenes and without an end). The deep voice of Andrew Brown, emerging from the car, although it originated more than two hundred miles away, was unstrained by distance. When you used to sit on the shore of your pond on Sunday morning, listening to the church bells of Acton and Concord, you were aware of the excellent filter of the intervening atmosphere. Science has attended to that, and sound now maintains its intensity without regard for distance. Properly sponsored, it goes on forever.

12 A fire engine, out for a trial spin, roared past Emerson's[22] house, hot with readiness for public duty. Over the barn roofs the martins dipped and chittered. A swarthy daughter of an asparagus grower, in culottes, shirt, and bandanna, pedalled past on her bicycle. It was indeed a delicious evening, and I returned to the inn (I believe it was your house once) to rock with the old ladies on the concrete veranda.

13 Next morning early I started afoot for Walden, out Main Street and down Thoreau, past the depot and the Minuteman[23] Chevrolet Company. The morning was fresh, and in a bean field along the way I flushed an agriculturalist, quietly studying his beans. Thoreau Street soon joined Number 126, an artery of the State. We number our highways nowadays, our speed being so great we can remember little of their quality or character and are lucky to remember their number. (Men have an indistinct notion that if they keep up this activity long enough all will at length ride somewhere, in next to no time.) Your pond is on 126.

14 I knew I must be nearing your woodland retreat when the Golden Pheasant lunchroom came into view—Sealtest ice cream, toasted sandwiches, hot frankfurters, waffles, tonics, and lunches. Were I the proprietor, I should add rice, Indian meal, and molasses—just for old time's sake. The Pheasant, incidentally, is for sale: a chance for some nature lover who wishes to set himself up beside a pond in the Concord atmosphere and live deliberately, fronting only the essential facts of life on Number 126. Beyond the Pheasant was a place called Walden Breezes, an oasis[24] whose porch pillars were made of old green shutters sawed into lengths. On the porch was a distorting mirror, to give the traveler a comical image of himself, who had miraculously learned to gaze in an ordinary glass without smiling. Behind the Breezes, in a sun-parched clearing, dwelt your philosophical descendants in their trailers, each trailer the size of your hut, but all grouped together for the sake of congeniality. Trailer people leave the city, as you did, to discover solitude and in any weather, at any hour of

the day or night, to improve the nick[25] of time; but they soon collect in villages and get bogged deeper in the mud than ever. The camp behind Walden Breezes was just rousing itself to the morning. The ground was packed hard under the heel, and the sun came through the clearing to bake the soil and enlarge the wry smell of cramped housekeeping. Cushman's bakery truck had stopped to deliver an early basket of rolls. A camp dog, seeing me in the road, barked petulantly.[26] A man emerged from one of the trailers and set forth with a bucket to draw water from some forest tap.

15 Leaving the highway I turned off into the woods toward the pond, which was apparent through the foliage. The floor of the forest was strewn with dried old oak leaves and *Transcripts*.[27] From beneath the flattened popcorn wrapper (*granum explosum*) peeped the frail violet. I followed a footpath and descended to the water's edge. The pond lay clear and blue in the morning light, as you have seen it so many times. In the shallows a man's waterlogged shirt undulated[28] gently. A few flies came out to greet me and convoy me to your cove, past the No Bathing signs on which the fellows and the girls had scrawled their names. I felt strangely excited suddenly to be snooping around your premises, tiptoeing along watchfully, as though not to tread by mistake upon the intervening century. Before I got to the cove I heard something which seemed to me quite wonderful: I heard your frog, a full, clear *troonk*, guiding me, still hoarse and solemn, bridging the years as the robins had bridged them in the sweetness of the village evening. But he soon quit, and I came on a couple of young boys throwing stones at him.

16 Your front yard is marked by a bronze tablet set in a stone. Four small granite posts, a few feet away, show where the house was. On top of the tablet was a pair of faded blue bathing trunks with a white stripe. Back of it is a pile of stones, a sort of cairn, left by your visitors as a tribute, I suppose. It is a rather ugly little heap of stones, Henry. In fact the hillside itself seems faded, browbeaten; a few tall skinny pines, bare of lower limbs, a smattering of young maples in suitable green, some birches and oaks, and a number of trees felled by the last big wind. It was from the bole of one of these fallen pines, torn up by the roots, that I extracted the stone which I added to the cairn—a sentimental act in which I was interrupted by a small terrier from a nearby picnic group, who confronted me and wanted to know about the stone.

17 I sat down for a while on one of the posts of your house to listen to the bluebottles and the dragonflies. The invaded glade[29] sprawled shabby and mean at my feet, but the flies were tuned to the old vibration.[30] There were the remains of a fire in your ruins, but I doubt that it was yours; also two beer bottles trodden into the soil and become part of earth. A young oak had taken root in your house, and two or three ferns, unrolling like the ticklers at a banquet. The only other furnishings were a DuBarry pattern sheet, a page torn from a picture magazine, and some crusts in wax paper.

18 Before I quit I walked clear round the pond and found the place where

you used to sit on the northeast side to get the sun in the fall, and the beach where you got sand for scrubbing your floor. On the eastern side of the pond, where the highway borders it, the State has built dressing rooms for swimmers, a float with diving towers, drinking fountains of porcelain, and rowboats for hire. The pond is in fact a State Preserve, and carries a twenty-dollar fine for picking wild flowers, a decree signed in all solemnity by your fellow-citizens Walter C. Wardell, Erson B. Barlow, and Nathaniel I. Bowditch. There was a smell of creosote where they had been building a wide wooden stairway to the road and the parking area. Swimmers and boaters were arriving; bodies splashed vigorously into the water and emerged wet and beautiful in the bright air. As I left, a boatload of town boys were splashing about in mid-pond, kidding and fooling, the young fellows singing at the tops of their lungs in a wild chorus:

> Amer-i-ca, Amer-i-ca, God shed his grace on thee,
> And crown thy good with brotherhood
> From sea to shi-ning sea!

19 I walked back to town along the railroad, following your custom. The rails were expanding noisily in the hot sun, and on the slope of the roadbed the wild grape and the blackberry sent up their creepers to the track.

20 The expense of my brief sojourn in Concord was

Canvas shoes .	$1.95	
Baseball bat . .	.25	gifts to take back to a boy
Left-handed fielder's glove	1.25	
Hotel and meals	4.25	
In all . . .	$7.70	

As you see, this amount was almost what you spent for food for eight months. I cannot defend the shoes or the expenditure for shelter and food: they reveal a meanness and grossness in my nature which you would find contemptible. The baseball equipment, however, is the sort of impediment[31] with which you were never on even terms. You must remember that the house where you practiced the sort of economy which I respect was haunted only by mice and squirrels. You never had to cope with a shortstop.[32]

Notes

[1] Thoreau (1817–1862), an American philosopher, essayist, and naturalist (see "Civil Disobedience"), built and lived in a cabin from March 1845, to September 1847. The cabin was situated on the shore of Walden Pond, near Concord, Mass. Here Thoreau lived alone, supplying his needs by his own labor and testing his beliefs in self-reliance, frugality, and simplicity. He freed himself from routine as much as possible so that he could study, think, and observe nature and himself.

[2] This beginning is whimsical, but is also direct, economical in words, and attention-getting—qualities important in all writing but especially in informal essays, where style is at least as important as subject matter. The deftness of this essay is well illustrated by the skillful integration of sentences from Thoreau's own writing into White's paragraphs.

[3] Hasty, violent.

[4] Stay.

[5] Applicability; direct bearing upon the matter at hand.

[6] *Transcendental* has several meanings. Here it suggests "surpassing" or "superior," a concept beyond the ordinary or accidental in human experience.

[7] Worthy of belief.

[8] Numbness, stupor.

[9] The pleasures and deeper meanings of White's essay will be most fully experienced by readers who trace the phrases deftly used to their source in Thoreau's writings.

[10] An agricultural implement with teeth or disks, drawn over land to level or break it up.

[11] An edition of Thoreau's *Walden*.

[12] Secret, hidden.

[13] Concentration, combination.

[14] Covered entrance.

[15] These lines are direct quotations from Thoreau, not subtly altered as on some other occasions in this selection.

[16] Extending back beyond memory or record.

[17] White's diction is notable for several reasons, two of which are that he avoids triteness and often forms a new expression from a commonplace word.

[18] Certain, necessary.

[19] A city in Massachusetts, not far from Concord.

[20] Simultaneous sound in several keys.

[21] Onomatopoeia is the formation of a word by imitation of a sound made by, or associated with, its referent. Both "toc toc" and the frog's "troonk" (later in the essay) are onomatopoeic expressions.

[22] Ralph Waldo Emerson (see "The American Scholar") lived in Concord for a time and was Thoreau's friend.

[23] A Minuteman was an American patriot before and during the Revolutionary War who held himself in instant readiness for military service; Minutemen fought in the opening skirmishes at Lexington and Concord.

[24] Place of refuge and relief.

[25] Vital moment.

[26] Impatiently, irritably.

[27] The Boston *Transcript*, a newspaper.

[28] Waved up and down.

[29] Open space.

[30] Rhythmic movement.

[31] Problem, obstacle.

[32] The author and his wife have one son, Joel.

THE COSMONAUTS' WHISKERS

Russell Baker

Russell Baker (1925–) was born in Loudon County, Virginia, and grew up in New Jersey and Maryland. He served with the Naval Air Force during World War II and was graduated from Johns Hopkins University in 1947. He began his career with the *Baltimore Sun* and later joined the Washington Bureau of *The New York Times*. Since 1962 he has been writing "Observer," a column of criticism and wit for the *Times* that also appears in newspapers throughout the country. Mr. Baker is author of *An American in Washington* (1961), *No Cause for Panic* (1964), *All Things Considered* (1965), *Poor Russell's Almanac* (1972).

1 When the Russian cosmonauts[1] Nikolayev and Popovich made the first overnight orbit around the earth[2] and returned from space, they needed a shave. It was too bad. These 5 o'clock shadows from the Buck Rogers future proved conclusively, for those who still had hopes, that something cosmic[3] out there is grinning at us.

2 When two men strike out for that wonderful universe next door, it is depressing to know that they are going to arrive with the same old burdens of trouble and sorrow they carried back here. And that is clearly the message of the cosmonauts' beards.

3 After all, if a man can't even expect to leave the shaving miseries back on earth, what likelihood is there that anything else is going to be better once he gets to the other worlds?

4 All the evidence of both Soviet and American space travel to date indicates that instead of solving anything, travel around the cosmos is only going to make the routine problems of coping with life harder than ever. John Glenn's[4] experiment with eating in space showed that cookies out there crumble just as cookies crumble down here. Down here they at least settle into sofa chinks and bedclothes. Out there, without gravity, they float suspended in space, where they can drift under eyelids and into delicate machinery. Add to the paraphernalia[5] required for future space ships: a cookie-crumb net.

5 Schoolboys everywhere will think twice about space careers since the Russians have shown that space travel is no excuse for ignoring their homework. Colonel Popovich reported that he was studying his English after his 500,000th mile and planned to get on with his physics after dinner.

6 Again these are difficult earth burdens made harder. Physics and English are hard enough to master under the most comfortable campus conditions. Imagine trying to come to grips with the dangling participle and adiabatic[6] expansion while encumbered with a pressurized suit, gloves, and glass helmet. And while watching a telephone that might ring any minute with a personal call from Leonid Brezhnev[7] or Lyndon B. Johnson.

7 A Congressional committee has recently held hearings on the feasibility of giving the ladies a role in the American astronaut program. It takes little imagination to guess the problems this will raise when the day comes, as it surely will. Powder blending with the cookie crumbs suspended in mid-capsule, bobby pins floating into the yaw stabilizer, gloves lost on remote planets.

8 Add to the paraphernalia required for future space ships: an interplanetary ladies' glove-finder.

9 The technologists can probably supply the gadgets needed to whip these problems. If they can shave sandpaper on television, they can shave an astronaut in weightless space without scattering whiskers all through the cookie crumbs.

10 They can probably devise ways to clear the cabin air of crumbs, bobby pins, face powder, and even man-woman tensions. On the grander level they can probably think up ways to transport all the commonplaces of earth life, from politics to war to traffic congestion, all over the solar system.

11 What they cannot do, however, is build man an escape hatch to that wonderful universe next door. As the cosmonauts' beards have shown, they can only help man lug his troubles along on the search.

12 No one can disparage[8] the instinct behind the search. It would be too bad, however, if it ended by blotting out the Milky Way[9] with a curtain of celestial debris composed of old whiskers, bobby pins, and face powder dumped from spaceship garbage ejectors.

Notes

[1] The word *cosmonaut*—from *cosmo-*, a learned borrowing meaning "world" or "universe," and *naut* ("sailing," "nautical")—was coined in Russia. A cosmonaut is an *astronaut,* one who travels outside the atmosphere of the earth. (In Greek, *astro* means "star.")

[2] On August 11 and 12, 1962.

[3] Vast, immeasurable.

[4] Glenn made the first American orbital flight in 1962.

[5] Belongings, equipment.

[6] Occurring without loss or gain of heat.

[7] Appointed First Secretary of the Soviet Communist Party in 1964.

[8] Belittle.

[9] The galaxy containing the earth, sun, and solar system.

OVERPOPULATED AMERICA

Wayne H. Davis

Wayne Harry Davis (1930–) was born in Morgantown, West Virginia, and was educated at the University of West Virginia and the University of Illinois. He has taught at the universities of Illinois and Minnesota and at Middlebury College. Since 1962, Dr. Davis has been teaching and doing research at the University of Kentucky. His special fields of interest are plant evolution and the taxonomy of mammals.

1 I define as most seriously overpopulated that nation whose people by virtue of their numbers and activities are most rapidly decreasing the ability of the land to support human life. With our large population, our affluence[1] and our technological monstrosities[2] the United States wins first place by a substantial margin.

2 Let's compare the U.S. to India, for example. We have 203 million people, whereas she has 540 million

on much less land. But look at the impact of people on the land.

3 The average Indian eats his daily few cups of rice (or perhaps wheat, whose production on American farms contributed to our one percent per year drain in quality of our active farmland), draws his bucket of water from the communal well and sleeps in a mud hut. In his daily rounds to gather cow dung to burn to cook his rice and warm his feet, his footsteps, along with those of millions of his countrymen, help bring about a slow deterioration[3] of the ability of the land to support people. His contribution to the destruction of the land is minimal.[4]

4 An American, on the other hand, can be expected to destroy a piece of land on which he builds a home, garage and driveway. He will contribute his share to the 142 million tons of smoke and fumes, seven million junked cars, 20 million tons of paper, 48 billion cans, and 26 billion bottles the overburdened environment must absorb each year. To run his air conditioner we will strip-mine a Kentucky hillside, push the dirt and slate down into the stream, and burn coal in a power generator, whose smokestack contributes to a plume of smoke massive enough to cause cloud seeding and premature precipitation from Gulf winds which should be irrigating the wheat farms of Minnesota.

5 In his lifetime he will personally pollute three million gallons of water, and industry and agriculture will use ten times this much water in his behalf. To provide these needs the US Army Corps of Engineers will build dams and flood farmland. He will also use 21,000 gallons of leaded gasoline containing boron,[5] drink 28,000 pounds of milk and eat 10,000 pounds of meat. The latter is produced and squandered in a life pattern unknown to Asians. A steer on a Western range eats plants containing minerals necessary for plant life. Some of these are incorporated into the body of the steer which is later shipped for slaughter. After being eaten by man these nutrients[6] are flushed down the toilet into the ocean or buried in the cemetery, the surface of which is cluttered with boulders called tombstones and has been removed from productivity. The result is a continual drain on the productivity of range land. Add to this the erosion of overgrazed lands, and the effects of the falling water table as we mine Pleistocene[7] deposits of groundwater to irrigate to produce food for more people, and we can see why our land is dying far more rapidly than did the great civilizations of the Middle East, which experienced the same cycle. The average Indian citizen, whose fecal material[8] goes back to the land, has but a minute fraction of the destructive effect on the land that the affluent American does.

6 Thus I want to introduce a new term, which I suggest be used in future discussions of human population and ecology.[9] We should speak of our numbers in "Indian equivalents." An Indian equivalent I define as the average number of Indian citizens required to have the same detrimental[10] effect on the land's ability to support human life as would the average American. This value is difficult to determine, but let's take an extremely conservative working figure of 25. To see how conservative this is,

imagine the addition of 1000 citizens to your town and 25,000 to an Indian village. Not only would the Americans destroy much more land for homes, highways and a shopping center, but they would contribute far more to environmental deterioration in hundreds of other ways as well. For example, their demand for steel for new autos might increase the daily pollution equivalent of 130,000 junk autos which *Life* tells us that US Steel Corp. dumps into Lake Michigan. Their demand for textiles would help the cotton industry destroy the life in the Black Warrior River in Alabama with endrin.[11] And they would contribute to the massive industrial pollution of our oceans (we provide one third to one half the world's share) which has caused the precipitous[12] downward trend in our commercial fisheries landings during the past seven years.

7 The per capita gross national product of the United States is 38 times that of India. Most of our goods and services contribute to the decline in the ability of the environment to support life. Thus it is clear that a figure of 25 for an Indian equivalent is conservative. It has been suggested to me that a more realistic figure would be 500.

8 In Indian equivalents, therefore, the population of the United States is at least four billion. And the rate of growth is even more alarming. We are growing at one percent per year, a rate which would double our numbers in 70 years. India is growing at 2.5 percent. Using the Indian equivalent of 25, our population growth becomes 10 times as serious as that of India. According to the Rienows in their recent book *Moment in the Sun,* just one year's crop of American babies can be expected to use up 25 billion pounds of beef, 200 million pounds of steel and 9.1 billion gallons of gasoline during their collective lifetime. And the demands on water and land for our growing population are expected to be far greater than the supply available in the year 2000. We are destroying our land at a rate of over a million acres a year. We now have only 2.6 agricultural acres per person. By 1975 this will be cut to 2.2, the critical point for the maintenance of what we consider a decent diet, and by the year 2000 we might expect to have 1.2.

9 You might object that I am playing with statistics in using the Indian equivalent on the rate of growth. I am making the assumption that today's American child will live 35 years (the average Indian life span) at today's level of affluence. If he lives an American 70 years, our rate of population growth would be 20 times as serious as India's.

10 But the assumption of continued affluence at today's level is unfounded. If our numbers continue to rise, our standard of living will fall so sharply that by the year 2000 any surviving Americans might consider today's average Asian to be well off. Our children's destructive effects on their environment will decline as they sink ever lower into poverty.

11 The United States is in serious economic trouble now. Nothing could be more misleading than today's affluence, which rests precariously[13] on a crumbling foundation. Our productivity, which had been increasing

steadily at about 3.2 percent a year since World War II, has been falling during 1969. Our export over import balance has been shrinking steadily from $7.1 billion in 1964 to $0.15 billion in the first half of 1969. Our balance of payments deficit for the second quarter was $3.7 billion, the largest in history. We are now importing iron ore, steel, oil, beef, textiles, cameras, radios and hundreds of other things.

12 Our economy is based upon the Keynesian[14] concept of a continued growth in population and productivity. It worked in an underpopulated nation with excess resources. It could continue to work only if the earth and its resources were expanding at an annual rate of 4 to 5 percent. Yet neither the number of cars, the economy, the human population, nor anything else can expand indefinitely at an exponential rate in a finite world. We must face this fact *now*. The crisis is here. When Walter Heller[15] says that our economy will expand by 4 percent annually through the latter 1970s he is dreaming. He is in a theoretical world totally unaware of the realities of human ecology. If the economists do not wake up and devise a new system for us now somebody else will have to do it for them.

13 A civilization is comparable to a living organism. Its longevity is a function of its metabolism.[16] The higher the metabolism (affluence), the shorter the life. Keynesian economics has allowed us an affluent but shortened life span. We have now run our course.

14 The tragedy facing the United States is even greater and more imminent[17] than that descending upon the hungry nations. The Paddock brothers in their book, *Famine 1975!*, say that India "cannot be saved" no matter how much food we ship her. But India will be here after the United States is gone. Many millions will die in the most colossal famines India has ever known, but the land will survive and she will come back as she always has before. The United States, on the other hand, will be a desolate tangle of concrete and ticky-tacky, of strip-mined moonscape and silt-choked reservoirs. The land and water will be so contaminated with pesticides, herbicides, mercury fungicides, lead, boron, nickel, arsenic and hundreds of other toxic substances, which have been approaching critical levels of concentration in our environment as a result of our numbers and affluence, that they may be unable to sustain human life.

15 Thus as the curtain gets ready to fall on man's civilization, let it come as no surprise that it shall first fall on the United States. And let no one make the mistake of thinking we can save ourselves by "cleaning up the environment." Banning DDT is the equivalent of the physician's treating syphilis by putting a bandaid over the first chancre[18] to appear. In either case you can be sure that more serious and widespread trouble will soon appear unless the disease itself is treated. We cannot survive by planning to treat the symptoms such as air pollution, water pollution, soil erosion, etc.

16 What can we do to slow the rate of destruction of the United States as a land capable of supporting human life? There are two approaches. First, we must reverse the population growth. We have far more people now

than we can continue to support at anything near today's level of affluence. American women average slightly over three children each. According to the *Population Bulletin* if we reduced this number to 2.5 there would still be 330 million people in the nation at the end of the century. And even if we reduced this to 1.5 we would have 57 million more people in the year 2000 than we have now. With our present longevity patterns it would take more than 30 years for the population to peak even when reproducing at this rate, which would eventually give us a net decrease in numbers.

17 Do not make the mistake of thinking that technology will solve our population problem by producing a better contraceptive. Our problem now is that people want too many children. Surveys show the average number of children wanted by the American family is 3.3. There is little difference between the poor and the wealthy, black and white, Catholic and Protestant. Production of children at this rate during the next 30 years would be so catastrophic in effect on our resources and the viability[19] of the nation as to be beyond my ability to contemplate. To prevent this trend we must not only make contraceptives and abortion readily available to everyone, but we must establish a system to put severe economic pressure on those who produce children and reward those who do not. This can be done within our system of taxes and welfare.

18 The other thing we must do is to pare down our Indian equivalents. Individuals in American society vary tremendously in Indian equivalents. If we plot Indian equivalents versus their reciprocal, the percentage of land surviving a generation, we obtain a linear regression.[20] We can then place individuals and occupation types on this graph. At one end would be the starving blacks of Mississippi; they would approach unity in Indian equivalents, and would have the least destructive effect on the land. At the other end of the graph would be the politicians slicing pork for the barrel, the highway contractors, strip-mine operators, real estate developers, and public enemy number one—the US Army Corps of Engineers.

19 We must halt land destruction. We must abandon the view of land and minerals as private property to be exploited in any way economically feasible[21] for private financial gain. Land and minerals are resources upon which the very survival of the nation depends, and their use must be planned in the best interests of the people.

20 Rising expectations for the poor is a cruel joke foisted upon[22] them by the Establishment.[23] As our new economy of use-it-once-and-throw-it-away produces more and more products for the affluent, the share of our resources available for the poor declines. Blessed be the starving blacks of Mississippi with their outdoor privies, for they are ecologically sound, and they shall inherit a nation. Although I hope that we will help these unfortunate people attain a decent standard of living by diverting war efforts to fertility control and job training, our most urgent task to assure this nation's survival during the next decade is to stop the affluent destroyers.

Notes

[1] Wealth; abundance of material goods and money.
[2] Hideous and frightening examples of engineering and the industrial arts.
[3] Weakening, lessening.
[4] Small, the least possible.
[5] A nonmetallic element; boron carbide is a hard, water-insoluble solid.
[6] Nourishing substances.
[7] An epoch beginning about one million years ago.
[8] Body wastes.
[9] The relations between organisms and their environment.
[10] Harmful, wasteful, damaging.
[11] A crystalline, poisonous solid.
[12] Steep, abrupt.
[13] Uncertainly, dangerously.
[14] Concerning the economic theories and programs of John Maynard Keynes (1883–1946), an English economist, and his followers. Keynesian economics places emphasis on maintaining full employment and controlling inflation by planned government intervention in the economy.
[15] An American economist.
[16] Physical and chemical processes by which energy is made available.
[17] Ready to occur at any moment.
[18] Sore, ulcer.
[19] Capability of living.
[20] In less exact terms, we can contrast "Indian equivalents" with their counterparts in the United States so as to obtain a graph showing worsening conditions.
[21] Used selfishly in any way that is economically suitable ("profitable").
[22] Fraudulently forced upon.
[23] The existing power structure in a society.

COMFORT

Aldous Huxley

ALDOUS (LEONARD) HUXLEY (1894–1963), English novelist, essayist, and poet, was a grandson of Thomas Henry Huxley and a grandnephew of Matthew Arnold. Undaunted by his imposing heritage, Aldous Huxley wrote a series of brilliantly satiric novels, including *Crome Yellow* (1921), *Mortal Coils* (1922), *Antic Hay* (1923), *Point Counter Point* (1928), *Brave New World* (1932), and *Ape and Essence* (1948). He also published a large number of trenchant essays and several distinguished volumes of poetry. The best single-volume collection of his writings is *The World of Aldous Huxley* (1947). Among his later books are *The Devils of Loudun* (1952), *The Doors of Perception* (1954), *Tomorrow and Tomorrow and Tomorrow* (1956), *Collected Essays* (1960), and *Island* (1962).

1 French hotel-keepers call it *Le confort moderne*, and they are right. For comfort is a thing of recent growth, younger than steam, a child when

telegraphy was born, only a generation older than radio. The invention of the means of being comfortable and the pursuit of comfort as a desirable end—one of the most desirable that human beings can propose to themselves—are modern phenomena, unparalleled in history since the time of the Romans. Like all phenomena with which we are extremely familiar, we take them for granted, as a fish takes the water in which it lives, not realizing the oddity and novelty of them, not bothering to consider their significance. The padded chair, the well-sprung bed, the sofa, central heating, and the regular hot bath—these and a host of other comforts enter into the daily lives of even the most moderately prosperous of the Anglo-Saxon bourgeoisie.[1] Three hundred years ago they were unknown to the greatest kings. This is a curious fact which deserves to be examined and analysed.

2 The first thing that strikes one about the discomfort in which our ancestors lived is that it was mainly voluntary.[2] Some of the apparatus of modern comfort is of purely modern invention; people could not put rubber tyres on their carriages before the discovery of South America and the rubber plant. But for the most part there is nothing new about the material basis of our comfort. Men could have made sofas and smoking-room chairs, could have installed bathrooms and central heating and sanitary plumbing any time during the last three or four thousand years. And as a matter of fact, at certain periods they did indulge themselves in these comforts. Two thousand years before Christ, the inhabitants of Knossos[3] were familiar with sanitary plumbing. The Romans had invented an elaborate system of hot-air heating, and the bathing facilities in a smart Roman villa were luxurious and complete beyond the dreams of modern man. There were sweating-rooms, massage-rooms, cold plunges, tepid drying-rooms with (if we may believe Sidonius Apollinaris)[4] improper frescoes[5] on the walls and comfortable couches where you could lie and get dry and talk to your friends. As for the public baths, they were almost inconceivably luxurious. "To such a height of luxury have we reached," said Seneca,[6] "that we are dissatisfied if, in our baths, we do not tread on gems." The size and completeness of the thermae[7] was proportionable to their splendour. A single room of the baths of Diocletian[8] has been transformed into a large church.

3 It would be possible to adduce many other examples showing what could be done with the limited means at our ancestors' disposal in the way of making life comfortable. They show sufficiently clearly that if the men of the Middle Ages and early modern epoch lived in filth and discomfort, it was not for any lack of ability to change their mode of life; it was because they chose to live in this way, because filth and discomfort fitted in with their principles and prejudices, political, moral, and religious.

COMFORT AND THE SPIRITUAL LIFE

4 What have comfort and cleanliness to do with politics, morals, and religion? At a first glance one would

say that there was and could be no causal connection between armchairs and democracies, sofas and the relaxation of the family system, hot baths and the decay of Christian orthodoxy. But look more closely and you will discover that there exists the closest connection between the recent growth of comfort and the recent history of ideas. I hope in this essay to make that connection manifest,[9] to show why it was not possible (not materially, but psychologically impossible) for the Italian princes of the quattrocento, for the Elizabethan, even for Louis XIV[10] to live in what the Romans would have called common cleanliness and decency, or enjoy what would be to us indispensable comforts.

5 Let us begin with the consideration of armchairs and central heating. These, I propose to show, became possible only with the breakdown of monarchical and feudal power and the decay of the old family and social hierarchies.[11] Smoking-room chairs and sofas exist to be lolled in. In a well-made modern armchair you cannot do anything but loll. Now, lolling is neither dignified nor respectful. When we wish to appear impressive, when we have to administer a rebuke to an inferior, we do not lie in a deep chair with our feet on the mantelpiece; we sit up and try to look majestical. Similarly, when we wish to be polite to a lady or show respect to the old or eminent, we cease to loll; we stand, or at least we straighten ourselves up. Now, in the past, human society was a hierarchy in which every man was always engaged in being impressive towards his inferiors or respectful to those above him. Lolling in such societies was utterly impossible. It was as much out of the question for Louis XIV to loll in the presence of his courtiers as it was for them to loll in the presence of their king. It was only when he attended a session of the Parlement that the King of France ever lolled in public. On these occasions he reclined in the Bed of Justice, while princes sat, the great officers of the crown stood, and the smaller fry knelt. Comfort was proclaimed as the appanage[12] of royalty. Only the king might stretch his legs. We may feel sure, however, that he stretched them in a very majestic manner. The lolling was purely ceremonial and accompanied by no loss of dignity. At ordinary times the king was seated, it is true, but seated in a dignified and upright position; the appearance of majesty had to be kept up. (For, after all, majesty is mainly a question of majestical appearance.) The courtiers, meanwhile, kept up the appearances of deference,[13] either standing, or else, if their rank was very high and their blood peculiarly blue, sitting, even in the royal presence, on stools. What was true of the king's court was true of the nobleman's household; and the squire was to his dependents, the merchant was to his apprentices and servants, what the monarch was to his courtiers. In all cases the superior had to express his superiority by being dignified, the inferior his inferiority by being deferential; there could be no lolling. Even in the intimacies of family life it was the same: the parents ruled like popes and princes, by divine right; the children were their subjects. Our fathers took the fifth commandment[14] very seriously—how seriously

may be judged from the fact that during the great Calvin's theocratic rule of Geneva[15] a child was publicly decapitated[16] for having ventured to strike its parents. Lolling on the part of children, though not perhaps a capital offence, would have been regarded as an act of the grossest disrespect, punishable by much flagellation,[17] starving, and confinement. For a slighter insult—neglect to touch his cap—Vespasiano Gonzaga[18] kicked his only son to death; one shudders to think what he might have been provoked to do if the boy had lolled. If the children might not loll in the presence of their parents, neither might the parents loll in the presence of their children, for fear of demeaning themselves in the eyes of those whose duty it was to honour them. Thus we see that in the European society of two or three hundred years ago it was impossible for any one—from the Holy Roman Emperor and the King of France down to the poorest beggar, from the bearded patriarch[19] to the baby—to loll in the presence of any one else. Old furniture reflects the physical habits of the hierarchical society for which it was made. It was in the power of mediaeval and Renaissance craftsmen to create armchairs and sofas that might have rivalled in comfort those of today. But society being what, in fact, it was, they did nothing of the kind. It was not, indeed, until the sixteenth century that chairs became at all common. Before that time a chair was a symbol of authority. Committee-men now loll, Members of Parliament are comfortably seated, but authority still belongs to a Chairman, still issues from a symbolical Chair. In the Middle Ages only the great had chairs. When a great man travelled, he took his chair with him, so that he might never be seen detached from the outward and visible sign of his authority. To this day the Throne no less than the Crown is the symbol of royalty. In mediaeval times the vulgar sat, whenever it was permissible for them to sit, on benches, stools, and settles. With the rise, during the Renaissance period, of a rich and independent bourgeoisie, chairs began to be more freely used. Those who could afford chairs sat in them, but sat with dignity and discomfort; for the chairs of the sixteenth century were still very throne-like and imposed upon those who sat in them a painfully majestic attitude. It was only in the eighteenth century, when the old hierarchies were seriously breaking up, that furniture began to be comfortable. And even then there was no real lolling. Armchairs and sofas on which men (and, later, women) might indecorously[20] sprawl were not made until democracy was firmly established, the middle classes enlarged to gigantic proportions, good manners lost from out of the world, women emancipated, and family restraints dissolved.

CENTRAL HEATING AND THE FEUDAL SYSTEM

6 Another essential component of modern comfort—the adequate heating of houses—was made impossible, at least for the great ones of the earth, by the political structure of ancient societies. Plebeians[21] were more fortunate in this respect than nobles. Living in small houses, they were able

to keep warm. But the nobleman, the prince, the king, and the cardinal inhabited palaces of a grandeur corresponding with their social position. In order to prove that they were greater than other men, they had to live in surroundings considerably more than life-size. They received their guests in vast halls like roller-skating rinks; they marched in solemn processions along galleries as long and as draughty as Alpine tunnels, up and down triumphal staircases that looked like the cataracts of the Nile frozen into marble. Being what he was, a great man in those days had to spend a great deal of his time in performing solemn symbolical charades and pompous ballets—performances which required a lot of room to accommodate the numerous actors and spectators. This explains the enormous dimensions of royal and princely palaces, even of the houses of ordinary landed gentlemen. They owed it to their position to live, as though they were giants, in rooms a hundred feet long and thirty high. How splendid, how magnificent! But oh, how bleak! In our days the self-made great are not expected to keep up their position in the splendid style of those who were great by divine right. Sacrificing grandiosity[22] to comfort, they live in rooms small enough to be heated. (And so, when they were off duty, did the great in the past; most old palaces contain a series of tiny apartments to which their owners retired when the charades of state were over. But the charades were long-drawn affairs, and the unhappy princes of old days had to spend a great deal of time being magnificent in icy audience-chambers and among the whistling draughts of interminable galleries.)

7 Driving in the environs of Chicago, I was shown the house of a man who was reputed to be one of the richest and most influential of the city. It was a medium-sized house of perhaps fifteen or twenty smallish rooms. I looked at it in astonishment, thinking of the vast palaces in which I myself have lived in Italy (for considerably less rent than one would have to pay for garaging a Ford in Chicago). I remembered the rows of bedrooms as big as ordinary ballrooms, the drawing-rooms like railway stations, the staircase on which you could drive a couple of limousines abreast. Noble *palazzi,*[23] where one has room to feel oneself a superman! But remembering also those terrible winds that blow in February from the Apennines,[24] I was inclined to think that the rich man of Chicago had done well in sacrificing the magnificences on which his counterpart in another age and country would have spent his riches.

BATHS AND MORALS

8 It is to the decay of monarchy, aristocracy, and ancient social hierarchy that we owe the two components of modern comfort hitherto discussed. The third great component—the bath—must, I think, be attributed, at any rate in part, to the decay of Christian morals. There are still on the continent of Europe, and, for all I know, elsewhere, convent schools in which young ladies are brought up to believe that human bodies are objects of so impure and obscene a character that it is sinful for them to see, not

merely other people's nakedness, but even their own. Baths, when they are permitted to take them (every alternate Saturday) must be taken in a chemise descending well below the knees. And they are even taught a special technique of dressing which guarantees them from catching so much as a glimpse of their own skin. These schools are now, happily, exceptional, but there was a time, not so long ago, when they were the rule. Theirs is the great Christian ascetic[25] tradition which has flowed on in majestic continuity from the time of St. Anthony[26] and the unwashed, underfed, sex-starved monks of the Thebaid,[27] through the centuries, almost to the present day. It is to the weakening of that tradition that women at any rate owe the luxury of frequent bathing.

9 The early Christians were by no means enthusiastic bathers; but it is fair to point out that Christian ascetic tradition has not at all times been hostile to baths as such. That the Early Fathers should have found the promiscuity[28] of Roman bathing shocking is only natural. But the more moderate of them were prepared to allow a limited amount of washing, provided that the business was done with decency. The final decay of the great Roman baths was as much due to the destructiveness of the Barbarians[29] as to Christian ascetic objections. During the Ages of Faith there was actually a revival of bathing. The Crusaders[30] came back from the East, bringing with them the oriental vapour bath, which seems to have had a considerable popularity all over Europe. For reasons which it is difficult to understand, its popularity gradually waned, and the men and women of the late sixteenth and early seventeenth centuries seem to have been almost as dirty as their barbarous ancestors. Medical theory and court fashions may have had something to do with these fluctuations.[31]

10 The ascetic tradition was always strongest where women were concerned. The Goncourts[32] record in their diary the opinion, which seems to have been current in respectable circles during the Second Empire,[33] that female immodesty and immorality had increased with the growth of the bath habit. "Girls should wash less" was the obvious corollary.[34] Young ladies who enjoy their bath owe a debt of gratitude to Voltaire[35] for his mockeries, to the nineteenth-century scientists for their materialism. If these men had never lived to undermine the convent school tradition, our girls might still be as modest and as dirty as their ancestresses.

COMFORT AND MEDICINE

11 It is, however, to the doctors that bath-lovers owe their greatest debt. The discovery of microbic infection has put a premium on cleanliness. We wash now with religious fervour, like the Hindus. Our baths have become something like magic rites to protect us from the powers of evil, embodied in the dirt-loving germ. We may venture to prophesy that this medical religion will go still further in undermining the Christian ascetic tradition. Since the discovery of the beneficial effects of sunlight, too much clothing has become, medically speaking, a sin. Immodesty is now a virtue. It is quite likely that the doctors, whose

prestige among us is almost equal to that of the medicine men among the savages, will have us stark naked before very long. That will be the last stage in the process of making clothes more comfortable. It is a process which has been going on for some time —first among men, later among women —and among its determining causes are the decay of hierarchic formalism[36] and of Christian morality. In his lively little pamphlet describing Gladstone's[37] visit to Oxford shortly before his death, Mr. Fletcher has recorded the Grand Old Man's comments on the dress of the undergraduates. Mr. Gladstone, it appears, was distressed by the informality and the cheapness of the students' clothes. In his day, he said, young men went about with a hundred pounds' worth of clothes and jewellery on their persons, and every self-respecting youth had at least one pair of trousers in which he never sat down for fear of spoiling its shape. Mr. Gladstone visited Oxford at a time when undergraduates still wore very high starched collars and bowler hats. One wonders what he would have said of the open shirts, the gaudily coloured sweaters, the loose flannel trousers of the present generation. Dignified appearances have never been less assiduously[38] kept up than they are at present; informality has reached an unprecedented pitch. On all but the most solemn occasions a man, whatever his rank or position, may wear what he finds comfortable.

12 The obstacles in the way of women's comforts were moral as well as political. Women were compelled not merely to keep up social appearances, but also to conform to a tradition of Christian ascetic morality. Long after men had abandoned their uncomfortable formal clothes, women were still submitting to extraordinary inconveniences in the name of modesty. It was the war[39] which liberated them from their bondage. When women began to do war work, they found that the traditional modesty in dress was not compatible[40] with efficiency. They preferred to be efficient. Having discovered the advantages of immodesty, they have remained immodest ever since, to the great improvement of their health and increase of their personal comfort. Modern fashions are the most comfortable that women have ever worn. Even the ancient Greeks were probably less comfortable. Their undertunic, it is true, was as rational a garment as you could wish for; but their outer robe was simply a piece of stuff wound round the body like an Indian *sari,*[41] and fastened with safety-pins. No woman whose appearance depended on safety-pins can ever have felt really comfortable.

COMFORT AS AN END IN ITSELF

13 Made possible by changes in the traditional philosophy of life, comfort is now one of the causes of its own further spread. For comfort has now become a physical habit, a fashion, an ideal to be pursued for its own sake. The more comfort is brought into the world, the more it is likely to be valued. To those who have known comfort, discomfort is a real torture. And the fashion which now

decrees the worship of comfort is quite as imperious[42] as any other fashion. Moreover, enormous material interests are bound up with the supply of the means of comfort. The manufacturers of furniture, of heating apparatus, of plumbing fixtures, cannot afford to let the love of comfort die. In modern advertisement they have means for compelling it to live and grow.

14 Having now briefly traced the spiritual origins of modern comfort, I must say a few words about its effects. One can never have something for nothing, and the achievement of comfort has been accompanied by a compensating loss of other equally, or perhaps more, valuable things. A man of means who builds a house today is in general concerned primarily with the comfort of his future residence. He will spend a great deal of money (for comfort is very expensive: in America they talk of giving away the house with the plumbing) on bathrooms, heating apparatus, padded furnishings, and the like; and having spent it, he will regard his house as perfect. His counterpart in an earlier age would have been primarily concerned with the impressiveness and magnificence of his dwelling—with beauty, in a word, rather than comfort. The money our contemporary would spend on baths and central heating would have been spent in the past on marble staircases, a grand façade,[43] frescoes, huge suites of gilded rooms, pictures, statues. Sixteenth-century popes lived in a discomfort that a modern bank manager would consider unbearable; but they had Raphael's[44] frescoes, they had the Sistine chapel,[45] they had their galleries of ancient sculpture. Must we pity them for the absence from the Vatican[46] of bathrooms, central heating, and smoking-room chairs?

15 I am inclined to think that our present passion for comfort is a little exaggerated. Though I personally enjoy comfort, I have lived very happily in houses devoid of almost everything that Anglo-Saxons deem indispensable. Orientals and even South Europeans, who know not comfort and live very much as our ancestors lived centuries ago, seem to get on very well without our elaborate and costly apparatus of padded luxury. I am old-fashioned enough to believe in higher and lower things, and can see no point in material progress except in so far as it subserves[47] thought. I like labour-saving devices, because they economize time and energy which may be devoted to mental labour. (But then I enjoy mental labour; there are plenty of people who detest it, and who feel as much enthusiasm for thought-saving devices as for automatic dishwashers and sewing-machines.) I like rapid and easy transport, because by enlarging the world in which men can live it enlarges their minds. Comfort for me has a similar justification: it facilitates mental life. Discomfort handicaps thought; it is difficult when the body is cold and aching to use the mind. Comfort is a means to an end. The modern world seems to regard it as an end in itself, an absolute good. One day, perhaps, the earth will have been turned into one vast feather-bed, with man's body dozing on top of it and his mind underneath, like Desdemona,[48] smothered.

Notes

[1] Members of the middle class; in Marxist theory, those opposed to the proletariat, or wage-earning class.

[2] By free choice, of one's own will.

[3] A ruined city in Crete, capital of the ancient Minoan civilization.

[4] A fifth-century Christian church figure and politician, author of nine books of letters and poems.

[5] Pictures or designs painted on moist plaster surfaces with colors ground in water.

[6] Roman philosopher and tragedian who died in A.D. 65.

[7] Hot baths (public bathing establishments).

[8] Emperor of Rome A.D. 284–305.

[9] Obvious, evident.

[10] Louis the Great, the "Sun King," 1638–1715, King of France 1643–1715. The *Italian princes of the quattrocento* is a reference to the fifteenth century (literally four hundred, short for fourteen hundred). *Elizabethan* refers to the reign of Queen Elizabeth I, 1558–1603.

[11] Ranks, orders.

[12] Right, privilege, possession.

[13] Submission, yielding.

[14] "Honour thy father and thy mother that thy days may be long upon the land which the Lord thy God giveth thee" (Exodus 20:12).

[15] John Calvin (1509–1564), a French Protestant theologian, began work in Geneva, Switzerland, in 1536. *Theocratic rule* refers to government by a representative of God.

[16] Beheaded.

[17] Whipping, flogging.

[18] A member of the princely Italian family that ruled certain provinces from the fourteenth century to the eighteenth.

[19] An elder or leading member of a community.

[20] Indecently, improperly.

[21] Common people.

[22] Grandness, impressiveness.

[23] Stately private residences or palaces.

[24] A mountain range in Italy extending across the length of the peninsula from northwest to southwest.

[25] Severe, strict.

[26] An Egyptian hermit (A.D. 251?–356?) known as the founder of Roman Catholic monasticism.

[27] An ancient region surrounding Thebes, in Egypt.

[28] Casual, irregular association or mingling.

[29] Savage, uncivilized people; for Romans, the term referred to people who lived outside the Roman Empire.

[30] Those who went from Europe on military expeditions during the 11th to 13th centuries to recover the Holy Land (Palestine) from the Muslims.

[31] Changes.

[32] French art critics, historians, and novelists of the nineteenth century.

[33] The empire established in France (1852–1870) by Louis Napoleon, the successor to the Second Republic.

[34] Natural consequence.

[35] Francois Marie Arouet (1694–1778), French philosopher, dramatist, novelist, and essayist.

[36] Strict following of prescribed or traditional forms.

[37] William Gladstone (1809–1898), British statesman, four times prime minister between 1868 and 1894.

[38] Diligently, constantly.
[39] World War I, July 1914–November 1918.
[40] Consistent.
[41] The principal garment of Hindu women, a long piece of cloth worn around the body with an end draped over the head or one shoulder.
[42] Commanding, overbearing.
[43] Front.
[44] Italian painter, 1483–1520.
[45] The chapel of the pope in the Vatican at Rome, decorated with frescoes by Michelangelo and others.
[46] The chief residence of the popes in Vatican City, an independent state within the city of Rome.
[47] Is useful in promoting.
[48] Othello's wife, murdered by her husband as a result of jealousy instilled by Iago (Shakespeare's tragedy *Othello*, 1604).

WHAT PRODUCED THOSE POT-SMOKING, REBELLIOUS, DEMONSTRATING KIDS?

Eliot Daley

ELIOT DALEY (1936–) was born in Melrose, Massachusetts. He was educated at Fresno State College, where he earned both bachelor's and master's degrees. The holder of a degree in divinity from San Francisco Theological Seminary, Mr. Daley has served as a chaplain at Middlebury College and as a minister in Princeton, New Jersey. In addition to his position with a company producing programs for children on educational television outlets, Mr. Daley is a free-lance writer on subjects dealing with educational psychology and mass media.

1 Whatever happened to some of these kids today? How come they smoke pot, sleep around, demonstrate, and drop out? And why won't they study in our schools, work at our jobs, and kill in our wars? What got into them?

2 Television did.

3 Those born within a few years of 1950 never experienced a reality that didn't include massive doses of television. They spent more time with TV than with their parents or teachers. For the first time, an unsanctioned[1] source taught our children most of what they learned about our culture. And they have been profoundly shaped by what they learned—and mislearned. Their slogans reveal how staggeringly different these TV kids really are.

4 They don't just think we're square or corny. That's not what many of them are saying. They are suspicious of our intentions. They do not *trust* us.

5 What an assertion! How can we have a society—or any relationship—without trust? What made them feel we didn't have their best interests at heart?

6 Well, for one thing, we let TV rob them of their childhood. Back in what should have been the simple intimacy[2] and security of preschool days, we let the world bust in on them. Adult banality,[3] precocious[4] commercialism, visions of evil all flooded their waking hours.

7 Most of the children's programming in the early '50s was originally produced for older audiences in theaters. Very young children must have been confused by the unmitigated mayhem[5] of the "cartoons." How was a 4-year-old sitting alone before the TV set supposed to know why big cats chased small birds and ate them? From Tweetie and Sylvester to Popeye or The Road Runner, virtually every cartoon swamped them with the same theme: for some totally obscure reason, the big people are just bent on beating hell out of the little people. With a little luck, a weapon and a trick, the small may survive *this* time. But there's always next time . . .

8 For thousands of hours these pre-Oedipal[6] kids watched the (wicked) Powerful incessantly harass the (innocent) Weak. Is it any wonder they don't trust the Establishment?[7]

9 But that's only part of it. Commercials really took their toll, too. Never before have advertisers so systematically assaulted the judgment and will power of preschoolers!

10 It worked, of course. Seventy per cent of children ask for stuff they see on TV—and 89 per cent of their parents buy it for them.

DO YOUR OWN THING

11 Who can blame them for wanting to escape "our thing"? Hard on the heels of the evening news, with its roster of victims of our civilization, came the prime-time hours of affluent indolence.[8] From Lucy and Desi onward, TV has held up both the exaggerated and the genuine banalities of middle-class existence. The result is many of the young are embarrassed to be what, in very fact, they are.

12 The specter of a middle-class life sent them scurrying for alternatives.[9] Through the glass eye of TV, our children saw "our thing" as the child saw the Emperor without any clothes:[10] bombastic,[11] mindless, naked and vain. In all these years, can you name more than a couple of adults on TV whose adulthood was depicted as significant and fulfilling? Men tended to rely on money or weapons for their strength; women were shrewish[12] or conveniently missing altogether.

13 Unfortunately, parents' own habits compounded the distorted vision of adulthood. They spent less time sharing with their children whatever satisfactions they enjoyed as adults —because they were too busy watching that new TV machine. In 1949, only about a third of U.S. homes even had a radio playing after supper on Sunday nights. But by 1958, almost two-thirds of American families were glued to the tube by 8 P.M. Something new had been added. And something else was lost.

NOW!

14 That's when the kids want things. Now. Yesterday would have been better. (Tomorrow? Out of the question!) What makes them so darned impatient? Don't they know that things take time?

15 No, they don't. In fact, TV taught them that things *don't* take time. They happened on cue. Every problem had a solution. Every program had a conclusion. There were no alternatives to explore (no time for that). There were no human idiosyncrasies[13] to consider (power or deceit will prevail). Opinions, rights, feelings of others? Irrelevant. Due process of law? What a laugh! The Eisenhower Commission on television violence reported that 80 per cent of all violent conflicts on TV are resolved without ever bothering with due process of law. Should we really wonder that some radicals ignore law—and then expect amnesty?[14]

16 It is a particular shame that this generation witnessed so much cut-rate "justice" and superficial "problem-solving." Because they also became more aware than anyone of the enormity of intolerable social problems. So they have more sense of outrage—and less sense of change-process—than preceding generations. TV never demonstrated the distinction between awareness and understanding, imperative[15] and strategy, product and process.

17 And because they spent tens of thousands of hours squatting before the set, they didn't find it out on their own. All the hours that previous generations spent fort-building, club-forming and friend-making, this bunch spent in relatively passive spectatorship. And so their passion for healing is frustrated by their procedural incompetence,[16] and "patience" becomes an intolerable luxury synonymous with the indifference over-indulged by their elders.

HELL, NO! WE WON'T GO!

18 Lots of these kids have no stomach for killing. Not for national honor or any other reason. They're holed up in colleges, graduate schools and foreign countries hoping to avoid the draft.

19 TV has been a major factor again. War used to be remote. It was easy to glorify. Combatants never saw the "enemy" until a split-second of kill-or-be-killed.

20 But the pathetic peasants of Vietnam have been in our homes every day for five or six years now. Holding mangled children. Scurrying for shelter. Being shot and chased and badgered by grotesque armies indistinguishable in their effect. All these kids have seen the ravages of war. Every single day. After day after day.

21 On top of that, they don't share many of our prejudices and stereotypes[17] about "foreigners." That's another legacy[18] of TV. Before these kids ever entered kindergarten, they had spent more time seeing people of other lands than we had in our first 20 years. And they came to know them as people, with faces and names and personalities and families—not as anonymous masses of "Japs" or "Russkies." Consequently, when they see people who live in other lands being killed, they react differently; sociologist Herbert Gans found that, on viewing TV films of the war in

Vietnam, 75 per cent of teen-agers surveyed said they felt "sick, horrible, badly"; but 75 per cent of adults felt "more hawkish"!

TOMORROW HAS BEEN CANCELED

22 The younger generation expects to die soon. The *majority of* collegians fear they'll be dead within the next two decades! (Surveys consistently reveal this.) How come? Is it The Bomb? Or is it The War?

23 Partly. But it's also television. Through TV they have been swept into a crescendo[19] of violence that castrates[20] confidence in a future. So much fictional and authentic violence has bombarded them that it becomes hard to distinguish between fiction and fact.

24 When this generation was preschool age, only one show (*Dragnet*) involving guns was among the Top 10 broadcast. Just five years later, seven of the Top 10 programs were saturated with killing. Listen to the titles: *Gunsmoke, Have Gun—Will Travel, The Rifleman, Maverick, Tales of Wells Fargo, Wagon Train, The Texan.*

25 Then a real live Texan devastated them once and for all. As the bullets crashed into John F. Kennedy, the hero-worshipping dreams and vicarious aspirations[21] of a whole generation were shattered. If this princely creature could be reduced to nothing by madness, on what could a future be built? *These youngsters plunged with their families into an average of 34 hours of immersion[22] in television coverage of the John F. Kennedy assassination and funeral.*

26 TV chronicled in minute detail the wreckage of their aspirations. It portrayed in anguished incredulity the utter insecurity and ultimate futility of what has been The American Dream, Camelot-come-true.[23]

27 No TV event, no public event, before or since, equaled that experience. Not in hours broadcast, personnel involved, expense incurred, viewers watching—or impact felt.

28 Things just never got any better. The next November they watched an earthy Lyndon B. Johnson ground the hawkish Barry Goldwater—and then fly off himself, escalating the horror of Vietnam and further foreclosing their future.

29 They came to know other public men, too. And just when TV had made them personally known, it showed them shot to death. These kids were there when towering men of the '60's fell.[24] Fiction became fact. Those more willing to kill than die survived and the kids had already had enough of killing.

LET IT ALL HANG OUT

30 Teen-agers avoid TV like the plague. No segment of our population watches less. The kids are out making music.

31 *Making* music, not just listening to it. They're playing guitars, kazoos, washtubs—anything they can get their hands on. They want to get into the act. They sat impassively[25] during their most formative[26] years, mesmerized[27] by TV. Now they've traded the meaningless picture of TV for the pictureless meaning of music.

32 No one should doubt the importance of their music. Sometimes

merely raucous and rapacious,[28] more often their music is profoundly searching, poignantly vulnerable.[29] It dignifies their humanity in a way television never did.

33 Then the films pick up the beat and visualize their new-found rhythm of life. "Blow-Up" and "Easy Rider" illustrated their perceptions and perplexities. "Elvira Madigan" and "Romeo and Juliet" celebrated their futility.

34 Both music and films have become occasions for communion among the young. Now hundreds of thousands of young pilgrims surge to a Woodstock music festival to be pressed together in the flesh. No more electronic images! They want to be where there's *life*.

TURN ON!

35 Teen-agers are the shock troops of a culture hooked on drugs. At a $100,000,000 annual clip, many TV commercials encourage us to expect miracles from drugs. The young apparently have been convinced. Soaring after Utopia or Nirvana[30] or Ultimate Reality, their crash landings have made lurid news.

36 Ironically, the last 20 years have been the age of genuine miracle drugs —including many of the Brand Name products. But some were deceptively advertised. Moreover, we deceived ourselves. We thought we could buy temporary relief indefinitely and would never have to grapple with the roots of our dissatisfaction. Now we're all reaping the whirlwind. (Same thing with sex. Teen-agers don't hold a sacrosanct[31] view of human sexuality. It's just sort of there. No particular value or virtue involved. And that's the way they saw it on TV. Sex is just another marketing tool. Use it to tease a would-be buyer of cat food or razor blades or something. Sex: use as needed to grease the Gross National Product.[32] Of *course* the kids don't value it. We didn't.)

THERE'S A NEW WORLD COMING

37 TV turned them on to more than drugs and sex, though. This younger generation is excitingly and energetically rejuvenating[33] our whole visual environment. They are flocking into art and filmmaking courses in record numbers. They are splashing psychedelic art everywhere, designing and wearing unique clothes, exercising our eyes with their graffiti[34] and optical poetry. Everywhere we turn, they stimulate our sight.

38 Eventually, they may even stimulate our vision, as well as our sight. For this generation was sent, when very young, on a prolonged pilgrimage in the twilight zone where reality and fantasy merge. TV obliterated[35] boundaries of mind and material for them.

39 Consequently, they don't settle for the mundane[36] definition of reality we swallowed unquestioningly. They're hungry to probe deeper. Hallucinogenic drugs, mysticism, hypnosis, astrology, religious agony and ecstasy. They are sometimes fearless and frequently foolish in their quest. But they are questing, like never before.

40 This pioneer TV generation has blazed new trails. True, television has taken its toll—trivializing adulthood, exploiting childhood, ignoring needs

while fabricating wants. But we also know that television is capable of decreasing prejudice, increasing wonder and anathematizing[37] war. And we've scarcely begun to take it seriously.

Notes

1 Unauthorized; not approved.
2 Closeness, warmth.
3 Triteness, staleness.
4 Premature, ahead of time.
5 Inflicting bodily injury on another so as to make him less able to defend himself.
6 A reference to the early years of childhood, before strong attachment is felt toward a parent of the opposite sex. The so-called Oedipus complex is the desire of a person for sexual gratification through a parent of the other sex. (Oedipus, a Greek legendary figure, unknowingly killed his father and married his mother.)
7 The existing power structure in a society; institutional authority.
8 Prosperous laziness.
9 Choices; other possibilities.
10 A reference to the fairy story in which a ruler is finally seen as he actually is.
11 Pretentious, inflated.
12 Violent in temper and speech.
13 Peculiarities, characteristic habits.
14 Pardon, forgiveness.
15 Obligation.
16 Inability to act; lack of ability brought about by fixed habits and customs.
17 Standardized and simplified conceptions or images.
18 Gift, something handed down from the past.
19 Rising force; increase in volume or loudness.
20 Removes.
21 Hopes felt, experienced, or enjoyed through someone else.
22 Deep engagement, absorption.
23 Camelot, the legendary site of King Arthur's court, has come to suggest any ideal place or type of government.
24 Both Martin Luther King, Jr., and Robert Kennedy were killed in 1968.
25 Unmoved, without emotion.
26 Shaping, molding.
27 Hypnotized, fascinated.
28 Loud and violent.
29 Distressingly weak; pitifully capable of being hurt.
30 Utopia, an imaginary island, suggests a place or state of perfection; Nirvana may be defined as a state or place where one is free from worry and pain.
31 Sacred, elevated.
32 The total monetary value of all services and goods produced in a country.
33 Restoring, renewing.
34 Words or phrases written in public places. *Optical poetry* appeals more to the eye than the ear.
35 Wiped out.
36 Common, ordinary.
37 Cursing, putting under a ban; detesting, loathing.

DARK GHETTO

Kenneth B. Clark

KENNETH BANCROFT CLARK (1914–) was born in the Panama Canal Zone and educated at Howard University (A.B. 1935) and Columbia (Ph.D. 1940). Dr. Clark has been a member of the psychology staff of the College (University) of the City of New York since 1942, a full professor since 1960. He has lectured widely at other universities and has served on numerous commissions dealing with social and educational problems throughout the United States. Among Clark's books are *Desegregation: An Appraisal of the Evidence* (1953), *Prejudice and Your Child* (1955), and *Dark Ghetto* (1965).

1 White America is basically a middle-class society; the middle class sets the mores[1] and the manners to which the upper class must, when it wishes influence, seek to conform, at least in appearances, and which the lower class struggles to attain or defensively rejects. But dark America, of the rural and of the urban Negro, has been automatically assigned to be a lower-class society; the lower class sets the mores and manners to which, if the Negro upper class wishes influence, it must appeal; and from which the Negro middle class struggles to escape. As long as this chasm between white and dark America is allowed to exist, racial tensions and conflict, hatred and fear will spread. The poor are always alienated[2] from normal society, and when the poor are Negro, as they increasingly are in American cities, a double trauma[3] exists—rejection on the basis of class and race is a danger to the stability of society as a whole. Even though Negroes are a minority in America—approximately one-tenth of the population—a minority that is sick with despair can poison the wellsprings from which the majority, too, must drink. The social dynamics[4] of the dark ghettos can be seen as the restless thrust of a lower-class group to rise into the middle class.[5]

* * *

2 The symptoms of lower-class society afflict the dark ghettos of America—low aspiration, poor education, family instability, illegitimacy, unemployment, crime, drug addiction and alcoholism, frequent illness and early death. But because Negroes begin with the primary affliction of inferior racial status, the burdens of despair and hatred are more pervasive.[6] Even initiative usually goes unrewarded as relatively few Negroes succeed in moving beyond menial[7] jobs, and those who do find racial discrimination everywhere they go.

3 The most concrete fact of the ghetto is its physical ugliness—the dirt, the filth, the neglect. In many stores walls are unpainted, windows are unwashed, service is poor, supplies are meager. The parks are seedy with lack of care. The streets are crowded with the people and refuse. In all of Harlem there is no museum,

no art gallery, no art school, no sustained "little theater" group; despite the stereotype[8] of the Negro as artist, there are only five libraries—but hundreds of bars, hundreds of churches, and scores of fortune tellers. Everywhere there are signs of fantasy, decay, abandonment, and defeat. The only constant characteristic is a sense of inadequacy. People seem to have given up in the little things that are so often the symbol of the larger things.

* * *

4 Given the chronic debasement and assaults on his ego, probably the most difficult feeling for any American Negro to maintain toward himself or any other Negro is that of stable and unqualified respect. His core of doubt about the qualifications and the price in integrity or honesty which the successful Negro must have paid, or even concerning his right to prominence in the face of the pervasive failure of his group, protrudes and contaminates the ability of one Negro to respect and to accept another Negro without ambivalence and skepticism.[9] This seems particularly true when the Negro seeks—and wins—recognition in fields not usually open to Negroes, and where competition and promotion are rigorously controlled by the most powerful whites of our society, e.g., diplomacy and the upper echelons[10] of the academic, business, and industrial world. It is less true in such fields as the arts, the theater, and athletics, where the talent and personal accomplishments of an individual Negro are not subject to ambiguous[11] interpretations: Marian Anderson met the clear test of a great singing voice; it is evident to all that Sidney Poitier and Sammy Davis, Jr., are great talents; that Jackie Robinson was a great ball player; and that Joe Louis knocked out nearly all of his opponents. But even in these cases of outstanding talent and skill among Negroes, it is possible for the masses of Negroes to obtain vicarious[12] satisfaction and release of their frustrations by identifying with them, admiring the talent without, ironically,[13] respecting the person who possesses it.

5 The effective use of the potential power of the Negro masses and the ability of Negro leaders to discipline and mobilize that power for constructive social change may well be determined by the ability of a critical mass of Negroes to control their ambivalence toward themselves and to develop the capacity for genuine and sustained respect for those Negroes who are worthy of confidence and respect. The present unrealities and distortions of ghetto life make it difficult to differentiate between empty flamboyance[14] and valid achievement; between hysterical, cynical, verbal manipulations and sound judgment.[15] It is difficult for the uneducated, exploited, and despised Negro to know whom he can trust and whom he must continue to suspect. He knows for sure only his own deep despair and resentment, and he sees that as long as the conditions which give rise to these feelings persist he will continue to be their victim. The compounded tragedy is that he will remain the chief victim also of himself. The real tragedy for the Negro is that he has not taken himself seriously because no one else has. The hope for the Negro is that now he is asserting that he really is a human being, and is demanding the rights

due to a human being. If he succeeds in winning these rights he will respect and trust himself, but he cannot win the right to human dignity without the ability to respect and cherish his own humanity in spite of pervasive white rejection.

* * *

6 Subtle tensions may result when whites themselves who harbor deep feelings of guilt about Negroes attempt prematurely and with exaggerated warmth to establish close relationships with them. This puts a strain on the Negro and makes it difficult for him to adjust normally. If the Negro rejects the overture[16] as an invasion of his individuality, the whites, in turn, may be bewildered and hurt, and regress[17] to a safe level of hostility and alienation. Few, if any, are capable of racelessness. But whites who try to be free must have the courage to accept the inevitable chaos and confusion of a changing society. There will be inevitable irrationalities[18] in any move to a higher stage of rationality and justice. Above all, one must not retreat in the face of pain. Anyone who cringes, who retreats to the insidious[19] conviction that things were more peaceful and, therefore, better when the Negro knew his place may find temporary security, but he has chosen the way of the past and instability.

7 The mistake is to seek for purity at all, and the white liberal no more than the Negro ought to expect of himself a superhuman response. Original innocence, if such a thing has meaning, can never be regained; in contemporary society, no one, Negro or white, can be totally without prejudice. No one should expect purity of himself or others. Any genuine relationship between Negro and white must face honestly all of the ambivalences both feel for each other. Each must identify with the other without sentiment. The white must resist the tendency to attribute all virtue to the underdog; he must respond insofar as he is able with a pure kind of empathy[20] that is raceless, that accepts and understands the frailties and anxieties and weaknesses that all men share, the common predicament of mankind.

8 Any white who dares to be free of the myths of race faces awkwardness and risk and a need to defend himself, even ironically, against Negroes themselves. For many Negroes prefer, unconsciously or not, a continuation of the double standard; their preference sometimes wears the guise[21] of an insistence on interpreting lack of prejudice as itself evidence of prejudice. Negroes are so accustomed to prejudice that many find it easier to deal with it than with a single standard of judgment for all men. It requires strength and courage for whites to persist in the face of such rejection. It is a temptation to retreat into sentimentality instead, and to be caught in the net of condescension, to say, "I would not want to hurt you because you are a Negro," and to suffocate the Negro with respect. Any white who refuses to be trapped into such an escape, and reaches the point of total liberation, will see and understand and act freely. He can never retreat, no matter what the threats, either to the sentimental lie or to the traditional racist lie; for the Negro is

watching and waiting, despite his cynicism and his suspicion, with the beginning of trust.

9 Those whites who are really committed to civil rights can make it clear to society at large that a significant minority of Americans will no longer accept equivocation and procrastination.[22] But it is far easier to deal with racial problems by writing letters to congressmen than to demonstrate one's own freedom. Every individual who rises above the constrictions of race is a demonstration that this is really possible. Every time a Negro sees a group of secretaries—white and Negro—chatting over lunch; or children—white and Negro—walking together to school, he feels that hope is possible. Every time his white friend shows he is not afraid to argue with him as with anyone else, he sees that freedom is possible, that there are some for whom race is irrelevant, who accept or reject a person not as a Negro or a white, but in terms of himself. Only so can the real confinements of the ghetto be broken. The Negro alone cannot win this fight that transcends[23] the "civil rights struggle." White and Negro must fight together for the rights of human beings to make mistakes and to aspire to human goals. Negroes will not break out of the barriers of the ghetto unless whites transcend the barriers of their own minds, for the ghetto is to the Negro a reflection of the ghetto in which the white lives imprisoned. The poetic irony of American race relations is that the rejected Negro must somehow also find the strength to free the privileged white.

Notes

1 Folkways, customs.
2 Turned away, cut off from.
3 Injury, shock, or startling experience.
4 Motivating or driving forces.
5 The excerpts that follow indicate that Clark has used Harlem, a section of New York City, as a symbol of the "dark" ghetto found in many areas throughout the Western world. A ghetto is a slum area thickly populated by one or more minority groups, often as a result of social or economic restrictions. The word *ghetto* is Italian in origin, possibly from "borghetto," a form of "borgo" meaning "a settlement outside the city wall."
6 Extended, spread widely.
7 Humble, degrading.
8 Simplified and standardized impression or image.
9 Positive and negative feelings combined with doubt or uncertainty.
10 Levels, ranks.
11 Open to various interpretations.
12 Felt through the experience of others.
13 In a contradictory way.
14 Showiness, display.
15 Between empty, exaggerated talk and reasoned thought.
16 Offer, proposal.
17 Go back, revert.
18 Absurd or illogical actions.
19 Deceitful, beguiling.

[20] Close identification with the feelings and thoughts of someone else.
[21] Appearance.
[22] Hedging (misleading) and delaying action.
[23] Rises above.

"THE OLD MAN'S WORDS WERE LIKE A CURSE"

Ralph Ellison

RALPH ELLISON (1914–) was born in Oklahoma City. He was a student at Tuskegee Institute, Alabama, 1933–1936. Ellison has received numerous honorary degrees and has lectured at several American universities. For many years he has been a prolific contributor of fiction and nonfiction to various magazines. *Invisible Man* (1952) is his major work, a powerful novel dealing with the growth and conflicts of a young American black.

1 It goes a long way back, some twenty years. All my life I had been looking for something, and everywhere I turned someone tried to tell me what it was. I accepted their answers too, though they were often in contradiction and even self-contradictory. I was naïve. I was looking for myself and asking everyone except myself questions which I, and only I, could answer. It took me a long time and much painful boomeranging of my expectations to achieve a realization everyone else appears to have been born with: That I am nobody but myself. But first I had to discover that I am an invisible man!

2 And yet I am no freak of nature, nor of history. I was in the cards, other things having been equal (or unequal) eighty-five years ago. I am not ashamed of my grandparents for having been slaves. I am only ashamed of myself for having at one time been ashamed. About eighty-five years ago they were told that they were free,[1] united with others of our country in everything pertaining to the common good, and, in everything social, separate like the fingers of the hand. And they believed it. They exulted[2] in it. They stayed in their place, worked hard, and brought up my father to do the same. But my grandfather is the one. He was an odd old guy, my grandfather, and I am told I take after him. It was he who caused the trouble. On his deathbed he called my father to him and said, "Son, after I'm gone I want you to keep up the good fight. I never told you, but our life is a war and I have been a traitor all my born days, a spy in the enemy's country ever since I give up my gun back in the Reconstruction.[3] Live with your head in the lion's mouth. I want you to overcome 'em with yeses, undermine 'em with grins, agree 'em to death and destruction, let 'em swoller you till they vomit

or bust wide open." They thought the old man had gone out of his mind. He had been the meekest of men. The younger children were rushed from the room, the shades drawn and the flame of the lamp turned so low that it sputtered on the wick like the old man's breathing. "Learn it to the younguns," he whispered fiercely; then he died.

3 But my folks were more alarmed over his last words than over his dying. It was as though he had not died at all, his words caused so much anxiety. I was warned emphatically to forget what he had said and, indeed, this is the first time it has been mentioned outside the family circle. It had a tremendous effect upon me, however. I could never be sure of what he meant. Grandfather had been a quiet old man who never made any trouble, yet on his deathbed he had called himself a traitor and a spy, and he had spoken of his meekness as a dangerous activity. It became a constant puzzle which lay unanswered in the back of my mind. And whenever things went well for me I remembered my grandfather and felt guilty and uncomfortable. It was as though I was carrying out his advice in spite of myself. And to make it worse, everyone loved me for it. I was praised by the most lily-white men of the town. I was considered an example of desirable conduct—just as my grandfather had been. And what puzzled me was that the old man had defined it as *treachery*. When I was praised for my conduct I felt a guilt that in some way I was doing something that was really against the wishes of the white folks, that if they had understood they would have desired me to act just the opposite, that I should have been sulky and mean, and that that really would have been what they wanted, even though they were fooled and thought they wanted me to act as I did. It made me afraid that some day they would look upon me as a traitor and I would be lost. Still I was more afraid to act any other way because they didn't like that at all. The old man's words were like a curse.[4]

Notes

[1] On January 1, 1863, President Lincoln signed the Emancipation Proclamation, freeing slaves in those territories in rebellion against the Union.

[2] Rejoiced.

[3] The period following the Civil War, 1865–1877.

[4] The "curse" to which the author refers is reflected in Ellison's own despairing comment: "There is no stability anywhere and there will not be for many years to come, and progress now insistently asserts its tragic side; the evil now stares out of the bright sunlight." This selection should be compared with that by James Baldwin later in this book.

ON THE BEACH

Caskie Stinnett

CASKIE STINNETT (1911–) was born in Remington, Virginia, and was graduated from the College of William and Mary in 1932. He began his career as a reporter for the Staunton, Virginia, *News-Leader* and in 1936 served with the U.S. government in Washington as an information specialist. In 1945 he entered magazine work; in 1967 he became editor of *Holiday Magazine.* He is author of *Will Not Run Feb. 22nd* (1956); *Out of the Red* (1960); and *Back to Abnormal* (1963), from which the following essay is taken. He contributes articles to many popular magazines and is a lecturer on humor.

1 For a long time (too long, it now appears) we watched with strained tolerance the struggle between men and women which, in retrospect, seems to have left the cold-war stage right after World War II. For a while it was fun to watch, the women being absurdly arrogant[1] as they got a better grip on their authority and the men being petulant[2] as they discovered no one was impressed any longer with their Clarence Day[3] attitudes, when suddenly the laughter left and the whole thing took on a life-and-death character. We used to think one of our finest moments was to lean an arm on a mantelpiece, swirl the olive in our glass, and tell our fellow dinner guests —in a first-rate Peter DeVries[4] manner—how we felt about the thing: "In the war between the sexes," we would say owlishly, "we are a conscientious objector." It was a good line, all right, but we don't say it any more, for the same reason, perhaps, that Chamberlain[5] suddenly stopped saying that all Hitler wanted to do was to take back the Fatherland. One day Man was the stronger sex, the next day he was just bewildered, groping through the reference books to see where nature, God, and his own philosophers had let him down.

2 In the first flush of their victory, the Women were generous. All they wanted was Equality, they said, nothing more. When they reached that point, though, they didn't pause long enough to touch up their lipstick. Oh, some things that were well established could go on, the victors said. Men could continue to die younger than women, the incidence[6] of widowhood could continue its ascent, construction work and stoop-labor could remain the right of man, and, if they wanted to, they could continue to paint the greatest pictures, write the greatest books, compose the greatest symphonies, and think the loftiest thoughts. None of that would be disturbed, they promised, if man recognized his place and kept in it. Any student of history knew this couldn't work; the victor can't grant the vanquished equality. It didn't work, and Women soon dropped the pretense.

3 Well, we've brooded about this a good bit, along with some other poor losers, and we're willing to concede the battle lost but hope something can

be salvaged from the reconstruction period that lies ahead. To that end, we've been reading the works of our leading traitors—D. H. Lawrence, Ashley Montagu,[7] and others who have supported Woman in her belief that she must control the world. From our reading has come a sort of pleasant confusion—exactly the kind of confusion which makes men so lovable and so frightening (wanting to believe what they read, but at the same time fighting every idea). More than anything else, the thing that really halts our progress is the image which emerges from these writings of Woman as a special creature, a creature of uncommon prescience,[8] of understanding of such depth that man can only estimate it, of such vision that, by comparison, Man is little more than a Cub Scout, of masterful intrigue and diplomacy, and, above all, a creature who is a victim of almost total misunderstanding.

4 It's that last we balk at. Women are understood much better than they think. It's an old stunt, when you're trying to get away with something, to take on an aura of mystery. Kids do it all the time, but with only moderate success, because other kids see through the trick instantly. We know what women want: they want tenderness, warmth, kindness, and compassion. But they shouldn't take it by force.

Notes

1 Haughty, overbearing.

2 Showing sudden, impatient irritation.

3 Clarence Day (1874–1935) was a sardonic American humorist whose *Life with Father* described a bossy, demanding individual.

4 An American novelist noted for witty and satirical observations about contemporary living.

5 Neville Chamberlain (1869–1940) was prime minister of England during Hitler's rise to power.

6 Rate.

7 English authors who have upheld and advanced the cause and role of women.

8 Foresight, advance understanding.

A REMARKABLE AND MARVELOUS SEX[1]

Estelle Ramey

ESTELLE R. RAMEY (1917–) was born in Detroit. She holds a master's degree from Columbia University and a Ph.D. from the University of Chicago. In 1965 she became a professor of physiology at the medical school of Georgetown University.

Dear God! What does a woman want?—DR. SIGMUND FREUD[2]

Every girl wants to be like her mother.—DR. BENJAMIN SPOCK[3]

What would have happened at the Bay of Pigs if a woman had been in control?
—DR. EDGAR BERMAN

1 When I first read the headline "Doctor Asserts Women Are Unfit for Top Jobs," I thought there must be some mistake. People just don't say things like that in public any more. But I was wrong. Dr. Edgar F. Berman, a former surgeon, a friend and adviser to Hubert Humphrey, and a onetime State Department consultant on Latin American health problems, had indeed said to fellow Democrats, to the press, and for all the world to hear that women, with their monthly "raging hormonal imbalances," turn into unstable creatures, too irrational to be trusted with the highest positions of responsibility.

2 Whenever men argue that women after all *are* biologically different, they really don't mean different; they mean inferior—in terms of stamina, stability, and cerebration.[4] The term "biologically different" has the neat effect of taking the whole subject out of the realm of personal masculine prejudice and landing it squarely in the lap of impartial science: it's not a man's fault that women are relegated to less important, less interesting occupations; it's just the way the evolutionary cookie crumbled. And, as Freud exclaimed, "Dear God! What does a woman want?" Why should some women get upset by this natural stacking of the deck when they have so many other attractive biologic attributes? Besides, they make such great wives and mothers.

3 As a child of my culture, I don't mind getting involved occasionally in the fun and games of being treated like a fragile flower. But as a physiologist[5] working with the unromantic scientific facts of life, I find it hard to delude myself about feminine frailty.

4 I know that when it comes to survival, it should have been a Frenchwoman rather than a Frenchman who cried: "*Vive la différence!*"[6] Men have big muscles; but in the game of durability their "delicate" wives hold the protoplasmic aces. Any insurance actuary knows that men collapse faster under the psychic and physical stresses of living. Men are a dear and wonderful tribe, and they often make great husbands and fathers; but we all must face the fact that genetically they are the weaker sex. That well-advertised Y chromosome[7] of theirs is, literally, almost a blank.

5 Contrary to current fashionable nonsense about the inborn defects of *female* physiology, women are, in fact, a remarkable and marvelous sex. Dear Dr. Berman: I think it's time to restate a plain old scientific truth: The female of the species, *any* species, is sturdier than the male from the moment of conception to the last hurrah.

6 Evidence collected by a well-known endocrinologist,[8] Dr. James B. Hamilton, shows that, from worms to humans, the male is less able to tolerate life's everyday stresses. Dr. Hamilton also notes: "There can be little doubt that the male has a higher mortality rate in almost all forms of animal life studied thus far."

7 In my work with Dr. Maurice S. Goldstein, of McGill University, we found that in such traumas[9] as hemorrhage and neurological shock male rats and rabbits suffered more than their female counterparts. I have no idea how male rats and rabbits feel about sharing responsibilities with female rats and rabbits; but whatever their attitudes, I doubt that it had much effect on the kind of data we obtained.

8 When I reviewed the available literature on how stress and disease affect males and females, I was struck by the fact that there has been astonishingly little basic research on the dismal survival record of the male —even though the phenomenon was noted at least as early as 1786. You might expect the subject to rate top priority, because, after all, it is a matter of life and death. But perhaps men, who constitute the vast majority of research scientists and physicians, would rather not think about the implications of such research. How disconcerting it would be to discover that evolution had reserved some of its choicest genetic gifts for the female!

9 Surprisingly, many more boys than girls are conceived, but about 12 percent more male than female fetuses die before delivery. Yet even with this early male attrition, 105 boys are born for every 100 girls. During the first week of life, the death rate is 32 percent greater for males than for females. Significantly, the sex difference in survival shows up long before society has a chance to impose its special stresses on boys and men. With every year, the dreary disparity[10] between male and female durability inexorably[11] increases. No wonder those retirement paradises have many more beauty salons than barbershops. And no wonder lonely widows find their genetic bonus a Pyrrhic victory.[12]

10 There are few scientific explanations for male fragility. The cardiovascular disorders, like coronary disease, have a much higher incidence in men even in early youth. Part of the problem may be the environmental stresses imposed on men by society —to compete, to produce, to succeed. Part of the problem may be hormonal. Dr. Hamilton's findings suggest that the male hormone testosterone induces a slightly higher metabolic rate in most tissues and that the male thus "burns out" faster. Other research indicates that the female's estrogen hormones may help retard the aging of blood vessels—something testosterone does not do. To be sure, testosterone is a delightful hormone, as hormones go, but I must say the estrogens seem to be much more helpful physiologically.

11 That is why I was startled to read Dr. Berman's attempt to give the ancient concept of woman's predestined inferiority a firm scientific basis. He suggested that if women, with their raging hormones, were allowed to make really important decisions, our perfect male-run society would be plunged into a female morass[13] of racial strife, air pollution, inflation, student riots, wars, famine, hijackings, and midi skirts. The mind boggles. What would have happened at the Bay of Pigs,[14] asked Dr. Berman, if a woman had been in control? All I can ask is what *did* happen? And who *was* in control?

12 Dr. Berman went on to suggest that most honest physicians secretly agree with him but are too chicken to speak out and antagonize the harridans[15] of the Women's Liberation Movement or their own rich women patients. One must admire Dr. Berman's self-sacrifice: he gladly suffered political martyrdom in order to protect society from women and women from society.

13 All this would be a teapot tempest[16] except that it strikes at the heart of human relations. If women are inevitably doomed to defective brain function because of their normal hormonal secretions, then they are indeed biologic seconds, and every roadblock should be placed in their way as they try to join men in making the vital decisions of the world. "Anatomy is destiny," Sigmund Freud once said, as he consigned women to the nursery. "Women are made to be concerned first and foremost with child care, husband care, and home care," Dr. Benjamin Spock said, fully concurring with Dr. Freud. "Genes are our fate and hormones our masters," Dr. Berman said, as he firmly closed the door of the White House executive suite to all people who have ovaries.[17]

14 I rather like the phrase "anatomy is destiny." It has a certain ring, and it happens to be true. It means that if you have ovaries, you'll never be a father. If you have testes,[18] you'll never be a mother. If you are a cocker spaniel, you might as well forget about becoming head of General Motors. And if my grandmother had wheels, she would have been a station wagon.

15 It does *not* mean that if you have ovaries instead of testes, you might as well forget about becoming a Senator, or a physicist, or a prime minister, or President of the United States. Or even a surgeon.

16 It is interesting that Dr. Berman latched onto the menstrual cycle to keep women at bay. Their cyclic bleeding has fascinated and repelled men ever since Homo sapiens[19] first started to assign social roles. Most primitive societies and religions reflected this awe and repugnance. Menstruating women were taboo and were temporarily expelled from the tribe, which considered them under a curse visited by the gods. These days we hear pseudoscientific terms about women's "raging hormonal imbalances," but atavistic[20] instincts are still whispering: "They are accursed."

17 Women themselves have accepted this distorted view of their own biology. They still call menstruation the curse. Many women do have some discomfort during their periods. But it is usually mild and seldom affects the efficiency of women who have responsibilities they feel strongly about. Some women get quite ill for a day or two; most don't. Despite popular belief that working women are home sick more frequently than men, extensive federal studies in every job category indicate that women take less time off from work—including *pregnancy leaves*—than men do.

18 Of course, men have endocrine problems, too. They may suffer thyroid disease, infertility, impotence, Addison's disease, diabetes, pituitary disease, and a host of other endocrine ailments to which we are all heir. But they often serve effectively in high

jobs and high office. John Kennedy had a serious hormonal disorder, adrenal insufficiency. Everyone who lives long enough deteriorates physically. By the time a man is old enough to be within hailing distance of the Presidency, you can be sure he has something the matter with him. His blood vessels, his stomach, and anything else aren't what they were when he was sixteen.

19 A woman of that age isn't in "perfect" health, either, but she has a better statistical chance of remaining sturdier. We hope for relative emotional and physical stability in our leaders, and sometimes we get it. Women, given the chance, might actually have a better track record than men, because their blood vessels don't narrow as fast with age, and the blood supply to their brains is therefore better maintained over a longer period of time.

20 None of this convinces the Dr. Bermans of the world that women may have the capacity for the highest leadership. Even when they act like men, they just aren't gentlemen. Don't they cry while men keep a stiff upper lip? Well, there are worse responses to life's problems than crying. Suicide, for example. U.S. Public Health data shows that females have a much lower suicidal death rate—about one third that of males. Although many more women seemingly attempt suicide, they often carefully stop short of dying, as if demanding help in the most dramatic way they know. Men make unsuccessful attempts less frequently; they just write off society and themselves. Maybe more men should cry.

21 I am often asked why so few women achieve professional distinction in this country. Why are only 6.7 percent of our practicing physicians and 3 percent of our lawyers and 1 percent of our United States Senators women? Could there be sex differences in IQs? No. The accumulated evidence shows that on all forms of standardized testing the female IQ is not significantly different from the male's. There are differences in various skills, but they seem to be directly related to the way we bring up boys and girls. We encourage even the smallest boy to innovate,[21] but we praise little girls for conforming. Creativity, by definition, is nonconformity, and brains need to be exercised. No major innate[22] differences have been documented.

22 Psychologist Lewis Terman's long-term study, started in 1920 with a matched group of extremely gifted boys and girls wth IQs over 150, showed that the gifted girls did not complete as many advanced-education courses as the gifted boys and did not use their education professionally to the same degree. As these women became less involved with intellectual pursuits and more involved with traditional female tasks, their performance on intelligence tests no longer matched the men's.

23 Few of these brilliant women tried to develop their intellectual talents simply because there has been a very small market for brilliant women in this country. Before a woman could become a full professor at Harvard, say, or a member of the National Academy of Sciences, she would first virtually need to receive a Nobel Prize. Besides, her professional tenac-

ity[23] might have discouraged prospective husbands—and that's serious.

24 The relatively few women who have bothered to develop their intellectual skills often find that society views them as oddballs. Men have told me more than once: "You certainly don't look like a woman scientist." I know exactly what they mean, and I thank them warmly. Their notion of a Woman Scientist is that horse-faced, flat-chested female in arch-support shoes who sublimates her sex starvation in a passionate pursuit of laboratory data and economy tours of European museums.

25 Such stereotypes[24] are bred in the marrow of our society and discourage most bright girls from the start. Medical-school admissions committees don't have to work hard to discriminate against women applicants. Not many women even bother to apply. We end up with fewer women physicians than almost any country except Spain, Madagascar, and South Vietnam. Even Switzerland, where women don't yet have the vote, has almost twice the percentage of women in medical school as we do. Yet we send more girls to college than does any other country in the world. Why? Because that's where the best husbands are to be found.

26 So we have a very large reserve of female human beings, superbly endowed physically and intellectually, but sharply limited in opportunities for social problem-solving in a society that desperately needs all the trained brains it can get. Many of these bright, accomplished, and frustrated women don't even try very hard to find out why their men are willing to pay any price, sometimes even their own life, for the privilege of getting out of the house, away from the wife and the kids, out into the world where the action is, to any job, however dull, anywhere but the security and comfort of the home.

27 Could it be possible that security and comfort are not the *ne plus ultra*[25] of human happiness? I think so. After all, women in harems have reached the ultimate in security and comfort—they don't have to worry about anything; they just have to wait their turn.

28 No society is so rich that it can afford to waste educated brain power. We cannot continue to underuse our expensively trained women while we overuse and casually expend our equally expensively trained men. It is not enough to advise an anxious wife to shovel the snow off the walk herself or to cook low-fat meals to protect her husband's heart. Given a man's greater innate susceptibility to life's stresses, we must stop compounding his problems of survival by insisting he carry society's managerial burdens like limpets on his shoulders. Men need protection, and women have been delinquent in not providing it by really sharing the burdens.

29 I don't expect that equality for women will necessarily bring manna[26] from above. Women are not that different from men, who, despite all their advantages, have only realized their full potential in painfully small numbers. Women's Liberation won't produce a million female Jeffersons and Einsteins. But just one such woman might change the world, and

we must make it easier for her to surface and for all her sisters to use the talents they have as they choose.

30 Dr. Berman and I are, after all, beating a dead horse. Societal roles cannot be assigned on the basis of some stereotype of male or female capacity for leadership. As a society, we must learn to answer as Samuel Johnson[27] did when he was asked the question, "Which is more intelligent, man or woman?" To which Dr. Johnson replied: "Which man and which woman?"

Notes

1 This article appeared in *McCall's Magazine* (January 1971) under the title "Well, Fellows, What Did Happen at the Bay of Pigs and Who Was in Control?"

2 An Austrian neurologist and founder of psychoanalysis (1856–1939).

3 American physician (pediatrician), born in 1903. Famous for his books on baby care and child-rearing, Dr. Spock is also active in politics.

4 Thinking; use of the mind.

5 A specialist in the functions of living organisms.

6 "Long live [Hooray for] the difference."

7 A sex chromosome (threadlike body in a cell nucleus carrying genes) that produces male characteristics in man and most mammals.

8 Specialist in the endocrine glands and their secretions. Among the endocrine glands are the pituitary, adrenal, and thyroid.

9 Bodily injury produced by violence; startling experience.

10 Inequality, difference.

11 Unalterably; not to be moved or changed.

12 A victory obtained at too great cost. The phrase is taken from the name of an ancient king, Pyrrhus, who won a battle but lost most of his army while doing so.

13 Bog, marsh.

14 The U.S.-supported Cuban invasion in April 1961 that failed and led to the strengthening of the Castro regime in Cuba. Later, President Kennedy ordered a naval quarantine of Cuba to eliminate a threat to American security.

15 Hags; scolding women.

16 A minor matter.

17 Female gonads (reproductive glands).

18 Male gonads (reproductive glands).

19 Man.

20 Reverting to or suggesting the characteristics or beliefs of a remote ancestor.

21 Introduce something new; make changes; experiment.

22 Inborn, native.

23 Act of holding fast, of hanging on.

24 Standardized, simplified opinions or images.

25 The highest point.

26 A gift from heaven. In Exodus 16, an account is provided of how food was miraculously supplied to Israelites in the wilderness.

27 Dr. Samuel Johnson (1709–1784), English critic and dictionary-maker.

HATRED

John Ciardi

JOHN CIARDI (1916–) was born in Boston and studied at Bates College and Tufts University. He received his master's degree from the University of Michigan in 1939. He has taught at the University of Kansas City, Harvard, and Rutgers. The author of several volumes of poetry, he became poetry editor of *The Saturday Review* in 1956. Among the books he has published are *Person to Person* (1964) and *An Alphabestiary* (1966).

1 Our local high school's graduation ceremonies were scheduled for the football stadium with the high school gym as a rain site.

2 Graduation day built up to a soggy swelter. My daughter was to graduate, en route to Swarthmore in September, and all day long she and her classmates were running in and out of the house, dripping excitement, plans, and sweat.

3 The graduating class planned the symbolic[1] release of two white doves during the ceremony, and the doves had to be visited and admired. One group had decided to wear armbands sporting a white dove. Another announced it would distribute small American flags to pin on the shoulder of their academic gowns. The intent of the flag-distributors was clearly to distinguish between patriotic Americans and peace doves, and the doves had to meet and discuss this affront[2] to their motives—which they solved by deciding to wear both insignia.

4 There were other momentous decisions. Mom had to be asked which ribbon looked best on the graduation dress that would in any case be covered by the blue imitation-academic gown. There would be many parties that night, and itineraries[3] had to be discussed if not planned. If they drew and donned their regalia early, Dad would have a chance to snap away with the Polaroid, and that, of course, had to be planned in frivolous[4] detail. There was more excitement than purpose in the discussions. Having decided weeks ago exactly how they would plan things, they had to reconvene every half-hour to discuss all the plans again.

5 At 5, with the interminables[5] set for 6:30, the swelter turned into a spurt of showers, the showers fading into a steady drizzle that managed to cool nothing while raising the humidity. We were in for it. The gym was an airless box with too few windows too high in one wall, and, as it turned out, the slant of the drizzle was such that even those inadequate vents had to be closed. Add about 300 graduates and more than a thousand parents and friends, and we were in for a Black Hole of Calcutta[6] painted an institutional beige.

6 A psychic year and two quarts of sweat later the class had death-

marched its way to its places, the band had ground out its approximate and endless tonalities,[7] the choir had piped distantly with that aggressive indifference to human suffering that motivates all music teachers given a chance to "offer their program," and after some blessedly brief and unrhetorical remarks by the class president, the salutatorian[8] came on, an earnest young man with a carefully compiled list of the issues of all our lives.

7 He began by condemning the school system for the endless flow of busy work it had handed out to him in place of a questing education, and he made firm points, though just a bit overfirmly. I found him honorable, refreshing, and relentless. Having just discovered the world, he had yet to discover any doubts about his discovery. Yet he was asking hard questions and asking them well. Some freshman instructor, I found myself thinking, would find in this lad his recompense[9] for the illiterate year. Once softened by a reasonable uncertainty, this would be an intellect. At the moment, however, he had won his honors by what he called "an unthinking docility,"[10] and he was in a mood to savor them.

8 Having categorized[11] the school system, he moved on to the war in Asia, to the race issue, to pollution, to the lack of confidence in the federal government, to the military-industrial complex, to unrest, to the dedication of the socially committed young. He had, as I recall, just mourned the deaths at Kent State as a sign of police repression when a voice from the audience called: "Is this a graduation or a rally?"

9 There were anger and hatred in that voice, and it was instantly joined by a chorus of jeers that seemed to have been waiting only for a signal. There was more than a physical swelter in the room. For a moment there seemed even to be the possibility of violence. Certainly there was a pent rancor[12] against anyone who would question, who declared a difference, who dared "rock the boat." I thought of the hardhats[13] invading Wall Street, righteous and truculent[14]—except, alas, that these were neighbors and parents, and they were disrupting their own children's chosen spokesman.

10 As noted, the boy was a bit gauche[15] in his sense of certainty. But it was not his rhetoric that had moved this hatred. The jeerers would have sat patiently through any number of round, smooth platitudes.[16] His offense had been to question established values, and the answer to such questioning had become a brawl of catcalls and red-faced shouts. Nor were the hecklers in a mood to quit. It took both the superintendent of schools and the president of the board of education, speaking in turn, to assert the boy's right to speak, and to restore a grumbling sort of order. The president's remarks on freedom of speech provided a countercue to those who identified with the boy, and a handful of parents and friends—perhaps as many as 3 per cent—stood up to applaud.

11 Then it happened. The few who stood in the audience to applaud passed on one of those indefinable crowd signals to the graduating class, and the class responded by standing to applaud. Perhaps as many as 60

or 70 per cent of the graduates rose—certainly well over half of them. For an instant then that sweat box contained an epiphany[17] of the generation gap.

12 On both sides, of course, there were dissenters, as there were those who would not get involved, as there were, I suppose, a few sheep who rose because those around them were rising.

13 Yet the difference in proportion was overwhelming: among the parents perhaps as many as 3 per cent declaring themselves, among the graduates a clear majority—one side and another of a mood, of a commitment, and of a climate of ideas; one side and another of a community's image of itself.

14 It will do me for a pictogram.[18] The line between the age groups has seldom been more clearly drawn. If I confess that what little is left of my hope rides with the young, the difference would be as visible to one with opposite views, so long as he is willing to open his eyes to a view. We are divided, the picture says, and I see small hope of a kindly tolerance across that division.

15 Yet, as nearly as I can sense the mood of a crowd—and I speak as an old manipulator[19] of audiences—the flow of hatred was all from the old to the young. The graduates rose not against but for, not in hatred of their parents and neighbors but in affirmation of their classmate's right to speak.

16 It is a mad world in which the young must be tolerant of the intolerant old, in which the young must accept the hatred of their elders and return not hatred but dissent.

17 Think, neighbors; for God's sake think. It may be righteously self-satisfying to ask—I have heard you ask it—"Why do they hate us?" It will be more useful to ask, "Why do we hate them?" You know why of course. They tell all of us that we have given our lives in tawdry[20] faith to tin gods. They dismiss our sacrifices and our hypocrisies as pointless. They cancel us. And we hate them for it. Even though they are probably right. Especially because they are probably right.

Notes

[1] Representational; the use of something to stand for something else. Here, doves are symbols of peace.

[2] Offense, challenge.

[3] Travel plans and routes.

[4] Unimportant, trifling.

[5] Lengthy (really, unending) events.

[6] In 1756, more than 100 Europeans were suffocated in a small prison cell in Calcutta, India.

[7] Sounds.

[8] A student, often the second-ranked person in a class, who delivers a "greeting" at commencement exercises.

[9] Reward.

[10] Capable of being managed, handled, and taught.

[11] Classified, defined.

[12] Resentment, hostility.

[13] Construction workers who wear protective helmets.
[14] Hostile, aggressive.
[15] Crude, tactless.
[16] Dull, trite remarks.
[17] A moment of insight, sudden understanding, or revelation.
[18] A pictorial representation of an idea.
[19] Handler, manager.
[20] Cheap, showy.

THE NEW COMPUTERIZED AGE: NO LIFE UNTOUCHED

David Sarnoff

DAVID SARNOFF (1891–1971) was born in Russia and was brought to America at the age of nine. He was educated in public schools in Brooklyn, New York, and at Pratt Institute. In 1919, he began his lifelong association with the Radio Corporation of America and was Chairman of the Board from 1947 until his death. His interest in science and engineering was intense and unflagging throughout his life.

1 In our increasingly complex world, information is becoming the basic building block of society. However, at a time when the acquisition of new scientific information alone is approaching a rate of 250 million pages annually, the tide of knowledge is overwhelming the human capability for dealing with it. So man must turn to a machine if he hopes to contain the tide and channel it to beneficial ends.

2 The electronic computer, handling millions of facts with the swiftness of light, has given contemporary meaning to Aristotle's[1] vision of the liberating possibilities of machines: "When looms weave by themselves, man's slavery will end." By transforming the way in which he gathers, stores, retrieves, and uses information, this versatile[2] instrument is helping man to overcome his mental and physical limitations. It is vastly widening his intellectual horizon, enabling him better to comprehend his universe, and providing the means to master that portion of it lying within his reach.

3 Although we are barely in the second decade of electronic data processing, the outlines of its influence on our culture are beginning to emerge. Far from depersonalizing the individual and dehumanizing his society, the computer[3] promises a degree of personalized service never before available to mankind.

4 By the end of the century, for the equivalent of a few dollars a month, the individual will have a vast complex of computer services at his command. Information utilities will make computing power available, like elec-

tricity, to thousands of users simultaneously. The computer in the home will be joined to a national and global computer system that provides services ranging from banking and travel facilities to library research and medical care. High-speed communications devices, linked to satellites in space, will transmit data to and from virtually any point on earth with the ease of a dial system. Students, businessmen, scientists, government officials, and housewives will converse with computers as readily as they now talk by telephone.

5 In the health field, computers will be employed to maintain a complete medical profile on every person in the country from the hour of birth. The record will be constantly updated by a regional computer for immediate access by doctors or hospital personnel. The computer also will maintain files on every known ailment, its symptoms, diagnosis, and treatment. A doctor will communicate a patient's symptoms to the computer center and within seconds receive suggestions for treatment based both on the symptoms and the patient's history.

6 Computers will handle the nation's fiscal transactions[4] from a central credit information exchange, to which all banks, business enterprises, and individuals will be connected. Purchases will be made, funds invested, and loans issued by transfers of credit within the computer without a dollar or penny physically exchanging hands. Even the soil will be computerized. The long-range outlook for agriculture includes new sensing devices that will be placed on larger farms, feeding information to the computer on soil moisture, temperature, weather outlook, and other details. The computer will calculate the best crops to plant, the best seeding times, the amount of fertilizer, and even the correct harvesting time for maximum yield.

7 Some of the most profound changes wrought by the computer will be in education. Here, the machine will do more than assist students to solve problems and to locate up-to-date information: It will fundamentally improve and enrich the entire learning process. The student's educational experience will be analyzed by the computer from the primary grades through university. Computer-based teaching machines, programed and operated by teachers thoroughly trained in electronic data processing[5] techniques, will instruct students at the rate best suited to each individual. The concept of mass education will give way to the concept of personal tutoring, with the teacher and the computer working as a team. Computers will bring many new learning dimensions to the classroom. For example, they will simulate nuclear reactors[6] and other complex, dangerous, or remote systems, enabling students to learn through a form of experience what could formerly be taught only in theory.

8 The computer's participation in the field of learning will continue long after the end of formal education. The government estimates that 50 per cent of the jobs to be held ten years from now do not even exist today. With this tremendous rate of occupational obsolescence,[7] future generations of Americans may pursue two or three careers during their lifetimes. The home computer will aid in develop-

ing career mobility by providing continuing self-instruction.

9 Just as it is recasting the educational process, the computer is also fundamentally changing the production and distribution of the printed word. Five centuries ago, Gutenberg[8] broke words into individual letters. Electronic composition now breaks the letters into tiny patterns of dots that are stored in the computer's memory. Any character can be called up by the computer, written on the face of a cathode ray tube,[9] and reproduced on film or paper in thousandths of a second. Nothing moves except the electrons.

10 When the electronic computer first appeared in composition rooms and printing shops several years ago, its job was to hyphenate words and justify text. But the computer, working at speeds of thousands of words a minute, was driving mechanical typesetting devices capable of setting only a few words per minute. Now, the development of computerized composition makes it possible to set text at hundreds of lines per minute. Photographs and drawings will be set the same way. Since the printed picture is itself a dot structure, the computer can electronically scan any photograph or drawing, reduce it to dots and store it, then retrieve it and beam it on a cathode ray tube for immediate reproduction.

11 In the future, electronics will develop processes that will make it possible to go from final copy and illustrations to printing in one integrated[10] electronic process. One result will be that newspapers, in the foreseeable future, will no longer be printed in a single location. Instead, they will be transmitted through computers in complete page form to regional electronic printing centers that will turn out special editions for the areas they govern. Local news and advertising will be inserted on the spot. Eventually, the newspaper can be reproduced in the home through a small copying device functioning as part of a home communications center.

12 Basic changes also will come to other areas of the printed word. For example, of the more than one billion books published every year, almost half are textbooks. The growth of knowledge and the factor of obsolescence mean that these texts must be supplemented by a professor's mimeographed notes. Today, these notes have a small distribution of only a few hundred copies. Computers will make it possible to catalogue this information and thus broaden its availability.

13 At the turn of the century, most large universities will not only have electronic composition systems that allow them to reprint original research, theses, or course notes upon demand; they will also have a computerized information retrieval[11] library. This process of information retrieval can be duplicated in almost any other field. The scientist will have the latest technical papers culled by the computer and reproduced in the laboratory or home. The computer will bring to the attorney all the pertinent[12] laws, decisions, and precedents on any case that concerns him. The business executive need not rush to the office every morning; most of the information he will need to conduct his business will be run off for

him at home, and he will have a two-way national and global closed-circuit television, via satellites for meetings and conferences.

14 Some of these developments are probabilities, some of them are certainties, and all of them are or soon will be within the capabilities of the computer art. But one fact is absolute: the incredible growth of the computer in numbers, power, and availability.

15 In just ten years, the typical electronic data processor has become ten times smaller, 100 times faster and 1,000 times less expensive to operate. These trends will continue, and our national computing power, which is doubling every year, will soon be sufficient to make the computer a genuinely universal tool.

16 In 1956, there were fewer than 1,000 computers in the United States. Today there are 30,000, or more than $11 billion worth; and by 1976 the machine population may reach 100,000. And these figures will, of course, be greatly increased through the growth of data processing in other nations.

17 A decade ago, our machines were capable of 12 billion computations per hour; today, they can do more than 20 trillion, and by 1976—a decade from now—they will attain 400 trillion—or about two billion computations per hour for every man, woman and child. Quite evidently the threshold of the computer age has barely been crossed.

18 Nevertheless, for all its potential to stretch the mind a thousandfold, it is perhaps necessary to point out that the computer is still a thing—that it cannot see, feel, or act unless first acted upon. Its value depends upon man's ability to use it with purpose and intelligence. If his postulates[13] are wrong, the computerized future can only be a massive enlargement of human error.

19 Ramsay MacDonald[14] once warned against "an attempt to clothe unreality in the garb of mathematical reality." Computers echo this warning. For they cannot usurp man's unique ability to blend intuition with fact, to feel as well as think. In the end, this remains the basis of human progress.

20 The task ahead will be to assign to the machine those things which it can best do, and reserve for man those things which he must provide and control. It is my conviction that society will adjust itself to the computer and work in harmony with it for the genuine betterment of life.

Notes

[1] Aristotle (384–322 B.C.) was a Greek philosopher, the pupil of Plato and tutor of Alexander the Great.

[2] Capable of many uses.

[3] This now-universal term may be defined in several ways. Basically, a *computer* is an apparatus which through mechanical or electronic processes is capable of carrying out complex mathematical and other kinds of operations at high speeds.

[4] Financial matters in general.

[5] The use of electronic computers in the handling of information.

[6] Apparatuses in which nuclear-fission chain reactions can be initiated or controlled for the purpose of generating heat and producing useful radiation.

7 Passed out of use; outdated, outmoded.
8 Johannes Gutenberg (1400–1468), a German printer credited with the invention of printing from movable type.
9 A vacuum tube that generates a beam of electrons.
10 United, tied together.
11 The systematic recovery of data; the memory bank of a computer.
12 Fitting, appropriate.
13 Assumptions, propositions.
14 British statesman and labor leader, 1866–1937.

THE COMPUTER AND THE POET

Norman Cousins

NORMAN COUSINS (1912–) was born in Union Hill, New Jersey, and was a student at Columbia University. He is the holder of honorary degrees from several American colleges and universities and is widely known as a lecturer on literary, cultural, and political subjects. From 1940 until 1971 he was connected with the *Saturday Review* as executive editor, editor, and president. In 1972, he founded *World*, a magazine concerned with ideas and the arts—cultural events on a world scale. Among Cousins's many books are *Modern Man Is Obsolete* (1945), *Talks with Nehru* (1951), *In Place of Folly* (1961).

1 The essential problem of man in a computerized age remains the same as it has always been. That problem is not solely how to be more productive, more comfortable, more content, but how to be more sensitive, more sensible, more proportionate,[1] more alive. The computer makes possible a phenomenal leap in human proficiency; it demolishes the fences around the practical and even the theoretical intelligence. But the question persists and indeed grows whether the computer will make it easier or harder for human beings to know who they really are, to identify their real problems, to respond more fully to beauty, to place adequate value on life, and to make their world safer than it now is.

2 Electronic brains can reduce the profusion[2] of dead ends involved in vital research. But they can't eliminate the foolishness and decay that come from the unexamined life.[3] Nor do they connect a man to the things he has to be connected to—the reality of pain in others; the possibilities of creative growth in himself; the memory of the race; and the rights of the next generation.

3 The reason these matters are important in a computerized age is that there may be a tendency to mistake data for wisdom, just as there has always been a tendency to confuse logic with values, and intelligence with insight. Unobstructed access to facts can produce unlimited good only if it is matched by the desire and ability

to find out what they mean and where they would lead.

4 Facts are terrible things if left sprawling and unattended. They are too easily regarded as evaluated certainties[4] rather than as the rawest of raw materials crying to be processed into the texture of logic. It requires a very unusual mind, Whitehead[5] said, to undertake the analysis of a fact. The computer can provide a correct number, but it may be an irrelevant number until judgment is pronounced.

5 To the extent, then, that man fails to make the distinction between the intermediate operations of electronic intelligence and the ultimate responsibilities of human decision and conscience, the computer could prove a digression.[6] It could obscure man's awareness of the need to come to terms with himself. It may foster the illusion that he is asking fundamental questions when actually he is asking only functional[7] ones. It may be regarded as a substitute for intelligence instead of an extension of it. It may promote undue confidence in concrete answers. "If we begin with certainties," Bacon[8] said, "we shall end in doubts; but if we begin with doubts, and we are patient with them, we shall end in certainties."

6 The computer knows how to vanquish error, but before we lose ourselves in celebration of the victory, we might reflect on the great advances in the human situation that have come about because men were challenged by error and would not stop thinking and probing until they found better approaches for dealing with it. "Give me a good fruitful error, full of seeds, bursting with its own corrections," Ferris Greenslet[9] wrote. "You can keep your sterile truth for yourself."

7 The biggest single need in computer technoloy is not for improved circuitry,[10] or enlarged capacity, or prolonged memory, or miniaturized containers, but for better questions and better use of the answers. Without taking anything away from the technicians, we think it might be fruitful to effect some sort of junction between the computer technologist and the poet. A genuine purpose may be served by turning loose the wonders of the creative imagination on the kinds of problems being put to electronic tubes and transistors. The company of poets may enable the men who tend the machines to see a larger panorama[11] of possibilities than technology alone may inspire.

8 A poet, said Aristotle,[12] has the advantage of expressing the universal; the specialist expresses only the particular. The poet, moreover, can remind us that man's greatest energy comes not from his dynamos[13] but from his dreams. The notion of where a man ought to be instead of where he is; the liberation from cramped prospects; the intimations of immortality[14] through art—all these proceed naturally out of dreams. But the quality of a man's dreams can only be a reflection of his subconscious. What he puts into his subconscious, therefore, is quite literally the most important nourishment in the world.

9 Nothing really happens to a man except as it is registered in the subconscious. This is where event and feeling become memory and where the proof of life is stored. The poet—and we use the term to include all those who have respect for and speak

to the human spirit—can help to supply the subconscious with material to enhance[15] its sensitivity, thus safeguarding it. The poet, too, can help to keep man from making himself over in the image of his electronic marvels. For the danger is not so much that man will be controlled by the computer as that he may imitate it.

10 The poet reminds men of their uniqueness. It is not necessary to possess the ultimate definition of this uniqueness. Even to speculate on it is a gain.

Notes

[1] Balanced.

[2] Abundance.

[3] In his *Apology,* Socrates (470–399 B.C.), a Greek philosopher, wrote, "The life which is unexamined is not worth living."

[4] Determined facts, known values.

[5] Alfred North Whitehead, 1861–1947, an English philosopher and mathematician who lived much of his life in the United States.

[6] Bypath, detour.

[7] Useful.

[8] Francis Bacon (1561–1626), English philosopher, essayist, and statesman.

[9] An American publisher and author (1875–1959), former associate editor of the *Atlantic Monthly.*

[10] The detailed plan of an electric network.

[11] View of wide scope.

[12] A Greek philosopher (384–322 B.C.) who was a pupil of Plato. His *Poetics* has remained an influential work through the centuries.

[13] Electric generators.

[14] A reference to a famed poem (1807) by William Wordsworth, "Intimations of Immortality from Recollections of Early Childhood."

[15] Magnify, increase.

FREUDIAN FOOTBALL

Thomas Hornsby Ferril

THOMAS HORNSBY FERRIL (1896–) was born in Denver and received an A.B. degree from Colorado College. Except for service during World War I he has spent his entire life in Denver, but his fame as poet and editor is national and even international. Copublisher (with his wife, Helen R. Ferril) of the famed *Rocky Mountain Herald,* he contributes an urbane and thoughtful weekly column to it. The paragraphs that follow illustrate the quality of his fertile, roving mind. His best-known volume of prose is *I Hate Thursday* (1946); his best collection of poetry is *New and Selected Poems* (1952). He was one of 31 poets commissioned by the Steuben Glass Company to participate in its "Poetry in Crystal" exhibition in New York City in 1963.

1 As I look back over the intellectual caprices[1] of the past quarter century, I am amazed that neither the Marxists nor the Freudians[2] ever took out after football. There's not a single book on the subject. It is now too late. In olympian cerebration,[3] Marx and Freud are obsolete; the atom has taken over, and football, for the moment, seems reasonably safe from encroachment,[4] although we may still see a few flurries; cobalt tracers, perhaps, for the study of the parabolas[5] of flat passes, but it won't amount to much because the atom is cut out for graver duties.

2 If the Marxists had been more alert, they could have made something out of football as brutal capitalistic exploitation of the working class.[6] They might have noted a few strikes for higher pay and a court decision entitling a college football player to workman's compensation benefits following injury.

3 But it was the Freudians who made the colossal blunder. You could argue that they overlooked football on the grounds that it was just too big to be noticed on those Saturday afternoons when the college library was free for their invasion of fiction, drama, poetry, painting, sculpture, music, and economics.

4 Yet why, when the whole town was roaring over their heads, did they pay no attention to the emotional frenzy? Frankly, I think they must have, but the Freudians were notoriously selfish fellows; they wanted everything whole-hog; they were always extremely jealous of anthropologists,[7] and, as you look back on their dilemma as far as football was concerned, their dog-in-the-manger attitude was perhaps justified, for no self-respecting Freudian could ever have done a full-dress job on football without cutting some detested anthropologist in on the gravy.

5 But had the Freudians been less self-centered and had they welcomed a bit of anthropological assistance, just think of the monumental treatises[8] by which the scientific literature of the period might have been enriched, great books wedding the wisdom of "Gesammelte Schriften" with the profundity of "The Golden Bough."[9]

6 Let me set down, in nostalgic[10] summary, some of the findings that might have been made, had the Freudians not been sulking in their tents.

7 Obviously, football is a syndrome[11] of religious rites symbolizing the struggle to preserve the egg of life through the rigors of impending winter. The rites begin at the autumn equinox and culminate on the first day of the New Year with great festivals identified with bowls of plenty; the festivals are associated with flowers such as roses, fruits such as oranges, farm crops such as cotton, and even-sun-worship and appeasement of great reptiles such as alligators.

8 In these rites the egg of life is symbolized by what is called "the oval," an inflated bladder covered with hog skin. The convention of "the oval" is repeated in the architectural oval-shaped design of the vast outdoor churches in which the services are held every Sabbath[12] in every town and city, also every Sunday in the greater centers of population

where an advanced priesthood performs. These enormous roofless churches dominate every college campus; no other edifice compares in size with them, and they bear witness to the high spiritual development of the culture that produced them.

9 Literally millions of worshipers attend the Sabbath services in these enormous open-air churches. Subconsciously, these hordes of worshipers are seeking an outlet from sex-frustration in anticipation of violent masochism and sadism[13] about to be enacted by a highly trained priesthood of young men. Football obviously arises out of the Oedipus complex.[14] Love of mother dominates the entire ritual. The churches, without exception, are dedicated to Alma Mater, Dear Mother. (Notre Dame[15] and football are synonymous.)

10 The rites are performed on a rectangular area of green grass orientated to the four directions. The grass, symbolizing summer, is striped with ominous white lines representing the knifing snows of winter. The white stripes are repeated in the ceremonial costumes of the four whistling monitors[16] who control the services through a time period divided into four quarters, symbolizing the four seasons.

11 The ceremony begins with colorful processions of musicians and semi-nude virgins who move in and out of ritualized patterns. This excites the thousands of worshipers to rise from their seats, shout frenzied poetry in unison, and chant ecstatic anthems through which runs the Oedipus theme of willingness to die for love of Mother.

12 The actual rites, performed by 22 young priests of perfect physique, might appear to the uninitiated as a chaotic[17] conflict concerned only with hurting the oval by kicking it, then endeavoring to rescue and protect the egg.

13 However, the procedure is highly stylized. On each side there are eleven young men wearing colorful and protective costumes. The group in so-called "possession" of the oval first arrange themselves in an egg-shaped "huddle," as it is called, for a moment of prayerful meditation and whispering of secret numbers to each other.

14 Then they rearrange themselves with relation to the position of the egg. In a typical "formation" there are seven priests "on the line," seven being a mystical number associated not, as Jung[18] purists might contend, with the "seven last words" but, actually, with sublimation[19] of the "seven deadly sins"[20] into "the seven cardinal principles of education."

15 The central priest crouches over the egg, protecting it with his hands while over his back quarters hovers the "quarter-back." The transposition of "back quarters" to "quarter-back" is easily explained by the Adler[21] school. To the layman the curious posture assumed by the "quarter-back," as he hovers over the central priest, immediately suggests the Cretan origins of Mycenaean[22] animal art, but this popular view is untenable.[23] Actually, of course, the "quarter-back" symbolizes the libido,[24] combining two instincts, namely (a) Eros,[25] which strives for even closer union and (b) the instinct for destruction of anything which lies in the path of Eros. Moreover, the "pleasure-pain" excitement of the hysterical worshipers focuses entirely on the

actions of the libido-quarter-back. Behind him are three priests representing the male triad.[26]

16 At a given signal, the egg is passed by sleight-of-hand to one of the members of the triad who endeavors to move it by bodily force across the white lines of winter. This procedure, up and down the enclosure, continues through the four quarters of the ritual.

17 At the end of the second quarter, implying the summer solstice, the processions of musicians and semi-nude virgins are resumed. After forming themselves into pictograms, representing alphabetical and animal fetishes,[27] the virgins perform a most curious rite requiring far more dexterity than the earlier phallic Maypole rituals[28] from which it seems to be derived. Each of the virgins carries a wand of shining metal which she spins on her fingertips, tosses playfully into the air, and with which she interweaves her body in most intricate gyrations.[29]

18 The virgins perform another important function throughout the entire service. This concerns the mystical rite of "conversion" following success of one of the young priests in carrying the oval across the last white line of winter. As the moment of "conversion" approaches, the virgins kneel at the edge of the grass, bury their faces in the earth, then raise their arms to heaven in supplication, praying that "the uprights will be split." "Conversion" is indeed a dedicated ceremony.

19 Freud and Breuer[30] in 1895 ("Studien über Hysteria") described "conversion" as hysterical symptoms originating through the energy of a mental process being withheld from conscious influence, and this precisely accounts for the behavior of the virgins in the football services.

20 The foregoing, I confess, scarcely scratches the surface. Space does not permit interpretation of football as related to dreams, or discussion of the great subconscious reservoirs of thwarted American energy that weekly seek expression through vicarious[31] enjoyment of ritualized violence and infliction of pain. To relate football to the Oedipus complex alone would require, as it well deserves, years of patient research by scholarly men such as we find in the Ford Foundation.[32]

21 I only regret that these studies were not undertaken a quarter century ago, when the Freudians were in full flower. It's just another instance, so characteristic of our culture, of too little and too late.

Notes

[1] Whims, notions.

[2] A *Marxist* is a follower (adherent) of Karl Marx (1818–1883), German economist and socialist; *Freudian* relates to the doctrines of an Austrian neurologist, Sigmund Freud (1856–1939), regarding his interpretations of dreams and treatment of mental illnesses.

[3] Lofty thinking. *Olympian* is derived from Mount Olympus, home of the gods of classical Greece.

[4] Trespass, being taken over.

[5] Plane curves (flight of the football).

[6] Those who, according to Marxist theory, perform the labor of society and thus are the producers of value; those exploited by the wealthy (the capitalists).

[7] Scientists who study the origins, customs, and beliefs of mankind.

[8] Formal papers; learned writings.

[9] *The Golden Bough* is a lengthy study by Sir James G. Frazer, a Scottish anthropologist (1854–1941), of the religions, folklore, and mythology of primitive man. *Gesammelte Schriften* is German for "complete or total writings."

[10] Desirous of returning in thought or fact to a former time.

[11] Pattern, or group, of circumstances applying to a particular condition or idea.

[12] The seventh day of the week (Saturday) or the first day of the week (Sunday); religious day of rest.

[13] Self-punishment and the causing of physical pain to others. (Look up the origins of these words; both come from proper names.)

[14] The desire of a child for sexual pleasure through its parent of the opposite sex; usually considered the sexual desire of a son for his mother.

[15] "Our Lady" (the Virgin Mary).

[16] Officials.

[17] Confused.

[18] Carl Jung (1875–1961), Swiss psychologist and psychiatrist.

[19] Diversion, changing.

[20] Pride, anger, lust, sloth, envy, gluttony, covetousness.

[21] Alfred Adler (1870–1937), Austrian psychiatrist and psychologist.

[22] The island of Crete and the Greek city of Mycenae were the sites of ancient civilizations.

[23] Incapable of being defended.

[24] The sexual instinct.

[25] The ancient Greek god of love.

[26] Group of three.

[27] Objects regarded as having magical qualities and deserving respect and devotion.

[28] Set forms of activity, ceremonies.

[29] Whirlings, circular or spiral motions.

[30] Josef Breuer (1842–1925), Austrian pioneer in psychoanalysis.

[31] Felt or enjoyed through imagined participation in the experience of others.

[32] An endowed institution, named for the American automobile manufacturer Henry Ford, that makes grants for studies, surveys, and varied researchers.

A FABLE

James Reston

JAMES BARRETT RESTON (1909–) was born in Scotland, was brought to the United States in 1910, and then returned to Scotland from 1914 to 1920 to attend school. A graduate of the University of Illinois (1932), he holds honorary degrees from Colgate, Oberlin, Rutgers, Dartmouth, New York University, and the University of Michigan, among others. Beginning his career on the Springfield, Ohio, *Daily News* in 1932, he did publicity work for Ohio State University and the Cincinnati Baseball Club, and in 1934 became a reporter for the Associated Press, based first in New York City and then in London. In 1939 he joined the London bureau of *The New*

York Times, was transferred to its Washington bureau in 1941, and has been a vice-president of the company since 1969. Mr. Reston won the 1945 Pulitzer Prize for news reporting.

1 Once upon a time,[1] all the creatures in the animal kingdom got to lying around drinking Olde Mead (120 proof) and making goo-goo eyes at every cute chick in the forest. All, that is, except the Bears.

2 The Beavers wouldn't cut down trees unless they had power saws, and the Rabbits wouldn't eat anything except icebox lettuce with thousand island dressing, and pretty soon the Bears started going around gobbling up all the other animals.

3 After a while, a horse named Gallup[2] took a poll which showed that 97.3 percent of the animals left were against being gobbled up, so the King Lion called them all together and made them a big speech about the need for sacrifices.

4 "Ask not what the forest can do for you," he said, "but what you can do for the forest."[3] Everybody from the Elephant to the Jackass was deeply impressed and began asking exactly that.

5 "What can we do to help?" asked the Chief Worker among the Ants.

INCENTIVES, ANYBODY?

6 "The trouble with you," replied the Lion, "is that you need more incentives.[4] You are not getting paid enough for your labor. I'm going to see to it that your minimum wage is raised from a dollar an hour to a dollar and a quarter an hour right away."

7 "But it is jobs we need more than anything else," said the Chief Ant.

8 "I know," replied the Lion. "It is a terrible thing to be an unemployed Ant, so I'm going to increase your unemployment compensation and stretch it out over a longer period."

9 "What about us?" asked the Fat Cat. "What can we do to help?"

10 "Produce," replied the Lion, "Production is what we need, and I promise that your depletion allowances will be maintained at a high level so that you continue to have more cream than anybody else."

11 "And what about us?" asked the farmer Jackass. "What shall we do?"

12 "Don't produce," said the Lion. "Farm production is what we don't need. Please don't produce any more and we'll pay you well. We'll do anything, but please take it easy."

13 Up then strode the Tiger, who had been watching the Bears from a missile gap on the fringe of the forest. "Give us our orders," said the Tiger. "We have seen the enemy and we want to help."

14 "I want you to be happy," said the Lion. "I know how it is out there without your women folk and your cubs. Go back to your post in peace and I'll send them all out to you at Government expense."

THE BEARS ARE HEARD FROM

15 At this point, there was a ghastly roar from the Bears in the forest. "Hearken to that," said the Lion. "We have never been in greater danger. The outcome of this struggle is very

much in doubt. Where are the volunteers?"

16 First to step up was a very old British Lion. "We must be sensible about this," he said. "We must talk things over with the Bears. It is all very tiresome, but we must not be rash or beastly in our attitude."

17 Next came the French Giraffe who said he hated Bears but pointed out that the Giraffes were all fighting among themselves and did not really have time to watch the Bears.

18 Finally, a German Police Dog offered to watch the Bears but complained that he could not afford to do very much and besides did not trust himself to get too close to the Bears. Whereupon the Lion called once more for volunteers.

19 "Let us help," said all the female animals. "You treat us like a bunch of useless ninnies while all the female Bears are working over there like mad."

20 "This is a male's world," said the Lion. "You are consumers, not fighters. You must consume more useless things, so that the workers can produce more useless things."

21 "What about us?" said all the young Oxen. "We are strong and willing."

22 "But you are dumb," roared the Lion. "You must educate yourselves. Everybody who is not dumber than an Ox must have a college education."

23 "But I am poor," said the Church Mouse.

24 "Don't give it a thought," said the Lion. "I'll get you a scholarship at Oberlin, or a Government job in Washington under the Harvard faculty."

25 So saying, the Lion lay down with the Lamb, and the Bears laughed and laughed, and the wise old Owl flew off in search of a safer perch.

26 *MORAL: ASK AND YE SHALL RECEIVE; ASK NOT, AND YE SHALL RECEIVE ANYWAY.*

Notes

1 This is a "fairy story" beginning, but the author calls this essay a "fable" (a brief tale narrated to point a moral or teach a lesson).

2 George H. Gallup, born 1901, an American statistician and pollster. A Gallup poll is a representative sampling of public opinion, belief, and awareness.

3 An allusion to the inaugural address of President John F. Kennedy in 1961.

4 Encouragements; rewards.

RIDERS ON EARTH TOGETHER, BROTHERS IN ETERNAL COLD[1]

Archibald MacLeish

ARCHIBALD MACLEISH (1892–) was born in Glencoe, Illinois, and was graduated from Yale University in 1915. The holder of numerous honorary degrees and one-time professor at Harvard, MacLeish has served as Librarian of Congress (1939–1944), and in several governmental departments and agencies. He is the author of many volumes of poetry, several books of prose, and a number of plays in verse.

1 Men's conception of themselves and of each other has always depended on their notion of the earth. When the earth was the World—all the world there was—and the stars were lights in Dante's heaven,[2] and the ground beneath men's feet roofed Hell, they saw themselves as creatures at the center of the universe, the sole, particular concern of God—and from that high place they ruled and killed and conquered as they pleased.

2 And when, centuries later, the earth was no longer the world but a small, wet spinning planet in the solar system of a minor star off at the edge of an inconsiderable galaxy[3] in the immeasurable distances of space—when Dante's heaven had disappeared and there was no Hell (at least no Hell beneath the feet)—men began to see themselves not as God-directed actors at the center of a noble drama, but as helpless victims of a senseless farce where all the rest were helpless victims also, and millions could be killed in worldwide wars or in blasted cities or in concentration camps without a thought or reason but the reason —if we call it one—of force.

3 Now, in the last few hours, the notion may have changed again. For the first time in all of time, men have *seen* the earth: seen it not as continents or oceans from the little distance of a hundred miles or two or three, but seen it from the depths of space; seen it whole and round and beautiful and small, as even Dante—that "first imagination of Christendom"—had never dreamed of seeing it; as the 20th-century philosophers of absurdity and despair were incapable of guessing that it might be seen. And seeing it so, one question came to the minds of those who looked at it. "Is it inhabited?" they said to each other and laughed—and then they did not laugh. What came to their minds a hundred thousand miles and more into space—"halfway to the moon" they put it—what came to their minds was the life on that little, lonely, floating planet, that tiny raft in the enormous empty night. "Is it inhabited?"

4 The medieval notion of the earth put man at the center of everything. The nuclear notion of the earth put him nowhere—beyond the range of reason even—lost in absurdity and war. The latest notion may have other consequences. Formed as it was in the

minds of heroic voyagers who were also men, it may remake our image of mankind. No longer that preposterous figure at the center, no longer that degraded and degrading victim off at the margins of reality and blind with blood, man may at last become himself.

5 To see the earth as it truly is, small and blue and beautiful in that eternal silence where it floats, is to see ourselves as riders on the earth together, brothers on that bright loveliness in the eternal cold—brothers who know now they are truly brothers.

Notes

[1] This selection first appeared in print on Christmas Day, 1968. Apollo 8 was launched on December 21 with Frank Borman, William Anders, and James A. Lovell aboard. These astronauts were the first to orbit the moon. Their flight lasted 147 hours.

[2] A reference to Dante's *Divine Comedy,* a narrative epic poem of the 14th century.

[3] A large system of stars held together by mutual gravitation and separated from other similar systems by vast regions of space.

Man's Mind and Judgment

THINKING AS A HOBBY

William Golding

William Gerald Golding (1911–) was born in Cornwall, England, and was educated at Oxford University. During World War II he served in the British Navy (1940–1945). In recent years he has devoted himself to writing and teaching, his hobbies being self-described as "thinking, classical Greek, sailing, and archaeology." Among his highly original writings are *Lord of the Flies* (1954), a symbolic narrative of schoolboys who revert to savagery when marooned on an island; *Pincher Martin* (1956); *The Spire* (1964); *The Pyramid* (1967); *The Scorpion God* (1972).

1 While I was still a boy, I came to the conclusion that there were three grades of thinking; and since I was later to claim thinking as my hobby, I came to an even stranger conclusion—namely, that I myself could not think at all.

2 I must have been an unsatisfactory child for grownups to deal with. I remember how incomprehensible[1] they appeared to me at first, but not, of course, how I appeared to them. It was the headmaster of my grammar school[2] who first brought the subject of thinking before me—though neither in the way, nor with the result he in-

tended. He had some statuettes in his study. They stood on a high cupboard behind his desk. One was a lady wearing nothing but a bath towel. She seemed frozen in an eternal panic lest the bath towel slip down any farther; and since she had no arms, she was in an unfortunate position to pull the towel up again. Next to her, crouched the statuette of a leopard, ready to spring down at the top drawer of a filing cabinet labeled A–AH. My innocence interpreted this as the victim's last, despairing cry. Beyond the leopard was a naked, muscular gentleman, who sat, looking down, with his chin on his fist and his elbow on his knee. He seemed utterly miserable.

3 Some time later, I learned about these statuettes. The headmaster had placed them where they would face delinquent children, because they symbolized[3] to him the whole of life. The naked lady was the Venus of Milo.[4] She was Love. She was not worried about the towel. She was just busy being beautiful. The leopard was Nature, and he was being natural. The naked, muscular gentleman was not miserable. He was Rodin's[5] Thinker, an image of pure thought. It is easy to buy small plaster models of what you think life is like.

4 I had better explain that I was a frequent visitor to the headmaster's study, because of the latest thing I had done or left undone. As we now say, I was not integrated. I was, if anything, disintegrated; and I was puzzled. Grownups never made sense. Whenever I found myself in a penal[6] position before the headmaster's desk, with the statuettes glimmering whitely above him, I would sink my head, clasp my hands behind my back and writhe one shoe over the other.

5 The headmaster would look opaquely[7] at me through flashing spectacles.

6 "What are we going to do with you?"

7 Well, what *were* they going to do with me? I would writhe my shoe some more and stare down at the worn rug.

8 "Look up, boy! Can't you look up?"

9 Then I would look up at the cupboard, where the naked lady was frozen in her panic and the muscular gentleman contemplated the hindquarters of the leopard in endless gloom. I had nothing to say to the headmaster. His spectacles caught the light so that you could see nothing human behind them. There was no possibility of communication.

10 "Don't you ever think at all?"

11 No, I didn't think, wasn't thinking, couldn't think—I was simply waiting in anguish for the interview to stop.

12 "Then you'd better learn—hadn't you?"

13 On one occasion the headmaster leaped to his feet, reached up and plonked Rodin's masterpiece on the desk before me.

14 "That's what a man looks like when he's really thinking."

15 I surveyed the gentleman without interest or comprehension.

16 "Go back to your class."

17 Clearly there was something missing in me. Nature had endowed the rest of the human race with a sixth sense and left me out. This must be so, I mused, on my way back to the class, since whether I had broken a window, or failed to remember Boyle's Law,[8] or been late for school, my teachers produced me one, adult answer: "Why can't you think?"

18 As I saw the case, I had broken the window because I had tried to hit Jack Arney with a cricket ball and missed him; I could not remember Boyle's Law because I had never bothered to learn it; and I was late for school because I preferred looking over the bridge into the river. In fact, I was wicked. Were my teachers, perhaps, so good that they could not understand the depths of my depravity?[9] Were they clear, untormented people who could direct their every action by this mysterious business of thinking? The whole thing was incomprehensible. In my earlier years, I found even the statuette of the Thinker confusing. I did not believe any of my teachers were naked, ever. Like someone born deaf, but bitterly determined to find out about sound, I watched my teachers to find out about thought.

19 There was Mr. Houghton. He was always telling me to think. With a modest satisfaction, he would tell me that he had thought a bit himself. Then why did he spend so much time drinking? Or was there more sense in drinking than there appeared to be? But if not, and if drinking were in fact ruinous to health—and Mr. Houghton was ruined, there was no doubt about that—why was he always talking about the clean life and the virtues of fresh air? He would spread his arms wide with the action of a man who habitually spent his time striding along mountain ridges.

20 "Open air does me good, boys—I know it!"

21 Sometimes, exalted by his own oratory, he would leap from his desk and hustle us outside into a hideous wind.

22 "Now, boys! Deep breaths! Feel it right down inside you—huge draughts of God's good air!"

23 He would stand before us, rejoicing in his perfect health, an open-air man. He would put his hands on his waist and take a tremendous breath. You could hear the wind, trapped in the cavern of his chest and struggling with all the unnatural impediments.[10] His body would reel with shock and his ruined face go white at the unaccustomed visitation. He would stagger back to his desk and collapse there, useless for the rest of the morning.

24 Mr. Houghton was given to high-minded monologues about the good life, sexless and full of duty. Yet in the middle of one of these monologues, if a girl passed the window, tapping along on her neat little feet, he would interrupt his discourse, his neck would turn of itself and he would watch her out of sight. In this instance, he seemed to me ruled not by thought but by an invisible and irresistible spring in his nape.[11]

25 His neck was an object of great interest to me. Normally it bulged a bit over his collar. But Mr. Houghton had fought in the First World War alongside both Americans and French, and had come—by who knows what illogic?—to a settled detestation[12] of both countries. If either country happened to be prominent in current affairs, no argument could make Mr. Houghton think well of it. He would bang the desk, his neck would bulge still further and go red. "You can say what you like," he would cry, "but I've thought about this—and I know what I think!"

26 Mr. Houghton thought with his neck.

27 There was Miss Parsons. She

assured us that her dearest wish was our welfare, but I knew even then, with the mysterious clairvoyance[13] of childhood, that what she wanted most was the husband she never got. There was Mr. Hands—and so on.

28 I have dealt at length with my teachers because this was my introduction to the nature of what is commonly called thought. Through them I discovered that thought is often full of unconscious prejudice, ignorance and hypocrisy. It will lecture on disinterested purity while its neck is being remorselessly twisted toward a skirt. Technically, it is about as proficient as most businessmen's golf, as honest as most politicians' intentions, or—to come near my own preoccupation—as coherent[14] as most books that get written. It is what I came to call grade-three thinking, though more properly, it is feeling, rather than thought.

29 True, often there is a kind of innocence in prejudices, but in those days I viewed grade-three thinking with an intolerant contempt and an incautious mockery. I delighted to confront a pious lady who hated the Germans with the proposition that we should love our enemies. She taught me a great truth in dealing with grade-three thinkers; because of her, I no longer dismiss lightly a mental process which for nine-tenths of the population is the nearest they will ever get to thought. They have immense solidarity.[15] We had better respect them, for we are outnumbered and surrounded. A crowd of grade-three thinkers, all shouting the same thing, all warming their hands at the fire of their own prejudices, will not thank you for pointing out the contradictions in their beliefs. Man is a gregarious[16] animal, and enjoys agreement as cows will graze all the same way on the side of a hill.

30 Grade-two thinking is the detection of contradictions. I reached grade two when I trapped the poor, pious lady. Grade-two thinkers do not stampede easily, though often they fall into the other fault and lag behind. Grade-two thinking is a withdrawal, with eyes and ears open. It became my hobby and brought satisfaction and loneliness in either hand. For grade-two thinking destroys without having the power to create. It set me watching the crowds cheering His Majesty the King and asking myself what all the fuss was about, without giving me anything postive to put in the place of that heady patriotism. But there were compensations. To hear people justify their habit of hunting foxes and tearing them to pieces by claiming that the foxes liked it. To hear our Prime Minister talk about the great benefit we conferred on India by jailing people like Pandit Nehru and Gandhi.[17] To hear American politicians talk about peace in one sentence and refuse to join the League of Nations[18] in the next. Yes, there were moments of delight.

31 But I was growing toward adolescence and had to admit that Mr. Houghton was not the only one with an irresistible spring in his neck. I, too, felt the compulsive[19] hand of nature and began to find that pointing out contradiction could be costly as well as fun. There was Ruth, for example, a serious and attractive girl. I was an atheist[20] at the time. Grade-two thinking is a menace to religion and knocks down sects[21] like skittles.[22]

I put myself in a position to be converted by her with an hypocrisy worthy of grade three. She was a Methodist—or at least, her parents were, and Ruth had to follow suit. But, alas, instead of relying on the Holy Spirit to convert me, Ruth was foolish enough to open her pretty mouth in argument. She claimed that the Bible (King James Version) was literally inspired. I countered by saying that the Catholics believed in the literal inspiration of Saint Jerome's *Vulgate*,[23] and the two books were different. Argument flagged.

32 At last she remarked that there were an awful lot of Methodists, and they couldn't be wrong, could they—not all those millions? That was too easy, said I restively (for the nearer you were to Ruth, the nicer she was to be near to) since there were more Roman Catholics than Methodists anyway; and they couldn't be wrong, could they—not all those hundreds of millions? An awful flicker of doubt appeared in her eyes. I slid my arm round her waist and murmured breathlessly that if we were counting heads, the Buddhists[24] were the boys for my money. But Ruth had *really* wanted to do me good, because I was so nice. She fled. The combination of my arm and those countless Buddhists was too much for her.

33 That night her father visited my father and left, red-cheeked and indignant. I was given the third degree[25] to find out what had happened. It was lucky we were both of us only fourteen. I lost Ruth and gained an undeserved reputation as a potential libertine.[26]

34 So grade-two thinking could be dangerous. It was in this knowledge, at the age of fifteen, that I remember making a comment from the heights of grade two, on the limitations of grade three. One evening I found myself alone in the school hall, preparing it for a party. The door of the headmaster's study was open. I went in. The headmaster had ceased to thump Rodin's Thinker down on the desk as an example to the young. Perhaps he had not found any more candidates, but the statuettes were still there, glimmering and gathering dust on top of the cupboard. I stood on a chair and rearranged them. I stood Venus in her bath towel on the filing cabinet, so that now the top drawer caught its breath in a gasp of sexy excitement. "A–ah!" The portentous[27] Thinker I placed on the edge of the cupboard so that he looked down at the bath towel and waited for it to slip.

35 Grade-two thinking, though it filled life with fun and excitement, did not make for content. To find out the deficiencies of our elders bolsters[28] the young ego but does not make for personal security. I found that grade two was not only the power to point out contradictions. It took the swimmer some distance from the shore and left him there, out of his depth. I decided that Pontius Pilate[29] was a typical grade-two thinker. "What is truth?" he said, a very common grade-two thought, but one that is used always as the end of an argument instead of the beginning. There is a still higher grade of thought which says, "What is truth?" and sets out to find it.

36 But these grade-one thinkers were few and far between. They did not visit my grammar school in the flesh though they were there in books. I

aspired to them, partly because I was ambitious and partly because I now saw my hobby as an unsatisfactory thing if it went no further. If you set out to climb a mountain, however high you climb, you have failed if you cannot reach the top.

37 I *did* meet an undeniably grade-one thinker in my first year at Oxford. I was looking over a small bridge in Magdalen Deer Park, and a tiny mustached and hatted figure came and stood by my side. He was a German who had just fled from the Nazis to Oxford as a temporary refuge. His name was Einstein.[30]

38 But Professor Einstein knew no English at that time and I knew only two words of German. I beamed at him, trying wordlessly to convey by my bearing all the affection and respect that the English felt for him. It is possible—and I have to make the admission—that I felt here were two grade-one thinkers standing side by side; yet I doubt if my face conveyed more than a formless awe. I would have given my Greek and Latin and French and a good slice of my English for enough German to communicate. But we were divided; he was as inscrutable[31] as my headmaster. For perhaps five minutes we stood together on the bridge, undeniable grade-one thinker and breathless aspirant. With true greatness, Professor Einstein realized that any contact was better than none. He pointed to a trout wavering in midstream.

39 He spoke: *"Fisch."*

40 My brain reeled. Here I was, mingling with the great, and yet helpless as the veriest grade-three thinker. Desperately I sought for some sign by which I might convey that I, too, revered pure reason. I nodded vehemently. In a brilliant flash I used up half of my German vocabulary.

41 *"Fisch. Ja. Ja."*

42 For perhaps another five minutes we stood side by side. Then Professor Einstein, his whole figure still conveying good will and amiability, drifted away out of sight.

43 I, too, would be a grade-one thinker. I was irreverent at the best of times. Political and religious systems, social customs, loyalties and traditions, they all came tumbling down like so many rotten apples off a tree. This was a fine hobby and a sensible substitute for cricket, since you could play it all the year round. I came up in the end with what must always remain the justification for grade-one thinking, its sign, seal and charter. I devised a coherent system for living. It was a moral system, which was wholly logical. Of course, as I readily admitted, conversion of the world to my way of thinking might be difficult, since my system did away with a number of trifles, such as big business, centralized government, armies, marriage. . . .

44 It was Ruth all over again. I had some very good friends who stood by me, and still do. But my acquaintances vanished, taking the girls with them. Young women seemed oddly contented with the world as it was. They valued the meaningless ceremony with a ring. Young men, while willing to concede the chaining sordidness[32] of marriage, were hesitant about abandoning the organizations which they hoped would give them a career. A young man on the first rung of the Royal Navy, while perfectly agreeable to doing away

with big business and marriage, got as red-necked as Mr. Houghton when I proposed a world without any battleships in it.

45 Had the game gone too far? Was it a game any longer? In those prewar days, I stood to lose a great deal, for the sake of a hobby.

46 Now you are expecting me to describe how I saw the folly of my ways and came back to the warm nest, where prejudices are so often called loyalties, where pointless actions are hallowed[33] into custom by repetition, where we are content to say we think when all we do is feel.

47 But you would be wrong. I dropped my hobby and turned professional.

48 If I were to go back to the headmaster's study and find the dusty statuettes still there, I would arrange them differently. I would dust Venus and put her aside, for I have come to love her and know her for the fair thing she is. But I would put the Thinker, sunk in his desperate thought, where there were shadows before him—and at his back, I would put the leopard, crouched and ready to spring.

Notes

1 Not understandable.

2 In Great Britain, a grammar school roughly corresponds to an American high school.

3 Stood for; represented. (A symbol is something used for, or regarded as representing, something else.)

4 A marble statue of Venus, carved about 200 B.C. The statue was found in 1820 on Melos, a Greek island in the Aegean Sea.

5 Auguste Rodin (1840–1917) was a French sculptor.

6 Involving punishment.

7 Not clearly; unseeingly.

8 A principle in chemistry (thermodynamics) relating the pressure of gases to their temperature and volume.

9 Wickedness, corruption.

10 Obstructions, obstacles.

11 The back of the neck.

12 Hatred.

13 Quick knowledge, intuition.

14 Logical, consistent.

15 Fellowship or union of feelings and beliefs; kindred attitudes.

16 Sociable.

17 Jawaharlal Nehru (1889–1964), a Hindu political leader, first Prime Minister of the Dominion of India, and the father of Indira Gandhi. Mohandas (Mahatma) Gandhi (1869–1948) was a Hindu religious leader and social reformer.

18 A peace-promoting organization of nations created in 1919, at the end of World War I, and dissolved in 1949.

19 Compelling.

20 One who denies the existence of God.

21 Religious denominations.

22 Ninepins (a form of bowling).

23 The Latin version of the Bible, prepared largely by St. Jerome at the end of the 4th century.

[24] Followers of Buddhism, a religion originated in India by Gautama Buddha, ca. 563–483 B.C.
[25] Intensive questioning.
[26] A freethinker; a morally unrestrained person.
[27] Significant, momentous.
[28] Supports, strengthens.
[29] The Roman official who tried and condemned Jesus Christ.
[30] Albert Einstein (1879–1955), physicist, formulator of the theory of relativity.
[31] Mysterious, not easily understood.
[32] Baseness, selfishness.
[33] Made sacred, honored.

THE MYTH OF THE MASS MIND

Joyce Cary

JOYCE CARY (1888–1957) was born in Londonderry, Ireland, and was educated at Oxford University. He joined the Nigerian Political Service in 1913 and lived for several years in Africa. Among his numerous books are *The African Witch* (1936); *Herself Surprised* (1941); *The Horse's Mouth* (1944); *A Fearful Joy* (1949); *The Captive and the Free* (1959).

1 Every age, they say, has its special bit of nonsense. The eighteenth century had its noble savage,[1] and the nineteenth, its automatic progress. Now we have this modern nonsense about the "mass man." We are all told constantly that people are becoming more and more standardized. That mass education, mass amusements, mass production, ready-made clothes, and a popular press are destroying all individuality—turning civilization into a nice, warmed, sterilized orphan asylum where all the little lost souls wear the same uniforms, eat the same meals, think the same thoughts, and play the same games.

2 This belief is now so completely accepted that it underlies half the writing and thinking of the time, like chalk under the downs.[2] You don't see it but it gives shape to what you do see. If you deny it you will get exactly the same response as Galileo[3] when he said that the earth moved through the sky. You will be told, "Use your eyes. And don't talk nonsense. Look at the crowds in the street or at any football match. Go to the films, read the newspapers. Consider the disappearance of national dress all over the world—the immense development of laws restricting individual liberty, standardizing our lives. Go on a tour to famous sights—year by year there will be bigger crowds of morons gaping at them and listening to the spiel[4] of some bored guide—a piece nicely designed to satisfy the mass mind."

3 And you will be referred to history and old travel accounts to learn how various and delightful the world was, in dress and thought and individu-

ality, one hundred or even fifty years ago.

4 I was convinced of all this myself till I went to administer the affairs of a primitive tribe in Africa. There I found that the tribal mind was much more truly a mass mind than anything I had known in Europe. The nearest approximation to it was among illiterate peasantry in remote country districts. Tribesmen and primitive peasants are intensely narrow and conservative. Their very simple ideas and reactions guide them in a mysterious and dangerous world.

5 I found that young chiefs with enterprise and ambition were keen to learn about the world outside the tribe. If they got away from it, they tended to put on European dress. To them, European dress was not a mark of the mass mind, but of the free and independent mind.

6 Likewise, when a European peasantry becomes educated and enterprising, it breaks away from the national dress which seems a badge of servitude and backwardness. To tourists, no doubt, this is a misfortune. As a keen tourist and sight-seer, I wish all Scotsmen would wear the kilt and all Turks the tarboosh.[5] I'm delighted that some are beginning to do so again. But these are individualists, eccentrics, nationalists—national dress is not a tribal uniform to them, but a proclamation of difference, an assertion of self.

7 Education, contact with other peoples, breaks up tribal uniformity of thought and custom, brings in new ideas. That is, it makes for difference. The celebrated eccentrics of former centuries were either lunatics—or educated men.

8 New ideas also make for conflict. Old African chiefs hated roads and railways: they said they brought in strangers who corrupted the young people with new ideas and made them rebellious. They were quite right. It is far easier to rule a primitive tribe than a modern democracy where every individual is ready to criticize the government, where everyone has his own ideas about politics and religion, and where dozens of societies, unions, religious sects claim independence and support ambitious leaders who are ready to fight at any time for their "rights."

9 The more education a man has the more likely he is to be independent in his views and obstinate in sticking to them. A committee of professors, I can assure you, is much harder to manage than a council of African chiefs.

10 And this throws light on another argument brought forward to prove that individuality is vanishing from the world—the enormous increase of law and regulation, the growing power of the police. In my primitive African tribe, law enforcement was in the hands of village chiefs. There was very little theft. I could leave my bungalow wide open and unguarded for three weeks at a time and nothing was ever taken. We had crimes of passion and crimes of witchcraft, but no criminal class, no crooks as you know them in the big city, no cranks, no anarchists[6]—so we did not require an elaborate structure of law.

11 You do not need traffic police where there is no wheeled traffic. You do not need postal bylaws[7] where no one knows how to write. But the modern state, simply because of the independence of its citizens, the complication of their demands, needs a huge machine of law and police. This

is not a proof of the mass mind but the exact opposite—of a growing number of people who think and act for themselves, and, rightly or wrongly, are ready to defy the old simple rules founded on custom.

12 Thus, the modern state has lost its mass mind in getting education. But, you will say, this education destroys the primitive mass mind only to replace it with a number of mob minds: in the crowds which queue[8] for the films or a match, read the same newspapers, and shout for the same spellbinders.[9] Mass education is driving out the sound, traditional culture to bring in a lot of half-baked slogans. It produces the shallow brain seeking only to be distracted from serious reflection.

13 But these "mobs" have no resemblance to those of the tribal world where every individual does the same thing at the same time—hunts, dances, drinks in the mass. Even if he had the will to do anything else, it would not be there to do. The modern individual has an immense choice of occupation and amusement. So that the "mass" of sight-seers at any show place today is actually composed of individuals who have freely chosen to join that crowd and will join a different one tomorrow. What looks like a proof of the mob mind is really evidence of spreading interests among the people and a variety of occupations. And if some of these interests are "popular," aimed at a crowd which is not very critical or reflective, they are a good deal more so than interests which were the only recourse of their ancestors—dog-fighting, bear-baiting, the fit-up melodrama[10] or one-night stand, once a year, and booze.

14 In the best educated countries, you find the biggest demand for something new in amusement as well as for instruction. Education enlarges all the interests of a man. Apart from what he learns, he acquires a general curiosity and a wider taste.

15 Compare the press of today with that of a hundred or even fifty years ago. You will find a far greater variety of subjects appealing to a greater variety of tastes. You will find instructive articles on matters formerly dealt with only in the special magazines. Perhaps they don't aim at a learned audience, but they help the general reader to get some idea of what the experts are doing in atomic research or medicine or even astronomy. If you want to write a best seller, your best subject nowadays is probably cosmology.[11]

16 But if a hundred thousand people are ready to buy a book on the nature of the universe, you have a mass demand at the bookshops. The mass demand is not a proof of falling standards: it means that millions are being educated who would formerly have been left in the illiterate mass. There are "masses" reading learned works just as there are other "masses" going to popular films. The number of people with a good university education is many hundred times what it was fifty years ago, and that explains the immense development of arts and literature in experimental forms that would have had no chance of appreciation before. And in the millions in the next category who have just become literate in the last generation, whose reactions to education have given rise to this illusion of an increasing "mass mind," what we are seeing is not a collapse of standards, but a very rapid improvement. The crowds at the

cinemas and the bus loads on the sight-seeing tours are on the way up. They have already left the mass; they are individuals seeking ideas for themselves.

17 The mass mind idea is not only a bit of nonsense, it is dangerous nonsense. It leads to a profound defeatism,[12] to the secret and unacknowledged belief that the dictators hold all the trumps.

18 The reasoning, when you bring it to light, is something like this. There are two kinds of education in the world: the free, which develops the individual according to his nature, and the specialized, which turns out doctors, scientists, mechanics—useful servants of the state or of industry. In a democracy each individual has both types. In the Soviet he gets only the specialized—the whole plan is to make him a state slave.

19 But it seems that free education merely debases[13] the standards of thought and life by producing mob minds without spiritual strength. Meanwhile the Soviet acquires millions of workers, docile[14] as serfs, yet skillful as our own craftsmen. Aiming deliberately at the creation of a mass mind it will easily defeat the free world, where opinions are shallow and divided.

20 But this is based on bad psychology. The West is not producing a mass mind, but a variety of strong minds with the richest sense of adventure and will for discovery. The East is not succeeding in obtaining a mass mind either—it is going in the opposite direction. Merely by process of education, it is producing every year people who can at least think a little more freely than illiterate peasants, who are very likely therefore to think critical thoughts, however much they may hide them. That is why the task of the dictatorship becomes constantly more difficult, why it is obliged to stiffen its grip, to hire more police, to bribe more spies, and to purge its own party, every year or so, of "deviators."[15]

21 What I suggest is that no kind of education, however narrow, can produce the mass mind. The reason is that minds are creative, that thoughts wander by themselves and cannot be controlled by the cleverest police. All education is free in this sense; it cannot be shut up within walls. To teach people to think, if only to make them more useful as soldiers and mechanics, is to open all thoughts to them—a whole world of new ideas. And though the dictator may wish to think of them as a proletariat,[16] they have already begun to leave the proletariat.

22 The "mass mind" is a delusion.[17] How many dictators have been amazed when their rule, which seemed so strong, has collapsed in a few hours, without a friend?

Notes

[1] A reference to the belief that "natural man" is both good and happy and that mankind is corrupted by society. This idea, strongly held in the eighteenth century, notably by the French philosopher Jean Jacques Rousseau (1712–1778), has persisted to the present day and has even intensified in the 1960s and 1970s among some Americans.

[2] Open, rolling country, the soil of which contains limestone.

[3] Italian physicist and astronomer (1564–1642).
[4] Extravagant speech.
[5] Cap of cloth or felt, usually red.
[6] Persons who wish to overturn by violence all forms of established government.
[7] Rules, regulations.
[8] Form a line.
[9] Speakers who fascinate their listeners.
[10] Contrived emotional and sentimental display.
[11] Study of the origin and general structure of the universe.
[12] Belief that effort and struggle are useless.
[13] Corrupts, pollutes.
[14] Easily managed.
[15] Persons who turn away from accepted beliefs, policies, and practices.
[16] Working classes; people without property.
[17] False belief.

HOW DO YOU KNOW IT'S GOOD?

Marya Mannes

MARYA MANNES (1904–) was born in New York City and was educated in private schools in that city. She has been an editor of *Vogue* and of *Glamour*. During World War II she served as an intelligence analyst for the United States and since then has occupied herself with varied magazine and television assignments. Among her books are *Message from a Stranger* (1948), a novel; *More in Anger* (1958); *Subverse* (1959); and *The New York I Know* (1961).

1 Suppose there were no critics to tell us how to react to a picture, a play, or a new composition of music. Suppose we wandered innocent as the dawn into an art exhibition of unsigned paintings. By what standards, by what values would we decide whether they were good or bad, talented or untalented, successes or failures? How can we ever know that what we think is right?

2 For the last fifteen or twenty years the fashion in criticism or appreciation of the arts has been to deny the existence of any valid criteria[1] and to make the words "good" or "bad" irrelevant, immaterial, and inapplicable. There is no such thing, we are told, as a set of standards, first acquired through experience and knowledge and later imposed on the subject under discussion. This has been a popular approach, for it relieves the critic of the responsibility of judgment and the public of the necessity of knowledge. It pleases those resentful of disciplines, it flatters the empty-minded by calling them open-minded, it comforts the confused. Under the banner of democracy and the kind of equality which our forefathers did *not* mean, it says, in effect, "Who are you to tell us what is good or bad?" This is the same cry used so long and

so effectively by the producers of mass media who insist that it is the public, not they, who decides what it wants to hear and see, and that for a critic to say that *this* program is bad and *this* program is good is purely a reflection of personal taste. Nobody recently has expressed this philosophy more succinctly than Dr. Frank Stanton, the highly intelligent president of CBS television. At a hearing before the Federal Communications Commission, this phrase escaped him under questioning: "One man's mediocrity[2] is another man's good program."

3 There is no better way of saying "No values are absolute."[3] There is another important aspect to this philosophy of *laissez faire:*[4] It is the fear, in all observers of all forms of art, of guessing wrong. This fear is well come by, for who has not heard of the contemporary outcries against artists who later were called great? Every age has its arbiters[5] who do not grow with their times, who cannot tell evolution from revolution or the difference between frivolous faddism, amateurish experimentation, and profound and necessary change. Who wants to be caught *flagrante delicto*[6] with an error of judgment as serious as this? It is far safer, and certainly easier, to look at a picture or a play or a poem and say "This is hard to understand, but it may be good," or simply to welcome it as a new form. The word "new"—in our country especially—has magical connotations. What is new must be good; what is old is probably bad. And if a critic can describe the new in language that nobody can understand, he's safer still. If he has mastered the art of saying nothing with exquisite complexity, nobody can quote him later as saying anything.

4 But all these, I maintain, are forms of abdication[7] from the responsibility of judgment. In creating, the artist commits himself; in appreciating, you have a commitment of your own. For after all, it is the audience which makes the arts. A climate of appreciation is essential to its flowering, and the higher the expectations of the public, the better the performance of the artist. Conversely, only a public ill-served by its critics could have accepted as art and as literature so much in these last years that has been neither. If anything goes, everything goes; and at the bottom of the junk-pile lie the discarded standards too.

5 But what are these standards? How do you get them? How do you know they're the right ones? How can you make a clear pattern out of so many intangibles,[8] including that greatest one, the very private I?

6 Well for one thing, it's fairly obvious that the more you read and see and hear, the more equipped you'll be to practice that art of association which is at the basis of all understanding and judgment. The more you live and the more you look, the more aware you are of a consistent pattern—as universal as the stars, as the tides, as breathing, as night and day—underlying everything. I would call this pattern and this rhythm an order. Not order—*an* order. Within it exists an incredible diversity of forms. Without it lies chaos. I would further call this order—this incredible diversity held within one pattern—health. And I would call chaos—the wild cells of destruction—sickness. It is in the

end up to you to distinguish between the diversity that is health and the chaos that is sickness, and you can't do this without a process of association that can link a bar of Mozart with the corner of a Vermeer painting, or a Stravinsky score with a Picasso abstraction; or that can relate an aggressive act with a Franz Kline painting and a fit of coughing with a John Cage composition.[9]

7 There is no accident in the fact that certain expressions of art live for all time and that others die with the moment, and although you may not always define the reasons, you can ask the questions. What does an artist say that is timeless; how does he say it? How much is fashion, how much is merely reflection? Why is Sir Walter Scott so hard to read now, and Jane Austen not? Why is baroque[10] right for one age and too effulgent for another?

8 Can a standard of craftsmanship apply to art of all ages, or does each have its own, and different, definitions? You may have been aware, inadvertently,[11] that craftsmanship has become a dirty word these years because, again, it implies standards—something done well or done badly. The result of this convenient avoidance is a plentitude[12] of actors who can't project their voices, singers who can't phrase their songs, poets who can't communicate emotion, and writers who have no vocabulary—not to speak of painters who can't draw. The dogma[13] now is that craftsmanship gets in the way of expression. You can do better if you don't know *how* you do it, let alone *what* you're doing.[14]

9 I think it is time you helped reverse this trend by trying to rediscover craft: the command of the chosen instrument, whether it is a brush, a word, or a voice. When you begin to detect the difference between freedom and sloppiness, between serious experimentation and egotherapy,[15] between skill and slickness, between strength and violence, you are on your way to separating the sheep from the goats, a form of segregation denied us for quite a while. All you need to restore it is a small bundle of standards and a Geiger counter[16] that detects fraud, and we might begin our tour of the arts in an area where both are urgently needed: contemporary painting.

10 I don't know what's worse: to have to look at acres of bad art to find the little good, or to read what the critics say about it all. In no other field of expression has so much double-talk flourished, so much confusion prevailed, and so much nonsense been circulated: further evidence of the close interdependence between the arts and the critical climate they inhabit. It will be my pleasure to share with you some of this double-talk so typical of our times.

11 Item one: preface for a catalogue of an abstract painter:

12 "Time-bound meditation experiencing a life; sincere with plastic piety at the threshold of hallowed arcana; a striving for pure ideation giving shape to inner drive; formalized patterns where neural balances reach a fiction."[17] End of quote. Know what this artist paints like now?

13 Item two: a review in the *Art News:*

14 ". . . a weird and disparate assortment of material, but the monstrosity which bloomed into his most recent

cancer of aggregations is present in some form everywhere. . . ." Then, later, "A gluttony of things and processes terminated by a glorious constipation."

15 Item three, same magazine, review of an artist who welds automobile fragments into abstract shapes:

16 "Each fragment . . . is made an extreme of human exasperation, torn at and fought all the way, and has its rightness of form as if by accident. *Any technique that requires order or discipline would just be the human ego.* No, these must be egoless, uncontrolled, undesigned and different enough to give you a bang—fifty miles an hour around a telephone pole. . . ."

17 "Any technique that requires order or discipline would just be the human ego." What does he mean—"just be"? What are they really talking about? Is this journalism? Is it criticism? Or is it that other convenient abdication from standards of performance and judgment practiced by so many artists and critics that they, like certain writers who deal only in sickness and depravity,[18] "reflect the chaos about them"? Again, whose chaos? Whose depravity?

18 I had always thought that the prime function of art was to create order *out* of chaos—again, not the order of neatness or rigidity or convention or artifice, but the order of clarity by which one will and one vision could draw the essential truth out of apparent confusion. I still do. It is not enough to use parts of a car to convey the brutality of the machine. This is as slavishly representative, and just as easy, as arranging dried flowers under glass to convey nature.

19 Speaking of which, i.e.,[19] the use of real materials (burlap, old gloves, bottletops) in lieu of pigment, this is what one critic had to say about an exhibition of Assemblage at the Museum of Modern Art last year:

20 "Spotted throughout the show are indisputable works of art, accounting for a quarter or even a half of the total display. But the remainder are works of non-art, anti-art, and art substitutes that are the aesthetic counterparts of the social deficiencies that land people in the clink on charges of vagrancy. These aesthetic bankrupts . . . have no legitimate ideological[20] roof over their heads and not the price of a square intellectual meal, much less a spiritual sandwich, in their pockets."

21 I quote these words of John Canaday of *The New York Times* as an example of the kind of criticism which puts responsibility to an intelligent public above popularity with an intellectual coterie.[21] Canaday has the courage to say what he thinks and the capacity to say it clearly: two qualities notably absent from his profession.

22 Next to art, I would say that appreciation and evaluation in the field of music is the most difficult. For it is rarely possible to judge a new composition at one hearing only. What seems confusing or fragmented at first might well become clear and organic[22] a third time. Or it might not. The only salvation here for the listener is, again, an instinct born of experience and association which allows him to separate intent from accident, design from experimentation, and pretense from conviction. Much of contemporary music is, like its

sister art, merely a reflection of the composer's own fragmentation: an absorption in self and symbols at the expense of communication with others. The artist, in short, says to the public: if you don't understand this, it's because you're dumb. I maintain that you are not. You may have to go part way or even halfway to meet the artist, but if you must go the whole way, it's his fault, not yours. Hold fast to that. And remember it too when you read new poetry, that estranged[23] sister of music.

23 "A multitude of causes, unknown to former times, are now acting with a combined force to blunt the discriminating powers of the mind, and, unfitting it for all voluntary[24] exertion, to reduce it to a state of almost savage torpor.[25] The most effective of these causes are the great national events which are daily taking place and the increasing accumulation of men in cities, where the uniformity of their occupations produces a craving for extraordinary incident, which the rapid communication of intelligence hourly gratifies. To this tendency of life and manners, the literature and theatrical exhibitions of the country have conformed themselves."

24 This startlingly applicable comment was written in the year 1800 by William Wordsworth in the preface to his "Lyrical Ballads"; and it has been cited by Edwin Muir in his recently published book "The Estate of Poetry." Muir states that poetry's effective range and influence have diminished alarmingly in the modern world. He believes in the inherent[26] and indestructible qualities of the human mind and the great and permanent objects that act upon it, and suggests that the audience will increase when "poetry loses what obscurity is left in it by attempting greater themes, for great themes have to be stated clearly." If you keep that firmly in mind and resist, in Muir's words, "the vast dissemination[27] of secondary objects that isolate us from the natural world," you have gone a long way toward equipping yourself for the examination of any work of art.

25 When you come to theatre, in this extremely hasty tour of the arts, you can approach it on two different levels. You can bring to it anticipation and innocence, giving yourself up, as it were, to the life on the stage and reacting to it emotionally, if the play is good, or listlessly, if the play is boring; a part of the audience organism[28] that expresses its favor by silence or laughter and its disfavor by coughing and rustling. Or you can bring to it certain critical faculties that may heighten, rather than diminish, your enjoyment.

26 You can ask yourselves whether the actors are truly in their parts or merely projecting themselves; whether the scenery helps or hurts the mood; whether the playwright is honest with himself, his characters, and you. Somewhere along the line you can learn to distinguish between the true creative act and the false arbitrary gesture; between fresh observation and stale cliché; between the avant-garde play that is pretentious drivel and the avant-garde play that finds new ways to say old truths.

27 Purpose and craftsmanship—end and means—these are the keys to your judgment in all the arts. What is this painter trying to say when he slashes a broad band of black across

a white canvas and lets the edges dribble down? Is it a statement of violence? Is it a self-portrait? If it is *one* of these, has he made you believe it? Or is this a gesture of the ego or a form of therapy? If it shocks you, what does it shock you into?

28 And what of this tight little painting of bright flowers in a vase? Is the painter saying anything new about flowers? Is it different from a million other canvases of flowers? Has it any life, any meaning, beyond its statement? Is there any pleasure in its forms or texture? The question is not whether a thing is abstract or representational, whether it is "modern" or conventional. The question, inexorably,[29] is whether it is good. And this is a decision which only you, on the basis of instinct, experience, and association, can make for yourself. It takes independence and courage. It involves, moreover, the risk of wrong decision and the humility, after the passage of time, of recognizing it as such. As we grow and change and learn, our attitudes can change too, and what we once thought obscure or "difficult" can later emerge as coherent and illuminating. Entrenched prejudices, obdurate[30] opinions are as sterile[31] as no opinions at all.

29 Yet standards there are, timeless as the universe itself. And when you have committed yourself to them, you have acquired a passport to that elusive but immutable[32] realm of truth. Keep it with you in the forests of bewilderment. And never be afraid to speak up.

Notes

[1] Standards of judgment.

[2] Ordinary quality; that which is adequate but neither good nor bad.

[3] Complete, perfect.

[4] A French term meaning "allow to act," this expression applies to noninterference in the affairs of others, to the practice of letting things alone. It is often used to refer to a kind of government economic policy.

[5] Judges, umpires.

[6] A Latin term meaning "while the crime is blazing." The expression popularly means "caught in the act."

[7] Renunciation, giving up, shirking.

[8] Things or ideas that are immaterial, not measurable, not definite or clear.

[9] The first four composers and artists mentioned have familiar names. Franz Kline (1910–1962) was an American painter; John Cage, American composer, was born in 1912.

[10] Ornate, extravagant, *Effulgent* means "radiant," "shining forth brilliantly."

[11] Unintentionally, by chance.

[12] Abundance, oversupply.

[13] Established opinion or belief.

[14] Ivor Brown in "The Case for Greater Clarity in Writing" (later in this book) develops this idea rather fully.

[15] Treatment of oneself; self-indulgence.

[16] A device for measuring radioactivity.

[17] Each of the words used here and in following quotations can be defined, but, as the author points out, their use here results in nonsense.

[18] Corruptness, wickedness, perversion.

19 *Id est* (that is).
20 Consisting of a group or body of ideas forming a thought system.
21 Group, clique.
22 Systematically arranged.
23 Alienated, kept at a distance.
24 Self-willed, of one's own accord.
25 Sluggishness.
26 Self-contained, inbred.
27 Spreading, broadcasting.
28 Form, group.
29 Unalterably, constantly.
30 Stubborn.
31 Lifeless.
32 Changeless, fixed.

THE METHOD OF SCIENTIFIC INVESTIGATION

Thomas Henry Huxley

THOMAS HENRY HUXLEY (1825–1895) was born at Ealing, England. In 1846 after receiving his medical degree from the University of London, he made a four-year voyage on the British naval vessel *Rattlesnake*. During this voyage he began scientific studies which led him to accept, in later years, the conclusions which Darwin's *On the Origin of Species* (1859) established. An early believer in the theory of evolution, Huxley wrote and lectured to popularize Darwin's ideas and other scientific thought of his time.

1 The method of scientific investigation is nothing but the expression of the necessary mode[1] of working of the human mind. It is simply the mode at which all phenomena[2] are reasoned about, rendered precise and exact. There is no more difference, but there is just the same kind of difference, between the mental operations of a man of science and those of an ordinary person as there is between the operations and methods of a baker or of a butcher weighing out his goods in common scales and the operations of a chemist in performing a difficult and complex analysis by means of his balance and finely graduated[3] weights. It is not that the action of the scales in the one case and the balance in the other differ in the principles of their construction or manner of working; but the beam of one is set on an infinitely finer axis than the other and of course turns by the addition of a much smaller weight.

2 You will understand this better, perhaps, if I give you some familiar example. You have all heard it repeated, I dare say, that men of science work by means of induction and deduction,[4] and that by the help of these

operations they, in a sort of sense, wring from nature certain other things which are called natural laws and causes, and that out of these, by some cunning skill of their own, they build up hypotheses[5] and theories. And it is imagined by many that the operations of the common mind can be by no means compared with these processes, and that they have to be acquired by a sort of special apprenticeship to the craft. To hear all these large words you would think that the mind of a man of science must be constituted differently from that of his fellow men; but if you will not be frightened by terms, you will discover that you are quite wrong and that all these terrible apparatus are being used by yourselves every day and every hour of your lives.

3 There is a well-known incident in one of Molière's[6] plays where the author makes the hero express unbounded delight on being told that he had been talking prose during the whole of his life. In the same way I trust that you will take comfort and be delighted with yourselves on the discovery that you have been acting on the principles of inductive and deductive philosophy during the same period. Probably there is not one here who has not in the course of the day had occasion to set in motion a complex train of reasoning of the very same kind, though differing of course in degree, as that which a scientific man goes through in tracing the causes of natural phenomena.

4 A very trivial circumstance will serve to exemplify this. Suppose you go into a fruiterer's shop, wanting an apple. You take up one, and on biting it you find it is sour; you look at it and see that it is hard and green. You take up another one, and that too is hard, green, and sour. The shopman offers you a third; but before biting it you examine it and find that it is hard and green, and you immediately say that you will not have it, as it must be sour like those that you have already tried.

5 Nothing can be more simple than that, you think; but if you will take the trouble to analyze and trace out into its logical elements what has been done by the mind, you will be greatly surprised. In the first place you have performed the operation of induction. You found that in two experiences hardness and greenness in apples go together with sourness. It was so in the first case, and it was confirmed by the second. True, it is a very small basis, but still it is enough to make an induction from; you generalize the facts, and you expect to find sourness in apples where you get hardness and greenness. You found upon that a general law that all hard and green apples are sour; and that, so far as it goes, is a perfect induction. Well, having got your natural law in this way, when you are offered another apple which you find is hard and green, you say, "All hard and green apples are sour; this apple is hard and green; therefore this apple is sour." That train of reasoning is what logicians call a syllogism and has all its various parts and terms—its major premise, its minor premise, and its conclusion. And by the help of further reasoning, which if drawn out would have to be exhibited in two or three other syllogisms, you arrive at your final determination, "I will not have that apple." So that, you see, you have, in

the first place, established a law by induction, and upon that you have founded a deduction and reasoned out the special conclusion of the particular case. Well now, suppose, having got your law, that at some time afterwards you are discussing the qualities of apples with a friend. You will say to him, "It is a very curious thing, but I find that all hard and green apples are sour!" Your friend says to you, "But how do you know that?" You at once reply, "Oh, because I have tried them over and over again and have always found them to be so." Well, if we were talking science instead of common sense, we should call that an experimental verification.[7] And if still opposed you go further and say, "I have heard from the people in Somersetshire and Devonshire,[8] where a large number of apples are grown, that they have observed the same thing. It is also found to be the case in Normandy and in North America. In short, I find it to be the universal experience of mankind wherever attention has been directed to the subject." Whereupon, your friend, unless he is a very unreasonable man, agrees with you and is convinced that you are quite right in the conclusion you have drawn. He believes, although perhaps he does not know he believes it, that the more extensive verifications are, that the more frequently experiments have been made and results of the same kind arrived at, that the more varied the conditions under which the same results have been attained the more certain is the ultimate conclusion, and he disputes the question no further. He sees that the experiment has been tried under all sorts of conditions as to time, place, and people with the same result; and he says with you, therefore, that the law you have laid down must be a good one and he must believe it.

6 In science we do the same thing; the philosopher exercises precisely the same faculties, though in a much more delicate manner. In scientific inquiry it becomes a matter of duty to expose a supposed law to every possible kind of verification, and to take care, moreover, that this is done intentionally and not left to mere accident as in the case of the apples. And in science, as in common life, our confidence in a law is in exact proportion to the absence of variation[9] in the result of our experimental verifications. For instance, if you let go your grasp of an article you may have in your hand, it will immediately fall to the ground. That is a very common verification of one of the best established laws of nature, that of gravitation. The method by which men of science established the existence of the law is exactly the same as that by which we have established the trivial[10] proposition about the sourness of hard and green apples. But we believe it in such an extensive, thorough, and unhesitating manner because the universal experience of mankind verifies[11] it, and we can verify it ourselves at any time; and that is the strongest possible foundation on which any natural law can rest.

7 So much by way of proof that the method of establishing laws in science is exactly the same as that pursued in common life. Let us now turn to another matter (though really it is but another phase of the same question), and that is the method by which from

the relations of certain phenomena we prove that some stand in the position of causes towards the others.

8 I want to put the case clearly before you, and I will therefore show you what I mean by another familiar example. I will suppose that one of you, on coming down in the morning to the parlor of your house, finds that a teapot and some spoons which had been left in the room on the previous evening are gone; the window is open, and you observe the mark of a dirty hand on the window-frame; and perhaps, in addition to that, you notice the impress of a hobnailed shoe[12] on the gravel outside. All these phenomena have struck your attention instantly, and before two seconds have passed you say, "Oh, somebody has broken open the window, entered the room, and run off with the spoons and the teapot!" That speech is out of your mouth in a moment. And you will probably add, "I know there has; I am quite sure of it." You mean to say exactly what you know; but in reality what you have said has been the expression of what is, in all essential particulars, an hypothesis. You do not *know* it at all; it is nothing but an hypothesis rapidly framed in your own mind! And it is an hypothesis founded on a long train of inductions and deductions.

9 What are those inductions and deductions, and how have you got at this hypothesis? You have observed, in the first place, that the window is open; but by a train of reasoning involving many inductions and deductions, you have probably arrived long before at the general law—and a very good one it is—that windows do not open of themselves; and you therefore conclude that something has opened the window. A second general law that you have arrived at in the same way is that teapots and spoons do not go out of a window spontaneously,[13] and you are satisfied that, as they are not now where you left them, they have been removed. In the third place, you look at the marks on the window and the shoe marks outside, and you say that in all previous experience the former kind of mark has never been produced by anything else but the hand of a human being; and the same experience shows that no other animal but a man at present wears shoes with hobnails on them such as would produce the marks in the gravel. I do not know, even if we could discover any of those "missing links"[14] that are talked about, that they would help us to any other conclusion! At any rate the law which states our present experience is strong enough for my present purpose. You next reach the conclusion that as these kinds of marks have not been left by any other animal than man, or are liable to be formed in any other way than by a man's hand and shoe, the marks in question have been formed by a man in that way. You have, further, a general law founded on observation and experience, and that too is, I am sorry to say, a very universal and unimpeachable[15] one—that some men are thieves; and you assume at once from all these premises—and that is what constitutes your hypothesis—that the man who made the marks outside and on the window sill opened the window, got into the room, and stole your teapot and spoons. You have now arrived at a *vera causa;*[16] you have assumed a

cause which it is plain is competent to produce all the phenomena you have observed. You can explain all these phenomena only by the hypothesis of a thief. But that is an hypothetical conclusion, of the justice of which you have no absolute proof at all; it is only rendered highly probable by a series of inductive and deductive reasonings.

10 I suppose your first action, assuming that you are a man of ordinary common sense and that you have established this hypothesis to your own satisfaction, will very likely be to go off for the police and set them on the track of the burglar with the view to the recovery of your property. But just as you are starting with this object, some person comes in and on learning what you are about says, "My good friend, you are going on a great deal too fast. How do you know that the man who really made the marks took the spoons? It might have been a monkey that took them, and the man may have merely looked in afterwards." You would probably reply, "Well, that is all very well, but you see it is contrary to all experience of the way teapots and spoons are abstracted;[17] so that, at any rate, your hypothesis is less probable than mine." While you are talking the thing over in this way, another friend arrives, one of that good kind of people that I was talking of a little while ago.

11 And he might say, "Oh, my dear sir, you are certainly going on a great deal too fast. You are most presumptuous.[18] You admit that all these occurrences took place when you were fast asleep, at a time when you could not possibly have known anything about what was taking place. How do you know that the laws of nature are not suspended during the night? It may be that there has been some kind of supernatural interference in this case." In point of fact, he declares that your hypothesis is one of which you cannot at all demonstrate the truth and that you are by no means sure that the laws of nature are the same when you are asleep as when you are awake.

12 Well, now, you cannot at the moment answer that kind of reasoning. You feel that your worthy friend has you somewhat at a disadvantage. You will feel perfectly convinced in your own mind, however, that you are quite right, and you will say to him, "My good friend, I can only be guided by the natural probabilities of the case, and if you will be kind enough to stand aside and permit me to pass, I will go and fetch the police." Well, we will suppose that your journey is successful and that by good luck you meet with a policeman; that eventually the burglar is found with your property on his person and the marks correspond to his hand and to his boots. Probably any jury would consider those facts a very good experimental verification of your hypothesis touching the cause of the abnormal phenomena observed in your parlor, and would act accordingly.

13 Now, in this supposititious[19] case I have taken phenomena of a very common kind in order that you might see what are the different steps in an ordinary process of reasoning, if you will only take the trouble to analyze it carefully. All the operations I have described, you will see, are involved in the mind of any man of sense in

leading him to a conclusion as to the course he should take in order to make good a robbery and punish the offender. I say that you are led, in that case, to your conclusion by exactly the same train of reasoning as that which a man of science pursues when he is endeavoring to discover the origin and laws of the most occult[20] phenomena. The process is, and always must be, the same; and precisely the same mode of reasoning was employed by Newton and Laplace[21] in their endeavors to discover and define the causes of the movements of the heavenly bodies as you, with your own common sense, would employ to detect a burglar. The only difference is that, the nature of the inquiry being more abstruse,[22] every step has to be most carefully watched so that there may not be a single crack or flaw in your hypothesis. A flaw or crack in many of the hypotheses of daily life may be of little or no moment as affecting the general correctness of the conclusions at which we may arrive; but in a scientific inquiry a fallacy,[23] great or small, is always of importance and is sure to be in the long run constantly productive of mischievous[24] if not fatal results.

14 Do not allow yourselves to be misled by the common notion that an hypothesis is untrustworthy simply because it is an hypothesis. It is often urged in respect to some scientific conclusion that, after all, it is only an hypothesis. But what more have we to guide us in nine-tenths of the most important affairs of daily life than hypotheses, and often very ill-based ones? So that in science, where the evidence of an hypothesis is subjected to the most rigid examination, we may rightly pursue the same course. You may have hypotheses and hypotheses. A man may say, if he likes, that the moon is made of green cheese; that is an hypothesis. But another man, who has devoted a great deal of time and attention to the subject and availed himself of the most powerful telescopes and the results of the observations of others, declares that in his opinion it is probably composed of materials very similar to those of which our own earth is made up; and that is also only an hypothesis. But I need not tell you that there is an enormous difference in the value of the two hypotheses. That one which is based on sound scientific knowledge is sure to have a corresponding value; and that which is a mere hasty random[25] guess is likely to have but little value. Every great step in our progress in discovering causes has been made in exactly the same way as that which I have detailed to you. A person observing the occurrence of certain facts and phenomena asks, naturally enough, what kind of operation known to occur in nature applied to the particular case, will unravel and explain the mystery. Hence you have the scientific hypothesis; and its value will be proportionate[26] to the care and completeness with which its basis has been tested and verified. It is in these matters as in the commonest affairs of practical life: the guess of the fool will be folly, while the guess of the wise man will contain wisdom. In all cases you see that the value of the result depends on the patience and faithfulness with which the investigator applies to his hypothesis every possible kind of verification.

Notes

[1] Way, manner, method.

[2] Occurrences, circumstances, or facts that can be observed; objects, situations, or persons that seem remarkable or extraordinary.

[3] Arranged in degrees.

[4] Forms of reasoning in which conclusions are reached by proceeding from specific items to general statements or by the reverse method (general ideas to particulars). Both methods of thinking are illustrated in paragraphs 4 and 5.

[5] Guides to thinking accepted as probable in the light of known facts; plausible interpretation subject to testing.

[6] Molière (1622–1673), French playwright and actor.

[7] Proof of truth by means of experimentation.

[8] Counties in southwest England.

[9] Sameness; lack of difference.

[10] Unimportant; minor.

[11] Proves.

[12] A shoe the sole of which is protected (covered) with large-headed nails.

[13] By natural impulse; of themselves.

[14] Something lacking for the completion of a series of thoughts, ideas, or explanations. Most important of all "missing links" is the hypothetical animal assumed to have formed a connecting link between the apes and man.

[15] Unquestionable, above suspicion, impossible to deny.

[16] True cause (information).

[17] Removed, stolen.

[18] Too quick to assume, too eager to jump to a conclusion.

[19] Hypothetical, not genuine.

[20] Mysterious, difficult to understand.

[21] Sir Isaac Newton (1642–1727), English mathematician and philosopher; Pierre Laplace (1749–1827), French astronomer and mathematician.

[22] Hard to understand.

[23] False and misleading belief, notion, step, or conclusion.

[24] Harmful.

[25] Without definite aim, reason, purpose.

[26] Related to.

THE ALLEGORY OF THE CAVE[1]

Plato

PLATO (427–347 B.C.) was born in Athens, Greece, studied under Socrates, and became one of the most influential thinkers of all time. His philosophy is largely expressed in his dialogues, the depth, range, and style of which have caused them to be considered among the masterpieces of world literature. Among his great works are the *Apology* (defense of Socrates), the *Symposium*, and, most celebrated of all, the *Republic*, a demonstration of justice by a discussion of the ideal state.

1 And now, I said, let me show in a figure how far our nature is enlightened or unenlightened: Behold! human beings living in an underground den, which has a mouth open towards the light and reaching all along the den; here they have been from their childhood, and have their legs and necks chained so that they cannot move, and can only see before them, being prevented by the chains from turning round their heads. Above and behind them a fire is blazing at a distance, and between the fire and the prisoners there is a raised way; and you will see, if you look, a low wall built along the way, like the screen which marionette players have in front of them, over which they show the puppets.

2 I see.

3 And do you see, I said, men passing along the wall carrying all sorts of vessels, and statues and figures of animals made of wood and stone and various materials, which appear over the wall? Some of them are talking, others silent.

4 You have shown me a strange image, and they are strange prisoners.

5 Like ourselves, I replied; and they see only their own shadows, or the shadows of one another, which the fire throws on the opposite wall of the cave?

6 True, he said; how could they see anything but the shadows if they were never allowed to move their heads?

7 And of the objects which are being carried in like manner they would only see the shadows?

8 Yes, he said.

9 And if they were able to converse with one another, would they not suppose that they were naming what was actually before them?

10 Very true.

11 And suppose further that the prison had an echo which came from the other side, would they not be sure to fancy[2] when one of the passers-by spoke that the voice which they heard came from the passing shadow?

12 No question, he replied.

13 To them, I said, the truth would be literally nothing but the shadows of the images.

14 That is certain.

15 And now look again, and see what will naturally follow if the prisoners are released and disabused[3] of their error. At first, when any of them is liberated and compelled suddenly to stand up and turn his neck round and walk and look towards the light, he will suffer sharp pains; the glare will distress him and he will be unable to see the realities of which in his former state he had seen the shadows; and then conceive some one saying to him, that what he saw before was an illusion,[4] but that now, when he is approaching nearer to being and his eye is turned towards more real existence, he has a clearer vision—what will be his reply? And you may further imagine that his instructor is pointing to the objects as they pass and requiring him to name them—will he not be perplexed? Will he not fancy that the shadows which he formerly saw are truer than the objects which are now shown to him?

16 Far truer.

17 And if he is compelled to look straight at the light, will he not have a pain in his eyes which will make him turn away to take refuge in the

objects of vision which he can see, and which he will conceive to be in reality clearer than the things which are now being shown to him?

18 True, he said.

19 And suppose once more, that he is reluctantly dragged up a steep and rugged ascent, and held fast until he is forced into the presence of the sun himself, is he not likely to be pained and irritated? When he approaches the light his eyes will be dazzled and he will not be able to see anything at all of what are now called realities.

20 Not all in a moment, he said.

21 He will require to grow accustomed to the sight of the upper world. And first he will see the shadows best, next the reflections of men and other objects in the water, and then the objects themselves; then he will gaze upon the light of the moon and the stars and the spangled[5] heaven; and he will see the sky and the stars by night better than the sun or the light of the sun by day?

22 Certainly.

23 Last of all he will be able to see the sun, and not mere reflections of him in the water, but he will see him in his own proper place, and not in another; and he will contemplate him as he is.

24 Certainly.

25 He will then proceed to argue that this is he who gives the season and the years, and is the guardian of all that is in the visible world, and in a certain way the cause of all things which he and his fellows have been accustomed to behold?

26 Clearly, he said, he would first see the sun and then reason about him.

27 And when he remembered his old habitation,[6] and the wisdom of the den and his fellow-prisoners, do you not suppose that he would felicitate[7] himself on the change, and pity them?

28 Certainly, he would.

29 And if they were in the habit of conferring honors among themselves on those who were quickest to observe the passing shadows and to remark which of them went before, and which followed after, and which were together; and who were therefore best able to draw conclusions as to the future, do you think that he would care for such honors and glories, or envy the possessors of them? Would he not say with Homer,[8]

> Better to be the poor servant of a poor master,

and to endure anything, rather than think as they do and live after their manner?

30 Yes, he said, I think that he would rather suffer anything than entertain these false notions and live in this miserable manner.

31 Imagine once more, I said, such an one coming suddenly out of the sun to be replaced in his old situation; would he not be certain to have his eyes full of darkness?

32 To be sure, he said.

33 And if there were a contest, and he had to compete in measuring the shadows with the prisoners who had never moved out of the den, while his sight was still weak, and before his eyes had become steady (and the time which would be needed to acquire this new habit of sight might be very considerable) would he not be ridiculous? Men would say of him that up he went and down he came without his eyes; and that it was better not even to think of ascending; and if any

one tried to loose another and lead him up to the light, let them only catch the offender, and they would put him to death.

34 No question, he said.

35 This entire allegory, I said, you may now append,[9] dear Glaucon, to the previous argument; the prison-house is the world of sight, the light of the fire is the sun, and you will not misapprehend me if you interpret the journey upwards to be the ascent of the soul into the intellectual world according to my poor belief, which, at your desire, I have expressed—whether rightly or wrongly God knows. But, whether true or false, my opinion is that in the world of knowledge the idea of good appears last of all, and is seen only with an effort; and, when seen, is also inferred to be the universal author of all things beautiful and right, parent of light and of the lord of light in this visible world, and the immediate source of reason and truth in the intellectual; and that this is the power upon which he who would act rationally either in public or private life must have his eye fixed.

36 I agree, he said, as far as I am able to understand you.

37 Moreover, I said, you must not wonder that those who attain to this beatific[10] vision are unwilling to descend to human affairs; for their souls are ever hastening into the upper world where they desire to dwell; which desire of theirs is very natural, if our allegory may be trusted.

38 Yes, very natural.

39 And is there anything surprising in one who passes from divine contemplations to the evil state of man, misbehaving himself in a ridiculous manner; if, while his eyes are blinking and before he has become accustomed to the surrounding darkness, he is compelled to fight in courts of law, or in other places, about the images or the shadows of images of justice, and is endeavouring to meet the conceptions of those who have never yet seen absolute justice?

40 Anything but surprising, he replied.

41 Any one who has common sense will remember that the bewilderments of the eyes are of two kinds, and arise from two causes, either from coming out of the light or from going into the light, which is true of the mind's eye, quite as much as of the bodily eye; and he who remembers this when he sees any one whose vision is perplexed and weak, will not be too ready to laugh; he will first ask whether that soul of man has come out of the brighter life, and is unable to see because unaccustomed to the dark, or having turned from darkness to the day is dazzled by excess of light. And he will count the one happy in his condition and state of being, and he will pity the other; or, if he have a mind to laugh at the soul which comes from below into the light, there will be more reason in this than in the laugh which greets him who returns from above out of the light into the den.

42 That, he said, is a very just distinction.

Notes

[1] *Allegory,* from Greek terms meaning "to speak so as to imply something else," is a representation of meaning through concrete form, a figurative treatment of one idea under the guise of another. In this title, *cave* symbolizes "darkness" or "unenlightenment."
[2] Suppose, picture to onself.
[3] Set right.
[4] False impression.
[5] Sprinkled with stars.
[6] Dwelling place.
[7] Compliment, congratulate.
[8] An 8th-century B.C. Greek poet, possibly the author of the *Iliad* and the *Odyssey.*
[9] Add.
[10] Blissful, blessed.

FASHIONS IN VULGARITY

Louis Kronenberger

LOUIS KRONENBERGER (1904–) was born in Cincinnati and was educated at the university there. At the beginning of his career he was an editor for two New York book publishers; later, he worked on *Fortune Magazine* and was a drama critic for other periodicals. Mr. Kronenberger has lectured and taught at numerous universities. He is the author of many books, among them *Company Manners* (1954), *A Month of Sundays* (1961), and *Quality: Its Image in the Arts* (1969).

I

1 Nothing, in a sense, would be easier to chronicle[1] than a history of bad taste. The past is strewn with horrible examples; we need only look at the drearier or declining sections of cities, or in junk or antique shops, or—since on occasion vulgarity begins at home—in our own family attics. There are McKinley-period[2] trophies in architecture, German-beermug-era trophies in décor.[3] Everywhere there are reminders of a false refinement; or novels that ladies quite as much as ladies' maids once wept over. Every age yields fictional accounts of moneyed upstarts—Trimalchio in ancient Rome, M. Jourdain in seventeenth-century France, the Veneerings in nineteenth-century England.[4] Was "bad taste" ever more rife[5] than among Victorian England's indigestible wedding-cakes in stone? Yet, was "vulgarity" ever so ridiculous as with the great Lord Chesterfield,[6] who deemed it vulgar to laugh aloud; or with the French classical drama, that forbade mention of the handkerchief, since on its exalted stage not noses were blown, but trumpets.

2 Yet, though nothing were more easily compiled than a chronicle of bad taste, nothing, after a time, calls

out more for revision. Let fifty years go by, and it is not the items in the catalogue that shriek bad taste; it is the cataloguer. Not what he excoriated[7] will seem vulgar, but what he extolled.[8] In the early 1920's a critic of décor, championing the most functional furniture, might have whacked away at the curlycued accessories of the Victorians. Today all too many people wish their keepsakes had been kept, sigh in vain for their grandparents' square pianos and rosewood sofas; and shudder at the metal frames and tubular stems that passed for furniture. Clearly, since taste began, one generation's fashion has become the next generation's fright.

3 In the degree, then, that it posits touchstones[9] and untouchables, proclaims What's Done and proscribes[10] What Will Never Do, every catalogue of bad taste is a comedy of overassurance. Virtually the same era that banished the handkerchief from the drama, and laughter from the drawing-room, cheerfully made butts of cuckolds[11] and sport of madmen. The Augustans, while thinking it effeminate for men to carry umbrellas, deemed it manly for them to carry muffs. The Victorians,[12] while forbidding mention of most illnesses and all sex, doted on rancid[13] practical jokes. Yet, for all such warnings of booby traps, there is perhaps some point in our trying to discover vulgarity's more permanent traits. From the past, we get at least a clue in its verbal alliances, in the company it kept. There was once constant reference to "vulgar display," to "vulgar curiosity," to "vulgar presumption." Vulgar display, probably the arch offender, calls up visions of too much finery and jewelry, of bric-a-brac[14] and be-silvered-and-china'd dining-room tables—or simply of too much dinner. All this particularly brings the last century to mind, for with it emerged large, prosperous middle-class families that, by requiring large houses, encouraged lavish living. Moreover, an age that admired plump, high-busted women put no tax on heavy meals. Then, too, so prudish an age banned so many other forms of indulgence as perhaps to make lavishness less an initial desire than a kind of last resort. A respectable matron dared not smoke a cigarette; on the other hand she could virtuously eat three slices of cake.

4 Actually, even the more tasteful Victorians never stigmatized[15] display in itself; they merely stigmatized this thing or that on display. Passing up, for the moment, any distinction between vulgarity and bad taste, we still might note that vulgarity isn't avoided merely through good taste in individual selection; there must also be a sense of proportion about the whole. Nor need we confine ourselves to the marble and plush atrocities of upstarts: the desire to exhibit on a vast scale has much ancient and aristocratic warrant.[16] Most lordly establishments impart a too strutting sense of ownership, of greedy heaping-up and senseless size. Measured against a perfect taste, the patrician's giving material form to his pride of rank can be just as vulgar as the parvenu's[17] proclaiming his lack of any.

5 There was that other once-common phrase, "vulgar presumption." It has largely fallen into disuse, not because people have stopped being presumptuous but because the phrase became

a caste reproof—something applied to whomever one deemed one's social inferior. The culprit might often be vulgar enough, whether from a bumptious[18] attempt to get on or a blatant attempt to dazzle; but he was hardly presumptuous: it was rather his detractors who presumed. But of course the class bias that stamps so many things vulgar goes very deep—indeed to the roots of the word itself, to *vulgus* or the common people. Something, in other words, was vulgar that had a lower-class stamp—or at least the stamp of a lower class than one's own.

6 This class bias is not uninstructive; but though we have still to define vulgarity, plainly in its subtler connotations today it has not just overflowed "lower class" banks; it has been rechanneled in a different direction. We might even contend that it is only the common people—along with some decidedly uncommon ones—who are not vulgar. What were once designated the lower orders may be coarse or crude, may indeed be common or cheap or disgusting. But the things they do that are most beyond the pale[19]—belch or spit, eat with their knives or sleep in their underwear—do not quite fit our current sense of "vulgar." It is crude to eat with your knife; what is vulgar is to drink tea with your little finger extended. It is disgusting to pick your teeth; what is vulgar is to use a gold toothpick. It is illiterate to say "ain't I"; what is vulgar is to say "aren't I." The common people, as a group, are not vulgar if only because they don't know enough or care enough to be.

7 It is among those who would once have been termed their betters that we encounter vulgarity full blast. We encounter it, that is, when signs of education have entered in; when there is a certain awareness of social or cultural or esthetic right and wrong; where there is a craving to attract notice or seem to belong. We are never, said La Rochefoucauld,[20] so ridiculous through the qualities we have as through those we pretend to; and we are never, he might have added, so cheap. For, together with such pretensions, there almost always goes the attempt to mask them—the coy tactic, the devious maneuver. Vulgarity, I would think, involves motivation. People are vulgar when, for self-interested reasons, they resort to unworthy methods—whenever they do something to falsify or floodlight their prestige or importance, their claims to position or talent or knowledge. They are equally vulgar when, from the same kind of motives, they fail to do something. One of the columnists told of a Broadway figure who displayed a new gold cigarette case. "I'm sick of gold," he remarked—"what I'd have really liked was a platinum cigarette case: but my friends would have thought it was silver."

8 At an innocuous[21] level, vulgarity is mere vanity—people's wanting to look their best, or better than their best. Oliver Cromwell[22] might exhort the portraitist to paint him warts and all; most of us desire to have the warts removed, and dimples added. Few of us speak as readily of the ancestor who was hanged as of the ancestor who was knighted. But if we weren't a little vulgar in matters of this sort we might be something much worse, we might be unbearably priggish.[23] It is not till people, in manifesting superiority, begin to seem sniffy and cheap—or no better than what they

disparage[24]—that vulgarity turns offensive. The well-placed have for generations made a vulgar ploy[25] of vulgarity: Jones, they will remark, had "the bad taste" to refer to something they didn't want mentioned; or Smith had "the insolence" to remind them of something they preferred to forget. This sort of high-handedness always has vulgar blood; high-handedness, indeed, must pass an esthetic test of being more stylish or witty than it is arrogant and rude. Equally, there are right and wrong snubs. The wrong ones can be as ill-bred as anything they wish to pulverize. For a nice snub, consider the very nobly born Frenchman to whom some one not half so well-born was bragging of his vast family mansion with its great high-domed dining-room. "With us," the Frenchman finally murmured, "it's just the other way. Our dining-room is so low that all we can eat is fried sole."

9 Obviously, there are ways in which human and artistic vulgarity differ. Vulgarity in life is not just an esthetic offense; it has a falseness or impurity about it, an *inner* cheapness. Vulgar people often display perfect form; can talk well, live smartly, even get discreetly ahead in the world. But as they grow superficially more presentable, they grow, if anything, inwardly more insensitive. There is even a kind of vulgarity so self-assured as to take pride in flaunting itself: a very famous theater personage sent out, as a Christmas card, a picture of himself posing for a beer ad. Vulgarity in art, on the other hand, usually involves form as well as substance, and questions of esthetic effect. But it, too, largely derives from a false or flashy motive, from a greater wish to be impressive than sound. Often in men of much talent we find a streak of it—of excess or exhibitionism, specious beauty or spurious virtue. Swinburne can be too lilting or lush; Wilde and Disraeli use too much pomade; Tennessee Williams can be lavishly sensational, William Saroyan ostentatiously humane.[26]

10 On the other hand, we must distinguish between styles in art and the vulgarization of a style. Thus, gingerbread architecture with its childlike Hansel-and-Gretel playfulness may be far less vulgar than "classical" mansions that look like U.S. subtreasuries. One may not respond to the baroque of Tiepolo's frescoes or Prandtauer's[27] architecture; but except where misapplied, baroque is not vulgar in the least. Indeed, the real test of taste perhaps only arises at the level of the ornamented or theatrical. Any one, by playing safe, by wearing only grey and navy blue, by sticking to the best Georgian[28] spoons, by reading Virgil or Racine, can be unassailably tasteful. The test of taste comes in one's particular use of bright paint and loud colors, or harps and trumpets, or marble and jewels. Almost any one can grasp the vulgarity in Liszt and the lack of it in Mozart; it is more difficult to grasp the vulgar lapses in Wagner and the lack of them in Berlioz. And certainly one great form of vulgarity is the fear of vulgarity; it flaws the work of even a Henry James.[29]

II

11 Vulgarity does not stand still: there are fashions in it, it shows progress, it gains on one front and loses on another. The world of today differs

strikingly from that of two centuries ago—machinery and mass production, literacy and mass communication, democracy and relatively classless living have proved banes[30] and blessings alike. Material display—the overmuch, the over-large, the over-stuffed, the over-shiny—has in great part been streamlined into submission. Our material tastes have not only learned from the excesses of the past, they are shaped by the exigencies[31] of the present. What with a general lack of space today, and lack of servants; with doctors and diets, with the rise of sport and decline of prudery,[32] most people eat, dress, live, travel, entertain more simply. To gorge or splurge is curiously unchic. Most people indeed live like most other people, in a world of deep-freezes, dishwashers, station wagons, casseroles and baby-sitters. A pantry maid is almost as remote as a coach-and-four; and a man may see the same dress on his secretary as on his wife. And with so much social and cultural leveling off, vulgar display has steeply declined.

12 The new vulgarity is different. The old vulgarity followed that classic rule for the playwright—always show rather than tell. The vulgar used to show how grand they were by the size of their houses, the massiness of their plate, the snootiness of their butlers; by how they over-dressed, over-tipped, overrode those about them. They never said they were rich; they never had to.

13 Today the old stage formula has been discarded for the blunter vulgarity of *announcing* one's importance. Self-display has passed over into self-advertisement; and it is not so much the business world that conducts itself so as the world of journalism, of Hollywood and Broadway, of TV and "the communication arts." In that world people, beyond frequently engaging paid publicists, distribute their own testimonials, write their own plugs, sing their own praises, stress their own good deeds. And when not patting their own backs, they are slapping—or stabbing—other people's. When they cannot command the limelight, they invade it. This is an age of name-dropping—and of last-name-dropping even more—when on meeting a famous man of sixty, a man of twenty-four straightway calls him Bill. And as the first name flourishes in speech, so does the first person in writing. Serious writers turn out waggish[33] pieces as a way of plugging their books. Columnists brag, when the most piffling news story breaks, how they had predicted it months before. Into the body of their newspaper stints people inject commercials about their TV appearances. Even all sense of occasion has vanished. At a small private New Year's Eve party, while the guests were watching, on TV, the crowds gathered in Times Square, one television man sang out loudly to another: "They wanted *me* to handle this—but we couldn't get together on the dough." The remark, to be sure, isn't much more vulgar than the sort of gathering that makes it possible. In the professional world today, entertainment tends to be the merest form of self-advancement, of blandly feeding the mouth that bites you, of managing to be seen, of striking up useful connections on sofas, of cooking up deals over drinks. Even those hostesses who are above the battle and imagine they

are exhibiting lions are actually racing rats.

14 All this, however appalling, is today perhaps inevitable. What with ratings and samplings, press-agentry and polls, people who are supposed to mold and influence others must more and more promote themselves, make shop-windows of their offices, show windows of their homes. Truman Capote, in his book about the visit of the *Porgy and Bess* troupe to the Soviet Union, told how, while most of those on board the train going into Russia relaxed and joked, a columnist was kidded for sitting in a compartment alone, pounding relentlessly away at his typewriter. "People don't get into my income-tax bracket," he explained, "by looking at scenery."

15 Furthermore, the whole fashion in entertaining, or interviewing, or "educating" mass audiences today tends to throw privacy to the winds, to make publicity not just an unreprehensible,[34] but a greatly respected, side of modern life. To use zoological terms once more—it keeps getting harder to use strictly human ones—there now goes on a kind of human horse show, in which blue-ribboned personalities are trotted up and down, are photographed, queried, televised; or are just put on view as distinguished hosts or pedigreed hostesses endorsing Scotch or bed-sheets or soap. For the amateurs in all this, the appeal to vanity may be enough: for the professionals, it is part of a fierce struggle to survive. Big-name feuding is no longer mere internecine strife; it is a spectator sport. Which of two feuders will come out ahead is on a par with which of two football teams.

16 The worst part of all this is that it has *become* such a spectator sport. It was said, long ago, that evil communications corrupt good manners: it might be said more pertinently[35] today that mass communication corrupts good manners, that we are all being gradually worn down, that without even being aware of it, we are acquiescing in what would have appalled us twenty-five years ago. And how not, with the very air we breathe commercialized, with the very lives we live treated as so much copy? Quite literally, it is the gossip columnist's business to write about what is none of his business. The quiz programs with their venal[36] lure and test-of-virtue stakes have vanished; but another kind of quiz program survives, where interviewers ask people—before millions of listeners—questions that their closest friends might hesitate to ask them when alone.

17 It is perfectly true that it takes two to make up such interviews—and millions, listening in, to make a go of them. Clearly, were there no people willing to be questioned, and no large audiences intent upon the answers, such programs could not exist. But, psychologically and sociologically, the thing is not so simple. With the person interviewed, vanity; love of the limelight; the fear that it will go elsewhere, are strong inducements; and in an age when publicity has become respectable and when psychiatry has licensed people to Tell All, fewer and fewer are those who when invited will say No. But what has happened to the performer is really less important than what has happened to the public. Of course, the average person is full of

curiosity and enjoys gossip. But to argue that—because he's something of a peeping tom—it's his inquisitiveness that produces such interviews, is pure peeping-tommyrot. We bring up our children, we order our lives, we regulate our society on the contrary principle that our shoddier instincts should not be deliberately pandered[37] to. Those most genuinely concerned for freedom of speech are no less concerned for the right of privacy; nor are they misled when sensationalism appears purporting to be the servant of truth, or when psychiatry is commercially invoked to chaperone smut. The motive of the scandal magazines is all too clear. It is where the motive is masked, when privacy is invaded on the pretext[38] of a sociological search warrant, that a more menacing vulgarization appears; and as the product of such corrupting alliances, what sort of children will inhabit the world of tomorrow? For in time values not only get tarnished: they even get turned around. A few years ago George S. Kaufman,[39] by complaining that *Stille Nacht*[40] was being turned into a kind of cheap Christmas commercial, roused a storm of furious protest against himself: in the face of such things, who shall dare to argue that people can distinguish God from Mammon?[41]

18 We live in a world where TV is now sovereign, is so enthroned that 50,000,000 Americans sit bareheaded before it for hours on end, enduring blare for the sake of glare, and forever plagued by those powers behind the throne—the sponsors with their intrusions. *Of course* there are good television programs; but that is sociologically beyond the point. The point is that for tens of millions of people TV has become habit-forming, brain-softening, taste-degrading; has altered for the worse the whole cultural climate of American life. Privacy was in sufficient danger before TV appeared; and TV has given it its death blow. And as all liking for privacy vanishes, all dislike for publicity must vanish too. Men that one would have supposed had distinction are nowadays Men of Distinction by way of the ads. Indeed, the better known a man is for his taste or good character, the more he is sought out, the more he is importuned,[42] to sully or betray them. When those who shape our manners shout at parties about not getting together over the dough, or send out their beer blurbs as Christmas cards, who shall maintain that the vulgarity that once featured a clock planted in a Venus de Milo's[43] belly has disappeared? Some of us might even put back the clock if we could.

Notes

1 Record, relate.

2 William McKinley was President of the United States, 1897–1901.

3 Style of decoration.

4 Trimalchio was a vulgar rich man in Petronius Arbiter's *The Satyricon,* a work of the first century; Monsieur Jourdain tried to pass as a gentleman by spending large sums of money (Molière's *The Bourgeois Gentleman,* 1670); Hamilton and Anastatia Veneering were social climbers in Dickens's *Our Mutual Friend* (1864–1866).

5 Common, abundant.

[6] A British statesman and author (1694–1773).
[7] Denounced, berated.
[8] Praised highly.
[9] Lays down standards or criteria of judgment.
[10] Prohibits.
[11] The husbands of unfaithful wives were made the objects of ridicule and contempt.
[12] Those who lived in Great Britain during the reign of Queen Victoria (1837–1901). "Augustans," indirectly a reference to the Augustan Age of Roman literature, here applies to those living in the eighteenth century in England.
[13] Unpleasant, stale.
[14] Small decorative articles.
[15] Branded with disgrace, defamed.
[16] Authorization, right.
[17] A *parvenu* is a newcomer, one who has recently acquired wealth or position; a *patrician* is a member of an influential ruling class.
[18] Offensive, rude.
[19] *Pale* has a meaning of "limits," "bounds." *Beyond the pale* means beyond the limits of courtesy, safety, or, as here, good taste and propriety.
[20] A French moralist and essayist (1613–1680).
[21] Harmless.
[22] Puritan statesman and British general (1599–1658).
[23] Fussy, self-righteous.
[24] Discredit, put down.
[25] Maneuver, trick.
[26] The first three persons named were English figures of the nineteenth century; Williams and Saroyan are 20th-century American playwrights.
[27] Prandtauer (or Prandauer) was an Austrian architect who died in 1826; Giovanni Tiepolo and his son were 18th-century Italian painters.
[28] A reference to a period of British history from the accession of George I in 1714 to the death of George IV in 1830.
[29] Every standard desk dictionary will identify the composers and authors listed in this passage.
[30] Poisons, deaths, destructions.
[31] Demands, needs.
[32] Excessive modesty.
[33] Jocular, roguish, merry.
[34] Blameless, innocent.
[35] More to the point, directly.
[36] Corrupt.
[37] Catered.
[38] Excuse; concealed reason.
[39] American dramatist and journalist, 1889–1961.
[40] "Silent Night."
[41] A personification of riches or material wealth.
[42] Pressed, begged.
[43] In 1820, an ancient Greek statue of Venus was found on the island of Melos (whence its name) and is now in the Louvre, Paris.

The Learning Game

OBSERVATION

Henry David Thoreau

HENRY DAVID THOREAU (1817–1862) was born to near poverty in the town of Concord, Massachusetts, and became at times a teacher, surveyor, odd-job man, speaker, and writer. Through diligence and thrift he was able to attend a local academy and Harvard College, where he made a lifelong friend of Emerson. Graduated in 1837, Thoreau taught in his brother's school and then worked for his father. In 1845, Thoreau was jailed for a day for refusing to pay the poll tax. He built a hut at Walden Pond, outside Concord, and lived there between 1845 and 1847. He lectured from Maine to Pennsylvania on transcendentalism and the abolition of slavery. The last years of Thoreau's life were plagued by tuberculosis, and he died at the age of forty-four.

1 There is no such thing as pure *objective* observation. Your observation, to be interesting, *i.e.*[1] to be significant, must be *subjective*.

2 The sum of what the writer of whatever class has to report is simply some human experience, whether he be poet or philosopher or man of science. The man of most science is the man most alive, whose life is the greatest event. Senses that take cognizance[2] of outward things merely are

of no avail. It matters not where or how far you travel—the farther commonly the worse—but how much alive you are. If it is possible to conceive of an event outside to humanity, it is not of the slightest significance, though it were the explosion of a planet. Every important worker will report what life there is in him. It makes no odds into what seeming deserts the poet is born. Though all his neighbors pronounce it a Sahara, it will be a paradise to him; for the desert which we see is the result of the barrenness of our experience. No mere willful activity whatever, whether in writing verses or collecting statistics, will produce true poetry or science. . . .

3 All that a man has to say or do that can possibly concern mankind, is in some shape or other to tell the story of his love—to sing, and, if he is fortunate and keeps alive, he will be forever in love. This alone is to be alive to the extremities.[3] It is a pity that this divine creature should ever suffer from cold feet; a still greater pity that the coldness so often reaches to his heart. I look over the report of the doings of a scientific association and am surprised that there is so little life to be reported; I am put off with a parcel of dry technical terms. Anything living is easily and naturally expressed in popular language. I cannot help suspecting that the life of these learned professors has been almost as inhuman and wooden as a rain-gauge or self-registering magnetic machine. They communicate no fact which rises to the temperature of blood-heat. It doesn't all amount to one rhyme.

Notes

1 *Id est,* that is.
2 Notice, awareness.
3 Limits, ends.

CONRAD'S "YOUTH"

Robert F. Haugh

ROBERT F. HAUGH (1910–) was born in Independence, Kansas, and was graduated from the University of Kansas in 1934. In 1948, he received the degree of Doctor of Philosophy from the University of Michigan, where he now teaches. Dr. Haugh's particular fields of interest and research are modern fiction and American literature.

1 "Youth" is a modest gem of a story with rare felicity of style and event.[1] Youth and the ancient East; youth and an old skipper in his first command; youth and an old rotting coaler —when one examines the story he is

astonished to find the magic in images of age which permeate[2] it. In a story of darkness, inspired attention to patterns of light; in a story of youth, inspired attention to patterns of age. Here is the key to Conrad's magnificent verve[3] and sparkle in "Youth." The reader finds youth in odd places, myriad[4] images of decay. Yet so deftly does Conrad manage point of view that his ancients are not weary, hopeless relics of lost vitality, but sprightly like a child's vision of Saint Nick. Conrad's squalor here is like Dickens': brightened by a sparkling spirit, forever young. Conrad creates a joyful world of sombre events by two methods: the dichromatic refraction of his style; and the *progression d'effet* which makes the tale vibrate with energy the more it plunges into disaster.[5]

2 "Youth" is a Marlow story, but barely so. Marlow appears at the opening curtain, reappears at intervals to say, "Pass the bottle," and the rest of the time remains in the anonymity of the "I" telling the story.

3 The skipper of the "*Judea:* London, 'Do or Die' " is a sixty-year-old neophyte[6] with cottony hair and blue eyes amazingly like a boy's. He is on his first cruise as captain—a boyish circumstance oddly matching Marlow's twenty years. His wife, whom we meet shortly, has "the figure of a young girl, with a face . . . wrinkled and ruddy like a winter apple." When the collision comes—one of the early disasters—Captain Beard snatches her up like a bride, runs nimbly across deck and down a ladder to a boat. What could be more youthful and surprising—more delightfully like the capering Saint Nick?

4 The second mate is elderly as well, white-bearded: "—between those two old chaps I felt like a small boy between two grandfathers." Like the skipper, the mate "had something wrong with his luck, and had never got on." But of course Marlow has a wondrous faith in his luck, and is certain with the immortal certitude[7] of youth, that he will get on, never fear.

5 The ship is old, all rust and grime, but it has "Do or die" under the scrollwork[8] of the stern, and to young Marlow it is the very spirit of adventure.

6 Another oldster is Jermyn, the North Sea pilot with the perpetual[9] tear on the end of his nose, whose ideas are hostile to hopeful young Marlow's dreams: "We either had been in trouble, or were in trouble, or expected to be in trouble." Scornful as the young seaman is, he recognizes trouble when it comes. First, the October gale that shifts the ballast of sand while underway for Tyne coal.[10] It was the famous gale of that year; it sends men into the cavernous[11] hold to shovel back the shifting sand, "falling down with a great flourish of shovels."

7 At Tyne, Mrs. Beard comes aboard while the ship is loaded. The grandmotherly old lady with the figure of a young girl mends Marlow's socks and shirts. The ship, tied alongside a dock, is rammed in a drizzle by sheer bad luck. In an astonishing sequence of events, the climax is the hail from the captain, out in a small boat even before the crew had wits enough to miss him.

8 After repairs they set out, loaded with coal. It is January in "beautiful sunny winter weather that has more

charm than in the summertime, because it is unexpected, and crisp, and you know it won't, can't last long." It is weather like youth in the company of wintry old men. In the channel a gale from the southwest punishes the *Judea* "with spite, without interval, without mercy." The ship begins to leak badly. Marlow and the others work at the pumps that wheeze like a bad heart, but work as they will, they barely keep even with the water. Young Marlow thinks, "What an adventure!" in exultation[12] at the test life is offering him.

9 They put into Falmouth[13] for repairs, take her out once more, and are back in a week with the crew refusing duty. Yet Marlow loves the ship more than ever. A third time they try it and come back. Now this adventurous craft, this white-winged bird of the seas, repository[14] of nomadic[15] youth's dreams—becomes a fixed museum freak, the familiar sight of townspeople, pointed out to tourists. Sailors become like citizens, known to grocers and tobacconists. Still young Marlow's love burgeons;[16] he defends her hotly from disparagement.[17]

10 Finally the *Judea* has a new copper bottom; the cargo is reshipped —then the rats leave her. But she breaks the spell of England at last and plunges ponderously[18] into southern latitudes. She lumbers through an interminable procession of days, while the gilt flashes her youthful slogan: "Do or die."

11 She is to die, but her death, climaxing other images of age in the story, illuminates magnificently the spirit of youth. The first signs of her mortality come in the Indian Ocean, when young Marlow notices a "funny smell." Soon the dread explanation is known—the cargo is afire. Spontaneous combustion[19] has occurred in coal made into powder by repeated loading and unloading.

12 Captain Beard is steadfast for Bangkok; no turning aside to Australia or closer ports. They try to smother the fire by cutting off air; they pump water into the hold.

> It was our fate to pump into that ship; to pump out of her; to pump into her; and after keeping water out of her to save ourselves from being drowned, we frantically poured water into her to save ourselves from being burned . . . the bright stream flashed in the sunshine . . . vanished on the black surface of the coal . . . a pestiferous[20] cloud, unclean vapors . . . defiling the splendor of sea and sky.

13 Yet the splendor and brightness are there, in young Marlow's heart. Trial by water, trial by fire, then trial by concussion—for the ship explodes after apparent and deceptive quiescence.[21]

14 Marlow finds himself sprawled on the black cargo after the blast. He clambers back to the unfamiliar deck to encounter the captain. "Where's the cabin table?" is Captain Beard's first inquiry. He must find the cabin table, center of his rational[22] life, before he can order his senses. Then, "Trim the yards," of that floating disaster, and trim them the crew does, to steer for Bangkok. Young Marlow thinks, "This is great. Now, this is something like. I wonder what will happen?"

15 A mail ship takes them in tow for Batavia,[23] but towing fans the fire, which now leaps high above the ship. The *Judea* must be abandoned. Not a

one of the crew but decides to stay with her to the last. The last of the *Judea* is a dazzling flame towering into the night sky, a Phoenix[24] flame to feed the spirit of young Marlow, eternal youth.

> Oh, the glamor of youth! Oh, the fire of it, more dazzling than the flames of the burning ship, throwing a magic light on the wide earth, leaping audaciously[25] to the sky—

First thought of the exultant Marlow is that he will first see the romantic East as skipper of his own craft—a small boat it is true, but what is that to youth?

16 Captain Beard wants to save precious mementoes of his first command—a length of old stream cable; a kedge anchor.[26] The crew says, "Aye, aye, sir" respectfully, then lets it slip over the side at first opportunity. Marlow stands off in his small command, but goes aboard one last time to fetch the captain. Where his imagination had created panic, shouting, terror, instead he finds the captain asleep on a settee, the mate and a few of the crew serenely eating cheese and bread and ale amidst the disaster.

17 The *Judea* burns in glorious triumph, her "magnificent death like a grave." The small boats set out under orders to keep together for safety. Not young Marlow.

> Do you know what I thought? I thought I would pull clear—part company as soon as I could. I wanted to have my first command all to myself.

18 Then come days of scorching sea, the boat seeming to stand still as if bewitched, with the men's mouths dry as tinder. They drag at oars with aching arms. Then one night, after the blistering desolation, comes an aromatic puff, laden with the strange odors of blossoms: "the mysterious East, perfumed like a flower." The youth sits, weary beyond expression at the journey's end, but exulting like a conqueror. Soon the captain follows. "I had a terrible time of it," he murmurs.

19 Marlow's first encounter with the people of the East finds him cursed for a native merchant as he approaches a ship in the harbor. Even this he thinks fascinating, and even a bit flattering.

20 "Youth" closes on a brilliant image of the jetty lined with exotic[27] faces, all attentive and silent in a blaze of color. They gaze without a sigh at the weary men, the old skipper who "looked as if he would never wake," old Mahon the mate, white beard upturned as though he had been shot, all sleeping "unconscious of the land and the people and the violence of sunshine." Youth, a blaze of color . . . the ancient East and the ancient men . . . these are the images that key the events in "Youth." They are events of disaster, defeat, frustration, deadly monotony, yet made to shine by the magic of style.

21 Conrad's design here has none of the menace of universal evil to be found in *Nigger of the Narcissus*.[28] But the split vision of his artistic consciousness permeates scene and event: age and youth; splendor and stifling fumes; frustration and exuberance; disaster and courage—these are the orderings of his matchless sensibility[29] for the materials and designs of his art.

Notes

[1] Although this is a clear and penetrating critical essay and review, it will be meaningful only when read in connection with the story itself (see under THE SHORT STORY).

[2] Saturate, penetrate, pervade.

[3] Vigor, enthusiasm.

[4] Numerous; in great number.

[5] This is a difficult sentence. *Dichromatic,* which means "having two colors," here suggests Conrad's awareness of light and dark, youth and age, life and death, good and evil—concepts that make up the story "Youth." *Progression d'effet* is a term from French which here means "enlargement and intensification."

[6] Beginner, novice, greenhorn.

[7] Undying confidence.

[8] Decoration.

[9] Permanent.

[10] Tyne, a river in northeast England, has long been famous as a center of the coaling industry.

[11] Deep.

[12] Joy, triumph.

[13] A seaport in southwest England.

[14] A place where things are stored.

[15] Wandering.

[16] Sprouts, grows.

[17] Reproach, discredit.

[18] Heavily, awkwardly.

[19] Ignition of a substance without heat from any external source.

[20] Evil, troublesome.

[21] Quiet, inactivity.

[22] Reasonable, sensible.

[23] A former name for Djakarta, a seaport on the northwest coast of Java.

[24] A *phoenix* was a mythical bird, fabled to burn itself on a funeral pyre and to rise from its ashes.

[25] Recklessly, boldly.

[26] A small anchor, the rope of which is used for pulling a boat along.

[27] Strange, exciting.

[28] A novel (1897) by Conrad.

[29] Feeling, perception.

MAN WILL PREVAIL

William Faulkner

WILLIAM FAULKNER (1897–1962) wrote from the background of his native Mississippi, where he lived most of his life. After service with the British Royal Air Force in 1918, he studied briefly at the University of Mississippi and then was postmaster of that college town (University, Mississippi) for two years. His more notable novels and collections of short stories are *The Sound and the Fury* (1929), *As I Lay Dying* (1930),

Sanctuary (1931), *These Thirteen* (1931), *Light in August* (1932), *The Unvanquished* (1938), *The Wild Palms* (1939), *Go Down, Moses* (1942), *Intruder in the Dust* (1948), *Collected Stories* (1950), *Requiem for a Nun* (1951), *A Fable* (1954, Pulitzer Prize), *Dr. Martino and Other Stories* (1959), and *The Reivers* (1962, Pulitzer Prize).

1 I feel that this award was not made to me as a man, but to my work—a life's work in the agony and sweat of the human spirit, not for glory and least of all for profit, but to create out of the materials of the human spirit something which did not exist before. So this award is only mine in trust. It will not be difficult to find a dedication for the money part of it commensurate[1] with the purpose and significance of its origin. But I would like to do the same with the acclaim[2] too, by using this moment as a pinnacle[3] from which I might be listened to by the young men and women already dedicated to the same anguish and travail,[4] among whom is already that one who will some day stand here where I am standing.

2 Our tragedy today is a general and universal physical fear so long sustained by now that we can even bear it. There are no longer problems of the spirit. There is only the question: When will I be blown up? Because of this, the young man or woman writing today has forgotten the problems of the human heart in conflict with itself which alone can make good writing because only that is worth writing about, worth the agony and the sweat.

3 He must learn them again. He must teach himself that the basest[5] of all things is to be afraid; and, teaching himself that, forget it forever, leaving no room in his workshop for anything but the old verities[6] and truths of the heart, the old universal truths lacking which any story is ephemeral[7] and doomed—love and honor and pity and pride and compassion and sacrifice. Until he does so, he labors under a curse. He writes not of love but of lust, of defeats in which nobody loses anything of value, of victories without hope and, worst of all, without pity or compassion. His griefs grieve on no universal bones, leaving no scars. He writes not of the heart but of the glands.

4 Until he relearns these things, he will write as though he stood among and watched the end of man. I decline to accept the end of man. It is easy enough to say that man is immortal simply because he will endure: that when the last ding-dong of doom has clanged and faded from the last worthless rock hanging tideless in the last red and dying evening, that even then there will still be one more sound: that of his puny inexhaustible[8] voice, still talking. I refuse to accept this. I believe that man will not merely endure: he will prevail. He is immortal, not because he alone among creatures has an inexhaustible voice, but because he has a soul, a spirit capable of compassion and sacrifice and endurance. The poet's, the writer's, duty is to write about these things. It is his privilege to help man endure by lifting his heart, by reminding him of the courage and honor and hope and pride and compassion and pity and sacrifice which have been the glory of his past. The poet's voice need not merely be the record of man, it can be one of the props, the pillars to help him endure and prevail.

Notes

[1] Having the same measure, corresponding in amount or degree.
[2] Approval, praise.
[3] Peak, highest point.
[4] Labor, toil, pain.
[5] Most cowardly, mean-spirited.
[6] Basic facts.
[7] Short-lived, insubstantial.
[8] Unfailing, tireless.

THE READING MACHINE

Morris Bishop

MORRIS (GILBERT) BISHOP (1893–) was born in Willard, New York, and educated at Cornell University, where he taught romance languages until 1960 and now is university historian. He has written several books, among them *A Gallery of Eccentrics* (1928); *Pascal, the Life of Genius* (1936); *Spilt Milk* (1942); *A Bowl of Bishop* (1954); *The Horizon Book of the Middle Ages* (1968); and *The Exotics* (1969). Mr. Bishop is also editor of *A Treasury of British Humor* (1942).

1 "I have invented a reading machine," said Professor Entwhistle, a strident energumen[1] whose violent enthusiasms are apt to infect his colleagues[2] with nausea or hot flashes before the eyes.

2 Every head in the smoking room of the Faculty Club bowed over a magazine, in an attitude of prayer. The prayer was unanswered as usual.

3 "It is obvious," said Professor Entwhistle, "that the greatest waste of our civilization is the time spent in reading. We have been able to speed up practically everything to fit the modern tempo—communication, transportation, calculation. But today a man takes just as long to read a book as Dante[3] did, or—"

4 "Great Caesar!" said the Professor of Amphibology,[4] shutting his magazine with a spank.

5 "Or great Caesar,"[5] continued Professor Entwhistle. "So I have invented a machine. It operates by a simple arrangement of photoelectric cells, which scan a line of type at lightning speed. The operation of the photoelectric cells is synchronized[6] with a mechanical device for turning the pages—rather ingenious.[7] I figure that my machine can read a book of three hundred pages in ten minutes."

6 "Can it read French?" said the Professor of Bio-Economics,[8] without looking up.

7 "It can read any language that is printed in Roman type. And by an alteration of the master pattern on which the photoelectric cells operate,

it can be fitted to read Russian, or Bulgarian, or any language printed in the Cyrillic alphabet.[9] In fact, it will do more. By simply throwing a switch, you can adapt it to read Hebrew, or Arabic, or any language that is written from right to left instead of from left to right."

8 "Chinese?" said the Professor of Amphibology, throwing himself into the arena. The others still studied their magazines.

9 "Not Chinese, as yet," said Professor Entwhistle. "Though by inserting the pages sidewise . . . Yes, I think it could be done."

10 "Yes, but when you say this contrivance[10] reads, exactly what do you mean? It seems to me—"

11 "The light waves registered by the photoelectric cells are first converted into sound waves."

12 "So you can listen to the reading of the text?"

13 "Not at all. The sound waves alter so fast that you hear nothing but a continuous hum. If you hear them at all. You can't, in fact, because they are on a wave length inaudible to the human ear."

14 "Well, it seems to me—"

15 "Think of the efficiency of the thing!" Professor Entwhistle was really warming up. "Think of the time saved! You assign a student a bibliography of fifty books. He runs them through the machine comfortably in a weekend. And on Monday morning he turns in a certificate from the machine. Everything has been conscientiously read!"

16 "Yes, but the student won't remember what he has read!"

17 "He doesn't remember what he reads now."

18 "Well, you have me there," said the Professor of Amphibology. "I confess you have me there. But it seems to me we would have to pass the machine and fail the student."

19 "Not at all," said Professor Entwhistle. "An accountant today does not think of doing his work by multiplication and division. Often he is unable to multiply and divide. He confides his problem to a business machine and the machine does his work for him. All the accountant has to know is how to run the machine. That is efficiency."

20 "Still, it seems to me that what we want to do is to transfer the contents of the book to the student's mind."

21 "In this mechanized age? My dear fellow! What we want is to train the student to run machines. An airplane pilot doesn't need to know the history of aerodynamics.[11] He needs to know how to run his machine. A lawyer doesn't want to know the development of theories of Roman law. He wants to win cases, if possible by getting the right answers to logical problems. That is largely a mechanical process. It might well be possible to construct a machine. It could begin by solving simple syllogisms, you know—drawing a conclusion from a major premise and a minor premise—"

22 "Here, let's not get distracted. This reading machine of yours, it must *do* something, it must make some kind of record. What happens after you get the sound waves?"

23 "That's the beauty of it," said Professor Entwhistle. "The sound waves are converted into light waves, of a different character from the original light waves, and these are communicated to an automatic type-

writer, working at inconceivable speed. This transforms the light impulses into legible typescript, in folders of a hundred pages each. It tosses them out the way a combine tosses out sacked wheat. Thus, everything the machine reads is preserved entire, in durable[12] form. The only thing that remains is to file it somewhere, and for this you would need only the services of a capable filing clerk."

24 "Or you could read it?" persisted the Professor of Amphibology.

25 "Why, yes, if you wanted to, you could read it," said Professor Entwhistle.

26 An indigestible[13] silence hung over the Faculty Club.

27 "I see where the Athletic Association has bought a pitching machine," said the Assistant Professor of Business Psychology (Retail). "Damn thing throws any curve desired, with a maximum margin of error of three centimeters over the plate. What'll they be thinking of next?"

28 "A batting machine, obviously," said Professor Entwhistle.

Notes

1 Loud enthusiast.
2 Associates, fellow-workers.
3 Italian poet (1265–1321), author of the *Divine Comedy*.
4 A humorously nonexistent professorship; *amphibology* means an uncertainty or ambiguity of speech.
5 Julius Caesar lived from about 100 B.C. to 44 B.C.
6 Fitted to operate exactly together.
7 Clever, original.
8 Another invention of the author; *bio* is a Greek prefix meaning "life."
9 Writing (script) later adopted for use in languages such as Russian.
10 Device, invention.
11 A science that deals with the motion of air and other gases.
12 Lasting.
13 Strained (not easily absorbed).

THE CASE FOR GREATER CLARITY IN WRITING

Ivor Brown

IVOR JOHN CARNEGIE BROWN (1891–) is one of London's most accomplished men of letters. His first novel was published when he was only 24; since then he has composed many books on politics, drama, and the art of writing. Among his better-known titles are *A Word in Your Ear* (1942), *No Idle Words* (1948), *Chosen Words* (1955), *London* (1960), *How Shakespeare Spent the Day* (1963), *What Is a Play?* (1964), *A Ring of Words* (1967), *Dickens and His World* (1970).

1 The literary fashion of these days is not to know what you mean and, if challenged, to shrug a careless shoulder and say that you write what you write and the reader must make his own interpretation. The author's observations are presumed to be pregnant;[1] the reader is to be midwife and bring the child to birth. It is no business of genius to make itself plain.

2 This was the line taken up by T. S. Eliot[2] in an interview given after the first production of *The Cocktail Party* at the Edinburgh Festival of Arts in 1949. The play later acted with immense success in London and New York was, I think, a simplified and improved version of the original. But that does not affect Eliot's reply to the charge of being obscure and his tenet[3] that the artist is under no obligation to be explicit.[4] He projects his thoughts, feelings, and fancies: on the task of interpretation the public must bring its own wits to bear.

3 I suggest in return that this attitude betrays either laziness or affectation.[5] It is the abdication[6] of authorship. It is the business of the literary artist to know his mind and to speak it. Mr. Eliot, after all, was dramatizing certain problems of conduct and of human relations and he presented a Psychotherapeutic Sage as moral preceptor.[7] He was not just fetching up thoughts that lie too deep for tears; he was informing us about destiny and salvation, important matters on which we have a right to clear instruction. In that case we surely are entitled to know what his opinions on these great matters are. The fact that the play was written in what might be called conversational verse does not affect the proposition that an author is evading his responsibilities if he is not intelligible.[8]

4 Swift[9] shrewdly said that the true definition of style is "proper words in proper places." To this I would add "proper thoughts in proper order." There is nothing impossible about that. The greatest prose writers of our time are in my estimation Bernard Shaw and Somerset Maugham.[10] Did either of them ever write a sentence that was vague?

5 If you are anti-Shavian you can accuse Shaw of writing every sort of nonsense, but you need never pause for a moment to wonder what sort of nonsense he intends. And as a model of lucid scrutiny[11] of a life's experience and a life's conclusions Maugham's *The Summing-Up* is unsurpassed. Again, you need not agree with his judgments and valuations, but you know precisely what those judgments are.

6 Now let us have some examples of the muddled writing for which in my opinion there is no excuse. Mr. Henry Green's[12] novels are now very much in the intellectual fashion, presumably because he so loftily disdains syntax, grammar, and punctuation. Here is a typical sentence from page 1 of his much-praised story, modestly called "Nothing":

> It was wet then, did she remember he was saying, so unlike this he said, and turned his face to its dazzle of window, it had been dark with sad tears on the panes and streets of canals as he sat by her fire for Jane liked dusk, would not turn on the lights until she couldn't see to move, while outside a single street lamp was yellow, reflected over a thousand raindrops on the glass, the fire was rose, and Penelope came in.

7 Could anything be untidier? A schoolboy would be in trouble for such infantile, turbid,[13] ill-punctuated stuff, with its flood of commas and contempt of all the rules of composition; those rules were not made to be a nuisance to writers but for the advantage of readers. As a reader I object to having this mess thrown at my head.

8 Then we have Mr. T. S. Eliot writing "Notes Towards a Definition of Culture." Note the timidity of the title. He is not offering to define culture; he is going to devote 124 pages to fidgeting round the edges of a definition. He includes sentences like this:

> The way of looking at culture and religion which I have been trying to adumbrate[14] is so difficult that I am not sure I grasp it myself except in flashes or that I comprehend all its implications.[15]

9 Now if an author can only "try to adumbrate" an opinion and then admits his own inability to understand his own point of view, I suggest that he should keep quiet until he has cleared up his own confusion. Can one imagine a master of thought and English faltering and fumbling in this way! But to cut one's way through mental fog is now to be called obvious, or trivial; to founder[16] in it, confessing one's impotence,[17] is taken to be profound.

10 Nobody can pretend that much of the poetry written in the last quarter of a century has not been obscure. That is one reason why in Great Britain the bulk of it has become unsalable. London publishers protest that, with the exception of Eliot and one or two others, it is ruin to print poetry, and the Arts Council, appealed to for help by the distraught bards,[18] is busily considering what to do about the wilting Muse.[19] Shall it endow with public funds publication of the poetry which the public is now so unwilling to read?

11 The defense of the Obscure poets who defy grammar, syntax, and meaning as they eject their strained imagery is a mixed one. Some pleaders merely deny the charge; those who do not understand the tangled products of the Spasmodist[20] Singers are accused of being lazy or stupid or both. The blame is laid on the boneheaded reader who will not puzzle the stuff out and work away at the verbal jigsaw provided. Another plea is that the contemporary world is so confused in its complex of economic, political, ethical, and psychological problems that nobody who is true to his time can be expected to be lucid in the exposition of the age and its dilemmas.[21]

12 The first excuse is a mere denial of guilt, which gets nowhere in a court of law. The second is an affirmation and defense of artistic impotence. Once more it is the abdication of the author. The more intricate the mass of our difficulties the greater is the need of minds able to cut into them like knives, get rid of jargon[22] and give us meaning.

13 One habit of those unable to express themselves is to take cover under a long word which happens to be in vogue. Existentialism is an obvious case in point. Whenever somebody tells me that So-and-So is an Existentialist, with the implication that I am therefore to bow my head in awe and admiration, I immediately challenge him for a definition of Existentialism.

I have never had the beginnings of a satisfactory reply.[23]

14 Producers and actors of Existentialist plays are completely flummoxed[24] if asked to cut the cackle and say exactly what they mean. So, in my experience, are literary critics. They wander off into some vague profundities[25] about Essence and when asked to say exactly what that means they do not know.

15 To be vague may often be a short cut to a certain kind of popularity. It provides a debating point, and man is an argumentative animal. To write a poem, a play, or a book which will become a dinner-table topic may be a profitable occupation. It is jam for the intellectual snobs who relish telling you what the author was really getting at. Because you do not know, and do not pretend to know, you are supposed to be a crude simpleton. The history of the Snob-Value of the Obscure deserves a book in itself. When Browning[26] remarked that only the author knew the meaning of his "Sordello" and that he had forgotten it, he gave enormous joy to the Browning Societies of his day, who then got to work on unravelment and so displayed their own surpassing acumen[27] and ingenuity.

16 Admittedly the poet is not quite in the same position as the writer of prose. He is working more on percept than on concept, more on feeling than on dialectic.[28] But there is no reason why he should not be able to give an exact image in words of his perceptions and his emotions. The best poets have managed to do so. Do we know just what Keats felt about the nightingale or the Grecian urn?[29] We do. He did not have to make war on syntax or turn his odes into a grammarian's funeral.

17 I have never had to scratch my head over the sweet melancholy of A. E. Housman or put wet towels round an aching brain in order to excavate the meanings from a poem of Tennyson.[30] Sometimes a creative mind works so rapidly that his thought outruns his hand and the images become telescoped like the railway carriages in an accident: Shakespeare's immense fecundity[31] sometimes led to this. But no great poet, at his best, is obscure.

18 The public as a whole—that is, the public barring the Intellectual Snobs—shows its sensible preference for having its artists in sufficient possession of their faculties to put us all, and immediately, in possession of their meaning. The artist who does not know his own intentions is a pretender. If he does know them and cannot express them he is merely incompetent.

19 I hope I have made myself plain.

Notes

1 Full of meaning, significant.

2 Thomas Stearns Eliot (1888–1964), an influential poet, critic, and playwright who was born in the United States and lived largely in England.

3 Opinion.

4 Fully clear.

5 Pretense, artificiality.

[6] Giving up, renouncing.
[7] A wise person using mental suggestion for teaching morality and ethics.
[8] Capable of being understood.
[9] Jonathan Swift (1667–1745), English essayist and satirist.
[10] For George Bernard Shaw, see *Arms and the Man,* later in this book; Maugham (1874–1965) was an English novelist, short-story writer, and dramatist.
[11] Clear examination, inquiry.
[12] An English novelist, born in 1905.
[13] Clouded, obscured.
[14] Outline, sketch.
[15] Suggestions.
[16] Fall, sink down.
[17] Weakness.
[18] Bewildered poets.
[19] A goddess or other power regarded as aiding a poet.
[20] A *spasmodic* person is one seized by spasms—sudden, violent attacks. Here, poets are seen as people suffering bursts of excitement.
[21] Problems, perplexities.
[22] Meaningless talk and writing.
[23] The author is not alone in his failure to understand; a partial definition of *existentialism:* "the doctrine that a person forms the inner being, the essence and core, of his life in the kind of existence (life) he chooses to lead."
[24] Confused, upset.
[25] "Deep" thoughts.
[26] Robert Browning (1812–1889), English poet.
[27] Acuteness of mind, insight.
[28] More on seeing than thinking, more on emotion than argumentation.
[29] See Keats's "Ode on a Grecian Urn" in this volume.
[30] See the selections by Housman and Tennyson in this volume.
[31] Fruitfulness, abundance.

STYLE

John Henry Newman

JOHN HENRY NEWMAN (1801–1890) was one of the truly notable literary and religious figures of the nineteenth century. Originally an Anglican vicar, he was received into the Roman Catholic Church in 1845 and in 1879 was created a Cardinal by Pope Leo XIII. His *Apologia Pro Vita Sua* (1864, 1865) is a well-wrought autobiography; many volumes of his sermons have continued to wield influence; his *The Idea of a University* (1852) is the rich outcome of his work as Rector of Catholic University, Dublin.

1 Thought and speech are inseparable from each other. Matter and expression are parts of one: style is a thinking out into language. This is what I have been laying down, and this is literature; not *things,* not the verbal symbols of things; not on the other hand mere *words;* but thoughts ex-

pressed in language. Call to mind, Gentlemen, the meaning of the Greek word which expresses this special prerogative[1] of man over the feeble intelligence of the inferior animals. It is called Logos: what does Logos mean? it stands both for *reason* and for *speech,* and it is difficult to say which it means more properly. It means both at once: Why? because really they cannot be divided,—because they are in a true sense one. When we can separate light and illumination, life and motion, the convex and the concave of a curve, then will it be possible for thought to tread speech under foot, and to hope to do without it—then will it be conceivable that the vigorous and fertile intellect should renounce its own double, its instrument of expression, and the channel of its speculations and emotions.

2 Critics should consider this view of the subject before they lay down such canons[2] of taste as the writer[3] whose pages I have quoted. Such men as he is consider fine writing to be an *addition from without* to the matter treated of,—a sort of ornament superimposed,[4] or a luxury indulged in, by those who have time and inclination for such vanities. They speak as if *one* man could do the thought, and *another* the style. We read in Persian travels of the way in which young gentlemen go to work in the East, when they would engage in correspondence with those who inspire them with hope or fear. They cannot write one sentence themselves; so they betake themselves to the professional letter-writer. They confide to him the object they have in view. They have a point to gain from a superior, a favour to ask, an evil to deprecate;[5] they have to approach a man in power, or to make court to some beautiful lady. The professional man manufactures words for them, as they are wanted, as a stationer sells them paper, or a schoolmaster might cut their pens. Thought and word are, in their conception, two things, and thus there is a division of labour. The man of thought comes to the man of words; and the man of words, duly instructed in the thought, dips the pen of desire into the ink of devotedness and proceeds to spread it over the page of desolation. Then the nightingale of affection is heard to warble to the rose of loveliness, while the breeze of anxiety plays around the brow of expectation. This is what the Easterns are said to consider fine writing; and it seems pretty much the idea of the school of critics to whom I have been referring.

3 We have an instance in literary history of this very proceeding nearer home, in a great University, in the latter years of the last century. I have referred to it before now in a public lecture elsewhere;[6] but it is too much in point here to be omitted. A learned Arabic scholar had to deliver a set of lectures before its doctors and professors on an historical subject in which his reading had lain. A linguist[7] is conversant with science rather than with literature; but this gentleman felt that his lectures must not be without style. Being of the opinion of the Orientals, with whose writings he was familiar, he determined to buy a style. He took the step of engaging a person, at a price, to turn the matter which he had got together into ornamental[8] English. Observe, he did not wish for

mere grammatical English, but for an elaborate, pretentious style. An artist was found in the person of a country curate,[9] and the job was carried out. His lectures remain to this day, in their own place in the protracted series of annual Discourses to which they belong, distinguished amid a number of heavyish compositions by the rhetorical and ambitious diction for which he went into the market. This learned divine, indeed, and the author I have quoted, differ from each other in the estimate they respectively form of literary composition; but they agree together in this,—in considering such composition a trick and a trade; they put it on a par with the gold plate and the flowers and the music of a banquet, which do not make the viands[10] better, but the entertainment more pleasurable; as if language were the hired servant, the mere mistress of the reason, and not the lawful wife in her own house.

Notes

1 Power, right.
2 Rules, laws.
3 Laurence Sterne (1713–1768), an English novelist and clergyman.
4 Set over or above; joined as an addition.
5 Disapprove, protest against.
6 In the third of a series of lectures entitled "The Position of Catholics in England."
7 A person skilled in several languages.
8 Showy, decorative.
9 A parish priest.
10 Food.

THE FIVE MAIN PURPOSES OF EDUCATION

Max Rafferty

Max Rafferty (1917–) was born in New Orleans and received his undergraduate education at the University of California, Los Angeles. He earned the degree of Doctor of Education from the University of Southern California (1955). In 1963, he became Superintendent of Public Instruction for the state of California. Among his books are *Suffer, Little Children* (1962) and *What They Are Doing to Your Children* (1964).

1 An old, old story is told of a certain philosopher who in a dream one night was visited by Minerva, goddess of wisdom. In partial repayment for a long life of dedication to philosophy, she offered him the answer to one question, with no strings attached.

2 "Tell me, O goddess," cagily quoth

the sage,[1] "how I may find the one unfailing path to truth, justice and virtue?"

3 "That's easy," quipped his Olympian visitant[2] briskly. "Just define your terms."

4 And with that she vanished in a flurry of ectoplasm,[3] after the annoying manner of goddesses.

5 I was reminded of old Min the other day when I received this letter from one of my less ecstatic correspondents.

6 "You're always talking about the strengths, weaknesses and problems of education. I notice, however, that you never quite get around to defining your terms. What is education or, rather, what should it be? What's the purpose of education anyway?"

7 It doesn't have one, sir. It has five, and here they are.

1—*To pursue the truth.*

8 Yes, sir. The truth. No matter where it may be or how cleverly it may be concealed. It is a never-ending chase, of course, and being mortal, erring humans, we may never quite catch up with truth and hold it cupped in our hands. The very search for it, though, cannot but ennoble[4] those who spend their lives in such a quest.

2—*To hand down the cultural heritage of the race.*

9 Otherwise each generation would have to spend its valuable time re-inventing the wheel. Or writing "Hamlet." Or splitting the atom. Education focuses the accumulated wisdom of the past upon the vexing problems of the present in order to make possible a better future. Or at least it should.

3—*To teach organized, disciplined, systematic subject matter.*

10 Not life adjustment, togetherness, in-groupness or happy, easy, comfortable acceptance by one's peer group. The only thing which enables man to dominate a savagely hostile environment is knowledge of specific subject matter and the ability to use it as a means of keeping said environment tamed and in its place. This old saw[5] is especially pertinent[6] for present-day America, whose planetary environment is currently so downright hostile as to be positively hair-raising.

4—*To help the individual realize his own potential.*

11 Until relatively recently, concern with the individual was the be-all and the end-all of my profession. Of late we've been plunging up all kinds of blind alleys labeled "group counseling," "group psychological testing" and an educator's version of "group therapy." We'd better get the individual back into the educational spotlight unless, of course, we want to opt for the ant-hill, mass-Pavlovian-reflex training which the Russians have substituted for real education.[7] The latter is cheaper, and more efficient. It just isn't education.

5—*To ensure the survival of our country.*

12 If Uncle Sam goes down the drain, so does our whole educational establishment with its practitioners. Something else would take its place, no

doubt, but it would be pretty unrecognizable, except perhaps to somebody like George Orwell.[8] In fact, we educators had better do whatever is necessary to see that Uncle Sam stays around a while longer. Unless we're ready to change our vocation,[9] that is.

13 There. I've defined my terms. For my money, these are the five purposes of education.

14 You will notice that none of them has much to do with adjustment to environment or with the achievement of popularity within one's group or even with making a fast buck. These things can be taught, all right, but the process is not real education.

Notes

1 Shrewdly asked the wise man.

2 Olympus, a mountain in Greece, was the mythical home of Greek gods.

3 The supposed outward flow from the body of a supernatural agency or being.

4 Elevate, exalt.

5 Saying.

6 Suitable, applicable.

7 Ivan Pavlov (1849–1936) was a Russian physiologist, famed for his experiments with the reactions of dogs to varied stimuli.

8 An English novelist and essayist (1903–1950), whose best-known work is *1984*, an anti-Utopian novel which appeared in 1949.

9 Business or profession.

WHAT IS WRONG WITH THE UNIVERSITY ACCORDING TO THE STUDENTS

Harold Taylor

HAROLD TAYLOR (1914–) was born in Toronto, Canada, and was educated at the University of Toronto and at the University of London (England). He came to the United States in 1939 and was naturalized in 1947. At the age of thirty, he became president of Sarah Lawrence College. Since leaving that position in 1959, Dr. Taylor has advanced educational experiments throughout the United States and abroad by teaching, lecturing, and writing. Among his books are *On Education and Freedom* (1954), *Art and the Intellect* (1960), *Students Without Teachers* (1969).

Here is a list of what activist students say is wrong with their education in the university. The list is not drawn from the radical literature or the action programs of the militants,[1] although most of them would agree with it. It is a summary of what most concerned students say on the basis of their own experience.[2]

1. The university has remained aloof from the moral, political and social issues of contemporary society and has simply acted as the servant of the status quo,[3] selling its services to the highest bidder and ignoring the true interest and needs of the students and the American people.
2. Students have no real part in making educational and social policy and are being programmed by others to fit into an unjust, undemocratic, and racist[4] society.
3. Faculty members, who control the curriculum and the teaching system, are concerned with following their own academic careers and not with the education of students.
4. The teaching has therefore been of low quality, dehumanized, mechanized, and organized in a system made to suit the convenience of the faculty.
5. The system consists of:
   (a) Professors lecturing to students in large classes three times a week, in fifty-minute periods, with one period a week for discussion sections and tests. Most of the lectures are boring and cover ground also covered in assigned textbooks written by other professors who are also boring.
   (b) Students taking required courses, either as general requirements for the B.A. degree or as special requirements of the subject matter departments, with few other options.[5] The student is locked into whatever courses the faculty decides he must take, and no matter how bad the course and the teacher, the student has no escape and has little chance to plan his own education. This results in low motivation,[6] or at the very least, no encouragement for developing a motivation on the part of those who are already unmotivated.
   (c) Five courses are to be taken as the regular number each semester in order to graduate in four years, with three units of academic credit for each course. This fragments the student's time and makes it impossible for him to do justice to any one subject, since with fifteen classes a week plus the discussion and test sections, with each class taught in the same way by lectures and reading assignments, there is no time left to think about what is being learned, and not enough is taught about any one thing.
   (d) An examination and grading apparatus which is used to measure and award credit for the way in which the student meets the expectations of the teacher. This means that the student is constantly and anxiously working to make a good grade rather than learning the subject, while the examinations, sometimes in the form of objective tests administered biweekly, measure what he has remembered rather than what he is capable of doing as a thinking person.
   (e) Departmental majors by which the student must take courses in the junior and senior year which are geared to the academic requirements of graduate school rather than to the development of the student's interests and intellectual ability.
6. The total effect of this system is therefore to divorce learning from life, to put the student in a passive role, and to force him through the study of materials which are irrelevant to his own interests and to the needs and problems of the society around him.
7. Both the curriculum and the admis-

sions policies are stacked in favor of white middle-income students from suburban or urban high schools where from eighty to ninety-five percent of all seniors go on to college. This means that when intelligent students whose academic preparation has been poor are admitted to college, they find it very hard to keep up in a competitive system which puts its primary emphasis on the skills of academic learning, and in a high proportion of cases are flunked out or drop out through discouragement.

8. The political and social pressures on the students and faculty in the public universities from boards of regents[7] and state legislatures are so great that student and faculty activism[8] is repressed, academic freedom is stifled, and campus dissent is met by police action, tear gas, clubs, and guns.
9. The social restrictions of campus life treat the student as a child rather than as a responsible young adult, and prevent him from enjoying the ordinary privileges of privacy and freedom which he would have if he were not in college.
10. University presidents and administrative officers are crisis managers, fund-raisers, politicians, and bureaucrats, not educators, and they have little knowledge of student realities and little respect for student opinion unless it coincides with their own or unless they are forced to pay attention to students and their views through student confrontations.[9] Since they are responsible to the conservative boards of trustees that appoint them to office, to alumni, to potential donors, and to state legislative bodies, and they are hired to carry out board policy, they seldom take stands on any political or social issues, and are faceless office-holders rather than cultural and educational leaders. They therefore have little influence on student opinion or on the quality of the students' education.

Notes

[1] The words *radical* and *militant* each have several meanings, but in general they refer to persons who are active and even violent in working for drastic changes in political, social, educational, or economic affairs.

[2] This selection does not fully represent the style of the book from which it is taken. *How To Change Colleges: Notes on Radical Reform* is a handbook, an "operating manual," on how to put educational changes into effect. It consists of seventeen chapters written in straightforward prose. This selection is a summary of the points at issue.

[3] The existing state or condition, things as they are now.

[4] A reference to the belief that human races have distinctive characteristics that determine their cultures and that one's own race is superior and therefore entitled to rule others.

[5] Choices.

[6] Incentive, encouragement.

[7] In some states, groups of persons are appointed or elected to supervise educational standards and to set requirements for all educational activities within their boundaries. A *regent* is one who has and who exercises "ruling power."

[8] Action, involvement.

[9] Direct meetings; opposition.

SURVIVAL U

John Fischer

JOHN FISCHER (1910–) was born in Oklahoma and was educated at the University of Oklahoma and at Oxford University (Rhodes Scholar). He began his career as a newspaper reporter. He was editor-in-chief of *Harper's Magazine* from 1953 to 1967. Among Mr. Fischer's books are *Master Plan U.S.A.* (1951) and *The Stupidity Problem and Other Harassments* (1964).

It gets pretty depressing to watch what is going on in the world and realize that your education is not equipping you to do anything about it.

—From a letter by a University of California senior

1 She is not a radical, and has never taken part in any demonstration. She will graduate with honors, and profound disillusionment. From listening to her—and a good many like-minded students at California and East Coast campuses—I think I am beginning to understand what they mean when they say that a liberal-arts education isn't relevant.

2 They mean it is incoherent. It doesn't cohere. It consists of bits and pieces which don't stick together, and have no common purpose. One of our leading Negro educators, Arthur Lewis of Princeton, recently summed it up better than I can. America is the only country, he said, where youngsters are required "to fritter away their precious years in meaningless peregrination[1] from subject to subject . . . spending twelve weeks getting some tidbits of religion, twelve weeks learning French, twelve weeks seeing whether the history professor is stimulating, twelve weeks seeking entertainment from the economics professor, twelve weeks confirming that one is not going to be able to master calculus."

3 These fragments are meaningless because they are not organized around any central purpose, or vision of the world. The typical liberal-arts college has no clearly defined goals. It merely offers a smorgasbord[2] of courses, in hopes that if a student nibbles at a few dishes from the humanities table, plus a snack of science, and a garnish of art or anthropology, he may emerge as "a cultivated man"—whatever that means. Except for a few surviving church schools, no university even pretends to have a unifying philosophy. Individual teachers may have personal ideologies—but since they are likely to range, on any given campus, from Marxism[3] to worship of the scientific method to exaltation of the irrational (*à la* Norman O. Brown), they don't cohere either. They often leave a student convinced at the end of four years that any given idea is probably about as valid as any other—and that none of them has much relationship

to the others, or to the decisions he is going to have to make the day after graduation.

4 Education was not always like that. The earliest European universities had a precise purpose: to train an elite[4] for the service of the Church. Everything they taught was focused to that end. Thomas Aquinas[5] had spelled it all out: what subjects had to be mastered, how each connected with every other, and what meaning they had for man and God.

5 Later, for a span of several centuries, Oxford and Cambridge had an equally clear function: to train administrators to run an empire. So too did Harvard and Yale at the time they were founded; their job was to produce the clergymen, lawyers, and doctors that a new country needed. In each case, the curriculum was rigidly prescribed. A student learned what he needed, to prepare himself to be a competent priest, district officer, or surgeon. He had no doubts about the relevance of his courses—and no time to fret about expanding his consciousness or currying his sensual awareness.

6 This is still true of our professional schools. I have yet to hear an engineering or medical student complain that his education is meaningless. Only in the liberal-arts colleges—which boast that "we are not trade schools"—do the youngsters get that feeling that they are drowning in a cloud of feathers.

7 For a long while some of our less complacent academies have been trying to restore coherence to American education. When Robert Hutchins was at Chicago, he tried to use the Great Books to build a comprehensible framework for the main ideas of civilized man. His experiment is still being carried on, with some modifications, at St. John's[6]—but it has not proved irresistibly contagious. Sure, the thoughts of Plato and Machiavelli are still pertinent, so far as they go—but somehow they don't seem quite enough armor for a world beset with splitting atoms, urban guerrillas, nineteen varieties of psychotherapists, amplified guitars, napalm, computers, astronauts, and an atmosphere polluted simultaneously with auto exhaust and TV commercials.

8 Another strategy for linking together the bits-and-pieces has been attempted at Harvard and at a number of other universities. They require their students to take at least two years of survey courses, known variously as core studies, general education, or world civilization. These too have been something less than triumphantly successful. Most faculty members don't like to teach them, regarding them as superficial and synthetic.[7] (And right they are, since no survey course that I know of has a strong unifying concept to give it focus.) Moreover, the senior professors shun such courses in favor of their own narrow specialities. Consequently, the core studies which are meant to place all human experience—well, at least the brightest nuggets—into One Big Picture usually end up in the perfunctory[8] hands of resentful junior teachers. Naturally the undergraduates don't take them seriously either.

9 Any successful reform of American education, I am now convinced, will

have to be far more revolutionary than anything yet attempted. At a minimum, it should be:

1. Founded on a single guiding concept—an idea capable of knotting together all strands of study, thus giving them both coherence and visible purpose.

2. Capable of equipping young people to do something about "what is going on in the world"—notably the things which bother them most, including war, injustice, racial conflict, and the quality of life.

Maybe it isn't possible. Perhaps knowledge is proliferating[9] so fast, and in so many directions, that it can never again be ordered into a coherent whole, so that molecular biology, Robert Lowell's poetry, and highway engineering will seem relevant to each other and to the lives of ordinary people. Quite possibly the knowledge explosion, as Peter F. Drucker has called it, dooms us to scholarship which grows steadily more specialized, fragmented, and incomprehensible.

10 The Soviet experience is hardly encouraging. Russian education is built on what is meant to be a unifying ideology: Marxism-Leninism. In theory, it provides an organizing principle for all scholarly activity—whether history, literature, genetics, or military science. Its purpose is explicit: to train a Communist elite for the greater power and glory of the Soviet state, just as the medieval universities trained a priesthood to serve the Church.

11 Yet according to all accounts that I have seen, it doesn't work very well. Soviet intellectuals apparently are almost as restless and unhappy as our own. Increasing numbers of them are finding Marxism-Leninism too simplistic,[10] too narrowly doctrinaire, too oppressive; the bravest are risking prison in order to pursue their own heretical visions of reality.

12 Is it conceivable, then, that we might hit upon another idea which could serve as the organizing principle for many fields of scholarly inquiry; which is relevant to the urgent needs of our time; and which would not, on the other hand, impose an ideological strait jacket, as both ecclesiastical and Marxist education attempted to do?

13 Just possibly it could be done. For the last two or three years I have been probing around among professors, college administrators, and students—and so far I have come up with only one idea which might fit the specifications. It is simply the idea of survival.

14 For the first time in history, the future of the human race is now in serious question. This fact is hard to believe, or even think about—yet it is the message which a growing number of scientists are trying, almost frantically, to get across to us. Listen, for example, to Professor Richard A. Falk of Princeton and of the Center for Advanced Study in the Behavioral Sciences:

> The planet and mankind are in grave danger of irreversible catastrophe . . . Man may be skeptical about following the flight of the dodo into extinction, but the evidence points increasingly to just such a pursuit. . . . There are four interconnected threats to the planet —wars of mass destruction, overpopulation, pollution, and the depletion of resources. They have a cumulative[11] effect. A problem in

> one area renders it more difficult to solve the problems in any other area. . . . The basis of all four problems is the inadequacy of the sovereign states to manage the affairs of mankind in the twentieth century.

15 Similar warnings could be quoted from a long list of other social scientists, biologists, and physicists, among them such distinguished thinkers as Rene Dubos, Buckminster Fuller, Loren Eiseley, George Wald, and Barry Commoner. They are not hopeless. Most of them believe that we still have a chance to bring our weapons, our population growth, and the destruction of our environment under control before it is too late. But the time is short, and so far there is no evidence that enough people are taking them seriously.

16 That would be the prime aim of the experimental university I'm suggesting here: to look seriously at the interlinking threats to human existence, and to learn what we can do to fight them off.

17 Let's call it Survival U. It will not be a multiversity, offering courses in every conceivable field. Its motto—emblazoned[12] on a life jacket rampant—will be: "What must we do to be saved?" If a course does not help to answer that question, it will not be taught here. Students interested in musicology, junk sculpture, the Theater of the Absurd, and the literary *dicta* of Leslie Fiedler can go somewhere else.

18 Neither will our professors be detached, dispassionate scholars. To get hired, each will have to demonstrate an emotional commitment to our cause. Moreover, he will be expected to be a moralist; for this generation of students, like no other in my lifetime, is hungering and thirsting after righteousness. What it wants is a moral system it can believe in—and that is what our university will try to provide. In every class it will preach the primordial[13] ethic of survival.

19 The biology department, for example, will point out that it is sinful for anybody to have more than two children. It has long since become glaringly evident that unless the earth's cancerous growth of population can be halted, all other problems—poverty, war, racial strife, uninhabitable cities, and the rest—are beyond solution. So the department naturally will teach all known methods of birth control, and much of its research will be aimed at perfecting cheaper and better ones.

20 Its second lesson in biological morality will be: "Nobody has a right to poison the environment we live in." This maxim will be illustrated by a list of public enemies. At the top will stand the politicians, scientists, and military men—of whatever country—who make and deploy atomic weapons; for if these are ever used, even in so-called defensive systems like the ABM, the atmosphere will be so contaminated with strontium 90 and other radioactive isotopes that human survival seems most unlikely. Also on the list will be anybody who makes or tests chemical and biological weapons—or who even attempts to get rid of obsolete nerve gas, as our Army recently proposed, by dumping the stuff in the sea.

21 Only slightly less wicked, our biology profs will indicate, is the farmer who drenches his land with

DDT. Such insecticides remain virulent[14] indefinitely, and as they wash into the streams and oceans they poison fish, water fowl, and eventually the people who eat them. Worse yet—as John Hay noted in his recently published *In Defense of Nature*—"The original small, diluted concentrations of these chemicals tend to build up in a food chain so as to end in a concentration that may be thousands of times as strong." It is rapidly spreading throughout the globe. DDT already has been found in the tissues of Eskimos and of Antarctic penguins, so it seems probable that similar deposits are gradually building up in your body and mine. The minimum fatal dosage is still unknown.

22 Before he finishes this course, a student may begin to feel twinges of conscience himself. Is his motorcycle exhaust adding carbon monoxide to the smog we breathe? Is his sewage polluting the nearest river? If so, he will be reminded of two proverbs. From Jesus: "Let him who is without sin among you cast the first stone." From Pogo: "We have met the enemy and he is us."

23 In like fashion, our engineering students will learn not only how to build dams and highways, but where *not* to build them. Unless they understand that it is immoral to flood the Grand Canyon or destroy the Everglades with a jetport, they will never pass the final exam. Indeed, our engineering graduates will be trained to ask a key question about every contract offered them: "What will be its effect on human life?" That obviously will lead to other questions which every engineer ought to comprehend as thoroughly as his slide rule. Is this new highway really necessary? Would it be wiser to use the money for mass transit—or to decongest traffic by building a new city somewhere else? Is an offshore oil well really a good idea, in view of what happened to Santa Barbara?

24 Our engineering faculty also will specialize in training men for a new growth industry: garbage disposal. Americans already are spending $4½ billion a year to collect and get rid of the garbage which we produce more profusely[15] than any other people (more than five pounds a day for each of us). But unless we are resigned to stifling in our own trash, we are going to have to come up with at least an additional $835 million a year. Any industry with a growth rate of 18 per cent offers obvious attractions to a bright young man—and if he can figure out a new way to get rid of our offal, his fortune will be unlimited.

25 Because the old ways no longer work. Every big city in the United States is running out of dumping grounds. Burning won't do either, since the air is dangerously polluted already—and in any case, 75 per cent of the incinerators in use are inadequate. For some 150 years Californians happily piled their garbage into San Francisco Bay, but they can't much longer. Dump-and-fill operations already have reduced it to half its original size, and in a few more decades it would be possible to walk dry-shod from Oakland to the Embarcadero. Consequently, San Francisco is now planning to ship garbage 375 miles to the yet uncluttered deserts of Lassen County by special train—known locally as "The Twentieth Stenchery Limited" and

"The Excess Express." The city may actually get away with this scheme, since hardly anybody lives in Lassen County except Indians, and who cares about them? But what is the answer for the metropolis that doesn't have an unspoiled desert handy?

26 A few ingenious[16] notions are cropping up here and there. The Japanese are experimenting with a machine which compacts garbage, under great heat and pressure, into building blocks. A New York businessman is thinking of building a garbage mountain somewhere upstate, and equipping it with ski runs to amortize the cost. An aluminum company plans to collect and reprocess used aluminum cans—which, unlike the old-fashioned tin can, will not rust away. Our engineering department will try to Think Big along these lines. That way lies not only new careers, but salvation.

27 Survival U's Department of Earth Sciences will be headed—if we are lucky—by Dr. Charles F. Park, Jr., now professor of geology and mineral engineering at Stanford. He knows as well as anybody how fast mankind is using up the world's supply of raw materials. In a paper written for the American Geographical Society he punctured one of America's most engaging (and pernicious)[17] myths: our belief that an ever-expanding economy can keep living standards rising indefinitely.

28 It won't happen; because, as Dr. Park demonstrates, the tonnage of metal in the earth's crust won't last indefinitely. Already we are running short of silver, mercury, tin, and cobalt—all in growing demand by the high-technology industries. Even the commoner metals may soon be in short supply. The United States alone is consuming one ton of iron and eighteen pounds of copper every year, for each of its inhabitants. Poorer countries, struggling to industrialize, hope to raise their consumption of these two key materials to something like that level. If they should succeed—and if the globe's population doubles in the next forty years, as it will at present growth rates—then the world will have to produce, somehow, *twelve times* as much iron and copper every year as it does now. Dr. Park sees little hope that such production levels can ever be reached, much less sustained indefinitely. The same thing, of course—doubled in spades—goes for other raw materials: timber, oil, natural gas, and water, to note only a few.

29 Survival U, therefore, will prepare its students to consume less. This does not necessarily mean an immediate drop in living standards—perhaps only a change in the yardstick by which we measure them. Conceivably Americans might be happier with fewer automobiles, neon signs, beer cans, supersonic jets, barbecue grills, and similar metallic fluff. But happy or not, our students had better learn how to live The Simpler Life, because that is what most of them are likely to have before they reach middle age.

30 To help them understand how very precious resources really are, our mathematics department will teach a new kind of bookkeeping: social accounting. It will train people to analyze budgets—both government and corporate—with an eye not merely to immediate dollar costs, but to the long-range costs to society.

31 By conventional bookkeeping methods, for example, the coal companies strip-mining away the hillsides of Kentucky and West Virginia show a handsome profit. Their ledgers, however, show only a fraction of the true cost of their operations. They take no account of destroyed land which can never bear another crop; of rivers poisoned by mud and seeping acid from the spoil banks; of floods which sweep over farms and towns downstream, because the ravaged slopes can no longer hold the rainfall. Although these costs are not borne by the mining firms, they are nevertheless real. They fall mostly on the taxpayers, who have to pay for disaster relief, flood-control levees, and the resettlement of Appalachian farm families forced off the land. As soon as our students (the taxpayers of tomorrow) learn to read a social balance sheet, they obviously will throw the strip miners into bankruptcy.

32 Another case study will analyze the proposal of the Inhuman Real Estate Corporation to build a fifty-story skyscraper in the most congested area of midtown Manhattan. If 90 per cent of the office space can be rented at $12 per square foot, it looks like a sound investment, according to antique accounting methods. To uncover the true facts, however, our students will investigate the cost of moving 12,000 additional workers in and out of midtown during rush hours. The first (and least) item is $8 million worth of new city buses. When they are crammed into the already clogged avenues, the daily loss of man-hours in traffic jams may run to a couple of million more. The fumes from their diesel engines will cause an estimated 9 per cent increase in New York's incidence[18] of emphysema and lung cancer; this requires the construction of three new hospitals. To supply them, plus the new building, with water—already perilously short in the city—a new reservoir has to be built on the headwaters of the Delaware River, 140 miles away. Some of the dairy farmers pushed out of the drowned valley will move promptly into the Bronx and go on relief. The subtraction of their milk output from the city's supply leads to a price increase of two cents a quart. For a Harlem mother with seven hungry children, that is the last straw. She summons her neighbors to join her in riot, seven blocks go up in flames, and the Mayor demands higher taxes to hire more police. . . .

33 Instead of a sound investment, Inhuman Towers now looks like criminal folly, which would be forbidden by any sensible government. Our students will keep that in mind when they walk across campus to their government class.

34 Its main goal will be to discover why our institutions have done so badly in their efforts (as Dr. Falk put it) "to manage the affairs of mankind in the twentieth century." This will be a compulsory course for all freshmen, taught by professors who are capable of looking critically at every political artifact, from the Constitution to the local county council. They will start by pointing out that we are living in a state of near-anarchy, because we have no government capable of dealing effectively with public problems.

35 Instead we have a hodgepodge of

80,000 local governments—villages, townships, counties, cities, port authorities, sewer districts, and special purpose agencies. Their authority is so limited, and their jurisdictions so confused and overlapping, that most of them are virtually impotent.[19] The states, which in theory could put this mess into some sort of order, usually have shown little interest and less competence. When Washington is called to help out—as it increasingly has been for the last thirty-five years—it often has proved ham-handed and entangled in its own archaic bureaucracy. The end result is that nobody in authority has been able to take care of the country's mounting needs. Our welfare rolls keep growing, our air and water get dirtier, housing gets scarcer, airports jam up, road traffic clots, railways fall apart, prices rise, ghettos burn, schools turn out more illiterates every year, and a war nobody wants drags on and on. Small wonder that so many young people are losing confidence in American institutions. In their present state, they don't deserve much confidence.

36 The advanced students of government at Survival U will try to find out whether these institutions can be renewed and rebuilt. They will take a hard look at the few places—Jacksonville, Minnesota, Nashville, Appalachia—which are creating new forms of government. Will these work any better, and if so, how can they be duplicated elsewhere? Can the states be brought to life, or should we start thinking about an entirely different kind of arrangement? Ten regional prefectures,[20] perhaps, to replace the fifty states? Or should we take seriously Norman Mailer's suggestion for a new kind of city-state to govern our great metropolises? (He merely called for New York City to secede from its state; but that isn't radical enough. To be truly governable, the new Republic of New York City ought to include chunks of New Jersey and Connecticut as well.) Alternatively, can we find some way to break up Megalopolis,[21] and spread our population into smaller and more livable communities throughout the continent? Why should we keep 70 per cent of our people crowded into less than 2 per cent of our land area, anyway?

37 Looking beyond our borders, our students will be encouraged to ask even harder questions. Are nation-states actually feasible,[22] now that they have power to destroy each other in a single afternoon? Can we agree on something else to take their place, before the balance of terror becomes unstable? What price would most people be willing to pay for a more durable kind of human organization—more taxes, giving up national flags, perhaps the sacrifice of some of our hard-won liberties?

38 All these courses (and everything else taught at Survival U) are really branches of a single science. Human ecology is one of the youngest disciplines, and probably the most important. It is the study of the relationship between man and his environment, both natural and technological. It teaches us to understand the consequences of our actions—how sulfur-laden fuel oil burned in England produces an acid rain that damages the forests of Scandinavia, why a well-meant farm subsidy can force millions of Negro tenants off the land and lead to Watts and Hough.[23] A graduate

who comprehends ecology will know how to look at "what is going on in the world," and he will be equipped to do something about it. Whether he ends up as a city planner, a politician, an enlightened engineer, a teacher, or a reporter, he will have had a relevant education. All of its parts will hang together in a coherent whole.

39 And if we can get enough such graduates, man and his environment may survive a while longer, against all the odds.

Notes

1 Travel, movement.
2 A buffet meal; any medley or conglomeration.
3 A system of thought developed by Karl Marx (1818–1883), a German economist and philosopher, involving his ideas about class struggle, exploitation of workers, and the downfall of capitalism.
4 Persons with authority and influence.
5 An Italian philosopher (1225–1274) and major theologian of the Roman Catholic Church.
6 A college in Annapolis, Maryland.
7 Not real or genuine; artificial.
8 Performing routinely or indifferently.
9 Growing by multiplication.
10 Overly simplified, made too easy.
11 Growing and increasing by constant addition.
12 Proclaimed, depicted.
13 Original, first-formed.
14 Deadly, poisonous, active.
15 Abundantly, freely.
16 Inventive, clever.
17 Harmful.
18 Rate of occurrence.
19 Without force or effectiveness; powerless.
20 Territories, areas.
21 An urban region consisting of several adjoining cities and their suburbs.
22 Suitable; capable of being accomplished or effected, or of surviving.
23 City ghetto areas occupied by large numbers of blacks.

THE AMERICAN SCHOLAR[1]

Ralph Waldo Emerson

RALPH WALDO EMERSON (1803–1882) was born in Boston, Massachusetts, and was reared by his widowed mother and a Puritan aunt. After education at Boston Latin School, at the Latin School in Concord, Massachusetts, and at Harvard, Emerson taught school and then was admitted to Harvard's Divinity School. By 1829, he was serving in the pulpit of the Second Unitarian Church of Boston. Having lost his first wife after a short marriage, and in doubt about his religious beliefs, he left to tour Europe in 1832 and 1833.

In 1835, Emerson remarried, settled in Concord, and wrote and lectured in this country and abroad. Much later, his mind began to fail, and the burning of his home in Concord in 1872 was a blow from which he never fully recovered. Among his numerous works are *Nature* (1836); *Poems* (1847); *English Traits* (1856); *Society and Solitude* (1870). His *Complete Works* appeared in 1903–1904.

Another sign of our times, also marked by an analogous[2] political movement, is the new importance given to the single person. Everything that tends to insulate the individual—to surround him with barriers of natural respect, so that each man shall feel the world as his, and man shall treat with man as a sovereign state with a sovereign state—tends to true union as well as greatness. "I learned," said the melancholy Pestalozzi,[3] "that no man in God's wide earth is either willing or able to help any other man." Help must come from the bosom alone. The scholar is that man who must take up into himself all the ability of the time, all the contributions of the past, all the hopes of the future. He must be a university of knowledges. If there be one lesson more than another which should pierce his ear, it is: the world is nothing, the man is all; in yourself is the law of all nature, and you know not yet how a globule[4] of sap ascends; in yourself slumbers the whole of reason; it is for you to know all, it is for you to dare all. Mr. President and gentlemen, this confidence in the unsearched might of man belongs, by all motives, by all prophecy, by all preparation, to the American scholar. We have listened too long to the courtly Muses of Europe. The spirit of the American freeman is already suspected to be timid, imitative, tame. Public and private avarice[5] make the air we breathe thick and fat. The scholar is decent, indolent, complaisant.[6] See already the tragic consequence. The mind of this country, taught to aim at low objects, eats upon itself. There is no work for any but the decorous and the complaisant.[7] Young men of the fairest promise, who begin life upon our shores, inflated by the mountain winds, shined upon by all the stars of God, find the earth below not in unison with these—but are hindered from action by the disgust which the principles on which business is managed inspire, and turn drudges, or die of disgust—some of them suicides. What is the remedy? They did not yet see, and thousands of young men as hopeful now crowding to the barriers for the career do not yet see, that if the single man plant himself indomitably[8] on his instincts, and there abide, the huge world will come round to him. Patience—patience—with the shades of all the good and great for company; and for solace, the perspective of your own infinite life; and for work, the study and the communication of principles, the making those instincts prevalent, the conversion of the world. Is it not the chief disgrace in the world, not to be a unit—not to be reckoned one character—not to yield that peculiar fruit which each man was created to bear, but to be reckoned in the gross, in the hundred, or the thousand, or the party, the section, to which we belong; and our opinion predicted geographically, as the North or the South? Not so, brothers and friends—please God, ours shall not be so. We will walk on our own feet; we will work with our own hands; we will speak our own minds. The study of letters shall be no longer a name for pity, for doubt, and for sensual indulgence. The dread of man and the love of man shall be a wall of defense and a wreath of joy around all. A nation of men will for the first time exist, because each believes himself inspired by the Divine Soul which also inspires all men.[9]

Notes

[1] This address, of which only the long final paragraph is here reprinted, was delivered before the Phi Beta Kappa Society of Harvard in August 1837. It was called "our intellectual Declaration of Independence" by Oliver Wendell Holmes and soon became widely influential. This idealistic appeal for active leadership in American society by homegrown thinkers left Emerson's audience divided between enthusiasm and dismay, for the talk was considered drastic and even incendiary by some listeners. Its message unquestionably had great influence in freeing American literary thought from its ties to English and European society and literature and started native writing on a course that has consistently become more self-reliant during succeeding decades.

[2] Corresponding, related, comparable. In preceding paragraphs, Emerson had been discussing, "as a sign of the times," the fact that a political movement that elevated persons of "the lowest class" also resulted in literature that dealt with "the near, the low." Emerson felt that this "sign" was a "great stride" forward.

[3] Johann Heinrich Pestalozzi (1746–1827) was a Swiss educational reformer, "melancholy" because of the apparent failure of his theories.

[4] Small sphere.

[5] Greed, desire.

[6] Inclined or disposed to please; agreeable.

[7] Those proper and obliging.

[8] In an unyielding, unconquerable way.

[9] Here, as in much of what he lectured about and wrote, Emerson is pleading for individualism, self-reliance, and, inevitably, a resulting spirit of hope and optimism.

Ideas That Influenced the Nation

Introductory note

The civilization and culture of modern man have been shaped and guided by the thoughts of a limited number of men and women. More than a century ago, Walt Whitman wrote:

> It is strictly true that a few first-class poets, philosophers, and authors have substantially settled and given status to the entire religion, education, law, sociology, and so forth of the hitherto civilized world, by tingeing and often creating the atmospheres out of which they have arisen.

Something of the same idea is expressed in these words by the late American author Clarence Day:

> The world of books is the most remarkable creation of man. Nothing else that he builds ever lasts. Monuments fall; nations perish; civilizations grow old and die out; and, after an era of darkness, new races build others. But in the world of books are volumes that have seen this happen again and again, and yet live on, still young, still as fresh as the day they were written, still telling men's hearts of the hearts of men centuries dead.

Some two or three hundred works might be listed as truly "seminal," books or essays that are genuinely original and that have deeply influenced events. The selections that follow, with some claim to being seminal, have a particular meaning for American students of the late twentieth century.

THE MAYFLOWER COMPACT

William Bradford

William Bradford (1590–1657) emigrated from England to Holland in 1609, arrived in the New World on the *Mayflower,* and was elected governor of Plymouth Colony. He held this office most of the time between 1622 and 1656. Bradford's life was closely bound up with the colonial settlement of which he was the leading authority in legislative, executive, and judicial affairs. In 1630, he began his *History of Plimouth Plantation,* a work completed in 1651.

In the Name of God, Amen.

1 We whose names are underwritten, the loyal subjects of our dread[1] Sovereign Lord King James, by the Grace of God of Great Britain, France, and Ireland King, Defender of the Faith, etc.[2]

2 Having undertaken, for the Glory of God and advancement of the Christian Faith and Honour of our King and Country, a Voyage to plant the First Colony in the Northern Parts of Virginia, do by these presents solemnly and mutually in the presence of God and one of another, Covenant and Combine ourselves together into a Civil Body Politic, for our better ordering and preservation and furtherance[3] of the ends aforesaid; and by virtue hereof to enact, constitute and frame such just and equal Laws, Ordinances, Acts, Constitutions and Offices, from time to time, as shall be thought most meet[4] and convenient for the general good of the Colony, unto which we promise all due submission and obedience. In witness whereof we have hereunder subscribed our names at Cape Cod, the 11th of November, in the year of the reign of our Sovereign Lord King James, of England, France and Ireland the eighteenth, and of Scotland the fifty-fourth. Anno Domini 1620.

Notes

[1] Feared, held in awe.

[2] This compact (agreement or covenant) was signed on board the *Mayflower* by the first settlers at Plymouth on November 11, 1620. The first of several such governments organized by religious groups in New England, this agreement focused on the idea of the consent of the people and remained the basis of government in Plymouth Colony until the colony was made a part of Massachusetts in 1691.

[3] Advancement, promotion.

[4] Suitable, proper.

THE DECLARATION OF INDEPENDENCE

Thomas Jefferson

THOMAS JEFFERSON (1743–1826) was born into a prominent Virginia family, studied at the College of William and Mary, and from 1767 to 1774 practiced law. He entered Virginia's House of Burgesses, and in 1775 and 1776, as a member of the Continental Congress, drafted the principles contained in the Declaration of Independence. He was elected Governor of Virginia in 1779, went abroad to help negotiate the Treaty of Paris, and in 1784 succeeded Benjamin Franklin as Minister to France.

Upon his return in 1789, Jefferson served as Washington's Secretary of State and urged adoption of the Bill of Rights. In 1796, he was narrowly defeated for the presidency of the United States, but in 1800 he was elected. After his retirement in 1809, he established the University of Virginia, designed the state capitol at Richmond and Monticello, his own notably beautiful home near Charlottesville, and wrote extensively.

In CONGRESS, July 4, 1776.

THE UNANIMOUS DECLARATION of the thirteen united STATES OF AMERICA.[1]

1 When in the Course of human events, it becomes necessary for one people to dissolve the political bands which have connected them with another, and to assume among the powers of the earth, the separate and equal station to which the Laws of Nature and of Nature's God entitle them, a decent respect to the opinions of mankind requires that they should declare the causes which impel them to the separation.———We hold these truths to be self-evident, that all men are created equal, that they are endowed by their Creator with certain unalienable[2] Rights, that among these are Life, Liberty and the pursuit of Happiness.[3]—That to secure these rights, Governments are instituted among Men, deriving their just powers from the consent of the governed,—That whenever any Form of Government becomes destructive of these ends, it is the Right of the People to alter or to abolish it, and to institute new Government, laying its foundation on such principles and organizing its powers in such form, as to them shall seem most likely to effect their Safety and Happiness. Prudence, indeed, will dictate that Governments long established should not be changed for light and transient[4] causes; and accordingly all experience hath shewn,[5] that mankind are more disposed to suffer, while evils are sufferable, than to right themselves by abolishing the forms to which they are accustomed. But when a long train of abuses and usurpations, pursuing invariably the same Object evinces a design to reduce them under absolute Despotism,[6] it is their right, it is their duty, to throw off such Government, and to provide new Guards for their future security.—Such has been the patient sufferance of these

Colonies; and such is now the necessity which constrains them to alter their former Systems of Government. The history of the present King of Great Britain[7] is a history of repeated injuries and usurpations, all having in direct object the establishment of an absolute Tyranny over these States. To prove this, let Facts be submitted to a candid[8] world.——He has refused his Assent to Laws, the most wholesome and necessary for the public good.——He has forbidden his Governors to pass Laws of immediate and pressing importance, unless suspended in their operation till his Assent should be obtained; and when so suspended, he has utterly neglected to attend to them.——He has refused to pass other Laws for the accommodation of large districts of people, unless those people would relinquish the right of Representation in the Legislature, a right inestimable[9] to them and formidable to tyrants only. ——He has called together legislative bodies at places unusual, uncomfortable, and distant from the depository[10] of their public Records, for the sole purpose of fatiguing them into compliance with his measures. ——He has dissolved Representative Houses repeatedly, for opposing with manly firmness his invasions on the rights of the people.——He has refused for a long time, after such dissolutions,[11] to cause others to be elected; whereby the Legislative powers, incapable of Annihilation, have returned to the People at large for their exercise;[12] the State remaining in the mean time exposed to all the dangers of invasion from without, and convulsions within.——He has endeavoured to prevent the population of these States; for that purpose obstructing the Laws for Naturalization of Foreigners; refusing to pass others to encourage their migrations hither, and raising the conditions of new Appropriations of Lands.——He has obstructed the Administration of Justice, by refusing his Assent to Laws for establishing Judiciary powers.——He has made Judges dependent on his Will alone, for the tenure[13] of their offices, and the amount and payment of their salaries.——He has erected a multitude of New Offices, and sent hither swarms of Officers to harass our people, and eat out their substance. ——He has kept among us, in times of peace, Standing Armies without the Consent of our legislatures.——He has affected to render the Military independent of and superior to the Civil power.——He has combined with others[14] to subject us to a jurisdiction foreign to our constitution, and unacknowledged by our laws; giving his Assent to their Acts of pretended Legislation:—For Quartering large bodies of armed troops among us:—For protecting them, by a mock Trial, from punishment for any Murders which they should commit on the Inhabitants of these States:—For cutting off our Trade with all parts of the world:—For imposing Taxes on us without our Consent:—For depriving us in many cases, of the benefits of Trial by Jury:—For transporting us beyond Seas to be tried for pretended offences:—For abolishing the free System of English Laws in a neighbouring Province,[15] establishing therein an Arbitrary government, and enlarging its Boundaries so as to render it at once an example and fit instrument for introducing the same absolute rule into these Colonies:—For taking away our Charters, abolishing our most valuable Laws, and altering fundamentally the Forms of our Governments:—For suspending our own Legislatures, and declaring themselves invested with power to legislate for us in all cases whatsoever.—He has abdicated Government here, by declaring us out of his Protection and waging War against us:—He has plundered our seas, ravaged our Coasts, burnt our towns, and destroyed the lives of our people.—He is at this time transporting large Armies of foreign Mercenaries[16] to compleat the works of death, desolation and tyranny, already begun with circumstances of Cruelty & perfidy scarcely paralleled in the most barbarous ages, and totally unworthy the Head of a civilized nation.—He has constrained our fellow Citizens taken Captive on the high Seas to bear Arms against their Country, to become the executioners of their friends and Brethren, or to fall themselves by their Hands.—He has excited domestic[17] insurrections amongst us, and has endeavoured to bring on the inhabitants of our frontiers, the merciless Indian Savages, whose known rule of warfare, is an undistinguished destruction of all ages, sexes and conditions. In every stage of these Oppressions We have Petitioned for Redress in the most humble terms: Our repeated Petitions have been answered only by repeated injury. A Prince, whose character is thus marked by every act which may define a Tyrant, is unfit to be the ruler of a free people. Nor have We been wanting in attentions to our British brethren. We have warned them from time to time of attempts by their legislature to extend an unwarrantable jurisdiction over us. We have reminded them of the circumstances of our emigration and settlement here. We have appealed to their native justice and magnanimity,[18] and we have conjured them by the ties of our common kindred to disavow these usurpations, which, would inevitably interrupt our connections and correspondence. They too have been deaf to the voice of justice and of consanguinity.[19] We must, therefore, acquiesce in the necessity, which denounces[20] our Separation, and hold them, as we hold the rest of mankind, Enemies in War, in Peace Friends.

2 We, therefore, the Representatives of the United States of America, in General Congress Assembled, appealing to the Supreme Judge of the world for the rectitude[21] of our intentions, do, in the Name and by Authority of the good People of these Colonies, solemnly publish and declare, That these United Colonies are, and of Right ought to be Free and Independent States; that they are Absolved from all Allegiance to the British Crown, and that all political connection between them and the State of Great Britain, is and ought to be totally dissolved; and that as Free and Independent States, they have full Power to levy War, conclude Peace, contract Alliances, establish Commerce, and to do all other Acts and Things which Independent States may of right do.——And for the support of this Declaration, with a firm reliance on the protection of divine Providence, we mutually pledge to each other our Lives, our Fortunes and our sacred Honor.

Notes

[1] Richard Henry Lee (of Virginia) proposed a resolution in Congress on June 7, 1776, that "these united Colonies are, and by right ought to be, free and independent States." Action was postponed, but on June 11 a committee was appointed, which on June 28 presented the draft of a Declaration of Independence. It was largely the work of Jefferson, although Franklin made contributions, and the influence of John Adams is evident. On July 2, Lee's original resolution was passed. On July 4, the Declaration was passed. The Liberty Bell then rang from the State House steeple in Philadelphia.

[2] Incapable of being transferred.

[3] The political and philosophical ideals expressed in the Declaration can be traced back in history for centuries. For instance, John Locke (1632–1704), an English philosopher, defined "natural rights" as being those of "life, liberty and estate." A major distinction of the Declaration is the substitution of "the pursuit of happiness" for "estate" (property).

[4] Brief, temporary.

[5] Has shown.

[6] Tyranny.

[7] George III, king from 1760 to 1820.

[8] Impartial.

[9] Too great to be estimated.

[10] Place for keeping, storing.

[11] Breakings up, dispersals.

[12] Performance.

[13] Holding, possessing.

[14] Members of the British Parliament.

[15] The Quebec Act of 1774 made concessions to French Catholics, established French law, and thus divided Quebec from seaboard colonies to the south.

[16] German soldiers, largely Hessians.

[17] Native, at home.

[18] Nobility, greatness of mind and spirit.

[19] Relationship because of common ancestry, blood ties.

[20] Proclaims.

[21] Rightness.

THE AMERICAN CRISIS

Thomas Paine

THOMAS PAINE (1737–1809) was born in Thetford, England. At the age of thirty-seven, bankrupt and separated from his second wife, he sailed for Philadelphia, where he became an editor, writer, and spokesman for the American cause. He served as a soldier in the Revolution from 1776 to 1783.

In 1787, he traveled to Paris and then to London, where his controversial writings led to an indictment for treason. Opposing the Reign of Terror, he was imprisoned in France and was released only through the intercession of James Monroe. On his return to America in 1802, he was denounced as an atheist. He lived from then on in obscurity on his farm in New Rochelle, New York; ten years after his death his remains were taken to England and reburied in an unknown location.

1 These are the times that try men's souls: The summer soldier and the sunshine patriot[1] will in this crisis, shrink from the service of his country; but he that stands it Now, deserves the love and thanks of man and woman. Tyranny, like hell, is not easily conquered; yet we have this consolation with us, that the harder the conflict, the more glorious the triumph. What we obtain too cheap, we esteem to[o] lightly:——'Tis dearness only that gives everything its value. Heaven knows how to put a proper price upon its goods; and it would be strange indeed, if so celestial an article as FREEDOM should not be highly rated. Britain, with an army to enforce her tyranny, has declared that she has a right (not only to) TAX but "to BIND *us in* ALL CASES WHATSOEVER," and if being *bound in that manner,* is not slavery, then is there not such a thing as slavery upon earth. Even the expression is impious for so unlimited a power can belong only to God. . . .[2]

2 I have as little superstition in me as any man living, but my secret opinion has ever been, and still is, that God Almighty will not give up a people to military destruction, or leave them unsupportedly[3] to perish, who have so earnestly and so repeatedly sought to avoid the calamities of war, by every decent method which wisdom could invent.[4] Neither have I so much of the infidel[5] in me, as to suppose that he has relinquished the government of the world, and given us up to the care of devils; and as I do not, I cannot see on what grounds the king of Britain can look up to heaven for help against us: a common murderer, a highwayman, or a house-breaker, has as good a pretence[6] as he.

3 'Tis surprising to see how rapidly a panic will sometimes run through a country. All nations and ages have been subject to them: Britain has trembled like an ague at the report of a French fleet of flat-bottomed boats; and in the fourteenth century the whole English army, after ravaging the kingdom of France, was driven back like men petrified with fear; and this brave exploit was performed by a few broken forces collected and headed by a woman, Joan of Arc.[7] Would that heaven might inspire some Jersey maid to spirit up her countrymen, and save her fair fellow sufferers from ravage and ravishment! Yet panics, in some cases, have their uses; they produce as much good as hurt. Their duration is always short; the mind soon grows through them, and acquires a firmer habit than before. But their peculiar advantage is, that they are the touchstones[8] of sincerity and hypocrisy, and bring things and men to light, which might otherwise have lain forever undiscovered. In fact, they have the same effect on secret traitors which an imaginary apparition[9] would have upon a private murderer. They sift out the hidden thoughts of man, and hold them up in public to the world. Many a disguised tory[10] has lately shown his head, that shall penitentially solemnize with curses the day on

which Howe arrived upon the Delaware. . . .[11]

4 America did not, nor does not want force; but she wanted a proper application of that force. Wisdom is not the purchase of a day, and it is no wonder that we should err at the first setting off. From an excess of tenderness, we were unwilling to raise an army, and trusted our cause to the temporary defence of a well-meaning militia.[12] A summer's experience has now taught us better; yet with those troops, while they were collected, we were able to set bounds to the progress of the enemy, and, thank God! they are again assembling. I always considered militia as the best troops in the world for a sudden exertion, but they will not do for a long campaign. Howe, it is probable, will make an attempt on this city;[13] should he fail on this side the Delaware, he is ruined. If he succeeds, our cause is not ruined. He stakes all on his side against a part on ours; admitting he succeeds, the consequence will be, that armies from both ends of the continent will march to assist their suffering friends in the middle states; for he cannot go everywhere, it is impossible. I consider Howe as the greatest enemy the tories have; he is bringing a war into their country, which, had it not been for him and partly for themselves, they had been clear of. Should he now be expelled, I wish with all the devotion of a Christian, that the names of whig[14] and tory may never more be mentioned; but should the tories give him encouragement to come, or assistance if he come, I as sincerely wish that our next year's arms may expel them from the continent, and the Congress appropriate their possessions to the relief of those who have suffered in well-doing. A single successful battle next year will settle the whole. America could carry on a two years' war by the confiscation of the property of disaffected[15] persons, and be made happy by their expulsion. Say not that this is revenge, call it rather the soft resentment of a suffering people, who, having no object in view but the GOOD of ALL, have staked their OWN ALL upon a seemingly doubtful event. Yet it is folly to argue against determined hardness; eloquence may strike the ear, and the language of sorrow draw forth the tear of compassion, but nothing can reach the heart that is steeled with prejudice.

5 Quitting this class of men, I turn with the warm ardor of a friend to those who have nobly stood, and are yet determined to stand the matter out: I call not upon a few, but upon all: not on THIS state or THAT state, but on EVERY state: up and help us; lay your shoulders to the wheel; better have too much force than too little, when so great an object is at stake. Let it be told to the future world, that in the depth of winter, when nothing but hope and virtue could survive, that the city and the country, alarmed at one common danger, came forth to meet and to repulse it. Say not that thousands are gone, turn out your tens of thousands; throw not the burden of the day upon Providence, but *"show your faith by your works,"* that God may bless you. It matters not where you live, or what rank of life you hold, the evil or the blessing will reach you all. The far and the near, the home counties and the back, the rich and the poor, will suffer or

rejoice alike. The heart that feels not now is dead; the blood of his children will curse his cowardice, who shrinks back at a time when a little might have saved the whole, and made *them* happy. I love the man that can smile in trouble, that can gather strength from distress, and grow brave by reflection. 'Tis the business of little minds to shrink; but he whose heart is firm, and whose conscience approves his conduct, will pursue his principles unto death. My own line of reasoning is to myself as straight and clear as a ray of light. Not all the treasures of the world, so far as I believe, could have induced me to support an offensive war, for I think it murder; but if a thief breaks into my house, burns and destroys my property, and kills or threatens to kill me, or those that are in it, and to *"bind me in all cases whatsoever"* to his absolute will, am I to suffer it? What signifies it to me, whether he who does it is a king or a common man; my countryman or not my countryman; whether it be done by an individual villain, or an army of them? If we reason to the root of things we shall find no difference; neither can any just cause be assigned why we should punish in the one case and pardon in the other. Let them call me rebel, and welcome, I feel no concern from it; but I should suffer the misery of devils, were I to make a whore of my soul by swearing allegiance to one whose character is that of a sottish, stupid, stubborn, worthless, brutish man. I conceive likewise a horrid idea in receiving mercy from a being, who at the last day shall be shrieking to the rocks and mountains to cover him, and fleeing with terror from the orphan, the widow, and the slain of America.

6 There are cases which cannot be overdone by language, and this is one. There are persons, too, who see not the full extent of the evil which threatens them; they solace[16] themselves with hopes that the enemy, if he succeed, will be merciful. It is the madness of folly, to expect mercy from those who have refused to do justice; and even mercy, where conquest is the object, is only a trick of war; the cunning of the fox is as murderous as the violence of the wolf, and we ought to guard equally against both. Howe's first object is, partly by threats and partly by promises, to terrify or seduce the people to deliver up their arms and receive mercy. The ministry recommended the same plan to Gage,[17] and this is what the tories call making their peace, *"a peace which passeth all understanding"*[18] *indeed!* A peace which would be the immediate forerunner of a worse ruin than any we have yet thought of. Ye men of Pennsylvania, do reason upon these things! Were the back counties to give up their arms, they would fall an easy prey to the Indians, who are all armed: this perhaps is what some tories would not be sorry for. Were the home counties to deliver up their arms, they would be exposed to the resentment of the back counties, who would then have it in their power to chastise their defection at pleasure. And were any one state to give up its arms, THAT state must be garrisoned by all Howe's army of Britons and Hessians[19] to preserve it from the anger of the rest. Mutual fear is the principal link in the chain of mutual

love, and woe be to that state that breaks the compact. Howe is mercifully inviting you to barbarous destruction, and men must be either rogues or fools that will not see it. I dwell not upon the vapors of imagination; I bring reason to your ears, and, in language as plain as A, B, C, hold up truth to your eyes.

7 I thank *God* that I fear not. I see no real cause for fear. I know our situation well, and can see the way out of it. While our army was collected, Howe dared not risk a battle; and it is no credit to him that he decamped from the White Plains[20] and waited a mean opportunity to ravage the defenceless Jerseys;[21] but it is great credit to us, that, with a handful of men, we sustained an orderly retreat for near an hundred miles, brought off our ammunition, all our fieldpieces, the greatest part of our stores, and had four rivers to pass. None can say that our retreat was precipitate, for we were near three weeks in performing it, that the country might have time to come in. Twice we marched back to meet the enemy and remained out till dark. The sign of fear was not seen in our camp, and had not some of the cowardly and disaffected inhabitants spread false alarms through the country, the Jersies had never been ravaged. Once more we are again collected and collecting, our new army at both ends of the continent is recruiting fast, and we shall be able to open the next campaign with sixty thousand men, well-armed and clothed. This is our situation, and who will may know it. By perseverance and fortitude we have the prospect of a glorious issue; by cowardice and submission, the sad choice of a variety of evils—a ravaged country—a depopulated city—habitations without safety, and slavery without hope—our homes turned into barracks and bawdy-houses for Hessians, and a future race to provide for, whose fathers we shall doubt of. Look on this picture and weep over it! and if there yet remains one thoughtless wretch who believes it not, let him suffer it unlamented.[22]

Notes

1 "Fair weather friends"; persons who are loyal and brave only in good times, when all goes well.

2 Paine was known as a freethinker and a believer in the existence of God on the evidence of reason and nature only. As a Deist, he rejected the idea of supernatural revelations. His religious thought was considered radical, or at least liberal, in his time, but he was not, as President Theodore Roosevelt later called him, "a filthy little atheist."

3 Without help.

4 Signs of the coming struggle had been appearing for many years—some say since the *Mayflower Compact* of 1620. A Declaration of Rights protesting "taxation without representation" had appeared in 1765. And it was also in 1765 that Patrick Henry had attacked the Stamp Act in a speech to the Virginia legislature: "Tarquin and Caesar each had his Brutus, Charles the First his Cromwell, and George the Third may profit by their example. . . . If this be treason, make the most of it."

5 Unbeliever; person without religious faith.

6 Justification, excuse.

[7] The Maid of Orleans (ca. 1412–1431), the French national heroine and martyr who raised the siege of Orleans.

[8] Tests, standards, criteria.

[9] Phantom.

[10] A Tory was a person who supported the British cause during the Revolution. Members of the Tory party in England from the late seventeenth century to about 1832 favored the authority of the King over Parliament. Today, the term frequently is used to mean "conservative" or "opposed to radicalism."

[11] In 1775, Lord William Howe had taken command of British troops in America.

[12] Bodies of men doing military duty only in emergencies.

[13] "This city" refers to Philadelphia, which Howe did indeed occupy in September 1777.

[14] During the Revolution, Whigs were members of the patriotic (rebel) party.

[15] Discontented, disloyal.

[16] Comfort.

[17] Thomas Gage (1721–1787), British general in America 1763–1776.

[18] An ironic reference to a Biblical passage: Philippians 4:7.

[19] A term for paid (professional) soldiers from Hesse, Germany, and elsewhere who served in the British army.

[20] At White Plains, Westchester County, New York, Howe had attacked successfully.

[21] In 1775, the colony was divided into East Jersey and West Jersey.

[22] According to tradition, Paine wrote this selection on a drumhead following the hasty retreat of General Greene's forces from North River (the Hudson) to Newark, New Jersey, on November 20, 1776. Some historians claim that Washington's forces were so inspired by hearing this appeal read that they were able successfully to strike across the Delaware at Trenton on Christmas night and shortly to attack at Princeton. Paine fought in both engagements.

A BILL FOR ESTABLISHING RELIGIOUS FREEDOM[1]

Thomas Jefferson

For comment on the life and work of Thomas Jefferson, see under the Declaration of Independence selection.

1 SECTION I. Well aware that the opinions and belief of men depend not on their own will, but follow involuntarily the evidence proposed to their minds; that Almighty God hath created the mind free, and manifested his supreme will that free it shall remain by making it altogether insusceptible[2] of restraint; that all attempts to influence it by temporal[3] punishments, or burthens,[4] or by civil incapacitations, tend only to beget habits of hypocrisy and meanness, and are a departure from the plan of the holy author of our religion, who being lord both of body and mind, yet chose not to propagate it by coercions on either, as was in his almighty power to do, but to exalt it by its influence on reason alone; that the impious presumption of legislature and ruler, civil as well as ecclesiasti-

cal, who, being themselves but fallible[5] and uninspired men, have assumed dominion over the faith of others, setting up their own opinions and modes of thinking as the only true and infallible, and as such endeavoring to impose them on others, hath established and maintained false religions over the greatest part of the world and through all time: that to compel a man to furnish contributions of money for the propagation[6] of opinions which he disbelieves and abhors is sinful and tyrannical; that even the forcing him to support this or that teacher of his own religious persuasion is depriving him of the comfortable liberty of giving his contributions to the particular pastor whose morals he would make his pattern and whose powers he feels most persuasive to righteousness, and is withdrawing from the ministry those temporary rewards which, proceeding from an approbation of their personal conduct, are an additional incitement to earnest and unremitting labors for the instruction of mankind; that our civil rights have no dependence on our religious opinions, any more than our opinions in physics or geometry; and therefore the proscribing[7] any citizen as unworthy the public confidence by laying upon him an incapacity of being called to offices of trust or emolument,[8] unless he profess or renounce this or that religious opinion, is depriving him injudiciously of those privileges and advantages to which, in common with his fellow citizens, he has a natural right; that it tends also to corrupt the principles of that very religion it is meant to encourage, by bribing with a monopoly of worldly honors and emoluments those who will externally profess and conform to it; that though indeed these are criminals who do not withstand such temptation, yet neither are those innocent who lay the bait in their way; that the opinions of men are not the object of civil government, nor under its jurisdiction; that to suffer the civil magistrate to intrude his powers into the field of opinion and to restrain the profession or propagation of principles on supposition of their ill tendency is a dangerous fallacy, which at once destroys all religious liberty, because he being of course judge of that tendency will make his opinions the rule of judgment and approve or condemn the sentiments of others only as they shall square with or suffer from his own; that it is time enough for the rightful purposes of civil government for its officers to interfere when principles break out into overt[9] acts against peace and good order; and finally, that truth is great and will prevail if left to herself; that she is the proper and sufficient antagonist to error, and has nothing to fear from the conflict unless by human interposition[10] disarmed of her natural weapons, free argument and debate; errors ceasing to be dangerous when it is permitted freely to contradict them.[11]

2 SECTION II. We the General Assembly of Virginia do enact that no man shall be compelled to frequent or support any religious worship, place, or ministry whatsoever, nor shall be enforced, restrained, molested, or burthened in his body or goods, or shall otherwise suffer, on account of his religious opinions or beliefs; but that all men shall be free to profess, and by argument to maintain, their

opinions in matters of religion, and that the same shall in no wise diminish, enlarge, or affect their civil capacities.

3 SECTION III. And though we well know that this Assembly, elected by the people for their ordinary purposes of legislation only, have no power to restrain the acts of succeeding Assemblies, constituted with powers equal to our own, and that therefore to declare this act to be irrevocable[12] would be of no effect in law; yet we are free to declare, and do declare, that the rights hereby asserted are of the natural rights of mankind, and that if any act shall be hereafter passed to repeal the present or to narrow its operations, such act will be an infringement of natural right.

Notes

[1] The memorable inscription that Jefferson prepared for his tombstone at Monticello contains no mention of the fact that he was President of the United States. Instead, it refers to the three acts of which he was proudest: "Here was buried Thomas Jefferson, author of The Declaration of Independence, of the Statute of Virginia for religious freedom, and father of the University of Virginia."

[2] Incapable of receiving or undergoing.

[3] Worldly.

[4] *Burthens* is an archaic form of "burdens."

[5] Liable to mistake or error.

[6] Reproduction, transmission.

[7] Denouncing, banishing, or exiling.

[8] Profit, compensation.

[9] Open, unconcealed.

[10] Erection of an obstacle or barrier; coming between.

[11] As is customary in such declarations, this preamble is one long "whereas"; what follows completes the thought of the "sentence." This extraordinary passage of 613 words still does not form a complete sentence, since its predicate is stated in Section II. It may be called a periodic "sentence" because its meaning is not fully clear until the period is reached. It is also a suspensive (or suspended) structure because it keeps the reader in suspense by holding back a statement of action (the predicate).

[12] Not to be revoked, recalled, or annulled.

A SOUTHERNER ON SLAVERY[1]

Thomas Jefferson

For comment on the author, see under the Declaration of Independence selection.

1 There must doubtless be an unhappy influence on the manners of our people produced by the existence of slavery among us. The whole commerce between master and slave is a perpetual exercise of the most boister-

ous passions, the most unremitting despotism on the one part, and degrading submissions on the other.[2] Our children see this and learn to imitate it, for man is an imitative animal. This quality is the germ of all education in him. From his cradle to his grave he is learning to do what he sees others do. If a parent could find no motive either in his philanthropy[3] or his self-love for restraining the intemperance of passion toward his slave, it should always be a sufficient one that his child is present. But generally it is not sufficient. The parent storms, the child looks on, catches the lineaments[4] of wrath, puts on the same airs in the circle of smaller slaves, gives a loose to the worst of passions, and thus nursed, educated, and daily exercised in tyranny, cannot but be stamped by it with odious[5] peculiarities. The man must be a prodigy who can retain his manners and morals undepraved by such circumstances. And with what execration[6] should the statesman be loaded who, permitting one-half of the citizens thus to trample on the rights of the other, transforms those into despots, and these into enemies, destroys the morals of the one part, and the *amor patriae*[7] of the other. For if a slave can have a country in this world, it must be any other in preference to that in which he is born to live and labor for another; in which he must lock up the faculties of his nature, contribute as far as depends on his individual endeavors to the evanishment[8] of the human race, or entail[9] his own miserable condition on the endless generations proceeding from him.

With the morals of the people, their industry also is destroyed. For in a warm climate, no man will labor for himself who can make another labor for him. This is so true that, of the proprietors of slaves, a very small proportion indeed are ever seen to labor. And can the liberties of a nation be thought secure when we have removed their only firm basis, a conviction in the minds of the people that these liberties are of the gift of God? That they are not to be violated but with His wrath? Indeed, I tremble for my country when I reflect that God is just; that His justice cannot sleep forever; that considering numbers, nature, and natural means only, a revolution of the wheel of fortune, an exchange of situation, is among possible events; that it may become probable by supernatural interference! The Almighty has no attribute which can take side with us in such a contest.

3 But it is impossible to be temperate and to pursue this subject through the various considerations of policy, of morals, of history natural and civil. We must be contented to hope they will force their way into everyone's mind. I think a change already perceptible, since the origin of the present revolution.[10] The spirit of the master is abating, that of the slave rising from the dust, his condition mollifying,[11] the way, I hope, preparing, under the auspices of heaven, for a total emancipation, and that this is disposed, in the order of events, to be with the consent of the masters, rather than by their extirpation.[12]

* * *

4 It is a problem[13] which I give to the master to solve, whether the religious precepts[14] against the violation

of property were not framed for him as well as his slave? And whether the slave may not as justifiably take a little from one who has taken all from him, as he may slay one who would slay him? That a change in the relations in which a man is placed should change his ideas of moral right and wrong, is neither new, nor peculiar to the color of the blacks. Homer tells us it was so two thousand six hundred years ago:

> Jove fix'd it certain, that whatever day
> Makes a man a slave, takes his worth away.

5 But the slaves of which Homer speaks were whites. Notwithstanding these considerations which must weaken their respect for the laws of property, we find among them numerous instances of the most rigid integrity, and as many as among their better instructed masters, of benevolence, gratitude, and unshaken fidelity. The opinion that they are inferior in the faculties of reason and imagination must be hazarded[15] with great diffidence.[16]

Notes

1 In the year of his retirement as governor of Virginia, Jefferson began writing answers to twenty-three questions dealing with matters of state and national interest, of which this comment on slavery is Number 18. In other "notes," Jefferson dealt with natural resources, education, social customs, religious freedom, civil rights, and the like. This "note" was written in 1784.

2 Jefferson insisted upon religious freedom, upon state-supported education, and upon the abolition of slavery. In his hatred of tyranny and outward symbols of power in whatever form, he relied upon the integrity of the common man.

3 Affection for mankind and contributions to socially useful purposes.

4 Features, outlines.

5 Hateful, detestable.

6 Detestation, abhorrence.

7 Love of country.

8 Disappearance.

9 A legal term meaning "to settle on an heir" by bequest or inheritance.

10 The American Revolution.

11 Softening, improving.

12 Destruction, extermination.

13 These related paragraphs are from Note 14 in this work by Jefferson.

14 Commandments, teachings.

15 Stated, offered.

16 Restraint, lack of confidence.

CIVIL DISOBEDIENCE

Henry David Thoreau

For comment on the life and work of Thoreau, see under the "Observation" selection.

1 I heartily accept the motto,—"That government is best which governs least"; and I should like to see it acted up to more rapidly and systematically.[2] Carried out, it finally amounts to this, which also I believe,—"That government is best which governs not at all"; and when men are prepared for it, that will be the kind of government which they will have. Government is at best but an expedient;[3] but most governments are usually, and all governments are sometimes, inexpedient. The objections which have been brought against a standing army, and they are many and weighty, and deserve to prevail, may also at last be brought against a standing government. The standing army is only an arm of the standing government. The government itself, which is only the mode which the people have chosen to execute their will, is equally liable to be abused and perverted before the people can act through it. Witness the present Mexican war, the work of comparatively a few individuals using the standing government as their tool; for, in the outset, the people would not have consented to this measure.[4]

2 This American government,—what is it but a tradition, though a recent one, endeavoring to transmit itself unimpaired to posterity, but each instant losing some of its integrity? It has not the vitality and force of a single living man; for a single man can bend it to his will. It is a sort of wooden gun to the people themselves. But it is not the less necessary for this; for the people must have some complicated machinery or other, and hear its din, to satisfy that idea of government which they have. Governments show thus how successfully men can be imposed on, even impose on themselves, for their own advantage. It is excellent, we must all allow. Yet this government never of itself furthered any enterprise, but by the alacrity with which it got out of its way. *It* does not keep the country free. *It* does not settle the West. *It* does not educate. The character inherent in the American people has done all that has been accomplished; and it would have done somewhat more, if the government had not sometimes got in its way. For government is an expedient by which men would fain[5] succeed in letting one another alone; and, as has been said, when it is most expedient, the governed are most let alone by it. Trade and commerce, if they were not made of india-rubber, would never manage to bounce over the obstacles which legislators are continually putting in their way; and, if one were to judge these men wholly by the effects of their actions and not partly by their intentions, they would deserve to be classed and punished with

those mischievous persons who put obstructions on the railroads.

3 But, to speak practically and as a citizen, unlike those who call themselves no-government men, I ask for, not at once no government, but *at once* a better government. Let every man make known what kind of government would command his respect, and that will be one step toward obtaining it.

4 After all, the practical reason why, when the power is once in the hands of the people, a majority are permitted, and for a long period continue, to rule is not because they are most likely to be in the right, nor because this seems fairest to the minority, but because they are physically the strongest. But a government in which the majority rule in all cases cannot be based on justice, even as far as men understand it. Can there not be a government in which majorities do not virtually decide right and wrong, but conscience?[6]—in which majorities decide only those questions to which the rule of expediency is applicable? Must the citizen ever for a moment, or in the least degree, resign his conscience to the legislator? Why has every man a conscience, then? I think that we should be men first, and subjects afterward. It is not desirable to cultivate a respect for the law, so much as for the right. The only obligation which I have a right to assume is to do at any time what I think right. It is truly enough said that a corporation has no conscience; but a corporation of conscientious men is a corporation *with* a conscience. Law never made men a whit more just; and, by means of their respect for it, even the well-disposed are daily made the agents of injustice. A common and natural result of an undue respect for law is, that you may see a file of soldiers, colonel, captain, corporal, privates, powder-monkeys,[7] and all, marching in admirable order over hill and dale to the wars, against their wills, ay, against their common sense and consciences, which makes it very steep marching indeed, and produces a palpitation of the heart. They have no doubt that it is a damnable business in which they are concerned; they are all peaceably inclined. Now, what are they? Men at all? or small movable forts and magazines, at the service of some unscrupulous man in power? Visit the Navy-Yard, and behold a marine, such a man as an American government can make, or such as it can make a man with its black arts,—a mere shadow and reminiscence of humanity, a man laid out alive and standing, and already, as one may say, buried under arms with funeral accompaniments, though it may be,—

> "Not a drum was heard, not a funeral note,
> As his corse to the rampart we hurried;
> Not a soldier discharged his farewell shot
> O'er the grave where our hero we buried."[8]

5 The mass of men serve the state thus, not as men mainly, but as machines, with their bodies. They are the standing army, and the militia, jailers, constables, *posse comitatus*,[9] etc. In most cases there is no free exercise whatever of the judgment or of the moral sense; but they put themselves on a level with wood and earth and stones; and wooden men can

perhaps be manufactured that will serve the purpose as well. Such command no more respect than men of straw or a lump of dirt. They have the same sort of worth only as horses and dogs. Yet such as these even are commonly esteemed good citizens. Others—as most legislators, politicians, lawyers, ministers, and office-holders—serve the state chiefly with their heads; and, as they rarely make any moral distinctions, they are as likely to serve the devil, without *intending* it, as God. A very few,—as heroes, patriots, martyrs, reformers in the great sense, and *men*—serve the state with their consciences also, and so necessarily resist it for the most part; and they are commonly treated as enemies by it. A wise man will only be useful as a man, and will not submit to be "clay," and "stop a hole to keep the wind away,"[10] but leave that office to his dust at least:—

> "I am too high-born to be propertied,
> To be a secondary at control,
> Or useful serving-man and instrument
> To any sovereign state throughout the world."[11]

6 He who gives himself entirely to his fellow-men appears to them useless and selfish; but he who gives himself partially to them is pronounced a benefactor and philanthropist.

7 How does it become a man to behave toward this American government to-day? I answer, that he cannot without disgrace be associated with it.[12] I cannot for an instant recognize that political organization as *my* government which is the *slave's* government also.

8 All men recognize the right of revolution; that is, the right to refuse allegiance to, and to resist, the government, when its tyranny or its inefficiency are great and unendurable. But almost all say that such is not the case now. But such was the case, they think, in the Revolution of '75. If one were to tell me that this was a bad government because it taxed certain foreign commodities brought to its ports, it is most probable that I should not make an ado about it, for I can do without them. All machines have their friction; and possibly this does enough good to counterbalance the evil. At any rate, it is a great evil to make a stir about it. But when the friction comes to have its machine, and oppression and robbery are organized, I say, let us not have such a machine any longer. In other words, when a sixth of the population of a nation which has undertaken to be the refuge of liberty are slaves, and a whole country[13] is unjustly overrun and conquered by a foreign army, and subjected to military law, I think that it is not too soon for honest men to rebel and revolutionize. What makes this duty the more urgent is the fact that the country so overrun is not our own, but ours is the invading army. . . .

9 Unjust laws exist: shall we be content to obey them, or shall we endeavor to amend them, and obey them until we have succeeded, or shall we transgress them at once? Men generally, under such a government as this, think that they ought to wait until they have persuaded the majority to alter them. They think that, if they should resist, the remedy would be worse than the evil. But it is the fault of the government itself that the remedy *is* worse than the evil. *It* makes it worse. Why is it not more apt

to anticipate and provide for reform? Why does it not cherish its wise minority? Why does it cry and resist before it is hurt? Why does it not encourage its citizens to be on the alert to point out its faults, and *do* better than it would have them? Why does it always crucify Christ, and excommunicate Copernicus and Luther,[14] and pronounce Washington and Franklin rebels?

10 One would think, that a deliberate and practical denial of its authority was the only offense never contemplated by government; else, why has it not assigned its definite, its suitable and proportionate penalty? If a man who has no property refuses but once to earn nine shillings for the State, he is put in prison for a period unlimited by any law that I know, and determined only by the discretion of those who placed him there; but if he should steal ninety times nine shillings from the State, he is soon permitted to go at large again.

11 If the injustice is part of the necessary friction of the machine of government, let it go, let it go: perchance it will wear smooth,—certainly the machine will wear out. If the injustice has a spring, or a pulley, or a rope, or a crank, exclusively for itself, then perhaps you may consider whether the remedy will not be worse than the evil; but if it is of such a nature that it requires you to be the agent of injustice to another, then, I say, break the law. Let your life be a counter friction to stop the machine. What I have to do is to see, at any rate, that I do not lend myself to the wrong which I condemn.

12 As for adopting the ways which the State has provided for remedying the evil, I know not of such ways. They take too much time and a man's life will be gone. I have other affairs to attend to. I came into this world, not chiefly to make this a good place to live in, but to live in it, be it good or bad. A man has not everything to do, but something; and because he cannot do *everything*, it is not necessary that he should do *something* wrong. It is not my business to be petitioning the Governor or the Legislature any more than it is theirs to petition me; and if they should not hear my petition, what should I do then? But in this case the State has provided no way: its very Constituton is the evil. This may seem to be harsh and stubborn and unconciliatory; but it is to treat with the utmost kindness and consideration the only spirit that can appreciate or deserves it. So is all change for the better, like birth and death, which convulse the body. . . .

13 The authority of government, even such as I am willing to submit to,—for I will cheerfully obey those who know and can do better than I, and in many things even those who neither know nor can do so well,—is still an impure one: to be strictly just, it must have the sanction[15] and consent of the governed. It can have no pure right over my person and property but what I concede to it. The progress from an absolute to a limited monarchy, from a limited monarchy to a democracy, is a progress toward a true respect for the individual. Even the Chinese philosopher was wise enough to regard the individual as the basis of the empire. Is a democracy, such as we know it, the last improvement possible in government? Is it not possible to take a step further towards recognizing and organizing the rights

of man? There will never be a really free and enlightened State until the State comes to recognize the individual as a higher and independent power, from which all its own power and authority are derived, and treats him accordingly. I please myself with imagining a State at last which can afford to be just to all men, and to treat the individual with respect as a neighbor; which even would not think it inconsistent with its own repose if a few were to live aloof from it, not meddling with it, nor embraced by it, who fulfilled all the duties of neighbors and fellow-men. A State which bore this kind of fruit, and suffered it to drop off as fast as it ripened, would prepare the way for a still more perfect and glorious State, which also I have imagined, but not yet anywhere seen.

Notes

1 This essay, originally delivered as a lecture, was published in 1849. The selection shown here consists of the opening paragraphs of the lecture-essay, a few from the center portion, and the conclusion. The complete work is several times as long as the part here reprinted.

2 In his First Inaugural Address, Jefferson supported "a wise and frugal government, which shall restrain men from injuring one another, shall leave them otherwise free to regulate their own pursuits of industry and improvement, and shall not take from the mouth of labor the bread it has earned." That is, Jefferson (and Thomas Paine as well) believed that government was, or should be, a social contract permitted solely by necessity and even then only to as slight a degree as possible. Thoreau was following not only the concepts of Jefferson and Paine but also those of Emerson, in whose essay on "Politics" appears this sentence: "Hence the less government we have the better—the fewer laws and the less confided power."

3 Means to an end.

4 The war was especially unpopular among those New Englanders who felt that it was being waged in the selfish interests of southern politicians and cotton planters and of northern cotton merchants eager to extend slave territory.

5 Gladly.

6 At the Constitutional Convention of 1787, the "Jeffersonians," who favored rule by the majority, won out over the conservative minority represented by John Adams, Alexander Hamilton, and others.

7 Boys or men on warships (or elsewhere) in charge of explosives.

8 These are the opening lines of Charles Wolfe's *The Burial of Sir John Moore at Coruna* (1817).

9 "Having the authority of the county"; citizens summoned by the sheriff to help in preserving peace; a posse.

10 These lines are in *Hamlet,* Act V, Scene I: "Imperious Caesar, dead and turned to clay/ Might stop a hole to keep the wind away."

11 These lines are from Shakespeare's *King John,* Act V, Scene 2. The word *propertied* means "made a chattel of," "enslaved."

12 Thoreau felt that the administration of President Polk (1845–1849) encouraged slavery by passing fugitive slave laws and by waging the Mexican War.

13 Mexico.

14 Copernicus' description of the solar system was banned by the Roman Catholic Church. Luther, a founder and leader of the German Reformation, was excommunicated in 1521.

15 Permission.

FINAL STATEMENT

John Brown

JOHN BROWN (1800–1859), born in Connecticut of old New England stock, became convinced that he had a mission from God to free all slaves in the United States. Dreaming of himself as leader of a band which would fall upon slaveholders to release blacks, he joined five of his sons in Kansas in 1855 and engaged in bloody guerrilla warfare. In 1859, he and his followers moved on Harpers Ferry, Virginia, where he raided the town to free what slaves were there and seized the United States armory as a base from which to free still others by force of arms. A company of marines led by Robert E. Lee stormed the arsenal and captured Brown, who was hanged on December 2, 1859.

1 I have, may it please the Court, a few words to say.

2 In the first place, I deny everything but what I have all along admitted—the design on my part to free the slaves. I intended certainly to have made a clear thing of that matter, as I did last winter, when I went into Missouri, and there took slaves without the snapping of a gun on either side, moved them through the country, and finally left them in Canada. I designed to have done the same thing again, on a larger scale. That was all I intended. I never did intend murder, or treason, or the destruction of property, or to excite or incite slaves to rebellion, or to make insurrection.

3 I have another objection: and that is, it is unjust that I should suffer such a penalty. Had I interfered in the manner which I admit, and which I admit has been fairly proved—(for I admire the truthfulness and candor of the greater portion of the witnesses who have testified in this case)—had I so interfered in behalf of the rich, the powerful, the intelligent, the so-called great, or in behalf of any of their friends, either father, mother, brother, sister, wife, or children, or any of that class, and suffered and sacrificed what I have in this interference,[1] it would have been all right, and every man in this Court would have deemed[2] it an act worthy of reward rather than punishment.

4 This Court acknowledges, as I suppose, the validity[3] of the Law of God. I see a book kissed here which I suppose to be the Bible, or, at least, the New Testament. That teaches me that all things "whatsoever I would that men should do unto me, I should do even so to them."[4] It teaches me, further, to "remember them that are in bonds as bound with them." I endeavored to act up to that instruction. I say, I am yet too young to understand that God is any respecter[5] of persons. I believe that to have interfered as I have done, as I have always freely admitted I have done, in behalf of His despised poor, was not wrong, but right. Now, if it is deemed necessary that I should forfeit my life for the furtherance[6] of the ends of justice, and mingle my blood further with the blood of my children, and with the

blood of millions in this slave country whose rights are disregarded by wicked, cruel, and unjust enactments, I submit: so let it be done!

Notes

[1] Opposition.
[2] Thought, judged.
[3] Soundness, rightness.
[4] A reference to the New Testament, Matthew 7:12.
[5] One improperly or incorrectly influenced.
[6] Advancement.

I HEAR THE MOURNFUL WAIL OF MILLIONS

Frederick Douglass

FREDERICK DOUGLASS (1817–1895) was born into slavery in Maryland, the son of an unidentified white man. As a youth, he escaped to Massachusetts and became an effective agent of the Anti-Slavery Society because of his powerful eloquence on the lecture platform. Fearing capture as a fugitive slave, he spent several years in Great Britain, where he continued his studies and public speaking. During the war, he organized two black regiments in Massachusetts; after the war, he continued to work for black causes until his death. His autobiography, published in 1845 and revised in 1892, is entitled *Narrative of the Life of Frederick Douglass.*

1 Fellow citizens, above your national, tumultuous joy,[1] I hear the mournful wail of millions whose chains, heavy and grievous yesterday, are, today, rendered more intolerable by the jubilee shouts that reach them. If I do forget, if I do not faithfully remember those bleeding children of sorrow this day, "may my right hand forget her cunning,[2] and may my tongue cleave to the roof of my mouth"! To forget them, to pass lightly over their wrongs, and to chime in with the popular theme would be treason most scandalous and shocking, and would make me a reproach before God and the world. My subject, then, fellow citizens, is *American slavery.* I shall see this day and its popular characteristics from the slave's point of view. Standing there identified with the American bondman,[3] making his wrongs mine, I do not hesitate to declare with all my soul that the character and conduct of this nation never looked blacker to me than on this Fourth of July! Whether we turn to the declarations of the past or to the professions[4] of the present, the conduct of the nation seems equally hideous and revolting. America is false to the past, false to the present,

and solemnly binds herself to be false to the future. Standing with God and the crushed and bleeding slave on this occasion, I will, in the name of humanity which is outraged, in the name of liberty which is fettered, in the name of the Constitution and the Bible which are disregarded and trampled upon, dare to call in question and to denounce, with all the emphasis I can command, everything that serves to perpetuate slavery—the great sin and shame of America! "I will not equivocate; I will not excuse";[5] I will use the severest language I can command; and yet not one word shall escape me that any man, whose judgment is not blinded by prejudice, or who is not at heart a slaveholder, shall not confess to be right and just.

2 But I fancy I hear someone of my audience say, "It is just in this circumstance that you and your brother abolitionists fail to make a favorable impression on the public mind. Would you argue more and denounce less, would you persuade more and rebuke less, your cause would be much more likely to succeed." But, I submit, where all is plain, there is nothing to be argued. What point in the anti-slavery creed would you have me argue? On what branch of the subject do the people of this country need light? Must I undertake to prove that the slave is a man? That point is conceded already. Nobody doubts it. The slaveholders themselves acknowledge it in the enactment of laws for their government. They acknowledge it when they punish disobedience on the part of the slave. There are seventy-two crimes in the state of Virginia which, if committed by a black man (no matter how ignorant he be), subject him to the punishment of death; while only two of the same crimes will subject a white man to the like punishment. What is this but the acknowledgment that the slave is a moral, intellectual, and responsible being? The manhood of the slave is conceded. It is admitted in the fact that Southern statute books are covered with enactments forbidding, under severe fines and penalties, the teaching of the slave to read or to write. When you can point to any such laws in reference to the beasts of the field, then I may consent to argue the manhood of the slave. When the dogs in your streets, when the fowls of the air, when the cattle on your hills, when the fish of the sea and the reptiles that crawl shall be unable to distinguish the slave from a brute, then will I argue with you that the slave is a man.

3 For the present, it is enough to affirm the equal manhood of the Negro race. Is it not astonishing that while we are plowing, planting, and reaping, using all kinds of mechanical tools, erecting houses, constructing bridges, building ships, working in metals of brass, iron, copper, silver, and gold; that while we are reading, writing, and ciphering,[6] acting as clerks, merchants, and secretaries, having among us lawyers, doctors, ministers, poets, authors, editors, orators, and teachers; that while we are engaged in all manner of enterprises common to other men, digging gold in California, capturing the whale in the Pacific, feeding sheep and cattle on the hillside, living, moving, acting, thinking, planning, living in families as husbands, wives, and children, and,

above all, confessing and worshiping the Christian's God, and looking hopefully for life and immortality beyond the grave, we are called upon to prove that we are men![7]

4 Would you have me argue that man is entitled to liberty? that he is the rightful owner of his own body? You have already declared it. Must I argue the wrongfulness of slavery? Is that a question for republicans?[8] Is it to be settled by the rules of logic and argumentation, as a matter beset with great difficulty, involving a doubtful application of the principle of justice, hard to be understood? How should I look today, in the presence of Americans, dividing and subdividing a discourse, to show that men have a natural right to freedom? speaking of it relatively and positively, negatively and affirmatively? To do so would be to make myself ridiculous and to offer an insult to your understanding. There is not a man beneath the canopy of heaven[9] that does not know that slavery is wrong for him.

5 What, am I to argue that it is wrong to make men brutes, to rob them of their liberty, to work them without wages, to keep them ignorant of their relations to their fellow men, to beat them with sticks, to flay their flesh with the lash, to load their limbs with irons, to hunt them with dogs, to sell them at auction, to sunder their families, to knock out their teeth, to burn their flesh, to starve them into obedience and submission to their masters? Must I argue that a system thus marked with blood, and stained with pollution, is wrong? No! I will not. I have better employment for my time and strength than such arguments would imply.

6 What, then, remains to be argued? Is it that slavery is not divine; that God did not establish it; that our doctors of divinity are mistaken? There is blasphemy in the thought. That which is inhuman cannot be divine! Who can reason on such a proposition? They that can may; I cannot. The time for such argument is past.

7 At a time like this, scorching iron, not convincing argument, is needed. O! had I the ability, and could I reach the nation's ear, I would today pour out a fiery stream of biting ridicule, blasting reproach, withering sarcasm, and stern rebuke. For it is not light that is needed, but fire; it is not the gentle shower, but thunder. We need the storm, the whirlwind, and the earthquake. The feeling of the nation must be quickened; the conscience of the nation must be roused; the propriety[10] of the nation must be startled; the hypocrisy of the nation must be exposed; and its crimes against God and man must be proclaimed and denounced.

8 What, to the American slave, is your Fourth of July? I answer: a day that reveals to him, more than all other days in the year, the gross injustice and cruelty to which he is the constant victim. To him, your celebration is a sham; your boasted liberty, an unholy license; your national greatness, swelling vanity; your sounds of rejoicing are empty and heartless; your denunciation of tyrants, brass-fronted impudence; your shouts of liberty and equality, hollow mockery; your prayers and hymns, your sermons and thanksgivings, with all your religious parade and solemnity, are, to him, mere bombast,[11] fraud, deception, impiety,

and hypocrisy—a thin veil to cover up crimes which would disgrace a nation of savages. There is not a nation of savages. There is not a nation on the earth guilty of practices more shocking and bloody than are the people of the United States at this very hour.

9 Go where you may, search where you will, roam through all the monarchies and despotisms of the Old World, travel through South America, search out every abuse, and when you have found the last, lay your facts by the side of the everyday practices of this nation, and you will say with me that, for revolting barbarity and shameless hypocrisy, America reigns without a rival.

Notes

[1] This oration was delivered in Rochester, New York, in 1852 at a ceremony commemorating the Declaration of Independence. "An address such as this," according to records in the Rochester Historical Society, "might have resulted in the mobbing of Douglass had it been delivered in many cities." Only excerpts from the oration are given in this selection.

[2] Psalm 137, verse 5: "If I forget thee, O Jerusalem, let my right hand forget her cunning."

[3] A male slave.

[4] Declarations, avowals.

[5] On January 1, 1831, William Lloyd Garrison (1805–1879), a leader in the abolition movement, declared: "I am in earnest. I will not equivocate: I will not excuse; I will not retreat a single inch; and I *will* be heard."

[6] Calculating, figuring.

[7] The rhetoric is impassioned, but the structure is firmly that of a periodic sentence.

[8] A republican favors a form of government in which the power rests in the body of citizens entitled to vote. A Republican (with a capital R) is a member of a political party so named. A related distinction should be made between a democrat and a Democrat.

[9] The sky. A canopy is a covering or overhanging projection.

[10] Sense of justice.

[11] Pompous speech; padding.

THE GETTYSBURG ADDRESS[1]

Abraham Lincoln

Abraham Lincoln (1809–1865) was born in a log cabin in Kentucky of a largely illiterate frontier family. He was inadequately educated and throughout his life continued to relish the colloquialisms, crudities, and tall tales of his native region. Through hard work, homespun integrity, dedication, and nobility of heart and mind, Lincoln became the sixteenth President of the United States and the nation's most eloquent and beloved statesman, the embodiment of a torn people's suffering and the rebirth of their nation.

The Civil War broke out while Lincoln was new in office, and within two years the executive powers of this man of political moderation were so extended that he became a virtual dictator. Beset by radical abolitionists on one side and on the other by defeatists within his own cabinet and party, plagued by military confusion and mounting expenditures, he managed to steer a middle course through chaotic events and, "showing malice toward none . . . charity for all," to bring the war to a close with the Union intact.

He was inaugurated the second time on March 4, 1865. A month later, General Lee surrendered Southern forces to General Grant at Appomattox. Less than a week afterward, in the early hours following Good Friday, Abraham Lincoln, the man, was dead of a bullet wound. His legend lives on.

1 Four score and seven years ago our fathers brought forth on this continent, a new nation, conceived in Liberty, and dedicated to the proposition that all men are created equal.

2 Now we are engaged in a great civil war; testing whether that nation, or any nation so conceived and so dedicated, can long endure. We are met on a great battlefield of that war. We have come to dedicate a portion of that field as a final resting-place for those who here gave their lives that that nation might live. It is altogether fitting and proper that we should do this.

3 But, in a larger sense, we cannot dedicate—we cannot consecrate—we cannot hallow—this ground. The brave men, living and dead, who struggled here have consecrated it, far above our poor power to add or detract. The world will little note, nor long remember, what we say here, but it can never forget what they did here. It is for us the living, rather, to be dedicated here to the unfinished work which they who fought here have thus far so nobly advanced. It is rather for us to be here dedicated to the great task remaining before us—that from these honored dead we take increased devotion to that cause for which they gave the last full measure of devotion; that we here highly resolve that these dead shall not have died in vain; that this nation, under God, shall have a new birth of freedom; and that government of the people, by the people, for the people,[2] shall not perish from the earth.

Notes

[1] Probably nothing Lincoln said or wrote better illustrated his nobility and democratic love of all mankind than the 260 words of what has become the best-known and most revered speech ever delivered in this country. See "Lincoln at Gettysburg," later in this book.

[2] Whether Lincoln knew it or not, a Boston clergyman, Theodore Parker, made an attack on slavery in 1850 in which he referred to democracy as "a government of all the people, by all the people, for all the people."

I DO NOT BELIEVE IN THE LAW OF HATE[1]

Clarence Darrow

CLARENCE DARROW (1857–1938) was born in Ohio. During his long legal career he was noted for his defense of labor organizations and as a criminal lawyer in numerous newsworthy cases. Among his books were *Farmington* (1904), an autobiographical novel; *The Story of My Life* (1932); and *Attorney for the Damned* (1957), a collection of thirteen speeches.

1 I do not believe in the law of hate. I may not be true to my ideals always, but I believe in the law of love, and I believe you can do nothing with hatred. I would like to see a time when man loves his fellow man and forgets his color or his creed. We will never be civilized until that time comes. I know the Negro race has a long road to go. I believe that the life of the Negro race has been a life of tragedy, of injustice, of oppression. The law has made him equal, but man has not. And, after all, the last analysis is: what has man done?—and not what has the law done? I know there is a long road ahead of him before he can take the place which I believe he should take. I know that before him there is sorrow, tribulation,[2] and death among the blacks, and perhaps the whites. I am sorry. I would do what I could to avert it. I would advise patience; I would advise tolerance; I would advise understanding; I would advise all those things which are necessary for men who live together.

2 Gentlemen, what do you think of your duty in this case? I have watched day after day these black, tense faces that have crowded this court. These black faces that now are looking to you twelve whites, feeling that the hopes and fears of a race are in your keeping.

3 This case is about to end, gentlemen. To them, it is life. Not one of their color sits on this jury. Their fate is in the hands of twelve whites. Their eyes are fixed on you, their hearts go out to you, and their hopes hang on your verdict.

4 This is all. I ask you, on behalf of this defendant, on behalf of these helpless ones who turn to you, and more than that—on behalf of this great state, and this great city, which must face this problem and face it fairly—I ask you, in the name of progress and of the human race, to return a verdict of not guilty in this case!

Notes

1 This excerpt consists of approximately one-third of Darrow's final plea to the jury on May 19, 1926, in the trial of a black who, in defense of his home, was accused of killing a white man. The speaker, 69 at the time he delivered this impassioned plea, later declared that

the verdict of "not guilty" meant that "the doctrine that a man's house is his castle applied to the black man as well as to the white man. If not the first time that a white jury had vindicated this principle, it was the first that ever came to my notice."

[2] Trouble, suffering.

I HAVE A DREAM

Martin Luther King, Jr.

MARTIN LUTHER KING, JR. (1929–1968) was born in Atlanta and educated at Morehouse University, Crozer Theological Seminary, and Boston University. He began his career by serving as pastor of a church in Montgomery, Alabama. During an active career, Dr. King lectured widely, was selected as one of ten outstanding personalities in the country in 1956, and won the Nobel Peace Prize for 1964. He was assassinated on April 4, 1968.

1 Five score years ago, a great American, in whose symbolic shadow we stand, signed the Emancipation Proclamation.[1] This momentous decree came as a great beacon light of hope to millions of Negro slaves who had been seared in the flames of withering injustice. It came as a joyous daybreak to end the long night of captivity.

2 But one hundred years later, we must face the tragic fact that the Negro is still not free. One hundred years later, the life of the Negro is still sadly crippled by the manacles[2] of segregation and the chains of discrimination. One hundred years later, the Negro lives on a lonely island of poverty in the midst of a vast ocean of material prosperity. One hundred years later, the Negro is still languished in the corners of American society and finds himself an exile in his own land. So we have come here today to dramatize an appalling condition.

3 In a sense we have come to our nation's Capital to cash a check. When the architects of our republic wrote the magnificent words of the Constitution and the Declaration of Independence, they were signing a promissory note[3] to which every American was to fall heir. This note was a promise that all men would be guaranteed the unalienable[4] rights of life, liberty, and the pursuit of happiness.

4 It is obvious today that America has defaulted on this promissory note insofar as her citizens of color are concerned. Instead of honoring this sacred obligation, America has given the Negro people a bad check; a check which has come back marked "insufficient funds." But we refuse to believe that the bank of justice is bankrupt. We refuse to believe that there are insufficient funds in the great vaults of opportunity of this nation. So we have come to cash this check—a check that will give us upon demand the riches of freedom and the

security of justice. We have also come to this hallowed[5] spot to remind America of the fierce urgency of *now.* This is no time to engage in the luxury of cooling off or to take the tranquilizing drug of gradualism.[6] *Now* is the time to make real the promises of Democracy. *Now* is the time to rise from the dark and desolate valley of segregation to the sunlit path of racial justice. *Now* is the time to open the doors of opportunity to all of God's children. *Now* is the time to lift our nation from the quicksands of racial injustice to the solid rock of brotherhood.

5 It would be fatal for the nation to overlook the urgency of the moment and to underestimate the determination of the Negro. This sweltering summer of the Negro's legitimate discontent will not pass until there is an invigorating autumn of freedom and equality. 1963 is not an end, but a beginning. Those who hope that the Negro needed to blow off steam and will now be content will have a rude awakening if the nation returns to business as usual. There will be neither rest nor tranquillity in America until the Negro is granted his citizenship rights. The whirlwinds of revolt will continue to shake the foundations of our nation until the bright day of justice emerges.

6 But there is something that I must say to my people who stand on the warm threshold which leads into the palace of justice. In the process of gaining our rightful place we must not be guilty of wrongful deeds. Let us not seek to satisfy our thirst for freedom by drinking from the cup of bitterness and hatred. We must forever conduct our struggle on the high plane of dignity and discipline. We must not allow our creative protest to degenerate into physical violence. Again and again we must rise to the majestic heights of meeting physical force with soul force. The marvelous new militancy[7] which has engulfed the Negro community must not lead us to a distrust of all white people, for many of our white brothers, as evidenced by their presence here today, have come to realize that their destiny is tied up with our destiny and their freedom is inextricably[8] bound to our freedom. We cannot walk alone.

7 And as we walk, we must make the pledge that we shall march ahead. We cannot turn back. There are those who are asking the devotees[9] of civil rights, "When will you be satisfied?" We can never be satisfied as long as the Negro is the victim of the unspeakable horrors of police brutality. We can never be satisfied as long as our bodies, heavy with the fatigue of travel, cannot gain lodging in the motels of the highways and the hotels of the cities. We cannot be satisfied as long as the Negro's basic mobility[10] is from a smaller ghetto to a larger one. We can never be satisfied as long as a Negro in Mississippi cannot vote and a Negro in New York believes he has nothing for which to vote. No, no, we are not satisfied, and we will not be satisfied until justice rolls down like waters and righteousness like a mighty stream.

8 I am not unmindful that some of you have come here out of great trials and tribulations.[11] Some of you have come fresh from narrow jail cells. Some of you have come from areas where your quest for freedom left you

battered by the storms of persecution and staggered by the winds of police brutality. You have been the veterans of creative suffering. Continue to work with the faith that unearned suffering is redemptive.[12]

9 Go back to Mississippi, go back to Alabama, go back to South Carolina, go back to Georgia, go back to Louisiana, go back to the slums and ghettos of our northern cities, knowing that somehow this situation can and will be changed. Let us not wallow in the valley of despair.

10 I say to you today, my friends, that in spite of the difficulties and frustrations of the moment I still have a dream. It is a dream deeply rooted in the American dream.

11 I have a dream that one day this nation will rise up and live out the true meaning of its creed: "We hold these truths to be self-evident; that all men are created equal."[13]

12 I have a dream that one day on the red hills of Georgia the sons of former slaves and the sons of former slaveowners will be able to sit down together at the table of brotherhood.

13 I have a dream that one day even the state of Mississippi, a desert state sweltering with the heat of injustice and oppression, will be transformed into an oasis of freedom and justice.

14 I have a dream that my four little children will one day live in a nation where they will not be judged by the color of their skin but by the content of their character.

15 I have a dream today.

16 I have a dream that one day the state of Alabama, whose governor's lips are presently dripping with the words of interposition and nullification,[14] will be transformed into a situation where little black boys and black girls will be able to join hands with little white boys and white girls and walk together as sisters and brothers.

17 I have a dream today.

18 I have a dream that one day every valley shall be exalted, every hill and mountain shall be made low, the rough places will be made plains, and the crooked places will be made straight, and the glory of the Lord shall be revealed, and all flesh shall see it together.[15]

19 This is our hope. This is the faith with which I return to the South. With this faith we will be able to hew out of the mountain of despair a stone of hope. With this faith we will be able to transform the jangling discords of our nation into a beautiful symphony of brotherhood. With this faith we will be able to work together, to pray together, to struggle together, to go to jail together, to stand up for freedom together, knowing that we will be free one day.

20 This will be the day when all of God's children will be able to sing with new meaning

> My country, 'tis of thee,
> Sweet land of liberty,
> Of thee I sing:
> Land where my fathers died,
> Land of the pilgrims' pride,
> From every mountain-side
> Let freedom ring.

21 And if America is to be a great nation this must become true. So let freedom ring from the prodigious[16] hilltops of New Hampshire. Let freedom ring from the mighty mountains of New York. Let freedom ring from the heightening Alleghenies of Pennsylvania!

22 Let freedom ring from the snow-capped Rockies of Colorado!

23 Let freedom ring from the curvaceous[17] peaks of California!

24 But not only that; let freedom ring from Stone Mountain of Georgia!

25 Let freedom ring from Lookout Mountain of Tennessee!

26 Let freedom ring from every hill and molehill of Mississippi. From every mountainside, let freedom ring.

27 When we let freedom ring, when we let it ring from every village and every hamlet, from every state and every city, we will be able to speed up that day when all of God's children, black men and white men, Jews and Gentiles, Protestants and Catholics, will be able to join hands and sing in the words of the old Negro spiritual, "Free at last! free at last! thank God almighty, we are free at last!"

Notes

[1] On January 1, 1863, President Lincoln signed a decree freeing slaves in those territories still in rebellion against the Union. Dr. King delivered this speech on August 28, 1963, in front of the Lincoln Memorial in Washington, D.C.

[2] Handcuffs, shackles.

[3] A written promise to pay a debt.

[4] Not to be transferred or taken away.

[5] Consecrated, holy.

[6] The principle of reaching a goal by gradual steps rather than by sudden or drastic change.

[7] Aggressiveness, combativeness.

[8] Not to be loosed or untied.

[9] Followers of, believers in.

[10] Capability of movement.

[11] Sorrows, troubles.

[12] Serving to redeem, to pay off or buy back.

[13] See paragraph 1 of the Declaration of Independence.

[14] States' rights and failure to enforce federal laws.

[15] The allusions in this paragraph are from the Bible.

[16] Lofty, immense.

[17] Curving, molded.

Toward the 21st Century

Introductory note

What living will be like in the twenty-first century, no one can be certain. The selections that follow provide scattered clues, a few guidelines to the ideas and ideals which thoughtful men and women feel will be required, and a few statements about the problems and demands of life during coming decades.

You may reflect that as free men who should be the masters of machines, we may be able to take charge of the revolution now in progress and effect sociological, political, and physical changes of enormous significance. Surely no question could conceivably be more significant than how a free and democratic people can and should set about controlling the revolution in living now occurring and certain to continue.

Questions that can be raised—and not really answered—deal with the problem of poverty amidst plenty; of unemployment that presumably will increase (or lessen) as machines and techniques wipe out certain jobs and create others; of air and water pollution; of the destruction of natural resources; of overpopulation and resultant food shortages and hunger; of the human and financial costs of education, medical care, public housing; of urban growth and the spread of slum areas; of the difficulties involved in restraining individual impulses in the name of collective welfare; of attitudes involving prejudice, religion, race, national aspirations, and the age-old problems of war and peace and the brotherhood of man.

A VISION OF THE YEAR 2000

Clare Boothe Luce

CLARE BOOTHE LUCE (1903–) was born in New York City and was educated at St. Mary's, in Garden City, L.I., and at The Castle, Tarrytown, New York. She holds degrees from Colby College and from Fordham, Temple, Creighton, and Georgetown universities. An associate editor of *Vogue* magazine in 1930, she became associate and then managing editor of *Vanity Fair* (1931–1934), was a newspaper columnist in 1934, and since 1935 has been a playwright whose works include *The Women* (1937), *Kiss the Boys Goodbye* (1938), *Margin for Error* (1939), and *Child of the Morning* (1951). Mrs. Luce was a Connecticut representative to the 78th and 79th Congresses and U.S. Ambassador to Italy, 1953–1957. She is a trustee of the Carnegie Endowment for International Peace and a director of the Museum of Modern Art. Her other writings include *Stuffed Shirts* (1933) and *Europe in the Spring* (1940).

1 As we enter the new year 1966, it is time to take stock of the fact that we are living through the greatest revolution in the history of mankind. It is not ideological[1] in character, though modern ideologies—capitalism, Communism, fascism, and socialism—have all played their parts in advancing or delaying it. Its origins are rooted in the ancient past—and in man's ancient yet ever modern thirst for knowledge and for power over his environment. This world-shaking revolution is the scientific and technological[2] revolution of the twentieth century.

2 The pace of science and of technology in the West had begun to quicken well before World War II. But it is their explosive rate of progress since then, especially in America, that now gives them their revolutionary character.

3 For example, the New York World's Fair of 1939 chose as its theme "The World of Tomorrow." Its most spectacular exhibit was a scale model of a futuristic civilization in which mankind had intercontinental rocketry and atomic power. Guides who conducted open-mouthed visitors through the exhibit informed them that the scientists and technologists who had designed it were confident rockets would come in one or two generations, though atomic power probably would be a matter of several centuries. Five years later, America had both.

4 During my first term in Congress (1942–44), if any Congressman had predicted that the United States would be spending billions within fewer than twenty years to land on the moon, the moonstruck solon[3] might

have landed back in private life after the next election. Unmanned spacecraft orbiting Mars; men walking in space, digging through the earth's crust on the ocean floor, perfecting "death rays" (lasers); submarines capable of firing intercontinental missiles from under water and cruising below polar floes; robot machines that not only could calculate production needs and consumer demands, but program their own work, make decisions, correct their own errors, digest and memorize millions of facts and figures and produce them in the twinkling of an eye—all such things, as we reached the midcentury mark, were still to be found only in science fiction and in Buck Rogers and Superman comic strips. Today they, and much else that was incredible a few years ago, are realities.

5 In the past quarter of a century, the scientific and technological revolution has radically changed our life. It has changed our landscape and architecture, our domestic politics, foreign policies, economics, sociology, manners, morals, ethics—the entire character and quality of our culture.

6 And yet scientists (and their computers) are telling us that the revolution has scarcely begun and that its rate of progress will be sixteen times greater each year than the year before.

7 Our wildest speculations, as 1966 is ushered in, may seem merely timid predictions as we near the end of this century. Submarines that can fly? Vertical passenger-plane takeoffs? Planes carrying a thousand people? These are already on the drawing boards. A device to supply man with "gills," so he can breathe as easily in the ocean as he does on land? Sport submarines that can cruise for a weekend on the ocean's bottom? Engineering methods that will permit us to erect houses and hotels on the bosom of the sea? Accurate medical checkups and diagnoses made by computers? New eyes for old? New ears, hearts, kidneys, livers, bones for outworn or diseased ones? A life expectancy of a hundred years? All quite possible in the lifetime of millions of Americans. The great breakthrough—the discovery of how to dissolve the field of gravity, so man can hover above the earth in giant aircraft or sky houses and observatories? A way to control volcanoes, so they will create new islands for our constantly expanding population to inhabit? Maybe not for centuries—but maybe before our children become grandparents.

8 Only one thing can we predict with any certainty: If the revolution is *not* stopped, life in America in the year 2000 will be as different from life here today as life today differs from life in 1800. And over fifty percent of our population will be living in the super-revolutionary year 2000!

9 We know, as free men who are (or ought to be) the masters of our machines, that the revolution *can* be stopped dead in its tracks—any time we deliberately choose to stop it. We could today launch a nuclear holocaust[4] that would end the revolution with a billion-trillion-horsepower bang.

10 There is another way we can turn the revolution into a nightmare for America, if not for the rest of the world. That is to continue to fail (as we are presently failing) to take

charge of it firmly, at the political, sociological, and physical levels where it is affecting our lives adversely.

11 How should a free and democratic people set about controlling this prodigious[5] revolution? That is a subject too vast for a columnist's limited pen. But already many American leaders are arguing the urgent need for control. The problem—and paradox[6]—of crushing poverty in an age of potentially limitless plenty challenges even the dullest political minds.

12 We are beginning to realize that unemployment among unskilled and semiskilled workers must steadily increase as automation and cybernation[7] phase out[8] their jobs. We know it is daily more necessary to plan jobs now for millions of idle hands who will otherwise be employed by the Devil.[9] We suspect that if we are to keep consumer dollars flowing into industry, we may have to guarantee an annual income for all our adults and may even have to pay our young people to go to college, so they won't turn to crime, for want of job opportunities. We are beginning to realize that we will have to shorten the workweek by days, not hours, if we are to maintain even nominal full employment.

13 But as a nation we are still far from aware of how tragically we have failed to control some of the pernicious[10] physical side effects of the revolution.

14 We have let our superb industrial plants dump their refuse into all our river systems and inland-ocean lakes, turning even the mighty Hudson and Mississippi into poisonous sewers and our Great Lakes into cesspools. We have let our industrial machines and proliferating[11] automobiles fill the skies over our cities with noxious[12] gases and industrial dirt of every kind. In a technological age that could easily provide disposal plants and filter systems for air and water pollutants, we have supinely[13] permitted the revolution to filter its noisome[14] wastes through our stomachs and lungs.

15 We have refused to make government, industry, or ourselves responsible for disposing decently of the corpses of our worn-out mechanical household slaves—refrigerators, television sets, and other equipment destined for the junkyard. The ugly, rusty, twisted bodies of our most idolized machine, the automobile, have piled up along our highways. We have increased the scandal of the automobile graveyard with the scandal of roadside litter. Every day, tons of bottles, cans, boxes, papers, food remnants, cigarette butts, and other rubbish are thrown out of car windows onto the roadside. (And to all this we annually contribute to our highways the bloody litter of more than 50,000 smashed bodies.)

16 It is as though, having a genie[15] under our national roof, a prodigious Santa Claus who showers us with luxuries and comforts and toys, we allow him to poison us with his breath and bury us in his filth, while we enjoy his gifts.

17 It has been estimated (by those miraculous computers) that an adequate program to provide clean air, clean water, and clean highways for citizens of the future will cost 50 billion dollars. But if we do not very soon undertake this program, by the year 2000, Americans will be living in an Augean stable.[16] At this point,

the country is likely to become a nation of emigrants. The tremendous population shift to the West in the past ten years is partially due to the desire of millions to escape the disgusting side effects of the revolution. But when, even in the West, people no longer can see the stars at night for the smog, they will begin to leave America itself—

18 Looking in the New Year's crystal ball, I see two pictures forming for the year 2000. In one, thousands of Americans are leaving in thousand-passenger planes (and hover ships) for lands—any lands, however "backward"—where there are green hills and blue skies and sweet waters. Australia, New Zealand, Africa, Latin America, islands where the winds broom white clouds and where birds sing in occasional parks and forests—such lands are beckoning Americans, in full flight from the vast slum made of their own country by their parents' indifference to the side effects of history's greatest revolution.

19 In the second picture, I see a fair land, full of shining buildings and extraordinary new machines and artifacts,[17] whose uses I am unable to imagine—any more than I could have imagined what a radio or television set was for, had I seen their forms in a crystal ball in my youth. In this picture, I also see sights I once was familiar with: old men fishing and young people swimming in the wide, clean rivers that flow through cities—small children playing in the shade of great trees along flower-bordered highways—lovers walking through green city parks under a clear midnight moon, unafraid of muggers.[18]

20 But I also see a new sight: magnificent universities with garden campuses, where the youth of our land is being trained to direct the revolution for the betterment of mankind. And I seem to hear a professor explaining that, along about 1966, the American people began energetically to fight the war against poverty. Not against material poverty only, but against poverty of spirit. "America," this professor is saying, "awoke somewhat late to the fact that it is not enough for a great nation of free men to be strong and rich in material things. It must be rich in spirit, rich in imagination, rich in courage—and it must desire to create a beautiful as well as a prosperous country. So, about 1966, the American people began to control the scientific and technological revolution. This revolution is still presenting us with many problems; but thanks to the actions begun thirty years ago, we of the twenty-first century know we can solve them."

Notes

1 Relating to *ideology*, a body of doctrines, beliefs, myths, and opinions.
2 Relating to science and industry.
3 Lawmaker, legislator.
4 Destruction, devastation.
5 Great, marvelous.
6 Self-contradiction.

[7] The technique of operating and controlling by automatic means, such as electronic devices; the application of mechanics to engineering, designed to replace human controls.
[8] Ease out of service.
[9] In the so-called Puritan ethic, work is noble, laziness and sloth are ignoble and even evil.
[10] Hurtful, deadly.
[11] Multiplying, growing.
[12] Injurious, harmful to health.
[13] Passively.
[14] Offensive, disgusting.
[15] A spirit; a wonder-worker.
[16] In mythology, King Augeas kept 3,000 oxen in stables that had not been cleaned for thirty years. Hercules turned a river through the stables and cleaned them thoroughly.
[17] Man-made objects.
[18] Those who rob and injure their victims.

A FUTURE THAT MAKES ECOLOGICAL SENSE

Garrett De Bell

Garrett De Bell (1940–) received a Bachelor of Science degree from Stanford University in 1961. He then continued his studies toward a doctorate in zoology at the University of California (Berkeley) but left school to devote full time to ecological and environmental problems.

1 For the last few years I've noticed two trends in literature about the future. Journals like *Audubon Magazine, Sierra Club Bulletin,* and *Cry California* are generally concerned about imminent[1] ecological disaster—the death of canyons and valleys, the end of whales, big cats, eagles, falcons, pelicans, and even man. The magazines popularizing science, such as *Popular Science* and *Popular Mechanics,* speak of the technological Utopia[2] of the future—a television screen attached to every telephone, a helicopter on every rooftop, and sleek supersonic transports for the fortunate few within them who cannot hear their sonic boom. The two kinds of journal seem oblivious of each other and mutually exclusive. Yet there is a connection: The more we strive to reach the popular science future, the more likely we are to achieve the ecological disaster.[3]

2 The production, use and disposal of technologically sophisticated gadgets is a big part of our ecological problem. The solution to the problem is not found in a simple banning of billboards and non-returnable bottles, nor in the promotion of anti-litter campaigns and highway beautification. Some of our best polluters encourage such useful activities with advertising that professes deep concern about environment. This kind of

effort is at worst cynical[4] and at best misguided. Dealing with our ecological crises in population, water and air pollution, pesticides, transportation and the quality of life requires more than mere palliatives.[5] It requires the restructuring of many aspects of society.

3 We need first to halt growth of the world's population and then work toward reducing the current three and a half billion people to something less than one billion people. This number, perhaps, could be supported at a standard of living roughly similar to that of countries such as Norway and the Netherlands at the present time. The absurdly affluent and destructive standard of living in a country like the United States could not be sustained for very long for a population of more than three or four hundred million people all over the world.

4 One of the main purposes of the teach-in[6] and the whole ecological movement in this country today is to direct attention to a new kind of thinking about our environmental problems, a search for options[7] so that we can decide the goals and the directions to take to provide for a future that makes ecological sense. What might such a future be like? Imagine your own.

5 You can imagine hearing someone say, "Remember the subdivision that used to be where that orange grove is?" You can see a web of parks throughout the cities replacing the freeways and streets that once dominated. You can see agriculture become diversified again, with a great variety of crops grown together, replacing the old reliance on mass-produced single crop operations that are highly dependent on pesticides,[8] machines, and cheap farm labor. The traditional American values of rural life come back, and many more people grow their own food on smaller holdings and with a better quality of existence for the farm workers—and for everyone else.

6 More fruits and vegetables have insects on them instead of poisons. They can be brushed off or swallowed accidentally without harm. They are not mutagenic.[9] They eat very little themselves, and because there is no mono-crop, they can't wipe it out.

7 We see an end to some of the contradictions in American life. Where we once burned fossil fuels and polluted the air to provide electricity to run the escalators and other labor-saving devices that fattened us and sent us to the electric exercise machines and calorie-free soft drinks, we can rediscover walking. Where we overheated or overconditioned our air, we rely again on the human adaptability to stress that shaped us and gave us our physical integrity over a million years of living. Although the small labor-saving devices did not use much power, their aggregate use increased the demand for electricity, and with it the need for more dams, more oxidizing of fossil fuel, and more proliferation[10] of nuclear power plants and their radionuclides.[11] We find that diminishing dependence upon electric devices diminishes the need to build dams on wild rivers, pollute the air and sea with fossil fuels, and poison the ecosphere[12] with dispersing nuclear waste.

8 With conspicuous consumption

eliminated, we have more leisure time and a shorter work week. There are fewer automobiles, less reliance upon wasteful packaging, and less need for the labor saving devices that exploited natural resources in order to save time to spend with little reward in our overdepleted[13] world. We produce what we need and not a surplus. We allocate limited resources. New economists adjust economic sights to accommodate the requirements of our space-ship Earth, limited closed system that it is. The economists rethink about growth and know that "growth for the sake of growth is the ideology of the cancer cell," as Edward Abbey pointed out.

9 There is less spectator sport and more participating. The American people, once a nation of watchers, are "do-it-yourself people" again. They ski where the snowmobiles took them, walk where trail bikes crudded the wilderness and swim where motorboats droned over lakes they oiled. The people buy less music and make more of their own. There is a world quiet enough to hear it in.

10 People are healthier. Fewer coronaries[14] strike them because walking and bicycling and swimming keep them fitter. There are fewer people in hospitals because the old murderous automobile-oriented transportation system has been brought under control. Even the former automobile manufacturers, salesmen, and service people live longer, better lives. One major change is that every product we buy includes in its price the cost of its ultimate disposal. The many products that once were cheap because they were dumped at will have become so expensive that they no longer end up cluttering the environment.

11 Many of the people who were producing automobiles have been shifted into the housing or building industry. Their main job is restructuring the urban wastes to planned cities, restoring land to good agricultural use, building high-quality clustered dwellings at the edges of the good agricultural land, using recycled[15] material from the old buildings. People ride the short distance to their work and have a chance to farm a little in the sun. There are legs and arms and abdomens where the flab was, and the air is once again transparent.

12 The idea that a steady state works is commonplace. The population is declining slowly toward a balance between man and the other living things upon which his own life depends. The need for, and number of, schools, doctors, highways, roads, public parks, recreational facilities, swimming pools, and other facilities is roughly the same from year to year. People work enough to service equipment and to replace things that wear out. They devote energy to increasing the quality of life rather than to providing more and more possessions. The job of the garbage man and junk man is elevated to the stature of recycling engineer, looping systems in such a way that materials cause no environmental deterioration. Many power plants and dams are dismantled as the amount of energy needed each year declines and people develop sensible ways of living that require much less power, pollution, and environmental disruption. There

is decentralization of many basic services. Ecologically sound food stores prosper, offering pesticide-free produce in returnable containers.

13 Advertising serves to inform, not to overstimulate, and is believable again. Wilderness areas are no longer under attack, and retread wilderness increases substantially each year; less land is needed for commercial timber production because of effective recycling of wood products, reduction of conspicuous consumption and the lessening of need as the population drops. Poisoning of the ecosystem[16] by the leaded automobile gasoline has ceased because engine redesign eliminates the need for lead additives.

14 Emphysema and lung cancer caused by smog are eliminated and the smog goes. People learn how to garden again, and allow the recovery to take place with the natural forms of "pest" control instead of heavy doses of pesticides.

15 People are learning progressively more about relying less on gadgets. They have long since refused to buy ten cents worth of food in a T.V. dinner on an aluminum platter that will outlast the food for generations.

16 Many of the things built in the past in the name of conservation are being unbuilt. The Army Corps of Engineers is spending its time undoing the damage it has done over the past decades. Cities no longer ask the Corps to build a dam to prevent flooding of houses unwisely built on a flood plain. Instead, they ask the Corps to restore the flood plain to a vegetative cover that accommodates floods—good creative work for engineers.

17 And that technological mistake, the supersonic transport, has long since been a strange delusion, the few that were built having been dismantled and forgotten.

18 So much for one view of the future—more Utopian[17] than likely, unless people want it that way. Many believe we cannot solve the environmental problems because of the powerful influence of vested interests.[18] Obviously we can't solve these problems unless we meet these interests directly in the political arena and demonstrate that survival—theirs and ours—requires continuing change. The massive grass-roots[19] political movement which we now see growing can bring this about. One of the major changes of the decade can come from an ecological-political movement that bridges the gap between Left and Right and young and old. This movement will get people together behind candidates who press for a healthy environment and will turn out of office those who only pretend to do so.

19 The thing people must realize above all is that the solution to our environmental crises involves simple, small measures by many people in accelerating sequence.[20] The changes needed will require a conversion like that required to win World World II and then to reconvert to peace. The reward is worth this kind of effort. Consider the alternative.

Notes

[1] Near at hand; coming soon.
[2] An imaginary land where life is perfect.

[3] *Ecology* may be defined as a branch of biology that deals with the relations between organisms (forms of animal and plant life) and their environment.
[4] Contemptuous, insincere.
[5] Excuses, apologies; relief without a cure.
[6] A lengthy series of lectures, speeches, and so on presented as a form of social protest.
[7] Choices, alternatives.
[8] Chemical preparations for destroying flies, mosquitoes, and so on.
[9] Capable of causing (inducing) a sudden change from the parent type.
[10] Multiplication, growth.
[11] Radioactive nuclides (atomic species in which all atoms have the same atomic and mass number).
[12] That part of the atmosphere in which one can breathe normally.
[13] Exhausted.
[14] Heart attacks.
[15] Passed through for further change, use, or treatment.
[16] A system formed by the interaction (reciprocal action) of a community of organisms (plant or animal life) with their environment.
[17] Visionary, idealistic.
[18] Special interest for personal reasons in an existing system, institution, or arrangement.
[19] Involving the common people, the masses.
[20] Faster and faster occurrence.

WHAT WOULD IT BE LIKE IF WOMEN WIN

Gloria Steinem

GLORIA STEINEM (1936–) was born in Toledo, Ohio, and was graduated from Smith College in 1956. She has contributed widely to various magazines and is the author of several books including *The Thousand Indias* (1957) and *The Beach Book* (1963).

1 Any change is fearful, especially one affecting both politics and sex roles, so let me begin these utopian[1] speculations with a fact. To break the ice.

2 Women don't want to exchange places with men. Male chauvinists,[2] science-fiction writers and comedians may favor that idea for its shock value, but psychologists say it is a fantasy based on the ruling-class ego and guilt. Men assume that women want to imitate them, which is just what white people assumed about blacks. An assumption so strong that it may convince the second-class group of the need to imitate, but for both women and blacks that stage has passed. Guilt produces the question. What if they could treat us as we have treated them?

3 That is not our goal. But we do want to change the economic system to one more based on merit. In Women's Lib Utopia, there will be free access to good jobs—and decent pay for the bad ones women have been performing all along, including housework. Increased skilled labor

might lead to a four-hour workday, and higher wages would encourage further mechanization of repetitive jobs now kept alive by cheap labor.

4 With women as half the country's elected representatives, and a woman President once in a while, the country's *machismo*[3] problems would be greatly reduced. The old-fashioned idea that manhood depends on violence and victory is, after all, an important part of our troubles in the streets, and in Viet Nam. I'm not saying that women leaders would eliminate violence. We are not more moral than men; we are only uncorrupted by power so far. When we do acquire power, we might turn out to have an equal impulse toward aggression. Even now, Margaret Mead[4] believes that women fight less often but more fiercely than men, because women are not taught the rules of the war game and fight only when cornered. But for the next 50 years or so, women in politics will be very valuable by tempering the idea of manhood into something less aggressive and better suited to this crowded, post-atomic planet. Consumer protection and children's rights, for instance, might get more legislative attention.

5 Men will have to give up ruling-class privileges, but in return they will no longer be the only ones to support the family, get drafted, bear the strain of power and responsibility. Freud[5] to the contrary, anatomy is not destiny,[6] at least not for more than nine months at a time. In Israel, women are drafted, and some have gone to war. In England, more men type and run switchboards. In India and Israel, a woman rules. In Sweden, both parents take care of the children. In this country, come Utopia, men and women won't reverse roles; they will be free to choose according to individual talents and preferences.

6 If role reform sounds sexually unsettling, think how it will change the sexual hypocrisy[7] we have now. No more sex arranged on the barter system, with women pretending interest, and men never sure whether they are loved for themselves or for the security few women can get any other way. (Married or not, for sexual reasons or social ones, most women still find it second nature to Uncle-Tom.[8]) No more men who are encouraged to spend a lifetime living with inferiors; with housekeepers, or dependent creatures who are still children. No more domineering wives, emasculating[9] women, and "Jewish mothers," all of whom are simply human beings with all their normal ambition and drive confined to the home. No more unequal partnerships that eventually doom love and sex.

7 In order to produce that kind of confidence and individuality, child rearing will train according to talent. Little girls will no longer be surrounded by air-tight, self-fulfilling prophecies of natural passivity, lack of ambition and objectivity, inability to exercise power, and dexterity[10] (so long as special aptitude for jobs requiring patience and dexterity is confined to poorly paid jobs; brain surgery is for males).

8 Schools and universities will help to break down traditional sex roles, even when parents will not. Half the teachers will be men, a rarity now at preschool and elementary levels; girls will not necessarily serve cookies or

boys hoist up the flag. Athletic teams will be picked only by strength and skill. Sexually segregated courses like auto mechanics and home economics will be taken by boys and girls together. New courses in sexual politics will explore female subjugation[11] as the model for political oppression, and women's history will be an academic staple, along with black history, at least until the white-male-oriented textbooks are integrated and rewritten.

9 As for the American child's classic problem—too much mother, too little father—that would be cured by an equalization of parental responsibility. Free nurseries, school lunches, family cafeterias built into every housing complex, service companies that will do household cleaning chores in a regular, businesslike way, and more responsibility by the entire community for the children: all these will make it possible for both mother and father to work, and to have equal leisure time with the children at home. For parents of very young children, however, a special job category, created by Government and unions, would allow such parents a shorter work day.

10 The revolution would not take away the option of being a housewife. A woman who prefers to be her husband's housekeeper and/or hostess would receive a percentage of his pay determined by the domestic relations courts. If divorced, she might be eligible for a pension fund, and for a job-training allowance. Or a divorce could be treated the same way that the dissolution of a business partnership is now.

11 If these proposals seem farfetched, consider Sweden, where most of them are already in effect. Sweden is not yet a working Women's Lib model; most of the role-reform programs began less than a decade ago, and are just beginning to take hold. But that country is so far ahead of us in recognizing the problem that Swedish statements on sex and equality sound like bulletins from the moon.

12 Our marriage laws, for instance, are so reactionary[12] that Women's Lib groups want couples to take a compulsory written exam on the law, as for a driver's license, before going through with the wedding. A man has alimony and wifely debts to worry about, but a woman may lose so many of her civil rights that in the U.S. now, in important legal ways, she becomes a child again. In some states, she cannot sign credit agreements, use her maiden name, incorporate a business, or establish a legal residence of her own. Being a wife, according to most social and legal definitions, is still a 19th century thing.

13 Assuming, however, that these blatantly[13] sexist laws are abolished or reformed, that job discrimination is forbidden, that parents share financial responsibility for each other and the children, and that sexual relationships become partnerships of equal adults (some pretty big assumptions), then marriage will probably go right on. Men and women are, after all, physically complementary.[14] When society stops encouraging men to be exploiters and women to be parasites,[15] they may turn out to be more complementary in emotion as well. Women's Lib is not trying to destroy the American family. A look at the statistics on divorce—plus the way in which old

people are farmed out with strangers and young people flee the home—shows the destruction that has already been done. Liberated women are just trying to point out the disaster, and build compassionate and practical alternatives from the ruins.

14 What will exist is a variety of alternative life-styles. Since the population explosion dictates that childbearing be kept to a minimum, parents-and-children will be only one of many "families": couples, age groups, working groups, mixed communes, blood-related clans, class groups, creative groups. Single women will have the right to stay single without ridicule, without the attitudes now betrayed by "spinster" and "bachelor." Lesbians or homosexuals will no longer be denied legally binding marriages, complete with mutual-support agreements and inheritance rights. Paradoxically,[16] the number of homosexuals may get smaller. With fewer overpossessive mothers and fewer fathers who hold up an impossibly cruel or perfectionist idea of manhood, boys will be less likely to be denied or reject their identity as males.

15 Changes that now seem small may get bigger:

MEN'S LIB

16 Men now suffer from more diseases due to stress, heart attacks, ulcers, a higher suicide rate, greater difficulty living alone, less adaptability to change and, in general, a shorter life span than women. There is some scientific evidence that what produces physical problems is not work itself, but the inability to choose which work, and how much. With women bearing half the financial responsibility, and with the idea of "masculine" jobs gone, men might well feel freer and live longer.

RELIGION

17 Protestant women are already becoming ordained ministers; radical nuns are carrying out liturgical[17] functions that were once the exclusive property of priests; Jewish women are rewriting prayers—particularly those that Orthodox Jews recite every morning thanking God they are not female. In the future, the church will become an area of equal participation by women. This means, of course, that organized religion will have to give up one of its great historical weapons: sexual repression. In most structured faiths, from Hinduism through Roman Catholicism, the status of women went down as the position of priests ascended. Male clergy implied, if they did not teach, that women were unclean, unworthy and sources of ungodly temptation, in order to remove them as rivals for the emotional forces of men. Full participation of women in ecclesiastical life might involve certain changes in theology, such as, for instance, a radical redefinition of sin.

LITERARY PROBLEMS

18 Revised sex roles will outdate more children's books than civil rights ever did. Only a few children had the problem of a *Little Black Sambo*, but most have the male-female stereotypes of "Dick and Jane." A boomlet of children's books about mothers who work has already begun, and liberated

parents and editors are beginning to pressure for change in the textbook industry. Fiction writing will change more gradually, but romantic novels with wilting heroines and swashbuckling[18] heroes will be reduced to historical value. Or perhaps to the sado-masochist[19] trade. (*Marjorie Morningstar,* a romantic novel that took the '50s by storm, has already begun to seem as unreal as its '20s predecessor, *The Sheik.*) As for the literary plots that turn on forced marriages or horrific[20] abortions, they will seem as dated as Prohibition stories. Free legal abortions and free birth control will force writers to give up pregnancy as the *deus ex machina.*[21]

MANNERS AND FASHION

19 Dress will be more androgynous,[22] with class symbols becoming more important than sexual ones. Pro- or anti-Establishment styles may already be more vital than who is wearing them. Hardhats are just as likely to rough up antiwar girls as antiwar men in the street, and police understand that women are just as likely to be pushers or bombers. Dances haven't required that one partner lead the other for years, anyway. Chivalry will transfer itself to those who need it, or deserve respect: old people, admired people, anyone with an armload of packages. Women with normal work identities will be less likely to attach their whole sense of self to youth and appearance; thus there will be fewer nervous breakdowns when the first wrinkles appear. Lighting cigarettes and other treasured niceties will become gestures of mutual affection. "I like to be helped on with my coat," says one Women's Lib worker, "but not if it costs me $2,000 a year in salary."

20 For those with nostalgia[23] for a simpler past, here is a word of comfort. Anthropologist Geoffrey Gorer studied the few peaceful human tribes and discovered one common characteristic: sex roles were not polarized.[24] Differences of dress and occupation were at a minimum. Society, in other words, was not using sexual blackmail as a way of getting women to do cheap labor, or men to be aggressve.

21 Thus Women's Lib may achieve a more peaceful society on the way toward its other goals. That is why the Swedish government considers reform to bring about greater equality in the sex roles one of its most important concerns. As Prime Minister Olof Palme explained in a widely ignored speech delivered in Washington this spring: "It is *human beings* we shall emancipate. In Sweden today, if a politician should declare that the woman ought to have a different role from man's, he would be regarded as something from the Stone Age." In other words, the most radical goal of the movement is egalitarianism.[25]

22 If Women's Lib wins, perhaps we all do.

Notes

[1] Involving imaginary or ideal perfection. Sir Thomas More's *Utopia* described an island where all aspects of life—government, the economy, and so on—approached the ideal.

[2] Persons devoted to a cause, especially those who are zealous and belligerent. The word comes from the name of a soldier in one of Napoleon's armies, a loud-mouthed patriot.

[3] A currently popular term of no particular meaning but referring generally to "method of operation."

[4] An American anthropologist and author born in 1901.

[5] Dr. Sigmund Freud (1856–1939), Austrian neurologist and psychoanalyst.

[6] A statement also singled out and commented upon by Dr. Estelle Ramey in another article in this volume.

[7] Pretense, deceit.

[8] To act meekly. The phrase comes from the title of Harriet Beecher Stowe's antislavery novel, *Uncle Tom's Cabin* (1852). "Uncle Tomism" is a relationship between whites and blacks in which the latter adopt a submissive attitude.

[9] Making others weaker; depriving of strength.

[10] Skill, agility.

[11] Submission, enslavement.

[12] Backward, overly conservative.

[13] Openly and offensively obvious.

[14] Completing; fulfilling each other.

[15] Those who receive support without making any return; leeches.

[16] Seemingly self-contradictory.

[17] Churchly, religious.

[18] Daring, adventurous.

[19] Sado-masochism is a disturbed personality condition marked by sadism (sexual gratification through causing physical pain) and masochism (gratification obtained from pain inflicted upon oneself).

[20] Causing horror.

[21] Any forced or artificial device used to resolve difficulties; literally, "god from a machine."

[22] Relating to both male and female.

[23] Longing to return.

[24] Made to show different properties; at opposite ends of a spectrum.

[25] Equality.

LOVE AND LIBERATION

Lisa Hobbs

Lisa Hobbs (1925–) was born in Melbourne, Australia, and was educated in that country. In the United States, she worked for ten years as a reporter on the San Francisco *Examiner* and later became a foreign correspondent for the San Francisco *Chronicle*. Mrs. Hobbs has lectured widely on college campuses in the United States and Canada. She is the author of *I Saw Red China* (1966) and *India, India* (1967).

1 I am a woman. But a woman in a man's world.

2 This means that my life thus far has been spent living within institutions and concepts[1] which men, not women, made. It means that I must act, feel, look and speak in ways which man has determined are "suitable" for me. These modes of behavior were determined thousands of years ago when woman, lacking any means of birth control, was condemned to

live her life within a narrow and limiting biological context.[2] They have survived because man established his "manhood" in direct proportion to his ability to override the female and sustain his ego-strength[3] through this process. Taking stock of this biological difference, he has exploited[4] it by initiating and supporting institutions and attitudes that gave the male ego an almost supreme power over the female ego. These institutions and attitudes remain intact[5] today and it is the aim of the women's liberation movement to destroy them. . . .[6]

3 If we look at the world around us, we see that love has become a rare commodity, spontaneous warmth all but quenched, laughter is heard only through the television tubes. We are bound together by our humanity yet dare not look one another in the eye for fear we will see some part of ourselves reflected there, some part in need that frightens and repels us. We give our help to the unemployed in the form of a check in the mails, our help to the sick aged in the form of drugs, our help to children in the form of gadgets, our help to one another in the form of alcohol, trinkets and gestures. Why is it that we can no longer be human and love and weep and laugh and relish making fools of ourselves? For we long to do these things, we long to be more human, to put more into life, get more out of life. It is as if we are going through life on tiptoe, never really experiencing it; life passes by like a painless and bland[7] movie when we long to sink our teeth into its being. Why can't we? What has happened to us? What has been done to us?

4 What has happened is simply that *our society has become one giant rational construct.*[8] It is an intellectual abstraction[9] and no longer relates to the warm, groping, shabby and sometimes hilarious realities of our human nature. These concepts under which we live, which force us to forever compete, to play sexually stereotyped roles, to marry as we do, raise children as we do, make war as we do, make love as we do, work as we do and relate as we do—these concepts have polluted our souls.

5 We can see what has been done to our land, rivers, beaches and forests. We can measure precisely how the face of our planet has been polluted and partially destroyed by false social and economic values. What is more difficult to measure is the extent to which man's nature has been polluted and lacerated[10] by the same kind of false social and economic values.

6 The task of women in the coming decades is to ruthlessly destroy these false constructs that dominate our life. Despite present conditions of unprecedented[11] strain, there is all the intelligence, goodness, strength and vision necessary to reconstruct our entire society. The initial step has already been undertaken—the disengagement[12] of woman from the historic programming of male and female roles. Once this disengagement is completed, women of the world will be free to tear apart all the rational constructs that do not relate to the reality of humanity.

7 It is no longer good enough to blame man for keeping woman ignorant. For man himself is ignorant and in the sum total no more capable or enlightened than woman.

Notes

[1] Notions, ideas.
[2] Set of circumstances or facts that surround an idea, event, or situation.
[3] Self-importance.
[4] Used selfishly.
[5] Whole, sound, unbroken.
[6] The subtitle of the book from which this selection was taken is "Up Front with the Feminists." A *feminist* is one who advances the cause of social and political rights for women equal to those for men. *Liberation* means "release," "freedom from bondage."
[7] Dull, insipid.
[8] A complex idea, structure, or image from a number of simpler ideas, structures, or images.
[9] General idea, unrealistic notion.
[10] Torn, mangled.
[11] Never before known.
[12] Withdrawal, release.

THE FIRE NEXT TIME

James Baldwin

James Baldwin (1924–) was born in New York City and was educated in local schools. He has been the recipient of numerous grants and fellowships in his active writing career and has lectured throughout the country on civil rights for blacks and other minority groups. Among his books are *Go Tell It on the Mountain* (1953), *Notes of a Native Son* (1955), *Nobody Knows My Name* (1960), *Tell Me How Long the Train's Been Gone* (1968), *No Name in the Street* (1972).

1 The American Negro has the great advantage of having never believed that collection of myths to which white Americans cling: that their ancestors were all freedom-loving heroes, that they were born in the greatest country the world has ever seen, or that Americans are invincible[1] in battle and wise in peace, that Americans have always dealt honorably with Mexicans and Indians and all other neighbors or inferiors, that American men are the world's most direct and virile, that American women are pure. Negroes know far more about white Americans than that; it can almost be said, in fact, that they know about white Americans what parents—or, anyway, mothers—know about their children, and that they very often regard white Americans that way. And perhaps this attitude, held in spite of what they know and have endured, helps to explain why Negroes, on the whole, and until lately, have allowed themselves to feel so little hatred. The tendency has really been, insofar as

this was possible, to dismiss white people as the slightly mad victims of their own brainwashing.[2] One watched the lives they led. One could not be fooled about that; one watched the things they did and the excuses that they gave themselves, and if a white man was really in trouble, deep trouble, it was to the Negro's door that he came. And one felt that if one had had that white man's worldly advantages, one would never have become as bewildered and as joyless and as thoughtlessly cruel as he. The Negro came to the white man for a roof or for five dollars or for a letter to the judge; the white man came to the Negro for love. But he was not often able to give what he came seeking. The price was too high; he had too much to lose. And the Negro knew this, too. When one knows this about a man, it is impossible for one to hate him, but unless he becomes a man—becomes equal—it is also impossible for one to love him. Ultimately,[3] one tends to avoid him, for the universal characteristic of children is to assume that they have a monopoly[4] on trouble, and therefore a monopoly on *you*. (Ask any Negro what he knows about the white people with whom he works. And then ask the white people with whom he works what they know about *him*.)

2 How can the American Negro past be used? It is entirely possible that this dishonored[5] past will rise up soon to smite all of us. There are some wars, for example (if anyone on the globe is still mad enough to go to war) that the American Negro will not support, however many of his people may be coerced[6]—and there is a limit to the number of people any government can put in prison, and a rigid limit indeed to the practicality of such a course. A bill is coming in that I fear America is not prepared to pay. "The problem of the twentieth century," wrote W. E. B. Du Bois[7] around sixty years ago, "is the problem of the color line." A fearful and delicate problem, which compromises, when it does not corrupt, all the American efforts to build a better world—here, there, or anywhere. It is for this reason that everything white Americans think they believe in must now be reexamined. What one would not like to see again is the consolidation[8] of peoples on the basis of their color. But as long as we in the West place on color the value that we do, we make it impossible for the great unwashed[9] to consolidate themselves according to any other principle. Color is not a human or a personal reality; it is a political reality. But this is a distinction so extremely hard to make that the West has not been able to make it yet. And at the center of this dreadful storm, this vast confusion, stand the black people of this nation, who must now share the fate of a nation that has never accepted them, to which they were brought in chains. Well, if this is so, one has no choice but to do all in one's power to change that fate, and at no matter what risk—eviction, imprisonment, torture, death. For the sake of one's children, in order to minimize[10] the bill that *they* must pay, one must be careful not to take refuge in any delusion—and the value placed on the color of the skin is always and everywhere and forever a delusion. I know that what I am asking is impossible. But in our time, as in every time, the

impossible is the least that one can demand—and one is, after all, emboldened[11] by the spectacle of human history in general, and American Negro history in particular, for it testifies to nothing less than the perpetual achievement of the impossible.

3 When I was very young, and was dealing with my buddies in those wine- and urine-stained hallways, something in me wondered, *What will happen to all that beauty?* For black people, though I am aware that some of us, black and white, do not know it yet, are very beautiful. And when I sat at Elijah's[12] table and watched the baby, the women, and the men, and we talked about God's—or Allah's[13]—vengeance, I wondered, when that vengeance was achieved, *What will happen to all that beauty then?* I could also see that the intransigence[14] and ignorance of the white world might make that vengeance inevitable—a vengeance that does not really depend on, and cannot really be executed by, any person or organization, and that cannot be prevented by any police force or army: historical vengeance, a cosmic[15] vengeance, based on the law that we recognize when we say, "Whatever goes up must come down." And here we are, at the center of the arc, trapped in the gaudiest, most valuable, and most improbable water wheel the world has ever seen. Everything now, we must assume, is in our hands; we have no right to assume otherwise. If we—and now I mean the relatively conscious whites and the relatively conscious blacks, who must, like lovers, insist on, or create, the consciousness of the others—do not falter in our duty now, we may be able, handful that we are, to end the racial nightmare, and achieve our country, and change the history of the world. If we do not now dare everything, the fulfillment of that prophecy, re-created from the Bible in song by a slave, is upon us: *God gave Noah the rainbow sign, No more water, the fire next time!*[16]

Notes

1 Unbeatable, not to be conquered.

2 A method for altering beliefs and changing attitudes through the use of stress techniques or torture. Here, the term is used to imply controlled, systematic indoctrination (teaching).

3 Finally.

4 Exclusive control or possession.

5 Shameful, disgraceful.

6 Compelled, forced.

7 A black American educator and writer, 1868–1963.

8 Grouping, combining.

9 The so-called lower class.

10 Reduce, lessen.

11 Encouraged.

12 Elijah Muhammad, leader of the Nation of Islam movement.

13 The Supreme Being of Islam, the religious faith of Muslims.

14 Unwillingness or inability to change or compromise.

[15] Vast, far-reaching.

[16] A reference to the Great Flood, a universal deluge recorded as having occurred in the days of Noah, the Hebrew patriarch who built a vessel (Noah's Ark) in which he, his family, and animals of many kinds survived (Genesis, chapters 5–9).

AN OPEN LETTER TO STUDENTS

Paul Amos Moody

PAUL AMOS MOODY (1903–) was born in Vermont and was educated at Morningside College and the University of Michigan. He began long service as a professor and researcher at the University of Vermont in 1927. His work has been largely concerned with evolution and human genetics.

1 Man has become so powerful in controlling his own social evolution, including the invention of means for his own destruction, that nothing short of complete cooperation by all peoples on our "shrinking planet" will suffice.[1] If any people or society finds itself unable to adapt to such cooperative living on a global scale we may predict that that people or society will go the way of the dinosaurs,[2] leaving the earth to those peoples who can make the adjustment. Natural selection[3] is not dead; but in the modern world natural selection is placing a premium on ability to live cooperatively, not competitively.

2 Each of us is naturally interested that *his* society shall be among the survivors. It is not pleasant to imagine a future in which our particular race or nation shall have no part. How can we help to insure that our group shall not be eliminated by natural selection? Evidently, since social evolution is so largely under human control, we can contribute most by supporting all measures which further cooperative living on this earth.

3 Perhaps all peoples will be able to make the adjustment to cooperative living on a global scale. On the other hand, being as pessimistic as possible for the moment, we may ask: What will happen if *no* peoples can make the necessary adaptation? Then we may feel sure that mankind as a whole will become as extinct as the dinosaurs (probably through self-destruction), leaving our environmental niches[4] free for exploitation[5] by some other form of life. What form of life? We should have as great difficulty predicting that as a dinosaur would have had predicting that the mammals would inherit his place on earth.

4 But such pessimism is untimely. Possibly the way of progress will be found to lie through some form other than man. We have reason to doubt that this will be the case, however. Increasingly man controls his own evolution, especially his social evolution. Development of cooperative

living is one process in that social evolution. We may feel confident that man, or at least some groups of men, will develop the qualities necessary for cooperation on the scale required. If so, there now seems no ascertainable[6] limit to man's supremacy. Each of us can make his own contribution toward creating a mental and spiritual climate in which the necessary cooperation can thrive. "Cooperation begins at home" but it must not end until it encompasses the earth. Each of us can contribute to this end.

5 In closing this letter on an optimistic note I may be laying myself open to the accusation of being a "Pollyanna."[7] After all, none of us can really foretell the future—most especially the distant future. But optimism seems at least as warranted as pessimism, especially when we recall the brief space in which our social evolution has been operative. [Previously] we spoke of a hypothetical[8] time-lapse movie of earth history. You will recall that the movie runs continuously for a year, but that of that year man has been in existence for only about twelve *hours,* and civilization has occupied only the last five or six *minutes.* Much social evolution has occurred in that five or six minutes; we may feel confident that much more will occur before man's time on earth equals that of many of his predecessors.[9] Our social evolution is near its beginning, not its ending. Knowledge of evolution, then, gives us the perspective[10] for optimism. We say that these are "dark days"; thoughtful reading of history will convince us that most days have been "dark" in the sense we have in mind. But out of the darkness has come progress in the past. That fact gives us optimism that progress will also characterize the long trends of the future.

Notes

[1] Be enough.

[2] Extinct land reptiles ranging in length up to 90 feet who lived in the Mesozoic Era, the fourth of five eras of zoologic time, approximately 70,000,000 to 200,000,000 years ago.

[3] A process in nature resulting in the survival and continuance of only those forms of plant and animal life that have characteristics enabling them to adapt to a specific environment; that is, "survival of the fittest."

[4] Recesses, corners, places.

[5] Selfish use.

[6] Clear-cut, readily determined.

[7] An overly optimistic person. The name is derived from that of a heroine created by Eleanor Porter (1868–1920), an American novelist.

[8] Supposed, assumed.

[9] Those who came (went) before.

[10] Mental view, prospect.

CULTURAL AND BIOLOGICAL EVOLUTION

William T. Keeton

William T. Keeton (1933–) was born in Roanoke, Virginia, and was educated at the University of Chicago, Virginia Polytechnic Institute, and Cornell University. In 1964, Dr. Keeton became an associate professor at Cornell. His work in the biological sciences is widely known.

1 One of the most interesting discoveries of recent years is that early hominids[1] used tools long before their brains were much larger than those of apes. Thus the old idea that a large brain and high intelligence were necessary prerequisites[2] for the use of tools has been discredited. Early man's use of tools may, in fact, have been an important factor in leading to evolution of higher intelligence. Once tool use and tool making began, individuals that excelled in these endeavors would surely have had an advantage over their less talented fellows. There would thus have been strong selection for neural mechanisms[3] making possible improved tool making and use. Thus perhaps, instead of considering culture the crown of man's fully evolved intelligence, we should regard early cultural development and increasing intelligence as two faces of the same coin; in a sense, the highly developed brain of modern man may be as much a consequence as a cause of culture.

2 Cultural evolution can proceed at a far more rapid pace than biological evolution. Words as units of inheritance are much more effective than genes[4] in spreading new developments and in giving dominance to new approaches originating with a few talented individuals. But the two types of evolution continue to be interwoven just as they were in tool use; they may well be even more so in the future.

3 Man now has the ability to alter deliberately some aspects of the future evolution of his species (and of other species). Modern medicine, by saving people with gross genetic defects[5] that would once have been fatal, permits perpetuation of genes that natural selection would formerly have eliminated. Man could, if he chose, practice eugenics[6]—deliberately restrict the perpetuation of some genetic traits and encourage the perpetuation of others. And the day will surely come when the DNA[7] of genes can deliberately be altered in order to design, at least in part, new human beings. When that day comes, how do we decide what to design? And who decides? And who controls the one who decides? And in the meantime, how do we handle the

problem of controlling the size of human populations, a problem becoming increasingly serious as a result of our interference with the action of many of the former regulating factors? These are important questions that are at once biological, economic, political, and moral. They must be faced soon. We have already gone too far toward modifying biological evolution to pull back. Like it or not, the next few generations of human beings must answer these and many similar questions. The answers they choose to give may well have as profound an influence on the future of life as anything that has happened since the first cells appeared in the primordial[8] seas.

Notes

1 A term in anthropology meaning members of a family consisting of man and his ancestors.

2 Items or things required beforehand.

3 Nervous systems.

4 Units of heredity.

5 Flaws or failures in heredity.

6 The science of improving qualities of the human race.

7 An abbreviation for deoxyribonucleic acid, any of a class of acids that functions in the transference of genetic (hereditary) characteristics and in the synthesis of protein.

8 Existing at or from the very beginning.

NOT QUITE UTOPIA

Stuart Chase

STUART CHASE (1888–) was born in New Hampshire and was graduated from Harvard in 1910. For several years he worked with his father's firm of public accountants in Boston and then began long service with various agencies of the United States government. He has contributed widely to magazines and is the author of many books, among them *The Tragedy of Waste* (1925), *Men and Machines* (1929), *Government in Business* (1935), *The Proper Study of Mankind* (1948), *The Power of Words* (1953), American Credos (1962), *Danger—Man Talking* (1969).

1 A faculty member of the Westchester State College,[1] let us say, walks out to his mailbox for the Sunday *New York Times* on a spring morning in the year 2001. The shad-blow[2] is almost over and the orioles are back. The *Times* weighs just half a pound, rather than the present eight. It is charged to his personal account in the computerized credit system to which every American citizen belongs. His salary is of course credited. Competitive advertising has largely disappeared, leaving chiefly news, reviews and comment.

2 As he looks up, the sky is a deep, unpolluted blue.

3 A squirrel is chattering, but he hears no thundering jets, no sonic booms,[3] no grinding trucks, roaring motorcycles, screeching station wagons, or grunting bulldozers.

4 Along the clear, almost transparent road, faintly luminous[4] at night, comes a fuel-cell car, small, quiet, easy to park, shockproof, fumeless. . . . An electric truck follows. Yellow daffodils are blooming by a roadside innocent of beer cans.

5 Water from the nuclear desalting plant at Greenwich is cold and free of chlorine, with plenty for lawn, garden, and community swimming pool. Private, unguarded pools are banned—too many children were drowned in this struggle for prestige. The fear of drought has disappeared forever—at least in coastal areas.

6 There are no commercials on television, a service now charged to citizens in the national credit system along with other public utilities.

7 The beaches of Long Island Sound are white and clean, and shore birds are thick in the wide salt marshes. Power boats with fuel cells are as silent as the sailboats, and water skiing is assigned a separate area, with stiff penalties for leaving it. The waters of the Sound are clear and clean. Great schools of shad are running up the Hudson and Connecticut rivers, shellfish are healthy and abundant. Even Lake Erie is slowly beginning to breathe again.

8 Through a gap in his tall pine grove, the professor can see on the horizon the towers of the New Town near White Plains. It is one of a dozen local centers in the New York urban field, helping to take the pressure off Manhattan. Its symphony orchestra, he recalls, won the recent All-American competition.

9 No private automobiles are now permitted in Manhattan, not even for the grandest politicos. Electric buses, electric trucks for night deliveries, plenty of fuel-cell taxis, bicycles on the special paths constitute the vehicles aboveground. The professor can go from a station near his home to Manhattan in 20 noiseless minutes underground. It takes him no longer to the international airport, where Stol-planes[5] rise and descend vertically with almost no noise. The supersonic liners have been abandoned, pending a solution of the sonic boom problem. The professor can get anywhere in the world comfortably in a few hours, as it is.

10 A good half of New York City's area is now open space, following the Great Demolition of the 1980's, and population is down to an unhurried five million. No crowds yell at a would-be suicide, "Go ahead and jump!" The parks are safe at night; the malls[6] with their fountains, flowers, and sidewalk cafés are pleasant for shopping or for meditation by day.

11 The United Nations has left New York for an island of its own in the Indian Ocean. It has a powerful legislative body responsible to no nation but to mankind, and the whole organization is intensively devoted to settling disputes between nations, enforcing disarmament, and balancing the world economy. Its lordly budget of over $100 billion a year comes from royalties on various supranational[7] resources, drawn from the sea, from

Antarctica, and from the earth's mantle. A cut in the tolls of the new sea-level canal across Nicaragua also helps.

12 The last substantial war, beyond UN control, ended in Southeast Asia in the early 1970's, when the governments of both belligerents were overwhelmingly displaced by their exasperated, bereaved, and impoverished citizens, and the UN was called in to mandate the whole devastated area. The explosion of several nuclear weapons on each side was the dreadful price for bringing permanent peace on earth.

13 The cold war between the U.S. and the U.S.S.R. was finally abandoned in the late 1970's. One reason was that Russian scientists discovered and gave to the world a cure for cancer. The impact even dissolved the John Birch Society.[8]

14 China and a reunited Germany are now strong supporters of the United Nations. As a result of the steady growth of the mixed economy, the opposing ideologies[9] of Communism and the Radical Right have all but withered away. Mr. William F. Buckley, Jr.[10] devotes his still energetic mind to raising delphiniums.

15 No human landings on Mars or Venus are now planned. The terrible disaster on the return from the moon by the first astronauts determined that.[11] Outer space is obviously inhospitable for long trips by earthlings; there are too many unknown variables. Exploration is still vigorously carried on, but by unmanned vehicles and instruments, under the direction of scientists in UNESCO.

16 Competition between nations is largely confined to advances in the arts, research, and the Olympic Games. Deprived of its military function, a nation is now a nostalgic[12] homeland, and a much more decent and friendly institution. Capital punishment has been abolished in most countries, the crime rate is down, and there is no point to stealing money in a society devoted to computerized credit.

17 Every child on earth now learns the world language—with its phonetic spelling and simple structure—through television lessons and plays. A little fiction and poetry have recently been written in this synthetic tongue, but its literary value remains to be proved, however excellent it may be for international conferences.

18 Nearly every child on earth receives all the education his genes[13] permit. He grows up an independent thinker, informed by the scientific attitude. This has gone far to heal race relations, but no final solution can yet be announced. There is however, no *Apartheid*[14] in South Africa and no "Black Power" in the United States.

19 The American population is growing at half of one percent a year, down from 1.6 percent in 1965. The world rate stands at 0.7 percent. Though birth control is universally available, with some extraordinary new techniques in both sterilization and tranquilizing[15] the sex drive, these growth rates are known to be too high. Planetary policy aims at a rate of *zero* by 2025, with world population thereafter never to exceed seven billion children, women, and men. That seems to be the maximum our living space can comfortably support.

It is no longer a question of the food supply setting the total, but elbow room.

20 The food supply in calories is now growing at 1.3 percent, almost twice the rate of population. Some African children are still undernourished, but the dreadful famines of the 1970's and 1980's will never come again, and the insidious[16] and deadly new variety of plague which then originated to balance births with deaths has at last been conquered by the World Health Organization.

21 Nuclear power plants, using the fusion process with hydrogen from all the oceans as raw material, are now beginning to raise living standards everywhere, and the area once known as the Hungry World—two-thirds of mankind—has lost its title. The battle now is with the temptations of material abundance rather than with the deprivations of scarcity. Economic textbooks are at last being rewritten on this principle.

22 Our professor walks back from his pleasant roadside, waving to a neighbor on horseback, hacking[17] along the parallel trail. He breathes deep of the fresh spring air, notes the dogwood buds almost ready to create their annual snowdrift, and enters his pleasant home, warmed and serviced by wireless pulsations of energy. He opens the Sunday *Times* to read the latest instrument analysis from Mars. Yes, once there were probably living creatures on Mars, and then . . . ?

Notes

[1] The college is imaginary in a sense, but Westchester is the name of a county just north of New York City.

[2] Annual migration of shad (deep-bodied herring) for the purpose of spawning.

[3] Loud noises caused by the shock wave of an aircraft moving at supersonic speed (greater than the speed of sound waves through air).

[4] Shining, bright.

[5] Short takeoff and landing aircraft.

[6] Areas lined with shrubbery and shade trees.

[7] Beyond the authority of one government.

[8] A conservative organization founded in 1958 to combat Communist activities in the United States.

[9] Bodies or sets of opinion, belief, and doctrine.

[10] Editor of the *National Review* and an articulate spokesman for conservatism.

[11] Remember, this selection appeared in 1968; even prophets can err.

[12] Referring to the desire to return to a former time or place in one's life.

[13] Units of heredity.

[14] Racial segregation and discrimination against blacks and other nonwhites.

[15] Calming, quieting.

[16] Treacherous, stealthy.

[17] Riding at an ordinary pace.

Profile, Portrait, and Autobiography

INTRODUCTORY NOTE

Biography has been a popular form of reading for centuries. Sketches of kings and members of the ruling class have long thrilled readers who by them vicariously experienced all sorts of adventures. Curiosity about others is as old as the human race, and its power and attraction have increased rather than decreased through the centuries. Within the past century our curiosity about others, great and small, has resulted in both a major industry and a major literary type. Biography and autobiography in books, magazines, motion pictures, television, and radio are a twentieth-century flood that shows no signs of receding.

Modern readers are not always so absorbed with literal accounts of striking deeds as readers and listeners were centuries ago. But eagerness to know the intimate details of others' lives, curiosity about people's attainments, about their strengths and weaknesses, their ways of speaking and thinking and acting, their human and their inhuman qualities are as dominant now as man's urge to escape or to live through fiction. This fascination with the lives of others has been cultivated as biography has become a more settled type, as it has come to be more appealingly written, as it has dealt more and more with ordinary people and less and less with contemporary kings and princes.

The present-day popularity of biographical writing also traces to the fact that readers have come to realize that truth is actually "stranger than fiction." Perhaps it would be more correct to say that "truth is stranger than fiction *dares* to be," for some of the complications, ironies, and coincidences in almost anyone's life would have to be discarded by a competent narrative writer. Put into fiction they would seem either impossible or improbable. The biographer is restrained by no such consideration. His whole work, if properly handled, seems credible, and its reader will willingly accept more hair-raising and heart-stopping episodes than any novelist or story writer could hope to employ. Good biographical and autobiographical writing is narrative and has not only appropriated the appealing techniques of narration but added to them.

Closely related to biography and autobiography is the *profile*. This type of writing is a combination of biographical material and interpretation of character. That is, the profile (as in *The New Yorker* and other periodicals) is biographical writing in a modern vein: superimposed upon an account of the subject's heredity, background, environment, and accomplishments is an attempted evaluation of his traits and characteristics—*Who's Who* detail plus anecdotal material plus character analysis. A profile is not a full-length portrait; it bears somewhat the relationship to a full biography that a short story does to a novel.

Biography and autobiography have a distinct limitation. Philip Guedalla, an English writer, was cynical when he remarked that biography is "a region bounded on the north by history, on the south by fiction, on the east by obituary, and on the west by tedium." But it is true that every age writes its own biography and emphasizes its own villains and heroes. It is necessary to remember that a biography may not deal with timeless truth, that it often merely reflects an attitude or point of view of an earlier day. Other genres—essays, stories, poems, novels, plays—can and often do state essential and ever-green truths. Biography may reveal such truths, but there are few undisputed and documented facts in anyone's life, and probably no biography or autobiography has ever been complete, unprejudiced, or impartial. "The proper study of mankind is man," but study unadorned and unaided by artistic creativeness may be faulty and fragmentary. And a long list of autobiographies, St. Augustine's, Cellini's, Casanova's, Rousseau's, and Franklin's among them, attest that it is even more difficult to know—and to tell—the truth about oneself. Novelist, short story writer, poet, and dramatist, under no such compulsion, create characters or narrate events that, at their best, seem "truer than truth." Thackeray once wrote that "fiction carries a greater amount of truth in solution than the volume which purports to be all true."

An attempt to view man's mind from the inside may be considered as appealing more to morbid inquisitiveness than to healthy curiosity. Guedalla has likened the new biography to a sport such as big-game hunting and suggests that it is as unfair as only such a sport can be. In an attempt not to become myth-makers, some biographers tend to become exhibitionists. Spice, not truth; abuse, not use; realism, not a single reticence—these are the credo of those whose aim is sensationalism and sales. However this may be, the penetrating discernment and sophisticated detachment of the new school of biographers have made the type a serious rival of fiction.

THE MONSTER

Deems Taylor

(JOSEPH) DEEMS TAYLOR (1885–1966) was a composer and critic who, after graduation from New York University, became a journalist. His love for music prevailed, and he became a music critic and editor of *Musical America.* As a composer he first won serious attention with cantatas based on the well-known poems, "The Highwayman" (Noyes) and "The Chambered Nautilus" (Holmes). Other compositions include "Through the Looking-Glass," an impressionistic suite based on Carroll's fantasy; *The King's Henchman,* a romantic opera of medieval England with libretto by Edna St. Vincent Millay; and *Peter Ibbetson,* an operatic work based on Du Maurier's novel. He also wrote music for plays by George S. Kaufman, Marc Connelly, and Elmer Rice. Books of criticism largely collected from Mr. Taylor's radio talks include *Of Men and Music* (1937), *The Well-Tempered Listener* (1940), and *Music to My Ears* (1949). Two later books are *Some Enchanted Evenings* (1953) and *The One-Track Mind* (1953).

1 He was an undersized little man, with a head too big for his body—a sickly little man. His nerves were bad. He had skin trouble. It was agony for him to wear anything next to his skin coarser than silk. And he had delusions of grandeur.[1]

2 He was a monster of conceit. Never for one minute did he look at the world or at people, except in relation to himself. He was not only the most important person in the world, to himself; in his own eyes he was the only person who existed. He believed himself to be one of the greatest dramatists in the world, one of the greatest thinkers, and one of the greatest composers. To hear him talk, he was Shakespeare, and Beethoven, and Plato, rolled into one. And you would have had no difficulty in hearing him talk. He was one of the most exhaustive[2] conversationalists that ever lived. An evening with him was an evening spent in listening to a monologue.[3] Sometimes he was brilliant; sometimes he was maddeningly tiresome. But whether he was being brilliant or dull, he had one sole topic of conversation: himself. What *he* thought and what *he* did.

3 He had a mania[4] for being in the right. The slightest hint of disagreement, from anyone, on the most trivial point, was enough to set him off on a harangue[5] that might last for hours, in which he proved himself right in so many ways, and with such exhausting volubility,[6] that in the end his hearer, stunned and deafened, would agree with him, for the sake of peace.

4 It never occurred to him that he and his doings were not of the most intense and fascinating interest to anyone with whom he came in contact. He had theories about almost any subject under the sun, including vegetarianism,[7] the drama, politics, and music; and in support of these

theories he wrote pamphlets, letters, books . . . thousands upon thousands of words, hundreds and hundreds of pages. He not only wrote these things, and published them—usually at somebody else's expense—but he would sit and read them aloud, for hours, to his friends and his family.

5 He wrote operas; and no sooner did he have the synopsis[8] of a story, but he would invite—or rather summon—a crowd of his friends to his house and read it aloud to them. Not for criticism. For applause. When the complete poem was written, the friends had to come again, and hear *that* read aloud. Then he would publish the poem, sometimes years before the music that went with it was written. He played the piano like a composer, in the worst sense of what that implies, and he would sit down at the piano before parties that included some of the finest pianists of his time, and play for them, by the hour—his own music, needless to say. He had a composer's voice. And he would invite eminent vocalists to his house, and sing them his operas, taking all the parts.

6 He had the emotional stability of a six-year-old child. When he felt out of sorts, he would rave and stamp, or sink into suicidal gloom and talk darkly of going to the East to end his days as a Buddist[9] monk. Ten minutes later, when something pleased him, he would rush out of doors and run around the garden, or jump up and down on the sofa, or stand on his head. He could be grief-stricken over the death of a pet dog, and he could be callous and heartless to a degree that would have made a Roman emperor shudder.

7 He was almost innocent of any sense of responsibility. Not only did he seem incapable of supporting himself, but it never occurred to him that he was under any obligation to do so. He was convinced that the world owed him a living. In support of this belief, he borrowed money from everybody who was good for a loan—men, women, friends, or strangers. He wrote begging letters by the score, sometimes groveling[10] without shame, at others loftily offering his intended benefactor the privilege of contributing to his support, and being mortally offended if the recipient declined the honor. I have found no record of his ever paying or repaying money to anyone who did not have a legal claim upon it.

8 What money he could lay his hands on he spent like an Indian rajah.[11] The mere prospect of a performance of one of his operas was enough to set him to running up bills amounting to ten times the amount of his prospective royalties. On an income that would reduce a more scrupulous[12] man to doing his own laundry, he would keep two servants. Without enough money in his pocket to pay his rent, he would have the walls and ceiling of his study lined with pink silk. No one will ever know —certainly he never knew—how much money he owed. We do know that his greatest benefactor[13] gave him $6,000 to pay the most pressing of his debts in one city, and a year later had to give him $16,000 to enable him to live in another city without being thrown into jail for debt.

9 He was equally unscrupulous in other ways. An endless procession of women marches through his life. His

first wife spent twenty years enduring and forgiving his infidelities.[14] His second wife had been the wife of his most devoted friend and admirer, from whom he stole her. And even while he was trying to persuade her to leave her first husband he was writing to a friend to inquire whether he could suggest some wealthy woman —*any* wealthy woman—whom he could marry for her money.

10 He was completely selfish in his other personal relationships. His liking for his friends was measured solely by the completeness of their devotion to him, or by their usefulness to him, whether financial or artistic. The minute they failed him—even by so much as refusing a dinner invitation—or began to lessen in usefulness, he cast them off without a second thought. At the end of his life he had exactly one friend left whom he had known even in middle age.

11 He had a genuis for making enemies. He would insult a man who disagreed with him about the weather. He would pull endless wires in order to meet some man who admired his work and was able and anxious to be of use to him—and would proceed to make a mortal enemy of him with some idiotic and wholly uncalled-for exhibition of arrogance[15] and bad manners. A character in one of his operas was a caricature[16] of one of the most powerful music critics of his day. Not content with burlesquing him, he invited the critic to his house and read him the libretto[17] aloud in front of his friends.

12 The name of this monster was Richard Wagner. Everything that I have said about him you can find on record—in newspapers, in police reports, in the testimony of people who knew him, in his own letters, between the lines of his autobiography. And the curious thing about this record is that it doesn't matter in the least.

13 Because this undersized, sickly, disagreeable, fascinating little man was right all the time. The joke was on us. He *was* one of the world's great dramatists; he *was* a great thinker; he *was* one of the most stupendous musical geniuses that, up to now, the world has ever seen. The world did owe him a living. People couldn't know those things at the time, I suppose; and yet to us, who know his music, it does seem as though they should have known. What if he did talk about himself all the time? If he talked about himself for twenty-four hours every day for the span of his life, he would not have uttered half the number of words that other men have spoken and written about him since his death.

14 When you consider what he wrote —thirteen operas and music dramas, eleven of them still holding the stage, eight of them unquestionably worth ranking among the world's great musico-dramatic masterpieces—when you listen to what he wrote, the debts and heartaches that people had to endure from him don't seem much of a price. Eduard Hanslick, the critic whom he caricatured in *Die Meistersinger* and who hated him ever after, now lives only because he was caricatured in *Die Meistersinger.* The women whose hearts he broke are long since dead; and the man who could never love anyone but himself has made them deathless atonement,[18]

I think, with *Tristan und Isolde*. Think of the luxury with which for a time, at least, fate rewarded Napoleon, the man who ruined France and looted Europe; and then perhaps you will agree that a few thousand dollars' worth of debts were not too heavy a price to pay for the *Ring* trilogy.[19]

15 What if he was faithless to his friends and to his wives? He had one mistress to whom he was faithful to the day of his death: Music. Not for a single moment did he ever compromise with what he believed, with what he dreamed. There is not a line of his music that could have been conceived by a little mind. Even when he is dull, or downright bad, he is dull in the grand manner. There is greatness about his worst mistakes. Listening to his music, one does not forgive him for what he may or may not have been. It is not a matter of forgiveness. It is a matter of being dumb with wonder that his poor brain and body didn't burst under the torment of the demon of creative energy that lived inside him, struggling, clawing, scratching to be released; tearing, shrieking at him to write the music that was in him. The miracle is that what he did in the little space of seventy years could have been done at all, even by a great genius. Is it any wonder that he had no time to be a man?

Notes

[1] False opinions of (his own) greatness.
[2] Detailed, thorough.
[3] Talk by a single speaker.
[4] Craze, exaggerated desire.
[5] Long, passionate speech.
[6] Flow of words.
[7] Practice of eating only vegetables, fruits, grain, and nuts.
[8] Brief summary.
[9] Follower of a religion that originated in India which holds that life is full of suffering caused by desire.
[10] Acting humbly or in fear.
[11] King or prince.
[12] Careful, principled, exact.
[13] Helper, patron.
[14] Adulteries.
[15] Overbearing pride, haughtiness.
[16] Exaggerated picture.
[17] The words of an opera.
[18] Amends, righting of a wrong.
[19] The Ring of the Nibelung. *Trilogy* means "three," but the Wagnerian Ring of music dramas is commonly referred to as a tetralogy (series of four): *Das Rheingold* (1869), *Die Walküre* (1870), *Siegfried* (1876), *Götterdämmerung* (1876).

THE STORY OF MY LIFE

Helen Keller

Helen (Adams) Keller (1880–1968) was born in Tuscumbia, Alabama. As a consequence of illness she was blind and deaf from the age of 19 months, but as the result of long training (the beginning of which is recounted in the selection that follows) she became a lecturer on behalf of the blind and deaf throughout the world. One of the great women of the twentieth (or any other) century, Miss Keller held numerous honorary degrees and received the acclaim of millions of people, high and low, during her long and useful lifetime.

1 The most important day I remember in all my life is the one on which my teacher, Anne Mansfield Sullivan, came to me. I am filled with wonder when I consider the immeasurable,[1] contrasts between the two lives which it connects. It was the third of March, 1887, three months before I was seven years old.

2 On the afternoon of that eventful day, I stood on the porch, dumb, expectant. I guessed vaguely from my mother's signs and from the hurrying to and fro in the house that something unusual was about to happen, so I went to the door and waited on the steps. The afternoon sun penetrated the mass of honeysuckle that covered the porch, and fell on my upturned face. My fingers lingered almost unconsciously on the familiar leaves and blossoms which had just come forth to greet the sweet southern spring. I did not know what the future held of marvel or surprise for me. Anger and bitterness had preyed upon me continually for weeks, and a deep languor[2] had succeeded this passionate struggle.

3 Have you ever been at sea in a dense fog, when it seemed as if a tangible[3] white darkness shut you in, and the great ship, tense and anxious, groped her way toward the shore with plummet and sounding-line, and you waited with beating heart for something to happen? I was like that ship before my education began, only I was without compass or sounding-line and had no way of knowing how near the harbour was. "Light! give me light!" was the wordless cry of my soul, and the light of love shone on me in that very hour.

4 I felt approaching footsteps. I stretched out my hand as I supposed to my mother. Some one took it, and I was caught up and held close in the arms of her who had come to reveal all things to me, and, more than all things else, to love me.

5 The morning after my teacher came she led me into her room and gave me a doll. The little blind children at the Perkins Institution[4] had sent it and Laura Bridgman had dressed it; but I did not know this until afterward. When I had played with it a little while, Miss Sullivan slowly spelled into my hand the word "d-o-l-l." I was at once interested in this finger play and tried to imitate

it. When I finally succeeded in making the letters correctly I was flushed with childish pleasure and pride. Running downstairs to my mother I held up my hand and made the letters for *doll.* I did not know that I was spelling a word or even that words existed; I was simply making my fingers go in monkey-like imitation. In the days that followed I learned to spell in this uncomprehending[5] way a great many words, among them *pin, hat, cup* and a few verbs like *sit, stand,* and *walk.* But my teacher had been with me several weeks before I understood that everything has a name.

6 One day, while I was playing with my new doll, Miss Sullivan put my big rag doll into my lap also, spelled "d-o-l-l" and tried to make me understand that "d-o-l-l" applied to both. Earlier in the day we had had a tussle over the words "m-u-g" and "w-a-t-e-r." Miss Sullivan had tried to impress it upon me that "m-u-g" is *mug* and that "w-a-t-e-r" is *water,* but I persisted in confounding the two. In despair she had dropped the subject for the time, only to renew it at the first opportunity. I became impatient at her repeated attempts and, seizing the new doll, I dashed it upon the floor. I was keenly delighted when I felt the fragments of the broken doll at my feet. Neither sorrow nor regret followed my passionate outburst. I had not loved the doll. In the still, dark world in which I lived there was no strong sentiment or tenderness. I felt my teacher sweep the fragments to one side of the hearth, and I had a sense of satisfaction that the cause of my discomfort was removed. She brought me my hat, and I knew I was going out into the warm sunshine. This thought, if a wordless sensation may be called a thought, made me hop and skip with pleasure.

7 We walked down the path to the well-house, attracted by the fragrance of the honeysuckle with which it was covered. Someone was drawing water, and my teacher placed my hand under the spout. As the cool stream gushed over one hand she spelled into the other the word *water,* first slowly, then rapidly. I stood still, my whole attention fixed upon the motions of her fingers. Suddenly I felt a misty consciousness as of something forgotten —a thrill of returning thought; and somehow the mystery of language was revealed to me. I knew then that "w-a-t-e-r" meant the wonderful cool something that was flowing over my hand. That living word awakened my soul, gave it light, hope, joy, set it free! There were barriers still, it is true, but barriers that could in time be swept away.

8 I left the well-house eager to learn. Everything had a name, and each name gave birth to a new thought. As we returned to the house, every object which I touched seemed to quiver with life. That was because I saw everything with the strange, new sight that had come to me. On entering the door I remembered the doll I had broken. I felt my way to the hearth and picked up the pieces. I tried vainly to put them together. Then my eyes filled with tears; for I realized what I had done, and for the first time I felt repentance[6] and sorrow.

9 I learned a great many new words that day. I do not remember what they all were; but I do know that *mother, father, sister, teacher* were

among them—words that were to make the world blossom for me, "like Aaron's rod, with flowers."[7] It would have been difficult to find a happier child than I was as I lay in my crib at the close of that eventful day and lived over the joys it had brought me, and for the first time longed for a new day to come.

10 I recall many incidents of the summer of 1887 that followed my soul's sudden awakening. I did nothing but explore with my hands and learn the name of every object that I touched; and the more I handled things and learned their names and uses, the more joyous and confident grew my sense of kinship with the rest of the world.

11 When the time of daisies and buttercups came, Miss Sullivan took me by the hand across the fields, where men were preparing the earth for the seed, to the banks of the Tennessee River, and there, sitting on the warm grass, I had my first lessons in the beneficence[8] of nature. I learned how the sun and the rain make to grow out of the ground every tree that is pleasant to the sight and good for food, how birds build their nests and live and thrive from land to land, how the squirrel, the deer, the lion, and every other creature finds food and shelter. As my knowledge of things grew, I felt more and more the delight of the world I was in. Long before I learned to do a sum in arithmetic or describe the shape of the earth, Miss Sullivan had taught me to find beauty in the fragrant woods, in every blade of grass, and in the curves and dimples of my baby sister's hand. She linked my earliest thoughts with nature and made me feel that "birds and flowers and I were happy peers."

12 But about this time I had an experience which taught me that nature is not always kind. One day my teacher and I were returning from a long ramble. The morning had been fine, but it was growing warm and sultry[9] when at last we turned our faces homeward. Two or three times we stopped to rest under a tree by the wayside. Our last halt was under a wild cherry tree a short distance from the house. The shade was grateful,[10] and the tree was so easy to climb that with my teacher's assistance I was able to scramble to a seat in the branches. It was so cool up in the tree that Miss Sullivan proposed that we have our luncheon there. I promised to keep still while she went to the house to fetch it.

13 Suddenly a change passed over the tree. All the sun's warmth left the air. I knew the sky was black, because all the heat, which meant light to me, had died out of the atmosphere. A strange odour came up from the earth. I knew it, it was the odour that always precedes a thunderstorm, and a nameless fear clutched at my heart. I felt absolutely alone, cut off from my friends and the firm earth. The immense, the unknown, enfolded me. I remained still and expectant; a chilling terror crept over me. I longed for my teacher's return; but above all things I wanted to get down from that tree.

14 There was a moment of sinister[11] silence, then a multitudinous[12] stirring of the leaves. A shiver ran through the tree, and the wind sent forth a blast that would have knocked me off had I not clung to the branch with

might and main. The tree swayed and strained. The small twigs snapped and fell about me in showers. A wild impulse to jump seized me, but terror held me fast. I crouched down in the fork of the tree. The branches lashed about me. I felt the intermittent[13] jarring that came now and then, as if something heavy had fallen and the shock had traveled up till it reached the limb I sat on. It worked my suspense up to the highest point, and just as I was thinking the tree and I should fall together, my teacher seized my hand and helped me down. I clung to her, trembling with joy to feel the earth under my feet once more. I had learned a new lesson—that nature "wages open war against her children, and under softest touch hides treacherous claws."

15 After this experience it was a long time before I climbed another tree. The mere thought filled me with terror. It was the sweet allurement[14] of the mimosa tree in full bloom that finally overcame my fears. One beautiful spring morning when I was alone in the summer-house, reading, I became aware of a wonderful subtle fragrance in the air. I started up and instinctively stretched out my hands. It seemed as if the spirit of spring had passed through the summer-house. "What is it?" I asked, and the next minute I recognized the odour of the mimosa blossoms. I felt my way to the end of the garden, knowing that the mimosa tree was near the fence, at the turn of the path. Yes, there it was, all quivering in the warm sunshine, its blossom-laden branches almost touching the long grass. Was there ever anything so exquisitely beautiful in the world before! Its delicate blossoms shrank from the slightest earthly touch; it seemed as if a tree of paradise had been transplanted to earth. I made my way through a shower of petals to the great trunk and for one minute stood irresolute;[15] then, putting my foot in the broad space between the forked branches, I pulled myself up into the tree. I had some difficulty in holding on, for the branches were very large and the bark hurt my hands. But I had a delicious sense that I was doing something unusual and wonderful, so I kept on climbing higher and higher, until I reached a little seat which somebody had built there so long ago that it had grown part of the tree itself. I sat there for a long, long time, feeling like a fairy on a rosy cloud. After that I spent many happy hours in my tree of paradise, thinking fair thoughts and dreaming bright dreams.

16 I had now the key to all language, and I was eager to learn to use it. Children who hear acquire language without any particular effort; the words that fall from others' lips they catch on the wing, as it were, delightedly, while the little deaf child must trap them by a slow and often painful process. But whatever the process, the result is wonderful. Gradually from naming an object we advance step by step until we have traversed the vast distance between our first stammered syllable and the sweep of thought in a line of Shakespeare.

17 At first, when my teacher told me about a new thing I asked very few questions. My ideas were vague, and my vocabulary was inadequate; but as my knowledge of things grew, and I learned more and more words, my

field of inquiry broadened, and I would return again and again to the same subject, eager for further information. Sometimes a new word revived an image that some earlier experience had engraved on my brain.

18 I remember the morning that I first asked the meaning of the word *love*. This was before I knew many words. I had found a few early violets in the garden and brought them to my teacher. She tried to kiss me: but at that time I did not like to have any one kiss me except my mother. Miss Sullivan put her arm gently round me and spelled into my hand, "I love Helen."

19 "What is love?" I asked.

20 She drew me closer to her and said, "It is here," pointing to my heart, whose beats I was conscious of for the first time. Her words puzzled me very much because I did not then understand anything unless I touched it.

21 I smelt the violets in her hand and asked, half in words, half in signs, a question which meant, "Is love the sweetness of flowers?"

22 "No," said my teacher.

23 Again I thought. The warm sun was shining on us.

24 "Is this not love?" I asked, pointing in the direction from which the heat came. "Is this not love?"

25 It seemed to me that there could be nothing more beautiful than the sun, whose warmth makes all things grow. But Miss Sullivan shook her head, and I was greatly puzzled and disappointed. I thought it strange that my teacher could not show me love.

26 A day or two afterward I was stringing beads of different sizes in symmetrical[16] groups—two large beads, three small ones, and so on. I had made many mistakes, and Miss Sullivan had pointed them out again and again with gentle patience. Finally I noticed a very obvious error in the sequence[17] and for an instant I concentrated my attention on the lesson and tried to think how I should have arranged the beads. Miss Sullivan touched my forehead and spelled with decided emphasis, "Think."

27 In a flash I knew that the word was the name of the process that was going on in my head. This was my first conscious perception[18] of an abstract idea.

28 For a long time I was still—I was not thinking of the beads in my lap, but trying to find a meaning for "love" in the light of this new idea. The sun had been under a cloud all day, and there had been brief showers; but suddenly the sun broke forth in all its southern splendour.

29 Again I asked my teacher, "Is this not love?"

30 "Love is something like the clouds that were in the sky before the sun came out," she replied. Then in simpler words than these, which at that time I could not have understood, she explained: "You cannot touch the clouds, you know; but you feel the rain and know how glad the flowers and the thirsty earth are to have it after a hot day. You cannot touch love either; but you feel the sweetness that it pours into everything. Without love you would not be happy or want to play."

31 The beautiful truth burst upon my mind—I felt that there were invisible lines stretched between my spirit and the spirits of others.

32 From the beginning of my educa-

tion Miss Sullivan made it a practice to speak to me as she would speak to any hearing child; the only difference was that she spelled the sentences into my hand instead of speaking them. If I did not know the words and idioms necessary to express my thoughts, she supplied them, even suggesting conversation when I was unable to keep up my end of the dialogue.

33 This process was continued for several years; for the deaf child does not learn in a month, or even in two or three years, the numberless idioms and expressions used in the simplest daily intercourse. The little hearing child learns these from constant repetition and imitation. The conversation he hears in his home stimulates his mind and suggests topics and calls forth the spontaneous[19] expression of his own thoughts. This natural exchange of ideas is denied to the deaf child. My teacher, realizing this, determined to supply the kinds of stimulus I lacked. This she did by repeating to me as far as possible, verbatim, what she heard, and by showing me how I could take part in the conversation. But it was a long time before I ventured to take the initiative and still longer before I could find something appropriate to say at the right time.

34 The deaf and the blind find it very difficult to acquire the amenities[20] of conversation. How much more this difficulty must be augmented[21] in the case of those who are both deaf and blind! They cannot distinguish the tone of the voice or, without assistance, go up and down the gamut[22] of tones that give significance to words; nor can they watch the expression of the speaker's face, and a look is often the very soul of what one says.

Notes

1 Limitless.
2 Weakness, lack of energy.
3 Real, actual, concrete.
4 An institution in Boston providing help for handicapped persons.
5 Not understanding, not fully grasping.
6 Regret, remorse.
7 A rod (staff) that miraculously blossomed and yielded almonds. See Numbers 17:8.
8 Goodness, kindness.
9 Damp and close.
10 Welcome, deeply appreciated.
11 Threatening.
12 Occurring in great numbers.
13 Stopping and beginning again.
14 Charm, appeal.
15 Undecided, doubtful.
16 Well-proportioned, regular in form.
17 Order of succession.
18 Understanding.
19 Unplanned, natural, impulsive.
20 Agreeable ways, courtesies.
21 Increased.
22 Entire range or scale.

GENERAL CASS'S MILITARY CAREER—AND MINE[1]

Abraham Lincoln

For comment on the life of Abraham Lincoln, see under The Gettysburg Address selection.

1 In my hurry, I was very near closing on the subject of military tails,[2] before I was done with it. There is one entire article of the sort I have not discussed yet; I mean the military tail you Democrats are now engaged in dove-tailing on to the great Michigander.[3] Yes, sir, all his biographers (and they are legion) have him in hand, tying him to a military tail, like so many mischievous boys tying a dog to a bladder of beans. True, the material they have is very limited; but they drive at it, might and main. He *in*vaded Canada[4] without resistance, and he *out*vaded it without pursuit. As he did both under orders, I suppose there was, to him, neither credit nor discredit in them; but they are made to constitute a large part of the tail. He was not at Hull's[5] surrender, but he was close by. He was volunteer aid to General Harrison on the day of the battle of the Thames; and, as you said in 1840, Harrison was picking whortleberries two miles off,[6] while the battle was fought, I suppose it is a just conclusion, with you, to say Cass was aiding Harrison to pick whortleberries. This is about all, except the mooted question of the broken sword. Some authors say he broke it; some say he threw it away; and some others, who ought to know, say nothing about it. Perhaps it would be a fair historical compromise to say, if he did not break it, he did not do anything else with it.

2 By the way, Mr. Speaker, did you know I am a military hero? Yes, sir, in the days of the Black Hawk[7] war, I fought, bled, and came away. Speaking of General Cass's career, reminds me of my own. I was not at Stillman's[8] defeat, but I was about as near it as Cass was to Hull's surrender; and, like him, I saw the place very soon afterwards. It is quite certain I did not break my sword, for I had none to break; but I bent a musket pretty badly on one occasion. If Cass broke his sword, the idea is, he broke it in desperation; I bent the musket by accident. If General Cass went in advance of me in picking whortleberries, I guess I surpassed him in charges upon the wild onions. If he saw any live fighting Indians, it was more than I did, but I had a good many bloody struggles with the mosquitoes; and although I never fainted from loss of blood, I can truly say I was often very hungry.[9]

3 Mr. Speaker, if I should ever con-

clude to doff[10] whatever our Democratic friends may suppose there is of black-cockade Federalism about me, and, thereupon, they shall take me up as their candidate for the Presidency, I protest they shall not make fun of me, as they have of General Cass, by attempting to write me into a military hero.

Notes

[1] This selection is an excerpt from a speech entitled "The Presidential Question" which Lincoln delivered in the House of Representatives on July 27, 1848.

[2] Lincoln was a vigorous and effective political party man. Lewis Cass (1782–1866), presented as a hero of the War of 1812, was the Democratic nominee for President in 1848 and was defeated by Zachary Taylor. In defending Whig principles and attacking the Democratic platform, Lincoln poked fun at the practice of tying a political party to a military man's coattails.

[3] General Cass was governor of the Michigan Territory, 1813–1831, while holding rank as a brigadier general in the United States Army.

[4] The present relationship of mutual confidence and friendship between the United States and Canada is of fairly recent origin. Up until 1815, issues between the United States and Great Britain produced a series of armed conflicts in North America; the United States made repeated and largely unsuccessful invasions of Canada, especially during the period 1812–1814.

[5] William Hull (1753–1825), an American territorial governor and army officer, surrendered after a futile attack upon the British in upper Canada. For supposed dereliction in duty, Hull was court-martialed, sentenced to death, and later vindicated.

[6] General William Henry Harrison (1773–1841) was the successful Whig candidate for President in 1840. The Democrats, of course, belittled the military record he had made in the War of 1812. The Battle of the Thames River on October 5, 1813, secured for the United States control of territory that Hull had lost the previous year; the victory helped to elevate Harrison to the Presidency.

[7] The Black Hawk War of 1832 was waged in Illinois and Wisconsin between the United States and a faction of Sauk and Fox Indians led by Chief Black Hawk. In 1804, spokesmen of the two tribes had ceded some 50 million acres of land to the government. Black Hawk and his followers resisted this transfer of the northwestern half of Illinois, much of southwest Wisconsin, and all of eastern Missouri. When squatters occupied Black Hawk's own village, war broke out. Victorious, the United States kept all the disputed territory and, for war damages, seized all of eastern Iowa.

[8] On May 14, 1832, Major Stillman led a group of 340 rangers on a scouting expedition against the Indians under Black Hawk. In a disgraceful engagement, the largely drunken rangers were repulsed and scattered by 40 braves.

[9] Altogether, Lincoln spent fifty-one days in the armed service of the United States. Carl Sandburg, one of Lincoln's biographers, has suggested that Lincoln enlisted for two reasons: he would soon lose his job as a clerk and, in running for the legislature, a war record of any kind would be helpful. This same biographer records that Lincoln, unable to recall the proper command for getting a company into a column, shouted "This company is dismissed for two minutes, when it will fall in again on the other side of the gate."

[10] Remove, take off.

LINCOLN AT GETTYSBURG

Paul McClelland Angle

PAUL MCCLELLAND ANGLE (1900–) is a noted Lincoln scholar and secretary of the Chicago Historical Society. Among his books are *Mary Lincoln, Wife and Widow* (with Carl Sandburg, 1932); *Here I Have Lived—A History of Lincoln's Springfield* (1935); *A Handbook of Illinois Society* (1943); *A Shelf of Lincoln Books* (1946); *The Living Lincoln* (with Earl S. Miers, 1955); *Tragic Years, 1860–1865* (1960); *The Civil War Years in Pictures* (1967); *Prairie State* (1968).

1 *Soon after the Battle of Chancellorsville, Lee took the exultant*[1] *Army of Northern Virginia across the Potomac and started north. Perhaps his ultimate*[2] *objective was Washington, perhaps it was the rich cities of Pennsylvania, where dwindling supplies might be replenished. No one knew. Hooker, whose army had not been demoralized by defeat, started north at the same time, skillfully disposing his troops so that they would stand as a shield between the Confederates and the national Capital.*

2 *Early in the morning of June 28, 1863, George Gordon Meade, commanding Hooker's Fifth Corps, was awakened by a messenger from the President placing him in command of the Army of the Potomac. Four days later his forward elements stumbled into Lee's advance guard, and the Battle of Gettysburg began. For three days Lee sent troops hitherto invincible*[3] *against blue lines that at first yielded and then stood firm. When it was over, his army, bled by 20,000 casualties, had lost one of the decisive battles of history.*

I

3 *Carl Sandburg recounts the first great victory of the Army of the Potomac:*

4 From day to day neither Meade nor Lee had been certain where the other was. Lee would rather have taken Harrisburg, its stores and supplies, and then battled Meade on the way to Philadelphia. In that case Lee would have had ammunition enough to keep his artillery firing with no letup, no orders during an infantry charge that ammunition was running low and must be saved.

5 Lee rode his horse along roads winding through bright summer landscapes to find himself suddenly looking at the smoke of a battle he had not ordered nor planned. Some of his own marching divisions had become entangled[4] with enemy columns, traded shots, and a battle had begun that Lee could draw away from or carry on. He decided to carry on. He said Yes. His troops in their last two battles and on general form looked unbeatable. Against him was an untried commander with a jealous staff that had never worked as smoothly as his own. If he could repeat his performances with his men at Fredericksburg and Chancellorsville, he could then march to Harrisburg, use the State Capitol for barracks, replenish his needs, march on to Philadelphia, Baltimore, and Washington, lay hold

of money, supplies, munitions, win European recognition and end of the war.

6 The stakes were immense, the chances fair. The new enemy commander had never planned a battle nor handled a big army in the wild upsets of frontal[5] combat on a wide line. Also, fifty-eight regiments of Northern veterans who had fought at Antietam, Fredericksburg, Chancellorsville, had gone home, their time up, their places filled by militia and raw recruits.

7 One factor was against Lee: he would have to tell his cannoneers to go slow and count their shells, while Meade's artillery could fire on and on from an endless supply. Another factor, too, was against Lee: he was away from his Virginia, where he knew the ground and the people, while Meade's men were fighting for their homes, women, barns, cattle, and fields against invaders and strangers, as Meade saw and felt it.

8 To Lee's words, "If the enemy is there, we must attack him," Longstreet, who now replaced Stonewall Jackson,[6] spoke sharply, "If he is there, it will be because he is anxious that we should attack him—a good reason, in my judgment, for not doing so." This vague and involved feeling Longstreet nursed in his breast; attack was unwise, and his advice rejected. It resulted in hours of delay and wasted time that might have counted.

9 Lee hammered at the Union left wing the first day, the right wing the second day, Meade on that day sending word to Lincoln that the enemy was "repulsed at all points." On the third day, July 3, 1863, Lee smashed at Meade's center. Under Longstreet's command, General George Edward Pickett, a tall arrow of a man, with mustache and goatee, with long ringlets of auburn hair flying as he galloped his horse, headed 15,000 men, who had nearly a mile to go up a slow slope of land to reach the Union center. Pickett might have had thoughts in his blanket under the stars some night that week of how long ago it was, twenty-one years, since he, a Virginia boy schooled in Richmond, had been studying law in his uncle's office in Quincy, Illinois, seeing men daily who tried cases with the young attorney Abraham Lincoln. And the Pickett boy had gone on to West Point, graduated at the bottom of his class, the last of all, though later he had been first to go over the parapets at Chapultepec in 1847,[7] and still later, in 1859, had taken possession of San Juan Island at Puget Sound on the delicate mission of accommodating officials of the Buchanan administration[8] in bringing on a war with Great Britain, with the hope of saving his country from a threatened civil war by welding its divided sections. British diplomacy achieved joint occupation of the island by troops of two nations and thus averted war. On the Peninsula,[9] Pickett's men had earned the nickname of "The Game Cock Brigade," and he considered love of woman second only to the passion for war.

10 Before starting his men on their charge to the Union center, Pickett handed Longstreet a letter to a girl in Richmond he was to marry if he lived. Longstreet had ordered Pickett to go forward and Pickett had penciled on the back of the envelope, "If Old Peter's (Longstreet's) nod means death, good-by, and God bless you, little one!" An officer held out a flask

of whiskey to Pickett: "Take a drink with me; in an hour you'll be in hell or glory." And Pickett said No; he had promised "the little girl" he wouldn't.

11 Across the long rise of open ground, with the blue flag of Virginia floating ahead, over field and meadow Pickett's 15,000 marched steadily and smoothly, almost as if on a drill ground. Solid shot, grape and canister,[10] from the Union artillery plowed through them, and later a wild rain of rifle bullets. Seven-eighths of a mile they marched in the open sunlight, every man a target for the Union marksmen behind stone fences and breastworks. They obeyed orders; Uncle Robert[11] had said they would go anywhere and do anything.

12 As men fell, their places were filled, the ranks closed up. As officers tumbled off horses it was taken as expected in battle.

13 Perhaps half who started reached the Union lines surmounting Cemetery Ridge.

14 Then came cold steel, the bayonet, the clubbed musket. The strongest and last line of the enemy was reached. "The Confederate battle flag waved over his defenses," said a Confederate major, "and the fighting over the wall became hand to hand, but more than half having already fallen, our line was too weak to rout the enemy."

15 Meade rode up white-faced to hear it was a repulse and cried, "Thank God!" Lee commented: "They deserved success as far as it can be deserved by human valor and fortitude. More may have been required of them than they were able to perform." To one of his colonels, Lee said, "This has been a sad day for us, a sad day, but we cannot expect always to gain victories."

16 As a heavy rainfall came on the night of July 4, Lee ordered a retreat toward the Potomac.[12]

II

17 *Cemeteries mark battlefields. How that at Gettysburg came to be created, and how Lincoln was invited to dedicate it, are related by Clark E. Carr, the Illinois member of the cemetery commission.*

18 Scarcely had the reverberations[13] of the guns of the battle died away when the Honorable David Wills, a citizen of Gettysburg, wrote to the Honorable Andrew G. Curtin, the great war Governor of Pennsylvania, suggesting that a plot of ground in the midst of the battlefield be at once purchased and set apart as a soldiers' national cemetery, and that the remains of the dead be exhumed[14] and placed in this cemetery. He suggested that the ground to be selected should be on what was known as Cemetery Hill, so called because adjoining it is the local cemetery of Gettysburg. . . .

19 Governor Curtin at once approved of the recommendation of Mr. Wills, and correspondence was opened with the governors of the loyal States whose troops had engaged in the battle, asking them to co-operate in the movement. The grounds proposed by Mr. Wills . . . were at once purchased. . . .

20 It was proposed, as the work proceeded, that memorial dedicatory exercises be held to consecrate this sacred ground, which was finally determined upon. The day first fixed

upon for these exercises was the twenty-third of October, 1863.

21 The Honorable Edward Everett, of Massachusetts, was then regarded as the greatest living American orator, and it was decided to invite him to deliver the oration; and this was done. But he replied that it was wholly out of his power to make the necessary preparation by the twenty-third of October. So desirous were we all to have Mr. Everett that the dedication was postponed to Thursday, the nineteenth of November, 1863—nearly a month—to suit Mr. Everett's convenience. The dedication took place on that day.

22 A formal invitation to be present was sent to the President of the United States and his Cabinet, to Major General George G. Meade . . . , and to the officers and soldiers who had participated in, and gained, the memorable victory. Invitations were also sent to the venerable Lieutenant General Winfield Scott and to Admiral Charles Stewart, the distinguished and time-honored representatives of the army and navy, to the diplomatic corps, representing foreign governments, to the members of both Houses of Congress, and to other distinguished personages.

23 All these invitations and all arrangements for the dedicatory exercises—as was the case with everything relating to the cemetery—were considered and decided upon by our Board of Commissioners, and were, insofar as he was able, under the direction of the Board, carried into effect by Mr. Wills, our president. As we were all representing and speaking for the governors of our respective States, by whom we were appointed, we made all the invitations in their names.

24 The proposition to ask Mr. Lincoln to speak at the Gettysburg ceremonies was an afterthought. The President of the United States had, like the other distinguished personages, been invited to be present, but Mr. Lincoln was not, at that time, invited to speak. In fact, it did not seem to occur to anyone that he could speak upon such an occasion.

25 Scarcely any member of the Board, excepting the member representing Illinois, had ever heard him speak at all, and no other member had ever heard, or read from him, anything except political discussions. When the suggestion was made that he be invited to speak, while all expressed high appreciation of his great abilities as a political speaker, as shown in his debates with Senator Douglas, and in his Cooper Institute address,[15] the question was raised as to his ability to speak upon such a grave and solemn occasion as that of the memorial services. Besides, it was said that, with his important duties and responsibilities, he could not possibly have the leisure to prepare an address for such an occasion. In answer to this it was urged that he himself, better than anyone else, could determine as to these questions, and that, if he were invited to speak, he was sure to do what, under the circumstances, would be right and proper. . . .

26 It was finally decided to ask President Lincoln "after the oration" (that is to say, after Mr. Everett's oration), as Chief Executive of the nation, "to set apart formally these grounds to their sacred use by a few appropriate remarks." This was done in the name

of the governors of the States, as was the case with others, by Mr. Wills; but the invitation was not settled upon and sent to Mr. Lincoln until the second of November, more than six weeks after Mr. Everett had been invited to speak, and but a little more than two weeks before the exercises were held.[16]

III

27 *Tardy as it was, the invitation to speak was promptly accepted by the President. On November 18, 1863, he and his party proceeded from Washington to Gettysburg by special train. Of that trip and the preliminaries of the dedicatory exercises, John Hay preserved much in his diary, at the same time demonstrating that a man with a finely developed literary instinct does not always recognize a masterpiece when he hears it.*

28 On our train were the President, Seward, Usher and Blair; Nicolay and myself; Mercier and Admiral Reynaud; Bertinatti and Capt. Isola and Lt. Martinez and Cora; Mrs. Wise; Wayne MacVeagh; McDougal of Canada, and one or two others.[17] We had a pleasant sort of trip. . . .

29 At Gettysburg the President went to Mr. Wills, who expected him, and our party broke like a drop of quicksilver spilled. MacVeagh, young Stanton, and I foraged[18] around for a while—walked out to the college, got a chafing dish of oysters, then some supper, and finally, loafing around to the Court House where Lamon was holding a meeting of marshals, we found Forney and went around to his place, Mr. Fahnestock's, and drank a little whisky with him. He had been drinking a good deal during the day and was getting to feel a little ugly and dangerous. He was particularly bitter on Montgomery Blair. MacVeagh was telling him that he pitched into the Tycoon[19] coming up, and told him some truths. He said the President got a good deal of that from time to time and needed it. . . .

30 We went out after a while following the music to hear the serenades.[20] The President appeared at the door and said half a dozen words meaning nothing and went in. Seward, who was staying around the corner at Harper's, was called out, and spoke so indistinctly that I did not hear a word of what he was saying. Forney and MacVeagh were still growling about Blair.

31 We went back to Forney's room, having picked up Nicolay, and drank more whisky. Nicolay sang his little song of the "Three Thieves," and we then sang "John Brown."[21] At last we proposed that Forney should make a speech and two or three started out, Shannon and Behan and Nicolay, to get a band to serenade him. I stayed with him. So did Stanton and MacVeagh. He still growled quietly and I thought he was going to do something imprudent.[22] He said, "If I speak, I will speak my mind." The music sounded in the street, and the fuglers[23] came rushing up imploring him to come down. He smiled quietly, told them to keep cool, and asked, "Are the recorders there?" "I suppose so of course," shouted the fugler. "Ascertain," said the imperturable[24] Forney. "Hay, we'll take a drink." They shouted and begged him to come down. The thing would be a failure—it would be his fault, etc.

"Are the recorders congenial?" he calmly insisted on knowing. Somebody commended prudence. He said sternly, "I am always prudent." I walked downstairs with him.

32 The crowd was large and clamorous. The fuglers stood by the door in an agony. The reporters squatted at a little stand in the entry. Forney stood on the threshold, John Young and I by him. The crowd shouted as the door opened. Forney said, "My friends, these are the first hearty cheers I have heard tonight. You gave no such cheers to your President down the street. Do you know what you owe to that great man? You owe your country—you owe your name as American citizens."

33 He went on blackguarding[25] the crowd for their apathy and then diverged to his own record, saying he had been for Lincoln in his heart in 1860—that open advocacy was not as effectual as the course he took—dividing the most corrupt organization that ever existed—the proslavery Democratic party. He dwelled at length on this question and then went back to the eulogy[26] of the President, that great, wonderful, mysterious, inexplicable man who holds in his single hands the reins of the Republic; who keeps his own counsels; who does his own purpose in his own way, no matter what temporizing[27] minister in his cabinet sets himself up in opposition to the progress of the age.

34 And very much of this.

35 After him Wayne MacVeagh made a most touching and beautiful speech of five minutes and Judge Shannon of Pittsburgh spoke effectively and acceptably to the people.

36 "That speech must not be written out yet," says Young. "He will see further about it when he gets sober," as we went upstairs. We sang more of "John Brown" and went home.

37 In the morning I got a beast and rode out with the President's suite to the Cemetery in the procession. The procession formed itself in an orphanly[28] sort of way and moved out with very little help from anybody, and after a little delay, Mr. Everett took his place on the stand—and Mr. Stockton made a prayer which thought it was an oration; and Mr. Everett spoke as he always does, perfectly—and the President, in a fine, free way, with more grace than is his wont,[29] said his half dozen words of consecration, and the music wailed and we went home through crowded and cheering streets. And all the particulars are in the daily papers.[30]

IV

38 *Here are the "half dozen words of consecration."*[31]

39 Fourscore and seven years ago our fathers brought forth on this continent a new nation, conceived in liberty, and dedicated to the proposition that all men are created equal.

40 Now we are engaged in a great civil war, testing whether that nation, or any nation so conceived and so dedicated, can long endure. We are met on a great battlefield of that war. We have come to dedicate a portion of that field as a final resting-place for those who here gave their lives that that nation might live. It is altogether fitting and proper that we should do this.

41 But in a larger sense, we cannot

dedicate—we cannot consecrate—we cannot hallow—this ground. The brave men, living and dead, who struggled here, have consecrated it far above our poor power to add or detract. The world will little note nor long remember what we say here, but it can never forget what they did here. It is for us, the living, rather, to be dedicated here to the unfinished work which they who fought here have thus far so nobly advanced. It is rather for us to be here dedicated to the great task remaining before us—that from these honored dead we take increased devotion to that cause for which they gave the last full measure of devotion; that we here highly resolve that these dead shall not have died in vain; that this nation, under God, shall have a new birth of freedom; and that government of the people, by the people, for the people, shall not perish from the earth.

V

42 *In prose only less memorable than Lincoln's own, Carl Sandburg has written the epilogue*[32] *to Gettysburg*:

43 After the ceremonies at Gettysburg, Lincoln lunched with Governor Curtin, Mr. Everett, and others at the Wills home, held a reception that had not been planned, handshaking nearly an hour, looking gloomy and listless but brightening sometimes as a small boy or girl came in line, and stopping one tall man for remarks as to just how high up he reached. At five o'clock he attended a patriotic meeting in the Presbyterian church, walking arm-in-arm with old John Burns, and listening to an address by Lieutenant Governor-elect Anderson of Ohio. At six-thirty he was on the departing Washington train. In the dining car his secretary, John Hay, ate with Simon Cameron and Wayne MacVeagh. Hay had thought Cameron and MacVeagh hated each other, but he noted: "I was more than usually struck by the intimate jovial relations that existed between men that hate and detest each other as cordially as do the Pennsylvania politicians."

44 The ride to Washington took until midnight. Lincoln was weary, talked little, stretched out on one of the side seats in the drawing room and had a wet towel laid across his eyes and forehead.

45 He had stood that day, the world's foremost spokesman of popular government, saying that democracy was yet worth fighting for. He had spoken as one in mist who might head on deeper yet into mist. He incarnated[33] the assurances and pretenses of popular government, implied that it could and might perish from the earth. What he meant by "a new birth of freedom" for the nation could have a thousand interpretations. The taller riddles[34] of democracy stood up out of the address. It had the dream touch of vast and furious events epitomized[35] for any foreteller to read what was to come. He did not assume that the drafted soldiers, substitutes, and bounty-paid privates had died willingly under Lee's shot and shell, in deliberate consecration of themselves to the Union cause. His cadences[36] sang the ancient song that where there is freedom men have fought and sacrificed for it, and that freedom is worth men's dying for. For the first time since he became President he had on a dramatic occasion

declaimed, howsoever it might be read, Jefferson's proposition which had been a slogan of the Revolutionary War—"All men are created equal"—leaving no other inference than that he regarded the Negro slave as a man.[37] His outwardly smooth sentences were inside of them gnarled and tough with the enigmas[38] of the American experiment.

46 Back at Gettysburg the blue haze of the Cumberland Mountains had dimmed till it was a blur in a nocturne.[39] The moon was up and fell with a bland golden benevolence[40] on the new-made graves of soldiers, on the sepulchers[41] of old settlers, on the horse carcasses of which the onrush of war had not yet permitted removal. The New York *Herald* man walked amid them and ended the story he sent his paper: "The air, the trees, the graves are silent. Even the relic hunters are gone now. And the soldiers here never wake to the sound of reveille."

47 In many a country cottage over the land, a tall old clock in a quiet corner told time in a tick-tock deliberation. Whether the orchard branches hung with pink-spray blossoms or icicles of sleet, whether the outside news was seedtime or harvest, rain or drouth, births or deaths, the swing of the pendulum was right and left and right and left in a tick-tock deliberation.

48 The face and dial of the clock had known the eyes of a boy who listened to its tick-tock and learned to read its minute and hour hands. And the boy had seen years measured off by the swinging pendulum, and grown to man size, had gone away. And the people in the cottage knew that the clock would stand there and the boy never again come into the room and look at the clock with the query, "What is the time?"

49 In a row of graves of the Unidentified the boy would sleep long in the dedicated final resting place at Gettysburg. Why he had gone away and why he would never come back had roots in some mystery of flags and drums, of national fate in which individuals sink as in a deep sea, of men swallowed and vanished in a man-made storm of smoke and steel.

50 The mystery deepened and moved with ancient music and inviolable consolation[42] because a solemn Man of Authority had stood at the graves of the Unidentified and spoken the words "We cannot consecrate—we cannot hallow—this ground. The brave men, living and dead, who struggled here, have consecrated it far above our poor power to add or detract. . . . From these honored dead we take increased devotion to that cause for which they gave the last full measure of devotion."

51 To the backward and forward pendulum swing of a tall old clock in a quiet corner they might read those cadenced words while outside the windows the first flurry of snow blew across the orchard and down over the meadow, the beginnings of winter in a gun-metal gloaming to be later arched with a star-flung sky.[43]

Notes

[1] Joyous, triumphant.
[2] Last, final.
[3] Incapable of being defeated.
[4] Snarled, mixed up.
[5] Head-on.
[6] James Longstreet (1821–1904), Confederate general; Thomas Jonathan Jackson (1824–1863), also a Confederate general and a cavalry leader.
[7] Chapultepec, a castle-fortress on the outskirts of Mexico City, captured by U.S. forces in the Mexican War. *Parapets* are defensive walls, or elevations.
[8] James Buchanan was the fifteenth President of the United States, 1857–1861.
[9] A district in southeastern Virginia between the York and James rivers.
[10] Grape shot is a cluster of small cast-iron balls shot from a cannon; *canister* is case shot, a collection of small projectiles in a case, also to be fired from a cannon.
[11] General Robert E. Lee.
[12] From *Abraham Lincoln: The War Years* by Carl Sandburg, copyright 1939 by Harcourt, Brace and Company, Inc.
[13] Reechoed sounds.
[14] Dug up.
[15] A free, privately supported college founded in 1859 by Peter Cooper, a New York inventor and philanthropist; Lincoln here delivered his first address in the East as a Presidential candidate (February 27, 1860). Senator Stephen Douglas (1813–1861) was a political rival of Lincoln's.
[16] Carr, *Lincoln at Gettysburg*, pp. 8–10, 18–25.
[17] Most of these persons were important at the time but need not be identified now. William Henry Seward was Secretary of State, 1861–1869.
[18] Wandered.
[19] A person with wealth and power. *Tycoon*, from Japanese, is a title formerly used for the *shogun* of Japan, who ruled the country in the emperor's name.
[20] Open-air performances of music at night.
[21] See John Brown's "Final Statement," earlier in this book.
[22] Rash, unwise.
[23] Soldiers on guard duty.
[24] Calm, unruffled.
[25] Cursing, reviling.
[26] High praise.
[27] Indecisive, yielding.
[28] Deserted, unprotected.
[29] Custom, practice, habit.
[30] Reprinted by permission of Dodd, Mead & Company from *Lincoln and the Civil War* by Tyler Dennett. Copyright 1939 by Dodd, Mead & Company, Inc.
[31] See "The Gettysburg Address," earlier in this book.
[32] Concluding part, final chapter.
[33] Personified, typified.
[34] Puzzles.
[35] Condensed, summarized.
[36] Rhythmic patterns.
[37] See Jefferson's "A Southerner on Slavery," earlier in this book.
[38] Hidden meanings, puzzles.
[39] Actually, music appropriate for the night; here, the meaning is that of a dreamy, pensive night scene.
[40] Kindliness.

[41] Graves.
[42] Comfort and solace that cannot be destroyed.
[43] From *Abraham Lincoln: The War Years* by Carl Sandburg, copyright 1939 by Harcourt, Brace and Company, Inc.

RALPH NADER: DEDICATED MAN

The Editors of Current Biography

CURRENT BIOGRAPHY, a valuable aid to libraries and research students, is a periodical appearing eleven times annually. It presents readable and authoritative biographical sketches of newsworthy persons in varied fields of human endeavor. The information collected by its editors is secured from biographees themselves and from newspaper accounts, magazine articles, and books.

1 Ralph Nader was born on February 27, 1934 in the small Connecticut town of Winsted, the youngest child of Nadra and Rose (Bouziane) Nader, who had both emigrated to the United States from Lebanon.[1] Nadra Nader established a restaurant and bakery in Winsted in 1925, which he still runs with the help of his son Shaffak. The Naders also have two daughters. One is a research scientist and the other teaches at the University of California at Berkeley. The Nader family have always been politically active in their town, and Nadra told a reporter for *Newsweek* (January 22, 1968) that Ralph had been brought up to "understand that working for justice in the country is a safeguard of our democracy."

2 On scholarships Ralph Nader attended the Gilbert School in Winsted and Princeton University's Woodrow Wilson School of Public and International Affairs, where he was elected to Phi Beta Kappa and graduated *magna cum laude*[2] in 1955 with a major in government and economics. At Princeton he displayed his nonconformity[3] by acts that ranged from a refusal to wear the ubiquitous[4] white buck shoes of that era to an unsuccessful campaign to prevent the campus trees from being sprayed with DDT. Although he belonged to a college generation notorious for its political and social apathy,[5] Nader stood apart. Appalled by the arbitrary power that the university administration exercised over his fellow students, he tried, without success, to interest them in defending their legal rights.

3 After graduation Nader went to Harvard Law School, which he has since described as a "high-priced tool factory" that only prepared its students to practise law in the service of a bank or corporation. Although he worked part-time, he found time to edit the *Harvard Law Record* and still managed to graduate with distinction in 1958. For several months he stayed on at Harvard after graduation, work-

ing as a research assistant to Professor Harold J. Berman, an authority on Russian law. Then followed a six-month stint in the United States Army and an extensive tour, on his own, of Latin America, Europe, and Africa. Nader then settled in Hartford, Connecticut, where he set up a private law practice. On the side he conducted an informal legal aid society, and from 1961 to 1963 he lectured in history and government at the University of Hartford.

4 It was at Harvard that Nader first became interested in auto safety. While studying auto injury cases, he gathered data on automobile technology[6] at Harvard and MIT and became convinced that the law unfairly put all the blame on driver failure and none on unsafe vehicle design. His first article on the subject, entitled "American Cars: Designed for Death," appeared in the *Harvard Law Record* in 1958. After graduation he campaigned for improved safety regulations in magazine articles, in speeches to civic groups, and in testimony before committees of the Massachusetts and Connecticut state legislatures. In early 1964, however, he decided that his efforts were being wasted on the local level and that he would have to carry his fight to Washington.

5 For several years Nader had been acquainted with urbanologist[7] Daniel P. Moynihan, who shared his own concern with auto safety. In 1964 Moynihan, then Assistant Secretary of Labor, provided Nader with an entrée[8] to Washington by inviting him to serve as a $50-a-day consultant at the Labor Department. Beginning in April 1964 Nader devoted his time to producing a 200-page study that called for the federal government to take far greater responsibility in promoting auto safety. During that period he also began to provide information to the staff of the Senate subcommittee on executive reorganization, chaired by Connecticut Senator Abraham A. Ribicoff, who had long been concerned with the "fantastic carnage" he saw taking place on the highways. Although he continued to collaborate with Ribicoff's staff, Nader left the Labor Department in May 1965 to devote most of his time to writing a book on auto safety.

6 Nader's book, *Unsafe at Any Speed: The Designed-in Dangers of the American Automobile,* was brought out by Grossman Publishers in November 1965. Although he attacked the whole Detroit automobile industry for its emphasis on profits and styling over safety, he concentrated his fire on the Chevrolet Corvair, "one of the nastiest-handling cars ever built," and claimed that General Motors took "four years of the model and 1,124,076 Corvairs before they decided to do something . . . to help control the car's handling hazards." The book became a best seller, and by the end of 1967 some 450,000 hard-cover and paperback copies had been sold. Nader has received around $50,000 in royalties from the book.

7 Meanwhile, Congressional support was growing for the passage of auto safety legislation. In July 1965 Senator Ribicoff's subcommittee opened its hearings, during the course of which representatives of the auto industry were asked what they were doing to promote greater vehicle safety. Presi-

dent Lyndon B. Johnson called for a highway safety act in his 1966 State of the Union address, and Congress appeared ready to draft even stronger legislation than that favored by the Administration. On February 10, 1966, Ralph Nader delivered an indictment[9] of the auto industry in testifying before the Ribicoff subcommittee.

8 Effective legislation would probably have been passed that year in any event, but within the next few weeks a news story broke that aroused public opinion to a point where swift passage was assured. On March 6, 1966, newspapers published Nader's complaint that for the past month he had been under investigation by private detectives hired by the auto industry. Furthermore, he asserted that he had received a series of harassing[10] telephone calls, and that women had tried to lure him into potentially compromising situations. Although auto company spokesmen at first denied Nader's charges, on March 9 General Motors conceded that it had initiated "a routine investigation" of Nader to find out if he had any connection with damage suits that had been filed against GM because of defects in the Corvair. The company denied that its investigation had included harassment or intimidation, but in a nationally televised hearing on March 22, General Motors President James M. Roche admitted to the Ribicoff subcommittee that there had been "some harassment," publicly apologized to Nader, and agreed with Senator Ribicoff that the inquiry had been "most unworthy of American business." He nevertheless denied that girls had been employed as "sex lures" and that the investigation had included any harassing telephone calls. At the same hearing Ribicoff told the subcommittee that, having read the complete text of the detectives' reports submitted by GM, he had been able to find little concerning Nader's possible connections with the Corvair litigation[11] and had reached the conclusion that most of the private investigation had evidently been "an attempt to downgrade and smear a man." He added that the detectives had been unable to find "a damn thing wrong" with Nader.

9 Alleging invasion of privacy and harassment, in November 1966 Nader filed a suit against General Motors and its private detective for $26,000,000 in damages. His case received spectacular support the following February, when the detective, Vincent Gillen, submitted a sworn statement admitting that his instructions from General Motors had been "to get something somewhere on this guy . . . get him out of their hair . . . shut him up." Gillen also swore that General Motors executives had made false statements at the subcommittee hearings as to the true nature of the Nader investigations. As of late 1968 Nader's suit was still pending.[12]

10 After Roche's appearance before the Senate subcommittee in March 1966, Nader continued his auto safety campaign. He accused Ford and General Motors of equipping their cars with unreliable seat belts, criticized Rolls-Royce and Volkswagen for faulty design, and called on Detroit to reveal all defects discovered in their models. When the final Senate version of the auto safety bill was under preparation, Nader and the auto industry lobbyist[13] sat

in separate rooms outside the Senate chamber, reading the draft as it was prepared. The National Traffic and Motor Vehicle Safety Act was passed by the Senate on June 24, 1966, and by the House on August 17, 1966. On August 30 the Washington *Post* editorialized: "Most of the credit for making possible this important legislation belongs to one man—Ralph Nader. . . . Through his book, *Unsafe at Any Speed*, his determination, and his seemingly limitless energy, he won; a one-man lobby for the public prevailed over the Nation's most powerful industry."

11 After President Johnson signed the act into law on September 9, Nader became the watchdog[14] of the National Traffic Safety Agency, the administrative organ it established. He contended in January 1967 that the agency showed "disturbing signs of being intimidated"[15] by Detroit and charged in February that the first set of auto safety regulations had been "considerably weakened" to meet industry protests. His assertions that the agency had developed a "protective attitude" toward the auto makers led in March to a review of its activities by the Senate Commerce Committee. Although the committee accepted the agency's defense of its new set of regulations, Nader has continued to monitor[16] and criticize its progress.

12 Having won his initial victory on auto safety, Nader turned his attention to mounting crusades in other areas where he felt the public interest was threatened. They have included drives to eliminate health hazards in mining, to upgrade the safety standards of natural gas pipelines, to improve the lot of the American Indian, and to reduce the indiscriminate[17] use of X-rays in dental examinations. His most significant contribution, however, was his role in the passage of the 1967 Wholesome Meat Act, which imposed federal inspection standards on almost all slaughterhouses and processing plants in the United States. The prospects for the legislation looked dim in the summer of 1967 when Nader obtained from the Department of Agriculture a forgotten study of conditions—some quite gruesome—in intrastate meat-processing plants not subject to federal inspection. He passed the report to the press, helped spark a Congressional letter-writing campaign, addressed groups in ten cities from coast to coast, and wrote several hard-hitting articles for the *New Republic*. The result was a bill with teeth in it.

13 Nader described for B. Drummond Ayres Jr. in an interview for *Coronet* (October 1967) the way he plans his tactics: "You've got to keep the opposition off balance. Once you get them tumbling, you can't let up. . . . That's the only way to get results." One of his critics, Thomas C. Mann, president of the Automobile Manufacturers Association, has complained that Nader has "launched a series of hit-and-run attacks" but that he refuses to make his comments in official proceedings where they must be supported by facts. Nader, however, denies that he makes rash charges: "The exact opposite is the case. I'm the one who can't afford to make mistakes." In getting his message across to the people and Congress, his excellent working relationship with the press is crucial.[18] Reporters like

him and respect his integrity. They also have learned to count on the depth and accuracy of his reports.

14 When asked by the late Senator Robert F. Kennedy why he was "doing all this," Nader replied, "If I were engaged in activities for the prevention of cruelty to animals, nobody would ask me that question." Patrick Anderson in the *New York Times Magazine* (October 29, 1967) explained Nader's devotion to causes in this way: "It stems from the social consciousness of an ultra-individualistic lawyer . . . instinctively opposed to any action he views as an arbitrary[19] exercise of power against the individual." Aware that many people dismiss him as a fanatic, Nader admits to being an idealist, but he adds that he knows how to translate his ideals into action. As he puts it, "I deal in the art of the possible." Evidently not motivated by the need for personal glory, Nader told his *Newsweek* interviewer (January 22, 1968), "If I can stay on the sidelines and get three senators to say something, that's better than if I said it myself."

15 Nader has defined his ultimate[20] goal as "nothing less than the qualitative reform of the industrial revolution," but he recognizes that working alone he can deal effectively with only a limited number of issues at any one time. To expand his crusade he has considered forming "a public-interest law firm," possibly with foundation backing, and staffed with both specialists in consumer affairs and lawyers. In the meantime, during the summer of 1968, he was assisted by seven young lawyers and students, all unpaid, who helped him to conduct an investigation of the Federal Trade Commission.

16 Spartan[21] in his personal habits, Ralph Nader usually works an eighteen-hour day. In Washington he rents a small $97-a-month office and sleeps in a $20-a-week furnished room. He has no secretary and must keep his address and telephone number confidential to prevent a deluge of callers. His only major expense is the office telephone that he uses to keep in touch with secret contacts in corporate offices and research laboratories. Aside from his dwindling book royalties, his income derives from fees for articles and speeches and from occassional teaching.

17 At Harvard he gave up the only car he ever owned because he had no need for it. He does not smoke, drinks only an occasional glass of wine or beer, and finds no time for a social life. All this, coupled with his lanky six-foot-four-inch frame and boyish face, reminded the *Newsweek* (January 22, 1968) writer of a "Jimmy Stewart hero in a Frank Capra movie."

18 Nader has black, curly hair and brown eyes. He has spoken Arabic since childhood and also has a working knowledge of Chinese, Portuguese, Spanish, and Russian. In 1967 he was voted one of the Ten Outstanding Young Men of the Year by the United States Junior Chamber of Commerce.

Notes

[1] A small republic at the eastern end of the Mediterranean, north of Israel and west of Syria.

[2] With great praise. Special honors for grades above average are *cum laude* (with honor); *magna cum laude;* and *summa cum laude* (with highest praise).

[3] Failure or refusal to comply with established customs.

[4] Present everywhere.

[5] Lack of concern or interest.

[6] Engineering, industrial design and construction.

[7] Student of cities and city life.

[8] Means of entering.

[9] Charge, accusation.

[10] Disturbing, tormenting.

[11] Contest at law; dispute.

[12] In August 1970, General Motors paid Nader $425,000 in an out-of-court settlement of the suit. Nader declared at the time that he would use the money to monitor General Motors' activities, but he has also used it to further other consumer campaigns.

[13] One who tries to influence legislation and opinion in favor of special interests.

[14] Guardian.

[15] Made timid, overawed.

[16] Observe and record.

[17] Haphazard, widespread.

[18] Decisive, all-important.

[19] Unreasonable, capricious.

[20] Final.

[21] Simple, frugal. The reference is to Sparta, an ancient city in southern Greece whose inhabitants were sternly disciplined and notably courageous.

SONG FOR A SMALL VOYAGER

Joan Baez

JOAN BAEZ (1941–) was born in New York City. She attended local schools and, for a brief time, Boston University. Her marriage in 1968 to David Harris did not interrupt her active career as a folk singer and lecturer. She is the author of *Daybreak* (1968), an informal autobiography.

1 When I leave the hospital, it will be cold out. Maybe raining. I'll be wearing my green cape, and the baby will be wrapped up in some soft thing that we got as a gift. Because David can't be here—he is in jail for refusing to fight in a senseless war—my friends Robert and Christi will help me into a car and drive us home. Christmas will be all around, and I'll put on the red robe my sister gave me and climb into bed. The robe has a separate hood that slips over my head, because the winter winds are fierce up here on

Struggle Mountain, and the windows not the best fitted in the world, and the drafts take over the house like old familiar tenants. At first, I'll probably just keep the baby next to me on the bed. That way I won't have to get up much for a while. . . .

2 I think about the crazy stretch of time last July when we were all sitting around in the dust and sun, waiting for the federal marshals to come and pick up David. I was four months pregnant, bulging out of my T-shirt, feeling much bigger than I looked. I spent my time trying to keep David's head and my head unjumbled during the limbo[1] of not knowing how long we'd be together. Friends came and went in droves, each trying in his own stumbling way to say good-by to David. David just went on smiling his great country and Western smile, saying, "All right! Too much. Brother, I'm ready!" and there was lots of laughter and hugging and loud music and drinking of juice and crunching of ice cubes. Once in a while David would walk off into the blazing hills with his beloved companion Moondog, our white Samoyed.[2] I couldn't take the heat, and would stay behind and wave to him, and think about what it would be like when he came home, and there would be three of us instead of two.

3 Robert and Christi were fixing themselves a place in the garage, and they were to stay on here with me. They have stayed, and I wonder now what I would have done without them. Robert is a carpenter, electrician, gardener, mechanic, plumber, can fix anything that's fixable and some things that aren't, and at the same time he's as shy as a miner's child. Christi is pregnant and beautiful, and on these splendid fall days, as she works in the yard with Robert, wearing Robert's oldest crumbling blue jeans, she turns and smiles when you call her name, and seems like some gloriously happy wayward madonna[3] whom somebody finally let play in the dirt.

4 Last night I had a bad dream. I dreamed that David was home and we had a terrible fight. I threw milk at him, and he got so mad that he tried to kill me and was taken away by some strangers. When I saw him next, he was strapped down to an operating table. He held up his hands, and all the fingers were burnt off and sealed at the palm. I said, "Oh, darling David! Everything will be all right!" but I was terrified, and his face was strange and fearful and reddish, and not to be touched.

5 When I woke up, my spine was gooseflesh, and it seemed that my hair was standing straight up. It was four o'clock, and I wrote down the dream and stayed awake until the sky began to lighten.

6 I struggled to interpret it, but my mind began to drift, and I found myself chewing on my lip, crumpling my forehead, and staring off into the dark, racing from fantasy to fantasy, all about being in the hospital in labor. . . . The whiteness of the sheets and gowns, the smell of antiseptic, the squeaking of the nurses' shoes coming and leaving, the pale-green walls. . . . The doctor with his mask on, me working, working. . . .

7 The little wrinkled pink face. . . . How long before the first yell? Will I get to hold it right away? Will it be

healthy? Will I get to feed it once before it gets the hospital formula? And back again to the start, over and over and around and around until, with the light of dawn, my frenzy abated[4] like the outgoing tide and I fell into an exhausted sleep.

8 In a couple of weeks I'll begin a Lamaze childbirth course.[5] I'll learn breathing techniques, exercises, how to recognize different stages of labor and what to do in each. I'll learn how to react to commands given by my doctor and by Christi, who will go through the course with me and then work by my side through labor and delivery. Perhaps most important of all, I will be trained how to relax. Maybe the classes will make some of the more obscure fears real, so that even if I can't conquer them, I can at least stand toe to toe with them when the time comes. I think Christi and I will have some funny times. I mean I think we'll have to laugh when I start my breathing exercises, lying on the floor, panting like a puffed-up blowfish. Christi timing my breathing and giving commands, the dogs and cats looking on in wonder. I think it's good for the baby when I laugh. . . .

9 As I sit here and write, I can look out the window to the east. It is evening, and the sky is very light blue, with pink angel hair strewn across it in lavish wisps. Out in the middle of a deserted sagebrush desert in Arizona, David is sitting in Safford Federal Prison Camp. He may be writing me a letter this very minute, as we are in the same time zone, and almost all of his letters begin with an extravagant verbal portrait of Arizona sunsets.

10 The sky over his prison is big. Big and open and clean and eternal. David's like that, too. He's six foot three, and his eyes are blue as crystal air at the ocean's edge. He reaches far. He is a brother to the sky. Things become quite easy when one sees them right. His Arizona sky is the same as the California sky I see when I look out the east window. It holds us both and watches us both, rains on our heads and delivers to us the sun and the moon. Those are the things I'll sing about when I'm standing at that window, holding the baby in my arms.

11 David is away in prison, but he is also here with me.

12 I am ecstatic that I am going to become a mother, and I am terrified.

13 To be truthful, my feelings about having a baby seldom get very philosophical, seldom go much beyond the anticipation of actually giving birth. When they do, they go in two directions. One, to all the atrocities[6] I take for granted in this century, and, two, to the everlasting beauties of the earth. Then I juggle. It comes out something like this.

14 I cannot tell if it is a sin of some kind to subject a yet-unborn soul to the disease which we call society, or if it is a sin of another kind, equal in wickedness, to deny any potential being the magnificence of one orange sunset.

15 The world, after what we've done to it, is barely fit for a cockroach to live in. It gasps for air and is dying. To state facts about the condition of mankind becomes hackneyed and boring, and we lose patience with hearing them. Not because they are not true, but because they are not real to us. They seem to be things out of our

control. The truth is simply that we are living in the most violent, reckless, and deadly era the world has ever known. And we, the human race, have chosen to be as blind as snakes, as stubborn as asses, and dumber than cows.

16 And yet to look into the eyes of any man who is open and vulnerable for as much as one second, the world seems to turn suddenly into an unmapped ocean of innocence, hope, and beauty. A world in which man recognizes that he has a choice of how to live his life. He does not have to be a snake, ass, or cow, but a whole person. If those moments can be nurtured, understood, and built upon rather than fearfully labeled and swept away, then there is truly hope for mankind's survival and the birth of brotherhood.

17 The odds? Against.

18 The risks? High.

19 The reason to bother? The joy of living and watching the flowering of love.

20 I cannot resist the urge to bring forth one more small voyager.

21 May God teach me the art of loving, and grant my child the gift of seeing.

Notes

[1] Place of confinement, condition of neglect or oblivion. Here, *limbo* means "state of uncertainty."

[2] A dog of a breed originally developed in northern Europe and Asia that has a thick, long white coat.

[3] This word has several specific meanings but here implies "mother." In Italian, *madonna* means "my lady"; it is also used for Mary, the mother of Jesus.

[4] Lessened, subsided.

[5] Fernand Lamaze, a 20th-century French physician, originated a method by which an expectant mother is prepared for childbirth by physical and psychological conditioning and training.

[6] Evils, vile happenings.

THE SHORT STORY

NOTES ON READING

Although little more than a century old, the short story traces its ancestry to earlier forms of prose fiction. The type has grown not only from the novel but, like the novel itself, from brief tales told by cavemen, from the fables of Aesop, and from ancient Oriental episodes and stories. Probably the oldest of all literary forms in origin, the short story certainly owes something to a famous medieval potpourri, the *Gesta Romanorum,* to Chaucer's *The Canterbury Tales,* to Boccaccio's *Decameron* and Cervantes' *Don Quixote,* to "novels" and "histories" of the Elizabethan age, and to many other influences.

From these ancestors of the short story has evolved a definite type of literature, a type really founded by Edgar Allan Poe (1809–1849). When Poe discarded the leisurely narrative methods of earlier writers and began to construct narratives notable for unity and compression, the modern short story was born. And yet Poe did not "invent" the short story; his contribution was the shaping and arranging of materials and elements known and used for centuries. When Nathaniel Hawthorne (1804–1864) followed Poe's stories with his somber, slowly paced fiction, the type may be said to have been not only born but weaned. It rapidly grew to adulthood, first in America and somewhat later in England.

It is impossible to give a satisfactory definition of the short story. One that is too restricting puts the short story form into a strait jacket that hampers its freedom of movement so that it does not include, as it must, certain types of successful experimental stories that do not conform to a rigid pattern. And a definition that is too broad is likely to mean little or nothing. The short story can be explained, however, in broad terms that cover all such imaginative writing as novels, plays, films, and many television and radio productions. Writing of this kind has four ingredients: character, action, setting, and a basic idea, or theme. That is, *characters* must *act* out a situation against a *setting* or background, and the way in which they act must mean something or convey an *idea* or *theme* to the reader.

The limitation of the short story is the limitation of space: it must be short. The average story, because generally it must not exceed 5,000 to 6,000 words, does not have the range of a novel. The short-story writer paints miniatures; the novelist paints murals. Because he must confine himself to a small canvas, the writer of the short story ordinarily observes certain principles. He knows, because his story must be short, that he must limit the number of characters in it and that usually its focus must fall on one character, or at most on a limited group of characters. He must similarly restrict the number of settings he uses; within a short space he cannot thoughtlessly move his characters from place to place. Also he must not allow his story to consume any more time than is necessary. And, finally, he knows that he must focus the reader's attention on a single situation, the climax of his story. Whereas a novel can build up a number of scenes before the climax is reached, the short story is restricted; its climax must be reached quickly.

The possibilities of the short story are the outgrowth of its limitations. Its assets capitalize on its liabilities. It can deal with certain situations that a novel could not handle effectively. Just because a story *is* short, the writer can concentrate his material most effectively, whereas the novelist may be more diffuse. A short story is like a newspaper editorial on a local tax problem; a novel resembles a treatise on economics. Each serves a need, but in a different way.

The great advantage of the short story is that it can focus sharply on a single character (or a very limited group of characters) in a single situation. Each of the stories in this volume builds to a climactic situation. All the incidents in the forepart of each story are calculated to focus the reader's attention on the ending. The novel, too, adopts this method of construction; but its subject is likely to be wider, its scope broader, its characters more numerous, its situations more varied and unrelated.

The guiding principle of the short story is *unity*. Short stories concentrate on a single unified situation; characters are reduced to a minimum number; the author usually focuses on only one person. Even when the spotlight of attention is spread over two or more, the focus is shared, not divided.

Here are some hints on what to look for in short stories. Not all these questions will apply to every narrative. Intelligent and continued reading will suggest further and more specific questions, but these will serve as a starting point for analysis.

1. Who is the central character of the story? (Or is there more than one central character? If so, how does the author preserve the unified focus?)
2. What are the dominant traits of the central character?
3. What forces make up the main conflict of the story?
4. How is this conflict resolved? If it is not resolved, what prevents a resolution?
5. What part does setting play in the story?
6. What is the theme, or idea, that underlies the story?
7. From what point of view is the story told? That is, from what angle or seat does the writer elect to view the characters and events of the story?
8. Does the author economize by shortening the actual elapsed time of the story? If so, how?
9. Which of the four basic elements of fiction dominates the story—character, action (plot), setting, or theme?
10. In what respects are the style and content of the story interrelated and mutually dependent upon one another?

THE CASK OF AMONTILLADO

Edgar Allan Poe

Edgar Allan Poe (1809–1849), whose sinister tales are reflective of his tragic life, was born in Boston and orphaned less than three years later. His unhappiness in the foster home of the Allans of Richmond, his brief attendance at the University of Virginia and West Point, his poverty-stricken and unstable later life are familiar legends. Poe's reputation as the founder of the modern short story stems from the meticulously fashioned, unified "single effect" which he devised. His stories and many of his poems are sustained studies in mystery and horror. Among his most famous short stories are "Ligeia," 1838; "The Fall of the House of Usher," 1839; "The Murders in the Rue Morgue," 1841; "The Masque of the Red Death," 1842; "The Black Cat," 1843; "The Gold-Bug," 1843; "The Tell-Tale Heart," 1843; and "The Purloined Letter," 1845.

The thousand injuries of Fortunato I had borne as I best could; but when he ventured upon insult, I vowed revenge. You, who so well know the nature of my soul, will not suppose, however, that I gave utterance to a threat. *At length* I would be avenged; this was a point definitively[1] settled—but the very definitiveness with which it was resolved precluded[2] the idea of risk. I must not only punish, but punish with impunity.[3] A wrong is unredressed when retribution overtakes its redresser. It is equally unredressed when the avenger fails to make himself felt as such to him who has done the wrong.

It must be understood that neither by word nor deed had I given Fortunato cause to doubt my good will. I continued, as was my wont,[4] to smile in his face, and he did not perceive that my smile *now* was at the thought of his immolation.[5]

He had a weak point—this Fortunato—although in other regards he was a man to be respected and even feared. He prided himself on his connoisseurship[6] in wine. Few Italians have the true virtuoso[7] spirit. For the most part their enthusiasm is adopted to suit the time and opportunity, to practice imposture[8] upon the British and Austrian millionaires. In painting and gemmary,[9] Fortunato, like his countrymen, was a quack, but in the matter of old wines he was sincere. In this respect I did not differ from him materially;—I was skillful in the Italian vintages myself, and bought largely whenever I could.

It was about dusk, one evening during the supreme madness of the carnival season, that I encountered my friend. He accosted[10] me with excessive warmth, for he had been drinking much. The man wore motley.[11] He had on a tight-fitting parti-striped dress, and his head was surmounted by the conical cap and bells. I was so pleased to see him that I thought I should never have done wringing his hand.

I said to him—"My dear Fortunato, you are luckily met. How remarkably well you are looking today. But I have received a pipe[12] of what passes for Amontillado,[13] and I have my doubts."

"How?" said he. "Amontillado? A pipe? Impossible! And in the middle of the carnival!"

"I have my doubts," I replied; "and I was silly enough to pay the full Amontillado price without consulting you in the matter. You were not to be found, and I was fearful of losing a bargain."

"Amontillado!"

"I have my doubts."

"Amontillado!"

"And I must satisfy them."

"Amontillado!"

"As you are engaged, I am on my way to Luchresi. If anyone has a critical turn, it is he. He will tell me—"

"Luchresi cannot tell Amontillado from Sherry."

"And yet some fools will have it that his taste is a match for your own."

"Come, let us go."

"Whither?"

"To your vaults."

"My friend, no; I will not impose upon your good nature. I perceive you have an engagement. Luchresi—"

"I have no engagement; come."

"My friend, no. It is not the engagement, but the severe cold with which I perceive you are afflicted. The vaults are insufferably damp. They are encrusted with nitre."[14]

"Let us go, nevertheless. The cold is merely nothing. Amontillado! You have been imposed upon. And as for Luchresi, he cannot distinguish Sherry from Amontillado."

Thus speaking, Fortunato possessed himself of my arm; and putting on a mask of black silk and drawing a *roquelaure*[15] closely about my person, I suffered him to hurry me to my palazzo.[16]

There were no attendants at home; they had absconded[17] to make merry in honor of the time. I had told them that I should not return until the morning, and had given them explicit[18] orders not to stir from the house. These orders were sufficient, I well knew, to insure their immediate disappearance, one and all, as soon as my back was turned.

I took from their sconces two flambeaux,[19] and giving one to Fortunato, bowed him through several suites of rooms to the archway that led into the vaults. I passed down a long and winding staircase, requesting him to be cautious as he followed. We came at length to the foot of the descent and stood together upon the damp ground of the catacombs[20] of the Montresors.

The gait of my friend was unsteady, and the bells upon his cap jingled as he strode.

"The pipe," he said.

"It is farther on," said I; "but observe the white web-work which gleams from these cavern walls."

He turned towards me and looked into my eyes with two filmy orbs that distilled the rheum of intoxication.

"Nitre?" he asked, at length.

"Nitre," I replied. "How long have you had that cough?"

"Ugh! ugh! ugh!—ugh! ugh! ugh! —ugh! ugh! ugh!—ugh! ugh! ugh!— ugh! ugh! ugh!"

My poor friend found it impossible to reply for many minutes.

"It is nothing," he said, at last.

"Come," I said, with decision, "we will go back; your health is precious. You are rich, respected, admired, beloved; you are happy, as once I was. You are a man to be missed. For me it is no matter. We will go back; you will be ill, and I cannot be responsible. Besides, there is Luchresi—"

"Enough," he said; "the cough is a mere nothing; it will not kill me. I shall not die of a cough."

"True—true," I replied; "and, indeed, I had no intention of alarming you unnecessarily—but you should use all proper caution. A draught of this Médoc[21] will defend us from the damps."

Here I knocked off the neck of a bottle which I drew from a long row of its fellows that lay upon the mold.

"Drink," I said, presenting him the wine.

He raised it to his lips with a leer. He paused and nodded to me familiarly, while his bells jingled.

"I drink," he said, "to the buried that repose around us."

"And I to your long life."

He again took my arm, and we proceeded.

"These vaults," he said, "are extensive."

"The Montresors," I replied, "were a great and numerous family."

"I forget your arms."

"A huge human foot d'or, in a field azure; the foot crushes a serpent rampant whose fangs are embedded in the heel."

"And the motto?"

"*Nemo me impune lacessit.*"[22]

"Good!" he said.

The wine sparkled in his eyes and the bells jingled. My own fancy grew warm with the Médoc. We had passed through long walls of piled skeletons, with casks and puncheons[23] intermingling, into the inmost recesses of the catacombs. I paused again, and this time I made bold to seize Fortunato by an arm above the elbow.

"The nitre!" I said; "see, it increases. It hangs like moss upon the vaults. We are below the river's bed. The drops of moisture trickle among the bones. Come, we will go back ere it is too late. Your cough—"

"It is nothing," he said; "let us go on. But first, another draught of the Médoc."

I broke and reached him a flagon of De Graves.[24] He emptied it at a breath. His eyes flashed with a fierce light. He laughed and threw the bottle upwards with a gesticulation[25] I did not understand.

I looked at him in surprise. He repeated the movement—a grotesque one.

"You do not comprehend?" he said.

"Not I," I replied.

"Then you are not of the brotherhood."

"How?"

"You are not of the masons."[26]

"Yes, yes," I said, "yes, yes."

"You? Impossible! A mason?"

"A mason," I replied.

"A sign," he said, "a sign."

"It is this," I answered, producing from beneath the folds of my *roquelaure,* a trowel.

"You jest," he exclaimed, recoiling a few paces. "But let us proceed to the Amontillado."

"Be it so," I said, replacing the tool beneath the cloak, and again offering him my arm. He leaned upon it heavily. We continued our route in search of the Amontillado. We passed through a range of low arches, descended, passed on, and, descending again, arrived at a deep crypt,[27] in which the foulness of the air caused our flambeaux rather to glow than flame.

At the most remote end of the crypt there appeared another less spacious. Its walls had been lined with human remains, piled to the vault overhead, in the fashion of the great catacombs of Paris. Three sides of this interior crypt were still ornamented in this manner. From the fourth the bones had been thrown down, and lay promiscuously[28] upon the earth, forming at one point a mound of some size. Within the wall thus exposed by the displacing of the bones, we perceived a still interior recess, in depth about four feet, in width three, in height six or seven. It seemed to have been constructed for no especial use within itself, but formed merely the interval between two of the colossal supports of the roof of the catacombs, and was backed by one of their circumscribing[29] walls of solid granite.

It was in vain that Fortunato, uplifting his dull torch, endeavored to pry into the depth of the recess. Its termination[30] the feeble light did not enable us to see.

"Proceed," I said; "herein is the Amontillado. As for Luchresi—"

"He is an ignoramus," interrupted my friend, as he stepped unsteadily forward, while I followed immediately at his heels. In an instant he had reached the extremity of the niche, and finding his progress arrested by the rock, stood stupidly bewildered. A moment more and I had fettered him to the granite. In its surface were two iron staples, distant from each other about two feet, horizontally. From one of these depended a short chain, from the other a padlock. Throwing the links about his waist, it was but the work of a few seconds to secure it. He was too much astounded to resist. Withdrawing the key I stepped back from the recess.

"Pass your hand," I said, "over the wall; you cannot help feeling the nitre. Indeed, it is *very* damp. Once more let me *implore* you to return. No? Then I must positively leave you. But I must first render you all the little attentions in my power."

"The Amontillado!" ejaculated my friend, not yet recovered from his astonishment.

"True," I replied; "the Amontillado."

As I said these words I busied myself among the pile of bones of which I have before spoken. Throwing them aside, I soon uncovered a quantity of building stone and mortar. With these materials and with the aid of my trowel, I began vigorously to wall up the entrance of the niche.

I had scarcely laid the first tier of the masonry when I discovered that the intoxication of Fortunato had in a great measure worn off. The earliest indication I had of this was a low moaning cry from the depth of the recess. It was *not* the cry of a drunken man. There was then a long and obstinate[31] silence. I laid the second tier, and the third, and the fourth; and then I heard the furious vibrations of the chain. The noise lasted for several minutes, during which, that I might hearken to it with the more satisfaction, I ceased my labors and sat down upon the bones. When at last the clanking subsided, I resumed the trowel, and finished without interruption the fifth, the sixth, and the seventh tier. The wall was now nearly upon a level with my breast. I again paused, and holding the flambeaux over the mason-work, threw a few feeble rays upon the figure within.

A succession of loud and shrill screams, bursting suddenly from the throat of the chained form, seemed to thrust me violently back. For a brief moment I hesitated, I trembled. Unsheathing my rapier,[32] I began to grope with it about the recess; but the thought of an instant reassured me. I placed my hand upon the solid fabric of the catacombs, and felt satisfied. I reapproached the wall; I replied to the yells of him who clamored. I reechoed, I aided, I surpassed them in volume and in strength. I did this, and the clamorer grew still.

It was now midnight, and my task was drawing to a close. I had completed the eighth, the ninth, and the tenth tier. I had finished a portion of the last and the eleventh; there remained but a single stone to be fitted and plastered in. I struggled with its weight; I placed it partially in its destined position. But now there came from out the niche a low laugh that erected the hairs upon my head. It was succeeded by a sad voice, which I had difficulty in recognizing as that of the noble Fortunato. The voice said—

"Ha! ha! ha!—he! he! he!—a very good joke, indeed—an excellent jest. We will have many a rich laugh about it at the palazzo—he! he! he!—over our wine—he! he! he!"

"The Amontillado!" I said.

"He! he! he!—he! he! he!—yes, the Amontillado. But is it not getting late? Will not they be awaiting us at the palazzo, the Lady Fortunato and the rest? Let us be gone."

"Yes," I said, "let us be gone."

"For the love of God, Montresor!"

"Yes," I said, "for the love of God!"

But to these words I hearkened in vain for a reply. I grew impatient. I called aloud—

"Fortunato!"

No answer. I called again—

"Fortunato!"

No answer still. I thrust a torch through the remaining aperture[33] and let it fall within. There came forth in return only a jingling of the bells. My heart grew sick—on account of the dampness of the catacombs. I hastended to make an end of my labor. I forced the last stone into its position; I plastered it up. Against the new masonry I re-erected the old rampart of bones. For the half of a century no mortal has disturbed them. *In pace requiescat.*[34]

Notes

[1] Completely.
[2] Prevented.
[3] Freedom from punishment.
[4] Custom, habit.
[5] Sacrifice (being killed).
[6] Taste and knowledge.
[7] Cultivated, skillful.
[8] Deception, fraud.
[9] Knowledge of precious gems (stones).
[10] Approached.
[11] Clothing of several colors, like that worn by jesters.
[12] A large cask.
[13] A pale-colored Spanish sherry (wine).
[14] White salt clinging to the walls.
[15] A cloak reaching to the knees.
[16] Palace, large private residence.
[17] Left suddenly.
[18] Clear and definite.
[19] Montresor took two flaming torches from their brackets.
[20] Underground cemeteries.
[21] A claret wine produced in southwestern France.
[22] "No one attacks me with impunity" (freedom from revenge).
[23] Large containers usually holding 80 gallons.
[24] A large bottle of French wine.
[25] Excited gesture (movement).
[26] A *freemason* is a member of a secret order, or brotherhood, having for its main purpose mutual help and the promotion of brotherly love.
[27] Underground chamber or vault; a pit.
[28] Carelessly, haphazardly.
[29] Enclosing, surrounding.
[30] Ending.
[31] Stubborn, unyielding.
[32] A sword with a long, narrow blade.
[33] Opening.
[34] May he rest in peace.

A ROSE FOR EMILY

William Faulkner

For comment on the life and writings of William Faulkner, see under "Man Will Prevail."

I

When Miss Emily Grieson died, our whole town went to her funeral: the men through a sort of respectful affection for a fallen monument, the women mostly out of curiosity to see the inside of her house, which no one save an old man-servant—a combined gardener and cook—had seen in at least ten years.

It was a big, squarish frame house that had once been white, decorated with cupolas[1] and spires and scrolled balconies in the heavily lightsome style of the Seventies, set on what had once been our most select street. But garages and cotton gins had encroached and obliterated even the august[2] names of that neighborhood; only Miss Emily's house was left, lifting its stubborn and coquettish[3] decay above the cotton wagons and the gasoline pumps—an eyesore among eyesores. And now Miss Emily had gone to join the representatives of those august names where they lay in the cedar-bemused cemetery among the ranked and anonymous graves of Union and Confederate soldiers who fell at the battle of Jefferson.

Alive, Miss Emily had been a tradition, a duty, and a care; a sort of hereditary obligation upon the town, dating from that day in 1894 when Colonel Sartoris, the mayor—he who fathered the edict[4] that no Negro woman should appear on the streets without an apron—remitted her taxes, the dispensation dating from the death of her father on into perpetuity.[5] Not that Miss Emily would have accepted charity. Colonel Sartoris invented an involved tale to the effect that Miss Emily's father had loaned money to the town, which the town, as a matter of business, preferred this way of repaying. Only a man of Colonel Sartoris' generation and thought could have invented it, and only a woman could have believed it.

When the next generation, with its more modern ideas, became mayors and aldermen, this arrangement created some little dissatisfaction. On the first of the year they mailed her a tax notice. February came, and there was no reply. They wrote her a formal letter, asking her to call at the sheriff's office at her convenience. A week later the mayor wrote her himself, offering to call or to send his car for her, and received in reply a note on paper of an archaic[6] shape, in a thin, flowing calligraphy[7] in faded ink, to the effect that she no longer went out at all. The tax notice was also enclosed, without comment.

They called a special meeting of the Board of Aldermen. A deputation waited upon her, knocked at the door through which no visitor had passed since she ceased giving china-painting lessons eight or ten years earlier. They were admitted by the old Negro into a dim hall from which a stairway mounted into still more shadow. It smelled of dust and disuse—a close, dank smell. The Negro led them into the parlor. It was furnished in heavy, leather-covered furniture. When the Negro opened the blinds of one window, they could see that the leather was cracked; and when they sat down, a faint dust rose sluggishly about their thighs, spinning with slow motes in the single sun-ray. On a tarnished gilt easel before the fireplace stood a crayon portrait of Miss Emily's father.

They rose when she entered—a small, fat woman in black, with a thin gold chain descending to her waist and vanishing into her belt, leaning on an ebony cane with a tarnished gold head. Her skeleton was small and spare; perhaps that was why what would have been merely plumpness in another was obesity in her. She looked bloated, like a body long submerged in motionless water, and of that pallid[8] hue. Her eyes, lost in the fatty ridges of her face, looked like two small pieces of coal pressed into a lump of dough as they moved from one face to another while the visitors stated their errand.

She did not ask them to sit. She just stood in the door and listened quietly until the spokesman came to a stumbling halt. Then they could hear the invisible watch ticking at the end of the gold chain.

Her voice was dry and cold. "I have no taxes in Jefferson. Colonel Sartoris explained it to me. Perhaps one of you can gain access to the city records and satisfy yourselves."

"But we have. We are the city authorities, Miss Emily. Didn't you get a notice from the sheriff, signed by him?"

"I received a paper, yes," Miss Emily said. "Perhaps he considers himself the sheriff . . . I have no taxes in Jefferson."

"But there is nothing on the books to show that, you see. We must go by the—"

"See Colonel Sartoris. I have no taxes in Jefferson."

"But, Miss Emily—"

"See Colonel Sartoris." (Colonel Sartoris had been dead almost ten years.) "I have no taxes in Jefferson. Tobe!" The Negro appeared. "Show these gentlemen out."

II

She vanquished them, horse and foot,[9] just as she had vanquished their fathers thirty years before about the smell. That was two years after her father's death and a short time after her sweetheart—the one we believed would marry her—had deserted her. After her father's death she went out very little; after her sweetheart went away, people hardly saw her at all. A few of the ladies had the temerity[10] to call but were not received, and the only sign of life about the place was the Negro man—a young man then—going in and out with a market basket.

"Just as if a man—any man—could keep a kitchen properly," the ladies said; so they were not surprised when the smell developed. It was another link between the gross, teeming world and the high and mighty Griersons.

A neighbor, a woman, complained to the mayor, Judge Stevens, eighty years old.

"But what will you have me do about it, madam?" he said.

"Why, send her word to stop it," the woman said. "Isn't there a law?"

"I'm sure that won't be necessary," Judge Stevens said. "It's probably just a snake or a rat that nigger of hers killed in the yard. I'll speak to him about it."

The next day he received two more complaints, one from a man who came in diffident deprecation.[11] "We really must do something about it, Judge. I'd be the last one in the world to bother Miss Emily, but we've got to do something." That night the Board of Aldermen met—three graybeards and one younger man, a member of the rising generation.

"It's simple enough," he said. "Send her word to have her place cleaned up. Give her a certain time to do it in, and if she don't . . ."

"Dammit, sir," Judge Stevens said, "will you accuse a lady to her face of smelling bad?"

So the next night, after midnight, four men crossed Miss Emily's lawn and slunk about the house like burglars, sniffing along the base of the brickwork and at the cellar openings while one of them performed a regular sowing motion with his hand out of a sack slung from his shoulder. They broke open the cellar door and sprinkled lime there, and in all the outbuildings. As they recrossed the lawn, a window that had been dark was lighted and Miss Emily sat in it, the light behind her, and her upright torso motionless as that of an idol. They crept quietly across the lawn and into the shadow of the locusts that lined the street. After a week or two the smell went away.

That was when people had begun to feel really sorry for her. People in our town, remembering how Old Lady Wyatt, her great-aunt, had gone completely crazy at last, believed that the Griersons held themselves a little too high for what they really were. None of the young men were quite good enough for Miss Emily and such. We had long thought of them as a tableau:[12] Miss Emily a slender figure in white in the background, her father a spraddled silhouette[13] in the foreground, his back to her and clutching a horse-whip, the two of them framed by the back-flung front door. So when she got to be thirty and was still single, we were not pleased exactly, but vindicated; even with insanity in the family she wouldn't have turned down all of her chances if they had really materialized.

When her father died, it got about that the house was all that was left to her; and in a way, people were glad. At last they could pity Miss Emily. Being left alone, and a pauper, she had become humanized. Now she too would know the old thrill and the old despair of a penny more or less.

The day after his death all the ladies prepared to call at the house and offer condolence and aid, as is our custom. Miss Emily met them at the door, dressed as usual and with no trace of grief on her face. She told them that her father was not dead. She did that for three days, with the ministers calling on her, and the doctors, trying to persuade her to let them dispose of the body. Just as they were about to resort to law and force, she broke down, and they buried her father quickly.

We did not say she was crazy then. We believed she had to do that. We remembered all the young men her father had driven away, and we knew that with nothing left, she would have to cling to that which had robbed her, as people will.

III

She was sick for a long time. When we saw her again, her hair was cut short, making her look like a girl, with a vague resemblance to those angels in colored church windows—sort of tragic and serene.

The town had just let the contracts for paving the sidewalks, and in the summer after her father's death they began the work. The construction company came with niggers and mules and machinery, and a foreman named Homer Barron, a Yankee—a big, dark, ready man, with a big voice and eyes lighter than his face. The little boys would follow in groups to hear him cuss the niggers, and the niggers singing in time to the rise and fall of picks. Pretty soon he knew everybody in town. Whenever you heard a lot of laughing anywhere about the square, Homer Barron would be in the center of the group. Presently we began to see him and Miss Emily on Sunday afternoons driving in the yellow-wheeled buggy and the matched team of bays[14] from the livery stable.

At first we were glad that Miss Emily would have an interest, because the ladies all said, "Of course a Grierson would not think seriously of a Northerner, a day laborer." But there were still others, older people, who said that even grief could not cause a real lady to forget *noblesse oblige*[15]—without calling it *noblesse oblige*. They just said, "Poor Emily. Her kinsfolk should come to her." She had some kin in Alabama; but years ago her father had fallen out with them over the estate of Old Lady Wyatt, the crazy woman, and there was no communication between the two families. They had not even been represented at the funeral.

And as soon as the old people said, "Poor Emily," the whispering began. "Do you suppose it's really so?" they said to one another. "Of course it is. What else could . . ." This behind their hands; rustling of craned silk and satin behind jalousies[16] closed upon the sun of Sunday afternoon as the thin, swift clop-clop-clop of the matched team passed: "Poor Emily."

She carried her head high enough —even when we believed that she was fallen. It was as if she demanded more than ever the recognition of her dignity as the last Grierson; as if it had wanted that touch of earthiness to reaffirm her imperviousness.[17] Like when she bought the rat poison, the arsenic. That was over a year after they had begun to say "Poor Emily," and while the two female cousins were visiting her.

"I want some poison," she said to the druggist. She was over thirty then, still a slight woman, though thinner than usual, with cold, haughty black eyes in a face the flesh of which was strained across the temples and about the eye-sockets as you imagine a lighthouse-keeper's face ought to look. "I want some poison," she said.

"Yes, Miss Emily. What kind? For rats and such? I'd recom—"

"I want the best you have. I don't care what kind."

The druggist named several. "They'll kill anything up to an elephant. But what you want is—"

"Arsenic," Miss Emily said. "Is that a good one?"

"Is . . . arsenic? Yes, ma'am. But what you want—"

"I want arsenic."

The druggist looked down at her. She looked back at him, erect, her face like a strained flag. "Why, of course," the druggist said. "If that's what you want. But the law requires you to tell what you are going to use it for."

Miss Emily just stared at him, her head tilted back in order to look him eye for eye, until he looked away and went and got the arsenic and wrapped it up. The Negro delivery boy brought her the package; the druggist didn't come back. When she opened the package at home there was written on the box, under the skull and bones: "For rats."

IV

So the next day we all said, "She will kill herself"; and we said it would be the best thing. When she had first begun to be seen with Homer Barron, we had said, "She will marry him." Then we said, "She will persuade him yet," because Homer himself had remarked—he liked men, and it was known that he drank with the younger men in the Elks' Club—that he was not a marrying man. Later we said "Poor Emily" behind the jalousies as they passed on Sunday afternoon in the glittering buggy, Miss Emily with her head high and Homer Barron with his hat cocked and a cigar in his teeth, reins and whip in a yellow glove.

Then some of the ladies began to say that it was a disgrace to the town and a bad example to the young people. The men did not want to interfere, but at last the ladies forced the Baptist minister—Miss Emily's people were Episcopal—to call upon her. He would never divulge what happened during that interview, but he refused to go back again. The next Sunday they again drove about the streets, and the following day the minister's wife wrote to Miss Emily's relations in Alabama.

So she had blood-kin under her roof again and we sat back to watch developments. At first nothing happened. Then we were sure that they were to be married. We learned that Miss Emily had been to the jeweler's and ordered a man's toilet set in silver, with the letters H.B. on each piece. Two days later we learned that she had bought a complete outfit of men's clothing, including a nightshirt, and we said, "They are married." We were really glad. We were glad because the two female cousins were even more Grierson than Miss Emily had ever been.

So we were not surprised when Homer Barron—the streets had been finished some time since—was gone. We were a little disappointed that there was not a public blowing-off, but we believed that he had gone on to prepare for Miss Emily's coming, or to give her a chance to get rid of the cousins. (By that time it was a cabal,[18] and we were all Miss Emily's allies to help circumvent[19] the cousins.) Sure enough, after another week they departed. And, as we had expected all along, within three days Homer Barron was back in town. A neighbor saw the Negro man admit him at the kitchen door at dusk one evening.

And that was the last we saw of Homer Barron. And of Miss Emily for some time. The Negro man went in and out with the market basket, but the front door remained closed. Now and then we would see her at a window for a moment, as the men did that night when they sprinkled the lime, but for almost six months she did not appear on the streets. Then we knew that this was to be expected too; as if that quality of her father which had thwarted her woman's life so many times had been too virulent[20] and too furious to die.

When we next saw Miss Emily, she had grown fat and her hair was turning gray. During the next few years it grew grayer and grayer until it attained an even pepper-and-salt iron-gray, when it ceased turning. Up to the day of her death at seventy-four it was still that vigorous iron-gray, like the hair of an active man.

From that time on her front door remained closed, save for a period of six or seven years, when she was about forty, during which she gave lessons in china-painting. She fitted up a studio in one of the downstairs rooms, where the daughters and granddaughters of Colonel Sartoris' contemporaries were sent to her with the same regularity and in the same spirit that they were sent to church on Sundays with a twenty-five-cent piece for the collection plate. Meanwhile her taxes had been remitted.

Then the newer generation became the backbone and the spirit of the town, and the painting pupils grew up and fell away and did not send their children to her with boxes of color and tedious brushes and pictures cut from the ladies' magazines. The front door closed upon the last one and remained closed for good. When the town got free postal delivery, Miss Emily alone refused to let them fasten the metal numbers above her door and attach a mailbox to it. She would not listen to them.

Daily, monthly, yearly we watched the Negro grow grayer and more stooped, going in and out with the market basket. Each December we sent her a tax notice, which would be returned by the post office a week later, unclaimed. Now and then we would see her in one of the downstairs windows—she had evidently shut up the top floor of the house—like the carven torso of an idol in a niche, looking or not looking at us, we could never tell which. Thus she passed from generation to generation—dear, inescapable, impervious, tranquil, and perverse.[21]

And so she died. Fell ill in the house filled with dust and shadows, with only a doddering[22] Negro man to wait on her. We did not even know she was sick; we had long since given up trying to get any information from the Negro. He talked to no one, probably not even to her, for his voice had grown harsh and rusty, as if from disuse.

She died in one of the downstairs

rooms, in a heavy walnut bed with a curtain, her gray head propped on a pillow yellow and moldy with age and lack of sunlight.

V

The Negro met the first of the ladies at the front door and let them in, with their hushed, sibilant[23] voices and their quick, curious glances, and then he disappeared. He walked right through the house and out the back and was not seen again.

The two female cousins came at once. They held the funeral on the second day, with the town coming to look at Miss Emily beneath a mass of bought flowers, with the crayon face of her father musing profoundly above the bier[24] and the ladies sibilant and macabre;[25] and the very old men—some in their brushed Confederate uniforms—on the porch and the lawn, talking of Miss Emily as if she had been a contemporary of theirs, believing that they had danced with her and courted her perhaps, confusing time with its mathematical progression, as the old do, to whom all the past is not a diminishing road but, instead, a huge meadow which no winter ever quite touches, divided from them now by the narrow bottle-neck of the most recent decade.

Already we knew that there was one room in that region above stairs which no one had seen in forty years, and which would have to be forced. They waited until Miss Emily was decently in the ground before they opened it.

The violence of breaking down the door seemed to fill this room with pervading dust. A thin, acrid pall[26] as of the tomb seemed to lie everywhere upon this room decked and furnished as for a bridal: upon the valance curtains of faded rose color, upon the rose-shaded lights, upon the dressing table, upon the delicate array of crystal and the man's toilet things backed with tarnished silver, silver so tarnished that the monogram was obscured. Among them lay a collar and tie, as if they had just been removed, which, lifted, left upon the surface a pale crescent in the dust. Upon a chair hung the suit, carefully folded; beneath it the two mute shoes and the discarded socks.

The man himself lay in the bed.

For a long while we just stood there, looking down at the profound and fleshless grin. The body had apparently once lain in the attitude of an embrace, but now the long sleep that outlasts love, that conquers even the grimace of love, had cuckolded[27] him. What was left of him, rotted beneath what was left of the nightshirt, had become inextricable from the bed in which he lay; and upon him and upon the pillow beside him lay that even coating of the patient and biding dust.

Then we noticed that in the second pillow was the indentation of a head. One of us lifted something from it, and leaning forward, that faint and invisible dust dry and acrid in the nostrils, we saw a long strand of iron-gray hair.

Notes

[1] Domes, belfries.
[2] Revered; important.
[3] Careless.
[4] Decree, order.
[5] Lasting forever.
[6] Ancient, old-fashioned.
[7] Penmanship, handwriting.
[8] Pale, faint.
[9] Defeated them completely (all soldiers on foot and horseback).
[10] Boldness.
[11] Apology, hesitation.
[12] Picture, scene.
[13] Outline, image.
[14] A pair of reddish-brown horses.
[15] Literally, "nobility obliges"; the obligation of rich or high-born people to act honorably and charitably.
[16] Blinds or shutters made with horizontal slats.
[17] Inability to be influenced or injured.
[18] Clique; group of plotters.
[19] Get around, bypass.
[20] Bitter, hostile, spiteful.
[21] Dear, unavoidable, unimpaired, calm, and cantankerous.
[22] Trembling, aged.
[23] Whistling, hissing.
[24] Stand on which a corpse (or coffin) is placed before burial.
[25] Ghastly, grim.
[26] Sharp, bitter gloom.
[27] Been unfaithful to.

THE OPEN WINDOW

"Saki" (H. H. Munro)

"SAKI" (HECTOR HUGH MUNRO, 1870–1916) was a British novelist, short-story writer, and political satirist who was killed in France during World War I. He was born in Burma but was largely educated in England and on tours with his father through continental Europe. His first, and most serious, book was *The Rise of the Russian Empire* (1900). He wrote many short stories, collections of which are variously entitled *Reginald* (1904), *Reginald in Russia* (1910), *The Chronicles of Clovis* (1911), and *Beasts and Super-Beasts* (1914). His novels are *The Unbearable Bassington* (1912) and *When William Came* (1913).

"My aunt will be down presently, Mr. Nuttel," said a very self-possessed young lady of fifteen; "in the meantime you must try to put up with me."

Framton Nuttel endeavoured to say the correct something which should duly flatter the niece of the moment without unduly discounting the aunt that was to come. Privately he doubted more than ever whether these formal visits on a succession of total strangers would do much toward helping the nerve cure which he was supposed to be undergoing.

"I know how it will be," his sister had said when he was preparing to migrate to this rural retreat; "you will bury yourself down there and not speak to a living soul, and your nerves will be worse than ever from moping. I shall just give you letters of introduction to all the people I know there. Some of them, as far as I can remember, were quite nice."

Framton wondered whether Mrs. Sappleton, the lady to whom he was presenting one of the letters of introduction, came into the nice division.

"Do you know many of the people round here?" asked the niece, when she judged that they had had sufficient silent communion.

"Hardly a soul," said Framton. "My sister was staying here, at the rectory,[1] you know, some four years ago, and she gave me letters of introduction to some of the people here."

He made the last statement in a tone of distinct regret.

"Then you know practically nothing about my aunt?" pursued the self-possessed young lady.

"Only her name and address," admitted the caller. He was wondering whether Mrs. Sappleton was in the married or widowed state. An indefinable something about the room seemed to suggest masculine habitation.

"Her great tragedy happened just three years ago," said the child; "that would be since your sister's time."

"Her tragedy?" asked Framton; somehow, in this restful country spot, tragedies seemed out of place.

"You may wonder why we keep that window wide open on an October afternoon," said the niece, indicating a large French window that opened on to a lawn.

"It is quite warm for the time of the year," said Framton; "but has that window got anything to do with the tragedy?"

"Out through that window, three years ago to a day, her husband and her two young brothers went off for their day's shooting. They never came back. In crossing the moor to their favourite snipe-shooting[2] ground they were all three engulfed in a treacherous piece of bog. It had been that dreadful wet summer, you know, and places that were safe in other years gave way suddenly without warning. Their bodies were never recovered. That was the dreadful part of it." Here the child's voice lost its self-possessed note and became falteringly human. "Poor aunt always thinks that they will come back some day, they and the little brown spaniel that was lost with them, and walk in at that window just as they used to do. That is why the window is kept open every evening till it is quite dusk. Poor dear aunt, she has often told me how they went out, her husband with his white water-proof coat over his arm, and Ronnie, her youngest brother, singing 'Bertie, why do you bound?' as he always did to tease her, because she said it got on her nerves. Do you know, sometimes on still, quiet evenings like this, I almost get a creepy feeling that they will all walk in through that window—"

She broke off with a little shudder. It was a relief to Framton when the aunt bustled into the room with a whirl of apologies for being late in making her appearance.

"I hope Vera has been amusing you?" she said.

"She has been very interesting," said Framton.

"I hope you don't mind the open window," said Mrs. Sappleton briskly; "my husband and brothers will be home directly from shooting, and they always come in this way. They've been out for snipe in the marshes today, so they'll make a fine mess over my poor carpets. So like you men-folk, isn't it?"

She rattled on cheerfully about the shooting and the scarcity of birds and the prospects for duck in the winter. To Framton it was all purely horrible. He made a desperate but only partially successful effort to turn the talk on to a less ghastly topic; he was conscious that his hostess was giving him only a fragment of her attention, and her eyes were constantly straying past him to the open window and the lawn beyond. It was certainly an unfortunate coincidence[3] that he should have paid his visit on this tragic anniversary.

"The doctors agree in ordering me complete rest, an absence of mental excitement, and avoidance of anything in the nature of violent physical exercise," announced Framton, who laboured under the tolerably widespread delusion that total strangers and chance acquaintances are hungry for the least detail of one's ailments and infirmities, their cause and cure. "On the matter of diet they are not so much in agreement," he continued.

"No?" said Mrs. Sappleton, in a voice which replaced a yawn only at the last moment. Then she suddenly brightened into alert attention—but not to what Framton was saying.

"Here they are at last!" she cried. "Just in time for tea, and don't they look as if they were muddy up to the eyes!"

Framton shivered slightly and turned toward the niece with a look intended to convey sympathetic comprehension. The child was staring out through the open window with dazed horror in her eyes. In a chill shock of nameless fear Framton swung round in his seat and looked in the same direction.

In the deepening twilight three figures were walking across the lawn toward the window; they all carried guns under their arms, and one of them was additionally burdened with a white coat hung over his shoulders. A tired brown spaniel kept close at their heels. Noiselessly they neared the house, and then a hoarse young voice chanted out of the dusk: "I said, Bertie, why do you bound?"

Framton grabbed wildly at his stick and hat; the hall-door, the gravel-drive, and the front gate were dimly-noted stages in his headlong retreat. A cyclist coming along the road had to run into the hedge to avoid imminent[4] collision.

"Here we are, my dear," said the bearer of the white mackintosh,[5] coming in through the window; "fairly muddy, but most of it's dry. Who was that who bolted out as we came up?"

"A most extraordinary man, a Mr.

Nuttel," said Mrs. Sappleton; "could only talk about his illness, and dashed off without a word of good-bye or apology when you arrived. One would think he had seen a ghost."

"I expect it was the spaniel," said the niece calmly; "he told me he had a horror of dogs. He was once hunted into a cemetery somewhere on the banks of the Ganges[6] by a pack of pariah[7] dogs and had to spend the night in a newly dug grave with the creatures snarling and grinning and foaming just above him. Enough to make anyone lose their nerve."

Romance at short notice was her specialty.

Notes

1 Parsonage, home of a minister.
2 Snipes are long-billed game birds found in marshy areas.
3 Occurrence by chance of two or more events at one time.
4 Likely to occur at any moment.
5 A raincoat made of cloth rendered waterproof by India rubber and named after its inventor, Charles Macintosh (1766–1843).
6 A river in India, sacred to the Hindus.
7 Outcast.

IN ANOTHER COUNTRY

Ernest Hemingway

Ernest (Miller) Hemingway (1898–1961), "the fictional laureate of the 'lost generation,'" spent his early years in his native Oak Park, Illinois, became a reporter on *The Kansas City Star*, and began writing fiction after serving on the Italian front in World War I. Much of his writing emphasizes the somewhat studied disillusionment of the American expatriates among whom he lived in Paris during the postwar period. Typical of "lost generation" attitudinizing is preoccupation with the macabre, with suffering, death, and loss of values in his first two novels, *The Sun Also Rises* (1926) and *A Farewell to Arms* (1929). Later novels, *To Have and Have Not* (1937) and *For Whom the Bell Tolls* (1940), show a more positive faith in values and organized society. *A Moveable Feast* (1964) is an interesting series of autobiographical sketches that reveals much about the author's early writing and his formative years abroad. He received the 1954 Nobel Prize in literature.

In the fall the war was always there, but we did not go to it any more. It was cold in the fall in Milan and the dark came very early. Then the electric lights came on, and it was pleasant along the streets looking in the windows. There was much game hanging outside the shops, and the snow powdered in the fur of the foxes and the wind blew their tails. The deer hung stiff and heavy and empty, and small birds blew in the wind and the wind turned their feathers. It was a cold fall and the wind came down from the mountains.

We were all at the hospital every afternoon, and there were different ways of walking across the town through the dusk to the hospital. Two of the ways were alongside canals, but they were long. Always, though, you crossed a bridge across a canal to enter the hospital. There was a choice of three bridges. On one of them a woman sold roasted chestnuts. It was warm, standing in front of her charcoal fire, and the chestnuts were warm afterward in your pocket. The hospital was very old and very beautiful, and you entered through a gate and walked across a courtyard and out a gate on the other side. There were usually funerals starting from the courtyard. Beyond the old hospital were the new brick pavilions, and there we met every afternoon and were all very polite and interested in what was the matter, and sat in the machines that were to make so much difference.

The doctor came up to the machine where I was sitting and said: "What did you like best to do before the war? Did you practice a sport?"

I said: "Yes, football."

"Good," he said. "You will be able to play football again better than ever."

My knee did not bend and the leg dropped straight from the knee to the ankle without a calf, and the machine was to bend the knee and make it move as in riding a tricycle. But it did not bend yet, and instead the machine lurched when it came to the bending part. The doctor said: "That will all pass. You are a fortunate young man. You will play football again like a champion."

In the next machine was a major who had a little hand like a baby's. He winked at me when the doctor examined his hand, which was between two leather straps that bounced up and down and flapped the stiff fingers, and said: "And will I too play football, captain-doctor?" He had been a very great fencer, and before the war the greatest fencer in Italy.

The doctor went to his office in a back room and brought a photograph which showed a hand that had been withered almost as small as the major's, before it had taken a machine course, and after was a little larger. The major held the photograph with his good hand and looked at it very carefully. "A wound?" he asked.

"An industrial accident," the doctor said.

"Very interesting, very interesting," the major said, and handed it back to the doctor.

"You have confidence?"

"No," said the major.[1]

There were three boys who came each day who were about the same age I was. They were all three from Milan, and one of them was to be a lawyer, and one was to be a painter, and one had intended to be a soldier, and after we were finished with the machines, sometimes we walked back together to the Café Cova, which was next door to the Scala. We walked the short way through the communist quarter because we were four together. The people hated us because we were officers, and from a wineshop someone would call out, "*A basso gli ufficiali!*"[2] as we passed. Another boy who walked with us sometimes and made us five wore a black silk handkerchief across his face because he had no nose then and his face was to be rebuilt. He had gone out to the front from the military academy and been wounded within an hour after he had gone into the front line for the first time. They rebuilt his face, but he came from a very old family and they could never get the nose exactly right. He went to South America and worked in a bank. But this was a long time ago, and then we did not any of us know how it was going to be afterward. We only knew then that there was always the war, but that we were not going to it any more.

We all had the same medals, except the boy with the black silk bandage across his face, and he had not been at the front long enough to get any medals. The tall boy with a very pale face who was to be a lawyer had been a lieutenant of Arditi and had three medals of the sort we each had only one of. He had lived a very long time with death and was a little detached. We were all a little detached, and there was nothing that held us together except that we met every afternoon at the hospital. Although, as we walked to the Cova through the tough part of town, walking in the dark, with light and singing coming out of the wineshops, and sometimes having to walk into the street when the men and women would crowd together on the sidewalk so that we would have had to jostle them to get by, we felt held together by there being something that had happened that they, the people who disliked us, did not understand.

We ourselves all understood the Cova, where it was rich and warm and not too brightly lighted, and noisy and smoky at certain hours, and there were always girls at the tables and the illustrated papers on a rack on the wall. The girls at the Cova were very patriotic, and I found that the most patriotic people in Italy were the café girls—and I believe they are still patriotic.

The boys at first were very polite about my medals and asked me what I had done to get them. I showed them the papers, which were written in very beautiful language and full of *fratellanza* and *abnegazione*,[3] but which really said, with the adjectives removed, that I had been given the medals because I was an American. After that their manner changed a little toward me, although I was their friend against outsiders. I was a friend, but I was never really one of them after they had read the citations,[4] because it had been different with them and they had done very different things to get their medals. I had been wounded, it was true; but we all knew that being wounded, after all, was really an accident. I was never ashamed of the ribbons, though, and sometimes, after the cocktail hour, I would imagine myself having done all the things they had done to get their medals; but walking home at night through the empty streets with the cold wind and all the shops closed, trying to keep near the street lights, I knew that I would never have done such things, and I was very much afraid to die, and often lay in bed at night by myself, afraid to die and wondering how I would be when I went back to the front again.

The three with the medals were

like hunting-hawks; and I was not a hawk, although I might seem a hawk to those who had never hunted; they, the three, knew better and so we drifted apart. But I stayed good friends with the boy who had been wounded his first day at the front, because he would never know now how he would have turned out; so he could never be accepted either, and I liked him because I thought perhaps he would not have turned out to be a hawk either.

The major, who had been the great fencer, did not believe in bravery, and spent much time while we sat in the machines correcting my grammar. He had complimented me on how I spoke Italian, and we talked together very easily. One day I had said that Italian seemed such an easy language to me that I could not take a great interest in it; everything was so easy to say. "Ah, yes," the major said. "Why, then do you not take up the use of grammar?" So we took up the use of grammar, and soon Italian was such a difficult language that I was afraid to talk to him until I had the grammar straight in my mind.

The major came very regularly to the hospital. I do not think he ever missed a day, although I am sure he did not believe in the machines. There was a time when none of us believed in the machines, and one day the major said it was all nonsense. The machines were new then and it was we who were to prove them. It was an idiotic idea, he said, "a theory, like another." I had not learned my grammar, and he said I was a stupid, impossible disgrace, and he was a fool to have bothered with me. He was a small man and he sat straight up in his chair with his right hand thrust into the machine and looked straight ahead at the wall while the straps thumped up and down with his fingers in them.

"What will you do when the war is over if it is over?" he asked me. "Speak grammatically!"

"I will go to the States."

"Are you married?"

"No, but I hope to be."

"The more of a fool you are," he said. He seemed very angry. "A man must not marry."

"Why, Signor Maggiore?"

"Don't call me 'Signor Maggiore.' "

"Why must not a man marry?"

"He cannot marry. He cannot marry," he said angrily. "If he is to lose everything, he should not place himself in a position to lose that. He should not place himself in a position to lose. He should find things he cannot lose."

He spoke very angrily and bitterly, and looked straight ahead while he talked.

"But why should he necessarily lose it?"

"He'll lose it," the major said. He was looking at the wall. Then he looked down at the machine and jerked his little hand out from between the straps and slapped it hard against his thigh. "He'll lose it," he almost shouted. "Don't argue with me!" Then he called to the attendant who ran the machines. "Come and turn this damned thing off."

He went back into the other room for the light treatment and the massage. Then I heard him ask the doctor if he might use his telephone and he shut the door. When he came back into the room, I was sitting in another machine. He was wearing his cape and had his cap on, and he came directly toward my machine and put his arm on my shoulder.

"I am so sorry," he said, and patted me on the shoulder with his good hand. "I would not be rude. My wife has just died. You must forgive me."

"Oh—" I said, feeling sick for him. "I am *so* sorry."

He stood there biting his lower lip. "It is very difficult," he said. "I cannot resign myself."

He looked straight past me and out through the window. Then he began to cry. "I am utterly unable to resign myself," he said and choked. And then, crying, his head up looking at nothing, carrying himself straight and soldierly, with tears on both his cheeks and biting his lips, he walked past the machines and out the door.

The doctor told me that the major's wife, who was very young and whom he had not married until he was definitely invalided out[5] of the war, had died of pneumonia. She had been sick only a few days. No one expected her to die. The major did not come to the hospital for three days. Then he came at the usual hour, wearing a black band on the sleeve of his uniform. When he came back, there were large framed photographs around the wall, of all sorts of wounds before and after they had been cured by the machines. In front of the machine the major used were three photographs of hands like his that were completely restored. I do not know where the doctor got them. I always understood we were the first to use the machines. The photographs did not make much difference to the major because he only looked out of the window.[6]

Notes

[1] Hemingway is famed for underwriting, for his cryptic, enigmatic style. He rarely elaborates an emotion or situation but leaves the reader with opportunities for reflection, for adding in his own mind what the author implies.

[2] Down with the officers!

[3] Comradeship and self-sacrifice.

[4] Statements telling of achievements.

[5] Removed from active service because of injury or illness.

[6] Hemingway expressed in many stories and several novels the feelings of war-wounded people, many of them disillusioned through loss of hope and faith of any kind and defeated by the disintegration of former values. Typical of the author's ideas about a stoic acceptance of primal emotions and defeats is this product of Hemingway's service on the Italian front. Some critics feel that the story reveals, as clearly and powerfully as anything he ever wrote, Hemingway's preoccupation with the macabre, with suffering, and with death. It is a terse, ironic, and bitter commentary on the aftermath of war.

VANKA

Anton Chekhov

Anton (Pavlovich) Chekhov (1860–1904) was born of peasant parents in southern Russia. He received a medical degree at the University of Moscow in 1884 but soon began to neglect the practice of medicine in order to write. His numerous stories and plays gave him a commanding position in literary Russia. Throughout much of the world today, he is considered a master writer because of his precision as a literary craftsman and the poignant illumination which he gives to such human experiences as loneliness, grief, hunger, and misery.

Nine-year-old Vanka Jukov, who had been apprentice to the shoemaker Aliakhine for three months, did not go to bed the night before Christmas. He waited till the master and mistress and the assistants had gone out to an early church-service, to procure from his employer's cupboard a small phial[1] of ink and a penholder with a rusty nib; then, spreading a crumpled sheet of paper in front of him, began to write.

Before, however, deciding to make the first letter, he looked furtively[2] at the door and at the window, glanced several times at the sombre ikon,[3] on either side of which stretched shelves full of lasts, and heaved a heart-rending sigh. The sheet of paper was spread on a bench, and he himself was on his knees in front of it.

"Dear Grandfather Constantin Makaritch," he wrote, "I am writing you a letter. I wish you a Happy Christmas and all God's holy best. I have no father or mamenka,[4] you are all I have."

Vanka gave a look toward the window in which shone the reflection of his candle and vividly pictured to himself his grandfather, Constantin Makaritch, who was night-watchman at Messrs. Jivarevev. He was a small, lean, unusually lively and active old man of sixty-five, always smiling and blear-eyed. All day he slept in the servants' kitchen or trifled with the cooks. At night, enveloped in an ample sheepskin coat, he strayed round the domain, tapping with his cudgel.[5] Behind him, each hanging its head, walked the old bitch Kashtanka, and Viune, so named because of his black coat and long body, and his resemblance to a loach.[6] Viune was an unusually civil and friendly dog, looking as kindly at a stranger as at his masters, but he was not to be trusted. Beneath his deference and humbleness was hid the most inquisitorial maliciousness.[7] No one better than he knew how to sneak up and take a bite at a leg, to slip into the larder or steal a moujik's[8] chicken. More than once they had nearly broken his hindlegs, twice he had been hung up, every week he was nearly flogged to death, but he recovered from it all.

At this moment, for certain, his

grandfather was standing at the gate, blinking his eyes at the bright red windows of the village church, stamping his feet in their high felt boots, and jesting with the people in the yard; his cudgel would be hanging from his belt, he would be hugging himself with cold, giving a little dry, old man's cough, and at times pinching a servant girl or a cook.

"Won't we take some snuff?" he asks, holding out his snuffbox to the women. The women take a pinch of snuff, and sneeze.

The old man goes into indescribable ecstasies, breaks into loud laughter, and cries:

"Off with it, it will freeze to your nose!"

He gives his snuff also to the dogs. Kashtanka sneezes, twitches her nose, and very offended walks away. Viune deferentially[9] refuses to sniff and wags his tail. It is glorious weather, not a breath of wind, clear, and frosty; it is a dark night, but the whole village, its white roofs, and streaks of smoke from the chimneys, the trees silvered with hoar-frost, and the snowdrifts, you can see it all. The sky scintillates[10] with bright twinkling stars, and the Milky Way stands out so clearly that it looks as if it had been polished and rubbed over with snow for the holidays. . . .

Vanka sighs, dips his pen in the ink, and continues to write:

"Last night I got a thrashing, the patron dragged me by my hair into the yard, belaboured me with a shoemaker's stirrup, because, while I was rocking their brat in its cradle, I unfortunately fell asleep. And during the week, my mistress told me to clean a herring, and I began by its tail, so she took the herring and thrust its phiz[11] into my face. The assistants tease me, send me to the tavern for vodka, make me steal the patron's cucumbers, and the patron beats me with whatever is handy. Food there is none; in the morning it's bread, at dinner 'gruel,' and in the evening again bread; as for tea or sour-cabbage soup, the patrons themselves guzzle that. They make me sleep in the vestibule, and when their brat cries I don't sleep at all but have to rock the cradle. Dear Grandpapa, for Heaven's sake take me away from here, home to our village, I can't bear this any more. . . . I bow to the ground to you, and will pray to God for ever and ever, take me from here or I shall die. . . ."

The corners of Vanka's mouth went down, he rubbed his eyes with his dirty fist, and sobbed.

"I'll grate your tobacco for you," he continued, "I pray to God for you, and if there is anything wrong, then flog me like the gray goat. And if you really think I shan't find work, then I'll ask the manager, for Christ's sake, to let me clean the boots, or I'll go instead of Fedia as underherdsman. Dear Grandpapa, I can't bear this any more, it'll kill me. . . . I wanted to run away to our village, but I have no boots, and I was afraid of the frost. And when I grow up I'll look after you, no one shall harm you, and when you die I'll pray for the repose of your soul, just like I do for mamma Pelagea.

"As for Moscow, it is a large town, there are all gentlemen's houses, lots of horses, no sheep, and the dogs are not vicious. The children don't come round at Christmas with a star, no one is allowed to sing in the choir, and once I saw in a shop window hooks on a line and fishing rods, all for sale, and for every kind of fish, awfully convenient. And there was one hook which would catch a sheatfish weighing a pound. And there are shops with guns, like the master's, and I am sure they must cost 100 roubles each. And in the meat-shops there are woodcocks, partridges, and hares, but who shot them or where they come from the shopman won't say.

"Dear Grandpapa, and when the masters give a Christmas tree, take a golden walnut and hide it in my green box. Ask the young lady, Olga Ignatievna, for it, say it's for Vanka."

Vanka sighed convulsively[12] and again stared at the window. He remembered that his grandfather always went through the forest for the Christmas tree and took his grandson with him. What happy times! The frost crackled, his grandfather crackled, and as they both did, Vanka did the same. Then before cutting down the Christmas tree his grandfather smoked his pipe, took a long pinch of snuff, and made fun of poor frozen little Vanka. . . . The young fir trees, wrapt in hoar-frost, stand motionless and wait; which of them will die? Suddenly a hare springing from somewhere darts over the snowdrift. . . . His grandfather could not help shouting:

"Catch it, catch it, catch it! Ah, short-tailed devil!"

When the tree was down, his grandfather dragged it to the master's house, and there they set about decorating it. The young lady, Olga Ignatievna, Vanka's great friend, busied herself most about it. When little Vanka's mother, Pelagea, was still alive, and was servant-woman in the house, Olga Ignatievna used to stuff him with sugar-candy, and, having nothing to do, taught him to read, write, count up to one hundred, and even to dance the quadrille.[13] When Pelagea died, they placed the orphan Vanka in the kitchen with his grandfather, and from the kitchen he was sent to Moscow, to Aliakhine, the shoemaker.

"Come quick, dear Grandpapa," continued Vanka, "I beseech you for Christ's sake take me from here. Have pity on a poor orphan, for here they all beat me, and I am frightfully hungry, and so bored that I can't tell you, I cry all the time. The other day the patron hit me on the head with a last; I fell to the ground, and only just returned to life. My life is a disaster, worse than any dog's. . . . I send greetings to Aliona, to one-eyed Egor, and the coachman, and don't let anyone have my harmonium.[14] I remain, your grandson, Ivan Jukov, dear Grandpapa, do come."

Vanka folded his sheet of paper in four and put it into an envelope, purchased the night before for a kopeck. He thought a little, dipped the pen into the ink, and wrote the address:

"The village, to my grandfather." He then scratched his head, thought again, and added: "Constantin Makaritch." Pleased at having been able to write without disturbance, he put on his cap, and, omitting his sheepskin coat, ran out in his shirt-sleeves into the street.

The shopman at the poulterer's, from whom he had inquired the night before, had told him that letters were to be put into post-boxes, and from thence they were conveyed over the whole earth in mail troikas[15] by drunken post-boys and to the sound of bells. Vanka ran to the first post-box and slipped his precious letter into the slit.

An hour afterwards, lulled by hope, he was sleeping soundly. In his dreams he saw a stove, by the stove sat his grandfather with his legs dangling down, barefooted, and reading a letter to the cooks. . . . Around the stove walked Viune, wagging his tail. . . .

Notes

1 Small glass container.
2 Slyly, secretly.
3 Picture of a sacred person.
4 Feminine guardian or nurse.
5 Club, thick stick.
6 A slender fish.
7 Prying meanness, spitefulness.
8 Peasant's.
9 Respectfully.
10 Sparkles.
11 Face (a slangy abbreviation of *physiognomy*).
12 Agitatedly; as in a spasm.
13 A square dance for four couples.
14 A small, organ-like keyboard musical instrument.
15 A wagon or carriage drawn by three horses abreast.

A TRIP TO CZARDIS

Edwin Granberry

EDWIN (PHILLIPS) GRANBERRY (1897–) was born in Meridian, Mississippi, and educated at the University of Florida, Columbia University (A.B., 1920), and the 47 Workshop (drama) at Harvard (1922–1924). He taught Romance languages at various colleges and engaged in free-lance newspaper work and creative writing before his appointment in 1933 to the staff of Rollins College, where he is now Irving Bacheller Professor of Creative Writing. Mr. Granberry is the author of several novels, among them *The Ancient Hunger* (1927), *Strangers and Lovers* (1928), and *The Erl King* (1930); he has contributed many articles and stories to various periodicals here and abroad.

It was still dark in the pine woods when the two brothers awoke. But it was plain that day had come, and in a little while there would be no more stars. Day itself would be in the sky and they would be going along the road. Jim waked first, coming quickly out of sleep and sitting up in the bed to take fresh hold of the things in his head, starting them up again out of the corners of his mind where sleep had tucked them. Then he waked Daniel and they sat up together in the bed. Jim put his arm around his young brother, for the night had been dewy and cool with the swamp wind. Daniel shivered a little and whimpered, it being dark in the room and his baby concerns still on him somewhat, making sleep heavy on his mind and slow to give understanding its way.

"Hit's the day, Dan'l. This day that's right here now, we are goen. You'll recollect it all in a minute."

"I recollect. We are goen in the wagon to see papa—"

"Then hush and don't whine."

"I were dreamen, Jim."

"What dreamen did you have?"

"I can't tell. But it were fearful what I dreamt."

"All the way we are goen this time. We won't stop at any places, but we will go all the way to Czardis[1] to see papa. I never see such a place as Czardis."

"I recollect the water tower—"

"Not in your own right, Dan'l. Hit's by my tellen it you see it in your mind."

"And lemonade with ice in it I saw—"

"That too I seen and told to you."

"Then I never see it at all?"

"Hit's me were there, Dan'l. I let you play like, but hits me who went to Czardis. Yet I never till this day told half how much I see. There's sights I never told."

They stopped talking, listening for their mother's stir in the kitchen. But the night stillness was unlifted. Daniel began to shiver again.

"Hit's dark," he said.

"Hit's your eyes stuck," Jim said. "Would you want me to drip a little water on your eyes?"

"Oh!" cried the young one, pressing his face into his brother's side, "don't douse me, Jim, no more. The cold aches me."

The other soothed him, holding him around the body.

"You won't have e're chill or malarie ache to-day, Dan'l. Hit's a fair day—"

"I won't be cold?"

"Hit's a bright day. I hear mournen doves[2] starten a'ready. The sun will bake you warm. . . . Uncle Holly might buy us somethen new to eat in Czardis."

"What would it be?"

"Hit ain't decided yet. . . . He hasn't spoke. Hit might be somethen sweet. Maybe a candy ball fixed on to a rubber string."

"A candy ball!" Daniel showed a stir of happiness. "Oh, Jim!" But it was a deceit of the imagination, making his eyes shine wistfully; the grain of his flesh was against it. He settled into a stillness by himself.

"My stomach would retch it up, Jim. . . . I guess I couldn't eat it."

"You might could keep a little down."

"No . . . I would bring it home and keep it. . . ."

Their mother when they went to bed had laid a clean pair of pants and a waist for each on the chair. Jim crept out of bed and put on his clothes, then aided his brother on with his. They could not hear any noise in the kitchen, but hickory firewood burning in the kitchen stove worked a smell through the house, and in the forest guinea fowls were sailing down from the trees and poking their way along the half-dark ground toward the kitchen steps, making it known the door was open and that within someone was stirring about at the getting of food.

Jim led his brother by the hand down the dark way of yellow-pine stairs that went narrowly and without banisters to the rooms below. The young brother went huddling in his clothes, ague-like,[3] knowing warmth was near, hungering for his place by the stove, to sit in peace on the bricks in the floor by the stove's side and watch the eating, it being his nature to have a sickness against food.

They came in silence to the kitchen, Jim leading and holding his brother by the hand. The floor was lately strewn with fresh bright sand that would sparkle when the daybreak got above the forest, though now it lay dull as hoarfrost and cold to the unshod feet of the brothers. The door to the firebox of the stove was open, and in front of it their mother sat in a chair, speaking low as they entered, muttering under her breath. The two boys went near and stood still, thinking she was blessing the food, there being mush dipped up and steaming in two bowls. And they stood cast down until she lifted her eyes to them and spoke.

"Your clothes on already," she said. "You look right neat." She did not rise, but kept her chair, looking cold and stiff, with the cloth of her black dress sagging between her knees. The sons stood in front of her and she laid her hand on first one head and then the other and spoke a little about the day, charging them to be sober and of few words, as she had raised them.

Jim sat on the bench by the table and began to eat, mixing dark molasses sugar through his bowl of mush. But a nausea began in Daniel's stomach at sight of the sweet and he lagged by the stove, gazing at the food as it passed into his brother's mouth.

Suddenly a shadow filled the back doorway and Holly, their uncle, stood there looking in. He was lean and big and dark from wind and weather, working in the timber as their father had done. He had no wife and children and would roam far off with the timber gangs in the Everglades.[4] This latter year he did not go far but stayed near them. Their mother stopped and looked at the man and he looked at her in silence. Then he looked at Jim and Daniel.

"You're goen to take them, after all?"

She waited a minute, seeming to get the words straight in her mind before bringing them out, making them say what was set there.

"He asked to see them. Nobody but God-Almighty ought to tell a soul hit can or can't have."

Having delivered her mind, she went out into the yard with the man and they spoke more words in an undertone, pausing in their speech.

In the silence of the kitchen, Daniel began to speak out and name what thing among his possessions he would take to Czardis to give his father. But the older boy belittled this and that and everything that was called up, saying one thing was of too little consequence for a man, and that another was of no account because it was food. But when the older boy had abolished the idea and silence had regained, he worked back to the thought, coming to it roundabout and making it new and as his own, letting it be decided that each of them would take their father a pomegranate[5] from the tree in the yard.

They went to the kitchen door. The swamp fog had risen suddenly. They saw their mother standing in the lot while their uncle hitched the horse to the wagon. Leaving the steps, Jim climbed to the first crotch of the pomegranate tree. The reddest fruits were on the top branches. He worked his way up higher. The fog was now curling up out of the swamp, making gray mountains and rivers in the air and strange ghost shapes. Landmarks disappeared in the billows, or half-seen, they bewildered the sight and an eye could so little mark the known or strange that a befuddlement took hold of the mind, like the visitations sailors beheld in the fogs of Okeechobee.[6] Jim could not find the ground. He seemed to have climbed into the mountains. The light was unnatural and dark and the pines were blue and dark over the mountains.

A voice cried out of the fog:

"Are worms gnawen you that you skin up a pomegranate tree at this hour? Don't I feed you enough?"

The boy worked his way down. At the foot of the tree he met his mother. She squatted and put her arm around him, her voice tight and quivering, and he felt tears on her face.

"We ain't come to the shame yet of you and Dan'l hunten your food off trees and grass. People seein' you gnawen on the road will say Jim Cameron's sons are starved, foragen[7] like cattle of the field."

"I were getten the pomegranates for papa," said the boy, resigned to his mother's concern. She stood up when he said this, holding him in front of her skirts. In a while she said:

"I guess we won't take any, Jim. . . . But I'm proud it come to you to take your papa somethin."

And after a silence, the boy said:

"Hit were Dan'l it come to, Mamma."

Then she took his hand, not looking down, and in her throat, as if in her bosom, she repeated:

"Hit were a fine thought and I'm right proud . . . though today we won't take anything. . . ."

"I guess there's better pomegranates in Czardis where we are goen—"

"There's no better pomegranates in Czardis than right here over your head," she said grimly. "If pomegranates were needed, we would take him his own. . . . You are older'n Dan'l, Jim. When we get to the place we are goen, you won't know your papa after so long. He will be pale and he won't be as bright as you recollect. So don't labor him with questions . . . but speak when it behooves[8] you and let him see you are upright."

When the horse was harnessed and all was ready for the departure, the sons were seated on a shallow bed of hay in the back of the wagon and the mother took the driver's seat alone. The uncle had argued for having the top up over the seat, but she refused the shelter, remarking that she had always driven under the sky and would do it still today. He gave in silently and got upon the seat of his own wagon, which took the road first, their wagon following. This was strange and the sons asked:

"Why don't we all ride in Uncle Holly's wagon?"

But their mother made no reply.

For several miles they traveled in silence through their own part of the woods, meeting no one. The boys whispered a little to themselves, but their mother and their uncle sat without speaking, nor did they turn their heads to look back. At last the narrow road they were following left the woods and came out to the highway, and it was seen that other wagons besides their own were going to Czardis. And as they got farther along, they began to meet many other people going to the town, and the boys asked their mother what day it was. It was Wednesday. And then they asked her why so many wagons were going along the road if it wasn't Saturday and a market day. When she told them to be quiet, they settled down to watching the people go by. Some of them were faces that were strange and some were neighbors who lived in other parts of the woods. Some who passed them stared in silence and some went by looking straight to the front. But there were none of them who spoke, for their mother turned her eyes neither right nor left, but drove the horses on like a woman in her sleep. All was silent as the wagons passed, except the squeaking of the wheels and the thud of the horses' hoofs on the dry, packed sand.

At the edge of the town, the crowds increased and their wagon got lost in the press of people. All were moving in one direction.

Finally they were going along by a high brick wall on top of which ran a barbed-wire fence. Farther along the way in the middle of the wall was a tall, stone building with many people in front. There were trees along the outside of the wall and in the branches of one of the trees Daniel saw a man. He was looking over the brick wall down into the courtyard. All the wagons were stopping here and hitching through the grove in front of the building. But their Uncle Holly's wagon and their own drove on, making way slowly as through a crowd at a fair, for under the trees knots of men were gathered, talking in undertones. Daniel pulled at his mother's skirts and whispered:

"What made that man climb up that tree?"

Again she told him to be quiet.

"We're not to talk today," said Jim. "Papa is sick and we're not to make him worse." But his high, thin voice made his mother turn cold. She looked back and saw he had grown pale and still, staring at the iron-barred windows of the building. When he caught her gaze, his chin began to quiver and she turned back front to dodge the knowledge of his eyes.

For the two wagons had stopped now and the uncle gotten down and left them sitting alone while he went to the door of the building and talked with a man standing there. The crowd fell silent, staring at their mother.

"See, Jim, all the men up the trees!" Daniel whispered once more, leaning close in to his brother's side.

"Hush, Dan'l. Be still."

The young boy obeyed this time, falling into a bewildered stare at all the things about him he did not understand, for in all the trees along the brick wall men began to appear perched high in the branches, and on the roof of a building across the way stood other men, all gaping at something in the yard back of the wall.

Their uncle returned and hitched his horse to a ring in one of the trees. Then he hitched their mother's horse and all of them got out and stood on the ground in a huddle. The walls of the building rose before them. Strange faces at the barred windows laughed aloud and called down curses at the men below.

Now they were moving, with a wall of faces on either side of them, their uncle going first, followed by their mother who held to each of them by a hand. They went up the steps of the building. The door opened and their uncle stepped inside. He came back in a moment and all of them went in and followed a man down a corridor and into a bare room with two chairs and a wooden bench. A man in a black robe sat on one of the chairs, and in front of him on the bench, leaning forward looking down between his arms, sat their father. His face was lean and gray, which made him look very tall. But his hair was black, and his eyes were blue and mild and strange as he stood up and held the two sons against his body while he stooped to kiss their mother. The man in black left the room and walked up and down outside in the corridor. A second stranger stood in the doorway with his back to the room. The father picked up one of the sons and then the other in his arms and looked at them and leaned their faces on his own. Then he sat down on the bench and held them against him. Their mother sat down by them and they were all together.

A few low words were spoken and then a silence fell over them all. And in a while the parents spoke a little more and touched one another. But the bare stone floor and the stone walls and the unaccustomed arms of their father hushed the sons with the new and strange. And when the time had passed, the father took his watch from his pocket:

"I'm goen to give you my watch, Jim. You are the oldest. I want you to keep it till you are a grown man. . . . And I want you to always do what mamma tells you. . . . I'm goen to give you the chain, Dan'l. . . ."

The young brother took the chain, slipped out of his father's arms, and went to his mother with it. He spread it out on her knee and began to talk to her in a whisper. She bent over him, and again all of them in the room grew silent.

A sudden sound of marching was heard in the corridor. The man rose up and took his sons in his arms, holding them abruptly. But their uncle, who had been standing with the man in the doorway, came suddenly and took them and went out and down through the big doorway by which they had entered the building. As the doors opened to let them pass, the crowd gathered around the steps pressed forward to look inside. The older boy cringed in his uncle's arms. His uncle turned and stood with his back to the crowd. Their mother came through the doors. The crowd fell back. Again through a passageway of gazing eyes, they reached the wagons. This time they sat on the seat beside their mother.

Leaving their uncle and his wagon behind, they started off on the road that led out of town.

"Is papa coming home with Uncle Holly?" Jim asked in a still voice.

His mother nodded her head.

Reaching the woods once more and the silence he knew, Daniel whispered to his brother:

"We got a watch and chain instead, Jim."

But Jim neither answered nor turned his eyes.

Notes

[1] The setting of this story is rural Florida; Czardis is the fictional name of a town, a seat of county government.

[2] Mourning doves, noted for their sorrowful cooing.

[3] An *ague* is a fit of fever or shaking chills.

[4] A swampy, partly forested region in southern Florida.

[5] An edible fruit with a red rind and acid-tasting flesh.

[6] A large lake in the Everglades.

[7] Foraging (searching, hunting).

[8] When it is necessary or proper.

THE SPOILER

Paul Brodeur

Paul Adrian Brodeur, Jr. (1931–) was born in Boston and attended Phillips Academy, Andover, and Harvard, from which he was graduated in 1953. A staff writer for *The New Yorker* since 1958, he is the author of *The Sick Fox* and *The Stunt Man,* novels, and of a collection of short stories, *Downstream,* published in 1972.

Stephen Drew saw the shaggy-haired skiers when he was riding up the chair lift for his first run of the day. They came hurtling toward him over the lip of a steep face—three of them, strung out across the trail that plunged down the mountain beside the liftline.[1] Hatless, wearing tattered Levis and baggy sweaters, and not deigning to make the slightest speed checks, they came straight on, skiing powerfully and gracelessly, bounding high into the air from the tops of moguls[2] and landing heavily and often wavering off balance until, exploding off other moguls, they seemed miraculously to regain their equilibrium in flight. Stephen turned his attention to one skier who was racing perilously close to the steel towers that supported the chair-lift cable, and saw the wind-burned face of a young man in his early twenties—a blunt, openmouthed face that was surrounded by a thick mane of red hair, which, covering his ears and most of his forehead, was kept out of his eyes only because it was streaming backward in the wake of his tremendous speed. The red-headed skier was past him in an instant, yet Stephen had the sensation that he had not passed beneath him but over him, like an avalanche or a jet plane. Turning in the chair, he watched the youth and his companions disappear over the lip of another face, emerge again as specks far down the mountain, and finally pass from view behind a screen of fir trees.

Stephen saw the shaggy-haired skiers again half an hour later, when he was halfway down the mountain. He had stopped to rest and was looking back to watch an instructor—a model of skiing grace—lead his class of students over a tortuous series of moguls when he heard a joyous shout from far above him and, glancing up the mountain, saw the red-headed skier silhouetted,[3] arms outflung and skis apart, against the blue January sky as he came over the lip of another face. This time, however, the youth caught an edge when he landed and, teetering out of control, plunged into the midst of the skiing class, narrowly missing a girl in yellow stretch pants before he finally righted himself and came to a ragged stop a few yards below Stephen. Now, ignoring his two companions, who, whooping at his plight, swept past and disappeared, the red-headed skier leaned forward, thrust his weight against his poles, which bent in protest, and, shaking his head as if to clear it, spat into the snow between the tips of his skis. An instant later, Stephen's view of him was interrupted as the ski instructor passed between them with a straight downhill plunge and two quick finishing waggles. Placing himself directly in front of the red-headed youth, the instructor also leaned forward on his poles and, in a shrill German accent, began to scream slowly spaced words that seemed to ricochet[4] off the hard-packed snow.

"If . . . I . . . effer . . . shall . . . see . . . such . . . foolishness . . . again . . . you . . . shall . . . be . . . taken . . . from . . . this . . . mount-a-a-ahn!" he shouted in a rising crescendo[5] of outrage. "Haff . . . you . . . a-ahnderstood . . . me?"

For a moment, the two figures remained motionless, bent toward one another like a pair of stags locked in combat; then the shaggy-haired skier lifted his head and looked the ski instructor in the face. For a long time, he simply stared at the instructor without the slightest expression, but just before he pushed off down the mountain he gave a faint grin that Stephen interpreted as a smirk of contempt.

With a surge of energy that seemed to be the residue[6] of anger, the ski instructor began sidestepping briskly up the mountain to rejoin his class. When he drew abreast of Stephen, however, he paused for breath and, in a voice still full of rage, shouted, "They care not for any thing, this kind of people! They haff no idea what means responsibility! If he has fallen, that one, he can only haff badly hurt this girl in my class!"

Stephen nodded in agreement, but made no reply. There was something in the instructor's shrilly enunciated Teutonic anger that seemed improbable and out of place on this tree-covered mountain in Vermont. Besides, Stephen had been watching the shaggy-haired skier, who was plummeting down the mountainside with the same reckless abandon as before, and, remembering that he himself had skied with a certain abandon at the age of twenty, had been thinking with regret that the sensation of such speed was something he would never come close to experiencing again. He had, in fact, been in the process of acknowledging to himself that there were certain things he was past doing, because of fear. Not that he really wanted to ski beyond the brink of control, but to admit that he was past it and afraid to try was something else again, for, at thirty-five, Stephen considered himself a young man whose courage was still intact. Now, resuming his train of thought as the instructor resumed his climb, he realized that he envied the shaggy-haired youth who, envying no one and emulating[7] nothing—not even the grace of ski instructors—skied only against himself, and in so doing conquered fear. Was it just a question of age? Stephen wondered. But once again the voice of the instructor intruded upon his reverie. It was a calm voice now, completely under control, and fading away as he called soothingly back to the students, who trailed him down the mountain.

"So remember, always in our linked turns we lock the knees together, and we dip up . . . and then down . . . and so-o-o-o . . ."

Stephen did not see the shaggy-haired skiers on the slopes again. At three o'clock, he took a final run down the mountain and found his wife, Marilyn, waiting for him outside the base lodge. She was sitting in the afternoon sun, looking very pretty in the new blue-and-white ski outfit he had bought her for the trip, and Stephen paused to admire her. Then, as he bent over to release his safety bindings, he realized that she had not brought the baby with her. "How's little Petey?" he asked.

"I left him with the sitter," Marilyn said proudly, as if she were announcing an achievement. "He's fine."

Stephen kicked his boots free of the bindings. Afterward, he strapped his skis together, placed them on his shoulder, and followed Marilyn through a parking lot to the place where she had left their car.

"Can we ski together tomorrow?" she asked, smiling.

"Of course!" he replied with a laugh. "Isn't that why we came up here—to ski?"

Marilyn nodded, but the smile had left her face. "The girl seems very good," she said somberly.[8] "Her name is Janice Pike. She's got funny bleached hair, but she's intelligent and competent, and Petey took to her right away. I spent the whole morning and most of the afternoon with them, and I've given her careful instructions about everything. I really don't think we have to worry."

"Then we won't worry," Stephen replied lightly. "Does the girl know we'll want her for the next few days?"

"Yes, and she's delighted about that. Evidently she needs the money."

They had reached the car, and after fastening his skis to the roof rack Stephen got inside, opened the door on Marilyn's side, and started up the engine. As they drove through the valley that led south, toward Worthington, Marilyn continued to tell him about the sitter.

"I've given Janice the telephone

number at the base lodge so we could be paged if we were needed," she went on. "She, of course, knows all the doctors in the vicinity. Oh, and she's familiar with the house we're staying in, which makes me especially happy because of the stove and everything. It turns out the caretaker often hires her to clean up the place after weekends."

"I'd say we were lucky," Stephen said, glancing carefully at his wife. She has become more and more like me, he thought. She tries to think of all the awful possibilities.

"One thing worries me, though," Marilyn was saying.

"What's that?"

"Where the house is," she replied. "I mean it's so isolated. Not that I think anything would happen, but what if it did?"

Stephen reached across the seat and touched her arm. "Don't give in to that, baby," he said gently. But as they drove on through the valley, he realized that his words of admonition[9] were a form of self-address. They had lost their first child—a boy of two—in an absurd accident, a year before. Little Peter had been born five months later, at the end of June, and except on rare occasions, when he had been safely tucked into his crib for the night and their neighbor, Mrs. Murphy, could come over to sit for them, they had never left him with anyone. Now, having been lent the use of a small chalet[10] by friends in Boston, they had come skiing with the idea of spelling one another at the task of caring for the baby. (He would ski in the mornings and she in the afternoons—not an ideal solution, perhaps, but all they hoped for.) When they arrived in Worthington, the night before, they telephoned the caretaker, who came to open up the house. The caretaker was friendly and garrulous[11]—a country handyman whose dealings with the winter sporting crowd had coated his native astuteness[12] with a certain veneer of assurance.

"Your wife ski, too?" he asked, glancing at the baby.

"Yes," Stephen answered.

"Then you're goin' to need a sitter, ain't you?"

"Yes," Stephen replied, though he and Marilyn had scarcely bothered to discuss the possibility. "It would be nice if we could ski together," he added, glancing at her.

"I know just the girl," the caretaker said. "She's nineteen and real experienced. Lives in town. Why'nt I have her call you in the morning?"

"Fine," said Stephen. "I'd appreciate that."

After the caretaker left, he turned to Marilyn. "There's no harm in trying her out, is there?" he said.

Now, turning off the highway at a point midway between the mountain and the town, Stephen drove over a dirt road that wound up the side of the valley through thick stands of spruce and pine trees. The road was a washboard affair, bordered by high snowbanks that had been thrown up by plows, and the heavy growth had plunged it into premature shadow. There were half a dozen forks and turnoffs on the way to the house, and realizing for the first time that none of them was marked, Stephen suddenly found himself wondering how the girl could possibly give directions to summon help. He imagined her trying to remember all the twists and turns as precious minutes slipped away. "Don't give in to that," he had told Marilyn, sitting beside him. But he had merely been talking to himself.

The chalet, a prefabricated structure with two sides consisting of panel picture windows, was hidden from the road by a wooded knoll, and was reached by a narrow, rutted driveway that first passed before a similar dwelling, fifty yards away, which was unoccupied. The driveway ended in a cul-de-sac[13] at the second house, where Stephen turned the car around and parked it. When he and Marilyn came through the door, they found the sitter watching television and Petey playing happily on the tile floor at her feet.

Ten minutes later, Stephen set out to drive Janice Pike home. As they descended over the washboard road toward the valley, the girl lit a cigarette, stubbed it out, and immediately lit another. To make conversation, Stephen asked her if she had always lived in Worthington.

Janice Pike shook her head, which tossed the bleached, teased mop of hair that crowned it, and blew out a cloud of smoke. "For a year after high school, I worked over to Brattleboro," she replied. "Waitressing."

"How did you like Brattleboro?"

"I liked it a lot. I have a boy friend there."

"What made you come back?"

"My family," she replied. "They want me to settle down, you know?"

"What about your boy friend?"

"Oh, he drives over to see me weekends. He's a plumber's apprentice and he got himself a car this year."

They had reached the valley highway and were driving past a series of ski lodges, restaurants, and roadhouses. "I suppose there's a lot doing here on weekends," Stephen said.

"Yeah, but we just seem to drive around," replied the girl morosely,[14] and looked out the window. "Saturday night, we were driving around and I never saw so many cars parked out in front of these places," she went on. "I guess people must really be having a swell time in them. I mean little bitsy joints with just a guitar player or something and about twenty cars out front!"

Stephen glanced sidewise at Janice Pike, and decided that her hair was teased into its absurd pile as an antidote[15] to boredom. Now he imagined her having worked over it for hours, only to drive around and look wistfully through the windshield of the apprentice plumber's car at lights in the windows of ski lodges. "You should get your boy friend to take you dancing in some of these places," he said.

"Yeah, but they're supposed to be kind of wild," she replied, with more yearning, however, than disapproval. "I mean a lot of the fellows who come skiing here are real maniacs, you know?"

"No kidding," Stephen said.

"Look, I wasn't going to say anything because your wife seems awful worried about leaving the baby and everything, but a whole carload of guys drove up to the house this afternoon. They sat out front awhile, honking and waving at me. Then they went over to the other house and left some skis and stuff inside and drove away. I'm pretty sure the caretaker doesn't know they're there, and I was a little worried 'cause they looked kind of wild, you know, but maybe they were just out for fun."

"Sure," Stephen said. "Probably a lark of some kind."

"Yeah, well, I kept the door locked anyway."

"That's a good idea," Stephen replied.

They had arrived in Worthington, a village built at the conjunction of two roads that crossed through the mountains, and packed with shabby frame houses. Following the girl's directions, Stephen drove to the lower end of town, where, next to a small stream and the gutted remnants of a factory that had once been used to manufacture wooden boxes, there stood a particularly ramshackle dwelling with a sagging roof, peeling shingles, and a veranda that was evolving into debris. For a moment, Stephen studied the house in silence; then, embarrassed, he took out his wallet and turned to the girl. "How much do we owe you, Janice?" he asked.

"Your wife picked me up at ten o'clock, so that would make about six hours I worked," she replied.

"And what do you charge by the hour?" Stephen asked.

"Fifty cents?"

Stephen looked again at the decrepit house, and winced. "Tell you what, Janice, let's call it eight hours," he said, handing her four one-dollar bills. "I'll come by for you tomorrow morning at nine."

"Oh, lovely!" she cried. "Thank you!" Now, jumping out of the car, she climbed the porch steps and, skirting a large hole where several rotten planks had fallen through, waved at Stephen and went into the house.

"Thank *you!*" Stephen called after her. A child of Appalachia,[16] he thought as he turned the car around and headed back through town. He drove more quickly on the return trip, anxious to take a bath, have a drink, and play with Petey before his bedtime. He was happy with anticipation. For the first time in a year, he sensed that he and Marilyn were on the brink of resuming life. He told himself that it was a good thing they had decided to come skiing, and that they had been able to bring themselves to leave little Petey with the girl. They must not give in to the temptation to overprotect him. Yes, above all, they must not allow his life and theirs to be forever colored by tragedy. Entangled in these thoughts, Stephen was surprised when, fifteen minutes later, he came upon a black Volkswagen sitting in the driveway that led up to the house. The Volkswagen was badly battered at the fenders and wore a bent Florida license plate, and it had been parked carelessly, in such a way that it half blocked the drive. Putting his car into second gear, Stephen drove slowly around it; then, glancing toward the porch of the other house, he saw that there were three young men sitting on it in deck chairs. The young men were drinking beer from cans, and, looking closer, Stephen saw that one of them was, unmistakably, the shaggy, red-headed youth he had seen on the mountain. None of the young men bothered to look at the passing car, but as Stephen drove by, the redhead gave a flip of his wrist that sent his beer can over the porch railing and into a snowbank.

When he drew up before the house of his friends, Stephen parked the car, got out, and stood beside it for several minutes as he tried to decide what the three shaggy-haired skiers were doing in the other chalet. Perhaps the caretaker is allowing them to stay there in return for some chores, he thought. Or perhaps the caretaker is making money on the side with an illicit[17] rental. But what if, as Janice Pike seemed to imply, the young men had simply broken into the place? Stephen thought of them catching sight of Janice's bleached hair through the picture window, and for a moment he toyed with the idea of telephoning the caretaker. Then he decided against it. Their honking at Janice was like their skiing, the parking of their car in the middle of the driveway, and the red-headed youth's disposal of his beer can. It was thoughtless, nothing more—just thoughtlessness. You're getting old, Stephen told himself. What's the point of spoiling other people's fun? But when he went into the house, he did not mention the presence of the shaggy-haired skiers to Marilyn.

In the morning, the sun was shining brilliantly in a cloudless sky. When Stephen left the house to pick up Janice Pike, the black Volkswagen was still parked before the other chalet. It was there when he returned with the girl, half an hour later, so he asked her if it was the same car that had honked at her the day before.

She took a deep drag on her cigarette, and nodded. "Yeah, that's the one," she replied. "I know from the dented fenders. They must be wild drivers, huh?"

Stephen looked quickly at Janice Pike. Had he detected a slight note of admiration in her voice, or was it his imagination? Everything was "wild" to this country girl, or was it simply that, out of sheer boredom, she hoped her life might become so? "Look, Janice," he said. "I don't want to mention anything about this to my wife, but on the other hand I don't want to spend my day worrying, either. So I'll speak frankly to you—O.K.?"

"Sure, but you don't have to worry, Mr. Drew. I'll keep the door locked—you can count on that."

"Fine," Stephen said, and glanced at her hair. "But maybe you'd better stay away from the window as much as possible. I mean, just don't be sitting too conspicuously next to it."

"Oh, sure," the girl replied. "O.K."

"And I'll phone you every couple of hours from the base lodge," Stephen said. "Just to make certain things are all right."

When they went into the house, Marilyn went over a list of things she had made out for Janice to do. "Petey's lunch is on the stove," she said. "You'll just have to heat it up. If he balks at eating the beef mush, dip each spoonful into his banana-dessert mush. It sometimes works. He woke up at seven this morning, which means he'll be ready for his nap any time now. After lunch, of course, he'll take another nap. If it's still sunny when he wakes up from that one, bundle him into his snowsuit and take him outside for some air."

"No," Stephen said quickly. "Don't have him go out today."

"But if it's nice and sunny—"

Stephen shook his head, picked up an armload of jackets, poles, and ski boots, and started out the door. "A day or two won't matter," he said over his shoulder. "And I'll feel better if he stays inside."

When Stephen reached the car, he

put the jackets, poles, and boots into the back and climbed in behind the wheel. He was about to start the engine when he heard the sharp crack of a rifle. The report sounded close by, but in the cold, dazzling brilliance of the morning light he could not be sure how close. Leaving the car door open, he listened intently, heard several more shots, and recognized the explicitly[18] neat sound of a .22-calibre rifle. The shots seemed to be coming from the far side of the next house, but he could detect no movement there. When Marilyn climbed into the car, he started up the engine and drove slowly down the driveway.

"Really, Stephen, you shouldn't interfere that way," Marilyn said. "Why on earth shouldn't the girl take Petey out for some air?"

"There's a reason," Stephen said absently, but they were drawing abreast of the other house, and he was not paying Marilyn any real attention, for at that moment the three young men, led by the shaggy red-headed youth, came around a corner from the back. The redhead was carrying a rifle, which, when he saw the car, he seemed to thrust out of sight between his body and the wall of the house. They must be there illegally, Stephen thought. He wondered if Marilyn had seen the weapon, but a moment later he realized that she had not.

"Goodness!" she exclaimed. "Who are *they*—beatniks?"[19]

Stephen nodded his head, and turned to study the young men as he drove past. Unshaven and bleary-eyed, they seemed to have recently risen after a night of heavy drinking, and now they gave the car bold looks of appraisal that, because of their brazenness,[20] also seemed to be defensive. Looking back, Stephen saw them duck quickly into the house. He was more certain than ever now that they had broken into it, but as he continued down the drive it was the rifle that stayed in his mind. He knew that it was against the law in almost every state to shoot a rifle so close to inhabited places. He wondered if he should not call the police.

"What's the matter?" Marilyn asked.

"Nothing," he told her.

His mind, however, was in ferment. The harsh vibrations of the washboard road that descended into the valley triggered his brain into conjuring up visions of catastrophe. Helplessly, he imagined the young men firing at a beer can, the bullet ricocheting off a rock, piercing the picture window behind which little Petey sat playing, or, perhaps, striking the girl and causing one of her interminable cigarettes to fall, smoldering, upon a scatter rug. . . . "They haff no idea what means responsibility," the outraged ski instructor had said. The sentence repeated itself within him endlessly.

"You're awfully silent," Marilyn remarked when they reached the highway.

"It's nothing," he told her again, and, stepping hard on the accelerator, drove quickly toward the mountain, already planning to telephone Janice Pike the moment they arrived. The miles seemed to pass slowly, however, and soon they found themselves behind a line of cars bearing other skiers to the slopes. When finally they reached the parking lot at the base lodge, he jumped from the car, unstrapped Marilyn's skis, and handed them to her. Then, as he reached inside the car for her boots and poles, he deliberately pushed his own boots out of sight beneath the seat.

"Damn!" he said, straightening up. "I've left my boots behind."

Marilyn made a grimace of sympathy and pain.

"Why don't you take a few runs on the beginner's slope," he told her. "It'll get you in the swing of things. I won't be more than half an hour—forty minutes at the most."

He scarcely waited to hear her assent, but, jumping into the car, started the engine, threw it into first gear, and tore away. There was no traffic on the road leading from the mountain, but the sun, rising higher in the sky, shed a brilliant light that, rebounding from the snow and glinting off the hood of the car, found its way into his eyes. The light—a sharp, metallic intrusion—cut into him, exposing his fear as a surgeon's scalpel lays open tissue to disclose a nerve, and now, as the valley broadened, so did the range of awful possibilities that haunted his mind.

When he swerved into the driveway, twenty minutes later, he jammed the car into second gear, topped the knoll[21] with a roar, and swept past the first chalet and the Volkswagen, which was still parked, half blocking the road, before it. He was squinting through the windshield, hoping to get a glimpse of Janice Pike's massive blond coiffure in the picture window, when, dead ahead, walking toward him down the middle of the drive, he saw the shaggy red-headed youth. Stephen slammed on the brakes and brought the car to an abrupt halt; then, taking a deep breath, he was amazed to find himself filling with a curious kind of relief—the kind of relief that comes when the worst is apparent and no longer in the realm of fantasy—for the shaggy-haired youth, who was standing just ahead of the front bumper and looking at him without expression, was holding a rifle over his shoulder with one hand and the hind legs of a blood-spattered snowshoe hare with the other. Stephen's gaze travelled along the barrel of the rifle that, draped carelessly over the young man's shoulder, was pointing in the direction of the picture window, where he could see Janice Pike, holding little Peter. He got out of the car, walked toward the red-headed youth, and stopped directly in front of him.

"Is the rifle loaded?" he asked. He was looking into the young man's eyes, which were deep blue, and the sound of his voice came back to him as an alien presence—a cold breath that was still as the icicles hanging perilously from the roof of the house.

The shaggy-haired youth made no reply, but gave the snowshoe hare a shake so that—as if gore[22] were in itself sufficient answer—its bloody carcass was swung ever so slightly in Stephen's direction.

"Look where the rifle's pointing," Stephen said. Every instinct in him wanted to make a lunge for it, but fear of causing the weapon to discharge deterred him, and this terrible fear, plus the studied unconcern of the young man's face, unnerved him. He felt his control unravelling like a ball of twine. "Damn you," he said in a hoarse whisper. *"Look where it's pointing!"*

The shaggy-haired youth gave a quick sidewise glance toward the picture window; then he looked at Stephen again and shrugged. "Relax," he said. "The safety's on."

Cursing him, Stephen told him to take the rifle off his shoulder.

For a moment, the shaggy-haired youth looked at Stephen with the same detachment with which he had stared into the face of the angry ski instructor; then, with taunting slowness, he swung the rifle from his shoulder in a lazy arc and rested the tip of the barrel against the top of his shoe. "Man, you've gone and lost your cool," he told Stephen, and calmly pulled the trigger. Afterward, he gave an insolent grin and, to further affirm the fact that the safety was on, allowed the weight of the rifle to be suspended from his forefinger, which was still curled around the trigger.

Stephen looked at the unafraid, contemptuous face before him and, a second later, struck it. The blow—a roundhouse swing—landed just in front of the ear on the sideburn and knocked the shaggy-haired youth into a sitting position in the middle of the driveway. The rifle fell to the ground, and, stooping quickly, Stephen picked it up and pushed the safety button off.

The shaggy-haired youth had not uttered a sound, but when he saw Stephen pick up the rifle and push the safety button off, his mouth fell open, and the look of fear that Stephen hoped to see—desperately *wanted* to see—came over his face and filled his eyes. Sitting there, rubbing the side of his head with one hand and still clutching the bloody hare with the other, he suddenly looked like a small boy about to cry.

"Listen, man," he said in a voice that croaked. "Like we're low on funds, you know, and the rabbit's just for eating."

"Shut up!" Stephen replied. He wanted silence simply because he was trying to figure out what he should do next.

"So maybe it's out of season," the young man went on. "What d'you care? You're not a game warden."

"Shut up!" Stephen said again, but as he looked down at the youth he felt some of the anger and hatred draining out of him.

"Look, the house wasn't even locked! It was just sitting there, like waiting for us, and the rifle was standing in the corner behind the door."

"The rabbit and the house have nothing to do with it," Stephen told him. "It's my *child,* you fool! You were pointing the rifle at my *child!*"

"But nothing *happened!*" said the shaggy-haired youth, shaking his head in puzzlement and protest. "I mean, like, if nothing's happened—"

"Something's going to happen now," Stephen told him quietly. "Here's what's going to happen. You and your friends are going to pack up and be out of here in five minutes. You are only going to have five minutes—d'you understand?—and if you are not, the lot of you, out of here for good in five minutes, I am going to make damn sure you'll be here when the state police arrive. Now get on your feet and get moving."

The shaggy-haired youth did as he was told and, still clutching the snowshoe hare, stumbled off down the driveway to the other house. A moment later, Stephen saw a curtain being parted in the kitchen window and a pair of disembodied[23] faces looking out at him. Suddenly he felt immensely weary. Glancing at his watch, he leaned against the fender of his car and waited.

Five minutes later, the young men had finished packing the Volkswagen. Stephen watched them in silence as, casting nervous glances in his direction like hired men anxious to please, they threw the last of their belongings into the back of the car. He was struck by the idea that they, who had skied without fear, were now dancing to the macabre[24] tune of his own fear, but he derived no satisfaction from it. Presently the red-headed youth came out of the house, closed the door behind him, and, picking up the hare from the porch, walked around the front of the car to the driver's side. At this point, he hesitated, as if debating with himself; then he tossed the hare into some bushes and looked toward Stephen. For several moments, he stood there, gazing at Stephen with profound reproach, as if what had happened between them was caused by a gulf of misunderstanding that was far too deep to ever be bridged. Then, with a sad shake of his head, he got in behind the wheel, started the engine, and drove away.

Leaning against his car, Stephen listened as the Volkswagen growled toward the valley in second gear. He continued listening until the sound of its engine faded into silence; then he turned and walked toward the house where Janice Pike, still holding the baby at the picture window, was looking out at him with horror and awe. He was thinking that he would not return the rifle to the other house until he and Marilyn and little Peter left for good. He was trembling slightly as he reached the door, but he did not know whether it was with the aftermath[25] of rage or with a mixture of relief and regret. He told himself, however, that even now the shaggy-haired skiers were probably heading for some other mountain, where, bounding high into the air with arms outflung and whoops of joy, they would continue to escape from care.

Notes

1 An apparatus for conveying skiers up the side of a slope.
2 Bumps or mounds of hard snow on a ski slope.
3 Outlined.
4 Bounce off, rebound.
5 Increasing loudness, force, and volume.
6 Remainder, that which is left.
7 Imitating, patterning after.
8 Gravely.
9 Advice, counsel.
10 A kind of farmhouse, low and with wide eaves, common in Alpine and other mountainous regions.
11 Talkative.
12 Shrewdness, cunning.
13 Blind alley, a street closed at one end.
14 Sullenly, gloomily.
15 Prevention, counteraction.

16 A mountainous region in the eastern United States, used here as a symbol of poverty and underprivilege.

17 Unlawful, unauthorized.

18 Clearly, unmistakably.

19 A member of the beat generation who rejects or avoids conventional behavior, dress, etc. The term is derived from *beat* and *nik,* a Russian suffix designating an agent or one concerned with something, as in *sputnik.*

20 Shamelessness, impudence.

21 Hill.

22 Clotted blood.

23 Without bodies.

24 Grim, gruesome.

25 Consequence, result.

INFLEXIBLE LOGIC

Russell Maloney

RUSSELL MALONEY (1910–1948) was born in Brookline, Massachusetts, and was graduated from Harvard in 1932. After graduation he began tutoring Harvard undergraduates and sending in jokes and short articles to *The New Yorker*. Editors of the magazine were impressed by his contributions, offered him a job, and he was a staff member, 1934–1945. He turned out prodigious amounts of magazine material under varied pseudonyms. He published only two books before his early death: *It's Still Maloney* (1946) and *Our Own Baedeker* (1947, with Eugene Kinkead).

When the six chimpanzees came into his life, Mr. Bainbridge was thirty-eight years old. He was a bachelor and lived comfortably in a remote part of Connecticut, in a large old house with a carriage drive, a conservatory,[1] a tennis court, and a well-selected library. His income was derived from impeccably[2] situated real estate in New York City, and he spent it soberly, in a manner which could give offense to nobody. Once a year, late in April, his tennis court was resurfaced, and after that anybody in the neighborhood was welcome to use it; his monthly statement from Brentano's[3] seldom ran below seventy-five dollars; every third year, in November, he turned in his old Cadillac coupé for a new one; he ordered his cigars, which were mild and rather moderately priced, in shipments of one thousand, from a tobacconist in Havana; because of the international situation he had canceled arrangements to travel abroad, and after due thought had decided to spend his traveling allowance on wines, which seemed likely to get scarcer and more expensive if the war lasted.[4] On the whole, Mr. Bainbridge's life was deliberately, and not too unsuccessfully, modeled after that of an English country gentleman of the late eighteenth century, a gentleman interested in the arts and in the expansion of science, and so sure of himself that he didn't care if some people thought him eccentric.

Mr. Bainbridge had many friends in New York, and he spent several days of the month in the city, staying at his club and looking around. Sometimes he called up a girl and took her out to a theater and a night club. Sometimes he and a couple of classmates got a little tight and went to a prizefight. Mr. Bainbridge also looked in now and then at some of the conservative art galleries, and liked occasionally to go to a concert. And he liked cocktail parties, too, because of the fine footling[5] conversation and the extraordinary number of pretty girls who had nothing else to do with the rest of their evening. It was at a New York cocktail party, however, that Mr. Bainbridge kept his preliminary appointment with doom. At one of the parties given by Hobie Packard, the stockbroker, he learned about the theory of the six chimpanzees.

It was almost six-forty. The people who had intended to have one drink and go had already gone, and the people who intended to stay were fortifying themselves with slightly dried canapés and talking animatedly. A group of stage and radio people had coagulated[6] in one corner, near Packard's Capehart,[7] and were wrangling about various methods of cheating the Collector of Internal Revenue. In another corner was a group of stockbrokers, talking about the greatest stockbroker of them all, Gauguin.[8] Little Marcia Lupton was sitting with a young man, saying earnestly, "Do you really want to know what my greatest ambition is? I want to be myself," and Mr. Bainbridge smiled gently, thinking of the time Marcia had said that to him. Then he heard the voice of Bernard Weiss, the critic, saying, "Of course he wrote one good novel. It's not surprising. After all, we know that if six chimpanzees were set to work pounding six typewriters at random, they would, in a million years, write all the books in the British Museum."

Mr. Bainbridge drifted over to Weiss and was introduced to Weiss's companion, a Mr. Noble. "What's this about a million chimpanzees, Weiss?" he asked.

"Six chimpanzees," Mr. Weiss said. "It's an old cliché[9] of the mathematicians. I thought everybody was told about it in school. Law of averages, you know, or maybe it's permutation and combination.[10] The six chimps, just pounding away at the typewriter keys, would be bound to copy out all the books ever written by man. There are only so many possible combinations of letters and numerals, and they'd produce all of them—see? Of course they'd also turn out a mountain of gibberish, but they'd work the books in, too. All the books in the British Museum."

Mr. Bainbridge was delighted; this was the sort of talk he liked to hear when he came to New York. "Well, but look here," he said, just to keep up his part in the foolish conversation, "what if one of the chimpanzees finally did duplicate a book, right down to the last period, but left that off? Would that count?"

"I suppose not. Probably the chimpanzee would get around to doing the book again, and put the period in."

"What nonsense!" Mr. Noble cried.

"It may be nonsense, but Sir James Jeans believes it," Mr. Weiss said, huffily. "Jeans or Lancelot Hogben.[11] I know I ran across it quite recently."

Mr. Bainbridge was impressed. He read quite a bit of popular science, and both Jeans and Hogben were in his library. "Is that so?" he murmured, no longer feeling frivolous.[12] "Wonder if it has ever actually been tried? I mean, has anybody ever put six chimpanzees in a room with six typewriters and a lot of paper?"

Mr. Weiss glanced at Mr. Bainbridge's empty cocktail glass and said dryly, "Probably not."

Nine weeks later, on a winter evening, Mr. Bainbridge was sitting in his study with his friend James Mallard, an assistant professor of mathematics at New Haven.[13] He was plainly nervous as he poured himself a drink and said, "Mallard, I've asked you to come here—brandy? cigar?—for a particular reason. You remember that I wrote you some time ago, asking your opinion of . . . of a certain mathematical hypothesis, or supposition."

"Yes," Professor Mallard said, briskly. "I remember perfectly. About the six chimpanzees and the British Museum. And I told you it was a perfectly sound popularization of a principle known to every schoolboy who had studied the science of probabilities."

"Precisely," Mr. Bainbridge said. "Well, Mallard, I made up my mind. . . . It was not difficult for me, because I have, in spite of that fellow in the White House,[14] been able to give something every year to the Museum of Natural History, and they were naturally glad to oblige me. . . . And after all, the only contribution a layman can make to the process of science is to assist with the drudgery of experiment. . . . In short, I—"

"I suppose you're trying to tell me that you have produced six chimpanzees and set them to work at typewriters in order to see whether they will eventually write all the books in the British Museum. Is that it?"

"Yes, that's it," Mr. Bainbridge said. "What a mind you have, Mallard. Six fine young males, in perfect condition. I had a—I suppose you'd call it a dormitory—built out in back of the stable. The typewriters are in the conservatory. It's light and airy in there, and I moved most of the plants out. Mr. North, the man who owns the circus, very obligingly let me engage one of his best animal men. Really, it was no trouble at all."

Professor Mallard smiled indulgently.[15] "After all, such a thing is not unheard of," he said. "I seem to remember that a man at some university put his graduate students to work flipping coins, to see if heads and tails came up an equal number of times. Of course they did."

Mr. Bainbridge looked at his friend very queerly. "Then you believe that any such principle of the science of probabilities will stand up under an actual test?"

"Certainly."

"You had better see for yourself." Mr. Bainbridge led Professor Mallard downstairs, along a corridor, through a disused music room, and into a large conservatory. The middle of the floor had been cleared of plants and was occupied by a row of six typewriter tables, each one supporting a hooded machine. At the left of each typewriter was a neat stack of yellow copy paper. Empty wastebaskets were under each table. The chairs were the unpadded, spring-backed kind favored by experienced stenographers. A large bunch of ripe bananas was hanging in one corner, and in another stood a Great Bear[16] water-cooler and a rack of Lily cups. Six piles of typescript, each about a foot high, were ranged along the wall on an improvised[17] shelf. Mr. Bainbridge picked up one of the piles, which he could just conveniently lift, and set it on a table before Professor Mallard. "The output to date of Chimpanzee A, known as Bill," he said simply.

"'*Oliver Twist*, by Charles Dickens,'" Professor Mallard read out. He read the first and second pages of the manuscript, then feverishly[18] leafed through to the end. "You mean to tell me," he said, "that this chimpanzee has written—"

"Word for word and comma for comma," said Mr. Bainbridge. "Young, my butler, and I took turns comparing it with the edition I own. Having finished *Oliver Twist*, Bill is, as you see, starting the sociological works of Vilfredo Pareto, in Italian. At the rate he has been going, it should keep him busy for the rest of the month."

"And all the chimpanzees—" Professor Mallard was pale, and enunciated[19] with difficulty—"they aren't all—"

"Oh, yes, all writing books which I have every reason to believe are in the British Museum. The prose of John Donne, some Anatole France, Conan Doyle, Galen, the collected plays of Somerset Maugham, Marcel Proust, the memoirs of the late Marie of Rumania, and a monograph by a Dr. Wiley on the marsh grasses of Maine and Massachusetts. I can sum it up for you, Mallard, by telling you that since I started this experiment, four weeks and some days ago, none of the chimpanzees has spoiled a single sheet of paper."

Professor Mallard straightened up, passed his handkerchief across his brow, and took a deep breath. "I apologize for my weakness," he said. "It was simply the sudden shock. No, looking at the thing scientifically—and I hope I am at least as capable of that as the next man—there is nothing marvelous about the situation. These chimpanzees, or a succession of similar teams of chimpanzees, would in a million years write all the books in the British Museum. I told you some time ago that I believed that statement. Why should my belief be altered by the fact that they produced some of the books at the very outset? After all, I should not be very much surprised if I tossed a coin a hundred times and it came up heads every time. I know that if I kept at it long enough, the ratio would reduce itself to an exact fifty percent. Rest assured, these chimpanzees will begin to compose gibberish quite soon. It is bound to happen. Science tells us so. Meanwhile, I advise you to keep this experiment secret. Uninformed people might create a sensation if they knew."

"I will, indeed," Mr. Bainbridge said. "And I'm very grateful for your rational analysis.[20] It reassures me. And now, before you go, you must hear the new Schnabel[21] records that arrived today."

During the succeeding three months, Professor Mallard got into the habit of telephoning Mr. Bainbridge every Friday afternoon at five-thirty, immediately after leaving his seminar room. The Professor would say, "Well?" and Mr. Bainbridge would reply, "They're still at it, Mallard. Haven't spoiled a sheet of paper yet." If Mr. Bainbridge had to go out on Friday afternoon he would leave a written message with his butler, who would read it to Professor Mallard: "Mr. Bainbridge says we now have Trevelyan's *Life of Macaulay,* the *Confessions of St. Augustine, Vanity Fair,* part of Irving's *Life of George Washington,* the *Book of the Dead,* and some speeches delivered in Parliament in opposition to the Corn Laws,[22] sir." Professor Mallard would reply, with a hint of a snarl in his voice, "Tell him to remember what I predicted," and hang up with a clash.

The eleventh Friday that Professor Mallard telephoned, Mr. Bainbridge said, "No change. I have had to store the bulk of the manuscript in the cellar. I would have burned it, except that it probably has some scientific value."

"How dare you talk of scientific value?" The voice from New Haven roared faintly in the receiver. "Scientific value! You—you—chimpanzee!" There were further inarticulate[23] sputterings, and Mr. Bainbridge hung up with a disturbed expression. "I am afraid Mallard is overtaxing himself," he murmured.

Next day, however, he was pleasantly surprised. He was leafing through a manuscript that had been completed the previous day by Chimpanzee D, Corky. It was the complete diary of Samuel Pepys, and Mr. Bainbridge was chuckling over the naughty passages, which were omitted in his own edition, when Professor Mallard was shown into the room. "I have come to apologize for my outrageous conduct on the telephone yesterday," the Professor said.

"Please don't think of it any more. I know you have many things on your mind," Mr. Bainbridge said. "Would you like a drink?"

"A large whisky, straight, please," Professor Mallard said. "I got rather cold driving down. No change, I presume?"

"No, none. Chimpanzee F, Dinty, is just finishing John Florio's translation of Montaigne's essays, but there is no other news of interest."

Professor Mallard squared his shoulders and tossed off his drink in one astonishing gulp. "I should like to see them at work," he said. "Would I disturb them, do you think?"

"Not at all. As a matter of fact, I usually look in on them around this time of day. Dinty may have finished his Montaigne by now, and it is always interesting to see them start a new work. I would have thought that they would continue on the same sheet of paper, but they don't, you know. Always a fresh sheet, and the title in capitals."

Professor Mallard, without apology, poured another drink and slugged it down. "Lead on," he said.

It was dusk in the conservatory, and the chimpanzees were typing by the light of student lamps clamped to their desks. The keeper lounged in a corner, eating a banana and reading *Billboard.*[24] "You might as well take an hour or so off," Mr. Bainbridge said. The man left.

Professor Mallard, who had not taken off his overcoat, stood with his hands in his pockets, looking at the busy chimpanzees, "I wonder if you know, Bainbridge, that the science of probabilities takes everything into account," he said, in a queer, tight voice. "It is certainly almost beyond the bounds of credibility[25] that these chimpanzees should write books without a single error, but that abnormality[26] may be corrected by—*these!*" He took his hands from his pockets, and each one held a .38 revolver. "Stand back out of harm's way!" he shouted.

"Mallard! Stop it!" The revolvers barked, first the right hand, then the left, then the right. Two chimpanzees fell, and a third reeled into a corner. Mr. Bainbridge seized his friend's arm and wrested one of the weapons from him.

"Now I am armed, too, Mallard, and I advise you to stop!" he cried. Professor Mallard's answer was to draw a bead on Chimpanzee E and shoot him dead. Mr. Bainbridge made a rush, and Professor Mallard fired at him. Mr. Bainbridge, in his quick death agony, tightened his finger on the trigger of his revolver. It went off, and Professor Mallard went down. On his hands and knees he fired at the two chimpanzees which were still unhurt, and then collapsed.

There was nobody to hear his last words. "The human equation . . . always the enemy of science . . ." he panted. "This time . . . vice versa . . . I, a mere mortal, . . . savior of science . . . deserve a Nobel . . ."

When the old butler came running into the conservatory to investigate the noises, his eyes were met by a truly appalling[27] sight. The student lamps were shattered, but a newly risen moon shone in through the conservatory windows on the corpses of the two gentlemen, each clutching a smoking revolver. Five of the chimpanzees were dead. The sixth was Chimpanzee F. His right arm disabled, obviously bleeding to death, he was slumped before his typewriter. Painfully, with his left hand, he took from the machine the completed last page of Florio's Montaigne. Groping for a fresh sheet, he inserted it, and typed with one finger, *"Uncle Tom's Cabin,* by Harriet Beecher Stowe. Chapte. . . ." Then he, too, was dead.

Notes

1 Greenhouse.
2 Perfectly.
3 A large bookstore in New York City.
4 World War II (1939–1945). This story, published in 1940, would now require a different reference to Havana, Cuba, as a source of cigars for American smokers.
5 Silly, foolish.
6 Thickened, clustered.
7 The name of an expensive line of musical and recording instruments.
8 A French painter (1848–1903), whose paintings now bring large prices.
9 Trite saying.
10 Steps in mathematics involving change in the order of elements in a series.

11 English scientists.
12 Light, trivial.
13 Several institutions of higher learning are situated in New Haven, Connecticut; the reference here is probably to the best-known of these, Yale University.
14 Franklin D. Roosevelt, President of the United States, 1933–1945.
15 Permissively, tolerantly.
16 Brand name of bottled drinking water.
17 Hastily erected; carelessly put together.
18 Excitedly.
19 Pronounced (spoke).
20 Sensible thinking.
21 Austrian pianist (1882–1951).
22 British laws regulating the trade of grain, the last of which was repealed in 1846.
23 Unclear, indistinct.
24 A magazine dealing with theatrical affairs.
25 Capability of belief; trustworthiness.
26 Irregularity.
27 Horrifying, dismaying.

CHICKEN ITZA

Robert F. Young

ROBERT F. YOUNG (1915–) was born in Silver Creek, New York, and attended school there. He has been writing short stories, largely science fiction, for many years. Among collections of his work are *The Worlds of Robert F. Young* (1965) and *A Glass of Stars* (1968).

It having been established that the quickest way to civilize a savage is by providing him with a civilized environment and bestowing upon him the blessings of technology,[1] the International Space Agency, when it came time to civilize the Siw of Sirius V, built a modern city for them in the big green plain where for centuries they had raised children, crops and chickens, and stocked it with all the technological goodies known to man.[2] It also having been established that civilized environments require efficient supervision, constant care and mechanical savoir-faire,[3] ISA recruited a civilian cadre[4] of experts to staff and maintain the city and to educate and train the Siw. Then, to teach the Siw technological self-reliance and to find out whether they were worth all the trouble, ISA put the city on an incommunicado[5] status and left it to shift for itself for five years. When the trial period ended, they sent an inspector to look things over and report back. The inspector's name was G. A. Firby, and technology was his tutor, his mistress and his god. He might question his tutor and have misgivings about his mistress, but he never doubted his god.

* * *

It was the first time Firby had seen the city, and his reaction upon being greeted by its mayor, who as head of the cadre had been alerted to his coming, was one of cautious surprise. The elevated apron against which he had berthed his one-man spaceship was near enough to the outskirts to afford him an excellent view of the south side. However, it wasn't the pleasant and practical layout of the buildings, streets and parking lots that occasioned his surprise, but their air of brand-newness. The buildings looked as though they had been built yesterday, the streets as though they had been laid that very morning and the parking lots as though they had been black-topped less than an hour ago. Moreover, the electric runabouts, both those cruising the streets and those parked in the lots, gave the impression they had just rolled off the assembly line.

"Sort of takes your breath away, doesn't it?" Mayor Henry Kobecker said. Despite the jaunty white feather he wore in his hat, he seemed nervous and ill at ease. His instructions were to conduct the tour without fanfare; he gave the impression that he didn't want to conduct it at all.

"It takes more than a view of a few housetops to take *my* breath away," Firby said.

"Quite so," the mayor agreed. "Quite so. Will you come this way, Mr. Firby?"

Firby accompanied his host down a ramp to where the latter's runabout and Siw chauffeur were waiting. He had no qualms[6] about leaving his ship unguarded. It was equipped with a special antiburglar device that made mayhem[7] of would-be intruders and sounded an alarm that was audible for a radius of ten miles.

The chauffeur's skin was the hue of varnished mahogany. After seating his two passengers in the rear of the runabout, he withdrew a handful of yellow pellets from a pocket in his mauve uniform and scattered them over the hood. Then he got behind the steering wheel and turned on the motor.

"What was that he threw on the hood?" Firby asked.

"Native corn," Mayor Kobecker replied. "According to Siw superstition, it brings good luck."

Firby gave his host a long look but made no comment.

The chauffeur rolled back the roof. "Which where, Mayhar?"

"I think we'll start with the Administration Building, Albert." The mayor faced Firby. "Is that agreeable with you, sir?"

Firby did not answer. His eyes had focused of their own accord on a distant high-rise apartment building that had just caught the rays of the morning sun. He had eyes like a hawk, and if there'd been a single crack in the synthibrick façade, a single sag in one of the balconies or a single pane missing from one of the windows, he would have seen it.

The tour began. Firby's eyes grew gradually larger. Broad avenues, lined with immaculate storefronts and fretted[8] with crystalline walkways, appeared. None of the walkways was closed for repairs, none of the storefronts needed refurbishing and not once did the wheels of the runabout encounter a chuckhole.

There were civilized Siw everywhere—riding in other runabouts, walking the walkways, coming out of shopping centers laden with packages. But what made Firby sit up and take notice had nothing to do with their numbers nor their apparent prosperity—nor even with the white feathers they wore in their hats. What struck him were their happy faces and carefree gaits.

The city dwellers he was familiar with had haunted faces and walked as though someone were chasing them.

"This," said Mayor Kobecker presently, "is the Administration Building."

Firby saw that Albert had parked the runabout in the morning shadow of a large dignified edifice. He accompanied the mayor inside, where he was conducted through room after room lined with busy computers, every one of which looked as though it had been delivered fresh from the factory that very morning. All of the programmers were Siw and all of them seemed happy in their civilized habiliments[9] and environment.

The mayor's office was in the center of the building. Four color-3V screens inset in the walls functioned as windows. In the center of the room stood the mayor's desk. On it was a vase filled with white flowers. Firby, a nature lover at heart, went over and smelled them, only to discover that they were chicken feathers.

Straightening, he gave the mayor another long look. The mayor shifted his weight from his left foot to his right, fiddled with his tie but offered no explanation.

Next, while the mayor was outlining how City Hall administered to the city, Firby inspected the color-3V screens. At first he thought they were malfunctioning.[10] This was because he was accustomed to color-3V screens that depicted people with blue faces and green teeth. The people in these screens, albeit[11] they had mahogany-hued faces and even though they were too far away for him to see their teeth, looked real.

For some reason, this annoyed him.

In swift succession, he inspected the Power Plant, the Sewage Disposal Plant, the Visiphone Building, the Department of Sanitation Shed and the Water Works. In not a single instance did he find a machine or a piece of equipment that needed repair.

Somehow he had the feeling that a vital ingredient was missing in each of the places he'd inspected, but it wasn't until Mayor Kobecker was wining and dining him in Siw City's most elite eatery that he realized what it was. Momentarily, he was stunned. Then, recovering himself, he said, "Why is it, Mayor, that I haven't seen a single mechanic, repairman or maintenance man since I've been here?"

"I'm—I'm afraid we have no need for them anymore," Mayor Kobecker said.

"Preposterous! For your city to be in the condition it's in, they must be working twenty-four hours a day. Where are they?"

"Some of them have gone into other trades. A few of them have taken up raising chickens. A——"

"Raising chickens!"

"Yes, sir. When our machines stopped breaking down and our appliances stopped malfunctioning and our streets and buildings no longer needed repairing, they had to do something, so——"

"All machines break down! All appliances malfunction! All streets and buildings need repairs!"

"Ours don't."

Firby looked at him. If he hadn't known better, he could have sworn that the mayor meant what he was saying.

He thought for a while. Whatever the reason behind it, there was no questioning the technological perfection he had seen thus far. But for all he knew, it might be a carefully contrived mask hiding the façade of a city-sized Penn Central railroad station. Streets, buildings, runabouts, color-3V sets, utilities—these were not reliable criteria.[12] There was only one foolproof way of taking a city's pulse and getting an accurate reading: by inspecting its major industries. Siw City had only one.

"Take me to Synthinc," Firby said.

* * *

After reseating his two passengers, Albert threw a second handful of corn over the runabout's hood before he got back behind the wheel. Firby ground his teeth. "Can't you stop him from doing that, Mayor?"

"I—I don't think it would be advisable, sir. We haven't had a traffic accident in years."

"Are you implying that *everybody* throws corn on their hood?"

"I'm—I'm afraid so."

For the first time, Firby realized that the feather in the mayor's hat was a chicken feather.

The runabout rolled smoothly past parks like Easter baskets, schools like birthday cakes and hospitals like blocks of spun sugar. From the front, Synthinc looked like a big brick of Neapolitan ice cream. Centered above the entrance were the letters S-Y-N-T-H-I-N-C. Just beneath them were two crossed chicken feathers molded in bronze.

Firby followed the mayor into the building.

A balding man advanced to meet them. The mayor introduced him as Fyodor Dubchek, the president and general manager. "I'll be delighted to show you around, Mr. Firby," Dubchek said.

"Just take me to the machines."

There were hundreds of them—thousands. All of them were set up for the various operations involved in turning a native plant called puwuwun into commercial synthifabric, and each was tended by a Siw.

Firby walked up and down the aisles, listening in vain for the rumble of a bad bearing or the telltale knocking of a worn shaft. Rounding a corner, he saw a Siw wearing striped mechanic's coveralls and carrying what appeared to be a large oilcan passing from machine to machine and depositing a few drops of oil on each. But Firby's elation was short-lived, for when the Siw came closer, he saw that what he'd thought was an oilcan was in reality a water sprinkler and that what he'd taken for oil was water.

For a moment, the enormity of the sacrilege[13] was too much for him to cope with. "Water," he babbled. "He's oiling the machines with water."

"Not *ordinary* water," said Dubchek, who with the mayor was standing just behind him. "Rain water."

"*Rain* water!"

"Not *ordinary* rain water, Mr. Firby," Mayor Kobecker said. "*Sacred* rain water. Sprinkling it on things is a Siw ritual[14] designed to ward off trouble."

"On the same order as scattering corn, no doubt," Firby said scathingly.

The mayor flinched slightly but held his ground. "Yes, sir."

"And using chicken feathers for talismans."[15]

The mayor nodded. "They're Siw stratagems—all of them. And they can be used both ways. The point is, they work. At first we were reluctant to permit such practices, but after we relented, our breakdown rate was cut in half, our——"

"Listen," Firby interrupted. "I know as well as anyone that keeping a city in shape is a never-ending problem. But you're not going to tell me that you solved it by allowing the people you were supposed to civilize to revert to such superstitious foolishness as scattering corn, sprinkling rain water and wearing chicken feathers! There's another reason why your roofs don't cave in, why your streets don't develop chuckholes, why your machines don't break down. There *has* to be!"

"As a matter of fact," Mayor Kobecker admitted with an air of resignation, "there is."

"Aha!—I knew science was lurking behind the scenes somewhere!"

"Well, not science exactly. But we do have a sort of—ah—supervising engineer."

"You do? Then why haven't I been introduced to him? Take me to him at once!"

"I'd—I'd rather not, Mr. Firby. I don't think you'll like him."

"Nonsense! Of course I'll like him. I've never wanted to meet anybody so much in all my life."

The mayor sighed. "All right, Mr. Firby. Since you insist."

Dubchek gasped. "But Henry, you can't——"

"I have no alternative, Fyodor. Come, Mr. Firby, I'll conduct you to his headquarters."

* * *

Reseated in the runabout and bound for the headquarters of the supervising engineer, Firby voiced his credo:[16] "It may well be doubted," said he, "whether technological ingenuity can give birth to a dilemma that technological ingenuity may not, by proper application, resolve. I say this, Mayor, in face of the glaring fact that our cities back on Earth leave much to be desired. Their tube trains run late, their walkways keep stalling, their visiphone service is a laugh, half the time they don't have electricity and their streets have as many chuckholes as the moon has craters. But I have always maintained that eventually our technology will find a way to avert mechanical breakdowns and minimize deterioration, that a roseate[17] day will dawn when the petty vexations that plague us from morning till night will be no more. Apparently, that day has already dawned for Siw City, Mayor, and I congratulate you. Maybe your supervising engineer can perform a similar miracle for us. Who is he, by the way? I knew ISA left some good men up here, but I had no idea any of them was *that* good."

The mayor didn't answer and Firby didn't press the question. He'd find out for himself who the supervising engineer was.

Presently, Albert brought the runabout to a halt in front of a one-story cement-block structure. A purple-and-green blanket functioned as a front door and there were no windows. Firby frowned but said nothing. The mayor held the blanket aside and followed Firby. The interior consisted of a single barnlike room. In the center of the floor stood a large block of discolored concrete. Flickering radiance came from a source somewhere behind it but provided little in the way of actual illumination. Hanging from rafters were miscellaneous articles of various shapes and sizes, none of which Firby could positively identify but one of which he could have sworn was a bundle of chicken feathers.

It doesn't mean a thing, he told himself. It doesn't mean a thing. Aloud, he said, as calmly as he could, "Well, where is this supervising engineer of yours, Mayor?"

"Right over here."

Mayor Kobecker led the way around the discolored concrete block, and presently Firby saw that the room contained a second curiosity—a pedestal. Upon it, flanked by two lighted tapers, stood a small doll. It had been carved out of mahoganylike wood, had agates for eyes, chicken down for hair, tiny pebbles for teeth, and was clad in striped mechanic's coveralls. Protruding from the center of its small forehead was the head of a nail.

"The coveralls were my idea," Mayor Kobecker said. "Rather appropriate, don't you think?"

"A fetish!"[18] Firby exploded. "A goddamn fetish!"

"He doesn't ask for much in the way of sacrifices. A pullet or two now and then. Once in a while, a goat. Sometimes a sheep. He's really quite reasonable when you consider what the union scale is these days. . . . Well, what else could we do, Mr. Firby? Our buildings were falling apart, our runabouts wouldn't run, our machines kept breaking down faster than we could fix them, our canned 3V programs had defective sound tracks, most of the sets themselves wouldn't work. We couldn't ask the personnel of the supply ships for help—we were forbidden even to talk to them while the trial period was in effect. We *had* to turn to the Siw. And, as things turned out, it was the wisest move we could have made. Civilized men have built things to fall to pieces for so long that they've now forgotten how to build them to stay together. The whole thing has gotten out of hand, as you know yourself. Ordinary measures of coping with the problem just aren't effective anymore."

"I don't believe it!" Firby shouted. "I don't believe it!"

"Shhh!—you'll offend him, sir. Please be careful. You must remember that the homunculus[19] is merely his focal point. Actually, he's everywhere. There's no end to the things he can make go wrong for you if you make him mad."

"I don't believe it!" Firby screamed. "I don't believe it!"

* * *

He still didn't believe it when the drive malfunctioned during blast-off and his ship nearly nose-dived into a mountain. He still didn't believe it when the air conditioner went out of whack during deorbiting and the interior temperature climbed to a blistering 110 degrees Fahrenheit. He still didn't believe it when the automatic pilot lost its bearings and took him 10,000 miles off course. When he finally got back to Earth, demoralized, dehydrated and half dead, the port mechanics found water in the fuel, corn in the air conditioner and chicken feathers in the automatic pilot.

Then he believed it.

Notes

1 The industrial arts, engineering and applied science.

2 It should be kept in mind that this somewhat tongue-in-cheek "spoof" of a story presumably derives its title from Chichén Itzá, the name of an ancient Mayan city that flourished more than a thousand years ago. Mayan civilization—that of American Indians in Yucatan, Mexico, Guatemala, and Honduras—was the most highly developed of all pre-Columbian (Christopher Columbus) societies. Among outstanding achievements of this civilization were architecture, an accurate calendar, knowledge of mathematics, and rich decoration of fabrics and stone.

3 Knowledge of what to do.

4 Group, unit.

5 Isolated, not to be communicated with.

6 Fears, uneasy feelings.

7 Crippling, mutilation, destruction.

8 Ornamented, decorated.

9 Furnishings, surroundings; dress.

10 Not performing properly.

11 Although.

12 Standards of judgment.

13 The size of the offense.

14 Custom, procedure.

15 Charms, lucky pieces.

16 Belief, creed.

17 Optimistic, happy.

18 An object housing a powerful spirit and requiring respect, awe, or reverence.

19 Midget; miniature body.

THE MOTH AND THE STAR

James Thurber

James Thurber (1894–1961) was born in Columbus, Ohio, and attended Ohio State University. He spent two years in diplomatic service in France, was a former staff member of *The New York Post,* and from 1926 until shortly before his death was a frequent contributor to *The New Yorker*. He wrote, among other books, *Is Sex Necessary?* (1929 and 1950, with E. B. White); *The Middle-Aged Man on the Flying Trapeze* (1935); *Let Your Mind Alone* (1937); *The Last Flower* (1939); *The Male Animal* (1940, a play, with Elliott Nugent); *Men, Women, and Dogs* (1943); *The Thurber Carnival*

(1945); *The Thirteen Clocks* (1950); *The Years with Ross* (1959); and *Credos and Curios* (1962). He is best known for keenly nonsensical and absurd essays and sketches which are often accompanied by his own thin-line drawings; their amused detachment and their sense of frustration combine to make them significant examples of contemporary American humor and satire.

A young and impressionable moth once set his heart on a certain star. He told his mother about this and she counselled him to set his heart on a bridge lamp instead. "Stars aren't the thing to hang around," she said; "lamps are the thing to hang around." "You get somewhere that way," said the moth's father. "You don't get anywhere chasing stars." But the moth would not heed the words of either parent. Every evening at dusk when the star came out he would start flying toward it and every morning at dawn he would crawl back home worn out with his vain endeavor. One day his father said to him, "You haven't burned a wing in months, boy, and it looks to me as if you were never going to. All your brothers have been badly burned flying around street lamps and all your sisters have been terribly singed flying around house lamps. Come on, now, get out of here and get yourself scorched! A big strapping moth like you without a mark on him!"

The moth left his father's house, but he would not fly around street lamps and he would not fly around house lamps. He went right on trying to reach the star, which was four and one-third light years, or twenty-five trillion miles, away. The moth thought it was just caught in the top branches of an elm. He never did reach the star, but he went right on trying, night after night, and when he was a very, very old moth he began to think that he really had reached the star and he went around saying so. This gave him a deep and lasting pleasure, and he lived to a great old age. His parents and his brothers and his sisters had all been burned to death when they were quite young.

Moral: Who flies afar from the sphere of our sorrow is here today and here tomorrow.

THE STORY OF RUTH

From the Bible[1]

The Bible has been, and still is, the most influential collection of literature in the world. For many centuries, it has shed a light in which the imaginations of countless men have sought inspiration, security, and guidance.

The word *Bible* comes from Greek *biblion,* which in its plural form (*biblia*) means "papyrus scrolls" (the customary book form of antiquity) or "little books." Thus, the

Bible, although called "the Book of Books," is not really a book at all but a library, a collection of little books of many kinds. It was written over a period of time extending from about 1200 B.C. to A.D. 150. Its various parts were set down in three languages (Hebrew, Aramaic, and Greek) in several regions adjoining the eastern shores of the Mediterranean Sea. Its authors were prophets, story tellers, philosophers, poets, teachers, and historians, many of whose names are unknown. It may be called a library of Hebrew literature that, in its slow production over many centuries, is actually an anthology or even a survey.

The nucleus of the Bible, the Old Testament, was formed by a collection of sacred writings to which ancient Jews appealed as the supreme authority in all moral and religious matters. The Hebrew Scripture forms a record of the life and spiritual growth of a small but influential people, recounted in language that is full of contrasting color and vitality. In the thirty-nine books that make up the Old Testament appear thousands of men and women who are weak and strong, noble and cruel, saintly and wicked. This nucleus of the Bible contains virtually every type of literature conceivable: prosy genealogies, songs, folk tales, legends, odes, laments, hymns, dramatic monologues, history, sermons, essays, myths, biographies, philosophy, and letters. It contains accounts of tribal customs and soaring visions, records of laws, and nuggets of universal wisdom. In short, the Old Testament is an absorbing recital of how a great people built from primitive notions of the Deity a lofty concept of religion and ethics.

The New Testament is a collection of books produced by the early Christian church. It contains the earliest documents extant on the life of Jesus, the work of apostles, and the establishment of the Christian faith.

Now it came to pass in the days when the judges ruled, that there was a famine in the land. And a certain man of Beth-lehem-judah went to sojourn in the country of Moab,[2] he, and his wife, and his two sons. And the name of the man was Elimelech, and the name of his life Naomi, and the name of his two sons Mahlon and Chilion, Ephrathites of Beth-lehem-judah. And they came into the country of Moab, and continued there. And Elimelech, Naomi's husband, died; and she was left, and her two sons. And they took them wives of the women of Moab; the name of the one was Orpah, and the name of the other Ruth: and they dwelled there about ten years. And Mahlon and Chilion died also both of them; and the woman was left[3] of her two sons and her husband.

Then she arose with her daughters-in-law, that she might return from the country of Moab: for she had heard in the country of Moab how that the Lord had visited his people in giving them bread. Wherefore she went forth out of the place where she was, and her two daughters-in-law with her; and they went on the way to return unto the land of Judah.

And Naomi said unto her two daughters-in-law, "Go, return each to her mother's house: the Lord deal kindly with you, as ye have dealt with the dead, and with me. The Lord grant you that ye may find rest, each of you in the house of her husband."

Then she kissed them; and they lifted up their voice, and wept. And they said unto her, "Surely we will return with thee unto thy people."

And Naomi said, "Turn again, my daughters: why will ye go with me? are there yet any more sons in my womb, that they may be your husbands? Turn again, my daughters, go your way; for I am too old to have a husband. If I should say, I have hope, if I should have a husband also to-night, and should also bear sons; would ye tarry for them till they were grown? would ye stay for them from having husbands? nay, my daughters; for it grieveth me much for your sakes that the hand of the Lord is gone out against me."[4]

And they lifted up their voice, and wept again: and Orpah kissed her mother-in-law; but Ruth cleaved[5] unto her. And she said, "Behold, thy sister-in-law is gone back unto her people, and unto her gods: return thou after thy sister-in-law."

And Ruth said, "Intreat[6] me not to leave thee, or to return from following after thee: for whither thou goest, I will go; and where thou lodgest, I will lodge: thy people shall be my people, and thy God my God: where thou diest, will I die, and there will I be buried: the Lord do so to me, and more also, if ought but death part thee and me."

When she saw that she was steadfastly minded to go with her, then she left speaking unto her.

So they two went until they came to Beth-lehem. And it came to pass, when they were come to Beth-lehem, that all the city was moved about them, and they said, "Is this Naomi?"

And she said unto them, "Call me not Naomi, call me Marah:[7] for the Almighty hath dealt very bitterly with me. I went out full, and the Lord hath brought me home again empty: why then call ye me Naomi, seeing the Lord hath testified against me and the Almighty hath afflicted me?"

So Naomi returned, and Ruth the Moabitess, her daughter-in-law, with her, which returned out of the country of Moab and they came to Beth-lehem in the beginning of barley harvest. And Naomi had a kinsman of her husband's, a mighty man of wealth, of the family of Elimelech; and his name was Boaz. And Ruth the Moabitess said unto Naomi, "Let me now go to the field, and glean ears of corn after him in whose sight I shall find grace." And she said unto her, "Go, my daughter." And she went, and came, and gleaned in the field after the reapers: and her hap[8] was to light on a part of the field belonging unto Boaz, who was of the kindred of Elimelech.

And, behold, Boaz came from Beth-lehem, and said unto the reapers, "The Lord be with you." And they answered him, "The Lord bless thee."

Then said Boaz unto his servant that was set over the reapers, "Whose damsel is this?"

And the servant that was set over the reapers answered and said, "It is the Moabitish damsel that came back with Naomi out of the country of Moab: and she said, 'I pray you, let me glean and gather after the reapers among the sheaves': so she came, and hath continued even from the morning until now, that she tarried a little in the house."

Then said Boaz unto Ruth, "Hearest thou not, my daughter? Go not to glean in another field, neither go from hence, but abide here fast by my maidens: let thine eyes be on the field that they do reap, and go thou after them: have I not charged the young men that they shall not touch thee? and when thou art athirst, go unto the vessels, and drink of that which the young men have drawn."

Then she fell on her face, and bowed herself to the ground, and said unto him, "Why have I found grace in thine eyes, that thou shouldest take knowledge of me, seeing I am a stranger?"

And Boaz answered and said unto her, "It hath fully been showed me all that thou hast done unto thy mother-in-law since the death of thine husband: and how thou hast left thy father and thy mother, and the land of thy nativity, and art come unto a people which thou knewest not heretofore. The Lord recompense thy work, and a full reward be given thee of the Lord God of Israel, under whose wings thou art come to trust."

Then she said, "Let me find favour in thy sight, my lord; for that thou hast comforted me, and for that thou hast spoken friendly unto thine handmaid, though I be not like unto one of thine handmaidens."

And Boaz said unto her, "At mealtime come thou thither, and eat of the bread, and dip thy morsel in the vinegar."

And she sat beside the reapers: and he reached her parched corn, and she did eat, and was sufficed,[9] and left. And when she was risen up to glean, Boaz commanded his young men, saying, "Let her glean even among the sheaves, and reproach her not: and let fall also some of the handfuls of purpose for her, and leave them, that she may glean them, and rebuke her not."[10]

So she gleaned in the field until even, and beat out that she had gleaned: and it was about an ephah[11] of barley. And she took it up, and went into the city: and her mother-in-law saw what she had gleaned: and she brought forth, and gave to her that she had reserved after she was sufficed.

And her mother-in-law said unto her, "Where hast thou gleaned to-day? and where wroughtest[12] thou? blessed be he that did take knowledge of thee."

And she showed her mother-in-law with whom she had wrought, and said, "The man's name with whom I wrought to-day is Boaz."

And Naomi said unto her daughter-in-law, "Blessed be he of the Lord, who hath not left off his kindness to the living and to the dead." And Naomi said unto her, "The man is near of kin unto us, one of our next kinsmen."

And Ruth the Moabitess said, "He said unto me also, 'Thou shalt keep fast by my young men, until they have ended all my harvest.' "

And Naomi said unto Ruth her daughter-in-law, "It is good, my daughter, that thou go out with his maidens, that they meet thee not in any other field."

So she kept fast by the maidens of Boaz to glean unto the end of barley harvest and of wheat harvest; and dwelt with her mother-in-law.

Then Naomi her mother-in-law said unto her, "My daughter, shall I not seek rest for thee, that it may be well with thee? And now is not Boaz of our kindred, with whose maidens thou wast? Behold, he winnoweth[13] barley to-night in the threshingfloor. Wash thyself therefore, and anoint thee, and put thy raiment upon thee, and get thee down to the floor: but make not thyself known unto the man, until he shall have done eating and drinking. And it shall be, when he lieth down, that thou shalt mark the place where he shall lie, and thou shalt go in, and uncover his feet, and lay thee down; and he will tell thee what thou shalt do."

And she said unto her, "All that thou sayest unto me I will do."

And she went down unto the floor, and did according to all that her mother-in-law bade her. And when Boaz had eaten and drunk, and his heart was merry, he went to lie down at the end of the heap of corn: and she came softly, and uncovered his feet, and laid her down. And it came to pass at midnight, that the man was afraid, and turned himself: and, behold, a woman lay at his feet.

And he said, "Who art thou?"

And she answered, "I am Ruth thine handmaid: spread therefore thy skirt over thine handmaid; for thou art a near kinsman."

And he said, "Blessed be thou of the Lord, my daughter: for thou hast showed more kindness in the latter end than at the beginning, inasmuch as thou followedst not young men, whether poor or rich. And now, my daughter, fear not; I will do to thee all that thou requirest: for all the city of my people doth know that thou art a virtuous woman. And now it is true that I am thy near kinsman: howbeit[14] there is a kinsman nearer than I. Tarry this night, and it shall be in the morning, that if he will perform unto thee the part of a kinsman, well; let him do the kinsman's part: but if he will not do the part of a kinsman to thee, then will I do the part of a kinsman to thee, as the Lord liveth: lie down until the morning."[15]

And she lay at his feet until the morning: and she rose up before one could know another.

And he said, "Let it not be known that a woman came into the floor." Also he said, "Bring the veil that thou hast upon thee, and hold it."

And when she held it, he measured six measures of barley, and laid it on[16] her: and she went into the city. And when she came to her mother-in-law, she said, "Who art thou, my daughter?"

And she told her all that the man had done to her. And she said, "These six measures of barley gave he me; for he said to me, 'Go not empty unto thy mother-in-law.' "

Then said she, "Sit still, my daughter, until thou know how the matter will fall: for the man will not be in rest, until he have finished the thing this day."

Then went Boaz up to the gate, and sat him down there: and, behold, the kinsman of whom Boaz spoke came by; unto whom he said, "Ho, such a one! turn aside, sit down here."

And he turned aside, and sat down. And he took ten men of the elders of the city, and said, "Sit ye down here." And they sat down.

And he said unto the kinsman, "Naomi, that is come again out of the country of Moab, selleth a parcel of land, which was our brother Elimelech's: and I thought to advertise thee, saying, 'Buy it before the inhabitants, and before the elders of my people. If thou wilt redeem it, redeem it': but if thou wilt not redeem it, then tell me, that I may know: for there is none to redeem it beside thee; and I am after thee."

And he said, "I will redeem it."

Then said Boaz, "What[17] day thou buyest the field of the hand of Naomi, thou must buy it also of Ruth the Moabitess, the wife of the dead, to raise up the name of the dead upon his inheritance."

And the kinsman said, "I cannot redeem it for myself, lest I mar mine own inheritance: redeem thou my right to thyself; for I cannot redeem it."

(Now this was the manner in former time in Israel concerning redeeming and concerning changing, for to confirm all things; a man plucked off his shoe, and gave it to his neighbour: and this was a testimony in Israel.) Therefore the kinsman said unto Boaz, "Buy it for thee." So he drew off his shoe.

And Boaz said unto the elders, and unto all the people, "Ye are witnesses this day, that I have bought all that was Elimelech's, and all that was Chilion's and Mahlon's, of the hand of Naomi. Moreover Ruth the Moabitess, the wife of Mahlon, have I purchased to be my wife, to raise up the name of the dead upon his inheritance, that the name of the dead be not cut off from among his brethren, and from the gate of his place: ye are witnesses this day."

And all the people that were in the gate, and the elders, said, "We are witnesses. The Lord make the woman that is come into thine house like Rachel and like Leah,[18] which two did build the house of Israel: and do thou worthily in Ephratah, and be famous in Beth-lehem: and let thy house be like the house of Pharez, whom Tamar bore unto Judah, of the seed which the Lord shall give thee of this young woman."

So Boaz took Ruth, and she was his wife: and when he went in unto her, the Lord gave her conception, and she bore a son.

And the women said unto Naomi, "Blessed be the Lord, which hath not left thee this day without a kinsman, that his name may be famous in Israel. And he shall be unto thee a restorer of thy life, and a nourisher of thine old age: for thy daughter-in-law which loveth thee, which is better to thee than seven sons, hath borne him."

And Naomi took the child, and laid it in her bosom, and became nurse unto it. And the women her neighbours gave it a name, saying, "There is a son born to Naomi; and they called his name Obed: he is the father of Jesse, the father of David."[19]

Notes

[1] This short story was written about 450 B.C., but the events it narrates occurred "in the days when judges ruled," or about 1100 B.C. In the King James Version (translation), the "Book of Ruth" consists of four chapters. Except for the last five verses (which contain merely names of persons) the entire story is reprinted here, although chapter and verse numbers have been omitted as an aid to reading.

[2] Moab, the grandson of Lot (who was Abraham's nephew), was the alleged ancestor of the Moabites, a warlike Semitic people dwelling east of the Dead Sea.

[3] Bereaved.

[4] That is, I regret for your sake that God is angry with me.

[5] Clung.

[6] Ask, beg. *Intreat* is an archaic form of *entreat;* the King James Version was published in 1611.

[7] Marah was a well of bitter water in the wilderness. The name *Ruth* means "the companion." *Naomi* denotes "pleasant."

[8] Luck, fate.

[9] Satisfied.

[10] Permission granted to the poor to glean leftover grain after harvesters had finished a field was commanded by Hebrew law. Boaz, however, was obviously exceeding the law because of his kindness and his respect for a dead kinsman.

[11] An ancient Hebrew unit of dry measure equal to a little over a bushel (8 gallons).

[12] Worked.

[13] Frees grain from chaff and dirt.

[14] Although.

[15] Boaz is acting according to the ancient Jewish custom whereby a childless widow could expect to be married by the closest kinsman of the deceased husband, thus preserving the family name and inheritance. The reason that the nearer kinsman of whom Boez speaks was unwilling to do his part is indicated by his reply, "lest I mar mine own inheritance." If he were to have a child by Ruth, the child would be accounted a son and heir of the deceased husband.

[16] Gave it to.

[17] The same.

[18] Rachel was Jacob's favorite wife, the mother of Joseph. Although Jacob had been promised Rachel in marriage if he worked seven years for her father, he was tricked into marrying Leah, an older sister. Jacob then had to work another seven years for Rachel.

[19] David, a shepherd boy who became King of the Hebrews, was a national hero. Under his rule, the Hebrew people formed a strong state from a loose confederation of tribes.

WALLACE

Richard H. Rovere

RICHARD ROVERE (1915–) was born in Jersey City, New Jersey, and was educated at Columbia University (A.B., 1937). His journalistic career has included editorial jobs on *The New Masses, The Nation, Common Sense,* and, since 1944, on *The New Yorker*. In addition, he has been a foreign correspondent and book critic. His works include *The General and The President* (1951), a study written with another author of the Truman-MacArthur conflict; *Senator Joe McCarthy* (1959); *The American Establishment* (1962); *The Goldwater Caper* (1965), an account of the 1964 Presidential campaign; and *Waist Deep in the Big Muddy* (1968).

As a schoolboy, my relations with teachers were almost always tense and hostile.[1] I disliked my studies and did very badly in them. There are, I have heard, inept students who bring out the best in teachers, who challenge their skill and move them to sympathy and affection. I seemed to bring out the worst in them. I think my personality had more to do with this than my poor classroom work. Anyway, something about me was deeply offensive to the pedagogic temperament.[2]

Often, it took a teacher no more than a few minutes to conceive a raging dislike for me. I recall an instructor in elementary French who shied a textbook at my head the very first day I attended his class. We had never laid eyes on each other until fifteen or twenty minutes before he assaulted me. I no longer remember what, if anything, provoked him to violence. It is possible that I said something that was either insolent or intolerably stupid. I guess I often did. It is also possible that I said nothing at all. Even my silence, my humility, my acquiescence,[3] could annoy my teachers. The very sight of me, the mere awareness of my existence on earth, could be unendurably irritating to them.

This was the case with my fourth-grade teacher, Miss Purdy. In order to make the acquaintance of her new students on the opening day of school, she had each one rise and give his name and address as she called the roll. Her voice was soft and gentle, her manner sympathetic, until she came to me. Indeed, up to then I had been dreamily entertaining the hope that I was at last about to enjoy a happy association with a teacher. When Miss Purdy's eye fell on me, however, her face suddenly twisted and darkened with revulsion. She hesitated for a few moments while she looked me up and down and thought of a suitable comment on what she saw. "Aha!" she finally said, addressing not me but my new classmates, in a voice that was now coarse and cruel. "I don't have to ask *his* name. There, boys and girls, is Mr. J. Pierpont Morgan, lounging back in his mahogany-lined office."[4] She held each syllable of the financier's name on her lips as long as she was able to, so that my fellow-students could savor the full irony of it. I imagine my posture was a bit relaxed for the occasion, but I know well that she would not have resented anyone else's sprawl as much as she did mine. I can even hear her making some friendly, schoolmarmish quip about too much summer vacation to any other pupil. Friendly quips were never for me. In some unfortunate and mysterious fashion, my entire being rubbed Miss Purdy and all her breed the wrong way. Throughout the fourth grade, she persisted in tormenting me with her idiotic Morgan joke. "And perhaps Mr. J. P. Revere can tell us all about Vasco da Gama[5] this morning," she would say, throwing in a little added insult by mispronouncing my surname.

The aversion I inspired in teachers might under certain circumstances have been turned to good account. It might have stimulated me to industry; it might have made me get high marks, just so I could prove to the world that my persecutors were motivated by prejudice and perhaps by a touch of envy; or it might have bred a monumental rebelliousness in me, a contempt for all authority, that could have become the foundation of a career as the leader of some great movement against all tyranny and oppression.

It did none of these things. Instead, I became, so far as my school life was concerned, a thoroughly browbeaten boy, and I accepted the hostility of my teachers as an inescapable condition of life. In fact, I took the absolutely disastrous view that my teachers were unquestionably right in their estimate of me as a dense and altogether noxious[6] creature who deserved, if anything, worse than he got. These teachers were, after all, men and women who had mastered the parts of speech, the multiplication tables, and a simply staggering number of imports and exports in a staggering number of countries. They could add up columns of figures the very sight of which made me dizzy and sick to the stomach. They could read "As You Like It" with pleasure—so they said, anyway, and I believed everything they said. I felt that if such knowledgeable people told me that I was stupid, they certainly must know what they were talking about. In consequence, my grades sank lower and lower, my face became more noticeably blank, my manner more mulish, and my presence in the classroom more aggravating to whoever presided over it. To be sure, I hated my teachers for their hatred of me, and I missed no chance to abuse them behind their backs, but fundamentally I shared with them the view that I was a worthless and despicable boy, as undeserving of an education as I was incapable of absorbing one. Often, on school days, I wished that I were dead.

This was my attitude, at least, until my second year in preparatory school, when, at fourteen, I fell under the exhilarating, regenerative influence of my friend Wallace Duckworth. Wallace changed my whole outlook on life. It was he who freed me from my terrible awe of teachers; it was he who showed me that they could be brought to book[7] and made fools of as easily as I could be; it was he who showed me that the gap between their knowledge and mine was not unbridgeable. Sometimes I think that I should like to become a famous man, a United States senator or something of that sort, just to be able to repay my debt to Wallace. I should like to be so important that people would inquire into the early influences on my life and I would be able to tell them about Wallace.

I was freshly reminded of my debt to Wallace not long ago when my mother happened to come across a packet of letters I had written to her and my father during my first two years in a boarding school on Long Island. In one of these, I reported that "There's a new kid in school who's supposed to be a scientifical genius." Wallace was this genius. In a series of intelligence and aptitude tests we all took in the opening week, he achieved some incredible score, a mark that, according to the people who made up the tests, certified him as a genius and absolutely guaranteed that in later life he would join the company of Einstein, Steinmetz, and Edison.[8] Naturally, his teachers were thrilled—but not for long.

Within a matter of weeks, it became clear that although Wallace was unquestionably a genius, or at least an exceptionally bright boy, he was disposed to use his considerable gifts not to equip himself for a career in the service of mankind but for purely anti-social undertakings. Far from making the distinguished scholastic record everyone expected of him, he made an altogether deplorable one. He never did a lick of schoolwork. He had picked up his scientific knowledge somewhere but evidently not from teachers. I am not sure about this, but I think Wallace's record, as long as he was in school, was even worse than mine. In my mind's eye there is a picture of the sheet of monthly averages thumbtacked to the bulletin board across the hall from the school post office; my name is one from the bottom, the bottom name being Wallace's.

As a matter of fact, one look at Wallace should have been enough to tell the teachers what sort of genius he was. At fourteen, he was somewhat shorter than he should have been and a good deal stouter. His face was round, owlish, and dirty. He had big, dark eyes, and his black hair, which hardly ever got cut, was arranged on his head as the four winds wanted it. He had been outfitted with attractive and fairly expensive clothes, but he changed from one suit to another only when his parents came to call on him and ordered him to get out of what he had on.

The two most expressive things about him were his mouth and the pockets of his jacket. By looking at his mouth, one could tell whether he was plotting evil or had recently accomplished it. If he was bent upon malevolence,[9] his lips were all puckered up, like those of a billiard player about to make a difficult shot. After the deed was done, the pucker was replaced by a delicate, unearthly smile. How a teacher who knew anything about boys could miss the fact that both expressions were masks of Satan I'm sure I don't know. Wallace's pockets were less interesting than his mouth, perhaps, but more spectacular in a way. The side pockets of his jacket bulged out over his pudgy haunches like burro hampers. They were filled with tools—screwdrivers, pliers, files, wrenches, wire cutters, nail sets, and I don't know what else. In addition to all this, one pocket always contained a rolled-up copy of *Popular Mechanics,* while from the top of the other protruded *Scientific American* or some other such magazine. His breast pocket contained, besides a large collection of fountain pens and mechanical pencils, a picket fence of drill bits, gimlets, kitchen knives, and other pointed instruments. When he walked, he clinked and jangled and pealed.[10]

Wallace lived just down the hall from me, and I got to know him one afternoon, a week or so after school started, when I was wrestling with an algebra lesson. I was really trying to get good marks at the time, for my father had threatened me with unpleasant reprisals[11] if my grades did not show early improvement. I could make no sense of the algebra, though, and I thought that the scientific genius, who had not as yet been unmasked, might be generous enough to lend me a hand.

It was a study period, but I found Wallace stretched out on the floor working away at something he was learning to make from *Popular Mechanics.* He received me with courtesy, but after hearing my request he went immediately back to his tinkering. "I could do that algebra, all right," he said, "but I can't be bothered with it. Got to get this dingbat going this afternoon. Anyway, I don't care about algebra. It's too twitchy. Real engineers never do any of that stuff. It's too twitchy for them." I soon learned that "twitch" was an all-purpose word of Wallace's. It turned up, in one form or another, in about every third sentence he spoke. It did duty as a noun, an adjective, a verb, and an adverb.

I was disappointed by his refusal of help but fascinated by what he was doing. I stayed on and watched him as he deftly cut and spliced wires, removed and replaced screws, referring, every so often, to his magazine for further instruction. He worked silently, lips fiendishly puckered, for some time, then looked up at me and said, "Say, you know anything about that organ in the chapel?"

"What about it?" I asked.

"I mean do you know anything about how it works?"

"No," I said. "I don't know anything about that."

"Too bad," Wallace said, reaching for a pair of pliers. "I had a really twitchy idea." He worked at his wires and screws for quite a while. After perhaps ten minutes, he looked up again. "Well, anyhow," he said, "maybe you know how to get in the chapel and have a look at the organ?"

"Sure, that's easy," I said. "Just walk in. The chapel's always open. They keep it open so you can go in and pray if you want to, and things like that."

"Oh" was Wallace's only comment.

I didn't at all grasp what he had in mind until church time the following Sunday. At about six o'clock that morning, several hours before the service, he tiptoed into my room and shook me from sleep. "Hey, get dressed," he said. "Let's you and I twitch over to the chapel and have a look at the organ."

Game for any form of amusement, I got up and went along. In the bright, not quite frosty October morning, we scurried over the lawns to the handsome Georgian chapel. It was an hour before the rising bell.

Wallace had brought along a flashlight as well as his usual collection of hardware. We went to the rear of the chancel,[12] where the organ was, and he poked the light underneath the thing and inside it for a few minutes. Then he got out his pliers and screwdrivers and performed some operations that I could neither see nor understand. We were in the chapel for only a few minutes. "There," Wallace said as he came up from under the keyboard. "I guess I got her twitched up just about right. Let's go." Back in my room, we talked softly until the rest of the school began to stir. I asked Wallace what, precisely, he had done to the organ. "You'll see," he said with that faint, faraway smile where the pucker had been. Using my commonplace imagination, I guessed that he had fixed the organ so it would give out peculiar noises or something like that. I didn't realize then that Wallace's tricks were seldom commonplace.

Church began as usual that Sunday morning. The headmaster delivered the invocation[13] and then announced the number and title of the first hymn. He held up his hymnal and gave the genteel, throat-clearing cough that was his customary signal to the organist to get going. The organist came down on the keys but not a peep sounded from the pipes. He tried again. Nothing but a click.

When the headmaster realized that the organ wasn't working, he walked quickly to the rear and consulted in whispers with the organist. Together they made a hurried inspection of the instrument, peering inside it, snapping the electric switch back and forth, and reaching to the base plug to make certain the juice was on. Everything seemed all right, yet the organ wouldn't sound a note.

"Something appears to be wrong with our organ," the headmaster said when he returned to the lectern. "I regret to say that for this morning's service we shall have to—"

At the first word of the announcement, Wallace, who was next to me in one of the rear pews, slid out of his seat and bustled noisily down the middle aisle. It was highly unusual conduct, and every eye was on him. His gaudy magazines flapped from his pockets, his portable workshop clattered and clanked as he strode importantly to the chancel and rose on tiptoe to reach the ear of the astonished headmaster. He spoke in a stage whisper that could be heard everywhere in the chapel. "Worked around organs quite a bit, sir," he said. "Think I can get this one going in a jiffy."

Given the chance, the headmaster would undoubtedly have declined Wallace's kind offer. Wallace didn't give him the chance. He scooted for the organ. For perhaps a minute, he worked on it, hands flying, tools tinkling.

Then, stuffing the tools back into his pockets, he returned to the headmaster. "There you are, sir," he said, smiling up at him. "Think she'll go all right now." The headmaster, with great doubt in his heart, I am sure, nodded to the organist to try again. Wallace stood by, looking rather like the inventor of a new kind of airplane waiting to see his brain child take flight. He faked a look of deep anxiety, which, when a fine, clear swell came from the pipes, was replaced by a faint smile of relief, also faked. On the second or third chord, he bustled back down the aisle, looking very solemn and businesslike and ready for serious worship.

It was a fine performance, particularly brilliant in its timing. If Wallace had had to stay at the organ even a few seconds longer—that is, if he had done a slightly more elaborate job of twitching it in the first place—he would have been ordered back to his pew before he had got done with the repairs. Moreover, someone would probably have guessed that it was he who had put it on the fritz in the first place. But no one did guess it. Not then, anyway. For weeks after that, Wallace's prestige in the school was enormous. Everyone had had from the beginning a sense of honor and pride at having a genius around, but no one up to then had realized how useful a genius could be. Wallace let on after church that Sunday that he was well up on the workings not merely of organs but also of heating and plumbing systems, automobiles, radios, washing machines, and just about everything else. He said he would be pleased to help out in any emergency. Everyone thought he was wonderful.

"That was a real good twitch, wasn't it?" he said to me when we were by ourselves. I said that it certainly was.

From that time on, I was proud

and happy to be Wallace's cup-bearer.[14] I find it hard now to explain exactly what his victory with the organ, and all his later victories over authority, meant to me, but I do know that they meant a very great deal. Partly, I guess, it was just the knowledge that he enjoyed my company. I was an authentic, certified dunce and he was an acknowledged genius, yet he liked being with me. Better yet was my discovery that this super-brain disliked schoolwork every bit as much as I did. He was bored silly, as I was, by "Il Penseroso" and completely unable to stir up any enthusiasm for "Silas Marner"[15] and all the foolish goings on over Eppie. Finally, and this perhaps was what made me love him most, he had it in his power to humiliate and bring low the very people who had so often humiliated me and brought me low.

As I spent the long fall and winter afternoons with Wallace, being introduced by him to the early novels of H. G. Wells,[16] which he admired extravagantly, and watching him make crystal sets, window-cleaning machines, automatic chair-rockers, and miniature steam turbines from plans in *Popular Mechanics,* I gradually absorbed bits of his liberating philosophy. "If I were you," he used to say, "I wouldn't be scared by those teachers. They don't know anything. They're twitches, those teachers, real twerpy, twitchy twitches." "Twerpy" was an adjective often used by Wallace to modify "twitch." It added several degrees of twitchiness to anything twitchy.

Although Wallace had refused at first to help me with my lessons, he later gave freely of his assistance. I explained to him that my father was greatly distressed about my work and that I really wanted to make him happier. Wallace was moved by this. He would read along in my Latin grammar, study out algebra problems with me, and explain things in language that seemed a lot more lucid than that of my teachers. Before long, I began to understand that half my trouble lay in my fear of my studies, my teachers, and myself. "Don't know why you get so twitched up over this stuff," Wallace would say a trifle impatiently as he helped me get the gist of a speech in "As You Like It." "There isn't anything hard about this. Fact, it's pretty good right in here. It's just those teachers who twitch it all up. I wish they'd all go soak their heads."

Wallace rode along for quite a while on the strength of his intelligence tests and his organ-fixing, but in time it became obvious that his disappointing classroom performance was not so much the result of failure to adjust to a new environment (as a genius, he received more tolerance in this respect than non-geniuses) as of out-and-out refusal to cooperate with the efforts being made to educate him. Even when he had learned a lesson in the course of helping me with it, he wouldn't give the teachers the satisfaction of thinking he had learned anything in their classes. Then, too, his pranks began to catch up with him. Some of them, he made no effort to conceal.

He was easily the greatest teacher-baiter I have ever known. His masterpiece, I think, was one he thought up for our algebra class. "Hey, you twitch," he called to me one day as I was passing his room on my way to the daily ordeal of "x"s and "y"s. "I got a good one for old twitch Potter." I went into his room, and he took down from his closet shelf a spool of shiny copper wire. "Now, watch this," he said. He took the free end of the wire and drew it up through the left sleeve of his shirt. Then he brought it across his chest, underneath the shirt, and ran it down the right sleeve. He closed his left fist over the spool and held the free end of the wire between right thumb and forefinger. "Let's get over to that dopey class," he said, and we went.

When the lesson was well started, Wallace leaned back in his seat and began to play in a languorous but ostentatious[17] manner with the wire. It glistened brightly in the strong classroom light, and it took Mr. Potter, the teacher, only a few seconds to notice that Wallace was paying no mind to the blackboard equations but was, instead, completely absorbed in the business of fingering the wire.

"Wallace Duckworth, what's that you're fiddling with?" Mr. Potter said.

"Piece of wire, sir."

"Give it to me this instant."

"Yes, sir," Wallace said, extending his hand.

Mr. Potter had, no doubt, bargained on getting a stray piece of wire that he could unceremoniously pitch into the wastebasket. Wallace handed him about eighteen inches of it. As Mr. Potter took it, Wallace released several inches more.

"I want *all* that wire, Wallace," Mr. Potter said.

"I'm giving it to you, sir," Wallace answered. He let go of about two feet more. Mr. Potter kept pulling. His rage so far overcame his reason that he couldn't figure out what Wallace was doing. As he pulled, Wallace fed him more and more wire, and the stuff began to coil up on the floor around his feet. Guiding the wire with the fingers of his right hand, Wallace created quite a bit of tension, so that eventually Mr. Potter was pulling hand over hand, like a sailor tightening lines in a high sea. When he thought the tension was great enough, Wallace let two or three feet slip quickly through his hands, and Mr. Potter toppled to the floor, landing in a terrible tangle of wire.

I no longer remember all of Wallace's inventions in detail. Once, I recall, he made, in the chemistry laboratory, some kind of invisible paint —a sort of shellac, I suppose—and covered every blackboard in the school with it. The next day, chalk skidded along the slate and left about as much impression as it would have made on a cake of ice. The dormitory he and I lived in was an old one of frame construction, and when we had fire drills, we had to climb down outside fire escapes. One night, Wallace tied a piece of flypaper securely around each rung of each ladder in the building, then rang the fire alarm. Still another time, he went back to his first love, the organ, and put several pounds of flour in the pipes, so that when the organist turned on the pumps, a cloud of flour filled the chapel. One of his favorite tricks was to take the dust jacket from a novel and wrap it around a textbook. In a Latin class, then, he would appear to be reading "Black April"[18] when he should have been reading about the campaigns in Gaul. After several of his teachers had discovered that he had the right book in the wrong cover (he piously explained that he put the covers on to keep his books clean), he felt free to remove the textbook and really read a novel in class.

Wallace was expelled shortly before the Easter vacation. As the winter had drawn on, life had become duller and duller for him, and to brighten things up he had resorted to pranks of larger conception and of an increasingly anti-social character. He poured five pounds of sugar into the gasoline tank of the basketball coach's car just before the coach was to start out, with two or three of the team's best players in his car, for a game with a school about twenty-five miles away. The engine functioned adequately until the car hit an isolated spot on the highway, miles from any service place. Then it gummed up completely. The coach and the players riding with him came close to frostbite, and the game had to be called off. The adventure cost Wallace's parents a couple of hundred dollars for automobile repairs. Accused of the prank, which clearly bore his trademark, Wallace had freely admitted his guilt. It was explained to his parents that he would be given one more chance in school; another trick of any sort and he would be packed off on the first train.

Later, trying to justify himself to me, he said, "You don't like that coach either, do you? He's the twerpiest twitch here. All teachers are twitchy, but coaches are the worst ones of all."

I don't recall what I said. Wallace had not consulted me about several of his recent escapades, and although I was still loyal to him, I was beginning to have misgivings about some of them.

As I recall it, the affair that led directly to his expulsion was a relatively trifling one, something to do with blown fuses or short circuits. At any rate, Wallace's parents had to come and fetch him home. It was a sad occasion for me, for Wallace had built in me the foundations for a sense of security. My marks were improving, my father was happier, and I no longer cringed at the sight of a teacher. I feared, though, that without Wallace standing behind me and giving me courage, I might slip back into the old ways. I was very near to tears as I helped him pack up his turbines, his tools, and his stacks of magazines. He, however, was quite cheerful. "I suppose my Pop will put me in another one of these places, and I'll have to twitch my way out of it all over again," he said.

"Just remember how dumb all those teachers are," he said to me a few moments before he got into his parents' car. "They're so twitchy dumb they can't even tell if anyone else is dumb." It was rather a sweeping generalization, I later learned, but it served me well for a number of years. Whenever I was belabored by a teacher, I remembered my grimy genius friend and his reassurances. I got through school somehow or other. I still cower a bit when I find that someone I've met is a schoolteacher, but things aren't too bad and I am on reasonably civil terms with a number of teachers, and even a few professors.

Notes

[1] The essential conflict of this story, one largely resolved by Wallace, is the narrator's strong feeling of insecurity, inexperience, and general worthlessness versus his confused recognition that he must try to meet adult standards. The irritation and hostility which the narrator firmly believes that he inspires in his elders is the outward expression of this conflict. Wallace serves as the *deus ex machina* (god from the machine) who relieves the narrator's feeling of insecurity and thus provides a traditional happy ending.

[2] This paragraph is an opening developed by deductive logic. It states the general situation, the basic conflict, of the story; the next four paragraphs amplify the beginning by providing specific instances and examples. The focus of these five paragraphs is wholly on the narrator, actually identified in the story as the author himself. The focus is then shifted to Wallace for the remainder of the story, except that toward the end the spotlight once again is turned on the narrator—at this stage, one strongly influenced by the lessons learned from Wallace's attitudes and behavior.

[3] Submission, acceptance.

[4] John Pierpont Morgan (1867–1943) was an immensely wealthy financier and philanthropist.

[5] A Portuguese navigator, discoverer of the sea route from Portugal around the continent of Africa to India. He lived from about 1460 to 1524.

[6] Harmful, injurious.

[7] An expression meaning "called to account" or "brought to justice."

[8] Comparison to these eminent and world-famed scientists is one of many examples of the exaggerated language that provides some part of the humorous content of the story.

[9] Malice, hatred, evil.

[10] An auditory appeal made in specific, forceful, even exaggerated diction.

[11] Retaliation, "getting back at."

[12] The usually enclosed space about the altar of a church, normally reserved for the clergy and other religious officials.

[13] A petition to God for His presence and aid.

[14] An attendant who fills and hands around the cups in which wine or other drink is served.

[15] "Il Penseroso" is a poem by John Milton (1608–1674). *Silas Marner* (1861) is a novel by George Eliot (Mary Ann Evans, 1819–1880), an Englishwoman.

[16] Herbert George Wells (1866–1946), English novelist and science-fiction writer.

[17] Lazy but showy; languid but obvious.

[18] A novel (1927) by Julia Peterkin (1880–1961), a South Carolina writer of stories about Gullah Negroes.

YOUTH

Joseph Conrad

Joseph Conrad (1857–1924) was born Jozef Teodor Konrad Korzeniowski in Poland, then under Russian rule. Following the death of his parents, both of whom suffered hardships and exile at the hands of the Russians, he was brought up under the guardianship of an uncle. At the age of fifteen, Conrad announced his desire to go to sea, and in 1874 he went to Marseilles, France, where he entered service in the French Mercantile Marine. In 1878, Conrad joined an English ship. In his twenty-first year, he set foot on English soil for the first time. During the next few years he spent all his spare moments on shipboard and in port learning the English language, largely from newspapers. He also stored up incidents, experiences, impressions, and observations of characters which he later used in short stories and novels. For fourteen years, Conrad served as one of the commanding officers of British merchant ships sailing to Africa, South America, Australia, and the Orient. In 1894 he left the sea and settled in London as a writer. In 1896 Conrad married an English girl. This son of Polish patriots turned merchant seaman turned writer was henceforth an English novelist, although to the end of his life Conrad spoke the language with a thick foreign accent.

This could have occurred nowhere but in England, where men and sea interpenetrate, so to speak—the sea entering into the life of most men, and the men knowing something or everything about the sea, in the way of amusement, of travel, or of bread-winning.[1]

We were sitting round a mahogany table that reflected the bottle, the claret glasses, and our faces as we leaned on our elbows. There was a director of companies, an accountant, a lawyer, Marlow, and myself. The director had been a *Conway*[2] boy, the accountant had served four years at sea, the lawyer—a fine crusted Tory, High Churchman, the best of old fellows, the soul of honor—had been chief officer in the P. & O.[3] service in the good old days when mail-boats were square-rigged at least on two masts, and used to come down the China Sea before a fair monsoon[4] with stun'sails[5] set alow and aloft. We all began life in the merchant service. Between the five of us there was the strong bond of the sea, and also the fellowship of the craft, which no amount of enthusiasm for yachting, cruising, and so on can give, since one is only the amusement of life and the other is life itself.

Marlow (at least I think that is how he spelt his name) told the story, or rather the chronicle, of a voyage:

"Yes, I have seen a little of the Eastern seas; but what I remember best is my first voyage there. You fellows know there are those voyages that seem ordered for the illustration of life, that might stand for a symbol of existence. You fight, work, sweat, nearly kill yourself, sometimes do kill yourself, trying to accomplish something—and you can't. Not from any fault of yours. You simply can do nothing, neither great nor little—not a thing in the world—not even marry an old maid, or get a wretched 600-ton cargo of coal to its port of destination.

"It was altogether a memorable affair. It was my first voyage to the East, and my first voyage as second mate; it was also my skipper's first command. You'll admit it was time. He was sixty if a day; a little man, with a broad, not very straight back, with bowed shoulders and one leg more bandy[6] than the other, he had that queer, twisted-about appearance you see so often in men who work in the fields. He had a nutcracker face—chin and nose trying to come together over a sunken mouth—and it was framed in iron-gray fluffy hair, that looked like a chinstrap of cotton-wool sprinkled with coal-dust. And he had blue eyes in that old face of his which were amazingly like a boy's, with that candid expression some quite common men preserve to the end of their days by a rare internal gift of simplicity of heart and rectitude of soul. What induced him to accept me was a wonder. I had come out of a crack Australian clipper, where I had been third officer, and he seemed to have a prejudice against crack clippers as aristocratic and high-toned. He said to me, 'You know, in this ship you will have to work.' I said I had to work in every ship I had ever been in. 'Ah, but this is different, and you gentlemen out of them big ships; . . . but there! I dare say you will do. Join tomorrow.'

"I joined tomorrow. It was twenty-two years ago; and I was just twenty. How time passes! It was one of the happiest days of my life. Fancy! Second mate for the first time—a really responsible officer! I wouldn't have thrown up my new billet[7] for a fortune. The mate looked me over carefully. He was also an old chap, but of another stamp. He had a Roman nose, a snow-white, long beard, and his name was Mahon, but he insisted that it should be pronounced Mann. He was well connected; yet there was something wrong with his luck, and he had never got on.

"As to the captain, he had been for years in coasters,[8] then in the Mediterranean, and last in the West Indian trade. He had never been round the Capes.[9] He could just write a kind of sketchy hand, and didn't care for writing at all. Both were thorough good seamen of course, and between those two old chaps I felt like a small boy between two grandfathers.

"The ship also was old. Her name was the *Judea*. Queer name, isn't it? She belonged to a man Wilmer, Wilcox—some name like that; but he has been bankrupt and dead these twenty years or more, and his name don't matter. She had been laid up in Shadwell basin for ever so long. You may imagine her state. She was all rust, dust, grime—soot aloft, dirt on deck. To me it was like coming out of a palace into a ruined cottage. She was about 400 tons, had a primitive windlass,[10] wooden latches to the doors, not a bit of brass about her, and a big square stern. There was on it, below her name in big letters, a lot of scrollwork, with the gilt off, and some sort of a coat of arms, with the motto 'Do or Die' underneath. I remember it took my fancy immensely. There was a touch of romance in it, something that made me love the old thing—something that appealed to my youth!

"We left London in ballast[11]—sand ballast—to load a cargo of coal in a northern port for Bangkok.[12] Bangkok! I thrilled. I had been six years at sea, but had only seen Melbourne and Sydney, very good places, charming places in their way—but Bangkok!

"We worked out of the Thames under canvas, with a North Sea pilot on board. His name was Jermyn, and he dodged all day long about the galley drying his handkerchief before the stove. Apparently he never slept. He was a dismal man, with a perpetual tear sparkling at the end of his nose, who either had been in trouble, or was in trouble, or expected to be in trouble—couldn't be happy unless something went wrong. He mistrusted my youth, my common sense, and my seamanship, and made a point of showing it in a hundred little ways. I dare say he was right. It seems to me I knew very little then, and I know not much more now; but I cherish a hate for that Jermyn to this day.

"We were a week working up as far as Yarmouth Roads, and then we got into a gale—the famous October gale of twenty-two years ago. It was wind, lightning, sleet, snow, and a terrific sea. We were flying light, and you may imagine how bad it was when I tell you we had smashed bulwarks[13] and a flooded deck. On the second night she shifted her ballast into the lee bow,[14] and by that time we had been blown off somewhere on the Dogger Bank. There was nothing for it but go below with shovels and try to right her, and there we were in that vast hold, gloomy like a cavern, the tallow dips stuck and flickering on the beams, the gale howling above, the ship tossing about like mad on her side; there we all were, Jermyn, the captain, everyone, hardly able to keep our feet, engaged on that gravedigger's work, and trying to toss shovelfuls of wet sand up to windward. At every tumble of the ship you could see vaguely in the dim light men falling down with a great flourish of shovels. One of the ship's boys (we had two), impressed by the weirdness of the scene, wept as if his heart would break. We could hear him blubbering somewhere in the shadows.

"On the third day the gale died out, and by and by a north-country tug picked us up. We took sixteen days in all to get from London to the Tyne![15] When we got into dock we had lost our turn for loading, and they hauled us off to a pier where we remained for a month. Mrs. Beard (the captain's name was Beard) came from Colchester to see the old man. She lived on board. The crew of runners had left, and there remained only the officers, one boy and the steward, a mulatto who answered to the name of Abraham. Mrs. Beard was an old woman, with a face all wrinkled and ruddy like a winter apple, and the figure of a young girl. She caught sight of me once, sewing on a button, and insisted on having my shirts to repair. This was something different from the captains' wives I had known on board crack clippers. When I brought her the shirts, she said: 'And the socks? They want mending, I am sure, and John's—Captain Beard's—things are all in order now. I would be glad of something to do.' Bless the old woman. She overhauled my outfit for me, and meantime I read for the first time *Sartor Resartus* and Burnaby's *Ride to Khiva*.[16] I didn't understand much of the first then; but I remember I preferred the soldier to the philosopher at the time; a preference which life has only confirmed. One was a man, and the other was either more—or less. However, they are both dead and Mrs. Beard is dead, and youth, strength, genius, thoughts, achievements, simple hearts —all dies. . . . No matter.

"They loaded us at last. We shipped a crew. Eight able seamen and two boys. We hauled off one evening to the buoys at the dock gates, ready to go out, and with a fair prospect of beginning the voyage next day. Mrs. Beard was to start for home by a late train. When the ship was fast we went to tea. We sat rather silent through the meal—Mahon, the old couple, and I. I finished first, and slipped away for a smoke, my cabin being in a deckhouse just against the poop.[17] It was high water, blowing fresh with a drizzle; the double dock gates were opened, and the steam colliers[18] were going in and out in the darkness with their lights burning bright, a great splashing of propellers, rattling of winches, and a lot of hailing on the pierheads. I watched the procession of headlights gliding high and of green lights gliding low in the night, when suddenly a red gleam flashed at me, vanished, came into view again, and remained. The fore end of a steamer loomed up close. I shouted down the cabin, 'Come up, quick!' and then heard a startled voice saying afar in the dark, 'Stop her, sir.' A bell jingled. Another voice cried warningly, 'We are going right into that bark, sir.' The answer to this was a gruff 'All right,' and the next thing was a heavy crash as the steamer struck a glancing blow with the bluff of her bow about our fore-rigging. There was a moment of confusion, yelling, and running about. Steam roared. Then somebody was heard saying, 'All clear, sir.' . . . 'Are you all right?' asked the gruff voice. I had jumped forward to see the damage, and hailed back, 'I think so.' 'Easy astern,' said the gruff voice. A bell jingled. 'What steamer is that?' screamed Mahon. By that time she was no more to us than a bulky shadow maneuvering a little way off. They shouted at us some name—a woman's name, Miranda or Melissa —or some such thing. 'This means another month in this beastly hole,' said Mahon to me, as we peered with lamps about the splintered bulwarks and broken braces. 'But where's the captain?'

"We had not heard or seen anything of him all that time. We went aft to look. A doleful voice arose hailing somewhere in the middle of the dock, '*Judea* ahoy!' . . . How the devil did he get there? . . . 'Hallo!' we shouted. 'I am adrift in our boat without oars,' he cried. A belated water-man offered his services, and Mahon struck a bargain with him for a half crown[19] to tow our skipper alongside; but it was Mrs. Beard that came up the ladder first. They had been floating about the dock in the mizzly[20] cold rain for nearly an hour. I was never so surprised in my life.

"It appears that when he heard my shout 'Come up' he understood at once what was the matter, caught up his wife, ran on deck, and across, and down into our boat, which was fast to the ladder. Not bad for a sixty-year-old. Just imagine that old fellow saving heroically in his arms that old woman—the woman of his life. He set her down on a thwart,[21] and was ready to climb back on board when the painter came adrift somehow, and away they went together. Of course in the confusion we did not hear him shouting. He looked abashed. She said cheerfully, 'I suppose it does not matter my losing the train now?' 'No, Jenny—you go below and get warm,' he growled. Then to us: 'A sailor has no business with a wife—I say. There I was, out of the ship. Well, no harm done this time. Let's go and look at what that fool of a steamer smashed.'

"It wasn't much, but it delayed us three weeks. At the end of that time, the captain being engaged with his agents, I carried Mrs. Beard's bag to the railway station and put her all comfy into a third-class carriage. She lowered the window to say, 'You are a good young man. If you see John—Captain Beard—without his muffler at night, just remind him from me to keep his throat well wrapped up.' 'Certainly, Mrs. Beard,' I said. 'You are a good young man; I noticed how attentive you are to John—to Captain—' The train pulled out suddenly; I took my cap off to the old woman: I never saw her again. . . . Pass the bottle.[22]

"We went to sea next day. When we made that start for Bangkok we had been already three months out of London. We had expected to be a fortnight or so—at the outside.

"It was January, and the weather was beautiful—the beautiful sunny winter weather that has more charm than in the summertime, because it is unexpected, and crisp, and you know it won't, it can't, last long. It's like a windfall, like a godsend, like an unexpected piece of luck.

"It lasted all down the North Sea, all down Channel; and it lasted till we were three hundred miles or so to the westward of the Lizards;[23] then the wind went round to the sou'west and began to pipe up. In two days it blew a gale. The *Judea,* hove to, wallowed on the Atlantic like an old candle-box. It blew day after day: it blew with spite, without interval, without mercy, without rest. The world was nothing but an immensity of great foaming waves rushing at us, under a sky low enough to touch with the hand and dirty like a smoked ceiling. In the stormy space surrounding us there was as much flying spray as air. Day after day and night after night there was nothing round the ship but the howl of the wind, the tumult of the sea, the noise of water pouring over her deck. There was no rest for her and no rest for us. She tossed, she pitched, she stood on her head, she sat on her tail, she rolled, she groaned, and we had to hold on while on deck and cling to our bunks when below, in a constant effort of body and worry of mind.

"One night Mahon spoke through the small window of my berth. It opened right into my very bed, and I was lying there sleepless, in my boots, feeling as though I had not slept for years, and could not if I tried. He said excitedly:

" 'You got the sounding rod[24] in here, Marlow? I can't get the pumps to suck. By God! It's no child's play.'

"I gave him the sounding rod and lay down again, trying to think of various things—but I thought only of the pumps. When I came on deck they were still at it, and my watch relieved at the pumps. By the light of the lantern brought on deck to examine the sounding rod I caught a glimpse of their weary, serious faces. We pumped all the four hours. We pumped all night, all day, all the week—watch and watch. She was working herself loose, and leaked badly—not enough to drown us at once, but enough to kill us with the work at the pumps. And while we pumped the ship was going from us piecemeal: the bulwarks went, the the stanchions[25] were torn out, the ventilators smashed, the cabin door burst in. There was not a dry spot in the ship. She was being gutted bit by bit. The long-boat[26] changed, as if by magic, into matchwood where she stood in her gripes.[27] I had lashed her myself, and was rather proud of my handiwork, which had withstood so long the malice of the sea. And we pumped. And there was no break in the weather. The sea was white like a sheet of foam, like a caldron of boiling milk; there was not a break in the clouds, no—not the size of a man's hand—no, not for so much as ten seconds. There was for us no sky, there were for us no stars, no sun, no universe—nothing but angry clouds and an infuriated sea. We pumped watch and watch, for dear life; and it seemed to last for months, for years, for all eternity, as though we had been dead and gone to a hell for sailors. We forgot the day of the week, the name of the month, what year it was, and whether we had ever been ashore. The sails blew away, she lay broadside on under a weather cloth, the ocean poured over her, and we did not care. We turned those handles, and had the eyes of idiots. As soon as we had crawled on deck I used to take a round turn with a rope about the men, the pumps, and the mainmast, and we turned, we turned incessantly, with the water to our waists, to our necks, over our heads. It was all one. We had forgotten how it felt to be dry.

"And there was somewhere in me the thought: By Jove! This is the deuce of an adventure—something you read about; and it is my first voyage as second mate—and I am only twenty—and here I am lasting it out as well as any of these men, and keeping my chaps up to the mark. I was pleased. I would not have given up the experience for worlds. I had moments of exultation. Whenever the old dismantled craft pitched heavily with her counter high in the air, she seemed to me to throw up, like an appeal, like a defiance, like a cry to the clouds without mercy, the words written on her stern: '*Judea,* London. Do or Die.'

"O youth! The strength of it, the faith of it, the imagination of it! To me she was not an old rattle-trap carting about the world a lot of coal for a freight—to me she was the endeavor, the test, the trial of life. I think of her with pleasure, with affection, with regret—as you would think of someone dead you have loved. I shall never forget her. . . . Pass the bottle.

"One night when tied to the mast, as I explained, we were pumping on, deafened with the wind, and without spirit enough in us to wish ourselves dead, a heavy sea crashed aboard and swept clean over us. As soon as I got my breath I shouted, as in duty bound, 'Keep on, boys!' when suddenly I felt something hard floating on deck strike the calf of my leg. I made a grab at it and missed. It was so dark we could not see each other's faces within a foot—you understand.

"After that thump the ship kept quiet for a while, and the thing, whatever it was, struck my leg again. This time I caught it—and it was a saucepan. At first, being stupid with fatigue and thinking of nothing but the pumps, I did not understand what I had in my hand. Suddenly it dawned upon me, and I shouted, 'Boys, the house on deck is gone. Leave this, and let's look for the cook.'

"There was a deckhouse forward, which contained the galley, the cook's berth, and the quarters of the crew. As we had expected for days to see it swept away, the hands had been ordered to sleep in the cabin—the only safe place in the ship. The steward, Abraham, however, persisted in clinging to his berth, stupidly, like a mule —from sheer fright, I believe, like an animal that won't leave a stable falling in an earthquake. So we went to look for him. It was chancing death, since once out of our lashings we were as exposed as if on a raft. But we went. The house was shattered as if a shell had exploded inside. Most of it had gone overboard—stove, men's quarters, and their property, all was gone; but two posts, holding a portion of the bulkhead to which Abraham's bunk was attached, remained as if by a miracle. We groped in the ruins and came upon this, and there he was, sitting in his bunk, surrounded by foam and wreckage, jabbering cheerfully to himself. He was out of his mind; completely and forever mad, with this sudden shock coming upon the fag-end of his endurance. We snatched him up, lugged him aft, and pitched him headfirst down the cabin companion.[28] You understand there was no time to carry him down with infinite precautions and wait to see how he got on. Those below would pick him up at the bottom of the stairs all right. We were in a hurry to go back to the pumps. That business could not wait. A bad leak is an inhuman thing.

"One would think that the sole purpose of that fiendish gale had been to make a lunatic of that poor devil of a mulatto. It eased before morning, and next day the sky cleared, and as the sea went down the leak took up. When it came to bending a fresh set of sails the crew demanded to put back—and really there was nothing else to do. Boats gone, decks swept clean, cabin gutted, men without a stitch but what they stood in, stores spoiled, ship strained. We put her head for home, and—would you believe it? The wind came east right in our teeth. It blew fresh, it blew continuously. We had to beat up every inch of the way, but she did not leak so badly, the water keeping comparatively smooth. Two hours' pumping in every four is no joke—but it kept her afloat as far as Falmouth.[29]

"The good people there live on casualties of the sea, and no doubt were glad to see us. A hungry crowd of shipwrights sharpened their chisels at the sight of that carcass of a ship. And, by Jove! they had pretty pickings off us before they were done. I fancy the owner was already in a tight place. There were delays. Then it was decided to take part of the cargo out and calk her topsides. This was done, the repairs finished, cargo reshipped; a new crew came on board, and we went out—for Bangkok. At the end of a week we were back again. The crew said they weren't going to Bangkok—a hundred and fifty days' passage—in a something hooker that wanted pumping eight hours out of the twenty-four; and the nautical papers inserted again the little paragraph: '*Judea.* Bark. Tyne to Bangkok; coals; put back to Falmouth leaky and with crew refusing duty.'

"There were more delays—more tinkering. The owner came down for a day, and said she was as right as a little fiddle. Poor old Captain Beard looked like the ghost of a Geordie[30] skipper—through the worry and humiliation of it. Remember, he was sixty, and it was his first command.

Mahon said it was a foolish business and would end badly. I loved the ship more than ever, and wanted awfully to get to Bangkok. To Bangkok! Magic name, blessed name. Mesopotamia wasn't a patch on it.[31] Remember, I was twenty, and it was my first second-mate's billet, and the East was waiting for me.

"We went out and anchored in the outer roads with a fresh crew—the third. She leaked worse than ever. It was as if those confounded shipwrights had actually made a hole in her. This time we did not even go outside. The crew simply refused to man the windlass.

"They towed us back to the inner harbor, and we became a fixture, a feature, an institution of the place. People pointed us out to visitors as 'That 'ere bark that's going to Bangkok—has been here six months—put back three times.' On holidays the small boys pulling about in boats would hail, '*Judea,* ahoy!' and if a head showed above the rail shouted, 'Where you bound to?—Bangkok?' and jeered. We were only three on board. The poor old skipper mooned in the cabin. Mahon undertook the cooking, and unexpectedly developed all a Frenchman's genius for preparing nice little messes. I looked languidly after the rigging. We became citizens of Falmouth. Every shopkeeper knew us. At the barber's or tobacconist's they asked familiarly, 'Do you think you will ever get to Bangkok?' Meantime the owner, the underwriters, and the charterers[32] squabbled amongst themselves in London, and our pay went on. . . . Pass the bottle.

"It was horrid. Morally it was worse than pumping for life. It seemed as though we had been forgotten by the world, belonged to nobody, would get nowhere; it seemed that, as if bewitched, we would have to live forever and ever in that inner harbor, a derision and a byword to generations of longshore loafers and dishonest boatmen. I obtained three months' pay and a five days' leave, and made a rush for London. It took me a day to get there and pretty well another to come back—but three months' pay went all the same. I don't know what I did with it. I went to a music hall, I believe, lunched, dined, and supped in a swell place in Regent Street, and was back on time, with nothing but a complete set of Byron's[33] works and a new railway rug to show for three months' work. The boatman who pulled me off to the ship said: 'Hallo! I thought you had left the old thing. *She* will never get to Bangkok.' 'That's all *you* know about it,' I said, scornfully—but I didn't like that prophecy at all.

"Suddenly a man, some kind of agent to somebody, appeared with full powers. He had grog-blossoms[34] all over his face, an indomitable energy, and was a jolly soul. We leaped into life again. A hulk came alongside, took our cargo, and then we went into dry dock to get our copper stripped. No wonder she leaked. The poor thing, strained beyond endurance by the gale, had, as if in disgust, spat out all the oakum of her lower seams. She was recalked, new-coppered, and made as tight as a bottle. We went back to the hulk and reshipped our cargo.

"Then, on a fine moonlight night, all the rats left the ship.

"We had been infested with them. They had destroyed our sails, consumed more stores than the crew, affably shared our beds and our dangers, and now, when the ship was made seaworthy, concluded to clear out. I called Mahon to enjoy the spectacle. Rat after rat appeared on our rail, took a last look over his shoulder, and leaped with a hollow thud into the empty hulk. We tried to count them, but soon lost the tale. Mahon said: 'Well, well! don't talk to me about the intelligence of rats. They ought to have left before, when we had that narrow squeak from foundering. There you have the proof how silly is the superstition about them. They leave a good ship for an old rotten hulk, where there is nothing to eat, too, the fools! . . . I don't believe they know what is safe or what is good for them, any more than you or I.'

"And after some more talk we agreed that the wisdom of rats had been grossly overrated, being in fact no greater than that of men.

"The story of the ship was known, by this, all up the Channel from Land's End to the Forelands, and we could get no crew on the south coast. They sent us one all complete from Liverpool, and we left once more—for Bangkok.

"We had fair breezes, smooth water right into the tropics, and the old *Judea* lumbered along in the sunshine. When she went eight knots[35] everything cracked aloft, and we tied our caps to our heads; but mostly she strolled on at the rate of three miles an hour. What could you expect? She was tired—that old ship. Her youth was where mine is—where yours is—you fellows who listen to this yarn; and what friend would throw your years and your weariness in your face? We didn't grumble at her. To us aft,[36] at least, it seemed as though we had been born in her, reared in her, had lived in her for ages, had never known any other ship. I would just as soon have abused the old village church at home for not being a cathedral.

"And for me there was also my youth to make me patient. There was all the East before me, and all life, and the thought that I had been tried in that ship and had come out pretty well. And I thought of men of old who, centuries ago, went that road in ships that sailed no better, to the land of palms, and spices, and yellow sands, and of brown nations ruled by kings more cruel than Nero the Roman, and more splendid than Solomon the Jew.[37] The old bark lumbered on, heavy with her age and the burden of her cargo, while I lived the life of youth in ignorance and hope. She lumbered on through an interminable[38] procession of days; and the fresh gilding flashed back at the setting sun, seemed to cry out over the darkening sea the words painted on her stern, '*Judea*, London. Do or Die.'

"Then we entered the Indian Ocean and steered northerly for Java Head. The winds were light. Weeks slipped by. She crawled on, do or die, and people at home began to think of posting us as overdue.

"One Saturday evening, I being off duty, the men asked me to give them an extra bucket of water or so—for washing clothes. As I did not wish to screw on the fresh-water pump so late, I went forward whistling, and with a key in my hand to unlock the forepeak scuttle,[39] intending to serve the water out of a spare tank we kept there.

"The smell down below was as unexpected as it was frightful. One would have thought hundreds of paraffin lamps[40] had been flaring and smoking in that hole for days. I was glad to get out. The man with me coughed and said, 'Funny smell, sir.' I answered negligently, 'It's good for the health, they say,' and walked aft.

"The first thing I did was to put my head down the square of the midship ventilator. As I lifted the lid a visible breath, something like a thin fog, a puff of faint haze, rose from the opening. The ascending air was hot, and had a heavy, sooty, paraffiny smell. I gave one sniff, and put down the lid gently. It was no use choking myself. The cargo was on fire.

"Next day she began to smoke in earnest. You see, it was to be expected, for though the coal was of a safe kind, that cargo had been so handled, so broken up with handling, that it looked more like smithy coal[41] than anything else. Then it had been wetted—more than once. It rained all the time we were taking it back from the hulk, and now with this long passage it got heated, and there was another case of spontaneous combustion.[42]

"The captain called us into the cabin. He had a chart spread on the table, and looked unhappy. He said, 'The coast of West Australia is near, but I mean to proceed to our destination. It is the hurricane month, too; but we will just keep her head for Bangkok, and fight the fire. No more putting back anywhere, if we all get roasted. We will try first to stifle this 'ere damned combustion by want of air.'

"We tried. We battened down[43] everything, and still she smoked. The smoke kept coming out through imperceptible crevices; it forced itself through bulkheads and covers; it oozed here and there and everywhere in slender threads, in an invisible film, in an incomprehensible manner. It made its way into the cabin, into the forecastle; it poisoned the sheltered places on the deck; it could be sniffed as high as the mainyard. It was clear that if the smoke came out the air came in. This was disheartening. This combustion refused to be stifled.

"We resolved to try water, and took the hatches off. Enormous volumes of smoke, whitish, yellowish, thick, greasy, misty, choking, ascended as high as the trucks. All hands cleared out aft. Then the poisonous cloud blew away, and we went back to work in a smoke that was no thicker now than that of an ordinary factory chimney.

"We rigged the force pump, got the hose along, and by and by it burst. Well, it was as old as the ship—a prehistoric hose, and past repair. Then we pumped with the feeble head pump, drew water with buckets, and in this way managed in time to pour lots of Indian Ocean into the main hatch. The bright stream flashed in sunshine, fell into a layer of white crawling smoke, and vanished on the black surface of coal. Steam ascended mingling with the smoke. We poured salt water as into a barrel without a bottom. It was our fate to pump in that ship, to pump out of her, to pump into her; and after keeping water out of her to save ourselves from being drowned, we frantically poured water into her to save ourselves from being burnt.

"And she crawled on, do or die, in the serene weather. The sky was a miracle of purity, a miracle of azure. The sea was polished, was blue, was pellucid, was sparkling like a precious stone, extending on all sides, all round to the horizon—as if the whole terrestrial globe had been one jewel, one colossal sapphire, a single gem fashioned into a planet. And on the luster of the great calm waters the *Judea* glided imperceptibly, enveloped in languid and unclean vapors, in a lazy cloud that drifted to leeward, light and slow; a pestiferous cloud defiling the splendor of sea and sky.

"All this time of course we saw no fire. The cargo smoldered at the bottom somewhere. Once Mahon, as we were working side by side, said to me with a queer smile: 'Now, if she only would spring a tidy leak—like that time when we first left the Channel—it would put a stopper on this fire. Wouldn't it?' I remarked irrelevantly,[44] 'Do you remember the rats?'

"We fought the fire and sailed the ship, too, as carefully as though nothing had been the matter. The steward cooked and attended on us. Of the other twelve men, eight worked while four rested. Everyone took his turn, captain included. There was equality, and if not exactly fraternity, then a deal of good feeling. Sometimes a man, as he dashed a bucketful of water down the hatchway, would yell out, 'Hurrah for Bangkok!' and the rest laughed. But generally we were taciturn[45] and serious—and thirsty. Oh! how thirsty! And we had to be careful with the water. Strict allowance. The ship smoked, the sun blazed. . . . Pass the bottle.

"We tried everything. We even made an attempt to dig down to the fire. No good, of course. No man could remain more than a minute below. Mahon, who went first, fainted there, and the man who went to fetch him out did likewise. We lugged them out on deck. Then I leaped down to show how easily it could be done. They had learned wisdom by that time, and contented themselves by fishing for me with a chainhook tied to a broom handle, I believe. I did not offer to go and fetch up my shovel, which was left down below.

"Things began to look bad. We put the longboat into the water. The second boat was ready to swing out. We had also another, a fourteen-foot thing, on davits[46] aft, where it was quite safe.

"Then, behold, the smoke suddenly decreased. We redoubled our efforts to flood the bottom of the ship. In two days there was no smoke at all. Everybody was on the broad grin. This was on a Friday. On Saturday no work, but sailing the ship, of course, was done. The men washed their clothes and their faces for the first time in a fortnight, and had a special dinner given them. They spoke of spontaneous combustion with contempt, and implied *they* were the boys to put out combustions. Somehow we all felt as though we each had inherited a large fortune. But a beastly smell of burning hung about the ship. Captain Beard had hollow eyes and sunken cheeks. I had never noticed so much before how twisted and bowed he was. He and Mahon prowled soberly about hatches and ventilators, sniffing. It struck me suddenly poor Mahon was a very, very old chap. As to me, I was pleased and proud as though I had helped to win a great naval battle. O youth!

"The night was fine. In the morning a homeward-bound ship passed us hull down—the first we had seen for months; but we were nearing the land at last, Java Head being about 190 miles off, and nearly due north.

"Next day it was my watch on deck from eight to twelve. At breakfast the captain observed, 'It's wonderful how that smell hangs about the cabin.' About ten, the mate being on the poop, I stepped down on the main deck for a moment. The carpenter's bench stood abaft the mainmast: I leaned against it sucking at my pipe, and the carpenter, a young chap, came to talk to me. He remarked, 'I think we have done very well, haven't we?' and then I perceived with annoyance the fool was trying to tilt the bench. I said curtly, 'Don't, Chips,' and immediately became aware of a queer sensation, of an absurd delusion—I seemed somehow to be in the air. I heard all round me like a pent-up breath released—as if a thousand giants simultaneously had said Phoo!—and felt a dull concussion which made my ribs ache suddenly. No doubt about it—I was in the air, and my body was describing a short parabola.[47] But short as it was, I had the time to think several thoughts in, as far as I can remember, the following order: 'This can't be the carpenter—What is it?—Some accident—Submarine volcano?—Coals, gas!—By Jove! We are being blown up—Everybody's dead—I am falling into the afterhatch—I see fire in it.'

"The coaldust suspended in the air of the hold had glowed dull-red at the moment of the explosion. In the twinkling of an eye, in an infinitesimal fraction of a second since the first tilt of the bench, I was sprawling full length on the cargo. I picked myself up and scrambled out. It was quick like a rebound. The deck was a wilderness of smashed timber, lying crosswise like trees in a wood after a hurricane; an immense curtain of solid rags waved gently before me—it was the mainsail blown to strips. I thought: the masts will be toppling over directly; and to get out of the way bolted on all fours towards the poop ladder. The first person I saw was Mahon, with eyes like saucers, his mouth open, and the long white hair standing straight on end round his head like a silver halo. He was just about to go down when the sight of the main deck stirring, heaving up, and changing into splinters before his eyes, petrified him on the top step. I stared at him in unbelief, and he stared at me with a queer kind of shocked curiosity. I did not know that I had no hair, no eyebrows, no eyelashes, that my young mustache was burnt off, that my face was black, one cheek laid open, my nose cut, and my chin bleeding. I had lost my cap, one of my slippers, and my shirt was torn to rags. Of all this I was not aware. I was amazed to see the ship still afloat, the poop deck whole—and, most of all, to see anybody alive. Also the peace of the sky and the serenity of the sea were distinctly surprising. I suppose I expected to see them convulsed with horror. . . . Pass the bottle.

"There was a voice hailing the ship from somewhere—in the air, in the sky—I couldn't tell. Presently I saw the captain—and he was mad. He asked me eagerly, 'Where's the cabin table?' and to hear such a question was a frightful shock. I had just been blown up, you understand, and vibrated with that experience—I wasn't quite sure whether I was alive. Mahon began to stamp with both feet and yelled at him, 'Good God! don't you see the deck's blown out of her?' I found my voice, and stammered out as if conscious of some gross neglect of duty, 'I don't know where the cabin table is.' It was like an absurd dream.

"Do you know what he wanted next? Well, he wanted to trim the yards. Very placidly,[48] and as if lost in thought, he insisted on having the foreyard squared.[49] 'I don't know if there's anybody alive,' said Mahon, almost tearfully. 'Surely,' he said, gently, 'there will be enough left to square the foreyard.'

"The old chap, it seems, was in his own berth winding up the chronometers,[50] when the shock sent him spinning. Immediately it occurred to him—as he said afterwards—that the ship had struck something, and ran out into the cabin. There, he saw, the cabin table had vanished somewhere. The deck being blown up, it had fallen down into the lazarette[51] of course. Where we had our breakfast that morning he saw only a great hole in the floor. This appeared to him so awfully mysterious, and impressed him so immensely, that what he saw and heard after he got on deck were mere trifles in comparison. And, mark, he noticed directly the wheel deserted and his bark off her course—and his only thought was to get that miserable, stripped, undecked, smoldering shell of a ship back again with her head pointing at her port of destination. Bangkok! That's what he was after. I tell you this quiet, bowed, bandy-legged, almost deformed little man was immense in the singleness of his idea and in his placid ignorance of our agitation. He motioned us forward with a commanding gesture, and went to take the wheel himself.

"Yes; that was the first thing we did—trim the yards of that wreck! No one was killed, or even disabled, but everyone was more or less hurt. You should have seen them! Some were in rags, with black faces, like coal heavers, like sweeps, and had bullet heads that seemed closely cropped, but were in fact singed to the skin. Others, of the watch below, awakened by being shot out from their collapsing bunks, shivered incessantly, and kept on groaning even as we went about our work. But they all worked. That crew of Liverpool hard cases had in them the right stuff. It's my experience they always have. It is the sea that gives it—the vastness, the loneliness surrounding their dark stolid souls. Ah, Well! We stumbled, we crept, we fell, we barked our shins on the wreckage, we hauled. The masts stood, but we did not know how much they might be charred down below. It was nearly calm, but a long swell ran from the west and made her roll. They might go at any moment.

We looked at them with apprehension. One could not foresee which way they would fall.

"Then we retreated aft and looked about us. The deck was a tangle of planks on edge, of planks on end, of splinters, of ruined woodwork. The masts rose from that chaos like big trees above a matted undergrowth. The interstices[52] of that mass of wreckage were full of something whitish, sluggish, stirring—of something that was like a greasy fog. The smoke of the invisible fire was coming up again, was trailing, like a poisonous thick mist in some valley choked with dead wood. Already lazy wisps were beginning to curl upwards amongst the mass of splinters. Here and there a piece of timber, stuck upright, resembled a post. Half of a fife rail[53] had been shot through the foresail, and the sky made a patch of glorious blue in the ignobly soiled canvas. A portion of several boards holding together had fallen across the rail, and one end protruded overboard, like a gangway leading upon nothing, like a gangway leading over the deep sea, leading to death—as if inviting us to walk the plank at once and be done with our ridiculous troubles. And still the air, the sky—a ghost, something invisible was hailing the ship.

"Someone had the sense to look over, and there was the helmsman,[54] who had impulsively jumped overboard, anxious to come back. He yelled and swam lustily like a merman, keeping up with the ship. We threw him a rope, and presently he stood amongst us streaming with water and very crestfallen. The captain had surrendered the wheel, and apart, elbow on rail and chin in hand, gazed at the sea wistfully. We asked ourselves, What next? I thought, Now, this is something like. This is great. I wonder what will happen. O youth!

"Suddenly Mahon sighted a steamer far astern. Captain Beard said, 'We may do something with her yet.' We hoisted two flags, which said in the international language of the sea, 'On fire. Want immediate assistance.' The steamer grew bigger rapidly, and by and by spoke with two flags on her foremast, 'I am coming to your assistance.'

"In half an hour she was abreast, to windward, within hail, and rolling slightly, with her engines stopped. We lost our composure, and yelled all together with excitement, 'We've been blown up.' A man in a white helmet, on the bridge, cried, 'Yes! All right! all right!' and he nodded his head, and smiled, and made soothing motions with his hand as though at a lot of frightened children. One of the boats dropped in the water, and walked towards us upon the sea with her long oars. Four Calashes pulled a swinging stroke. This was my first sight of Malay seamen. I've known them since, but what struck me then was their unconcern: they came alongside, and even the bowman standing up and holding to our main chains with the boathook did not deign to lift his head for a glance. I thought people who had been blown up deserved more attention.

"A little man, dry like a chip and agile like a monkey, clambered up. It was the mate of the steamer. He gave one look, and cried, 'O boys—you had better quit!'

"We were silent. He talked apart with the captain for a time—seemed to argue with him. Then they went away together to the steamer.

"When our skipper came back we learned that the steamer was the *Somerville,* Captain Nash, from West Australia to Singapore via Batavia with mails, and that the agreement was she should tow us to Anjer or Batavia, if possible, where we could extinguish the fire by scuttling,[55] and then proceed on our voyage—to Bangkok! The old man seemed excited. 'We will do it yet,' he said to Mahon, fiercely. He shook his fist at the sky. Nobody else said a word.

"At noon the steamer began to tow. She went ahead slim and high, and what was left of the *Judea* followed at the end of seventy fathom of towrope—followed her swiftly like a cloud of smoke with mastheads protruding above. We went aloft to furl the sails. We coughed on the yards, and were careful about the bunts.[56] Do you see the lot of us there, putting a neat furl on the sails of that ship doomed to arrive nowhere? There was not a man who didn't think that at any moment the masts would topple over. From aloft we could not see the ship for smoke, and they worked carefully, passing the gaskets[57] with even turns. 'Harbor furl—aloft there!' cried Mahon from below.

"You understand this? I don't think one of those chaps expected to get down in the usual way. When we did I heard them saying to each other, 'Well, I thought we would come down overboard, in a lump—sticks and all—blame me if I didn't.' 'That's what I was thinking to myself,' would answer wearily another battered and bandaged scarecrow. And, mind, these were men without the drilled-in habit of obedience. To an onlooker they would be a lot of profane scallawags[58] without a redeeming point. What made them do it—what made them obey me when I, thinking consciously how fine it was, made them drop the bunt of the foresail twice to try and do it better? What? They had no professional reputation—no examples, no praise. It wasn't a sense of duty; they all knew well enough how to shirk, and laze, and dodge—when they had a mind to it—and mostly they had. Was it the two pounds ten[59] a month that sent them there? They didn't think their pay half good enough. No; it was something in them, something inborn and subtle and everlasting. I don't say positively that the crew of a French or German merchantman wouldn't have done it, but I doubt whether it would have been done in the same way. There was a completeness in it, something solid like a principle, and masterful like an instinct—a disclosure of something secret—of that hidden something, that gift of good or evil that makes racial difference, that shapes the fate of nations.

"It was that night at ten that, for the first time since we had been fighting it, we saw the fire. The speed of the towing had fanned the smoldering destruction. A blue gleam appeared forward, shining below the wreck of the deck. It wavered in patches, it seemed to stir and creep like the light of a glow-worm. I saw it first, and told Mahon. 'Then the game's up,' he said. 'We had better stop this towing, or she will burst out suddenly fore and aft before we can clear out.' We set up a yell; rang bells to attract their attention; they towed on. At last Mahon and I had to crawl forward and cut the rope with an axe. There was no time to cast off the lashings. Red tongues could be seen licking the wilderness of splinters under our feet as we made our way back to the poop.

"Of course they very soon found out in the steamer that the rope was gone. She gave a loud blast of her whistle, her lights were seen sweeping in a wide circle, she came up ranging close alongside, and stopped. We were all in a tight group on the poop looking at her. Every man had saved a little bundle or a bag. Suddenly a conical flame with a twisted top shot up forward and threw upon the black sea a circle of light, with the two vessels side by side and heaving gently in its center. Captain Beard had been sitting on the gratings still and mute for hours, but now he rose slowly and advanced in front of us, to the mizzen-shrouds.[60] Captain Nash hailed: 'Come along! Look sharp. I have mailbags on board. I will take you and your boats to Singapore.'

" 'Thank you! No!' said our skipper. 'We must see the last of the ship.'

" 'I can't stand by any longer," shouted the other. 'Mails—you know.'

" 'Ay! ay! We are all right.'

" 'Very well! I'll report you in Singapore. . . . Good-by!'

"He waved his hand. Our men dropped their bundles quietly. The steamer moved ahead, and passing out of the circle of light, vanished at once from our sight, dazzled by the fire which burned fiercely. And then I knew that I would see the East first as commander of a small boat. I thought it fine; and the fidelity to the old ship was fine. We should see the last of her. Oh, the glamor of youth! Oh, the fire of it, more dazzling than the flames of the burning ship, throwing a magic light on the wide earth, leaping audaciously to the sky, presently to be quenched by time, more cruel, more pitiless, more bitter than the sea—and like the flames of the burning ship surrounded by an impenetrable night.

"The old man warned us in his gentle and inflexible way that it was part of our duty to save for the underwriters as much as we could of the ship's gear. Accordingly we went to work aft, while she blazed forward to give us plenty of light. We lugged out a lot of rubbish. What didn't we save? An old barometer fixed with an absurd quantity of screws nearly cost me my life: a sudden rush of smoke came upon me, and I just got away in time. There were various stores, bolts of canvas, coils of rope; the poop looked like a marine bazaar, and the boats were lumbered to the gunwales.[61] One would have thought the old man wanted to take as much as he could of his first command with him. He was very, very quiet, but off his balance evidently. Would you believe it? He wanted to take a length of old stream-cable and a kedge anchor with him in the longboat. We said, 'Ay, ay, sir,' deferentially,[62] and on the quiet let the things slip overboard. The heavy medicine chest went that way, two bags of green coffee, tins of paint—fancy, paint!—a whole lot of things. Then I was ordered with two hands into the boats to make a stowage and get them ready against the time it would be proper for us to leave the ship.

"We put everything straight, stepped the longboat's mast for our skipper, who was to take charge of her, and I was not sorry to sit down for a moment. My face felt raw, every limb ached as if broken, I was aware of all my ribs, and would have sworn to a twist in the backbone. The boats, fast astern, lay in a deep shadow, and all around I could see the circle of the sea lighted by the fire. A gigantic flame arose forward straight and clear. It flared fierce, with noises like the whirr of wings, with rumbles as of thunder. There were cracks, detonations, and from the cone of flame the sparks flew upwards, as man is born to trouble,[63] to leaky ships, and to ships that burn.

"What bothered me was that the ship, lying broadside to the swell and to such wind as there was—a mere breath—the boats would not keep astern where they were safe, but persisted, in a pigheaded way boats have, in getting under the counter and then swinging alongside. They were knocking about dangerously and coming near the flame, while the ship rolled on them, and, of course, there was always the danger of the masts going over the side at any moment. I and my two boatkeepers kept them off as best we could, with oars and boathooks; but to be constantly at it became exasperating, since there was no reason why we should not leave at once. We could not see those on board, nor could we imagine what caused the delay. The boatkeepers were swearing feebly, and I had not only my share of the work but also had to keep at it two men who showed a constant inclination to lay themselves down and let things slide.

"At last I hailed, 'On deck there,' and someone looked over. 'We're ready here,' I said. The head disappeared, and very soon popped up again. 'The captain says, All right, sir, and to keep the boats well clear of the ship.'

"Half an hour passed. Suddenly there was a frightful racket, rattle, clanking of chain, hiss of water, and millions of sparks flew up into the shivering column of smoke that stood leaning slightly above the ship. The catheads[64] had burned away, and the two red-hot anchors had gone to the bottom, tearing out after them two hundred fathom[65] of red-hot chain. The ship trembled, the mass of flame swayed as if ready to collapse, and the fore-topgallant mast fell. It darted down like an arrow of fire, shot under, and instantly leaping up within an oar's length of the boats, floated quietly, very black on the luminous sea. I hailed the deck again. After some time a man in an unexpectedly cheerful but also muffled tone, as though he had been trying to speak with his mouth shut, informed me, 'Coming directly, sir,' and vanished. For a long time I heard nothing but the whirr and roar of the fire. There were also whistling sounds. The boats jumped, tugged at the painters, ran at each other playfully, knocked their sides together, or, do what we would, swung in a bunch against the ship's side. I couldn't stand it any longer, and swarming up a rope, clambered aboard over the stern.

"It was as bright as day. Coming up like this, the sheet of fire facing me was a terrifying sight, and the heat seemed hardly bearable at first. On a settee cushion dragged out of the cabin Captain Beard, his legs drawn up and one arm under his head, slept with the light playing on him. Do you know what the rest were busy about? They were sitting on deck right aft, round an open case, eating bread and cheese and drinking bottled stout.[66]

"On the background of flames twisting in fierce tongues above their heads they seemed at home like salamanders,[67] and looked like a band of desperate pirates. The fire sparkled in the whites of their eyes, gleamed on patches of white skin seen through the torn shirts. Each had the marks as of a battle about him—bandaged heads, tied-up arms, a strip of dirty rag round a knee—and each man had a bottle between his legs and a chunk of cheese in his hand. Mahon got up. With his handsome and disreputable head, his hooked profile, his long white beard, and with an uncorked bottle in his hand, he resembled one of those reckless sea robbers of old making merry amidst violence and disaster. 'The last meal on board,' he explained solemnly. 'We had nothing to eat all day, and it was no use leaving all this.' He flourished the bottle and indicated the sleeping skipper. 'He said he couldn't swallow anything, so I got him to lie down,' he went on; and as I stared, 'I don't know whether you are aware, young fellow, the man had no sleep to speak of for days—and there will be dam' little sleep in the boats.' 'There will be no boats by and by if you fool about much longer,' I said, indignantly. I walked up to the skipper and shook him by the shoulder. At last he opened his eyes, but did not move. 'Time to leave her, sir,' I said quietly.

"He got up painfully, looked at the flames, at the sea sparkling round the ship, and black, black as ink farther away; he looked at the stars shining dim through a thin veil of smoke in a sky black, black as Erebus.[68]

" 'Youngest first,' he said.

"And the ordinary seaman, wiping his mouth with the back of his hand, got up, clambered over the taffrail, and vanished. Others followed. One, on the point of going over, stopped short to drain his bottle, and with a great swing of his arm flung it at the fire. 'Take this!' he cried.

"The skipper lingered disconsolately, and we left him to commune alone for a while with his first command. Then I went up again and brought him away at last. It was time. The ironwork on the poop was hot to the touch.

"Then the painter[69] of the longboat was cut, and the three boats, tied together, drifted clear of the ship. It was just sixteen hours after the explosion when we abandoned her. Mahon had charge of the second boat, and I had the smallest—the fourteen-foot thing. The longboat would have taken the lot of us; but the skipper said we must save as much property as we could—for the underwriters—and so I got my first command. I had two men with me, a bag of biscuits, a few tins of meat, and a breaker of water. I was ordered to keep close to the longboat, that in case of bad weather we might be taken into her.

"And do you know what I thought? I thought I would part company as soon as I could. I wanted to have my first command all to myself. I wasn't going to sail in a squadron if there were a chance for independent cruising. I would make land by myself. I would beat the other boats. Youth! Ah, youth! The silly, charming, beautiful youth.

"But we did not make a start at once. We must see the last of the ship. And so the boats drifted about that night, heaving and setting on the swell. The men dozed, waked, sighed, groaned. I looked at the burning ship.

"Between the darkness of earth and heaven she was burning fiercely upon a disc of purple sea shot by the blood-red play of gleams; upon a disc of water glittering and sinister. A high, clear flame, an immense and lonely flame, ascended from the ocean, and from its summit the black smoke poured continuously at the sky. She burned furiously; mournful and imposing like a funeral pile kindled in the night, surrounded by the sea, watched over by the stars. A magnificent death had come like a grace, like a gift, like a reward to that old ship at the end of her laborious days. The surrender of her weary ghost to the keeping of stars and sea was stirring like the sight of a glorious triumph. The masts fell just before daybreak, and for a moment there was a burst and turmoil of sparks that seemed to fill with flying fire the night patient and watchful, the vast night lying silent upon the sea. At daylight she was only a charred shell, floating still under a cloud of smoke and bearing a glowing mass of coal within.

"Then the oars were got out, and the boats forming in a line moved round her remains as if in procession —the longboat leading. As we pulled across her stern a slim dart of fire shot out viciously at us, and suddenly she went down, head first, in a great hiss of steam. The unconsumed stern was the last to sink; but the paint had gone, had cracked, had peeled off, and there were no letters, there was no word, no stubborn device that was like her soul, to flash at the rising sun her creed and her name.

"We made our way north. A breeze sprang up, and about noon all the boats came together for the last time. I had no mast or sail in mine, but I made a mast out of a spare oar and hoisted a boat-awning for a sail, with a boathook for a yard. She was certainly over-masted, but I had the satisfaction of knowing that with the wind aft I could beat the other two. I had to wait for them. Then we all had a look at the captain's chart, and, after a sociable meal of hard bread and water, got our last instructions. These were simple: steer north, and keep together as much as possible. 'Be careful with the jury-rig,[70] Marlow,' said the captain; and Mahon, as I sailed proudly past his boat, wrinkled his curved nose and hailed, 'You will sail that ship of yours under water, if you don't look out, young fellow.' He was a malicious[71] old man —and may the deep sea where he sleeps now rock him gently, rock him tenderly to the end of time!

"Before sunset a thick rain-squall passed over the two boats, which were far astern, and that was the last I saw of them for a time. Next day I sat steering my cockle-shell—my first command—with nothing but water and sky round me. I did sight in the afternoon the upper sails of a ship far away, but said nothing, and my men did not notice her. You see I was afraid she might be homeward bound, and I had no mind to turn back from the portals of the East. I was steering for Java—another blessed name—like Bangkok, you know. I steered many days.

"I need not tell you what it is to be knocking about in an open boat. I remember nights and days of calm, when we pulled, we pulled, and the boat seemed to stand still, as if bewitched within the circle of the sea horizon. I remember the heat, the deluge of rain-squalls that kept us bailing for dear life (but filled our water cask), and I remember sixteen hours on end with a mouth dry as a cinder and a steering oar over the stern to keep my first command head on to a breaking sea. I did not know how good a man I was till then. I remember the drawn faces, the dejected figures of my two men, and I remember my youth and the feeling that will never come back any more—the feeling that I could last forever, outlast the sea, the earth, and all men; the deceitful feeling that lures us on to joys, to perils, to love, to vain effort—to death; the triumphant conviction of strength, the heat of life in the handful of dust, the glow in the heart that with every year grows dim, grows cold, grows small, and expires—and expires, too soon, too soon—before life itself.

"And this is how I see the East. I have seen its secret places and have looked into its very soul; but now I see it always from a small boat, a high outline of mountains, blue and afar in the morning; like faint mist at noon; a jagged wall of purple at sunset. I have the feel of the oar in my hand, the vision of a scorching blue sea in my eyes. And I see a bay, a wide bay, smooth as glass and polished like ice, shimmering in the dark. A red light burns far off upon the gloom of the land, and the night is soft and warm. We drag at the oars with aching arms, and suddenly a puff of wind, a puff faint and tepid[72] and laden with strange odors of blossoms, of aromatic[73] wood, comes out of the still night—the first sigh of the East on my face. That I can never forget. It was impalpable[74] and enslaving, like a charm, like a whispered promise of mysterious delight.

"We had been pulling this finishing spell for eleven hours. Two pulled, and he whose turn it was to rest sat at the tiller. We had made out the red light in that bay and steered for it, guessing it must mark some small coasting port. We passed two vessels, outlandish and high-sterned, sleeping at anchor, and, approaching the light, now very dim, ran the boat's nose against the end of a jutting wharf. We were blind with fatigue. My men dropped the oars and fell off the thwarts as if dead. I made fast to a pile. A current rippled softly. The scented obscurity of the shore was grouped into vast masses, a density of colossal clumps of vegetation, probably—mute and fantastic shapes. And at their foot the semicircle of a beach gleamed faintly, like an illusion. There was not a light, not a stir, not a sound. The mysterious East faced me, perfumed like a flower, silent like death, dark like a grave.

"And I sat weary beyond expression, exulting like a conqueror, sleepless and entranced as if before a profound, a fateful enigma.[75]

"A splashing of oars, a measured dip reverberating on the level of water, intensified by the silence of the shore into loud claps, made me jump up. A boat, a European boat, was coming in. I invoked the name of the dead; I hailed: '*Judea* ahoy!' A thin shout answered.

"It was the captain. I had beaten the flagship by three hours, and I was glad to hear the old man's voice again, tremulous and tired. 'Is it you, Marlow?' 'Mind the end of that jetty, sir,' I cried.

"He approached cautiously, and brought up with the deep-sea lead line which we had saved—for the underwriters. I eased my painter and fell alongside. He sat, a broken figure at the stern, wet with dew, his hands clasped in his lap. His men were asleep already. 'I had a terrible time of it,' he murmured. 'Mahon is behind —not very far.' We conversed in whispers, in low whispers, as if afraid to wake up the land. Guns, thunder, earthquakes would not have awakened the men just then.

"Looking round as we talked, I saw away at sea a bright light traveling in the night. 'There's a steamer passing the bay,' I said. She was not passing, she was entering, and she even came close and anchored. 'I wish,' said the old man, 'you would find out whether she is English. Perhaps they could give us a passage somewhere.' He seemed nervously anxious. So by dint of punching and kicking I started one of my men into a state of somnambulism,[76] and giving him an oar, took another and pulled towards the lights of the steamer.

"There was a murmur of voices in her, metallic hollow clangs of the engine room, footsteps on the deck. Her ports shone, round like dilated eyes. Shapes moved about, and there was a shadowy man high up on the bridge. He heard my oars.

"And then, before I could open my lips, the East spoke to me, but it was in a Western voice. A torrent of words was poured into the enigmatical, the fateful silence; outlandish, angry words, mixed with words and even whole sentences of good English, less strange but even more surprising. The voice swore and cursed violently; it riddled the solemn peace of the bay by a volley of abuse. It began by calling me Pig, and from that went crescendo[77] into unmentionable adjectives—in English. The man up there raged aloud in two languages, and with a sincerity in his fury that almost convinced me I had, in some way, sinned against the harmony of the universe. I could hardly see him, but began to think he would work himself into a fit.

"Suddenly he ceased, and I could hear him snorting and blowing like a porpoise. I said:

" 'What steamer is this, pray?'

" 'Eh? What's this? And who are you?'

" 'Castaway crew of an English bark burnt at sea. We came here tonight. I am the second mate. The captain is in the longboat, and wishes to know if you would give us a passage somewhere.'

" 'Oh, my goodness! I say. . . . This is the *Celestial* from Singapore on her return trip. I'll arrange with your captain in the morning, . . . and, . . . I say, . . . did you hear me just now?'

" 'I should think the whole bay heard you.'

" 'I thought you were a shoreboat. Now, look here—this infernal lazy scoundrel of a caretaker has gone to sleep again—curse him. The light is out, and I nearly ran foul of the end of this damned jetty. This is the third time he plays me this trick. Now, I ask you, can anybody stand this kind of thing? It's enough to drive a man out of his mind. I'll report him. . . . I'll get the Assistant Resident to give him the sack, by—! See—there's no light. It's out, isn't it? I take you to witness the light's out. There should be a light, you know. A red light on the—'

"'There was a light,' I said, mildly.

"'But it's out, man! What's the use of talking like this? You can see for yourself it's out—don't you? If you had to take a valuable steamer along this Godforsaken coast you would want a light, too. I'll kick him from end to end of his miserable wharf. You'll see if I don't. I will—'

"'So I may tell my captain you'll take us?' I broke in.

"'Yes, I'll take you. Good night,' he said, brusquely.

"I pulled back, made fast again to the jetty, and then went to sleep at last. I had faced the silence of the East. I had heard some of its language. But when I opened my eyes again the silence was as complete as though it had never been broken. I was lying in a flood of light, and the sky had never looked so far, so high, before. I opened my eyes and lay without moving.

"And then I saw the men of the East—they were looking at me. The whole length of the jetty was full of people. I saw brown, bronze, yellow faces, the black eyes, the glitter, the color of an Eastern crowd. And all these beings stared without a murmur, without a sigh, without a movement. They stared down at the boats, at the sleeping men who at night had come to them from the sea. Nothing moved. The fronds of palms stood still against the sky. Not a branch stirred along the shore, and the brown roofs of hidden houses peeped through the big leaves that hung shining and still like leaves forged of heavy metal. This was the East of the ancient navigators, so old, so mysterious, resplendent[78] and somber, living and unchanged, full of danger and promise. And these were the men. I sat up suddenly. A wave of movement passed through the crowd from end to end, passed along the heads, swayed the bodies, ran along the jetty like a ripple on the water, like a breath of wind on a field—and all was still again. I see it now—the wide sweep of the bay, the glittering sands, the wealth of green infinite and varied, the sea blue like the sea of a dream, the crowd of attentive faces, the blaze of vivid color—the water reflecting it all, the curve of the shore, the jetty, the high-sterned outlandish craft floating still, and the three boats with the tired men from the West sleeping, unconscious of the land and the people and of the violence of sunshine. They slept thrown across the thwarts, curled on bottom-boards, in the careless attitudes of death. The head of the old skipper, leaning back in the stern of the longboat, had fallen on his breast, and he looked as though he would never wake. Farther out old Mahon's face was upturned to the sky, with the long white beard spread out on his breast, as though he had been shot where he sat at the tiller; and a man, all in a heap in the bows of the boat, slept with both arms embracing the stemhead and with his cheek laid on the gunwale. The East looked at them without a sound.

"I have known its fascination since; I have seen the mysterious shores, the still water, the lands of brown nations, where a stealthy Nemesis[79] lies in wait, pursues, overtakes so many of the conquering race, who are proud of their wisdom, of their knowledge, of their strength. But for me all the East is contained in that vision of my youth. It is all in that moment when I opened my young eyes on it. I came upon it from a tussle with the sea—and I was young—and I saw it looking at me. And this is all that is left of it! Only a moment; a moment of strength, of romance, of glamor—of youth! . . . A flick of sunshine upon a strange shore, the time to remember, the time for a sigh, and—good-by!—Night—Good-by . . . !"

He drank.

"Ah! The good old time—the good old time. Youth and the sea. Glamor and the sea! The good, strong sea, the salt, bitter sea, that could whisper to you and roar at you and knock your breath out of you."

He drank again.

"By all that's wonderful it is the sea, I believe, the sea itself—or is it youth alone? Who can tell? But you here—you all had something out of life: money, love—whatever one gets on shore—and, tell me, wasn't that the best time, that time when we were young at sea; young and had nothing, on the sea that gives nothing, except hard knocks—and sometimes a chance to feel your strength—that only—that you all regret?"

And we all nodded at him: the man of finance, the man of accounts, the man of law, we all nodded at him over the polished table that like a still sheet of brown water reflected our faces, lined, wrinkled; our faces marked by toil, by deceptions, by success, by love; our weary eyes looking still, looking always, looking anxiously for something out of life, that while it is expected is already gone—has passed unseen, in a sigh, in a flash—together with the youth, with the strength, with the romance of illusions.

Notes

1 This story is at least partly autobiographical. In an "author's note" composed nearly twenty years after he wrote the story, Conrad said "*Youth* is a feat of memory. It is a record of experience; but that experience, in its facts, in its inwardness and in its outward coloring, begins and ends in myself." Conrad changed the real name of the ship (*Palestine*) to *Judea.* He kept unchanged the names of the real captain and mate, Beard and Mahon.

2 The *Conway* was a training ship on which student officers gained experience.

3 A British line shipping to the Far East, the Pacific and Oriental.

4 Seasonal winds of the Indian Ocean accompanied by heavy rains.

5 Studding sails (light sails extended by poles or spars).

6 Bowed, crooked.

7 Job.

8 Ships engaged in coastwise trade.

9 The Cape of Good Hope (southwestern tip of Africa) and Cape Horn (southernmost point of South America).

[10] A device for raising or hauling objects; here a cable device for handling an anchor.

[11] Any heavy material (here, sand) carried to provide stability and desired draft.

[12] A fabled seaport, the capital of Siam (now Thailand).

[13] Solid structures extending above deck level for the protection of persons and cargo.

[14] The forward part of the ship toward which the wind blows.

[15] A river in the northeast of England that flows into the North Sea some three hundred miles north of London.

[16] *Sartor Resartus* ("the tailor retailored") is a satirical work (1833–1834) by Thomas Carlyle. *Ride to Khiva* is a travel book (1876) by an English soldier; it describes his long winter journey on horseback across the Russian steppes.

[17] Raised deck at the stern of a ship that usually forms the roof of the ship's cabin.

[18] Ships for carrying coal.

[19] A coin equal to 2s6d, at the time equivalent to some 50 cents.

[20] Drizzly (a coinage from "mist" and "drizzle").

[21] A seat across a boat, especially one used by an oarsman.

[22] This is the first of several instances in which the narrator breaks into the story he is telling with a direct request to those listening to him. Such "breaks" in the narrative serve to remind the reader of the circumstances under which the story is being told and provide instances of how a skilled writer can "stage manage" his characters.

[23] Lizard Head is a peninsula in southwest England, terminating in Lizard Point, the southernmost point in England.

[24] Measuring stick.

[25] Upright posts, supports.

[26] The largest boat then carried on a sailing vessel.

[27] Grips, fastenings.

[28] A stair within the hull of a vessel.

[29] A seaport in southwestern England.

[30] A "Geordie" is a native of Tyneside in northeast England.

[31] David Garrick, an 18th-century English actor, said that "that blessed word Mesopotamia" had the power to make people laugh or cry if it were spoken by George Whitefield, a famous preacher and orator.

[32] Persons who had leased the ship; underwriters are insurers.

[33] George Gordon, Lord Byron (1788–1824), English poet.

[34] Swelling and skin discoloration caused by excessive use of alcohol.

[35] A knot is a unit of speed equal to one nautical mile (about 1.15 statute miles) an hour.

[36] Toward or at the stern (back) of a vessel.

[37] Nero was emperor of Rome A.D. 54–68. Solomon was a 10th-century B.C. king of Israel, the son of David and an extraordinarily wise man.

[38] Unending.

[39] A covered hatchway (opening) in the deck of a ship.

[40] Paraffin is a solid substance obtained from crude petroleum, used in candlemaking and for waterproofing. In England, kerosene is called paraffin oil.

[41] Coal used by a blacksmith.

[42] The ignition of a substance from the rapid oxidation of its own constituents without heat from any external source.

[43] Covered.

[44] Not pertinent, related.

[45] Silent.

[46] Devices for supporting, raising, and lowering boats.

[47] Curve, arc.

[48] Calmly, serenely.

[49] That is, to set the sails on the lower mast ready for sailing.

[50] Timepieces.

[51] Space between decks.

[52] Intervening spaces.

[53] A rail surrounding the mast of a sailing vessel.

[54] Person who steers a ship.

[55] Cutting a hole in the side or bottom.

[56] The middle part of a sail gathered into a bunch.

[57] Rings for making a joint watertight.

[58] Rascals.

[59] At the time, about $12.

[60] Taut lines (ropes) from the third mast.

[61] Packed with useless articles to the upper edges of the boat.

[62] Respectfully.

[63] Job 5:7: "Yet man is born unto trouble [just] as [surely as] the sparks fly upward."

[64] Timbers to which an anchor is secured.

[65] A fathom is 6 feet.

[66] A dark, sweet brew made of roasted malt.

[67] Lizards or other reptiles once thought to be able to live in fire.

[68] In classical mythology, the entrance to Hades, the underworld; here the meaning is "total darkness."

[69] Rope for fastening or towing a vessel.

[70] Temporary rig (arrangement of sails).

[71] Spiteful.

[72] Lukewarm.

[73] Sweet-scented.

[74] Not definite or clear, intangible.

[75] Riddle; baffling problem.

[76] Sleepwalking.

[77] Increasing volume.

[78] Gleaming, shining brilliantly.

[79] In classical mythology, the goddess of divine retribution; hence, an agent of punishment.

PLAYS

NOTES ON READING

Drama and fiction (short stories and novels) are alike in several ways. Each presents a series of related actions that form a plot (*what* happens?). Each is concerned with characterization (*who* is involved in the action?). Each places some emphasis upon setting (*where* does the action occur?). Each develops a central theme (what is the *meaning* and *significance* of the selection?).

The basic distinction between fiction and drama is that the former is written to be read, the latter nearly always to be acted. In a short story or novel, we *read* what characters say and do. In an acted play we *hear* what characters say and *see* what they do. A play tells its own story through dialogue and action and is restricted by the physical means of its presentation and by certain dramatic conventions.

Out of people, dialogue, and action set against a backdrop come elements of the drama scheme of life: motives, morals, causes, and conflicts. Place all this in a building called a theater, add lighting effects, music effects, costume, trained actors—and a version of some fable of human life will always emerge. This is drama in a technical—indeed, a magical—sense.

Everyone's life is surrounded by drama in some form or other—whether it be the quiet drama of daily living, the excitement of the latest TV or movie thriller, a human interest story from today's newspaper, or a scene in a village or city street witnessed from a nearby window. When people meet, talk, and move, new behavior patterns result. And because people the world over are ruled by much the same emotions and passions, have much the same frustrations, want alike to be appreciated and loved, hope for happiness, cherish dreams, and possess ideals and goals, they are understandably interested in the successes and failures—the drama—of other people's lives.

If these "other people" live far back in history, if they are great and powerful, if they take great risks—that is, if they illuminate the universal pattern—they provide exciting vicarious experience for the amusement, horror, and education of less-publicized fellow human beings. The plays of Shakespeare bring to life such majestic or arresting figures as Antony, Cleopatra, Hamlet, Juliet, Macbeth, Henry the Eighth, Falstaff, Lear, Ophelia, Julius Caesar, and Othello and cause them to live before our eyes as flesh-and-blood people with whom we can identify or, at worst, interpret with some degree of human understanding.

A printed play is only an approximate sketch of what the author intended the acted play to be. He must depend on the skills of actors and director, the imagination and adroitness of scene designers, the ingenuity of electricians, the efficiency of stagehands. The playwright also must depend on his audience to see, to hear, and to reflect on what is presented.

Drama on the printed page is so different from its effect on the stage that it places upon the reader a heavier responsibility than does fiction. When one reads a play imaginatively and thoughtfully, he serves as actor, director, scene designer, and stagehand. The reader should be able to "see" a play. He can compensate for the loss of live actors by an opportunity to study stage directions at leisure and to reread dialogue that reveals the physical, mental, and emotional actions and reactions of characters.

In reading and analyzing a play, keep in mind the values implicit in all effective drama:

1. *Factual values.* Summarize the play in two or three sentences. What elements in the summary seem familiar? Unfamiliar? Does any part of the factual value of the play depend on its familiarity or unfamiliarity?
2. *Technical values.* Divide the play into its parts. Indicate the time, place, and content of each part; state for each part whether the action is past, present, or to come. Is the structure of the play designed to bring out its theme? Upon what conventions of staging (lighting, scene shifting, and so on) do technical values depend?
3. *Psychological values.* Certain values of a play may be classified as sensory, emotional, empathetic, and analytical. The sensory values of a play involve experiencing a series of images. Emotional values can be noted by making a diagram representing the succession of feelings and emotions experienced by major characters in the play. As a reader, do you identify with (strongly sympathize with, favorably react to) any one character in the play? What analysis of a major character is made by others in the play through what they say, appear to think, and actually do? If a character is not analyzed by other players, make your own analysis.

4. *Symbolical values.* Effective plays achieve added significance by the use of elements created as symbols. Identify and describe the major symbols (persons, objects, actions) appearing in the plays by Sophocles, Shaw, and Wilder. Symbolical values are less important, less central, in many plays than in these three, but every worthwhile dramatic effort relies to some extent on the use of symbols.
5. *Thematic values.* Every drama states or implies an ethical and philosophical attitude. What is the *theme* of the play? Is this ideational value explicit or implicit? What is the author's apparent attitude toward the ethical and philosophical values stated or suggested? How important are these values in shaping your overall opinion of the play?

ANTIGONE

Sophocles

Sophocles (ca. 496 B.C.–ca. 406) was born at Colonus in Attica, near Athens, and thus lived, of course, during the great Periclean Age of Athens. Little is authoritatively known of his life, but it is thought that he moved in the best society of his day and it is known that he was an important public and military figure. He certainly knew Herodotus, and he studied the art of writing tragedy with Aeschylus. It is reported that he was handsome, popular, and well versed in music and gymnastics.

It is generally agreed that *Antigone* was the first of his seven surviving plays to be produced. Probably written about 442 B.C., it is one of three dramas dealing with the Theban saga: *Oedipus the King* interprets the early part of the story; *Oedipus at Colonus* deals with the final hours and death of Oedipus; and *Antigone* treats of the last events of this famous legend.

According to the story, which Sophocles occasionally altered for dramatic purposes, Eteocles, son of Oedipus and now king of Thebes, had exiled his brother, Polyneices, who also coveted the vacated throne. Polyneices had secured aid and had led a host of warriors against the city of Thebes in order to seize the throne. In an ensuing battle, Eteocles and Polyneices had killed each other and thus fulfilled a curse which had been called down upon them by their now-dead father. The invaders were repulsed and Creon had become king. He issued a proclamation that the body of Eteocles should be given honorable burial but that Polyneices' corpse should lie unburied. The action of *Antigone* opens at this point on the day after the battle.

The translation given here is by Sir Richard C. Jebb (1841–1905), British scholar and the great authority of all time on Sophocles.

PRINCIPAL CHARACTERS

ANTIGONE, ISMENE — *daughters of Oedipus*

CREON *king of Thebes, brother of Jocasta*

HAEMON *son of Creon*

TEIRESIAS *a blind prophet*

EURYDICE *wife of Creon*

CHORUS OF THEBAN ELDERS

SCENE:

An open space before the royal palace, once that of Oedipus, at Thebes. The backscene represents the front of the palace, with three doors, of which the central and largest is the principal entrance into the house. The time is at daybreak on the morning after the fall of the two brothers, Eteocles and Polyneices, and the flight of the defeated Argives. ANTIGONE *calls* ISMENE *forth from the palace, in order to speak to her alone.*

ANTIGONE. Ismene, sister, mine own dear sister, knowest thou what ill there is, of all bequeathed by Oedipus, that Zeus fulfils not for us twain while we live? Nothing painful is there, nothing fraught with ruin, no shame, no dishonour, that I have not seen in thy woes and mine.

And now what new edict is this of which they tell, that our Captain hath just published to all Thebes? Knowest thou aught? Hast thou heard? Or is it hidden from thee that our friends are threatened with the doom of our foes?[1]

ISMENE. No word of friends, Antigone, gladsome or painful, hath come to me, since we two sisters were bereft of brothers twain, killed in one day by a twofold blow; and since in this last night the Argive host hath fled, I know no more, whether my fortune be brighter, or more grievous.

ANTIGONE. I knew it well, and therefore sought to bring thee beyond the gates of the court, that thou mightest hear alone.

ISMENE. What is it? 'Tis plain that thou are brooding on some dark tidings.

ANTIGONE. What, hath not Creon destined our brothers, the one to honoured burial, the other to unburied shame? Eteocles, they say, with due observance of right and custom, he hath laid in the earth, for his honour among the dead below. But the hapless corpse of Polyneices—as rumour saith, it hath been published to the town that none shall entomb him or mourn, but leave unwept, unsepulchred, a welcome store for the birds, as they espy him, to feast on at will.

Such, 'tis said, is the edict that the good Creon hath set forth for thee and for me,—yes, for *me*,—and is coming hither to proclaim it clearly to those who know it not; nor counts the matter light, but, whoso disobeys in aught, his doom is death by stoning before all the folk. Thou knowest it now; and thou wilt soon show whether thou art nobly bred, or the base daughter of a noble line.

ISMENE. Poor sister,—and if things stand thus, what could I help to do or undo?

ANTIGONE. Consider if thou wilt share the toil and the deed.

ISMENE. In what venture? What can be thy meaning?

ANTIGONE. Wilt thou aid this hand to lift the dead?

ISMENE. Thou wouldst bury him,—when 'tis forbidden to Thebes?

ANTIGONE. I will do my part,—and

thine, if thou wilt not,—to a brother. False to him will I never be found.

ISMENE. Ah, over-bold! when Creon hath forbidden?

ANTIGONE. Nay, he hath no right to keep me from mine own.

ISMENE. Ah me! think, sister, how our father perished, amid hate and scorn, when sins bared by his own search had moved him to strike both eyes with self-blinding hand; then the mother wife, two names in one, with twisted noose did despite unto her life; and last, our two brothers in one day,—each shedding, hapless one, a kinsman's blood,—wrought out with mutual hands their common doom. And now *we* in turn—we two left all alone—think how we shall perish, more miserably than all the rest, if, in defiance of the law, we brave a king's decree or his powers. Nay, we must remember, first, that we were born women, as who should not strive with men; next, that we are ruled of the stronger, so that we must obey in these things, and in things yet sorer. I, therefore, asking the Spirits Infernal to pardon, seeing that force is put on me herein, will hearken to our rulers; for 'tis witless to be over busy.

ANTIGONE. I will not urge thee,—no, nor, if thou yet shouldst have the mind, wouldst thou be welcome as a worker with *me*. Nay, be what thou wilt; but I will bury him: well for me to die in doing that. I shall rest, a loved one with him whom I have loved, sinless in my crime; for I owe a longer allegiance to the dead than to the living: in that world I shall abide for ever. But if *thou* wilt, be guilty of dishonouring laws which the gods have stablished in honour.

ISMENE. I do them no dishonour; but to defy the State,—I have no strength for that.

ANTIGONE. Such be thy plea:—I, then, will go to heap the earth above the brother whom I love.

ISMENE. Alas, unhappy one! How I fear for thee!

ANTIGONE. Fear not for me: guide thine own fate aright.

ISMENE. At least, then, disclose this plan to none, but hide it closely,—and so, too, will I.

ANTIGONE. Oh, denounce it! Thou wilt be far more hateful for thy silence, if thou proclaim not these things to all.

ISMENE. Thou hast a hot heart for chilling deeds.

ANTIGONE. I know that I please where I am most bound to please.

ISMENE. Aye, if thou canst; but thou wouldst what thou canst not.

ANTIGONE. Why, then, when my strength fails, I shall have done.

ISMENE. A hopeless quest should not be made at all.

ANTIGONE. If thus thou speakest, thou wilt have hatred from me, and will justly be subject to the lasting hatred of the dead. But leave me, and the folly that is mine alone, to suffer this dread thing; for I shall not suffer aught so dreadful as an ignoble death.

ISMENE. Go, then, if thou must; and of this be sure,—that, though thine errand is foolish, to thy dear ones thou art truly dear.

[*Exit* ANTIGONE *on the spectators' left.* ISMENE *retires into the palace by one of the two side-doors. When they have departed, the* CHORUS OF THEBAN ELDERS *enters.*][2]

CHORUS [*singing*] [*strophe 1*]. Beam of the sun, fairest light that ever dawned on Thebe of the seven gates, thou hast shone forth at last, eye of golden day, arisen above Dirce's streams! The warrior of the white shield, who came from Argos in his panoply, hath been stirred by thee to headlong flight, in swifter career;

LEADER OF THE CHORUS [*systema 1*]. who set forth against our land by reason of the vexed claims of Polyneices; and, like shrill-screaming eagle, he flew over into our land, in snow-white pinion sheathed, with an armèd throng, and with plumage of helms.

CHORUS [*antistrophe 1*]. He paused above our dwellings; he ravened around our sevenfold portals with spears athirst for blood; but he went hence, or ever his jaws were glutted with our gore, or the Fire-god's pine-fed flame had seized our crown of towers. So fierce was the noise of battle raised behind him, a thing too hard for him to conquer, as he wrestled with his dragon foe.

LEADER [*systema 2*]. For Zeus utterly abhors the boasts of a proud tongue; and when he beheld them coming on in a great stream, in the haughty pride of clanging gold, he smote with brandished fire one who was now hasting to shout victory at his goal upon our ramparts.

CHORUS [*strophe 2*]. Swung down, he fell on the earth with a crash, torch in hand, he who so lately, in the frenzy of the mad onset, was raging against us with the blasts of his tempestuous hate. But those threats fared not as he hoped; and to other foes the mighty War-god dispensed their several dooms, dealing havoc around, a mighty helper at our need.

LEADER [*systema 3*]. For seven captains at seven gates, matched against seven, left the tribute of their panoplies to Zeus who turns the battle; save those two of cruel fate, who, born of one sire and one mother, set against each other their twain conquering spears, and are sharers in a common death.

CHORUS [*antistrophe 2*]. But since Victory of glorious name hath come to us, with joy responsive to the joy of Thebe whose chariots are many, let us enjoy forgetfulness after the late wars, and visit all the temples of the gods with night-long dance and song; and may Bacchus be our leader, whose dancing shakes the land of Thebe.

LEADER [*systema 4*]. But lo, the king of the land comes yonder, Creon, son of Menoeceus, our new ruler by the new fortunes that the gods have given; what counsel is he pondering, that he hath proposed this special conference of elders, summoned by his general mandate?

[*Enter* CREON, *from the central doors of the palace, in the garb of king, with two attendants.*]

CREON. Sirs, the vessel of our State, after being tossed on wild waves, hath once more been safely steadied by the gods: and ye, out of all the folk, have been called apart by my summons, because I knew, first of all, how true and constant was your reverence for the royal power of Laïus; how, again, when Oedipus was ruler of our land, and when he had perished, your steadfast loyalty still upheld their children. Since, then, his sons have fallen in one day by a twofold doom,—each smitten by the other, each stained with a brother's blood,—I now possess the throne and all its powers, by nearness of kinship to the dead.

No man can be fully known, in soul and spirit and mind, until he hath been seen versed in rule and law-giving. For if any, being supreme guide of the State, cleaves not to the best counsels, but, through some fear, keeps his lips locked, I hold, and have ever held, him most base; and if any makes a friend of more account than his fatherland, that man hath no place in my regard. For I—be Zeus my witness, who sees all things always—would not be silent if I saw ruin, instead of safety, coming to the citizens; nor would I ever deem the country's foe a friend to myself; remembering this, that our country is the ship that bears us safe, and that only while she prospers in our voyage can we make true friends.

Such are the rules by which I guard this city's greatness. And in accord with them is the edict which I have now published to the folk touching the sons of Oedipus;—that Eteocles, who hath fallen fighting for our city, in all renown of arms, shall be entombed, and crowned with every rite that follows the noblest dead to their rest. But for his brother, Polyneices,—who came back from exile, and sought to consume utterly with fire the city of his fathers and the shrines of his fathers' gods,—sought to taste of kindred blood, and to lead the remnant into slavery;—touching this man, it hath been proclaimed to our people that none shall grace him with sepulture or lament, but leave him unburied, a corpse for birds and dogs to eat, a ghastly sight of shame.

Such the spirit of my dealing; and never, by deed of mine, shall the wicked stand in honour before the just; but whoso hath good will to Thebes, he shall be honoured of me, in his life and in his death.

LEADER OF THE CHORUS. Such is thy pleasure, Creon, son of Menoeceus, touching this city's foe, and its friend; and thou hast power, I ween, to take what order thou wilt, both for the dead, and for all us who live.

CREON. See, then, that ye be guardians of the mandate.

LEADER. Lay the burden of this task on some younger man.

CREON. Nay, watchers of the corpse have been found.

LEADER. What, then, is this further charge that thou wouldst give?

CREON. That ye side not with the breakers of these commands.

LEADER. No man is so foolish that he is enamoured of death.

CREON. In sooth, that is the meed; yet lucre hath oft ruined men through their hopes.

[*A* GUARD *enters from the spectators' left.*]

GUARD. My liege, I will not say that I come breathless from speed, or that I have plied a nimble foot; for often did my thoughts make me pause, and wheel round in my path, to return. My mind was holding large discourse with me; "Fool, why goest thou to thy certain doom?" "Wretch, tarrrying again? And if Creon hears this from another, must not thou smart for it?" So debating, I went on my way with lagging steps, and thus a short road was made long. At last, however, it carried the day that I should come hither—to thee; and, though my tale be nought, yet will I tell it; for I come with a good grip on one hope,—that I can suffer nothing but what is my fate.

CREON. And what is it that disquiets thee thus?

GUARD. I wish to tell thee first about myself—I did not do the deed—I did not see the doer—it were not right that I should come to any harm.

CREON. Thou hast a shrewd eye for thy mark; well dost thou fence thyself round against the blame; clearly thou hast some strange thing to tell.

GUARD. Aye, truly; dread news makes one pause long.

CREON. Then tell it, wilt thou, and so get thee gone?

GUARD. Well, this is it.—The corpse—some one hath just given it burial, and gone away,—after sprinkling thirsty dust on the flesh, with such other rites as piety enjoins.

CREON. What sayest thou? What living man hath dared this deed?

GUARD. I know not; no stroke of pickaxe was seen there, no earth thrown up by mattock; the ground was hard and dry, unbroken, without track of wheels; the doer was one who had left no trace. And when the first day-watchman showed it to us, sore wonder fell on all. The dead man was veiled from us; not shut within a tomb, but lightly strewn with dust, as by the hand of one who shunned a curse. And no sign met the eye as though any beast of prey or any dog had come nigh to him, or torn him.

Then evil words flew fast and loud among us, guard accusing guard; and it would e'en have come to blows at last, nor was there any to hinder. Every man was the culprit, and no one was convicted, but all disclaimed knowledge of the deed. And we were ready to take red-hot iron in our hands;—to walk through fire;—to make oath by the gods that we had not done the deed,—that we were not privy to the planning or the doing.

At last, when all our searching was fruitless, one spake, who made us all bend our faces on the earth in fear; for we saw not how we could gainsay him, or escape mischance if we obeyed. His counsel was that this deed must be reported to thee, and not hidden. And this seemed best; and the lot doomed my hapless self to win this prize. So here I stand,—as unwelcome as unwilling, well I wot; for no man delights in the bearer of bad news.

LEADER. O king, my thoughts have long been whispering, can this deed, perchance, be e'en the work of gods?

CREON. Cease, ere thy words fill me utterly with wrath, lest thou be found at once an old man and foolish. For thou sayest what is not to be borne, in saying that the gods have care for this corpse. Was it for high reward of trusty service that they sought to hide his nakedness, who came to burn their pillared shrines and sacred treasures, to burn their land, and scatter its laws to the winds? Or dost thou behold the gods honouring the wicked? It cannot be. No! From the first there were certain in the town that muttered against me, chafing at this edict, wagging their heads in secret; and kept not their necks duly under the yoke, like men contented with my sway.

'Tis by them, well I know, that these have been beguiled and bribed to do this deed. Nothing so evil as money ever grew to be current among men. This lays cities low, this drives men from their homes, this trains and warps honest souls till they set themselves to works of shame; this still teaches folk to practise villainies, and to know every godless deed.

But all the men who wrought this thing for hire have made it sure that, soon or late, they shall pay the price. Now, as Zeus still hath my reverence, know this—I tell it thee on my oath:—If ye find not the very author of this burial, and produce him before mine eyes, death alone shall not be enough for you, till first, hung up alive, ye have revealed this outrage,—that henceforth ye may thieve with better knowledge whence lucre should be won, and learn that it is not well to love gain from every source. For thou wilt find that ill-gotten pelf brings more men to ruin than to weal.

GUARD. May I speak? Or shall I just turn and go?

CREON. Knowest thou not that even now thy voice offends?

GUARD. Is thy smart in the ears, or in the soul?

CREON. And why wouldst thou define the seat of my pain?

GUARD. The doer vexes thy mind, but I, thine ears.

CREON. Ah, thou art a born babbler, 'tis well seen.

GUARD. May be, but never the doer of this deed.

CREON. Yea, and more,—the seller of thy life for silver.

GUARD. Alas! 'Tis sad, truly, that he who judges should misjudge.

CREON. Let thy fancy play with "judgment" as it will;—but, if ye show me not the doers of these things, ye shall avow that dastardly gains work sorrows.

[CREON *goes into the palace.*]

GUARD. Well, may he be found! so 'twere best. But, be he caught or be he not—fortune must settle that —truly thou wilt not see me here again. Saved, even now, beyond hope and thought, I owe the gods great thanks.

[*The* GUARD *goes out on the spectators' left.*]

CHORUS [*singing*] [*strophe 1*]. Wonders are many, and none is more wonderful than man; the power that crosses the white sea, driven by the stormy south-wind, making a path under surges that threaten to engulf him; and Earth, the eldest of the gods, the immortal, the unwearied, doth he wear, turning the soil with the offspring of horses, as the ploughs go to and fro from year to year.

[*antistrophe 1*]. And the light-hearted race of birds, and the tribes of savage beasts, and the sea-brood of the deep, he snares in the meshes of his woven toils, he leads captive, man excellent in wit. And he masters by his arts the beast whose lair is in the wilds, who roams the hills; he tames the horse of shaggy mane, he puts the yoke upon its neck, he tames the tireless mountain bull.

[*strophe 2*]. And speech, and wind-swift thought, and all the moods that mould a state, hath he taught himself; and how to flee the arrows of the frost, when 'tis hard lodging under the clear sky, and the arrows of the rushing rain; yea, he hath resource for all; without resource he meets nothing that must come: only against Death shall he call for aid in vain; but from baffling maladies he hath devised escapes.

[*antistrophe 2*]. Cunning beyond fancy's dream is the fertile skill which brings him, now to evil, now to good. When he honours the laws of the land, and that justice which he hath sworn by the gods to uphold, proudly stands his city: no city hath he who, for his rashness, dwells with sin. Never may he share my hearth, never think my thoughts, who doth these things!

[*Enter the* GUARD *on the spectators' left, leading in* ANTIGONE.]

LEADER OF THE CHORUS. What portent from the gods is this?—my soul is amazed. I know her—how can I deny that yon maiden is Antigone?

O hapless, and child of hapless sire,—of Oedipus! What means this? Thou brought a prisoner?—thou, disloyal to the king's laws, and taken in folly?

GUARD. Here she is, the doer of the deed:—we caught this girl burying him:—but where is Creon?

[CREON *enters hurriedly from the palace.*]

LEADER. Lo, he comes forth again from the house, at our need.

CREON. What is it? What hath chanced, that makes my coming timely?

GUARD. O king, against nothing should men pledge their word; for the afterthought belies the first intent. I could have vowed that I should not soon be here again,—scared by thy threats, with which I had just been lashed: but,—since the joy that surprises and transcends our hopes is like in fulness to no other pleasure,—I have come, though 'tis in breach of my sworn oath, bringing this maid; who was taken showing grace to the dead. This time there was no casting of lots; no, this luck hath fallen to me, and to none else. And now, sire, take her thyself, question her, examine her, as thou wilt; but I have a right to free and final quittance of this trouble.

CREON. And thy prisoner here—how and whence hast thou taken her?

GUARD. She was burying the man; thou knowest all.

CREON. Dost thou mean what thou sayest? Dost thou speak aright?

GUARD. I saw her burying the corpse that thou hadst forbidden to bury. Is that plain and clear?

CREON. And how was she seen? how taken in the act?

GUARD. It befell on this wise. When we had come to the place,—with those dread menaces of thine upon us,—we swept away all the dust that covered the corpse, and bared the dank body well; and then sat us down on the brow of the hill, to windward, heedful that the smell from him should not strike us; every man was wide awake, and kept his neighbour alert with torrents of threats, if anyone should be careless of this task.

So went it, until the sun's bright orb stood in mid heaven, and the heat began to burn: and then suddenly a whirlwind lifted from the earth a storm of dust, a trouble in the sky, and filled the plain, marring all the leafage of its woods; and the wide air was choked therewith: we closed our eyes, and bore the plague from the gods.

And when, after a long while, this storm had passed, the maid was seen; and she cried aloud with the sharp cry of a bird in its bitterness,—even as when, within the empty nest, it sees the bed stripped of its nestlings. So she also, when she saw the corpse bare, lifted up a voice of wailing, and called down curses on the doers of that deed. And straightway she brought thirsty dust in her hands; and from a shapely ewer of bronze, held high, with thrice-poured drink-offering she crowned the dead.

We rushed forward when we saw it, and at once closed upon our quarry, who was in no wise dismayed. Then we taxed her with her past and present doings; and she stood not on denial of aught,—at once to my joy and to my pain. To have escaped from ills one's self is a great joy; but 'tis painful to bring friends to ill. Howbeit, all such things are of less account to me than mine own safety.

CREON. Thou—thou whose face is bent to earth—dost thou avow, or disavow, this deed?

ANTIGONE. I avow it; I make no denial.

CREON [*to* GUARD]. Thou canst betake thee whither thou wilt, free and clear of a grave charge. [*Exit* GUARD.] [*to* ANTIGONE]. Now, tell me thou—not in many words, but briefly—knewest thou that an edict had forbidden this?

ANTIGONE. I knew it: could I help it? It was public.

CREON. And thou didst indeed dare to transgress that law?

ANTIGONE. Yes; for it was not Zeus that had published me that edict; not such are the laws set among men by the Justice who dwells with the gods below; nor deemed I that thy decrees were of such force, that a mortal could override the unwritten and unfailing statutes of heaven. For their life is not of to-day or yesterday, but from all time, and no man knows when they were first put forth.

Not through dread of any human pride could I answer to the gods for breaking *these*. Die I must,—I knew that well (how should I not?)—even without thy edicts. But if I am to die before my time, I count that a gain: for when any one lives, as I do, compassed about with evils, can such a one find aught but gain in death?

So for me to meet this doom is trifling grief; but if I had suffered my mother's son to lie in death an unburied corpse, that would have grieved me; for this, I am not grieved. And if my present deeds are foolish in thy sight, it may be that a foolish judge arraigns my folly.

LEADER OF THE CHORUS. The maid shows herself passionate child of passionate sire, and knows not how to bend before troubles.

CREON. Yet I would have thee know that o'er-stubborn spirits are most often humbled; 'tis the stiffest iron, baked to hardness in the fire, that thou shalt oftenest see snapped and shivered; and I have known horses that show temper brought to order by a little curb; there is no room for pride, when thou art thy neighbour's slave.—This girl was already versed in insolence when she transgressed the laws that had been set forth; and, that done, lo, a second insult,—to vaunt of this, and exult in her deed.

Now verily I am no man, she is the man, if this victory shall rest with her, and bring no penalty. No! be she sister's child, or nearer to me in blood than any that worships Zeus at the altar of our house,—she and her kinsfolk shall not avoid a doom most dire; for indeed I charge that other with a like share in the plotting of this burial.

And summon her—for I saw her e'en now within,—raving, and not mistress of her wits. So oft, before the deed, the mind stands self-convicted in its treason, when folks are plotting mischief in the dark. But verily this, too, is hateful,—when one who hath been caught in wickedness then seeks to make the crime a glory.

ANTIGONE. Wouldst thou do more than take and slay me?

CREON. No more, indeed; having that, I have all.

ANTIGONE. Why then dost thou delay? In thy discourse there is nought that pleases me,—never may there be!—and so my words must needs be unpleasing to thee. And yet, for glory—whence could I have won a nobler, than by giving burial to mine own brother? All here would own that they thought it well, were not their lips sealed by fear. But royalty, blest in so much besides, hath the power to do and say what it will.

CREON. Thou differest from all these Thebans in that view.

ANTIGONE. These also share it; but they curb their tongues for thee.

CREON. And art thou not ashamed to act apart from them?

ANTIGONE. No; there is nothing shameful in piety to a brother.

CREON. Was it not a brother, too, that died in the opposite cause?

ANTIGONE. Brother by the same mother and the same sire.

CREON. Why, then, dost thou render a grace that is impious in his sight?

ANTIGONE. The dead man will not say that he so deems it.

CREON. Yea, if thou makest him but equal in honour with the wicked.

ANTIGONE. It was his brother, not his slave, that perished.

CREON. Wasting this land; while *he* fell as its champion.

ANTIGONE. Nevertheless, Hades desires these rites.

CREON. But the good desires not a like portion with the evil.

ANTIGONE. Who knows but this seems blameless in the world below?

CREON. A foe is never a friend—not even in death.

ANTIGONE. 'Tis not my nature to join in hating, but in loving.

CREON. Pass, then, to the world of the dead, and, if thou must needs love, love them. While I live, no woman shall rule me.

[*Enter* ISMENE *from the house, led in by two attendants.*]

CHORUS [*chanting*]. Lo, yonder Ismene comes forth, shedding such tears as fond sisters weep; a cloud upon her brow casts its shadow over her darkly-flushing face, and breaks in rain on her fair cheek.

CREON. And thou, who, lurking like a viper in my house, wast secretly draining my life-blood, while I knew not that I was nurturing two pests, to rise against my throne—come, tell me now, wilt thou also confess thy part in this burial, or wilt thou forswear all knowledge of it?

ISMENE. I have done the deed,—if she allows my claim,—and share the burden of the charge.

ANTIGONE. Nay, justice will not suffer thee to do that: thou didst not consent to the deed, nor did I give thee part in it.

ISMENE. But, now that ills beset thee, I am not ashamed to sail the sea of trouble at thy side.

ANTIGONE. Whose was the deed, Hades and the dead are witnesses: a friend in words is not the friend that I love.

ISMENE. Nay, sister, reject me not, but let me die with thee, and duly honour the dead.

ANTIGONE. Share not thou my death, nor claim deeds to which thou hast not put thy hand: my death will suffice.

ISMENE. And what life is dear to me, bereft of thee?

ANTIGONE. Ask Creon; all thy care is for him.

ISMENE. Why vex me thus, when it avails thee nought?

ANTIGONE. Indeed, if I mock, 'tis with pain that I mock thee.

ISMENE. Tell me,—how can I serve thee, even now?

ANTIGONE. Save thyself: I grudge not thy escape.

ISMENE. Ah, woe is me! And shall I have no share in thy fate?

ANTIGONE. Thy choice was to live; mine, to die.

ISMENE. At least thy choice was not made without my protest.

ANTIGONE. One world approved thy wisdom; another, mine.

ISMENE. Howbeit, the offense is the same for both of us.

ANTIGONE. Be of good cheer; thou livest; but my life hath long been given to death, that so I might serve the dead.

CREON. Lo, one of these maidens hath newly shown herself foolish, as the other hath been since her life began.

ISMENE. Yea, O king, such reason as nature may have given abides not with the unfortunate, but goes astray.

CREON. Thine did, when thou chosest vile deeds with the vile.

ISMENE. What life could I endure, without her presence?

CREON. Nay, speak not of her "presence"; she lives no more.

ISMENE. But wilt thou slay the betrothed of thine own son?

CREON. Nay, there are other fields for him to plough.

ISMENE. But there can never be such love as bound him to her.

CREON. I like not an evil wife for my son.

ANTIGONE. Haemon, beloved! How thy father wrongs thee!

CREON. Enough, enough of thee and of thy marriage!

LEADER OF THE CHORUS. Wilt thou indeed rob thy son of this maiden?

CREON. 'Tis Death that shall stay these bridals for me.

LEADER. 'Tis determined, it seems, that she shall die.

CREON. Determined, yes, for thee and for me.—[*to the two attendants*] No more delay—servants, take them within! Henceforth they must be women, and not range at large; for verily even the bold seek to fly, when they see Death now closing on their life.

[*Exeunt attendants, guarding* ANTIGONE *and* ISMENE.—CREON *remains.*]

CHORUS [*singing*] [*strophe 1*]. Blest are they whose days have not tasted of evil. For when a house hath once been shaken from heaven, there the curse fails nevermore, passing from life to life of the race; even as, when the surge is driven over the darkness of the deep by the fierce breath of Thracian sea-winds, it rolls up the black sand from the depths, and there is a sullen roar from wind-vexed headlands that front the blows of the storm.

[*antistrophe 1*]. I see that from olden time the sorrows in the house of the Labdacidae are heaped upon the sorrows of the dead; and generation is not freed by generation, but some god strikes them down, and the race hath no deliverance.

For now that hope of which the light had been spread above the last root of the house of Oedipus—that hope, in turn, is brought low—by the blood-stained dust due to the gods infernal, and by folly in speech, and frenzy at the heart.

[*strophe 2*]. Thy power, O Zeus, what human trespass can limit? That power which neither Sleep, the all-ensnaring, nor the untiring months of the gods can master; but thou, a ruler to whom time brings not old age, dwellest in the dazzling splendour of Olympus.

And through the future, near and far, as through the past, shall this law hold good: Nothing that is vast enters into the life of mortals without a curse.

[*antistrophe 2*]. For that hope whose wanderings are so wide is to many men a comfort, but to many a false lure of giddy desires; and the disappointment comes on one who knoweth nought till he burn his foot against the hot fire.

For with wisdom hath some one given forth the famous saying, that evil seems good, soon or late, to him whose mind the god draws to mischief; and but for the briefest space doth he fare free of woe.

LEADER OF THE CHORUS. But lo, Haemon, the last of thy sons;—comes he grieving for the doom of his promised bride, Antigone, and bitter for the baffled hope of his marriage?

[*Enter* HAEMON.]

CREON. We shall know soon, better than seers could tell us.—My son, hearing the fixed doom of thy betrothed, art thou come in rage against thy father? Or have I thy good will, act how I may?

HAEMON. Father, I am thine; and thou, in thy wisdom, tracest for me rules which I shall follow. No marriage shall be deemed by me a greater gain than thy good guidance.

CREON. Yea, this, my son, should be thy heart's fixed law,—in all things to obey thy father's will. 'Tis for this that men pray to see dutiful children grow up around them in their homes,—that such may requite their father's foe with evil, and honour, as their father doth, his friend. But he who begets unprofitable children—what shall we say that he hath sown, but troubles for himself, and much triumph for his foes? Then do not thou, my son, at pleasure's beck, dethrone thy reason for a woman's sake; knowing that this is a joy that soon grows cold in clasping arms,—an evil woman to share thy bed and thy home. For what wound could strike deeper than a false friend? Nay, with loathing, and as if she were thine enemy, let this girl go to find a husband in the house of Hades. For since I have taken her, alone of all the city, in open disobedience, I will not make myself a liar to my people—I will slay her.

So let her appeal as she will to the majesty of kindred blood. If I am to nurture mine own kindred in naughtiness, needs must I bear with it in aliens. He who does his duty in his own household will be found righteous in the State also. But if any one transgresses, and does violence to the laws, or thinks to dictate to his rulers, such an one can win no praise from me. No, whomsoever the city may appoint, that man must be obeyed, in little things and great, in just things and unjust; and I should feel sure that one who thus obeys would be a good ruler no less than a good subject, and in the storm of spears would stand his ground where he was set, loyal and dauntless at his comrade's side.

But disobedience is the worst of evils. This it is that ruins cities; this makes homes desolate; by this, the ranks of allies are broken into headlong rout; but, of the lives whose course is fair, the greater part owes safety to obedience. Therefore we must support the cause of order, and in no wise suffer a woman to worst us. Better to fall from power, if we must, by a man's hand; then we should not be called weaker than a woman.

LEADER. To us, unless our years have stolen our wit, thou seemest to say wisely what thou sayest.

HAEMON. Father, the gods implant reason in men, the highest of all things that we call our own. Not mine the skill—far from me be the quest!—to say wherein thou speakest not aright; and yet another man, too, might have some useful thought. At least, it is my natural office to watch, on thy behalf, all that men say, or do, or find to blame. For the dread of thy frown forbids the citizen to speak such words as would offend thine ear; but I can hear these murmurs in the dark, these moanings of the city for this maiden; "no woman," they say, "ever merited her doom less,—none ever was to die so shamefully for deeds so glorious as hers; who, when her own brother had fallen in bloody strife, would not leave him unburied, to be devoured by carrion dogs, or by any bird:—deserves not *she* the meed of golden honour?"

Such is the darkling rumour that spreads in secret. For me, my father, no treasure is so precious as thy welfare. What, indeed, is a nobler ornament for children than a prospering sire's fair fame, or for sire than son's? Wear not, then, one mood only in thyself; think not that thy word, and thine alone, must be right. For if any man thinks that he alone is wise,—that in speech, or in mind, he hath no peer,—such a soul, when laid open, is ever found empty.

No, though a man be wise, 'tis no shame for him to learn many things, and to bend in season. Seest thou, beside the wintry torrent's course, how the trees that yield to it save every twig, while the stiff-necked perish root and branch? And even thus he who keeps the sheet of his sail taut, and never slackens it, upsets his boat, and finishes his voyage with keel uppermost.

Nay, forego thy wrath; permit thyself to change. For if I, a younger man, may offer my thought, it were far best, I ween, that men should be all-wise by nature; but, otherwise—and oft the scale inclines not so—'tis good also to learn from those who speak aright.

LEADER. Sire, 'tis meet that thou shouldest profit by his words, if he speaks aught in season, and thou, Haemon, by thy father's; for on both parts there hath been wise speech.

CREON. Men of my age—are we indeed to be schooled, then, by men of his?

HAEMON. In nothing that is not right; but if I am young, thou shouldest look to my merits, not to my years.

CREON. Is it a merit to honour the unruly?

HAEMON. I could wish no one to show respect for evil-doers.

CREON. Then is not she tainted with that malady?

HAEMON. Our Theban folk, with one voice, denies it.

CREON. Shall Thebes prescribe to me how I must rule?

HAEMON. See, there thou hast spoken like a youth indeed.

CREON. Am I to rule this land by other judgment than mine own?

HAEMON. That is no city which belongs to one man.

CREON. Is not the city held to be the ruler's?

HAEMON. Thou wouldst make a good monarch of a desert.

CREON. This boy, it seems, is the woman's champion.

HAEMON. If thou art a woman; indeed, my care is for thee.

CREON. Shameless, at open feud with thy father!

HAEMON. Nay, I see thee offending against justice.

CREON. Do I offend, when I respect mine own prerogatives?

HAEMON. Thou dost not respect them,

when thou tramplest on the gods' honours.

CREON. O dastard nature, yielding place to woman!

HAEMON. Thou wilt never find me yield to baseness.

CREON. All thy words, at least, plead for that girl.

HAEMON. And for thee, and for me, and for the gods below.

CREON. Thou canst never marry her, on this side the grave.

HAEMON. Then she must die, and in death destroy another.

CREON. How! doth thy boldness run to open threats?

HAEMON. What threat is it, to combat vain resolves?

CREON. Thou shalt rue thy witless teaching of wisdom.

HAEMON. Wert thou not my father, I would have called thee unwise.

CREON. Thou woman's slave, use not wheedling speech with me.

HAEMON. Thou wouldest speak, and then hear no reply?

CREON. Sayest thou so? Now, by the heaven above us—be sure of it—thou shalt smart for taunting me in this opprobrious strain. Bring forth that hated thing, that she may die forthwith in his presence—before his eyes—at her bridegroom's side!

HAEMON. No, not at my side—never think it—shall she perish; nor shalt thou ever set eyes more upon my face:—rave, then, with such friends as can endure thee.

[*Exit* HAEMON.]

LEADER. The man is gone, O king, in angry haste; a youthful mind, when stung, is fierce.

CREON. Let him do, or dream, more than man—good speed to him!—But he shall not save these two girls from their doom.

LEADER. Dost thou indeed purpose to slay both?

CREON. Not her whose hands are pure: thou sayest well.

LEADER. And by what doom mean'st thou to slay the other?

CREON. I will take her where the path is loneliest, and hide her, living, in a rocky vault, with so much food set forth as piety prescribes, that the city may avoid a public stain. And there, praying to Hades, the only god whom she worships, perchance she will obtain release from death; or else will learn, at last, though late, that it is lost labour to revere the dead.

[CREON *goes into the palace.*]

CHORUS [*singing*] [*strophe*]. Love, unconquered in the fight, Love, who makest havoc of wealth, who keepest thy vigil on the soft cheek of a maiden; thou roamest over the sea, and among the homes of dwellers in the wilds; no immortal can escape thee, nor any among men whose life is for a day; and he to whom thou hast come is mad. [*antistrophe*]. The just themselves have their minds warped by thee to wrong, for their ruin: 'tis thou that hast stirred up this present strife of kinsmen; victorious is the love-kindling light from the eyes of the fair bride; it is a power enthroned in sway beside the eternal laws; for there the goddess Aphrodite is working her unconquerable will.

[ANTIGONE *is led out of the palace by two of* CREON'S *attendants who are about to conduct her to her doom.*]

But now I also am carried beyond the bounds of loyalty, and can no more keep back the streaming tears, when I see Antigone thus passing to the bridal chamber where all are laid to rest.

[*The following lines between* ANTIGONE *and the* CHORUS *are chanted responsively.*]

ANTIGONE [*strophe 1*]. See me, citizens of my fatherland, setting forth on my last way, looking last on the sunlight that is for me no more; no, Hades who gives sleep to all leads me living to Acheron's shore; who have had no portion in the chant that brings the bride, nor hath any song been mine for the crowning of bridals; whom the lord of the Dark Lake shall wed.

CHORUS [*systema 1*]. Glorious, therefore, and with praise, thou departest to that deep place of the dead: wasting sickness hath not smitten thee; thou hast not found the wages of the sword; no, mistress of thine own fate, and still alive, thou shalt pass to Hades, as no other of mortal kind hath passed.

ANTIGONE [*antistrophe 1*]. I have heard in other days how dread a doom befell our Phrygian guest, the daughter of Tantalus, on the Sipylian heights,[3] how, like clinging ivy, the growth of stone subdued her; and the rains fail not, as men tell, from her wasting form, nor fails the snow, while beneath her weeping lids the tears bedew her bosom; and most like to hers is the fate that brings me to my rest.

CHORUS [*systema 2*]. Yet she was a goddess, thou knowest, and born of gods; we are mortals, and of mortal race. But 'tis great renown for a woman who hath perished that she should have shared the doom of the godlike, in her life, and afterward in death.

ANTIGONE [*strophe 2*]. Ah, I am mocked! In the name of our fathers' gods, can ye not wait till I am gone,—must ye taunt me to my face, O my city, and ye, her wealthy sons? Ah, fount of Dirce, and thou holy ground of Thebe whose chariots are many; ye, at least, will bear me witness, in what sort, unwept of friends, and by what laws I pass to the rock-closed prison of my strange tomb, ah me unhappy! who have no home on the earth or in the shades, no home with the living or with the dead.

CHORUS [*strophe 3*]. Thou hast rushed forward to the utmost verge of daring; and against that throne where Justice sits on high thou hast fallen, my daughter, with a grievous fall. But in this ordeal thou art paying, haply, for thy father's sin.

ANTIGONE [*antistrophe 2*]. Thou hast touched on my bitterest thought,—awaking the ever-new lament for my sire and for all the doom given to us, the famed house of Labdacus. Alas for the horrors of the mother's bed! alas for the wretched mother's slumber at the side of her own son,—and my sire! from what manner of parents did I take my miserable being! And to them I go thus, accursed, unwed, to share their home. Alas, my brother, ill-starred in thy marriage, in thy death thou hast undone my life!

CHORUS [*antistrophe 3*]. Reverent action claims a certain praise for reverence; but an offense against power cannot be brooked by him who hath power in his keeping. Thy self-willed temper hath wrought thy ruin.

ANTIGONE. Unwept, unfriended, without marriage-song, I am led forth in my sorrow on this journey that can be delayed no more. No longer, hapless one, may I behold yon day-star's sacred eye; but for my fate no tear is shed, no friend makes moan.

[CREON *enters from the palace.*]

CREON. Know ye not that songs and wailings before death would never cease, if it profited to utter them? Away with her—away! And when ye have enclosed her, according to my word, in her vaulted grave, leave her alone, forlorn—whether she wishes to die, or to live a buried life in such a home. Our hands are clean as touching this maiden. But this is certain—she shall be deprived of her sojourn in the light.

ANTIGONE. Tomb, bridal-chamber, eternal prison in the caverned rock, whither I go to find mine own, those many who have perished, and whom Persephone[4] hath received among the dead! Last of all shall I pass thither, and far most miserably of all, before the term of my life is spent. But I cherish good hope that my coming will be welcome to my father, and pleasant to thee, my mother, and welcome, brother, to thee; for, when ye died, with mine own hands I washed and dressed you, and poured drink-offerings at your graves; and now, Polyneices, 'tis for tending thy corpse that I win such recompense as this.

And what law of heaven have I transgressed? Why, hapless one, should I look to the gods any more, —what ally should I invoke,—when by piety I have earned the name of impious? Nay, then, if these things are pleasing to the gods, when I have suffered my doom, I shall come to know my sin; but if the sin is with my judges, I could wish them no fuller measure of evil than they, on their part, mete wrongfully to me.

CHORUS. Still the same tempest of the soul vexes this maiden with the same fierce gusts.

CREON. Then for this shall her guards have cause to rue their slowness.

ANTIGONE. Ah me! that word hath come very near to death.

CREON. I can cheer thee with no hope that this doom is not thus to be fulfilled.

ANTIGONE. O city of my fathers in the land of Thebe! O ye gods, eldest of our race!—they lead me hence—now, now—they tarry not! Behold me, princes of Thebes, the last daughter of the house of your kings,—see what I suffer, and from whom, because I feared to cast away the fear of Heaven!

[ANTIGONE *is led away by the guards.*]

CHORUS [*singing*] [*strophe 1*]. Even thus endured Danae[5] in her beauty to change the light of day for brass-bound walls; and in that chamber, secret as the grave, she was held close prisoner; yet was she of a proud lineage, O my daughter, and charged with the keeping of the seed of Zeus, that fell in the golden rain.

But dreadful is the mysterious power of fate: there is no deliverance from it by wealth or by war, by fenced city, or dark, sea-beaten ships.

[*antistrophe 1*]. And bonds tamed the son of Dryas,[6] swift to wrath, that king of the Edonians; so paid he for his frenzied taunts, when, by the will of Dionysus, he was pent in a rocky prison. There the fierce exuberance of his madness slowly passed away. That man learned to know the god, whom in his frenzy he had provoked with mockeries; for he had sought to quell the god-possessed women, and the Bacchanalian fire; and he angered the Muses that love the flute.

[*strophe 2*]. And by the waters of the Dark Rocks, the waters of the twofold sea, are the shores of Bosporus, and Thracian Salmydessus; where Ares, neighbour to the city, saw the accurst, blinding wound dealt to the two sons of Phineus by his fierce wife,—the wound that brought darkness to those vengeance-craving orbs, smitten with her bloody hands, smitten with her shuttle for a dagger.

[*antistrophe 2*]. Pining in their misery, they bewailed their cruel doom, those sons of a mother hapless in her marriage; but she traced her descent from the ancient line of the Erechtheidae; and in far-distant caves she was nursed amid her father's storms, that child of Boreas, swift as a steed over the steep hills, a daughter of gods; yet upon her also the gray Fates bore hard, my daughter.[7]

[*Enter* TEIRESIAS, *led by a Boy, on the spectators' right.*]

TEIRESIAS. Princes of Thebes, we have come with linked steps, both served by the eyes of one; for thus, by a guide's help, the blind must walk.

CREON. And what, aged Teiresias, are thy tidings?

TEIRESIAS. I will tell thee; and do thou hearken to the seer.

CREON. Indeed, it has not been my wont to slight thy counsel.

TEIRESIAS. Therefore didst thou steer our city's course aright.

CREON. I have felt, and can attest, thy benefits.

TEIRESIAS. Mark that now, once more, thou standest on fate's fine edge.

CREON. What means this? How I shudder at thy message!

TEIRESIAS. Thou wilt learn, when thou hearest the warnings of mine art. As I took my place on mine old seat of augury, where all birds have been wont to gather within my ken, I heard a strange voice among them; they were screaming with dire, feverish rage, that drowned their language in a jargon; and I knew that they were rending each other with their talons, murderously; the whirr of wings told no doubtful tale.

Forthwith, in fear, I essayed burnt-sacrifice on a duly kindled altar: but from my offerings the Fire-god showed no flame; a dank moisture, oozing from the thigh-flesh, trickled forth upon the embers, and smoked, and sputtered; the gall was scattered to the air; and the streaming thighs lay bared of the fat that had been wrapped round them.

Such was the failure of the rites by which I vainly asked a sign, as from this boy I learned; for he is my guide, as I am guide to others. And 'tis thy counsel that hath brought this sickness on our State. For the altars of our city and of our hearths have been tainted, one and all, by birds and dogs, with carrion from the hapless corpse, the son of Oedipus: and therefore the gods no more accept prayer and sacrifice at our hands, or the flame of meat-offering; nor doth any bird give a clear sign by its shrill cry, for they have tasted the fatness of a slain man's blood.

Think, then, on these things, my son. All men are liable to err; but when an error hath been made, that man is no longer witless or unblest who heals the ill into which he hath fallen, and remains not stubborn.

Self-will, we know, incurs the charge of folly. Nay, allow the claim of the dead; stab not the fallen; what prowess is it to slay the slain anew? I have sought thy good, and for thy good I speak: and never is it sweeter to learn from a good counsellor than when he counsels for thine own gain.

CREON. Old man, ye all shoot your shafts at me, as archers at the butts;—ye must needs practise on me with seer-craft also;—aye, the seer-tribe hath long trafficked in me, and made me their merchandise. Gain your gains, drive your trade, if ye list, in the silver-gold of Sardis and the gold of India; but ye shall not hide that man in the grave,—no, though the eagles of Zeus should bear the carrion morsels to their Master's throne—no, not for dread of that defilement will I suffer his burial:—for well I know that no mortal can defile the gods. —But, aged Teiresias, the wisest fall with a shameful fall, when they clothe shameful thoughts in fair words, for lucre's sake.

TEIRESIAS. Alas! Doth any man know, doth any consider . . .

CREON. Whereof? What general truth dost thou announce?

TEIRESIAS. How precious, above all wealth, is good counsel.

CREON. As folly, I think, is the worst mischief.

TEIRESIAS. Yet thou art tainted with that distemper.

CREON. I would not answer the seer with a taunt.

TEIRESIAS. But thou dost, in saying that I prophesy falsely.

CREON. Well, the prophet-tribe was ever fond of money.

TEIRESIAS. And the race bred of tyrants loves base gain.

CREON. Knowest thou that thy speech is spoken of thy king?

TEIRESIAS. I know it; for through me thou hast saved Thebes.

CREON. Thou art a wise seer; but thou lovest evil deeds.

TEIRESIAS. Thou wilt rouse me to utter the dread secret in my soul.

CREON. Out with it!—Only speak it not for gain.

TEIRESIAS. Indeed, methinks, I shall not,—as touching thee.

CREON. Know that thou shalt not trade on my resolve.

TEIRESIAS. Then know thou—aye, know it well—that thou shalt not live through many more courses of the sun's swift chariot, ere one begotten of thine own loins shall have been given by thee, a corpse for corpses; because thou hast thrust children of the sunlight to the shades, and ruthlessly lodged a living soul in the grave; but keepest in this world one who belongs to the gods infernal, a corpse unburied, unhonoured, all unhallowed. In such thou hast no part, nor have the gods above, but this is a violence done to them by thee. Therefore the avenging destroyers lie in wait for thee, the Furies of Hades and of the gods, that thou mayest be taken in these same ills.

And mark well if I speak these things as a hireling. A time not long to be delayed shall awaken the wailing of men and of women in thy house. And a tumult of hatred against thee stirs all the cities whose mangled sons had the burial-rite from dogs, or from wild beasts, or from some winged bird that bore a polluting breath to each city that contains the hearths of the dead.[8]

Such arrows for thy heart—since thou provokest me—have I launched at thee, archer-like, in my anger,—sure arrows, of which thou shalt not escape the smart.—Boy, lead me home, that he may spend his rage on younger men, and learn to keep a tongue more temperate, and to bear within his breast a better mind than now he bears.

[*The Boy leads* TEIRESIAS *out.*]

LEADER OF THE CHORUS. The man hath gone, O King, with dread prophecies. And, since the hair on this head, once dark, hath been white, I know that he hath never been a false prophet to our city.

CREON. I, too, know it well, and am troubled in soul. 'Tis dire to yield; but, by resistance, to smite my pride with ruin—this, too, is a dire choice.

LEADER. Son of Menoeceus, it behoves thee to take wise counsel.

CREON. What should I do, then? Speak, and I will obey.

LEADER. Go thou, and free the maiden from her rocky chamber, and make a tomb for the unburied dead.

CREON. And this is thy counsel? Thou wouldst have me yield?

LEADER. Yea, King, and with all speed; for swift harms from the gods cut short the folly of men.

CREON. Ah me, 'tis hard, but I resign my cherished resolve,—I obey. We must not wage a vain war with destiny.

LEADER. Go, thou, and do these things; leave them not to others.

CREON. Even as I am I'll go:—on, on, my servants, each and all of you,—take axes in your hands, and hasten to the ground that ye see yonder! Since our judgment hath taken this turn, I will be present to unloose her, as I myself bound her. My heart misgives me, 'tis best to keep the established laws, even to life's end.

[CREON *and his servants hasten out on the spectators' left.*]

CHORUS [*singing*][9] [*strophe 1*]. O thou of many names, glory of the Cadmeian bride, offspring of loud-thundering Zeus! thou who watchest over famed Italia, and reignest, where all guests are welcomed, in the sheltered plain of Eleusinian Deo! O Bacchus, dweller in Thebe, mother-city of Bacchants, by the softly-gliding stream of Ismenus, on the soil where the fierce dragon's teeth were sown!

[*antistrophe 1*]. Thou hast been seen where torch-flames glare through smoke, above the crests of the twin peaks, where move the Corycian nymphs, thy votaries, hard by Castalia's stream.

Thou comest from the ivy-mantled slopes of Nysa's hills, and from the shore green with many-clustered vines, while thy name is lifted up on strains of more than mortal power, as thou visitest the ways of Thebe:

[*strophe 2*]. Thebe, of all cities, thou holdest first in honour, thou, and thy mother whom the lightning smote; and now, when all our people is captive to a violent plague, come thou with healing feet over the Parnassian height, or over the moaning strait!

[*antistrophe 2*]. O thou with whom the stars rejoice as they move, the stars whose breath is fire; O master of the voices of the night; son begotten of Zeus; appear, O king, with thine attendant Thyiads, who in night-long frenzy dance before thee, the giver of good gifts, Iacchus!

[*Enter* MESSENGER, *on the spectators' left.*]

MESSENGER. Dwellers by the house of Cadmus and of Amphion, there is no estate of mortal life that I would ever praise or blame as settled. Fortune raises and Fortune humbles the lucky or unlucky from day to day, and no one can prophesy to men concerning those things which are established. For Creon was blest once, as I count bliss; he had saved this land of Cadmus from its foes; he was clothed with sole dominion in the land; he reigned, the glorious sire of princely children. And now all hath been lost. For when a man hath forfeited his pleasures, I count him not as living,—I hold him but a breathing corpse. Heap up riches in thy house, if thou wilt; live in kingly state; yet, if there be no gladness therewith, I would not give the shadow of a vapour for all the rest, compared with joy.

LEADER OF THE CHORUS. And what is this new grief that thou hast to tell for our princes?

MESSENGER. Death; and the living are guilty for the dead.

LEADER. And who is the slayer? Who the stricken? Speak.

MESSENGER. Haemon hath perished; his blood hath been shed by no stranger.

LEADER. By his father's hand, or by his own?

MESSENGER. By his own, in wrath with his sire for the murder.

LEADER. O prophet, how true, then, hast thou proved thy word!

MESSENGER. These things stand thus; ye must consider of the rest.

LEADER. Lo, I see the hapless Eurydice, Creon's wife, approaching; she comes from the house by chance, haply,—or because she knows the tidings of her son.

[*Enter* EURYDICE *from the palace.*]

EURYDICE. People of Thebes, I heard your words as I was going forth, to salute the goddess Pallas with my prayers. Even as I was loosing the fastenings of the gate, to open it, the message of a household woe smote on mine ear: I sank back, terror-stricken, into the arms of my handmaids, and my senses fled. But say again what the tidings were; I shall hear them as one who is no stranger to sorrow.

MESSENGER. Dear lady, I will witness of what I saw, and will leave no word of the truth untold. Why, indeed, should I soothe thee with words in which I must presently be found false? Truth is ever best. —I attended thy lord as his guide to the furthest part of the plain, where the body of Polyneices, torn by dogs, still lay unpitied. We prayed the goddess of the roads, and Pluto,[10] in mercy to restrain their wrath; we washed the dead with holy washing; and with freshly-plucked boughs we solemnly burned such relics as there were. We raised a high mound of his native earth; and then we turned away to enter the maiden's nuptial chamber with rocky couch, the caverned mansion of the bride of Death. And, from afar off, one of us heard a voice of loud wailing at that bride's unhallowed bower; and came to tell our master Creon.

And as the king drew nearer, doubtful sounds of a bitter cry floated around him; he groaned, and said in accents of anguish, "Wretched that I am, can my foreboding be true? Am I going on the woefullest way that ever I went? My son's voice greets me.—Go, my servants,—haste ye nearer, and when ye have reached the tomb, pass through the gap, where the stones have been wrenched away, to the cell's very mouth,—and look, and see if 'tis Haemon's voice that I know, or if mine ear is cheated by the gods."

This search, at our despairing master's word, we went to make; and in the furthest part of the tomb we descried *her* hanging by the neck, slung by a thread-wrought halter of fine linen: while *he* was embracing her with arms thrown around her waist,—bewailing the loss of his bride who is with the dead, and his father's deeds, and his own ill-starred love.

But his father, when he saw him, cried aloud with a dread cry and went in, and called to him with a voice of wailing:—"Unhappy, what a deed hast thou done! What thought hath come to thee? What manner of mischance hath marred thy reason? Come forth, my child! I pray thee—I implore!" But the boy glared at him with fierce eyes, spat in his face, and, without a word of answer, drew his cross-hilted sword:—as his father rushed forth in flight, he missed his aim;— then, hapless one, wroth with himself, he straightway leaned with all his weight against his sword, and drove it, half its length, into his side; and, while sense lingered, he clasped the maiden to his faint embrace, and, as he gasped, sent forth on her pale cheek the swift stream of the oozing blood.

Corpse enfolding corpse he lies; he hath won his nuptial rites, poor youth, not here, yet in the halls of Death; and he hath witnessed to mankind that, of all curses which cleave to man, ill counsel is the sovereign curse.

[EURYDICE *retires into the house.*]

LEADER. What wouldst thou augur from this? The lady hath turned back, and is gone, without a word, good or evil.

MESSENGER. I, too, am startled; yet I nourish the hope that, at these sore tidings of her son, she cannot deign to give her sorrow public vent, but in the privacy of the house will set her handmaids to mourn the household grief. For she is not untaught of discretion, that she should err.

LEADER. I know not; but to me, at least, a strained silence seems to portend peril, no less than vain abundance of lament.

MESSENGER. Well, I will enter the house, and learn whether indeed she is not hiding some repressed purpose in the depths of a passionate heart. Yea, thou sayest well: excess of silence, too, may have a perilous meaning.

[*The* MESSENGER *goes into the palace. Enter* CREON, *on the spectators' left, with attendants, carrying the shrouded body of* HAEMON *on a bier. The following lines between* CREON *and the* CHORUS *are chanted responsively.*]

CHORUS. Lo, yonder the king himself draws near, bearing that which tells too clear a tale,—the work of no stranger's madness,—if we may say it,—but of his own misdeeds.

CREON [*strophe 1*]. Woe for the sins of a darkened soul, stubborn sins, fraught with death! Ah, ye behold us, the sire who hath slain, the son who hath perished! Woe is me, for the wretched blindness of my counsels! Alas, my son, thou hast died in thy youth, by a timeless doom, woe is me!—thy spirit hath fled,—not by thy folly, but by mine own!

CHORUS [*strophe 2*]. Ah me, how all too late thou seemest to see the right!

CREON. Ah me, I have learned the bitter lesson! But then, methinks, oh then, some god smote me from above with crushing weight, and hurled me into ways of cruelty, woe is me,—overthrowing and trampling on my joy! Woe, woe, for the troublous toils of men!

[*Enter* MESSENGER *from the house.*]

MESSENGER. Sire, thou hast come, methinks, as one whose hands are not empty, but who hath store laid up besides; thou bearest yonder burden with thee; and thou art soon to look upon the woes within thy house.

CREON. And what worse ill is yet to follow upon ills?

MESSENGER. Thy queen hath died, true mother of yon corpse—ah, hapless lady!—by blows newly dealt.

CREON [*antistrophe 1*]. Oh Hades, all-receiving, whom no sacrifice can appease! Hast thou, then, no mercy for me? O thou herald of evil, bitter tidings, what word dost thou utter? Alas, I was already as dead, and thou hast smitten me anew! What sayest thou, my son? What is this new message that thou bringest—woe, woe is me!—of a wife's doom,—of slaughter heaped on slaughter?

CHORUS. Thou canst behold: 'tis no longer hidden within.

[*The doors of the palace are opened, and the corpse of* EURYDICE *is disclosed.*]

CREON [*antistrophe 2*]. Ah me,—yonder I behold a new, a second woe! What destiny, ah what, can yet await me? I have but now raised my son in my arms,—and there, again, I see a corpse before me! Alas, alas, unhappy mother! Alas, my child!

MESSENGER. There, at the altar, self-stabbed with a keen knife, she suffered her darkening eyes to close, when she had wailed for the noble fate of Megareus[11] who died before, and then for his fate who lies there,—and when, with her last breath, she had invoked evil fortunes upon thee, the slayer of thy sons.

CREON [*strophe 3*]. Woe, woe! I thrill with dread. Is there none to strike me to the heart with two-edged sword?—O miserable that I am, and steeped in miserable anguish!

MESSENGER. Yea, both this son's doom, and that other's, were laid to thy charge by her whose corpse thou seest.

CREON. And what was the manner of the violent deed by which she passed away?

MESSENGER. Her own hand struck her to the heart, when she had learned her son's sorely lamented fate.

CREON [*strophe 4*]. Ah me, this guilt can never be fixed on any other of mortal kind, for my acquittal! I, even I, was thy slayer, wretched that I am—I own the truth. Lead me away, O my servants, lead me hence with all speed, whose life is but as death!

CHORUS. Thy counsels are good, if there can be good with ills; briefest is best, when trouble is in our path.

CREON [*antistrophe 3*]. Oh, let it come, let it appear, that fairest of fates for me, that brings my last day,—aye, best fate of all! Oh, let it come, that I may never look upon to-morrow's light.

CHORUS. These things are in the future; present tasks claim our care: the ordering of the future rests where it should rest.

CREON. All my desires, at least, were summed in that prayer.

CHORUS. Pray thou no more; for mortals have no escape from destined woe.

CREON [*antistrophe 4*]. Lead me away, I pray you; a rash, foolish man; who have slain thee, ah my son, unwittingly, and thee, too, my wife—unhappy that I am! I know not which way I should bend my gaze, or where I should seek support; for all is amiss with that which is in my hands,—and yonder, again, a crushing fate hath leapt upon my head.

[*As* CREON *is being conducted into the palace, the* LEADER OF THE CHORUS *speaks the closing verses.*]

LEADER. Wisdom is the supreme part of happiness; and reverence towards the gods must be inviolate. Great words of prideful men are ever punished with great blows, and, in old age, teach the chastened to be wise.[12]

Notes

[1] The central conflict of this play depends, in part, upon the conventional Greek attitude toward the ritual of burial. The punishment Creon had inflicted upon the dead Polyneices was

looked upon with horror and terror not only by Antigone but by all others in Thebes at the time. What happens to a dead body may seem of comparatively little importance today, but to Thebans it was a matter of supreme importance. Sophocles has used this basic situation to explore the question of whether man-made and dictatorially enforced law should take precedence over an individual's concept of what he thinks is divine law. Thus, Creon seeks to impose his human law upon an Antigone who rebels and disobeys because of her respect for what she considers a higher law. This conflict is as modern as tomorrow's newspaper and plays a part in the daily lives of everyone now living in the twentieth century. The potentiality of men and women to be and to remain free spiritual beings is tested every day now just as it was in the days of legendary Thebes.

[2] In ancient Greece, the chorus was originally a group of men who performed at religious festivals; Greek drama may be said to have evolved from choral rites. At first, choral songs made up the bulk of a play, but later the chorus became somewhat subordinate. In this play, for example, the words and dancing of the chorus are intended largely to comment on the action rather than to develop it; Sophocles in *Antigone* primarily uses the chorus to comment upon the universality and paramount significance of the action and does not permit these masked characters to play an active role. The movement of a Greek chorus was highly stylized: as it sang the *strophe,* it moved from right to left; in singing the *antistrophe,* it retraced its steps and returned to the original position. The word *systema* is a Greek term meaning "methodical in procedure and plan" and refers to a specific portion of the choral group's singing and dancing. The chorus here celebrates the victory over the Argive forces and Polyneices. (*Dirce* is a river on the Theban plain; the phrase *dragon foe* is a reference to the legend that Thebans sprang from dragon's teeth sown by Cadmus.)

[3] A Phrygian princess married to a Theban king boasted that she had had more children than Leto, mother of Apollo and Artemis. These latter two murdered her offspring, and the princess herself was turned into a rock on Mount Sipylus. Melted snow on the mountain caused "tears" to flow down the rock formation.

[4] Persephone: the queen of the underworld.

[5] Danae was the daughter of the king of Argos. It was prophesied that he would be slain by his daughter's sons; he shut up his daughter in a bronze tower. Zeus came to her "in the form of a shower" and she conceived a son, Perseus, who did indeed kill his grandfather.

[6] The son of Dryas was Lycurgus, a king who opposed introduction of the Dionysiac religion and was consequently imprisoned by the god.

[7] This allusion is difficult to follow. A daughter of an Athenian princess was married to Phineus, the Thracian king, and bore him two sons. Phineus abandoned his wife and married another woman who, while Ares, the god of war, looked on, put out the eyes of her stepsons.

[8] Creon had exposed the bodies of all seven warriors, not just that of Polyneices.

[9] This is a hymn to the god Dionysus (Bacchus), whose mother was a Theban princess, Semele. When pregnant by her lover, Zeus, Semele asked him to appear to her in his own shape. When he complied with her request, she was "blinded by his lightning."

[10] The goddess of the roads (Hecate) and Pluto are divinities of the underworld.

[11] Megareus was killed during the siege of the city.

[12] Now that you have read *Antigone,* consider this comment by Edith Hamilton, acknowledged authority on Greek and Roman life and literature and inspired writer on classical subjects: "In every way Sophocles is the embodiment of what we know as Greek, so much so that all definitions of the Greek spirit and Greek art are first of all definitions of his spirit and his art. He has imposed himself upon the world as the quintessential Greek . . . he is direct, lucid, simple, reasonable . . . a great tragedian, a supremely gifted poet, and yet a detached observer of life."

THE LONG CHRISTMAS DINNER

Thornton Wilder

THORNTON [NIVEN] WILDER (1897–) was born in Madison, Wisconsin, studied at Oberlin, and was graduated from Yale in 1920. He has studied abroad and taught and lectured widely in this country. Among his more noted plays and novels are *The Bridge of San Luis Rey* (1927), *The Woman of Andros* (1930), *Heaven's My Destination* (1935), *Our Town* (1938), *The Skin of Our Teeth* (1942), *The Ides of March* (1948), *The Matchmaker* (1954), *The Eighth Day* (1967). *Hello Dolly,* a musical comedy, is based on *The Matchmaker.*

Mr. Wilder has frequently shown in his work a distaste for realism. *The Long Christmas Dinner* is a highly imaginative play in which the action, directions for costuming, and stage business do not treat life with photographic reality. The play exhibits some of the most sophisticated techniques and strategies of playmaking within the range of modern theatrical art. The noted critic John Gassner has hailed it as "the most beautiful one-act play in English prose."

THE CAST

LUCIA
MOTHER BAYARD
RODERICK
COUSIN BRANDON
CHARLES
GENEVIEVE } *children of Roderick and Lucia*
THE NURSE
LEONORA, *wife of Charles*
ERMENGARDE
SAM
LUCIA II
RODERICK II } *children of Charles and Leonora*

The dining-room of the Bayard home. Close to the footlights a long dining table is handsomely spread for Christmas dinner. The carver's place with a great turkey before it is at the spectator's right.

A door, left back, leads into the hall.

At the extreme left, by the proscenium[1] pillar, is a strange portal trimmed

---

with garlands[2] of fruits and flowers. Directly opposite is another edged and hung with black velvet. The portals denote birth and death.

Ninety years are to be traversed in this play which represents in accelerated motion ninety Christmas dinners in the Bayard household. The actors are dressed in inconspicuous clothes and must indicate their gradual increase in years through their acting. Most of them carry wigs of white hair which they adjust upon their heads at the indicated moment, simply and without comment. The ladies may have shawls concealed beneath the table that they gradually draw up about their shoulders as they grow older.

Throughout the play the characters continue eating imaginary food with imaginary knives and forks.

There is no curtain. The audience arriving at the theatre sees the stage set and the table laid, though still in partial darkness. Gradually the lights in the auditorium become dim and the stage brightens until sparkling winter sunlight streams through the dining room windows.

Enter LUCIA. *She inspects the table, touching here a knife and there a fork. She talks to a servant girl who is invisible to us.*

LUCIA. I reckon we're ready now, Gertrude. We won't ring the chimes to-day. I'll just call them myself. [*She goes into the hall and calls.*] Roderick. Mother Bayard. We're all ready. Come to dinner.

[*Enter* RODERICK *from the hall, pushing* MOTHER BAYARD *in a wheel chair, which he places at his Left at the table.*]

MOTHER BAYARD. . . . and a new horse too, Roderick. I used to think that only the wicked owned two horses. A new horse and a new house and a new wife!

LUCIA. Here, Mother Bayard, you sit between us.

[LUCIA *ties a napkin around* MOTHER BAYARD's *neck.* RODERICK *sits in chair Right,* LUCIA *in chair Left of table.*]

RODERICK. Well, Mother, how do you like it? Our first Christmas dinner in the new house, hey?

MOTHER BAYARD. Tz-Tz-Tz! I don't know what your dear father would say! [RODERICK *says a murmured grace and then begins to carve in pantomime[3] the turkey.*] My dear Lucia, I can remember when there were still Indians on this very ground, and I wasn't a young girl either. I can remember when we had to cross the Mississippi on a new-made raft. I can remember when St. Louis and Kansas City were full of Indians.

LUCIA. Imagine that! What a wonderful day for our first Christmas dinner: a beautiful sunny morning, snow, a splendid sermon. Dr. McCarthy preaches a splendid sermon. I cried and cried.

RODERICK [*Extending an imaginary carving-fork*]. Come now, what'll you have, Mother? A little sliver of white? [*He serves the turkey during the following speeches with the help of the imaginary servant.*]

LUCIA. Every least twig is wrapped around with ice. You almost never see that. [*Over her shoulder.*] Gertrude, I forgot the jelly. You know, —on the top shelf.—Mother Bayard,

I found your mother's gravy-boat while we were moving. What was her name, dear? What were all your names? You were . . . a . . . Genevieve Wainright. Now your mother——

MOTHER BAYARD [*As they eat*]. Yes, you must write it down somewhere. I was Genevieve Wainright. My mother was Faith Morrison. She was the daughter of a farmer in New Hampshire who was something of a blacksmith too. And she married young John Wainright——

LUCIA [*Memorizing on her fingers*]. Genevieve Wainright. Faith Morrison.

RODERICK. It's all down in a book somewhere upstairs. We have it all. All that kind of thing is very interesting. Come, Lucia, just a little wine. Mother, a little red wine for Christmas day. Full of iron. "Take a little wine for thy stomach's sake."[4]

LUCIA. Really, I can't get used to wine! What would my father say? But I suppose it's all right.

[*Enter* COUSIN BRANDON *from the hall. He draws up a chair and takes his place by* LUCIA.]

COUSIN BRANDON [*Rubbing his hands*]. Well, well, I smell turkey. My dear cousins, I can't tell you how pleasant it is to be having Christmas dinner with you all. I've lived out there in Alaska so long without relatives. Let me see, how long have you had this new house, Roderick?

RODERICK. Why, it must be . . .

MOTHER BAYARD. Five years. It's five years, children. You should keep a diary. This is your sixth Christmas dinner here.[5]

LUCIA. Think of that, Roderick. We feel as though we had lived here twenty years.

COUSIN BRANDON. At all events it still looks as good as new.

RODERICK [*Over his carving*]. What'll you have, Brandon, light or dark? —Frieda,[6] fill up Cousin Brandon's glass.

LUCIA. Oh, dear, I can't get used to these wines. I don't know what my father'd say, I'm sure. What'll you have, Mother Bayard?

MOTHER BAYARD. Yes, I can remember when there were Indians on this very land.

LUCIA [*Softly*]. Mother Bayard hasn't been very well lately, Roderick.

[MOTHER BAYARD'S *chair, without any visible propulsion,*[7] *starts to draw away from the table, turns toward the Right, and slowly goes toward the dark portal.*]

MOTHER BAYARD. My mother was a Faith Morrison. And in New Hampshire she married a young John Wainright, who was a Congregational minister. He saw her in his congregation one day . . .

LUCIA [*Rising and coming to Center stage*]. Mother Bayard, hadn't you better lie down, dear?

MOTHER BAYARD. . . . and right in the middle of his sermon he said to himself: "I'll marry that girl." And he did, and I'm their daughter.

[RODERICK *rises, turns to Right with concern.*]

LUCIA [*Looking after her with anxiety*]. Just a little nap, dear?

MOTHER BAYARD. I'm all right. Just go on with your dinner. [*Exit down Right.*] I was ten, and I said to my brother——

[*A very slight pause, during which* RODERICK *sits and* LUCIA *returns to her seat. All three resume eating.*][8]

COUSIN BRANDON [*Genially*]. It's too bad it's such a cold dark day to-day. We almost need the lamps. I spoke to Major Lewis for a moment after church. His sciatica[9] troubles him, but he does pretty well.

LUCIA [*Dabbing her eyes*]. I know Mother Bayard wouldn't want us to grieve for her on Christmas day, but I can't forget her sitting in her wheel chair right beside us, only a year ago. And she would be so glad to know our good news.

RODERICK. Now, now. It's Christmas. [*Formally.*] Cousin Brandon, a glass of wine with you, sir.

COUSIN BRANDON [*Half rising, lifting his glass gallantly*]. A glass of wine with you, sir.

LUCIA. Does the Major's sciatica cause him much pain?

COUSIN BRANDON. Some, perhaps. But you know his way. He says it'll be all the same in a hundred years.

LUCIA. Yes, he's a great philosopher.

RODERICK. His wife sends you a thousand thanks for her Christmas present.

LUCIA. I forget what I gave her.—Oh, yes, the workbasket! [*Slight pause. Characters look toward Left portal. Through the entrance of birth comes a* NURSE *holding in her arms an imaginary baby.* LUCIA *rushes toward it, the men following.*] O my darling baby! Who ever saw such a child! Quick, Nurse, a boy or a girl? A boy! Roderick, what shall we call him?

RODERICK. We'll call him Charles after your father and grandfather.

LUCIA. But there are no Charleses in the Bible, Roderick.

RODERICK. Of course, there are. Surely there are.

LUCIA. Roderick!—Very well, but he will always be Samuel[10] to me.

COUSIN BRANDON. Really, Nurse, you've never seen such a child.

[NURSE *starts up stage to Center door.*]

LUCIA. What miraculous hands he has! Really, they are the most beautiful hands in the world. All right, Nurse. Have a good nap, my darling child.

[*Exit* NURSE *in the hall.* LUCIA *and* COUSIN BRANDON *to seats.*]

RODERICK [*Calling through Center door*]. Don't drop him, Nurse. Brandon and I need him in our firm. [*He returns to his chair and starts to carve.*] Lucia, a little white meat? Some stuffing? Cranberry sauce, anybody?

LUCIA [*Over her shoulder*]. Margaret, the stuffing is very good to-day.—Just a little, thank you.

RODERICK. Now something to wash it down. [*Half rising.*] Cousin Brandon, a glass of wine with you, sir. To the ladies, God bless them.

LUCIA. Thank you, kind sirs.

COUSIN BRANDON. Pity it's such an overcast day to-day. And no snow.

LUCIA. But the sermon was lovely. I cried and cried. Dr. Spaulding does preach such a splendid sermon.

RODERICK. I saw Major Lewis for a moment after church. He says his rheumatism comes and goes. His wife says she has something for Charles and will bring it over this afternoon.

[*Again they turn to portal down Left. Enter* NURSE as before. LUCIA *rushes to her.* RODERICK *comes to*

Center of stage below table. COUSIN BRANDON *does not rise.*]

LUCIA. O my lovely new baby! Really, it never occurred to me that it might be a girl. Why, Nurse, she's perfect.

RODERICK. Now call her what you choose. It's your turn.

LUCIA. Loolooloolooo. Aië. Aië. Yes, this time I shall have my way. She shall be called Genevieve after your mother. Have a good nap, my treasure. [*Exit* NURSE *into the hall.*] Imagine! Sometime she'll be grown up and say, "Good-morning, Mother. Good-morning, Father."—Really, Cousin Brandon, you don't find a baby like that every day.

[*They return to their seats and again begin to eat.* RODERICK *carves as before, standing.*]

COUSIN BRANDON. *And* the new factory.[11]

LUCIA. A new factory? Really? Roderick, I shall be very uncomfortable if we're going to turn out to be rich. I've been afraid of that for years.—However, we mustn't talk about such things on Christmas day. I'll just take a little piece of white meat, thank you. Roderick, Charles is destined for the ministry. I'm sure of it.

RODERICK. Woman, he's only twelve. Let him have a free mind. *We* want him in the firm, I don't mind saying. [*He sits. Definitely shows maturity.*] Anyway, no time passes as slowly as this when you're waiting for your urchins to grow up and settle down to business.

LUCIA. I don't want time to go any faster, thank you. I love the children just as they are.—Really, Roderick, you know what the doctor said: One glass a meal. No, Margaret, that will be all.

RODERICK [*Glass in hand*]. Now I wonder what's the matter with me.

LUCIA. Roderick, do be reasonable.

RODERICK [*Rises, takes a few steps Right, with gallant irony*]. But, my dear, statistics show that we steady, moderate drinkers . . .

LUCIA [*Rises, rushes to Center below table*]. Roderick! My dear! What . . . ?

RODERICK [*Returns to his seat with a frightened look of relief; now definitely older*]. Well, it's fine to be back at table with you again. [LUCIA *returns to her seat.*] How many good Christmas dinners have I had to miss upstairs? And to be back at a fine bright one, too.

LUCIA. O my dear, you gave us a very alarming time! Here's your glass of milk.—Josephine, bring Mr. Bayard his medicine from the cupboard in the library.

RODERICK. At all events, now that I'm better I'm going to start doing something about the house.

LUCIA. Roderick! You're not going to change the house?

RODERICK. Only touch it up here and there. It looks a hundred years old.[12]

[CHARLES *enters casually from the hall.*]

CHARLES. It's a great blowy morning, Mother. The wind comes over the hill like a lot of cannon. [*He kisses his mother's hair.*]

LUCIA. Charles, you carve the turkey, dear. Your father's not well.

RODERICK. But—but not yet.

CHARLES. You always said you hated carving.

[CHARLES *gets a chair from Right*

wall and puts it Right end of table where MOTHER BAYARD *was.* RODERICK *sits.* CHARLES *takes his father's former place at end of table.* CHARLES, *sitting, begins to carve.*]

LUCIA [*Showing her years*]. And such a good sermon. I cried and cried. Mother Bayard loved a good sermon so. And she used to sing the Christmas hymns all around the year. Oh, dear, oh, dear, I've been thinking of her all morning!

CHARLES. Sh, Mother. It's Christmas day. You mustn't think of such things.—You mustn't be depressed.

LUCIA. But sad things aren't the same as depressing things. I must be getting old: I like them.

CHARLES. Uncle Brandon, you haven't anything to eat. Pass his plate, Hilda . . . and some cranberry sauce . . .

[*Enter* GENEVIEVE *from the hall.*]

GENEVIEVE. It's glorious. [*Kisses father's temple, gets chair and sits Center between her father and* COUSIN BRANDON.] Every least twig is wrapped around with ice. You almost never see that.

LUCIA. Did you have time to deliver those presents after church, Genevieve?

GENEVIEVE. Yes, Mama. Old Mrs. Lewis sends you a thousand thanks for hers. It was just what she wanted, she said. Give me lots, Charles, lots.

RODERICK. Statistics, ladies and gentlemen, show that we steady, moderate . . .

CHARLES. How about a little skating this afternoon, Father?

RODERICK. I'll live till I'm ninety. [*Rising and starting toward Right portal.*]

LUCIA. I really don't think he ought to go skating.

RODERICK [*At the very portal, suddenly astonished*]. Yes, but . . . but . . . not yet!

[*Exit down Left.*]

LUCIA [*Dabbing her eyes*]. He was so young and so clever, Cousin Brandon. [*Raising her voice for* COUSIN BRANDON'S *deafness.*] I say he was so young and so clever.—Never forget your father, children. He was a good man.—Well, he wouldn't want us to grieve for him to-day.

CHARLES. White or dark, Genevieve? Just another sliver, Mother?

LUCIA [*Drawing on her shawl*]. I can remember our first Christmas dinner in this house, Genevieve. Twenty-five years ago to-day.[13] Mother Bayard was sitting here in her wheel chair. She could remember when Indians lived in this very spot and when she had to cross the river on a new-made raft.

CHARLES. She couldn't have, Mother.

GENEVIEVE. That can't be true.

LUCIA. It certainly was true—even I can remember when there was only one paved street. We were very happy to walk on boards. [*Louder, to* COUSIN BRANDON.] We can remember when there were no sidewalks, can't we, Cousin Brandon?

COUSIN BRANDON [*Delighted*]. Oh, yes! And those were the days.

CHARLES and GENEVIEVE [*Sotto voce. This is a family refrain*]. Those were the days.[14]

LUCIA. . . . and the ball last night, Genevieve? Did you have a nice time? I hope you didn't *waltz*, dear. I think a girl in our position ought to set an example. Did Charles keep an eye on you?

GENEVIEVE. He had none left. They were all on Leonora Banning. He can't conceal it any longer, Mother. I think he's engaged to marry Leonora Banning.

CHARLES. I'm not engaged to marry anyone.

LUCIA. Well, she's very pretty.

GENEVIEVE. I shall never marry, Mother—I shall sit in this house beside you forever, as though life were one long, happy Christmas dinner.

LUCIA. O my child, you mustn't say such things!

GENEVIEVE [*Playfully*]. You don't want me? You don't want me? [LUCIA *bursts into tears.* GENEVIEVE *rises and goes to her.*] Why, Mother, how silly you are! There's nothing sad about that—what could possibly be sad about that?

LUCIA [*Drying her eyes*]. Forgive me. I'm just unpredictable, that's all.

[CHARLES *goes to the door and leads in* LEONORA BANNING *from the hall.*]

CHARLES. Leonora!

LEONORA. Good-morning, Mother Bayard. [LUCIA *rises and greets* LEONORA *near door.* COUSIN BRANDON *also rises.*] Good-morning, everybody. Mother Bayard, you sit here by Charles. [*She helps her into chair formerly occupied by* RODERICK. COUSIN BRANDON *sits in Center chair.* GENEVIEVE *sits on his Left, and* LEONORA *sits at foot of the table.*] It's really a splendid Christmas day to-day.

CHARLES. Little white meat? Genevieve, Mother, Leonora?

LEONORA. Every least twig is encircled with ice.—You never see that.

CHARLES [*Shouting*]. Uncle Brandon, another?—Rogers, fill my uncle's glass.

LUCIA [*To* CHARLES]. Do what your father used to do. It would please Cousin Brandon so. You know—[*pretending to raise a glass*] "Uncle Brandon, a glass of wine——"

CHARLES [*Rising*]. Uncle Brandon, a glass of wine with you, sir.

COUSIN BRANDON [*Not rising*]. A glass of wine with you, sir. To the ladies, God bless them every one.

THE LADIES. Thank you, kind sirs.

GENEVIEVE. And if I go to Germany for my music I promise to be back for Christmas. I wouldn't miss that.

LUCIA. I hate to think of you over there all alone in those strange pensions.[15]

GENEVIEVE. But, darling, the time will pass so fast that you'll hardly know I'm gone. I'll be back in the twinkling of an eye.

[LEONORA *looks toward Left portal, rises, takes several steps.* NURSE *enters, with baby, down Left.*]

LEONORA. Oh, what an angel! The darlingest baby in the world. Do let me hold it, Nurse. [*The* NURSE *resolutely has been crossing the stage and now exits at the Right portal.* LEONORA *follows.*] Oh, I did love it so.

[CHARLES *rises, puts his arm around his wife, whispering, and slowly leads her back to her chair.*]

GENEVIEVE [*To her mother as the other two cross—softly*]. Isn't there anything I can do?

LUCIA [*Raises her eyebrows, ruefully*]. No, dear. Only time, only the passing of time can help in these things. [CHARLES *returns to his seat. Slight pause.*] Don't you think we could ask Cousin Ermengarde to come and live with us here? There's plenty for everyone and there's no reason why she should go on teaching the First Grade for ever and ever. She wouldn't be in the way, would she, Charles?

CHARLES. No, I think it would be fine.—A little more potato and gravy, anybody? A little more turkey, Mother?

[COUSIN BRANDON *rises and starts slowly toward the dark portal.* LUCIA *rises and stands for a moment with her face in her hands.*]

COUSIN BRANDON [*Muttering*]. It was great to be in Alaska in those days . . .

GENEVIEVE [*Half rising, and gazing at her mother in fear*]. Mother, what is . . . ?

LUCIA [*Hurriedly*]. Hush, my dear. It will pass.—Hold fast to your music, you know. [*As* GENEVIEVE *starts toward her.*] No, no. I want to be alone for a few minutes.

CHARLES. If the Republicans collected all their votes instead of going off into cliques[16] among themselves, they might prevent his getting a second term.

[LUCIA *turns and starts after* COUSIN BRANDON *toward the Right.*]

GENEVIEVE. Charles, Mother doesn't tell us, but she hasn't been very well these days.

CHARLES. Come, Mother, we'll go to Florida for a few weeks. [GENEVIEVE *rushes toward her mother.*]

[*Exit* COUSIN BRANDON, *Right.*]

LUCIA [*By the portal, smiling at* GENEVIEVE *and waving her hand*]. Don't be foolish. Don't grieve. [*She clasps her hands under her chin; her lips move, whispering; she walks serenely through the portal.*]

GENEVIEVE [*Stares after her*]. But what will I do? What's left for me to do? [*She returns to her seat.*]

[*At the same moment the* NURSE, *with two babies, enters from the Left.* LEONORA *rushes to them.*]

LEONORA. O my darlings . . . twins . . . Charles, aren't they glorious! Look at them. Look at them.

[CHARLES *crosses to down Left.*]

GENEVIEVE [*Sinks down on the table, her face buried in her arms*]. But what will I do? What's left for me to do?

CHARLES [*Bending over the basket*]. Which is which?

LEONORA. I feel as though I were the first mother who ever had twins.—Look at them now!—But why wasn't Mother Bayard allowed to stay and see them!

GENEVIEVE [*Rising suddenly distraught, loudly*]. I don't want to go on. I can't bear it.

CHARLES [*Goes to her quickly. He whispers to her earnestly, taking both her hands*]. But, Genevieve, Genevieve! How frightfully Mother would feel to think that . . . Genevieve!

GENEVIEVE [*Wildly*]. I never told her how wonderful she was. We all treated her as though she were just a friend in the house. I thought she'd be here forever. [*Sits.*]

LEONORA [*Timidly*]. Genevieve darling, do come one minute and hold my babies' hands. [GENEVIEVE *collects herself and goes over to the* NURSE. *She smiles brokenly into the basket.*] We shall call the girl Lucia after her grandmother,—will that please you? Do just see what adorable little hands they have.

GENEVIEVE. They are wonderful, Leonora.

LEONORA. Give him your finger, darling. Just let him hold it.

CHARLES. And we'll call the boy Samuel.—Well, now everybody come and finish your dinners. [*The women take their places.* CHARLES *calls out into the hall.*] Don't drop them, Nurse; at least don't drop the boy. We need him in the firm. [*He returns to his place.*]

LEONORA. Some day they'll be big. Imagine! They'll come in and say, "Hello, Mother!"

CHARLES [*Now forty, dignified*]. Come, a little wine, Leonora, Genevieve? Full of iron. Eduardo, fill the ladies' glasses. It certainly is a keen, cold morning. I used to go skating with Father on mornings like this and Mother would come back from church saying ——

GENEVIEVE [*Dreamily*]. I know—saying, "Such a splendid sermon. I cried and cried."

LEONORA. Why did she cry, dear?

GENEVIEVE. That generation all cried at sermons. It was their way.

LEONORA. Really, Genevieve?

GENEVIEVE. They had had to go since they were children and I suppose sermons reminded them of their fathers and mothers, just as Christmas dinners do us. Especially in an old house like this.

LEONORA. It really is pretty old, Charles. And so ugly, with all that ironwork filigree and that dreadful cupola.[17]

GENEVIEVE. Charles! You aren't going to change the house!

CHARLES. No, no. I won't give up the house, but great heavens! it's fifty years old. This spring we'll remove the cupola and build a new wing toward the tennis courts.

[*From now on* GENEVIEVE *is seen to change. She sits up more straightly. The corners of her mouth become fixed. She becomes a forthright and slightly disillusioned spinster.* CHARLES *becomes the plain business man and a little pompous.*]

LEONORA. And then couldn't we ask your dear old Cousin Ermengarde to come and live with us?[18] She's really the self-effacing[19] kind.

CHARLES. Ask her now. Take her out of the First Grade.

GENEVIEVE. We only seem to think of it on Christmas day with her Christmas card staring us in the face.

[*Enter Left,* NURSE *and baby.*]

LEONORA [*Rising and crossing down Left*]. Another boy! Another boy! Here's a Roderick for you at last.

CHARLES [*Crossing to down Left*]. Roderick Brandon Bayard. A regular little fighter.

LEONORA. Good-bye, darling. Don't grow up too fast. Yes, yes. Aië, aië, aië—stay just as you are.—Thank you, Nurse.

GENEVIEVE [*Who has not left the table, repeats dryly*]. Stay just as you are.

[*Exit* NURSE *into hall.* CHARLES *and* LEONORA *return to their places.*]

LEONORA. Now I have three children. One, two, three. Two boys and a girl. I'm collecting them. It's very exciting. [*Over her shoulder.*]

What, Hilda? Oh, Cousin Ermengarde's come! Come in, Cousin. [*She goes to the hall door and welcomes* COUSIN ERMENGARDE, *already an elderly woman.*]

ERMENGARDE [*Shyly*]. It's such a pleasure to be with you all.

CHARLES [*Pulling out the center chair for her*]. The twins have taken a great fancy to you already, Cousin.

LEONORA. The baby went to her at once.

CHARLES. Exactly how are we related, Cousin Ermengarde?—There, Genevieve, that's your specialty.—First a little more turkey and stuffing, Mother? Cranberry sauce, anybody?

GENEVIEVE. I can work it out: Grandmother Bayard was your . . .

ERMENGARDE. Your Grandmother Bayard was a second cousin of my Grandmother Haskins through the Wainrights.

CHARLES. Well, it's all in a book somewhere upstairs. All that kind of thing is awfully interesting.

GENEVIEVE. Nonsense. There are no such books. I collect my notes off gravestones, and you have to scrape a good deal of moss—let me tell you—to find one great-grandparent.

CHARLES. There's a story that my Grandmother Bayard crossed the Mississippi on a raft before there were any bridges or ferry-boats. She died before Genevieve or I were born. Time certainly goes very fast in a great new country like this. Have some more cranberry sauce, Cousin Ermengarde.

ERMENGARDE [*Timidly*]. Well, time must be passing very slowly in Europe with this dreadful, dreadful war going on.[20]

CHARLES. Perhaps an occasional war isn't so bad after all. It clears up a lot of poisons that collect in nations. It's like a boil.

ERMENGARDE. Oh, dear, oh, dear!

CHARLES [*With relish*]. Yes, it's like a boil.—Ho! ho! Here are your twins. [*The twins appear at the hall door.* SAM *is wearing the uniform of an ensign or lieutenant.* LUCIA *is fussing over some detail on it.*]

LUCIA. Isn't he wonderful in it, Mother?

CHARLES. Let's get a look at you.

SAM. Mother, don't let Roderick fool with my stamp album while I'm gone. [*Crosses to Right.*]

LEONORA. Now, Sam, do write a letter once in a while. Do be a good boy about that, mind.

SAM. You might send some of those cakes of yours once in a while, Cousin Ermengarde.

[LEONORA *rises.*]

ERMENGARDE [*In a flutter*]. I certainly will, my dear boy.

[LEONORA *crosses to Center;* SAM *crosses down Right.*]

CHARLES [*Rising and facing* SAM]. If you need any money, we have agents in Paris and London, remember.

[LEONORA *crossing down Right.*]

LEONORA. Do be a good boy, Sam.

SAM. Well, good-bye . . .

[SAM *kisses his mother without sentimentality and goes out briskly through the dark portal.*[21] *They all return to their seats,* LUCIA *sitting at her father's left.*]

ERMENGARDE [*In a low, constrained voice, making conversation*]. I spoke to Mrs. Fairchild for a moment coming out of church. Her rheumatism's a little better, she says. She sends you her warmest thanks for the Christmas present. The workbasket, wasn't it?—[*Slight pause.*] It was an admirable sermon. And our stained-glass window looked so beautiful, Leonora, so beautiful. Everybody spoke of it and so affectionately of Sammy. [LEONORA'S *hand goes to her mouth.*] Forgive me, Leonora, but it's better to speak of him than not to speak of him when we're all thinking of him so hard.

LEONORA [*Rising, in anguish*]. He was a mere boy. He was a mere boy, Charles.

CHARLES. My dear, my dear.

LEONORA. I want to tell him how wonderful he was. We let him go so casually. I want to tell him how we all feel about him.—Forgive me, let me walk about a minute.—Yes, of course, Ermengarde—it's best to speak of him.

LUCIA [*In a low voice to* GENEVIEVE]. Isn't there anything I can do?

GENEVIEVE. No, no. Only time, only the passing of time can help in these things.

[LEONORA, *straying about the room, finds herself near the door to the hall at the moment that her son* RODERICK *enters. He links his arm with hers and leads her back to the table. He looks up and sees the family's dejection.*][22]

RODERICK. What's the matter, anyway? What are you all so glum about? The skating was fine to-day.

CHARLES. Roderick, I have something to say to you.

RODERICK [*Standing below his mother's chair*]. Everybody was there. Lucia skated in the corners with Dan Creighton the whole time. When'll it be, Lucia, when'll it be?

LUCIA. I don't know what you mean.

RODERICK. Lucia's leaving us soon, Mother. Dan Creighton, of all people.

CHARLES [*Ominously*].[23] Young man, I have something to say to you.

RODERICK. Yes, Father.

CHARLES. Is it true, Roderick, that you made yourself conspicuous last night at the Country Club—at a Christmas Eve dance, too?

LEONORA. Not now, Charles, I beg of you. This is Christmas dinner.

RODERICK [*Loudly*]. No, I didn't.

LUCIA. Really, Father, he didn't. It was that dreadful Johnny Lewis.

CHARLES. I don't want to hear about Johnny Lewis. I want to know whether a son of mine . . .

LEONORA. Charles, I beg of you . . .

CHARLES. The first family of this city!

RODERICK [*Crossing below table to Left Center*]. I hate this town and everything about it. I always did.

CHARLES. You behaved like a spoiled puppy, sir, an ill-bred spoiled puppy.

RODERICK. What did I do? What did I do that was wrong?

CHARLES [*Rising*]. You were drunk and you were rude to the daughters of my best friends.

GENEVIEVE [*Striking the table*]. Nothing in the world deserves an ugly scene like this. Charles, I'm ashamed of you.

RODERICK. Great God, you gotta get drunk in this town to forget how dull it is. Time passes so slowly here that it stands still, that's what's the trouble. [*Turns and walks toward the hall door.*]

CHARLES. Well, young man, we can employ your time. You will leave the university and you will come into the Bayard factory on January second.

RODERICK [*At the door into the hall*]. I have better things to do than to go into your old factory. I'm going somewhere where time passes, my God! [*He goes out into the hall.*]

LEONORA [*Rising and rushing to door*]. Roderick, Roderick, come here just a moment.—Charles, where can he go?

LUCIA [*Rising*]. Sh, Mother. He'll come back. [*She leads her mother back to chair, then starts for the hall door.*] Now I have to go upstairs and pack my trunk.

LEONORA. I won't have any children left! [*Sits.*]

LUCIA [*From the door*]. Sh, Mother. He'll come back. He's only gone to California or somewhere.—Cousin Ermengarde has done most of my packing—thanks a thousand times, Cousin Ermengarde. [*She kisses her mother as an afterthought.*] I won't be long [*She runs out into the hall.*]

ERMENGARDE [*Cheerfully*]. It's a very beautiful day. On the way home from church I stopped and saw Mrs. Foster a moment. Her arthritis comes and goes.

LEONORA. Is she actually in pain, dear?

ERMENGARDE. Oh, she says it'll all be the same in a hundred years!

LEONORA. Yes, she's a brave little stoic.

CHARLES. Come now, a little white meat, Mother?—Mary, pass my cousin's plate.

LEONORA. What is it, Mary?—Oh, here's a telegram from them in Paris! "Love and Christmas greetings to all." I told them we'd be eating some of their wedding cake and thinking about them to-day. It seems to be all decided that they will settle down in the East, Ermengarde. I can't even have my daughter for a neighbor. They hope to build before long somewhere on the shore north of New York.

GENEVIEVE. There is no shore north of New York.

LEONORA. Well, east or west or whatever it is.

[*Pause.*]

CHARLES [*Now sixty years old*]. My, what a dark day. [*Pause.*] How slowly time passes without any young people in the house.

LEONORA. I have three children somewhere.

CHARLES [*Blunderingly offering comfort*]. Well, one of them gave his life for his country.

LEONORA [*Sadly*]. And one of them is selling aluminum in China.

GENEVIEVE [*Slowly working herself up to a hysterical crisis*]. I can stand everything but this terrible soot everywhere. We should have moved long ago. We're surrounded by factories. We have to change the window curtains every week.

LEONORA. Why, Genevieve!

GENEVIEVE. I can't stand it. [*Rising.*] I can't stand it any more. I'm going abroad. It's not only the soot that comes through the very walls of this house; it's the *thoughts*, it's the thought of what has been and what might have been here. And the feeling about this house of the years *grinding away*. My mother died yesterday—not twenty-five years ago. Oh, I'm going to live and die abroad! [CHARLES *rises.*] Yes, I'm going to be the American old maid living and dying in a pension in Munich or Florence.

ERMENGARDE. Genevieve, you're tired.

CHARLES. Come, Genevieve, take a good drink of cold water. Mary, open the window a minute.

GENEVIEVE. I'm sorry. I'm sorry.

[*She hurries tearfully out into the hall.* CHARLES *sits.*]

ERMENGARDE. Dear Genevieve will come back to us, I think. [*She rises and starts toward the dark portal.*] You should have been out to-day, Leonora. It was one of those days when everything was encircled with ice. Very pretty, indeed.

CHARLES. Leonora, I used to go skating with Father on mornings like this.—I wish I felt a little better. [CHARLES *rises and starts following* ERMENGARDE *toward the Right.*]

LEONORA [*Rising*]. What! Have I got two invalids on my hands at once? Now, Cousin Ermengarde, you must get better and help me nurse Charles.

ERMENGARDE. I'll do my best. [ERMENGARDE *turns at the very portal and comes back to the table.*]

CHARLES. Well, Leonora, I'll do what you ask. I'll write the puppy a letter of forgiveness and apology. It's Christmas day. I'll cable it. That's what I'll do. [*He goes out the portal Right. Slight pause.*]

LEONORA [*Drying her eyes*]. Ermengarde, it's such a comfort having you here with me. [*Sits in place at left of* ERMENGARDE, *formerly occupied by* GENEVIEVE.] Mary, I really can't eat anything. Well, perhaps a sliver of white meat.

ERMENGARDE [*Very old*]. I spoke to Mrs. Keene for a moment coming out of church. She asked after the young people.—At church I felt very proud sitting under our windows, Leonora, and our brass tablets. The Bayard aisle,—it's a regular Bayard aisle and I love it.

LEONORA. Ermengarde, would you be very angry with me if I went and stayed with the young people a little this spring?

ERMENGARDE. Why, no. I know how badly they want you and need you. Especially now that they're about to build a new house.

LEONORA. You wouldn't be angry? This house is yours as long as you want it, remember.

ERMENGARDE. I don't see why the rest of you dislike it. I like it more than I can say.

LEONORA. I won't be long. I'll be back in no time and we can have some more of our readings-aloud in the evening.

[*She kisses her and goes into the hall.* ERMENGARDE, *left alone, eats slowly and talks to* MARY.]

ERMENGARDE. Really, Mary, I'll change my mind. If you'll ask Bertha to be good enough to make me a little eggnog. A dear little eggnog. —Such a nice letter this morning from Mrs. Bayard, Mary. Such a nice letter. They're having their first Christmas dinner in the new house. They must be very happy. They call her Mother Bayard, she says, as though she were an old lady. And she says she finds it more comfortable to come and go in a wheel chair.—Such a dear letter. . . . And, Mary, I can tell you a secret. It's still a great secret, mind! They're expecting a grandchild. Isn't that good news! Now I'll read a little. [*She props a book up before her, still dipping a spoon into a custard from time to time. She grows from very old to immensely old. She sighs. She finds a cane beside her, and totters out of the Right portal, murmuring:*] Dear little Roderick and little Lucia.

[*The audience gazes for a space of time at the table before the lights slowly dim out.*]

CURTAIN

Notes

1 An arch, sometimes including a wall, that separates the stage from the auditorium.

2 Wreaths.

3 Acting out; mute gesture.

4 A quotation from the Bible, I Timothy, 5:23.

5 The author uses several devices for noting the passage of time. Here, the return of Cousin Brandon from Alaska indicates that five years have slipped by.

6 Gertrude, the imaginary servant at the first Christmas dinner, has been replaced by Frieda. This is a device used here, and later, to indicate the passage of time and, perhaps, is also a comment on the impermanence of domestic service.

7 Moving force.

8 Mother Bayard's is the first death in this procession. Others at the table resume eating after she passes through the portal of death, but we soon learn that they are really at dinner one year later.

9 A painful disorder usually extending from the hip down the back of the thigh.

10 A reference to the birth of Samuel, an Old Testament judge and prophet of Israel. Samuel's mother, Hannah, was childless until she prayed to God for the birth of a son. See I Samuel, chapter 1.

11 An abrupt change in the topic of conversation shortly indicates that twelve years have passed since the birth of Charles.

12 An exaggeration, but one that calls to mind that the house was new at the time of the first Christmas dinner.

13 A more direct statement about time than is usually employed in this nonrealistic play.

14 In a low voice. In Italian, the phrase means "under the voice."

15 Boardinghouses.

16 Groups.

17 Ornamental work and dome.

18 This relative had been considered as a person to join the family circle before the deaths of Cousin Brandon and Lucia, but as happens with such proposals, the invitation had been delayed. Note Genevieve's next remark.

19 Humble.

20 World War I lasted from July 1914 to November 1918.

21 Sam's exit foretells his death in war, a fact confirmed by Ermengarde in the next speech.

22 Low spirits.

23 Threateningly.

ARMS AND THE MAN[1]

George Bernard Shaw

GEORGE BERNARD SHAW (1856–1950) was an Irish-born dramatist, critic, and tract writer, considered by some the greatest English (British) playwright since Shakespeare. Certainly he was a master of razor-edged utterance that has provided audiences and readers keen intellectual satisfaction for many years. Paradox in Shaw's plays, a kind of perversity, is a suitable term for his favorite dramatic technique: the introduction of a character or situation that appears to be one thing and is subsequently revealed as quite another.

Born in Dublin of English stock, Shaw left school at the age of fourteen, worked in a government real estate office for five years, and, when twenty, joined his mother, who had gone to London to work as a music teacher. He began his writing career as an unsuccessful novelist. Shaw became interested in the Fabian Society, an organization founded in 1884 to seek the gradual spread of socialism by peaceful means, but he never became a conventional socialist. Although he wrote economic and political tracts for the Fabians, he believed throughout his life in what he termed "the Life Force," active, individually willed evolution dependent upon each man's vitality and sense of personal power.

By inheritance and through association with his mother, Shaw became a lover of music, especially the work of Mozart and Richard Wagner. He soon became a newspaper critic of music, and in this role, and later as a drama critic for a London magazine, he wrote provocative reviews that wittily mocked conventional tastes and fashionable preferences. Shaw especially admired the Norwegian dramatist Henrik Ibsen (1828–1906), whom he considered a realistic and reforming playwright. Ibsen dealt with modern life and presented what Shaw called "genuine discussion" in his plays.

Shaw's training in music and dramatic criticism, his interest in reform, and his admiration for Mozart, Wagner, and Ibsen helped to make him a playwright who knew theatrical techniques and conventions and who was determined to shake audiences out of their hypocrisies, complacencies, and unthinking acceptance of the status quo. "I must warn my readers," he once wrote, "that my attacks are directed against themselves, not against my stage figures." Beginning with his first play in 1892, he continued throughout a long life to show his unorthodox turn of mind and his distrust of accepted institutions and conventions in dozens of plays and other writings designed to teach, to tease, and to provoke.

PRINCIPAL CHARACTERS

RAINA PETKOFF, *a young Bulgarian lady*
CATHERINE PETKOFF, *her mother*
LOUKA, *the Petkoff's maid*
CAPTAIN BLUNTSCHLI, *a Swiss officer in the Serbian army*
NICOLA, *the Petkoff's butler*
PAUL PETKOFF, *a major in the Bulgarian army, Raina's father*
SERGIUS SARANOFF, *a major in the Bulgarian army, Raina's fiancé*

Act I

Night: A lady's bedchamber in Bulgaria, in a small town near the Dragoman Pass, late in November in the year 1885. Through an open window with a little balcony a peak of the Balkans, wonderfully white and beautiful in the starlit snow, seems quite close at hand, though it is really miles away.[2] *The interior of the room is not like anything to be seen in the west of Europe. It is half rich Bulgarian, half cheap Viennese. Above the head of the bed, which stands against a little wall cutting off the left-hand corner of the room, is a painted wooden shrine, blue and gold, with an ivory image of Christ, and a light hanging before it in a pierced metal ball suspended by three chains. The principal seat, placed towards the other side of the room and opposite the window, is a Turkish ottoman. The counterpane and hangings of the bed, the window curtains, the little carpet, and all the ornamental textile fabrics in the room are oriental and gorgeous; the paper on the walls is occidental and paltry. The washstand, against the wall on the side nearest the ottoman and window, consists of an enamelled iron basin with a pail beneath it in a painted metal frame, and a single towel on the rail at the side. The dressing table, between the bed and the window, is a common pine table, covered with a cloth of many colours, with an expensive toilet mirror on it. The door is on the side nearest the bed; and there is a chest of drawers between. This chest of drawers is also covered by a variegated*[3] *native cloth; and on it there is a pile of paper-backed novels, a box of chocolate creams, and a miniature easel with a large photograph of an extremely handsome officer, whose lofty bearing and magnetic glance can be felt even from the portrait. The room is lighted by a candle on the chest of drawers, and another on the dressing table with a box of matches beside it.*

The window is hinged doorwise and stands wide open. Outside, a pair of wooden shutters, opening outwards, also stand open. On the balcony a young lady, intensely conscious of the romantic beauty of the night, and of the fact that her own youth and beauty are part of it, is gazing at the snowy Balkans. She is in her nightgown, well covered by a long mantle of furs, worth, on a moderate estimate, about three times the furniture of the room.

Her reverie is interrupted by her mother, Catherine Petkoff, a woman over forty, imperiously energetic, with magnificent black hair and eyes, who might be a very splendid specimen of the wife of a mountain farmer, but is determined to be a Viennese lady, and to that end wears a fashionable tea gown on all occasions.

CATHERINE [*entering hastily, full of good news*]. Raina! [*She pronounces it Rah-eena, with the stress on the ee.*] Raina! [*She goes to the bed, expecting to find* RAINA *there.*] Why, where—? [RAINA *looks into the room.*] Heavens, child! are you out in the night air instead of in your bed? Youll[4] catch your death. Louka told me you were asleep.

RAINA [*dreamily*]. I sent her away. I wanted to be alone. The stars are so beautiful! What is the matter?

CATHERINE. Such news! There has been a battle.

RAINA [*her eyes dilating*]. Ah! [*She comes eagerly to* CATHERINE.]

CATHERINE. A great battle at Slivnitza! A victory! And it was won by Sergius.

RAINA [*with a cry of delight*]. Ah! [*They embrace rapturously*] Oh, mother! [*Then, with sudden anxiety*] Is father safe?

CATHERINE. Of course: he sends me the news. Sergius is the hero of the hour, the idol of the regiment.

RAINA. Tell me, tell me. How was it? [*Ecstatically*] Oh, mother! mother! mother! [*She pulls her mother down on the ottoman; and they kiss one another frantically.*]

CATHERINE [*with surging enthusiasm*]. You cant guess how splendid it is. A cavalry charge! think of that! He defied our Russian commanders—acted without orders—led a charge on his own responsibility—headed it himself—was the first man to sweep through their guns. Cant you see it, Raina: our gallant splendid Bulgarians with their swords and eyes flashing, thundering down like an avalanche and scattering the wretched Serbs and their dandified Austrian officers like chaff. And you! you kept Sergius waiting a year before you would be betrothed to him. Oh, if you have a drop of Bulgarian blood in your veins, you will worship him when he comes back.

RAINA. What will he care for my poor little worship after the acclamations of a whole army of heroes? But no matter: I am so happy! so proud! [*She rises and walks about excitedly.*] It proves that all our ideas were real after all.

CATHERINE [*indignantly*]. Our ideas real! What do you mean?

RAINA. Our ideas of what Sergius would do. Our patriotism. Our heroic ideals. I sometimes used to doubt whether they were anything but dreams. Oh, what faithless little creatures girls are! When I buckled on Sergius's sword he looked so noble: it was treason to think of disillusion or humiliation or failure. And yet—and yet—[*She sits down again suddenly*] Promise me youll never tell him.

CATHERINE. Dont ask me for promises until I know what I'm promising.

RAINA. Well, it came into my head just as he was holding me in his arms and looking into my eyes, that perhaps we only had our heroic ideas because we are so fond of reading Byron and Pushkin,[5] and because we were so delighted with the opera that season at Bucharest. Real life is so seldom like that! indeed never, as far as I knew it then. [*Remorsefully*] Only think, mother: I doubted him: I wondered whether all his heroic qualities and his soldiership might not prove mere imagination when he went into a real battle. I had an uneasy fear that he might cut a poor figure there beside all those clever officers from the Tsar's court.

CATHERINE. A poor figure! Shame on you! The Serbs have Austrian officers who are just as clever as the Russians; but we have beaten them in every battle for all that.

RAINA [*laughing and snuggling against her mother*]. Yes: I was only a prosaic little coward. Oh, to think that it was all true! that Sergius is just as splendid and noble as he looks! that the world is really a glorious world of women who can see its glory and men who can act its romance! What happiness! what unspeakable fulfilment!

[*They are interrupted by the entry of* LOUKA, *a handsome proud girl in a pretty Bulgarian peasant's dress with double apron, so defiant that her servility to* RAINA *is almost insolent. She is afraid of* CATHERINE, *but even with her goes as far as she dares.*]

LOUKA. If you please, madam, all the windows are to be closed and the shutters made fast. They say there may be shooting in the streets. [RAINA *and* CATHERINE *rise together, alarmed.*] The Serbs are being chased right back through the pass; and they say they may run into the town. Our cavalry will be after them; and our people will be ready for them, you may be sure, now theyre running away. [*She goes out on the balcony, and pulls the outside shutters to; then steps back into the room.*]

CATHERINE [*businesslike, housekeeping instincts aroused*]. I must see that everything is made safe downstairs.

RAINA. I wish our people were not so cruel. What glory is there in killing wretched fugitives?

CATHERINE. Cruel! Do you suppose they would hesitate to kill you—or worse?

RAINA [*to* LOUKA]. Leave the shutters so that I can just close them if I hear any noise.

CATHERINE [*authoritatively, turning on her way to the door*]. Oh no, dear: you must keep them fastened. You would be sure to drop off to sleep and leave them open. Make them fast, Louka.

LOUKA. Yes, madam. [*She fastens them.*]

RAINA. Dont be anxious about me. The moment I hear a shot, I shall blow out the candles and roll myself up in bed with my ears well covered.

CATHERINE. Quite the wisest thing you can do, my love. Goodnight.

RAINA. Goodnight. [*Her emotion comes back for a moment.*] Wish me joy [*They kiss.*] This is the happiest night of my life—if only there are no fugitives.

CATHERINE. Go to bed, dear; and dont think of them. [*She goes out.*]

LOUKA [*secretly to* RAINA]. If you would like the shutters open, just give them a push like this [*she pushes them: they open: she pulls them to again*]. One of them ought to be bolted at the bottom; but the bolt's gone.

RAINA [*with dignity, reproving her*]. Thanks, Louka; but we must do what we are told. [LOUKA *makes a grimace.*] Goodnight.

LOUKA [*carelessly*]. Goodnight. [*She goes out, swaggering.*]

[RAINA, *left alone, takes off her fur cloak and throws it on the ottoman. Then she goes to the chest of drawers, and adores the portrait there with feelings that are beyond all expression. She does not kiss it or press it to her breast, or shew it any mark of bodily affection; but she takes it in her hands and elevates it, like a priestess.*]

RAINA [*looking up at the picture*]. Oh, I shall never be unworthy of you any more, my soul's hero: never,

never, never. [*She replaces it reverently. Then she selects a novel from the little pile of books. She turns over the leaves dreamily; finds her page; turns the book inside out at it; and, with a happy sigh, gets into bed and prepares to read hersel; to sleep. But before abandoning herself to fiction, she raises her eyes once more, thinking of the blessed reality, and murmurs*] My hero! my hero!

[*A distant shot breaks the quiet of the night. She starts, listening; and two more shots, much nearer, follow, startling her so that she scrambles out of bed, and hastily blows out the candle on the chest of drawers. Then, putting her fingers in her ears, she runs to the dressing table, blows out the light there, and hurries back to bed in the dark, nothing being visible but the glimmer of the light in the pierced ball before the image, and the starlight seen through the slits at the top of the shutters. The firing breaks out again: there is a startling fusillade quite close at hand. Whilst it is still echoing, the shutters disappear, pulled open from without; and for an instant the rectangle of snowy starlight flashes out with the figure of a man silhouetted in black upon it. The shutters close immediately; and the room is dark again. But the silence is now broken by the sound of panting. Then there is a scratch; and the flame of a match is seen in the middle of the room.*]

RAINA [*crouching on the bed*]. Who's there? [*The match is out instantly.*] Who's there? Who is that?

A MAN'S VOICE [*in the darkness, subduedly, but threateningly*]. Sh—sh! Dont call out; or youll be shot. Be good; and no harm will happen to you. [*She is heard leaving her bed, and making for the door.*] Take care: it's no use trying to run away.

RAINA. But who—

THE VOICE [*warning*]. Remember: if you raise your voice my revolver will go off. [*Commandingly*] Strike a light and let me see you. Do you hear. [*Another moment of silence and darkness as she retreats to the chest of drawers. Then she lights a candle; and the mystery is at an end. He is a man about 35, in a deplorable plight, bespattered with mud and blood and snow, his belt and the strap of his revolver case keeping together the torn ruins of the blue tunic of a Serbian artillery officer. All that the candlelight and his unwashed unkempt condition make it possible to discern is that he is of middling stature and undistinguished appearance, with strong neck and shoulders, roundish obstinate looking head covered with short crisp bronze curls, clear quick eyes and good brows and mouth, hopelessly prosaic*[6] *nose like that of a strong minded baby, trim soldierlike carriage and energetic manner, and with all his wits about him in spite of his desperate predicament: even with a sense of the humor of it, without, however, the least intention of trifling with it or throwing away a chance. Reckoning up what he can guess about* RAINA: *her age, her social position, her character, and the extent to which she is frightened, he continues, more politely but still most determinedly*] Excuse my disturbing you; but you recognize my uniform? Serb! If I'm caught I shall be killed. [*Menacingly*] Do you understand that?

RAINA. Yes.

THE MAN. Well, I dont intend to get killed if I can help it. [*Still more formidably*] Do you understand that? [*He locks the door quickly but quietly.*]

RAINA [*disdainfully*]. I suppose not. [*She draws herself up superbly, and looks him straight in the face, adding, with cutting emphasis*] Some soldiers, I know, are afraid to die.[7]

THE MAN [*with grim goodhumor*]. All of them, dear lady, all of them, believe me. It is our duty to live as long as we can. Now, if you raise an alarm—

RAINA [*cutting him short*]. You will shoot me. How do you know that *I* am afraid to die?

THE MAN [*cunningly*]. Ah; but suppose I dont shoot you, what will happen then? A lot of your cavalry will burst into this pretty room of yours and slaughter me here like a pig; for I'll fight like a demon: they shant get me into the street to amuse themselves with: I know what they are. Are you prepared to receive that sort of company in your present undress?[8] [RAINA, *suddenly conscious of her nightgown, instinctively shrinks and gathers it more closely about her neck. He watches her and adds pitilessly*] Hardly presentable, eh? [*She turns to the ottoman. He raises his pistol instantly, and cries*] Stop! [*She stops.*] Where are you going?

RAINA [*with dignified patience*]. Only to get my cloak.

THE MAN [*passing swiftly to the ottoman and snatching the cloak*]. A good idea! I'll keep the cloak; and youll take care that nobody comes in and sees you without it. This is a better weapon than the revolver: eh? [*He throws the pistol down on the ottoman.*]

RAINA [*revolted*]. It is not the weapon of a gentleman!

THE MAN. It's good enough for a man with only you to stand between him and death. [*As they look at one another for a moment,* RAINA *hardly able to believe that even a Serbian officer can be so cynically and selfishly unchivalrous, they are startled by a sharp fusillade in the street. The chill of imminent death hushes the man's voice as he adds*] Do you hear? If you are going to bring those blackguards in on me you shall receive them as you are.

[*Clamor and disturbance. The pursuers in the street batter at the house door, shouting* Open the door! Open the door! Wake up, will you! *A man servant's voice calls to them angrily from within* This is Major Petkoff's house: you cant come in here; *but a renewal of the clamor, and a torrent of blows on the door, end with his letting a chain down with a clank, followed by a rush of heavy footsteps and a din of triumphant yells, dominated at last by the voice of* CATHERINE, *indignantly addressing an officer with* What does this mean, sir? Do you know where you are? *The noise subsides suddenly.*]

LOUKA [*outside, knocking at the bedroom door*]. My lady! my lady! get up quick and open the door. If you dont they will break it down.

[*The fugitive throws up his head with the gesture of a man who sees that it is all over with him, and drops the manner he has been assuming to intimidate* RAINA.]

THE MAN [*sincerely and kindly*]. No use, dear: I'm done for. [*Flinging the cloak to her*] Quick! wrap yourself up: theyre coming.

RAINA. Oh, thank you. [*She wraps herself up with intense relief.*]

THE MAN [*between his teeth*]. Dont mention it.

RAINA [*anxiously*]. What will you do?

THE MAN [*grimly*]. The first man in will find out. Keep out of the way; and dont look. It wont last long; but it will not be nice. [*He draws his sabre and faces the door, waiting.*]

RAINA [*impulsively*]. I'll help you. I'll save you.

THE MAN. You cant.

RAINA. I can. I'll hide you. [*She drags him towards the window.*] Here! behind the curtains.

THE MAN [*yielding to her*]. Theres just half a chance, if you keep your head.

RAINA [*drawing the curtain before him*]. S-sh! [*She makes for the ottoman.*]

THE MAN [*putting out his head*]. Remember—

RAINA [*running back to him*]. Yes?

THE MAN. —nine soldiers out of ten are born fools.

RAINA. Oh! [*She draws the curtain angrily before him.*]

THE MAN [*looking out at the other side*]. If they find me, I promise you a fight: a devil of a fight.

[*She stamps at him. He disappears hastily. She takes off her cloak, and throws it across the foot of the bed. Then, with a sleepy, disturbed air, she opens the door.* LOUKA *enters excitedly.*]

LOUKA. One of those beasts of Serbs has been seen climbing up the waterpipe to your balcony. Our men want to search for him; and they are so wild and drunk and furious. [*She makes for the other side of the room to get as far from the door as possible.*] My lady says you are to dress at once and to— [*She sees the revolver lying on the ottoman, and stops, petrified.*[9]]

RAINA [*as if annoyed at being disturbed*]. They shall not search here. Why have they been let in?

CATHERINE [*coming in hastily*]. Raina, darling, are you safe? Have you seen anyone or heard anything?

RAINA. I heard the shooting. Surely the soldiers will not dare come in here?

CATHERINE. I have found a Russian officer, thank Heaven: he knows Sergius. [*Speaking through the door to someone outside*] Sir: will you come in now. My daughter will receive you.

[*A young Russian officer, in Bulgarian uniform, enters, sword in hand.*]

OFFICER [*with soft feline politeness and stiff military carriage*]. Good evening, gracious lady. I am sorry to intrude; but there is a Serb hiding on the balcony. Will you and the gracious lady your mother please to withdraw whilst we search?

RAINA [*petulantly*]. Nonsense, sir: you can see that there is no one on the balcony. [*She throws the shutters wide open and stands with her back to the curtain where* THE MAN *is hidden, pointing to the moonlit balcony. A couple of shots are fired right under the window; and a bullet shatters the glass opposite* RAINA, *who winks and gasps, but stand her ground; whilst* CATHERINE *screams, and* THE OFFICER, *with a cry of* Take care! *rushes to the balcony.*]

THE OFFICER [*on the balcony, shouting savagely down to the street*]. Cease firing there, you fools: do you hear? Cease firing, damn you! [*He glares down for a moment; then turns to* RAINA, *trying to resume his polite manner.*] Could anyone have got in without your knowledge? Were you asleep?

RAINA. No: I have not been to bed.

THE OFFICER [*impatiently, coming back into the room*]. Your neighbors have their heads so full of runaway Serbs that they see them everywhere. [*Politely*] Gracious lady: a thousand pardons. Goodnight. [*Military bow, which* RAINA *returns coldly. Another to* CATHERINE, *who follows him out.*]

[RAINA *closes the shutters. She turns and sees* LOUKA, *who has been watching the scene curiously.*]

RAINA. Dont leave my mother, Louka, until the soldiers go away.

[LOUKA *glances at* RAINA, *at the ottoman, at the curtain; then purses her lips secretively, laughs insolently, and goes out.* RAINA, *highly offended by this demonstration, follows her to the door, and shuts it behind her with a slam, locking it violently.* THE MAN *immediately steps out from behind the curtain, sheathing his sabre. Then, dismissing the danger from his mind in a businesslike way, he comes affably to* RAINA.]

THE MAN. A narrow shave; but a miss is as good as a mile. Dear young lady: your servant to the death. I wish for your sake I had joined the Bulgarian army instead of the other one. I am not a native Serb.

RAINA [*haughtily*]. No: you are one of the Austrians who set the Serbs on to rob us of our national liberty, and who officer their army for them. We hate them!

THE MAN. Austrian! not I. Dont hate me, dear young lady. I am a Swiss, fighting merely as a professional soldier. I joined the Serbs because they came first on the road from Switzerland. Be generous: youve beaten us hollow.

RAINA. Have I not been generous?

THE MAN. Noble! Heroic! But I'm not saved yet. This particular rush will soon pass through; but the pursuit will go on all night by fits and starts. I must take my chance to get off in a quiet interval. [*Pleasantly*] You dont mind my waiting just a minute or two, do you?

RAINA [*putting on her most genteel society manner*]. Oh, not at all. Wont you sit down?

THE MAN. Thanks. [*He sits on the foot of the bed.*]

[RAINA *walks with studied elegance to the ottoman and sits down. Unfortunately she sits on the pistol, and jumps up with a shriek.* THE MAN, *all nerves, shies like a frightened horse to the other side of the room.*]

THE MAN [*irritably*]. Dont frighten me like that. What is it?

RAINA. Your revolver! It was staring that officer in the face all the time. What an escape![10]

THE MAN [*vexed at being unnecessarily terrified*]. Oh, is that all?

RAINA [*staring at him rather superciliously as she conceives a poorer and poorer opinion of him, and feels proportionately more and more at her ease*]. I am sorry I frightened you. [*She takes up the pistol and hands it to him.*] Pray take it to protect yourself against me.

THE MAN [*grinning wearily at the sarcasm as he takes the pistol*]. No use, dear young lady: theres nothing in it. It's not loaded. [*He makes a grimace at it, and drops it disparagingly into his revolver case.*]

RAINA. Load it by all means.

THE MAN. Ive no ammunition. What use are cartridges in battle? I always carry chocolate instead; and I finished the last cake of that hours ago.

RAINA [*outraged in her most cherished ideals of manhood*]. Chocolate! Do you stuff your pockets with sweets—like a schoolboy—even in the field?

THE MAN [*grinning*]. Yes: isnt it contemptible? [*Hungrily*] I wish I had some now.

RAINA. Allow me. [*She sails away scornfully to the chest of drawers, and returns with the box of confectionery in her hand.*] I am sorry I have eaten them all except these. [*She offers him the box.*]

THE MAN [*ravenously*]. Youre an angel! [*He gobbles the contents.*] Creams! Delicious! [*He looks anxiously to see whether there are any more. There are none: he can only scrape the box with his fingers and suck them. When that nourishment is exhausted he accepts the inevitable with pathetic goodhumor, and says, with grateful emotion*] Bless you, dear lady! You can always tell an old soldier by the inside of his holsters and cartridge boxes. The young ones carry pistols and cartridges: the old ones, grub. Thank you. [*He hands back the box. She snatches it contemptuously from him and throws it away. He shies again, as if she had meant to strike him.*] Ugh! Dont do things so suddenly, gracious lady. It's mean to revenge yourself because I frightened you just now.

RAINA [*loftily*]. Frighten me! Do you know, sir, that though I am only a woman, I think I am at heart as brave as you.

THE MAN. I should think so. You havnt been under fire for three days as I have. I can stand two days without shewing it much; but no man can stand three days: I'm as nervous as a mouse. [*He sits down on the ottoman, and takes his head in his hands.*] Would you like to see me cry?

RAINA [*alarmed*]. No.

THE MAN. If you would, all you have to do is to scold me just as if I were a little boy and you my nurse. If I were in camp now, theyd play all sorts of tricks on me.

RAINA. [*a little moved*]. I'm sorry. I wont scold you. [*Touched by the sympathy in her tone, he raises his head and looks gratefully at her: she immediately draws back and says stiffly*] You must excuse me: our soldiers are not like that. [*She moves away from the ottoman.*]

THE MAN. Oh yes they are. There are only two sorts of soldiers: old ones and young ones. Ive served fourteen years: half of your fellows never smelt powder before. Why, how is it that youve just beaten us? Sheer ignorance of the art of war, nothing else. [*Indignantly*] I never saw anything so unprofessional.

RAINA [*ironically*]. Oh! was it unprofessional to beat you?

THE MAN. Well, come! is it professional to throw a regiment of cavalry on a battery of machine guns, with the dead certainty that if the guns go off not a horse or man will ever get within fifty yards of the fire? I couldnt believe my eyes when I saw it.

RAINA [*eagerly turning to him, as all her enthusiasm and her dreams of glory rush back on her*]. Did you see the great cavalry charge? Oh, tell me about it. Describe it to me.

THE MAN. You never saw a cavalry charge, did you?

RAINA. How could I?

THE MAN. Ah, perhaps not. No: of course not! Well, it's a funny sight. It's like slinging a handful of peas against a window pane: first one comes; then two or three close behind him; and then all the rest in a lump.

RAINA [*her eyes dilating as she raises her clasped hands ecstatically*]. Yes, first One! the bravest of the brave!

THE MAN [*prosaically*]. Hm! you should see the poor devil pulling at his horse.

RAINA. Why should he pull at his horse?

THE MAN [*impatient of so stupid a question*]. It's running away with him, of course: do you suppose the fellow wants to get there before the others and be killed? Then they all come. You can tell the young ones by their wildness and their slashing. The old ones come bunched up under the number one guard: they know that theyre mere projectiles, and that it's no use trying to fight. The wounds are mostly broken knees, from the horses cannoning together.

RAINA. Ugh! But I dont believe the first man is a coward. I know he is a hero!

THE MAN [*goodhumoredly*]. Thats what youd have said if youd seen the first man in the charge today.

RAINA [*breathless, forgiving him everything*]. Ah, I knew it! Tell me. Tell me about him.

THE MAN. He did it like an operatic tenor. A regular handsome fellow, with flashing eyes and lovely moustache, shouting his war-cry and charging like Don Quixote at the windmills.[11] We did laugh.

RAINA. You dared to laugh!

THE MAN. Yes; but when the sergeant ran up as white as a sheet, and told us theyd sent us the wrong ammunition, and that we couldnt fire a round for the next ten minutes, we laughed at the other side of our mouths. I never felt so sick in my life; though Ive been in one or two very tight places. And I hadnt even a revolver cartridge: only chocolate. We'd no bayonets: nothing. Of course, they just cut us to bits. And there was Don

Quixote flourishing like a drum major, thinking he'd done the cleverest thing ever known, whereas he ought to be courtmartialled for it. Of all the fools ever let loose on a field of battle, that man must be the very maddest. He and his regiment simply committed suicide; only the pistol missed fire: thats all.

RAINA [*deeply wounded, but steadfastly loyal to her ideals*]. Indeed! Would you know him again if you saw him?

THE MAN. Shall I ever forget him! [*She again goes to the chest of drawers. He watches her with a vague hope that she may have something more for him to eat. She takes the portrait from its stand and brings it to him.*]

RAINA. That is a photograph of the gentleman—the patriot and hero—to whom I am betrothed.

THE MAN [*recognizing it with a shock*]. I'm really very sorry. [*Looking at her*] Was it fair to lead me on? [*He looks at the portrait again*] Yes: thats Don Quixote: not a doubt of it. [*He stifles a laugh.*]

RAINA [*quickly*]. Why do you laugh?

THE MAN [*apologetic, but still greatly tickled*]. I didnt laugh I assure you. At least I didnt mean to. But when I think of him charging the windmills and imagining he was doing the finest thing—[*He chokes with suppressed laughter.*]

RAINA [*sternly*]. Give me back the portrait, sir.

THE MAN [*with sincere remorse*]. Of course. Certainly. I'm really very sorry. [*He hands her the picture. She deliberately kisses it and looks him straight in the face before returning to the chest of drawers to replace it. He follows her, apologizing.*] Perhaps I'm quite wrong, you know: no doubt I am. Most likely he had got wind of the cartridge business somehow, and knew it was a safe job.

RAINA. That is to say, he was a pretender and a coward! You did not dare say that before.

THE MAN [*with comic gesture of despair*]. It's no use, dear lady: I cant make you see it from the professional point of view. [*As he turns away to get back to the ottoman, a couple of distant shots threaten renewed trouble.*]

RAINA [*sternly, as she sees him listening to the shots*]. So much the better for you!

THE MAN [*turning*]. How?

RAINA. You are my enemy; and you are at my mercy. What would I do if I were a professional soldier?

THE MAN. Ah, true, dear young lady: youre always right. I know how good youve been to me: to my last hour I shall remember those three chocolate creams. It was unsoldierly; but it was angelic.

RAINA [*coldly*]. Thank you. And now I will do a soldierly thing. You cannot stay here after what you have just said about my future husband; but I will go out on the balcony and see whether it is safe for you to climb down into the street. [*She turns to the window.*]

THE MAN [*changing countenance*]. Down that waterpipe! Stop! Wait! I cant! I darent! The very thought of it makes me giddy. I came up it fast enough with death behind me. But to face it now in cold blood—!

[*He sinks on the ottoman.*] It's no use: I give up: I'm beaten. Give the alarm. [*He drops his head on his hands in the deepest dejection.*]

RAINA [*disarmed by pity*]. Come: dont be disheartened. [*She stoops over him almost maternally: he shakes his head.*] Oh, you are a very poor soldier: a chocolate cream soldier! Come, cheer up! it takes less courage to climb down than to face capture: remember that.

THE MAN [*dreamily, lulled by her voice*]. No: capture only means death; and death is sleep: oh, sleep, sleep, sleep, undisturbed sleep! Climbing down the pipe means doing something—exerting myself—thinking! Death ten times over first.

RAINA [*softly and wonderingly, catching the rhythm of his weariness*]. Are you as sleepy as that?

THE MAN. Ive not had two hours undisturbed sleep since I joined. I havnt closed my eyes for forty-eight hours.

RAINA [*at her wit's end*]. But what am I to do with you?

THE MAN [*staggering up, roused by her desperation*]. Of course. I must do something. [*He shakes himself; pulls himself together; and speaks with rallied vigor and courage.*] You see, sleep or no sleep, hunger or no hunger, tired or not tired, you can always do a thing when you know it must be done. Well, that pipe must be got down: [*he hits himself on the chest*] do you hear that, you chocolate cream soldier? [*He turns to the window.*]

RAINA [*anxiously*]. But if you fall?

THE MAN. I shall sleep as if the stones were a feather bed. Goodbye. [*He makes boldly for the window; and his hand is on the shutter when there is a terrible burst of firing in the street beneath.*]

RAINA [*rushing to him*]. Stop! [*She seizes him recklessly, and pulls him quite round.*] Theyll kill you.

THE MAN [*coolly, but attentively*]. Never mind: this sort of thing is all in my day's work. I'm bound to take my chance. [*Decisively*] Now do what I tell you. Put out the candle; so that they shant see the light when I open the shutters. And keep away from the window, whatever you do. If they see me theyre sure to have a shot at me.

RAINA [*clinging to him*]. Theyre sure to see you: it's bright moonlight. I'll save you. Oh, how can you be so indifferent! You want me to save you, dont you?

THE MAN. I really don't want to be troublesome. [*She shakes him in her impatience.*] I am not indifferent, dear young lady, I assure you. But how is it to be done?

RAINA. Come away from the window. [*She takes him firmly back to the middle of the room. The moment she releases him he turns mechanically towards the window again. She seizes him and turns him back, exclaiming*] Please! [*He becomes motionless, like a hypnotized rabbit, his fatigue gaining fast on him. She releases him, and addresses him patronizingly.*][12] Now listen. You must trust to our hospitality. You do not yet know in whose house you are. I am a Petkoff.

THE MAN. A pet what?

RAINA [*rather indignantly*]. I mean that I belong to the family of the Petkoffs, the richest and best known in our country.

THE MAN. Oh yes, of course. I beg your pardon. The Petkoffs, to be sure. How stupid of me!

RAINA. You know you never heard of them until this moment. How can you stoop to pretend!

THE MAN. Forgive me: I'm too tired to think; and the change of subject was too much for me. Dont scold me.

RAINA. I forgot. It might make you cry. [*He nods, quite seriously. She pouts and then resumes her patronizing tone.*] I must tell you that my father holds the highest command of any Bulgarian in our army. He is [*proudly*] a Major.

THE MAN [*pretending to be deeply impressed*]. A Major! Bless me! Think of that!

RAINA. You shewed great ignorance in thinking that it was necessary to climb up to the balcony because ours is the only private house that has two rows of windows. There is a flight of stairs inside to get up and down by.

THE MAN. Stairs! How grand! You live in great luxury indeed, dear young lady.

RAINA. Do you know what a library is?

THE MAN. A library? A roomful of books?

RAINA. Yes. We have one, the only one in Bulgaria.

THE MAN. Actually a real library! I should like to see that.

RAINA [*affectedly*]. I tell you these things to shew you that you are not in the house of ignorant country folk who would kill you the moment they saw your Serbian uniform, but among civilized people. We go to Bucharest every year for the opera season; and I have spent a whole month in Vienna.

THE MAN. I saw that, dear young lady. I saw at once that you knew the world.

RAINA. Have you ever seen the opera of Ernani?[13]

THE MAN. Is that the one with the devil in it in red velvet, and a soldiers' chorus?

RAINA [*contemptuously*]. No!

THE MAN [*stifling a heavy sigh of weariness*]. Then I dont know it.

RAINA. I thought you might have remembered the great scene where Ernani, flying from his foes just as you are tonight, takes refuge in the castle of his bitterest enemy, an old Castilian noble. The noble refuses to give him up. His guest is sacred to him.

THE MAN [*quickly, waking up a little*]. Have your people got that notion?

RAINA [*with dignity*]. My mother and I can understand that notion, as you call it. And if instead of threatening me with your pistol as you did you had simply thrown yourself as a fugitive on our hospitality, you would have been as safe as in your father's house.

THE MAN. Quite sure?

RAINA [*turning her back on him in disgust*]. Oh, it is useless to try to make you understand.

THE MAN. Dont be angry: you see how awkward it would be for me if there was any mistake. My father is a very hospitable man: he keeps six hotels; but I couldnt trust him as far as that. What about your father?

RAINA. He is away at Slivnitza fighting for his country. I answer for your safety. There is my hand in pledge of it. Will that reassure you? [*She offers him her hand.*]

THE MAN [*looking dubiously at his own hand*]. Better not touch my hand, dear young lady. I must have a wash first.

RAINA [*touched*]. That is very nice of you. I see that you are a gentleman.

THE MAN [*puzzled*]. Eh?

RAINA. You must not think I am surprised. Bulgarians of really good standing—people in our position—wash their hands nearly every day. So you see I can appreciate your delicacy. You may take my hand. [*She offers it again.*]

THE MAN [*kissing it with his hands behind his back*]. Thanks, gracious young lady: I feel safe at last. And now would you mind breaking the news to your mother? I had better not stay here secretly longer than is necessary.

RAINA. If you will be so good as to keep perfectly still whilst I am away.

THE MAN. Certainly. [*He sits down on the ottoman.*]

[RAINA *goes to the bed and wraps herself in the fur cloak. His eyes close. She goes to the door. Turning for a last look at him, she sees that he is dropping off to sleep.*]

RAINA [*at the door*]. You are not going asleep, are you? [*He murmurs inarticulately: she runs to him and shakes him.*] Do you hear? Wake up: you are falling asleep.

THE MAN. Eh? Falling aslee—? Oh no: not the least in the world: I was only thinking. It's all right: I'm wide awake.

RAINA [*severely*]. Will you please stand up while I am away. [*He rises reluctantly.*] All the time, mind.

THE MAN [*standing unsteadily*]. Certainly. Certainly: you may depend on me.

[RAINA *looks doubtfully at him. He smiles weakly. She goes reluctantly, turning again at the door, and almost catching him in the act of yawning. She goes out.*]

THE MAN [*drowsily*]. Sleep, sleep, sleep, sleep, slee—[*The words trail off into a murmur. He wakes again with a shock on the point of falling.*] Where am I? Thats what I want to know: where am I? Must keep awake. Nothing keeps me awake except danger: remember that: [*intently*] danger, danger, danger, dan—[*trailing off again: another shock*] Wheres danger? Mus' find it. [*He starts off vaguely round the room in search of it.*] What am I looking for? Sleep—danger—dont know. [*He stumbles against the bed.*] Ah yes: now I know. All right now. I'm to go to bed, but not to sleep. Be sure not to sleep, because of danger. Not to lie down either, only sit down. [*He sits on the bed. A blissful expression comes into his face.*] Ah! [*With a happy sigh he sinks back at full length; lifts his boots into the bed with a final effort; and falls fast asleep instantly.*]

[CATHERINE *comes in, followed by* RAINA.]

RAINA [*looking at the ottoman*]. He's gone! I left him here.

CATHERINE. Here! Then he must have climbed down from the—

RAINA [*seeing him*]. Oh! [*She points.*]

CATHERINE [*scandalized*]. Well! [*She strides to the bed,* RAINA *following until she is opposite her on the other side.*] He's fast asleep. The brute!

RAINA [*anxiously*]. Sh!

CATHERINE [*shaking him*]. Sir! [*Shaking him again, harder*] Sir!! [*Vehemently, shaking very hard*] Sir!!!

RAINA [*catching her arm*]. Dont, mamma; the poor darling is worn out. Let him sleep.

CATHERINE [*letting him go, and turning amazed to* RAINA]. The poor darling! Raina!!! [*She looks sternly at her daughter.*]

The man sleeps profoundly.

Act II

The sixth of March, 1886. In the garden of Major Petkoff's house. It is a fine spring morning: the garden looks fresh and pretty. Beyond the paling the tops of a couple of minarets[14] *can be seen, shewing that there is a valley there, with the little town in it. A few miles farther the Balkan mountains rise and shut in the landscape. Looking towards them from within the garden, the side of the house is seen on the left, with a garden door reached by a little flight of steps. On the right the stable yard, with its gateway, encroaches on the garden. There are fruit bushes along the paling and house, covered with washing spread out to dry. A path runs by the house, and rises by two steps at the corner, where it turns out of sight. In the middle, a small table, with two bent wood chairs at it, is laid for breakfast with Turkish coffee pot, cups, rolls, etc.; but the cups have been used and the bread broken. There is a wooden garden seat against the wall on the right.*

LOUKA, *smoking a cigaret, is standing between the table and the house, turning her back with angry disdain on a man servant who is lecturing her. He is a middle-aged man of cool temperament and low but clear and keen intelligence, with the complacency of the servant who values himself on his rank in servitude, and the imperturbability of the accurate calculator who has no illusions. He wears a white Bulgarian costume: jacket with embroidered border, sash, wide knickerbockers, and decorated gaiters. His head is shaved up to the crown, giving him a high Japanese forehead. His name is* NICOLA.

NICOLA. Be warned in time, Louka: mend your manners. I know the mistress. She is so grand that she never dreams that any servant could dare be disrespectful to her; but if she once suspects that you are defying her, out you go.

LOUKA. I do defy her. I will defy her. What do I care for her?

NICOLA. If you quarrel with the family, I never can marry you. It's the same as if you quarrelled with me!

LOUKA. You take her part against me, do you?

NICOLA [*sedately*]. I shall always be dependent on the good will of the family. When I leave their service and start a shop in Sofia, their custom will be half my capital: their bad word would ruin me.

LOUKA. You have no spirit. I should like to catch them saying a word against me!

NICOLA [*pityingly*]. I should have expected more sense from you, Louka. But youre young; youre young!

LOUKA. Yes; and you like me the better for it, dont you? But I know some family secrets they wouldnt care to have told, young as I am. Let them quarrel with me if they dare!

NICOLA [*with compassionate superiority*]. Do you know what they would do if they heard you talk like that?

LOUKA. What could they do?

NICOLA. Discharge you for untruthfulness. Who would believe any stories you told after that? Who would give you another situation? Who in this house would dare be seen speaking to you ever again? How long would your father be left on his little farm? [*She impatiently throws away the end of her cigaret, and stamps on it.*] Child: you dont know the power such high people have over the like of you and me when we try to rise out of our poverty against them. [*He goes close to her and lowers his voice.*] Look at me, ten years in their service. Do you think I know no secrets? I know things about the mistress that she wouldnt have the master know for a thousand levas.[15] I know things about him that she wouldnt let him hear the last of for six months if I blabbed them to her. I know things about Raina that would break off her match with Sergius if—

LOUKA [*turning on him quickly*]. How do you know? I never told you!

NICOLA [*opening his eyes cunningly*]. So thats your little secret, is it? I thought it might be something like that. Well, you take my advice and be respectful; and make the mistress feel that no matter what you know or dont know, she can depend on you to hold your tongue and serve the family faithfully. Thats what they like; and thats how youll make most out of them.

LOUKA [*with searching scorn*]. You have the soul of a servant, Nicola.

NICOLA [*complacently*]. Yes: thats the secret of success in service.

[*A loud knocking with a whip handle on a wooden door is heard from the stable yard.*]

MALE VOICE OUTSIDE. Hollo! Hollo there! Nicola!

LOUKA. Master! back from the war!

NICOLA [*quickly*]. My word for it, Louka, the war's over. Off with you and get some fresh coffee. [*He runs out into the stable yard.*]

LOUKA [*as she collects the coffee pot and cups on the tray, and carries it into the house*]. Youll never put the soul of a servant into me.

[MAJOR PETKOFF *comes from the stable yard, followed by Nicola. He is a cheerful, excitable, insignificant, unpolished man of about 50, naturally unambitious except as to his income and his importance in local society, but just now greatly pleased with the military rank which the war has thrust on him as a man of consequence in his town. The fever of plucky patrio-*

tism which the Serbian attack roused in all the Bulgarians has pulled him through the war; but he is obviously glad to be home again.]

PETKOFF [*pointing to the table with his whip*]. Breakfast out here, eh?

NICOLA. Yes, sir. The mistress and Miss Raina have just gone in.

PETKOFF [*sitting down and taking a roll*]. Go in and say Ive come; and get me some fresh coffee.

NICOLA. It's coming, sir. [*He goes to the house door.* LOUKA, *with fresh coffee, a clean cup, and a brandy bottle on her tray, meets him.*] Have you told the mistress?

LOUKA. Yes: she's coming.

[NICOLA *goes into the house.* LOUKA *brings the coffee to the table.*]

PETKOFF. Well: the Serbs havnt run away with you, have they?

LOUKA. No, sir.

PETKOFF. Thats right. Have you brought me some cognac?

LOUKA [*putting the bottle on the table*]. Here, sir.

PETKOFF. Thats right. [*He pours some into his coffee.*]

[CATHERINE, *who, having at this early hour made only a very perfunctory toilet, wears a Bulgarian apron over a once brilliant but now half worn-out dressing gown, and a colored handkerchief tied over her thick black hair, comes from the house with Turkish slippers on her bare feet, looking astonishingly handsome and stately under all the circumstances.* LOUKA *goes into the house.*]

CATHERINE. My dear Paul: what a surprise for us! [*She stoops over the back of his chair to kiss him.*] Have they brought you fresh coffee?

PETKOFF. Yes: Louka's been looking after me. The war's over. The treaty was signed three days ago at Bucharest; and the decree for our army to demobilize was issued yesterday.

CATHERINE [*springing erect, with flashing eyes*]. Paul: have you let the Austrians force you to make peace?

PETKOFF [*submissively*]. My dear: they didnt consult me. What could I do? [*She sits down and turns away from him.*] But of course we saw to it that the treaty was an honorable one. It declares peace—

CATHERINE [*outraged*]. Peace!

PETKOFF [*appeasing her*].—but not friendly relations: remember that. They wanted to put that in; but I insisted on its being struck out. What more could I do?

CATHERINE. You could have annexed Serbia and made Prince Alexander[16] Emperor of the Balkans. Thats what I would have done.

PETKOFF. I dont doubt it in the least, my dear. But I should have had to subdue the whole Austrian Empire first; and that would have kept me too long away from you. I missed you greatly.

CATHERINE [*relenting*]. Ah! [*She stretches her hand affectionately across the table to squeeze his.*]

PETKOFF. And how have you been, my dear?

CATHERINE. Oh, my usual sore throats: thats all.

PETKOFF [*with conviction*]. That comes from washing your neck every day. Ive often told you so.

CATHERINE. Nonsense, Paul!

PETKOFF [*over his coffee and cigaret*]. I dont believe in going too far with these modern customs. All this washing cant be good for the health: it's not natural. There was an Englishman at Philippopolis who used to wet himself all over with cold water every morning when he got up. Disgusting! It all comes from the English: their climate makes them so dirty that they have to be perpetually washing themselves. Look at my father! he never had a bath in his life; and he lived to be ninety-eight, the healthiest man in Bulgaria. I dont mind a good wash once a week to keep up my position; but once a day is carrying the thing to a ridiculous extreme.

CATHERINE. You are a barbarian at heart still, Paul. I hope you behaved yourself before all those Russian officers.

PETKOFF. I did my best. I took care to let them know that we have a library.

CATHERINE. Ah; but you didnt tell them that we have an electric bell in it? I have had one put up.

PETKOFF. Whats an electric bell?

CATHERINE. You touch a button; something tinkles in the kitchen; and then Nicola comes up.

PETKOFF. Why not shout for him?

CATHERINE. Civilized people never shout for their servants. Ive learnt that while you were away.

PETKOFF. Well, I'll tell you something Ive learnt too. Civilized people dont hang out their washing to dry where visitors can see it; so youd better have all that [*indicating the clothes on the bushes*] put somewhere else.

CATHERINE. Oh, thats absurd, Paul: I I dont believe really refined people notice such things.

SERGIUS [*knocking at the stable gates*]. Gate, Nicola!

PETKOFF. Theres Sergius. [*Shouting*] Hollo, Nicola!

CATHERINE. Oh, dont shout, Paul: it really isnt nice.

PETKOFF. Bosh! [*He shouts louder than before*] Nicola!

NICOLA [*appearing at the house door*]. Yes, sir.

PETKOFF. Are you deaf? Dont you hear Major Saranoff knocking? Bring him round this way. [*He pronounces the name with the stress on the second syllable: Sarahnoff*].

NICOLA. Yes, major. [*He goes into the stable yard.*]

PETKOFF. You must talk to him, my dear, until Raina takes him off our hands. He bores my life out about our not promoting him. Over my head, if you please.

CATHERINE. He certainly ought to be promoted when he marries Raina. Besides, the country should insist on having at least one native general.

PETKOFF. Yes; so that he could throw away whole brigades instead of regiments. It's no use, my dear: he hasnt the slightest chance of promotion until we're quite sure that the peace will be a lasting one.

NICOLA [*at the gate, announcing*]. Major Sergius Saranoff! [*He goes into the house and returns presently with a third chair, which he places at the table. He then withdraws.*] [MAJOR SERGIUS SARANOFF, *the original of the portrait in* RAINA'S *room, is a tall romantically hand-*

some man, with the physical hardihood, the high spirit, and the susceptible imagination of an untamed mountaineer chieftain. But his remarkable personal distinction is of a characteristically civilized type. The ridges of his eyebrows, curving with an interrogative twist round the projections at the outer corners; his jealously observant eye; his nose, thin, keen, and apprehensive in spite of the pugnacious high bridge and large nostril; his assertive chin would not be out of place in a Parisian salon, shewing that the clever imaginative barbarian has an acute critical faculty which has been thrown into intense activity by the arrival of western civilization in the Balkans. The result is precisely what the advent of nineteenth century thought first produced in England: to wit, Byronism. By his brooding on the perpetual failure, not only of others, but of himself, to live up to his ideals; by his consequent cynical scorn for humanity; by his jejune credulity as to the absolute validity of his concepts and the unworthiness of the world in disregarding them; by his wincings and mockeries under the sting of the petty disillusions which every hour spent among men brings to his sensitive observation, he has acquired the half tragic, half ironic air, the mysterious moodiness, the suggestion of a strange and terrible history that has left nothing but undying remorse, by which Childe Harold[17] *fascinated the grandmothers of his English contemporaries. It is clear that here or nowhere is* RAINA'S *ideal hero.* CATHERINE *is hardly less enthusiastic about him than her daughter, and much less reserved in shewing her enthusiasm. As he enters from the stable gate, she rises effusively to greet him.* PETKOFF *is distinctly less disposed to make a fuss about him.*]

PETKOFF. Here already, Sergius! Glad to see you.

CATHERINE. My dear Sergius! [*She holds out both her hands.*]

SERGIUS [*kissing them with scrupulous gallantry*]. My dear mother, if I may call you so.

PETKOFF [*drily*]. Mother-in-law, Sergius: mother-in-law! Sit down; and have some coffee.

SERGIUS. Thank you: none for me. [*He gets away from the table with a certain distaste for* PETKOFF'S *enjoyment of it, and posts himself with conscious dignity against the rail of the steps leading to the house.*]

CATHERINE. You look superb. The campaign has improved you, Sergius. Everybody here is mad about you. We were all wild with enthusiasm about that magnificent cavalry charge.

SERGIUS [*with grave irony*]. Madam: it was the cradle and the grave of my military reputation.

CATHERINE. How so?

SERGIUS. I won the battle the wrong way when our worthy Russian generals were losing it the right way. In short, I upset their plans, and wounded their self-esteem. Two Cossack colonels had their regiments routed on the most correct principles of scientific warfare. Two major-generals got killed strictly according to military etiquette. The two colonels are now major-generals; and I am still a simple major.

CATHERINE. You shall not remain so, Sergius. The women are on your side; and they will see that justice is done you.

SERGIUS. It is too late. I have only waited for the peace to send in my resignation.

PETKOFF [*dropping his cup in his amazement*]. Your resignation!

CATHERINE. Oh, you must withdraw it!

SERGIUS [*with resolute measured emphasis, folding his arms*]. I never withdraw.

PETKOFF [*vexed*]. Now who could have supposed you were going to do such a thing?

SERGIUS [*with fire*]. Everyone that knew me. But enough of myself and my affairs. How is Raina; and where is Raina?

RAINA [*suddenly coming round the corner of the house and standing at the top of the steps in the path*]. Raina is here.

[*She makes a charming picture as they turn to look at her. She wears an underdress of pale green silk, draped with an overdress of thin ecru canvas embroidered with gold. She is crowned with a dainty eastern cap of gold tinsel.* SERGIUS *goes impulsively to meet her. Posing regally, she presents her hand: he drops chivalrously on one knee and kisses it.*]

PETKOFF [*aside to* CATHERINE, *beaming with parental pride*]. Pretty, isnt it? She always appears at the right moment.

CATHERINE [*impatiently*]. Yes; she listens for it. It is an abominable habit.

[SERGIUS *leads* RAINA *forward with splendid gallantry. When they arrive at the table, she turns to him with a bend of the head: he bows; and thus they separate, he coming to his place and she going behind her father's chair.*]

RAINA [*stooping and kissing her father*]. Dear father! Welcome home!

PETKOFF [*patting her cheek*]. My little pet girl. [*He kisses her. She goes to the chair left by* NICOLA *for* SERGIUS, *and sits down.*]

CATHERINE. And so youre no longer a soldier, Sergius.

SERGIUS. I am no longer a soldier. Soldiering, my dear madam, is the coward's art of attacking mercilessly when you are strong, and keeping out of harm's way when you are weak. That is the whole secret of successful fighting. Get your enemy at a disadvantage; and never, on any account, fight him on equal terms.

PETKOFF. They wouldnt let us make a fair stand-up fight of it. However, I suppose soldiering has to be a trade like any other trade.

SERGIUS. Precisely. But I have no ambition to shine as a tradesman; so I have taken the advice of that bagman of a captain that settled the exchange of prisoners with us at Pirot, and given it up.

PETKOFF. What! that Swiss fellow? Sergius, Ive often thought of that exchange since. He over-reached us about those horses.

SERGIUS. Of course he over-reached us. His father was a hotel and livery stable keeper; and he owed his first step to his knowledge of horse-dealing. [*With mock enthusiasm*] Ah, he was a soldier: every inch a soldier! If only I had bought the horses for my regiment instead of foolishly leading it into danger, I should have been a field-marshal now!

CATHERINE. A Swiss? What was he doing in the Serbian army?

PETKOFF. A volunteer, of course: keen on picking up his profession. [*Chuckling*] We shouldnt have been able to begin fighting if these foreigners hadnt shewn us how to do it: we knew nothing about it; and neither did the Serbs. Egad, thered have been no war without them!

RAINA. Are there many Swiss officers in the Serbian Army?

PETKOFF. No. All Austrians, just as our officers were all Russians. This was the only Swiss I came across. I'll never trust a Swiss again. He humbugged us into giving him fifty ablebodied men for two hundred worn out chargers. They werent even eatable!

SERGIUS. We were two children in the hands of that consummate soldier, major: simply two innocent little children.

RAINA. What was he like?

CATHERINE. Oh, Raina, what a silly question!

SERGIUS. He was like a commercial traveller in uniform. Bourgeois to his boots!

PETKOFF [*grinning*]. Sergius: tell Catherine that queer story his friend told us about how he escaped after Slivnitza. You remember. About his being hid by two women.

SERGIUS [*with bitter irony*]. Oh yes: quite a romance! He was serving in the very battery I so unprofessionally charged. Being a thorough soldier, he ran away like the rest of them, with our cavalry at his heels. To escape their sabres he climbed a water-pipe and made his way into the bedroom of a young Bulgarian lady. The young lady was enchanted by his persuasive commercial traveller's manners. She very modestly entertained him for an hour or so, and then called in her mother lest her conduct should appear unmaidenly. The old lady was equally fascinated; and the fugitive was sent on his way in the morning, disguised in an old coat belonging to the master of the house, who was away at the war.

RAINA [*rising with marked stateliness*]. Your life in the camp has made you coarse, Sergius. I did not think you would have repeated such a story before me. [*She turns away coldly.*]

CATHERINE [*also rising*]. She is right, Sergius. If such women exist, we should be spared the knowledge of them.

PETKOFF. Pooh! nonsense! what does it matter?

SERGIUS [*ashamed*]. No, Petkoff: I was wrong. [*To* RAINA, *with earnest humility*] I beg your pardon. I have behaved abominably. Forgive me, Raina. [*She bows reservedly.*] And you too, madam. [CATHERINE *bows graciously and sits down. He proceeds solemnly, again addressing* RAINA] The glimpses I have had of the seamy side of life during the last few months have made me cynical; but I should not have brought my cynicism here: least of all into your presence, Raina. I— [*Here, turning to the others, he is evidently going to begin a long speech when the Major interrupts him.*]

PETKOFF. Stuff and nonsense, Sergius! Thats quite enough fuss about nothing: a soldier's daughter should be able to stand up without flinching to a little strong conversation. [*He rises.*] Come: it's time for us to get to business. We have to make up our minds how those three regiments are to get back to Philippopolis: theres no forage for them on the Sofia route. [*He goes towards the house.*] Come along. [SERGIUS *is about to follow him when* CATHERINE *rises and intervenes.*]

CATHERINE. Oh, Paul, cant you spare Sergius for a few moments? Raina has hardly seen him yet. Perhaps I can help you to settle about the regiments.

SERGIUS [*protesting*]. My dear madam, impossible: you—

CATHERINE [*stopping him playfully*]. You stay here, my dear Sergius: theres no hurry. I have a word or two to say to Paul. [SERGIUS *instantly bows and steps back.*] Now, dear [*taking* PETKOFF's *arm*]: come and see the electric bell.

PETKOFF. Oh, very well, very well.

[*They go into the house together affectionately.* SERGIUS, *left alone with* RAINA, *looks anxiously at her, fearing that she is still offended. She smiles, and stretches out her arms to him.*]

SERGIUS [*hastening to her*]. Am I forgiven?

RAINA [*placing her hands on his shoulders as she looks up at him with admiration and worship*]. My hero! My king!

SERGIUS. My queen! [*He kisses her on the forehead.*]

RAINA. How I have envied you, Sergius! You have been out in the world, on the field of battle, able to prove yourself there worthy of any woman in the world; whilst I have had to sit at home inactive—dreaming—useless—doing nothing that could give me the right to call myself worthy of any man.

SERGIUS. Dearest: all my deeds have been yours. You inspired me. I have gone through the war like a knight in a tournament with his lady looking down at him!

RAINA. And you have never been absent from my thoughts for a moment. [*Very solemnly*] Sergius: I think we two have found the higher love. When I think of you, I feel that I could never do a base deed, or think an ignoble thought.

SERGIUS. My lady and my saint! [*He clasps her reverently.*]

RAINA [*returning his embrace*]. My lord and my—

SERGIUS. Sh—sh! Let me be the worshipper, dear. You little know how unworthy even the best man is of a girl's pure passion!

RAINA. I trust you. I love you. You will never disappoint me, Sergius. [LOUKA *is heard singing within the house. They quickly release each other.*] I cant pretend to talk indifferently before her: my heart is too full. [LOUKA *comes from the house with her tray. She goes to the table, and begins to clear it, with her back turned to them.*] I will get my hat; and then we can go out until lunch time. Wouldnt you like that?

SERGIUS. Be quick. If you are away five minutes, it will seem five hours. [RAINA *runs to the top of the steps, and turns there to exchange looks with him and wave him a kiss with both hands. He looks after her with emotion for a moment; then turns slowly away, his face radiant with the loftiest exaltation. The movement shifts his field of vision, into the corner of which there now comes the tail of* LOUKA's *double apron. His attention is arrested at once. He takes a stealthy look at her, and begins to twirl his moustache mischievously, with his left hand akimbo on his hip. Finally, striking the ground with his heels in something of a cavalry swagger, he strolls over to the other side of the table, opposite her, and says*] Louka: do you know what the higher love is?

LOUKA [*astonished*]. No, sir.

SERGIUS. Very fatiguing thing to keep up for any length of time, Louka. One feels the need of some relief after it.

LOUKA [*innocently*]. Perhaps you would like some coffee, sir? [*She stretches her hand across the table for the coffee pot.*]

SERGIUS [*taking her hand*]. Thank you, Louka.

LOUKA [*pretending to pull*]. Oh, sir, you know I didnt mean that. I'm surprised at you!

SERGIUS [*coming clear of the table and drawing her with him*]. I am surprised at myself, Louka. What would Sergius, the hero of Slivnitza, say if he saw me now? What would Sergius, the apostle of the higher love, say if he saw me now? What would the half dozen Sergiuses who keep popping in and out of this handsome figure of mine say if they caught us here? [*Letting go her hand and slipping his arm dexterously round her waist*] Do you consider my figure handsome, Louka?

LOUKA. Let me go, sir. I shall be disgraced. [*She struggles: he holds her inexorably.*] Oh, will you let go?

SERGIUS [*looking straight into her eyes*]. No.

LOUKA. Then stand back where we cant be seen. Have you no common sense?

SERGIUS. Ah! thats reasonable. [*He takes her into the stableyard gateway, where they are hidden from the house.*]

LOUKA [*plaintively*]. I may have been seen from the windows: Miss Raina is sure to be spying about after you.

SERGIUS [*stung: letting her go*]. Take care, Louka. I may be worthless enough to betray the higher love; but do not you insult it.

LOUKA [*demurely*]. Not for the world, sir, I'm sure. May I go on with my work, please, now?

SERGIUS [*again putting his arm round her*]. You are a provoking little witch, Louka. If you were in love with me, would you spy out of windows on me?

LOUKA. Well, you see, sir, since you say you are half a dozen different gentlemen all at once, I should have a great deal to look after.

SERGIUS [*charmed*]. Witty as well as pretty. [*He tries to kiss her.*]

LOUKA [*avoiding him*]. No: I dont want your kisses. Gentlefolk are all alike: you making love to me behind Miss Raina's back; and she doing the same behind yours.

SERGIUS [*recoiling a step*]. Louka!

LOUKA. It shews how little you really care.

SERGIUS [*dropping his familiarity, and speaking with freezing politeness*]. If our conversation is to continue, Louka, you will please remember that a gentleman does not discuss the conduct of the lady he is engaged to with her maid.

LOUKA. It's so hard to know what a gentleman considers right. I thought from your trying to kiss me that you had given up being so particular.

SERGIUS [*turning from her and striking his forehead as he comes back into the garden from the gateway*]. Devil! devil!

LOUKA. Ha! ha! I expect one of the six of you is very like me, sir; though I am only Miss Raina's maid. [*She goes back to her work at the table, taking no further notice of him.*]

SERGIUS [*speaking to himself*]. Which of the six is the real man? thats the question that torments me. One of them is a hero, another a buffoon, another a humbug, another perhaps a bit of a blackguard. [*He pauses, and looks furtively at* LOUKA *as he adds, with deep bitterness*] And one, at least, is a coward: jealous, like all cowards. [*He goes to the table.*] Louka.

LOUKA. Yes?

SERGIUS. Who is my rival?

LOUKA. You shall never get that out of me, for love or money.

SERGIUS. Why?

LOUKA. Never mind why. Besides, you would tell that I told you; and I should lose my place.

SERGIUS [*holding out his right hand in affirmation*]. No! on the honor of a—[*He checks himself; and his hand drops, nerveless, as he concludes sardonically*]—of a man capable of behaving as I have been behaving for the last five minutes. Who is he?

LOUKA. I dont know. I never saw him. I only heard his voice through the door of her room.

SERGIUS. Damnation! How dare you?

LOUKA [*retreating*]. Oh, I mean no harm: youve no right to take up my words like that. The mistress knows all about it. And I tell you that if that gentleman ever comes here again, Miss Raina will marry him, whether he likes it or not. I know the difference between the sort of manner you and she put on before one another and the real manner.

[SERGIUS *shivers as if she had stabbed him. Then, setting his face like iron, he strides grimly to her, and grips her above the elbows with both hands.*]

SERGIUS. Now listen you to me.

LOUKA [*wincing*]. Not so tight: youre hurting me.

SERGIUS. That doesn't matter. You have stained my honor by making me a party to your eavesdropping. And you have betrayed your mistress.

LOUKA [*writhing*]. Please—

SERGIUS. That shews that you are an abominable little clod of common clay, with the soul of a servant. [*He lets her go as if she were an unclean thing, and turns away, dusting his hands of her, to the bench by the wall, where he sits down with averted head, meditating gloomily.*]

LOUKA [*whimpering angrily with her hands up her sleeves, feeling her bruised arms*]. You know how to hurt with your tongue as well as with your hands. But I dont care, now Ive found out that whatever clay I'm made of, youre made of the same. As for her, she's a liar; and her fine airs are a cheat; and I'm worth six of her. [*She shakes the pain off hardily; tosses her head; and sets to work to put the things on the tray.*]

[*He looks doubtfully at her. She finishes packing the tray, and laps the cloth over the edges, so as to carry all out together. As she stoops to lift it, he rises.*]

SERGIUS. Louka! [*She stops and looks defiantly at him.*] A gentleman has no right to hurt a woman under any circumstances. [*With profound humility, uncovering his head*] I beg your pardon.

LOUKA. That sort of apology may satisfy a lady. Of what use is it to a servant?

SERGIUS [*rudely crossed in his chivalry, throws it off with a bitter laugh, and says slightingly*]. Oh! you wish to be paid for the hurt! [*He puts on his shako, and takes some money from his pocket.*]

LOUKA [*her eyes filling with tears in spite of herself*]. No: I want my hurt made well.

SERGIUS [*sobered by her tone*]. How? [*She rolls up her left sleeve; clasps her arm with the thumb and fingers of her right hand; and looks down at the bruise. Then she raises her head and looks straight at him. Finally, with a superb gesture, she presents her arm to be kissed. Amazed, he looks at her; at the arm; at her again; hesitates; and then, with shuddering intensity, exclaims* Never! *and gets away as far as possible from her.*

Her arm drops. Without a word, and with unaffected dignity, she takes her tray, and is approaching the house when RAINA *returns, wearing a hat and jacket in the height of the Vienna fashion of the previous year, 1885. Louka makes way proudly for her, and then goes into the house.*]

RAINA. I'm ready. Whats the matter? [*Gaily*] Have you been flirting with Louka?

SERGIUS [*hastily*]. No, no. How can you think such a thing?

RAINA [*ashamed of herself*]. Forgive me, dear: it was only a jest. I am so happy today.

[*He goes quickly to her, and kisses her hand remorsefully.* CATHERINE *comes out and calls to them from the top of the steps.*]

CATHERINE [*coming down to them*]. I am sorry to disturb you, children; but Paul is distracted over those three regiments. He doesnt know how to send them to Philippopolis; and he objects to every suggestion of mine. You must go and help him, Sergius. He is in the library.

RAINA [*disappointed*]. But we are just going out for a walk.

SERGIUS. I shall not be long. Wait for me just five minutes. [*He runs up the steps to the door.*]

RAINA [*following him to the foot of the steps and looking up at him with timid coquetry*]. I shall go round and wait in full view of the library windows. Be sure you draw father's attention to me. If you are a moment longer than five minutes, I shall go in and fetch you, regiments or no regiments.

SERGIUS [*laughing*]. Very well. [*He goes in.*]

[RAINA *watches him until he is out of her sight. Then, with a perceptible relaxation of manner, she begins to pace up and down the garden in a brown study.*]

CATHERINE. Imagine their meeting that Swiss and hearing the whole story! The very first thing your father asked for was the old coat we sent him off in. A nice mess you have got us into!

RAINA [*gazing thoughtfully at the gravel as she walks*]. The little beast!

CATHERINE. Little beast! What little beast?

RAINA. To go and tell! Oh, if I had him here, I'd cram him with chocolate creams til he couldnt ever speak again!

CATHERINE. Dont talk such stuff. Tell me the truth, Raina. How long was he in your room before you came to me?

RAINA [*whisking round and recommencing her march in the opposite direction*]. Oh, I forget.

CATHERINE. You cannot forget! Did he really climb up after the soldiers were gone; or was he there when that officer searched the room?

RAINA. No. Yes: I think he must have been there then.

CATHERINE. You think! Oh, Raina! Raina! Will anything ever make you straightforward? If Sergius finds out, it will be all over between you.

RAINA [*with cool impertinence*]. Oh, I know Sergius is your pet. I sometimes wish you could marry him instead of me. You would just suit him. You would pet him, and spoil him, and mother him to perfection.

CATHERINE [*opening her eyes very widely indeed*]. Well, upon my word!

RAINA [*capriciously: half to herself*]. I always feel a longing to do or say something dreadful to him—to shock his propriety—to scandalize the five senses out of him. [*To* CATHERINE, *perversely*] I dont care whether he finds out about the chocolate cream soldier or not. I half hope he may. [*She again turns and strolls flippantly away up the path to the corner of the house.*]

CATHERINE. And what should I be able to say to your father, pray?

RAINA [*over her shoulder, from the top of the two steps*]. Oh, poor father! As if he could help himself! [*She turns the corner and passes out of sight.*]

CATHERINE [*looking after her, her fingers itching*]. Oh, if you were only ten years younger! [LOUKA *comes from the house with a salver, which she carries hanging down by her side.*] Well?

LOUKA. Theres a gentleman just called, madam. A Serbian officer.

CATHERINE [*flaming*]. A Serb! And how dare he—[*checking herself bitterly*] Oh, I forgot. We are at peace now. I suppose we shall have them calling every day to pay their compliments. Well: if he is an officer why dont you tell your master? He is in the library with Major Saranoff. Why do you come to me?

LOUKA. But he asks for you, madam. And I dont think he knows who you are: he said the lady of the house. He gave me this little ticket for you. [*She takes a card out of her bosom; puts it on the salver; and offers it to* CATHERINE.]

CATHERINE [*reading*]. "Captain Bluntschli"? Thats a German name.

LOUKA. Swiss, madam, I think.

CATHERINE [*with a bound that makes* LOUKA *jump back*]. Swiss! What is he like?

LOUKA [*timidly*]. He has a big carpet bag, madam.

CATHERINE. Oh Heavens! he's come to return the coat. Send him away: say we're not at home: ask him to leave his address and I'll write to him. Oh stop: that will never do. Wait! [*She throws herself into a chair to think it out.* LOUKA *waits.*] The master and Major Saranoff are busy in the library, arnt they?

LOUKA. Yes, madam.

CATHERINE [*decisively*]. Bring the gentleman out here at once. [*Peremptorily*] And be very polite to him. Dont delay. Here [*impatiently snatching the salver from her*]: leave that here; and go straight back to him.

LOUKA. Yes, madam [*going*].

CATHERINE. Louka!

LOUKA [*stopping*]. Yes, madam.

CATHERINE. Is the library door shut?

LOUKA. I think so, madam.

CATHERINE. If not, shut it as you pass through.

LOUKA. Yes, madam [*going*].

CATHERINE. Stop [LOUKA *stops*]. He will have to go that way [*indicating the gate of the stableyard*]. Tell Nicola to bring his bag here after him. Dont forget.

LOUKA [*surprised*]. His bag?

CATHERINE. Yes: here: as soon as possible. [*Vehemently*] Be quick! [LOUKA *runs into the house.* CATHERINE *snatches her apron off and throws it behind a bush. She then takes up the salver and uses it as a mirror, with the result that the handkerchief tied round her head follows the apron. A touch to her hair and a shake to her dressing gown make her presentable.*] Oh, how? how? how can a man be such a fool! Such a moment to select! [LOUKA *appears at the door of the house, announcing* CAPTAIN BLUNTSCHLI. *She stands aside at the top of the steps to let him pass before she goes in again. He is the man of the midnight adventure in* RAINA'*s room, clean, well brushed, smartly uniformed, and out of trouble, but still unmistakably the same man. The moment* LOUKA'*s back is turned,* CATHERINE *swoops on him with impetuous, urgent, coaxing appeal.*] Captain Bluntschli: I am very glad to see you; but you must leave this house at once. [*He raises his eyebrows.*] My husband has just returned with my future son-in-law; and they know nothing. If they did, the consequences would be terrible. You are a foreigner: you do not feel our national animosities as we do. We still hate the Serbs: the effect of the peace on my husband has been to make him feel like a lion baulked of his prey. If he discovers our secret, he will never forgive me; and my daughter's life will hardly be safe. Will you, like the chivalrous gentleman and soldier you are, leave at once before he finds you here?

BLUNTSCHLI [*disappointed, but philosophical*]. At once, gracious lady. I only came to thank you and return the coat you lent me. If you will allow me to take it out of my bag and leave it with your servant as I pass out, I need detain you no further. [*He turns to go into the house.*]

CATHERINE [*catching him by the sleeve*]. Oh, you must not think of going back that way. [*Coaxing him across to the stable gates*] This is the shortest way out. Many thanks. So glad to have been of service to you. Good-bye.

BLUNTSCHLI. But my bag?

CATHERINE. It shall be sent on. You will leave me your address.

BLUNTSCHLI. True. Allow me. [*He takes out his cardcase, and stops to write his address, keeping* CATHERINE *in an agony of impatience. As he hands her the card,* PETKOFF, *hatless, rushes from the house in a fluster of hospitality, followed by* SERGIUS.]

PETKOFF [*as he hurries down the steps*]. My dear Captain Bluntschli—

CATHERINE. Oh Heavens! [*She sinks on the seat against the wall.*]

PETKOFF [*too preoccupied to notice her as he shakes* BLUNTSCHLI'*s hand heartily*] Those stupid people of mine thought I was out here, instead of in the—haw!—library [*he cannot mention the library without betraying how proud he is of it*]. I saw you through the window. I was wondering why you didnt come in. Saranoff is with me: you remember him, dont you?

SERGIUS [*saluting humorously, and then offering his hand with great charm of manner*]. Welcome, our friend the enemy!

PETKOFF. No longer the enemy, happily. [*Rather anxiously*] I hope youve called as a friend, and not about horses or prisoners.

CATHERINE. Oh, quite as a friend, Paul. I was just asking Captain Bluntschli to stay to lunch; but he declares he must go at once.

SERGIUS [*sardonically*]. Impossible, Bluntschli. We want you here badly. We have to send on three cavalry regiments to Philippopolis; and we dont in the least know how to do it.

BLUNTSCHLI [*suddenly attentive and businesslike*]. Philippopolis? The forage is the trouble, I suppose.

PETKOFF [*eagerly*]. Yes: thats it. [*To* SERGIUS] He sees the whole thing at once.

BLUNTSCHLI. I think I can shew you how to manage that.

SERGIUS. Invaluable man! Come along! [*Towering over Bluntschli, he puts his hand on his shoulder and takes him to the steps,* PETKOFF *following.*]

[RAINA *comes from the house as* BLUNTSCHLI *puts his foot on the first step.*]

RAINA. Oh! The chocolate cream soldier!

[BLUNTSCHLI *stands rigid.* SERGIUS, *amazed, looks at* RAINA, *then at* PETKOFF, *who looks back at him and then at his wife.*]

CATHERINE [*with commanding presence of mind*]. My dear Raina, dont you see that we have a guest here? Captain Bluntschli: one of our new Serbian friends.

[RAINA *bows:* BLUNTSCHLI *bows.*]

RAINA. How silly of me! [*She comes

down into the centre of the group, between BLUNTSCHLI *and* PETKOFF.] I made a beautiful ornament this morning for the ice pudding; and that stupid Nicola has just put down a pile of plates on it and spoilt it. [*To* BLUNTSCHLI, *winningly*] I hope you didn't think that you were the chocolate cream soldier, Captain Bluntschli.

BLUNTSCHLI [*laughing*]. I assure you I did. [*Stealing a whimsical glance at her*] Your explanation was a relief.

PETKOFF [*suspiciously, to* RAINA]. And since when, pray, have you taken to cooking?

CATHERINE. Oh, whilst you were away. It is her latest fancy.

PETKOFF [*testily*]. And has Nicola taken to drinking? He used to be careful enough. First he shews Captain Bluntschli out here when he knew quite well I was in the library; and then he goes downstairs and breaks Raina's chocolate soldier. He must—[NICOLA *appears at the top of the steps with the bag. He descends; places it respectfully before* BLUNTSCHLI; *and waits for further orders. General amazement.* NICOLA, *unconscious of the effect he is producing, looks perfectly satisfied with himself. When* PETKOFF *recovers his power of speech, he breaks out at him with*] Are you mad, Nicola?

NICOLA [*taken aback*]. Sir?

PETKOFF. What have you brought that for?

NICOLA. My lady's orders, major. Louka told me that—

CATHERINE [*interrupting him*]. My orders! Why should I order you to bring Captain Bluntschli's luggage out here? What are you thinking of, Nicola?

NICOLA [*after a moment's bewilderment, picking up the bag as he addresses* BLUNTSCHLI *with the very perfection of servile discretion*]. I beg your pardon, captain, I am sure. [*To* CATHERINE] My fault, madam: I hope youll overlook it. [*He bows, and is going to the steps with the bag, when* PETKOFF *addresses him angrily.*]

PETKOFF. Youd better go and slam that bag, too, down on Miss Raina's ice pudding! [*This is too much for* NICOLA. *The bag drops from his hand almost on his master's toes, eliciting a roar of*] Begone, you butter-fingered donkey.

NICOLA [*snatching up the bag, and escaping into the house*]. Yes, major.

CATHERINE. Oh, never mind. Paul: dont be angry.

PETKOFF [*blustering*]. Scoundrel! He's got out of hand while I was away. I'll teach him. Infernal blackguard! The sack next Saturday! I'll clear out the whole establishment—[*He is stifled by the caresses of his wife and daughter, who hang round his neck, petting him*].

CATHERINE. } RAINA } [*together*].

{ Now, now, now, it mustnt be angry. He meant no harm. Be good to please me, dear.

{ Wow, wow, wow: not on your first day at home. I'll make another ice pudding. Tch-Sh-sh-sh-sh!

PETKOFF [*yielding*]. Oh well, never

mind. Come, Bluntschli: lets have no more nonsense about going away. You know very well youre not going back to Switzerland yet. Until you do go back youll stay with us.

RAINA. Oh, do, Captain Bluntschli.

PETKOFF [*to* CATHERINE]. Now, Catherine: it's of you he's afraid. Press him: and he'll stay.

CATHERINE. Of course I shall be only too delighted if [*appealingly*] Captain Bluntschli really wishes to stay. He knows my wishes.

BLUNTSCHLI [*in his driest military manner*]. I am at madam's orders.

SERGIUS [*cordially*]. That settles it!

PETKOFF [*heartily*]. Of course!

RAINA. You see you must stay.

BLUNTSCHLI [*smiling*]. Well, if I must, I must.

[*Gesture of despair from* CATHERINE.]

Act III

In the library after lunch. It is not much of a library. Its literary equipment consists of a single fixed shelf stocked with old paper covered novels, broken backed, coffee stained, torn and thumbed; and a couple of little hanging shelves with a few gift books on them: the rest of the wall space being occupied by trophies of war and the chase. But it is a most comfortable sitting room. A row of three large windows shews a mountain panorama, just now seen in one of its friendliest aspects in the mellowing afternoon light. In the corner next the right-hand window a square earthenware stove, a perfect tower of glistening pottery, rises nearly to the ceiling and guarantees plenty of warmth. The ottoman is like that in RAINA'*s room, and similarly placed; and the window seats are luxurious with decorated cushions. There is one object, however, hopelessly out of keeping with its surroundings. This is a small kitchen table, much the worse for wear, fitted as a writing table with an old canister full of pens, an eggcup filled with ink, and a deplorable scrap of heavily used pink blotting paper.*

At the side of this table, which stands to the left of anyone facing the window, BLUNTSCHLI *is hard at work with a couple of maps before him, writing orders. At the head of it sits* SERGIUS, *who is supposed to be also at work, but is actually gnawing the feather of a pen, and contemplating* BLUNTSCHLI'*s quick, sure, businesslike progress with a mixture of envious irritation at his own incapacity and awestruck wonder at an ability which seems to him almost miraculous, though its prosaic character forbids him to esteem it.* THE MAJOR *is comfortably established on the ottoman, with a newspaper in his hand and the tube of his hookah*[18] *within easy reach.* CATHERINE *sits at the stove, with her back to them, embroidering.* RAINA, *reclining on the divan, is gazing in a daydream out at the Balkan landscape, with a neglected novel in her lap.*

The door is on the same side as the stove, farther from the window. The button of the electric bell is at the opposite side, behind BLUNTSCHLI.

PETKOFF [*looking up from his paper to watch how they are getting on at the table*]. Are you sure I cant help in any way, Bluntschli?

BLUNTSCHLI [*without interrupting his writing or looking up*]. Quite sure, thank you. Saranoff and I will manage it.

SERGIUS [*grimly*]. Yes: we'll manage it. He finds out what to do; draws up the orders; and I sign em. Division of labor! [BLUNTSCHLI *passes him a paper.*] Another one? Thank you. [*He plants the paper squarely before him; sets his chair carefully parallel to it; and signs with his cheek on his elbow and his protruded tongue following the movements of his pen.*] This hand is more accustomed to the sword than to the pen.

PETKOFF. It's very good of you, Bluntschli: it is indeed, to let yourself be put upon in this way. Now are you quite sure I can do nothing?

CATHERINE [*in a low warning tone*]. You can stop interrupting, Paul.

PETKOFF [*starting and looking round at her*]. Eh? Oh! Quite right, my love: quite right. [*He takes his newspaper up again, but presently lets it drop.*] Ah, you havnt been campaigning, Catherine: you dont know how pleasant it is for us to sit here, after a good lunch, with nothing to do but enjoy ourselves. Theres only one thing I want to make me thoroughly comfortable.

CATHERINE. What is that?

PETKOFF. My old coat. I'm not at home in this one: I feel as if I were on parade.

CATHERINE. My dear Paul, how absurd you are about that old coat! It must be hanging in the blue closet where you left it.

PETKOFF. My dear Catherine, I tell you Ive looked there. Am I to believe my own eyes or not? [CATHERINE *rises and crosses the room to press the button of the electric bell.*] What are you shewing off that bell for? [*She looks at him majestically, and silently resumes her chair and her needlework.*] My dear: if you think the obstinacy of your sex can make a coat out of two old dressing gowns of Raina's, your waterproof, and my mackintosh, youre mistaken. Thats exactly what the blue closet contains at present.

[NICOLA *presents himself.*]

CATHERINE. Nicola: go to the blue closet and bring your master's old coat here: the braided one he wears in the house.

NICOLA. Yes, madam. [*He goes out.*]

PETKOFF. Catherine.

CATHERINE. Yes, Paul.

PETKOFF. I bet you any piece of jewellery you like to order from Sofia against a week's housekeeping money that the coat isnt there.

CATHERINE. Done, Paul!

PETKOFF [*excited by the prospect of a gamble*]. Come: heres an opportunity for some sport. Wholl bet on it? Blunschli: I'll give you six to one.

BLUNTSCHLI [*imperturbably*]. It would be robbing you, major. Madame is sure to be right. [*Without looking up, he passes another batch of papers to* SERGIUS.]

SERGIUS [*also excited*]. Bravo, Switzerland! Major: I bet my best charger against an Arab mare for Raina that Nicola finds the coat in the blue closet.

PETKOFF [*eagerly*]. Your best char—

CATHERINE [*hastily interrupting him*]. Dont be foolish, Paul. An Arabian mare will cost you 50,000 levas.

RAINA [*suddenly coming out of her picturesque revery*]. Really, mother, if you are going to take the jewellery, I dont see why you should grudge me my Arab. [NICOLA *comes back with the coat, and brings it to* PETKOFF, *who can hardly believe his eyes.*]

CATHERINE. Where was it, Nicola?

NICOLA. Hanging in the blue closet, madam.

PETKOFF. Well, I am d—

CATHERINE [*stopping him*]. Paul!

PETKOFF. I could have sworn it wasnt there. Age is beginning to tell on me. I'm getting hallucinations.[19] [*To* NICOLA] Here: help me to change. Excuse me, Bluntschli. [*He begins changing coats,* NICOLA *acting as valet.*] Remember: I didnt take that bet of yours, Sergius. Youd better give Raina that Arab steed yourself, since youve roused her expectations. Eh, Raina? [*He looks round at her; but she is again rapt in the landscape. With a little gush of parental affection and pride, he points her out to them, and says*] She's dreaming, as usual.

SERGIUS. Assuredly she shall not be the loser.

PETKOFF. So much the better for her. *I* shant come off so cheaply, I expect. [*The change is now complete.* NICOLA *goes out with the discarded coat.*] Ah, now I feel at home at last. [*He sits down and takes his newspaper with a grunt of relief.*]

BLUNTSCHLI [*to* SERGIUS, *handing a paper*]. Thats the last order.

PETKOFF [*jumping up*]. What! Finished?

BLUNTSCHLI. Finished.

PETKOFF [*with childlike envy*]. Havnt you anything for me to sign?

BLUNTSCHLI. Not necessary. His signature will do.

PETKOFF [*inflating his chest and thumping it*]. Ah well, I think weve done a thundering good day's work. Can I do anything more?

BLUNTSCHLI. You had better both see the fellows that are to take these. [SERGIUS *rises*] Pack them off at once; and shew them that Ive marked on the orders the time they should hand them in by. Tell them that if they stop to drink or tell stories—if theyre five minutes late, theyll have the skin taken off their backs.

SERGIUS [*stiffening indignantly*]. I'll say so. [*He strides to the door.*] And if one of them is man enough to spit in my face for insulting him, I'll buy his discharge and give him a pension. [*He goes out.*]

BLUNTSCHLI [*confidentially*]. Just see that he talks to them properly, major, will you?

PETKOFF [*officiously*]. Quite right, Bluntschli, quite right. I'll see to it. [*He goes to the door importantly, but hesitates on the threshold.*] By the bye, Catherine, you may as well come too. Theyll be far more frightened of you than of me.

CATHERINE [*putting down her embroidery*]. I daresay I had better. You would only splutter at them. [*She goes out,* PETKOFF *holding the door for her and following her.*]

BLUNTSCHLI. What an army! They make cannons out of cherry trees; and the officers send for their wives to keep discipline! [*He begins to fold and docket the papers.*]

[RAINA, *who has risen from the divan, marches slowly down the room with her hands clasped behind her, and looks mischievously at him.*]

RAINA. You look ever so much nicer than when we last met. [*He looks up, surprised.*] What have you done to yourself?

BLUNTSCHLI. Washed; brushed; good night's sleep and breakfast. Thats all.

RAINA. Did you get back safely that morning?

BLUNTSCHLI. Quite, thanks.

RAINA. Were they angry with you for running away from Sergius's charge?

BLUNTSCHLI [*grinning*]. No: they were glad; because theyd all just run away themselves.

RAINA [*going to the table, and leaning over it towards him*]. It must have made a lovely story for them: all that about me and my room.

BLUNTSCHLI. Capital story. But I only told it to one of them: a particular friend.

RAINA. On whose discretion you could absolutely rely?

BLUNTSCHLI. Absolutely.

RAINA. Hm! He told it all to my father and Sergius the day you exchanged the prisoners. [*She turns away and strolls carelessly across to the other side of the room.*]

BLUNTSCHLI [*deeply concerned, and half incredulous*]. No! You dont mean that, do you?

RAINA [*turning, with sudden earnestness*]. I do indeed. But they dont know that it was in this house you took refuge. If Sergius knew, he would challenge you and kill you in a duel.

BLUNTSCHLI. Bless me! then dont tell him.

RAINA. Please be serious, Captain Bluntschli. Can you not realize what it is to me to deceive him? I want to be quite perfect with Sergius: no meanness, no smallness, no deceit. My relation to him is the one really beautiful and noble part of my life. I hope you can understand that.

BLUNTSCHLI [*sceptically*]. You mean that you wouldnt like him to find out that the story about the ice pudding was a—a—a—You know.

RAINA [*wincing*]. Ah, dont talk of it in that flippant way. I lied: I know it. But I did it to save your life. He would have killed you. That was the second time I ever uttered a falsehood. [BLUNTSCHLI *rises quickly and looks doubtfully and somewhat severely at her.*] Do you remember the first time?

BLUNTSCHLI. I! No. Was I present?

RAINA. Yes; and I told the officer who was searching for you that you were not present.

BLUNTSCHLI. True. I should have remembered it.

RAINA [*greatly encouraged*]. Ah, it is natural that you should forget it first. It cost you nothing: it cost me a lie! A lie!

[*She sits down on the ottoman, looking straight before her with her hands clasped around her knee.* BLUNTSCHLI, *quite touched, goes to the ottoman with a particularly reassuring and considerate air, and sits down beside her.*]

BLUNTSCHLI. My dear young lady, dont let this worry you. Remember: I'm a soldier. Now what are the two things that happen to a soldier so often that he comes to think nothing of them? One is hearing people tell lies [RAINA *recoils*]: the other is getting his life saved in all sorts of ways by all sorts of people.

RAINA [*rising in indignant protest*]. And so he becomes a creature incapable of faith and of gratitude.

BLUNTSCHLI [*making a wry face*]. Do you like gratitude? I dont. If pity is akin to love, gratitude is akin to the other thing.

RAINA. Gratitude! [*Turning on him*] If you are incapable of gratitude you are incapable of any noble sentiment. Even animals are grateful. Oh, I see now exactly what you think of me! You were not surprised to hear me lie. To you it was something I probably did every day! every hour! That is how men think of women. [*She paces the room tragically.*]

BLUNTSCHLI [*dubiously*]. Theres reason in everything. You said youd told only two lies in your whole life. Dear young lady: isnt that rather a short allowance? I'm quite a straightforward man myself; but it wouldnt last me a whole morning.

RAINA [*staring haughtily at him*]. Do you know, sir, that you are insulting me?

BLUNTSCHLI. I cant help it. When you strike that noble attitude and speak in that thrilling voice, I admire you; but I find it impossible to believe a single word you say.

RAINA [*superbly*]. Captain Bluntschli!

BLUNTSCHLI [*unmoved*]. Yes?

RAINA [*standing over him, as if she could not believe her senses*]. Do you mean what you said just now? Do you know what you said just now?

BLUNTSCHLI. I do.

RAINA [*gasping*]. I! I!!! [*She points to herself incredulously, meaning "I, RAINA PETKOFF, tell lies!" He meets her gaze unflinchingly. She suddenly sits down beside him, and adds, with a complete change of manner from the heroic to a babyish familiarity*] How did you find me out?

BLUNTSCHLI [*promptly*]. Instinct, dear young lady. Instinct, and experience of the world.

RAINA [*wonderingly*]. Do you know, you are the first man I ever met who did not take me seriously?

BLUNTSCHLI. You mean, dont you, that I am the first man that has ever taken you quite seriously?

RAINA. Yes: I suppose I do mean that. [*Cosily, quite at her ease with him*] How strange it is to be talked to in such a way! You know, Ive always gone on like that.

BLUNTSCHLI. You mean the—?

RAINA. I mean the noble attitude and the thrilling voice. [*They laugh together.*] I did it when I was a tiny child to my nurse. She believed in it. I do it before my parents. They believe in it. I do it before Sergius. He believes in it.

BLUNTSCHLI. Yes: he's a little in that line himself, isnt he?

RAINA [*startled*]. Oh! Do you think so?

BLUNTSCHLI. You know him better than I do.

RAINA. I wonder—I wonder is he? If I thought that—! [*Discouraged*] Ah, well: what does it matter? I suppose, now youve found me out, you despise me.

BLUNTSCHLI [*warmly, rising*]. No, my dear young lady, no, no, no a thousand times. It's part of your youth: part of your charm. I'm like all the rest of them: the nurse, your parents, Sergius: I'm your infatuated admirer.

RAINA [*pleased*]. Really?

BLUNTSCHLI [*slapping his breast smartly with his hand, German fashion*] Hand aufs Herz![20] Really and truly.

RAINA [*very happy*]. But what did you think of me for giving you my portrait?

BLUNTSCHLI [*astonished*]. Your portrait! You never gave me your portrait.

RAINA [*quickly*]. Do you mean to say you never got it?

BLUNTSCHLI. No. [*He sits down beside her, with renewed interest, and says, with some complacency*] When did you send it to me?

RAINA [*indignantly*]. I did not send it to you. [*She turns her head away, and adds, reluctantly*] It was in the pocket of that coat.

BLUNTSCHLI [*pursing his lips and rounding his eyes*]. Oh-o-oh! I never found it. It must be there still.

RAINA [*springing up*]. There still! for my father to find the first time he puts his hand in his pocket! Oh, how could you be so stupid?

BLUNTSCHLI [*rising also*]. It doesnt matter: I suppose it's only a photograph: how can he tell who it was intended for? Tell him he put it there himself.

RAINA [*bitterly*]. Yes: that is so clever! isnt it? [*Distractedly*] Oh! what shall I do?

BLUNTSCHLI. Ah, I see. You wrote something on it. That was rash.

RAINA [*vexed almost to tears*]. Oh, to have done such a thing for you, who care no more—except to laugh at me—oh! Are you sure nobody has touched it?

BLUNTSCHLI. Well, I cant be quite sure. You see, I couldnt carry it about with me all the time: one cant take much luggage on active service.

RAINA. What did you do with it?

BLUNTSCHLI. When I got through to Pirot I had to put it in safe keeping somehow. I thought of the railway cloak room; but thats the surest place to get looted in modern warfare. So I pawned it.

RAINA. Pawned it!!!

BLUNTSCHLI. I know it doesnt sound nice; but it was much the safest plan. I redeemed it the day before yesterday. Heaven only knows whether the pawnbroker cleared out the pockets or not.

RAINA [*furious: throwing the words right into his face*]. You have a low shopkeeping mind. You think of things that would never come into a gentleman's head.

BLUNTSCHLI [*phlegmatically*]. Thats the Swiss national character, dear lady. [*He returns to the table.*]

RAINA. Oh, I wish I had never met you. [*She flounces away, and sits at the window fuming.*]

[LOUKA *comes in with a heap of letters and telegrams on her salver, and crosses, with her bold free gait, to the table. Her left sleeve is looped up to the shoulder with a brooch, shewing her naked arm, with a broad gilt bracelet covering the bruise.*]

LOUKA [*to* BLUNTSCHLI]. For you. [*She empties the salver with a fling on to the table.*] The messenger is waiting. [*She is determined not to be civil to an enemy, even if she must bring him his letters.*]

BLUNTSCHLI [*to* RAINA]. Will you excuse me: the last postal delivery that reached me was three weeks ago. These are the subsequent accumulations. Four telegrams: a week old. [*He opens one.*] Oho! Bad news!

RAINA [*rising and advancing a little remorsefully*]. Bad news?

BLUNTSCHLI. My father's dead. [*He looks at the telegram with his lips pursed, musing on the unexpected change in his arrangements.* LOUKA *crosses herself hastily.*]

RAINA. Oh, how very sad!

BLUNTSCHLI. Yes: I shall have to start for home in an hour. He has left a lot of big hotels behind him to be looked after. [*He takes up a fat letter in a long blue envelope.*] Here's a whacking letter from the family solicitor. [*He puts out the enclosures and glances over them.*] Great Heavens! Seventy! Two Hundred! [*In a crescendo*[21] *of dismay*] Four hundred! Four thousand!! Nine thousand six hundred!!! What on earth am I to do with them all?

RAINA [*timidly*]. Nine thousand hotels?

BLUNTSCHLI. Hotels! nonsense. If you only knew! Oh, it's too ridiculous! Excuse me: I must give my fellow orders about starting. [*He leaves the room hastily, with the documents in his hand.*]

LOUKA [*knowing instinctively that she can annoy* RAINA *by disparaging* BLUNTSCHLI]. He has not much heart, that Swiss. He has not a word of grief for his poor father.

RAINA [*bitterly*]. Grief! A man who has been doing nothing but killing people for years! What does he care? What does any soldier care? [*She goes to the door, restraining her tears with difficulty.*]

LOUKA. Major Saranoff has been fighting too; and he has plenty of heart left. [RAINA, *at the door, draws herself up haughtily and goes out.*] Aha! I thought you wouldnt get much feeling out of your soldier. [*She is following* RAINA *when* NICOLA *enters with an armful of logs for the stove.*]

NICOLA [*grinning amorously at her*]. Ive been trying all the afternoon to get a minute alone with you, my girl. [*His countenance changes as he notices her arm.*] Why, what fashion is that of wearing your sleeve, child?

LOUKA [*proudly*]. My own fashion.

NICOLA. Indeed! If the mistress catches you, she'll talk to you. [*He puts the logs down, and seats himself comfortably on the ottoman.*]

LOUKA. Is that any reason why you should take it on yourself to talk to me?

NICOLA. Come! dont be so contrairy with me. Ive some good news for you. [*She sits down beside him. He take out some paper money.* LOUKA, *with an eager gleam in her eyes, tries to snatch it; but he shifts it quickly to his left hand, out of her reach.*] See! a twenty leva bill! Sergius gave me that, out of pure swagger. A fool and his money are soon parted. Theres ten levas more. The Swiss gave me that for backing up the mistress's and Raina's lies about him. He's no fool, he isnt. You should have heard old Catherine downstairs as polite as you please to me, telling me not to mind the Major being a little impatient; for they knew what a good servant I was—after making a fool and a liar of me before them all! The twenty will go to our savings; and you shall have the ten to spend if youll only talk to me so as to remind me I'm a human being. I get tired of being a servant occasionally.

LOUKA. Yes: sell your manhood for 30 levas, and buy me for 10! [*Rising scornfully*] Keep your money. You were born to be a servant. I was not. When you set up your shop you will only be everybody's servant instead of somebody's servant. [*She goes moodily to the table and seats herself regally in Sergius's chair.*]

NICOLA [*picking up his logs, and going to the stove*]. Ah, wait til you see. We shall have our evenings to ourselves; and I shall be master in my own house, I promise you. [*He throws the logs down and kneels at the stove.*]

LOUKA. You shall never be master in mine.

NICOLA [*turning, still on his knees, and squatting down rather forlornly on his calves, daunted by her implacable disdain*] You have a great ambition in you, Louka. Remember: if any luck comes to you, it was I that made a woman of you.

LOUKA. You!

NICOLA [*scrambling up and going to her*]. Yes, me. Who was it made you give up wearing a couple of pounds of false black hair on your head and reddening your lips and cheeks like any other Bulgarian girl! I did. Who taught you to trim your nails, and keep your hands clean, and be dainty about yourself, like a fine Russian lady! Me: do you hear that? me! [*She tosses her head defiantly; and he turns away, adding more coolly*] Ive often thought that if Raina were out of the way, and you just a little less of a fool and Sergius just a little more of one, you might come to be one of my grandest customers, instead of only being my wife and costing me money.

LOUKA. I believe you would rather be my servant than my husband. You would make more out of me. Oh, I know that soul of yours.

NICOLA [*going closer to her for greater emphasis*]. Never you mind my soul; but just listen to my advice. If you want to be a lady, your present behaviour to me wont do at all, unless when we're alone. It's too sharp and impudent; and impudence is a sort of familiarity: it shews affection for me. And dont you try being high and mighty with me, either. Youre like all country girls: you think it's genteel to treat a servant the way I treat a stable-boy. Thats only your ignorance; and dont you forget it. And dont be so ready to defy everybody. Act as if you expected to have your own way, not as if you expected to be ordered about. The way to get on as a lady is the same as the way to get on as a servant: youve got to know your place: thats the secret of it. And you may depend on me to know my place if you get promoted. Think over it, my girl. I'll stand by you: one servant should always stand by another.

LOUKA [*rising impatiently*]. Oh, I must behave in my own way. You take all the courage out of me with your cold-blooded wisdom. Go and put those logs in the fire: thats the sort of thing you understand. [*Before* NICOLA *can retort,* SERGIUS *comes in. He checks himself a moment on seeing* LOUKA; *then goes to the stove.*]

SERGIUS [*to* NICOLA]. I am not in the way of your work, I hope.

NICOLA [*in a smooth, elderly manner*]. Oh no, sir: thank you kindly. I was only speaking to this foolish girl about her habit of running up here to the library whenever she gets a chance, to look at the books. Thats the worst of her education, sir: it gives her habits above her station. [*To* LOUKA] Make that table tidy, Louka, for the Major. [*He goes out sedately.*]

[LOUKA, *without looking at* SERGIUS, *pretends to arrange the papers on the table. He crosses slowly to her, and studies the arrangement of her sleeve reflectively.*]

SERGIUS. Let me see: is there a mark there? [*He turns up the bracelet and sees the bruise made by his grasp. She stands motionless, not looking at him: fascinated, but on her guard*] Ffff! Does it hurt?

LOUKA. Yes.

SERGIUS. Shall I cure it?

LOUKA [*instantly withdrawing herself proudly, but still not looking at him*]. No. You cannot cure it now.

SERGIUS [*masterfully*]. Quite sure? [*He makes a movement as if to take her in his arms.*]

LOUKA. Dont trifle with me, please. An officer should not trifle with a servant.

SERGIUS [*indicating the bruise with a merciless stroke of his forefinger*]. That was no trifle, Louka.

LOUKA [*flinching; then looking at him for the first time*]. Are you sorry?

SERGIUS [*with measured emphasis, folding his arms*]. I am never sorry.

LOUKA [*wistfully*]. I wish I could believe a man could be as unlike a woman as that. I wonder are you really a brave man?

SERGIUS [*unaffectedly, relaxing his attitude*]. Yes: I am a brave man. My heart jumped like a woman's at the first shot; but in the charge I found that I was brave. Yes: that at least is real about me.

LOUKA. Did you find in the charge that the men whose fathers are poor like mine were any less brave than the men who are rich like you?

SERGIUS [*with bitter levity*]. Not a bit. They all slashed and cursed and yelled like heroes. Psha! the courage to rage and kill is cheap. I have an English bull terrier who has as much of that sort of courage as the whole Bulgarian nation, and the whole Russian nation at its back. But he lets my groom thrash him, all the same. Thats your soldier all over! No, Louka: your poor men can cut throats; but they are afraid of their officers; they put up with insults and blows; they stand by and see one another punished like children: aye, and help to do it when they are ordered. And the officers!!! Well [*with a short harsh laugh*] *I* am an officer. Oh, [*fervently*] give me the man who will defy to the death any power on earth or in heaven that sets itself up against his own will and conscience: he alone is the brave man.

LOUKA. How easy it is to talk! Men never seem to me to grow up: they all have schoolboy's ideas. You dont know what true courage is.

SERGIUS [*ironically*]. Indeed! I am willing to be instructed. [*He sits on the ottoman, sprawling magnificently.*]

LOUKA. Look at me! How much am I allowed to have my own will? I have to get your room ready for you: to sweep and dust, to fetch and carry. How could that degrade me if it did not degrade you to have it done for you? But [*with subdued passion*] if I were Empress of Russia, above everyone in the world, then!! Ah then, though according to you I could shew no courage at all, you should see, you should see.

SERGIUS. What would you do, most noble Empress?

LOUKA. I would marry the man I loved, which no other queen in Europe has the courage to do. If I loved you, though you would be as far beneath me as I am beneath you, I would dare to be the equal of my inferior. Would you dare as much if you loved me? No: if you felt the beginnings of love for me you would not let it grow. You would not dare: you would marry a rich man's daughter because you would be afraid of what other people would say of you.

SERGIUS [*bounding up*]. You lie: it is not so, by all the stars! If I loved you, and I were the Tsar himself, I would set you on the throne by my side. You know that I love another woman, a woman as high above you as heaven is above earth. And you are jealous of her.

LOUKA. I have no reason to be. She will never marry you now. The man I told you of has come back. She will marry the Swiss.

SERGIUS [*recoiling*]. The Swiss!

LOUKA. A man worth ten of you. Then you can come to me; and I will refuse you. You are not good enough for me. [*She turns to the door.*]

SERGIUS [*springing after her and catching her fiercely in his arms*]. I will kill the Swiss; and afterwards I will do as I please with you.

LOUKA [*in his arms, passive and steadfast*]. The Swiss will kill you, perhaps. He has beaten you in love. He may beat you in war.

SERGIUS [*tormentedly*]. Do you think I believe that she—she! whose worst thoughts are higher than your best ones, is capable of trifling with another man behind my back?

LOUKA. Do you think she would believe the Swiss if he told her now that I am in your arms?

SERGIUS [*releasing her in despair*]. Damnation! Oh, damnation! Mockery! mockery everywhere! everything I think is mocked by everything I do. [*He strikes himself frantically on the breast.*] Coward! liar! fool! Shall I kill myself like a man, or live and pretend to laugh at myself? [*She again turns to go.*] Louka! [*She stops near the door.*] Remember: you belong to me.

LOUKA [*turning*]. What does that mean? An insult?

SERGIUS [*commandingly*]. It means that you love me, and that I have had you here in my arms, and will perhaps have you there again. Whether that is an insult I neither know nor care: take it as you please. But [*vehemently*] I will not be a coward and a trifler. If I choose to love you, I dare marry you, in spite of all Bulgaria. If these hands ever touch you again, they shall touch my affianced bride.

LOUKA. We shall see whether you dare keep your word. And take care. I will not wait long.

SERGIUS [*again folding his arms and standing motionless in the middle of the room*]. Yes: we shall see. And you shall wait my pleasure. [BLUNTSCHLI, *much preoccupied, with his papers still in his hand, enters, leaving the door open for* LOUKA *to go out. He goes across to the table, glancing at her as he passes.* SERGIUS, *without altering his resolute attitude, watches him steadily.* LOUKA *goes out, leaving the door open.*]

BLUNTSCHLI [*absently, sitting at the table as before, and putting down his papers*]. Thats a remarkable looking young woman.

SERGIUS [*gravely, without moving*]. Captain Bluntschli.

BLUNTSCHLI. Eh?

SERGIUS. You have deceived me. You are my rival. I brook no rivals. At six o'clock I shall be in the drilling-ground on the Klissoura road, alone, on horseback, with my sabre. Do you understand?

BLUNTSCHLI [*staring, but sitting quite at his ease*]. Oh, thank you: thats a cavalry man's proposal. I'm in the artillery; and I have the choice of weapons. If I go, I shall take a machine gun. And there shall be no mistake about the cartridges this time.

SERGIUS [*flushing, but with deadly coldness*]. Take care, sir. It is not our custom in Bulgaria to allow invitations of that kind to be trifled with.

BLUNTSCHLI [*warmly*]. Pooh! dont talk to me about Bulgaria. You dont know what fighting is. But have it your own way. Bring your sabre along. I'll meet you.

SERGIUS [*fiercely delighted to find his opponent a man of spirit*]. Well said, Switzer. Shall I lend you my best horse?

BLUNTSCHLI. No: damn your horse! thank you all the same, my dear fellow. [RAINA *comes in, and hears the next sentence.*] I shall fight you on foot. Horseback's too dangerous; I dont want to kill you if I can help it.

RAINA [*hurrying forward anxiously*]. I have heard what Captain Bluntschli said, Sergius. You are going to fight. Why? [SERGIUS *turns away in silence, and goes to the stove, where he stands watching her as she continues, to* BLUNTSCHLI] What about?

BLUNTSCHLI. I dont know: he hasnt told me. Better not interfere, dear young lady. No harm will be done: Ive often acted as sword instructor. He wont be able to touch me; and I'll not hurt him. It will save explanations. In the morning I shall be off home; and youll never see me or hear of me again. You and he will then make it up and live happily ever after.

RAINA [*turning away deeply hurt, almost with a sob in her voice*]. I never said I wanted to see you again.

SERGIUS [*striding forward*]. Ha! That is a confession.

RAINA [*haughtily*]. What do you mean?

SERGIUS. You love that man!

RAINA [*scandalized*]. Sergius!

SERGIUS. You allow him to make love to you behind my back, just as you treat me as your affianced husband behind his. Bluntschli: you knew our relations; and you deceived me. It is for that that I call you to account, not for having received favors *I* never enjoyed.

BLUNTSCHLI [*jumping up indignantly*]. Stuff! Rubbish! I have received no favors. Why, the young lady doesnt even know whether I'm married or not.

RAINA [*forgetting herself*]. Oh! [*Collapsing on the ottoman*] Are you?

SERGIUS. You see the young lady's concern, Captain Bluntschli. Denial is useless. You have enjoyed the privilege of being received in her own room, late at night—

BLUNTSCHLI [*interrupting him pepperily*]. Yes, you blockhead! she received me with a pistol at her head. Your cavalry were at my heels. I'd have blown out her brains if she'd uttered a cry.

SERGIUS [*taken aback*]. Bluntschli! Raina: is this true?

RAINA [*rising in wrathful majesty*]. Oh, how dare you, how dare you?

BLUNTSCHLI. Apologize, man: apologize. [*He resumes his seat at the table.*]

SERGIUS [*with the old measured emphasis, folding his arms*]. I never apologize!

RAINA [*passionately*]. This is the doing of that friend of yours, Captain Bluntschli. It is he who is spreading this horrible story about me. [*She walks about excitedly.*]

BLUNTSCHLI. No: he's dead. Burnt alive!

RAINA [*stopping, shocked*]. Burnt alive!

BLUNTSCHLI. Shot in the hip in a woodyard. Couldnt drag himself out. Your fellows' shells set the timber on fire and burnt him, with half a dozen other poor devils in the same predicament.

RAINA. How horrible!

SERGIUS. And how ridiculous! Oh, war! war! the dream of patriots and heroes! A fraud, Bluntschli. A hollow sham, like love.

RAINA [*outraged*]. Like love! You say that before me!

BLUNTSCHLI. Come, Saranoff: that matter is explained.

SERGIUS. A hollow sham, I say. Would you have come back here if nothing had passed between you except at the muzzle of your pistol? Raina is mistaken about your friend who was burnt. He was not my informant.

RAINA. Who then? [*Suddenly guessing the truth*] Ah, Louka! my maid! my servant! You were with her this morning all that time after—after—Oh, what sort of god is this I have been worshipping! [*He meets her gaze with sardonic enjoyment of her disenchantment. Angered all the more, she goes closer to him, and says, in a lower, intenser tone*] Do you know that I looked out of the window as I went upstairs, to have another sight of my hero; and I saw something I did not understand then. I know now that you were making love to her.

SERGIUS [*with grim humor*]. You saw that?

RAINA. Only too well. [*She turns away, and throws herself on the divan under the centre window, quite overcome.*]

SERGIUS [*cynically*]. Raina: our romance is shattered. Life's a farce.

BLUNTSCHLI [*to Raina, whimsically*]. You see: he's found himself out now.

SERGIUS [*going to him*]. Bluntschli: I have allowed you to call me a blockhead. You may now call me a coward as well. I refuse to fight you. Do you know why?

BLUNTSCHLI. No; but it doesnt matter. I didnt ask the reason when you cried on; and I dont ask the reason now that you cry off. I'm a professional soldier! I fight when I have to, and am very glad to get out of it when I havnt to. Youre only an amateur: you think fighting's an amusement.

SERGIUS [*sitting down at the table, nose to nose with him*]. You shall hear the reason all the same, my professional. The reason is that it takes two men—real men—men of heart, blood and honor—to make a genuine combat. I could no more fight with you than I could make love to an ugly woman. Youve no magnetism: youre not a man: youre a machine.

BLUNTSCHLI [*apologetically*]. Quite true, quite true. I always was that sort of chap. I'm very sorry.

SERGIUS. Psha!

BLUNTSCHLI. But now that youve found that life isnt a farce, but something quite sensible and serious, what further obstacle is there to your happiness?

RAINA [*rising*]. You are very solicitous about my happiness and his. Do you forget his new love—Louka? It is not you that he must fight now, but his rival, Nicola.

SERGIUS. Rival!! [*bounding half across the room*]

RAINA. Dont you know that theyre engaged?

SERGIUS. Nicola! Are fresh abysses opening? Nicola!!

RAINA [*sarcastically*]. A shocking sacrifice, isnt it? Such beauty! such intellect! such modesty! wasted on a middle-aged servant man. Really, Sergius, you cannot stand by and allow such a thing. It would be unworthy of your chivalry.

SERGIUS [*losing all self-control*]. Viper! Viper! [*He rushes to and fro, raging.*]

BLUNTSCHLI. Look here, Saranoff: youre getting the worst of this.

RAINA [*getting angrier*]. Do you realize what he has done, Captain Bluntschli? He has set this girl as a spy on us; and her reward is that he makes love to her.

SERGIUS. False! Monstrous!

RAINA. Monstrous! [*Confronting him*] Do you deny that she told you about Captain Bluntschli being in my room?

SERGIUS. No; but—

RAINA [*interrupting*]. Do you deny that you were making love to her when she told you?

SERGIUS. No; but I tell you—

RAINA [*cutting him short contemptuously*]. It is unnecessary to tell us anything more. That is quite enough for us. [*She turns away from him and sweeps majestically back to the window.*]

BLUNTSCHLI [*quietly, as* SERGIUS, *in an agony of mortification, sinks on the ottoman, clutching his averted head between his fists*]. I told you you were getting the worst of it, Saranoff.

SERGIUS. Tiger cat!

RAINA [*running excitedly to* BLUNTSCHLI]. You hear this man calling me names, Captain Bluntschli?

BLUNTSCHLI. What else can he do, dear lady? He must defend himself somehow. Come [*very persuasively*]: dont quarrel. What good does it do?

[RAINA, *with a gasp, sits down on the ottoman, and after a vain effort to look vexedly at* BLUNTSCHLI, *falls a victim to her sense of humor, and actually leans back babyishly against the writhing shoulder of* SERGIUS.]

SERGIUS. Engaged to Nicola! Ha! ha! Ah well, Bluntschli, you are right to take this huge imposture of a world coolly.

RAINA [*quaintly to* BLUNTSCHLI, *with an intuitive guess at his state of mind*]. I daresay you think us a couple of grown-up babies, dont you?

SERGIUS [*grinning savagely*]. He does: he does. Swiss civilization nursetending Bulgarian barbarism, eh?

BLUNTSCHLI [*blushing*]. Not at all, I assure you. I'm only very glad to get you two quieted. There! there! let's be pleasant and talk it over in a friendly way. Where is this other young lady?

RAINA. Listening at the door, probably.

SERGIUS [*shivering as if a bullet had struck him, and speaking with quiet but deep indignation*]. I will prove that that, at least, is a calumny. [*He goes with dignity to the door and opens it. A yell of fury bursts from him as he looks out. He darts into the passage, and returns dragging in* LOUKA, *whom he flings violently against the table, exclaiming*] Judge her, Bluntschli. You, the cool impartial man: judge the eavesdropper.

[LOUKA *stands her ground, proud and silent.*]

BLUNTSCHLI [*shaking his head*]. I mustnt judge her. I once listened myself outside a tent when there was a mutiny brewing. It's all a question of the degree of provocation. My life was at stake.

LOUKA. My love was at stake. I am not ashamed.

RAINA [*contemptuously*]. Your love! Your curiosity, you mean.

LOUKA [*facing her and returning her contempt with interest*]. My love, stronger than anything you can feel, even for your chocolate cream soldier.

SERGIUS [*with quick suspicion, to* LOUKA]. What does that mean?

LOUKA [*fiercely*]. I mean—

SERGIUS [*interrupting her slightingly*]. Oh, I remember: the ice pudding. A paltry taunt, girl!

[MAJOR PETKOFF *enters, in his shirtsleeves.*]

PETKOFF. Excuse my shirtsleeves, gentlemen. Raina: somebody has been wearing that coat of mine: I'll swear it. Somebody with a differently shaped back. It's all burst open at the sleeve. Your mother is mending it. I wish she'd make haste: I shall catch cold. [*He looks more attentively at them.*] Is anything the matter?

RAINA. No. [*She sits down at the stove, with a tranquil air.*]

SERGIUS. Oh no. [*He sits down at the end of the table, as at first.*]

BLUNTSCHLI [*who is already seated*]. Nothing. Nothing.

PETKOFF [*sitting down on the ottoman in his old place*]. Thats all right. [*He notices* LOUKA.] Anything the matter, Louka?

LOUKA. No, sir.

PETKOFF [*genially*]. Thats all right. [*He sneezes.*] Go and ask your mistress for my coat, like a good girl, will you?

[NICOLA *enters with the coat.* LOUKA *makes a pretence of having business in the room by taking the little table with the hookah away to the wall near the windows.*]

RAINA [*rising quickly as she sees the coat on* NICOLA'S *arm*]. Here it is, papa. Give it to me, Nicola; and do you put some more wood on the fire. [*She takes the coat, and brings it to the Major, who stands up to put it on.* NICOLA *attends to the fire.*]

PETKOFF [*to* RAINA, *teasing her affectionately*]. Aha! Going to be very good to poor old papa just for one day after his return from the wars, eh?

RAINA [*with solemn reproach*]. Ah, how can you say that to me, father?

PETKOFF. Well, well, only a joke, little one. Come: give me a kiss. [*She kisses him.*] Now give me the coat.

RAINA. No: I am going to put it on for you. Turn your back. [*He turns his back and feels behind him with his arms for the sleeves. She dexterously takes the photograph from the pocket and throws it on the table before* BLUNTSCHLI, *who covers it with a sheet of paper under the very nose of* SERGIUS, *who looks on amazed, with his suspicions roused in the highest degree. She then helps* PETKOFF *on with his coat.*] There, dear! Now are you comfortable?

PETKOFF. Quite, little love. Thanks. [*He sits down; and* RAINA *returns to her seat near the stove.*] Oh, by the bye, Ive found something funny. Whats the meaning of this? [*He puts his hand into the picked pocket.*] Eh? Hallo! [*He tries the other pocket.*] Well, I could have sworn—! [*Much puzzled, he tries the breast pocket.*] I wonder—[*trying the original pocket*] Where can it—? [*He rises, exclaiming*] Your mother's taken it!

RAINA [*very red*]. Taken what?

PETKOFF. Your photograph, with the inscription: "Raina, to her Chocolate Cream Soldier: a Souvenir." Now you know theres something more in this than meets the eye; and I'm going to find it out. [*Shouting*] Nicola!

NICOLA [*coming to him*]. Sir!

PETKOFF. Did you spoil any pastry of Miss Raina's this morning?

NICOLA. You heard Miss Raina say that I did, sir.

PETKOFF. I know that, you idiot. Was it true?

NICOLA. I am sure Miss Raina is incapable of saying anything that is not true, sir.

PETKOFF. Are you? Then I'm not. [*Turning to the others*] Come: do you think I dont see it all? [*He goes to* SERGIUS, *and slaps him on the shoulder.*] Sergius: youre the chocolate cream soldier, arnt you?

SERGIUS [*starting up*]. I! A chocolate cream soldier! Certainly not.

PETKOFF. Not! [*He looks at them. They are all very serious and very conscious.*] Do you mean to tell me that Raina sends things like that to other men?

SERGIUS [*enigmatically*]. The world is not such an innocent place as we used to think, Petkoff.

BLUNTSCHLI [*rising*]. It's all right, major. I'm the chocolate cream soldier. [PETKOFF *and* SERGIUS *are equally astonished.*] The gracious young lady saved my life by giving me chocolate creams when I was starving: shall I ever forget their flavour! My late friend Stolz told you the story at Pirot. I was the fugitive.

PETKOFF. You! [*He gasps.*] Sergius: do you remember how those two women went on this morning when we mentioned it? [SERGIUS *smiles cynically.* PETKOFF *confronts* RAINA *severely.*] Youre a nice young woman, arnt you?

RAINA [*bitterly*]. Major Saranoff has changed his mind. And when I wrote that on the photograph, I did not know that Captain Bluntschli was married.

BLUNTSCHLI [*startled into vehement protest*]. I'm not married.

RAINA [*with deep reproach*]. You said you were.

BLUNTSCHLI. I did not. I positively did not. I never was married in my life.

PETKOFF [*exasperated*]. Raina: will you kindly inform me, if I am not asking too much, which of these gentlemen you are engaged to?

RAINA. To neither of them. This young lady [*introducing* LOUKA, *who faces them all proudly*] is the object of Major Saranoff's affections at present.

PETKOFF. Louka! Are you mad, Sergius? Why, this girl's engaged to Nicola.

NICOLA. I beg your pardon, sir. There is a mistake. Louka is not engaged to me.

PETKOFF. Not engaged to you, you scoundrel! Why, you had twenty-five levas from me on the day of your betrothal; and she had that gilt bracelet from Miss Raina.

NICOLA [*with cool unction*]. We gave it out so, sir. But it was only to give Louka protection. She had a soul above her station; and I have been no more than her confidential servant. I intend, as you know, sir, to set up a shop later on in Sofia; and I look forward to her custom and recommendation should she marry into the nobility. [*He goes out with impressive discretion, leaving them all staring after him.*]

PETKOFF [*breaking the silence*]. Well, I am—hm!

SERGIUS. This is either the finest heroism or the most crawling baseness. Which is it, Bluntschli?

BLUNTSCHLI. Never mind whether it's heroism or baseness. Nicola's the ablest man Ive met in Bulgaria.

I'll make him manager of a hotel if he can speak French and German.

LOUKA [*suddenly breaking out at* SERGIUS]. I have been insulted by everyone here. You set them the example. You owe me an apology. [SERGIUS, *like a repeating clock of which the spring has been touched, immediately begins to fold his arms.*]

BLUNTSCHLI [*before he can speak*]. It's no use. He never apologizes.

LOUKA. Not to you, his equal and his enemy. To me, his poor servant, he will not refuse to apologize.

SERGIUS [*approvingly*]. You are right. [*He bends his knee in his grandest manner*] Forgive me.

LOUKA. I forgive you. [*She timidly gives him her hand, which he kisses.*] That touch makes me your affianced wife.

SERGIUS [*springing up*]. Ah! I forgot that.

LOUKA [*coldly*]. You can withdraw if you like.

SERGIUS. Withdraw! Never! You belong to me. [*He puts his arm about her.*]

[CATHERINE *comes in and finds* LOUKA *in* SERGIUS'S *arms, with all the rest gazing at them in bewildered astonishment.*]

CATHERINE. What does this mean? [SERGIUS *releases* LOUKA.]

PETKOFF. Well, my dear, it appears that Sergius is going to marry Louka instead of Raina. [*She is about to break out indignantly at him: he stops her by exclaiming testily*] Dont blame me: Ive nothing to do with it. [*He retreats to stove.*]

CATHERINE. Marry Louka! Sergius: you are bound by your word to us!

SERGIUS [*folding his arms*]. Nothing binds me.

BLUNTSCHLI [*much pleased by this piece of common sense*]. Saranoff: your hand. My congratulations. These heroics of yours have their practical side after all. [*To* LOUKA] Gracious young lady: the best wishes of a good Republican! [*He kisses her hand, to* RAINA'S *great disgust, and returns to his seat.*]

CATHERINE. Louka: you have been telling stories.

LOUKA. I have done Raina no harm.

CATHERINE [*haughtily*]. Raina! [RAINA, *equally indignant, almost snorts at the liberty.*]

LOUKA. I have a right to call her Raina: she calls me Louka. I told Major Saranoff she would never marry him if the Swiss gentleman came back.

BLUNTSCHLI [*rising, much surprised*]. Hallo!

LOUKA [*turning to* RAINA]. I thought you were fonder of him than of Sergius. You know best whether I was right.

BLUNTSCHLI. What nonsense! I assure you, my dear major, my dear madame, the gracious young lady simply saved my life, nothing else. She never cared two straws for me. Why, bless my heart and soul, look at the young lady and look at me. She, rich, young, beautiful, with her imagination full of fairy princes and noble natures and cavalry charges and goodness knows what! And I, a commonplace Swiss soldier who hardly knows what a decent life is after fifteen years of barracks and battles: a vagabond, a man who has spoiled all his chances in life through an incurably romantic disposition, a man—

SERGIUS [*starting as if a needle had pricked him and interrupting* BLUNTSCHLI *in incredulous amazement*]. Excuse me, Bluntschli: what did you say had spoiled your chances in life?

BLUNTSCHLI [*promptly*]. An incurably romantic disposition. I ran away from home twice when I was a boy. I went into the army instead of into my father's business. I climbed the balcony of this house when a man of sense would have dived into the nearest cellar. I came sneaking back here to have another look at the young lady when any other man of my age would have sent the coat back—

PETKOFF. My coat!

BLUNTSCHLI. —yes: thats the coat I mean—would have sent it back and gone quietly home. Do you suppose I am the sort of fellow a young girl falls in love with? Why, look at our ages! I'm thirty-four: I dont suppose the young lady is much over seventeen. [*This estimate produces a marked sensation, all the rest turning and staring at one another. He proceeds innocently*] All that adventure which was life or death to me, was only a schoolgirl's game to her—chocolate creams and hide and seek. Heres the proof! [*He takes the photograph from the table.*] Now, I ask you, would a woman who took the affair seriously have sent me this and written on it "Raina, to her Chocolate Cream Soldier: a Souvenir"? [*He exhibits the photograph triumphantly, as if it settled the matter beyond all possibility of refutation.*]

PETKOFF. Thats what I was looking for. How the deuce did it get there? [*He comes from the stove to look at it, and sits down on the ottoman.*]

BLUNTSCHLI [*to* RAINA, *complacently*]. I have put everything right, I hope, gracious young lady.

RAINA [*going to the table to face him*]. I quite agree with your account of yourself. You are a romantic idiot. [BLUNTSCHLI *is unspeakably taken aback.*] Next time, I hope you will know the difference between a schoolgirl of seventeen and a woman of twenty-three.

BLUNTSCHLI [*stupefied*]. Twenty-three!

[RAINA *snaps the photograph contemptuously from his hand; tears it up; throws the pieces in his face; and sweeps back to her former place.*]

SERGIUS [*with grim enjoyment of his rival's discomfiture*]. Bluntschli: my one last belief is gone. Your sagacity is a fraud, like everything else. You have less sense than even I!

BLUNTSCHLI [*overwhelmed*]. Twenty-three! Twenty-three!! [*He considers.*] Hm! [*Swiftly making up his mind and coming to his host*] In that case, Major Petkoff, I beg to propose formally to become a suitor for your daughter's hand, in place of Major Saranoff retired.

RAINA. You dare!

BLUNTSCHLI. If you were twenty-three when you said those things to me this afternoon, I shall take them seriously.

CATHERINE [*loftily polite*]. I doubt, sir, whether you quite realize either my daughter's position or that of Major Sergius Saranoff, whose place you propose to take. The Petkoffs and the Saranoffs are known as the richest and most important families in the country. Our position is almost historical: we can go back for twenty years.

PETKOFF. Oh, never mind that, Catherine. [*To* BLUNTSCHLI] We should be most happy, Bluntschli, if it were only a question of your position; but hang it, you know, Raina is accustomed to a very comfortable establishment. Sergius keeps twenty horses.

BLUNTSCHLI. But who wants twenty horses? We're not going to keep a circus.

CATHERINE [*severely*]. My daughter, sir, is accustomed to a first-rate stable.

RAINA. Hush, mother: youre making me ridiculous.

BLUNTSCHLI. Oh well, if it comes to a question of an establishment, here goes! [*He darts impetuously to the table; seizes the papers in the blue envelope; and turns to* SERGIUS.] How many horses did you say?

SERGIUS. Twenty, noble Switzer.

BLUNTSCHLI. I have two hundred horses. [*They are amazed.*] How many carriages?

SERGIUS. Three.

BLUNTSCHLI. I have seventy. Twenty-four of them will hold twelve inside, besides two on the box, without counting the driver and conductor. How many tablecloths have you?

SERGIUS. How the deuce do I know?

BLUNTSCHLI. Have you four thousand?

SERGIUS. No.

BLUNTSCHLI. I have. I have nine thousand six hundred pairs of sheets and blankets, with two thousand four hundred eider-down quilts. I have ten thousand knives and forks, and the same quantity of dessert spoons. I have three hundred servants. I have six palatial establishments, besides two livery stables, a tea garden, and a private house. I have four medals for distinguished services; I have the rank of an officer and the standing of a gentleman; and I have three native languages. Shew me any man in Bulgaria that can offer as much!

PETKOFF [*with childish awe*]. Are you Emperor of Switzerland?

BLUNTSCHLI. My rank is the highest known in Switzerland: I am a free citizen.

CATHERINE. Then, Captain Bluntschli, since you are my daughter's choice—

RAINA [*mutinously*]. He's not.

CATHERINE [*ignoring her*].—I shall not stand in the way of her happiness. [PETKOFF *is about to speak*] That is Major Petkoff's feeling also.

PETKOFF. Oh, I shall be only too glad. Two hundred horses! Whew!

SERGIUS. What says the lady?

RAINA [*pretending to sulk*]. The lady says that he can keep his tablecloths and his omnibuses. I am not here to be sold to the highest bidder. [*She turns her back on him.*]

BLUNTSCHLI. I wont take that answer. I appealed to you as a fugitive, a beggar, and a starving man. You accepted me. You gave me your hand to kiss, your bed to sleep in, and your roof to shelter me.

RAINA. I did not give them to the Emperor of Switzerland.

BLUNTSCHLI. Thats just what I say. [*He catches her by the shoulders and turns her face-to-face with him.*] Now tell us whom you did give them to.

RAINA [*succumbing with a shy smile*]. To my chocolate cream soldier.

BLUNTSCHLI [*with a boyish laugh of delight*]. Thatll do. Thank you. [*He looks at his watch and suddenly becomes businesslike.*] Time's up, major. Youve managed those regiments so well that youre sure to be asked to get rid of some of the infantry of the Timok division. Send them home by way of Lom Palanka. Saranoff: dont get married until I come back: I shall be here punctually at five in the evening on Tuesday fortnight. Gracious ladies [*his heels click*] good evening. [*He makes them a military bow, and goes.*]

SERGIUS. What a man! Is he a man?

Notes

1 The title comes from the first line of Virgil's *Aeneid:* "Arma virumque cano" (Arms and the man I sing). The setting of the play is Bulgaria, a country which to Victorian Englishmen seemed an exotic, distant, and somewhat comical land constantly embroiled in small but colorful wars. Act I takes place during the last days of the Serbo-Bulgarian War (November 1885), and Acts II and III during the ensuing Treaty of Bucharest (March 1886). Before the play opens, a part of Bulgaria had achieved independence after five centuries of Turkish rule; another part, loyal to the Turkish sultan, sought to unite the country. A neighboring country, Serbia, fearful of civil war in Bulgaria, proclaimed war and was defeated by Bulgarians shortly before the play opens.

2 This view provides a key image in the play; it parallels the occupant's (Raina's) view of human ideals, one of romantic idealism. Descriptions of stage settings as well as all dramatic directions within an effective play deserve careful study because they are integral parts of characterization and action. For example, the description of the room that follows suggests that, in the process of Westernization, Bulgaria has lost something of its own beauty and also symbolizes the union of East and West at the end of the play.

3 Many-colored.

4 Shaw was interested in phonetics (*Pygmalion,* later adapted into *My Fair Lady,* is a presentation of the effect of accent on social classes), in a reformed alphabet, and in spelling reform (for example, "shew" for "show" throughout *Arms and the Man*). Shaw also considered the apostrophe a "useless" mark and retained it only when omission would be confusing (*I'll,* not *Ill*) and when it affected pronunciation (*he's* not *hes*).

5 Alexander Pushkin (1799–1873), Russian poet, short-story writer, and dramatist, was influenced by Byron.

6 Commonplace, undistinguished.

7 Raina is an idealist who clings to the romantic idea that most soldiers are unafraid to die. The response to this remark is one that Shaw obviously considered practical and healthy.

8 An instance of what the playwright considered prudishness and false modesty.

9 Rigid (converted into stone).

10 The revolver was in plain view of stage figures and of the audience; that the investigating soldiers did not notice it is Shaw's commentary on soldierly intelligence and training.

11 The hero of Cervantes' romance was inspired by lofty, chivalrous, and impractical ideals—such as tilting at windmills.

[12] Condescendingly.

[13] An opera by Giuseppe Verdi (1813–1901), Italian composer.

[14] Towers attached to Muslim mosques (places of worship) from which people are called to prayer.

[15] The *lev* is a Bulgarian monetary unit, at the time (1886) worth about one cent. The correct plural is *levs,* not *levas.*

[16] The first elected ruler of Bulgaria, Prince Alexander of Battenberg, reigned 1879–1886.

[17] Hero of Byron's *Childe Harold.*

[18] A tobacco pipe with a long, flexible tube by which smoke is drawn through a jar of water.

[19] Illusions, false notions.

[20] German for "hand on heart."

[21] Increase in force, volume, or loudness.

POETRY

NOTES ON READING

Poetry offers advantages in learning to read and write well. Because good poets use language with precision, making words serve their purposes exactly, careful reading of poetry helps you to see how language works. Such reading is useful as vocabulary study and is also an excellent means of discovering how the meaning and effect of words are controlled by the contexts in which they appear. Good poets use language for immediate and intense effects. Understanding poetry, where "each word must carry twenty other words upon its back," requires effort that will be repaid by an increase in reading and writing skills.

Certain resources of language have a special importance in poetry. For instance, the rhythm of a poem is a means of communication, reinforcing and combining with the meaning of words, often suggesting or representing the attitude of a poem. But most of all, poetry calls for active contribution from you. The poet makes use of what you know and what you have felt. Good poetry blends sense and sound in ways that extend one's imagination, memory, and experience beyond the physical limits of one's life. The poetry selections in this book should stimulate reflection and curiosity and encourage the beginnings of an understanding of, and respect for, the power of expression in meter, rhyme, and other poetic devices.

A poem is to a piece of prose as an abstract painting is to a realistic portrait. From the same material the poet or artist intensifies by selecting parts or fragments of an idea or image, which he heightens (colors) by sound (or pigments) and rearranges in order to suggest a more sensitive, frequently more *accurate,* expression of the whole subject. Poetry is the quintessence of written feeling. The poet, departing from strict syntax and the literal sense of every word, discovers new powers of expression and often enriches our language with new words for concepts we could not express or did not realize before.

Modern poems, in particular, employ techniques such as abrupt shifts in point of view, omissions, and juxtapositions (placement together of words and phrases for contrast or comparison). Not all good poems necessarily proceed sequentially and logically; they can be grasped with richer and deeper responses only after repeated readings.

Now let's get to some particulars. These statements about poetry may be helpful:

1. Poetry is a language phenomenon—a way of saying things. Whether to teach, preach, or simply thrill; to paint, inform, or spellbind, this is not the language of over-the-counter existence, although many of the words are the same. A new blend of sound and sense is here, rich in connotation, imagery, impression, music, and offering new problems in meaning.

2. Poetry extends over a wide range of subject matter and experience, familiar and unfamiliar. One age may sing of sea battle, another of a lady's eyes. Or in the same age one man may ponder the skylark while another weaves nightmarish dream fantasies. The modern poet may use conventional topics, new topics, or apparently no topics at all, remaining content with patterns of sound and rhythm. In any period the gamut may be marked at one end by folk song and at the other by metaphysics.

3. Poetry has organization and purpose, but methods of presentation vary from period to period, century to century.

4. Poetry, like music and other arts, has appeals that vary with the experience and personality of the audience. A passage may jog your memory suddenly and help you reenjoy a lost moment. It may startle you into action or a new belief. It may help you escape reality for a moment's peace. It may offer you new illusions to replace the old. But it will not sledgehammer a skeptic into belief. You must meet the poet halfway, then suspend disbelief for a time. Of course, if after reading and thinking, you honestly feel that your original poor impression of a poet, a poem, or poetry itself remains, maintain it stoutly; you will at least know by then why you feel the way you do—that knowledge itself is a step ahead.

5. Poetry comes in various shapes and forms, types and subtypes. Although matter is more important than form, the two are linked, and it is obvious that you should pick up a little information on ballads, sonnets, and so on. Certain terms that you will need in studying poetry are briefly defined at the end of this introductory note. Do not memorize these definitions, but do refer to them as your need or your instructor suggests.

6. Poetry has pronounced rhythms, generally arranged in metrical patterns.

It often has rhyme, and rhyme also comes in varied patterns. It often is musical. It relies heavily on figurative language and allusion. Quick study, as needed, of terms in the following glossary will provide what help you need in dealing with such matters, but a further word on rhyme and meter may be useful.

When two words rhyme (see definition of *rhyme* in the glossary), each is noted in what is called a *rhyme scheme* by use of the same letter of the alphabet. For example, if the first and third lines of a stanza rhyme and the second and fourth do likewise, the scheme is referred to as *abab*. But be certain not to confuse true rhyme and *assonance* (see the glossary).

Metrical analysis is only one aspect of the study of poetry, but it is important. It involves both rhythm and accent. Perhaps the best way to begin a study of metrics is to realize that you are familiar with rhythm, a characteristic of such activities as breathing, walking, talking, singing, and dancing. Possibly some of you are familiar with laboratory experiments in psychology that have demonstrated man's basic need for rhythm. You may have observed the passage of regular or nearly equivalent time elements between specific activities involved in a crew's digging a ditch, marching, or even strolling down the street. You are not unaware of the recurrence of specific sounds and kinds of sounds in the music that delights you. You are familiar with the *beat* of music, a time division chosen by the composer (or performer) that ranges from a fraction of a second to several seconds. Your minds and your feet understand that a succession of equal beats produces a regularly recurring pulsation comparable to the ticking of a clock. The *tempo* of a given piece of music is determined by the duration of its beat.

Of rhythm in poetry and prose you may be less conscious. All language, whether in verse or prose, whether spoken or written, has a natural tendency to fall into metrical patterns that any ear can detect if its owner is properly directed. In English poetry, a rhythmic pattern is established by a combination of *accent* and *number of syllables* that forms a line which is repeated over and over.

In English prose, the recurrence of accent and occasionally of a measured number of syllables also occurs. That is, prose, too, has its rhythms, sometimes irregular, sometimes clearly marked, but rarely sustained for any prolonged period. In prose, rhythm is primarily a quality of style. All effective prose avoids a jerky staccato as well as the sing-song monotony of unchanging regularity. It does, however, often secure a fairly regular flow of accent that harmonizes with the sense and mood of what is being expressed. Prose rhythm has a much wider choice than rhythm in poetry because it is free to place accents with greater irregularity, no line of prose ever having to be forced into a specific rhythmic pattern.

To understand the basic rhythm of prose, consider this opening paragraph of Hemingway's "In Another Country":

> In the fall the war was always there, but we did not go to it any more. It was cold in the fall in Milan and the dark came very early. Then the electric lights came on, and it was pleasant along the streets looking in the windows. There was much game hanging outside the shops, and the snow powdered in the fur of the foxes and the wind blew their tails. The deer hung stiff and heavy and empty, and small birds

blew in the wind and the wind turned their feathers. It was a cold fall and the wind came down from the mountains.

In this passage, the accents approximate a regular pattern. Had Hemingway continued the pattern of this paragraph throughout the story, the effect would have become monotonous. Yet the rise and fall of movement, the metered phrases and clauses, should reveal something about the nature and function of rhythm in writing. In prose, and especially in poetry, rhythm lends pleasure and heightened emotional response to the reader; more important, it contributes to the mood and meaning of writing.

The term *meter* in English poetry refers to the pattern of stressed and unstressed syllables in a line, or verse, of a poem. The number of syllables in a line may be fixed and the number of stresses may vary, or the stresses may be fixed and the number of unstressed syllables may change. The number of stresses and syllables is fixed and definite in the most frequent forms of meter in English verse, although actually this basic pattern occasionally varies so as to avoid sounding like a metronome. In some modern poetry, regular meter is largely forsaken, and *cadences* (see the glossary) are employed to approximate the flow of speech. These are the meters most commonly used in English poetry: *iambic, trochaic, anapestic, dactylic,* and *spondaic.* Each is defined and illustrated in the glossary. Every such metrical unit, or group of syllables, is called a *foot;* the number of feet in a line of poetry determines its name as, for example, a verse of three feet is called *trimeter* and one of five feet is called *pentameter.*

With this information at hand in addition to that which is supplied in the glossary, what can you make of this part of Byron's "The Destruction of Sennacherib"?

> The Assyrian came down like a wolf on the fold,
> And his cohorts were gleaming in purple and gold;
> And the sheen of their spears was like stars on the sea,
> Where the blue wave rolls nightly on deep Galilee.

It is impossible to read this material without hearing its music. Technically, the four lines, or verses, constitute a kind of stanza called a *quatrain;* the rhyme scheme is *aabb;* the meter is *anapestic tetrameter:*

> And the sheen/ of their spears/ was like stars/ on the sea

As has been mentioned, not every line of poetry is so definitely accented as this one, but your ear, properly attuned, and your mind, filled with basic knowledge about meter, should enable you to read other poetry with understanding allowance for subtly altered rhythmic effects.

For your guidance in studying selections that follow, here are further examples of metrical structure:

Blank Verse (Iambic Pentameter)

EMERSON, *THE SNOW-STORM*

> Announced/ by all/ the trum/ pets of/ the sky,
> Arrives/ the snow,/ and, driv/ ing o'er/ the fields,
> Seems no/ where to/ alight:/ the whit/ ed air

Hides hills/ and woods,/ the riv/ er, and/ the heaven,
And veils/ the farm-/ house at/ the gar/ den's end.

[*Note:* Line 4 has a feminine ending, an unaccented syllable.]

Iambic Tetrameter

BRYANT, *TO THE FRINGED GENTIAN*

Thou blos/ som bright/ with au/ tumn dew
And col/ ored with/ the heaven's/ own blue
That open/ est when/ the qui/ et light
Succeeds/ the keen/ and fros/ ty night—

Anapestic Trimeter

POE, *ULALUME*

The skies/ they were ash/ en and sober
The leaves/ they were crisp/ ed and sere—
The leaves/ they were wither/ ing and sere:
It was night,/ in the lone/ some October
Of my most/ immemor/ ial year

Trochaic Octameter

POE, *THE RAVEN*

Once up/ on a/ midnight/ dreary,/ while I/ pondered/ weak and/ weary.
Over/ many a/ quaint and/ curious/ volume/ of for/ gotten/ lore—
While I/ nodded,/ nearly/ napping,/ sudden/ ly there/ came a/ tapping,
As of/ some one/ gently/ rapping,/ rapping/ at my/ chamber/ door.

Because free verse is free to be regular as well as to be free, it is difficult to define. Some free verse employs alliteration, assonance, rhyme, and occasionally regular meter. A typical free verse poem, however, shows no such devices throughout and is unrhymed. It has form, however: the arrangement of syllables and words, line lengths, and spacing of pauses fit the meaning at every point. Robert Frost once said that free verse was "like playing tennis with the net down." Theodore Roethke has answered this statement by writing: "The net is stretched even tighter. Since the poet has neither stanza form nor rhyme to rely on, he has to be more cunning than ever. . . . He has to depend more on his ear."

Most verse in English naturally falls into an iambic pattern, so that if you can recognize and understand this foot you should have little difficulty in scanning much of the poetry in this section. You should know, however, that not all the feet in a given line are necessarily identical and that a line is named by the prevailing kind of foot it contains. It will also help to remember that poets occasionally vary line length as well as metrical pattern within the same poem. For example, each of the three stanzas of Emily Dickinson's *I Died for Beauty* contains two kinds of lines: iambic tetrameter alternating with iambic trimeter:

I died/ for beau/ ty, but/ was scarce
Adjust/ ed in/ the tomb,
When one/ who died/ for truth/ was lain
In an/ adjoin/ ing room.

* * *

The poems that follow are arranged in three groups. Narrative poetry focuses on "what happens" and resembles an incident, anecdote, or even short story.

The second group, light verse and songs, is designed to show that poetry is not always serious, grim, and somber. Much light verse is gay and bantering, but it is carefully constructed and suggests an underlying theme that is as often sober and satiric as it is fun-provoking and amusing. Literally hundreds of native American songs and ballads have contributed to the social and literary history of the United States. Many of them now seem simple and even naive, but two points about them should be remembered: first, songs and ballads are intended not so much for reading as for singing; second, however unliterary they may appear, many songs and ballads are genuine records of the interests, yearnings, and troubles of a nation and its people.

The third group, lyric poems, resembles the second in the sense that each selection has something of the form and musical quality of a song. Lyric poems may be called songlike outpourings of their authors' innermost feelings, ideas, and yearnings.

Reading any kind of poetry requires the same skills and perceptions as reading prose. But since poetry may not be so familiar a form to you, these questions should suggest useful approaches.

1. Study the vocabulary of the poem. What passages are obscure? What key allusions must you check in a reference book? What ordinary words are employed in apparently unusual meanings? What other words must you look up and add to your reading vocabulary? Your writing vocabulary?
2. Who is speaking in the poem? To whom? What is the occasion? (A poem is often dramatic. Do not assume that "I" is the poet speaking in his own person.)
3. What is the attitude in the poem? (Answering this question is not primarily a matter of describing how the poet felt; it is a matter of describing the attitude that arises for you.)
4. What part of the effect of the poem is accounted for by its rhythm? Does the rhythm represent or suggest any sort of movement? Is the effect of the rhythm consistent with, and does it reinforce, the emotion of the poem?
5. What words or expressions in the poem are so used that, beyond any function they may have in making a statement, they evoke in you images and feelings?
6. Does the poem have a theme that may be stated outside the terms of the poem itself? Is there a line or a short passage that states the theme? Is the theme implicit—suggested instead of being directly stated and left for you to formulate?

GLOSSARY

Alliteration. The close repetition of consonant sounds, usually at the beginnings of words (*she sells seashells by the seashore*). The first line of Whitman's "Beat! Beat! Drums!" illustrates alliteration: "Beat! beat! drums!—blow! bugles! blow!"

Anapest. A metrical foot of two short syllables followed by one long syllable. (A syllable is a segment of speech produced by a single pulse of air pressure from the lungs; in writing, a syllable is a character or set of characters representing such an element of speech.) The phrase "to the end" consists of three syllables, the first two of which are unstressed (short) and the third long (stressed): *tŏ thĕ ēnd* or, marked in another way, *tŏ thĕ énd.*

Assonance. Similarity in sound between vowels. Assonance is to vowels what alliteration (see above) is to consonants. Assonance differs from rhyme (which see, below) in that final consonants are not identical, although the accented vowels are: *wine, lime.*

Blank verse. Unrhymed iambic pentameter; that is, verse consisting of unrhymed lines of ten syllables each, the second, fourth, sixth, eighth, and tenth syllables bearing the accents. It is called "blank" because it is void of rhyme and for no other reason. It has been used for lofty dignified passages of epic poetry, drama, and the like, but it is comparatively rare in American verse.

Cadence. The recognizable beat and rhythmic flow of phrase in both verse and prose, but without a formal and definite stress pattern. Cadence is related to rhythm, but it appears usually in larger and looser units of syllables than the metrical movement of regular verse or poetry. Cadence is an essential ingredient of *free verse* (which see) and appears often in carefully phrased and balanced prose.

Conceit. A term applied to a strained or involved comparison of ideas, a figure of speech that frequently determines the *form* of a piece of literature. Originally, the word meant an "idea," or "notion" and was applied to something conceived in one's mind, something made up, fabricated.

Couplet. A pair of successive lines of verse, especially such as rhyme together and are of identical length.

Dactyl. A metrical foot consisting of an accented syllable followed by two unaccented ones (*mūrmŭrĭng*).

Dimeter. A line of poetry made up of two feet.

Foot. The basic rhythmic unit in a recognizable metric pattern. In English the commonest feet are iambic, trochaic, anapestic, and dactylic (which see).

Free verse. Verse that has no regular metrical pattern, but that does have cadence, often set up irregularly as to length of line to "look like" poetry. It employs imagery and figures of conventional verse and definitely has organization and over-all unity of effect. Another term for free verse is *vers libre* (free line); neither should be confused with *blank verse.*

Heroic couplet. A pair of rhyming lines in iambic pentameter; such a couplet may be a "closed" couplet, with an organization of its own, or one unit with other continuous "open" couplets, with "run-on" lines.

Hexameter. A line of poetry having six feet.

Iambic. Common type of foot with an unaccented syllable followed by an accented one (*ŏmīt*).

Lyric. Originally a poem to be sung to lyre accompaniment, hence melodic; today, however, generally a short poem with strong emotional basis and marked individual personality.

Metaphysical poetry. Loosely, poetry dealing with reasoning processes and philosophical complexities; marked by intellectual pyrotechnics, conceits, subtleties, unusual comparisons.

Meter. A term used to designate the number of feet to a line (pentameter equals five-foot line, and so on). The term also refers to any formal arrangement of rhythm.

Monometer. A line of poetry having only one foot.

Pentameter. A line of poetry having five feet.

Prosody. The study of metrical structure.

Quatrain. A four-line stanza or a unit group of four lines in a long poem.

Refrain. The repeated portion of a poem, ballad, or song used for choral effect or audience participation.

Rhyme. Repetition of sound at the end of poetic lines (or at the middle and end of a line—"internal" rhyme). Stressed vowels and following consonants should be identical (*wine-mine*). (See *Assonance.*)

Run-on line. A verse (line) having a thought that carries over to the next line without a break.

Scansion. The act of dividing a line of poetry into feet, placing accent marks, deciding meter, and perhaps reading aloud. The commonest lines in English are tetrameter, pentameter, and hexameter; the four most familiar patterns are iambic, trochaic, anapestic, and dactylic.

Spondee. A foot consisting of two accented syllables (*dāybrēak*).

Stanza. A stanza is the equivalent in a poem to the paragraph in prose. That is, a stanza is a unit of verse marked by distinct meter, subject, pattern, or rhyme. In some poems, stanzas indicate separate topics or divisions of thought, but the rhyme scheme, metrical pattern, and typographical spacing are distinctive marks of the stanza. Only loosely can a stanza be called a verse, since the latter (see below) is really one line of poetry. The most common stanza forms in poetry are the couplet (see above), the tercet (three lines), the quatrain (see above). Somewhat rarer stanza forms in American verse are rime royal (seven lines of iambic pentameter, rhyming *ababbcc*), ottava rima (eight lines of iambic pentameter, rhyming *abababcc*), and the Spenserian stanza (eight lines of iambic pentameter, one of iambic hexameter). The sonnet is sometimes referred to as a stanza, but actually it is a complete verse form in itself, consisting of fourteen lines.

Tetrameter. A line of poetry having four feet.

Trimeter. A line of poetry having three feet.

Trochee. A metrical foot consisting of an accented (stressed) syllable followed by an unaccented one (*trĭppiňg*).

Verse. A verse is a single line of poetry. The term is also a loose synonym for poetry, presumably because verse is patterned language. And yet a form that is merely rhythmical may be doggerel: "Here lie the remains of Daniel Blank / He dropped a match in a gasoline tank." Poetry is patterned language, but it is language that exhibits imagination, emotion, and genuine thought. All poetry is verse of a sort, but not all verse is poetry. Distinguishing one from the other is a part of the process of learning to read with understanding. Also, in modern songs, verse is another name for stanza (which see).

Narrative Poems

LORD RANDALL[1]

"Oh where ha'e ye been, Lord Randall my son?
O where ha'e ye been, my handsome young man?"
"I ha'e been to the wild wood: mother, make my bed soon,
For I'm weary wi' hunting, and fain wald[2] lie down."

"Where gat ye your dinner, Lord Randall my son?
Where gat ye your dinner, my handsome young man?"
"I dined wi' my true love; mother, make my bed soon,
For I'm weary wi' hunting, and fain wald lie down."

"What gat ye to your dinner, Lord Randall my son?
What gat ye to your dinner, my handsome young man?"
"I gat eels boiled in broo:[3] mother, make my bed soon,
For I'm weary wi' hunting and fain wald lie down."

"What became of your bloodhounds, Lord Randall my son?
What became of your bloodhounds, my handsome young man?"
"O they swelled and they died: mother, make my bed soon,
For I'm weary wi' hunting and fain wald lie down."

"O I fear ye are poisoned, Lord Randall my son!
O I fear ye are poisoned, my handsome young man!"
"O yes, I am poisoned: mother, make my bed soon,
For I'm sick at the heart, and I fain wald lie down."

THE TWA CORBIES

As I was walking all alane,
I herd twa corbies making a mane;[4]
The tane unto the t'other say,
"Where sall we gang and dine to-day?"

"In behint yon auld fail[5] dyke,
I wot there lies a new slain knight;
And naebody kens that he lies there,
But his hawk, his hound, and lady fair.

"His hound is to the hunting gane,
His hawk to fetch the wild-fowl hame,
His lady's ta'en another mate,
So we may mak our dinner sweet.

"Ye'll sit on his white hause-bane,[6]
And I'll pike out his bonny blue een;
Wi ae lock o his gowden hair
We'll theek[7] our nest when it grows bare.

"Mony a one for him makes mane,
But nane sall ken where he is gane;
Oer his white banes when they are bare,
The wind sall blaw for evermair."

BONNY BARBARA ALLAN

It was in and about the Martinmas[8] time,
When the green leaves were a falling,
That Sir John Graeme, in the West Country,
Fell in love with Barbara Allan.

He sent his men down through the town
To the place where she was dwelling:
"O haste and come to my master dear,
Gin[9] ye be Barbara Allan."

O hooly,[10] hooly rose she up,
To the place where he was lying,
And when she drew the curtain by,
"Young man, I think you're dying."

"O it's I'm sick, and very, very sick,
And it's a' for Barbara Allan;
O the better for me ye's never be,
Tho your heart's blood were a spilling."

"O dinna ye mind,[11] young man," said she,
"When ye was in the tavern a drinking,
That ye made the healths gae round and round,
And slighted Barbara Allan?"

He turned his face unto the wall,
And death was with him dealing;
"Adieu, adieu, my dear friends all,
And be kind to Barbara Allan."

And slowly, slowly raise she up,
And slowly, slowly left him,
And sighing said she could not stay,
Since death of life had reft him.

She had not gane a mile but twa,
When she heard the dead-bell ringing,
And every jow that the dead-bell geid,[12]
It cry'd, Woe to Barbara Allan!

"O mother, mother, make my bed!
O make it saft and narrow!
Since my love died for me today,
I'll die for him tomorrow."

John Keats

LA BELLE DAME SANS MERCI[13]

O what can ail thee, Knight at arms,
Alone and palely loitering?
The sedge[14] has withered from the Lake,
And no birds sing!

O what can ail thee, Knight at arms,
So haggard and so woe-begone?
The Squirrel's granary is full,
And the harvest's done.

I see a lily on thy brow,
With anguish moist and fever dew;
And on thy cheeks a fading rose
Fast withereth too.

I met a Lady in the Meads.
Full beautiful, a faery's child;
Her hair was long, her foot was light,
And her eyes were wild.

I made a Garland for her head,
And bracelets, too, and fragrant Zone,[15]

She look'd at me as she did love,
And made sweet moan.

I set her on my pacing steed,
And nothing else saw, all day long;
For sidelong would she bend, and sing
A faery's song.

She found me roots of relish sweet,
And honey wild, and manna dew;
And sure in language strange she said,
"I love thee true."

She took me to her elfin grot,[16]
And there she wept and sigh'd full sore;
And there I shut her wild, wild eyes
With kisses four.

And there she lulled me asleep,
And there I dreamed, ah woe betide!
The latest[17] dream I ever dreamt,
On the cold hill side.

I saw pale Kings, and Princes too,
Pale warriors, death pale were they all;
They cried, "La belle dame sans merci
Thee hath in thrall!"[18]

I saw their starv'd lips in the gloam[19]
With horrid warning gaped wide—
And I awoke, and found me here,
On the cold hill's side.

And this is why I sojourn here,
Alone and palely loitering;
Though the sedge is withered from the Lake,
And no birds sing.

Alfred, Lord Tennyson

ULYSSES[20]

It little profits that an idle king,
By this still hearth, among these barren crags,
Matched with an agèd wife, I mete and dole
Unequal laws[21] unto a savage race,
That hoard, and sleep, and feed, and know not me.
I cannot rest from travel; I will drink
Life to the lees.[22] All times I have enjoyed
Greatly, have suffered greatly, both with those
That loved me, and alone; on shore, and when
Through scudding drifts[23] the rainy Hyades[24]
Vexed the dim sea. I am become a name;
For always roaming with a hungry heart
Much have I seen and known—cities of men,
And manners, climates, councils, governments,
Myself not least, but honored of them all—
And drunk delight of battle with my peers,
Far on the ringing plains of windy Troy.
I am a part of all that I have met;
Yet all experience is an arch wherethrough
Gleams that untraveled world, whose margin fades
Forever and forever when I move.
How dull it is to pause, to make an end,
To rust unburnished,[25] not to shine in use!
As though to breathe were life! Life piled on life
Were all too little, and of one to me
Little remains: but every hour is saved
From that eternal silence, something more,
A bringer of new things; and vile it were
For some three suns to store and hoard myself,
And this gray spirit yearning in desire
To follow knowledge like a sinking star,
Beyond the utmost bound of human thought.
This is my son, my own Telemachus,
To whom I leave the scepter and the isle—
Well-loved of me, discerning to fulfill
This labor, by slow prudence to make mild
A rugged people, and through soft degrees
Subdue them to the useful and the good.
Most blameless is he, centered in the sphere

Of common duties, decent not to fail
In offices of tenderness, and pay
Meet[26] adoration to my household gods,
When I am gone. He works his work, I mine.
There lies the port; the vessel puffs her sail;
There gloom the dark broad seas. My mariners,
Souls that have toiled, and wrought, and thought with me,—
That ever with a frolic welcome took
The thunder and the sunshine, and opposed
Free hearts, free foreheads,—you[27] and I are old;
Old age hath yet his honor and his toil.
Death closes all; but something ere the end,
Some work of noble note, may yet be done,
Not unbecoming men that strove with gods.
The lights begin to twinkle from the rocks;
The long day wanes; the slow moon climbs; the deep
Moans round with many voices. Come, my friends,
'Tis not too late to seek a newer world.
Push off, and sitting well in order smite
The sounding furrows; for my purpose holds
To sail beyond the sunset, and the baths
Of all the western stars,[28] until I die.
It may be that the gulfs will wash us down;
It may be we shall touch the Happy Isles,[29]
And see the great Achilles, whom we knew.
Though much is taken, much abides; and though
We are not now that strength which in old days
Moved earth and heaven; that which we are, we are;
One equal temper of heroic hearts,
Made weak by time and fate, but strong in will
To strive, to seek, to find, and not to yield.

Robert Browning

MY LAST DUCHESS[30]

That's my last Duchess painted on the wall,
Looking as if she were alive; I call
That piece a wonder, now: Fra Pandolf's[31] hands
Worked busily a day, and there she stands.
Will't please you sit and look at her? I said
"Fra Pandolf" by design, for never read
Strangers like you that pictured countenance,
The depth and passion of its earnest glance,
But to myself they turned (since none puts by
The curtain I have drawn for you, but I)
And seemed as they would ask me, if they durst,[32]
How such a glance came there; so, not the first
Are you to turn and ask thus. Sir, 'twas not
Her husband's presence only, called that spot
Of joy into the Duchess' cheek: perhaps
Fra Pandolf chanced to say, "Her mantle laps
Over my Lady's wrist too much," or "Paint
Must never hope to reproduce the faint
Half-flush that dies along her throat"; such stuff
Was courtesy, she thought, and cause enough
For calling up that spot of joy. She had
A heart . . . how shall I say? . . . too soon made glad,
Too easily impressed; she liked whate'er
She looked on, and her looks went everywhere.
Sir, 'twas all one! My favor at her breast,
The dropping of the daylight in the West,
The bough of cherries some officious fool
Broke in the orchard for her, the white mule

She rode with round the terrace—all and each
Would draw from her alike the approving speech,
Or blush, at least. She thanked men,—good; but thanked
Somehow . . . I know not how . . . as if she ranked
My gift of a nine-hundred-years-old name
With anybody's gift. Who'd stoop to blame
This sort of trifling? Even had you skill
In speech—(which I have not)—to make your will
Quite clear to such an one, and say, "Just this
Or that in you disgusts me; here you miss
Or there exceed the mark"—and if she let
Herself be lessoned so, nor plainly set
Her wits to yours, forsooth,[33] and made excuse,
—E'en then would be some stooping, and I choose
Never to stoop. Oh, Sir, she smiled, no doubt,
Whene'er I passed her; but who passed without
Much the same smile? This grew; I gave commands,[34]
Then all smiles stopped together. There she stands
As if alive. Will't please you rise? We'll meet
The company below, then. I repeat,
The Count your Master's known munificence[35]
Is ample warrant that no just pretence[36]
Of mine for dowry will be disallowed;
Though his fair daughter's self, as I avowed
At starting, is my object. Nay, we'll go
Together down, Sir! Notice Neptune, though,
Taming a sea-horse, thought a rarity,
Which Claus of Innsbruck[37] cast in bronze for me.

Rudyard Kipling

DANNY DEEVER

"What are the bugles blowin' for?" said Files-on-Parade.[38]
"To turn you out, to turn you out,"[39] the Color-Sergeant[40] said.
"What makes you look so white, so white?" said Files-on-Parade.
"I'm dreadin' what I've got to watch," the Color-Sergeant said.
For they're hangin' Danny Deever, you can 'ear the Dead March play,
The regiment's in 'ollow square[41]—they're hangin' him today;
They've taken of his buttons off an' cut his stripes away,[42]
An' they're hangin' Danny Deever in the mornin'.

"What makes the rear-rank breathe so 'ard?" said Files-on-Parade.
"It's bitter cold, it's bitter cold," the Color-Sergeant said.
"What makes that front-rank man fall down?" says Files-on-Parade.
"A touch of sun, a touch of sun," the Color-Sergeant said.
They are hangin' Danny Deever, they are marchin' of 'im round.
They 'ave 'alted Danny Deever by 'is coffin on the ground:
An 'e'll swing in 'arf a minute for a sneakin' shootin' hound—
O they're hangin' Danny Deever in the mornin'!

" 'Is cot was right-'and cot to mine," said Files-on-Parade.
" 'E's sleepin' out an' far tonight," the Color-Sergeant said.
"I've drunk 'is beer a score o' times," said Files-on-Parade.
" 'E's drinkin' bitter beer[43] alone," the Color-Sergeant said.
They are hangin' Danny Deever, you must mark 'im to 'is place,
For 'e shot a comrade sleepin'—you must look 'im in the face;
Nine 'undred of 'is county an' the regiment's disgrace,

While they're hangin' Danny Deever in the mornin'.

"What's that so black agin' the sun?" said Files-on-Parade.
"It's Danny fightin' 'ard for life," the Color-Sergeant said.
"What's that that whimpers over'ead?" said Files-on-Parade.
"It's Danny's soul that's passin' now," the Color-Sergeant said.
For they're done with Danny Deever, you can 'ear the quickstep[44] play,
The regiment's in column, an' they're marchin' us away;
Ho! the young recruits are shakin', an' they'll want their beer today,
After hangin' Danny Deever in the mornin'.

Edgar Lee Masters

LUCINDA MATLOCK[45]

I went to the dances at Chandlerville,
And played snap-out at Winchester.
One time we changed partners,
Driving home in the moonlight of middle June,
And then I found Davis.
We were married and lived together for seventy years,
Enjoying, working, raising the twelve children,
Eight of whom we lost
Ere I had reached the age of sixty.
I spun, I wove, I kept the house, I nursed the sick,
I made the garden, and for holiday
Rambled over the fields where sang the larks,
And by Spoon River gathering many a shell,
And many a flower and medicinal weed—
Shouting to the wooded hills, singing to the green valleys.
At ninety-six I had lived enough, that is all,
And passed to a sweet repose.
What is this I hear of sorrow and weariness,
Anger, discontent and drooping hopes?
Degenerate sons and daughters,
Life is too strong for you—
It takes life to love Life.[46]

Edwin Arlington Robinson

RICHARD CORY[47]

Whenever Richard Cory went down town,
We people on the pavement looked at him:
He was a gentleman from sole to crown,
Clean favored, and imperially slim.[48]

And he was always quietly arrayed,
And he was always human when he talked;
But still he fluttered pulses when he said,
"Good-morning," and he glittered when he walked.

And he was rich—yes, richer than a king—
And admirably schooled in every grace:
In fine, we thought that he was everything
To make us wish that we were in his place.

So on we worked, and waited for the light,
And went without the meat, and cursed the bread;
And Richard Cory, one calm summer night,
Went home and put a bullet through his head.

T. S. Eliot

JOURNEY OF THE MAGI[49]

"A cold coming we had of it,
Just the worst time of the year
For a journey, and such a long journey:

The ways deep and the weather sharp,
The very dead of winter."[50]
And the camels galled, sore-footed, refractory,
Lying down in the melting snow.
There were times we regretted
The summer palaces on slopes, the terraces,
And the silken girls bringing sherbet.
Then the camel men cursing and grumbling
And running away, and wanting their liquor and women,
And the night-fires going out, and the lack of shelters,
And the cities hostile and the towns unfriendly
And the villages dirty and charging high prices:
A hard time we had of it.
At the end we preferred to travel all night,
Sleeping in snatches,
With the voices singing in our ears, saying
That this was all folly.

Then at dawn we came down to a temperate[51] valley,
Wet, below the snow line, smelling of vegetation;
With a running stream and a water mill beating the darkness,
And three trees on the low sky,
And an old white horse galloped away in the meadow.
Then we came to a tavern with vine-leaves over the lintel,
Six hands at an open door dicing for pieces of silver,
And feet kicking the empty wineskins.[52]
But there was no information, and so we continued
And arrived at evening, not a moment too soon
Finding the place; it was (you may say) satisfactory.[53]

All this was a long time ago, I remember,
And I would do it again, but set down
This set down
This: were we led all that way for
Birth or Death? There was a Birth, certainly,
We had evidence and no doubt. I had seen birth and death,
But had thought they were different; this Birth was
Hard and bitter agony for us, like Death, our death.
We returned to our place, these Kingdoms,
But no longer at ease here, in the old dispensation,
With an alien people clutching their gods.
I should be glad of another death.

W. H. Auden

BALLAD[54]

O what is that sound which so thrills the ear
  Down in the valley drumming, drumming?
Only the scarlet soldiers, dear,
  The soldiers coming.

O what is that light I see flashing so clear
  Over the distance brightly, brightly?
Only the sun on their weapons, dear,
  As they step lightly.

O what are they doing with all that gear;
  What are they doing this morning, this morning?
Only the usual maneuvers, dear,
  Or perhaps a warning.

O why have they left the road down there;
  Why are they suddenly wheeling, wheeling?
Perhaps a change in the orders, dear;
  Why are you kneeling?

O haven't they stopped for the doctor's care;
  Haven't they reined their horses, their horses?

Why, they are none of them wounded, dear,
None of these forces.
O is it the parson they want, with white hair;
Is it the parson, is it, is it?
No, they are passing his gateway, dear,
Without a visit.

O it must be the farmer who lives so near;
It must be the farmer, so cunning, cunning;
They have passed the farm already, dear,
And now they are running.

O where are you going? stay with me here.
Were the vows you swore me deceiving?
No, I promised to love you, my dear,
But I must be leaving.

O it's broken the lock and splintered the door,
O it's the gate where they're turning, turning;
Their feet are heavy on the floor
And their eyes are burning.

Randall Jarrell

A CAMP IN THE PRUSSIAN FOREST[55]

I walk beside the prisoners to the road.
Load on puffed load,
Their corpses, stacked like sodden wood,
Lie barred or galled with blood

By the charred warehouse. No one comes today
In the old way
To knock the fillings from their teeth;
The dark, coned, common wreath

Is plaited for their grave—a kind of grief.
The living leaf
Clings to the planted profitable[56]
Pine if it is able;

The boughs sigh, mile on green, calm, breathing mile,
From this dead file
The planners ruled for them. . . . One year
They sent a million here:

Here men were drunk like water, burnt like wood.
The fat of good
And evil, the breast's star of hope
Were rendered into soap.

I paint the star I sawed from yellow pine—
And plant the sign
In soil that does not yet refuse
Its usual Jews

Their first asylum.[57] But the white, dwarfed star—
This dead white star—
Hides nothing, pays for nothing; smoke
Fouls it, a yellow joke,

The needles of the wreath are chalked with ash,
A filmy trash
Litters the black woods with the death
Of men; and one last breath

Curls from the monstrous chimney. . . . I laugh aloud
Again and again;
The star laughs from its rotting shroud
Of flesh. O star of men![58]

Notes

[1] This poem and the two succeeding ones are popular ballads. The term *popular ballad* applies to narrative songs that originated not at the courts of kings and in the homes of nobles but among "the people." (The word *popular* is derived from Latin "populus," meaning "people.") The ballads of England and Scotland were probably composed during the five centuries between 1200 and 1700, although none was written down until late in the thirteenth century and few were printed before the eighteenth.

[2] Gladly would.

[3] Broth.

[4] Two ravens (crows) complaining (talking).

[5] Turf.

[6] Neck bone.

[7] Thatch.

[8] The feast of St. Martin (November 11).

[9] If.

[10] Slowly.

[11] Don't you remember?

[12] Made.

[13] The subject matter of this selection (although not the title, which means "The lovely lady without pity") was adapted from a medieval poem. The plight of a mortal destroyed by love for a supernatural *femme fatale* has often been told in fairy tale, ballad, and myth. Keats's treatment is highly romantic.

[14] Coarse marsh grass.

[15] Girdle (sash).

[16] Grotto, cave.

[17] Last.

[18] In bondage, under a spell.

[19] Gloaming (twilight).

[20] A legendary Greek hero, Ulysses is the hero of Homer's *Odyssey,* a major figure in Homer's *Iliad,* and a minor one in Dante's *Divine Comedy.* After ten years at the siege of Troy, Ulysses sailed for home, but he was forced to wander for ten more years before reaching his home (Ithaca), his wife, and his son. According to Dante, Ulysses became restless and bored and wished to set out on another voyage. In his old age, he persuaded some of his subjects to accompany him on a voyage of exploration. *The Inferno,* 36: "Consider your origin; ye were not formed to live like brutes but to follow virtue and knowledge."

[21] Measure out rewards and punishments.

[22] Dregs, sediment (that is, the end).

[23] Driving showers of spray and rain.

[24] A group of seven stars in the constellation Taurus; they were associated with the rainy season.

[25] Unpolished, dull from lack of use.

[26] Suitable, proper.

[27] Ulysses' companions.

[28] The outer ocean or stream which, in ancient Grecian ideas of the structure of the universe, surrounded the flat surface of the earth and into which the stars descended.

[29] Elysium, or the Islands of the Blessed, where heroes such as Achilles (line 64) were thought to enjoy life after death. These islands were imagined as being in a far western ocean.

[30] This poem is based on incidents in the life of the Duke of Ferrara (an old and proud city in northern Italy). The Duke's first wife, Lucrezia, a young girl, died in 1561 after three years of marriage. Following her death, the Duke negotiated through an agent to marry a niece of the Count of Tyrol, who lived in Innsbruck.

[31] Brother Pandolph, an imaginary artist-monk.

[32] Dared.

[33] In fact.

[34] Browning said that he meant "the commands were that she should be put to death, or he might have had her shut up in a convent."

[35] Generosity.

[36] Claim.

[37] An imaginary sculptor, mentioned here as having cast in bronze a statue of the god of the sea.

[38] A private soldier, one assigned to close up the files (ranks).

[39] To assemble (muster).

[40] Noncommissioned officer who carried the regimental colors (flag).

[41] The soldiers, facing inwards, have formed the four sides of a square.

[42] Customs applied to a disgraced soldier.

[43] In English pubs, "bitter beer" is a favorite drink. Here, "bitter" is a grim play on words.

[44] A lively air played after the funeral march.

[45] This is one of the "free verse" poems published in the author's *Spoon River Anthology* (1915). Masters presents a series of frank, realistic epitaphs in which some 250 persons buried in a small Midwestern town speak from their graves and tell the stories of their lives.

[46] A vigorous, courageous woman, Lucinda Matlock has only scorn for persons she considers too weak to embrace life and live it to the full.

[47] The name "Richard Cory" is both romantic and aristocratic, characteristics reflecting the central figure and Robinson's life-long interest in romance. The poet's elliptical style is so sparse and economical that we can only surmise the causes of Richard Cory's disillusionment and despair.

[48] Robinson's diction does not often belong to the language of common speech. It is precise, chiseled, and image-provoking: "gentleman from sole to crown," "clean favored," "imperially slim," "fluttered pulses," "glittered when he walked."

[49] This poem is "spoken" by one of the three wise men (the Magi) who came "from the east" to Bethlehem (near Jerusalem) to pay homage to the infant Jesus. For a Biblical account, see Matthew 11.

[50] The first lines of this poem are adapted from a sermon on the Nativity preached by Lancelot Andrewes (1555–1626) on Christmas Day, 1622. The appropriate lines:

> It was no summer progress. A cold coming they had of it at this time of the year, just the worst time of the year to take a journey, and especially a long journey. The ways deep, the weather sharp, the days short, the sun farthest off, . . . the very dead of winter.

[51] The second stanza begins with a series of images suggesting freshness, rebirth, renewal. Gone are the cold, the long distances, the hardships of the first stanza. Gone are the regrets over ease and luxury left behind; gone are the discouragements, the lack of support for their journey, their doubt and suspicion. The first stanza consists of simple enumeration (count the number of *ands*) without any suggestion of hope for success and fulfillment. But now, the rhythm flows more easily. Dawn and moisture and a smell of vegetation meet the travelers. Running water brings a sense of vitality; this, the trees, the galloping horse, and the vine-leaves suggest fruitfulness, freedom, and hope.

[52] Behind the narrator's statement of facts, the reader knows that the symbols and images Eliot uses have particular significance. The "three trees" may connote the three crosses upon the center one of which Christ was crucified. The "six hands" suggest three men playing dice, that is, the soldiers "casting lots" for Christ's garments. The "pieces of silver" recall Judas' betrayal of Christ for thirty pieces of silver. The Christian symbolism of the vine ("I am the true Vine," said Jesus) is contradicted by, and contrasted with, "feet kicking the empty wineskins." The "temperate valley" is filled with ironic signs.

[53] The quest ends not in failure but in a sense of frustration, of bewilderment. The word "satisfactory" suggests "merely adequate" and conveys a tone of disappointment, a feeling that something momentous has happened but the narrator is not certain just what.

[54] A ballad is a simple narrative of folk origin. A literary, or art, ballad is one of known authorship that presents a romantic story situation with some degree of literary polish and sophistication. This selection uses the question-and-answer technique of the popular ballad; it is written in strongly rhythmic iambic tetrameter; it employs much repetition.

[55] Although it is not necessary for an understanding of the poem, Jarrell's note is illuminating: "An American soldier is speaking after the capture of one of the great German

death camps. The Jews, under the Nazis, were made to wear the badge of a yellow star. The white star of David is set over Jewish graves just as the cross is set over Christian graves."

[56] Useful, beneficial.

[57] Refuge, retreat.

[58] This selection is a questioning of human guilt in wartime. The greatest loss, the poet feels, is the individual's forfeiture of his humanity, not necessarily his life, whether the loss is caused by free choice or by force.

Light Verse and Songs

Edward Lear[1]

THE OWL AND THE PUSSYCAT

The Owl and the Pussy-Cat went to sea
In a beautiful pea-green boat;
They took some honey, and plenty of money
Wrapped up in a five-pound note.
The Owl looked up to the stars above,
And sang to a small guitar,
"O lovely Pussy, O Pussy, my love,
What a beautiful Pussy you are,
You are,
You are!
What a beautiful Pussy you are!"

Pussy said to the Owl, "You elegant fowl,
How charmingly sweet you sing!
Oh! let us be married; too long we have tarried;
But what shall we do for a ring?"
They sailed away, for a year and a day,
To the land where the bong-tree[2] grows;
And there in a wood a Piggy-wig stood,
With a ring at the end of his nose,
His nose,
His nose,
With a ring at the end of his nose.

"Dear Pig, are you willing to sell for one shilling
Your ring?" Said the Piggy, "I will."
So they took it away, and were married next day
By the Turkey who lives on the hill.
They dined on mince and slices of quince,
Which they ate with a runcible spoon;[3]
And hand in hand, on the edge of the sand,
They danced by the light of the moon,
The moon,
The moon,
They danced by the light of the moon.

Lewis Carroll[4]

THE CROCODILE[5]

How doth the little crocodile
Improve his shining tail,
And pour the waters of the Nile
On every shining scale!

How cheerfully he seems to grin,
How neatly spreads his claws,
And welcomes little fishes in
With gently smiling jaws.

FATHER WILLIAM[6]

"You are old, Father William," the young man said,
"And your hair has become very white,
And yet you incessantly stand on your head—
Do you think, at your age, it is right?"

"In my youth," Father William replied to his son,
"I feared it might injure the brain;
But now that I'm perfectly sure I have none,
Why, I do it again and again."

"You are old," said the youth, "as I mentioned before,
And have grown uncommonly fat;
Yet you turned a back-somersault in at the door—
Pray, what is the reason of that?"

"In my youth," said the sage, as he shook his gray locks,
"I kept all my limbs very supple
By the use of this ointment—one shilling the box—
Allow me to sell you a couple."

"You are old," said the youth, "and your jaws are too weak
For anything tougher than suet;[7]
Yet you finished the goose, with the bones and the beak;
Pray, how did you manage to do it?"

"In my youth," said his father, "I took to the law,
And argued each case with my wife;
And the muscular strength which it gave to my jaw
Has lasted the rest of my life."

"You are old," said the youth, "one would hardly suppose
That your eye was as steady as ever;
Yet you balanced an eel on the end of your nose—
What made you so awfully clever?"

"I have answered three questions, and that is enough,"
Said his father; "don't give yourself airs!
Do you think I can listen all day to such stuff?
Be off, or I'll kick you downstairs!"

JABBERWOCKY[8]

'Twas brillig, and the slithy[9] toves
Did gyre and gimble in the wabe;
All mimsy were the borogoves,
And the mome raths outgrabe.

"Beware the Jabberwock, my son!
The jaws that bite, the claws that catch!
Beware the Jubjub bird, and shun
The frumious Bandersnatch!"

He took his vorpal sword in hand;
Long time the manxome foe he sought—
So rested he by the Tumtum tree,
And stood awhile in thought.

And, as in uffish thought he stood,
The Jabberwock, with eyes of flame,
Came whiffling through the tulgey wood,
And burbled as it came!

One, two! One, two! And through and through
The vorpal blade went snicker-snack!
He left it dead, and with its head
He went galumphing back.

"And hast thou slain the Jabberwock?
Come to my arms, my beamish boy!
O frabjous day! Callooh! Callay!"
He chortled in his joy.

'Twas brillig, and the slithy toves
Did gyre and gimble in the wabe;
All mimsy were the borogoves,
And the mome raths outgrabe.

HUMPTY DUMPTY'S EXPLANATION OF "JABBERWOCKY"[10]

"You seem very clever at explaining words, Sir," said Alice. "Would you kindly tell me the meaning of the poem *Jabberwocky?*"

"Let's hear it," said Humpty Dumpty. "I can explain all the poems that ever were invented—and a good many that haven't been invented just yet."

This sounded very hopeful, so Alice repeated the first verse:

" 'Twas brillig, and the slithy toves
    Did gyre and gimble in the wabe;
All mimsy were the borogoves,
    And the mome raths outgrabe."

"That's enough to begin with," Humpty Dumpty interrupted: "there are plenty of hard words there. 'Brillig' means four o'clock in the afternoon—the time when you begin *broiling* things for dinner."

"That'll do very well," said Alice: "and 'slithy'?"

"Well, 'slithy' means 'lithe and slimy.' 'Lithe' is the same as 'active.' You see it's like a portmanteau—there are two meanings packed up into one word."

"I see it now," Alice remarked thoughtfully: "and what are 'toves'?"

"Well, 'toves' are something like badgers—they're something like lizards—and they're something like corkscrews."

"They must be very curious creatures."

"They are that," said Humpty Dumpty: "also they make their nests under sundials—also they live on cheese."

"And what's to 'gyre' and to 'gimble'?"

"To 'gyre' is to go round and round like a gyroscope. To 'gimble' is to make holes like a gimlet."

"And the 'wabe' is the grass plot round a sundial, I suppose?" said Alice, surprised at her own ingenuity.

"Of course it is. It's called 'wabe,' you know, because it goes a long way before it, and a long way behind it——"

"And a long way beyond it on each side," Alice added.

"Exactly so. Well then, 'mimsy' is 'flimsy and miserable' (there's another portmanteau for you). And a 'borogove' is a thin shabby-looking bird with its feathers sticking out all round—something like a live mop."

"And then 'mome raths'?" said Alice. "If I'm not giving you too much trouble."

"Well, a 'rath' is a sort of green pig: but 'mome' I'm not certain about. I think it's short for 'from home'—meaning that they'd lost their way, you know."

"And what does 'outgrabe" mean?"

"Well, 'outgribing' is something between bellowing and whistling, with a kind of sneeze in the middle: however, you'll hear it done, maybe—down in the wood yonder—and when you've once heard it you'll be *quite* content. Who's been repeating all that hard stuff to you?"

"I read it in a book," said Alice.

William Schwenck Gilbert[11]

THE AESTHETE[12]

If you're anxious for to shine in the high
    aesthetic line as a man of culture rare,
You must get up all the germs of the
    transcendental terms, and plant
    them everywhere.
You must lie upon the daisies, and discourse in novel phrases of your
    complicated state of mind,
The meaning doesn't matter if it's only
    idle chatter of a transcendental
    kind.
        And everyone will say,
        As you walk your mystic way,
"If this young man expresses himself in
    terms too deep for *me*,
Why, what a very singularly deep young
    man this deep young man must
    be!"

Be eloquent in praise of the very dull old
    ways which have long since
    passed away,
And convince 'em, if you can, that the
    reign of good Queen Anne was
    Culture's palmiest day.[13]

Of course you will pooh-pooh whatever's fresh and new, and declare it's crude and mean,
For Art stopped short in the cultivated court of the Empress Josephine.[14]
And everyone will say,
As you walk your mystic way,
"If that's not good enough for him which is good enough for *me*,
Why, what a very cultivated kind of youth this kind of youth must be!"

Then a sentimental passion of a vegetable fashion[15] must excite your languid spleen,
An attachment *à la* Plato[16] for a bashful young potato, or a not-too-French French bean!
Though the Philistines[17] may jostle, you will rank as an apostle in the high aesthetic band,
If you walk down Piccadilly[18] with a poppy or a lily in your medieval hand.
And everyone will say,
As you walk your flowery way,
"If he's content with a vegetable love, which would certainly not suit *me*,
Why, what a most particularly pure young man this pure young man must be!"

❁

Agnes Rogers Allen

LINES TO A DAUGHTER—ANY DAUGHTER[19]

One of the things that you really should know
Is when to say "yes," and when to say "no."
It's terribly, terribly risky to guess
At when to say "no" and when to say "yes."
Girls who are slaving for Woolworth and Kress
Lament for the day when they might have said "yes,"
Others are crying at night apropos
Of moments when clearly they should have said "no."

There aren't any textbooks, there aren't many rules,
The subject's neglected in orthodox schools.
Experience helps, but you seldom remember
Your April mistakes by the first of November.
You can't be consistent; there's often a reason
For changing your mind with a change in the season.
You may be quite right in accepting at seven
Suggestions you'd better refuse at eleven.

Perhaps you'll consider these tentative hints:
"No" to a dirndl of highly glazed chintz,
"Yes" to the bashful young man at the dance,
"No" to the man who's been living in France,
"Yes" to a walk in the park in the rain,
"Yes" if he asks for a chance to explain,
"No" to all slacks unless you're too thin,
"No" to that impulse to telephone him,
"Yes" to a baby, and "no" to a bore,
"No" if you're asked if you've heard it before,
"Yes" to the friend when she says, "Don't you think
Rabbit is just as becoming as mink?"
"Yes" to a Saturday, "no" to a Monday,
"Yes" to a salad and "no" to a sundae,
"No" to a wastrel and "yes" to a ranger,
"No" to a toady, and "yes" to a stranger

(That is, providing you use some discretion),
"No" to three cocktails in rapid succession,
"No" to magenta and chocolate brown,
"Yes" to a whisper and "no" to a frown,
"No" if he's misunderstood by his wife,
"Yes" if you want it the rest of your life.

Remember, my darling, careers and caresses
Depend on our choices of "noes" and of "yesses."

Dorothy Parker

RÉSUMÉ

Razors pain you;
Rivers are damp;
Acids stain you;
And drugs cause cramp.
Guns aren't lawful;
Nooses give;
Gas smells awful;
You might as well live.

E. E. Cummings

OLD AGE STICKS

old age sticks
up Keep
Off
signs) &

youth yanks them
down (old
age
cries No

Tres) & (pas)
youth laughs
(sing
old age

scolds Forbid
den Stop
Must
n't Don't

&) youth goes
right on
gr
owing old

SWING LOW, SWEET CHARIOT[20]

Swing low, sweet chariot,
Comin' for to carry me home;
Swing low, sweet chariot,
Comin' for to carry me home.
(*Repeat as Refrain*)

I looked over Jordan[21] and what did I see,
Comin' for to carry me home?
A band of angels comin' aftah me,
Comin' for to carry me home.
(*Refrain*)

If you git there before I do,
Comin' for to carry me home,
Tell all my frien's I'm a-comin', too,
Comin' for to carry me home.
(*Refrain*)

The brightes' day that ever I saw,
Comin' for to carry me home,
When Jesus washed my sins away
Comin' for to carry me home.
(*Refrain*)

I'm sometimes up an' sometimes down,
Comin' for to carry me home,
But still my soul feel heavenly-boun',
Comin' for to carry me home.
(*Refrain*)

NOBODY KNOWS DE TROUBLE I'VE SEEN

Nobody knows de trouble I've seen;
Nobody knows but Jesus.
Nobody knows de trouble I've seen;
Oh yes, Lord.

Sometimes I'm up, sometimes I'm down;
Oh yes, Lord.
Sometimes I'm almost to de groun',
Oh yes, Lord.

Although you see me gettin' 'long so,
Oh, yes, Lord.
I got my troubles here below—
Oh yes, Lord.

Nobody knows de trouble I've seen;
Nobody knows but Jesus.
Nobody knows de trouble I've seen;
Oh yes, Lord.

JESSE JAMES[22]

Jesse James was a lad that killed a-many a man;
He robbed the Danville train.
But that dirty little coward that shot Mr. Howard
Has laid poor Jesse in his grave.

Poor Jesse had a wife to mourn for his life
Three children, they were brave.
But that dirty little coward that shot Mr. Howard
Has laid poor Jesse in his grave.

It was Robert Ford, that dirty little coward,
I wonder how he does feel,
For he ate of Jesse's bread and he slept in Jesse's bed,
Then laid poor Jesse in his grave.

Jesse was a man, a friend to the poor,
He never would see a man suffer pain;
And with his brother Frank he robbed the Chicago bank,
And stopped the Glendale train.

It was his brother Frank that robbed the Gallatin bank,
And carried the money from the town;
It was in this very place that they had a little race,
For they shot Captain Sheets to the ground.

They went to the crossing not very far from there,
And there they did the same;
With the agent on his knees, he delivered up the keys
To the outlaws, Frank and Jesse James.

It was on Wednesday night, the moon was shining bright,
They robbed the Glendale train;
The people they did say, for many miles away,
It was robbed by Frank and Jesse James.

It was on Saturday night, Jesse was at home
Talking with his family brave,
Robert Ford came along like a thief in the night
And laid poor Jesse in his grave.

The people held their breath when they heard of Jesse's death,
And wondered how he ever came to die.
It was one of the gang called little Robert Ford,
He shot poor Jesse on the sly.

Jesse went to his rest with his hand on his breast,
The devil will be upon his knee.
He was born one day in the county of Clay
And came of a solitary race.

This song was made by Billy Gashade,
As soon as the news did arrive;
He said there was no man with the law in his hand
Who could take Jesse James when alive.

THE BIG ROCK CANDY MOUNTAIN[23]

One ev'ning as the sun went down
And the jungle fire was burning,
Down the track came a hobo humming,
And he said, "Boys, I'm not turning.
I'm headed for a land that's far away,
Beside the crystal fountain.
I'll see you all this coming fall
On the Big Rock Candy Mountain."

Chorus

On the Big Rock Candy Mountain,
There's a land that's fair and bright,
Where the handouts grow on bushes
And you sleep out ev'ry night,
Where the boxcars all are empty
And the sun shines ev'ry day—
Oh, the birds and the bees and the cigaret trees,
The rock-and-rye springs where the whang-doodle sings,
On the Big Rock Candy Mountain.

On the Big Rock Candy Mountain,
All the cops have wooden legs,
And the bulldogs all have rubber teeth,
And the hens lay softboiled eggs.
The farmers' trees are full of fruit,

And the barns are full of hay.
Oh, I'm bound to go where there ain't no snow,
Where the sleet don't fall and the wind don't blow,
On the Big Rock Candy Mountain.

On the Big Rock Candy Mountain,
You never change your socks,
And the little streams of alkyhol
Come trickling down the rocks.
The shacks all have to tip their hats
And the railroad bulls are blind,
There's a lake of stew and of whisky, too,
You can paddle all around in a big canoe,
On the Big Rock Candy Mountain.

On the Big Rock Candy Mountain,
The jails are made of tin,
And you can bust right out again
As soon as they put you in.
There ain't no shorthandled shovels,
No axes, saws or picks—
I'm a-going to stay where you sleep all day—
Oh, they boiled in oil the inventor of toil
On the Big Rock Candy Mountain.

Oh, come with me, and we'll go see
The Big Rock Candy Mountain.

THE OLD CHISHOLM TRAIL[24]

Come along, boys, and listen to my tale,
I'll tell you of my troubles on the old Chisholm Trail.

(*Refrain*)
Coma ti yi youpy, youpy yea, youpy yea,
Coma ti yi youpy, youpy yea.

I started up the trail October twenty-third,
I started up the trail with the 2-U[25] herd.

Oh, a ten-dollar hoss and a forty-dollar saddle,
And I'm goin' to punchin' Texas cattle.

I woke up one morning on the old Chisholm Trail,
Rope in my hand and a cow by the tail.

I'm up in the mornin' afore daylight
And afore I sleep the moon shines bright.

Old Ben Bolt was a blamed good boss,
But he'd go to see the girls on a sore-backed hoss.

Old Ben Bolt was a fine old man
And you'd know there was whiskey wherever he'd land.

It's cloudy in the West, a-looking like rain,
And my damned old slicker's in the wagon again.

Crippled my hoss, I don't know how,
Ropin' at the horns of a 2-U cow.

We hit Caldwell and we hit her on the fly,
We bedded down the cattle on the hill close by.

No chaps, no slicker, and it's pouring down rain,
And I swear, by god, I'll never night-herd again.

Feet in the stirrups and seat in the saddle,
I hung and rattled with them long-horn cattle.

Last night I was on guard and the leader broke the ranks,
I hit my horse down the shoulders, and I spurred him in the flanks.

The wind commenced to blow, and the rain began to fall,
Hit looked, by grab, like we was goin' to lose 'em all.

Foot in the stirrup and hand on the horn,
Best damned cowboy ever was born.

We rounded 'em up and put 'em on the cars,
And that was the last of the old Two Bars.

Oh it's bacon and beans most every day,—
I'd as soon be a-eatin' prairie hay.

I'm on my best horse and I'm goin' at a run,
I'm the quickest shootin' cowboy that ever pulled a gun.

I went to the wagon to get my roll,
To come back to Texas, dad-burn my soul.

I went to the boss to draw my roll,
He had it figgered out I was nine dollars in the hole.

With my knees in the saddle and my seat in the sky,
I'll quit punching cows in the sweet by and by.

Coma ti yi youpy, youpy yea, youpy yea,
Coma ti yi youpy, youpy yea.

GIT ALONG, LITTLE DOGIES[26]

As I was a-walking one morning for pleasure,
I spied a cow-puncher a-riding along;
His hat was throwed back and his spurs were a-jinglin',
As he approached me a-singin' this song:

(*Refrain*)
Whoopee ti yi yo, git along, little dogies,
It's your misfortune and none of my own;
Whoopee ti yi yo, git along, little dogies,
For you know Wyoming will be your new home.

Early in the springtime we'll round up the dogies,
Slap on their brands, and bob off their tails;[27]
Round up our horses, load up the chuck wagon,[28]
Then throw those dogies upon the trail.

It's whooping and yelling and driving the dogies,
Oh, how I wish you would go on;
It's whooping and punching and go on, little dogies,
For you know Wyoming will be your new home.

Some of the boys goes up the trail for pleasure,
But that's where they git it most awfully wrong;
For you haven't any idea the trouble they give us
When we go driving them dogies along.

When the night comes on and we hold them on the bed-ground,
These little dogies that roll on so slow;
Roll up the herd and cut out the strays,
And roll the little dogies that never rolled before.

Your mother she was raised way down in Texas,
Where the jimson weed and sand burrs grow;
Now we'll fill you up on prickly pear and cholla[29]
Till you are ready for the trail to Idaho.

Oh, you'll be soup for Uncle Sam's Injuns;[30]
"It's beef, heap beef," I hear them cry.
Git along, git along, git along, little dogies,
You're going to be beef steers by and by.

BUFFALO SONG[31]

In this way came the buffalo tracks
the buffalo tracks that we see
that everywhere we see

the tracks of those feet were made by life in this way
life that came
in this way

Life to the unborn
first in the belly of the mother
life to the unborn nose
to the unborn face, to the unborn eyes,
life to the unborn horns
life to the living being

Now the little calf is born
filled with life and motion
born filled with life and motion
born the newborn yellow calf
standing on its feet and walks

leaving tracks
leaving footprints
buflalo buffalo
leaving tracks

Notes

[1] Edward Lear was a landscape painter and a constant writer of easy, rollicking, humorous verses and limericks. He classified all of his writing as "nonsense pure and absolute," although readers continue to find good sense in the drollery, fantasy, and absurdity of his verse. Some of his work, including "The Owl and the Pussy-Cat," has attained the status of nursery classics.

[2] A nonsensical word coined by the author.

[3] A spoon-shaped fork with a cutting edge.

[4] Charles Lutwidge Dodgson is better known by his pen name of Lewis Carroll. He was a lay officer of the Anglican church and a lecturer on mathematics at Oxford University. Despite his scholarly treatises, Dodgson has been forgotten, but Lewis Carroll had a streak of whimsy and a fertility of imagination that provided his stories and poems with a charm and individuality that are now considered classic. Carroll knew poetry as well as he knew mathematics or the imaginative world of children; he was adept at writing caricatures of the kinds of poems his little real-life friend Alice Liddell had to learn to "make her good." When he put his friend into *Alice in Wonderland* (1865) and *Through the Looking-Glass* (1871), he immortalized her and himself.

[5] These two quatrains are a parody of a poem by Isaac Watts (1674–1748), an English theologian and hymn writer. The first four lines of Watts's poem:

How doth the little busy bee
Improve each shining hour,
And gather honey all the day
From every opening flower!

[6] This selection is a parody of *The Old Man's Comforts and How He Gained Them,* by Robert Southey, 1774–1843. Stanzas 1 and 4 of Southey's poem:

"You are old, Father William," the young man cried,
"The few locks which are left you are gray;
You are hale, Father William, a hearty old man,—
Now tell me the reason, I pray."

"In the days of my youth," Father William replied,
"I remembered that youth could not last;
I thought of the future, whatever I did,
That I never might grieve for the past."

[7] Fatty tissue used in cookery or processed to yield tallow.

[8] This classic example of nonsense verse is from *Through the Looking-Glass,* Chapter 1. It exhibits a mathematician's fondness for puzzles and a literary person's delight in word games.

[9] Concerning pronunciation, Carroll later wrote: "The *i* in *slithy* is long, as in *writhe;* and *toves* is pronounced so as to rhyme with *groves.* Again, the first *o* in *borogroves* is pronounced like the *o* in *borrow.*"

[10] From Chapter 6 of *Through the Looking-Glass.*

[11] William Schwenck Gilbert (1836–1919) is best known for the whimsical light operas he wrote in collaboration with Sir Arthur Sullivan (1842–1900). He was an attorney, but at the age of twenty-five he began to publish humorous verse that was soon to make him famous. "All humor," Gilbert once remarked, "is based upon a grave and quasi-respectful treatment of the ludicrous." The rollicking songs from his comic operas satirized Victorian attitudes toward the navy, the legal profession, the church, and other institutions. Underneath the surface absurdity of Gilbert's verse lies a substantial amount of logic and common sense.

[12] This selection is a caricature of such Victorian aesthetes as Oscar Wilde (1854–1900), Irish dramatist, wit, and critic. An aesthete is one who has, or claims to have, a high degree of sensitivity toward the beauties of art and nature, together with a scornful indifference to

practical matters. This selection is sung by Bunthorne, a fleshly poet, in Gilbert and Sullivan's *Patience* (1881).

[13] Literature and social customs in the reign of Queen Anne (1703–1714) were marked by an insistence on form that Gilbert found tedious and boring.

[14] The wife of Napoleon I and Empress of the French (1763–1814).

[15] Wilde was a vegetarian.

[16] A Platonic love, one that involves only a spiritual comradeship.

[17] Persons lacking culture and refinement.

[18] A London street.

[19] This poem, light and rollicking in tone, has undertones and meanings of some significance. Choosing the offered "suggestions" for individual selection and rejection should concern every reader.

[20] The words and music of this song go back to a camp meeting hymn entitled "Roll Call," the first stanza of which resembles the third stanza of this spiritual:

If you get there before I do,
When the gen'ral roll is call'd we'll be there;
Look out for me, I'm coming too,
When the gen'ral roll is called we'll be there.

Unable to express their feelings directly and openly, Negroes often stated their hopes and frustrations in Biblical terms, stories, and lyrics. Chariots are many times mentioned in the Bible; possibly the closest parallel to this spiritual is found in 2 Kings, 2:11: "There appeared a chariot of fire, and horses of fire . . . and Elijah went up by a whirlwind into heaven."

[21] A river that flows between Israel and Jordan through a part of its two-hundred-mile course, a symbol of the dividing line between this life and the next.

[22] Jesse Woodson James (1847–1882) was born and reared on a Missouri farm. After the Civil War, he and his brother, Frank, led what became the most notorious gang of robbers in American history. They robbed banks and held up trains in several Midwestern states, but popular sentiment was in their favor. However, a large reward was offered for their capture, dead or alive. Jesse James assumed the name of Thomas Howard and hid out, but he was killed by one of his accomplices, Robert Ford. (Frank, never convicted, later became a respectable citizen.) Jesse, murdered and thus a martyr, has become a legendary American hero.

[23] Among people constantly along railroad tracks in earlier days were hobos, who had their own songs. Some of these songs were modifications of popular tunes and ballads; others were mockingly sung to the music of revival hymns which these tramps, or vagrants, heard upon their infrequent stays in mission shelters. In this selection, an uncouth but imaginative singer narrates his vision of a far away place where good weather, an absence of policemen and railroad "dicks," and plentiful food and drink make a paradise for hobos.

[24] The Chisholm Trail ran from the Red River basin in Texas through Indian Territory to various railheads in Kansas. It was a main route for cattle bound for market on new transcontinental railways.

[25] A cattle brand.

[26] The term *dogie,* sometimes spelled "dogy," refers to a young bull calf.

[27] Rounded-up calves were gelded and identified by brand before being driven off to market.

[28] The cowboy slang term for food was "chuck"; a chuck wagon was the commissary of cattle herders on the move.

[29] Spiny, treelike cacti common to the southwestern United States.

[30] Government purchase of beef cattle for Indians on reservations provided a steady market for ranchers.

[31] It is easy to forget that the first Americans were Indians who had lived in what is now the United States long before the settlements of 1607 and 1620 or even before the discovery of 1492. This selection, translated from an Indian tongue, is a truly "native" American song, lyrical in its plaintive comment on creatures who preceded even Indians on western plains.

Lyric Poems

Sir Philip Sidney

WITH HOW SAD STEPS (FROM "ASTROPHEL AND STELLA")

31

With how sad steps, O Moon, thou climb'st the skies!
How silently, and with how wan[1] a face!
What, may it be that even in heavenly place
That busy archer[2] his sharp arrows tries?
Sure, if that long-with-love-acquainted eyes
Can judge of love, thou feel'st a lover's case.
I read it in thy looks; thy languished grace,
To me that feel the like, thy state descries.[3]
Then, even of fellowship, O Moon, tell me,
Is constant love deemed there but want of wit?[4]
Are beauties there as proud as here they be?
Do they above love to be loved, and yet
Those lovers scorn whom that love doth possess?
Do they call virtue there ungratefulness?

Christopher Marlowe

THE PASSIONATE SHEPHERD TO HIS LOVE

Come live with me, and be my love;
And we will all the pleasures prove
That hills and valleys, dales[5] and fields,
Woods, or steepy mountain yields.

And we will sit upon the rocks,
Seeing the shepherds feed their flocks
By shallow rivers, to whose falls
Melodious birds sing madrigals.[6]

And I will make thee beds of roses,
And a thousand fragrant posies;
A cap of flowers, and a kirtle[7]
Embroidered all with leaves of myrtle;

A gown made of the finest wool
Which from our pretty lambs we pull;
Fair-lined slippers for the cold,
With buckles of the purest gold;

A belt of straw and ivy-buds,
With coral clasps and amber studs;
And if these pleasures may thee move,
Come live with me, and be my love.

The shepherd-swains[8] shall dance and sing
For thy delight each May morning;
If these delights thy mind may move,
Then live with me, and be my love.

Sir Walter Raleigh

THE NYMPH'S REPLY TO THE SHEPHERD

If all the world and love were young,
And truth in every shepherd's tongue,
These pretty pleasures might me move,
To live with thee and be thy love.

But time drives flocks from field to fold,
When rivers rage, and rocks grow cold;
And Philomel[9] becometh dumb;
The rest complains of cares to come.

The flowers do fade, and wanton[10] fields
To wayward Winter reckoning yields;
A honey tongue, a heart of gall,[11]
Is fancy's spring, but sorrow's fall.

Thy gowns, thy shoes, thy beds of roses,
Thy cap, thy kirtle, and thy posies,[12]
Soon break, soon wither, soon forgotten,
In folly ripe, in reason rotten.

Thy belt of straw and ivy buds,
Thy coral clasps and amber studs,
All these in me no means can move,
To come to thee and be thy love.

But could youth last, and love still breed,
Had joys no date, nor age no need,
Then these delights my mind might move,
To live with thee and be thy love.

William Shakespeare

XV

When I consider every thing that grows
Holds in perfection but a little moment,
That this huge stage presenteth naught[13] but shows
Whereon the stars in secret influence[14] comment;
When I perceive that men as plants increase,
Cheered and checked[15] even by the self-same sky,
Vaunt[16] in their youthful sap, at height decrease,
And wear their brave state out of memory;
Then the conceit[17] of this inconstant stay
Sets you most rich in youth, before my sight,
Where wasteful Time debateth with Decay,
To change your day of youth to sullied[18] night;
And, all in war with Time for love of you,
As he takes from you, I engraft[19] you new.

XVIII

Shall I compare thee to a summer's day?
Thou art more lovely and more temperate:[20]
Rough winds do shake the darling buds of May,
And summer's lease hath all too short a date:

Sometimes too hot the eye of heaven shines,
And often is his gold complexion dimmed;
And every fair[21] from fair sometimes declines,
By chance or nature's changing course untrimmed;[22]
But thy eternal summer shall not fade,
Nor lose possession of that fair thou owest[23]
Nor shall Death brag thou wander'st in his shade,
When in eternal lines to time thou growest:
  So long as men can breathe or eyes can see,
  So long lives this,[24] and this gives life to thee.

XXIX

When, in disgrace with fortune and men's eyes,
I all alone beweep my outcast state,
And trouble deaf heaven with my bootless[25] cries,
And look upon myself and curse my fate,
Wishing me like to one more rich in hope,
Featured like him, like him with friends possessed,
Desiring this man's art and that man's scope,
With what I most enjoy contented least;
Yet in these thoughts myself almost despising,
Haply[26] I think on thee,—and then my state,[27]
Like to the lark at break of day arising
From sullen earth, sings hymns at heaven's gate;
  For thy sweet love remembered such wealth brings
  That then I scorn to change my state with kings.

CVI

When in the chronicle of wasted[28] time
I see descriptions of the fairest wights,[29]
And beauty making beautiful old rhyme
In praise of ladies dead and lovely knights,
Then, in the blazon[30] of sweet beauty's best,
Of hand, of foot, of lip, of eye, of brow,
I see their antique pen would have expressed
Even such a beauty as you master now.
So all their praises are but prophecies
Of this our time, all you prefiguring;
And, for[31] they looked but with divining eyes,
They had not skill enough your worth to sing:
  For we, which now behold these present days,
  Have eyes to wonder, but lack tongues to praise.

CXVI

Let me not to the marriage of true minds
Admit impediments.[32] Love is not love
Which alters when it alteration finds,
Or bends with the remover to remove:
O, no! it is an ever-fixèd mark
That looks on tempests and is never shaken;
It is the star to every wandering bark,
Whose worth's unknown, although his height be taken.[33]
Love's not Time's fool, though rosy lips and cheeks
Within his[34] bending sickle's compass[35] come;
Love alters not with his brief hours and weeks,
But bears it out even to the edge of doom.[36]
  If this be error and upon me proved,
  I never writ, nor no man ever loved.

Thomas Campion

NEVER LOVE UNLESS YOU CAN

Never love unless you can
Bear with all the faults of man;

Men sometimes will jealous be,
Though but little cause they see,
And hang the head, as discontent,
And speak what straight they will repent.

Men that but one saint adore
Make a show of love to more;
Beauty must be scorned in none,
Though but truly served in one;
For what is courtship but disguise?
True hearts may have dissembling[37] eyes.

Men when their affairs require
Must a while themselves retire,
Sometimes hunt, and sometimes hawk,
And not ever sit and talk.
If these and such like you can bear,
Then like, and love, and never fear.

John Donne[38]

THE BAIT

Come live with me and be my love,
And we will some new pleasures prove,
Of golden sands and crystal brooks,
With silken lines and silver hooks.

There will the river whispering run,
Warmed by thy eyes more than the sun.
And there th' enamored[39] fish will stay,
Begging themselves they may betray.

When thou wilt swim in that live bath,
Each fish, which every channel hath,
Will amorously to thee swim,
Gladder to catch thee, than thou him.

If thou, to be so seen, beest loath,[40]
By sun or moon, thou darkenest both;
And if myself have leave to see,
I need not their light, having thee.

Let others freeze with angling reeds,
And cut their legs with shells and weeds,
Or treacherously poor fish beset
With strangling snare, or windowy net.

Let coarse bold hands from slimy nest
The bedded fish in banks out-wrest,
Or curious traitors, sleave-silk flies,[41]
Bewitch poor fishes' wandering eyes.

For thee, thou needest no such deceit,
For thou thyself art thine own bait;
That fish that is not catched thereby,
Alas, is wiser far than I.

Robert Herrick

DELIGHT IN DISORDER

A sweet disorder in the dress
Kindles in clothes a wantonness;[42]
A lawn[43] about the shoulders thrown
Into a fine distraction;
An erring[44] lace, which here and there
Enthrals the crimson stomacher;[45]
A cuff neglectful, and thereby
Ribbons to flow confusèdly;
A winning wave (deserving note)
In the tempestuous petticoat;
A careless shoe-string, in whose tie
I see a wild civility:[46]
Do more bewitch me, than when art
Is too precise in every part.

UPON JULIA'S CLOTHES

Whenas[47] in silks my Julia goes,
Then, then, methinks, how sweetly flows
The liquefaction[48] of her clothes.

Next, when I cast mine eyes, and see
That brave[49] vibration, each way free,
O, how that glittering taketh me!

TO THE VIRGINS, TO MAKE MUCH OF TIME

Gather ye rosebuds while ye may,
Old Time is still a-flying,
And this same flower that smiles today
Tomorrow will be dying.

The glorious lamp of heaven, the sun,
The higher he's a-getting,
The sooner will his race be run,
And nearer he's to setting.

That age is best which is the first,
When youth and blood are warmer;

But being spent, the worse, and worst
Times still succeed the former.

Then be not coy, but use your time,
And while ye may, go marry;
For having lost but once your prime,
You may forever tarry.

George Herbert

THE COLLAR[50]

I struck the board[51] and cried, No more!
I will abroad.
What? Shall I ever sigh and pine?
My lines and life are free, free as the road,
Loose as the wind, as large as store.[52]
Shall I be still in suit?[53]
Have I no harvest but a thorn
To let me blood, and not restore
What I have lost with cordial[54] fruit?
Sure there was wine
Before my sighs did dry it; there was corn
Before my tears did drown it.
Is the year only lost to me?
Have I no bays[55] to crown it?
No flowers, no garlands gay? All blasted?
All wasted?
Not so, my heart! But there is fruit,
And thou hast hands.
Recover all thy sigh-blown age
On double pleasures. Leave thy cold dispute
Of what is fit and not. Forsake thy cage,
Thy rope of sands,
Which petty thoughts have made, and made to thee
Good cable, to enforce and draw,[56]
And be thy law,
While thou didst wink[57] and wouldst not see.

Away! Take heed!
I will abroad.
Call in thy death's head[58] there. Tie up thy fears.
He that forbears
To suit and serve his need
Deserves his load.
But as I raved and grew more fierce and wild
At every word,
Methought I heard one calling, Child!
And I replied, My Lord.

Edmund Waller

ON A GIRDLE

That which her slender waist confined,
Shall now my joyful temples bind;
No monarch but would give his crown,
His arms might do what this has done.

It was my heaven's extremest sphere,[59]
The pale[60] which held that lovely deer;
My joy, my grief, my hope, my love,
Did all within this circle move!

A narrow compass! and yet there
Dwelt all that's good, and all that's fair;
Give me but what this ribband bound,
Take all the rest the sun goes round!

GO, LOVELY ROSE!

Go, lovely rose!
Tell her that wastes her time and me
That now she knows,
When I resemble[61] her to thee,
How sweet and fair she seems to be.

Tell her that's young,
And shuns to have her graces spied,
That hadst thou sprung
In deserts, where no men abide,
Thou must have uncommended died.

Small is the worth
Of beauty from the light retired;
Bid her come forth,
Suffer herself to be desired,
And not blush so to be admired.

Then die! that she
The common fate of all things rare
May read in thee;

How small a part of time they share
That are so wondrous sweet and fair!

John Milton

ON HIS HAVING ARRIVED AT THE AGE OF TWENTY-THREE

How soon hath Time, the subtle thief of youth,
Stolen on his wing my three and twentieth year!
My hasting days fly on with full career,
But my late spring no bud or blossom shew'th.
Perhaps my semblance[62] might deceive the truth
That I to manhood am arrived so near;
And inward ripeness doth much less appear,
That some more timely-happy spirits endu'th.[63]
Yet be it less or more, or soon or slow,
It shall be still in strictest measure even[64]
To that same lot, however mean or high,
Toward which Time leads me, and the will of Heaven;
All is, if I have grace to use it so,
As ever in my great Task-Master's eye.[65]

ON HIS BLINDNESS

When I consider how my light is spent
Ere half my days,[66] in this dark world and wide,
And that one talent[67] which is death to hide
Lodged with me useless, though my soul more bent[68]
To serve therewith my Maker, and present
My true account, lest he returning chide;
"Doth God exact day-labor, light denied?"
I fondly[69] ask. But Patience, to prevent[70]
That murmur, soon replies, "God doth not need
Either man's work or his own gifts. Who best
Bear his mild yoke,[71] they serve him best. His state
Is kingly: thousands at his bidding speed,
And post o'er land and ocean without rest;
They also serve who only stand and wait."

Sir John Suckling

THE CONSTANT LOVER

Out upon it, I have loved
Three whole days together!
And am like to love three more,
If it prove fair weather.

Time shall moult[72] away his wings,
Ere he shall discover
In the whole wide world again
Such a constant lover.

But the spite on't is, no praise
Is due at all to me:
Love with me had made no stays,[73]
Had it any been but she.

Had it any been but she,
And that very face,
There had been at least ere this
A dozen dozen in her place.

Andrew Marvell

TO HIS COY MISTRESS

Had we but world enough, and time,
This coyness, Lady, were no crime.
We would sit down, and think which way
To walk, and pass our long love's day.
Thou by the Indian Ganges' side
Shouldst rubies find; I by the tide
Of Humber would complain.[74] I would

Love you ten years before the Flood,[75]
And you should, if you please, refuse
Till the conversion of the Jews.[76]
My vegetable[77] love should grow
Vaster than empires and more slow;
An hundred years should go to praise
Thine eyes, and on thy forehead gaze;
Two hundred to adore each breast,
But thirty thousand to the rest;
An age at least to every part,
And the last age should show your heart.
For, Lady, you deserve this state,[78]
Nor would I love at lower rate.

But at my back I always hear
Time's wingèd chariot hurrying near;
And yonder all before us lie
Deserts of vast eternity.
Thy beauty shall no more be found,
Nor, in thy marble vault, shall sound
My echoing song; then worms shall try
That long-preserved virginity,
And your quaint[79] honor turn to dust,
And into ashes all my lust:
The grave's a fine and private place,
But none, I think, do there embrace.

Now therefore, while the youthful hue
Sits on thy skin like morning dew,
And while thy willing soul transpires[80]
At every pore with instant fires,[81]
Now let us sport us while we may,
And now, like amorous birds of prey,
Rather at once our time devour
Than languish in his slow-chapped[82] power.
Let us roll all our strength and all
Our sweetness up into one ball,
And tear our pleasures with rough strife
Thorough[83] the iron gates of life;
Thus, though we cannot make our sun
Stand still, yet we will make him run.

William Blake

THE LAMB

Little Lamb, who made thee?
Dost thou know who made thee?
Gave thee life, and bid thee feed
By the stream and o'er the mead;
Gave thee clothing of delight,
Softest clothing, woolly, bright;
Gave thee such a tender voice,
Making all the vales rejoice?
Little Lamb, who made thee?
Dost thou know who made thee?

Little Lamb, I'll tell thee,
Little Lamb, I'll tell thee:
He is callèd by thy name,
For he calls himself a Lamb.[84]
He is meek, and he is mild;
He became a little child.
I a child, and thou a lamb,
We are callèd by his name.
Little Lamb, God bless thee!
Little Lamb, God bless thee!

THE CLOD AND THE PEBBLE

"Love seeketh not Itself to please,
Nor for itself hath any care,
But for another gives its ease,
And builds a Heaven in Hell's despair."

So sang a little Clod of Clay
Trodden with the cattle's feet,
But a Pebble of the brook
Warbled out these meters meet:

"Love seeketh only Self to please,
To bind another to Its delight,
Joys in another's loss of ease,
And builds a Hell in Heaven's despite."

THE TIGER

Tiger! Tiger! burning bright
In the forests of the night,
What immortal hand or eye
Could frame thy fearful symmetry?

In what distant deeps or skies
Burnt the fire of thine eyes?
On what wings dare he aspire?
What the hand dare seize the fire?

And what shoulder, and what art,
Could twist the sinews of thy heart?
And when thy heart began to beat,
What dread hand? and what dread feet?

What the hammer? what the chain?
In what furnace was thy brain?

What the anvil? what dread grasp
Dare its deadly terrors clasp?

When the stars threw down their spears,
And watered heaven with their tears,
Did he smile his work to see?
Did he who made the Lamb make thee?

Tiger! Tiger! burning bright
In the forests of the night,
What immortal hand or eye
Dare frame thy fearful symmetry?

A POISON TREE

I was angry with my friend:
I told my wrath, my wrath did end.
I was angry with my foe:
I told it not, my wrath did grow.

And I watered it in fears,
Night and morning with my tears;
And I sunnéd it with smiles,
And with soft deceitful wiles.

And it grew both day and night,
Till it bore an apple bright;
And my foe beheld it shine,
And he knew that it was mine,

And into my garden stole
When the night had veiled the pole:
In the morning glad I see
My foe outstretched beneath the tree.

William Wordsworth

COMPOSED UPON WESTMINSTER BRIDGE, SEPTEMBER 3, 1802[85]

Earth has not anything to show more fair:
Dull would he be of soul who could pass by
A sight so touching in its majesty:
This City now doth like a garment wear
The beauty of the morning: silent, bare,
Ships, towers, domes, theatres, and temples lie
Open unto the fields, and to the sky,—
All bright and glittering in the smokeless air.
Never did sun more beautifully steep
In his first splendor, valley, rock, or hill;
Ne'er saw I, never felt, a calm so deep!
The river glideth at his own sweet will:
Dear God! the very houses seem asleep;
And all that mighty heart is lying still!

THE WORLD IS TOO MUCH WITH US

The world is too much with us: late and soon,
Getting and spending, we lay waste our powers.
Little we see in nature that is ours;
We have given our hearts away, a sordid boon![86]
This sea that bares her bosom to the moon,
The winds that will be howling at all hours,
And are up-gathered now like sleeping flowers;
For this, for everything, we are out of tune;
It moves us not.—Great God! I'd rather be
A pagan suckled in a creed outworn;
So might I, standing on this pleasant lea,
Have glimpses that would make me less forlorn;
Have sight of Proteus rising from the sea;
Or hear old Triton blow his wreathèd horn.[87]

Lord Byron

SHE WALKS IN BEAUTY[88]

She walks in beauty, like the night
  Of cloudless climes[89] and starry skies;
And all that's best of dark and bright
  Meet in her aspect and her eyes:
Thus mellowed to that tender light
  Which heaven to gaudy day denies.

One shade the more, one ray the less,
Had half impaired the nameless grace
Which waves in every raven tress,
Or softly lightens o'er her face;
Where thoughts serenely sweet express
How pure, how dear their dwelling-place.

And on that cheek, and o'er that brow,
So soft, so calm, yet eloquent,
The smiles that win, the tints that glow,
But tell of days in goodness spent,
A mind at peace with all below,
A heart whose love is innocent!

WHEN A MAN HATH NO FREEDOM TO FIGHT FOR AT HOME[90]

When a man hath no freedom to fight for at home,
Let him combat for that of his neighbors;
Let him think of the glories of Greece and of Rome,
And get knocked on his head for his labors.

To do good to mankind is the chivalrous plan,
And is always as nobly requited;[91]
Then battle for freedom wherever you can,
And, if not shot or hanged, you'll get knighted.

John Keats

WHEN I HAVE FEARS THAT I MAY CEASE TO BE

When I have fears that I may cease to be
Before my pen has gleaned my teeming brain,
Before high-piled books, in charact'ry,[92]
Hold like rich garners the full-ripened grain;
When I behold, upon the night's starred face,
Huge cloudy symbols of a high romance,
And think that I may never live to trace
Their shadows, with the magic hand of chance;
And when I feel, fair creature of an hour,
That I shall never look upon thee more,
Never have relish in the faery power
Of unreflecting love—then on the shore
Of the wide world I stand alone, and think,
Till love and fame to nothingness do sink.

ODE ON A GRECIAN URN[93]

1

Thou still unravished bride of quietness,
Thou foster-child of Silence and slow Time,
Sylvan[94] historian, who canst thus express
A flowery tale more sweetly than our rhyme:
What leaf-fringed legend haunts about thy shape
Of deities or mortals, or of both,
In Tempe or the dales of Arcady?[95]
What men or gods are these? What maidens loth?
What mad pursuit? What struggle to escape?
What pipes and timbrels? What wild ecstasy?

2

Heard melodies are sweet, but those unheard
Are sweeter; therefore, ye soft pipes,[96] play on;
Not to the sensual ear,[97] but, more endeared,
Pipe to the spirit ditties of no tone:
Fair youth, beneath the trees, thou canst not leave
Thy song, nor ever can those trees be bare;
Bold Lover, never, never canst thou kiss,
Though winning near the goal—yet, do not grieve;

She cannot fade, though thou hast not thy bliss,
For ever wilt thou love, and she be fair!

3

Ah, happy, happy boughs! that cannot shed
Your leaves, nor ever bid the Spring adieu;
And, happy melodist, unwearied,
For ever piping songs for ever new.
More happy love! more happy, happy love!
For ever warm and still to be enjoyed,
For ever panting, and for ever young;
All breathing human passion far above,
That leaves a heart high-sorrowful and cloyed,[98]
A burning forehead, and a parching tongue.

4

Who are these coming to the sacrifice?
To what green altar, O mysterious priest,
Lead'st thou that heifer lowing at the skies,
And all her silken flanks with garlands drest?
What little town by river or sea shore,
Or mountain-built with peaceful citadel,
Is emptied of this folk, this pious[99] morn?
And, little town, thy streets for evermore
Will silent be; and not a soul to tell
Why thou art desolate, can e'er return.

5

O Attic[100] shape! Fair attitude! with brede
Of marble men and maidens overwrought,[101]
With forest branches and the trodden weed;
Thou, silent form! dost tease us out of thought
As doth eternity: Cold Pastoral![102]
When old age shall this generation waste,
Thou shalt remain, in midst of other woe
Than ours, a friend to man, to whom thou say'st,
"Beauty is truth, truth beauty,"[103]—that is all
Ye know on earth, and all ye need to know.

Percy Bysshe Shelley

OZYMANDIAS[104]

I met a traveler from an antique land
Who said: "Two vast and trunkless legs of stone
Stand in the desert. Near them, on the sand,
Half sunk, a shattered visage lies, whose frown,
And wrinkled lip, and sneer of cold command,
Tell that its sculptor well those passions read
Which yet survive, stamped on these lifeless things,
The hand that mocked them, and the heart that fed:[105]
And on the pedestal these words appear:
'My name is Ozymandias, King of Kings:
Look on my works, ye Mighty, and despair!'
Nothing beside remains. Round the decay
Of that colossal wreck, boundless and bare
The lone and level sands stretch far away."

MUSIC, WHEN SOFT VOICES DIE

Music, when soft voices die,
Vibrates in the memory—
Odors, when sweet violets sicken,

Live within the sense they quicken.
Rose leaves, when the rose is dead,
Are heaped for the belovéd's bed;[106]
And so thy thoughts,[107] when thou art gone,
Love itself shall slumber on.

Elizabeth Barrett Browning

HOW DO I LOVE THEE?[108]

How do I love thee? Let me count the ways.
I love thee to the depth and breadth and height
My soul can reach, when feeling out of sight
For the ends of Being and ideal Grace.
I love thee to the level of everyday's
Most quiet need, by sun and candle light.
I love thee freely, as men strive for Right;
I love thee purely, as they turn from Praise.
I love thee with the passion put to use
In my old griefs, and with my childhood's faith.
I love thee with a love I seemed to lose
With my lost saints—I love thee with the breath,
Smiles, tears, of all my life!—and, if God choose,
I shall but love thee better after death.

Henry Wadsworth Longfellow

DIVINA COMMEDIA[109]

1

Oft have I seen at some cathedral door
A laborer, pausing in the dust and heat,
Lay down his burden, and with reverent feet
Enter, and cross himself, and on the floor
Kneel to repeat his paternoster[110] o'er;
Far off the noises of the world retreat;
The loud vociferations[111] of the street
Become an undistinguishable roar.
So, as I enter here from day to day,
And leave my burden at this minster[112] gate,
Kneeling in prayer, and not ashamed to pray,
The tumult of the time disconsolate
To inarticulate[113] murmurs dies away,
While the eternal ages watch and wait.

Walt Whitman

WHEN I HEARD THE LEARN'D ASTRONOMER[114]

When I heard the learn'd astronomer,
When the proofs, the figures, were ranged in columns before me,
When I was shown the charts and diagrams, to add, divide, and measure them,
When I sitting heard the astronomer where he lectured with much applause in the lecture-room,
How soon unaccountable[115] I became tired and sick,
Till rising and gliding out I wander'd off by myself,
In the mystical moist night-air, and from time to time,
Look'd up in perfect silence at the stars.

A NOISELESS PATIENT SPIDER

A noiseless patient spider,
I mark'd where on a little promontory[116] it stood isolated,
Mark'd how to explore the vacant vast surrounding,
It launch'd forth filament, filament, filament,[117] out of itself,
Ever unreeling them, ever tirelessly speeding them.

And you O my soul where you stand,
Surrounded, detached, in measureless oceans of space,
Ceaselessly musing, venturing, throwing, seeking the spheres to connect them,
Till the bridge you will need be form'd, till the ductile[118] anchor hold,
Till the gossamer[119] thread you fling catch somewhere, O my soul.[120]

Matthew Arnold

DOVER BEACH[121]

The sea is calm to-night,
The tide is full, the moon lies fair
Upon the Straits;—on the French coast, the light
Gleams and is gone; the cliffs of England stand,
Glimmering and vast, out in the tranquil bay.
Come to the window, sweet is the night air!
Only, from the long line of spray
Where the sea meets the moon-blanch'd[122] land,
Listen! you hear the grating roar
Of pebbles which the waves draw back, and fling,
At their return, up the high strand,
Begin, and cease, and then again begin,
With tremulous cadence slow, and bring
The eternal note of sadness in.

Sophocles[123] long ago
Heard it on the Aegean, and it brought
Into his mind the turbid[124] ebb and flow
Of human misery;[125] we
Find also in the sound a thought,
Hearing it by this distant northern sea.

The sea of faith
Was once, too, at the full, and round earth's shore
Lay like the folds of a bright girdle furl'd;[126]
But now I only hear
Its melancholy, long, withdrawing roar,
Retreating to the breath
Of the night-wind down the vast edges drear
And naked shingles[127] of the world.

Ah, love, let us be true
To one another! for the world, which seems
To lie before us like a land of dreams,
So various, so beautiful, so new,
Hath really neither joy, nor love, nor light,
Nor certitude,[128] nor peace, nor help for pain;
And we are here as on a darkling plain
Swept with confused alarms of struggle and flight,
Where ignorant armies[129] clash by night.

Emily Dickinson

I LIKE TO SEE IT LAP THE MILES

I like to see it lap the miles,
And lick the valleys up,
And stop to feed itself at tanks;
And then, prodigious, step

Around a pile of mountains,
And, supercilious, peer
In shanties by the sides of roads;
And then a quarry pare

To fit its sides, and crawl between,
Complaining all the while
In horrid, hooting stanza;
Then chase itself down hill

And neigh like Boanerges;[130]
Then, punctual as a star,
Stop—docile and omnipotent—
At its own stable door.[131]

SUCCESS IS COUNTED SWEETEST

Success is counted sweetest
By those who ne'er succeed.
To comprehend a nectar[132]
Requires sorest need.

Not one of all the purple host
Who took the flag today
Can tell the definition,
So clear, of victory,

As he, defeated, dying,
On whose forbidden ear
The distant strains of triumph
Break, agonized and clear.

HE ATE AND DRANK THE PRECIOUS WORDS

He ate and drank the precious words,
His spirit grew robust;[133]
He knew no more that he was poor,
Nor that his frame was dust.

He danced along the dingy days,
And this bequest of wings
Was but a book. What liberty
A loosened spirit brings!

Gerard Manley Hopkins

HURRAHING IN HARVEST

Summer ends now; now, barbarous in beauty, the stooks[134] arise
Around; up above, what wind-walks! what lovely behaviour
Of silk-sack clouds! has wilder, wilful-wavier
Meal-drift moulded ever and melted across skies?

I walk, I lift up, I lift up heart, eyes,
Down all that glory in the heavens to glean our Saviour;
And, éyes, heárt, what looks, what lips yet gave you a
Rapturous love's greeting of realer, of rounder replies?

And the azurous[135] hung hills are his world-wielding shoulder
Majestic—as a stallion stalwart, very-violet-sweet!—
These things, these things were here and but the beholder
Wanting; which two when they once meet,
The heart réars wíngs bold and bolder
And hurls for him, O half hurls earth for him off under his feet.[136]

GOD'S GRANDEUR

The world is charged with the grandeur of God.
It will flame out, like shining from shook foil;[137]
It gathers to a greatness, like the ooze of oil
Crushed.[138] Why do men then now not reck his rod?[139]
Generations have trod, have trod, have trod;
And all is seared with trade; bleared, smeared with toil;
And wears man's smudge and shares man's smell: the soil
Is bare now, nor can foot feel, being shod.
And for[140] all this, nature is never spent;
There lives the dearest freshness deep down things;
And though the last lights off the black West went
Oh, morning, at the brown brink eastward, springs—
Because the Holy Ghost over the bent
World broods with warm breast and with ah! bright wings.

A. E. Housman

OH, WHEN I WAS IN LOVE WITH YOU

Oh, when I was in love with you,
Then I was clean and brave,
And miles around the wonder grew
How well did I behave.

And now the fancy passes by,
And nothing will remain,

And miles around they'll say that I
Am quite myself again.

WHEN I WAS ONE-AND-TWENTY

When I was one-and-twenty
I heard a wise man say,
"Give crowns and pounds and guineas[141]
But not your heart away;
Give pearls away and rubies
But keep your fancy free."
But I was one-and-twenty—
No use to talk to me.

When I was one-and-twenty
I heard him say again,
"The heart out of the bosom
Was never given in vain;
'Tis paid with sighs a plenty
And sold for endless rue."[142]
And I am two-and-twenty,
And, oh, 'tis true, 'tis true.

WITH RUE MY HEART IS LADEN

With rue[143] my heart is laden
For golden friends I had,
For many a rose-lipt maiden
And many a lightfoot lad.

By brooks too broad for leaping
The lightfoot boys are laid;
The rose-lipt girls are sleeping
In fields where roses fade.

"TERENCE, THIS IS STUPID STUFF:"[144]

"Terence, this is stupid stuff:
You eat your victuals[145] fast enough;
There can't be much amiss, 'tis clear,
To see the rate you drink your beer.
But oh, good Lord, the verse you make,
It gives a chap the belly-ache.
The cow, the old cow, she is dead;
It sleeps well, the hornèd head:
We poor lads, 'tis our turn now
To hear such tunes as killed the cow.
Pretty friendship 'tis to rhyme
Your friends to death before their time
Moping melancholy mad:
Come, pipe a tune to dance to, lad."

Why, if 'tis dancing you would be,
There's brisker pipes than poetry.
Say, for what were hop-yards[146] meant,
Or why was Burton built on Trent?[147]
Oh many a peer of England[148] brews
Livelier liquor than the Muse,
And malt does more than Milton can
To justify God's ways to man.[149]
Ale, man, ale's the stuff to drink
For fellows whom it hurts to think:
Look into the pewter pot
To see the world as the world's not.
And faith, 'tis pleasant till 'tis past:
The mischief is that 'twill not last.
Oh I have been to Ludlow[150] fair
And left my necktie God knows where,
And carried half-way home, or near,
Pints and quarts of Ludlow beer:
Then the world seemed none so bad,
And I myself a sterling lad;
And down in lovely muck[151] I've lain,
Happy till I woke again.
Then I saw the morning sky:
Heigho, the tale was all a lie;
The world, it was the old world yet,
I was I, my things were wet,
And nothing now remained to do
But begin the game anew.

Therefore, since the world has still
Much good, but much less good than ill,
And while the sun and moon endure
Luck's a chance, but trouble's sure,
I'd face it as a wise man would,
And train for ill and not for good.
'Tis true, the stuff I bring for sale
Is not so brisk a brew as ale:
Out of a stem that scored[152] the hand
I wrung it in a weary land.
But take it: if the smack[153] is sour,
The better for the embittered hour;
It should do good to heart and head
When your soul is in my soul's stead;[154]
And I will friend you, if I may,
In the dark and cloudy day.

There was a king reigned in the East:
There, when kings will sit to feast,
They get their fill before they think
With poisoned meat and poisoned drink.

He gathered all that springs to birth
From the many-venomed[155] earth;
First a little, thence to more,
He sampled all her killing store;
And easy, smiling, seasoned sound
Sate[156] the king when healths went round.
They put arsenic in his meat
And stared aghast to watch him eat;
They poured strychnine in his cup
And shook to see him drink it up:
They shook, they stared as white's their shirt:
Them it was their poison hurt.
—I tell the tale that I heard told.
Mithridates, he died old.[157]

William Butler Yeats

WHEN YOU ARE OLD

When you are old and gray and full of sleep,
And nodding by the fire, take down this book,
And slowly read, and dream of the soft look
Your eyes had once, and of their shadows deep;

How many loved your moments of glad grace,
And loved your beauty with love false or true;
But one man loved the pilgrim[158] soul in you,
And loved the sorrows of your changing face.

And bending down beside the glowing bars[159]
Murmur, a little sadly, how love fled
And paced upon the mountains overhead
And hid his face amid a crowd of stars.

THE LAKE ISLE OF INNISFREE[160]

I will arise and go now, and go to Innisfree,
And a small cabin build there, of clay and wattles[161] made;
Nine bean rows will I have there, a hive for the honey bee,
And live alone in the bee-loud glade.

And I shall have some peace there, for peace comes dropping slow,
Dropping from the veils of the morning to where the cricket sings;
There midnight's all a glimmer, and noon a purple glow,
And evening full of the linnet's[162] wings.

I will arise and go now, for always night and day
I hear lake water lapping with low sounds by the shore;
While I stand on the roadway, or on the pavements gray,
I hear it in the deep heart's core.

Edgar Lee Masters

PETIT, THE POET[163]

Seeds in a dry pod, tick, tick, tick,
Tick, tick, tick, like mites[164] in a quarrel—
Faint iambics that the full breeze wakens—
But the pine tree makes a symphony thereof.
Triolets, villanelles, rondels, rondeaus,
Ballades[165] by the score with the same old thought:
The snows and roses of yesterday are vanished;
And what is love but a rose that fades?[166]
Life all around me here in the village:
Tragedy, comedy, valor and truth,
Courage, constancy, heroism, failure—
All in the loom, and oh what patterns!
Woodlands, meadows, streams and rivers—
Blind to all of it all my life long.
Triolets, villanelles, rondels, rondeaus,
Seeds in a dry pod, tick, tick, tick,
Tick, tick, tick, what little iambics,
While Homer and Whitman roared in the pines?[167]

Robert Frost

MENDING WALL[168]

Something there is that doesn't love a wall,
That sends the frozon-ground-swell under it,
And spills the upper boulders in the sun;
And makes gaps even two can pass abreast.
The work of hunters is another thing:
I have come after them and made repair
Where they have left not one stone on a stone,
But they would have the rabbit out of hiding,
To please the yelping dogs. The gaps I mean,
No one has seen them made or heard them made,
But at spring mending-time we find them there.
I let my neighbor know beyond the hill;
And on a day we meet to walk the line
And set the wall between us once again.
We keep the wall between us as we go.
To each the boulders that have fallen to each.
And some are loaves and some so nearly balls
We have to use a spell to make them balance:
"Stay where you are until our backs are turned!"
We wear our fingers rough with handling them.
Oh, just another kind of out-door game,
One on a side. It comes to little more:
There where it is we do not need the wall:
He is all pine and I am apple orchard.
My apple trees will never get across
And eat the cones under his pines, I tell him.
He only says, "Good fences make good neighbors."
Spring is the mischief in me, and I wonder
If I could put a notion in his head:
"*Why* do they make good neighbors? Isn't it
Where there are cows? But here there are no cows.
Before I built a wall I'd ask to know
What I was walling in or walling out,
And to whom I was like to give offense.
Something there is that doesn't love a wall,
That wants it down." I could say "Elves" to him,
But it's not elves exactly, and I'd rather
He said it for himself. I see him there
Bringing a stone grasped firmly by the top
In each hand, like an old-stone savage armed.
He moves in darkness as it seems to me,
Not of woods only and the shade of trees.
He will not go behind his father's saying,
And he likes having thought of it so well
He says again, "Good fences make good neighbors."[169]

THE ROAD NOT TAKEN[170]

Two roads diverged in a yellow[171] wood,
And sorry I could not travel both
And be one traveler, long I stood
And looked down one as far as I could
To where it bent in the undergrowth;

Then took the other, as just as fair,
And having perhaps the better claim,
Because it was grassy and wanted wear;
Though as for that the passing there
Had worn them really about the same,

And both that morning equally lay
In leaves no step had trodden black.
Oh, I kept the first for another day!
Yet knowing how way leads on to way,
I doubted if I should ever come back.

I shall be telling this with a sigh
Somewhere ages and ages hence:
Two roads diverged in a wood, and I—
I took the one less traveled by,
And that has made all the difference.

MY OBJECTION TO BEING STEPPED ON

At the end of the row
I stepped on the toe
Of an unemployed[172] hoe.
It rose in offence
And struck me a blow
In the seat of my sense.
It wasn't to blame
But I called it a name.
And I must say it dealt
Me a blow that I felt
Like malice prepense.[173]
You may call me a fool,
But *was* there a rule
The weapon should be
Turned into a tool?
And what do we see?
The first tool I step on
Turned into a weapon.

Carl Sandburg

COOL TOMBS

When Abraham Lincoln was shovelled into the tombs, he forgot the copperheads[174] and the assassin . . . in the dust, in the cool tombs.

And Ulysses Grant lost all thought of con men[175] and Wall Street, cash and collateral turned ashes . . . in the dust, in the cool tombs.

Pocahontas' body, lovely as a poplar, sweet as a red haw in November or a pawpaw in May, did she wonder? does she remember? . . . in the dust, in the cool tombs?[176]

Take any streetful of people buying clothes and groceries, cheering a hero or throwing confetti and blowing tin horns . . . tell me if the lovers are losers . . . tell me if any get more than the lovers . . . in the dust . . . in the cool tombs.

CHICAGO

Hog Butcher for the World,
Tool Maker, Stacker of Wheat,
Player with Railroads and the Nation's Freight Handler;
Stormy, husky, brawling,
City of the Big Shoulders:
They tell me you are wicked, and I believe them; for I have seen your painted women under the gas lamps luring the farm boys.
And they tell me you are crooked, and I answer: Yes, it is true I have seen the gunman kill and go free to kill again.
And they tell me you are brutal, and my reply is: On the faces of women and children I have seen the marks of wanton[177] hunger.
And having answered so I turn once more to those who sneer at this my city, and I give them back the sneer and say to them:
Come and show me another city with lifted head singing so proud to be alive and coarse and strong and cunning.
Flinging magnetic[178] curses amid the toil of piling job on job, here is a tall bold slugger set vivid against the little soft cities;
Fierce as a dog with tongue lapping for action, cunning as a savage pitted against the wilderness,
    Bareheaded,
    Shovelling,
    Wrecking,
    Planning,
    Building, breaking, rebuilding,
Under the smoke, dust all over his mouth, laughing with white teeth,
Under the terrible burden of destiny laughing as a young man laughs,
Laughing even as an ignorant fighter laughs who has never lost a battle,
Bragging and laughing that under his wrist is the pulse, and under his ribs the heart of the people,
        Laughing!
Laughing the stormy, husky, brawling laughter of Youth, half-naked, sweating, proud to be Hog Butcher,

Tool Maker, Stacker of Wheat,
Player with Railroads and Freight
Handler to the Nation.

Marianne Moore

SILENCE[179]

My father used to say,
"Superior people never make long visits,
have to be shown Longfellow's grave
or the glass flowers at Harvard.[180]
Self-reliant like the cat—
that takes its prey to privacy,
the mouse's limp tail hanging like a shoe-
lace from its mouth—
they sometimes enjoy solitude,
and can be robbed of speech
by speech which has delighted them.
The deepest feeling always shows itself
in silence;
not in silence, but restraint."
Nor was he insincere in saying, "Make
my house your inn."
Inns are not residences.

POETRY[181]

I, too, dislike it: there are things that
are important beyond all this
fiddle.
Reading it, however, with a perfect
contempt for it, one discovers
in
it after all, a place for the genuine.
Hands that can grasp, eyes
that can dilate, hair that can rise
if it must, these things are important not because a

high-sounding interpretation can be put
upon them but because they
are
useful. When they become so deriv-
ative as to become unintelligible,
the same thing may be said for all of
us, that we
do not admire what
we cannot understand: the bat
holding on upside down or in
quest of something to

eat, elephants pushing, a wild horse
taking a roll, a tireless wolf
under
a tree, the immovable critic twitching
his skin like a horse that feels
a flea, the base-
ball fan, the statistician—
nor is it valid
to discriminate against 'business
documents and

school-books';[182] all these phenomena are
important. One must make a
distinction
however: when dragged into prominence by half poets, the result
is not poetry,
nor till the poets among us can be
'literalists of
the imagination'[183]—above
insolence and triviality and can
present

for inspection, imaginary gardens with
real toads in them, shall we
have
it. In the meantime, if you demand on
the one hand,
the raw material of poetry in
all its rawness and
that which is on the other hand
genuine, then you are interested
in poetry.

Countee Cullen

YET DO I MARVEL

I doubt not that God is good, well-
meaning, kind,
And did He stoop to quibble[184] could tell
why
The little buried mole continues blind.
Why flesh that mirrors Him must some
day die;

Make plain the reason tortured Tantalus[185]
Is baited by the fickle fruit, declare
If merely brute caprice[186] dooms Sisyphus[187]
To struggle up a never-ending stair.
Inscrutable His ways are, and immune
To catechism[188] by a mind too strewn
With petty cares to slightly understand
What awful brain compels His awful hand.
Yet do I marvel at this curious thing:
To make a poet black and bid him sing.

Langston Hughes

DREAM VARIATIONS

To fling my arms wide
In some place of the sun,
To whirl and to dance
Till the white day is done.
Then rest at cool evening
Beneath a tall tree
While night comes on gently,
Dark like me—
That is my dream!

To fling my arms wide
In the face of the sun,
Dance! Whirl! Whirl!
Till the quick day is done.
Rest at pale evening . . .
A tall, slim tree . . .
Night coming tenderly
Black like me.

REFUGEE IN AMERICA

There are words like *Freedom*
Sweet and wonderful to say.
On my heart-strings freedom sings
All day everyday.

There are words like *Liberty*
That almost make me cry.
If you had known what I knew
You would know why.

W. H. Auden

MUSÉE DES BEAUX ARTS[189]

About suffering they were never wrong,
The Old Masters:[190] how well they understood
Its human position; how it takes place
While someone else is eating or opening a window or just walking dully along;
How, when the aged are reverently, passionately waiting
For the miraculous birth,[191] there always must be
Children who did not specially want it to happen, skating
On a pond at the edge of the wood:
They[192] never forgot
That even the dreadful martyrdom[193] must run its course
Anyhow in a corner, some untidy spot
Where the dogs go on with their doggy life and the torturer's horse
Scratches its innocent behind on a tree.

In Breughel's *Icarus,*[194] for instance: how everything turns away
Quite leisurely from the disaster; the ploughman may
Have heard the splash, the forsaken cry,
But for him it was not an important failure; the sun shone
As it had to on the white legs disappearing into the green
Water; and the expensive delicate ship that must have seen
Something amazing, a boy falling out of the sky,
Had somewhere to get to and sailed calmly on.

Edna St. Vincent Millay

LOVE IS NOT ALL: IT IS NOT MEAT NOR DRINK

Love is not all: it is not meat nor drink
Nor slumber nor a roof against the rain;

Nor yet a floating spar[195] to men that sink
And rise and sink and rise and sink again;
Love can not fill the thickened lung with breath,
Nor clean the blood, nor set the fractured bone;
Yet many a man is making friends with death
Even as I speak, for lack of love alone.
It well may be that in a difficult hour,
Pinned down by pain and moaning for release,
Or nagged by want past resolution's power,[196]
I might be driven to sell your love for peace,
Or trade the memory of this night for food.
It well may be. I do not think I would.

Stephen Spender

DAYBREAK

At dawn she lay with her profile at that angle
Which, sleeping, seems the stone face of an angel;[197]
Her hair a harp the hand of a breeze follows
To play, against the white cloud of the pillows.
Then in a flush of rose she woke, and her eyes were open
Swimming with blue through the rose flesh of dawn.
From her dew of lips, the drop of one word
Fell, from a dawn of fountains, when she murmured
"Darling"—upon my heart the song of the first bird.
"My dream glides in my dream," she said, "come true.
I waken from you to my dream of you."
O, then my waking dream dared to assume
The audacity[198] of her sleep. Our dreams
Flowed into each other's arms, like streams.

OH YOUNG MEN OH YOUNG COMRADES[199]

Oh young men oh young comrades
it is too late now to stay in those houses
your fathers built where they built you to build to breed
money on money it is too late
to make or even to count what has been made
Count rather those fabulous possessions
which begin with your body and your fiery soul:—
the hairs on your head the muscles extending
in ranges with their lakes across your limbs
Count your eyes as jewels and your valued sex
then count the sun and the innumerable coined light
sparkling on waves and spangled[200] under trees
It is too late to stay in great houses where the ghosts are prisoned
—those ladies like flies perfect in amber[201]
those financiers like fossils of bones in coal.
Oh comrades, step beautifully from the solid wall
advance to rebuild and sleep with friend on hill
advance to rebel and remember what you have
no ghost ever had, immured[202] in his hall.

Wallace Stevens

THE EMPEROR OF ICE-CREAM[203]

Call the roller of big cigars,[204]
The muscular one, and bid him whip
In kitchen cups concupiscent[205] curds.
Let the wenches dawdle in such dress
As they are used to wear, and let the boys

Bring flowers in last month's newspapers.
Let be be finale of seem.
The only emperor is the emperor of ice-cream.[206]

Take from the dresser of deal,[207]
Lacking the three glass knobs, that sheet
On which she embroidered fantails once
And spread it so as to cover her face.
If her horny[208] feet protrude, they come
To show how cold she is, and dumb.
Let the lamp affix its beam.[209]
The only emperor is the emperor of ice-cream.[210]

Karl Shapiro

BUICK

As a sloop with a sweep of immaculate wing on her delicate spine
And a keel as steel as a root that holds in the sea as she leans,[211]
Leaning and laughing, my warmhearted beauty, you ride, you ride,
You tack on the curves with parabola[212] speed and a kiss of goodbye,
Like a thoroughbred sloop, my new high-spirited spirit, my kiss.

As my foot suggests that you leap in the air with your hips of a girl,
My finger that praises your wheel and announces your voices of song,[213]
Flouncing your skirts, you blueness of joy, you flirt of politeness,
You leap, you intelligence, essence[214] of wheelness with silvery nose,
And your platinum clocks of excitement stir like the hairs of a fern.

But how alien you are from the booming belts of your birth and the smoke
Where you turned on the stinging lathes of Detroit and Lansing at night
And shrieked at the torch in your secret parts and the amorous tests,
But now with your eyes that enter the future of roads you forget;
You are all instinct with your phosphorous[215] glow and your streaking hair.

And now when we stop it is not as the bird from the shell that I leave
Or the leathery pilot who steps from his bird with a sneer of delight,
And not as the ignorant beast do you squat and watch me depart,
But with exquisite breathing you smile, with satisfaction of love,
And I touch you again as you tick in the silence and settle in sleep.

Richard Eberhart

1934[216]

Caught upon a thousand thorns, I sing,
Like a rag in the wind,
Caught in the blares of the automobile horns
And on the falling airplane's wing.
Caught napping in my study
Among a thousand books of poetry.

Doing the same thing over and over again
Brings about an obliteration[217] of pain.
Each day dies in a paper litter
As the heart becomes less like a rapier.
In complexity, feeling myself absurd
Dictating an arbitrary word,

My self my own worst enemy,
Hunting the past through all its fears,
That on the brain that glory burst
Bombing a ragged future's story,
Caught in iron individuality
As in the backwash of a sea

Knowing not whether to fight out,
Or keep silent; to talk about the weather,
Or rage again through wrong and right,
Knowing knowledge is a norm of nothing,
And I have been to the Eastern seas
And walked on all the Hebrides.[218]

Ashamed of loving a long-practised self-hood,
Lost in a luxury of speculation,

At the straight grain of a pipe I stare
And spit upon all worlds of Spain;[219]
Time like a certain sedative
Quelling the growth of the purpose tree.

Aware of the futility of action,
Of the futility of prayer aware,
Trying to pry from the vest of poetry
The golden heart of mankind's deep despair,
Unworthy of a simple love
In august,[220] elected worlds to move

Stern, pliant in the modern world, I sing,
Afraid of nothing and afraid of everything,
Curtailing joy, withholding irony,
Pleased to condemn contemporaneity[221]
Seeking the reality, skirting
The dangerous absolutes[222] of fear and hope,

And I have eased reality and fiction
Into a kind of intellectual fruition[223]
Strength in solitude, life in death,
Compassion by suffering, love in strife,
And ever and still the weight of mystery
Arrows a way between my words and me.

Dylan Thomas

ESPECIALLY WHEN THE OCTOBER WIND

Especially when the October wind
With frosty fingers punishes my hair,
Caught by the crabbing[224] sun I walk on fire
And cast a shadow crab upon the land,
By sea's side, hearing the noise of birds,

Hearing the raven cough in winter sticks,[225]
My busy heart who shudders as she talks
Sheds the syllabic blood and drains her words.

Shut, too, in a tower of words, I mark
On the horizon walking like the trees
The wordy shapes of women, and the rows
Of the star-gestured children in the park.
Some let me make you of the vowelled beeches,
Some of the oaken voices, from the roots
Of many a thorny shire[226] tell you notes,
Some let me make you of the water's speeches.

Behind a pot of ferns the wagging clock
Tells me the hour's word, the neural[227] meaning
Flies on the shafted disc,[228] declaims the morning
And tells the windy weather in the cock.
Some let me make you of the meadow's signs;
The signal grass that tells me all I know
Breaks with the wormy winter through the eye.
Some let me tell you of the raven's sins.

Especially when the October wind
(Some let me make you of autumnal spells,
The spider-tongued, and the loud hill of Wales)
With fist of turnips punishes the land,
Some let me make you of the heartless words.
The heart is drained that, spelling in the scurry[229]
Of chemic blood, warned of the coming fury.
By the sea's side hear the dark-vowelled birds.

AND DEATH SHALL HAVE NO DOMINION[230]

And death shall have no dominion.
Dead men naked they shall be one
With the man in the wind and the west moon;
When their bones are picked clean and the clean bones gone,
They shall have stars at elbow and foot;
Though they go mad they shall be sane,
Though they sink through the sea they shall rise again;
Though lovers be lost love shall not;
And death shall have no dominion.

And death shall have no dominion.
Under the windings of the sea

They lying long shall not die windily;
Twisting on racks[231] when sinews give way,
Strapped to a wheel, yet they shall not break;
Faith in their hands shall snap in two,
And the unicorn[232] evils run them through;
Split all ends up they shan't crack;
And death shall have no dominion.

And death shall have no dominion.
No more may gulls cry at their ears
Or waves break loud on the seashores;
Where blew a flower may a flower no more
Lift its head to the blows of the rain;
Though they be mad and dead as nails,
Heads of the characters hammer through daisies;
Break in the sun till the sun breaks down,
And death shall have no dominion.

Theodore Roethke

HER LONGING[233]

Before this longing,
I lived serene as a fish,
At one with the plants in the pond,
The mare's tail, the floating frogbit,[234]
Among my eight-legged friends,
Open like a pool, a lesser parsnip,
Like a leech, looping myself along,
A bug-eyed edible one,
A mouth like a stickleback,—[235]
A thing quiescent![236]

But now—
The wild stream, the sea itself cannot contain me:
I dive with the black hag, the cormorant,[237]
Or walk the pebbly shore with the humpbacked heron,
Shaking out my catch in the morning sunlight,
Or rise with the gar-eagle, the great-winged condor,[238]
Floating over the mountains,
Pitting my breast against the rushing air,
A phoenix,[239] sure of my body,
Perpetually rising out of myself,
My wings hovering over the shorebirds,
Or beating against the black clouds of the storm,
Protecting the sea-cliffs.[240]

I WAITED

I waited for the wind to move the dust;
But no wind came.
I seemed to eat the air;
The meadow insects made a level[241] noise.
I rose, a heavy bulk, above the field.

It was as if I tried to walk in hay,
Deep in the mow, and each step deeper down,
Or floated on the surface of a pond,
The slow long ripples winking in my eyes.
I saw all things through water, magnified,
And shimmering. The sun burned through a haze,
And I became all that I looked upon.
I dazzled in the dazzle of a stone.

And then a jackass brayed. A lizard leaped my foot.
Slowly I came back to the dusty road;
And when I walked, my feet seemed deep in sand.
I moved like some heat-weary animal.
I went, not looking back. I was afraid.

The way grew steeper between stony walls,
Then lost itself down through a rocky gorge.
A donkey path led to a small plateau.
Below, the bright sea was, the level waves,
And all the winds came toward me. I was glad.

W. S. Merwin

THE BONES[242]

It takes a long time to hear what the sands

Seem to be saying, with the wind nudging them,
And then you cannot put it in words nor tell
Why these things should have a voice. All kinds
Of objects come in over the tide-wastes
In the course of a year, with a throaty
Rattle: weeds, driftwood, the bodies of birds
And of fish, shells. For years I had hardly
Considered shells as being bones, maybe
Because of the sound they could still make, though
I knew a man once who could raise a kind
Of wailing tune out of a flute he had,
Made from a fibula:[243] it was much the same
Register[244] as the shells'; the tune did not
Go on when his breath stopped, though you thought it would.
Then that morning, coming on the wreck,
I saw the kinship. No recent disaster
But an old ghost from under a green buoy,
Brought in by the last storm, or one from which
The big wind had peeled back the sand grave
To show what was still left: the bleached, chewed-off
Timbers like the ribs of a man or the jaw-bone
Of some extinct beast. Far down the sands its
Broken cage leaned out, casting no shadow
In the veiled light. There was a man sitting beside it
Eating out of a paper, littering the beach
With the bones of a few more fish, while the hulk
Cupped its empty hand high over him. Only he
And I had come to those sands knowing
That they were there. The rest was bones, whatever
Tunes they made. The bones of things; and of men too
And of man's endeavors whose ribs he had set
Between himself and the shapeless tides. Then
I saw how the sand was shifting like water,
That once could walk. Shells were to shut out the sea,
The bones of birds were built for floating
On air and water, and those of fish were devised
For their feeding depths, while a man's bones were framed
For what? For knowing the sands are here,
And coming to hear them a long time; for giving
Shapes to the sprawled sea, weight to its winds,
And wrecks to plead for its sands. These things are not
Limitless: we know there is somewhere
An end to them, though every way you look
They extend farther than a man can see.

Gwendolyn Brooks

THE PREACHER: RUMINATES[245] BEHIND THE SERMON

I think it must be lonely to be God.
Nobody loves a master. No. Despite
The bright hosannas, bright dear-Lords, and bright
Determined reverence of Sunday eyes.

Picture Jehovah striding through the hall
Of His importance, creatures running out
From servant-corners to acclaim, to shout
Appreciation of His merit's glare.

But who walks with Him?—dares to take His arm,
To slap Him on the shoulder, tweak His ear,
Buy Him a Coca-Cola or a beer,
Pooh-pooh His politics, call Him a fool?

Perhaps—who knows?—He tires of looking down.
Those eyes are never lifted. Never straight.
Perhaps sometimes He tires of being great
In solitude. Without a hand to hold.[246]

Adrienne Rich

THE ROOFWALKER

for Denise Levertov[247]

Over the half-finished houses
night comes. The builders
stand on the roof. It is
quiet after the hammers,
the pulleys hang slack.
Giants, the roofwalkers,
on a listing deck, the wave
of darkness about to break
on their heads. The sky
is a torn sail where figures
pass magnified, shadows
on a burning deck.

I feel like them up there:
exposed, larger than life,
and due to break my neck.

Was it worth while to lay—
with infinite exertion—
a roof I can't live under?
—All those blueprints,
closings of gaps,
measurings, calculations?
A life I didn't choose
chose me: even
my tools are the wrong ones
for what I have to do.
I'm naked, ignorant,
a naked man fleeing
across the roofs
who could with a shade of difference
be sitting in the lamplight
against the cream wallpaper
reading—not with indifference—
about a naked man
fleeing across the roofs.

Anne Sexton

THE ADDICT

Sleepmonger,[248]
deathmonger,
with capsules in my palms each night,
eight at a time from sweet pharmaceutical[249] bottles
I make arrangements for a pint-sized journey.
I'm the queen of this condition.
I'm an expert on making the trip
and now they say I'm an addict.
Now they ask why.
Why!

Don't they know
that I promised to die!
I'm keeping in practice.
I'm merely staying in shape.
The pills are a mother, but better,
every color and as good as sour balls.
I'm on a diet from death.

Yes, I admit
it has gotten to be a bit of a habit—
blows eight at a time, socked in the eye,
hauled away by the pink, the orange,
the green and the white goodnights.
I'm becoming something of a chemical
mixture.
That's it!

My supply
of tablets
has got to last for years and years.
I like them more than I like me.
Stubborn as hell, they won't let go.
It's a kind of marriage.
It's a kind of war
where I plant bombs inside
of myself.

Yes
I try
to kill myself in small amounts,
an innocuous[250] occupation.
Actually I'm hung up on it.
But remember I don't make too much noise.
And frankly no one has to lug me out
and I don't stand there in my winding sheet.
I'm a little buttercup in my yellow nightie
eating my eight loaves in a row
and in a certain order as in
the laying on of hands
or the black sacrament.[251]

It's a ceremony
but like any other sport

it's full of rules.
It's like a musical tennis match where
my mouth keeps catching the ball.
Then I lie on my altar
elevated by the eight chemical kisses.

What a lay me down this is
with two pink, two orange,
two green, two white goodnights.
Fee-fi-fo-fum—
Now I'm borrowed.
Now I'm numb.

LeRoi Jones

PREFACE TO A TWENTY-VOLUME SUICIDE NOTE

(*For Kellie Jones, Born 16 May, 1959*)
Lately, I've become accustomed to the way
The ground opens up and envelops me
Each time I go out to walk the dog.
Or the broad-edged silly music the wind
Makes when I run for a bus . . .

Things have come to that.

And now, each night I count the stars,
And each night I get the same number.
And when they will not come to be counted,
I count the holes they leave.

Nobody sings anymore.

And then last night, I tiptoed up
To my daughter's room and heard her
Talking to someone, and when I opened
The door, there was no one there . . .
Only she on her knees, peeking into

Her own clasped hands.

John Moffitt

SEEING NEW

Every once in a while you see a known word thoroughly
New: something like 'Easter egg' or 'mushroom' you look at
Unprepossessed[252] and taste of it fresh depths of flavor such as
A perceptive first-year student of an ancient tongue might.

That is just how I should wish to savor objects of
Everyday attention: I'd like, every now and then, as I go
Hurriedly down the street or even as I sit working at my
Desk, to look up and feel as if I was suddenly seeing some
Long-familiar shape dished up to me for the first
Time—as if, say, I was spending my first afternoon in
A boisterous Slavic city[253] where, from now on, I was going to
Make my home, happily taking in all the quick, enchanted
Newnesses sandwiched[254] unexpectedly here and there.

I like to imagine that once you have finally
Arrived at the point we're all of us some-how or other
Moving toward, every single object you come upon will
Strike you precisely that way every time you
Come upon it: as something utterly fresh and strange and
Revealing—a long-familiar noun or verb or adjective or
Preposition conjured up[255] new for your own special
Relish out of life's rich, unrepetitious vocabulary.

Notes

[1] Pale, lacking color.
[2] Cupid.
[3] Discerns, makes out.
[4] Sense, intelligence.
[5] Valleys.
[6] Short lyric poems designed for singing.
[7] Loose gown.
[8] Country lads, gallants.
[9] In classical mythology a princess who was changed into a nightingale, a bird noted for melodious song.
[10] Luxuriant, lush.
[11] Bitterness.
[12] Flowers.
[13] That the whole world presents nothing.
[14] Power.
[15] Encouraged and stopped.
[16] Boast, brag.
[17] False notion, whim.
[18] Stained, darkened.
[19] Graft; that is, add by this poem what Time takes from you.
[20] Moderate.
[21] Every beautiful thing.
[22] Stripped of gay clothing.
[23] Ownest (owns).
[24] This sonnet. Such a statement suggests faith in the endurance of poetry rather than the poet's egotism.
[25] Futile, useless.
[26] By chance.
[27] State of mind. In line 14, "state" is used to mean "throne" (chair of state).
[28] Past.
[29] Persons, sprites.
[30] Display or description.
[31] Because. That is, they were able only ("but") to foresee you prophetically.
[32] Obstacles.
[33] The star's value is unknown, although the star's "height" (altitude) may be known and actually used in navigation.
[34] Time's.
[35] Sweep, range.
[36] Brink of the Last Judgment (Judgment Day).
[37] Concealing, false-appearing.
[38] This is Donne's response to the poems earlier by Marlowe and Raleigh.
[39] Captivated, charmed.
[40] Are unwilling, reluctant.
[41] Flies of unraveled silk.
[42] Provocativeness, recklessness. The terms used in this lyric to describe clothing have an ethical, or social, connotation.
[43] A linen scarf.
[44] Floating, wandering.
[45] The lower part of the bodice (waist or fitted vest).
[46] Courtesy, politeness. In praising feminine disarray, Herrick is defining the "careless" grace of his own poetry—which was never careless.

[47] Archaic term for "when."

[48] The act or process of making liquid.

[49] Glorious.

[50] The collar is a symbol of spiritual restraint.

[51] Table.

[52] In abundance.

[53] Be always required to beg.

[54] Health-giving.

[55] The poet's wreath, here a symbol of festivity.

[56] Christian restrictions on behavior, which the "petty thoughts" of the meek believer have made strong ("good cable").

[57] Close your eyes (to the true weakness of the Church's teachings).

[58] The skull is a reminder of approaching death.

[59] The lady's outermost garment. (In Ptolemaic astronomy, nine concentric spheres made up the universe.)

[60] Fence enclosing a park. Obviously, "deer" is a pun.

[61] Compare.

[62] Appearance.

[63] Persons whose spiritual and intellectual development and achievements have an appropriate agreement with their physical appearance and age.

[64] Adequate, equal. Whenever it appears and whatever it amounts to, the poet's inner growth will be appropriate to the plans that time and heaven are getting ready.

[65] The general meaning seems to be "all service ranks alike with God." The "all" of line 13 can refer to either *time* or *talent*. Possibly the clue to these two lines may be found in line 14 of the next sonnet.

[66] Milton was forty-three when he became totally blind.

[67] The allusion is to Jesus's parable of the talents. An "unprofitable servant" hid his talent in the earth (Matthew 25).

[68] Eager, ready.

[69] Foolishly.

[70] Forestall.

[71] An allusion to the words of Jesus, "My yoke is easy" (Matthew 11:29–30).

[72] Shed, cast away.

[73] Stops, pauses.

[74] The Ganges is a long river flowing from the Himalayas into the Bay of Bengal; the Humber is a small estuary on the east coast of England. The word *complain* suggests the uttering of love complaints.

[75] The deluge referred to in Genesis 6, 7.

[76] According to the then popular belief, Jews were to be converted just before the Last Judgment (doomsday).

[77] Increasing, expanding.

[78] Esteem, dignity.

[79] Proud, defiant.

[80] Breathes forth, pours out.

[81] Immediate enthusiasm, hot interest.

[82] Slowly crushing. *Slow-chapped* literally means "slow-jawed"; time is seen as chewing up the world and everyone in it.

[83] An archaic word here, meaning "extending or passing through."

[84] Jesus Christ is sometimes referred to as "the Lamb" and "the Lamb of God." The metaphor is derived from the qualities of a lamb: meekness, gentleness, innocence.

[85] Wordsworth's note: "Composed on the roof of a coach, on my way to France." The conflict of feelings brought about by the poet's brief return to France, where he had once been a revolutionist and the lover of a Frenchwoman, evoked the personal tone of this sonnet.

[86] Gift. Giving the heart away is a sordid act.

87 Proteus, an old man of the sea, who, in the *Odyssey,* can assume a variety of shapes in his service of Neptune, mythical god of the sea. Triton, a deity of the sea, is usually represented as blowing on a conch shell.

88 This is one of the lyrics in *Hebrew Melodies* (1815), a collection of short poems dealing with incidents, largely from the Old Testament, meant to be set to music. Byron composed this lyric the day after he had seen his cousin by marriage, Mrs. Robert Wilmot, at a ball to which she had worn a black mourning gown brightened with spangles.

89 Regions.

90 Toward the end of his short life, Byron organized an expedition to help in the Greek war for independence from the Turks. In various writings he had helped to foster European belief in the Greek cause, and now he sought action as an honorable outlet to his beliefs. While living a Spartan existence in the Grecian town of Missolonghi and helping to train Greek troops for fighting, he succumbed to a series of feverish attacks (malaria? meningitis?) and died just after his thirty-sixth birthday.

91 Repaid.

92 Characters; written or printed letters of the alphabet.

93 According to one tradition, the urn (decorative vase) that inspired this selection was preserved in the garden of an English mansion, but there were, and are, many such treasures in the British Museum, marble urns carved with figures in relief. The vase described by Keats existed in all its particulars only in the poet's imagination.

94 Rustic, representing a woodland scene.

95 Tempe is a valley in Thessaly, Greece. The "dales of Arcady" are the valleys of Arcadia, an ancient Greek state. Keats uses the names as symbols of a pastoral ideal.

96 Wind instruments.

97 The ear of actual sense as opposed to that of imagination.

98 Surfeited, satiated.

99 Sacred.

100 Attica was the region of Greece in which Athens is located.

101 Ornamented all over with an interwoven pattern.

102 A pastoral story in marble.

103 Critics have long argued whether this quotation was uttered by the urn, by the poet, or by an invented lyric speaker. Similarly, they have debated whether the *ye* of the last line is addressed to the lyric speaker, to the urn, to readers, or to figures on the urn.

104 Ozymandias was Ramses II of Egypt, who lived in the 13th century, B.C. According to a Greek historian of the 1st century B.C., the largest statue in Egypt bore the inscription: "I am Ozymandias, King of Kings; if any man wishes to know where I lie, let him surpass me in some of my achievements."

105 That is, the sculptured passions outlast the hand of the sculptor who had "mocked" (both created and derided) them, as well as the heart of the king (Ozymandias), which had been their source.

106 Fallen petals make a bed for the dead rose.

107 That is, my thoughts of thee.

108 This poem is one of a sequence of forty-four sonnets inspired by the poet's love for her husband, Robert Browning.

109 This poem is the first of a series of six sonnets designed to precede and follow Longfellow's translation of parts of Dante's *Divine Comedy.* In this first sonnet, Dante's great poem is likened to a cathedral that the poet enters daily for prayer and for escape from the cares that he leaves outside. This figure (image) is continued in succeeding sonnets in the series.

110 The Lord's Prayer.

111 Noises, clamor.

112 Church, cathedral.

113 Unuttered, muffled.

114 Whitman was aware of the limitations of science and the scientific mind. Yet he was interested in scientific inquiry—and even in pseudosciences, such as phrenology. However, he

tended to think of science as intellectual and cold when contrasted with his faith in a divine purpose. He felt that man was an observer, at one with nature.

[115] Unexplained, mysterious.

[116] A high point of land or rock.

[117] Fine thread.

[118] Malleable; capable of being hammered or pressed (drawn out) thin.

[119] Thin, filmy cobweb or thread. Here a noun is used in an adjectival function.

[120] Certain critics have pointed out that the "I" of the poem may or may not refer to the author, but that Whitman himself, unlike the spider, was neither "noiseless" nor "patient."

[121] Dover is the closest point in England, about 20 miles, to the continent. The cliffs near Dover are white, high, and precipitous. As line 6 suggests, the poet and his wife are at a hotel in Dover; they are setting out on a journey abroad.

[122] Whitened (made light) by the moon.

[123] Greek tragic playwright of the fifth century B.C.

[124] Clouded, obscured.

[125] The opening of a chorus of Sophocles' *Antigone* is as follows: "Blest are they whose days have not tasted of evil. For when a house hath once been shaken from heaven, there the curse fails nevermore, passing from life to life of the race; even as, when the surge is driven over the darkness of the deep by the fierce breath of Thracian sea-winds, it rolls up the black sand from the depths, and there is a sullen roar from the wind-vexed headlands that front the blows of the storm."

[126] At high tide, the sea closely envelops the land. In its flow, the sea's forces are gathered like the "folds" of clothing ("bright girdle") that have been compressed ("furled"). As the sea retreats, it is unfurled (spread out).

[127] Beaches covered with pebbles and larger stones.

[128] Confidence, certainty.

[129] Possibly a reference to the siege of Rome by France in 1849 or to other warfare on the continent. One guess is that Arnold was referring to battles recounted by Thucydides (an ancient Greek writer) in his *History of the Peloponnesian War,* an edition of which the poet's father had published (1835).

[130] A name given by Jesus to two of his disciples; it means "sons of thunder" and refers to loud preachers and orators.

[131] This poem is possibly a caricature of the age of steam. Miss Dickinson creates a toy, a plaything, an iron horse. The poem employs one subject and one predicate: *I like,* followed by a series of infinitives: *lap, lick, stop, feed, step, peer, pare, crawl, chase, neigh, stop.* While the poet looks, from a distance, the string of toy cars is pulled along in a rhythmic, ongoing movement similar to that of a speeding train which finally halts at its terminal.

[132] In classical mythology, nectar is the life-giving drink or food of the gods.

[133] Strong, invigorated.

[134] Sheaves of grain (corn) placed upright so as to support each other for drying.

[135] Of a sky-blue color.

[136] Hopkins disdained several of the contemporary expectations of what poetry should be. He wished to bring alive the language of poetry and resorted to numerous verbal eccentricities, poetic tricks, and examples of obscure imagery in his attempts to do so. He often used word clusters instead of conventional phraseology; he used older or dialect words on many occasions; he coined new phrases by analogy with existing ones.

[137] In a comment on this poem the author wrote: "I mean *foil* in the sense of leaf or tinsel. . . . Shaken goldfoil gives off broad glares like sheet lightning and also, and this is true of nothing else, owing to its zigzag dents and creasings and network of small many-cornered facets, a sort of fork lightning too."

[138] Oil from crushed olives.

[139] Take heed or care about His authority.

[140] In spite of.

[141] The value of English money has changed over the years. At the time of writing, a

crown (five shillings) was worth about one dollar in United States money; the other coins mentioned, about five dollars.

142 Regret, sorrow.

143 This word, a favorite of the poet's, here means "compassion" or "pity."

144 Housman's poetic name for himself was "Terence." The author's proposed title for *A Shropshire Lad* was *The Poems of Terence Hearsay.* The work of a Roman playwright named Terence (Publius Terentius Afer) who lived in the second century B.C. was well known to Housman, a classical scholar.

145 Food.

146 Fields of hops; plants the dried, ripe cones of which are used in brewing. Malt (line 21) is another principal ingredient of beer and ale.

147 An English city famous for its breweries.

148 "Beer barons," brewery magnates raised to the peerage.

149 In the invocation of his epic poem *Paradise Lost,* John Milton states that his purpose is to "justify the ways of God to man."

150 A market town in Shropshire.

151 Dung, manure, filth.

152 Cut.

153 Kiss (taste).

154 Place.

155 Poisoned.

156 Sat.

157 The story of Mithridates, King of Pontus and a contemporary of Julius Caesar, is told in Pliny's *Natural History* (A.D. first century).

158 Journeying, wandering.

159 Of the fireplace.

160 Of the origin of this poem, Yeats wrote: "I had still the ambition . . . formed in my teens, of living in imitation of Thoreau [Henry David Thoreau, American essayist and naturalist, 1817–1862] on Innisfree [a small island in a lake in County Sligo] . . . When walking through Fleet Street, [in central London, the location of many newspaper offices] very homesick, I heard a little tinkle of water and saw a fountain in a shopwindow . . . and began to remember lake water. From the sudden remembrance came my poem *Innisfree.*"

161 Interwoven sticks and twigs.

162 A small songbird's.

163 For comment on the work from which this selection is taken, see "Lucinda Matlock."

164 A very small parasite. The author's purpose is to indicate the pettiness and unimportance of what the speaker (Petit) wrote during his lifetime.

165 These are minor verse forms, stanzaic arrangements that usually exhibit poetry that is light, trivial, or relatively unimportant.

166 Snows, yesterday's roses, and love are objects or concepts that have appeared in much trite, as well as great, poetry.

167 The poet says that during life he was blind to such great themes as those written about by Homer and Whitman and was content to turn out delicate, minor lyrics.

168 The springtime ritual of repairing stone walls separating adjacent properties, characteristic of the reputed neatness and good husbandry of New England farmers, provides the poet with a means of contrasting two kinds of Yankees, two kinds of men everywhere, and two kinds of attitude toward customs and tradition. The narrator is unconvinced of the need for keeping up boundary lines; his neighbor doggedly accepts as essential an act unquestioningly performed by his forebears.

169 "Good fences make good neighbors," but "Something there is that doesn't love a wall." This two-sided situation possibly typifies the paradox facing human society. In one view, walls are essential; and yet walls, and any artificial barrier, prevent progress toward brotherhood.

170 None of Frost's poems better illustrates his puzzling approach than this one. The word "road" involves synecdoche, a figure of speech in which a part is used for the whole or the

whole for a part. The term also involves using the special for the general or the general for the special.

[171] Autumn.

[172] Discarded, tossed aside.

[173] Intended or planned in advance.

[174] Copperheads were northern sympathizers with the Confederates during the Civil War; the term is derived from the name of a venomous snake. The assassin was John Wilkes Booth (1838–1865), an American actor.

[175] Confidence men, swindlers. Grant's administration was notorious for corruption in business and government.

[176] Pocahontas was an Indian maiden, daughter of Chief Powhatan, born about 1595, who died in 1617. The haw and pawpaw (papaw) to which she is compared are fruits of various bushes or small trees, notably the hawthorn.

[177] Deliberate, careless.

[178] Powerful.

[179] The belief that guests should not overstay their welcome is ancient: in the third century B.C., Plautus, the Roman dramatist, wrote: "No one can be so welcome a guest that he will not annoy his host after three days." An English poet (John Lyly) wrote in the sixteenth century that "Fish and guests in three days are stale."

[180] These references are to Cambridge, Massachusetts, and to a notable museum at Harvard College. The speaker's (poet's) father is represented as living in this area; his idea of "superior" people was that they were self-reliant and did not need to be shown sights.

[181] For Marianne Moore, poetry is a means of identifying the genuine: it is where one starts from, just that and no more. The "genuine," remarkably defined later as "imaginary gardens with real toads in them," is the main concern of this poem and of this poet. She was impatient with "half poets" and with what they drag into prominence in their work.

[182] This phrase, according to Miss Moore, was quoted from *The Diaries of Leo Tolstoy:* "Where the boundary between prose and poetry lies, I shall never be able to understand. . . . Poetry is verse; prose is not verse. Or else poetry is everything with the exception of business documents and schoolbooks."

[183] This phrase, again according to the poet, is from William Butler Yeats' *Ideas of Good and Evil:* "The limitation of his view was from the very intensity of his vision; he was a too literal realist of imagination. . . ." Yeats was referring to William Blake. If real poets, "literalists of the imagination," convey a genuine imagined experience, it is because vivid and authentic details (even "business documents and school-books") have been effectively used.

[184] Evade the point at issue.

[185] In classical mythology, Tantalus was a king in Asia Minor who for his crimes was doomed to remain in Tartarus, a sunless abyss below Hades (hell). Here, hungry and thirsty, he was condemned to stand in chin-deep water with fruit-laden branches above his head. Whenever Tantalus attempted to drink or eat, water or fruit receded out of reach. The word *tantalize* (meaning "to torment," "to tease") is derived from his name and predicament.

[186] Whim, strange notion.

[187] A figure in classical mythology, Sisyphus, former ruler of Corinth, was condemned to punishment in the same regions as Tantalus. His never-ending task was to roll a stone to the top of a slope; at the top of the incline, the stone always escaped Sisyphus' grasp and rolled down again.

[188] Series of questions and answers. In this sentence *inscrutable* means "mysterious," *immune* means "exempt."

[189] Museum of Fine Arts. The reference is to the Museum of Fine Arts in Brussels, which contains the painting (referred to in Line 14) by the Flemish painter Pieter Breughel (ca. 1525–1569).

[190] Eminent artists of earlier periods, especially of the fifteenth to eighteenth centuries.

[191] That is, the release and relief provided by death.

[192] The Old Masters.

[193] The suffering of life.

[194] Icarus was the son of Daedalus, a cunning craftsman and architect in classical mythology. Father and son flew on artificial wings fastened to their shoulders with wax. Icarus ventured near the sun, which melted the wax and caused him to fall and drown. In Breughel's painting, Icarus' legs are disappearing into the sea in one corner of the picture; the remainder of the painting has nothing to do with the mishap.

[195] A stout pole such as is used for a mast.

[196] That is, forced by need beyond one's will power to resist.

[197] That is, in complete peace and rest.

[198] Boldness, daring. The speaker and his freshly-awakened love act out what the girl had been dreaming.

[199] This title could refer to youthful companions, but it is true that Spender was influenced by radical (communist) ideas when this poem was written in the 1930s.

[200] Glittering, shining.

[201] Resin. That is, women of fashion are caught in their fixed and sterile ways of life just as flies are caught in glue.

[202] Confined, imprisoned.

[203] This seems an odd, whimsical, or nonsensical title for a poem discussing death and how we should deal with it. Start with the second stanza on a second reading; the actuality of the opening lines of this stanza and the clear images that follow "set the stage" and indicate the original intention of the poem.

Stevens' kind of poetic vision and its contrast and conflict with perception of the plain facts of life (and death) seeks here to find some relationship between imagination and reality. The speaker suggests that we see things precisely as they are: "Let be be the finale of seem." That is, let the state of things as they are (being, existing) be the concluding act (finale) of seeming (imagination).

[204] The muscular cigar-maker can be considered an undertaker, a caterer, or merely a person still alive who is unconcerned with death.

[205] The derivation of this word suggests lust or desire. The concept of a dairy product (curds) possessing sexual desire is surprising. Possibly the phrase has an ironic overtone in its reference to the kind of life the "emperor of ice-cream" presides over and one's understandable resentment at the intrusion of such attitudes into the presence of death. If this be true, then the lord of existence is a materialistic force, a kind of pleasure-seeking human greed symbolized by ice-cream.

[206] The presence of death (again, read the second stanza before the first in close analysis) is an excuse to have a party. Therefore, let the girls wear ordinary clothes, not mourning raiment; let the boys bring faded flowers. Then, send for the vulgar cigar-maker to prepare some party food. Have fun; there is no need to respect the dead woman's (girl's?) body. If her feet protrude from under the sheet, why worry? She's beyond objecting to this or to anything. The "ruler of the revels" (the emperor) is the spirit of materialism.

[207] A board or plank, especially of pine or fir. Two lines down, "fantails" means a tail, end, or part shaped like a fan.

[208] Calloused, horn-like through hardening.

[209] The death scene, in reality, is stripped of all fantasy. Look at the dead person steadily and clearly in light provided: death has no majesty, no mystery, no terror.

[210] The physical revelation of the real in all its ugliness and coldness is symbolized by the "horny feet"; the "coming" (or "being") of those feet grows out of this real scene and fuses reality and fantasy into an intense imaginative moment. The ironic contrast between those partying and the one lying dead is subtle and, for some readers, merely fanciful.

[211] In this extended simile, the poet is comparing his new automobile to a sleek, trim sailing vessel.

[212] A plane curve. Use of this word to suggest "sweep" is highly imaginative.

[213] Steering wheel and horn.

[214] Basic nature, true substance.

215 Shining, luminous.

216 This poem is a despairing, bitter comment on the inner turmoil of a poet as he reflects on the world about him. What precisely caused the author to feel as he indicates is not clear. Perhaps he was sensing the approach of world conflict: in 1934, Italy (Mussolini) refused to arbitrate debates with Ethiopia and invaded that country the following year. In 1934, Adolf Hitler became the Fuehrer of Germany. Also in 1934, the Chancellor of Austria (Dollfuss) was shot to death by Nazi plotters.

217 Removal.

218 It is unclear exactly what these references imply. "Eastern seas" may refer to the waters (seas) mentioned in the *Iliad* and *Odyssey* or to "Mare Orientalis," a dark plain on the face of the moon, also called the Eastern Sea. The Hebrides, islands off the west coast of Scotland, are also known as the "Western Islands." Apparently these allusions suggest a wide range of travel, knowledge, reading, and understanding.

219 A conservative reaction set in in Spain in 1933; shortly thereafter, Franco received help from Italy and Germany in the civil war that followed.

220 Important, dignified.

221 Present time, what is happening now.

222 Fixed positions, positives.

223 Realization, attainment.

224 Grouchy, ill-natured. The speaker walks in sunshine (fire) and casts a halting shadow.

225 Branches.

226 Region (county).

227 Inner, real. *Neural* applies to the nervous system.

228 Timepiece.

229 Rush.

230 Power, right, authority.

231 Instruments of torture.

232 A unicorn is a mythical creature resembling a horse, with a single horn in its forehead. *Unicorn* here means "unworldly," "mysterious."

233 Few modern statements about the miraculous power of love, of passion, to change an individual have been made in stronger, more concrete, or more lyrical terms than the two stanzas of this poem.

234 Water plants.

235 A spiny-backed fish.

236 The imagery of this selection and its concentrated power depend heavily upon the specific natural objects and living things mentioned. This first stanza, by contrast with the second, describes a quiet, resigned, slothful existence.

237 A fierce, greedy, gluttonous sea bird.

238 A vulture, the largest flying bird in the Western Hemisphere.

239 A mythical bird of great beauty, fabled to live for several hundred years and then to rise from its own ashes in the freshness of youth.

240 The contrast between the inactivity of Stanza 1 and the powerful action of Stanza 2 is now fully clear.

241 Even, uniform.

242 This selection deals with vast themes of life and death, the impermanence of man, the fate and final destiny of everything and everyone.

243 A bone of the leg extending from knee to ankle.

244 The compass and range of a voice or musical instrument.

245 *Ruminates* means to ponder, to meditate on, to chew over and over in one's mind. That is, a preacher who talks about God to his congregation reflects on Him as a man and not only as the subject of a sermon.

246 Despite unusual punctuation and apparent differences in length of line, this selection consists of four quatrains in iambic pentameter.

247 A prominent poet, born in England in 1923, long resident in the United States.

[248] A *monger* is a dealer or trader. A *sleepmonger* busies himself (itself) with sleep, a *deathmonger* with death.

[249] Relating to the preparation and dispensing of drugs.

[250] Inoffensive, harmless.

[251] A black sacrament is a Black Mass, a ceremony that mocks the Christian Mass and is performed by worshipers of the devil.

[252] Unprejudiced; without prior opinion or knowledge.

[253] A city in eastern or southeastern Europe, possibly in Russia (Soviet Republic) or Poland.

[254] Inserted; stuck in.

[255] Raised up, called forth.

INDEX OF AUTHORS IN PART FOUR

INDEX TO PARTS ONE, TWO, AND THREE

75 76 9 8 7 6 5 4 3